Abdelghani Benali

Sommaire

Introduction

L'écriture arabe en quelques mots

Ce cahier d'écriture s'adresse à toutes celles et tous ceux qui s'engagent dans l'apprentissage de la langue arabe.

Outre les habituelles pages de graphie pure, vous y trouverez une présentation de l'alphabet arabe et des principes généraux de ce système d'écriture, une présentation des signes diacritiques primaires et secondaires, des exercices de consolidation, de conversation et quelques exercices corrigés.

Mais avant de commencer, cela vaut peut-être la peine de s'attarder un moment pour mieux comprendre l'origine de la langue arabe dont l'accès à l'écriture et à la lecture est quelque peu ardu...

Nous vous proposons pour cela un petit voyage dans le temps...

Histoire de la langue arabe

La langue arabe est la plus jeune des langues sémitiques. Ce mot « sémitique » est très ancien dans la mesure où il découle du prénom Sem, un des fils du prophète Noé. Son nom a donc été donné à certaines familles de langues parlées autrefois en Asie et en Afrique.

Naturellement, l'hébreu, l'akkadien, le phénicien et l'araméen en font partie. La langue arabe est une langue qui s'écrit de la droite vers la gauche contrairement au français. Les lignes sont écrites à l'horizontale comme le français.

Comme toutes les langues du monde, l'arabe a d'abord été parlé avant d'être écrit.

Les habitants de la péninsule arabique s'exprimaient en arabe avant l'avènement de l'Islam.

Environ 150 ans avant l'avènement de l'Islam, les poètes de la période préislamique *(Jâhiliyya)* composèrent des odes très célèbres en arabe classique qui sont restées longtemps suspendues aux murs de la Ka'ba[1].

C'est la raison pour laquelle nous pouvons dater les premières occurrences de graphie arabe au troisième siècle après Jésus-Christ.

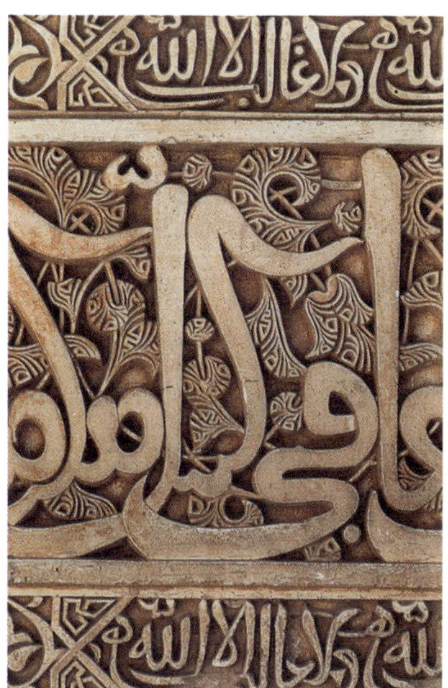

Origines de l'écriture arabe

En ce qui concerne les origines de la graphie arabe, une divergence existe entre les historiens : nabatéennes pour certains, syriaques pour d'autres.

Quoi qu'il en soit, l'araméen est indubitablement, l'origine première de la langue arabe. Les Arabes ont longtemps utilisé les systèmes d'écritures d'autres langues de la péninsule arabique avant de parvenir à la graphie de l'arabe classique qui sera progressivement améliorée et simplifiée jusqu'à devenir, dès le VIIe siècle, la graphie que l'on utilise encore aujourd'hui.

L'arabe, l'écriture d'une civilisation

L'expansion de l'Islam va jouer un rôle prépondérant pour la diffusion de la langue arabe. En effet, dès le VIIIe siècle, sous les Omeyyades, puis sous les Abbassides, l'Empire islamique adoptera la langue arabe comme langue officielle de l'administration. Au regard des échanges diplomatiques, commerciaux et militaires de l'époque, l'écriture de l'arabe se développera très vite sans jamais changer les fondamentaux graphiques de l'alphabet arabe. Ce sont les styles d'écriture qui varieront, et jamais l'alphabet.

[1] Le cube noir à la Mecque qui est le temple sacré pour les musulmans et en direction duquel ils se dirigent pour accomplir leurs cinq prières rituelles quotidiennes.

Par ailleurs, étant la langue du texte coranique, l'arabe sera la langue liturgique des musulmans ; elle deviendra rapidement un vecteur important dans le domaine de la recherche scientifique. Surtout après la fondation, à Bagdad, de la Maison de la sagesse par le Calife Haroun Al-Rachid, ami et contemporain de Charlemagne. Enfin, l'Empire Ottoman, dès le XIIIe siècle, permettra l'essor de la calligraphie arabe sur tous les supports et avec une grande variété de styles.

L'alphabet arabe

L'arabe utilise un alphabet consonantique (*abjad* en arabe) et s'écrit de droite à gauche. Il s'agit d'un alphabet qui ne note que les consonnes (28). Notez que parmi ces 28 consonnes, 3 sont, en outre, utilisées pour indiquer les voyelles longues. Enfin, les voyelles brèves sont des petits signes diacritiques sur ou sous les consonnes.

Au début de l'Islam, les premières copies du Coran étaient écrites avec l'alphabet arabe et ses 28 consonnes. Les lettres de l'alphabet arabe n'étaient pas ponctuées et leur forme était simple. Plusieurs sons s'écrivaient alors de la même manière. Suite à des lectures erronées, voire blasphématoires de certains versets coraniques, les Califes ont missionné les grands poètes et hommes de lettres afin de trouver une solution à ces problèmes de lecture.

Les points et signes diacritiques étaient nés. La forme actuelle de l'alphabet arabe date du XIIIe siècle.

En résumé :

- L'arabe est la plus jeune des **langues sémitiques** (hébreu, syriaque, araméen…)
- Depuis son origine, il utilise un **alphabet consonantique de 28 lettres**.
- L'arabe s'écrit **de droite à gauche**.
- L'arabe dispose de **trois voyelles brèves** et **trois voyelles longues.**
- Les voyelles brèves sont de simples **signes diacritiques placés <u>sur</u>** ou **<u>sous</u>** les consonnes.
- Il existe 3 voyelles longues qui **s'écrivent, mais ne se prononcent pas**.
- L'absence de voyelle est marquée par un petit **« zéro »** placé sur la lettre et appelé ***soukoun.***
- Le redoublement d'une consonne sera marqué par un petit signe appelé ***chadda.***

Présentation de l'alphabet

ا ب ت ث

ج ح خ

د ذ ر ز

س ش ص ض ط ظ

ع غ ف ق

ك ل م ن

ه و ي

La forme des lettres

SENS D'ÉCRITURE EN ARABE : ← ← ← (de droite à gauche).

La forme (ou graphie) des 28 lettres de l'alphabet arabe change selon qu'elles sont **isolées** ou placées au **début**, au **milieu** ou à la **fin** du mot.

	prononciation	isolée	finale	médiane	initiale
1	alif ['a]	ا	ـا	ـا	ا
2	bâ' [ba]	ب	ـب	ـبـ	بـ
3	tâ' [ta]	ت	ـت	ـتـ	تـ
4	thâ' [tha]	ث	ـث	ـثـ	ثـ
5	jîm [ja]	ج	ـج	ـجـ	جـ
6	hâ' [ha]	ح	ـح	ـحـ	حـ
7	khâ' [kha]	خ	ـخ	ـخـ	خـ
8	dâl [da]	د	ـد	ـد	د
9	dhâl [dha]	ذ	ـذ	ـذ	ذ
10	râ' [ra]	ر	ـر	ـر	ر
11	zây [za]	ز	ـز	ـز	ز
12	sîn [sa]	س	ـس	ـسـ	سـ

	prononciation	isolée	finale	médiane	initiale
13	chîn [cha]	ش	ـش	ـشـ	شـ
14	s̲âd [s̲a]	ص	ـص	ـصـ	صـ
15	d̲âd [d̲a]	ض	ـض	ـضـ	ضـ
16	t̲â' [t̲a]	ط	ـط	ـطـ	طـ
17	d̲h̲â' [d̲h̲a]	ظ	ـظ	ـظـ	ظـ
18	ᶜayn [ᶜa]	ع	ـع	ـعـ	عـ
19	rayn [ra]	غ	ـغ	ـغـ	غـ
20	fâ' [fa]	ف	ـف	ـفـ	فـ
21	q̲âf [q̲a]	ق	ـق	ـقـ	قـ
22	kâf [ka]	ك	ـك	ـكـ	كـ
23	lâm [la]	ل	ـل	ـلـ	لـ
24	mîm [ma]	م	ـم	ـمـ	مـ
25	noun [na]	ن	ـن	ـنـ	نـ
26	hâ' [ha]	ه	ـه	ـهـ	هـ
27	wâw [wa]	و	ـو	ـو	و
28	yâ' [ya]	ي	ـي	ـيـ	يـ

Remarques sur le tableau

- Le chiffre figurant dans la première colonne du tableau pages 8-9 indique le rang de chaque lettre dans l'alphabet.
- **Il faut apprendre l'alphabet dans l'ordre**, car les racines des mots sont classées par ordre alphabétique.
- On observera que les lettres de l'alphabet arabe peuvent comprendre les éléments suivants :
  - **Un corps principal :** une boucle, une ou plusieurs dents, un ou plusieurs points.
  - **Un trait de liaison** qui attache la lettre à la suivante et/ou à la précédente. Attention : certaines lettres ne s'attachent jamais à la suivante et ne peuvent donc avoir qu'un seul trait de liaison ; ce sont les lettres : و ز ر ذ د ا (n° 1, 8, 9, 10, 11 et 27).
  - **Un appendice décoratif** qui n'apparaît que quand la lettre est en fin de mot ou isolée.

Indications sur la prononciation des consonnes

Avant de travailler la graphie et l'écriture proprement dites, il convient de parler un peu de la prononciation, c'est-à-dire de la phonétique.

1. Consonnes qui ont un équivalent phonétique en français

2	ب	bâ' [ba]	= b	
3	ت	tâ' [ta]	= t	
8	د	dâl [da]	= d	
11	ز	zây [za]	= z	
12	س	sîn [sa]	= s	Comme dans ***sauter*** et ***singe***, jamais comme dans ***rose***.
19	غ	rayn [ra]	= r	Grasseyé du parler parisien.

20	ف	fâ' [fa]	= f	
22	ك	kâf [ka]	= k	
23	ل	lâm [la]	= l	
24	م	mîm [ma]	= m	
25	ن	noun [na]	= n	
27	و	wâw [wa]	= w	Comme dans ***kilowatt*** ou dans ***ouate***.
28	ي	yâ' [ya]	= y	Comme dans ***yole*** ou ***payer***.

2. Consonnes qui peuvent engendrer une difficulté

☞ n° 1 bis : ء hamza, ou « occlusive glottale »

La hamza peut être **l'attaque d'une voyelle**. Pour mieux comprendre de quoi il s'agit, prononcez isolément et avec assez d'énergie les mots ***avion*** – ***assez*** – ***idée*** : vous attaquez la voyelle initiale de ces mots par une consonne que le français n'écrit pas mais qui, phonétiquement, existe bel et bien, c'est **l'hiatus**. Cette consonne, l'arabe l'écrit : c'est la **hamza**.

Quand la hamza n'attaque pas une voyelle, elle devient un simple « coup de glotte », une sorte de léger hoquet.

Exemple : dans رَأْسٌ, ra'sun (à syllaber : ra'/sun), le signe « **'** » est la transcription de la hamza.

☞ n° 4 et 9 : ث thâ' et ذ dhâl

Le ث thâ' équivaut au ***th*** anglais sourd, comme dans ***thing*** ou ***think***.

Le ذ thâl équivaut au ***th*** anglais sonore, comme dans ***the*** ou ***that***.

Pour appréhender la différence entre une sourde et une sonore, faites l'expérience suivante : bouchez-vous les oreilles et prononcez « sss… », puis « zzz… » Dans le cas de « sss… », vous n'entendez qu'un bruit de sifflement très localisé. **Les cordes vocales ne vibrent pas**, on dit que ***s*** est **sourd**. Dans le cas de « zzz… », vous entendez une résonance en plus du bruit de sifflement, parce que **les cordes vocales vibrent**. On dit que ***z*** est **sonore**.

Faites la même expérience pour différencier les lettres n° 4 ث thâ' et n° 9 ذ dhâl.

☞ n° 5 : ج jîm

Actuellement, il existe trois prononciations différentes de cette lettre selon les régions :

- **dj** comme dans ***budget***.
- **j** comme dans ***jeûne***.
- **g** comme dans ***gare***.

☞ n° 6 et 26 : ح **ḫâ'** et ه **hâ'**

Le ه hâ' est l'équivalent du ***h*** dit « aspiré » – en réalité expiré – de l'anglais ***house*** ou de l'allemand ***Haus***. C'est un souffle qui frotte légèrement les parois de la glotte entrouverte.

Le ح ḫâ' est très différent. C'est un ***h*** fortement expiré. Le souffle vient directement de la poitrine, sans rencontrer d'obstacle dans la gorge. C'est un son qui n'existe pas en français moderne, sauf dans quelques exclamations vigoureuses, comme dans ***hum !*** Il s'entend plus qu'il ne se prononce. C'est un souffle plus énergique que celui du ه hâ', qui produit un frottement sur les parois assez fortement contractées du pharynx ; il s'articule donc davantage que le ه hâ'.

☞ n° 7 : خ **k͟hâ'**

C'est l'équivalent du ***ch*** allemand de **Buch** ou **Bach**, et de la ***jota*** espagnole.

Si l'on éprouve des difficultés à réaliser cette consonne, on partira du غ rayn (n° 19). Le غ rayn ressemble au ***r*** « grasseyé » des Parisiens, le ***r*** le plus couramment prononcé dans les villes françaises de nos jours. Il se réalise par le frottement de l'air expiré entre le voile du palais et la partie postérieure de la langue : il est sonore.

Le خ k͟hâ' (= ***ch*** allemand dur, ***jota***) se réalise au même endroit et de la même façon, mais avec cette différence qu'il est sourd. Faites l'expérience proposée pour les lettres n° 4 et 9, mais en partant cette fois du ***r*** « grasseyé » (rrr... = rayn) et en tâchant d'éliminer la résonance. Vous obtenez alors le خ k͟hâ'.

Pour l'articuler, il faut produire une sorte de raclement au fond de la gorge, comme si l'on voulait cracher.

☞ n° 10 : ر **r̠â'**.

C'est un ***r*** « roulé » – ou plus exactement vibré – du bout de la langue, celui des Espagnols et des Italiens.

On les distinguera sans difficulté du غ rayn (n° 19), voir ci-dessus (n° 7).

☞ n° 14 : ص **sâd**

Le ص sâd est un س sîn (n° 12) emphatique, c'est-à-dire prononcé avec plus de force.

☞ n° 15 : ض **dâd**

Le ض dâd se prononce de deux façons différentes selon les régions :

C'est soit l'emphatique du ذ dhâl (n° 9). Il est alors exactement semblable phonétiquement au ظ dhâ' (n° 17) dans une de ses deux prononciations. On devrait alors en toute rigueur le transcrire par un ***dhâ'***. C'est ainsi que le prononcent de très nombreux Arabes.

Soit l'emphatique du د dâl (n° 8). C'est ainsi que le prononcent les Égyptiens, entre autres, et c'est cette prononciation que rend sa transcription la plus courante en ***d***.

☞ n° 16 : ط **tâ'**

C'est l'emphatique du ت tâ' (n° 3).

☞ n° 17 : ظ **dhâ'**

Le ظ dhâ' se prononce de deux façons différentes selon les régions :

Comme un ذ thâl (n° 9) emphatique. Il se confond alors avec la première prononciation de ض dâd (n° 15) et devrait être transcrit par un ***d***. C'est la prononciation la plus répandue et la plus classique.

Ou comme un ز zây (n° 11) emphatique. C'est ainsi que le prononcent les Égyptiens, et c'est cette prononciation que rend sa transcription la plus courante en ***z***.

☞ n° 18 : ع **cayn**

Ce son est émis du plus profond de la gorge, en contractant la partie inférieure du larynx et en faisant vibrer des cordes vocales.

☞ n° 21 : ق **qâf**

Consonne gutturale par excellence, le ق qâf (n° 21) est émis par une explosion sourde se produisant à l'extrême fond de la gorge. C'est en quelque sorte un ***k*** prononcé avec un fort relâchement au niveau du voile du palais, donc sensiblement plus bas que le ك kâf (n° 22) qui, lui, est réalisé sur le palais osseux.

Distinguez donc bien cette consonne ق qâf (n° 21) du ك kâf (n° 22).

Les lettres isolées

ا **alif** ['a]

ب bâ' [ba]

ت tâ' [ta]

ث thâ' [tha]

ث ث ث

4 3 2 1

ث

ث

ث

ج jîm [ja]

1 2 3

ج ج ج

ج

ج

ج

1
2

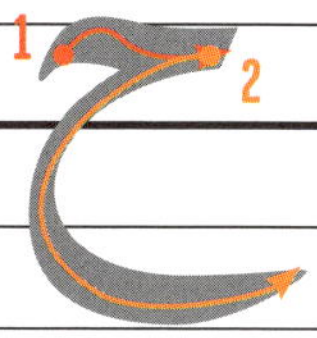

خ **khâ'** [kha]

خ خ خ

1 2 3

خ

خ

خ

د **dâl** [da]

د د د

د

د

د

ذ dhâl [dha]

ذ ذ ذ
2
1

ذ

ذ

ذ

ر
rā' [ra]

ز zây [za]

ز ز ز

1 2

ز

ز

ز

س **sîn** [sa]

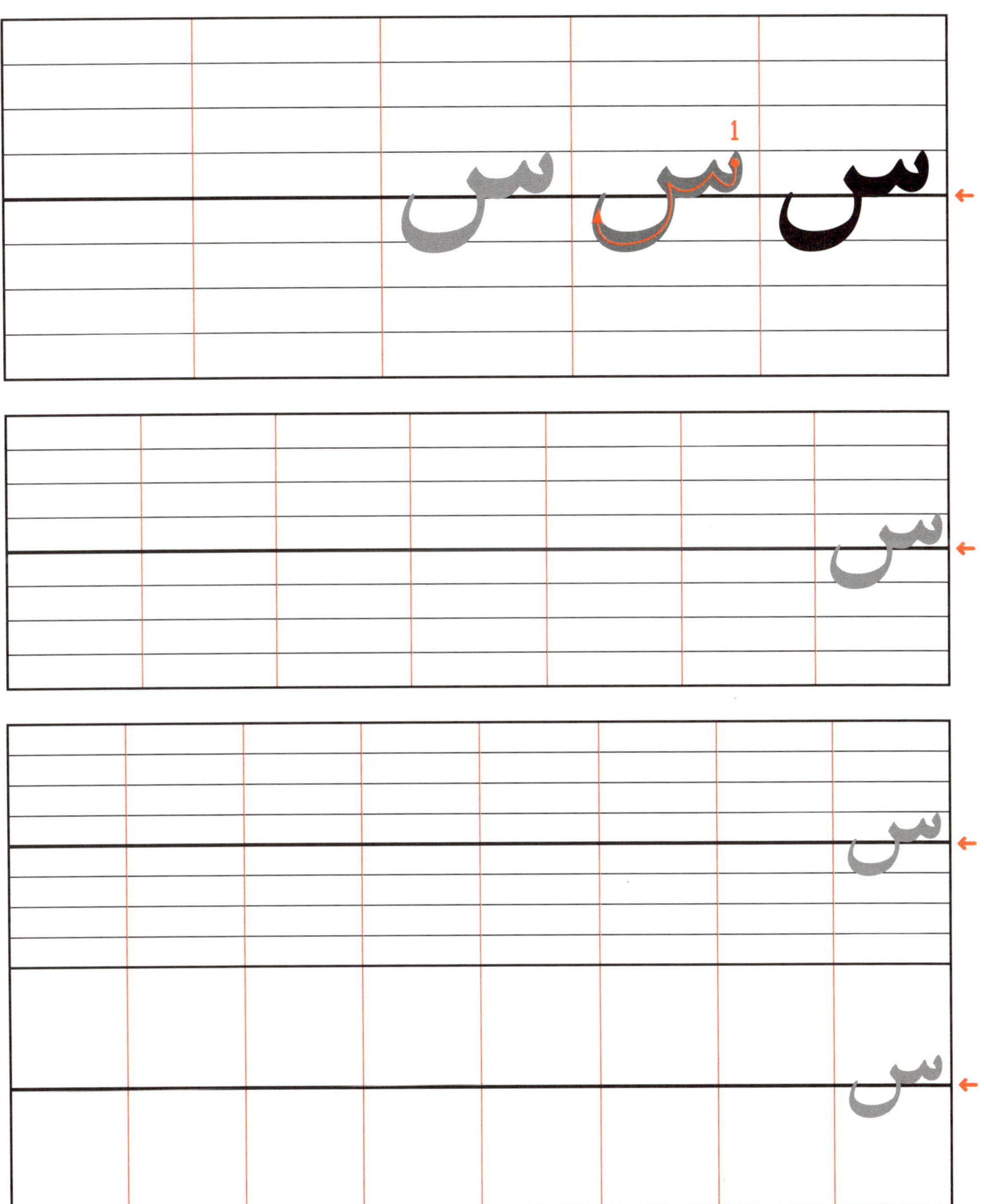

ش **chîn** [cha]

ش ش ش

4
3 2
1

ش

ش

ش

ص sâd [sa]

ض **d̲âd** [d̲a]

ط
ṯâ’ [ṯa]

ظ dhâ' [dha]

ظ ظ ظ

1 2 3

ظ

ظ

ظ

ع ᶜayn [ᶜa]

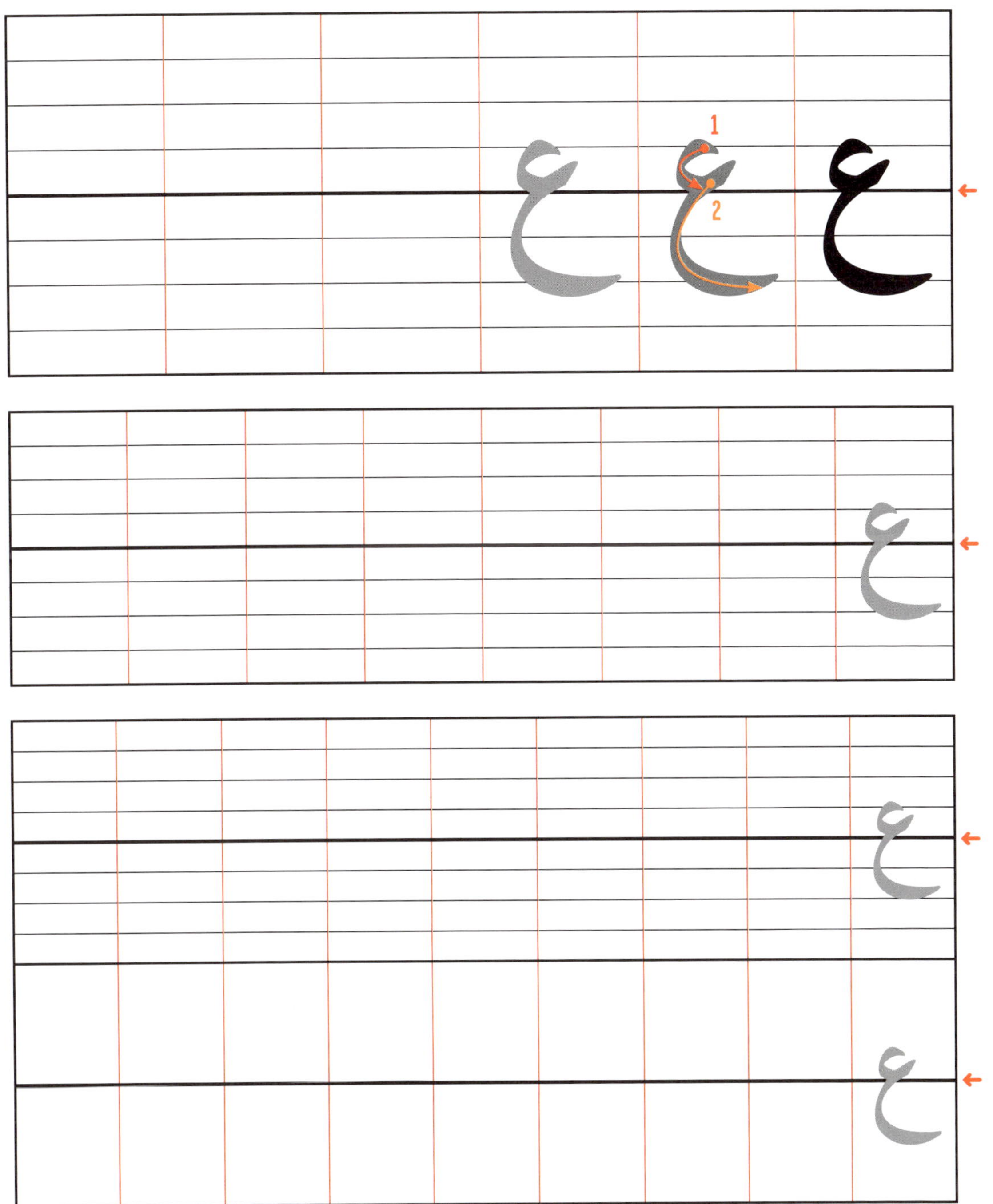

3
1
2

ف **fâ’** [fa]

ق gâf [qa]

ق ق ق

3 2 1

ق

ق

ق

ك kâf [ka]

2 1

ك ك ك

ك

ك

ك

ل lâm [la]

ل ل ل

ل

ل

ل

م mîm [ma]

1 2

ن noun [na]

ن ن ن

2 1

ن

ن

ن

ه hâ' [ha]

و wâw [wa]

			و	و	و

						و

							و
							و

ي **yâ'** [ya]

ي ي ي

1 2 3

ي

ي

ي

Voyelles brèves et longues, et signes diacritiques

Attention !

Vous avez remarqué que certaines lettres de l'alphabet arabe s'écrivent avec un, deux ou trois points placés au-dessus, dans ou sous la lettre. Ces points ne sont ni des signes diacritiques ni des marqueurs de voyelle.
Ces lettres peuvent toutefois comporter, en plus de leur(s) point(s), des signes diacritiques ou des marqueurs de voyelle.

L'alphabet arabe contient un total de **15 caractères** pointillés.

Les trois voyelles brèves اَلْحَرَكَاتُ الثَّلَاثُ al harakât aththalâth

1. Les voyelles arabes

Il y a, en arabe, 3 voyelles brèves et 3 voyelles longues :

– **a bref**, transcrit **a** : ـَ

– **i bref**, transcrit **i** : ـِ

– **u bref**, transcrit **u***: ـُ

– **a** long, transcrit **â**

– **i** long, transcrit **î**

– **u** long, transcrit **û***

* Les voyelles arabes transcrites par **u** et **û** se prononcent comme le **ou** français.

2. Écriture des voyelles brèves

☞ Le « a » :

Une voyelle brève ne peut pas s'écrire sans consonne. Le **a bref** s'écrit donc **au-dessus** de la consonne grâce au signe ـَ appelé *fatha*.

Exemple : la consonne ب **bâ'** (n° 2 de l'alphabet) additionnée d'un a bref devient بَ **ba**.

Recopiez ces autres exemples et lisez-les à haute voix :

ذَ

هَ

بَ

دَ

رَ

سَ

يَ

☞ Le « i » :

Le **i bref**, quant à lui, s'écrit **sous** la consonne grâce au signe ـِ appelé *kasra.*

Exemple : la consonne ب **bâ'** (n° 2 de l'alphabet) additionnée d'un i bref devient بِ **bi**.

Recopiez ces autres exemples et lisez-les à haute voix :

إِ

عِ

بِ

مِ

زِ

فِ

دِ

☞ **Le « ou » :**

Le **u bref**, enfin, s'écrit donc **au-dessus** de la consonne grâce au signe ـُ appelé *damma.*

Exemple : la consonne ب **bâ'** (n° 2 de l'alphabet) additionnée d'un u bref devient بُ **bou**.

Recopiez ces autres exemples et lisez-les à haute voix :

					تُ
					سُ
					لُ
					كُ
					طُ
					رُ
					نُ

Les voyelles longues

☞ Le « â » :

La lettre ا **alif** (n° 1 de l'alphabet) sert de signe de prolongation au **a bref**. Elle doit donc nécessairement être précédée d'une voyelle **a**.

Exemple : additionnée d'un **a bref**, la lettre ج s'écrit جَ et se prononce **[ja]**.

Mais additionnée d'un **â long**, elle s'écrie جَا et se prononce **[jâ]**.

Exemple : جَامِعَة **jâmi**ᶜ**a**, *université.*

☞ Le « î » :

La lettre ي **yâ** (n° 28 de l'alphabet) sert de signe de prolongation au **i bref**. Elle doit donc nécessairement être précédée d'une voyelle **i**.

Exemple : additionnée d'un **i bref**, la lettre ج s'écrit جِ et se prononce **[ji]**.

Mais additionnée d'un **î long**, elle s'écrie جِي et se prononce **[jî]**.

Exemple : عَبْدُ الْمَجِيد ᶜ**Abdoulmajîd**, le prénom masculin *Abdelmajid.*

☞ Le « û » :

La lettre و **wâw** (n° 27 de l'alphabet) sert de signe de prolongation au **u bref**. Elle doit donc nécessairement être précédée d'une voyelle **u**.

Exemple : additionnée d'un **u bref**, la lettre ج s'écrit جُ et se prononce **[jou]**.

Mais additionnée d'un **û long**, elle s'écrie جُو et se prononce **[joû]**.

Exemple : مَوْجُود **mawjoûd**, *il y en a (pour les choses)/il est là (pour les humains).*

L'absence de voyelle ou « sukûn » (repos) السُّكُونُ

L'absence de voyelle ou **quiescence** est notée par le signe ْ suscrit au-dessus de la lettre, nommé **sukûn**, *repos*. On prononce alors la lettre sans voyelle.

Exemple : dans le mot **maktabî** *mon bureau*, la **lettre k** n'a pas de voyelle :

مَ + كْ + تَ + بِ + ي = مَكْتَبِي

Écrivez ces mots et prononcez-les à haute voix :

ismî *mon (pré)nom*

اِ + سْ + مِ + ي = اِسْمِي

Ahmad *(prénom masculin)*

أَ + حْ + مَ + دْ = أَحْمَدْ

anta *tu (masculin)*

أَ + نْ + تَ = أَنْتَ

anti *tu (féminin)*

أَ + نْ + تِ = أَنْتِ

min *de/originaire de*

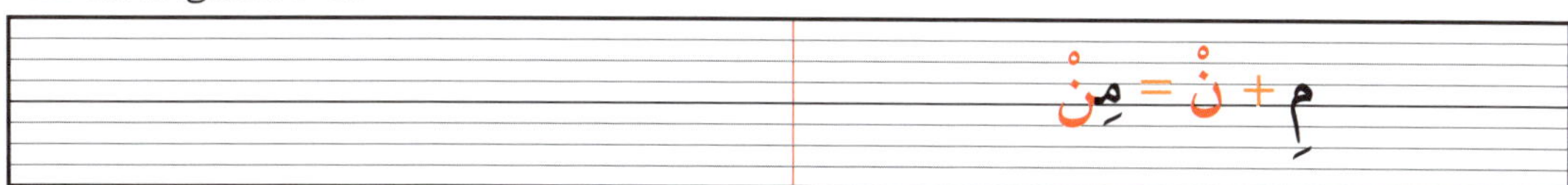

مِ + نْ = مِنْ

misr *Égypte*

مِ + صْ + ر = مِصْر

La gémination ou « chadda » (intensification) الشَّدَّةُ

En surmontant une consonne par le signe ـّ nommé **chadda**, *tension*, *intensification*, on indique ainsi sa ***gémination*** *(ou renforcement)*.

Remarque : ce signe, par sa forme, est la lettre س **sîn** amputée de sa boucle terminale.

Exemple : سُكَّر **soukkar**, *sucre*

Écrivez les mots suivants et prononcez-les à haute voix :

sallama *saluer*

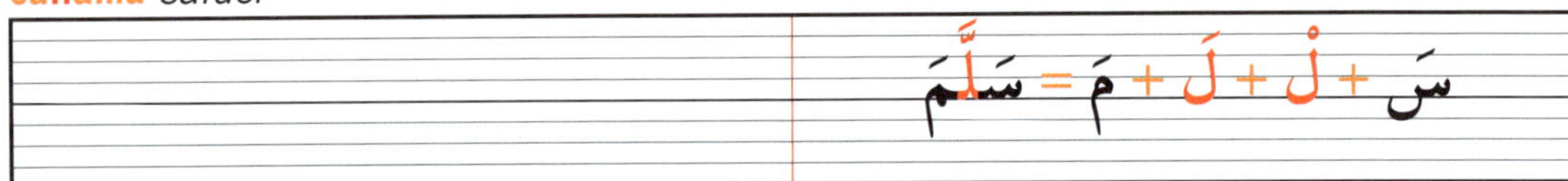

darraça *enseigner*

ᶜarabiyya *arabe*

taᶜallama *apprendre*

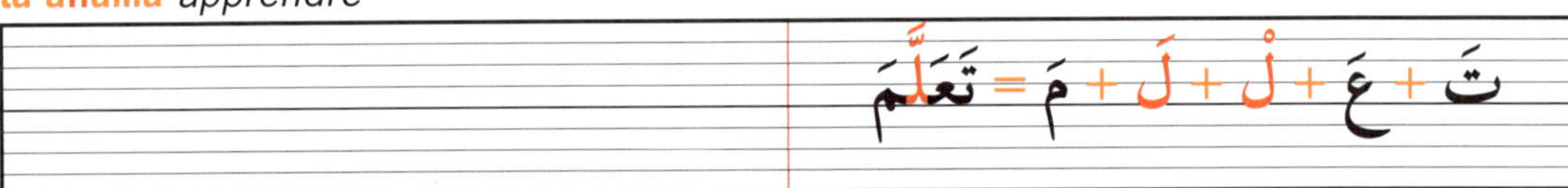

La double voyelle finale ou « tanwîn » التَّنْوِينُ

Le **tanwîn** correspond à la prononciation de la lettre **noûne** à la fin du mot.

Il y a trois formes du tanwîn :

– **tanwîn** avec *fatha* : il est constitué d'un ا **alif** ajouté à la fin du mot, qui est purement orthographique, et de deux fatha situées au-dessus de cette dernière lettre.
La prononciation consistera donc à ajouter -**ANE** à la fin du mot.
Exemple : كِتَابًا **kitâb-ane**, un livre

NB : pour le tanwîn de la fatha, on ajoutera un ا **alif** purement orthographique à la fin du mot. Sauf pour la ة fermée et la hamza ء.

– **tanwîn** avec *Kasra* : il est constitué de deux kasra situées au-dessous de la dernière lettre du mot.
La prononciation consistera donc à ajouter -**INE** à la fin du mot.
Exemple : كِتَابٍ **kitâb-ine**, un livre

– **tanwîn** avec *damma* : il est constitué de deux damma situées au-dessus de la dernière lettre du mot.
La prononciation consistera donc à ajouter -**OUNE** à la fin du mot.
Exemple : كِتَابٌ **kitâb-oune**, un livre

Note

Vous remarquerez que la signification ne change pas ; le mot *(un livre)* garde le même sens indépendamment du **tanwîn** en -**ANE**, -**INE** ou -**OUNE**.

En fait, le **tanwîn** marque l'indéfini ou l'indéterminé (*un*, *une* ou *des* en français). La différence est exclusivement grammaticale : c'est selon la fonction grammaticale du mot que l'on choisit tel ou tel **tanwîn**.

En général : on utilise le -**ANE** pour les compléments (cas direct ou accusatif), le -**INE** pour les cas indirects (ou génitif) et le -**OUNE** pour les sujets (cas sujet ou nominatif).

L'article défini التَّعْرِيفُ بِـ : اَلْـ...

L'article indique la détermination d'un mot : **le**, **la**, **l'**, **les** en français.

En arabe, l'article défini se compose du **alif-lam** qu'il faut ajouter en début de mot : الـ...

Nous allons voir que le **lam**, ل, ne sera pas toujours prononcé (voir pages 51 et 52 sur les lettres lunaires et les lettres solaires).

Un mot défini ne peut évidemment pas avoir de **tanwîn** (marque de l'indéfini) à la fin et vice versa.

Quelques exemples :
Reprenons le mot « livre » **kitâb** vu précédemment...

كِتَابًا **kitâb-ane**, un livre

الكِتَابَ **al kitâba**, le livre

كِتَابٍ **kitâb-ine**, un livre

الكِتَابِ **al kitâbi**, le livre

كِتَابٌ **kitâb-oune**, un livre

الكِتَابُ **al kitâbou**, le livre

Note

Dans le premier exemple en **a**, vous remarquerez que l'**alif** purement orthographique ajouté après tous les **tanwîn** en -**ANE** disparaît dès lors qu'il n'y a plus de **tanwîn** !

Les lettres lunaires et solaires

Pour des raisons phonétiques, les lettres de l'alphabet arabe sont classées en deux groupes : **les lettres lunaires** et **les lettres solaires**.

Les 28 lettres de l'alphabet sont réparties en deux groupes égaux : 14 lettres solaires et 14 lettres lunaires.

La différence entre les lettres solaires et lunaires ne se fait sentir qu'à la prononciation. Graphiquement, c'est-à-dire à l'écriture, rien ne change, et cette distinction n'a pas non plus d'incidence sur la grammaire.

1. Les lettres lunaires

ا ب ج ح خ ع غ ف ق ك م ه و ي

En début de mot, elles sont précédées par l'article défini الـ. Il faut également prononcer l'article défini **al** avant le mot.

Exemples : اَلْقَمَرُ **al qamarou**, *la lune*
اَلْعَرَبِيَّةُ **al ^{c}arabiyyatou**, *l'arabe*
اَلْمَطَارُ **al maṯârou**, *l'aéroport*

2. Les lettres solaires

ت ث د ذ ر ز س ش ص ض ط ظ ل ن

En début de mot, elles sont elles aussi précédées par l'article défini الـ. Ici, le لـ de l'article défini est purement orthographique et ne se prononce pas. La consonne qui suit le لـ est redoublée, ce qui est indiqué à l'écrit par une chadda (vue en page 49) ـّ.

Exemples : اَلشَّمْسُ **a-chchamsou**, *le soleil*
اَلسَّلاَمُ **a-ssalâmou**, *la paix, le salut*
اَلدَّرْسُ **a-ddarsou**, *la leçon, le cours*

Solaires	Lunaires
التَّمْرَة = la datte	الأُسْبُوعُ = la semaine
الثِّيَابُ = les vêtements	الْبَابُ = la porte
الدَّرْسُ = la leçon	الْجَمَالُ = la beauté
الذَّكَاءُ = l'intelligence	الْحَمَّامُ = le hammam
الرِّيَاضُ = Ryad	الْخُبْزُ = le pain
الزَّيْتُ = l'huile	الْعِلْمُ = la science
السَّاعَةُ = l'heure	الْغَابَةُ = la forêt
الشَّمْسُ = le soleil	الْفَجْرُ = l'aube
الصُّورَة = l'image	الْقَمَرُ = la lune
الضَّحِكُ = le rire	الْكِتَابُ = le livre
الطَّبِيبُ = le médecin	الْمَلِكُ = le roi
الظَّهْرُ = le dos	الْهَرَمُ = la pyramide
اللَّيْلُ = la nuit	الْوَرْدَةُ = la rose
النَّوْمُ = le sommeil	الْيَدُ = la main

Le â long ou « madda » الْمَدَّةُ

La combinaison du **a prolongé** en **â long** devrait s'écrire : اَا

Pour des raisons esthétiques et orthographiques, on écrira toujours le phonème **[â]** de la manière suivante : آ. Le petit signe flottant sur l'**alif** est appelé « **madda** ».

Il ne s'écrira que sur cette lettre pour la prolonger en **â**.

Exemple :
آكُلُ تُفَّاحَةً الآنَ **âkoulou touffâha alâna**, *Je mange une pomme maintenant.*

Alif tawîla (ou mamdoûda) et maqsoûra الأَلِفُ الْمَمْدُودَةُ وَالأَلِفُ الْمَقْصُورَةُ

L'**alif tawîla** *(tawîla = long)* **ou mamdoûda** est celui qui est représenté dans notre tableau des lettres page 8 (n° 1 de l'alphabet).

L'**alif maqsoûra** *(maqsoûra = bref)* se trace comme un **yâ** sans points ى.

Il apparaît seulement comme dernière lettre de certains mots :

ذِكْرَى **dhikrâ**, *souvenir*

عَلَى **ᶜalâ**, *sur*

Il sert seulement au premier usage de l'**alif tawîla** : signe graphique notant la prolongation du **a bref**. L'ensemble **fatha** + **alif maqsoûra** se note **â**.

Lâm-alif

La **lettre lâm** suivie d'un **alif** s'écrit لا ou ـــلا si le tout est précédé d'un trait de liaison.

Ce caractère est appelé **lâm-alif** لام أَلِف.

En fait, il s'agit d'une sorte de ligature* comme celle qui se trouve en français pour le groupe de lettres : **æ.**

lâ *non*

	ل + ا = لا ...

salâm *paix, salut*

	س + ل + ا + م = سلام ...

al islâm *soumission, Islam*

	اَ + لْ + إِ + سْ + لَ + ا + مُ = الإِسْلاَمُ ...

* Trait reliant deux lettres. Ensemble de lettres liées qui forment un caractère unique.

La « hamza » et ses supports الْهَمْزَةُ

La hamza est une consonne à part entière qui se réalise **sous forme d'attaque vocalique.**

Sa particularité est d'ordre graphique. Elle requiert un support d'écriture purement orthographique qui aura la forme de la lettre و **wâw**, de la lettre ى **yâ** sans les points (ou **alif bref**) ou de lettre ا **alif.**

Elle se vocalise comme les autres lettres et peut même être redoublée.

Le choix du support est fonction de plusieurs éléments, dont sa place dans le mot. Dans certains cas, elle peut s'écrire sans support.

Quant à sa prononciation, elle est strictement identique aux sons **a**, **i**, **ou** français respectivement pour une *hamza* + *fatha*, *hamza* + *kasra* et *hamza* + *damma*.

Il en est de même pour les hamza finales qui portent un **tanwîn** et qui se prononceront : -**ANE**, -**INE** ou -**OUNE**.

Note

Lorsque la **hamza** est **initiale dans un mot**, son support est **obligatoirement la lettre alif**. On placera la hamza sous le support si elle porte la voyelle **i** et au-dessus du support dans les deux autres cas (voyelles **a** et **u**).

Exemples à recopier :

anâ *moi/je*

	أَنَا

oustâdh *professeur*

	أُسْتَاذ

ilâ *vers, à, en direction de...*

	إِلَى

ayna ? *où ?*

	أَيْنَ

D'autres positions de la hamza :

أَكَلَ **akala**, *manger*

سَأَلَ **sa'ala**, *interroger*

قَرَأَ **qara'a**, *lire*

مَاءٌ **mâ'oun**, *de l'eau*

سُؤَالٌ **sou'âloun**, *une question*

قِرَاءَةٌ **qirâ'atoun**, *une lecture*

Lettres, autres positions

ا

Initiale				

Médiane				

Finale				

Note

Cette lettre est l'une des 6 lettres **non liées** [و ز ر ذ د ا] de l'alphabet arabe, c'est-à-dire qu'elle ne s'attache jamais avec la lettre suivante à l'aide d'une ligature ou trait de liaison ـ .

Initiale

Médiane

Finale

Liée

Initiale

Médiane

2 1

Finale

2 1

Liée

3 2 1

Ta fermée ة ou ـة

Il existe une seconde graphie de cette lettre, en position finale seulement : ة. On l'appelle **ta fermée** (marboûta) par opposition à la lettre normale ت, que l'on nomme **ta ouverte** (maftoûha).

Vous remarquerez que cette **ta** finale fermée s'écrit comme la lettre n° 26 ه ou ـه à laquelle sont ajoutés deux points, comme pour la lettre **ta** classique ت.

Cette lettre est le **marqueur du féminin** des noms et des adjectifs le plus courant.

Attention : aucun verbe ne peut se terminer par une **ta** fermée !

Initiale

ثـ

1

Médiane

ـثـ

2 1

Finale

ـث

2 1

Liée

ثثث

3 2 1

Initiale

1
2

Médiane

2
3 1

Finale

2
1
3

Liée

3 2 1
4

Initiale

1 2

Médiane

2 3 1

Finale

2 1 3

Liée

3 2 1 4

Initiale

1
2

Médiane

2
3
1

Finale

2
1
3

Liée

3 2 1
4

د

Initiale

د

Médiane

ـد
2 1

Finale

ـد
2 1

Note

Cette lettre est l'une des 6 lettres **non liées** [ا د ذ ر ز و] de l'alphabet arabe, c'est-à-dire qu'elle ne s'attache jamais avec la lettre suivante à l'aide d'une ligature ou trait de liaison ـ .

Initiale

ذ

Médiane

ـذ

2 1

Finale

ـذ

2 1

Note

Cette lettre est l'une des 6 lettres **non liées** [ا د ذ ر ز و] de l'alphabet arabe, c'est-à-dire qu'elle ne s'attache jamais avec la lettre suivante à l'aide d'une ligature ou trait de liaison ـ .

ر

Initiale

ر

Médiane

ـر

Finale

ـر

Note

Cette lettre est l'une des 6 lettres **non liées** [و ز ر ذ د ا] de l'alphabet arabe, c'est-à-dire qu'elle ne s'attache jamais avec la lettre suivante à l'aide d'une ligature ou trait de liaison ـ .

Initiale

Médiane

Finale

Note

Cette lettre est l'une des 6 lettres **non liées** [و ز ر ذ د ا] de l'alphabet arabe, c'est-à-dire qu'elle ne s'attache jamais avec la lettre suivante à l'aide d'une ligature ou trait de liaison ـ .

Initiale

سـ

Médiane

ـسـ

Finale

ـس

Liée

سسس

Initiale				ﺷ

Médiane				ـﺸـ

Finale				ـش

Liée		ششش

Initiale

Médiane

2 1

Finale

2 1

Liée

3 2 1

Initiale

ـضـ

Médiane

ـضـ

2 1

Finale

ـض

2 1

Liée

ضضض

3 2 1

Initiale

				1 2

Médiane

				2 3 1

Finale

				2 3 1

Liée

		3 2 1

Initiale

1 2

Médiane

2 3 1

Finale

3 1

Liée

3 2 1

Initiale

1 2

Médiane

2 3 1

Finale

2 1 3

Liée

3 2 1

Initiale

1 2

Médiane

2 3 1

Finale

2 1 3

Liée

3 2 1

Initiale

ﻓ

Médiane

ﻔ

Finale

ﻒ

Liée

ففف

3 2 1

Initiale

ﻗ

Médiane

ﻘ

Finale

ﻖ

Liée

ققق

3 2 1

Initiale

Médiane

Finale

Liée

Initiale

Médiane

2 1

Finale

1
2

Liée

3 2 1

Initiale

1 2

Médiane

3 2 1

Finale

3 2 1

Liée

5 4 3 2 1

6

Initiale

1

Médiane

2 1

Finale

1
2

Liée

2 1
3

ه

Initiale

هـ

2 1

Médiane

ـهـ

3 2 1

Finale

ـه

2 1

Liée

هـهـه

4 3 2 1

و

Initiale

و

Médiane

ـو

Finale

ـو

Note

Cette lettre est l'une des 6 lettres **non liées** [و ز ر ذ د ا] de l'alphabet arabe, c'est-à-dire qu'elle ne s'attache jamais avec la lettre suivante à l'aide d'une ligature ou trait de liaison ـ .

Initiale

Médiane

Finale

Liée

Consolidation

1 Recopier les lettres suivantes :

1. L'alphabet avec la fatha [a] اَلْفَتْحَةُ

1re partie

أَ بَ تَ ثَ جَ حَ خَ دَ ذَ رَ زَ سَ شَ صَ ضَ

2e partie

طَ ظَ عَ غَ فَ قَ كَ لَ مَ نَ هَ وَ يَ

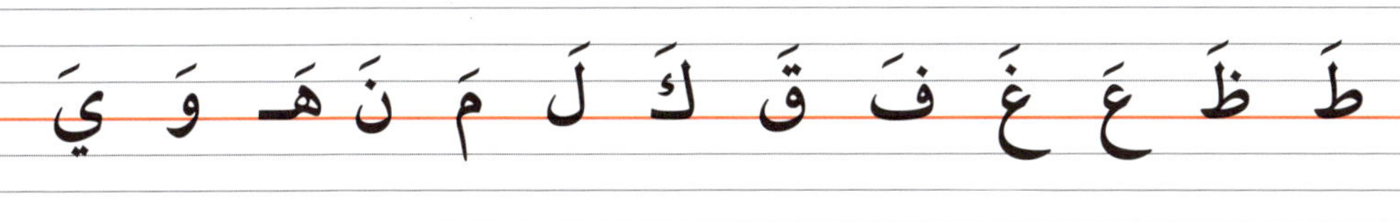

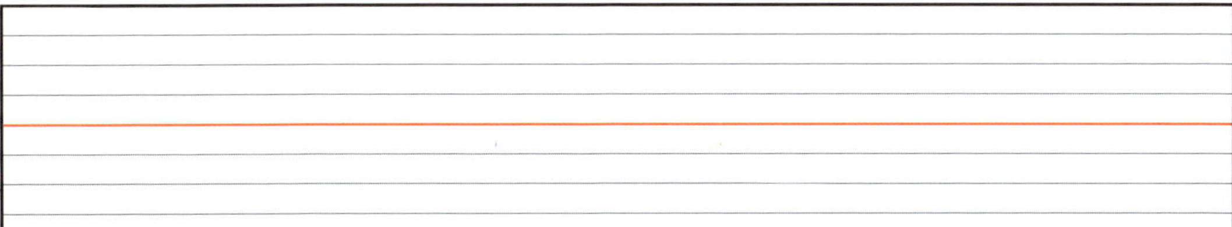

2. L'alphabet avec la kasra [i] اَلْكَسْرَةُ

1re partie

إِ بِ تِ ثِ جِ حِ خِ دِ ذِ رِ زِ سِ شِ صِ ضِ

2e partie

طِ ظِ عِ غِ فِ قِ كِ لِ مِ نِ هِـ وِ يِ

3. L'alphabet avec la damma [ou] اَلضَّمَّةُ

1re partie

أُ بُ تُ ثُ جُ حُ خُ دُ ذُ رُ زُ سُ شُ صُ ضُ

2e partie

طُ ظُ عُ غُ فُ قُ كُ لُ مُ نُ هُـ وُ يُ

4. L'alphabet avec le tanwîn de la fatha تَنْوِينُ الْفَتْحَةِ

1re partie

أً بًا تًا ثًا جًا حًا خًا دًا ذًا رًا زًا سًا شًا صًا ضًا

2e partie

طًا ظًا عًا غًا فًا قًا كًا لاً مًا نًا هًا وًا يًا

Note

Le tanwîn de la fatha implique l'ajout d'un **alif** purement orthographique ; c'est-à-dire que cet **alif** s'écrit mais ne se prononce pas. Les deux seules exceptions sont : la **ta marboûta (ta fermée)** et la **hamza** sous certaines conditions.

5. L'alphabet avec le tanwîn de la kasra تَنْوِينُ الْكَسْرَةِ

1re partie

إٍ بٍ تٍ ثٍ جٍ حٍ خٍ دٍ ذٍ رٍ زٍ سٍ شٍ صٍ ضٍ

2e partie

طٍ ظٍ عٍ غٍ فٍ قٍ كٍ لٍ مٍ نٍ هٍ وٍ يٍ

6. L'alphabet avec le tanwîn de la damma تَنْوِينُ الضَّمَّةِ

1re partie

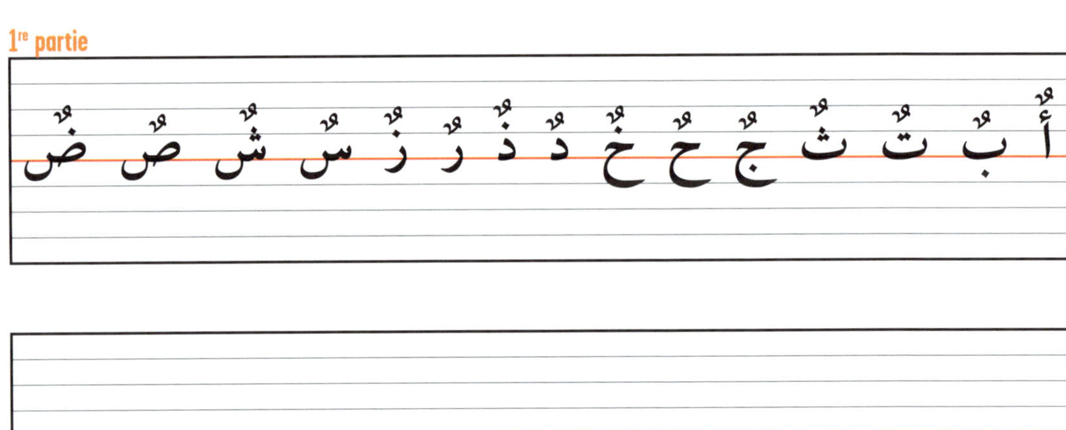

2e partie

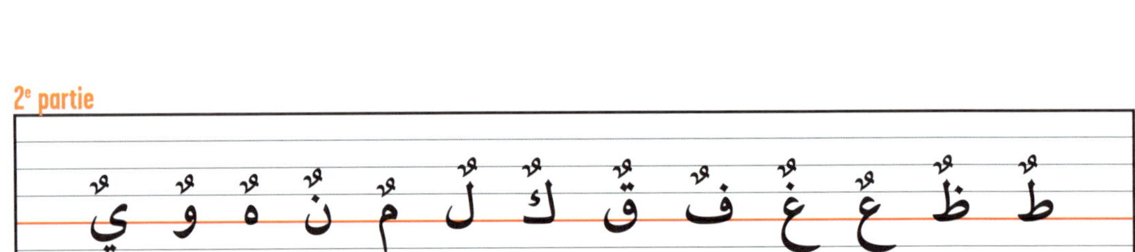

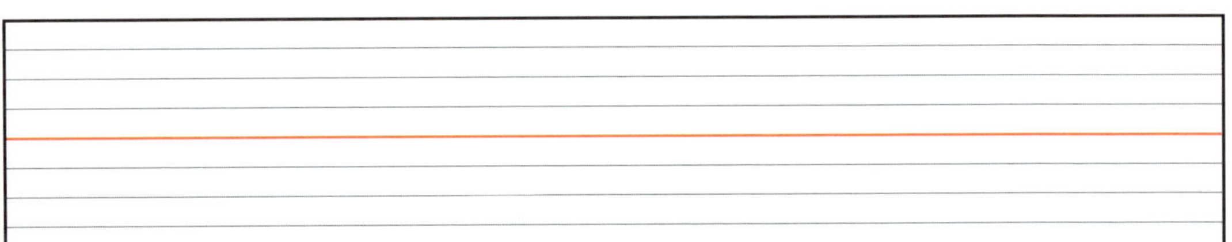

2 **Lier, s'il y a lieu, les lettres des mots suivants :**

1
أ + ك + ل
2
ش + ر + ب
3
ج + ل + س
4
و + ق + ف
5
ر + ك + ب
6
د + خ + ل
7
غ + ض + ب
8
ذ + ه + ب

9 غ + س + ل

10 س + ا + ل

11 ذ + ا + ب

12 ق + ا + ل

13 ع + ا + د

14 س + ا + ر

15 ن + ا + م

16 ص + ا + ح

17 ك + ا + ن

18 ا + ل + أ + ا + ن

19 ش + ك + ر + ا

20 ب + ي + ت

21 و + ر + د + ة

22 ع + ي + ن

23 ق + م + ر

24 م + س + ج + د

25 خ + ب + ز

26 م + ك + ت + ب + ة

27 م + ط + ا + ر

28 ج + ا + م + ع + ة

29 ج + م + ل

30 م + ح + طّ + ة

31 د + رّ + س

32 ت + ع + لّ + م

33 ق + ط + ا + ر

34 ج + م + ي + ل + ة

35 ا + ل + د + ر + س
36 ا + ل + ش + م + س
37 ط + ا + ئـ + ر + ة
38 ز + ا + ئـ + ر
39 ب + ا + ئـ + ع
40 م + م + ت + ل + ئ
41 ش + يـ + ئ
42 ع + ش + ا + ء
43 م + س + ا + ء
44 ر + أ + س
45 ر + ئ + ي + س
46 ل + ؤ + ل + ؤ
47 م + س + ؤ + و + ل

48 ← س + ؤ + ا + ل

49 ← ش + ؤ + و + ن

50 ← أ + ن + ي + س + ة

51 ← ف + ؤ + ا + د

52 ← ز + م + ل + ا + ؤ + ه

53 ← م + ؤ + ل + م

54 ← م + س + أ + ل + ة

55 ← ش + ا + ر + ع

56 ← ل + ق + ا + ء

57 ← ج + رّ + ي + ء

58 ← ج + ر + ي + د + ة

59 ← ش + ا + ي

60 ← ق + ه + و + ة

61 ق + ب + ل

62 ب + ع + د

63 ل + م + ا + ذ + ا

64 أَ + يْ + نَ

65 نَ + عَ + مْ

66 كَ + يْ + فَ

67 أ + ل + طّ + ا + ل + بُ

68 مَ + تَ + ى

69 مَ + دْ + ر + سَ + ة

70 ا + ل + س + م + ا + ء

71 ا + ل + ب + ل + د

72 أ + ل + أ + وّ + لُ

73 ا + ل + أ + خ + ي + ر

3 Décomposer les mots suivants :

1	←	دَرَّسَ
2	←	أَخْبَرَ
3	←	تَعَلَّمَ
4	←	تَرَاسَلَ
5	←	اِنْفَتَحَ
6	←	اِسْتَمَعَ

4 Mettre l'article défini الـ aux mots suivants en effectuant les modifications nécessaires :

ظَرْفٌ   وَرَقَةً   بَحْرٍ   مَكْتَبٌ   كِتَابًا

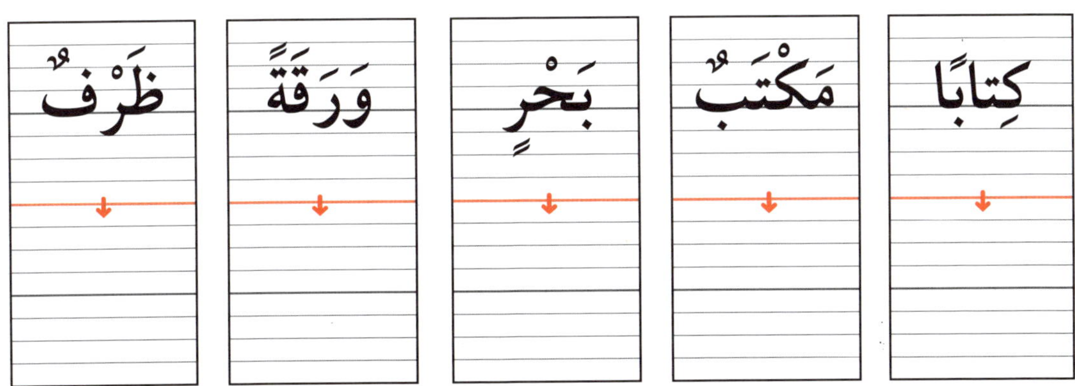

5 Décomposer les mots suivants :

1	←	يـخرج
2	←	يدخل
3	←	مغلق
4	←	مفتوح
5	←	يعوم
6	←	يـمشي
7	←	يطيـر
8	←	البنت
9	←	الـمرأة
10	←	رسالتـي

Groupes de lettres

Objectif : bien distinguer les sons qui se ressemblent !

Tantôt anagrammes, tantôt proches phonétiquement mais graphiquement différents, ou l'inverse, les mots suivants vous permettront de bien consolider vos acquis.

1 Copiez les groupes de lettres suivants, puis lisez-les à haute voix :

1 أَبَا – أَنَا

2 أَمَا – أَمَّا

3 قَلْبٌ – كَلْبٌ

4 صَيْفٌ – سَيْفٌ

5 شَيْءٌ – شَايٌ

6 صُورَةٌ – سُورَةٌ

7 عَمِلَ – لَمَعَ

8 عَسَلٌ – لَسَعَ

9 رَئِيسٌ – رَأْسٌ

10 سَأَلَ – سَالَ

11 هَوَاءٌ – هَوًى

12 حَوْلَ – لَوْحٌ

13 سَارَ – صَارَ

14 لَبِسَ – لَبِثَ

15 أَثَاثٌ – أَسَاسٌ

16 حَارِسٌ – حَارِثٌ

Copiez les groupes de lettres suivants, puis lisez-les à haute voix :

1 أَرَاكَ – عَلاَقَةٌ

2 جَدِيدٌ – حَدِيدٌ

3 سَمِينٌ – ثَمِينٌ

4 أُرِيدُ – أُدِيرُ

5 سَالِمٌ – سَلِيمٌ

6 مُشْمِسٌ – مُؤْمِنٌ

7 عَالِمٌ – عَالَمٌ

8 عِلْمٌ – عَلَمٌ

9 مَثَلٌ – مِثَالٌ

10 طِينٌ – تِيـنٌ

3 Liez, s'il y a lieu, les lettres suivantes :

Exemple	كَتَبَ ←	كَ + تَ + بَ
1	←	دَ + رَ + سَ
2	←	وَ + صَ + لَ
3	←	دَ + خَ + لَ
4	←	خَ + رَ + جَ
5	←	فَ + عَ + لَ
6	←	نَ + زَ + لَ
7	←	أَ + كَ + لَ
8	←	شَ + رِ + بَ
9	←	ذَ + هَ + بَ
10	←	بَ + عَ + ثَ

4 Ajoutez l'article défini aux mots suivants et lisez-les à haute voix :

Rappel

Si la première lettre du mot est « lunaire », l'article sera prononcé intégralement, si elle est « solaire », alors la lettre ل de l'article est purement orthographique et une chadda devra être dessinée au-dessus.

اَلْقَمَرُ al qamarou, *la lune*   اَلشَّمْسُ achchamsou, *le soleil*

1		ال + أَرْضَ
2		ال + بَارِدُ
3		ال + ظَبْيُ
4		ال + بَشَر
5		ال + غَار
6		ال + صَدِيقُ
7		ال + نُجُومُ
8		ال + حَقُّ

9 ال + عَدْل ←

10 ال + قَلَمُ ←

11 ال + مَاءُ ←

12 ال + ضَيْفُ ←

13 ال + شَايُ ←

14 ال + لُغَةُ ←

15 ال + ذَهَب ←

16 ال + سَمَكُ ←

17 ال + حَافِلَةُ ←

18 ال + هَاتِفُ ←

5 **Décomposez les mots suivants sous forme de lettres isolées :**

1 بتث
2 ملح
3 قنص
4 نصب
5 قطب
6 سوي
7 فهم
8 وَسَهْلاً
9 حَسَنًا
10 جِدًّا
11 عَفْوًا
12 فكر
13 حجج
14 سيط
15 ضلع
16 كفي
17 جيدًا
18 أَهْلاً
19 مَرْحَبًا
20 حَسَن
21 فَقَطْ
22 مُهِمًّا

Conversation et expressions

1 Recopiez ces phrases courantes et lisez-les à haute voix :

assalâmou ᶜalaykoum *Que la paix soit sur vous.*

اَلسَّلاَمُ عَلَيْكُمْ

اَلسَّلاَمُ عَلَيْكُمْ

wa ᶜalaykoumou assalâm *Que la paix soit sur vous.*

وَعَلَيْكُمُ السَّلاَمُ

وَعَلَيْكُمُ السَّلاَمُ

kayfa hâloukoum *Comment allez-vous ?*

كَيْفَ حَالُكُمْ؟

كَيْفَ حَالُكُمْ؟

lâ ba'sa *ça va (littéralement : point de misère).*

لاَ بَأْسَ

لاَ بَأْسَ

anâ bi-khair *Je vais bien.*

أَنَا بِخَيْرٍ

أَنَا بِخَيْرٍ

bi koulli souroûr *Avec plaisir !*

بِكُلِّ سُرُورٍ !

بِكُلِّ سُرُورٍ !

tafa<u>dd</u>al *Je t'en prie !*

تَفَضَّلْ !

تَفَضَّلْ !

tafa<u>dd</u>aloû *Je vous en prie !*

تَفَضَّلُوا !

تَفَضَّلُوا !

ilalliqâ' *Au revoir !*

إِلَى اللِّقَاءِ !

إِلَى اللِّقَاءِ !

ma^cassalâma *Au revoir !*

مَعَ السَّلاَمَةِ !

مَعَ السَّلاَمَةِ !

kamissâ^catou *Quelle heure est-il ?*

كَمِ السَّاعَةُ ؟

كَمِ السَّاعَةُ ؟

ᶜafwan *Pardon, excusez-moi, de rien !*

عَفْوًا !

عَفْوًا !

fîmâ baᶜd *Plus tard.*

فِيمَا بَعْدُ

فِيمَا بَعْدُ

sahratan saᶜîdatan *Bonne soirée !*

سَهْرَةً سَعِيدَةً !

سَهْرَةً سَعِيدَةً !

layla saᶜîdatan *Bonne nuit !*

لَيْلَةً سَعِيدَةً !

لَيْلَةً سَعِيدَةً !

chahiyyatan tayyibatan *Bon appétit !*

شَهِيَّةً طَيِّبَةً !

شَهِيَّةً طَيِّبَةً !

ma smouk ? *Comment t'appelles-tu ?*

مَا اسْمُكَ ؟

مَا اسْمُكَ ؟

isml mahmoud *Je m'appelle Mahmoud.*

اِسْمِي مَحْمُود

اِسْمِي مَحْمُود

anâ tâlib/tilmîdh *Je suis étudiant/élève.*

أَنَا طَالِب/ تِلْمِيذ

أَنَا طَالِب/ تِلْمِيذ

anâ tâliba/ tilmîdha *Je suis étudiante/élève.*

أَنَا طَالِبَة/ تِلْمِيذَة

أَنَا طَالِبَة/ تِلْمِيذَة

al hamdou lillâh *Que Dieu soit loué (littéralement : louange à Dieu).*

اَلْحَمْدُ لِلَّهِ

اَلْحَمْدُ لِلَّهِ

2 Recopiez ces chiffres et lisez-les à haute voix :

sifr *Zéro*

صِفْر

صِفْر

wâhid *Un*

وَاحِد

وَاحِد

ithnân *Deux*

اِثْنَان

اِثْنَان

thalâtha *Trois*

ثَلاَثَة

ثَلاَثَة

arbaᶜa *Quatre*

أَرْبَعَة

أَرْبَعَة

khamsa *Cinq*

خَمْسَة

خَمْسَة

sitta *Six*

سِتَّة

سِتَّة

sabᶜa *Sept*

سَبْعَة

سَبْعَة

thamâniya *Huit*

ثَمَانِيَة

ثَمَانِيَة

tis[c]a *Neuf*

تِسْعَة

تِسْعَة

[c]achra *Dix*

عَشَرَة

عَشَرَة

 **Recopiez ces proverbes et lisez-les à haute voix :**

man jadda wajada wa man zara^{c}a h̲as̲ada *Qui cherche trouve ! Qui travaille sérieusement récoltera le fruit de ses efforts. (Littéralement : qui travaille avec sérieux trouve ou qui sème récolte)*

مَنْ جَدَّ وَجَدَ وَمَنْ زَرَعَ حَصَدَ

مَنْ جَدَّ وَجَدَ وَمَنْ زَرَعَ حَصَدَ

al jâr qabla addâr warrafiq qabla attarîq *Choisis ta maison en fonction du voisinage et ne voyage qu'en bonne compagnie. (Littéralement : le voisin avant la maison et le compagnon avant le chemin)*

اَلْجَار قَبْلَ الدَّار وَالرَّفِيق قَبْلَ الطَّرِيق

اَلْجَار قَبْلَ الدَّار وَالرَّفِيق قَبْلَ الطَّرِيق

Calligraphie

Qu'est-ce qu'un calame ?

Le mot Calame vient de l'arabe pour certains (avec le sens de plume ou crayon) ou du latin pour d'autres *(calamus)*. Quoi qu'il en soit, le calame est un roseau que l'on taille en pointe et dont on se sert pour l'écriture.

Les premières calligraphies arabes étaient écrites avec le calame. On retrouve d'ailleurs beaucoup d'occurrences de ce mot dans la poésie arabe classique ainsi que dans le Coran.

Il existe plusieurs types de roseaux et par conséquent plusieurs types de calames avec des différences en termes de qualité et de longévité en fonction de l'origine de ces roseaux.

De nos jours, de grandes marques proposent des stylos, munis de pointes biseautées, qui sont dédiés à la calligraphie.

Les différents styles de la calligraphie arabe

Voici une liste non exhaustive des styles de la calligraphie arabe

- **Hijâzî :**
  L'un des styles les plus utilisés dès le début du VIIIe siècle est le style HIJÂZÎ en référence à la partie de la péninsule arabique qui comprend les villes sacrées de l'Islam que sont la Mecque et Médine ainsi que la ville de Djeddah : ***le Hijâz.***

- **Le Koufique (relatif à la ville irakienne de Koufa) :**
  Existe avec des variétés : fleuri, géométrique…
  Style d'écriture autrefois appelé « Hiri » et issu de l'écriture syriaque.

- **Thuluth (relatif au mot arabe thulth = un tiers) :**
  Le Thuluth est une écriture essentiellement utilisée pour la décoration et les finitions. C'est le style le plus ornemental qui existe. L'Andalousie a permis la diffusion de ce style grâce aux prouesses architecturales.

- **Le Naskhi (relatif au mot arabe Nâsikh = copiste) :**
  Le Naskhi est le style par défaut pour les correspondances et circulaires administratives sous les abbasides et plus tard, chez les Ottomans qui le développeront pour le rendre plus élégant. L'arrivée du papier permettra à ce style de devenir le style coranique pendant de nombreux siècles.

- **Le Diwani (relatif à l'arabe diwân = bureau ou administration ayant donné le mot français divan) :**
  Style particulier et très lisible utilisé par l'administration ottomane pour les correspondances et circulaires. La chancellerie l'utilisera aussi plus tard.

Note

La lettre **d̲âd** est la dernière lettre à avoir rejoint l'alphabet arabe. Par ailleurs, aucun autre alphabet ne contient cette lettre. Voilà pourquoi la langue arabe est connue dans le monde comme étant la langue du **D̲ÂD**.

La même expression (la langue arabe اَللُّغَةُ الْعَرَبِيَّةُ) est ici écrite de plusieurs façons différentes :

اللغة العربيّة

اللغة العربيّة

اللغة العربيّة

اللغة العربية

L'expression « au nom de dieu clément et miséricordieux » écrite en diverses calligraphies ornementales :

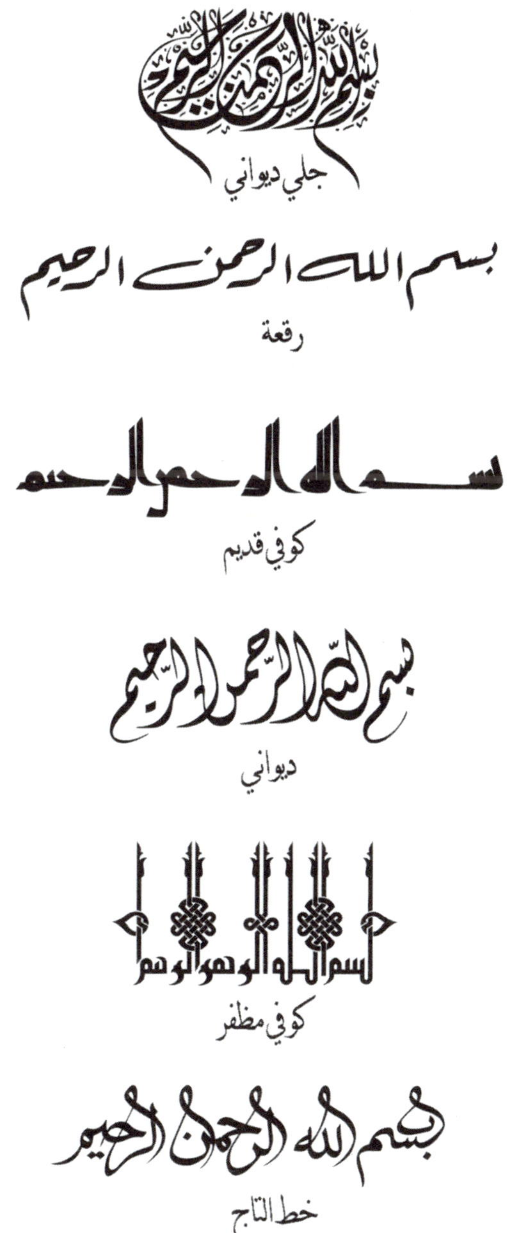

جلي ديواني

رقعة

كوفي قديم

ديواني

كوفي مظفر

خط التاج

خط الثلث

كوفي

كوفي مورق

كوفي معماري

كوفي كلاسيكي

خط الثلث

Bonne chance !

حَظّاً
سَعِيداً

١٤٣٤هـ
عبد الغني بنعلي

Merci beaucoup !

شُكْرًا جَزِيلًا

١٤٣٤هـ

Solutions

Consolidation

Exercice 2 pages 91-96

1 أكل akala *(manger)*
2 شرب chariba *(boire)*
3 جلس jalasa *(s'asseoir)*
4 وقف waqafa *(se lever ou s'arrêter)*
5 ركب rakiba *(monter, prendre)*
6 دخل dakhala *(entrer)*
7 غضب radiba *(s'énerver, se mettre en colère)*
8 ذهب dhahaba (aller)
9 غسل rasala *(laver)*
10 سال sâla *(couler)*
11 ذاب dhâba *(fondre)*
12 قال qâla *(dire)*
13 عاد ᶜâda *(revenir ou rendre visite)*
14 سار sâra *(marcher)*
15 نام nâma *(dormir)*
16 صاح sâha *(crier)*
17 كان kâna *(être)*
18 الآن al'âna *(maintenant)*
19 شكرا choukran *(merci)*
20 بيت bayt *(maison)*
21 وردة warda *(rose)*
22 عين ᶜayn *(œil)*
23 قمر qamar *(lune)*
24 مسجد masjid *(mosquée)*
25 خبز khoubz *(pain)*
26 مكتبة maktaba *(bibliothèque ou librairie)*
27 مطار matâr *(aéroport)*
28 جامعة jâmi'a *(université)*
29 جمل jamal *(dromadaire)*
30 محطّة mahatta *(gare ou station)*
31 درّس darrasa *(enseigner)*
32 تعلّم taᶜallama *(apprendre)*
33 قطار qitâr *(train)*
34 جميلة jamîla *(belle)*
35 الدّرس addars *(la leçon)*
36 الشّمس achchamsou *(le soleil)*
37 طائرة tâ'ira *(avion)*
38 زائر zâ'ir *(visiteur)*
39 بائع bâ'iᶜ *(vendeur)*
40 ممتلئ moumtali' *(plein, rempli)*
41 شيء chay' *(chose)*
42 عشاء ᶜachâ *(dîner)*
43 مساء masâ' *(soir)*
44 رأس ra's *(tête)*
45 رئيس ra'îs *(président)*
46 لؤلؤ lou'lou' *(perle)*
47 مسؤول mas'ûl *(responsable)*
48 سؤال sou'âl *(question)*
49 شؤون chou'ûn *(affaires)*

50 أنيسة anîsa *(prénom féminin qui signifie : bonne compagnie)*

51 فؤاد fouâd *(prénom masculin qui signifie : cœur)*

52 زملاؤه zoumalâouhou *(ses collègues)*

53 مؤلم mou'lim *(douloureux)*

54 مسألة mas'ala *(question = affaire)*

55 شارع chârі^{c} *(rue, avenue, boulevard)*

56 لقاء liqâ' *(rencontre)*

57 جرّيء jirrî' *(audacieux)*

58 جريدة jarîda *(journal)*

59 شاي chây *(thé)*

60 قهوة qahwa *(café)*

61 قبل qabla *(avant)*

62 بعد ba^{c}da *(après)*

63 لـماذا limâdhâ *(pourquoi)*

64 أَيْنَ ayna *(où)*

65 نَعَمْ na^{c}am *(oui)*

66 كَيْفَ kayfa *(comment)*

67 أَلطَّالِبُ attâlibou *(l'étudiant)*

68 مَتَى matâ *(quand)*

69 مَدْرَسَة madrasa *(école)*

70 أَلسَّمَاء assamâ' *(le ciel)*

71 أَلْبَلَد albalad *(le pays)*

72 أَلأَوَّلُ al awwal *(le premier)*

73 أَلأَخِيرُ al akhîr *(le dernier)*

Exercice ❸ page 97 :

1 دَ + رَّ + سَ
2 أَ + خْ + بَ + رَ
3 تَ + عَ + لَّ + مَ
4 تَ + رَ + ا + سَ + لَ
5 اِ + نْ + فَ + تَ + حَ
6 اِ + سْ + تَ + مَ + عَ

Exercice ❹ page 97 :

اَلْكِتابَ al kitâb *(le livre)*

اَلْمَكْتَبُ al maktab *(le bureau)*

اَلْبَحْرِ al bahr *(la mer)*

اَلْوَرَقَةَ al waraqa *(la feuille)*

اَلظَّرْفُ adhdharf *(l'enveloppe)*

Exercice ❺ page 98 :

1 ي + خ + ر + ج
2 ي + د + خ + ل
3 م + غ + ل + ق
4 م + ف + ت + و + ح
5 ي + ع + و + م
6 ي + م + ش + ي
7 ي + ط + ي + ر
8 ا + ل + ب + ن + ت
9 ا + ل + م + ر + أ + ة
10 ر + س + ا + ل + ت + ي

Groupes de lettres

Exercice 3 page 102 :

1	دَرَسَ	2	وَصَلَ
3	دَخَلَ	4	خَرَجَ
5	فَعَلَ	6	نَزَلَ
7	أَكَلَ	8	شَرِبَ
9	ذَهَبَ	10	بَعَثَ

Exercice 4 page 103 :

1 اَلْأَرْض *la terre*

2 اَلْبَارِدُ *le froid*

3 اَلظَّبْيُ *la gazelle*

4 اَلْبَشَرُ *l'humain*

5 اَلْغَارُ *la grotte*

6 اَلصَّدِيقُ *l'ami*

7 اَلنُّجُومُ *les étoiles*

8 اَلْحَقُّ *la vérité*

9 اَلْعَدْلُ *la justice*

10 اَلْقَلَمُ *le stylo / le crayon*

11 اَلْمَاءُ *l'eau*

12 اَلضَّيْفُ *l'invité*

13 اَلشَّايُ *le thé*

14 اَللُّغَةُ *la langue (pas l'organe)*

15 اَلذَّهَبُ *l'or*

16 اَلسَّمَكُ *le poisson*

17 اَلْحَافِلَةُ *l'autobus*

18 اَلْهَاتِفُ *le téléphone*

Exercice 5 page 105 :

1	ب + ت + ث	12	ف + ك + ر
2	م + ل + ح	13	ح + ج + ج
3	ق + ن + ص	14	س + ي + ط
4	ن + ص + ب	15	ض + ل + ع
5	ق + ط + ب	16	ك + ف + ي
6	س + و + ي	17	ج + ي + دً + ا
7	ف + ه + م	18	أَ + هْ + ل + اً
8	وَ + سَ + هْ + ل + اً	19	مَ + رْ + حَ + بً + ا
9	حَ + سَ + نً + ا	20	حَ + سَ + ن
10	جِ + دًّ + ا	21	ف + قَ + طْ
11	عَ + ف + وً + ا	22	مُ + هِ + مًّ + ا

Crédits : © Abdelghani Benali.

Création et réalisation : MediaSarbacane

Dépôt légal : mars 2013

N° d'édition : 4357 - août 2024

ISBN : 978-2-7005-8155-3

www.assimil.com

Imprimé en Roumanie par Master Print

LA 411®

PRODUCTION RESOURCE • VOL. 31 2010 EDITION

WWW.LA411.COM

THE PROFESSIONAL REFERENCE GUIDE FOR FILM, TELEVISION, COMMERCIAL AND MUSIC VIDEO PRODUCTION

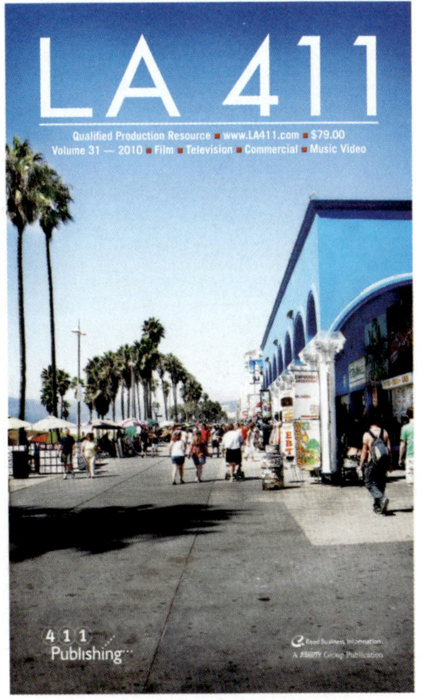

Cover photo by Michael Rueter
Michael Rueter Photography/L.A.-N.Y.

411 Publishing Company, 5900 Wilshire Boulevard, 31st Fl., Los Angeles, California 90036 USA
411 Publishing Book Sales
(323) 617-9400
411 Publishing Editorial
(323) 617-9402 FAX (323) 617-9534
411 Publishing Advertising Sales:
(323) 617-9415
www.la411.com

A VARIETY Group Publication

Letter From the Publisher and Editorial Staff

LA 411

Dear Customer,

Despite the hardships on the local film, TV and commercial production community due to recession and runaway production throughout 2009, Los Angles remains the unequivocal leader when it comes to production facilities, support services, richness of locations and most importantly, a skilled and experienced crew base.

And although there are other directories that can give you information on production services, 411 remains the only "Qualified" directory, in which every company and individual is required to submit professional references that are contacted by our editorial staff for verification.

To emphasize L.A.'s continued status as the world's film center, we've chosen "Classic L.A. Movie Locations" as the theme for our tab features. We've matched some of the areas most unique and iconic locations with great scenes from films or TV shows that were shot at those locations. We start with L.A.'s City Hall and Jack Webb's 1950s "Dragnet" introduction and end with a scene from 2009 indie favorite "(500) Days of Summer," shot inside downtown L.A.'s architectural gem, The Bradbury Building.

Recognizing the technical advancements taking place in the industry, we've expanded our High-Def section to include 3D and Digital Cinema, adding new categories such as Digital Cinema/3D Exhibition and Digital Cinema Packages & Post Production. Other new categories that have recently been added or expanded are: Prop Houses, DVD/Blu-Ray Authoring & Replication, Green Screens, Traffic Control & Barricades, Budgeting & Scheduling, Tax Incentive Services, Aerial Picture Vehicles, Firearms & Weapons and Steadicam Operators.

On our website, check out some of our latest features which include a "Request for Quote" service and "Tech Tips," short video primers that highlight the latest developments affecting the film production community. And be sure to sign up to receive our monthly "411 Newsletter," which in the past year has featured articles on the below-the-line talent behind such films and TV shows as "Mad Men," "Breaking Bad" and "G-Force."

Please know that we are here to support the Los Angeles production community. If you have suggestions for new categories, comments on our print & online directories or general feedback, please drop them in our e-suggestion box: suggestions@411publishing.com.

Thank you,

Sean Killebrew
Publisher

Steve Atinsky
Senior Editor

The listings are organized into 10 general tabbed sections and divided within the sections by category. The section Advertising Agencies and Production Companies, for example, contains categories relating to pre-production, such as Commercial Directors and Storyboard Artists, while the Post Production tab contains categories such as Post Houses and Duplication. Descriptions have been included in those categories and listings where the editors felt that additional information was needed. These descriptions are included soley at the discretion of the editors of LA 411.

Some of the categories in LA 411 are 'built' from other categories. For example, the listings in Composers & Sound Designers are drawn from the composer and sound designer rosters of the Music Production & Sound Design category. This makes it easier to find a composer, editor, commercial or music video director, because they are built into their own index of sorts. The 'built' categories are: Commercial Directors, Music Video Directors, Composers & Sound Designers and Editors; these categories also contain freelancers.

You will find three indices bound at the front of the book. The General Index uses keywords and cross-referencing to help you find whatever service or item you require. The Company/Crew index has the companies and crew who are listed in the book. And, of course, an Advertiser's Index is included.

LA 411 has several charts, digests and miscellaneous resources that may come in handy during your production. Look to the back of the Crew Section to find employment guidelines for child and adult players, as well as your trusty crew. In Sets & Stages, you'll find our extensive stage chart and a handy standing sets chart. In the front matter, you'll find sunrise and sunset times, holidays, festival and awards dates and a list of charitable organizations, some of which will accept your production's excess food. There is also a list of bookstores that sell our directories.

Information about listing, advertising and ordering LA 411 can be found in the front of the book. You can always call our office at (323) 617-9402 for guidance or user assistance.

How to Advertise in LA 411

411 Publishing offers a variety of ad packages in our print and online directories.

Because we strive to maintain a balance of editorial content and advertising in our print directories, ad space is limited. Additionally, since key spots, including tabs, go quickly, we recommend that you reserve space early for the 2011 edition.

Among the options that will increase your company's prominence in our online directory are:

IPL or Impact Listing: Puts you in the blue section at the top of all searches. Also includes 10 search terms.

EDP or Enhanced Dedicated Page: A listing page on which you can provide expanded copy about your company, as well download images and documents. Includes a red arrow next to your name on the list.

Premium IPL: This is a combination of the IPL and EDP options.

411 Features: Have you produced a video showcasing your products and/or services? 411 Features will give you the opportunity to display that video exclusively in your category, on your listing page and on the Home Page (in rotation with other videos).

To become an online advertiser or to learn more about our print and online advertising programs please call us at (323) 617-9415.

To Update Your Current Listing

LA 411 sends out an e-mail in the summer to every company listed in the book prompting you to make changes to your existing listing. If at any time you wish to update your current listing, please send us an e-mail at 411update@reedbusiness.com.

You can also go to **www.la411.com** and click the "Edit Your Listing" tab in the upper right corner where you will be prompted to enter your User Name and password for verification. Your User Name is the e-mail address that you have provided us for contacting you. If you are unsure what your User Name is, or if you need to be issued one, please e-mail us at 411update@reedbusiness.com. If you are unsure what your password is, use the "Forgot Password" link and we'll send this information to you. Please note: the e-mail you enter to request your password must match your User Name e-mail.

Unless you are applying for a NEW CATEGORY please do not fill out a new application, as you will be charged for something you already have. There is no charge for changes to existing listings. You may also download an application or apply online at **www.la411.com.**

How to Get Listed in LA 411

LA 411

Since our first edition in 1980, 411's editorial staff has meticulously researched and verified that every listing is qualified to be included in our directories and on our Web sites. We reserve the right to remove and/or requalify listings at any time.

Listing Requirements:

1. For LA 411: Applicants must be located in Southern California (Los Angeles, Orange, Riverside, Santa Barbara, San Bernardino, San Diego or Ventura counties). For the majority of our categories, work must be performed in the aforementioned areas.

For New York 411: Applicants must be located in the Tri State (New York, New Jersey and Connecticut) or Philadelphia areas. For the majority of our categories, work must be performed in the aforementioned areas.

2. You are allowed to apply for up to five (5) categories.

3. All applicants must include a current resume or letter on company letterhead OR you may create a text version in our online application process.

4. You must complete the application in full including three (3) local references for each category for which you believe you are qualified and in which you would like to appear. Call sheets, contracts or pay stubs are also acceptable.

5. 411 reserves the right to ask for additional references if those given are not verifiable or do not meet our professional guidelines.

6. References must be for film, television or commercials:
- Films must have a minimum two-week theatrical release.
- TV & commercials must be for Broadcast or Cable Networks. Local cable credits are not acceptable

Internet credits are only acceptable when produced for AMPTP affiliated companies--Studios, Broadcast Networks, certain Cable Networks and Independent Producers.

- Film & TV references are preferred but not required for a limited number of Location & Production Support categories such as Car Rentals, Travel Agencies, Notaries, etc.

7. All applicants must pay an application fee of $200 for a new application and $50 for each additional category. Applicants can pay by credit card or business check. **All application fees are non-refundable regardless of whether an application is eventually accepted or not**. Listings are editorial content and have no monetary value.

8. A separate application must be submitted for each 411 directory you wish to be listed in.

9. Advertising with 411 has no bearing on listing approvals. As you do not have to be a qualified listee to advertise, advertisers do not automatically qualify for listings.

10. No special provisions—such as additional text—can be provided in listings. No exceptions.

11. We only list companies by their actual business name. You may be asked to provide a copy of your state/city business license to confirm your name. A DBA or fictitious business name statement is NOT acceptable.

12. You may apply at any time. However, to be included in the next book, completed applications must be received prior to the advertised deadline. 411 will process your application as fast as possible. During season, this may take upwards of several weeks. Please be patient.

13. Applicants may be required to complete a phone interview with our editors.

14. The 411 Publishing editorial staff has final say in all matters regarding what goes into our directories and our Web sites. 411 Publishing reserves the right to review, confirm, edit and/or omit any listing or Enhanced Dedicated Page in whole or in part at our discretion.

15. NOT ALL APPLICANTS WILL QUALIFY.

16. You must provide at least three references per category AND pay your application fee BEFORE we can begin processing your application.

Applications can be found on our website la411.com. Select the "Apply to Be Listed" tab at the top of the Hompage and download a PDF of our application. You can also submit an application using our online system.

Submit your completed application and any additional materials you need to send for verification to: Application Dept., LA 411 Publishing Co., 5900 Wilshire Blvd., 31st Fl., Los Angeles, CA 90036

Or fax it to us at: (303) 265-2852

If you have questions call us at: (323) 617-9404

Application for LA 411® Freelance or Business Listing

SUBMITTING AN APPLICATION DOES NOT GUARANTEE A LISTING.

PRINT BOOK DEADLINE: FRIDAY JULY 16, 2010

The application fee for LA411 is $200 for the first category and $50 for each additional category.* **The fee is non-refundable. Submitting an application does not guarantee a listing.** Listings have no monetary value. You are allowed to apply for up to five categories. You may apply at any time, however to be considered for the next printed book we must have your completed materials by Friday, July 16, 2010. Listings will appear both in print and online. ***Application fee waived for advertisers.**

☐ Enclosed is my application fee for $________ for my listing(s) ($200 First/$50 ea. addl.) Number of Listings:______ (Limit 5)

☐ Please send me________ copies of the 2010 LA 411 for $49 plus 9.25% sales tax & s/h ($7 per copy) $________

(This is a special rate that is $30 off the regular price!)

Payment Info (Check or credit card only. No cash.) Total:________

☐Visa ☐MC ☐Amex Card#____________ Expires______ Name on Card__________

Cardholder Signature____________ or Check#____________

(make checks payable to 411 Publishing)

☐ Please contact me regarding display advertising or enhanced listing advertising

General Information Required

First Name ________ Last Name ________

Company Name ________ Type of Business ________

Street Address ________ Apt./Suite Number ________

City ________ ZIP Code ________ Print This Address? Yes ☐ or No ☐

( ) Local Phone Number ______ ( ) Additional Phone ______ ( ) Fax Number ______

@ E-mail Address (To be published) ________ www. Web Address ________

@ E-mail Address (For our contact purposes) ________

All information contained in every listing appears in print and online without exception

Requirements for Listing With L.A. 411

Three Recent Project References Required per Category

- Advertising with 411 has no bearing on listing approvals. You do not have to be a qualified listee to advertise. Advertisers do not automatically qualify for listings. Listings are editorial content and have no monetary value.
- You must complete this application—**ONLY COMPLETE APPLICATIONS WITH PAYMENT WILL BE CONSIDERED—**and **mail** it to: Application Dept., LA 411 Publishing Co., 5900 Wilshire Blvd., 31st Fl., Los Angeles, CA 90036.
- You must be located in Southern California (Los Angeles, Orange, Riverside, San Diego, Santa Barbara, San Bernardino, and Ventura counties).
- Please enclose a current resume and/or a letter written on your company letterhead explaining who you are, the services your company provides, why you belong in the categories you are applying for and how long you've been in business.
- **References are required** and must be from a variety of local advertising agencies, film, TV, commercial production companies or music video production companies for work you we hired to perform in the past twelve months. References will be contacted by phone. Call sheets, contracts, invoices or pay stubs are also acceptable.
- **You must submit three references for each category that you are applying for.** References may be repeated if you performed more than one service for a particular company.
- Applicants may be required to complete an interview with our editors. 411 editorial staff has final say in all matters regarding what goes into our directories and on our Web sites. **Not all applicants will qualify.** For a complete list of application requirements go to www.la411.com and click on the "Apply to be Listed" tab at the top of the page.

LA 411 Publishing Co., 5900 Wilshire Blvd., 31st Fl., Los Angeles, CA 90036 TEL (323) 617-9404 FAX (323) 617-9534

List categories for which you are applying: ______________________________

____

LA 411® CATEGORY LIST BY TAB SECTION

AD AGENCIES & PRODUCTION COS.
Advertising Agencies
Advertising Agency Freelance Producers
Animation Production Companies
Bidders
Commercial Directors
Commercial Production Companies
Corporate & Video Production Companies
Independent Sales Reps
Infomercial Production Companies
Movie & TV Marketing Companies
Music Video Directors
Music Video Production Companies
Production Offices
Promo Production Companies
Public Relations
Storyboard Artists
Trailer Production Companies

POST PRODUCTION
Audio Post Facilities
Commercial Editorial Houses
Composers/Sound Designers & Sound Editors
Computer Graphics & Visual FX
Digital Intermediates
Duplication
DVD/Blu-Ray, Authoring & Replication
Editing Equipment Rentals & Sales
Editors
Film & Tape Storage
Film Laboratories—Motion Picture
Film Laboratories—Still Photography
Mobile Video Units, Satellite & Transmission Services
Music Libraries & Publishing
Music Production & Sound Design
Opticals
Post Houses
Post Production Supervisors
Quality Control (QC)
Screening Rooms
Stock Footage & Photos
Titling, Captioning & Broadcast Design
Visual FX Artists
Visual FX Supervisors & Producers

SETS & STAGES
Backings & Scenic Artists
Green Screens
Set Design, Construction & Rentals
Set Sketchers
Stages
Stages—Portable
Standing Sets
TV Studios

LOCATION SERVICES & EQUIPMENT
Air Charters
Air Freight & Courier Services
Airlines
Airport Shuttles
Airports
Bus Charters
Car Dealerships
Car Rentals
Caterers
Communications Equipment
Consulates General
Crating & Packing
Custom Brokers & Carnets
Film Commissions & Permit Offices—California
Film Commissions—International
Film Commissions—North America
Hotels & Short-Term Housing
Limousine & Car Services
Location Libraries
Location Management & Scouts
Locations
Motorhomes & Portable Dressing Rooms
Moving, Storage & Transportation
Permit Services
Portable Restrooms
Production Services—International
Production Services—North America
Ranches
Security & Bodyguards
Specialty Transportation
Theaters & Stadiums
Traffic Control & Barricades
Travel Agencies
Weather

PRODUCTION SUPPORT
Acting/Dialect Coaches
Animals & Trainers
Budgeting & Scheduling
Casting Directors
Casting Facilities
Choreographers
Computer Consultants & Software
Computers, Office Equipment & Supplies
Digital Casting & Video Conferencing
Directories & Trade Publications
Entertainment Attorneys
Extras Casting Agencies
Finance
Hand & Leg Models
Insurance Brokers & Guarantors
Janitorial & Strike Services
Large Scale Event Planning
Libraries, Research & Clearance
Massage Therapists
Messenger Services
Nautical Film Services & Coordination
Notaries
Payroll & Production Accountants
Promotional Products
Stunt Coordinators—Aerial & Specialty
Stunt Coordinators & Performance Drivers
Stunt Equipment
Talent & Modeling Agencies
Tax Incentive Services
Technical Advisors
Transcription & Secretarial Services
Translation & Interpretation Services
Wrap Party Locations

CAMERA & SOUND EQUIPMENT
Aerial Equipment
Aerial—Fixed Wing & Helicopter Pilots
Camera Cars & Tracking Vehicles
Camera Rentals—Motion Picture
Camera Rentals—Still Photography
Motion Control
Music Playback Services
Raw Stock
Sound Equipment Rentals & Sales
Teleprompting Services & Cue Cards
Video Assist Services
Video Cameras & Equipment
Video Display, Playback & Projection

HIGH DEF, DIGITAL CINEMA & 3D
Digital Cinema/3D Exhibition
Digital Cinema Content Mgmt. & Storage Manufacturers
Digital Cinema Packages/Post
HD/3D Cameras & Equipment
HD Duplication
HD Editing Equipment
HD Equipment Manufacturers
HD Post Houses
HD Screening Rooms
HD Stock Footage
HD Tape Stock

GRIP & LIGHTING EQUIPMENT
Booms, Cranes & Camera Support
Climate Control Systems
Construction & Yard Equipment Rentals
Grip & Lighting Expendables
Grip Equipment
Hoisting & Lift Equipment/ Cherry Pickers
Lighting Equipment & Generators
Production Equipment & Accessories
Trucks & Vans

PROPS & WARDROBE
Aerial Picture Vehicles
Animatronics, Puppets & Makeup FX
Art Fabrication, Licensing & Rentals
Arts & Crafts Supplies
Atmospheric/Lighting FX & Pyrotechnics
Boats & Nautical Props
Building/Surface Materials & Hardware
Canopies & Tents
Car Prep, Rigging & Prototypes
Color-Correct Props
Costume Makers & Rentals
Draperies & Window Treatments
Dry Cleaners
Eyewear & Jewelry
Fabrics
Firearms & Weapons
Flags, Graphics & Signage
Flowers, Greens & Plants
Foam
Furniture Rentals & Accessories
Games, Toys & Amusements
Glass
Hair, Makeup & Wardrobe Supplies
Ice
Medical & Scientific Props
Musical Instrument Rentals
Neon
Photo, Video & Electronic Props
Picture Vehicles
Plastics, Plexiglas & Fiberglass
Product Placement
Prop Fabrication & Mechanical FX
Prop Houses
Restaurant & Kitchen Equipment
Specialty Props
Sport Vehicle Rentals
Sporting Goods
Studio Prop Rentals
Studio Services
Tailoring & Alterations
Uniforms & Surplus
Vintage Clothing & Accessories
Water Trucks

CREW
Agents, Reps & Job Referral Services
Ambulance/Paramedics & Nurses
Art Directors/Production Designers
Baby Wranglers
Camera Assistants
Camera Operators
Camera Operators—Steadicam
Craft Service
Digital Imaging Technicians
Directors of Photography
First Assistant Directors
Food Stylists & Home Economists
Gaffers & Lighting Directors
Grips
Hair & Makeup Artists
Producers
Production Coordinators
Production Managers
Production Stills Photographers
Prop Masters
Prosthetics
Script Supervisors
Second Assistant Directors
Set Decorators
Sound Mixers
Studio Teachers/Welfare Workers
Trade Associations/Unions
Transportation Captains
Underwater Technicians
VTR Operators
Wardrobe Stylists/ Costume Designers

CITY GUIDE (ONLINE ONLY)
Attractions
Bars and Clubs
Bookstores
Car Rentals
Domestic Personnel
Flowers and Gifts
Grocery Stores and Farmers Markets
Health and Fitness
Home Rental and Online Leasing Resources
Hotels
Limousine Services
Movie Theaters
Party Resources
Pet Services
Real Estate Agents and Agencies
Restaurant Delivery Services
Restaurant Roundup
Short-Term Furnished & Corporate Housing
Spas & Salons

For detailed information about reference requirements please call: (323) 617-9404 or go to www.LA411.com & click on the Apply to Be Listed tab.

Ordering Information

Complete this form and send with your payment to:
Attn: Book Sales Dept. 411 Publishing, 5900 Wilshire Blvd., 31st Fl., Los Angeles, CA 90036
or order through our online store at www.la411.com

For credit card orders, air and international shipments or questions call: (323) 617-9400 or contact Juliette Nichols at jnichols@reedbusiness.com. Credit card orders received by 12:00 noon PST will be shipped via FedEx that day. Please allow five working days for delivery on all orders.

Quantity	Item		Price	Tax	Shipping	Total
	LA 411 2010	(CA or NY orders)	$79.00	$7.30	$7.00	
		(Elsewhere)		$0.00	$7.00	
	New York 411 2009/2010	(CA or NY orders)	$59.00	$4.94	$6.00	
		(Elsewhere)		$0.00	$6.00	

Make checks payable to 411 Publishing Company.

____
Name/Title

____
Company/Profession

____
Address (No P.O. Boxes Please) City

____
State Zip Code Telephone

Retail Outlets Where 411 Directories Can Be Purchased

Biz Books	302 W. Cordova, Vancouver, BC	(604) 669-6431
Book Soup	8818 Sunset Blvd., West Hollywood, CA	(310) 659-3110
Cinema Books	4753 Roosevelt Way, Seattle, WA	(206) 547-7667
Diesel, A Bookstore	3890 Cross Creek Rd., Malibu, CA	(310) 456-9961
Diesel, A Bookstore	225 26th St., Ste. 33, Brentwood, CA	(310) 576-9960
The Drama Bookshop	250 W. 40th St., New York, NY	(212) 944-0595
Hennessey & Ingalls	1520 N. Cahuenga Blvd., Hollywood, CA	(323) 466-1256
Larry Edmunds Bookshop	6644 Hollywood Blvd., Hollywood, CA	(323) 463-3273
McNally Robinson Booksellers	1090 Don Mills Road, Toronto, ON	(416) 384-0084
New York University Book Center	18 Washington Pl., New York, NY	(212) 998-4667
Samuel French	7623 Sunset Blvd., Hollywood, CA	(323) 876-0570
Shakespeare & Co.	716 Broadway, New York, NY	(212) 529-1330
Showbiz Solutions	500 S. Sepulveda Blvd., Los Angeles, CA	(310) 440-9600
Skylight Books	1818 N. Vermont Ave., Los Angeles, CA	(323) 660-1175
University Bookstore, USC	840 Childsway, Los Angeles, CA	(213) 740-0066
Tattered Cover Book Store	1628 16th St., Denver, CO	(303) 436-1070
Vroman's Bookstore	695 E. Colorado Blvd., Pasadena, CA	(626) 449-5320
World Book & News	1652 N. Cahuenga Blvd., Hollywood, CA	(323) 465-4352
The Writer's Store	2040 Westwood Blvd., Los Angeles, CA	(310) 441-5151

Our directories are also available at the following major chains:

Amazon
Barnes & Noble
Borders

Call your local store to check on availability or to place an order.

* For more immediate service, order now at http://store.resource411.com/ or contact Juliette Nichols at (323) 917-9400 or jnichols@reedbusiness.com

The Los Angeles region is the entertainment production capital of the world—with good reason. No other area can match the talent of L.A.'s casts and crews, industry resources, diverse locations and great weather. Add to this a permit coordination process streamlined by FilmL.A. and it's no wonder why the region sees more days of film production than anywhere else.

Working with FilmL.A., Inc.

FilmL.A. is a private, nonprofit organization that coordinates and processes permits for on-location motion picture, television and commercial production under contract to the City of Los Angeles, Los Angeles County, and the cities of Diamond Bar, La Habra Heights, Lancaster, Palmdale, South Gate and The City of Industry. Non-municipal clients include the Angeles National Forest, the Burbank Unified School District, La Cañada Unified School District, Lawndale Elementary School District, Los Angeles Unified School District and San Gabriel Unified School District.

Ongoing community relations is a key component of the service FilmL.A. provides. The organization works to strike a balance between the needs and interests of the entertainment industry and the neighborhoods affected by on-location production.

FilmL.A.'s services help the region stay competitive in today's global entertainment production market. In 2008 alone, FilmL.A. coordinated nearly 48,000 days of on-location production.

Determining if You Need a Permit to Film

A permit is required for filming any commercial, motion picture, television program, advertisement, music video, or other similar production outside of the confines of a certified studio. A permit is also required for commercial still photography.

Obtaining a Permit

FilmL.A.'s website (www.filmla.com) provides the most up-to-date source of information on how to obtain an on-location production permit. A short guide highlighting key elements of the permit process is reprinted here for your convenience. Comprehensive process guides are also available on the "Film Permits" page in the "For Filmmakers" section of FilmL.A.'s website.

Insurance

Every permit application must include a valid certificate of insurance naming specific "additional insureds." Minimum coverage requirements are specified by City, County or other permit jurisdictions. FilmL.A. staff members are available to help you identify your film insurance needs.

Application

Film permit applicants may apply for permits online through FilmL.A.'s state-of-the-art Online Permit System (OPS), which allows users to track permit progress and status of agency approvals in real-time and download paid-for and finalized permits at their convenience. Applications may also be submitted in person, via fax or by email.

Your Production Coordinator

Once your application has been accepted, a FilmL.A. Production Coordinator will be assigned to your project. Your coordinator will be available to assist you from pre-production through wrap on the last day of your permit. He/she will collaborate with local authorities, making every effort to ensure that your permit is fulfilled, while minimizing the impact your activities could cause to the surrounding community.

Other Planning Resources

FilmL.A.'s Production Planning Team is available to help filmmakers navigate a host of pre-permitting location issues. Staffed by experienced production coordinators, the team is standing by to help you deal with planning issues long before you're ready to apply for your next permit. The team can provide immediate answers to questions involving: parking, lane and street closures, reservations at City Hall, Lincoln Heights Jail, Los Angeles County Beaches and many other issues. FilmL.A. also maintains LocoScout, an online location library focused on schools and publicly-owned properties available for filming.

Special Accommodations

In the areas served by FilmL.A., standard production days are Monday through Friday, and the normal hours of film activity are from 7 a.m. to 10 p.m. in areas where people live. The hours noted on every film permit specify arrival and departure times for production company personnel. Any filming activity outside of normal production hours usually requires that affected residents be surveyed to identify specific concerns or problems with the proposed activities. Surveys may also be required when filmmakers request to film on weekends in residential areas, seek permits to film at locations for extended durations, close streets or potentially interfere with merchant activity, or conduct exceptional activities (e.g., gunfire, explosions, aerial work, etc.). FilmL.A. does not provide survey services but does require that surveys are performed with specific forms. Typically, a production company will have its staff go door-to-door in the affected area and collect the surrounding neighbors' specific concerns, which will then be addressed in the permit process.

Application Fees

The easiest way to pay for and take delivery of your permit is to take advantage of FilmL.A.'s Permits on Account program, which allows credit-worthy customers to receive permits and be invoiced at a later time. FilmL.A.'s coordination fees, as well as fees required for official personnel (e.g., Fire Department staff) may be paid together in a single transaction, and non-credit customers can pay by cash, cashier's check, or money order. Business checks are also accepted from production companies that hold long-term insurance.

Neighborhood Notification

FilmL.A.'s permit coordination service includes notifying local residents and businesses about upcoming on-location production. In addition, FilmL.A. serves as a central contact for all neighborhood inquiries and complaint resolution.

FilmL.A. employs a team of experienced notification personnel, many of whom are bilingual. They make sure that FilmL.A.'s familiar door hangers are distributed to every neighbor within 500 feet of permitted filming activity and within 200 feet of production-related parking. Unusual activities such as gunfire, explosions and helicopter work often require notification on a larger scale, depending on the extent of the activities requested. FilmL.A. also offers eNotification in select areas for those who prefer to receive notices electronically.

FilmL.A.'s goal is to perform notification two days before production activity is scheduled to begin. This includes any substantial prep work that requires more than one large equipment vehicle parked on the street.

Other Locations

Some incorporated cities within L.A. County operate their own film offices, while others coordinate filming through their respective city departments. Requirements for filming in these areas differ. As a courtesy to the industry, FilmL.A. provides contact information for Southern California film offices outside its service area.

FilmL.A., Inc.
1201 W. 5th St., Ste. T-800
Los Angeles, CA 90017
Tel: (213) 977-8600
Fax: (213) 977-8610
Fax (permits): (213) 977-8601
www.filmla.com

Please see the FilmL.A. web site for driving directions and parking options.

Charities

This is just a small sampling of groups that offer assistance to those in need in the L.A area. Some of these organizations work to get excess food to the area's hungry. With the help of this list, if there is more food on set than your crew could eat, you can give one of these organizations a call.

AIDS Project Los Angeles
(213) 201-1600
www.apla.org

American Humane Association
(800) 227-4645
www.americanhumane.org/film

Angel Harvest
(323) 256-6881
www.angelharvest.org

Audrey Hepburn Children's Fund
(310) 393-5331
www.audreyhepburn.com

Autism Speaks
(212) 252-8584
www.autismspeaks.org

Camp Laurel
(626) 683-0800
www.camplaurel.org

Children of the Night
(818) 908-4474
www.childrenofthenight.org

Childrens Hospital Los Angeles
(323) 660-2450
www.childrenshospitalla.org

City of Hope
(800) 720-6824
(626) 256-4673
www.cityofhope.org

Covenant House California
(323) 461-3131
www.covdove.org

Daniel Pearl Foundation
(310) 441-1400
(877) 968-7429
www.danielpearl.org

Food Forward
(818) 530-4125
www.foodforward.org

Elizabeth Glaser Pediatric AIDS Foundation
(310) 314-1459
www.pedaids.org

Heal the Bay
(310) 451-1500
www.healthebay.org

Hollywood for Habitat for Humanity
(310) 323-4663
www.hollywoodforhabitat.com

The Humane Society of the United States
(202) 452-1100
www.hsushollywood.org

Inner-City Arts
(213) 627-9621
www.inner-cityarts.org

Jewish Family Service of Los Angeles (JFS)
(323) 761-8800
www.jfsla.org

The Leeza Gibbons Memory Foundation
(888) OK-Leeza
www.leezasplace.org

Literacy Network of Greater Los Angeles
(213) 237-6643
www.literacynetwork.org

Make-a-Wish Foundation of Greater Los Angeles
(310) 788-9474
(800) 322-9474
www.wishla.org

Much Love Animals Rescue
(310) 636-9115
www.muchlove.org

National Multiple Sclerosis Society (Southern CA Chapter)
(310) 479-4456
www.nationalmssociety.org/cal or
www.msevents.com

PAWS/LA
(323) 464-7297
www.pawsla.org

A Place Called Home (APCH)
(323) 232-7653
www.apch.org

Project Angel Food
922 Vine St.
(323) 845-1800
www.projectangelfood.org

St. Jude Children's Research Hospital
(800) 822-6344
www.stjude.org

spcaLA (Society for the Prevention of Cruelty to Animals LA)
(323) 730-5300, (888) SPCA-LA1
www.spcaLA.com

Union Rescue Mission
(213) 347-6300
www.unionrescuemission.org

Variety—The Children's Charity of the United States
(323) 655-1547
www.usvariety.org

2010 Sunrises & Sunsets/Pacific Standard Time

This table is based on sunrise and sunset times for Los Angeles, California. LA 411 recommends that the reader double-check any sunrise or sunset time with the day's local newspaper or with a weather service.

	JANUARY		FEBRUARY		MARCH		APRIL		MAY		JUNE	
	Rise A.M.	Set P.M.	Rise A.M.	Set P.M.	Rise A.M.	Set P.M.	Rise A.M.	Set P.M.	Rise A.M.	Set P.M.	Rise A.M.	Set P.M.
1	6:59	4:55	6:51	5:24	6:22	5:50	6:41	7:14	6:04	7:37	5:43	8:00
2	6:59	4:56	6:50	5:25	6:21	5:51	6:39	7:15	6:03	7:38	5:43	8:00
3	7:00	4:57	6:49	5:26	6:20	5:52	6:38	7:16	6:02	7:39	5:42	8:01
4	7:00	4:58	6:48	5:27	6:18	5:52	6:37	7:17	6:01	7:40	5:42	8:02
5	7:00	4:58	6:47	5:28	6:17	5:53	6:35	7:17	6:00	7:41	5:42	8:02
6	7:00	4:59	6:47	5:29	6:16	5:54	6:34	7:18	5:59	7:41	5:42	8:03
7	7:00	5:00	6:46	5:30	6:14	5:55	6:33	7:19	5:58	7:42	5:42	8:03
8	7:00	5:01	6:45	5:31	6:13	6:56	6:31	7:20	5:57	7:43	5:42	8:04
9	7:00	5:02	6:44	5:32	6:12	6:56	6:30	7:20	5:57	7:44	5:42	8:04
10	7:00	5:03	6:43	5:33	6:11	6:57	6:29	7:21	5:56	7:44	5:41	8:05
11	7:00	5:04	6:42	5:34	6:08	6:58	6:27	7:22	5:55	7:45	5:41	8:05
12	6:59	5:05	6:41	5:35	6:08	6:59	6:26	7:23	5:54	7:46	5:41	8:05
13	6:59	5:05	6:40	5:36	6:07	6:00	6:25	7:23	5:53	7:47	5:41	8:06
14	6:59	5:06	6:39	5:36	7:05	7:00	6:24	7:24	5:53	7:47	5:41	8:06
15	6:59	5:07	6:38	5:37	7:04	7:01	6:22	7:25	5:52	7:48	5:42	8:07
16	6:59	5:08	6:37	5:38	7:03	7:02	6:21	7:26	5:51	7:49	5:42	8:07
17	6:58	5:09	6:36	5:39	7:01	7:03	6:20	7:27	5:50	7:50	5:42	8:07
18	6:58	5:10	6:35	5:40	7:00	7:04	6:19	7:27	5:50	7:50	5:42	8:07
19	6:58	5:11	6:34	5:41	6:58	7:04	6:18	7:28	5:49	7:51	5:42	8:08
20	6:57	5:12	6:33	5:42	6:57	7:05	6:16	7:29	5:48	7:52	5:42	8:08
21	6:57	5:13	6:32	5:43	6:56	7:06	6:15	7:30	5:48	7:53	5:42	8:08
22	6:56	5:14	6:31	5:44	6:54	7:07	6:14	7:30	5:47	7:53	5:43	8:08
23	6:56	5:15	6:29	5:45	6:53	7:07	6:13	7:31	5:47	7:54	5:43	8:09
24	6:56	5:16	6:28	5:46	6:52	7:08	6:12	7:32	5:46	7:55	5:43	8:09
25	6:55	5:17	6:27	5:46	6:50	7:09	6:11	7:33	5:46	7:55	5:43	8:09
26	6:54	5:18	6:26	5:47	6:49	7:10	6:09	7:34	5:45	7:56	5:44	8:09
27	6:54	5:19	6:25	5:48	6:48	7:11	6:08	7:34	5:45	7:57	5:44	8:09
28	6:53	5:20	6:23	5:49	6:46	7:11	6:07	7:35	5:44	7:57	5:44	8:09
29	6:53	5:21			6:45	7:12	6:06	7:36	5:44	7:58	5:45	8:09
30	6:52	5:22			6:43	7:13	6:05	7:37	5:44	7:59	5:45	8:09
31	6:51	5:23			6:42	7:14			5:43	7:59		

2010 Sunrises & Sunsets/Pacific Standard Time

This table is based on sunrise and sunset times for Los Angeles, California. LA 411 recommends that the reader double-check any sunrise or sunset time with the day's local newspaper or with a weather service.

	JULY		AUGUST		SEPTEMBER		OCTOBER		NOVEMBER		DECEMBER	
	Rise A.M.	Set P.M.	Rise A.M.	Set P.M.	Rise A.M.	Set P.M.	Rise A.M.	Set P.M.	Rise A.M.	Set P.M.	Rise A.M.	Set P.M.
1	5:46	8:09	6:05	7:54	6:27	7:19	6:48	6:38	7:13	6:00	6:41	4:44 PM
2	5:46	8:09	6:06	7:53	6:28	7:18	6:49	6:36	7:14	6:00	6:42	4:44 PM
3	5:47	8:09	6:06	7:53	6:28	7:17	6:49	6:35	7:15	5:59	6:43	4:44 PM
4	5:47	8:09	6:07	7:52	6:29	7:15	6:50	6:33	7:16	5:58	6:44	4:44 PM
5	5:48	8:08	6:08	7:51	6:30	7:14	6:51	6:32	7:17	5:57	6:44	4:44 PM
6	5:48	8:08	6:08	7:50	6:31	7:12	6:52	6:31	7:18	5:56	6:45	4:44 PM
7	5:49	8:08	6:09	7:49	6:31	7:11	6:52	6:29	6:19	4:55	6:46	4:44 PM
8	5:49	8:08	6:10	7:48	6:32	7:10	6:53	6:28	6:20	4:54	6:47	4:44 PM
9	5:50	8:08	6:11	7:47	6:33	7:08	6:54	6:27	6:21	4:54	6:48	4:44 PM
10	5:50	8:07	6:11	7:46	6:33	7:07	6:55	6:26	6:22	4:53	6:48	4:44 PM
11	5:51	8:07	6:12	7:45	6:34	7:06	6:56	6:24	6:22	4:52	6:49	4:45 PM
12	5:51	8:07	6:13	7:44	6:35	7:04	6:56	6:23	6:23	4:52	6:50	4:45 PM
13	5:52	8:06	6:14	7:43	6:35	7:03	6:57	6:22	6:24	4:51	6:50	4:45 PM
14	5:53	8:06	6:14	7:41	6:36	7:01	6:58	6:20	6:25	4:50	6:51	4:45 PM
15	5:53	8:05	6:15	7:40	6:37	7:00	6:59	6:19	6:26	4:50	6:52	4:46 PM
16	5:54	8:05	6:16	7:39	6:37	6:58	7:00	6:18	6:27	4:49	6:52	4:46 PM
17	5:54	8:05	6:16	7:38	6:38	6:57	7:00	6:17	6:28	4:49	6:53	4:46 PM
18	5:55	8:04	6:17	7:37	6:39	6:56	7:01	6:16	6:29	4:48	6:54	4:47 PM
19	5:56	8:04	6:18	7:36	6:39	6:54	7:02	6:14	6:30	4:47	6:54	4:47 PM
20	5:56	8:03	6:19	7:34	6:40	6:53	7:03	6:13	6:31	4:47	6:55	4:48 PM
21	5:57	8:02	6:19	7:33	6:41	6:51	7:04	6:12	6:32	4:47	6:55	4:48 PM
22	5:58	8:01	6:20	7:32	6:42	6:50	7:04	6:11	6:33	4:46	6:56	4:49 PM
23	5:58	8:01	6:21	7:31	6:43	6:49	7:05	6:10	6:34	4:46	6:56	4:49 PM
24	5:59	8:00	6:21	7:30	6:43	6:47	7:06	6:09	6:35	4:45	6:57	4:50 PM
25	6:00	8:00	6:22	7:28	6:44	6:46	7:07	6:08	6:36	4:45	6:57	4:50 PM
26	6:01	7:59	6:23	7:27	6:44	6:44	7:08	6:07	6:37	4:45	6:57	4:51 PM
27	6:01	7:58	6:24	7:26	6:45	6:43	7:09	6:05	6:37	4:45	6:58	4:52 PM
28	6:02	7:58	6:24	7:24	6:46	6:42	7:10	6:04	6:38	4:44	6:58	4:52 PM
29	6:03	7:57	6:25	7:23	6:47	6:40	7:11	6:03	6:39	4:44	6:58	4:53 PM
30	6:03	7:56	6:26	7:22	6:48	6:39	7:11	6:02	6:40	4:44	6:59	4:54 PM
31	6:04	7:55	6:26	7:21			7:12	6:01			6:59	4:54 PM

2010 Holidays

January 1. . . . . New Year's Day (IA/SAG)
January 18. . . . . Martin Luther King, Jr. Day (IA/SAG)
February 15. . . . . President's Day (IA/SAG)
February 17. . . . . Ash Wednesday
March 30 . . . . Passover
April 2 . . . . Good Friday (SAG)
April 4 . . . . Easter Sunday
May 9 . . . . Mother's Day
May 31 . . . . Memorial Day (IA/SAG)
June 20 . . . . Fathers Day
July 4. . . . . Independence Day (IA/SAG)
August 11 . . . . Ramadan Begins
September 6 . . . . Labor Day (IA/SAG)
September 8* . . . . Rosh Hashanah
September 17* . . . . Yom Kippur
October 11. . . . . Columbus Day
October 31. . . . . Halloween
November 11. . . . . Veterans Day
November 25. . . . . Thanksgiving (IA/SAG)
December 1* . . . . Chanukah
December 7. . . . . Muharrama/Islamic New Year
December 25. . . . . Christmas (IA/SAG)

* Begins at sundown

Academy Awards (310) 247-3000
Academy of Motion Picture FAX (310) 859-9619
Arts & Sciences
8949 Wilshire Blvd.
Beverly Hills, CA 90211
www.oscars.org/awards/academyawards/index.html
March 7, 2010

AFCI Locations Trade Show 2009 (307) 367-4422
(323) 461-2324
Association of Film FAX (413) 375-2903
Commissioners Int'l www.afci.org
109 E. 17th St., Ste. 18
Cheyenne, WY 82001
April 15-17, 2010, Santa Monica

AFI Los Angeles Int'l Film Festival (323) 856-7600
The American Film Institute FAX (323) 467-4578
2021 N. Western Ave. www.afi.com
Los Angeles, CA 90027
November, 2010

AICP Shows (323) 960-4763
National LA FAX (323) 960-4766
650 N. Bronson Ave., Ste. 223B www.aicp.com
Los Angeles, CA 90004
Check Web site for dates

American Film Market (310) 446-1000
c/o IFTA FAX (310) 446-1600
10850 Wilshire Blvd., Ninth Fl. www.ifta-online.org/afm
Los Angeles, CA 90024
Managing Director: Jonathan Wolf
Check Web site for dates

Ann Arbor Film Festival (734) 995-5356
308 1/2 S. State St., Ste. 22 FAX (734) 995-5396
Ann Arbor, MI 48104 www.aafilmfest.org
March 23-28, 2010

Annie Awards (818) 842-8330
ASIFA-Hollywood FAX (818) 842-5645
2114 Burbank Blvd. www.annieawards.org
Burbank, CA 91502
February 6, 2010

Artios Awards 323-463-1925
Castin Society of America FAX (323)463-5753
606 N. Larchmont Blvd. www.castingsociety.com
Ste. 4-B
Los Angeles, CA 90004
Check Web site for dates

ASC Awards (323) 969-4333
c/o American Society FAX (323) 882-6391
of Cinematographers www.theasc.com/awards
P.O. Box 2230
Los Angeles, CA 90078
February 27, 2010

Aspen ShortFest (970) 925-6882
Aspen FilmFest FAX (970) 925-1967
110 E. Hallam St., Ste. 102 www.aspenfilm.org
Aspen, CO 81611
April 7-11, 2010

BAFTA Awards 44 20 7734 0022
British Academy of Film & TV Arts FAX 44 20 7734 1792
195 Piccadily www.bafta.org/awards
London, W1J 9LN
United Kingdom
February 21, 2010

Berlinale/ Berlin Int'l Film Festival 49 30 259 20 0
Potsdamer Straße 5 FAX 49 30 259 20 299
10785 Berlin www.berlinale.de
Germany
February 11-21, 2010

The Black Maria Film & Video Festival (201) 200-2043
c/o Media Arts Department FAX (201) 200-3490
Fries Hall www.blackmariafilmfestival.org
New Jersey City University
2039 Kennedy Blvd.
Jersey City, NJ 07305
February, 2010

Cannes Film Festival 33 1 53 59 61 00
3, rue Amélie FAX 33 1 53 59 61 10
Paris, F-75007 France www.festival-cannes.org
May 12–23, 2010

Cannes Lions Int'l Advertising Festival 44 20 7728 4040
Greater London House FAX 44 20 7728 4030
Hampstead Rd. www.canneslions.com
London, NW17EJ
United Kingdom
June 20-26, 2010

Chicago Int'l Children's Film Festival (773) 281-9075
c/o Facets Multi-Media FAX (773) 929-0266
1517 W. Fullerton Ave. www.cicff.org
Chicago, IL 60614
Check Web site for dates

A **Cine Gear Expo** (310) 472-0809
P.O. Box 492296 FAX (310) 471-8973
Los Angeles, CA 90049 www.cinegearexpo.com
June 3-6, 2010, Los Angeles

CineQuest (408) 295-3378
P.O. Box 720040 FAX (408) 995-5713
San Jose, CA 95172 www.cinequest.org
February 25-March 8, 2010

CineVegas Film Festival (702) 952-5555
170 S. Green Valley Pkwy, Ste. 120 FAX (702) 952-5556
Henderson, NV 89012 www.cinevegas.com
Check Web site for dates

Clio Awards (212) 683-4300
770 Broadway, Sixth Fl. FAX (212) 683-4796
New York, NY 10003 www.clioawards.com
May, 2010

Comic-Con (619) 491-2475
P.O. Box 128458 FAX (619) 414-1022
San Diego, CA 92112 www.comic-con.org
July 22-25, 2010

Creative Arts Emmy Awards (818) 754-2800
Academy of Television FAX (818) 761-2827
Arts & Sciences www.emmys.org
5220 Lankershim Blvd.
North Hollywood, CA 91601
September, 2010

Directors Guild of America Awards (310) 289-2000
7920 Sunset Blvd. FAX (310) 289-2029
Los Angeles, CA 90046 www.dga.org
January 30, 2010

DV Expo, West (212) 378-0400
Pasadena www.dvexpo.org
NewBay Media
810 Seventh Ave, 27th Fl.
New York, NY 10019
Check Web site for dates

Emmy Awards (818) 754-2800
Academy of Television FAX (818) 761-2827
Arts & Sciences www.emmys.org
5220 Lankershim Blvd.
North Hollywood, CA 91601
September, 2010

Film Independent Los Angeles Film Festival (310) 432-1240 / (866) 345-6337
9911 W. Pico Blvd. FAX **(310) 432-1203**
Los Angeles, CA 90035 **www.lafilmfest.com**
Check Web site for dates

Film Independent's Spirit Awards (310) 432-1240
Film Independent/Los Angeles FAX **(310) 432-1234**
9911 W. Pico Blvd., 11th Fl. **www.spiritawards.com**
Los Angeles, CA 90035
March 5, 2010

Florida Media Market (305) 372-4563
25 SE Second Ave., Ste. 1148 FAX **(305) 372-4564**
Miami, FL 33131 **www.floridamediamarket.com**
October, 2010

Golden Globes (310) 657-1731
c/o Hollywood Foreign FAX **(310) 657-5576**
Press Association **www.goldenglobes.org**
646 N. Robertson Blvd.
West Hollywood, CA 90069
January 17, 2010

Gotham Independent Film Awards (212) 465-8200
IFP/ New York FAX **(212) 465-8525**
68 Jay St., Ste. 425 **www.gothamifp.org**
Brooklyn, NY 11201
December, 2010

GRAMMY Awards (310) 392-3777
The Recording Academy FAX **(310) 392-2306**
3402 Pico Blvd. **www.grammy.com**
Santa Monica, CA 90405
January 31, 2010

The Hamptons Int'l Film Festival (631) 747-7978
Three Newtown Mews FAX **(631) 607-0444**
East Hampton, NY 11937 **www.hamptonsfilmfest.org**
October, 2010

Heartland Film Festival (317) 464-9405
200 S. Meridian St., Ste. 220 FAX **(317) 464-8409**
Indanapolis, IN 46225 **www.heartlandfilmfestival.org**
October, 2010

A **High Def Expo - Los Angeles** (818) 842-6611
3727 W. Magnolia Blvd., Ste. 729 FAX **(818) 842-6624**
Burbank, CA 91505 **www.createasphere.com**
Check Web site for dates

Hollywood Film Festival (310) 288-1882
433 N. Camden Dr. FAX **(310)-288-0060**
Ste. 600 **www.hollywoodfestival.com**
Beverly Hills, CA 90210
October, 2010

Independent Film Week (212) 465-8200
IFP/New York FAX **(212) 465-8525**
68 Jay St. Ste. 425 **www.ifp.org**
Brooklyn, NY 11201
September 18-23, 2010

Int'l CINDY Competitions (469) 464-4180
The CINDY Competitions FAX **(469) 464-4170**
P.O. Box 270779 **www.cindys.com**
Flower Mound, TX 75022
Check Web site for dates

Just for Laughs (514) 845-3155
2101 St-Laurent Blvd. FAX **(514) 845-4140**
Montreal, Quebec **www.hahaha.com**
Canada H2X 2T5
Check Web site for dates

Long Island Int'l Film Expo (516) 783-3199
c/o Bellmore Movies **www.liifilmexpo.org**
222 Petit Ave., Side Entrance
Bellmore, NY 11710
July 9-18, 2010

Method Fest (310) 535-9230
840 Apollo St., Ste. 314 FAX **(310) 535-9128**
El Segundo, CA 90245 **www.methodfest.com**
March 25-April 1, 2010

Miami International Film Festival (305) 237-3456
Miami Dade College FAX **(305) 257-7344**
25 NE Second St. **www.miamifilmfestival.com**
Ste. 5501-5
Miami, FL 33132
March 4-15, 2010

Mill Valley Film Festival (415) 383-5256
1001 Lootens Pl. FAX **(415) 383-8606**
Ste. 220 **www.mvff.com**
San Rafael, CA 94901
October, 2010

MTV Movie Awards (212) 258-8000 / (310) 752-8000
1515 Broadway FAX **(212) 846-1804**
New York, NY 10036 **www.mtv.com/ontv/movieawards**
June, 2010

MTV Video Music Awards (212) 258-8000 / (310) 752-8000
1515 Broadway FAX **(212) 846-1804**
New York, NY 10036 **www.mtv.com/ontv/vma**
September, 2010

NABSHOW/ National Association of Broadcasters (202) 429-5300 / (800) 342-2460
1771 N St. NW FAX **(202) 429-5493**
Washington, DC 20036 **www.nab.org/conventions**
April 10–15, 2010

NATPE Market & Conference (310) 453-4440
5757 Wilshire Blvd. FAX **(310) 453-5258**
Los Angeles, CA 90036 **www.natpe.org**
January 25–28, 2010, Las Vegas

Nashville Film Festival (615) 742-2500
P.O. Box 24330 FAX **(615) 742-1004**
Nashville, TN 37202 **www.nashvillefilmfestival.org**
April 15-22, 2010

New Directors/New Films (212) 875-5367
The Film Society @ Lincoln Center **www.filmlinc.com**
70 Lincloln Center Plaza
New York, NY 10023
Check Web site for dates

New York Emmy Awards (212) 459-3630
Nat'l Academy of Television FAX **(212) 459-9772**
Arts and Sciences **www.nynatas.org**
1375 Broadway, Ste. 2103
New York, NY, 10018
April 18, 2010

New York Festivals Int'l Television & Film Awards (212) 643-4800
260 W. 39th St., Tenth Fl. FAX **(212) 643-0170**
New York, NY 10018 **www.newyorkfestivals.com**
Check Web site for dates

New York Festivals Int'l Advertising In All Media Awards (212) 643-4800
260 W. 39th St., Tenth Fl. FAX **(212) 643-0170**
New York, NY 10018 **www.newyorkfestivals.com**
Check Web site for dates

New York Film Festival (212) 875-5610
The Film Society of Lincoln Center **www.filmlinc.com**
70 Lincoln Center Plaza
New York, NY 10023
Check Web site for dates

The One Show Festival (212) 979-1900
The One Club For Art & Copy FAX **(212) 979-5006**
21 E. 26th St., Fifth Fl. **www.oneclub.com**
New York, NY 10010
Check Web site for dates

Palm Springs Int'l Film Festival (760) 322-2930
1700 E. Tahquitz Canyon Way, Ste. 3 FAX **(760) 322-4087**
Palm Springs, CA 92262 **www.psfilmfest.org**
January 5-18, 2010

Producers Guild Awards (310) 358-9020
8530 Wilshire Blvd., Ste. 450 FAX **(310) 358-9520**
Beverly Hills, CA 90211 **www.producersguild.org**
January 24, 2010

Rhode Island Int'l Film Festival (401) 861-4445
P.O. Box 162 FAX **(401) 490-6735**
Newport, RI 02840 **www.film-festival.org**
August 10-15, 2010

Rocky Mountain VidExpo (303) 771-2000
8002 S. Oneida Court **www.vidxpo.com**
Centennial, CO 80112
October, 2010

San Francisco Int'l Film Festival (415) 561-5020
39 Mesa St., Ste. 110
The Presido
San Francisco, CA 94129
www.sffs.org/sf-intl-film-festival.aspx
April 22-May 6, 2010

Santa Barbara Int'l Film Festival (805) 963-0023
1528 Chapala St., Ste. 203 FAX **(805) 962-2524**
Santa Barbara, CA 93101 **www.sbfilmfestival.org**
February 4-14, 2010

Santa Monica Film Festival (310) 264-4274
P.O. Box 5236 FAX **(310) 264-4220**
Santa Monica, CA 90409 **www.smfilmfestival.com**
Check Web site for dates

Seattle Int'l Film Festival (206) 464-5830
400 Ninth Ave. N. FAX **(206) 264-7919**
Seattle, WA 98109 **www.siff.net**
May 20-June 13, 2010

ShoWest (646) 654-7680
770 Braodway FAX **(646) 654-7694**
New York, NY 10003 **www.showest.com**
March 15-18, 2010, Las Vegas

SIGGRAPH (212) 869-7440
July 27-29, 2010, Los Angeles **www.siggraph.org**

Slamdance Int'l Film Festival (323) 466-1786
5634 Melrose Ave. FAX **(323) 466-1784**
Los Angeles, CA 90038 **www.slamdance.com**
January 21-28, 2010

South By Southwest Film Conference & Festival (512) 467-7979
SXSW Headquarters, Box 4999 FAX **(512) 451-0754**
Austin, TX 78765 **www.sxsw.com**
March 12-20, 2010

Sundance Film Festival (435) 658-3456 (310) 360-1981
P.O. Box 684429 FAX **(801) 575-5175**
Salt Lake City, UT 84068 **www.sundance.org**
January 21–31, 2010

Telluride Film Festival (510) 665-9494
800 Jones St. FAX **(510) 665-9589**
Berkeley, CA 94710 **www.telluridefilmfestival.org**
September 3-6, 2010

Toronto Int'l Film Festival (416) 967-7371 (877) 968-3456
Two Carlton St. **www.tiff.net**
Toronto, ON M5B 1J3
September, 2010

Tribeca Film Festival (212) 941-2305
375 Greenwich St. FAX **(212) 941-3939**
New York, NY 10013 **www.tribecafilm.com/festival**
April 21-May 2, 2010

UNAFF (650) 724-5544
P.O. Box 19369 **www.unaff.org**
Stanford, CA 94309
Check Web site for dates

U.S. Int'l Film & Video Festival (310) 540-0959
713 S. Pacific Coast Hwy, Ste. A FAX **(310) 316-8905**
Redondo Beach, CA 90277 **www.filmfestawards.com**
Check Web site for dates

Visual Effects Society (VES) Awards (818) 981-7861
5535 Balboa Blvd., Ste. 205 FAX **(818) 981-0179**
Encino, CA 91316 **www.vesawards.com/awards**
February 28, 2010

Woods Hole Film Festival (508) 495-3456
87B Water St. FAX **(508) 495-3456**
Woods Hole, MA 02543 **www.woodsholefilmfestival.org**
July 31-August 7, 2010

WorldFest/ Houston Int'l Film & Video Fest. (713) 965-9955
9898 Bissonet, Ste., 650 FAX **(713) 965-9960**
Houston, TX 77036 **www.worldfest.org**
April 9-18, 2010

NOTES:

NOTES:

LA 411

LOS ANGELES CITY HALL

DRAGNET

TITLE CARD - L.A. Police Badge #714 with "Dragnet" superimposed.

SFX - Dragnet Theme

EXT. LOS ANGLES - DAY

Sweeping aerial shots of the city as Sgt Joe Friday (Jack Webb) speaks.

FRIDAY (V.O.)
This is the city, one of the largest in the United States.
It spreads out in all four directions like a broadroom rug.
From south and west to downtown business districts.
In the east, the industrial areas. Los Angeles, California,
pretty much like your town.

EXT. STATUE OF FATHER JUNIPERO SERRA

FRIDAY (V.O.)
This is a Spanish priest, one of the city's founders.

EXT. TROLLY CAR YARD

FRIDAY (V.O.)
It's changed a lot since then. It's got high-tension
wires bringing in the power for bus lines to get
you where you're going.

EXT. FREIGHT YARD

FRIDAY (V.O.)
It's got railroads and freight yards.

EXT. CHURCH

FRIDAY (V.O.)
Churches.

EXT. ANOTHER CHURCH

FRIDAY (V.O.)
Any kind you want.

EXT. MACARTHUR PARK

FRIDAY (V.O.)
Public parks and lakes.

EXT. CITY HALL

FRIDAY (V.O.)
It's got a police department and a City Hall.

Camera PANS up to the top of City Hall.

FRIDAY (V.O.)
This is where I work. My name is Friday.
I'm a cop.

SERIES CREATED BY:
Jack Webb

ALSO FILMED AT L.A. CITY HALL:
The Adventures of Superman, Barton Fink

LA 411
Qualified Production Resource • www.LA411.com • $79.00
Volume 31 — 2010 • Film • Television • Commercial • Music Video
411 Publishing

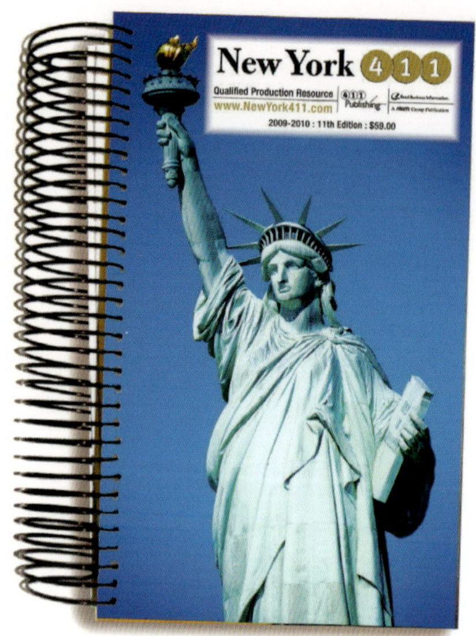
New York 411
Qualified Production Resource
www.NewYork411.com
2009-2010 : 11th Edition : $59.00

Advertiser Index

Covers & Tabs

NOTES:

LA 411

GRIFFITH PARK OBSERVATORY

REBEL WITHOUT A CAUSE

EXT. GRIFFITH OBSERVATORY PARKING LOT - DAY

Buzz, having taunted Jim (James Dean) into a game of knife sticking sees a museum administrator approaching. Buzz folds up his knife and puts it away. So does Jim.

Judy (Natalie Wood) and the rest of the gang look on. Plato (Sal Mineo) stands behind Jim.

JIM
You satisfied or you want more?

BUZZ
How 'bout you? Say the word and you're cold, Jack--you're dead.

JUDY
Buzzie--we better get out of here.

BUZZ
What's eating you, Judy? You want him alive?

JIM
Where can we meet?

BUZZ
Know the Millertown bluff?

COOKIE
The bluff, Buzz! That's dangerous up there.

BUZZ
Draw him a picture, Chicken Little. Eight o'clock.
Cookie, you call Moose and get a couple cars.
We're going to have us some real kicks.
Little chickie-run. You been on chickie-runs before?

JIM
Sure--that's all I do.

They are gone. Jim looks down at his shirt. There are spots of blood. Plato opens it, spits on a handkerchief and starts to wipe the blood away.

PLATO
Are you really going to meet them?

JIM
Who knows. Plato?

PLATO
What?

JIM
What's a chickie-run?

SCREENPLAY BY:
Stewart Stern & Irving Shulman from a story by Nicholas Ray

ALSO FILMED AT THE GRIFFITH PARK OBSERVATORY:
Terminator, Devil in a Blue Dress

LA 411

www.LA411.com

PICTURED:
Griffith Observatory

LOCATION:
Los Angeles

PHOTOGRAPHER:
Michael Rueter
Michael Rueter Photography/L.A.-N.Y.
www.michaelrueter.com

Supporting production in Southern California for 31 years

General Index

A

B

C

D

E

F

G

H

I

J

K

L

M

N

O

P

Q

R

S

T

U

V

W

X

Y

Z

SANTA MONICA PIER

THE STING

INT. CHICAGO - CAROUSEL - DAY

Hooker (Robert Redford) enters a building which contains a carousel on the bottom two floors and what appear to be apartments on the third floor. A 35 year-old woman, Billie, appears in her bathrobe on the second floor landing and descends the stairs to get the morning paper.

HOOKER
Excuse me, I'm looking for a guy named Henry Gondorff. You know him?

BILLIE
You Hooker?

HOOKER
Yeah.

BILLIE
Why didn't you say so. I thought maybe you was a copper or somethin'.

She goes to a side door and unlocks it.

BILLIE
It's the room in the back. He wasn't expecting you so soon though.

Hooker walks past the now motionless carousel to the room in the back and knocks on the door.

No answer. He gives the door a little push and it swings open.

INT. GONDORFF'S ROOM - DAY

The room inside is small and cluttered, consisting of a bed, a sink, and a bathroom, all covered by a layer of books, dirty clothes and beer bottles. Draped over a chair, fully dressed, but completely passed out is the one and only Henry Gondorff (Paul Newman).

HOOKER
The great Henry Gondorff.

INT. SHOWER - MINUTES LATER

Water blasting out of the fixture. Gondorff, fully clothed, is sitting in the bottom of the shower, the spray streaming off his face. Hooker, sitting on the floor between the toilet and the sink, watches listlessly.

GONDORFF
Turn the goddamn thing off, will ya.

HOOKER
You sober?

GONDORFF
I can talk, can't I?

Hooker makes no move to get up. Gondorff struggles to his knees, turns off the water, and slumps back against the wall.

GONDORFF
Glad to meet ya, kid. You're a real horse's ass.

SCREENPLAY BY:
David S. Ward

ALSO FILMED AT THE SANTA MONICA PIER:
Forrest Gump, Thank You for Smoking, They Shoot Horses Don't They?

Company/Crew Index

www.LA411.com

PICTURED:
Santa Monica Pier

LOCATION:
Santa Monica

PHOTOGRAPHER:
Michael Rueter
Michael Rueter Photography/L.A.-N.Y.
www.michaelrueter.com

Supporting production in Southern California for 31 years

Company/Crew Index

Company/Crew Index

Numbers

A

B

C

D

E

F

G

H

I

J

K

L

M

N

O

P

Q

R

S

T

U

V

W

X

Y

Z

NOTES:

LA 411

NOTES:

LA 411

NOTES:

CHINATOWN

EXT. CHINATOWN - STREET - NIGHT

Evelyn (Faye Dunaway) gets in the car. She starts it.
Gittes (Jack Nicholson) lets Escobar go.

ESCOBAR
I'll just have her followed. She's not going anywhere.

There's a single GUNSHOT. Both men look surprised.
Down the block a uniformed officer has fired.
Gittes rushes to the car. He opens it. Evelyn falls out, inert.

GITTES
No!

He holds onto Evelyn as Escobar and others hurry up.
Cross (John Huston) elbows through.

GITTES (Cont.)
Where is he? I'll kill him, I'll kill the son of a bitch.

Several officers contain Gittes.

ESCOBAR
Take it easy, take it easy, it was an accident.

GITTES
An accident.

Gittes looks down. What he sees horrifies him.
Cross is on the ground, holding Evelyn's body, crying.

GITTES
Get him away from her. He's responsible
for everything. Get him away from her!

ESCOBAR
Jake, you're very disturbed. You're crazy.
That's her father.

Walsh and Duffy elbow through the crowd.

ESCOBAR
(to them)
You wanna do your partner the biggest
favor of his life? Take him home.
Just get him the hell out of here!

Duffy bear hugs the protesting Gittes, along with Walsh, literally dragging him away from the scene, with Gittes trying to shake free.

Through the crowd noises, Walsh can be heard saying...

WALSH
Forget it, Jake. It's Chinatown.

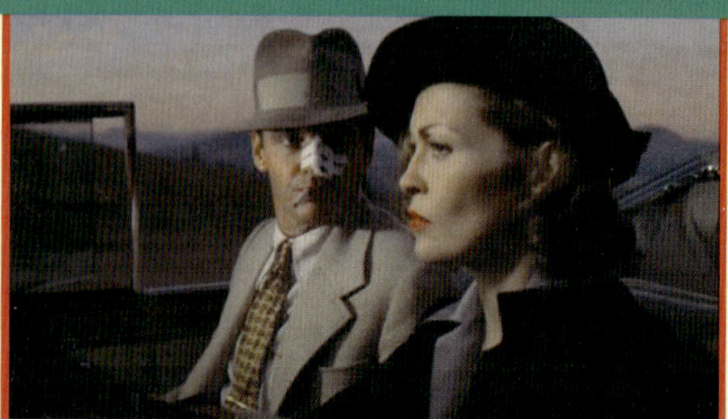

SCREENPLAY BY:
Robert Towne

ALSO FILMED IN CHINATOWN:
Lethal Weapon 4, Rush Hour

LA 411

www.LA411.com

■ PICTURED:
Chinatown

■ LOCATION:
Downtown Los Angeles

■ PHOTOGRAPHER:
Michael Rueter
Michael Rueter Photography/L.A.-N.Y.
www.michaelrueter.com

Supporting production in Southern California for 31 years

Advertising Agencies & Production Companies

Ⓐ ADVERTISER SYMBOL

Refer to the General Index for cross-referencing items in this section.

1124 Design Advertising (310) 821-1775 (310) 902-0808
323 Culver Blvd. FAX (310) 821-1972
Playa del Rey, CA 90293 www.1124design.com

72andSunny (310) 215-9009
6300 Arizona Circle FAX (310) 215-9012
Los Angeles, CA 90045 www.72andsunny.com

Abehsera & Partners (323) 931-1391

Admarketing, Inc. (310) 203-8400
1801 Century Park East, Ste. 2000 FAX (310) 277-7621
Century City, CA 90067 www.admarketing.com

Bramson + Associates (323) 938-3595

Campbell-Ewald (818) 526-1060
3120 W. Empire Ave. FAX (818) 556-5286
Burbank, CA 91504 www.cecom.com

Campbell-Ewald (310) 231-2900
11444 W. Olympic Blvd., 11th Fl. FAX (310) 473-3856
Los Angeles, CA 90064 www.cecom.com

cruz/kravetz: Ideas (888) 528-6658
2600 W. Olive Ave., Ste. 910 www.ckideas.com
Burbank, CA 91505

Dailey (310) 360-3100
8687 Melrose Ave., Ste. G300 FAX (310) 360-0810
West Hollywood, CA 90069 www.daileyideas.com

davidandgoliath (310) 445-5200
909 N. Sepulveda FAX (310) 445-5201
El Segundo, CA 90245 www.dng.com

DavisElen (213) 688-7000
865 S. Figueroa St., 12th Fl. FAX (213) 688-7288
Los Angeles, CA 90017 www.daviselen.com

DDB Worldwide Communications Group, Inc. (310) 907-1500
340 Main St. www.ddb.com
Venice, CA 90291

Dentsu America (310) 586-5600
2001 Wilshire Blvd., Ste. 600 FAX (310) 586-5894
Santa Monica, CA 90403 www.dentsuamerica.com

Deutsch, Inc. (310) 862-3000
FAX (310) 862-3100
www.deutschinc.com

DNA Studio (323) 463-2826
6535 Santa Monica Blvd. FAX (323) 463-2535
Hollywood, CA 90038 www.dnala.com

Draft FCB (949) 851-3050
17600 Gillette Ave. FAX (949) 567-9465
Irvine, CA 92614 www.fcb.com

Dreamentia, Inc. (213) 347-6000
453 S. Spring St., Ste. 808 FAX (213) 347-6001
Los Angeles, CA 90013 www.dreamentia.com

The Gary Group/2g Studios (310) 264-1800 (310) 264-1700
2048 Broadway FAX (310) 264-9744
Santa Monica, CA 90404 www.2gstudios.com

Ground Zero (310) 881-8000
4235 Redwood Ave. FAX (310) 881-8080
Los Angeles, CA 90066 www.groundzero.net

Kovel/Fuller (310) 841-4444
9925 Jefferson Blvd. FAX (310) 841-4599
Culver City, CA 90232 www.kovelfuller.com

La Agencia de Orci & Asociados (310) 444-7300
11620 Wilshire Blvd., Ste. 600 FAX (310) 478-3587
West Los Angeles, CA 90025 www.laagencia.com

LatinSphere Advertising, LLC (562) 983-5103
115 Pine Ave., Ste. 200 FAX (562) 983-5167
Long Beach, CA 90802 www.latinsphere.com

LBC Advertising (310) 656-1500
501 Santa Monica Blvd., Ste. 600 FAX (310) 656-1300
Santa Monica, CA 90401 www.lbcad.com

Leo Burnett, USA (323) 866-6020
6500 Wilshire Blvd., Ste. 1950 FAX (323) 866-6033
Los Angeles, CA 90048

McCann-Erickson, Inc. (323) 900-7100
5700 Wilshire Blvd., Ste. 225 www.universalmccann.com
Los Angeles, CA 90036

MeadsDurket, Inc. (619) 574-0808
6863 Friars Rd. FAX (619) 574-1664
San Diego, CA 92108 www.meadsdurket.com

Mendelsohn/Zien Advertising (310) 444-1990
FAX (310) 444-9888
www.mzad.com

The Miller Group Advertising, Inc. (310) 442-0101
1516 S. Bundy Dr., Ste. 200 FAX (310) 442-0107
Los Angeles, CA 90025 www.millergroup.net

MOB Media Inc./MOB Media Studios (949) 222-0220
27121 Towne Centre Dr., Ste. 260 FAX (949) 222-0243
Foothill Ranch, CA 92610 www.mobmedia.com

Motta Company (310) 348-9955
909 N. Sepulveda Blvd., Ste. 800 FAX (310) 322-3329
El Segundo, CA 90245 www.motta.com

Ogilvy & Mather, Inc. (310) 280-2200
3530 Hayden Ave. FAX (310) 280-2699
Culver City, CA 90232 www.ogilvy.com

Planet 3 Entertainment Group, LLC (310) 392-4600
1832 Franklin St. www.planet3entertainment.com
Santa Monica, CA 90404

Project X Media (858) 792-9685
320 S. Cedros Ave., Ste. 500 www.projectxmedia.com
Solana Beach, CA 92075

Red Marketing (310) 227-8200 (310) 678-7601
345 Richmond St. FAX (310) 227-8205
El Segundo, CA 90245 www.redm33.com

Riester (310) 392-4244
11833 Mississippi Ave., Ste. 101 FAX (310) 392-2595
Los Angeles, CA 90025 www.riester.com

Rubin Postaer and Associates (310) 394-4000
2525 Colorado Ave. www.rpa.com
Santa Monica, CA 90404

Saatchi & Saatchi/LA (310) 214-6000
3501 Sepulveda Blvd. FAX (310) 214-6160
Torrance, CA 90505 www.saatchila.com

Saeshe, Inc. (213) 683-2100
FAX (213) 683-2103
www.saeshe.com

Sagon-Phior (310) 575-4441 (818) 262-1838
2107 Sawtelle Blvd. FAX (310) 575-4995
Los Angeles, CA 90025 www.sagon-phior.com

TBWA Chiat/Day Advertising (310) 305-5000
5353 Grosvenor Blvd. FAX (310) 305-6000
Los Angeles, CA 90066 www.tbwachiat.com

Team One Advertising (310) 615-2000
1960 E. Grand Ave., Ste. 700 FAX (310) 322-7565
El Segundo, CA 90245 www.teamone-usa.com

TVA Marketing & Advertising (818) 505-8300
FAX (818) 505-8370
www.tvaproductions.com

Wongdoody (310) 280-7800
8500 Steller Dr., Ste. 5 FAX (310) 280-7780
Culver City, CA 90232 www.wongdoody.com

Young & Rubicam Brands (949) 754-2000
7535 Irvine Center Dr. FAX (949) 754-2001
Irvine, CA 92618 www.yr.com

LA 411 Advertising Agency Freelance Producers LA 411

Christine Anthony (323) 376-6463

Linda Arett (323) 650-5605

Bryan Barker (310) 869-9765
web.mac.com/bbarker/

Shari Becker (310) 254-6794
web.mac.com/sharibecker

Jackie Bombeck (310) 701-5898

John Brooks (310) 418-6708

Patrick Collins (310) 474-5330
FAX (310) 474-2780

Jackye Cruz (323) 460-4432

Bill Curran (310) 392-1035
(310) 729-4701

Juliet Diamond (310) 994-7935

Brian Donnelly (310) 880-9400

Carole Ferrari (626) 824-0240

Marla Friedler (949) 813-2450
www.bluetangoproductions.com

Bruce Fritzberg (323) 822-7881
(818) 231-2260

Debbie Galloway (818) 424-2353

Ellen J. Goldfarb (818) 342-9026
FAX (818) 342-9827

Jerry Grant (818) 882-3990
(503) 914-9672

Joan M. Gringer (310) 842-3281
(954) 609-6435
www.myspace.com/JGringer

Eric Herrmann (310) 854-3380
(310) 739-8330
FAX (310) 854-3358

Chantal Houle (310) 953-9166
(French) www.chantalhoule.com

Brad Johnson (949) 302-3318
web.mac.com/bradspace

Lisa Jokanovich (323) 876-6489
FAX (323) 845-9427

Erwin Kramer (310) 446-1866
(310) 266-8146
FAX (310) 446-1856
www.erwinkramer.com

Ilene Kramer (310) 446-1866
FAX (310) 446-1856

Rick Lieberman (310) 709-4832
(305) 321-3556

Jane Liepshutz (310) 365-9998
FAX (310) 859-1116
www.seejaneproduce.tv

Stephania Lipner (310) 739-1469

Lynn M. Luckoff (310) 463-2201

Patty Lum (310) 376-8088
(310) 989-7003

Pamela Mahan (310) 266-1400
www.pamelamahan.com

Patricia Matus (310) 216-7268

Kathy McGoff (310) 493-2718

Melanie Coventry McKinnell (818) 957-0708
(626) 688-2956

Jim Miller (213) 503-5448

Tena Montoya (310) 733-7369

Michele Morris (310) 663-5230
FAX (310) 827-5231

Tony Osiecki (310) 600-5823
(310) 558-8005

Derik Parrent (310) 995-0601

Ronnie Reade (310) 820-7939

Randy Rennolds (818) 846-2334
FAX (818) 567-1123

Rickmon Media (310) 503-5402
www.rickmonmedia.com

Lyra Rider (323) 309-7800

Kristin Roberts (310) 397-8850

Nancy Rose (818) 439-2126

Michael Shores (323) 791-9433
www.heavenanimage.com

Nancy Skenderian (310) 373-5665
(310) 753-1962

Brian Stashick (310) 858-1979
(310) 487-6044
FAX (310) 275-6995

Jason Stewart (310) 994-7600
(212) 796-4982

Dan Tarver (310) 433-5143

Mandi Tinsley (818) 501-2831
FAX (818) 986-9124

Steven Tobenkin (310) 621-1122
FAX (310) 388-1403

Kathie Van Kerckhoven (310) 395-9899
(310) 968-6875
FAX (310) 395-3471
web.mac.com/kathievan/iweb/site

Susan Vogelfang (310) 306-2648

Ree Whitford (818) 424-9988
(818) 505-1060

Allen Williams (310) 652-1393
(213) 308-8466

Kelly Wood (310) 600-1035
www.kellywoodproducer.com

Kathleen Yip (818) 386-0883
(310) 746-6302
web.mac.com/kathleenyip/iweb/site/
kathleen%20yip.html

Randall Zook (310) 753-5733

Leslie Zurla (818) 762-4346
(818) 207-1743
FAX (818) 506-8483

Acme Filmworks, Inc. (323) 464-7805
6525 Sunset Blvd., Ste. G-10 FAX (323) 464-6614
Hollywood, CA 90028 www.acmefilmworks.com
(2D/3D Animation, Character Cel Animation & Stop-Motion)
Executive Producers: Ron Diamond & David Schmier
Producer: Pernille D'Avolio
Directors: Gil Alkabetz, Garri Bardine, Jim Blashfield, Leslie Cabraga, Evert de Beijer, Paul and Menno De Nooijer, Michael Dudok De Wit, John Dilworth, Paul Driessen, Piotr Dumala, Stephen Flint-Muller, Daniel Guyonnet, Oliver Harrison, Anna Henckle-Donnersmarck, Chris Hinton, Greg Holfeld, Aleksandra Korejwo, Igor Kovalyov, Raimund Krumme, Chris Landreth, Christopher and Wolfgang Lauenstein, Caroline Leaf, Ashley Lenz, Susan Loughlin, Sean McBride, Frank and Caroline Mouris, Priit Parn, Luc Perez, Janet Perlman, Bill Plympton, Barry Purves, Joanna Quinn, Rosto, Erica Russell, Pam Stalker, Wendy Tilby and Amanda Forbis, Gianluigi Toccafondo, Miklos Varga, Solweig von Kleist, David Wasson, JC Wegman & Koji Yamamura
East Coast Sales Rep: David Schmier
Midwest Sales Rep: Tim Harwood
West Coast Sales Reps: Toni Saarinen & Jennifer Spencer

Acorn Entertainment (323) 238-4650
5777 W. Century Blvd., www.acornentertainment.com
10th Fl.
Los Angeles, CA 90045
(2D/3D Animation & Character Design)
Executive Producers: Evan Ricks & Thad Weinlein
Producer: Mary Wall

Animax Entertainment (818) 787-4444
6627 Valjean Ave. FAX (818) 374-9140
Van Nuys, CA 91406 www.animaxent.com
(2D/3D Computer Animation, Character Animation, Character Design, Compositing & Motion Graphics)

Associates & Yamashita (310) 664-9500
13600 Marina Pointe Dr., Ste. 1007 FAX (310) 664-9977
Marina del Rey, CA 90292 www.aayamashita.com
(3D Computer Animation, Cel Animation, Compositing & Live Action Integration)
President/Creative Director: Allen Yamashita

Berkos & Associates (818) 788-8246
(2D and 3D Animation & Stop-Motion Animation)

Bill Melendez Productions, Inc. (818) 382-7382
13400 Riverside Dr., Ste. 201 www.billmelendez.tv
Sherman Oaks, CA 91463
(2D/3D & Character Animation)
Business Affairs: Joanna Coletta
Animation Supervisor: Larry Leichliter
Sales Rep: Jeff Arnold

Bling Imaging (323) 874-3003
1011 N. Fuller Ave., Ste. B www.blingimaging.com
West Hollywood, CA 90046
VFX Supervisor: Paal Anand
VFX Producers: Kelle Holland & Fernando Zorrilla

DUCK Studios, a.k.a. Duck Soup Studios (310) 478-0771
2205 Stoner Ave. FAX (310) 478-0773
Los Angeles, CA 90064 www.duckstudios.com
(2D/3D Computer Animation, Cel Animation, Character and Illustrative Design, Compositing, Digital Ink and Paint, Live Action Integration & Stop Motion)
Executive Producer: Mark Medernach
President/Director: Roger Chouinard
Directors: Gints Apsits, Richard Borge, Jamie Caliri, Richard Cullen, Delicatessen, Eric Deutschman, Barbara Di Pasquale, Docter Twins, Evil Cat Land, Faivre Brothers, Eric Goldberg, James Hackett, Chris Harding, Laura Heit, JL Design, Peter Kaboth, Piotr Karwas, Stephen Kirklys, Amica Kubo, Lane and Jan, Miwa Matreyek, Graham Morris, Yorico Murakami, Andy Murdock, The Mushroom Company, Takahiro Okubo, Ritxi Ostariz, Nina Paley, Hsin Ping Pan, Plankton Art Co., Corky Quakenbush, Chris Romano, Maureen Selwood, Kang Seong, Steve Sonnenleiter, Shy the Sun AKA The Blackheart Gang, Theodore Ushev, YELLOW SHED & Ryan Zunkley
Sales Rep: Andrew Halpern
Music Video Rep: Randi Wilens

Duncan Studio (626) 578-1587
87 N. Raymond Ave., Ste. 900 FAX (626) 578-1327
Pasadena, CA 91103 www.duncanstudio.com

Elektrashock, Inc. (310) 399-4985
1320 Main St. FAX (310) 399-4972
Venice, CA 90291 www.elektrashock.com
(3D Animation)

Epoch Ink Animation (310) 823-7719
2918 Grayson Ave. www.epochinkanimation.com
Venice, CA 90291

Fred Wolf Films (818) 846-0611
4222 W. Burbank Blvd. FAX (818) 846-0979
Burbank, CA 91505 www.fredwolffilms.com
(Cel Animation)

Hornet, Inc. (917) 351-0520
(310) 641-9464
3962 Ince Blvd. FAX (917) 314-2117
Culver City, CA 90232 www.hornetinc.com
(2D/3D Computer Animation)
CEO: Jon Slusser
President: Greg Harvey
Vice President: Greg Bedard
Executive Producer: Michael Feder

ka-chew! (323) 468-3020
6353 Sunset Blvd. FAX (323) 468-3021
Los Angeles, CA 90028 www.kachew.com

Klasky Csupo, Inc. (323) 468-2600
1248 Highland Ave. FAX (323) 468-2675
Los Angeles, CA 90038 www.klaskycsupo.com

Kurtz & Friends (818) 841-8188
2312 W. Olive Ave. FAX (818) 841-6263
Burbank, CA 91506 www.kurtzandfriends.com
(2D/3D Computer Animation, Cel Animation, Character Design, Compositing, Digital Ink and Paint, Live Action Integration & Storyboards)
Producer: Boo Lopez
Director: Bob Kurtz

The Orphanage (323) 469-6700
6725 Sunset Blvd., Ste. 220 FAX (323) 469-6701
Los Angeles, CA 90028 www.theorphanage.com
(2D/3D Animation and FX, 3D Modeling & Character Animation)

Prana Studios, Inc. (323) 645-6500
1145 N. McCadden Pl. www.pranastudios.com
Los Angeles, CA 90038

Renegade Animation, Inc. (818) 551-2351
116 N. Maryland Ave., Lower Level FAX (818) 551-2350
Glendale, CA 91206 www.renegadeanimation.com
(Cel Animation)
Producer: Ashley Postlewaite
Animation Director: Darrell Van Citters
Sales Rep: Andy Arkin

Rhythm + Hues Design (310) 448-7500
5404 Jandy Pl. FAX (310) 448-7600
Los Angeles, CA 90066 www.rhythm.com
(Cel and Character Animation)
Executive Producer: Paul Babb
Head of Production, Commercial Digital: Lisa White
Animation/FX Directors: Clark Anderson, John-Mark Austin, Steve Beck, Robert Caruso, Mark Dippé, Bill Kroyer, Craig Talmy & Michael Wright
Visual FX Supervisors: Eric DeHaven, John Heller, Tim Miller & Bill Westenhofer
East Coast Sales Rep: Henry Hagerty
Midwest/Detroit Sales Rep: Marci Miles
Los Angeles Sales Rep: Connie Mellors

Ring of Fire (310) 966-5055
1538 20th St. FAX **(310) 966-5056**
Santa Monica, CA 90404 **www.ringoffire.com**
(2D/3D Computer Animation, Compositing, HD Visual FX & Visual FX Supervision)

Shadedbox, Inc. (626) 356-3663
1137 Huntington Dr., Bldg. D **www.shadedbox.com**
South Pasadena, CA 91030
(3D Animation, 3D Modeling, Animatics, CGI, Character Animation, Character Design, Computer Animation, Previsualizations & Stop-Motion Animation)

STEELE Studios (310) 656-7770
5737 Mesmer Ave. FAX **(310) 656-7771**
Culver City, CA 90230 **www.steelevfx.com**
(2D/3D Animation, 3D Modeling & Character Animation)
President/Creative Director: Jerry Steele
CEO/Sr. Executive Producer: Jo Steele

Storyheads Entertainment (323) 337-9062
8335 Sunset Blvd., Ste. 333 **www.storyheads.com**
West Hollywood, CA 90069
(2D/3D Animation, Cel Animation & Character Animation)
Founder/Creative Director: David Smith
Co-Founder/Executive Producer: Donna Smith

Synthespian Studios (818) 753-1822
(413) 664-8176
5355 Cartwright Ave., Ste. 117 FAX **(323) 576-5396**
North Hollywood, CA 91601 **www.synthespians.net**
President: Diana Walczak
COO: Michael Van Himbergen
Executive Producer: Amanda Roth
Producers: Wendy Gipp & Tom Leeser
Directors: Jeff Kleiser & Diana Walczak

Toon Makers, Inc. (818) 832-8666
17333 Ludlow St. **www.toonmakers.com**
Granada Hills, CA 91344
(Cel Animation, CGI & Character Design)
Producer: Rocky Solotoff

Wit Animation (310) 305-4790
1717 Lincoln Blvd. FAX **(310) 439-2530**
Venice, CA 90291 **www.witanimation.com**

Karen Anderson (310) 815-8897
FAX (310) 815-1269
www.epiphanypictures.com

Madelyn Curtis (310) 459-8976

Marcia Deliberto (818) 753-0262

Kat Dillon (310) 399-7839

Dale Dreher (310) 600-5020
www.hazardtown.com

Peggy Dunn (310) 398-4867
(310) 200-3979

Leslie M. Evers (310) 600-7373

Franny Faull (310) 614-0992

Katy Greene (310) 406-8800

Tracy Hauser (310) 293-2752

Lisa Hollingshead (310) 880-7556
(323) 828-5780

Craig Houchin (818) 951-5959
www.craighouchin.com

Holly D. Hughes (818) 951-6889

Alexis Ignatieff (323) 664-6417

Jan Katz (310) 821-2221
(310) 804-0913
FAX (310) 821-4106

Jodi Kemper (213) 507-8045

Brooke Lawrence (310) 560-9787

Darcy Leslie-Parsons (310) 963-6629
(310) 837-2817

Martha Lucas (213) 481-7109
(323) 376-9699

Judy May (818) 883-4909

Susan McGonigle (310) 770-7715
(858) 467-1494

Colleen O'Donnell (818) 591-1953
(818) 437-1133

Lynn Reynolds (323) 851-4662
(541) 601-7913
FAX (541) 552-0852

Kim Shapiro (818) 389-6888

Kathleen E. Simons (818) 497-8889
(423) 239-4949
FAX (423) 239-2232

Jay Sisson (213) 820-3075
(213) 210-1961
(Spanish)

Lindsay Skutch (805) 687-9852
(805) 341-3554

Debby Timmons (818) 906-2093

Susan Vogelfang (310) 306-2648

Allan Wachs (310) 589-4841
(310) 467-5131

Ree Whitford (818) 424-9988
(818) 505-1060

300ml (310) 264-3000
www.hungryman.com

Abdul Malik Abbott (323) 466-1171
www.1171.com

Charles Abehsera (323) 931-1782
www.backhomepictures.com

Nasar Abich Jr. (310) 652-8778
www.lspagency.net

John Adams (323) 653-0404
www.form.tv

Brian Ades (310) 503-8080

Casey Affleck (310) 659-1577
www.rsafilms.com

Agustin Alberdi (310) 823-5400
www.carbofilms.com

Jaron Albertin (323) 817-3300
www.smugglersite.com

Alex and Martin (323) 468-0123
www.partizan.com

Leslie Ali (323) 468-0123
www.partizan.com

Gil Alkabetz (323) 464-7805
www.acmefilmworks.com

Debbie Allen (310) 315-1750
www.30secondfilms.com

Ambitious Entertainment (818) 990-8993
(Reps for Commercial Directors) www.ambitiousent.com

Clark Anderson (310) 448-7900
www.rhythm.com

Wes Anderson (310) 857-1000
www.moxiepictures.com

Philippe Andre (310) 277-7001
www.companyfilms.net

Daniel Andreas (310) 986-3370
www.24pcine.com

Steve Andrich (310) 822-6367
www.ladybug-la.com

Anouk (323) 850-0690
(310) 917-9191
www.celsiusfilms.com

Chris Applebaum (310) 656-4646
www.reactorfilms.com

Gints Apsits (310) 478-0771
www.duckstudios.com

Dante Ariola (310) 826-6200
www.mjz.com

Adam Arkin (310) 399-9600
www.nonfictionspots.com

Alan Arkin (310) 399-9600
www.nonfictionspots.com

Ken Arlidge (310) 396-3636
www.aerofilm.tv

Janet Arlotta (310) 558-8755
www.fueldesign.com

Bozena Armstrong (310) 289-6650
FAX (310) 289-6658

Arni and Kinski (323) 969-0555
www.awhitelabelproduct.com

Fernando Arrioja (310) 823-5400
www.carbofilms.com

Renato Assad (818) 788-0153
www.fjproductions.com

Atanas (323) 790-1732
www.maneaterproductions.com

Shona Auerbach (310) 899-1700
www.gartner.tv

Enrique Aular (323) 932-6588
www.acatch22production.com

Sam Auster (818) 843-5040
www.austerproductions.com

Jesse Austin (323) 464-2406
www.47pictures.com

The AV Club (323) 465-5299
www.thedirectorsbureau.com

Mazik-Self Aviary (310) 288-8000
www.paradigmagency.com

Pedro Avila (310) 823-5400
www.carbofilms.com

Steve Ayson (323) 817-3300
www.smugglersite.com

Moh Azina (818) 985-9905
www.factoryfeatures.com

Mister Babbage (323) 957-1454
www.cmpictures.tv

Brian Baderman (310) 392-7333
www.thomaswintercooke.com

Matthew Badger (310) 275-9333
www.epochfilms.com

Rebecca Baehler (310) 656-4900
www.greendotfilms.com

Robert E Bailey (310) 458-0663
www.beachhousefilms.com

Grant Baird (310) 260-6100
www.motivfilms.com

Natalie Barandes (310) 360-7180
www.getitpictures.com

Joe Baratelli (310) 899-0335
www.tuesdayfilms.com

Hector Barboza (323) 932-6588
www.acatch22production.com

Garri Bardine (323) 464-7805
www.acmefilmworks.com

Antoine Bardou-Jacquet (323) 468-0123
www.partizan.com

Geoff Barish (310) 917-9191
www.untitled.tv

Howard Barish (818) 789-6777
www.kandoofilms.com

Raymond Bark (310) 899-1700
www.gartner.tv

Nicholas Barker (323) 860-8030
www.chelsea.com

Thomas Barron (818) 761-6644
www.imageg.com

Jim Barton (310) 315-1949
www.picturepk.com

Matt Bass (818) 985-9905
www.factoryfeatures.com

Gabriel Bassio (310) 305-8200
www.900frames.tv

Russell Bates (310) 659-6220
www.crossroadsfilms.com

Brian Baugh (310) 871-1506
www.i40films.com

Samuel Bayer (323) 969-0555
www.awhitelabelproduct.com

Christopher Bean (310) 550-6990
www.macguffin.com

Kevan Bean (310) 550-6990
www.macguffin.com

Jon Bekemeier (310) 315-1949
www.picturepk.com

Marina Belaustegui (323) 932-6588
www.acatch22production.com

Brian Belefant (503) 715-2852
(310) 854-2458
www.belefant.com

Brian Beletic (323) 817-3300
www.smugglersite.com

Martin Bell (310) 899-6979
www.cohnandco.com

Trudy Bellinger (310) 659-6220
www.crossroadsfilms.com

Chuck Bennett (310) 451-4148
www.biglawnfilms.com

Mark Raymon Bennett (310) 899-6979
(310) 917-9191
www.cohnandco.com

Anthea Benton (323) 645-1000
www.believemedia.com

Adam Berg (323) 817-3300
www.smugglersite.com

Stu Berg (310) 827-3336

Evan Bernard (323) 860-8030
(323) 465-9494
www.chelsea.com

Adam Bernstein (310) 275-9333
www.epochfilms.com

Kenneth Berris (805) 963-6776
www.berris.com

Fabio Berutti (323) 937-4182
www.legacyfilms.net

Anouk Besson (310) 275-9333
www.epochfilms.com

Nico Beyer (310) 659-6220
www.crossroadsfilms.com

Scott Bibo (323) 461-0101
www.altavistafilms.com

Tim Bieber (310) 399-9910
www.mrbigfilm.com

Big Machine (818) 906-0006
www.thedirectorsnetwork.com

Michael Bigelow (310) 899-1700
www.gartner.tv

bigtv (310) 453-2600
www.harvestfilms.com

Scott Billups (818) 990-8993
www.ambitiousent.com

Rob Bindler (310) 399-9600
www.nonfictionunlimited.com

Henry Bjoin (818) 846-1650
www.bjoinfilms.com

Robert Black (323) 653-0404
www.form.tv

Richard Black (818) 760-8707

Robert Blalack (323) 460-4393

Jim Blashfield (323) 464-7805
www.acmefilmworks.com

Adam Bleibtreu (310) 451-4112

Irv Blitz (310) 558-7100
www.hsiproductions.com

Neill Blomkamp (310) 659-1577
www.rsafilms.com

Blue Source (310) 826-6200
www.mjz.com

Armando Bo (310) 558-3667
www.anonymouscontent.com

David Bojorquez (310) 986-3370
www.24pcine.com

Fredrik Bond (310) 826-6200
www.mjz.com

Gillian Bonner (323) 874-8888
www.blackdragon.com

Richard Borge (310) 478-0771
www.duckstudios.com

Daniel Börjesson (323) 465-9494
www.helloandcompany.com

Kevin Bourland (310) 305-8200
www.900frames.tv

Patrick Bowyer (323) 464-3080
www.moostudios.com

Jordan Brady (323) 860-8686
www.ubercontent.com

Mike Brady (310) 338-0580
www.utopiafilms.com

Zach Braff (323) 937-3007
www.spaceprogram.tv

Eddie Brakha (310) 288-8000
www.paradigmagency.com

Moshe Brakha (323) 658-6541
(310) 288-8000
www.commercialhead.com

Marco Brambilla (323) 463-2826
www.dnala.com

Nick Brandt (323) 645-1000
www.believemedia.com

Kevin Brey (310) 558-3667
www.anonymouscontent.com

Larry Bridges (310) 828-7500
www.redcar.com

David Briggs (866) 711-5195
www.jspcreative.com

Wilfred Brimo (310) 659-6220
www.crossroadsfilms.com

Mark Brinster (818) 990-8993
www.ambitiousent.com

David Brooks (818) 985-9905
www.factoryfeatures.com

J Brown (323) 962-7855
www.tombofilm.com

Jerry Brown (323) 790-0440
www.sticks.tv

Kerry Shaw Brown (310) 453-1115
www.millenniumpictures.tv

Phil Brown (310) 828-8989
www.tateusa.com

PR Brown (323) 465-9494
www.helloandcompany.com

Bryan Buckley (310) 264-3000
www.hungryman.com

Frank Budgen (310) 558-3667
www.anonymouscontent.com

Jeffrey Burke (323) 257-4400
www.burketriolo.com

Nanette Burstein (323) 645-1000
www.believemedia.com

Matthaus Bussmann (310) 854-0647
www.sandwickmedia.com

Eric Bute (310) 260-6100
www.motivfilms.com

Adam Byrd (323) 464-3080
www.moostudios.com

Scott Caan (310) 288-8000
www.paradigmagency.com

Leslie Cabarga (323) 464-7805
www.acmefilmworks.com

Nelson Cabrera (310) 699-3133

Paul Cade (310) 899-6979
www.cohnandco.com

Marc Cadieux (310) 880-2493
FAX (818) 788-4168
www.sirreelfilms.com

Sam Cadman (310) 453-9244
www.toolofna.com

Reto Caduff (310) 986-3370
www.24pcine.com

Joshua Caine (323) 874-8888
www.blackdragon.com

Jamie Caliri (310) 478-0771
www.duckstudios.com

Adam Cameron (310) 277-7001
www.companyfilms.net

David Cameron (323) 650-4722

Don Cameron (323) 969-0555
www.awhitelabelproduct.com

Kenneth Cappello (310) 558-7100
www.hsiproductions.com

Peter Care (310) 396-7333
www.bobcentral.com

Rey Carlson (323) 465-9494
www.helloandcompany.com

Bob Carmichael (310) 739-0650
FAX (303) 955-7064
www.bobcarmichael.com

Joe Carnahan (310) 659-1577
www.rsafilms.com

Larry Carroll (310) 546-9515
(310) 372-4502
www.larrycarroll.net

Carter and Blitz (310) 558-3667
www.anonymouscontent.com

Tom Carty (310) 558-3667
www.anonymouscontent.com

Gerald V. Casale (310) 315-1949
www.picturepk.com

Bruce Caulk (310) 882-2100
www.intelliscape.com

Chamaco (310) 822-6367
www.ladybug-la.com

Jerry Chan (310) 295-4660
www.ringleaderproductions.com

Christian Charles (323) 850-0690
www.celsiusfilms.com

Steve Chase (310) 656-4646
www.reactorfilms.com

Carolyn Chen (323) 645-1000
www.believemedia.com

Spencer Chinoy (310) 857-1000
www.moxiepictures.com

Steven Chivers (323) 957-1454
www.cmpictures.tv

Lisa Cholodenko (323) 468-0123
www.partizan.com

Dana Christiaansen (310) 260-6100
www.motivfilms.com

Samuel Christopher (310) 264-3000
www.hungryman.com

Andrew Christou (310) 857-1000
www.moxiepictures.com

Curtis Clark (323) 460-4767
www.jacobandkoleagency.com

Duane Clark (818) 907-7111

Chuck Clemens (310) 305-8200
www.900frames.tv

Harry Cocciolo (310) 453-9244
www.toolofna.com

The Coen Brothers (310) 277-7001
www.companyfilms.net

Isabel Coixet (310) 823-5400
www.carbofilms.com

Barney Cokeliss (310) 659-1577
www.rsafilms.com

Charlie Cole (310) 899-6979
www.cohnandco.com

Nigel Cole (310) 395-5022

Simon Cole (310) 558-7100
www.hsiproductions.com

Jim Collins (310) 550-6990
www.macguffin.com

Marino Colmano (818) 362-5170

Colombo (323) 790-1732
www.maneaterproductions.com

Michel Comte (323) 653-0404
www.form.tv

Buddy Cone (310) 289-1232
www.fabricationfilms.com

Kevin Connolly (310) 558-7100
www.hsiproductions.com

Gil Cope (323) 460-2077
www.darklightpictures.com

Roman Coppola (323) 465-5299
www.thedirectorsbureau.com

Sofia Coppola (323) 465-5299
www.thedirectorsbureau.com

Mark Coppos (310) 656-4900
www.greendotfilms.com

Ericson Core (310) 314-1122
www.backyard.com

Trevor Cornish (310) 392-7333
www.thomaswintercooke.com

Allen Coulter (310) 264-3000
www.hungryman.com

Nathan Karma Cox (310) 315-1949
www.picturepk.com

Brian Coyne (818) 906-0006
www.thedirectorsnetwork.com

Eli Craig (310) 295-4660
www.ringleaderproductions.com

Pablo Croce (323) 932-6588
www.acatch22production.com

Tony Croll (310) 288-4545

Jeff Cronenweth (310) 917-9191
www.untitled.tv

Tim Cronenweth (310) 917-9191
www.untitled.tv

Paul Crowder (310) 399-9600
www.nonfictionunlimited.com

Cameron Crowe (310) 857-1000
www.moxiepictures.com

Bill Cuccinello (310) 315-1949
www.picturepk.com

Michael Cuesta (323) 650-4722

Richard Cullen (310) 478-0771
www.duckstudios.com

Dean Cundey (626) 584-4000
www.danwolfe.com

John Curran (310) 854-0647
www.sandwickfilms.com

Victor Currie (866) 368-6501
www.robinsoncurrie.com

Skip D'Amico (323) 650-4722

Tim Damon (310) 453-1115
www.millenniumpictures.tv

Randall P. Dark (323) 969-8822
www.illuminatehollywood.com

Camp David (310) 854-0647
www.sandwickfilms.com

Jonathan David (323) 860-5400
www.gofilm.net

Jonathan Dayton (310) 396-7333
www.bobcentral.com

Charlie Deaux (310) 652-8778
www.lspagency.net

Evert de Beijer (323) 464-7805
www.acmefilmworks.com

Tom De Cerchio (310) 566-6733
www.incubatorfilms.com

Jeffrey DeChausse (310) 559-8333
www.boxerfilms.net

Michael J. DeCourcey (310) 480-4031
www.decourcey.com

Leslie Dektor (323) 466-3455
www.dektorfilm.com

Mark Dektor (323) 466-3455
www.dektorfilm.com

Paul Dektor (323) 466-3455
www.dektorfilm.com

Delicatessen (310) 478-0771
www.duckstudios.com

Tom DeLonge (323) 466-1171
www.1171.com

David Denneen (323) 653-0404
www.form.tv

Paul and Menno De Nooijer (323) 464-7805
www.acmefilmworks.com

Mark de Paola (310) 550-5910
www.filmfilmfilminc.com

Scott Derrickson (310) 392-7333
www.thomaswintercooke.com

Christopher Desantis (310) 917-9191
www.untitled.tv

Caleb Deschanel (323) 460-2077
www.darklightpictures.com

Martin De Thurah (323) 465-9494
www.helloandcompany.com

Erik Deutschman (310) 478-0771
www.duckstudios.com

Patricia Mtz. De Velasco (310) 858-7204
www.labandafilms.com

Rob Devor (310) 399-9600
www.nonfictionunlimited.com

Michael Dudok De Wit (323) 464-7805
www.acmefilmworks.com

Tom Dey (310) 659-1577
www.rsafilms.com

Jun Diaz (323) 817-3300
www.smugglersite.com

Ben Dickinson (310) 659-1577
(323) 951-4400
www.rsafilms.com

Devon Dickson (818) 906-0006
www.thedirectorsnetwork.com

Carl Diebold (310) 576-4992
www.agogofilms.com

Steven Diller (310) 396-4333
(310) 826-6200
www.mjz.com

Ray Dillman (310) 826-6200
www.mjz.com

John Dilworth (323) 464-7805
www.acmefilmworks.com

Barbara Di Pasquale (310) 478-0771
www.duckstudios.com

Mark Dippé (310) 448-7900
www.rhythm.com

The Directors Network (818) 906-0006
3685 Motor Ave., Ste. 220 FAX (818) 906-0007
Los Angeles, CA 90034 www.thedirectorsnetwork.com
(Reps for Commercial Directors)

Abby Dix (818) 906-0006
www.thedirectorsnetwork.com

Jon Dixon (310) 288-8000
www.paradigmagency.com

Chris Do (310) 314-1618
www.blind.com

David Dobkin (323) 860-5400
www.gofilm.net

Docter Twins (310) 478-0771
www.duckstudios.com

James Dodson (310) 828-8989
www.tateusa.com

John Dolan (310) 558-3667
www.anonymouscontent.com

Kevin Dole (310) 470-0491
FAX (310) 475-9041

Andrew Dominik (310) 659-1577
www.rsafilms.com

Kevin Donovan (310) 395-5022
(323) 653-0404

Lenard Dorfman (310) 857-1000
www.moxiepictures.com

Tony Dow (310) 315-1750
www.30secondfilms.com

Bruce Dowad (310) 899-1720
(310) 956-3500
www.tightfilms.com

Dr. Garry (310) 857-7745
www.attackads.tv

Rebecca Dreyfus (323) 465-9494
www.helloandcompany.com

Pau Driessen (323) 464-7805
www.acmefilmworks.com

Shawn Driscoll (213) 385-5082
www.rightbrain.tv

David Dryer (310) 450-1220
(818) 906-0006
www.thedirectorsnetwork.com

Rick Dublin (323) 240-6736
www.motelfilms.com

Danny Ducovny (310) 396-7778
www.cucoloris.com

Jerry Dugan (213) 385-5082
(310) 822-6367
www.rightbrain.tv

Barry Dukoff (310) 399-9600
www.nonfictionspots.com

Piotr Dumala (323) 464-7805
www.acmefilmworks.com

Scott Duncan (323) 937-3007
www.spaceprogram.tv

Laurence Dunmore (310) 659-1577
www.rsafilms.com

Cheryl Dunn (323) 465-9494
www.helloandcompany.com

Steve Dunning (818) 906-0006
www.thedirectorsnetwork.com

Rob Dupear (310) 652-8778
www.lspagency.net

Alex Duplan (310) 858-7204
www.labandafilms.com

The Duplass Brothers (310) 659-1577
www.rsafilms.com

Claudio Duran (323) 932-6588
www.acatch22production.com

Richard E. (323) 464-5111
www.showreel.com

Timothy Eaton (866) 535-1972
www.veritestudios.com

Robert Eberlein (310) 277-0070

Ryan Ebner (310) 558-7100
www.hsiproductions.com

Paul Edwards (310) 288-8000
www.paradigmagency.com

Eagle Egilsson (310) 857-7745
www.attackads.tv

Sean Ehringer (310) 453-9244
www.toolofna.com

Breck Eisner (323) 860-8030
www.chelsea.com

Sean Ellis (310) 659-1577
www.rsafilms.com

Mona El Monsouri (310) 888-8900
(310) 277-7001
www.villains.com

The Elvis (323) 468-0123
www.partizan.com

Filip Engstrom (323) 817-3300
www.smugglersite.com

Jesper Ericstam (310) 314-1122
www.backyard.com

Christopher Erskin (323) 937-4182
www.legacyfilms.net

Steve Eshelman (310) 659-6220
www.crossroadsfilms.com

Will Eubank (310) 288-8000
www.paradigmagency.com

Bill Everett (310) 314-8770
www.wyomingfilms.net

Evil Cat Land (310) 478-0771
www.duckstudios.com

Todd Factor (310) 395-5022

Lauri Faggioni (310) 659-1577
www.rsafilms.com

Tenney Fairchild (310) 899-9100
www.m80films.com

Faivre Brothers (310) 478-0771
www.duckstudios.com

Adriano Falconi (213) 385-5082
www.rightbrain.tv

Trey Fanjoy (310) 260-6100
www.motivfilms.com

Darren Fanton (310) 295-4660
(650) 380-0972

Valerie Faris (310) 396-7333
www.bobcentral.com

Caitlin Felton (323) 860-5400
www.gofilm.net

Piper Ferguson (310) 656-9100
www.epixfilms.com

Rafael Fernandez (310) 656-4900
www.greendotfilms.com

Rod Findley (310) 208-2324
www.c-2k.com

Mo Fitzgibbon (323) 469-6800
www.walkerfitzgibbon.com

Miles Flannigan (323) 790-1732
www.maneaterproductions.com

Jeffrey Fleisig (323) 860-8686
www.ubercontent.com

Fritz Flieder (323) 463-2826
www.dnala.com

Stephen Flint-Muller (323) 464-7805
www.acmefilmworks.com

E.J. Foerster (310) 448-7900
www.rhythm.com

Richard Foley (818) 402-0707
FAX (818) 729-9033
www.explodedviewla.com

Steve Fong (310) 578-9383
www.kaboomproductions.com

Brett Foraker (310) 659-1577
www.rsafilms.com

Amanda Forbis (323) 464-7805
www.acmefilmworks.com

Claudia Forsthoevel (310) 399-3456
www.cwuw.com

Martin Fougerol (323) 464-3080
www.moostudios.com

Ken Fox (323) 930-0101
www.altavistafilms.com

Jeff France (310) 392-7333
www.thomaswintercooke.com

Justin Francis (310) 558-7100
www.hsiproductions.com

David Frankham (323) 817-3300
www.smugglersite.com

Thor Freudenthal (310) 656-4646
www.reactorfilms.com

Larry Frey (310) 664-4500
(323) 860-8030
www.chelsea.com

Rick Friedberg (818) 990-8993
www.ambitiousent.com

Liz Friedlander (323) 463-2826
www.dnala.com

Paul Fuentes (818) 990-8993
www.ambitiousent.com

Michael Fueter (310) 392-7333
www.thomaswintercooke.com

Nicolai Fuglsig (310) 826-6200
www.mjz.com

Damian Fulton (310) 394-0110
www.movingtargetla.com

Peter Fuszard (310) 581-5445
www.novemberfilms.com

Tony G (310) 458-0663
www.beachhousefilms.com

Jim Gable (310) 979-4333
www.gandb.tv

Leo Gabriadze (323) 876-3331
www.wildindigo.tv

David Gaddie (323) 468-0123
www.partizan.com

Jorge Gaggero (310) 823-5400
www.carbofilms.com

Stephen Gaghan (323) 653-0404
www.form.tv

Mark Galanty (310) 451-2525

Sidney Galanty (310) 451-2525

Andy Gallerani (310) 399-6630

Pico Garcez (818) 788-0153
www.fjproductions.com

Elma Garcia (323) 937-3007
www.spaceprogram.tv

Rodrigo Garcia (310) 858-7204
www.labandafilms.com

Rodrigo Garcia Saiz (323) 461-0101
www.altavistafilms.com

Victor Garcia (310) 826-6200
www.mjz.com

Anthony Garth (323) 790-1732
www.maneaterproductions.com

James Gartner (310) 899-1700
www.gartner.tv

Paul Gay (310) 396-4333
(310) 264-3000
www.omahapictures.com

Larry Gebhardt (818) 906-0006
www.thedirectorsnetwork.com

Kim Gehrig (323) 465-9494
www.helloandcompany.com

Kim Geldenhuys (310) 396-7333
www.bobcentral.com

Tryan George (323) 645-1000
www.believemedia.com

Luis Gerard (323) 860-8686
www.ubercontent.com

Richard Gibson (323) 860-8030
www.chelsea.com

Mark Gilbert (323) 465-9494
www.helloandcompany.com

Stuart Gillard (310) 288-8000
www.paradigmagency.com

Craig Gillespie (310) 826-6200
www.mjz.com

Bob Giraldi (310) 274-6102
www.giraldi.com

Maxime Giroux (310) 526-7703
www.instantkarmafilms.tv

Michael Givens (310) 444-7055
www.blueyedpictures.com

Jonathan Glazer (323) 465-9494
www.helloandcompany.com

Tim Godsall (310) 275-9333
(323) 856-9200
www.biscuitfilmworks.com

Goetz Brothers (310) 396-5796
www.detourfilms.com

Eric Goldberg (310) 478-0771
www.duckstudios.com

Paul Goldman (323) 468-0123
www.partizan.com

Adam Goldstein (310) 659-1577
www.rsafilms.com

Adam Goldstein (310) 453-2600
www.harvestfilms.com

Fabio Golombek (818) 788-0153
www.fjproductions.com

Michel Gondry (323) 468-0123
www.partizan.com

Olivier Gondry (323) 468-0123
www.partizan.com

Sunu Gonera (310) 288-8000
www.paradigmagency.com

Alejandro González Inárritu (310) 558-3667
www.anonymouscontent.com

Nick Gordon (323) 465-9494
www.helloandcompany.com

Robert Gordon (323) 782-7125
www.ftfilms.com

Jeff Gorman (310) 854-0647
www.sandwickfilms.com

Neil Gorring (310) 857-1000
www.moxiepictures.com

Chris Gosch (818) 729-0000
www.goschproductions.com

Fred Goss (310) 277-7001
www.companyfilms.net

Jean-Paul Goude (323) 969-0555
www.awhitelabelproduct.com

Johnny B. Graham (818) 906-0006
www.thedirectorsnetwork.com

Martin Granger (310) 857-1000
www.moxiepictures.com

Evin Grant (310) 444-7055
www.blueyedpictures.com

Grapefruit (818) 906-0006
www.thedirectorsnetwork.com

Joe Grasso (323) 957-1454
www.cmpictures.tv

Michael Grasso (310) 396-4333
www.omahapictures.com

David Gordon Green (323) 860-8030
www.chelsea.com

Steph Green (310) 659-1577
www.littleminx.tv

Howard Greenhalgh (323) 645-1000
www.believemedia.com

Paula Grief (310) 275-9333
www.epochfilms.com

James Griffiths (310) 857-1000
www.moxiepictures.com

Robert Groenwold (310) 559-8333
www.boxerfilms.net

Ron Gross (323) 658-6893
www.bluegoose.tv

Sebastien Grousset (310) 659-6220
www.crossroadsfilms.com

The Guard Brothers (310) 888-8900
(323) 817-3300
www.villains.com

Christopher Guest (323) 860-5400
www.gofilm.net

Guillaume (323) 650-4722

Sanjay Gupta (818) 906-0006
www.thedirectorsnetwork.com

Max Gutierrez (310) 295-4660
(310) 809-1778
www.ringleaderproductions.com

Daniel Guyonnet (323) 464-7805
www.acmefilmworks.com

H5 (310) 659-1577
www.littleminx.com

Jorn Haagen (323) 645-1000
www.believemedia.com

James Hackett (310) 478-0771
www.duckstudios.com

Jeremy Haft (323) 790-1732
www.maneaterproductions.com

Tom Haines (323) 465-9494
www.helloandcompany.com

Francois Halard (323) 464-3080
www.moostudios.com

Robert Hales (310) 558-7100
www.hsiproductions.com

Anders Hallberg (323) 645-1000
www.believemedia.com

Jim Hallowes (310) 390-4767
www.jimhallowes.com

Ron Hamad (818) 906-0006
(310) 823-5400
www.thedirectorsnetwork.com

Tim Hamilton (323) 860-5400
www.gofilm.net

Sanaa Hamri (310) 558-3667
www.anonymouscontent.com

Sean Hanish (310) 375-0593
www.cannoballproduction.com

Henrik Hansen (310) 396-3636
(310) 659-1577
www.aerofilm.tv

Pamela Hanson (323) 464-3080
www.moostudios.com

Andrew Hardaway (310) 559-8333
www.boxerfilms.net

Phil Harder (310) 396-7333
www.bobcentral.com

Chris Harding (310) 478-0771
www.duckstudios.com

Johnny Hardstaff (310) 659-1577
www.littleminx.com

Corin Hardy (323) 465-9494
www.helloandcompany.com

Varda Hardy (310) 264-0402

Rachel Harms (323) 650-4722

Jason Harrington (323) 645-1000
www.believemedia.com

Neil Harris (323) 817-3300
www.smugglersite.com

Oliver Harrison (323) 464-7805
www.acmefilmworks.com

Harvey and Carolyn (310) 659-6220
www.crossroadsfilms.com

Alfred Hau (310) 526-7703
www.instantkarmafilms.tv

Michael Haussman (310) 558-7100
www.hsiproductions.com

Haxan (323) 860-8030
www.chelsea.com

Blair Hayes (323) 653-0404
www.form.tv

Sian Heder (323) 464-2406
www.47pictures.com

Laura Heit (310) 478-0771
www.duckstudios.com

Hannah Hempstead (310) 306-3088
FAX (310) 306-3089

Anna Henckle-Donnersmarck (323) 464-7805
www.acmefilmworks.com

Stewart Hendler (310) 396-4333
(323) 860-8686
www.omahapictures.com

Graham Henman (323) 465-9494
www.helloandcompany.com

Doug Henry (323) 466-2490
www.kavichreynolds.com

Marshall Herskovitz (310) 395-5022

Dale Heslip (310) 260-6100
www.motivfilms.com

Jared Hess (310) 857-1000
www.moxiepictures.com

George Hickenlooper (213) 385-5082
www.rightbrain.tv

Thom Higgins (310) 395-5022
(310) 656-4900

Eric Hillenbrand (310) 558-7100
www.hsiproductions.com

Chris Hinton (323) 464-7805
www.acmefilmworks.com

Steven M. Hirohama (310) 204-0520
FAX (310) 202-1386
www.applebox.com

Kris Hixson (310) 871-1506
www.i40films.com

Hobby (310) 659-1577
www.rsafilms.com

Hobos with Guns (818) 985-9905
www.factoryfeatures.com

Matthias Hoene (323) 468-0123
www.partizan.com

The Hoffman Brothers (310) 453-2600
www.harvestfilms.com

Andreas Hoffman (310) 558-7100
www.hsiproductions.com

WD Hogan (310) 295-4660
www.ringleaderproductions.com

Greg Holfeld (323) 464-7805
www.acmefilmworks.com

King Hollis (323) 665-4198
www.alteregofilms.com

James Holt (323) 860-8030
www.chelsea.com

Chris Hooper (310) 396-7333
www.bobcentral.com

Cameron Hopkins (323) 464-2406
www.47pictures.com

Peter Horton (310) 395-5022

Jim Hosking (323) 856-9200
www.biscuitfilmworks.com

Arturo Hoyos (310) 338-0580
www.utopiafilms.com

Ricardo Hoyos (310) 338-0580
www.utopiafilms.com

Andy Huang (323) 464-3080
(323) 465-9494
www.moostudios.com

Bill Hudson (323) 650-4722

John Huet (310) 315-1949
www.picturepk.com

Hughes Brothers (310) 558-7100
www.hsiproductions.com

Greg Hughs (310) 305-8200
www.900frames.tv

Bruce Hunt (323) 856-9200
www.biscuitfilmworks.com

Bruce Hurwit (310) 659-6220
www.crossroadsfilms.com

Illegal Artists (310) 823-5400
(310) 453-6210
www.carbofilms.com

Wayne Isham (310) 659-6220
www.crossroadsfilms.com

Michael Ivey (310) 314-8770
www.wyomingfilms.net

James Ivory (310) 395-5022

Jack and Carol (310) 314-8770
www.wyomingfilms.net

Eric Jackson (323) 464-5111
www.showreel.com

Jesse Jacobs (310) 656-9100
www.epixfilms.com

Jacobs/Briere (323) 465-9494
www.helloandcompany.com

Enno Jacobsen (213) 385-5082
(310) 659-0010
www.newhousefilms.com

JAM (310) 659-6220
www.crossroadsfilms.com

Steve James (310) 399-9600
www.nonfictionunlimited.com

Michael Patrick Jann (323) 465-9494
www.helloandcompany.com

Mikael Jansson (323) 969-0555
www.awhitelabelproduct.com

Julia Jason (310) 659-6220
www.crossroadsfilms.com

Jaume (323) 645-1000
www.believemedia.com

The Jay and Tony Show (310) 315-1949
www.picturepk.com

David Jellison (310) 392-7333
www.thomaswintercooke.com

Andrews Jenkins (323) 860-5400
www.gofilm.net

Garth Jennings (310) 558-3667
(323) 465-9494
www.anonymouscontent.com

Norman Jewison (310) 395-5022

Robert Jitzmark (310) 264-3000
www.hungryman.com

JL Design (310) 478-0771
www.duckstudios.com

Phil Joanou (310) 826-6200
www.mjz.com

Gary Johns (323) 467-8252
www.a-film-by.com

Bryan Johnson (323) 938-8080

Cooper Johnson (818) 985-9905
www.factoryfeatures.com

Hugh Johnson (310) 659-1577
www.rsafilms.com

Erich Joiner (310) 453-9244
www.toolofna.com

Brent Jones (310) 396-3636
(323) 465-9494
www.aerofilm.tv

Bronston Jones (310) 857-7745
www.attackads.tv

Jeff Jones (818) 906-0006
www.thedirectorsnetwork.com

Sam Jones (310) 453-9244
www.toolofna.com

Toni Jones (310) 578-9383
www.kaboomproductions.com

Arni Thor Jonsson (310) 899-6979
www.cohnandco.com

Spike Jonze (310) 826-6200
www.mjz.com

Josh and Xander (310) 899-1720
www.tightfilms.com

Michael Joy (323) 860-8030
www.chelsea.com

Jaci Judelson (310) 558-7100
www.hsiproductions.com

Alex Juliá (310) 823-5400
www.carbofilms.com

Gil Junger (310) 288-8000
www.paradigmagency.com

Peter Kaboth (310) 478-0771
www.duckstudios.com

Peter Kagan (323) 850-0690
www.celsiusfilms.com

Joseph Kahn (310) 558-7100
www.hsiproductions.com

Scott Kalvert (310) 315-1949
www.picturepk.com

Adam Kane (818) 907-7111

Michael Karbelnikoff (323) 465-9494
www.helloandcompany.com

Jeffrey Karoff (310) 314-1122
www.backyard.com

Dean Karr (323) 876-3331
www.wildindigo.tv

Piotr Karwas (310) 478-0771
www.duckstudios.com

David Katz (310) 699-9760

Jeff Kaumeyer (310) 396-5796
www.detourfilms.com

Tony Kaye (310) 956-3500
www.supplyanddemand.tv

Walter Kehr (323) 465-9494
www.helloandcompany.com

Lance Kelleher (323) 653-0404
www.form.tv

Rory Kelleher (310) 558-3667
www.anonymouscontent.com

Kelley (323) 790-1732
www.maneaterproductions.com

Timothy Kendall (310) 448-7900
www.rhythm.com

Robby Kenner (310) 399-9600
www.nonfictionunlimited.com

Kenny FX (323) 790-1732
www.maneaterproductions.com

Billy Kent (818) 906-0006
www.thedirectorsnetwork.com

Bob Kerstetter (323) 860-8030
www.chelsea.com

Rolf Kestermann (323) 344-8905
www.stratofilms.com

Jim Kimura (323) 559-1110
FAX (626) 398-1387
www.tdnartists.com

Eric King (310) 828-8989
www.tateusa.com

Stephen Kirklys (310) 478-0771
www.duckstudios.com

Richard Kizu-Blair (310) 289-1232
www.fabricationfilms.com

Justin Klarenbeck (310) 392-7333
(310) 917-9191
www.thomaswintercooke.com

Steven Klein (310) 558-3667
www.anonymouscontent.com

Nikita Kleverov (323) 620-6925
www.halfelement.com

Isaac Klotz (323) 620-6925
www.halfelement.com

Rick Knief (310) 917-9191
www.untitled.tv

Rene Kock (310) 399-3456
www.cwuw.com

Albert Kodagolian (323) 645-1000
www.believemedia.com

Tom Koh (310) 314-1618
www.blind.com

Mark Kohl (310) 301-3313
www.zystar.com

Jason Kohn (323) 860-8686
www.ubercontent.com

Mark Kohr (310) 396-7333
www.bobcentral.com

Konwiser Brothers (323) 467-8252
www.a-film-by.com

Barbara Kopple (310) 399-9600
www.nonfictionunlimited.com

Aleksandra Korejwo (323) 464-7805
www.acmefilmworks.com

Harmony Korine (310) 826-6200
www.mjz.com

Joe Kosinski (310) 558-3667
www.anonymouscontent.com

Jesper Kouthoofd (310) 659-1577
www.littleminx.tv

Igor Kovalyov (323) 464-7805
www.acmefilmworks.com

Rob Kraetsch (323) 620-6925
www.halfelement.com

Brandon Kraines (310) 288-8000
www.paradigmagency.com

Randy Krallman (323) 817-3300
www.smugglersite.com

Johan Kramer (323) 860-8030
www.chelsea.com

Bob Kronovet (310) 315-1750
www.30secondfilms.com

Raimund Krumme (323) 464-7805
www.acmefilmworks.com

Amica Kubo (310) 478-0771
www.duckstudios.com

Chuck Kuhn (310) 314-8770
www.wyomingfilms.net

Tom Kuntz (310) 826-6200
www.mjz.com

Mauricio Kuri (323) 937-4182
www.legacyfilms.net

Warren Kushner (310) 656-4646
www.reactorfilms.com

David LaChapelle (310) 558-7100
www.hsiproductions.com

Dave Laden (323) 860-8686
www.ubercontent.com

Brian Lai (310) 526-7703
www.instantkarmafilms.tv

Andy Lambert (310) 558-7100
www.hsiproductions.com

Lou La Monte (310) 656-9100
www.epixfilms.com

Russ Lamoureux (323) 856-9200
www.biscuitfilmworks.com

Chris Landreth (323) 464-7805
www.acmefilmworks.com

Lane and Jan (310) 478-0771
www.duckstudios.com

Evan Lane (323) 790-1732
www.maneaterproductions.com

Rocky Lane (818) 906-0006
www.thedirectorsnetwork.com

Axel Laubscher (310) 888-8900
www.villains.com

Christoph and Wolfgang Lauenstein (323) 464-7805
www.acmefilmworks.com

Francis Lawrence (323) 463-2826
www.dnala.com

Caroline Leaf (323) 464-7805
www.acmefilmworks.com

John Le Blanc (323) 257-8881
FAX (323) 258-9549

Ringan Ledwidge (323) 817-3300
www.smugglersite.com

Virginia Lee (310) 656-4900
www.greendotfilms.com

Gregory Lemkin (310) 450-1220
www.oceanparkpix.com

David Lena (323) 937-4182
www.legacyfilms.net

Ashley Lenz (323) 464-7805
www.acmefilmworks.com

Dana Leshem (310) 986-3370
www.24pcine.com

Daniel Levi (310) 558-3667
www.anonymouscontent.com

James Levine (310) 775-6616
(818) 554-8019
FAX (310) 478-2100
www.typecastinginc.com

Dan Levinson (310) 857-1000
www.moxiepictures.com

Elyse Lewin (818) 788-4214

Nick Lewin (310) 659-6220
www.crossroadsfilms.com

Taron Lexton (310) 288-8000
www.paradigmagency.com

Leslie Libman (323) 653-0404
www.form.tv

Michel Lichtenstein (310) 822-6367
www.ladybug-la.com

Ron Lieberman (323) 653-0404
www.form.tv

John Lindauer (323) 645-1000
www.believemedia.com

Peter Lindbergh (323) 969-0555
www.awhitelabelproduct.com

Scott Evans Lindsay (310) 291-4999
www.slindsay.com

William Linsman (310) 450-1220
www.oceanparkpix.com

Nick Livesey (310) 659-1577
www.rsafilms.com

Walt Lloyd (818) 729-0000
www.goschproductions.com

Ken Locsmandi (310) 699-9760
www.ambitiousfilms.com

Brent Loefke (866) 711-5195
www.jspcreative.com

Robert Logevall (310) 558-3667 (323) 930-5900
www.anonymouscontent.com

Jeff Long (310) 301-3313
www.zystar.com

Peter Long (323) 957-5400
www.picrow.com

Save Lorenzo (323) 790-1732
www.maneaterproductions.com

Susan Loughlin (323) 464-7805
www.acmefilmworks.com

Henry Lu (310) 857-1000
www.moxiepictures.com

Suzanne Luna (310) 289-1232
www.fabricationfilms.com

Joe Lynch (323) 466-1171
www.1171.com

Eric Lynne (323) 468-0123
www.partizan.com

Peter Mack (323) 790-1732
www.maneaterproductions.com

Iain MacKenzie (310) 899-1720
www.tightfilms.com

Kenn MacRae (323) 937-3007
www.spaceprogram.tv

Asa Mader (323) 465-9494
www.helloandcompany.com

Michael Maher (213) 385-5082
www.rightbrain.tv

Max Malkin (310) 558-7100
www.hsiproductions.com

Malloys (310) 558-7100
www.hsiproductions.com

Luis Mandoki (310) 858-7204
www.labandafilms.com

Rudy Manning (310) 396-5796
www.detourfilms.com

Maurice Marable (323) 645-1000
www.believemedia.com

Joaquin Marques (310) 823-5400
www.carbofilms.com

Gregory Marquette (818) 990-8993
www.ambitiousent.com

Stephen Marro (310) 305-8200
www.900frames.tv

Rob Marshall (310) 857-1000
www.moxiepictures.com

Glenn Martin (323) 962-7855 (310) 917-9191
www.tombofilm.com

Alan Martinez (323) 240-6736
www.motelfilms.com

Vanessa Marzaroli (310) 314-1618
www.blind.com

Stu Maschwitz (323) 469-6700
www.theorphanage.com

Renny Maslow (323) 817-3300
www.smugglersite.com

Adam Massey (310) 917-9191
www.untitled.tv

Domenic Mastrippolito (310) 458-0663
www.beachhousefilms.com

John Mastromonaco (323) 782-3416
www.argylebrothers.com

Gregg Masuak (310) 458-0663
www.beachhousefilms.com

Zach Math (310) 396-7333
www.bobcentral.com

Nic Mathieu (310) 558-3667 (310) 659-6220
www.anonymouscontent.com

Camilo Matiz (323) 932-6588
www.acatch22production.com

Miwa Matreyek (310) 478-0771
www.duckstudios.com

Joe Maxwell (310) 260-6100
www.motivfilms.com

George Mays (310) 396-5796
www.detourfilms.com

Sean McBride (323) 464-7805
www.acmefilmworks.com

Ross McCanse (818) 506-4715

Michael McClary (310) 858-8878

Marcus McCollum (310) 659-6220
www.crossroadsfilms.com

Harry McCoy (310) 315-1949
www.picturepk.com

Scott McCullough (310) 437-3518
www.scottmccullough.com

Melodie McDaniel (323) 465-5299
www.thedirectorsbureau.com

Kevin McDonald (323) 860-8030
www.chelsea.com

Francine McDongall (310) 305-8200
www.900frames.tv

Keir McFarlane (323) 463-2826 (310) 854-0647
www.dnala.com

Geoff McFetridge (323) 465-5299
www.thedirectorsbureau.com

Tuesday McGowen (310) 315-1949
www.picturepk.com

Gary McKendry (323) 653-0404
www.form.tv

David McNally (310) 396-4333 (310) 277-7001
www.companyfilms.net

Tony McNamara (213) 385-5082
www.rightbrain.tv

Simon McQuoid (323) 860-5400
www.gofilm.net

James McTeigue (213) 385-5082
www.rightbrain.tv

Teresa Medina (323) 937-4182
www.legacyfilms.net

Charles Mehling (323) 860-8030
www.chelsea.com

Robert Mehnert (626) 584-4000
www.danwolfe.com

Theodore Melfi (310) 899-1700
www.gartner.tv

Nicholas Melillo (818) 990-8993
www.ambitiousent.com

Melina (310) 659-1577
www.rsafilms.com

Rob Meltzer (323) 466-2490
www.kavichreynolds.com

Sam Mendes (310) 659-1577
www.rsafilms.com

Nick Mendoza (323) 876-5123
(323) 842-3004
www.mendozagomez.com

Stan Mendoza (310) 314-8770
www.wyomingfilms.net

Salmon Higo Menduiña (310) 823-5400
www.carbofilms.com

Simon Mestel (310) 581-5445
www.novemberfilms.com

David Michalek (323) 969-0555
www.awhitelabelproduct.com

Paul Middleditch (323) 969-0555
www.awhitelabelproduct.com

Thomas Mignone (310) 927-6661
www.doominc.com

Michal Mihail (323) 466-1171
www.1171.com

Cousin Mike (323) 466-1171
www.1171.com

Bennett Miller (323) 817-3300
www.smugglersite.com

Josh Miller (310) 659-1577
www.littleminx.com

Mike Miller (818) 990-8993
www.ambitiousent.com

Mike Mills (323) 465-5299
www.thedirectorsbureau.com

Monty Miranda (310) 458-0663
www.beachhousefilms.com

Mister Boom Boom (323) 645-1000
www.believemedia.com

Adrian Moat (310) 659-1577
www.rsafilms.com

Francis Mohajerin (310) 727-2600
www.megahertzpictures.com

Terry Moloney (818) 907-7111

Jean-Baptiste Mondino (323) 463-2826
www.dnala.com

Cesario (Block) Montano (310) 699-9760
www.ambitiousfilms.com

Geoff Moore (310) 396-5796
www.detourfilms.com

Alexandre Moors (323) 465-9494
www.helloandcompany.com

Ben Mor (310) 659-1577
www.littleminx.tv

Flavia Moraes (310) 581-1100
www.filmplanet.com

Erik Morales (310) 823-5400
www.carbofilms.com

Alberto Moretorio (323) 937-4182
www.legacyfilms.net

Brett Morgan (310) 558-3667
www.anonymouscontent.com

Jay P. Morgan (818) 957-9002

Errol Morris (310) 857-1000
www.moxiepictures.com

Graham Morris (310) 478-0771
www.duckstudios.com

Phil Morrison (310) 275-9333
www.epochfilms.com

David R. Morton (323) 665-4198
www.alteregofilms.com

Rocky Morton (310) 826-6200
www.mjz.com

Caroline Mouris (323) 464-7805
www.acmefilmworks.com

Frank Mouris (323) 464-7805
www.acmefilmworks.com

Jayson Moyer (310) 659-6220
www.crossroadsfilms.com

David Mueller (310) 727-2600
www.megahertzpictures.com

Des Mullan (310) 458-0663
www.beachhousefilms.com

Sean Mullens (323) 790-0440
www.sticks.tv

Alan Munro (310) 394-0110
www.movingtargetla.com

Yorico Murakami (310) 478-0771
www.duckstudios.com

Steven Murashige (323) 650-4722

Andy Murdoch (310) 478-0771
www.duckstudios.com

Dom Murgia (818) 906-0006
www.thedirectorsnetwork.com

Dominic Murphy (323) 468-0123
www.partizan.com

Scott Murphy (866) 711-5195
www.jspcreative.com

Joe Murray (310) 559-8333
www.boxerfilms.net

Noam Murro (323) 856-9200
www.biscuitfilmworks.com

Ken Musen (310) 208-2324
www.c-2k.com

The Mushroom Company (310) 478-0771
www.duckstudios.com

George Muskens (310) 444-7055
www.blueyedpictures.com

Mike Myerburg (818) 985-9905
www.factoryfeatures.com

Thomas Napper (310) 558-7100
www.hsiproductions.com

Miguel Navarro (310) 823-5400
www.carbofilms.com

Neistat Brothers (310) 558-7100
www.hsiproductions.com

Mike Nelesen (310) 659-6220
www.crossroadsfilms.com

Rich Newey (310) 288-8000
www.paradigmagency.com

Nic and Sune (310) 854-0647
www.sandwickfilms.com

Doug Nichol (323) 468-0123
www.partizan.com

Amy Nicholson (310) 264-3000
www.hungryman.com

Dewey Nicks (310) 275-9333
(310) 888-8900
www.villains.com

Nicolas (310) 338-0580
www.utopiafilms.com

Marcus Nispel (310) 826-6200
www.mjz.com

nObrain (323) 969-0555
www.awhitelabelproduct.com

Nagi Noda (323) 468-0123
www.partizan.com

Nobuhito Noda (310) 752-7183

Christopher Nolan (310) 656-9100
www.epixfilms.com

Mehdi Norowzian (323) 465-9494
www.helloandcompany.com

Ace Norton (323) 468-0123
www.partizan.com

Joao Nuno (310) 823-5400
www.carbofilms.com

Peter Nydrle (310) 659-8844
www.nydrle.com

Klaus Obermeyer (310) 396-3636
www.aerofilm.tv

John O'Hagan (310) 659-1577
www.rsafilms.com

Takashiro Okubo (310) 478-0771
www.duckstudios.com

Jarl Olsen (323) 240-6736
www.motelfilms.com

James O'Neil (323) 876-6853

Jim O'Neil (310) 470-0491

Bill Orisich (323) 937-4182
www.legacyfilms.net

Ritxi Ostariz (310) 478-0771
www.duckstudios.com

Otis (323) 650-4722

Angelo Pacifici (310) 313-3762
(818) 990-8993
FAX (310) 745-1949
www.ambitiousent.com

Nina Paley (310) 478-0771
www.duckstudios.com

Hsin-Ping Pan (310) 478-0771
www.duckstudios.com

Ago Panini (310) 828-8989
www.tateusa.com

Scott Papera (310) 809-1910
www.alteregofilms.tv/scottpapera

Brian Papierski (310) 305-8200
www.900frames.tv

Priit Parn (323) 464-7805
www.acmefilmworks.com

Harry Patramanis (323) 653-0404
(310) 277-7001
www.form.tv

Chris Patterson (310) 209-8974
www.ranchexitfilms.com

Alexander Paul (310) 453-1115
www.millenniumpictures.tv

Charlie Paul (323) 464-2406
www.47pictures.com

Bruce Paynter (310) 444-7055
www.blueyedpictures.com

Rob Pearlstein (323) 860-5400
www.gofilm.net

Stephen Pearson (310) 264-3000
www.hungryman.com

Barbara Peeters (818) 729-0000
www.goschproductions.com

Mark Pellington (310) 659-6220
www.crossroadsfilms.com

Stacy Peralta (310) 399-9600
www.nonfictionunlimited.com

Vadim Perelman (310) 828-8989
www.tateusa.com

Jesse Peretz (310) 659-1577
www.rsafilms.com

Luc Perez (323) 464-7805
www.acmefilmworks.com

Hank Perlman (310) 264-3000
www.hungryman.com

Janet Perlman (323) 464-7805
www.acmefilmworks.com

Suthon Petchsuwan (310) 392-7333
www.thomaswintercooke.com

George Peters (323) 957-1454
www.cmpictures.tv

Barry Peterson (310) 656-4646
www.reactorfilms.com

Adria Petty (310) 453-2600
www.harvestfilms.com

Todd Philips (310) 857-1000
www.moxiepictures.com

Jeffrey Phillips (310) 444-7055
(310) 450-1220
www.blueyedpictures.com

Sean MacLeod Phillips (310) 395-4739

Kevin Pike (818) 808-9321
www.filmtrix.com

James Pilkington (323) 969-0555
www.awhitelabelproduct.com

Nick Piper (310) 314-1122
www.backyard.com

Pitof (310) 448-7900
www.rhythm.com

Martin Pitts (323) 876-6186

Mark Piznarski (310) 395-5022

Plankton Art Co. (310) 478-0771
www.duckstudios.com

Jeffery Plansker (310) 956-3500
www.supplyanddemand.tv

Aaron Platt (323) 465-9494
www.helloandcompany.com

Bo Platt (310) 392-7333
(323) 856-9200
www.thomaswintercooke.com

Bill Plympton (323) 464-7805
www.acmefilmworks.com

Tim Pope (310) 659-6220
www.crossroadsfilms.com

Greg Popp (310) 956-3500
www.supplyanddemand.tv

Popular Society (323) 464-2406
www.47pictures.com

William Powloski (310) 376-7870
www.velocityfx.com

Jose Antonio Pratt (310) 956-3500
www.supplyanddemand.tv

Doug Pray (323) 466-1171
www.1171.com

Jeff Preiss (310) 275-9333
www.epochfilms.com

Leland Price (310) 915-0366

Rodrigo Prieto (310) 858-7204
(310) 659-1577
www.labandafilms.com

Rob Pritts (310) 314-1122
www.backyard.com

Gillean Proctor (310) 659-6220
www.crossroadsfilms.com

Joel Pront (323) 645-1000
www.believemedia.com

Kathi Prosser (323) 860-8030
www.chelsea.com

Alex Proyas (310) 558-3667
www.anonymouscontent.com

Psyop (323) 817-3300
www.smugglersite.com

Pucho (323) 645-1000
www.believemedia.com

Bob Purman (310) 857-1000
www.moxiepictures.com

Barry Purves (323) 464-7805
www.acmefilmworks.com

Joe Pytka (310) 392-9571

Quad U.S.A. (323) 645-1000
www.believemedia.com

Corky Quakenbush (310) 478-0771
www.duckstudios.com

The Brothers Quay (323) 645-1000
(323) 465-9494
www.believemedia.com

Christopher Quinn (323) 860-8030
www.chelsea.com

Joanna Quinn (323) 464-7805
www.acmefilmworks.com

Nick Rafter (310) 854-0647
www.sandwickfilms.com

Paul Raimondi (760) 837-1093
www.raimondifilms.com

Ramon and Pedro (323) 468-0123
www.partizan.com

Lynne Ramsay (323) 465-9494
www.helloandcompany.com

David Ramser (323) 650-4722

Steven Ramser (310) 659-0010
www.newhousefilms.com

Greg Ramsey (323) 850-0690
www.celsiusfilms.com

Scott Randall (323) 930-0101
www.altavistafilms.com

Rankin and Chris (310) 558-7100
www.hsiproductions.com

Don Rase (310) 314-1122
www.backyard.com

Mark Rasmussen (323) 224-9051

Brett Ratner (310) 558-7100
www.hsiproductions.com

Juston Reardon (310) 558-3667
www.anonymouscontent.com

Adam Reed (310) 917-9191
www.untitled.tv

Peyton Reed (310) 857-1000
www.moxiepictures.com

Richard Reens (818) 906-0006
www.thedirectorsnetwork.com

Kai Regan (323) 465-9494
www.helloandcompany.com

Richard Reiss (818) 906-0006
www.thedirectorsnetwork.com

Jason Reitman (310) 828-8989
www.tateusa.com

Leonardo Ricagni (310) 289-1232
www.fabricationfilms.com

Paul Riccio (310) 854-0647
www.sandwickmedia.com

Tony Richards (818) 990-8993
www.ambitiousent.com

Robert Richardson (310) 453-9244
www.toolofna.com

Tim Richardson (323) 969-0555
www.awhitelabelproduct.com

Branscombe Richmond (310) 315-1750
www.30secondfilms.com

Jeff Richter (310) 822-6367
www.ladybug-la.com

Thomas Richter (310) 559-8333
www.boxerfilms.net

Riess/Hill (310) 899-1700
www.gartner.tv

Terry Rietta (310) 888-8900
www.villains.com

Patricia Riggen (323) 876-3331
www.wildindigo.tv

Carl Erik Rinsch (310) 659-1577
www.rsafilms.com

Nick Robertson (323) 969-0555
www.awhitelabelproduct.com

Fatima Robinson (310) 558-7100
www.hsiproductions.com

Gary Robinson (310) 247-0818
FAX (310) 858-2254
www.sharpcut.com

Roenberg (310) 854-0647
www.sandwickfilms.com

Steve Rogers (323) 856-9200
www.biscuitfilmworks.com

Chris Romano (310) 478-0771
www.duckstudios.com

Anthony Rose (323) 464-3080
www.moostudios.com

Rosto (323) 464-7805
www.acmefilmworks.com

Roger Roth (818) 901-1178
(310) 963-4812
FAX (818) 901-1179

Tom Routson (310) 453-9244
www.toolofna.com

Michael Rowles (323) 930-5900
www.frankmediausa.com

Jorge Rubia (323) 932-6588
www.acatch22production.com

Henry-Alex Rubin (323) 817-3300
www.smugglersite.com

Lisa Rubisch (310) 396-7333
www.bobcentral.com

Ondrej Rudavsky (818) 990-8993
www.ambitiousent.com

Aaron Ruell (323) 856-9200
www.biscuitfilmworks.com

George Marshall Ruge (310) 288-8000
www.paradigmagency.com

Mark Russel (310) 260-6100
www.motivfilms.com

Erica Russell (323) 464-7805
www.acmefilmworks.com

Alex Rutterford (310) 659-1577
www.rsafilms.com

Jim Rygiel (310) 453-1115
www.millenniumpictures.tv

Vittorio Sacco (310) 899-6979
www.cohnandco.com

Jorge Salinas (323) 932-6588
www.acatch22production.com

Saline Project (310) 558-7100
www.hsiproductions.com

Salzy (818) 985-9905
www.factoryfeatures.com

Kevin Samuels (310) 659-6220
(323) 937-3007
www.crossroadsfilms.com

Jessica Sanders (310) 399-9600
www.nonfictionunlimited.com

Rob Sanders (310) 314-1122
www.backyard.com

Rupert Sanders (310) 396-4333
(310) 826-6200
www.mjz.com

Paul Santana (323) 930-5900
www.frankmediausa.com

Esteban Sapir (310) 260-6100
www.motivfilms.com

Fernando Sarinana (323) 461-0101
www.altavistafilms.com

Michael Sarna (323) 466-1171
www.1171.com

Malik H. Sayeed (310) 659-1577
www.littleminx.com

Joe Schaak (323) 650-4722

Rocky Schenck (323) 463-2826
www.dnala.com

Marc Schölermann (323) 860-8686
www.ubercontent.com

Ed Schumacher (310) 652-8778
www.lspagency.net

Bob Schwartz (323) 851-5151

Bradley Scott (323) 790-1732
www.maneaterproductions.com

Jake Scott (310) 659-1577
www.rsafilms.com

Jordan Scott (310) 659-1577
www.rsafilms.com

Luke Scott (310) 659-1577
www.rsafilms.com

Ridley Scott (310) 659-1577
www.rsafilms.com

Tony Scott (310) 659-1577
www.rsafilms.com

Richard Sears (310) 656-4900
www.greendotfilms.com

Kosai Sekine (818) 906-0006
www.thedirectorsnetwork.com

Mark Seliger (310) 659-1577
www.littleminx.com

Shaun Sewter (323) 464-3080
www.moostudios.com

Dawn Shadforth (310) 659-1577
www.littleminx.com

Gary Shaffer (310) 578-9383
www.kaboomproductions.com

Jerry Shanks (818) 506-0502
FAX (818) 506-0502

Michael Shapiro (323) 937-3007
www.spaceprogram.tv

Munier Sharrieff (310) 289-1232
www.fabricationfilms.com

Bobby Sheehan (323) 850-0690
www.celsiusfilms.com

Guy Shelmerdine (323) 817-3300
www.smugglersite.com

Jim Sheridan (310) 857-1000
www.moxiepictures.com

Pat Sherman (310) 558-3667
www.anonymouscontent.com

Boyd Shermis (818) 347-2515
FAX (818) 347-2529
www.fxtc.com

Larry Shiu (310) 526-7703
www.instantkarmafilms.tv

Shynola (323) 465-5299
www.thedirectorsbureau.com

Si & Ad (323) 465-9494
www.helloandcompany.com

Lex Sidon (323) 466-1171
www.1171.com

Andre Siebert (818) 990-8993
www.ambitiousent.com

Marcos Siega (310) 264-3000
www.hungryman.com

Thomas Sigel (310) 854-0647
www.sandwickfilms.com

Floria Sigismondi (323) 645-1000
www.believemedia.com

Carlo Sigon (323) 962-7855
www.tombofilm.com

Brian Silva (323) 620-6925
www.halfelement.com

Tim Silver (310) 739-7356
(310) 399-5122

Jay Silverman (323) 466-6030
www.jaysilverman.com

Melissa Silverman (323) 645-1000
www.believemedia.com

Sabrina D. Simmons (323) 939-5711

Skee.tv (323) 465-9494
www.helloandcompany.com

Holly Goldberg Sloan (310) 450-1220
www.oceanparkpix.com

Adam Smith (310) 659-1577
www.rsafilms.com

Baker Smith (310) 453-2600
www.harvestfilms.com

Chris Smith (323) 817-3300
www.smugglersite.com

Jason Smith (310) 396-7333
(310) 558-7100
www.bobcentral.com

Kevin Smith (310) 314-1122
(310) 857-1000
www.backyard.com

Landis Smithers (310) 956-3500
www.supplyanddemand.tv

Roberto Sneider (310) 858-7204
www.labandafilms.com

Skott Snider (818) 906-0006
www.thedirectorsnetwork.com

Zack Snyder (323) 645-1000
www.believemedia.com

Patrick Solomon (310) 659-0010
www.newhousefilms.com

Michael Somoroff (310) 550-6990
www.macguffin.com

Jung Son (310) 526-7703
www.instantkarmafilms.tv

Jim Sonzero (323) 645-1000
www.believemedia.com

Kevin Spacey (310) 659-1577
www.rsafilms.com

Randy Spear (310) 822-6367
www.ladybug-la.com

Speck/Gordon (310) 396-4333
www.omahapictures.com

Scott Speer (310) 558-7100
www.hsiproductions.com

Pam Stalker (323) 464-7805
www.acmefilmworks.com

John Stanier (310) 209-8974
www.ranchexitfilms.com

Jerry Stanley (866) 711-5195
www.jspcreative.com

Bruce St. Clair (323) 653-0404
www.form.tv

Stefano (323) 466-1171
www.1171.com

David Steinberg (323) 460-2077
www.darklightpictures.com

David P. Stern (818) 788-7876
(818) 907-7012

Walter Stern (323) 465-9494
www.helloandcompany.com

Marcus Stevens (310) 395-5022

Nzingha Stewart (323) 463-2826
www.dnala.com

Scott Stewart (323) 469-6700
www.theorphanage.com

Susan Stitt (310) 453-1115
www.millenniumpictures.tv

Aaron Stoller (310) 314-1122
www.backyard.com

Nick Stoller (323) 856-9200
www.biscuitfilmworks.com

The Brothers Strause (310) 899-1720
www.tightfilms.com

Paul Street (323) 645-1000
www.believemedia.com

Streeter and Davis (310) 315-1949
www.picturepk.com

Chace Strickland (310) 314-1122
www.backyard.com

Stylewar (323) 817-3300
www.smugglersite.com

Patricia Sullivan (323) 969-8822
www.illuminatehollywood.com

Spencer Susser (310) 396-7333
www.bobcentral.com

Christian Swegal (818) 985-9905
www.factoryfeatures.com

Syd/Eric (310) 396-7333
www.bobcentral.com

Jeremy Sykes (619) 435-0888
www.sykesfilm-tv.com

Cary Symmons (310) 656-9100
www.epixfilms.com

Syndrome (323) 465-9494
www.helloandcompany.com

Marcelo Szechtman (310) 858-7204
www.labandafilms.com

Josh Taft (310) 956-3500
www.hsiproductions.com

Picky Talarico (310) 581-1100
www.filmplanet.com

Hideyuki Tanaka (310) 264-3000
www.hungryman.com

Johan Tappert (310) 854-0647
www.sandwickmedia.com

Pierre Tatarka (310) 858-7204
www.labandafilms.com

Ben Taylor (310) 659-6220
www.crossroadsfilms.com

Jonathan Taylor (310) 652-8778
www.lspagency.net

Jonathan Teplitzky (310) 828-8989
www.tateusa.com

Dinh Long Thai (626) 688-5818
(818) 906-0006
www.chopstickninja.com

Gary Thieltges (310) 449-1300

Brent Thomas (310) 656-4900
www.greendotfilms.com

Pam Thomas (310) 857-1000
www.moxiepictures.com

John Thompson (310) 295-4660
www.ringleaderproductions.com

Virgil P. Thompson (310) 838-7783
www.addressone.tv

Sean Thonson (310) 956-3500
www.supplyanddemand.tv

Three Legged Legs (310) 656-4900
www.greendotfilms.com

Peter Thwaites (310) 558-3667
www.anonymouscontent.com

Mark Tiedemann (323) 850-0690
www.celsiusfilms.com

Wendy Tilby (323) 464-7805
www.acmefilmworks.com

Terri Timely (310) 659-6220
www.crossroadsfilms.com

Ondi Timoner (310) 399-9600
www.nonfictionunlimited.com

Gianluigi Toccafondo (323) 464-7805
www.acmefilmworks.com

Frank Todaro (310) 857-1000
www.moxiepictures.com

Damien Toogood (323) 860-8030
www.chelsea.com

Salvatore Totino (310) 659-6220
www.crossroadsfilms.com

Stacy Toyama (310) 581-5445
www.novemberfilms.com

Jim Tozzi (818) 995-8629
www.stationwagonfilms.com

Traktor (323) 468-0123
www.partizan.com

Henry Trettin (818) 990-1038

Joachim Trier (310) 659-1577
www.rsafilms.com

Tronic (310) 558-7100
www.hsiproductions.com

Yu Tsai (213) 385-5082
www.rightbrain.tv

Steven Tsuchida (323) 860-8686
www.ubercontent.com

Tudor (323) 790-1732
www.maneaterproductions.com

Dana Tynan (310) 396-5796
www.detourfilms.com

Type2error (310) 659-6220
www.crossroadsfilms.com

Frank Underwood (818) 729-0000
www.goschproductions.com

Albert Uria (310) 823-5400
www.carbofilms.com

Antonio Urrutia (310) 858-7204
www.labandafilms.com

Theodore Ushev (310) 478-0771
www.duckstudios.com

Fernando Vallejo (310) 395-5022

Phillip Van (310) 659-1577
www.littleminx.com

Matthijs Van Heijningen (310) 826-6200
www.mjz.com

Miklos Varga (323) 464-7805
www.acmefilmworks.com

Tom Vaughan (323) 860-8686
www.ubercontent.com

Matthew Vaughn (310) 558-7100
www.hsiproductions.com

Alvaro Velarde (310) 822-6367
www.ladybug-la.com

Gore Verbinski (310) 558-3667
www.anonymouscontent.com

Vogel Villar-Rios (323) 645-1000
www.believemedia.com

Scott Vincent (310) 264-3000
www.hungryman.com

Max Vitali (310) 558-7100
www.hsiproductions.com

Art Vitarelli (949) 548-4524
www.reelorange.com

Solweig von Kleist (323) 464-7805
www.acmefilmworks.com

Christoffer Von Reis (310) 854-0647
www.sandwickfilms.com

Ellen Von Unwerth (323) 464-3080
www.moostudios.com

David Wagreich (310) 652-8778
www.lspagency.net

James Wahlberg (310) 289-1232
(310) 448-7900
www.fabricationfilms.com

Paula Walker (323) 344-8905
www.stratofilms.com

Robert W. Walker (323) 469-6800
www.walkerfitzgibbon.com

Stacy Wall (310) 275-9333
www.epochfilms.com

Kieran Walsh (310) 659-6220
www.crossroadsfilms.com

Markus Walter (323) 860-5400
www.gofilm.net

Derek Wan (323) 788-3883
FAX (323) 780-8887
www.allinone-usa.com

Kevin Ward (310) 453-1115
(818) 995-8629
www.millenniumpictures.tv

Jeremy Warshaw (310) 899-6979
www.cohnandco.com

David Wasson (323) 464-7805
www.acmefilmworks.com

John Waters (310) 857-1000
www.moxiepictures.com

Jon Watts (323) 817-3300
www.smugglersite.com

Jamie Way (310) 453-1115
www.millenniumpictures.tv

Marc Webb (323) 463-2826
www.dnala.com

Jim Weedon (310) 899-1700
www.gartner.tv

JC Wegman (323) 464-7805
www.acmefilmworks.com

Curtis Wehrfritz (310) 526-7703
www.instantkarmafilms.tv

Clay Weiner (323) 856-9200
www.biscuitfilmworks.com

Greg Weinschenker (310) 656-9100
(310) 470-0491
www.epixfilms.com

Danny Weisberg (310) 578-9383
(310) 458-0663
www.kaboomproductions.com

Jeff Weiser (818) 906-0006
www.thedirectorsnetwork.com

Martin Weisz (323) 465-9494
www.helloandcompany.com

James Weitz (310) 558-7100
www.hsiproductions.com

Eric Welch (310) 656-9100
www.epixfilms.com

Doug Werby (310) 578-9383
www.kaboomproductions.com

Michael Werk (310) 301-3313
(310) 209-8974
www.ranchexitfilms.com

Julian West (310) 550-6990
www.macguffin.com

Bill White (818) 400-9878
FAX (818) 845-1756
www.billwhitemedia.com

Charlie White (310) 396-4333
www.omahapictures.com

Declan Whitebloom (310) 659-1577
www.rsafilms.com

Whitey (323) 645-1000
www.believemedia.com

Kenneth Wiatrak (818) 985-1582
(818) 425-8310
FAX (818) 766-4584
www.wiatrak.us

Wiebke (323) 645-1000
www.believemedia.com

Christopher Wilcha (323) 860-8030
www.chelsea.com

Clay Williams (310) 826-6200
www.mjz.com

Hype Williams (310) 558-7100
www.hsiproductions.com

Peyton Wilson (310) 399-9600
www.nonfictionunlimited.com

Theresa Wingert (310) 550-6990
www.macguffin.com

Henning Winkelmann (310) 444-7055
(310) 550-6990
www.blueyedpictures.com

David Winning (818) 729-0000
www.goschproductions.com

Dan Wolfe (626) 584-4000
www.danwolfe.com

Bille Woodruff (323) 653-0404
www.form.tv

Jason Wulfsohn (310) 581-5445
www.novemberfilms.com

Koji Yamamura (323) 464-7805
www.acmefilmworks.com

Jon Yarbrough (310) 899-0335
www.tuesdayfilms.com

Eugene Yelchin (310) 289-1232
www.fabricationfilms.com

Yellow Shed (310) 478-0771
www.duckstudios.com

Jessica Yu (310) 399-9600
www.nonfictionunlimited.com

Bill Yukich (818) 985-9905
www.factoryfeatures.com

Ivan Zacharias (323) 817-3300
www.smugglersite.com

Leo Zahn (818) 981-0252
FAX (818) 788-2759
www.picturepalaceprod.com

Zissimos and Rowan (310) 264-3000
www.hungryman.com

Jim Zoolalian (310) 559-8333
www.boxerfilms.net

David Zucker (310) 395-5022

Ryan Zunkley (310) 478-0771
www.duckstudios.com

Harald Zwart (310) 277-7001
www.companyfilms.net

Edward Zwick (310) 395-5022

1171 Production Group (323) 466-1171
1680 N. Vine St., Ste. 300 FAX (323) 466-1136
Hollywood, CA 90028 www.1171.com
Executive Producers: Grant Cihlar & Nancy Cihlar
Directors: Abdul Malik Abbott, Cousin Mike, Tom DeLonge, Joe Lynch, Michal Mihail, Doug Pray, Michael Sarna, Lex Sidon & Stefano

24pCine (310) 986-3370
Executive Producer: Daniel Andreas www.iconspots.com
Vice President: Josh Kameyer
Directors: Daniel Andreas, David Bojorquez, Reto Caduff & Dana Leshem

30 Second Films (310) 315-1750
3019 Pico Blvd. FAX (310) 315-1757
Santa Monica, CA 90405 www.30secondfilms.com
Executive Producer: Alan J. Stamm
Directors: Debbie Allen, Tony Dow, Bob Kronovet & Branscombe Richmond

47 Pictures (323) 464-2406
6525 Sunset Blvd., Penthouse FAX (323) 464-2426
Hollywood, CA 90028 www.47pictures.com
Executive Producer: Doug Kluthe
Directors: Jesse Austin, Sian Heder, Cameron Hopkins, Charlie Paul & Popular Society

900 Frames (310) 305-8200
12910 Culver Blvd., Ste. G www.900frames.tv
Los Angeles, CA 90066
Executive Producer: Sam Najah
Directors: Gabriel Bassio, Kevin Bourland, Chuck Clemens, Greg Hughs, Stephen Marro, Francine McDongall & Brian Papierski

Acme Filmworks, Inc. (323) 464-7805
6525 Sunset Blvd., Ste. G-10 FAX (323) 464-6614
Hollywood, CA 90028
Executive Producers: Ron Diamond & David Schmier
Producer: Pernille D'Avolio
Directors: Gil Alkabetz, Garri Bardine, Jim Blashfield, Leslie Cabarga, Evert de Beijer, Paul and Menno De Nooijer, John Dilworth, Pau Driessen, Piotr Dumala, Michael Dudok De Wit, Stephen Flint-Muller, Daniel Guyonnet, Oliver Harrison, Anna Henckle-Donnersmarck, Chris Hinton, Greg Holfeld, Aleksandra Korejwo, Igor Kovalyov, Raimund Krumme, Chris Landreth, Christoph and Wolfgang Lauenstein, Caroline Leaf, Ashley Lenz, Susan Loughlin, Sean McBride, Frank and Caroline Mouris, Priit Parn, Janet Perlman, Luc Perez, Bill Plympton, Barry Purves, Joanna Quinn, Rosto, Erica Russell, Pam Stalker, Wendy Tilby and Amanda Forbis, Gianluigi Toccafondo, Miklos Varga, Solweig von Kleist, David Wasson, JC Wegman & Koji Yamamura
East Coast Sales Rep: David Schmier
Midwest Sales Rep: Tim Harwood
West Coast Sales Reps: Toni Saarinen & Jennifer Spencer

Address One LLC (310) 838-7783
468 N. Camden Dr., Ste. 385 www.addressone.tv
Beverly Hills, CA 90210
Producer: Tess Gallagher Thompson
Director: Virgil P. Thompson

Aéro Film (310) 396-3636
3000 31st St. FAX (310) 396-5636
Santa Monica, CA 90405 www.aerofilm.tv
President: Skip Short
Executive Producer: Lance O'Connor
Head of Production: Rob Helphand
Directors: Ken Arlidge, Henrik Hansen, Brent Jones & Klaus Obermeyer

All In One Productions (323) 780-8880
1111 Corporate Dr. FAX (323) 780-8887
Monterey Park, CA 91754 www.allinone-usa.com
Producer: Joanna Or
Director/Camerman: Derek Wan

Alta Vista Films (323) 930-0101
6615 Melrose Ave., Ste. 1 FAX (323) 935-8181
Hollywood, CA 90038 www.altavistafilms.com
Executive Producer: David Lozano
Directors: Scott Bibo, Gonzalo Guzman, Rodrigo Garcia Saiz & Fernando Sariñana
Director/Cameramen: Ken Fox & Scott Randall

Alter Ego Films (310) 809-1910
FAX (310) 356-3397
www.alteregofilms.com
Executive Producers: Karl Kimbrough & Scott Papera
Directors: King Hollis, Karl Kimbrough, David R. Morton & Scott Papera

Alturas Films (310) 230-6100
21700 Oxnard St., Ste. 2050 www.alturasfilms.com
Woodland Hills, CA 91367
Owner/Executive Producer: Marshall Rawlings
Executive Producer/ Music Videos: Lanette Phillips
Commercial/Film Development Executive: Dannikke Walkker
Executive Producer: Roger Hunt

Ambitious (310) 699-9760
523 Colorado Ave. FAX (310) 395-8895
Santa Monica, CA 90401 www.ambitiousfilms.com
Executive Producer/Director: David Katz
Directors: David Katz, Ken Locsmandi & Cesario "Block" Montano

American Video Group (310) 477-1535
2542 Aiken Ave. www.americanvideogroup.com
Los Angeles, CA 90064
President: John Berzner

Anonymous Content (310) 558-3667
3532 Hayden Ave. FAX (310) 558-2724
Culver City, CA 90232 www.anonymouscontent.com
Executive Producers: Jeff Baron, Cassie Hulen, Dave Morrison & Andy Traines
Head of Production: Sue Ellen Clair
Directors: Armando Bo, Kevin Brey, Frank Budgen, Carter and Blitz, Tom Carty, John Dolan, Andrew Douglas, David Fincher, Sunu Gonera, Sanaa Hamri, Alejandro González Iñárritu, Garth Jennings, Rory Kelleher, David Kellogg, Steven Klein, Joe Kosinski, Daniel Levi, Robert Logevall, Nic Mathieu, Brett Morgan, Chris Palmer, Alex Proyas, Juston Reardon, Mark Romanek, Pat Sherman, Peter Thwaites, Malcolm Venville, Gore Verbinski & Wong Kar Wai

Apple Box Productions, Inc. (310) 204-0520
10736 Jefferson Blvd., Ste. 415 FAX (310) 202-1386
Culver City, CA 90230 www.applebox.com
Director: Steven M. Hirohama

Argyle Brothers (323) 782-3416
8330 W. Third St. FAX (323) 782-4971
Los Angeles, CA 90048 www.argylebrothers.com
Director: John Mastromonaco
Managing Director: Craig Rodgers
Executive Producer: Suzie Greene-Tedesco

The Artists Company (323) 650-4722
(212) 679-7199
1015 N. Fairfax Ave. FAX (323) 650-4706
Los Angeles, CA 90046
Executive Producers: Roberto Cecchini & Lori Lober
Vice President: Sally Antonacchio
Head of Production: Susan Burton
Directors: David Cameron, Michael Cuesta, Skip D'Amico, Guillaume, Rachel Harms, Bill Hudson, Steven Murashige, Otis, David Ramser & Joe Schaak
Sales Rep: Dawn Clarke

The Association, Inc. (818) 841-9660
135 N. Screenland Dr. FAX (818) 841-8370
Burbank, CA 91505 www.theassociation.tv
Executive Producer: Randall Stith
Producers: Tim Melchior & Fletcher Murray
Head of Production: Jeffrey Murphy

Attack Ads, Inc. (310) 857-7745
578 Washington Blvd., Ste. 594 **www.attackads.tv**
Marina Del Rey, CA 90292
E.P.: Roberts Jones
Director/E.P.: Bronston Jones
Directors: Eagle Egilsson & Dr. Garry

Auster Productions, Inc. (818) 843-5040
2607 W. Magnolia Blvd. FAX **(818) 843-5041**
Burbank, CA 91505 **www.austerproductions.com**
Director/Cameraman: Sam Auster

Back Home Pictures (323) 931-1782
Director: Charles Abehsera **www.backhomepictures.com**
Production
Office Manager: Karen Beller
VP Business Affairs: Alix de Izaguirre

Backyard Productions (310) 314-1122
(847) 583-7000
248 Main St. FAX **(310) 314-1123**
Venice, CA 90291 **www.backyard.com**
President/Executive Producer: Blair Stribley
Executive Producers: Eriks Krumins, Kris Mathur & Peter Steinzeig
Head of Production: Peter Steinzeig
Producers: Carr Donald & Peter Keenan
Directors: Ericson Core, Jesper Ericstam, Jeffrey Karoff, Nick Piper, Rob Pritts, Don Rase, Rob Sanders,.Kevin Smith, Aaron Stoller & Chace Strickland
Partner/Director of Sales and Marketing: Roy Skillicorn
Sales Reps: The Family, Them Reps & Brad Grubaugh

BeachHouse Films (310) 458-0663
1557 Seventh St. FAX **(310) 458-9692**
Santa Monica, CA 90401 **www.beachhousefilms.com**
Executive Producers: David Coulter & Patti Coulter
Directors: Robert E Bailey, Larry Carroll, Tony G, Domenic Mastrippolito, Gregg Masuak, Monty Miranda, Des Mullan & Danny Weisberg
West Coast Sales Rep: Chuck Silverman
East Coast Sales Rep: Cindy Velsor
Midwest Sales Rep: Julie Vargo, Julie Vargo & Associates
South Eastern Sales Rep: Cindy Velsor
Detroit Sales Rep: Chuck Silverman

Beard Boy Productions (714) 734-0372
14451 Chambers Rd., Ste. 250 FAX **(714) 734-6031**
Tustin, CA 92780 **www.beardboy.com**
Executive Producer: Mike Smith
Producer: Steven Rey
Writer/Producer: Joe Dinki

The Bedford Falls Group (310) 395-5022
409 Santa Monica Blvd. FAX **(310) 394-2512**
Santa Monica, CA 90401
Executive Producer: Nancy Fishelson
Directors: Nigel Cole, Kevin Donovan, Todd Factor, Marshall Herskovitz, Thom Higgins, Peter Horton, James Ivory, Norman Jewison, Mark Piznarski, Marcus Stevens, Fernando Vallejo, David Zucker & Edward Zwick
Sales Reps: Delores Hively, Amy Jones, Robin Pickett & Lori Youmans

Believe Media (323) 645-1000
1040 N. Las Palmas Ave., Bldg. 10 FAX **(323) 645-1001**
Los Angeles, CA 90038 **www.believemedia.com**
Executive Producers: Gerard Cantor, Betsy Kelley, Liz Silver & Luke Thornton
Directors: Anthea Benton, Mister Boom Boom, Nick Brandt, Nanette Burstein, Carolyn Chen, Tryan George, Howard Greenhalgh, Jorn Haagen, Anders Hallberg, Jason Harrington, Jaume, Albert Kodagolian, John Lindauer, Maurice Marable, Joel Pront, Pucho, Quad U.S.A., The Brothers Quay, Floria Sigismondi, Melissa Silverman, Zack Snyder, Jim Sonzero, Paul Street, Vogel Villar-Rios, Whitey & Wiebke

Berris Pictures (805) 963-6776
1187 Coast Village Rd., Ste. 1320 **www.berris.com**
Santa Barbara, CA 93108
Executive Producer/Director of Sales: Everett Blake
President: Lauren Berris
Director: Kenneth Berris

Big Lawn Films (310) 451-4148
1207 Fourth St., PH 2 FAX **(310) 451-8822**
Santa Monica, CA 90401 **www.biglawnfilms.com**
Executive Producer: Andrew Denyer
Director: Chuck Bennett

Bill White Productions (818) 400-9878
3625 Pacific Ave. FAX **(818) 845-1756**
Burbank, CA 91505 **www.billwhitemedia.com**
Producer/Production Manager: Amy Shomer
Director/Writer/Producer: Bill White

Biscuit Filmworks (323) 856-9200
7026 Santa Monica Blvd. FAX **(323) 856-9300**
Los Angeles, CA 90038 **www.biscuitfilmworks.com**
Sr. Executive Producer: Shawn Lacy
Directors: Tim Godsall, Jim Hosking, Bruce Hunt, Russ Lamoureux, Noam Murro, Bo Platt, Steve Rogers, Aaron Ruell, Nick Stoller & Clay Weiner
West Coast Sales Reps: Dana Balkin & Renee Krumweide
Executive Producers: Colleen O'Donnell & Holly Vega
Midwest Sales Reps: Gay Guthrey & Assoc.
East Coast Sales Reps: Zeigler Jakubowicz Management Group

Bjoin Films (818) 846-1650
121 E. Linden Ave. FAX **(818) 846-1670**
Burbank, CA 91502 **www.bjoinfilms.com**
Director/Cameraman: Henry Bjoin

Black Dragon Entertainment, Inc. (323) 874-8888
FAX **(323) 874-1058**
www.blackdragon.com
Executive Producer/Directors: Gillian Bonner & Joshua Caine

Blind (310) 314-1618
1702 Olympic Blvd. FAX **(310) 314-1718**
Santa Monica, CA 90404 **www.blind.com**
Executive Producer: Tino Sladavic
Directors: Chris Do, Tom Koh & Vanessa Marzaroli

Blue Cow Creative (323) 469-8200
6500 Sunset Blvd. FAX **(323) 464-4100**
Los Angeles, CA 90028 **www.bluecowcreative.com**
Producers: Paul Geffre, Warren Ostergard & Tony Wise

Blue Goose Productions (323) 658-6893
8350 Melrose Ave., Ste. 204 **www.bluegoose.tv**
Los Angeles, CA 90069
Executive Producer: Bill Hoare
Director: Ron Gross

Blueyed Pictures, Inc. (310) 444-7055
10960 Wilshire Blvd., Ste. 1750 FAX **(310) 444-7050**
Los Angeles, CA 90024 **www.blueyedpictures.com**
Executive Producer: Jamee Natella
Directors: Michael Givens, Evin Grant, George Muskens, Bruce Paynter, Jeffrey Phillips & Henning Winkelmann

Bob Industries (310) 396-7333
1313 Fifth St. FAX **(310) 396-0202**
Santa Monica, CA 90401 **www.bobcentral.com**
Executive Producers: TK Knowles, John O'Grady & Chuck Ryant
Directors: Peter Care, Jonathan Dayton/Valerie Faris, Kim Geldenhuys, Phil Harder, Chris Hooper, Mark Kohr, Zach Math, Lisa Rubisch, Jason Smith, Spencer Susser & Syd/Eric

Boxer Films (310) 559-8333
3453 S. La Cienega Blvd., Bldg. B FAX **(310) 559-6226**
Los Angeles, CA 90016 **www.boxerfilms.net**
CEO: Kelly Clark
President: John Clark
Directors: John Allardice, Jeffrey deChausse, Robert Groenwold, Joe Murray, Claudio Prestia, Thomas Richter, David Adam Roth, Guy Sagy, Jim Zoolalian & Jason Wulfsohn
Sales Reps: Ann McKallagat, Jill Reehl & Reber-Covington

Brownstone Films (310) 399-9600
905 Olympic Blvd. FAX **(310) 581-9690**
Santa Monica, CA 90404 **www.nonfictionunlimited.com**
Executive Producer: Michael Degan
Directors: Adam Arkin, Alan Arkin & Barry Dukoff

Bucks Boys Productions, Inc. (310) 437-0914
3900 Grand View Blvd. FAX (310) 437-0919
Los Angeles, CA 90066 www.bucksboys.com
Executive Producers: Jonathan Becker & Joshua Greenberg
Executive Assistant to Producers: Tova Dann
Head of Production: Mercedes Allen
General Counsel: Carra Greenberg

Bully Pictures (310) 745-1635 (310) 871-0385
858 Burrell St. FAX (310) 745-1645
Marina Del Rey, CA 90292 www.bullypictures.com

Burke/Triolo Productions (323) 257-4400
99 Pasadena Ave. www.burketriolo.com
South Pasadena, CA 91030
Producer: Alison Armstrong
Director/Cameraman: Jeffrey Burke

c.2K Entertainment (310) 208-2324
1067 Gayley Ave. FAX (310) 208-2414
Los Angeles, CA 90024 www.c-2k.com
Directors: Rod Findley & Ken Musen

Cannonball Productions (310) 375-0593
4212 Via Nivel FAX (310) 375-0692
Palos Verdes Estates, CA 90274
www.cannoballproduction.com
President/Owner: Sean Hanish
Director: Sean Hanish
Producer: Chris Sias

Carbo Films (310) 823-5400
530 Wilshire Blvd., Ste. 308 FAX (310) 451-7416
Santa Monica, CA 90401 www.carbofilms.com
Executive Producers: Javier Carbo & Dora Medrano
Producer: Soledad Ramos
Directors: Agustin Alberdi, Fernando Arrioja, Pedro Avila, Isabel Coixet, Jorge Gaggero, Ron Hamad, Illegal Artists, Alex Juliá, Joaquin Marques, Salmon Higo Menduiña, Erik Morales, Miguel Navarro, Joao Nuno & Albert Uria

Carey Melcher Productions, Inc./ CMP (213) 598-3457 (818) 222-9817
Executive Producer: Carey Melcher

Castle Creek Productions (310) 979-7170
12233 W. Olympic Blvd., Ste. 314 FAX (310) 979-7173
Los Angeles, CA 90064 www.castlecreekproductions.com
President/Executive Producer: John Dietsch
Development Coordinator: Zach Evans

A Catch 22 Production (323) 932-6588 (310) 863-6909
5478 Wilshire Blvd., Ste. 300 FAX (323) 932-6598
Los Angeles, CA 90036 www.acatch22production.com
Executive Producer: Todd Harter
VP of Production: Valerie Mayer
Directors: Enrique Aular, Hector Barboza, Marina Belaustegui, Pablo Croce, Claudio Duran, Camilo Matiz, Jorge Rubia & Jorge Salinas

CatchLight Films (310) 295-0071
FAX (310) 341-3806
www.catchlightfilms.com
Producers: Rick A. Osako & Jeanette Volturno-Brill

Caviar Content (310) 396-3400
900 Pacific Ave. FAX (310) 396-3410
Venice, CA 90291 www.caviarcontent.com
Executive Producers: Michael Sagol & Tom Weissferdt
Executive Producer, Features & Branded Content: Rosanne Korenberg
Executive Producer, Hispanic Market: Ileana Goldenstein
Producer: Eric Brown & BP Cooper

Celsius Films (323) 850-0690 (212) 253-7400
1011 N. Fuller Ave., Ste. I FAX (323) 850-0696
West Hollywood, CA 90046 www.celsiusfilms.com
President/Executive Producer: Robert Fisher
Executive Producers: Jonathan Gribetz & Stephanie Oakley
Head of Production: Holly Jenkins
Directors: Anouk, Christian Charles, Peter Kagan, Greg Ramsey, Mark Tiedemann & Harvey Wang
Director/Cameramen: Greg Ramsey & Bobby Sheehan
Head of Sales: Jack Fahey
Sales Reps: Liz Laine & Courtenay Smith

Chelsea Pictures (323) 860-8030 (212) 431-3434
1040 N. Las Palmas Ave., Bldg. 15 FAX (323) 860-8035
Hollywood, CA 90038 www.chelsea.com
Partner & Executive Producers: Allison Amon, Lisa Mehling & Steve Wax
Executive Producers: Katy Greene & Sam Penfield
Head of Production: John LaChapelle
Directors: Nicholas Barker, Evan Bernard, Breck Eisner, Larry Frey, Richard Gibson, David Gordon Green, Haxan, James Holt, Michael Joy, Bob Kerstetter, Johan Kramer, Kevin McDonald, Charles Mehling, Kathi Prosser, Christopher Quinn, Damien Toogood & Christopher Wilcha
Sales Reps: Mark Andrews, Jim Robison, Kari Romeo, Jared Shapiro & Astrid Steel

Cinevative Productions (323) 852-8903
8271 Melrose Ave., Ste. 203 FAX (323) 852-0349
Los Angeles, CA 90046 www.cinevative.com
Executive Producers: Mark Ciglar & Carrie Dobro

Coast Media Teleproductions, Inc. (949) 417-0300
17062 Murphy Ave., Bldg. B www.coastmedia.com
Irvine, CA 92614

Commercial Head/Films (323) 658-6541
1049 S. Alfred St. FAX (323) 655-7650
Los Angeles, CA 90035 www.commercialhead.com
Executive Producer: Buddy Joe
Director: Moshe Brakha

Commercials While-U-Wait, Inc. (310) 399-3456
218 Grand Blvd. FAX (310) 396-1614
Venice, CA 90291 www.cwuw.com
Executive Producer/Directors: Claudia Forsthoevel & Rene Kock

A Common Thread, Inc. (310) 823-7300 (310) 798-9007
4081 Redwood Ave. FAX (310) 823-7305
Los Angeles, CA 90066 www.acommonthread.tv
Executive Producers: Tristan Drew & J.P. McMahon

Company (310) 277-7001
1551 S. Robertson Blvd. FAX (310) 277-7004
Los Angeles, CA 90035 www.companyfilms.net
Owner/Executive Producer: Robin Benson
Executive Producer: Richard Goldstein
Head of Production: Robert Nackman
Directors: Philippe Andre, Adam Cameron, The Coen Brothers, Mona El Mansouri, Fred Goss, David McNally, Harry Patramanis & Harald Zwart
East Coast Sales: Laura Dane
Mid West Sales: Rich Newman
West Coast Sales: Keith Quinn

Creative Chaos (310) 451-4112
425 19th St. FAX (310) 451-8069
Santa Monica, CA 90402
Executive Producer: Suzanne Bleibtreu
Producer: Harley Hoff
Director: Adam Bleibtreu

Crossroads Films (310) 659-6220 / (212) 647-1300
8630 Pine Tree Pl. FAX **(310) 659-3105**
West Hollywood, CA 90069 **www.crossroadsfilms.com**
Executive Producers: Carole Hughes & Camille Taylor
Directors: Russell Bates, Trudy Bellinger, Wilfred Brimo, Steve Eshelman, Sebastien Grousset, Harvey and Carolyn, Bruce Hurwit, Wayne Isham, JAM, Julia Jason, Nick Lewin, Nic Mathieu, Marcus McCollum, Jayson Moyer, Mike Nelesen, Mark Pellington, Tim Pope, Gillean Proctor, Kevin Samuels, Ben Taylor, Type2error & Kieran Walsh
Head of Sales/East Coast Sales Rep: Sharon Lew
Midwest Sales Rep: Janice Harryman
West Coast Rep: Tanya Cohen

Cucoloris Films, Inc. (310) 396-7778
72 Windward Ave. FAX **(310) 399-2182**
Venice, CA 90291 **www.cucoloris.com**
Executive Producer: Linda Stewart
Director: Danny Ducovny
East Coast Sales Rep.: Drew Miller
Midwest Sales Rep: Kevin Smith
West Coast Sales Rep: Rachel Finn
Southern Sales Rep: Ann Asprotites

Custom Video (310) 543-4901
707 Torrance Blvd., Ste. 105 **www.customvideo.tv**
Redondo Beach, CA 90277
Founder & Producer: Joe Jennings
President: Michael Ude
Producers: Hugh Malay, Geoff Nathanson & Rob Vouna

Dark Light Pictures (323) 460-2077
812 N. Highland Ave. FAX **(323) 460-7097**
Los Angeles, CA 90038 **www.darklightpictures.com**
Executive Producer: Vincent Arcaro
Head of Production: Sheila Flaherty
Director: David Steinberg
Director/Cameramen: Gil Cope & Caleb Deschanel
Sales Reps: Lauran McNamara, Connie Mellors & Schaffer Rogers

Dektor Film (323) 466-3455
1151 N. Highland Ave. FAX **(323) 856-8187**
Hollywood, CA 90038 **www.dektorfilm.com**
Executive Producers: Faith Dektor & Sven Shelgren
Director: Paul Dektor
Director/Cameramen: Leslie Dektor & Mark Dektor

Detour (310) 396-5796
1026 Cedar St. FAX **(310) 450-4345**
Santa Monica, CA 90405 **www.detourfilms.com**
Executive Producer: Josh Canova
Directors: Goetz Brothers, Jeff Kaumeyer, Rudy Manning, George Mays, Geoff Moore & Dana Tynan
Sales Rep: Michael Eha
Midwest Rep: Hillary Herbst
West Rep: Rachel Finn & Mary Saxon

Digital Studios West, Inc. (714) 842-1505 / (877) 379-7058
P.O. Box 614 **www.digitalstudioswest.com**
Huntington Beach, CA 92648

The Directors Bureau (323) 465-5299 / (323) 663-0500
1641 N. Ivar Ave. FAX **(323) 465-5547**
Hollywood, CA 90028 **www.thedirectorsbureau.com**
Directors: The AV Club, Roman Coppola, Sofia Coppola, Melodie McDaniel, Geoff McFetridge, Mike Mills & Shynola

DNA Studio (323) 463-2826
6535 Santa Monica Blvd. FAX **(323) 463-2535**
Hollywood, CA 90038 **www.dnala.com**
Executive Producer: Patricia Judice
Directors: Marco Brambilla, Fritz Flieder, Liz Friedlander, Francis Lawrence, Keir McFarlane, Jean-Baptiste Mondino, Rocky Schenck, Nzingha Stewart & Marc Webb
Sales Rep: Michel Waxman

DOOM, Inc. (310) 927-6661
818 S. Grand Ave., Ste. 804 FAX **(310) 496-2666**
Los Angeles, CA 90017 **www.doominc.com**
Head of Production/Producer: Darci Oltman
Director: Thomas Mignone

DUCK Studios, a.k.a. Duck Soup Studios (310) 478-0771
2205 Stoner Ave. FAX **(310) 478-0773**
Los Angeles, CA 90064 **www.duckstudios.com**
Executive Producer: Mark Medernach
President/Director: Roger Chouinard
Directors: Gints Apsits, Richard Borge, Jamie Caliri, Richard Cullen, Delicatessen, Eric Deutschman, Barbara Di Pasquale, Docter Twins, Evil Cat Land, Faivre Brothers, Eric Goldberg, James Hackett, Chris Harding, Laura Heit, JL Design, Peter Kaboth, Piotr Karwas, Stephen Kirklys, Amica Kubo, Lane and Jan, Miwa Matreyek, Graham Morris, Yorico Murakami, Andy Murdock, The Mushroom Company, Takahiro Okubo, Ritxi Ostariz, Nina Paley, Hsin Ping Pan, Plankton Art Co., Corky Quakenbush, Chris Romano, Maureen Selwood, Kang Seong, Steve Sonnenleiter, Shy the Sun AKA The Blackheart Gang, Theodore Ushev, YELLOW SHED & Ryan Zunkley
Sales Rep: Andrew Halpern
Music Video Rep: Randi Wilens

DuckPunk Productions (310) 836-3818
1861 S. Bundy Dr., Ste. 218 **www.duckpunk.net**
Los Angeles, CA 90025

Encore Media LLC (310) 823-9233
5301 Beethoven St., Ste. 290 FAX **(310) 823-9211**
Los Angeles, CA 90066 **www.encoremediallc.com**

Epix (310) 656-9100
23852 Pacific Coast Hwy, Ste. 379 FAX **(310) 656-9104**
Malibu, CA 90265 **www.epixfilms.com**
Executive Producer/Director: Lou La Monte
Producer: Laraine Gregory

Epoch Films, Inc. (310) 275-9333 / (310) 275-7938
9290 Civic Center Dr. FAX **(310) 275-7696**
Beverly Hills, CA 90210 **www.epochfilms.com**
Executive Producers: Mindy Goldberg & Jerry Solomon
Head of Production: John Duffin
Directors: Matthew Badger, Adam Bernstein, Anouk Besson, Tim Godsall, Paula Grief, Phil Morrison, Dewey Nicks, Jeff Preiss & Stacy Wall
Sales Rep: Mal Ward

Exeter Road Films (310) 503-8080
9200 Sunset Blvd., Second Fl. **www.exeterroadfilms.com**
Los Angeles, CA 90069

Exploded View (818) 729-9000 / (818) 402-0706
743 N. Keystone St. FAX **(818) 729-9033**
Burbank, CA 91506 **www.explodedviewla.com**
Executive Producer: Therese Sherman
Director: Richard Foley

Eyestorm Productions (310) 582-3937
1559 Seventh St. FAX **(310) 582-3939**
Santa Monica, CA 90401 **www.eyestormproductions.com**
Creative Directors: Michael Klima & Kyle Ruddick

F. J. Productions, Inc. (818) 788-0153
14900 Ventura Blvd., Ste. 350 FAX **(818) 788-0186**
Sherman Oaks, CA 91403 **www.fjproductions.com**
Directors: Renato Assad, Pico Garcez & Fabio Golombek
Production Coordinator: Tanira Lebedeff

Fabrication Films (310) 289-1232
8701 W. Olympic Blvd. FAX **(310) 289-1292**
Los Angeles, CA 90035 **www.fabricationfilms.com**
CEO: Kjehl Rasmussen
Executive Producer: Marc Siegel
Directors: Buddy Cone, Richard Kizu-Blair, Suzanne Luna, Leonardo Ricagni, Munier Sharrieff, James Wahlberg & Eugene Yelchin
West Coast Sales Rep: Ellen Knable
Midwest Sales Rep: Donna D'Aguanno
East Coast Sales Reps: Richard Fink & Robin Fried

Factory Features (818) 985-9905
111684 Ventura Blvd. FAX **(818) 474-7001**
Studio City, CA 91604 **www.factoryfeatures.com**
Executive Producer: Steven Johnson
Directors: Moh Azina, Matt Bass, David Brooks, Hobos with Guns, Cooper Johnson, Mike Myerburg, Salzy, Christian Swegal & Bill Yukich

Film Planet (310) 581-1100
1317 Innes Pl. FAX (310) 581-1130
Venice, CA 90291 www.filmplanet.com
Executive Producers: Robyn Bensinger & Karin Stuckenschmidt
Directors: Flavia Moraes & Picky Talarico

Film Réalité, Inc. (310) 883-8801
2017 Pacific Ave., Second Fl. FAX (310) 822-0835
Venice, CA 90291 www.filmrealite.com
Executive Producer: Richard Epstein
Head of Production: Marla Whittaker
Sales Rep: Andrew Hall Management

The Film Syndicate (323) 938-8080
7214 Melrose Ave. FAX (323) 938-8183
Los Angeles, CA 90046
Producer/Director: Bryan Johnson

FilmFilmFilm (310) 500-5773
P.O. Box 5445 www.filmfilmfilminc.com
Santa Monica, CA 90409
Executive Producer: Doris Bettencourt
Director: Mark de Paola

Flip Films, Inc. (310) 401-6140
1617 Broadway, Ste. A FAX (310) 401-6149
Santa Monica, CA 90404 www.flipfilms.com

Flying Tiger Films (323) 782-7125
8330 W. Third St. FAX (323) 782-7128
Los Angeles, CA 90048 www.ftfilms.com
Executive Producers: Rossi Cannon & Craig Rodgers
Director: Robert Gordon
Production Manager: Jeff Martin
East Coast Sales Rep: Chris Messiter
Midwest Sales Rep: Tracy Bernard
West Coast Sales Rep: Carol Biedermann

Form (323) 653-0404
8330 W. Third St. FAX (323) 653-0194
Los Angeles, CA 90048 www.form.tv
Executive Producers: Rossi Cannon & Craig Rodgers
Directors: John Adams, Robert Black, Michel Comte, David Cornell, David Denneen, Kevin Donovan, Jesse Dylan, Stephen Gaghan, Blair Hayes, Lance Kelleher, Ron Lieberman, Leslie Libman, Gary McKendry, Harry Patramanis, Bruce St. Clair, Bill Timmer & Bille Woodruff
Sales Reps: Tracy Bernard, Carol Biedermann, Andrew Hall & Chris Messiter

FRANKmedia (323) 930-5900
6374 Arizona Circle FAX (323) 930-5909
Los Angeles, CA 90045 www.frankmediausa.com
Managing Partner: Charles Salice
Executive Producer/Partner: Alex Blum
Directors: Robert Logevall, Michael Rowles & Paul Santana
West Coast Sales Rep: Connie Mellors & Co.
East Coast Sales Rep: Eby I Dickson
Midwest Sales Rep: Richard Miller Associates
Canada Sales Rep: Sparks Productions
Visual FX: Disorder

Fuel (310) 558-8755
1040 N. Sycamore Ave. www.fueldesign.com
Hollywood, CA 90038
Executive Producer/Director: Janet Arlotta
President: John Vernon Reid

Galanty & Company, Inc. (310) 451-2525
1640 Fifth St., Ste. 202
Santa Monica, CA 90401
Executive Producers: Mark Galanty & Sidney Galanty
Senior Producer: Steve Rood
Directors: Mark Galanty & Sidney Galanty

GARTNER (310) 899-1700
1531 Colorado Ave. FAX (310) 899-1710
Santa Monica, CA 90404 www.gartner.tv
Executive Producers: Don Block & Rich Carter
Head of Production: Elaine Strom Behnken
Directors: Shona Auerbach, Raymond Bark, Michael Bigelow, James Gartner, Theodore Melfi, Riess/Hill & Jim Weedon
East Coast Rep: Phillip Alden, The PTA
Midwest Rep: Renee Case & Co.
West Coast Reps: Andrea Andrews & Mark Andrews

Get It... Pictures (323) 462-7180
931 Cole Ave., Second Fl. FAX (323) 462-7190
West Hollywood, CA 90038 www.getitpictures.com
President: Natalie Barandes
Executive Producer: Steven Ward
Director: Natalie Barandes

Giraldi Media (310) 274-6102
(212) 966-1212
510 N. Hillcrest Rd. FAX (310) 274-6192
Beverly Hills, CA 90210 www.giraldi.com
Executive Producer: Debbie Merlin
Director: Bob Giraldi
West Coast Sales Rep: Wil LaFayette
Midwest Rep: Robin Pickett
East Coast Sales Rep: Samantha Tuttlebee

Go Film (323) 860-5400
(212) 677-7500
1040 N. Las Palmas Ave., Bungalow C FAX (323) 860-5401
Los Angeles, CA 90038 www.gofilm.net
Executive Producers: Gary Rose & Jonathan Weinstein
Heads of Production: Sandy Newman & Lisa Tauscher
Production Coordinators: Emily Malito & Christiane Sabo
Directors: Ric Cantor, David Dobkin, Caitlin Felton, Christopher Guest, Tim Hamilton, Andrews Jenkins, Rob Pearlstein, Rad-Ish, Jakob Strom, Markus Walter & Benjamin Weinstein
East Coast Sales Reps: Amy Jones & Michael Lobikis
West Coast Sales Rep: Stephanie Stephens
Mid West Sales Rep: Tracy Bernard

A Gosch Production (818) 729-0000
2227 W. Olive Ave. www.goschproductions.com
Burbank, CA 91506
CEO: Rob Gosch
Executive Producer: Pat Gosch
Directors: Chris Gosch, Walt Lloyd, Barbara Peeters, Frank Underwood & David Winning

Graying & Balding, Inc. (310) 979-4333
Executive Producer: Ann Kim FAX (310) 979-4334
Director: Jim Gable www.gandb.tv

Great Guns USA (310) 451-8150
63 Market St. FAX (310) 452-6323
Venice, CA 90291 www.greatgunsusa.com
President/Executive Producer: Tom Korsan
Executive Producer: Mary Sanders
Head of Production: Ellen DeVine

Green Dot Films, Inc. (310) 656-4900
1554 16th St. FAX (310) 656-0444
Santa Monica, CA 90404 www.greendotfilms.com
Managing Director: Rick Fishbein
Directors: Rebecca Baehler, Mark Coppos and Virginia Lee, Rafael Fernandez, GOLD, Richard Sears, Brent Thomas, & Three Legged Legs
Executive Producer/Head of Production: Rich Pring
Executive Producer/Head of Sales: Darren Foldes
Controller: Beth Clark
Vault Manager: Brady Spear
Office Manager: Kirby Coleman

Habana Avenue (310) 857-6678
1158 26th St., Ste. 374 www.habanaavenue.com
Santa Monica, CA 90403

Half Element Productions (323) 620-6925
1911 17th St., Ste. 5 www.halfelement.com
Santa Monica, CA 90404
Producers: Kim Daniels & Des Escober
Directors: Nikita Kleverov, Isaac Klotz & Brian Silva
Director/Cameraman: Rob Kraetsch

Hallowes Productions and Advertising (310) 390-4767
(310) 753-9381
11260 Regent St. FAX (310) 745-1107
Los Angeles, CA 90066 www.jimhallowes.com
Producer: Harry Mathias
Producer/Director: Jim Hallowes

harvest (310) 453-2600
3002 Pennsylvania Ave. FAX (310) 453-2602
Santa Monica, CA 90404 www.harvestfilms.com
Executive Producers: Bonnie Goldfarb & Scott Howard
Directors: bigtv, Adam Goldstein, The Hoffman Brothers, Adria Petty & Baker Smith
East Coast Rep: Michael Arkin
Midwest Rep: David Wagner
West Coast Reps: Brooke Covington & Rebecca Reber
Head of Production: Rob Sexton

Hello! (323) 465-9494
1641 N. Ivar Ave. FAX (323) 465-4203
Hollywood, CA 90028 www.helloandcompany.com
Owners: Graham Henman & Michael Karbelnikoff
Managing Director: Line Postmyr
Executive Producer: Carl Swan
Head of Production: Alexandra Chamberlain
Directors: Evan Bernard, Daniel Börjesson, Brothers Quay, PR Brown, Rey Carlson, Martin De Thurah, Rebecca Dreyfus, Cheryl Dunn, Kim Gehrig, Mark Gilbert, Jonathan Glazer, Nick Gordon, Tom Haines, Corin Hardy, Graham Henman, Andrew Huang, JacobsBriere, Michael Patrick Jann, Garth Jennings, Brent Jones, Michael Karbelnikoff, Walter Kehr, Asa Mader, Alexandre Moors, Mehdi Norowzian, Aaron Platt, Lynne Ramsay, Kai Regan, Si and Ad, Skee.tv, Walter Stern, Syndrome & Martin Weisz
Sales Reps: Michael Arkin, Marguerite Juliusson, Vicky Miller & Anna Triggs
EP of Music Videos/Intergrated Media: Sheira Rees-Davies
Music Video Rep: Jamie Kohn
Office Manager: Marissa Gallien

Hokus Pokus Productions, Inc. (818) 879-2200
23679 Calabasas Rd., Ste. 552 www.tvadvertising.com
Calabasas, CA 91302
Executive Producer: Robert Haukoos

Horizon Shine, Inc. (310) 392-5881
1810 14th St., Ste. 210 FAX (310) 392-5889
Santa Monica, CA 90404 www.horizonshine.com
Owner & Executive Producer: Robert Nackman

House of Usher Films (310) 586-0055
2014 Broadway FAX (310) 586-0065
Santa Monica, CA 90404 www.usherfilms.com

The House Production Company (323) 851-5151
1429 N. Spaulding Ave. FAX (323) 851-9598
Los Angeles, CA 90046
Executive Producer: Bonnie Matchinga
Producer: Sue Berry
Director: Bob Schwartz

HSI Productions, Inc. (310) 558-7100
(212) 627-3600
3630 Eastham Dr. FAX (310) 558-7101
Culver City, CA 90232 www.hsiproductions.com
President: Stavros Merjos
Executive Producer: Michael McQuhae
Directors: Irv Blitz, Kenneth Cappello, Simon Cole, Kevin Connolly, Gerard De Thame, Ryan Ebner, Justin Francis, Robert Hales, Michael Haussman, Eric Hillenbrand, Andreas Hoffmann, Hughes Brothers, Jaci Judelson, Joseph Kahn, David LaChapelle, Andy Lambert, Max Malkin, Malloys, Thomas Napper, Neistat Brothers, Rankin and Chris, Brett Ratner, Fatima Robinson, Saline Project, Jason Smith, Scott Speer, Tronic, Matthew Vaughn, Max Vitali, James Weitz & Hype Williams
Sales Rep: Michelle Ross
Executive Producer/VP: Rebecca Skinner

Hu-Man Element Productions, Inc. (213) 534-3700
1201 W. Fifth St., Ste. F-240A FAX (775) 667-1064
Los Angeles, CA 90017 www.hu-manelement.com

Hungry Man (310) 264-3000
(212) 625-5600
1517 20th St. FAX (310) 264-3001
Santa Monica, CA 90404 www.hungryman.com
Managing Partner: Kevin Byrne
Partners/Directors: Bryan Buckley & Hank Perlman
Executive Producer: Dan Duffy
Executive Producer/Head of Production: Cindy Becker
Directors: 300ml, Bryan Buckley, Samuel Christopher, Allen Coulter, Paul Gay, Robert Jitzmark, Bennett Miller, Amy Nicholson, Hank Perlman, Marcos Siega, Hideyuki Tanaka, Scott Vincent, Stephen Pearson & Zissimos and Rowan
East Coast Sales Reps: Mary French & Stacie Gillman
Midwest Sales Rep: Monaghan/Halpine

I-40 Films (310) 871-1506
11301 W. Olympic Blvd., Ste. 595 FAX (919) 832-3274
Los Angeles, CA 90064 www.i40films.com
Executive Producer: Kris Hixson
Senior VP of Production: David Mahanes
Directors: Brian Baugh & Kris Hixson

an ideal world (714) 953-9501
209 N. Bush St. FAX (714) 953-1195
Santa Ana, CA 92701 www.anidealworld.com
Executive Producer/Director: Robb Hart
Production Manager: Molly Talbot Hart

Illuminate – Arts, Media & Entertainment (323) 969-8822
3575 Cahuenga Blvd. West, Fourth Fl. FAX (323) 969-8840
Los Angeles, CA 90068 www.illuminatehollywood.com
Executive Producers: Eric Geisler, Patricia Sullivan & AJ Ullman
Directors: Randall P. Dark & Patricia Sullivan

Image G (818) 761-6644
10900 Ventura Blvd. www.imageg.com
Studio City, CA 91604
Director: Thomas Barron

Imaginary Forces (323) 957-6868
6526 Sunset Blvd. FAX (323) 957-9577
Los Angeles, CA 90028 www.imaginaryforces.com
Presidents: Peter Frankfurt & Chip Houghton
Head of Production: Ben Apley

Incubator (310) 566-6733
3303 Pico Blvd. FAX (310) 566-6739
Santa Monica, CA 90405 www.incubatorfilms.com
Director: Tom De Cerchio
Executive Producer: Billy Baughman

Independent Media, Inc. (310) 659-3503
3000 Olympic Blvd. FAX (310) 659-3520
Santa Monica, CA 90404 www.independentmediainc.com

Instant Karma Films (310) 526-7703
212 Marine St. FAX (310) 526-7076
Santa Monica, CA 90405 www.instantkarmafilms.tv
President: Tanya Hunger
Executive Producer: Craig Farkas
Directors: Maxime Giroux, Alfred Hau, Larry Shiu, Jung Son & Curtis Wehrfritz
Director/Cameraman: Brian Lai

Intelliscape Films, LLC (310) 882-2100
(800) 422-5996
11601 Wilshire Blvd., Fifth Fl. FAX (310) 575-1890
Los Angeles, CA 90025 www.intelliscape.com
Director: Bruce Caulk

IPS Productions (818) 755-0525
4705 Laurel Canyon Blvd., Ste. 200 FAX (818) 755-0526
Valley Village, CA 91607 www.ipsproductions.com
Executive Producer: Jim Sommers

Japanese Monster (310) 883-7800
2347 Ocean Ave. FAX (310) 883-7880
Venice, CA 90291 www.japanesemonster.com
Executive Producer: Tod Feaster
Head of Production: Paula Williams
Director: Craig Tanimoto

Jay Silverman Productions (323) 466-6030
1541 N. Cahuenga Blvd. FAX (323) 466-7139
Hollywood, CA 90028 www.jaysilverman.com
Director: Jay Silverman
Producer: Neil Gabriel

Jeffrey Markowitz Productions, Inc. (877) 297-8887
3366 Troy Dr. www.jeffproductions.com
Los Angeles, CA 90068

JSP Creative (866) 711-5195
(714) 288-6005
229 N. Glassell St. FAX (714) 288-6014
Orange, CA 92866 www.jspcreative.com
Producers: Brian FitzGerald & Jerry Stanley
Directors: David Briggs, Brent Loefke, Scott Murphy & Jerry Stanley

ka-chew! (323) 468-3020
6353 Sunset Blvd. FAX **(323) 468-3021**
Los Angeles, CA 90028 **www.kachew.com**
Executive VP: Richard Marlis
Sr. VP/Creative Director of Animation & Design: John Andrews
Executive Producer of Animation: Liz Seidman
Sr. Producer: Nathalie Renard

Kaboom Productions (310) 578-9383
2898 Glencoe Ave. **www.kaboomproductions.com**
Venice, CA 90291
Executive Producer: Lauren Schwartz
Head of Production: Mallary Weintraub
Directors: Steve Fong, Toni Jones, Gary Shaffer, Doug Werby & Danny Weisberg
East Coast Sales Rep: Mary Ford & Co.
Midwest Sales Rep: Julie Vargo & Assoc.
West Coast Sales Rep: Connie Mellors & Co.

Kabuki Productions, Inc. (310) 715-6480
P.O. Box 2226 FAX **(310) 715-6481**
Redondo Beach, CA 90278 **www.kabukipro.com**

Kandoo Films, Inc. (818) 789-6777
4515 Van Nuys Blvd., Ste. 100 FAX **(818) 789-2299**
Sherman Oaks, CA 91403 **www.kandoofilms.com**
Executive Producer/Director: Howard Barish
Producer: Al Smith
Sales Rep: Rhonda Kinosian

Karma Kollective (310) 836-5100
5870-D W. Jefferson FAX **(310) 836-5106**
Culver City, CA 90016 **www.karmakollective.tv**

Kavich Reynolds Productions, Inc. (323) 466-2490
6381 Hollywood Blvd., Ste. 580 FAX **(323) 466-3655**
Hollywood, CA 90028 **www.kavichreynolds.com**
President/Executive Producer: John Reynolds
Senior Executive Producer: Steve Kavich
Directors: Doug Henry & Rob Meltzer

Kommitted Films (310) 394-2416
631 Wilshire Blvd., Ste. 2A FAX **(310) 576-1384**
Santa Monica, CA 90401 **www.kommittedfilms.com**

La Banda Films (310) 858-7204
329 N. Wetherly Dr., Ste. 205 FAX **(310) 858-7206**
Beverly Hills, CA 90211 **www.labandafilms.com**
President: Roberto Sneider
Executive Producers: Paco Cossio, Carlos Estrada, David Phillips & Nadia Voukitchevitch
Directors: Patricia Mtz. De Velasco, Alex Duplan, Rodrigo Garcia, Luis Mandoki, Rodrigo Prieto, Roberto Sneider, Marcelo Szechtman, Pierre Tatarka & Antonio Urrutia

Ladybug Creative Digital Studio (310) 822-6367
1180 Nelrose Ave., Ste. 3 FAX **(310) 943-2190**
Venice, CA 90291 **www.ladybug-la.com**
Directors: Steve Andrich, Chamaco, Jerry Dugan, Michel Lichtenstein, Jeff Richter, Randy Spear & Alvaro Velarde
Executive Producers: David M. Bando
Sales Rep: Mira Reps

Lambo (310) 301-7700
4096 Glencoe Ave. FAX **(949) 376-5593**
Marina Del Rey, CA 90292 **www.lambo.la**

Legacy Films (323) 937-4182
6230 Wilshire Blvd., Ste. 227 FAX **(323) 937-7316**
Los Angeles, CA 90048 **www.legacyfilms.net**
Executive Producer: Michelle Colbert
Directors: Fabio Berutti, Christopher Erskin, Mauricio Kuri, David Lena, Teresa Medina, Alberto Moretorio & Bill Orisich

Lewin Pictures (818) 788-4214
4423 Firmament Ave. FAX **(818) 442-0014**
Encino, CA 91436
Director: Elyse Lewin

Lightning Bolt PIX (310) 828-8239
1653 18th St., Ste. 3B FAX **(310) 828-1923**
Santa Monica, CA 90404 **www.boltpix.com**
President: Michael Barnard
Designer/Director: Morgan Barnard
Designer/Editor: Christian Knudsen

Little Minx (310) 659-1577
634 N. LaPeer Dr. FAX **(310) 659-1377**
West Hollywood, CA 90069 **www.littleminx.tv**
President: Rhea Scott
Directors: Steph Green, H5, Johnny Hardstaff, Jesper Kouthoofd, Josh Miller, Ben Mor, Rodrigo Prieto, Malik Sayeed, Mark Seliger, Dawn Shadforth & Phillip Van

Locksmith (310) 287-1022
8500 Steller Dr., Bldg. 3 FAX **(310) 287-1208**
Culver City, CA 90232 **www.locksmithcontent.com**

Lucid Media (818) 362-5170
13139 Azores Ave. **www.marinocolmano.com**
Sylmar, CA 91342
Director/Cameraman: Marino Colmano

M Creative Group (818) 225-1541
23123 Ventura Blvd., Ste. 211 FAX **(818) 225-1476**
Woodland Hills, CA 91364 **www.mcreativegroup.net**
Creative Director/CEO: Seth Pinsker
Executive Producer/Sr. VP: Diane Glezerman

M-80 Films (310) 899-9100
701 Santa Monica Blvd. FAX **(310) 395-1750**
Santa Monica, CA 90401 **www.m80films.com**
Executive Producer: Marc Segiel
Director: Tenney Fairchild
Sales Reps: Stacey Altman, Marci Miles & Jennifer Warren

MacGuffin Films, Ltd. (310) 550-6990
350 N. Crescent Dr., Ste. 304 FAX **(310) 550-6237**
Beverly Hills, CA 90212 **www.macguffin.com**
President: Michael Salzer
Executive Producers: Gloria Colangelo & Sam Wool
Directors: Christopher Bean, Kevan Bean, Jim Collins, Michael Somoroff, Julian West, Theresa Wingert & Henning Winkelmann
East Coast Sales Reps: Vanessa Moseley & Maria Stenz
Office Head: Greg Pappas
Midwest Sales Rep: Jay Anderson
West Coast Sales Rep: Claire Worch
Regional Sales Rep: Sarah Lange

Make It Happen Productions, Inc. (818) 981-2327
13557 Ventura Blvd., Second Fl. FAX **(818) 981-2440**
Sherman Oaks, CA 91423 **www.mihp.tv**

Maneater Productions (323) 790-1732
(323) 327-2793
6860 Lexington Ave. FAX **(323) 460-6063**
Hollywood, CA 90038 **www.maneaterproductions.com**
Executive Producers: Christina Perri & Jed James
Directors: Atanas, Colombo, Miles Flannigan, Anthony Garth, Jeremy Haft, Kelley, Kenny FX, Evan Lane, Save Lorenzo, Peter Mack, Bradley Scott & Tudor

Megahertz Pictures (310) 727-2600
1600 Rosecrans Ave., Bldg. 2B FAX **(310) 727-2601**
Manhattan Beach, CA 90266 **www.megahertzpictures.com**
Executive Producer: John Harris
Director: David Mueller
Director/Cameraman: Francis Mohajerin

Mesita (818) 760-8707
11333 Moorpark Ave., Ste. 446
Studio City, CA 91602
Executive Producer: L.D. James
Director/Cameraman: Richard E. Black
Sales Rep: Darr Hawthorne

Millennium Pictures Productions, Inc. (310) 453-1115
2050 Broadway **www.millenniumpictures.tv**
Santa Monica, CA 90404
Executive Producers: Richard Gagon & Caroline Von Weyher
Managing Director: Caroline Von Weyher
Producer: Kellee Cragin
Directors: Kerry Shaw Brown, Tim Damon, Alexander Paul, Jim Rygiel, Boyd Shermis, Susan Stitt, Kevin Ward & Jamie Way
Midwest Rep: Cathi Connors/Connor Group
West Coast Reps: Ellen Dempsey & Connie Mellors
East Coast Rep: Mary Ford

Minerva Media Group, LLC (310) 647-5604
840 Apollo St., Ste. 324 FAX **(310) 647-5605**
El Segundo, CA 90245 **www.minervamg.com**

MJZ, Inc. (310) 826-6200
2201 Carmelina Ave. FAX (310) 826-6219
Los Angeles, CA 90064 www.mjz.com
President: David Zander
Sr. Executive Producer: Jeff Scruton
Executive Producers: Lisa Margulis & Eric Stern
Directors: Dante Ariola, Fredrik Bond, Steven Diller, Ray Dillman, Nicolai Fuglsig, Victor Garcia, Craig Gillespie, Phil Joanou, Spike Jonze, Harmony Korine, Tom Kuntz, Rocky Morton, Marcus Nispel, Pleix, Rupert Sanders, Blue Source, Matthijs Van Heijningen & Clay Williams

Mohr, Gallerani & More Films (310) 399-6630
1011 Pico Blvd., Ste. 9 FAX (310) 399-4876
Santa Monica, CA 90405
Executive Producer: Cay Mohr
Director: Andy Gallerani
Head of Production: Margot Ott
Producer: Melodie Woods

MonsterEye Films, LLC. (310) 442-0393
(310) 720-1456
12340 Santa Monica Blvd., Ste. 220 FAX (310) 733-1810
Los Angeles, CA 90025 www.monstereyefilms.com

Monument Television & Film Company (617) 771-7277
(323) 422-9980
(323) 462-2184
www.monumenttelevisionandfilm.com

Moo Studios (323) 464-3080
746 N. Cahuenga Blvd. FAX (323) 464-3699
Hollywood, CA 90038 www.moostudios.com
Executive Producer: David Lyons
Directors: Patrick Bowyer, Adam Byrd, Martin Fougerol, Francois Halard, Pamela Hanson, Andy Huang, Anthony Rose, Shaun Sewter & Ellen von Unwerth
Head Of Sales: Erika Sheldon
Head Of Production: Rebecca Donaghe

Morningstar Entertainment Inc. (714) 978-2266
571 N. Poplar, Ste. I FAX (714) 978-7858
Orange, CA 92868 www.morningstarhd.com

Mortar Inc. (323) 462-1220
931 N. Cole Ave., Ste. 200 FAX (323) 462-7190
Hollywood, CA 90038 www.mortarinc.com

Motel Films (323) 240-6736
Executive Producer: Rick Dublin www.motelfilms.com
Directors: Rick Dublin, Alan Martinez & Jarl Olsen
East Coast Sales Rep.: John Naitove
Midwest Sales Rep: Tim Harwood

Motion Theory (310) 396-9433
321 Hampton Dr., Ste. 101 FAX (310) 396-7883
Venice, CA 90291 www.motiontheory.com
Executive Producer: Javier Jimenez
West Coast Sales Rep: Boss Talent
East Coast Sales Rep: Blah! Blah? (Blah..)

Motiv Films (310) 260-6100
1630 Stewart St., Studio B1 FAX (310) 260-6111
Santa Monica, CA 90404 www.motivfilms.com
Executive Producer/Partner: Jim Rutherford
Directors: Grant Baird, Eric Bute, Dana Christiaansen, Trey Fanjoy, Dale Heslip, Joe Maxwell, Mark Russel & Esteban Sapir
Executive Producer/Commercials: Beth Pearson

Moving Target (310) 394-0110
P.O. Box 5367 www.movingtargetla.com
Santa Monica, CA 90409
Executive Producer: Brian Jochum
Directors: Alan Munro & Damian Fulton

Moxie Pictures (310) 857-1000
5890 W. Jefferson Blvd., Ste. J FAX (310) 857-1004
Los Angeles, CA 90016 www.moxiepictures.com
Executive Producers: Robby Fernandez & Lizzie Schwartz
Directors: Wes Anderson, Spencer Chinoy, Andrew Christou, Cameron Crowe, Lenny Dorfman, Neil Gorring, Martin Granger, James Griffiths, Jared Hess, Dan Levinson, Henry Lu, Rob Marshall, Errol Morris, Todd Philips, Bob Purman, Peyton Reed, Jim Sheridan, Kevin Smith, Pam Thomas, Frank Todaro & John Waters

Mr. Big Film (310) 399-9910
(310) 452-3583
1434 Abbot Kinney Blvd. FAX (310) 399-3454
Venice, CA 90291 www.mrbigfilm.com
Director/Cinematographer: Tim Bieber
Executive Producer: Kate Zimmer
Producer: Lisa DeLeo
East Coast Sales Rep: Judy Wolff
West Coast/Midwest Sales Rep: Ellen Knable

MRB Productions (323) 965-8881
FAX (323) 965-8882
www.mrbproductions.com

Newhouse Films (310) 659-0010
8630 Pine Tree Pl. FAX (310) 659-3105
Los Angeles, CA 90069 www.newhousefilms.com
Executive Producer: Heidi Nolting
Directors: Enno Jacobsen, Steven Ramser & Patrick Solomon
East Coast Sales Rep: Roxanne & Co.
Midwest Sales Rep: Robin Pickett & Assoc.
West Coast Sales Rep: Stacey & Co.

Nobody Productions (323) 662-7976
President: Adele Baughn www.nobodyproductions.com
Sr. VP of Marketing: Tom Wilson
Development: Anadel Baughn & Craig Lachman

Noda Films, Inc. (310) 866-1594
171 Pier Ave., Ste. 259
Santa Monica, CA 90405
Director/Cameraman: Nobuhito Noda

Nonfiction Unlimited (310) 399-9600
905 Olympic Blvd. www.nonfictionunlimited.com
Santa Monica, CA 90404
Executive Producers: Michael Degan & LJ/Loretta Jeneski
Directors: Rob Bindler, Paul Crowder, Rob Devor, Steve James, Robby Kenner, Barbara Kopple, Stacy Peralta, Jessica Sanders, Ondi Timoner, Peyton Wilson & Jessica Yu

November Films (310) 581-5445
17751 Tramonto Dr. FAX (310) 581-6114
Pacific Palisades, CA 90272 www.novemberfilms.com
Executive Producer: Alan Siegel
Producer: Chris Sheffield
Head of Production: Matthew Hensley
Directors: Peter Fuszard, Simon Mestel, Stacy Toyama & Jason Wulfsohn
Sales Rep: Andrew Halpern

Nydrle, Inc. (310) 659-8844
670 N. La Peer Dr. FAX (310) 659-7733
West Hollywood, CA 90069 www.nydrle.com
Executive Producer: Garner Kinmond
Director: Peter Nydrle

Ocean Park Pictures (310) 450-1220
741A 10th St. FAX (310) 319-1392
Santa Monica, CA 90403 www.oceanparkpix.com
Executive Producer: Tim Goldberg
Directors: David Dryer, Gregory Lemkin, William Linsman & Holly Goldberg Sloan
Director/Cameraman: Jeffrey Phillips

Oceangate Productions (323) 224-9051
660 S. Ave. 21, Ste. 3
Los Angeles, CA 90031
Executive Producer/Director: Mark Rasmussen

ODM Inc. (323) 933-1614
5820 Wilshire Blvd., Ste. 306 www.odmproductions.com
Los Angeles, CA 90036

Omaha Pictures (310) 396-4333
1040 N. Las Palmas Ave. FAX (310) 396-4323
Los Angeles, CA 90038 www.omahapictures.com
Managing Director: Diane McArter
Executive Producer: Eric Stern
Directors: Steven Diller, Paul Gay, Michael Grasso, Stewart Hendler, David McNally, Rupert Sanders, Speck/Gordon & Charlie White

O'Neil & Associates (323) 876-6853
1158 N. Curson Ave.
West Hollywood, CA 90046
Director: James O'Neil
Storyboards: Justice O'Neil

Onyx Productions Direct, Inc. (323) 692-9830
2355 Westwood Blvd., Ste. 401 FAX **(310) 470-0190**
Los Angeles, CA 90064 **www.onyxprod.com**
President/Executive Producer: Joan Renfrow

Original Film, Inc. (310) 445-9000
4223 Glencoe Ave., Ste. B119 FAX **(310) 445-9191**
Marina del Rey, CA 90292 **www.originalfilm.com**
Executive Producers: Jeff Devlin & Bruce Mellon
Head of Production: Robbyn Foxx
Sales Rep: Jeff Devlin

The Outfit Media Group (310) 477-5900
2148 Federal Ave., Ste. B FAX **(310) 477-5944**
Los Angeles, CA 90025 **www.theoutfitmg.com**

PAC (323) 931-9962
Producer/Director: Martin Pitts

Parlay Productions (310) 733-4430 (310) 270-7526
8500 Steller Dr., Bldg. 8 FAX **(310) 733-4439**
Culver City, CA 90232 **www.parlayproductions.com**

Partizan (323) 468-0123
7083 Hollywood Blvd., Ste. 401 FAX **(323) 468-0129**
Hollywood, CA 90028 **www.partizan.com**
Executive Producer & CEO: Sheila Stepanek
East Coast Sales Rep: Melanie McEvoy
Midwest Sales Rep: Tracy Bernard
West Coast Sales Rep: Tracy Fetterman
Directors: Alex and Martin, Leslie Ali, Agust Baldursson, Antoine Bardou-Jacquet, Lisa Cholodenko, David Gaddie, Paul Goldman, Michel Gondry, Olivier Gondry, Matthias Hoene, Illegal Artists, Eric Lynne, Dominic Murphy, Doug Nichol, Nagi Noda, Ace Norton, Ramon and Pedro, The Elvis & Traktor

Picture Park (310) 315-1949 (617) 457-1949
2940 Nebraska Ave. FAX **(310) 315-9749**
Santa Monica, CA 90404 **www.picturepk.com**
Executive Producers: Mark Hankey, Bill Near & Raub Shapiro
Directors: Jim Barton, Jon Bekemeier, Gerald V. Casale, Bill Cuccinello, John Huet, The Jay and Tony Show, Scott Kalvert, Nathan Karma Cox, Tuesday McGowen, Harry McCoy & Streeter and Davis
Sales Reps: Lisa Gimenez, Cindy Moran, Keith Quinn, Jeanne Rashford, Corey Rogers & Perry Schaeffer

Pictures In A Row (323) 957-5400
736 Seward St. FAX **(323) 957-5405**
Los Angeles, CA 90038 **www.picrow.com**
Director: Peter Lang

Playroom Creative (714) 969-3938
412 Indianapolis Ave. **www.playroomcreative.com**
Huntington Beach, CA 92648

Praxis Films (323) 460-4393
c/o R. Sirott, 17324 Partheia St. FAX **(323) 460-4181**
Northridge, CA 91325
Director: Robert Blalack

Precision Productions + Post (310) 839-4600
10718 McCune Ave. FAX **(310) 839-4601**
Los Angeles, CA 90034 **www.precisionpost.com**

Proscenium Pictures, Ltd. (323) 650-6767
8840 Wilshire Blvd. FAX **(323) 650-1345**
Beverly Hills, CA 90211 **www.prosceniumpictures.com**
Executive Producer: Jeff McQueen

Pusher Media (310) 576-1344
969 Colorado Ave. **www.pushermedia.com**
Santa Monica, CA 90401
Executive Producer: Ben Dossett

Pytka (310) 392-9571
916 Main St. FAX **(310) 392-5873**
Venice, CA 90291
Executive Producer: Tara Fitzpatrick
Director: Joe Pytka

@radical.media (310) 664-4500 (212) 462-1500
1630 12th St. FAX **(310) 664-4600**
Santa Monica, CA 90404 **www.radicalmedia.com**
Executive Producers: Jon Kamen, Donna Portaro & Frank Scherma
Sales Rep: Dominic Bernacchi

Raimondi Films, Inc. (760) 837-1093
75387 Stardust Ln. FAX **(760) 837-1879**
Indian Wells, CA 92210 **www.raimondifilms.com**
Executive Producer: Jane Raimondi
Director/Cameraman: Paul Raimondi

Raintree Productions (310) 827-3336
President/Executive Producer: Bob Wollin
Director: Stu Berg

Ranch Exit Films, Inc. (310) 209-8974
2216 Main St., PH 3 FAX **(310) 577-9207**
Santa Monica, CA 90405 **www.ranchexitfilms.com**
Executive Producer: Christopher Raser
Directors & Cameramen: Richard Carlson, Chris Patterson, John Stanier & Michael Werk

Rapport Films, Inc. (818) 980-4483
12652 Killion St.
Valley Village, CA 91607
Producer: D Cassidy

Raymond Entertainment Direct (323) 785-4700
3459 Cahuenga Blvd. FAX **(323) 785-4701**
Los Angeles, CA 90068 **www.raymondentertainment.com**

Reactor Films (310) 656-4646
1330 Fourth St. FAX **(310) 656-4649**
Santa Monica, CA 90401 **www.reactorfilms.com**
Executive Producer: Michael Romersa
COO: Nancy Novokmet
Directors: Chris Applebaum, Steve Chase, Thor Freudenthal, Warren Kushner & Barry Peterson
Head of Production: Tracy Hauser
Staff Production Manager: MaryBeth Ferensic
Vault Editor: Sean Stender
East Coast Sales Reps: Jessica Courter & Peter McCann
Midwest Sales Rep: Dave Dakich
West Coast Sales Rep: Tommy Romersa

RebelRobot (310) 399-6630
1011 Pico Blvd., Ste. 9 FAX **(310) 399-4876**
Santa Monica, CA 90405
Producer: Melodie Woods
Head of Production: Margot Ott
Director: Andy G.

rednavel flmworx (323) 467-7778
1670 Beverly Blvd., Ste. 10 **www.rednavel.com**
Los Angeles, CA 90038
President: Mitchell Welch

Reel Orange (949) 548-4524
316 La Jolla Dr. FAX **(949) 548-0749**
Newport Beach, CA 92663 **www.reelorange.com**
Director/Cameraman: Art Vitarelli

Revolver Films (310) 827-2441
4040 Del Rey Ave., Ste. 5 FAX **(310) 827-2661**
Marina del Rey, CA 90292 **www.revolverfilmsla.com**
Producer: Mark Priola

Rhythm + Hues Commercial Studios (310) 448-7900
5404 Jandy Pl. FAX **(310) 448-7601**
Los Angeles, CA 90066 **www.rhythm.com**
Executive Producer: Paul Babb
Head of Production, Live Action: Kat Dillon
Head of Production, Commercial Digital: Lisa White
Directors: Clark Anderson, Mark Dippé, EJ Foerster, Timothy Kendall, Pitof & James Wahlberg
East Coast Sales Rep: Carolyn Hill
Midwest/Detroit Sales Reps: Julie Ford, Kristina "KK" Kovacevic & Marci Miles
Western/Texas Sales Rep: Char Noonan
United Kingdom/Europe Sales Rep: Georgina Poushkine

Ringleader Productions (310) 295-4660
11155 Massachusetts Ave. FAX **(310) 945-5912**
Los Angeles, CA 90025 **www.ringleaderproductions.com**
Directors: Jerry Chan, Darren Fanton, David Hogan & Max Gutierrez

Ross McCanse & Associates, Inc. (818) 506-4715
3315 Oakdell Rd. FAX **(818) 506-4587**
Studio City, CA 91604
Director: Ross McCanse

RSA Films, Inc. (310) 659-1577
(212) 343-2020
634 N. La Peer Dr. FAX **(310) 659-1377**
West Hollywood, CA 90069 **www.rsafilms.com**
President: Jules Daly
VP & Executive Producer: Marjie Abrahams
Executive Producers: Philip Fox-Mills & Tracie Norfleet
Directors: Casey Affleck, Neill Blomkamp, Joe Carnahan, Barney Cokeliss, Tom Dey, Ben Dickinson, Andrew Dominik, Laurence Dunmore, The Duplass Brothers, Lauri Faggioni, Brett Foraker, Sean Ellis, Adam Goldstein, Hobby, Henrik Hansen, Hugh Johnson, Nick Livesey, Melina, Sam Mendes, Adrian Moat, John O'Hagan, Jesse Peretz, Carl Erik Rinsch, Alex Rutterford, The Russo Brothers, Jake Scott, Jordan Scott, Luke Scott, Ridley Scott, Tony Scott, Adam Smith, Kevin Spacey, Joachim Trier & Declan Whitebloom
East Coast Sales Reps: Philip Fox-Mills & Victoria Venantini
Midwest Sales Reps: Chris Karabas & Rob Mueller
West Coast Sales Rep: Holly Ross

Rumpus Creative (310) 437-0902
www.rumpuscreative.com

Sandwick (212) 647-1310
(310) 854-0647
8630 Pine Tree Pl. **www.sandwickmedia.com**
Los Angeles, CA 90069
President: Bill Sandwick
Directors: Matthaus Bussmann, Camp David, John Curran, Jeff Gorman, Keir McFarlane, Nic and Sune, Nick Rafter, Paul Riccio, Roenberg, Thomas Sigel, Johan Tappert & Christoffer Von Reis
East Coast Sales Rep: Jared Shapiro
Midwest Sales Rep: Janice Harryman
West Coast Sales Rep: Andrew Hall

Serial Dreamer Productions, Inc. (323) 848-7000
928 N. Fairfax Ave. FAX **(323) 848-7003**
Los Angeles, CA 90046 **www.serialdreamer.net**
Executive Producer: Paulina Hatoupis
Business Development: Michelle Hott

Sharpcut Productions (310) 247-0088
Director: Gary Robinson FAX **(310) 858-2254**
www.sharpcut.com

Shine (323) 937-7470
5410 Wilshire Blvd., Ste. 900 FAX **(323) 937-7420**
Los Angeles, CA 90036 **www.shinestudio.tv**
Creative Director: Michael Riley
Executive Producer: Bob Swensen

Showreel International, Inc. (323) 464-5111
1021 N. McCadden Pl. FAX **(323) 464-4216**
Hollywood, CA 90038 **www.showreel.com**
Directors: Richard E. & Eric Jackson
Executive Producer: Lynne Jackson

Sincbox (310) 566-6700
11601 Wilshire Blvd., Ste. 2150 FAX **(310) 566-6719**
Los Angeles, CA 90025 **www.sincbox.com**

Smith and Jones Films, Inc. (310) 948-5751
4123 Lankershim Blvd. FAX **(310) 496-2635**
Los Angeles, CA 91602 **www.smithandjonesfilms.net**

Smuggler (323) 817-3300
1715 N. Gower St. FAX **(323) 817-3333**
Los Angeles, CA 90028 **www.smugglersite.com**
Executive Producers: Brian Carmody & Patrick Milling Smith
Heads of Production: Allison Kunzman & Laura Thoel
Directors: Jaron Albertin, Steve Ayson, Brian Beletic, Adam Berg, Jun Diaz, Filip Engstrom, David Frankham, Guard Brothers, Neil Harris, Randy Krallman, Ringan Ledwidge, Renny Maslow, Bennett Miller, Psyop, Henry-Alex Rubin, Guy Shelmerdine, Chris Smith, Stylewar, Jon Watts & Ivan Zacharias
Chief Operating Officer: Lisa Rich

Sonic Films, Inc. (310) 785-9100
(212) 744-5333
73 Market St. FAX **(310) 564-7500**
Venice, CA 90291 **www.sonicfilmsinc.com**
Executive Producer: David Stoltz

Space Program (323) 937-3007
110 S. Fairfax Ave., Ste. 255 **www.spaceprogram.tv**
Los Angeles, CA 90036
Executive Producer: Bill Reilly
Directors: Zach Braff, Scott Duncan, Elma Garcia, Kenn MacRae, Kevin Samuels & Michael Shapiro
Sales Reps: Robin Pickett and Associates, Simpatico & Stacey and Company
Head of Production: Mora Killeen Walker

Sports Cinematography Group (310) 785-9100
(212) 744-5333
73 Market St. FAX **(310) 564-7500**
Venice, CA 90291 **www.sportscinematographygroup.com**
Executive Producer: David Stoltz

Squeeze (818) 906-0006
www.thedirectorsnetwork.com

Stardust Studios (310) 399-6047
1920 Main St., Ste. A FAX **(310) 399-7486**
Santa Monica, CA 90405 **www.stardust.tv**
Executive Producer: Eileen Doherty
Creative Director: Jake Banks

Station Wagon Films (818) 995-8629
4650 Greenbush Ave. **www.stationwagonfilms.com**
Sherman Oaks, CA 91423
Executive Producer: Anthony Mosa
Director: Jim Tozzi
Director/Cameraman: Kevin Ward
Head of Production: Allan Telias
Production Manager: Dawn Hoffman
Sales Reps: Michael Ella & Toni Saarinen

Steam (310) 636-4620
3021 Airport Ave., Ste. 201 FAX **(310) 636-4621**
Santa Monica, CA 90405 **www.steamshow.com**
Contact: Scott Bryant

Sticks + Stones Studios (323) 790-0440
6615 Melrose Ave., Loft 2 FAX **(323) 790-0450**
Los Angeles, CA 90038 **www.sticks.tv**
Executive Producer: Marlon Staggs
Coordinator: Erick Varillas
Directors: Jerry Brown & Sean Mullens
Producer: Gabrielle Yuro

Strato Films (323) 344-8905
Director: Paula Walker **www.stratofilms.com**
Director/Cameraman: Rolf Kestermann

Subliminal Pictures (818) 841-2550
FAX **(818) 450-0559**

superstudio (310) 582-1111
1508 17th St. FAX **(310) 582-1113**
Santa Monica, CA 90404 **www.superstudio.tv**
President/Executive Producer: Dana Garman Jacobsen
Staff Producer: Nathan de la Rionda

Supply & Demand, Inc. (310) 956-3500
6374 Arizona Circle FAX **(310) 956-3501**
Los Angeles, CA 90045 **www.supplyanddemand.tv**
Founder/Executive Producer: Tim Case
Co-Founder/Executive Producer: Kent Eby
Directors: Bruce Dowad, Tony Kaye, Jeffery Plansker, Greg Popp, Jose Antonio Pratt, Landis Smithers, Josh Taft & Sean Thonson
East Coast Rep: Katy Dickson & Kent Eby
West Coast Sales Rep: Reber/Covington
Executive Producer/Managing Director: Kira Carstensen
Head of Production: Kristen Wageman
Mid-West Sales Rep: Richard Miller & Assoc.

Tate USA (310) 828-8989
1913 Centinela Ave. FAX **(310) 828-0707**
Santa Monica, CA 90404 **www.tateusa.com**
Executive Producers: Hugh Bacher & David Tate
Directors: Phil Brown, James Dodson, Eric King, Ago Panini, Vadim Perelman, Jason Reitman & Jonathan Teplitzky

Tempered Entertainment, LLC (323) 252-6774
5810 W. Olympic Blvd., Ste. 202 FAX **(323) 655-5820**
Los Angeles, CA 90036 **www.temperedentertainment.com**

Tool of North America (310) 453-9244
2210 Broadway FAX **(310) 453-4185**
Santa Monica, CA 90404 **www.toolofna.com**
Executive Producer: Jennifer Siegel
Head of Production: Amy Delossa
Directors: Sam Cadman, Harry Cocciolo, Sean Ehringer, Erich Joiner, Sam Jones, Robert Richardson & Tom Routson

Trettin/Rodenbush + Partners (818) 990-1038
3900 Hollyline Ave. FAX **(818) 990-1038**
Sherman Oaks, CA 91423
Executive Producer: Ken Rodenbush
Director/Cameraman: Henry Trettin

trio films (310) 207-7800
2023 S. Westgate Ave. FAX **(310) 207-7807**
Los Angeles, CA 90025 **www.triofilms.com**
Executive Producers: Taylor Ferguson & Erin Tauscher

Tuesday Films (310) 899-0335
1450 20th St. FAX **(310) 828-4278**
Santa Monica, CA 90404 **www.tuesdayfilms.com**
Executive Producer: Mardi Minogue
Directors: Joe Baratelli & Jon Yarbrough
Production Supervisor: Neil Daniels

TWC (310) 392-7333
1655 Euclid St. FAX **(310) 392-7323**
Santa Monica, CA 90404 **www.thomaswintercooke.com**
Executive Producer/Partner: Mark Thomas
Partners: Philip Cooke & Ralph Winter
Head of Production: Jeff Snyder
Directors: Brian Baderman, Trevor Cornish, Scott Derrickson, Jeff France, Michael Fueter, David Jellison, Justin Klarenbeck, Suthon Petchsuwan & Bo Platt
West Coast Sales Rep: Michel Waxman

Über Content (323) 860-8686
1040 N. Las Palmas Ave., Bldg. 7 FAX **(323) 860-8689**
Los Angeles, CA 90038 **www.ubercontent.com**
Executive Producers: Phyllis Koenig, Preston Lee & Steve Wi
Directors: Jordan Brady, Jeffrey Fleisig, Luis Gerard, Stewart Hendler, Jason Kohn, Dave Laden, Marc Schölermann, Steven Tsuchida, & Tom Vaughan
East Coast Rep: Miss Smith, Inc.
West Coast Rep: Reber/Covington
Midwest Rep: Renee and Melissa
Hispanic Rep: Envision It

Untitled (310) 917-9191
2241 Corinth Ave. FAX **(310) 231-7612**
Los Angeles, CA 90064 **www.untitled.tv**
Executive Producer: Jim Evans
General Manager: Larry Edwards
Head of Production: Geoff Campbell
Directors: Geoffrey Barish, Mark Bennett, Anouk Besson, The Cronenweths, Christopher Desantis, Justin Klarenbeck, Rick Knief, Glenn Martin, Adam Massey & Adam Reed
West Coast Sales Rep: Siobhan McCafferty
Midwest Sales Rep: Nikki Weiss
East Coast Sales Rep: Ann McKallagat

Uptown 6 (323) 274-2552
6460 Odin St. FAX **(310) 497-7954**
Los Angeles, CA 90068 **www.uptown6.com**

Utopia Films, Inc. (310) 338-0580
7300 Lenox Ave., Ste. I23 FAX **(313) 557-0580**
Los Angeles, CA 91405 **www.utopiafilms.com**
Directors: Mike Brady, Arturo Hoyos, Ricardo Hoyos & Nicolas

Valiant Films (415) 989-5700
164 Townsend St., Studio 5 FAX **(415) 989-5701**
San Francisco, CA 94107 **www.valiantfilms.com**

Velocity Visuals, Inc. (310) 376-7870
Producer/Director: William Powloski **www.velocityfx.com**
Producer: Matt Gore

Verité Studios (866) 535-1972
708 Westmont Rd. **www.veritestudios.com**
Santa Barbara, CA 93108
Director: Timothy Eaton

Vihlene & Associates, Inc. (949) 582-0937
28241 Crown Valley Pkwy, Ste. F187 FAX **(949) 582-5070**
Laguna Niguel, CA 92677 **www.vihlene.com**
Executive Producer: Vern Vihlene Jr.

Villains (310) 888-8900
1746 N. Ivar Ave. FAX **(310) 888-8444**
Hollywood, CA 90028 **www.villains.com**
Owner: John Marshall
Directors: Mona El Monsouri, The Guard Brothers, Axel Laubscher, Dewey Nicks & Terry Rietta
Sales Reps: Lynn Mutchler & Dana Roberts

Vision Mixer Films (310) 344-3337
15332 Antioch St., Ste. 506 FAX **(310) 573-1077**
Pacific Palisades, CA 90272 **www.visionmixerfilms.com**

Vivus Media (213) 989-6884
www.vivusmedia.com
Executive Producers: Adam Fox & Wendy Shuey

Walker/Fitzgibbon Television/ Film Productions (323) 469-6800
6565 Sunset Blvd., Ste. 417 FAX **(323) 469-6801**
Los Angeles, CA 90028 **www.walkerfitzgibbon.com**
Executive Producer: Mo Fitzgibbon
Directors: Mo Fitzgibbon & Robert W. Walker
Producer: Fernando Viquez
Production: Elissa Slovin

Waterline Pictures, Inc. (818) 901-1178 (310) 963-4812
P.O. Box 56387 FAX **(818) 901-1179**
Sherman Oaks, CA 91413
Director: Roger Roth

a WhiteLabel product (323) 969-0555
1820 Industrial St., Ste. 106 FAX **(323) 512-7007**
Los Angeles, CA 90021 **www.awhitelabelproduct.com**
Executive Producers: Annique DeCaestecker, Oliver Hicks & Ellen Jacobson-Clarke
Directors: Arni and Kinski, Samuel Bayer, Don Cameron, Jean-Paul Goude, Mikael Jansson, Peter Lindbergh, David Michalek, Paul Middleditch, James Pilkington, Tim Richardson & Nick Robertson
Head of Production: Lynn Zekanis

Wild Indigo, LLC (323) 876-3331
Executive Producer: Arthur Gorson **www.wildindigo.tv**
Directors: Moses Edinborough, Leo Gabriadze, Dean Karr & Patricia Riggen

William Moffitt Associates (818) 495-3106
785 New York Dr. FAX **(626) 345-0673**
Altadena, CA 91001 **www.wmadigital.com**
President: Will Moffitt
Executive Producer: Lynne Moffitt
Sales Rep: Brooke Rothman

Windowseat Pictures (310) 535-3650
121 Sheldon St. **www.windowseatpictures.com**
El Segundo, CA 90245

Wit Animation (310) 305-4790
1717 Lincoln Blvd. FAX **(310) 439-2530**
Venice, CA 90291 **www.witanimation.com**

Wolfe and Company Films (626) 584-4000
39 E. Walnut St. FAX **(626) 584-4099**
Pasadena, CA 91103 **www.danwolfe.com**
Directors: Dean Cundey, Robert Mehnert & Dan Wolfe
Sales Rep: Tony Luna

Wright Banks/Tag Team (310) 470-0491
1334 Westwood Blvd., Ste. 9 FAX **(310) 388-0399**
Los Angeles, CA 90024
Executive Producer: Cindie Wright
Directors: Kevin Dole, Jim O'Neil, & Greg Weinschenker

WSR Creative (310) 391-9181
(310) 391-9182
12023 Venice Blvd., Ste. A FAX **(310) 391-9183**
Los Angeles, CA 90066 **www.wsrcreative.com**

Wyoming Films (310) 798-6332
1726 Manhattan Beach Blvd., Ste. J FAX **(310) 798-6344**
Manhattan Beach , CA 90266 **www.wyomingfilms.com**
Executive Producer: Mark West
Directors: Michael Ivey, Jack and Carol, Chuck Kuhn & Stan Mendoza
Director/Cameraman: Bill Everett
Head of Sales: Mike West

XOVR, LLC (310) 459-8080
8222 Melrose Ave., Ste. 203 FAX **(310) 459-1715**
Los Angeles, CA 90046 **www.xovr.com**

Z Group Films (310) 883-3304
(312) 738-2222
2017 Pacific Ave., Ste. 5 FAX **(310) 882-9804**
Venice, CA 90291 **www.zgroupfilms.com**
Executive Producer: Dan Zigulich

Zoo Film (323) 871-9000
6427 W. Sunset Blvd. FAX **(323) 962-8028**
Hollywood, CA 90028 **www.zoofilm.net**
Executive Producers: Gower Frost & Jan Wieringa
Head of Production: Kes Trester
Media Director: Matt Sarnecki

Zystar Films, Inc. (310) 301-3313
FAX **(310) 301-9433**
www.zystar.com
President/Executive Producer: Meryl Wallis Chase
Producers: Kent Gates & Carmen Silva
Directors: Mark Kohl, Jeff Long & Michael Werk

24pCine (310) 986-3370
1247 Lincoln Blvd., Ste. 151 www.24pcine.com
Santa Monica, CA 90401
Contact: Daniel Pfisterer

2K4K Talking Pictures (310) 447-8575
www.2k4ktalkingpictures.com

30 Second Films (310) 315-1750
3019 Pico Blvd. FAX (310) 315-1757
Santa Monica, CA 90405 www.30secondfilms.com
Contact: Alan J. Stamm

360° Live (619) 884-6821
P.O. Box 2033 www.360degreeslive.com
Manhattan Beach, CA 90267
Contact: Richard Crow

5th Wall Entertainment (323) 461-0600
6311 Romaine St., Ste. 7135 www.5thwall.tv
Hollywood, CA 90038

Acme Events (818) 767-8888
11001 Fleetwood St. www.acme-events.com
Sun Valley, CA 91352

Ad-Lib Marketing & Advertising (909) 629-1995
One Blacksmith Circle FAX (909) 629-1995
Phillips Ranch, CA 91766
Contact: Keith N. Underwood

Alex Pitt Photography (323) 665-4492
www.alexpittphotography.com

All In One Productions (323) 780-8880
1111 Corporate Dr. FAX (323) 780-8887
Monterey Park, CA 91754 www.allinone-usa.com
Contact: Joanna Or

Almost Midnight Productions (310) 313-4046
12240 Venice Blvd., Ste. 18 FAX (310) 313-4048
Los Angeles, CA 90066 www.almostmidnight.com

Alter Ego Creative Entertainment (323) 937-3348
7280 Melrose Ave., Ste. 3 FAX (323) 937-3334
Los Angeles, CA 90046 www.alteregoce.com

Alter Ego Films (310) 809-1910
FAX (310) 356-3397
www.alteregofilms.com

American Video Group (310) 477-1535
2542 Aiken Ave. www.americanvideogroup.com
Los Angeles, CA 90064
Contact: John Berzner

Anyes Galleani Images & Film (213) 626-6260
912 E. Third St., Ste. 203 www.galleani.com
Los Angeles, CA 90013

Arclight Productions (323) 464-7791
732 N. Highland Ave. FAX (323) 464-7406
Hollywood, CA 90038 www.arclightprods.com
Contacts: Karlo David, Steven Kochones & Steven Morales

ASP Media (661) 297-5176
FAX (916) 314-9256
www.aspmedia.tv

The Association, Inc. (818) 841-9660
135 N. Screenland Dr. FAX (818) 841-8370
Burbank, CA 91505 www.theassociation.tv
Contacts: Tim Melchior & Randy Stith

Auster Productions, Inc. (818) 843-5040
2607 W. Magnolia Blvd. FAX (818) 843-5041
Burbank, CA 91505 www.austerproductions.com
Contacts: Nona Friedman & Jennifer Wetzel

Automat Pictures (213) 351-0444
3255 Wilshire Blvd., Ste. 615 FAX (213) 351-0445
Los Angeles, CA 90010 www.automatpictures.com

Barcon Video Productions (818) 248-9161
3653 Mesa Lila Ln. FAX (818) 249-8884
Glendale, CA 91208 www.barcon.com

BCProductions, Inc./ BCTV Productions (949) 495-1500
(615) 495-0045
Contact: Bud W. Connell FAX (501) 851-7303
www.bctv.us

Bianco-Scott Productions (323) 467-6936
1438 Gower St., Box 52 www.biancoscott.com
Hollywood, CA 90028
Contact: Eric Scott

Blue Tango Productions (949) 813-2450
668 N. Coast Hwy, Ste. 226
Laguna Beach, CA 92651
Contact: Marla Friedler www.bluetangoproductions.com

Bluth Enterprises, Inc. (818) 502-1414
517 Commercial St. FAX (818) 500-1137
Glendale, CA 91203 www.bluthenterprises.com

A Broad Vision Productions (323) 848-9411
(323) 401-4157
FAX (866) 247-8610
www.abroadvisionproductions.com

Cinevative Productions (323) 852-8903
8271 Melrose Ave., Ste. 203 FAX (323) 852-0349
Los Angeles, CA 90046 www.cinevative.com
Contacts: Mark Ciglar & Carrie Dobro

Coast Media Teleproductions, Inc. (949) 417-0300
17062 Murphy Ave., Bldg. B www.coastmedia.com
Irvine, CA 92614
Contact: Joyce Smith

Combat Film Productions (818) 618-2527
www.combatfilmproductions.com

Crash Productions (310) 489-6848
713 N. Mansfield Ave. FAX (323) 939-9622
Los Angeles, CA 90038 www.crashproductions.com

Cresta West (323) 939-7003
6815 Willoughby Ave., Ste. 102 FAX (323) 939-7002
Los Angeles, CA 90038 www.crestagroup.com
Contact: Sara Beugen

Crystal Pyramid Productions (619) 644-3000
(800) 365-8433
7323 Rondel Court FAX (619) 644-3001
San Diego, CA 92119 www.crystalpyramid.com
Contacts: Patty Mooney & Mark Schulze

Custom Video (310) 543-4901
707 Torrance Blvd., Ste. 105 www.customvideo.tv
Redondo Beach, CA 90277
Contact: Michael Ude

A Cutt Studios (323) 466-7499
6519 Fountain Ave. www.worldtalentshowcase.com
Los Angeles, CA 90028
Contacts: Ricky Clay & Freeman White III

Dalrymple Productions (626) 963-5588
150 E. Meda Ave., Ste. 100 FAX (626) 963-0679
Glendora, CA 91741 www.dalpro.com

Defy Agency (310) 204-2340
5883 Blackwelder St., Ste. B FAX (310) 204-2341
Culver City, CA 90232 www.defyagency.com

Diligent, LLC (323) 661-0391
4216 Santa Monica Blvd. FAX (435) 579-7878
Los Angeles, CA 90029 www.dodiligent.com

Documentary Makers (213) 570-9500
FAX (213) 985-3001
www.documentarymakers.com

Dogmatic, Inc. (310) 450-3884
320 Sunset Ave. FAX (310) 452-3464
Venice, CA 90291 www.dogmatic.com

The Dreaming Tree (818) 845-3230
2817 W. Magnolia Blvd., Ste. A FAX (818) 688-8180
Burbank, CA 91505 www.dreamingtreeproductions.com

Dynasty Films (310) 913-7700
(818) 823-6088
www.dynastyfilms.com

Earl J. Beadle Productions, Inc. (626) 792-5626
(626) 688-5266
www.ejbproductions.com

Edward Pacio & Associates (818) 880-1586
(310) 995-6037
26931 Deerweed Trail FAX (818) 880-1001
Agoura Hills, CA 91301
Contact: Edward Pacio

Epiphany Media (323) 960-4092
(323) 819-1001
5300 Melrose Ave. FAX (323) 960-4073
Hollywood, CA 90038 www.epiphanymedia.com

Eric Blum Productions, Inc. (818) 707-4524
(818) 707-4526
31139 Via Colinas, Ste. 210 FAX (818) 707-0071
Thousand Oaks, CA 91362 www.ebproductions.com

Evolution L.A. Inc. (310) 587-9191
(310) 587-9116
1510 11th St., Ste. 101 FAX (310) 564-7717
Santa Monica, CA 90401 www.evolutionla.com
Contact: Mark Shockley

eVox Productions, LLC (310) 605-1400
2363 E. Pacifica Pl. FAX (310) 605-1429
Rancho Dominguez, CA 90220 www.evox.com

FilmCrafter (310) 773-1431
www.filmcrafter.com

Filmstyle Productions (818) 993-1099
FAX (818) 993-0062

Firestone Productions (323) 461-7500
(323) 377-9494
Contact: Scott Firestone www.firestoneproductions.com

Fovea Video Productions (310) 675-8822
1600 Rosecrans Ave. FAX (310) 675-8556
Manhattan Beach, CA 90266 www.foveavideo.com
Contact: Steven Schmidt

Frame Productions, Inc. (800) 495-4705
645 W. Ninth St., Ste. 110-661 www.frameproductions.com
Los Angeles, CA 90015

Galanty & Company, Inc. (310) 451-2525
1640 Fifth St., Ste. 202
Santa Monica, CA 90401
Contact: Mark Galanty

Gallagher/Thompson Productions (310) 838-7783
662 N. Van Ness Ave., Ste. 301 FAX (323) 960-4961
Los Angeles, CA 90004
Contact: Tess Gallagher Thompson

Glory Productions (818) 730-4900
www.gloryproductions.com

Golden Eagle Pix (805) 381-9095
(805) 208-1658
Contact: Peter Good FAX (805) 381-9096
www.goldeneaglepix.com

A Gosch Production (818) 729-0000
2227 W. Olive Ave. www.goschproductions.com
Burbank, CA 91506
Contact: Pat Gosch

GSM Entertainment (310) 205-0370
309 S. Sherbourne Dr., Ste. 108 FAX (310) 205-0123
Los Angeles, CA 90048 www.gsmentertainment.com

HD Wave (818) 415-1869
3650 Dark Canyon Rd., Ste. 223 FAX (952) 912-0519
Los Angeles, CA 90068 www.amfebious.com

Healthcare Communications Group (310) 606-5700
909 N. Sepulveda Blvd., Ste. 550 FAX (310) 606-5705
El Segundo, CA 90245 www.hcg.com
Contact: Linda Kilpatrick

HighDefVisions (415) 383-1007
www.highdefvisions.com

Hu-Man Element Productions, Inc. (213) 534-3700
1201 W. Fifth St., Ste. F-240A FAX (775) 667-1064
Los Angeles, CA 90017 www.hu-manelement.com

Image Factory (818) 841-1515
2029 Verdugo Blvd., Ste. 1030 FAX (818) 841-2395
Montrose, CA 91020
Contact: Machiko Kobayashi

Image Line Productions, Inc. (818) 762-2900
5320 Laurel Canyon Blvd. FAX (818) 762-2992
Valley Village, CA 91607 www.imagelinemedia.com
Contact: Brad D. White

Imagecraft (818) 954-0187
99 E. Providencia Ave. FAX (818) 954-0189
Burbank, CA 91502 www.imagecraft.tv

Imaginaut Entertainment (323) 665-5274
908 Parkman Ave. FAX (323) 693-5320
Los Angeles, CA 90026 www.imaginaut.com
Contact: Clay Westervelt

Intelliscape Films, LLC (310) 882-2100
(800) 422-5996
11601 Wilshire Blvd., Fifth Fl. FAX (310) 575-1890
Los Angeles, CA 90025 www.intelliscape.com
Contact: Bruce Caulk

International Television Group (ITG) (310) 656-9100
23852 Pacific Coast Hwy, Ste. 379 FAX (310) 656-9104
Malibu, CA 90265
Contact: Laraine Gregory & Lou La Monte

Jam Media, LLC (310) 289-4466
1800 Century Park East, Ste. 600 FAX (310) 289-2199
Los Angeles, CA 90067 www.jam-media.net

Jeffrey Markowitz Productions, Inc. (877) 297-8887
3366 Troy Dr. www.jeffproductions.com
Los Angeles, CA 90068

JM Digital Works (760) 476-1783
2460 Impala Dr. FAX (760) 476-1788
Carlsbad, CA 92008 www.jmdigitalworks.com
Contact: Ken Kebow

JSP Creative (866) 711-5195
(714) 288-6005
229 N. Glassell St. FAX (714) 288-6014
Orange, CA 92866 www.jspcreative.com
Contact: Jerry Stanley

Kandoo Films, Inc. (818) 789-6777
4515 Van Nuys Blvd., Ste. 100 FAX (818) 789-2299
Sherman Oaks, CA 91403 www.kandoofilms.com

LeTo Entertainment, LLC (310) 358-3282
(310) 621-1122
8840 Wilshire Blvd., Third Fl. FAX (310) 388-1403
Beverly Hills, CA 90211 www.letoentertainment.com

Lewis Lipstone Productions (310) 979-3500
12233 W. Olympic Blvd., Ste. 152 www.wmgmedia.com
Los Angeles, CA 90064
Contact: Lewis Lipstone

M Creative Group (818) 225-1541
23123 Ventura Blvd., Ste. 211 FAX (818) 225-1476
Woodland Hills, CA 91364 www.mcreativegroup.net
Contact: Seth Pinsker

Main Street Media, Inc. (310) 450-1846
(213) 509-7798
185 Pier Ave., Ste. 105 FAX (310) 399-9227
Santa Monica, CA 90405 www.mainstreetmediainc.com
Contacts: Chris Blakely & Rob Newell

Make It Happen Productions, Inc. **(818) 981-2327**
13557 Ventura Blvd., Second Fl. FAX **(818) 981-2440**
Sherman Oaks, CA 91423 **www.mihp.tv**

Master Communication **(310) 832-3303**
445 W. Seventh St. FAX **(310) 832-0296**
San Pedro, CA 90731 **www.bestmedia.com**
Contact: Mary Jo Masters

Matrix Communications **(310) 782-8400**
2522 Torrance Blvd.
Torrance, CA 90503

McNulty Nielsen, Inc. **(310) 704-1713**
6930½ Tujunga Ave. FAX **(323) 372-3768**
North Hollywood, CA 91605 **www.mcnultynielsen.com**

Media Fishtank **(818) 883-6092**
22738 Roscoe Blvd. FAX **(818) 883-6013**
West Hills, CA 91304 **www.mediafishtank.com**

Minerva Media Group, LLC **(310) 647-5604** **(310) 642-5659**
840 Apollo St., Ste. 324 FAX **(310) 642-5605**
El Segundo, CA 90245 **www.minervamg.com**

MOB Media Inc./MOB Media Studios **(949) 222-0220**
27121 Towne Centre Dr., Ste. 260 FAX **(949) 222-0243**
Foothill Ranch, CA 92610 **www.mobmedia.com**

Morningstar Entertainment Inc. **(714) 978-2266**
571 N. Poplar, Ste. I FAX **(714) 978-7858**
Orange, CA 92868 **www.morningstarhd.com**

Motion City Films **(310) 434-1272**
www.motioncity.com

New West Productions **(949) 717-3444**
P.O. Box 11418 FAX **(949) 717-0012**
Newport Beach, CA 92658 **www.newwest-inc.com**

Pat Blessing Productions **(213) 705-6978**
755 N. Lafayette Park Pl.
Los Angeles, CA 90026
Contact: Pat Blessing

Patterson Avenue Productions **(818) 567-1308**
238 S. Lamer St. **www.pattersonavenue.com**
Burbank, CA 91506

Point of Origin **(818) 392-8735**
www.pointoforiginmedia.com

Precision Productions + Post **(310) 839-4600**
10718 McCune Ave. FAX **(310) 839-4601**
Los Angeles, CA 90034 **www.precisionpost.com**

Quest Pictures **(213) 534-3620**
1201 W. Fifth St., Ste. T-230 **www.questpictures.com**
Los Angeles, CA 90017

Rickmon Media **(310) 503-5402**
www.rickmonmedia.com

RPM/Rigdon Production and Media **(310) 339-8382** **(310) 922-7197**
Contact: Dickie Rigdon FAX **(310) 424-7105**
www.rpmstudios.tv

Screen Door Entertainment, Inc. **(818) 781-5600**
15223 Burbank Blvd. FAX **(818) 781-5601**
Sherman Oaks, CA 91411 **www.sdetv.com**

Seven Pictures **(323) 462-0987**
6072 Franklin Ave. **www.sevenpictures.com**
Los Angeles, CA 90028

Silver Lining Productions, Inc. **(310) 289-6650**
149 South Barrington Ave., Ste. 770 FAX **(310) 289-6658**
Los Angeles, CA 90049 **www.silverliningp.com**
Contact: Bozena Armstrong

Slingshot Productions **(818) 999-2539** **(818) 999-3233**
8309 Ponce Ave. **www.slingshotpro.com**
West Hills, CA 91304
Contact: Alessandro Machi

Solana Productions **(858) 759-7983** **(800) 745-8225**
249 S. Highway 101, Ste. 225
Solana Beach, CA 92075

SplendidLight Media Productions **(949) 722-8485**
177 Riverside St. **www.splendidlight.com**
Newport Beach, CA 92663
Contacts: Lynn Splendid & Clayton Light

Standard **(323) 224-3944**
2020 N. Main St., Ste. 227 FAX **(323) 225-6226**
Los Angeles, CA 90031 **www.standardsite.com**
Contact: Adrian Velicescu

Staylor-Made Communications, Inc. **(858) 679-9303** **(800) 711-6699**
11835 Carmel Mountain Rd., FAX **(858) 679-9373**
Ste. 1304-365 **www.staylor-made.com**
San Diego, CA 92128

Steam **(310) 636-4620**
3021 Airport Ave., Ste. 201 **www.steamshow.com**
Santa Monica, CA 90405

Sterling Productions **(626) 675-0994**
600 N. Louise St., Ste. 8 **www.sterlingproductionstv.com**
Glendale, CA 91206

StormMaker Productions, Inc. **(818) 760-4111**
10551 Burbank Blvd. FAX **(818) 760-4111**
North Hollywood, CA 91601
www.stormmakerproductions.com

TVP Studios **(818) 843-3188**
1539 W. Magnolia Blvd. **www.tvpstudiosburbank.com**
Burbank, CA 91506
Contact: Richard Tamayo

Upper Diamond **(310) 862-9252**
5225 Wilshire Blvd., 12th Fl. **www.upperdiamond.com**
Los Angeles, CA 90036

Verité Studios **(866) 535-1972**
708 Westmont Rd. **www.veritestudios.com**
Santa Barbara, CA 93108
Contact: Timothy Eaton

The Video Agency, Inc./ TVA Productions **(818) 505-8300** **(888) 322-4296**
3950 Vantage Ave. FAX **(818) 505-8370**
Studio City, CA 91604 **www.tvaproductions.com**
Contact: Jeffery Goddard

Video Production Specialists (VPS) **(866) 447-3877**
FAX **(310) 577-0850**
www.videoproductionspecialists.com

Videowerks **(310) 393-8754** **(310) 780-4156**
3435 Ocean Park Blvd., Ste. 107 FAX **(310) 399-1829**
Santa Monica, CA 90405 **www.videowerks.com**

Vihlene & Associates, Inc. **(949) 582-0937**
28241 Crown Valley Pkwy, Ste. F187 FAX **(949) 582-5070**
Laguna Niguel, CA 92677 **www.vihlene.com**
Contact: Debbie Stolpp

Visual Concepts **(619) 291-2403**
FAX **(619) 291-2475**
www.visualconcepts.tv

William Moffitt Associates **(818) 495-3106**
785 New York Dr. FAX **(626) 345-0673**
Altadena, CA 91001 **www.wmadigital.com**
Contact: Lynne Moffitt

WSR Creative **(310) 391-9181** **(310) 391-9182**
12023 Venice Blvd., Ste. A FAX **(310) 391-9183**
Los Angeles, CA 90066 **www.wsrcreative.com**

Yada/Levine Video Productions **(323) 461-1616**
1253 Vine St., Ste. 21A FAX **(323) 461-2288**
Hollywood, CA 90038 **www.yadalevine.com**
Contact: Michael Yada

Boardalicious/Lisa Schreiber-Naber (310) 376-8656
www.boardalicious.com

Char & Associates/Char Noonan (805) 338-1301
www.char-associates.com

Kelley Class/Class Represents (310) 823-9808
(310) 650-5357

Connie Mellors & Company (818) 761-4520
FAX (818) 763-2248

Directors Management (818) 783-9772
FAX (818) 783-9702

Ellen Knable & Associates, Inc. (310) 829-3269
FAX (310) 453-4035
www.ekareps.com

The Everett Group/Patty Everett (818) 887-6633
FAX (818) 887-6655

Finn Saxon Represents/
Rachel Finn & Mary Saxon (310) 317-4449
(415) 398-9998
FAX (310) 317-1448
www.finnsaxon.com

Fresh Perspective (310) 415-6320
1123 11th St., Ste. 5
Santa Monica, CA 90403
FAX (310) 496-3228
www.freshperspective.tv

Janet Gilson (818) 708-8101
(310) 488-8055
FAX (818) 708-1609

Hardtribe/Maria V. Elgar (323) 793-3996
FAX (323) 936-9553
www.hardtribe.com

Darr Hawthorne (818) 906-8222
(818) 424-6656
FAX (818) 990-7422
www.burningmotorhome.com

Ron Hoffman (323) 960-3422
FAX (323) 960-3405

Howell Associates (310) 399-7477
2601 Ocean Park Blvd., Ste. 120
Santa Monica, CA 90405

Lee+Lou Productions, Inc. (310) 374-1918
(310) 480-5475
211 N. Dianthus St.
Manhattan Beach, CA 90266
www.leelou.com

Yvette Lubinsky (310) 827-2626
FAX (310) 827-4774

Tony Luna (818) 842-5490
FAX (818) 842-5490

Lynda Woodward & Associates, Inc. (818) 784-2168
FAX (818) 784-8507

Nikki Weiss & Co. (323) 651-1414
754 N. La Jolla Ave.
Los Angeles, CA 90046
FAX (323) 651-2525
www.nikkiweissandco.com

Novick & Assoc., Inc
TV and Digital Reps (415) 460-1626
(415) 860-1055
1010 B St., Ste. 219
San Rafael, CA 94901
FAX (415) 460-1646

Patricia O'Hara (805) 895-0267

Reber/Covington (310) 459-9711
(415) 398-4944
FAX (310) 459-4482

Red Iron/Michael Coronado (949) 474-5390
(310) 800-0543
86 Agostino
Irvine, CA 92614
FAX (949) 474-1513
www.red-iron.com

Red/Holly Ross (323) 850-0073
(310) 659-1577
FAX (323) 850-1525

Saarinen (323) 460-2320
FAX (323) 460-2323
www.saarinen.tv

Tom Scott (310) 230-9932
FAX (310) 230-9932

Shoreline Entertainment, Inc. (310) 551-2060
1875 Century Park East
Los Angeles, CA 90067
FAX (310) 201-0729
www.shorelineentertainment.com

Stacey & Company (310) 551-0050
10369 Tennessee Ave.
Los Angeles, CA 90064

Visual EFX, Inc./Gilles de Bonfilhs (818) 788-3309
FAX (818) 788-1680

Joan Webb (818) 344-1092
(213) 703-9769

Claire Worch/Claire & Company (310) 318-8700
FAX (310) 318-8762
www.claireandcompany.net

30 Second Films (310) 315-1750
3019 Pico Blvd. FAX (310) 315-1757
Santa Monica, CA 90405 www.30secondfilms.com
Contact: Alan J. Stamm

American Video Group (310) 477-1535
2542 Aiken Ave. www.americanvideogroup.com
Los Angeles, CA 90064
President: John Berzner

Custom Video (310) 543-4901
707 Torrance Blvd., Ste. 105 www.customvideo.tv
Redondo Beach, CA 90277
Contact: Michael Ude

dapTV associates (310) 867-5881
820 Westbourne Dr., Ste. 4 www.daptv.com
West Hollywood, CA 90069
Contact: Don Azars

FilmFilmFilm (310) 500-5773
P.O. Box 5445 www.filmfilmfilminc.com
Santa Monica, CA 90409
Contact: Doris Bettencourt

Hu-Man Element Productions, Inc. (213) 534-3700
1201 W. Fifth St., Ste. F-240A FAX (775) 667-1064
Los Angeles, CA 90017 www.hu-manelement.com

Infomercial Solutions, Inc. (818) 879-1140
30748 Davey Jones Dr. FAX (818) 879-1148
Agoura Hills, CA 91301 www.infomercialsolutions.com
Contact: David Schwartz

Kathy Kelly Productions, Inc. (805) 434-5100
P.O. Box 5262 FAX (805) 434-5355
Paso Robles, CA 93447 www.kellyprods.com
Contact: Kathy Kelly

Launch DRTV (310) 305-8342
12910 Culver Blvd., Ste. G FAX (310) 305-8240
Los Angeles, CA 90066 www.launchdrtv.com

Onyx Productions Direct, Inc. (323) 692-9830
2355 Westwood Blvd., Ste. 401 FAX (310) 470-0190
Los Angeles, CA 90064 www.onyxprod.com
Contact: Joan Renfrow

Raymond Entertainment Direct (323) 785-4700
3459 Cahuenga Blvd. FAX (323) 785-4701
Los Angeles, CA 90068 www.raymondentertainment.com

Script to Screen, Inc. (714) 558-3971
(800) 453-0003
200 N. Tustin Ave., Ste. 200 FAX (714) 558-1759
Santa Ana, CA 92705 www.scripttoscreen.com
Contact: Tony Kerry

Three and Two Films, Inc. (818) 700-8725
21363 Lassen St., Ste. 101 FAX (818) 700-8758
Chatsworth, CA 91311 www.threeandtwofilms.com

Two-D Productions (818) 224-2097
23945 Calabasas Rd., Ste. 112 FAX (818) 224-2098
Calabasas, CA 91302 www.two-d.com

The Video Agency, Inc./ TVA Productions (818) 505-8300
(888) 322-4296
3950 Vantage Ave. FAX (818) 505-8370
Studio City, CA 91604 www.tvaproductions.com
Contact: Jeffery Goddard

Video Production Specialists (VPS) (866) 447-3877
FAX (310) 577-0850
www.videoproductionspecialists.com

Videowerks (310) 393-8754
(310) 780-4156
3435 Ocean Park Blvd., Ste. 107 FAX (310) 399-1829
Santa Monica, CA 90405 www.videowerks.com
Contact: David Werk

Waldorf Crawford LLC (951) 659-2580
(951) 659-6399
P.O. Box 771, 52965 Cedar Crest Dr. FAX (951) 659-3700
Idyllwild, CA 92549 www.waldorfcrawford.com

Ant Farm (323) 850-0700
110 S. Fairfax Ave., Ste. 200 FAX **(323) 932-6797**
Los Angeles, CA 90036 **www.theantfarm.net**
(Print, Trailers & TV Spots)

Artphase, LLC (310) 943-9208
FAX **(310) 441-9606**
www.artphase.com

BLT & Associates (323) 860-4000
6430 Sunset Blvd., Eighth Fl. FAX **(323) 860-0890**
Los Angeles, CA 90028 **www.bltomato.com**
(DVD Packaging, Interactive, Motion Graphics, Print & Trailers)

Cimarron Group (323) 337-0300
6855 Santa Monica Blvd. FAX **(323) 337-0333**
Hollywood, CA 90038 **www.cimarrongroup.com**
(Interactive, Motion Graphics, Packaging, Print, Radio and TV Spots, Trailers & Web-Based)

CMP Burbank (818) 729-0800
2717 W. Olive Ave. **www.craigmurrayproductions.com**
Burbank, CA 91505
(Trailers)

Creative Impact Agency (818) 981-7656
(310) 613-3438
15315 Magnolia Blvd., Ste. 110 FAX **(818) 981-7643**
Sherman Oaks, CA 91403 **www.cia-adv.com**
(Interactive, Packaging, Posters, Print & Web-Based)

Crew Creative (323) 468-3636
7966 Beverly Blvd. FAX **(323) 468-3633**
Los Angeles, CA 90048 **www.crewcreative.com**
(Contests, Events, Print & Web-Based)

Firestone Productions (323) 461-7500
(323) 377-9494
www.firestoneproductions.com

Framework Studio, LLC (310) 815-1245
3535 Hayden Ave., Ste. 300 FAX **(310) 815-9821**
Culver City, CA 90232 **www.frameworkla.com**

GSM Entertainment (310) 205-0370
309 S. Sherbourne Dr., Ste. 108 FAX **(310) 205-0123**
Los Angeles, CA 90048 **www.gsmentertainment.com**
(Interactive, Trailers & Web-Based)

Haley Miranda Group (310) 842-7369
8654 Washington Blvd. FAX **(310) 842-8932**
Culver City, CA 90232 **www.haleymiranda.com**
(Contests, Print & Web-Based)

Hammer Creative (323) 463-9156
(323) 606-4700
6311 Romaine St., Third Fl. FAX **(323) 463-8130**
Hollywood, CA 90038 **www.hammercreative.com**
(Motion Graphics, Print, Trailers & TV Spots)

Insight EPK (818) 665-5451
5621 Slicers Circle FAX **(866) 339-3959**
Agoura Hills, CA 91301 **www.insightepk.com**

KO Creative (310) 288-3820
9300 Wilshire Blvd., Ste. 400 FAX **(310) 285-2095**
Beverly Hills, CA 90212 **www.ko-creative.com**
(Interactive, Motion Graphics, Network Promotions, Packaging, Posters, Print, Trailers & TV Spots)

Mark Woollen & Associates (310) 399-2690
207 Ashland Ave. FAX **(310) 399-2670**
Santa Monica, CA 90405 **www.markwoollen.com**
(Trailers, TV Spots & Web-Based)

Mighty Oak Media, Inc. (818) 990-2385
4118 Davana Rd. FAX **(818) 990-6085**
Sherman Oaks, CA 91423 **www.mightyoakmedia.com**
(Motion Graphics, Network Promotions, Radio Spots, Trailers, TV Spots & Web-based)

MOB Media Inc./MOB Media Studios (949) 222-0220
27121 Towne Centre Dr., Ste. 260 FAX **(949) 222-0243**
Foothill Ranch, CA 92610 **www.mobmedia.com**
(Contests, Events, Interactive, Motion Graphics, Network Promotions, Packaging, Posters, Print, Radio Spots, Trailers, TV Spots & Web-based)

mOcean (310) 481-0808
2440 S. Sepulveda Blvd., Ste. 150 FAX **(310) 481-0807**
Los Angeles, CA 90064 **www.moceanla.com**
(Interactive, Network Promotions, Print, Promos, Trailers & TV Spots)

New Wave Entertainment (818) 295-5000
2660 W. Olive Ave. FAX **(818) 295-5002**
Burbank, CA 91505 **www.nwe.com**
(Motion Graphics, Network Promotions, Packaging & Print)

Parkour Media (310) 846-8051
(212) 845-9089
P.O. Box 1442 FAX **(310) 846-8051**
Los Angeles, CA 90078 **www.parkourmedia.com**
(Interactive, Motion Graphics, Network Promotions, Online Marketing Strategies, Packaging, Posters, Print, TV Spots & Web-based)

Playground Media Group (310) 315-3800
1813 Centinela Ave. FAX **(310) 315-3801**
Santa Monica, CA 90404 **www.playgroundla.com**

Studio 27 (818) 216-9026
6860 Lexington Ave. FAX **(415) 621-1875**
Hollywood, CA 90038 **www.studio27inc.com**
(Web-Based)

Trailer Park (310) 845-3000
6922 Hollywood Blvd., 12th Fl. **www.trailerpark.com**
Hollywood, CA 90028
(Motion Graphics, Print, Trailers & TV Spots)

Winston Davis Associates (323) 930-8535
955 S. Carrillo Dr., Ste. 200 FAX **(323) 930-8545**
Los Angeles, CA 90048 **www.winstondavis.com**
(Motion Graphics, Radio and TV Spots & Trailers)

Abdul Malik Abbott (323) 466-1171 (310) 860-1771
www.1171.com

Timothy Agoglia (626) 442-6454
www.absolutefilms.net

Jonas Åkerlund (310) 659-1577
www.blackdogfilms.com

Jaron Albertin (323) 817-3300
www.smugglersite.com

Alex and Martin (323) 468-0123
www.partizan.com

Don Allen (323) 644-5552
www.revolverfilms.com

Jeff Alley (310) 860-1771
www.banditfilms.com

Philip Andelman (323) 468-0123
www.partizan.com

Chris Applebaum (323) 468-0123
www.partizan.com

Paul Ardolino (323) 469-8991
www.palardo.com

Matt Aselton (310) 275-9333
www.epochfilms.com

Daniel Askill (323) 463-2826
www.dnala.com

Associates In Science (323) 468-0123
www.partizan.com

Atanas (323) 790-1732
www.maneaterproductions.com

The AV Club (323) 465-5299
www.thedirectorsbureau.com

Meiert Avis (310) 576-1344
www.pushermedia.com

Moh Azina (818) 985-9905
www.factoryfeatures.com

Matt Badger (310) 275-9333
www.epochfilms.com

Eddie Barber (818) 982-7775

Antoine Bardou-Jacquet (323) 468-0123
www.partizan.com

Bill Barminski (310) 659-7659
www.mergefilms.com

Matt Bass (818) 985-9905
www.factoryfeatures.com

Ed Bell (310) 860-1771
www.banditfilms.com

Anthea Benton (323) 645-1000
www.believemedia.com

bigtv (323) 463-2826
www.dnala.com

Richard Bowen (310) 576-1344
www.pushermedia.com

Brand New School (323) 468-0123
www.partizan.com

Nick Brandt (323) 645-1000
www.believemedia.com

David Brooks (818) 985-9905
www.factoryfeatures.com

Art Brown (310) 576-4992
www.agogofilms.com

Paul Brown (310) 558-3667
www.anonymouscontent.com

Nanette Burstein (323) 645-1000
www.believemedia.com

Peter Byck (323) 252-5272
www.ralphtheroadie.com

Jim Canty (310) 558-7100
www.hsiproductions.com

Kenneth Cappello (310) 558-7100
www.hsiproductions.com

Peter Care (310) 396-7333
www.bobcentral.com

Romeo Carey (626) 442-6454
www.absolutefilms.net

Rey Carlson (310) 275-9333
www.epochfilms.com

Russell Carpenter (323) 469-8991
www.palardo.com

Carter and Blitz (310) 558-3667
www.anonymouscontent.com

Tom Carty (310) 558-3667
www.anonymouscontent.com

Gerald V. Casale (310) 828-8557
www.badcofilms.com

Cassius (323) 468-0123
www.partizan.com

Herbert Chan (626) 442-6454
www.absolutefilms.net

Carolyn Chen (323) 645-1000
www.believemedia.com

Les Claypool (310) 828-8557
www.badcofilms.com

Danny Clinch (323) 468-0123
www.partizan.com

Colombo (323) 790-1732
www.maneaterproductions.com

Kevin Connolly (310) 558-7100
www.hsiproductions.com

Roman Coppola (323) 465-5299
www.thedirectorsbureau.com

Sofia Coppola (323) 465-5299
www.thedirectorsbureau.com

Nathan Cox (310) 659-7659
www.mergefilms.com

Lisa Crook (323) 650-4722

Alisa Daglio (310) 576-4992
www.agogofilms.com

Dayo (323) 468-0123
www.partizan.com

Jonathan Dayton (310) 396-7333
www.bobcentral.com

Tom DeLonge (323) 466-1171
www.1171.com

Chad Denning (310) 576-4992
www.agogofilms.com

Ben Dickinson (310) 659-1577
www.blackdogfilms.com

E. Bernard Dixon (310) 860-1771
www.banditfilms.com

Diamond Dogs (310) 558-7100
www.hsiproductions.com

Andrew Dosunmu (323) 650-4722

Andrew Douglas (310) 558-3667
www.anonymouscontent.com

Tony Dow (310) 315-1750
www.30secondfilms.com

Shane Drake (310) 659-7659
www.mergefilms.com

Michael Eckhardt (626) 442-6454
www.absolutefilms.net

Moses Edinborough (323) 876-3331
www.wildindigo.tv

Charles Eganstein (626) 442-6454
www.absolutefilms.net

Filip Engstrom (323) 817-3300
www.smugglersite.com

Sam Erickson (310) 659-7659
www.mergefilms.com

Fernando Escovar (818) 726-7269

Lauri Faggioni (310) 659-1577
www.blackdogfilms.com

Valerie Faris (310) 396-7333
www.bobcentral.com

Paul Fedor (310) 558-3667
www.anonymouscontent.com

David Fincher (310) 558-3667
www.anonymouscontent.com

Miles Flannigan (323) 790-1732
www.maneaterproductions.com

Justin Francis (310) 558-7100
www.hsiproductions.com

Liz Friedlander (323) 463-2826
www.dnala.com

Jim Gable (310) 979-4333
www.gandb.tv

Leo Gabriadze (323) 876-3331
www.wildindigo.tv

Anthony Garth (323) 790-1732
www.maneaterproductions.com

Kim Geldenhuys (310) 396-7333
www.bobcentral.com

Tryan George (323) 645-1000
(323) 463-2826
www.believemedia.com

Andrea Giacobbe (310) 558-3667
www.anonymouscontent.com

Ed Gill (323) 463-2826
www.dnala.com

Jonathan Glazer (323) 463-2826
www.dnala.com

Gobi (310) 860-1771
www.banditfilms.com

Michel Gondry (323) 468-0123
www.partizan.com

Olivier Gondry (323) 468-0123
www.partizan.com

Nick Gordon (323) 463-2826
www.dnala.com

Gil Green (323) 468-0123
www.partizan.com

Steph Green (310) 659-1577
www.littleminx.com

Howard Greenhalgh (323) 645-1000
www.believemedia.com

Paula Grief (310) 275-9333
www.epochfilms.com

James Griffiths (323) 463-2826
www.dnala.com

The Guard Brothers (310) 888-8900
www.villains.com

Andrew Gura (323) 468-0123
www.partizan.com

H5 (310) 659-1577
www.littleminx.com

Jorn Haagen (323) 645-1000
www.believemedia.com

Jeremy Haft (323) 790-1732
www.maneaterproductions.com

Robert Hales (310) 558-7100
www.hsiproductions.com

Anders Hallberg (323) 645-1000
www.believemedia.com

Steve Hanft (310) 828-8557
www.badcofilms.com

Johnny Hardstaff (310) 659-1577
www.littleminx.com

Jason Harrington (323) 645-1000
www.believemedia.com

Michael Haussman (310) 558-7100
www.hsiproductions.com

Eric Haywood (323) 937-4182
www.legacyfilms.net

Simon Henwood (310) 558-7100
www.hsiproductions.com

Fluorescent Hill (323) 644-5552
www.revolverfilms.com

Hobos with Guns (818) 985-9905
www.factoryfeatures.com

Patrick Hoelck (310) 659-7659
www.mergefilms.com

Honey (323) 468-0123
www.partizan.com

Chris Hooper (310) 396-7333
www.bobcentral.com

Chris Hopewell (310) 558-3667
www.anonymouscontent.com

Illegal Artists (323) 468-0123
www.partizan.com

Wayne Isham (310) 659-7659
www.mergefilms.com

Mari Ito (626) 442-6454
www.absolutefilms.net

Jaume (323) 645-1000
www.believemedia.com

Garth Jennings (310) 558-3667
www.anonymouscontent.com

Bryan Johnson (323) 938-8080

Cooper Johnson (818) 985-9905
www.factoryfeatures.com

Noble Jones (323) 644-5552
www.revolverfilms.com

Byron Jost (626) 442-6454
www.absolutefilms.net

Miranda July (310) 275-9333
www.epochfilms.com

Joseph Kahn (310) 558-7100
www.hsiproductions.com

Wong Kar Wai (310) 558-3667
www.anonymouscontent.com

Dean Karr (323) 876-3331
www.wildindigo.tv

David Katz (310) 699-9760

Kelley (323) 790-1732
www.maneaterproductions.com

David Kellogg (310) 558-3667
www.anonymouscontent.com

Kenny FX (323) 790-1732
www.maneaterproductions.com

Kevin Kerslake (310) 659-7659
www.mergefilms.com

Nikita Kleverov (323) 620-6925
www.halfelement.com

Isaac Klotz (323) 620-6925
www.halfelement.com

Albert Kodagolian (323) 645-1000
www.believemedia.com

Mark Kohr (310) 396-7333
www.bobcentral.com

Jesper Kouthoofd (310) 659-1577
www.littleminx.tv

Rob Kraetsch (323) 620-6925
www.halfelement.com

Bob Kronovet (310) 315-1750
www.30secondfilms.com

David LaChapelle (310) 558-7100
www.hsiproductions.com

Evan Lane (323) 790-1732
www.maneaterproductions.com

Francis Lawrence (323) 463-2826
www.dnala.com

Nancy Leiviska (310) 454-0109
www.stefanino.com

Dom Leung (310) 558-3667
www.anonymouscontent.com

Drew Lightfoot (323) 644-5552
www.revolverfilms.com

John Lindauer (323) 645-1000
www.believemedia.com

Ken Locsmandi (310) 699-9760
www.ambitiousfilms.com

Save Lorenzo (323) 790-1732
www.maneaterproductions.com

Joe Lynch (323) 466-1171
www.1171.com

Peter Mack (323) 790-1732
www.maneaterproductions.com

Andrew MacNaughtan (323) 644-5552
www.revolverfilms.com

David Mallet (310) 659-7659
www.mergefilms.com

Malloys (310) 558-7100
www.hsiproductions.com

Mike Maloy (323) 937-4182
www.legacyfilms.net

Lisa Mann (323) 644-5552
www.revolverfilms.com

Maurice Marable (323) 645-1000
www.believemedia.com

Scott Marshall (310) 828-8557
www.badcofilms.com

Diane Martel (310) 558-7100
www.hsiproductions.com

Stu Maschwitz (323) 469-6700
www.theorphanage.com

Benny Mathews (310) 860-1771
www.banditfilms.com

Nic Mathieu (310) 558-3667
www.anonymouscontent.com

Enda McCallion (310) 275-9333
www.epochfilms.com

John McCrea (310) 828-8557
www.badcofilms.com

Melodie McDaniel (323) 465-5299
www.thedirectorsbureau.com

Keir McFarlane (323) 463-2826
www.dnala.com

Geoff McFetridge (323) 465-5299
www.thedirectorsbureau.com

Micah Meisner (323) 644-5552
www.revolverfilms.com

Melina (310) 659-1577
www.blackdogfilms.com

Thomas Mignone (310) 927-6661
www.doominc.com

Michal Mihail (323) 466-1171
www.1171.com

Cousin Mike (323) 466-1171
www.1171.com

Bennett Miller (323) 817-3300
www.smugglersite.com

Josh Miller (310) 659-1577
www.littleminx.com

Mike Mills (323) 465-5299
www.thedirectorsbureau.com

Mister Boom Boom (323) 645-1000
www.believemedia.com

Jean-Baptiste Mondino (323) 463-2826
www.dnala.com

Darrin Monroe (310) 860-1771
www.banditfilms.com

Cesario (Block) Montano (310) 699-9760
www.ambitiousfilms.com

Ben Mor (310) 659-1577
www.littleminx.tv

Wendy Morgan (323) 644-5552
www.revolverfilms.com

Phil Morrison (310) 275-9333
www.epochfilms.com

David Mould (310) 558-3667
www.anonymouscontent.com

Steven Murashige (323) 650-4722

Mike Myerburg (818) 985-9905
www.factoryfeatures.com

Tony (Nako) Nakonechnyj (323) 848-7293
www.reconfilms.com

Doug Nichol (323) 468-0123
www.partizan.com

Dewey Nicks (310) 888-8900
www.villains.com

Gareth O'Neil (323) 848-7293
www.reconfilms.com

Leslie Otis (323) 650-4722

Chris Palmer (310) 558-3667
www.anonymouscontent.com

Mike Palmieri (323) 644-5552
www.revolverfilms.com

Travis Payne (323) 665-6680
(323) 957-6680
FAX (323) 665-6681
www.travispayne.net

Mark Pellington (310) 659-7659
www.mergefilms.com

Jesse Peretz (310) 659-7659
www.mergefilms.com

Mike Piscitelli (323) 468-0123
www.partizan.com

Martin Pitts (323) 876-6186

Doug Pray (323) 466-1171
www.1171.com

Jeff Preiss (310) 275-9333
www.epochfilms.com

David Preizler (310) 275-9333
www.epochfilms.com

Rodrigo Prieto (310) 659-1577
www.littleminx.tv

Joel Pront (323) 645-1000
www.believemedia.com

Pucho (323) 645-1000
www.believemedia.com

Quad U.S.A. (323) 645-1000
www.believemedia.com

The Brothers Quay (323) 645-1000
www.believemedia.com

Ramon and Pedro (323) 468-0123
www.partizan.com

Rankin and Chris (310) 558-7100
www.hsiproductions.com

Brett Ratner (310) 558-7100
www.hsiproductions.com

Johan Renck (310) 659-1577
www.blackdogfilms.com

Matty Rich (310) 860-1771
www.banditfilms.com

Branscombe Richmond (310) 315-1750
www.30secondfilms.com

Carl Erik Rinsch (310) 659-1577
www.blackdogfilms.com

Fatima Robinson (310) 558-7100
www.hsiproductions.com

Roboshobo (323) 644-5552
www.revolverfilms.com

Wade Robson (310) 558-3667
www.anonymouscontent.com

Mark Romanek (310) 558-3667
www.anonymouscontent.com

Lisa Rubisch (310) 396-7333
www.bobcentral.com

George Marshall Ruge (310) 288-8000
www.paradigmagency.com

Saline Project (310) 558-7100
www.hsiproductions.com

Salzy (818) 985-9905
www.factoryfeatures.com

Miguel Sapochnik (323) 463-2826
www.dnala.com

Michael Sarna (323) 466-1171
www.1171.com

Hank Saroyan (323) 848-7293
www.reconfilms.com

Malik H. Sayeed (310) 659-1577
www.littleminx.com

Rocky Schenck (323) 463-2826
www.dnala.com

Keith Schofield (818) 985-9905
www.factoryfeatures.com

Bradley Scott (323) 790-1732
www.maneaterproductions.com

Jake Scott (310) 659-1577
www.blackdogfilms.com

Jordan Scott (310) 659-1577
www.blackdogfilms.com

Luke Scott (310) 659-1577
www.blackdogfilms.com

Ridley Scott (310) 659-1577
www.blackdogfilms.com

Rod S. Scott (818) 501-3000

Tony Scott (310) 659-1577
www.blackdogfilms.com

Mark Seliger (310) 659-1577
www.blackdogfilms.com

Nick Semmens (323) 848-7293
www.reconfilms.com

Dawn Shadforth (310) 659-1577
www.littleminx.com

Guy Shelmerdine (323) 817-3300
www.smugglersite.com

Graydon Sheppard (323) 644-5552
www.revolverfilms.com

Pat Sherman (310) 558-3667
www.anonymouscontent.com

Shynola (323) 465-5299
www.thedirectorsbureau.com

Lex Sidon (323) 466-1171
www.1171.com

Adam Sidy (323) 463-2826
www.dnala.com

Floria Sigismondi (323) 644-5552
(323) 645-1000
www.revolverfilms.com

Brian Silva (323) 620-6925
www.halfelement.com

Shaun Silva (310) 659-7659
www.mergefilms.com

Melissa Silverman (323) 645-1000
www.believemedia.com

David Slade (310) 659-1577
www.blackdogfilms.com

Slick (310) 828-8557
www.badcofilms.com

Alex Smith (310) 659-1577
www.blackdogfilms.com

Jason Smith (310) 396-7333
(310) 558-7100
www.bobcentral.com

Ryan Smith (310) 659-7659
www.mergefilms.com

Matt Smukler (310) 275-9333
www.epochfilms.com

Zack Snyder (323) 645-1000
www.believemedia.com

Jim Sonzero (323) 645-1000
www.believemedia.com

Speedway Films (323) 644-5552
www.revolverfilms.com

Scott Speer (310) 558-7100
www.hsiproductions.com

Stardust (323) 644-5552
www.revolverfilms.com

Stefano (323) 466-1171
www.1171.com

Walter Stern (323) 463-2826
www.dnala.com

Nzingha Stewart (323) 463-2826
www.dnala.com

Scott Stewart (323) 469-6700
www.theorphanage.com

Paul Street (323) 645-1000
www.believemedia.com

Stylewar (323) 817-3300
www.smugglersite.com

Spencer Susser (310) 396-7333
www.bobcentral.com

Christian Swegal (818) 985-9905
www.factoryfeatures.com

Syd/Eric (310) 396-7333
www.bobcentral.com

Tarsem (323) 650-4722

Terri Timely (310) 659-7659
www.mergefilms.com

Traktor (323) 468-0123
www.partizan.com

Tronic (310) 558-7100
www.hsiproductions.com

Tudor (323) 790-1732
www.maneaterproductions.com

Phillip Van (310) 659-1577
www.littleminx.com

Malcolm Venville (310) 558-3667
www.anonymouscontent.com

Gore Verbinski (310) 558-3667
www.anonymouscontent.com

Robert Villalobos (626) 442-6454
www.absolutefilms.net

Vogel Villar-Rios (323) 645-1000
www.believemedia.com

Rupert Wainwright (310) 576-1344
www.pushermedia.com

Stacy Wall (310) 275-9333
www.epochfilms.com

Jon Watts (323) 817-3300
www.smugglersite.com

Marc Webb (323) 463-2826
www.dnala.com

Declan Whitebloom (310) 659-7659
www.mergefilms.com

Whitey (323) 645-1000
www.believemedia.com

Wiebke (323) 645-1000
www.believemedia.com

Hype Williams (310) 558-7100
www.hsiproductions.com

Scott Winig (310) 659-7659
www.mergefilms.com

Masaki Yokochi (323) 848-7293
www.reconfilms.com

Bill Yukich (818) 985-9905
www.factoryfeatures.com

Lili Zanuck (323) 463-2826
www.dnala.com

1171 Production Group (323) 466-1171
1680 N. Vine St., Ste. 300 FAX (323) 466-1136
Hollywood, CA 90028 www.1171.com
Executive Producers: Grant Cihlar & Nancy Cihlar
Directors: Abdul Malik Abbott, Cousin Mike, Tom DeLonge, Joe Lynch, Michal Mihail, Doug Pray, Michael Sarna, Lex Sidon & Stefano

30 Second Films (310) 315-1750
3019 Pico Blvd. FAX (310) 315-1757
Santa Monica, CA 90405 www.30secondfilms.com
Executive Producer: Alan J. Stamm
Directors: Tony Dow, Bob Kronovet & Branscombe Richmond

Absolute Films (626) 442-6454 (323) 692-1010
1441 Huntington Dr., Bldg. 301 FAX (626) 448-1930
South Pasadena, CA 91030 www.absolutefilms.net
Executive Producer/Director: Romeo Carey
Producers: Charles Egan, Tom Franklin, Dino Lee, Josh Oacha & Saul Silver
Directors: Timothy Agoglia, Herbert Chan, Michael Eckhardt, Charles Eganstein, Mari Ito, Byron Jost & Robert Villalobos

Ali Zeus Corp. (310) 779-9603
6250 Canoga Ave., Ste. 474 www.azfilmstudios.com
Woodland Hills, CA 91367

Almost Midnight Productions (310) 313-4046
12240 Venice Blvd., Ste. 18 FAX (310) 313-4048
Los Angeles, CA 90066 www.almostmidnight.com

Ambitious (310) 699-9760
523 Colorado Ave. FAX (310) 395-8895
Santa Monica, CA 90401 www.ambitiousfilms.com
Executive Producer/Director: David Katz
Directors: David Katz, Ken Locsmandi & Cesario "Block" Montano

Anonymous Content (310) 558-3667
3532 Hayden Ave. FAX (310) 558-2724
Culver City, CA 90232 www.anonymouscontent.com
Executive Producer: Sheira Rees-Davis
Directors: Paul Brown, Carter and Blitz, Tom Carty, Andrew Douglas, Paul Fedor, David Fincher, Andrea Giacobbe, Chris Hopewell, Garth Jennings, David Kellogg, Dom Leung, Nic Mathieu, David Mould, Chris Palmer, Wade Robson, Mark Romanek, Pat Sherman, Malcolm Venville, Gore Verbinski & Wong Kar Wai
Sales Rep: Molly Bohas

The Artists Company (323) 650-4722 (212) 679-7199
1015 N. Fairfax Ave. FAX (323) 650-5150
Los Angeles, CA 90046
Executive Producer: Roberto Cecchini
Vice President: Sally Antonacchio
Directors: Lisa Crook, Andrew Dosunmu, Steven Murashige, Otis & Tarsem
Sales Rep: Laure Scott Representation

The Association, Inc. (818) 841-9660
135 N. Screenland Dr. FAX (818) 841-8370
Burbank, CA 91505 www.theassociation.tv
Executive Producer: Tim Melchior
Producers: Fletcher Murray & Randall Stith

Bad Company Films (310) 828-8557 (415) 550-6662
2940 Nebraska Ave. FAX (310) 315-9749
Santa Monica, CA 90404 www.badcofilms.com
Executive Producer: Raub Shapiro
Directors: Gerald V. Casale, Les Claypool, Steve Hanft, Scott Marshall, John McCrea & Slick
Sales Reps: Rosser Goodman & Karrie Wimberly

Bandit Films (818) 723-9831
www.banditfilms.com
Producers: Lisa M. Neal & Bruce Spears
Directors: Abdul Malik Abbott, Jeff Alley, Ed Bell, E. Bernard Dixon, Gobi, Benny Mathews, Darrin Monroe & Matty Rich
Director of Creative Affairs: Alison Cooper
Sales Rep: Carmen Jordan

Barber Tech Video Products (818) 982-7775 (877) 887-6388
40125 20th St. West FAX (661) 339-3235
Palmdale, CA 93551 www.barbertvp.com
Executive Producer/Director: Eddie Barber

Believe Media (323) 645-1000
1040 N. Las Palmas Ave., Bldg. 10 FAX (323) 645-1001
Los Angeles, CA 90038 www.believemedia.com
Executive Producers: Gerard Cantor, Betsy Kelley, Liz Silver & Luke Thornton
Directors: Anthea Benton, Mister Boom Boom, Nick Brandt, The Brothers Quay, Nanette Burstein, Carolyn Chen, Tryan George, Howard Greenhalgh, Jorn Haagen, Anders Hallberg, Jason Harrington, Jaume, Albert Kodagolian, John Lindauer, Maurice Marable, Joel Pront, Pucho, Quad U.S.A., Floria Sigismondi, Melissa Silverman, Zack Snyder, Jim Sonzero, Paul Street, Vogel Villar-Rios, Whitey & Wiebke

Black Dog Films (RSA Films) (310) 659-1577 (212) 343-2020
634 N. La Peer Dr. FAX (310) 659-1377
Los Angeles, CA 90069 www.blackdogfilms.com
Executive Producer: Kim Dellara
Directors: Jonas Åkerlund, Ben Dickinson, Lauri Faggioni, Melina, Johan Renck, Carl Erik Rinsch, Jake Scott, Jordan Scott, Luke Scott, Ridley Scott, Tony Scott, Mark Seliger, David Slade & Alex Smith

Black Dragon Entertainment, Inc. (323) 874-8888
FAX (323) 874-1058
www.blackdragon.com

Bob Industries (310) 396-7333
1313 Fifth St. FAX (310) 396-0202
Santa Monica, CA 90401 www.bobcentral.com
Executive Producers: TK Knowles, John O'Grady & Chuck Ryant
Directors: Peter Care, Jonathan Dayton, Valerie Faris, Kim Geldenhuys, Chris Hooper, Mark Kohr, Lisa Rubisch, Jason Smith, Spencer Susser & Syd/Eric

A Broad Vision Productions (323) 848-9411 (323) 401-4157
FAX (866) 247-8610
www.abroadvisionproductions.com

Bucks Boys Productions, Inc. (310) 437-0914
3900 Grand View Blvd. FAX (310) 437-0919
Los Angeles, CA 90066 www.bucksboys.com
Executive Producers: Jonathan Becker & Joshua Greenberg
Executive Assistant to Producers: Tova Dann
General Counsel: Carra Greenberg
Head of Production: Mercedes Allen

A Common Thread, Inc. (310) 823-7300 (310) 798-9007
4081 Redwood Ave. FAX (310) 823-7305
Los Angeles, CA 90066 www.acommonthread.tv
Executive Producers: Tristan Drew & J.P. McMahon

Devil's Night (310) 584-1086
3435 Ocean Park Blvd., Ste. 107-666 FAX (310) 584-1087
Santa Monica, CA 90405 www.devilsnight.com

Dice Films (818) 726-7269 (818) 762-1555
13222 Saticoy St. www.dicefilms.com
North Hollywood, CA 91605
Director: Fernando Escovar

The Directors Bureau (323) 465-5299 (323) 663-0500
1641 N. Ivar Ave. FAX (323) 465-5547
Hollywood, CA 90028 www.thedirectorsbureau.com
Executive Producer: Cayce Cole
Head of Production: Lana Kim
Directors: The AV Club, Roman Coppola, Sofia Coppola, Melodie McDaniel, Geoff McFetridge, Mike Mills & Shynola

DNA Studio (323) 463-2826
6535 Santa Monica Blvd. FAX **(323) 463-2535**
Hollywood, CA 90038 **www.dnala.com**
President/Executive Producer: David Naylor
VP/Executive Producer: Sam Aslanian
Executive Producer: Missy Galanida
Directors: Daniel Askill, BigTV!, Liz Friedlander, Tryan George, Ed Gill, Jonathan Glazer, Nick Gordon, James Griffiths, Francis Lawrence, Keir McFarlane, Jean-Baptiste Mondino, Miguel Sapochnik, Rocky Schenck, Adam Sidy, Walter Stern, Nzingha Stewart, Marc Webb & Lili Zanuck

DOOM, Inc. (310) 927-6661
308 N. Kenwood St., Ste. D FAX **(310) 496-2666**
Burbank, CA 91505 **www.doominc.com**
Head of Production/Producer: Darci Oltman
Director: Thomas Mignone
Producer: Natasha Noramly

Epoch Films, Inc. (310) 275-9333 / (310) 275-7938
9290 Civic Center Dr. FAX **(310) 275-7696**
Beverly Hills, CA 90210 **www.epochfilms.com**
Executive Producers: Mindy Goldberg & Jerry Solomon
Directors: Matt Aselton, Matt Badger, Rey Carlson, Paula Grief, Miranda July, Enda McCallion, Phil Morrison, Jeff Preiss, David Preizler, Matt Smukler & Stacy Wall
Sales Rep: Mal Ward

Eyestorm Productions (310) 582-3937
1559 Seventh St. FAX **(310) 582-3939**
Santa Monica, CA 90401 **www.eyestormproductions.com**
Creative Directors: Michael Klima & Kyle Ruddick

Factory Features (818) 985-9905
111684 Ventura Blvd. FAX **(818) 474-7001**
Studio City, CA 91604 **www.factoryfeatures.com**
Executive Producer: Steven Johnson
Directors: Moh Azina, Matt Bass, David Brooks, Hobos with Guns, Cooper Johnson, Mike Myerburg, Salzy, Keith Schofield, Christian Swegal & Bill Yukich

The Film Syndicate (323) 938-8080
7214 Melrose Ave. FAX **(323) 938-8183**
Los Angeles, CA 90046
Producer/Director: Bryan Johnson

Gallagher/Thompson Productions (310) 838-7783
662 N. Van Ness Ave., Ste. 301 FAX **(323) 960-4961**
Los Angeles, CA 90004
Producer: Tess Gallagher Thompson

A Go Go Films (310) 576-4992
927 Fourth St. FAX **(310) 576-7756**
Santa Monica, CA 90403 **www.agogofilms.com**
Director & Cameraman: Art Brown
Directors: Alisa Daglio, Chad Denning & Carl Diebold

Graying & Balding, Inc. (310) 979-4333
Executive Producers: Ann Kim FAX **(310) 979-4334**
Director: Jim Gable **www.gandb.tv**

Half Element Productions (323) 620-6925
1911 17th St., Ste. 5 **www.halfelement.com**
Santa Monica, CA 90404
Producers: Kim Daniels & Des Escober
Directors: Nikita Kleverov, Isaac Klotz & Brian Silva
Director/Cameraman: Rob Kraetsch

Highway 114 Pictures (213) 623-2577
810 S. Flower St., Ste. 706 FAX **(213) 627-0757**
Los Angeles, CA 90017 **www.highway114.com**

HSI Productions, Inc. (310) 558-7100 / (212) 627-3600
3630 Eastham Dr. FAX **(310) 558-7101**
Culver City, CA 90232 **www.hsiproductions.com**
President: Stavros Merjos
Executive Producers: Coleen Haynes & Rebecca Skinner
Directors: Jim Canty, Kenneth Cappello, Kevin Connolly, Diamond Dogs, Justin Francis, Robert Hales, Michael Haussman, Simon Henwood, Joseph Kahn, David LaChapelle, Malloys, Diane Martel, Rankin and Chris, Brett Ratner, Fatima Robinson, Saline Project, Jason Smith, Scott Speer, Tronic & Hype Williams
Music Video Sales: Christopher Clavadetscher

Karma Kollective (310) 836-5100
5870-D W. Jefferson FAX **(310) 836-5106**
Culver City, CA 90016 **www.karmakollective.tv**

Legacy Films (323) 937-4182
6230 Wilshire Blvd., Ste. 227 FAX **(323) 937-7316**
Los Angeles, CA 90048 **www.legacyfilms.net**
Executive Producer: Michelle Colbert
Directors: Eric Haywood & Mike Maloy

Little Minx (310) 659-1577
634 N. La Peer Dr. FAX **(310) 659-1377**
Los Angeles, CA 90069 **www.littleminx.tv**
President: Rhea Scott
Directors: Steph Green, H5, Johnny Hardstaff, Jesper Kouthoofd, Josh Miller, Ben Mor, Rodrigo Prieto, Malik Sayeed, Mark Seliger, Dawn Shadforth & Phillip Van
Executive Producer: Kim Dellara

Maneater Productions (323) 790-1732 / (323) 327-2793
6860 Lexington Ave. FAX **(323) 460-6063**
Hollywood, CA 90038 **www.maneaterproductions.com**
Directors: Atanas, Colombo, Miles Flannigan, Anthony Garth, Jeremy Haft, Kelley, Kenny FX, Evan Lane, Save Lorenzo, Peter Mack, Bradley Scott & Tudor
Executive Producers: Jed James & Christina Perri

Merge@Crossroads (310) 659-7659 / (212) 647-1310
8630 Pine Tree Pl. FAX **(310) 659-3105**
West Hollywood, CA 90069 **www.mergefilms.com**
Executive Producer: Joseph Uliano
Directors: Bill Barminski, Nathan Cox, Shane Drake, Sam Erickson, Patrick Hoelck, Wayne Isham, Kevin Kerslake, David Mallet, Mark Pellington, Jesse Peretz, Shaun Silva, Ryan Smith, Terri Timely, Declan Whitebloom & Scott Winig
Head of Production & Sales: Neil Maiers

Motion Theory (310) 396-9433
321 Hampton Dr., Ste. 101 FAX **(310) 396-7883**
Venice, CA 90291 **www.motiontheory.com**
Executive Producer: Javier Jimenez
Sales Rep: Caroline Gomez

PAC (323) 931-9962
Producer/Director: Martin Pitts

Palardo Productions (323) 469-8991 / (203) 387-0741
1807 Taft Ave., Ste. 4 **www.palardo.com**
Hollywood, CA 90028
President/Director: Paul Ardolino
Senior VP of Production: Michael Ward
Production Designer: Tom Ardolino
Sound Editor: Michael Goldblatt
Music Director: Bjorn Englen
Production Manager: Tim Wilson
Director/Cameraman: Russell Carpenter
VP of Sales: Catherine Taylor
Production Assistant: Chip Clements
Public Relations: Deanna Palfrey
Sound Mixer Engineer: Paul Mittenberg

Partizan (323) 468-0123
7083 Hollywood Blvd., Ste. 401 FAX **(323) 468-0129**
Hollywood, CA 90028 **www.partizan.com**
Executive Producer & CEO: Sheila Stepanek
Executive Producer: Jeff Pantaleo
Sales Representative: Danielle Hinde
Directors: Alex and Martin, Philip Andelman, Chris Applebaum, Associates In Science, Antoine Bardou-Jacquet, Brand New School, Cassius, Danny Clinch, Dayo, Michel Gondry, Olivier Gondry, Gil Green, Andrew Gura, Honey, Illegal Artists, Doug Nichol, Mike Piscitelli, Ramon and Pedro & Traktor

Peter Nydrle Productions (310) 659-8844
672 N. La Peer Dr. FAX **(310) 659-7733**
West Hollywood, CA 90069 **www.nydrle.com**
Head of Production: Garner Kinmond

Pusher Media (310) 576-1344
969 Colorado Ave. **www.pushermedia.com**
Santa Monica, CA 90401
Executive Producer: Ben Dossett
Directors: Richard Bowen, Meiert Avis & Rupert Wainwright

Reconnaissance Entertainment, Inc. (323) 848-7293
8286 Santa Monica FAX **(323) 848-7297**
West Hollywood, CA 90046 **www.reconfilms.com**
Head: David B. Baron
Executive Producer: Melissa Holmes
Directors: Tony "Nako" Nakonechnyj, Gareth O'Neil, Hank Saroyan, Nick Semmens & Masaki Yokochi

The Revolver Film Co. (323) 644-5552
1710 N. Vermont Ave., Ste. 108 FAX **(323) 644-5557**
Los Angeles, CA 90027 **www.revolverfilms.com**
Executive Producer: Kelly Norris Sarno
Directors: Don Allen, Fluorescent Hill, Noble Jones, Drew Lightfoot, Andrew MacNaughtan, Lisa Mann, Micah Meisner, Wendy Morgan, Mike Palmieri, Roboshobo, Graydon Sheppard, Floria Sigismondi, Speedway Films & Stardust
Directors' Rep: Justine Smith

Rockhard Films (310) 659-4400
1022 Palm Ave., Ste. 1 FAX **(310) 659-4402**
West Hollywood, CA 90069 **www.rhfilms.com**

Serial Dreamer Productions, Inc. (323) 848-7000
928 N. Fairfax Ave. FAX **(323) 848-7003**
Los Angeles, CA 90046 **www.serialdreamer.net**
Executive Producer: Paulina Hatoupis
Business Development: Michelle Hott

Sleeping Giant Films (310) 710-6525
www.sleepinggiantfilms.com

Smuggler (323) 817-3300
1715 N. Gower St. FAX **(323) 817-3333**
Los Angeles, CA 90028 **www.smugglersite.com**
Executive Producers: Brian Carmody & Patrick Milling Smith
Heads of Production: Allison Kunzman & Laura Thoel
Directors: Jaron Albertin, Filip Engstrom, Bennett Miller, Guy Shelmerdine, Stylewar & Jon Watts
Chief Operating Officer: Lisa Rich

Sound Matrix Studios (714) 437-9595 (714) 402-7450
18060 Newhope St. **www.videopromatrix.com**
Orange County, CA 92708

Stefanino Productions (310) 454-0109
15515 Sunset Blvd., Ste. 101 **www.stefanino.com**
Pacific Palisades, CA 90272
Director: Nancy Leiviska
Head of Music: Stefan Gordy
Executive Producer: Stuart Jemesen

trio films (310) 207-7800
2023 S. Westgate Ave. FAX **(310) 207-7807**
Los Angeles, CA 90025 **www.triofilms.com**
Executive Producers: Taylor Ferguson & Erin Tauscher

Viewpoint Creative (310) 822-3013
4079B Redwood Ave. FAX **(310) 822-3959**
Los Angeles, CA 90066 **www.viewpointcreative.com**
Executive Producers: Dave Shilale
Business Development: Amy Coblenz

Villains (310) 888-8900
1746 N. Ivar Ave. FAX **(310) 888-8444**
Hollywood, CA 90028 **www.villains.com**
President: John Marshall
Executive Producer/Director's Rep: Tommy LaBuda
Directors: The Guard Brothers & Dewey Nicks

Vivus Media (213) 989-6884
www.vivusmedia.com
Executive Producers: Adam Fox & Wendy Shuey

Waterline Pictures, Inc. (818) 901-1178 (310) 963-4812
P.O. Box 56387 FAX **(818) 901-1179**
Sherman Oaks, CA 91413
President/Director: Roger Roth

Wild Eyed Entertainment (213) 741-9301 (310) 466-1040
2222 S. Figueroa St., PH30 FAX **(213) 741-2303**
Los Angeles, CA 90007 **www.wildeyedent.com**

Wild Indigo, LLC (323) 876-3331
www.wildindigo.tv
Directors: Moses Edinborough, Leo Gabriadze & Dean Karr
Executive Producer: Arthur Gorson

1st Wave Productions (310) 474-2439
(310) 883-8800
2017 Pacific Ave. FAX (310) 474-5282
Venice, CA 90291 www.1stwaveproductions.com

4-Production Space (310) 566-6710
(310) 918-6896
3303 Pico Blvd., Second Fl. FAX (310) 943-1705
Santa Monica, CA 90405 www.4-productionspace.com

Albuquerque Studios (505) 227-2000
5650 University Blvd. SE FAX (505) 227-2001
Albuquerque, NM 87106 www.abqstudios.com

ANA Special Effects, Inc. (818) 909-6999
7021 Hayvenhurst Ave. FAX (818) 782-0635
Van Nuys, CA 91406 www.anaspecialeffects.com

Bedrock Studios (213) 413-7625
(323) 573-0705
1623 Allesandro St. FAX (213) 413-7632
Los Angeles, CA 90026 www.myspace.com/bedrockla

Bill Rentals (310) 396-5937
(323) 715-5499
73 Market St. FAX (310) 450-4988
Venice, CA 90291

BPR Investment (818) 347-4434
7050 Valjean Ave. FAX (818) 347-7565
Van Nuys, CA 91406

California Independent Production Center (818) 567-6190
4119 W. Burbank Blvd. www.ca-ipc.com
Burbank, CA 91505

CatchLight Films (310) 295-0071
413 E. Sycamore Ave. FAX (310) 341-3806
El Segundo, CA 90245 www.catchlightfilms.com

Century Studio Corporation (310) 287-3600
(888) 878-2437
8660 Hayden Pl., Ste. 100 FAX (310) 287-3608
Culver City, CA 90232 www.centurystudio.com

Costume Rentals Corporation (818) 753-3700
11149 Vanowen St. FAX (818) 753-3737
North Hollywood, CA 91605
www.costumerentalscorp.com

The Culver Studios (310) 202-1234
9336 W. Washington Blvd. FAX (310) 202-3201
Culver City, CA 90232 www.theculverstudios.com

Digital Jungle Post Production (323) 962-0867
6363 Santa Monica Blvd. FAX (323) 962-9960
Los Angeles, CA 90038 www.digijungle.com

Entertainment Post (818) 846-0411
639 S. Glenwood Pl. FAX (818) 846-1542
Burbank, CA 91506 www.entpost.com

eOfficeSuites, Inc. (310) 566-7000
13101 Washington Blvd., Ste.100 FAX (310) 566-7400
Los Angeles, CA 90066 www.eofficesuites.com

GoTV Studios, Inc. (818) 933-2100
(818) 933-2122
14144 Ventura Blvd., Ste. 300 FAX (818) 704-9386
Sherman Oaks, CA 91423
studiorentals.gotvnetworks.com

Hollywood Center Studios (323) 860-0000
1040 N. Las Palmas Ave. FAX (323) 860-8105
Hollywood, CA 90038 www.hollywoodcenter.com

Hollywood Production Center (323) 785-2100
1149 N. Gower St. FAX (323) 462-8179
Los Angeles, CA 90038 www.hollywoodpc.com

Hollywood Production Center 2 (818) 480-3100
121 W. Lexington Dr. FAX (818) 480-3199
Glendale, CA 91203 www.hollywoodpc.com

Line 204 (323) 960-0113
1034 N. Seward St. FAX (323) 960-8509
Hollywood, CA 90038 www.line204.com

Los Angeles Center Studios (213) 534-3000
www.lacenterstudios.com

The Lot (323) 850-3180
(323) 850-2832
1041 N. Formosa Ave. www.skyepartners.com
West Hollywood, CA 90046

Motiv Films (310) 260-6100
1630 Stewart St., Studio B1 FAX (310) 260-6111
Santa Monica, CA 90404 www.motivfilms.com

The Studios at Paramount (323) 956-4407
The Studios at Paramount Tenant Services
5555 Melrose Ave.
Hollywood, CA 90038
www.thestudiosatparamount.com

Pasadena Production Studios (626) 584-4090
39 E. Walnut St. FAX (626) 584-4099
Pasadena, CA 91103 www.danwolfe.com

Production Bays West (323) 656-0905
7920 Santa Monica Blvd. FAX (323) 375-1711
West Hollywood, CA 90046

Production Space (323) 469-2195
6427 Sunset Blvd. FAX (323) 962-8028
Hollywood, CA 90028 www.productionspace.net

Quixote Studios (323) 851-5030
1011 N. Fuller Ave. FAX (323) 851-5029
West Hollywood, CA 90046 www.quixote.com

Raleigh Studios (323) 960-3456
5300 Melrose Ave. FAX (323) 871-5600
Hollywood, CA 90038 www.raleighstudios.com

Ren-Mar Studios (323) 463-0808
846 N. Cahuenga Blvd. FAX (323) 465-8173
Hollywood, CA 90038 www.renmarstudios.com

Santa Monica Production Suites (310) 395-4620

Silverlake Production Annex (323) 661-0391
4216 Santa Monica Blvd. www.fancyfilm.com
Los Angeles, CA 90029

SOsuites division, Studio e Valencia (800) 298-1928
28005 Smyth Dr. FAX (661) 702-9705
Valencia, CA 91355 www.sosuites.com

SOsuites division, Sunset 8335 (323) 656-7100
8335 Sunset Blvd. FAX (323) 656-7155
West Hollywood, CA 90069 www.sosuites.com

Sunset Bronson Studios (323) 460-5858
5800 W. Sunset Blvd. FAX (323) 460-3844
Los Angeles, CA 90028 www.sgsandsbs.com

Sunset Gower Studios (323) 467-1001
1438 N. Gower St. www.sgsandsbs.com
Los Angeles, CA 90028

Team Halprin, Inc. (310) 842-7000
9190 W. Olympic Blvd., Ste. 304 FAX (310) 842-7014
Beverly Hills, CA 90212 www.teamhalprin.com

TMD Productions, Inc. (310) 202-1272
6725 W. Sunset Blvd., Ste. 350
Hollywood, CA 90028

Video Assist Systems, Inc. (818) 606-8901
FAX (818) 222-5862
www.videoassistsystems.com

7ate9 Entertainment (323) 464-6789
740 N. La Brea Ave. FAX (323) 464-7979
Hollywood, CA 90038 www.7ate9.com

Alternate Reality Entertainment (818) 742-7208
5701 Cantaloupe Ave. FAX (818) 782-0826
Sherman Oaks, CA 91401 www.alternatereality.tv
Contact: Michael Marconi

Army (323) 466-7600
6150 Santa Monica Blvd. FAX (323) 466-7601
Los Angeles, CA 90038 www.army.tv

The Association, Inc. (818) 841-9660
135 N. Screenland Dr. FAX (818) 841-8370
Burbank, CA 91505 www.theassociation.tv
Contacts: Tim Melchior & Randy Stith

Attack Ads, Inc. (310) 857-7745
578 Washington Blvd., Ste. 594 www.attackads.tv
Marina Del Rey, CA 90292
Contacts: Eagle Egilsson, Dr. Garry, Bronston Jones & Roberts Jones

Autonomy, Inc. (323) 662-7048
www.autonomy.tv

Barcon Video Productions (818) 248-9161
3653 Mesa Lila Ln. FAX (818) 249-8884
Glendale, CA 91208 www.barcon.com

Beantown Productions, Inc. (323) 960-0290
5707 Melrose Ave. FAX (310) 278-1009
Los Angeles, CA 90038 www.beantown.tv
Contacts: David Carr, David Comtois & Judie Stillman

BloomFilm (323) 850-5575

Brainwaves Media (310) 702-6374
223 E. Thousand Oaks Blvd. FAX (801) 720-2090
Thousand Oaks, CA 91362 www.brainwavesmedia.com

Bungalow 3 (818) 760-1333
11136 Chandler Blvd. FAX (818) 760-2334
North Hollywood, CA 91601 www.bungalow3.com
Contact: Rosemond Perdue-Cranner

Cinevative Productions (323) 852-8903
8271 Melrose Ave., Ste. 203 FAX (323) 852-0349
Los Angeles, CA 90046 www.cinevative.com
Contacts: Mark Ciglar & Carrie Dobro

Evolution Film and Tape, Inc. (818) 260-0300
3310 W. Vanowen St. FAX (818) 260-1333
Burbank, CA 91505 www.evolutionusa.com
Contact: Lisa Lettunich

Evolution L.A. Inc. (310) 587-9191
1510 11th St., Ste. 101 FAX (310) 564-7717
Santa Monica, CA 90401 www.evolutionla.com
Contact: Mark Shockley

Framework Studio, LLC (310) 815-1245
3535 Hayden Ave., Ste. 300 FAX (310) 815-9821
Culver City, CA 90232 www.frameworkla.com

Gross Productions (818) 557-7335
One Skyline Dr. FAX (818) 557-7336
Burbank, CA 91501
Contact: Chris Gross

Hammer Creative (323) 606-4700
(323) 463-9156
6311 Romaine St., Third Fl. FAX (323) 463-8130
Los Angeles, CA 90038 www.hammercreative.com
Contact: Mark Pierce

Idea Asylum Productions, Inc. (323) 634-0434
6100 Wilshire Blvd., Ste. 1550 FAX (323) 634-0575
Los Angeles, CA 90048 www.ideaasylum.com

Jay Silverman Productions (323) 466-6030
1541 N. Cahuenga Blvd. FAX (323) 466-7139
Hollywood, CA 90028 www.jaysilverman.com

Kandoo Films, Inc. (818) 789-6777
4515 Van Nuys Blvd., Ste. 100 FAX (818) 789-2299
Sherman Oaks, CA 91403 www.kandoofilms.com
Contacts: Howard Barish & Rhonda Kinosian

Make It Happen Productions, Inc. (818) 981-2327
13557 Ventura Blvd., Second Fl. FAX (818) 981-2440
Sherman Oaks, CA 91423 www.mihp.tv

MFI (866) 639-9804

Mighty Oak Media, Inc. (818) 990-2385
4118 Davana Rd. FAX (818) 990-6085
Sherman Oaks, CA 91423 www.mightyoakmedia.com

Monument Television & Film Company (617) 771-7277
(323) 422-9980
(323) 462-2184
www.monumenttelevisionandfilm.com

Morningstar Entertainment Inc. (714) 978-2266
571 N. Poplar, Ste. I FAX (714) 978-7858
Orange, CA 92868 www.morningstarhd.com

Moving Parts, Inc. (818) 738-7015
4111 W. Alameda Ave., Second Fl. FAX (818) 738-7040
Burbank, CA 91505 www.movingpartsinc.com
Contacts: Chad Cooperman & Matt Van Buren

Planet 3 Entertainment Group, LLC (310) 392-4600
1832 Franklin St. www.planet3entertainment.com
Santa Monica, CA 90404

Play Editorial, Inc. (323) 465-3500
6464 Sunset Blvd., Ste. 600 FAX (323) 465-3511
Hollywood, CA 90028 www.playeditorial.com

Point of Origin (818) 392-8735
www.pointoforiginmedia.com

Pongo Productions (323) 850-3333
Contacts: Tom McGough & Jon Mingle FAX (323) 850-3334
www.gopongo.com

Precision Productions + Post (310) 839-4600
10718 McCune Ave. FAX (310) 839-4601
Los Angeles, CA 90034 www.precisionpost.com

Proscenium Pictures, Ltd. (323) 650-6767
8840 Wilshire Blvd. FAX (323) 650-1345
Beverly Hills, CA 90211 www.prosceniumpictures.com

Psychic Bunny (310) 862-4262
453 S. Spring St., Ste. 922 FAX (213) 614-9046
Los Angeles, CA 90013 www.psychicbunny.com

Randemonium, Inc. (818) 505-0400
4555 Radford Ave. FAX (818) 505-0599
Studio City, CA 91607
Contact: Kenton Rand

Revolver Films (310) 827-2441
4040 Del Rey Ave., Ste. 5 FAX (310) 827-2661
Marina del Rey, CA 90292 www.revolverfilmsla.com
Contact: Mark Priola

Richmel Productions, Inc. (818) 719-9920
4829 Topanga Canyon Blvd., Ste. 208
Woodland Hills, CA 91364

Rickmon Media (310) 503-5402
www.rickmonmedia.com

Rumpus Creative (310) 437-0902
www.rumpuscreative.com

Silver Lining Productions, Inc. (310) 289-6650
149 S. Barrington Ave., Ste. 770 FAX **(310) 289-6658**
Los Angeles, CA 90049 **silverliningp.com**
Contact: Bozena Armstrong

The Spark Factory (626) 397-2719
10 E. Colorado Blvd. FAX **(626) 397-2732**
Pasadena, CA 91105 **www.sparkfactory.com**
Contacts: Susan Hunter & Tim Street

Splat Pictures (310) 403-4267
Contact: Rob Hampton FAX **(310) 231-1113**
www.splatpictures.com

Studio City (818) 557-7777
4705 Laurel Canyon Blvd., Ste. 400 FAX **(818) 557-6777**
Studio City, CA 91607 **www.studiocity.com**

Super 78 (323) 464-7878
6900 Santa Monica Blvd. FAX **(323) 464-7879**
Hollywood, CA 90038 **www.super78.com**
Contact: Laurie Leitzel

Thumbwar (310) 910-9030
5700 Melrose Ave., Ste. 302 FAX **(310) 910-9031**
Los Angeles, CA 90038 **thumbwar.tv**

Video Production Specialists (VPS) (866) 447-3877
FAX **(310) 577-0850**
www.videoproductionspecialists.com

Viewpoint Creative (310) 822-3013
4079B Redwood Ave. FAX **(310) 822-3959**
Los Angeles, CA 90066 **www.viewpointcreative.com**
Contacts: Dave Shilale

Vision Mixer Films (310) 344-3337
15332 Antioch St., Ste. 506 FAX **(310) 573-1077**
Pacific Palisades, CA 90272 **www.visionmixerfilms.com**
Contact: Erik Press

Wholly Cow Productions, Inc. (310) 545-8222
3770 Highland Ave., Ste. 202 FAX **(310) 545-0144**
Manhattan Beach, CA 90266 **www.whollycow.tv**

(310) 391-9181
WSR Creative (310) 391-9182
12023 Venice Blvd., Ste. A FAX **(310) 391-9183**
Los Angeles, CA 90066 **www.wsrcreative.com**

Artisans Public Relations (310) 837-6008
2530 Wilshire Blvd., Ste. 300 FAX **(310) 837-2286**
Santa Monica, CA 90403 **www.artisanspr.com**

Bender/Helper Impact (310) 473-4147
11500 W. Olympic Blvd., Ste. 655 FAX **(310) 478-7914**
West Los Angeles, CA 90064 **www.bhimpact.com**

Bragman Nyman Cafarelli, LLC (310) 854-4800
8687 Melrose Ave., Eighth Fl. FAX **(310) 854-4848**
Los Angeles, CA 90069 **www.bncpr.com**

Costa Communications (323) 650-3588
8265 Sunset Blvd., Ste. 101 FAX **(323) 654-5207**
Los Angeles, CA 90046 **www.costacomm.com**

Ed Baran Publicity (213) 482-4696
1114 Echo Park Ave. FAX **(213) 482-4616**
Los Angeles, CA 90026 **www.edbaran.com**

Goldfish Public Relations (818) 688-1502
124 N. Florence St. **www.goldfishpr.com**
Burbank, CA 91505

Henri Bollinger Associates (818) 784-0534
P.O. Box 57227 FAX **(818) 789-8862**
Sherman Oaks, CA 91413 **www.bollingerpr.com**

The Honig Company (818) 986-4300
3500 W. Olive Ave., Ste. 300 FAX **(818) 688-8047**
Burbank, CA 91505 **www.honigcompany.com**

Hype (323) 938-8363
6380 Wilshire Blvd., Ste. 1010 **www.hypeworld.com**
Los Angeles, CA 90048

Julian Myers Public Relations (310) 827-9089
13900 Panay Way, Ste. R217 FAX **(310) 827-9838**
Marina del Rey, CA 90292 **www.julianmyerspr.com**

Kallista (818) 566-9769
FAX **(310) 356-7234**
www.kallistapr.com

PMK, Inc. (310) 289-6200
700 N. San Vicente Blvd., Ste. 910 FAX **(310) 289-6677**
West Hollywood, CA 90069 **www.pmkhbh.com**

PReacher Reputation Management/PR (213) 683-9701
1308 Factory Pl., Ste. 009 FAX **(213) 683-9701**
Los Angeles, CA 90013 **www.preacherpub.com**

Press Kitchen PR (310) 821-1698
610 Venice Blvd., Ste. B FAX **(310) 821-1748**
Venice, CA 90291 **www.presskitchen.com**

Public Relations Associates (323) 653-0380
8455 Beverly Blvd., Ste. 303 FAX **(323) 653-0381**
Los Angeles, CA 90048

Rogers & Cowan, Inc. (310) 854-8100
8687 Melrose Ave., Seventh Fl. FAX **(310) 854-8101**
Los Angeles, CA 90069 **www.rogersandcowan.com**

SmartPR (323) 656-1068
8033 Sunset Blvd., Ste. 1033 FAX **(323) 656-8827**
Los Angeles, CA 90046 **www.smartprla.com**

Smoke & Mirrors Public Relations, Inc. (213) 250-4603
1825 Park Dr., Ste. 4 **www.sampr.net**
Los Angeles, CA 90026

Spelling Communications (213) 415-7400
865 S. Figueroa St., Ste. 1100 FAX **(213) 415-7405**
Los Angeles, CA 90017 **www.spellcom.com**

Teresa Conboy P.R. (323) 660-7748
P.O. Box 27766 **www.myspace.com/teresaconboypr**
Los Angeles, CA 90027

Wolfson Entertainment, Inc. (818) 615-0499
22201 Ventura Blvd., Ste. 207 FAX **(818) 615-0498**
Woodland Hills, CA 91364 **www.wolfsonent.com**

411 Creatives (310) 568-2733
10736 Jefferson Blvd., Ste. 820 www.411creatives.com
Culver City, CA 90230
(Reps for Storyboard Artists)

Ace Storyboards on Demand (949) 499-9964
(949) 677-0973
FAX (949) 499-9964
www.markpacella.com

Action Artists (323) 337-4666
1444¼ Glendale Blvd. FAX (323) 395-5663
Los Angeles, CA 90026 www.action-artists.com
(Reps for Storyboard Artists)

Hovig Alahaidoyan (310) 568-2733
www.411creatives.com

Mike Alden (310) 581-4050
www.storyboardsinc.com

Cassie R. Anderson (310) 943-9208
FAX (310) 441-9606
www.artphase.com

Don Anderson (310) 568-2733
www.411creatives.com

Andy Lee Storyboards (818) 585-7719
(818) 991-9186
www.andyleestoryboards.com

Animatic Media, Inc. (818) 842-0800
(954) 462-4000
1907 W. Burbank Blvd., Second Fl. FAX (818) 842-0864
Burbank, CA 91506 www.animaticmedia.com
(Animated Test Spots)

Katherine Arion (310) 936-5572
www.artarion.com

Dave Arkle (310) 581-4050
www.storyboardsinc.com

Daniel Auber (310) 568-2733
www.411creatives.com

Andrew Baron (310) 339-9558
(626) 795-0289
www.baronstudio.com

Patrick Barrett (818) 489-9465
www.patrickbarrettart.com

Richard Bennett (310) 568-2733
www.411creatives.com

Kathy Berry (310) 642-2721
www.famousframes.com

Paul Binkley (310) 642-2721
www.famousframes.com

Mark Bloom (310) 642-2721
www.famousframes.com

Jarid Boyce (310) 642-2721
www.famousframes.com

Georgia Bragg (310) 398-8150
(310) 345-8817
FAX (310) 398-4340

BrainForest Digital (818) 865-8333
5743 Corsa Ave., Ste. 220 FAX (818) 865-9333
Westlake Village, CA 91362 www.brain4est.com
(Animatics)

Tim Burgard (310) 581-4050
www.storyboardsinc.com

Ray Cadd (310) 581-4050
www.storyboardsinc.com

Dan Caplan (310) 581-4050
www.storyboardsinc.com

Peter Carpenter (310) 581-4050
www.storyboardsinc.com

Ivan Cat (310) 581-4050
(800) 289-0109
www.storyboardsinc.com

Bernard Chang (310) 642-2721
www.famousframes.com

Kevin Chin (310) 642-2721
www.famousframes.com

Jiye Choi (310) 581-4050
www.storyboardsinc.com

Donna Cline (310) 568-2733
www.411creatives.com

Jeff Coatney (310) 642-2721
www.famousframes.com

Phillipe Collot (310) 642-2721
www.famousframes.com

Elizabeth Colomba (310) 581-4050
www.storyboardsinc.com

Ronald M. Croci (310) 642-2721
www.famousframes.com

Federico D'Alessandro (310) 581-4050
www.storyboardsinc.com

Tony Daniel (310) 581-4050
www.storyboardsinc.com

Danelle Davenport (818) 590-8586
www.danelledavenport.com

Malcomb Davis (562) 433-7273
www.malcomb.com

Joe Dea (818) 990-8993
www.ambitiousent.com

Stephen DeBonrepos (310) 642-2721
www.famousframes.com

Gus DeGuzman (310) 642-2721
www.famousframes.com

Alex DeLeon (310) 985-1733
(310) 473-0775
FAX (310) 473-0775
www.stayup.com/artwork.html

Kristen Denton (310) 568-2733
www.411creatives.com

Shannon Denton (310) 568-2733
www.411creatives.com

Maurice DePas (818) 292-6531

Juan Diaz (310) 642-2721
www.famousframes.com

Paul Didier (310) 642-2721
www.famousframes.com

Hugo Dipietro (310) 642-2721
www.famousframes.com

Cash Donovan (310) 642-2721
www.famousframes.com

Warren Drummond (310) 568-2733
www.411creatives.com

Alex Echevarria (310) 581-4050
www.storyboardsinc.com

Tomoki Echigo (310) 642-2721
www.famousframes.com

Edward Cook Storyboards (818) 620-8624
(818) 567-0157
edcookstoryboards.blogspot.com

Famous Frames, Inc. (310) 642-2721
(800) 530-3375
5839 Green Valley Circle, Ste. 104 FAX (310) 642-2728
Culver City, CA 90230 www.famousframes.com
(Reps for Storyboard Artists)

Gabriella Farkas (310) 642-2721
www.famousframes.com

Kevin Farrell (310) 642-2721
www.famousframes.com

John Fox (310) 383-3773
www.johnfoxart.com

Frameworks Storyboards (323) 665-7736
983 Manzanita St. www.frameworks-la.com
Los Angeles, CA 90029
(Reps for Storyboard Artists)

Matt Fuller (310) 581-4050
www.storyboardsinc.com

Roger Gana (310) 581-4050
www.storyboardsinc.com

Jonathan Gesinski (310) 642-2721
www.famousframes.com

Craig Gilmore (310) 642-2721
www.famousframes.com

Chad Glass (310) 581-4050
www.storyboardsinc.com

Tony Gleeson (310) 568-2733
www.411creatives.com

Lyle Grant (310) 581-4050
www.storyboardsinc.com

Zack Grossman (310) 581-4050
www.storyboardsinc.com

Eric Hamlin (323) 350-2578
www.erichamlin.com

Ray Harris (818) 219-8970
www.rayharrisstudio.com

Todd Harris (310) 568-2733
www.411creatives.com

Josh Hayes (310) 581-4050
www.storyboardsinc.com

Jeff Henderson (310) 642-2721
www.famousframes.com

Trevor Hoier (310) 422-0596
s76.photobucket.com/albums/j39/thoier/

David Hudnut (310) 642-2721
www.famousframes.com

Robert Hunt/Studio E Design (310) 641-9319
(310) 486-8551
FAX (310) 641-3926
www.setsketch.com

Mark Hurtado (310) 642-2721
www.famousframes.com

Peter Ivanoff (310) 642-2721
www.famousframes.com

Mark Jackson (310) 568-2733
www.411creatives.com

Patrick James (310) 581-4050
www.storyboardsinc.com

Zeke Johnson (310) 581-4050
www.storyboardsinc.com

Robert Kalafut (310) 642-2721
www.famousframes.com

Merle Keller (310) 642-2721
www.famousframes.com

Ken Muth Storyboards (877) 903-3663
(352) 895-1145
www.kenmuthstoryboards.com

Cecil Kim (310) 568-2733
www.411creatives.com

Gordon Kljucec (310) 568-2733
www.411creatives.com

Brian Koons (310) 581-4050
www.storyboardsinc.com

Jeff Kronen (310) 642-2721
www.famousframes.com

David Larks (310) 642-2721
www.famousframes.com

Lance Leblanc (310) 581-4050
www.storyboardsinc.com

Jason Lee (310) 642-2721
www.famousframes.com

Michael Lee (310) 642-2721
www.famousframes.com

Anthony Liberatore (310) 581-4050
www.storyboardsinc.com

Wes Louie (310) 642-2721
www.famousframes.com

Franck Louis-Marie (310) 642-2721
www.famousframes.com

Salvatore Lucido (310) 642-2721
www.famousframes.com

Vincent Lucido (310) 568-2733
www.411creatives.com

Jim Magdaleno (714) 356-3765

Ernie Marjoram (310) 581-4050
www.storyboardsinc.com

Adolfo Martinez (310) 581-4050
www.storyboardsinc.com

Steven Martinez (310) 642-2721
www.famousframes.com

Eddy Mayer (310) 383-3152
FAX (310) 209-8480
www.eddymayer.com

Philip Mayor (310) 591-9910
www.philipmayor.com

Chad McCown (310) 642-2721
www.famousframes.com

Colin McGreal (310) 642-2721
www.famousframes.com

David Mellon (310) 642-2721
www.famousframes.com

Martin Mercer (323) 441-8876
(310) 415-7535
www.martinmercer.com

Marc Michelon (949) 497-6336
(949) 290-5066
FAX (949) 497-6336
www.michelondrawings.com

Mark Millicent (310) 642-2721
www.famousframes.com

Yori Mochizuki (310) 642-2721
www.famousframes.com

Alex Morris (310) 642-2721
www.famousframes.com

Brian Murray (310) 642-2721
www.famousframes.com

John Killian Nelson (310) 642-2721
www.famousframes.com

Rick Newsome (310) 581-4050
www.storyboardsinc.com

Quan Ngo (310) 642-2721
www.famousframes.com

Jude Nielson (310) 581-6677
(310) 739-0280
www.artwrist.com

Patrick O'Neal (310) 568-2733
www.411creatives.com

Mark S. Pacella (818) 990-8993
www.ambitiousent.com

Neal Parrow (310) 642-2721
www.famousframes.com

Ivan Pavlovits (310) 642-2721
www.famousframes.com

Chris Pechin/Peach Productions (818) 763-0995
(818) 903-2560
11274 La Maida St., Ste. 100
West Toluca Lake, CA 91601
FAX (818) 763-0995
www.peachprods.com

Elizabeth Perez (323) 666-5452

Richard Poulain (323) 307-1490

Charles Ratteray (310) 642-2721
www.famousframes.com

Bruce Rauffenbart (212) 226-4006
FAX (212) 219-3408
www.tvboards.com

Renee Reeser (310) 642-2721
www.famousframes.com

Reinman Illustration/Design (805) 640-7393
4612 Thacher Rd.
Ojai, CA 93023

Robin Richesson (562) 491-3501
(310) 633-0306

Rosenthal Represents (818) 222-5445
(Reps for Storyboard Artists)
FAX (818) 222-5650

David Russell (310) 568-2733
www.411creatives.com

Marc Sandroni (310) 581-4050
www.storyboardsinc.com

Mark Sasway (310) 642-2721
www.famousframes.com

Gerry Schelly (213) 687-3720
www.geocities.com/gerryschelly

Mitt Seely (323) 316-6809
(310) 455-7279
www.mittseely.com

David Selvadurai (310) 581-4050
www.storyboardsinc.com

Daniel Senties (310) 642-2721
www.famousframes.com

Josh Sheppard (323) 573-1234
(323) 258-4661
www.thestoryboardartist.com

Joseph Simon (818) 206-0144
www.allcrewagency.com

Aaron Sowd (310) 642-2721
www.famousframes.com

Timothy Spain (818) 240-0500
FAX (818) 240-5515

Eric Stewart (310) 581-4050
www.storyboardsinc.com

Chris Stiles (310) 642-2721
www.famousframes.com

Storyboards, Inc. (310) 581-4050
(800) 289-0109
100 Market St., Ste. E
Venice, CA 90291
FAX (310) 581-4060
www.storyboardsinc.com

Storyboards Online (818) 842-0800
1907 W. Burbank Blvd., Second Fl.
Burbank, CA 91506
FAX (818) 842-0864
www.storyboardsonline.com

Mike Swift (213) 944-9120
www.mikeswiftart.com

TellAVision (310) 230-5303
1060 20th St., Ste. 8
Santa Monica, CA 90403
(Reps for Storyboard Artists)
FAX (310) 388-5550
www.tellavisionagency.com

David Threadgold (310) 642-2721
www.famousframes.com

Bob Towner (310) 642-2721
www.famousframes.com

Transcontinuity Studios, Inc. (818) 980-8852
4710 W. Magnolia Blvd.
Burbank, CA 91505
FAX (818) 980-8974
www.nealadamsentertainment.com

Keith Turner (310) 569-5444
www.keithturner.info

Brad Vancata (310) 642-2721
www.famousframes.com

Joel Venti (310) 581-4050
www.storyboardsinc.com

Fred Warter (310) 642-2721
www.famousframes.com

John Watkiss (310) 568-2733
www.411creatives.com

Kaleo Welborn (310) 642-2721
www.famousframes.com

Eric Weldon (310) 568-2733
www.411creatives.com

Steve Werblum (310) 642-2721
www.famousframes.com

Nathaniel West (310) 568-2733
www.411creatives.com

Shari Wickstrom (310) 642-2721
www.famousframes.com

Jonathan Woods (310) 642-2721
www.famousframes.com

Nob Yamashita (310) 642-2721
www.famousframes.com

Jeff Zugale (310) 642-2721
www.famousframes.com

Alkemi Entertainment (323) 525-1155
706 N. Citrus Ave. FAX **(323) 525-1150**
Los Angeles, CA 90038 **www.alkemient.com**

Alternate Reality Entertainment (818) 742-7208
5701 Cantaloupe Ave. FAX **(818) 782-0826**
Sherman Oaks, CA 91401 **www.alternatereality.tv**
Contact: Michael Marconi

Ant Farm (323) 850-0700
110 S. Fairfax Ave., Ste. 200 FAX **(323) 932-6797**
Los Angeles, CA 90036 **www.theantfarm.net**

BloomFilm (323) 850-5575
Contact: Jon Bloom

BLT AV (323) 860-4000
6430 Sunset Blvd., Eighth Fl. FAX **(323) 860-0890**
Los Angeles, CA 90028 **www.bltomato.com**

Buddha Jones (323) 962-5100
910 N. Sycamore Ave. FAX **(323) 962-5105**
Los Angeles, CA 90038 **www.buddhajonestrailers.com**

Cimarron Group (323) 337-0300
6855 Santa Monica Blvd. FAX **(323) 337-0333**
Hollywood, CA 90038 **www.cimarrongroup.com**
Contact: Bob Farina

CMP Burbank (818) 729-0800
2717 W. Olive Ave. **www.craigmurrayproductions.com**
Burbank, CA 91505

Eyestorm Productions (310) 582-3937
1559 Seventh St. FAX **(310) 582-3939**
Santa Monica, CA 90401 **www.eyestormproductions.com**
Contacts: Michael Klima & Kyle Ruddick

Firestone Productions (323) 461-7500, (323) 377-9494
Contact: Scott Firestone **www.firestoneproductions.com**

Fix It In Post, Inc. (818) 344-7944
www.fixitinpost.net

Gas Station Zebra (818) 762-2150
4217 Coldwater Canyon Ave. FAX **(818) 762-2110**
Studio City, CA 91604 **www.gasstationzebra.com**

Goodspot (310) 453-5550
2932 Nebraska Ave. FAX **(310) 453-5580**
Santa Monica, CA 90404 **www.goodspot.com**

The Grossmyth Company (310) 390-4898
3114 Purdue Ave. FAX **(310) 437-5205**
Los Angeles, CA 90066 **www.grossmyth.com**
Contact: Caddie Hastings

Hammer Creative (323) 606-4700, (323) 463-9156
6311 Romaine St., Third Fl. FAX **(323) 463-8130**
Los Angeles, CA 90038 **www.hammercreative.com**
Contact: Mark Pierce

Ignition Creative (310) 315-6300
3211 Olympic Blvd. FAX **(310) 315-6399**
Santa Monica, CA 90404 **www.ignitionla.com**

Illusion Factory (818) 598-8400
21800 Burbank Blvd., Ste. 225 **www.illusionfactory.com**
Woodland Hills, CA 91367
Contact: Brian Weiner

In Sync Advertising (323) 965-4810
6135 Wilshire Blvd. FAX **(323) 965-8155**
Los Angeles, CA 90048 **www.insyncad.com**

Intralink Film (310) 859-7001
155 N. LaPeer Dr. FAX **(310) 859-0738**
Los Angeles, CA 90048 **www.intralinkfilm.com**

Kandoo Films, Inc. (818) 789-6777
4515 Van Nuys Blvd., Ste. 100 FAX **(818) 789-2299**
Sherman Oaks, CA 91403 **www.kandoofilms.com**
Contacts: Howard Barish & Rhonda Kinosian

KO Creative (310) 288-3820
9300 Wilshire Blvd., Ste. 400 FAX **(310) 285-2095**
Beverly Hills, CA 90212 **www.ko-creative.com**
Contact: Kristi Kilday

Mark Woollen & Associates (310) 399-2690
207 Ashland Ave. FAX **(310) 399-2670**
Santa Monica, CA 90405 **www.markwoollen.com**

mOcean (310) 481-0808
2440 S. Sepulveda Blvd., Ste. 150 FAX **(310) 481-0807**
Los Angeles, CA 90064 **www.moceanla.com**

Mojo, LLC (323) 932-7700
5750 Wilshire Blvd., Ste. 600 FAX **(323) 932-7701**
Los Angeles, CA 90036 **www.mojohouse.com**

Precision Productions + Post (310) 839-4600
10718 McCune Ave. FAX **(310) 839-4601**
Los Angeles, CA 90034 **www.precisionpost.com**

Reality Check Studios, Inc. (323) 465-3900, (323) 908-7000
6100 Melrose Ave. FAX **(323) 465-3600**
Los Angeles, CA 90038 **www.realityx.com**

Seismic Productions (323) 957-3350
7010 Santa Monica Blvd. **www.seismicproductions.com**
Los Angeles, CA 90038

Studio 27 (818) 216-9026
6860 Lexington Ave. FAX **(415) 621-1875**
Hollywood, CA 90038 **www.studio27inc.com**

Trailer Park (323) 461-4232
6922 Hollywood Blvd., 12th Fl. **www.trailerpark.com**
Los Angeles, CA 90028

TriCoast Studios (310) 458-7707
1547 10th St. FAX **(310) 458-7701**
Santa Monica, CA 90401 **www.tricoast.com**

Winston Davis Associates (323) 930-8535
955 S. Carrillo Dr., Ste. 200 FAX **(323) 930-8545**
Los Angeles, CA 90048 **www.winstondavis.com**

CLASSIC LOS ANGELES FILM LOCATIONS

ENNIS HOUSE

BLADE RUNNER

INT. DECKARD'S APARTMENT - NIGHT

The place is a mess. Deckard (Harrison Ford) walks in. He goes into the kitchen, comes out with a towel, drying his hair. He walks to the cocktail cabinet and pours himself a drink.

Deckard takes off his wet raincoat and throws it on a chair.

RACHAEL
Look.

Rachael (Sean Young) goes to him holding a picture in her hand. Deckard looks at it.

It's an old snapshot, a little girl with a mother and father.

RACHAEL (Cont.)
It's me with my parents.

Deckard hands it back to her slowly.

DECKARD
You remember when you were about six and you and your brother snuck into an empty building.... through the basement window?

RACHAEL
What? Y-yes....

DECKARD
You were going to play Doctor. He showed you his, then you chickened and ran out. Remember the bush outside your window with the spider in it. Green body, orange legs... you watched her build a web all summer.

RACHAEL
Yes.

DECKARD
One day there was an egg in the webb.

RACHAEL
After a while, the egg hatched and hundreds of baby spiders came out and ate her. That made quite an impression on me, Mr. Deckard.

DECKARD
You still don't get it?

RACHAEL
No.. I... I .... don't.

DECKARD
Implants. They are not your memories, they belong to Tyrell's sixteen year old niece.

Rachael just stares at him, stunned and barely holding on.

DECKARD
Wanna drink?

SCREENPLAY BY:
Hampton Fancher, David Peoples based on a novel by Philip K. Dick

ALSO FILMED AT ENNIS HOUSE: *Buffy the Vampire Slayer, Rush Hour*

LA 411

www.LA411.com

■ PICTURED:
Ennis House

■ LOCATION:
Los Angeles

■ PHOTOGRAPHER:
Michael Rueter
Michael Rueter Photography/L.A.-N.Y.
www.michaelrueter.com

Supporting production in Southern California for 31 years

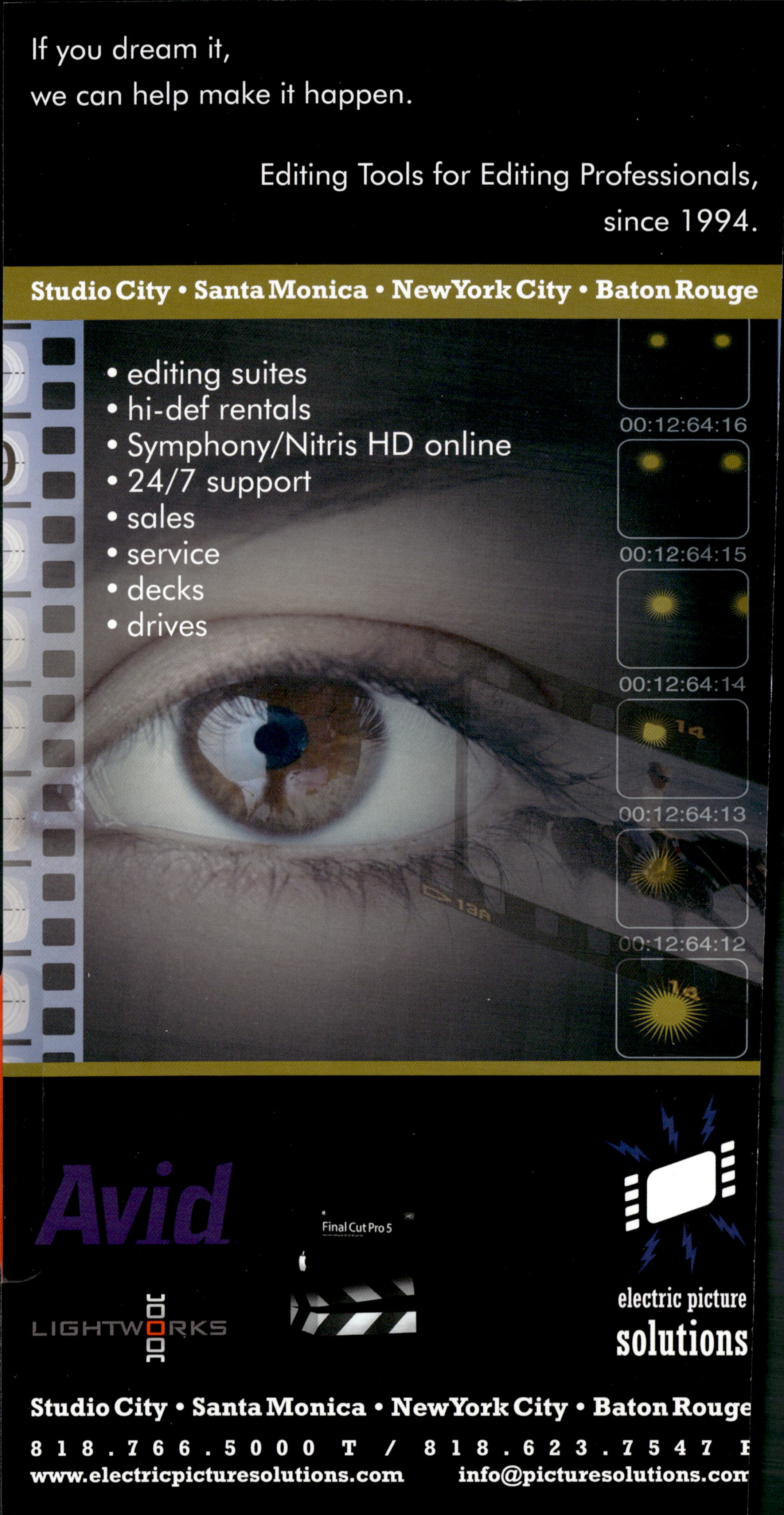

Ⓐ ADVERTISER SYMBOL

Refer to the General Index for cross-referencing items in this section.

1 Mix Productions (310) 237-6438
www.1mixproductions.com
(5.1 Surround, ADR, Archiving, Audio Laybacks, Dialogue Cleanup/Advanced NR (LB Labs), Digital Editing, Domestic Dubbing, Dubbing, Foley, Foreign Dubbing, Foreign Language, ISDN, Mastering, Mixing, Pre-Dubbing, Sound Design, Synching & Voice Over Services)

48 Windows Music and Mix (310) 392-9545
1661 Lincoln Blvd., Ste. 220 FAX (310) 392-9445
Santa Monica, CA 90404 www.48windows.com
(ADR, Audio Laybacks, Digital Sound Editing, Dubbing, Foley, Sound FX Library, Synching & Transmission Services)

5.1 Audio/iPost LLC (323) 932-7081
(818) 985-5000
5757 Wilshire Blvd., Ste. 360 FAX (323) 932-7084
Los Angeles, CA 90036 www.ipost-inc.com
(5.1 Surround, ADR, Audio Laybacks, Audio Laybacks to High Def, Digital Editing, Dolby Surround, ISDN, Laybacks, Mastering, Mixing, Music, Music Composition, Sound Design, Sound Editing, Sound FX Editing & Voice Over Services)
Contacts: Bob Grey, Michael Kross, Justin Lebens Laurence, Michael Senescu & Sheldon II

A B Audio Visual (562) 429-1042
(877) 222-8346
FAX (562) 429-2401
www.abaudio.com
(ADR, Audio Laybacks, Digital Sound Editing, Dubbing, Foley, Mastering, Music, Sound FX Library, Synching, Transfers & Voice Over Services)

Absolute Post (818) 842-7966
2633 N. San Fernando Blvd. FAX (818) 842-8815
Burbank, CA 91504 www.absolutepost.tv
(ADR, Foley, Mixing, Sound Editing, Synching & Transfers)
Contact: Misty Tamburelli

Action Audio & Visual (323) 461-4290
(888) 406-8164
10834 Burbank Blvd., Ste. A-100 FAX (323) 461-4292
North Hollywood, CA 91601 www.actionaudioandvisual.com
(5.1 Surround, ADR, Audio Laybacks, Audio Restoration Services, Digital Sound Editing, Dolby Surround, Domestic Dubbing, Dubbing, ISDN, Foley, Foreign Dubbing, Laybacks, Mixing, Music, Music Composition, Pre-Dubbing, Remote Sessions, Restoration, Sound Design, Sound Editing, Sound FX Editing, Sound FX Library, Synching, Transfers & Voice Over Services)

Advantage Audio/Jim Hodson (818) 566-8555
1026 N. Hollywood Way FAX (818) 566-8963
Burbank, CA 91505 www.advantageaudio.com
(Digital Sound Editing, Dubbing, Foley, Laybacks, Mixing & Sound FX Library)
Contacts: Jim Hodson, Heather Holbrook, Bob Poole & Paca Thomas

Aftershock Digital (323) 658-5700
8222 Melrose Ave., Ste. 304 FAX (323) 658-5200
Los Angeles, CA 90046 www.editkings.com
(Sound FX Library)
Contact: Fritz Feick

Alan Audio Works (310) 753-1564
(323) 906-8700
4222 Santa Monica Blvd. FAX (562) 408-6822
Los Angeles, CA 90029 www.alanaudioworks.com
(5.1 Surround, ADR, Audio Laybacks, Dolby Surround, Dubbing, Foley, Foreign Dubbing, Mastering, Mixing, Music, Music Composition, Music/Sound FX Library, Pre-Dubbing, Restoration, Sound Design, Sound Editing, Synching & Voice Over Services)

Allied Post Audio (310) 392-8280
1642 17th St. www.alliedpost.com
Santa Monica, CA 90404
(ADR, Audio Laybacks, Foley, Mixing, Pre-Dubbing, Sound Design, Sound Editing, Sound FX Library & Voice Over Services)

Alphadogs, Inc. (818) 729-9262
1612 W. Olive Ave., Ste. 200 FAX (818) 729-8537
Burbank, CA 91506 www.alphadogs.tv

AMP Studios (805) 955-7742
(805) 955-7770
101 W. Cochran St. FAX (805) 955-7705
Simi Valley, CA 93065 www.ampstudios.com
(Dolby Surround, Laybacks, Mixing, Music/Sound FX Library, Remote Sessions, Sound Editing, Synching & Transfers)

Anarchy Post (818) 334-3300
1811 Victory Blvd. FAX (818) 334-3305
Glendale, CA 91201 www.anarchypost.net
(5.1 Surround, ADR, Dialogue Cleanup/Advanced NR [LB Labs], Digital Editing, Dolby Surround, Domestic Dubbing, Dubbing, Foley, Foreign Dubbing, Mixing, Pre-Dubbing, Sound Design, Sound Editing, Sound FX Editing, Sound FX Library, Synching, THX Certified 5.1 Mixing & Voice Over Services)

The Andrita Media Center (323) 344-4500
3030 Andrita St. FAX (323) 344-4800
Los Angeles, CA 90065 www.andritastudios.com
(ADR, Audio Laybacks, Digital Sound Editing, Dubbing, Foley, Foreign and Domestic Dubbing, Laybacks, Mastering, Mixing, Sound Editing, Sound FX Library, Synching, Transfers, Transmission Services & Voice Over Services)

at&t Recording/Duplicating (323) 466-9000
402 N. Arden Blvd. FAX (323) 467-6615
Los Angeles, CA 90004
(Digital Sound Editing, Dubbing, Mixing & Sound FX Library)
Contact: Sheyna Smith

Atlantis Group (310) 458-9098
429 Santa Monica Blvd., Ste. 250 FAX (310) 458-9048
Santa Monica, CA 90401
www.atlantisgrouprecording.com
(5.1 Surround, ADR, Audio Laybacks, Digital Sound Editing, ISDN, Mixing, Music, Restoration, Sound Design, Sound Editing, Sound FX Editing, Synching & Voice Over Services)

Audio Gadgets (818) 567-2080
210 N. Pass Ave., Ste. 106 FAX (818) 567-2011
Burbank, CA 91505
(5.1 Surround, ADR, Digital Editing, Dolby Surround, Laybacks, Mixing, Sound Editing, Sound FX Editing, Remote Sessions, Sound FX Library & Voice Over Services)
Contact: John Jackson

Audio Mechanics (818) 846-5525
1200 W. Magnolia Blvd. FAX (818) 846-5501
Burbank, CA 91506 www.audiomechanics.com
(Digital Sound Editing, Mastering, Mixing, Restoration, Synching & Transfers)

Audio Post & Picture (818) 562-6444
3619 W. Magnolia Blvd. www.audiopostpicture.com
Burbank, CA 91505

AudioBanks (310) 581-1660
1660 Ninth St. FAX (310) 581-1661
Santa Monica, CA 90404 www.audiobanks.com
(ADR, Audio Laybacks, Digital Sound Editing, Dubbing, Foley, Mixing, Music/Sound FX Library & Synching)
Contacts: Amy Lyngos & Charlie Pomykal

AudioVision Production Services (714) 731-8883
(888) 731-8883
14731 Franklin Ave., Ste. D FAX (714) 731-8976
Tustin, CA 92780 www.audiovisionps.com
(5.1 Surround, ADR, Archiving, Audio Laybacks, Dolby Surround, Domestic Dubbing, Dubbing, Foley, Foreign Dubbing, ISDN, Laybacks, Mastering, Mixing, Music, Music Composition, Music FX Library, Pre-Dubbing, Preservation, Remote Sessions, Restoration, Sound Design, Sound Editing, Sound FX Editing, Sound FX Library, Synching, Transfers, Transmission Services & Voice Over Services)

Ⓐ **Bell Sound Studios** (323) 461-3036
916 N. Citrus Ave. FAX (323) 461-8764
Hollywood, CA 90038 www.bellsound.com
(ADR, Audio Laybacks, Digital Sound Editing, Mixing, Sound FX Library, Synching & Transfers)
Contact: Beth Quimby

The Bennett Group (310) 979-0191
2017 S. Westgate Ave. FAX (310) 207-2587
West Los Angeles, CA 90025
www.bennettproductions.com
(ADR, Audio Laybacks, Digital Sound Editing, Dubbing, Mixing, Music/Sound FX Library, Transfers & Transmission Services)
Contact: Cindy Casillas

Blague Communications (866) 769-5661
11417 Moorpark St. FAX (818) 769-5996
North Hollywood, CA 91602 www.blague-studio.com
(ADR, Dubbing, Foreign Dubbing, Mixing, Remote Sessions, Sound Design, Sound Editing, Synching & Voice Over Services)
Contacts: Mariela Fernandez & Jesús Guevara

Blue Tango Productions (949) 813-2450
668 N. Coast Hwy, Ste. 226
Laguna Beach, CA 92651
www.bluetangoproductions.com
(ADR, Audio Laybacks, Dubbing, Mixing, Synching & Transfers)

BluWave Audio (818) 777-3171
100 Universal City Plaza FAX (818) 866-2274
Bldg. 1220-LL www.bluwaveaudio.com
Universal City, CA 91608
(Digital and Analog Archiving, Digital Mastering, Mixing, Preservation, Restoration & Transfers)
Contact: Richard LeGrand

Ⓐ **Buzzy's Recording** (323) 931-1867
6900 Melrose Ave. FAX (323) 931-9681
Los Angeles, CA 90038 www.buzzysrecording.com
(ADR, Digital Sound Editing, Interactive Voice-Over, Mixing & Music/Sound FX Library)
Contact: Andrew Morris

Capitol Studios (323) 871-5001
1750 N. Vine St. FAX (323) 871-5058
Hollywood, CA 90028 www.capitolstudios.com
(Audio Laybacks, Digital Sound Editing, Dubbing, Mixing, Scoring/Sound Stage, Sound FX Library, Synching & Transfers)

CCI Digital, Inc. (818) 562-6300
2921 W. Alameda Ave. FAX (818) 562-8222
Burbank, CA 91505 www.ccidigital.com
(ADR, Dubbing, Laybacks, Mixing, Music/Sound FX Library & Sound Editing)

Chace Audio (818) 842-8346
(800) 842-8346
201 S. Victory Blvd. FAX (818) 842-8353
Burbank, CA 91502 www.chace.com
(5.1 Surround, 6.1 Surround, 7.1 Surround, ADR, AC3/dts Encoding [LB Labs], ADR, Archiving, Audio Laybacks, Audio Laybacks to High Def, Dialogue Cleanup/Advanced NR [LB Labs], Digital Editing, Digital Sound Editing, Dolby E, Dolby Surround, Domestic Dubbing, Dubbing, Foley, Foreign Dubbing, ISDN, Laybacks, Mastering, Mixing, Restoration, Sound Editing, Sound FX Editing, Synching, THX Certified 5.1 Mixing & Transfers)

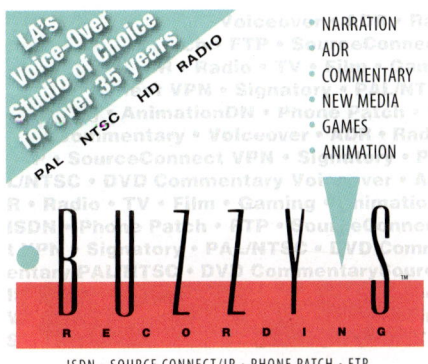

Cine Magnetics
Digital & Video Laboratories **(818) 623-2560**
3765 Cahuenga Blvd. West **www.cinemagnetics.com**
Studio City, CA 91604
(ADR, Audio Laybacks, Digital Sound Editing, Dolby Surround, Dubbing, Foreign and Domestic Dubbing, Laybacks, Mastering, Mixing, Sound Editing, Sound FX Library, Synching, THX Certified 5.1 Mixing, Transfers & Transmission Services)

Coast Media Teleproductions, Inc. **(949) 417-0300**
17062 Murphy Ave., Bldg. B **www.coastmedia.com**
Irvine, CA 92614
(ADR, Audio Laybacks, Digital Sound Editing, Dubbing, Foley, Mixing, Scoring/Sound Stage, Sound FX Library, Synching & Transfers)
Contact: Joyce Smith

Command Post **(818) 882-3300**
(818) 882-1315
8400 Keokuk Ave. FAX **(818) 886-1514**
Winnetka, CA 91306 **www.command-post.com**
(ADR, Dolby Surround, Dubbing, Foley, Laybacks, Mixing, Music/Sound FX Library, Sound Editing, Synching & Transfers)

The Complex Studios **(310) 477-1938**
2323 Corinth Ave. FAX **(310) 607-9631**
West Los Angeles, CA 90064 **www.thecomplexstudios.com**
(ADR, Mixing, Sound Editing & Transmission Services)

Costa Mesa Studios **(949) 515-9942**
711 W. 17th St., Ste. D10 FAX **(949) 515-4230**
Costa Mesa, CA 92627 **www.costamesastudios.com**
(Digital Sound Editing, ISDN, Foley, Mastering, Mixing, Mobile Facilities, Music, Music Composition, Music/Sound FX Library, Remote Sessions, Scoring/Sound Stage, Sound Design, Sound Editing, Sound FX Library & Voice Over Services)

Creative Media Recording **(714) 892-9469**
11105 Knott Ave., Ste. G **www.creativemediarecording.com**
Cypress, CA 90630
(ADR, Audio Laybacks, Digital Sound Editing, Dubbing, Foley, ISDN Capabilities, Mixing, Music, Sound FX Library & Translation and Transmission Services)
Contact: Tim Keenan

Daily Post **(310) 417-4844**
6701 Center Dr. West, Ste. 1111 FAX **(310) 410-1543**
Los Angeles, CA 90045 **www.dailypost.tv**

Danetracks, Inc. **(323) 512-8160**
7356 Santa Monica Blvd. FAX **(323) 512-8163**
West Hollywood, CA 90046 **www.danetracks.com**
(Editing, Mixing & Sound Design)
Contact: Ann Marie Wachel

Dangerous Waters Music **(310) 839-9444**
www.dwmusic.com
(Dialogue Cleanup/Advanced NR [LB Labs], Digital Editing, Dubbing, Mastering, Music, Music FX Library, Sound Design, Sound Editing & Voice Over Services)

Different by Design **(310) 689-2470**
12233 W. Olympic Blvd., Ste. 120 FAX **(310) 689-2471**
Los Angeles, CA 90064 **www.dxdproductions.com**
(ADR, Audio Laybacks, Digital Sound Editing & Mixing)
Contact: Matt Radecki

Digital Jungle Post Production **(323) 962-0867**
6363 Santa Monica Blvd. FAX **(323) 962-9960**
Hollywood, CA 90038 **www.digijungle.com**
(5.1 Surround, ADR, Archiving, Audio Laybacks to High Def, Dolby Surround, ISDN, Mastering, Mixing, Pre-Dubbing, Sound Editing, Sound FX Editing, Sound FX Library, Synching, Transfers & Voice Over Services)

Digital Sound Recording **(323) 258-6741**
607 N. Ave. 64 **www.vanwebster.com**
Los Angeles, CA 90042
(Archiving, Digital Editing, Mastering, Mixing, Music, Preservation, Restoration, Sound Editing, Sound FX Library & Voice Over Services)
Contact: Van Webster

DVCarney **(310) 595-4562**
www.dvcarney.com
(ADR, Archiving, Audio Laybacks, Digital Editing, Domestic Dubbing, Dubbing, Foley, Foreign Dubbing, Laybacks, Mastering, Mixing, Mobile Facilities, Music, Pre-Dubbing, Remote Sessions, Restoration, Sound Design, Sound FX Editing, Sound FX Library, Synching, Transfers & Voice Over Services)

Eleven **(310) 526-2911**
1231 Lincoln Blvd. FAX **(310) 526-2929**
Santa Monica, CA 90401 **www.elevensound.com**
(ADR, Dolby Surround, Dubbing, Foley, ISDN, Laybacks, Mixing, Music/Sound FX Library, Sound Editing, Synching & Transfers)
Contacts: Kristin Felt & D. J. Fox-Engstrom

Fox Studios **(310) 369-7678**
(310) 369-4636
10201 W. Pico Blvd. FAX **(310) 369-4407**
Los Angeles, CA 90035 **www.foxpost.com**

Gold Street **(818) 567-1911**
649 Bethany Rd. **www.goldstreetpost.com**
Burbank, CA 91504
(5.1 Surround, ADR, Dialogue/Music Editing, Domestic/ Foreign Dubbing, Mastering, Mixing, Music Composition, Noise Reduction, Sound Design/Editing & Voice Over Services)
Contact: Eric Michael Cap

Gray Martin Studios **(310) 449-4007**
3000 Olympic Blvd., Ste. 2520 FAX **(310) 449-4008**
Santa Monica, CA 90404 **www.graymartinstudios.com**
(5.1 Surround, ADR, Audio Laybacks, Digital Editing, ISDN, Mixing, Sound Design & Sound FX Library)

Hollywood Voice Over Service **(323) 899-1998**
8033 Sunset Blvd., Ste. 431 **www.myvoiceoverguy.com**
West Hollywood, CA 90046
(Voice Over Services)

iProbe Multilingual Solutions, Inc. **(888) 489-6035**
www.iprobesolutions.com
(5.1 Surround, ADR, Audio Laybacks, Audio Laybacks to High Def, Digital Editing, Dolby Surround, Domestic Dubbing, Dubbing, Foley, Foreign Dubbing, ISDN, Laybacks, Mastering, Mixing, Pre-Dubbing, Remote Sessions, Restoration, Sound Design, Sound Editing, Sound FX Editing, Sound FX Library, Sound Stage, Synching, Transfers, Transmission Services & Voice Over Services)

J.E. Sound Productions **(323) 850-0765**
1755 El Cerrito Pl., Ste. 304 **www.jesound.com**
Hollywood, CA 90028
(Mixing, Scoring/Sound Stage & Sound Editing)

Jet Stream Sound **(323) 883-0123**
3610 W. Magnolia Blvd. FAX **(818) 531-0401**
Burbank, CA 91505 **www.jetstreamsound.com**
(5.1 Surround, AC3/dts Encoding (LB Labs), ADR, Archiving, Audio Laybacks, Audio Laybacks to High Def, Dialogue Cleanup/Advanced NR (LB Labs), Digital Editing, Dolby Surround, Domestic Dubbing, Dubbing, Foley, Foreign Dubbing, Laybacks, Mastering, Mixing, Music, Music Composition, Music FX Library, Pre-Dubbing, Preservation, Remote Sessions, Restoration, Scoring Stage, Sound Design, Sound Editing, Sound FX Editing, Sound FX Library, Synching, Transfers & Voice Over Services)

Juice (310) 460-7830
1648 10th St. FAX **(310) 460-7845**
Santa Monica, CA 90404
Contact: Oscar Morales

Juniper Post (818) 841-1244
801 Main St. FAX **(818) 972-4966**
Burbank, CA 91506 **www.juniperpost.com**
(ADR, Foley, Mixing & Sound Editing)

Kappa Studios, Inc. (818) 843-3400
3619 W. Magnolia Blvd. FAX **(818) 559-5684**
Burbank, CA 91505 **www.kappastudios.com**
(ADR, Digital Sound Editing, Mixing, Restoration, Sound FX Library, Sound Stage & Transfers)
Contact: Paul Long

LA Recording (818) 425-2992
264 S. Oxford Ave., Ste. B **www.losangelesrecording.com**
Los Angeles, CA 90004
(5.1 Surround, AC3/dts Encoding [LB Labs], ADR, Audio Laybacks, Audio Laybacks to High Def, Dialogue Cleanup/ Advanced NR [LB Labs], Digital Editing, Dolby Surround, Domestic Dubbing, Dubbing, Foley, Foreign Dubbing, Laybacks, Mastering, Mixing, Music, Music Composition, Music FX Library, Pre-Dubbing, Restoration, Sound Design, Sound Editing, Sound FX Editing, Sound FX Library, Synching, Transfers, Transmission Services & Voice Over Services)

LA Studios, Inc. (323) 851-6351
3453 Cahuenga Blvd. West FAX **(323) 876-5347**
Los Angeles, CA 90068 **www.lastudios.com**
(ADR, Audio Laybacks, Digital Sound Editing, Dubbing, ISDN, Mixing, Music/Sound FX Library, Synching, Transfers & Transmission Services)
Contact: Jane Curry

Larson Studios (323) 469-3986
6520 Sunset Blvd. FAX **(323) 469-8507**
Hollywood, CA 90028 **www.larson.com**
(ADR, Audio Laybacks, Digital Sound Editing, Dubbing, Foley, Mixing, Music/Sound FX Library, Synching & Transfers)
Contact: Scott Turner

Latté Mix (310) 260-9838
1548 Ninth St. FAX **(310) 260-3978**
Santa Monica, CA 90401 **www.lattemix.com**
(ADR, Audio Laybacks, ISDN, Mixing, Music/Sound FX Library, Sound Design, Synching, Transfers & Transmission Services)

LB Labs (818) 363-9395
12126 Woodley Ave. **www.lb-labs.com**
Granada Hills, CA 91344
(7.1 Surround, Mastering, Mixing & Restoration)

Levels Audio (323) 461-3333
1026 N. Highland Ave. FAX **(323) 461-3364**
Los Angeles, CA 90028 **www.levelsaudio.com**

Lightpost Productions (818) 955-7678
1701 W. Burbank Blvd., Ste. 201 FAX **(818) 955-5181**
Burbank, CA 91506 **www.renthd.com**
(5.1 Surround, ADR, Audio Laybacks, Audio Laybacks to High Def, Digital Sound Editing, Foley, Foreign and Domestic Dubbing, Laybacks, Mastering, Mixing, Sound Design & Sound Editing)

Lime Studios (310) 829-5463
1528 20th St. FAX **(310) 829-5048**
Santa Monica, CA 90404 **www.limestudios.tv**
(5.1 Surround, ADR, Archiving, Audio Laybacks, Audio Laybacks to High Def, Digital Editing, Dolby Surround, Domestic/Foreign Dubbing, ISDN, Laybacks, Mixing, Music, Music Composition, Music FX Library, Pre-Dubbing, Remote Sessions, Sound Design, Sound Editing, Sound FX Editing, Sound FX Library, Synching, Transfers,Transmission Services & Voice Over Services)

Margarita Mix de Santa Monica (310) 396-3333
1661 Lincoln Blvd., Ste. 101 FAX **(310) 396-9633**
Santa Monica, CA 90404 **www.lastudios.com**
(5.1 Surround Sound, ADR, Audio Laybacks, Digital Encoding, Digital Sound Editing, Dubbing, Foley, High Def, ISDN, Mixing, Sound Design, Sound FX Network, Synching, Transfers & Transmission Services)
Contacts: Michele Millard & Whitney Warren
Mixers: Jack Aurora, Jimmy Hite, Jeff Levy & Jonathan Whitehead

Margarita Mix Hollywood (323) 962-6565
6838 Romaine St. FAX **(323) 962-8662**
Hollywood, CA 90038 **www.lastudios.com**
(5.1 Surround Sound, ADR, Audio Laybacks, Digital Sound Editing, Dubbing, High Def, ISDN, Mixing, Sound FX Library & Transfers)
Contact: Veneta Butler

Media City Sound (818) 508-3311
12711 Ventura Blvd., Ste. 110 FAX **(818) 508-3314**
Studio City, CA 91604 **www.mcsound.com**
(7.1 Surround, AC3/dts Encoding [LB Labs], ADR, Audio Laybacks, Audio Laybacks to High Def, Digital Sound Editing, Dubbing, Mixing, Music/Sound FX Library, Sound Design, Synching, Transmission Services & Voice Over Services)
Contact: Lisa Blackwood & Gloria Coronado

Mercury Sound Studios (818) 545-8090
632 Thompson Ave. FAX **(818) 545-8641**
Glendale, CA 91201 **www.mercurysoundstudios.com**
(5.1 Surround, ADR, Digital Editing, Dolby Surround, Domestic Dubbing, Dubbing, Foley, Foreign Dubbing, Mixing, Pre-Dubbing, Sound FX Library, Sound Design, Sound Editing, Sound FX Editing, THX Certified 5.1 Mixing & Transfers)

Mesmer, Inc. (310) 410-1900
6080 Center Dr., Ste. 210 FAX **(310) 410-1901**
Los Angeles, CA 90045 **www.mesmerav.com**
(ADR, Digital Sound Editing, Dubbing, Foley, Mixing, Scoring Stage, Sound FX Library & Synching)
Contacts: David Blau & Jeff Sudakin

Michael Hamilton Co. (818) 779-1006
(818) 205-3246
5801 Murietta Ave. **spikey01.com/hamilton_audio/**
Van Nuys, CA 91401 **hamilton_audio_home.html**
(5.1 Surround, ADR, Audio Laybacks, Audio Laybacks to High Def, Digital Editing, Dolby Surround, Dubbing, Foreign Dubbing, ISDN, Laybacks, Mastering, Mixing, Music FX Library, Restoration, Sound Design, Sound Editing, Sound FX Editing, Sound FX Library, Synching, Transfers & Voice Over Services)

Mint Mix (323) 804-1993
(310) 301-1800
316 S. Venice Blvd. **www.mintmix.net**
Venice, CA 90291
(5.1 Surround, AC3/dts Encoding [LB Labs], ADR, Audio Laybacks, Audio Laybacks to High Def, Dialogue Cleanup/ Advanced NR [LB Labs], Digital Editing, Dolby Surround, Domestic Dubbing, Dubbing, Foley, Foreign Dubbing, ISDN, Laybacks, Mastering, Mixing, Pre-Dubbing, Remote Sessions, Restoration, Sound Design, Sound Editing, Sound FX Editing, Sound FX Library, Sound Stage, Synching, Transfers & Voice Over Services)

Mix Magic Post Sound (323) 466-2442
839 N. Highland Ave. FAX **(323) 463-1677**
Los Angeles, CA 90038 **www.mixmagic.com**
(ADR, Audio Laybacks, Digital Sound Editing, Dubbing, Foley, Mixing, Music/Sound FX Library, Synching, Transfers & Transmission Services)
Contact: Sara Corbett

Monkeyland Audio, Inc. (818) 553-0955
4620 W. Magnolia Blvd. FAX **(818) 553-1155**
Burbank, CA 94505 **www.monkeylandaudio.com**
(ADR, Dolby Surround, Dubbing, Foley, Laybacks, Mixing, Sound Editing, Sound FX Library & Transfers)
Contact: Melissa Strater

NL3 Audio (213) 268-4226
1984 N. Main St., Ste. 300 FAX **(323) 227-1498**
Los Angeles, CA 90031 **www.nl3audio.com**
(ADR, Digital Sound Editing, Dolby Surround, Dubbing, Foley, Laybacks, Mastering, Mixing, Music, Music/Sound FX Library, Predubbing, Remote Sessions, Restoration, Scoring Stage, Scoring/Soundstage, Sound Editing, Sound FX Library, Synching & THX Certified 5.1 Mixing)

Novastar Digital Sound Services (323) 467-5020
6430 Sunset Blvd., Ste. 103 FAX **(323) 957-8707**
Hollywood, CA 90028 **www.novastarpost.com**
(ADR, Audio Laybacks, Digital Sound Editing, Foley, Restoration, Sound Design, Sound FX Library, Synching, THX Certified 5.1 Mixing & Transfers)
Contact: Bob Sky

Oasis Digital (323) 464-6858
215 N. Larchmont Blvd. FAX **(323) 464-6857**
Los Angeles, CA 90004 **www.oasisdigitalpost.com**
(5.1 Surround, ADR, Audio Laybacks, Digital Sound Editing, Foley, Mixing, Sound Design, Sound FX Editing & Voice Over Services)

ON Music and Sound (310) 264-0407
2042-A Broadway FAX **(310) 264-0381**
Santa Monica, CA 90404 **www.onmusicandsound.com**
(ADR, Dolby Surround, Dubbing, Foley, Laybacks, Mixing, Music/Sound FX Library, Remote Systems & Sound Editing)

OneWorld Language Solutions (323) 848-7993
FAX **(323) 848-7995**
www.oneworldlanguage.com

Oracle Post (818) 752-2800
4720 W. Magnolia Blvd. FAX **(818) 769-2624**
Burbank, CA 91505 **www.oraclepost.com**
(AC3/dts Encoding [LB Labs], ADR, Audio Laybacks, Digital Mixing, Dolby Surround, Digital Sound Editing, Foley, Mixing, Music FX Library, Scoring Stage, Sound Design, Sound FX Library, THX Certified 5.1 Mixing & Transfers)
Contacts: James Lifton & Paulette Lifton

Oracle Post (310) 449-5550
3232 Nebraska Ave. FAX **(310) 449-5554**
Santa Monica, CA 90404 **www.oraclepost.com**
(AC3/dts Encoding [LB Labs], ADR, Audio Laybacks, Digital Mixing, Dolby Surround, Digital Sound Editing, Foley, Mixing, Music FX Library, Scoring Stage, Sound Design, Sound FX Library, THX Certified 5.1 Mixing & Transfers)
Contacts: James Lifton & Paulette Lifton

Outlaw Sound (323) 462-1873
1608 N. Argyle Ave. FAX **(323) 957-2733**
Hollywood, CA 90028 **www.outlawsound.com**
(ADR, Digital Sound Editing & Transmission Services)
Contact: Allen Roth

The Outpost Sound Mixing Company (323) 466-7937
1037 N. Cole Ave. **www.outpostsound.com**
Hollywood, CA 90038
(5.1 Surround, ADR, ISDN, Laybacks, Mastering, Mixing, Music Composition, Sound Design, Sound Editing & Transfers)

Paramount Recording Studios (323) 465-4000
6245 Santa Monica Blvd. FAX **(323) 469-1905**
Hollywood, CA 90038 **www.paramountrecording.com**
(Mixing, Scoring Stage, Sound Editing, Sound FX Library & Transfers)
Contacts: Adam Beilenson & Mike Kerns

The Studios at Paramount (323) 956-1445
The Studios at Paramount FAX **(323) 862-2242**
Post Production Services **www.thestudiosatparamount.com**
5555 Melrose Ave.
Los Angeles, CA 90038
(5.1 Surround, ADR, Archiving, Audio Laybacks, Audio Laybacks to High Def, Digital Editing, Dolby Surround, Domestic Dubbing, Dubbing, ISDN, Foley, Laybacks, Mastering, Mixing, Pre-Dubbing, Remote Sessions, Restoration, Sound Editing, Sound FX Editing, Sound FX Library, Sound Stage, Transfers, Transmission Services & Voice Over Services)

Pixel Plantation (818) 566-7777
4111 W. Alameda Ave., Ste. 301 **www.pixelplantation.com**
Burbank, CA 91505
(5.1 Surround, Audio Laybacks, Audio Laybacks to High Def, ISDN, Mixing, Sound Design, Sound Editing & Voice Over Services)

Play (310) 576-0066
1447 Second St., Fourth Fl. FAX **(310) 576-0063**
Santa Monica, CA 90401 **www.playsound.com**
(5.1 Surround, ADR, Audio Laybacks, Audio Laybacks to High Def, Digital Editing, Dolby Surround, Domestic Dubbing, Dubbing, Foley, ISDN, Laybacks, Mastering, Mixing, Music, Music Composition, Music FX Library, Remote Sessions, Sound Design, Sound Editing, Sound FX Editing, Sound FX Library, Synching, Transfers & Voice Over Services)

Point360 (818) 556-5700
(866) 968-4336
1133 N. Hollywood Way FAX **(818) 556-5753**
Burbank, CA 91505 **www.point360.com**
(ADR, Audio Laybacks, Audio Restoration, Digital Sound Editing, Foley, Foreign Language Dubbing, Mixing, Sound FX Library, Synching & Transfers)

Point360 (310) 481-7000
12421 W. Olympic Blvd. FAX **(310) 207-8408**
Los Angeles, CA 90064 **www.point360.com**
(ADR, Audio Laybacks, Digital Sound Editing, Dubbing, Foley, Mixing, Sound FX Library, Synching & Transfers)

POP Sound (310) 458-9192
625 Arizona Ave. FAX **(310) 587-1222**
Santa Monica, CA 90401 **www.popsound.com**
(ADR, Digital Sound Editing & Mixing)

The Post Group (323) 462-2300
6335 Homewood Ave. FAX **(323) 462-0836**
Hollywood, CA 90028 **www.postgroup.com**
(Digital Sound Editing, Mixing, Sound FX Library & Transfers)
Contact: Ken Blaustein

Post Haste Media, Inc. (818) 232-7556
11115 Magnolia Blvd., Second Fl. FAX **(818) 237-5838**
North Hollywood, CA 91601 **www.posthastemedia.com**
(5.1 Surround, Audio Laybacks, Audio Restoration Services, Digital Sound Editing, Domestic Dubbing, Foley, Foreign Dubbing, ISDN, Laybacks, Mixing, Music Composition, Music FX Library, Pre-Dubbing, Sound Design, Sound Editing, Sound FX Library & Voice Over Services)

Post Logic Studios (323) 461-7887
1800 N. Vine St., Ste. 100 FAX **(323) 461-7790**
Los Angeles, CA 90028 **www.postlogic.com**
(ADR, Digital Sound Editing, Dubbing, Foley, Mixing, Sound FX Library & Transfers)

Post Modern Creative, LLC (949) 608-8700
2941 Alton Pkwy FAX **(949) 608-8729**
Irvine, CA 92606 **www.postmoderncreative.com**
(5.1 Surround, AC3/dts Encoding [LB Labs], ADR, Archiving, Audio Laybacks, Audio Laybacks to High Def, Dialogue Cleanup/Advanced NR [LB Labs], Digital Editing, Dolby Surround, Domestic and Foreign Dubbing, Laybacks, Mastering, Mixing, Music/Sound FX Library, Remote Sessions, Sound Editing, Sound Stage, Synching, Transmission Services, Transfers & Voice Over Services)
Contacts: Paul Both, Michael Boyd, Kathy Liddy, Rich O'Neill & Mike Pearce

Post Plus Sound, Inc. (818) 842-0191
2315 W. Burbank Blvd. FAX **(818) 842-0195**
Burbank, CA 91506 **www.postplussound.com**

Private Island Trax (323) 856-8729
6671 Sunset Blvd., Ste. 1518 FAX **(323) 856-0309**
Los Angeles, CA 90028 **www.privateislandtrax.com**

Ⓐ **Race Horse Studios** (310) 280-0175
3780 Selby Ave. FAX **(310) 280-0176**
Los Angeles, CA 90034 **www.racehorsestudios.com**
(5.1 Surround, ADR, Digital Editing, Dubbing, Foley, Laybacks, Mastering, Mixing, Music Composition, Restoration, Sound Design, Sound Editing, Sound FX Editing, Synching, Transfers, Transmission Services & Voice Over Services)

RavensWork (310) 392-2542
1611 Electric Ave. FAX **(310) 314-6774**
Venice, CA 90291 **www.ravenswork.com**
(5.1 Mixing, ADR, Audio Laybacks, Digital Sound Editing, Dubbing, Mixing, Music Composition, Sound Design, Sound FX Library, Synching, Transfers & Transmission Services)

Room (310) 450-7070
1426 Main St. FAX **(310) 450-5010**
Venice, CA 90291 **www.room.tv**
(5.1 Surround Sound, ADR, Audio Laybacks, Digital Sound Editing, Dubbing, Foley, High Def, Mixing, Sound FX Network & Synching)

Rusk Sound Studios (323) 462-6477
1556 N. La Brea Ave.
Hollywood, CA 90028
(ADR, Audio Laybacks, Digital Sound Editing, Dubbing, Foley, Mixing, Scoring/Sound Stage, Sound FX Library & Synching)

ScreenMusic International (818) 789-2954
18034 Ventura Blvd., Ste. 450 FAX **(818) 789-5801**
Encino, CA 91316 **www.screenmusic.com**
(Digital Sound Editing, Dubbing, Mixing, Synching & Transfers)

Serafine Inc. (310) 399-9279
P.O. Box 1798 **www.serafinecollective.com**
Simi Valley, CA 93065
(ADR, Digital Sound Editing, Dubbing, Foley, Mixing & Music/Sound FX Library)

Shoreline Studios (310) 394-4932
100 Wilshire Blvd., Ste. 150 FAX **(310) 458-7802**
Santa Monica, CA 90401 **www.shorelinestudios.com**
(ADR, Audio Laybacks, Digital Sound Editing, Mixing, Music/Sound FX Library & Transmission Services)
Contact: Gary Zacuto

Skyline Sound (818) 754-0194
12419 Valleyheart Dr. FAX **(818) 754-0194**
Studio City, CA 91604 **www.skylinesound.com**
(5.1 Surround, AC3/dts Encoding [LB Labs], ADR, Dialogue Cleanup/Advanced NR [LB Labs], Digital Editing, Dolby Surround, Mastering, Mixing, Restoration & Sound Editing)

Sonic Pool (323) 460-4649
6860 Lexington Ave. FAX **(323) 460-6063**
Los Angeles, CA 90038 **www.sonicpool.com**
(ADR, Digital Sound Editing, Dubbing, Foley, Mixing & Sound FX Library)

Sony Pictures Studios (310) 244-5722
10202 W. Washington Blvd. FAX **(310) 244-2303**
Culver City, CA 90232 **www.sonypicturesstudios.com**
Contact: Richard Branca

The Sound Shop, Inc. (310) 479-7049
1315½ Westwood Blvd. FAX **(310) 734-6900**
Los Angeles, CA 90024 **www.postsoundshop.com**
(ADR, Digital Sound Editing, Dubbing, Mixing, Music and Sound FX Library, Synching & Transfers)

Soundelux (323) 603-3200
7080 Hollywood Blvd., Ste. 1100 FAX **(323) 603-3233**
Hollywood, CA 90028 **www.soundelux.com**
(ADR, Digital Sound Editing, Dubbing, Foley, Laybacks, Mixing, Music/Sound FX Library, Restoration, Sound Design, Sound Editing, Sound FX Editing, Sound FX Library, Synching & Transfers)
Contacts: Jeffrey Eisner & Becky Sullivan

Soundmine (818) 767-4226
8457 Petaluma Dr. **www.soundmine.com**
Sun Valley, CA 91352

Soundscape Productions (818) 456-1052
7543 Loma Verde Ave. FAX **(818) 456-1046**
Canoga Park, CA 91303 **www.soundscapepost.com**
(5.1 Surround, AC3/dts Encoding [LB Labs], ADR, Audio Laybacks, Dialogue Cleanup/Advanced NR [LB Labs], Digital Sound Editing, Dubbing, Mixing, Mobile Facilities, Remote Sessions, Restoration, Sound Design, Sound FX Library, Transfers, Transmission Services & Voice Over Services)
Contact: Gregg Hall

SSI/Advanced Post Services (323) 874-9344
(818) 986-3255
7155 Santa Monica Blvd. FAX **(323) 850-7189**
Los Angeles, CA 90046 **www.ssipost.com**
(ADR, Audio Laybacks, Digital Sound Editing, Dubbing, Foley, Mixing, Sound FX Library, Synching, Transfers & Transmission Services)
Contact: Stuart Bartell

Stampede Post Productions (323) 463-8000
931 N. Citrus Ave. FAX **(323) 463-8010**
Hollywood, CA 91104 **www.stampedepost.com**
(ADR, Dubbing & MIxing)

Station 22 Edit & Effects (310) 488-7726
3614 Overland Ave. **www.station22.com**
Los Angeles, CA 90034

Ⓐ **Stewart Sound** (714) 973-3030
204 N. Broadway, Ste. N FAX **(714) 973-2530**
Santa Ana, CA 92701 **www.stewartsound.com**
(5.1 Surround, ADR, Audio Laybacks, Audio Laybacks to High Def, Audio Restoration Services, Digital Sound Editing, Dolby Surround, Domestic and Foreign Dubbing, Foley, ISDN, Laybacks, Mastering, Mixing, Music, Music Composition, Music FX Library, Remote Sessions, Restoration, Sound Design, Sound Editing, Sound FX Editing, Sound FX Library, Synching, THX Certified 5.1 Mixing, Transfers & Voice Over Services)

STS Foreign Language Services/
a division of STS Media Services, Inc. (818) 563-3004
P.O. Box 10213 **www.stsforeignlanguage.com**
Burbank, CA 91510
(5.1 Surround, ADR, Audio Laybacks, Digital Sound Editing, Dolby Surround, Dubbing, Foley, Mixing, Foreign Dubbing, Scoring/Sound Stage, Sound FX Library, Synching, Transfers & Voice Over Services)

Studio City Sound (818) 505-9368
4412 Whitsett Ave. FAX **(818) 761-4744**
Studio City, CA 91604 **www.studiocitysound.com**
(ADR, Audio Laybacks, Audio Restoration Services, Digital Sound Editing, Dolby Surround, Dubbing, ISDN, Foley, Foreign and Domestic Dubbing, Laybacks, Mastering, Mixing, Mobile Facilities, Music, Music Composition, Music/Sound FX Library, Pre-Dubbing, Remote Sessions, Restoration, Scoring Stage, Scoring/Sound Stage, Sound Design, Sound Editing, Sound FX Library, Synching, Transfers & Voice Over Services)

Studiopolis (818) 753-2680
11700 Ventura Blvd. FAX **(818) 753-7830**
Studio City, CA 91604 **www.studiopolisinc.com**
(ADR, Audio/Video Editing, Dialogue Record, Dubbing, Foley, ISDN, Laybacks, Mixing, Music/Sound FX Library, Remote Sessions, Sound Editing, Synching & Transfers)
Contacts: Laura Lopez & Jamie Simone

Sunwave Audio (310) 815-9375
10800 Rose Ave., Ste. 23 **home.netcom.com/~sunwave**
Los Angeles, CA 90034
(Digital Sound Editing, Mixing & Sound FX Library)

The Surround Factory (818) 760-3600
(818) 620-3030
FAX **(818) 578-8767**
www.surroundfactory.com
(5.1 Surround, ADR, Audio Laybacks, Digital Editing, Dolby Surround, Domestic and Foreign Dubbing, Foley, ISDN, Laybacks, Mastering, Mixing, Music, Music Composition, Music FX Library, Pre-Dubbing, Restoration, Sound Design, Sound Editing, Sound FX Editing, Sound FX Library, Synching & Voice Over Services)

Switch Studios (310) 301-1800
316 S. Venice Blvd. FAX **(310) 496-1964**
Venice, CA 90291 **www.switch-studios.com**
(5.1 Surround, ADR, Audio Laybacks to High Def, Dolby Surround, Laybacks, Mixing, Sound Design, Sound Editing, Sound FX Editing, Sound FX Library & Voice Over Services)

Technicolor Creative Services - Glendale (818) 500-9090
1631 Gardena Ave. FAX **(818) 500-4099**
Glendale, CA 91204 **www.technicolor.com**
(Audio Restoration Services)
Contact: Jim Feeney

Technicolor Creative Services - Hollywood (323) 860-7600
(323) 860-7816
1438 N. Gower St., Box 50, Bldg. 48 FAX **(323) 860-7801**
Hollywood, CA 90028 **www.technicolor.com**
(ADR, Foley, Laybacks, Mixing, Sound Editing, Synching & Transfers)
Contact: Mark Kaplan

Damon A. Tedesco/ Mobile Disc Music Inc. (310) 670-6155
8726 S. Sepulveda Blvd. **www.scoringmixer.com**
Los Angeles, CA 90045
(Digital Sound Editing, Mixing, Mobile Facilities & Scoring Stage)

Terra Vista Media, Inc. (562) 437-0393
216 The Promenade, Ste. 206 FAX **(562) 437-0395**
Long Beach, CA 90802 **www.terravistamedia.com**
(Audio Laybacks, Audio Laybacks to High Def, Audio Restoration Services, Digital Sound Editing, Foreign and Domestic Dubbing, ISDN, Laybacks, Mastering, Mixing, Music, Music/Sound FX Library, Restoration, Sound Design, Sound Editing, Synching, Transfers & Voice Over Services)

Threshold Sound + Vision (310) 571-0500
2114 Pico Blvd. FAX **(310) 571-0505**
Santa Monica, CA 90405 **www.thresholdsound.com**
(Mixing & Sound Design)

Thunder Recording + Sound Design (310) 829-4765
3211 Olympic Blvd. FAX **(310) 315-6399**
Santa Monica, CA 90404 **www.thunder-sound.com**
(5.1 Surround, ADR, Audio Laybacks, Digital Sound Editing, ISDN, Mixing, Sound Design, Sound FX Library, Transfers, Transmission Services & Voice Over Services)

Todd-AO Burbank (818) 295-5300
2901 W. Alameda Ave., Second Fl. **www.toddao.com**
Burbank, CA 91505
(5.1 Surround, ADR, Audio Laybacks, Dubbing, Mixing, Pre-Dubbing, Sound Design, Sound Editing, Sound FX Editing, Sound FX Library, Synching, Transfers & Voice Over Services)
Contact: Steve Bartkowicz

Todd-AO Hollywood (323) 962-4000
900 N. Seward FAX **(323) 466-2327**
Hollywood, CA 90038 **www.toddao.com**
(5.1 Surround, ADR, Audio Laybacks, Digital Editing, Dubbing, ISDN, Laybacks, Mixing, Pre-Dubbing, Sound Design, Sound Editing & Transfers)
Contact: Richard Burnette

Todd-AO West (310) 315-5000
3000 Olympic Blvd., Bldg. 1 FAX **(310) 315-5099**
Santa Monica, CA 90404 **www.toddao.com**
(5.1 Surround, ADR, Dubbing & Foley)
Contact: Matt Dubin

Tree Falls Post (323) 851-0299
3131 Cahuenga Blvd. West FAX **(323) 851-0277**
Los Angeles, CA 90068 **www.tfpost.com**
(5.1 Surround, ADR, Audio Laybacks, Audio Laybacks to High Def, Digital Editing, Dolby Surround, Dubbing, ISDN, Laybacks, Mixing, Pre-Dubbing, Sound Design, Sound Editing, Sound FX Library, Synching, Transfers, Transmission Services & Voice Over Services)

Union Editorial (310) 481-2200
12200 W. Olympic Blvd., Ste. 140 FAX **(310) 481-2248**
Los Angeles, CA 90064 **www.unioneditorial.com**
(ADR, Dolby Surround, Laybacks, Mixing, Music/Sound FX Library, Remote Sessions & Sound Editing)
Contact: Dona Richardson

Ⓐ **Universal Studios Sound** (818) 777-0169
(800) 892-1979
100 Universal City Plaza FAX **(818) 866-1494**
Universal City, CA 91608 **www.filmmakersdestination.com**
(ADR, Audio Layback, Audio Restoration and Preservation, Digital and Analog Archiving, Digital Mastering, Foley, Mix Stages, Mixing, Sound Design and Editing & Sound Transfers)
Contacts: Chris Jenkins & Steve Williams

Unreal Audio (818) 840-0304
1150 W. Olive Ave. FAX **(818) 840-0394**
Burbank, CA 91506 **www.unrealaudio.net**
(ADR, Dubbing, Foley, Laybacks, Mixing, Music/Sound FX Library, Sound Editing, Synching & Transfers)

The Village Recorder (310) 478-8227
1616 Butler Ave. FAX **(310) 479-1142**
Los Angeles, CA 90025 **www.villagestudios.com**
(ADR & Mixing)
Contact: Darren Frank

Virtual Hoedown (323) 254-4883
(ADR, Mixing & Sound Editing) FAX **(866) 433-6158**
www.virtualhoedown.com

Virtual Mix (818) 209-6176
www.virtualmix.com
(ADR, Digital Editing, Dolby Surround, Domestic Dubbing, Dubbing, Foley, Foreign Dubbing, Mixing, Pre-Dubbing, Restoration, Sound Design, Sound Editing, Sound FX Editing, Sound Stage, Synching, THX Certified 5.1 Mixing & Transfers)

Vitello Productions (818) 955-9930
1150 W. Olive Ave. FAX **(818) 955-9926**
Burbank, CA 91506 **www.vitello.com**
(ADR, Foley, Mixing & Sound Editing)
Contact: Paul Vitello

Walt Disney Studios (818) 560-2731
500 S. Buena Vista St. FAX **(818) 562-3262**
Burbank, CA 91521 **www.buenavistapost.com**

Warner Bros. Studio Facilities - Post Production Services (818) 954-1625
(818) 954-2515
4000 Warner Blvd. FAX **(818) 954-4138**
Burbank, CA 91522 **www.wbpostproduction.com**
(ADR, Digital Sound Editing, Dubbing, Foley, Mixing, Sound FX Library, Synching & Transfers)

Warrenwood Sound Studios (818) 563-1263
3825 W. Burbank Blvd. FAX **(818) 526-8963**
Burbank, CA 91505 **www.warrenwood.com**
(ADR, Dolby Surround, Foley, Laybacks, Mixing, Re-Recording Stage, Sound Editing & Sound FX Library)

Widget Post Production (310) 558-3941
2700 S. La Cienega Blvd. FAX **(310) 558-3951**
Los Angeles, CA 90034 **www.widgetpost.com**
(ADR, Digital Sound Editing, Dolby Surround, Foley, ISDN, Laybacks, Mixing, Restoration, Sound FX Library & Transfers)
Contacts: Anne Slack & Ray Vecchiola

Widget Post Production (323) 850-2500
c/o The Lot, 1041 N. Formosa Ave. **www.widgetpost.com**
Los Angeles, CA 90046
(ADR, Digital Sound Editing, Dolby Surround, Foley, ISDN, Laybacks, Mixing, Restoration, Sound FX Library & Transfers)

Wildfire Studios (323) 951-1700
640 S. San Vicente Blvd. **www.wildfirepost.com**
Los Angeles, CA 90048
(ADR & Foley)

William Sound Service (323) 461-5321
1343 N. Highland Ave.
Hollywood, CA 90028
(ADR, Audio Laybacks, Digital Sound Editing, Dubbing, Foley, Mixing, Sound FX Library, Synching & Transfers)
Contact: William Wang

Zach Seivers Sound Services (818) 749-1776
4640 Lankershim Blvd., Ste. 400 **www.zseivers.com**
North Hollywood, CA 91602

30 Second Films (310) 315-1750
3019 Pico Blvd. FAX (310) 315-1757
Santa Monica, CA 90405 www.30secondfilms.com
(Non-Linear Offline and Online)
Contact: Alan J. Stamm

47 Pictures (323) 464-2406
6525 Sunset Blvd., Penthouse FAX (323) 464-2426
Hollywood, CA 90028 www.47pictures.com
(Computer Animation, Computer Graphics, Film Editing, Non-Linear Offline, Post Production Supervision & Sound Design)

5th Wall Entertainment (323) 461-0600
6311 Romaine St., Ste. 7135 www.5thwall.tv
Hollywood, CA 90038
Editor: Michael Garber

60Hz, Inc. (310) 264-8498
1660 Stanford St. FAX (310) 264-8497
Santa Monica, CA 90404 www.60-hz.com
Editor: Oliver Power

Aaron & Le Duc (310) 452-2034
2210 Third St., Ste. 316 www.leducdesign.com
Santa Monica, CA 90405
(Digital Online & Linear/Non-Linear Offline)
Editors: Bruce Abrams, Arlan Boll & Greg Le Duc

Address One (310) 838-7783
(323) 465-4415
c/o Raleigh Studios FAX (323) 960-4961
662 N. Van Ness Ave., Ste. 301 www.addressone.tv
Los Angeles, CA 90004
(Computer Animation & Non-Linear Offline and Online)
Contact: Tess Thompson

Aftershock Digital (323) 658-5700
8222 Melrose Ave., Ste. 304 FAX (323) 658-5200
Los Angeles, CA 90046 www.editkings.com
(Non-Linear Offline and Online)
Editors: Fritz Feick & Scott Tetti

All In One Productions (323) 780-8880
1111 Corporate Dr. FAX (323) 780-8887
Monterey Park, CA 91754 www.allinone-usa.com
(Non-Linear Offline and Online)
Post Production Supervisor: Joanna Or

The Alliance Group (310) 338-0580
(310) 490-1436
5250 W. Century Blvd., Ste. 432 FAX (310) 337-1181
Los Angeles, CA 90045 www.alliancegroupllc.com
Editor: Mike Goodman

Alternate Reality Entertainment (818) 742-7208
5701 Cantaloupe Ave. FAX (818) 782-0826
Sherman Oaks, CA 91401 www.alternatereality.tv
(Computer Animation, Computer Graphics, Digital Offline, Digital Online, DVD Authoring, HD Editing, Non-Linear Offline, Non-Linear Online & Sound Design)
President: Michael Marconi

American Video Group (310) 477-1535
2542 Aiken Ave. www.americanvideogroup.com
Los Angeles, CA 90064
(Digital Non-Linear Offline and Online)
Executive Producer: John Berzner

Atomic Post (310) 315-7245
3025 W. Olympic Blvd., Ste. 128 www.atomicpost.us
Santa Monica, CA 90404
(Non-Linear Offline and Online)
Editor: Paul Belanger

Beam Universal (213) 908-5106
1338 McCollum St. www.beamuniversal.com
Los Angeles, CA 90026
(Non-Linear Offline & Post-Production Supervision)
Executive Producers/Editors: Bella Erikson & Stuart Robertson

Beast (310) 576-6300
1222 Sixth St. FAX (310) 576-6305
Santa Monica, CA 90401 www.beast.tv
(Digital Offline, HD Editing, Linear Offline, Non-Linear Offline & Post Production Supervision)
Executive Producer: Valerie Petrusson
Producers: Amburr Farls & Ann Martini
Editors: Rebecca Beluk, David Blackburn, Tim Brooks, Gordon Carey, Chris Chynoweth, Jonathan Del Gatto, John Dingfield, Michael Elliot, Lucas Eskin, Tim Fender, Kevin Garcia, Paul Kelly, Igor Kovalik, Brian Lagerhausen, Charlie Lee, Connor McDonald, Amanda Moreau, Paul Norling, Livio Sanchez, Adam Schwartz, Sam Selis, Stewart Shevin, Richard Smith, Adam Svatek, Derek Swanson, Val Thasher, Jim Ulbrich, Angelo Valencia, Doug Walker & Rob Watzke

Blissium (310) 453-7070
1630 Stewart St., Ste. B1 FAX (310) 260-6111
Santa Monica, CA 90404 www.blissium.com
(Compositing, Computer Animation, Computer Graphics, Digital, Digital Offline, Digital Online, DVD Authoring, HD Editing, Non-Linear Offline, Non-Linear Online & Visual FX)

Burbank Post (818) 953-8919
3619 W. Magnolia Blvd. www.burbankpost.tv
Burbank, CA 91505
(Non-Linear Offline and Online)
Executive Producer/Editor: Jim Settlemoir

BUTCHER editorial (310) 829-9333
1631 21st St. FAX (310) 829-5157
Santa Monica, CA 90404 www.butcheredit.com
Executive Producer: Rob Van
Producer: Chrissy Hamilton
Editors: Megan Bee, Jack Douglas, Dave Henegar & Mark Rees

Cake (310) 264-5551
1545 26th St., Ste. 300 FAX (310) 264-5552
Santa Monica, CA 90404 www.cakeshop.tv
(Compositing, Computer Graphics, Digital Linear/Non-Linear Offline and Online, HD Editing, Linear Offline and Online, Non-Linear Offline, Post Production Supervision & Visual FX)
President/Executive Producer: Tatiana Derovanessian
Producer: Patty Gaskey
Editors: Jarred Buck, Rick Lobo, Bob Mori, Jay Rogers & Mark Sanders
Visual Effects Artist/Designers: Josh Kirschenbaum & Brian Dickett

Chainsaw (323) 785-1550
940 N. Orange Dr., 2nd Fl. FAX (323) 785-1555
Hollywood, CA 90038 www.chainsawedit.com
(Analog, Compositing, Digital, Digital Offline and Online, Duplication, DVD Authoring, HD Editing, Non-Linear Offline and Online, Post Production Supervision & Standards Conversions)

chrome (310) 264-9700
2044 Broadway FAX (310) 264-9701
Santa Monica, CA 90404 www.chrome.tv
Executive Producer: Deanne Mehling
Editors: Hal Honigsberg, Adam Parker & Lance Pereira

Cosmo Street (310) 828-6666
2036 Broadway FAX (310) 453-9699
Santa Monica, CA 90404 www.cosmostreet.com
(Non-Linear Offline)
Executive Producer: Yvette Cobarrubias
Editors: Tessa Davis, Christjan Jordan, Katz, Ben Longland & Steve Prestemon

Cut + Run (310) 450-1116
1635 12th St. FAX (310) 450-1166
Santa Monica, CA 90404 www.cutandrun.tv
(Non-Linear Offline and Online)
Producers: Ashley Carrier, Chris Girard & Carr Schilling
Editors: David Checel, Marc D'Andre, Frank Effron, Steve Gandolfi, Jeff Grippe, Jay Nelson & Dan Swietlik
Managing Director/Executive Producer: Michelle Burke

Cutters Editorial (310) 309-3780
2110 Main St., Ste. 207 FAX (310) 309-3779
Santa Monica, CA 90405 **www.cutters.com**
(HD Editing & Non-Linear Offline)
Executive Producer: Nicole Visram
Los Angeles Editors: Christine Brown, Addison James, Nadav Kurtz, Rick Lobo, Ryan McGuire, Lenny Mesina & Richard Mettler
Sales Rep: Whitney Warren

DaveOneal.com (818) 640-2941
www.daveoneal.com
(Compositing, Computer Graphics, Digital Offline, Duplication, DVD Authoring, Linear Offline and Online & Visual FX)
Editor: Dave Oneal

The Edit Bay (714) 978-7878
571 N. Poplar St., Ste. I FAX (714) 978-7858
Orange, CA 92868 **www.theeditbay.com**

Editropolis, Inc. (818) 730-4905
24374 Welby Way **www.editropolis.com**
West Hills, CA 91307
(Non-Linear Offline and Online)
Contact: Joseph Conarkov
Editors: Joseph Conarkov & Rob Meltzer

Fortitude Editorial, Inc (323) 337-1175
940 N. Orange Dr., Ste. 150 FAX (323) 337-1439
Los Angeles, CA 90038 **www.fortitudeeditorial.com**
(Compositing, Computer Graphics, Digital, Digital Offline and Online, Duplication, Film Editing, HD Editing, Linear/Non-Linear Offline and Online, Post Production Supervision & Visual FX)

Foundation (424) 238-0381
1669 19th St. **www.foundationcontent.com**
Santa Monica, CA 90404
(Linear Online, Non-Linear Offline and Online & Post Production Supervision)
Owner/Editor: James Lipetzky
Executive Producer: Samantha Hart

A Gosch Production (818) 729-0000
2227 W. Olive Ave. **www.goschproductions.com**
Burbank, CA 91506
(Non-Linear Offline and Online)
Contact: Pat Gosch
Executive Producer: Rob Gosch
Directors/Editors: Cindia Perez & Jimmie Rhee
Producer: Barbara Peeters

Hyena Editorial, Inc. (310) 394-1048
725 Arizona Ave., Ste. 100 FAX (310) 395-5868
Santa Monica, CA 90401
Executive Producer: Kim Sprouse Higgins
Editors: Jamie Proctor, Kiran Rouzie & Keith Salmon

an ideal world (714) 953-9501
209 N. Bush St. FAX (714) 953-1195
Santa Ana, CA 92701 **www.anidealworld.com**
(Compositing, Computer Animation, Computer Graphics, Digital Offline, Digital Online, HD Editing, Non-Linear Offline, Non-Linear Online, Post Production Supervision & Visual FX)

Ignition Post (818) 762-2210
11108 Riverside Dr. **www.ignition-post.com**
Toluca Lake, CA 91602

JM Digital Works (760) 476-1783
2460 Impala Dr. FAX (760) 476-1788
Carlsbad, CA 92008 **www.jmdigitalworks.com**
(Digital Offline and Online)
Contact: Ken Kebow
Editor: Dave Graack

JR Post (818) 557-0200
2501 W. Burbank Blvd., Ste. 311 FAX (818) 557-0201
Burbank, CA 91505 **www.jrmediaservices.com**
(Negative Cutting & Non-Linear Offline)
Post Supervisor: Robert Troy

King Cut (310) 399-2040
1656 Abbot Kinney Blvd. FAX (310) 399-2134
Venice, CA 90291 **www.kingcut.com**
(Computer Graphics & Non-Linear Offline and Online)
Executive Producer: James Taylor
Editors: Enrique Aguirre, Tim Anderson, Johnny Bachelier, Kelly McClean & Aaron Neitz
Visual FX Artist: Philip Ineno

Lost Planet Editorial, Inc. (310) 396-7272
2515 Main St. FAX (310) 450-8696
Santa Monica, CA 90405 **www.lostplanet.com**
(Digital Online, Film Editing, HD Editing, Offline, Post Production Supervision & Sound Design)
Editors: Hank Corwin, Jennifer Dean, Bruce Herrman, Saar Klein, Paul Snyder & Jaime Valdueza

Lux Edit (310) 399-5959
(415) 393-9435
2403 Main St. FAX (310) 399-0012
Santa Monica, CA 90405 **www.luxedit.com**
(Compositing, Computer Animation & Digital Non-Linear Offline and Online)
Executive Producer: Tatianna Derovanessian
Editors: David Burghardt, Bob Gingg, Tracy Hof, Rick Lobo, Luis Ruiz, Nick Senser, Peter Tartar & Doug Werby
Creative Director: Scott Williams
Visual FX Artist: Josh Kirschenbaum

Migrant Editors (310) 345-1301
Editor: Nate Hubbard FAX (310) 545-2744
www.migranteditors.com

Miller Wishengrad Post/MWP (310) 587-3300
1335 Fourth St., Ste. 400 FAX (310) 587-3387
Santa Monica, CA 90401 **www.mwpost.com**
(Compositing, Computer Graphics, Film Editing, HD Editing, Non-Linear Offline and Online & Sound Design)
Executive Producer: Gary Le Vine
Editors: Sean Leute, Mike Miller & Jeff Wishengrad
Graphics: Josh Oram

Mind Over Eye, LLC (310) 396-4663
(310) 968-4259
1639 11th St., Ste. 117 FAX (310) 396-0663
Santa Monica, CA 90404 **www.mindovereye.com**
(HD and SD Offline and Online & Standards Conversions)

Minerva Media Group, LLC (310) 647-5604
(310) 642-5659
840 Apollo St., Ste. 324 FAX (310) 642-5605
El Segundo, CA 90245 **www.minervamg.com**
(Analog, Digital, Digital Offline, DVD Authoring, Non-Linear Offline, Non-Linear Online & Post Production Supervision)

Module Zero Media (310) 306-2600
(310) 621-5622
12804 Washington Blvd. FAX (310) 306-2661
Los Angeles, CA 90066 **www.modulezeromedia.com**
(Computer Graphics & Non-Linear Offline)
Contact: Maggie Zulovic

Nitestar Productions (323) 468-8089
6671 Sunset Blvd., Bldg. 1509, Ste. 104 FAX (323) 468-8094
Los Angeles, CA 90028 **www.nitestar.com/avid/**

Nomad Editing Company (310) 828-4999
1661 19th St. FAX (310) 828-3950
Santa Monica, CA 90404 **www.nomadedit.com**
(Non-Linear Offline)
Contact: Susye Idema

Oasis Editorial (310) 458-9661
725 Arizona Ave., Ste. 102 FAX (310) 458-7828
Santa Monica, CA 90401 **www.oasiseditorial.com**
(Film Editing & Linear/Non-Linear Offline)
Executive Producer: Nano Galloway
Editor: Brendan O'Carroll

Optimus (310) 917-2761
1237 Seventh St. FAX (310) 917-2762
Santa Monica, CA 90401 **www.optimus.com**
(Non-Linear Offline)
Executive Producer: Therese Hunsberger
Editors: Justin Amore, Grant MacDowell & Jim Staskauskas

Oracle Post (310) 449-5550
3232 Nebraska Ave. FAX (310) 449-5554
Santa Monica, CA 90404 **www.oraclepost.com**
(Digital Non-Linear Offline and Online)
Executive Producer: James Lifton
CEO/Post Supervisor: Paulette Lifton

Oracle Post (818) 752-2800
4720 W. Magnolia Blvd. FAX (818) 769-2624
Burbank, CA 91505 www.oraclepost.com
(Digital Non-Linear Offline and Online)
Executive Producer: James Lifton
CEO/Post Supervisor: Paulette Lifton

Pistolera Post (310) 451-9499
530 Wilshire Blvd., Ste. 308 FAX (310) 451-7416
Santa Monica, CA 90401 www.pistolerapost.com
(Analog, Compositing, Computer Graphics, Digital, Digital Online and Offline, Non-Linear Online and Offline, Post Production Supervision, Standards Conversions & Visual FX)

PlasterCITY Digital Post Facility (323) 469-9800
6500 Sunset Blvd. FAX (323) 462-4620
Los Angeles, CA 90028 www.plastercitypost.com
(Digital Offline and Online, HD Editing, Linear Online, Linear/Non-Linear Offline & Post Supervision)

Play Editorial, Inc. (323) 469-3500
6464 Sunset Blvd., Ste. 600 FAX (323) 469-3511
Hollywood, CA 90028 www.playeditorial.com
(Compositing, Digital Offline and Online, Film Editing, Non-Linear Offline and Online, Post Production Supervision & Visual FX)

Playroom Creative (714) 969-3938
412 Indianapolis Ave. www.playroomcreative.com
Huntington Beach, CA 92648

Point360 (310) 481-7000
12421 W. Olympic Blvd. www.point360.com
Los Angeles, CA 90064
(Compositing, Computer Animation, HD Editing, Non-Linear Offline, Non-Linear Online, Post Production Supervision, Sound Design & Visual FX)

Post Factory (714) 705-6099
(877) 411-4446
630 The City Dr., Ste. 100 FAX (714) 705-6090
Orange, CA 92868 www.postfactory.com
(Compositing, Computer Animation, Computer Graphics, Digital, Digital Offline, Digital Online, Duplication, DVD Authoring, Film Editing, HD Editing, Non-Linear Offline, Non-Linear Online, Post Production Supervision, Sound Design, Standards Conversions & Visual FX)
Avid/FCP/Smoke/Editor & Colorist: Chris Gendrin
Executive Producer: Jeremy Kientz

Post Modern (626) 584-4050
39 E. Walnut St. FAX (626) 584-4099
Pasadena, CA 91103 www.postmodernedits.com
Executive Producer: Steve Miles

Post Modern Creative, LLC (949) 608-8700
2941 Alton Pkwy FAX (949) 608-8729
Irvine, CA 92606 www.postmoderncreative.com
(Analog, Compositing, Computer Graphics, Digital, Duplication, DVD Authoring, HD Editing, Linear Online, Non-Linear Offline and Online, Post Production Supervision, Sound Design, Standards Conversions & Visual FX)
SVP Operations & Director of Creative Services: Mike Pearce
Editors: Jim Hancock, Chris Lovett, Marcelo Nonaca, Sergio Palermo, Jim Reed, Mary Riggin & Derek Seelig
Producer: Rich O'Neill
Executive Producer: Michael Boyd

Precision Productions + Post (310) 839-4600
10718 McCune Ave. FAX (310) 839-4601
Los Angeles, CA 90034 www.precisionpost.com
(Non-Linear Offline and Online)
Executive Producer: Joseph Arnao

Razor Edits (310) 968-1172
2996 Hyperion Ave. www.razoredits.com
Los Angeles, CA 90026
(Non-Linear Offline)
Executive Producer: Woody Pobiega
Editor: David Frame

The Reel Thing, Inc. (310) 828-9555
2425 Colorado Ave., Ste. 100 FAX (310) 828-9544
Santa Monica, CA 90404 www.thereelthinginc.com
(HD Editing & Non-Linear Offline and Online)
Executive Producer: & Doug Klekner
Editors: Sally Banta Todd Betts &
Smoke Artist: Mutalib Glasgow

ReX Edit (310) 314-8110
221 Rose Ave. FAX (310) 314-8115
Venice, CA 90291 www.rexedit.com
(Non-Linear Offline)
Executive Producer: Bill Fortney
Producer: Chanel Boyd
Editors: Kevin Anderson, Paul Bertino, Adriana Legay, Bill Marmor, Igor Patalas & Drew Thompson
Director of Marketing & Sales: Jeanie DiMaggio

Rock Paper Scissors (310) 586-0600
2308 Broadway FAX (310) 586-0601
Santa Monica, CA 90404 www.rockpaperscissors.com
(Linear/Non-Linear Offline)
CEO/Owner: Linda Carlson
Executive Producer: Carol Lynn Weaver
Editors: Kirk Baxter, David Brodie, Terence "Biff" Butler, Damion Clayton, Adam Pertofsky & Angus Wall

Roush Media (818) 559-8648
84 E. Santa Anita Ave. www.roush-media.com
Burbank, CA 91502
(Computer Graphics, Digital Non-Linear Offline and Online & Duplication)
Contact: Keith Roush

Rye (213) 361-1391
10523 Kling St. FAX (818) 760-7855
Toluca Lake, CA 91602 www.ryefilms.com
(Computer Graphics & Non-Linear Offline)
Editor: Rye Dahlman

S2 Editorial (310) 202-6668
13114 W. Washington Blvd. FAX (310) 202-6662
Culver City, CA 90066 www.adeditor.com
Editors: Michael Alberts & Steve Swersky

Shelter Post (949) 809-2150
18500 Von Karman Ave., Ste. 140 FAX (949) 809-2152
Irvine, CA 92612 www.shelterpost.com

Special Blend (310) 909-7338
13020 Pacific Promenade, Ste. 107 FAX (310) 909-7343
Playa Vista, CA 90094 www.specialblend.tv

Spot Welders, Inc. (310) 399-3350
825 Hampton Dr. FAX (310) 399-1228
Venice, CA 90291 www.spotwelders.com
(Non-Linear)
CEO: David Glean
Editors: Catherine Bull, Tanis Darling, Robert Duffy, Dick Gordon, Haines Hall, Dahkil Hausif, Michael Heldman, Dan Maloney, Pam Martin, Lucas Spaulding, Jon Stefansson & Brad Waskewich

Standard (323) 224-3944
2020 N. Main St., Ste. 227 FAX (323) 225-6226
Los Angeles, CA 90031 www.standardsite.com
(Computer Graphics & Non-Linear Offline and Online)

Sunset Edit (323) 467-8550
(818) 679-4014
849 N. Seward St. FAX (323) 467-8545
Los Angeles, CA 90038 www.sunsetedit.com
(Audio, HD Editing, Offline, Online & Visual FX)
Editors: David Baum, David Blackburn, Ed Cardenas, Farah, Kevin Filippini, Dean Gonzalez, Lenny, Ken Mowe, Steve Rees & Chris Wright
VFX: Howard Shur

TEDS (310) 237-6438
www.tedsla.com
(Compositing, DVD Authoring, Non-Linear Offline and Online, Post Production Supervision, Sound Design, Standards Conversions, Telecine & Visual FX)

Tonawanda Pictures, Inc. (323) 525-0151
8075 W. Third St., Ste. 406 FAX (323) 395-5574
Los Angeles, CA 90048
(Computer Graphics & Non-Linear Offline)

Undertow Productions (310) 497-8020
(DVD Authoring & Non-Linear Offline and Online)
Contact: Dave Poncia

Union Editorial (310) 481-2200
12200 W. Olympic Blvd., Ste. 140 FAX **(310) 481-2248**
Los Angeles, CA 90064 **www.unioneditorial.com**
(Non-Linear Offline and Online)
President/Executive Producer: Michael Raimondi
President of Entertainment: Jijo Reed
Vice President/Snr. Producer: Megan Dahlman
Editors: Nico Alba, Einar, Jay Friedkin, Nicholas Wayman Harris, Nick Lofting & Scott Trembley

Venice Beach Editorial (310) 305-5777
5353 Grosvenor St. FAX **(310) 305-4892**
Los Angeles, CA 90066 **www.venicebeacheditorial.com**
(Linear/Non-Linear Offline)
Executive Producer: Hunter Conner
Producer: Cristy Pacheco
Editors: Dan Bootzin, Bill Chessman, Billy Sacdalan, Rick Shambaugh, Peter Smith, Ethan Wells & Greg Young

Via Verde Productions & Post (310) 358-7685
23852 Pacific Coast Hwy, Ste. 480 FAX **(419) 735-9520**
Malibu, CA 90265 **www.viaverdedigital.com**
(Non-Linear Offline & Post Supervision)
Executive Producer: Mari Ciravolo

Victory Studios LA (818) 769-1776
10911 Riverside Dr., Ste. 100 FAX **(818) 760-1280**
North Hollywood, CA 91602 **www.victorystudiosla.com**
(Digital Offline, Digital Online, HD Editing, Non-Linear Offline, Non-Linear Online & Sound Design)

Visual Concepts (619) 291-2403
FAX **(619) 291-2475**
www.visualconcepts.tv
(Compositing, Computer Graphics, Digital, Digital Offline and Online, DVD Authoring, HD Editing, Non-Linear Offline and Online & Post Production Supervision)
Director of Photography: Mark Nelson
Post-Production Manager: Leslie Nelson

Vivus Media (213) 989-6884
www.vivusmedia.com
Executive Producers: Adam Fox & Wendy Shuey
Editor: Wendy Shuey

Waterline Pictures, Inc. (818) 901-1178
(310) 963-4812
P.O. Box 56387 FAX **(818) 901-1179**
Sherman Oaks, CA 91413
Editor: Roger Roth

Wheelhouse Editorial & Effects (310) 314-1950
www.wheelhouseedit.com
(Compositing, Computer Animation, Computer Graphics, Digital Offline and Online, HD Editing, Post Production Supervision & Sound Design)
Executive Producer: CJ Edwards

the Whitehouse (310) 319-9908
530 Wilshire Blvd., Ste. 400 FAX **(310) 319-9905**
Santa Monica, CA 90401 **www.whitehousepost.com**
Director of Post Production: Sue Dawson
Editors: Nick Allix, Heidi Black, Josh Bodnar, David Brixton, Ian Davies, Corky DeVault, Trish Fuller, Sam Gunn, Lisa Gunning, Grant Gustafson, Steve Hamilton, Russell Icke, Stephen Jess, Alaster Jordan, Meg Kubicka, Marc Langley, Rick Lawley, Carlos Lowenstein, Adam Marshall, Gareth McEwen, Crandall Miller, Dan Oberle, Steve Prestemon, Adam Robinson, John Smith, Ben Stephens, Christina Stumpf, Nikki Vapensky, Matt Walsh, Christophe Williams, Matthew Wood & Kevin Zimmerman
Represented Editors: Sven Budelmann, Paul Hardcastle, Jack Hutchings, Richard Learoyd, Filip Malasek, Colby Parker Jr., Alex Rodriguez & Greg Snider

Why Not Coco, Inc. (323) 798-4497
7959 Hollywood Blvd. FAX **(323) 798-4497**
Los Angeles, CA 90046 **www.whynotcoco.com**
(Computer Graphics, Digital Offline, Digital Online, Post Production Supervision & Sound Design)
Executive Producer: Angela Galletta
Editors: George Artope & Robert Levy

Wild Pictures (310) 526-7225
100 Market St., Third Fl. **www.wildpictures.com**
Venice, CA 90291
(Compositing, Computer Animation, Computer Graphics, Digital, Digital Offline, Digital Online, Duplication, DVD Authoring, Film Editing, HD Editing, Non-Linear Offline, Non-Linear Online, Post Production Supervision, Sound Design & Visual FX)

William Moffitt Associates (818) 495-3106
785 New York Dr. FAX **(626) 345-0673**
Altadena, CA 91001 **www.wmadigital.com**
(DVD Authoring, Computer Graphics, Digital Online, DVD Authoring, HD Editing & Non-Linear Editing)
Post Production Supervisor: Will Moffitt
Executive Producer: Lynne Moffitt

WinterWorks (310) 991-2464
20968 Waveview Dr.
Topanga, CA 90290
Executive Producer/Editor: Dave Winter
Editor: Jose Pedillo

WSR Creative (310) 391-9181
(310) 391-9182
12023 Venice Blvd., Ste. A FAX **(310) 391-9183**
Los Angeles, CA 90066 **www.wsrcreative.com**
Editors: Jose Delgado, Pablo Garrahan & John Rantz

740 Sound Design (310) 574-0740
12509 Beatrice St. FAX (310) 306-0744
Los Angeles, CA 90066 www.740sounddesign.com
(Dialogue Editor, Sound Designer, Sound Editor, Sound Effects Editor, Supervising Sound Editor & Voice Over Editor)

John Adair (310) 399-6900
www.emotomusic.com

Tori Amos (310) 572-4646
www.grooveaddicts.com

Michael Anastasi (310) 460-0123
www.stimmung.tv

The Angel (310) 285-0303
www.marshbest.com

Neil Argo (323) 854-2555
(818) 505-9600
www.neilargo.com

Craig Armstrong (310) 572-4646
www.grooveaddicts.com

David Arnold (310) 572-4646
www.grooveaddicts.com

Norman Arnold (310) 654-4060
www.amimusicgroup.com

Pam Aronoff (323) 960-9139
(Sound Designer & Voice Over Editor) www.moxymusic.net

Shane August (310) 651-6233
www.halfpipemusic.com

Laura B. (818) 505-8787
www.mixinpixls.com
(ADR Editor, Dialogue Editor, Sound Editor, Sound Effects Editors & Voice Over Editor)

Angelo Badalamenti (310) 572-4646
www.grooveaddicts.com

Klaus Badelt (310) 478-8227
www.primalscreammusic.com

Luis Balcov (310) 572-4646
www.grooveaddicts.com

Brian Banks (310) 581-1660
www.eartoear.com

John Barry (310) 572-4646
www.grooveaddicts.com

Steve Bartek (310) 572-4646
www.grooveaddicts.com

James Barth (818) 903-3680
www.jamesbarth.com
(Composer, Music Editor, Re-Recording Mixer, Sound Designer & Supervising Sound Editor)

Hugh Barton (310) 478-2120
FAX (310) 478-2130
www.bartonholt.com

Tyler Bates (310) 572-4646
www.grooveaddicts.com

Tom Batoy (323) 466-4696
www.monadavis.com

John Beal (818) 762-1640
www.composerjohnbeal.com

Michael Bearden (310) 285-0303
www.marshbest.com

Christophe Beck (310) 572-4646
www.grooveaddicts.com

Chris Bell (707) 363-1000

Michael Benghiat (661) 338-4749
www.themusickitchen.com

Scott Bennett (323) 857-7299
(323) 851-9623
www.blastmanagement.com

Joe Berardi (323) 222-1082
www.jhuck.com

Paul Bessenbacher (310) 399-6900
www.emotomusic.com

Garret Bever (818) 505-8787
(Sound Editor) www.kingklong.com

Dain Blair (310) 572-4646
www.grooveaddicts.com

Onnalee Blank (310) 210-6769
(310) 393-5340
www.fingermusic.tv
(Re-Recording Mixer, Sound Designer, Sound Effects Editor & Supervising Sound Editor)

David S. Blau (310) 410-1900
www.mesmerav.com

Blue Jay Productions/Bill Johnson (310) 306-7968
(Composer)

Bill Bodine (310) 459-6500
www.billbodinemusic.com

Rick Boston (323) 857-7299
(310) 393-5340
www.blastmanagement.com

Roddy Bottum (323) 222-1082
www.jhuck.com

Brad Breeck (323) 481-4581
www.audibleshift.com

Danny Brin (323) 655-2560

Jon Brion (310) 572-4646
www.grooveaddicts.com

Byron Brizuela (310) 572-4646
www.grooveaddicts.com

Bill Brown (323) 603-3203
www.soundeluxdmg.com

Benedikt Brydern (310) 451-8075
www.consordino.com

BT (310) 572-4646
www.grooveaddicts.com

Scott Burton (310) 478-8227
www.primalscreammusic.com
(Sound Designer & Supervising Sound Editor)

Cadesky/Dyer (323) 857-7299
www.blastmanagement.com

Dustin Camilleri (310) 392-8393
(Sound Designer) www.machinehead.com

Chris Campanaro (310) 581-6500
www.eliasarts.com

Al Capps (310) 572-4646
www.grooveaddicts.com

Marc Cashman (661) 222-9300
www.cashmancommercials.com

Teddy Castellucci (310) 572-4646
www.grooveaddicts.com

Sonia Castro (310) 392-9545
www.48windows.com

Stephen Thomas Cavit (310) 285-0303
www.marshbest.com

Michael Chandler (310) 392-9545
www.48windows.com

Francois Eudes Chanfrault (310) 652-8778
www.lspagency.net

Garron Chang (310) 392-0369
www.soundbath.com

Simon Changer (310) 285-0303
(Music Editor) www.marshbest.com

Brad Chiet (310) 640-3435
www.ifuelmusic.com

Meredith Chinn (310) 651-6233
www.halfpipemusic.com

Kim B. Christensen (310) 572-4646
www.grooveaddicts.com
(Sound Designer, Sound Editor, & Sound Effects Editor)

Stanley Clarke (310) 572-4646
www.grooveaddicts.com

George Clinton (310) 572-4646
www.grooveaddicts.com

Harry Cody (310) 572-4646
www.grooveaddicts.com

Contraband (323) 933-1614
5820 Wilshire Blvd., Ste. 306 www.contrabandusa.com
Los Angeles, CA 90036

Bruno Coon (323) 857-7299
(Composer & Music Editor) www.blastmanagement.com

Stewart Copeland (310) 572-4646
www.grooveaddicts.com

Julio Reyes Copello (310) 285-0303
www.marshbest.com

Chris Corner (310) 842-3891
www.musicfuzz.com

Bruno Coulais (310) 285-0303
www.marshbest.com

Michael Coulter (310) 393-7577
www.confidencehead.com

Hal Cragin (310) 568-3355
www.bluemusicla.com

Dan Crane (323) 222-1082
www.jhuck.com

Bobby Crew (858) 254-6779
(Sound Editor)

Lee Curreri (310) 410-1900
www.mesmerav.com

Raja Das (323) 481-4581
www.audibleshift.com

Don Davis (310) 572-4646
www.grooveaddicts.com

Steve Davis (310) 260-9838
www.themixsantamonica.com

John Debney (310) 572-4646
www.grooveaddicts.com

Reinhard Denke (310) 460-0123
www.stimmung.tv

Richard Devine (310) 393-5340
www.fingermusic.tv

Stephen Dewey (310) 392-8393
(Sound Designer) www.machinehead.com

Warren Dewey (310) 392-6392
(Sound Effects Editor)

Rich Dickerson (323) 856-3000
www.thegelleragency.com

James DiSalvio (310) 393-5340
www.fingermusic.tv

Ramin Djuadi (310) 478-8227
www.primalscreammusic.com

Gunnard Doboze (310) 285-0303
www.marshbest.com

Dom and Ant (310) 393-5340
www.fingermusic.tv

Rob Dougan (310) 572-4646
www.grooveaddicts.com

Nathan Dubin (310) 396-3333
www.lastudios.com
(Re-Recording Mixer & Supervising Sound Editor)

Ann Dudley (310) 572-4646
www.grooveaddicts.com

Larry Dunn (818) 990-8993
www.ambitiousent.com

Duran Duran (310) 842-3891
www.musicfuzz.com

The Dust Brothers (310) 572-4646
www.grooveaddicts.com

Josh Eichenbaum (310) 260-9838
(Sound Designer) www.themixsantamonica.com

Cliff Eidelman (310) 572-4646
www.grooveaddicts.com

Ryan Elder (310) 399-6900
www.emotomusic.com

Danny Elfman (310) 572-4646
www.grooveaddicts.com

Jeff Elmassian (310) 566-1463
www.endlessnoise.com

The Engine Room (310) 478-8227
www.primalscreammusic.com

Jim Ervin (800) 579-9157
www.laeg.net

Lucas Eskin (310) 410-1900
www.mesmerav.com

Charles Etienne (818) 399-6992
www.charlesetienne.com

Alan Ett (818) 508-3303
www.aemg.com

Lynn Fainchtein (310) 652-8778
(Music Supervisor) www.lspagency.net

Christopher Faizi (310) 651-6233
www.halfpipemusic.com

Gina Felicetta (818) 382-4792
www.garymyrick.com

Chad Fischer (310) 842-3891
www.musicfuzz.com

Joe Fischer (310) 285-0303
(Music Supervisor) www.marshbest.com

Mitchell Forman (310) 568-3355
www.bluemusicla.com

Carey Fosse (323) 222-1082
www.jhuck.com

Jill Fraser (818) 908-9083
www.jillfrasermusic.com

Mike Freedman (310) 597-3600
www.bigears.com

Eddie Freeman (562) 925-4514
www.icarusmusic.com

Freescha (310) 285-0303
www.marshbest.com

Christopher Garcia (310) 478-8227
www.primalscreammusic.com

Eric Garcia (310) 392-9545
www.48windows.com

Michelle Garuik (818) 565-5565
www.grindinc.com
(Re-Recording Mixer, Sound Designer, Sound Editor, & Sound Effects Editor)

Carlo Giacco (310) 285-0303
www.marshbest.com

Adam Giorgoni (310) 568-3355
www.bluemusicla.com

Sam Glaser (310) 204-6111
www.samglaser.com

Scott Glenn (310) 260-4949
www.humit.com

Nick Glenne-Smith (310) 572-4646
www.grooveaddicts.com

Godhead (310) 478-8227
www.primalscreammusic.com

Rich Goldman (310) 437-4380
(Music Supervisor) www.riptidemusic.com

Joel Goldsmith (310) 572-4646
www.grooveaddicts.com

Manoj Gopinath (818) 505-8787
www.kingklong.com

Brett Grant-Grierson (818) 606-5700
(Sound Editor) www.ears4hire.com

John Graves (818) 882-3300
(818) 882-1315
FAX (818) 886-1514
www.command-post.com/music
(Foley Artist, Re-Recording Mixer, Sound Designer, Sound Effects Editor & Supervising Sound Editor)

Robert Grieve (310) 788-3918
www.d-a-a.com
(ADR Editor, Sound Designer & Supervising Sound Editor)

Grizzly Bear (310) 652-8778
www.lspagency.net

Andrew Hagen (310) 828-5189
(Composer & Sound Designer) www.schtungmusic.com

Marlene Hajdu (818) 762-0635

Wes Hambright (818) 448-9262
www.orangedogmusic.com

Johannes Hammers (310) 392-8393
www.machinehead.com

Steve Hampton (310) 399-6900
www.emotomusic.com

Craig Harris (323) 851-8510
(Sound Effects Editor) www.craigharrismusic.com

Dan Hart (310) 260-4949
www.humit.com

Jud Haskins (310) 260-9939
www.horriblemusic.net

Paul Haslinger (310) 572-4646
www.grooveaddicts.com

Jimmy Haun (310) 581-6500
www.eliasarts.com

Emanuel Heinstein (310) 435-9499
(323) 327-2703
www.heinstein.com

Sean Hennessy (310) 651-6233
www.halfpipemusic.com

Jeffrey Hepker (818) 955-5268
www.zoostreet.com

Martin Hernandez (310) 652-8778
www.lspagency.net

Dino Herrmann (323) 222-1082
www.jhuck.com
(Re-Recording Mixer & Supervising Sound Editor)

Peter Himmelman (310) 478-8227
www.primalscreammusic.com

Dave Hodge (310) 393-5340
www.fingermusic.tv

Jim Hodson (818) 566-8555
www.advantageaudio.com
(Re-Recording Mixer & Sound Effects Editor)

Paul Hoffman (310) 568-3355
www.bluemusicla.com

Heather Holbrook (818) 566-8555
www.advantageaudio.com

Sean Holt (310) 478-2120
FAX (310) 478-2130
www.bartonholt.com

Les Hooper (818) 501-2727

Hein Hoven (310) 393-5340
www.fingermusic.tv

Jon Huck (323) 222-1082
(Music Supervisor) www.jhuck.com

John Hunter (310) 285-0303
www.marshbest.com

Mark Isham (310) 572-4646
www.grooveaddicts.com

Marc Jackson (818) 955-5268
FAX (818) 295-5001
www.zoostreet.com

Barry Jamieson (310) 450-7070
www.room.tv

Alexander Janko (310) 572-4646
www.grooveaddicts.com

Maurice Jarre (310) 572-4646
www.grooveaddicts.com

Mark Jasper (310) 264-0407
www.onmusicandsound.com
(Re-Recording Mixer, Sound Designer & Sound Effects Editor)

Chip Jenkins (310) 581-6500
www.eliasarts.com

Jason Johnson (310) 460-0123
www.stimmung.tv

Tobias Johnston (310) 393-7577
www.confidencehead.com

Jeffery Alan Jones (310) 753-1564
(323) 906-8700
FAX (562) 408-6822
www.jeffjonesmusic.com
(Foley Artist, Sound Designer, Re-Recording Mixer & Supervising Sound Editor)

dj JUN (310) 651-6233
www.halfpipemusic.com

Matt & Bubba Kadane (310) 652-8778
www.lspagency.net

Loren N. Kaplan (310) 472-7775
FAX (310) 472-7775
www.mamalahoapublishing.com

Andreas Kapsalis (310) 285-0303
www.marshbest.com

Kent Karlsson (310) 651-6233
www.halfpipemusic.com

Christopher Kemp (310) 581-6500
www.eliasarts.com

Rolfe Kent (310) 572-4646
www.grooveaddicts.com

Wojciech Kilar (310) 572-4646
www.grooveaddicts.com

Kinky (310) 842-3891
www.musicfuzz.com

David Klotz (310) 285-0303
(Music Editor) www.marshbest.com

Daniel Kolton (323) 857-7299
(310) 651-6233
www.blastmanagement.com

Kathryn Korniloff (310) 291-1122
(Sound Editor & Sound Effects Editor) www.sonicfruit.com

Gus Koven (310) 460-0123
(Sound Editor & Sound Effects Editor) www.stimmung.tv

Kadet Kuhne (323) 481-4581
(Sound Designer) www.audibleshift.com

Steve Kutay (818) 926-6704
www.radius360.com
(Dialogue Editor, Sound Designer & Supervising Sound Editor)

Hao Lam (310) 566-1463
www.endlessnoise.com

Garron R. Larcombe (310) 477-7195
www.soundtrackstudio.com

Bernie Larsen (323) 856-3000
www.thegelleragency.com

Latin Music Artist Alliance (323) 857-7299
www.blastmanagement.com

Chris Lennertz (310) 578-9686
(310) 572-4646
www.sonicfuel.net

Daniel Lenz (310) 393-5340
www.fingermusic.tv

Geoff Levin (818) 841-6607
www.geofflevin.com

Marc Levisohn (310) 597-3600
(ADR Supervisor & Dialogue Editor) www.bigears.com

Tony Lewis (310) 285-0303
(Music Editor) www.marshbest.com

Scott Liggett (818) 508-3303
(818) 645-2364
www.aemg.com

Ted Lobinger (310) 260-9838
www.themixsantamonica.com
(Dialogue Editor & Sound Designer)

David A. Logan (310) 393-5340
www.fingermusic.tv

Robert Lopez (310) 260-4949
www.humit.com

Vincenzo Lorusso (310) 450-7070
www.room.tv

Steve Love (310) 568-3355
www.bluemusicla.com

Joseph Ma (310) 396-6731
www.jamesobrienmusic.com

Curt Macdonald (805) 241-9940
(805) 390-1910
members.aol.com/cmacdon101/cmmp/cmmp.html
(Dialogue Editor & Sound Editor)

Wendy MaHarry (323) 857-7299
www.blastmanagement.com

Anthony Marinelli (323) 461-4646
www.musicforever.com

Elad Marish (310) 450-7070
(Music Editor) www.room.tv

Ric Markmann (818) 505-8505
www.mattermusic.com

Jeff Martin (310) 651-6233
www.halfpipemusic.com

John Massari (323) 573-2896
www.johnmassari.com
(Composer, Music Editor & Music Supervisor)

Hirotaka Matsuoka (310) 260-4949
www.humit.com

John McCarthy (323) 466-7056
www.mccarthymusic.com

Stephen McCarthy (310) 651-6233
www.halfpipemusic.com

Steve McClure (323) 481-4581
www.audibleshift.com

Dan McNamara (818) 789-0226
www.jinglefactory.com

Joel McNeely (310) 572-4646
www.grooveaddicts.com

Cyrus Melchor (818) 541-1760

Alex Menck (323) 466-4696
www.monadavis.com
(Composer, Music Editor & Music Supervisor)

Dean Menta (310) 337-9727
(310) 285-0303
(Music Editor) www.bendymusic.com

Mark Mercury (323) 349-5580
(Composer & Sound Designer) www.markmercury.com

Gigi Meroni (323) 856-3000
www.thegelleragency.com

Nick Michaud (310) 260-9838
(Sound Designer) www.themixsantamonica.com

Brian Miller (310) 410-1900
www.mesmerav.com
(Dialogue Editor, Foley Editor & Sound Editor)

Bryan E. Miller (818) 985-3300
www.sensory-overload.com

Jonathan Miller (310) 572-4646
www.grooveaddicts.com
(Re-Recording Mixer & Supervising Sound Editor)

Scott Miller (310) 378-8633
www.thehithouse.com
(Re-Recording Mixer & Sound Designer)

The Millionaire (323) 222-1082
www.jhuck.com

Bruce Millstein/End of Music (323) 823-1784
www.hear4more.com

Paul Mirkovich (310) 572-4646
www.grooveaddicts.com

Monster Music (323) 857-7299
www.blastmanagement.com

Guy Moon (310) 568-3355
www.bluemusicla.com

Mophonics (310) 452-0331
200 Westminister Ave. FAX (310) 452-0356
Venice, CA 90291 www.mophonics.com

Tony Morales (310) 399-6900
www.emotomusic.com

Sean Morris (323) 852-9991
www.seanmorris.com

Sebastian Arocha Morton (310) 285-0303
www.marshbest.com

Tim Mosher (323) 656-0197
www.mosherandstoker.com

Mark Mothersbaugh (310) 360-0561
www.mutato.com

Gary Myrick (818) 382-4792
www.garymyrick.com

Naughty G (310) 450-7070
www.room.tv

David Newman (310) 572-4646
www.grooveaddicts.com

The Newton Brothers (310) 651-6233
www.halfpipemusic.com

John O (310) 651-6233
www.halfpipemusic.com

James O'Brien (310) 396-6731
www.jamesobrienmusic.com

Tommy O'Brien (310) 397-3115
(310) 902-4784

Gregg Orenstein (310) 488-7726
www.station22.com

John Ottman (310) 572-4646
www.grooveaddicts.com

John Paesano (323) 857-7299
www.blastmanagement.com

Tom Page (310) 670-4999
www.dasoundmusic.com

dj Chris Paul (323) 857-7299
www.blastmanagement.com

Joey Peters (310) 651-6233
www.halfpipemusic.com

Howard Pfeifer (310) 572-4646
(818) 505-8787
www.grooveaddicts.com

Phil-X (310) 572-4646
www.grooveaddicts.com

Tony Phillips (310) 572-4646
www.grooveaddicts.com

Photek (310) 393-5340
www.fingermusic.tv

Nicholas Pike (310) 572-4646
www.grooveaddicts.com

Dan Pinella (818) 505-8505
www.mattermusic.com

Nicola Piovani (310) 572-4646
www.grooveaddicts.com

Basil Poledouris (310) 572-4646
www.grooveaddicts.com

Bob Poole (818) 566-8555
www.advantageaudio.com

Popular Beat Combo (323) 857-7299
www.blastmanagement.com

Michael Portis (818) 216-2841

Rachel Portman (310) 572-4646
www.grooveaddicts.com

Alan Porzio (310) 410-1900
www.mesmerav.com
(ADR Editor, Re-Recording Mixer, Sound Designer & Sound Effects Editor)

John Powell (310) 572-4646
www.grooveaddicts.com

Trevor Rabin (310) 572-4646
www.grooveaddicts.com

Dan Radlauer (310) 440-0055

Amine Ramer (310) 285-0303
(Music Supervisor) www.marshbest.com

Scott Rea (866) 630-6372
www.scottreamusic.com

Andy Rehfeldt (310) 566-1463
www.endlessnoise.com

Luis Resto (323) 857-7299
www.blastmanagement.com

Graeme Revell (310) 572-4646
www.grooveaddicts.com

Eddie Reyes (310) 828-5189
www.schtungmusic.com

Stan Ridgeway (310) 572-4646
www.grooveaddicts.com

David Rolfe (310) 568-3355
www.bluemusicla.com

Spookey Ruben (310) 460-0123
(310) 393-5340
www.stimmung.tv

Joey Rubenstien (310) 393-5340
www.fingermusic.tv

Jason Ruder (310) 285-0303
(Music Editor) www.marshbest.com

Joe Rudge (310) 285-0303
(Music Supervisor) www.marshbest.com

Keith Ruggiero (310) 633-4187
(310) 989-4814
www.soundsred.la

Boris Salchow (323) 876-7366
www.borissalchow.com

Adam Sanborne (310) 312-3329
www.s3mx.com

Andrea Saparoff (310) 455-1950
www.saparoffmusic.com

Adam Schiff (310) 392-8393
www.machinehead.com

Lalo Schifrin (310) 572-4646
www.grooveaddicts.com

Erik Schuiten (310) 566-1463
(Supervising Sound Editor) www.endlessnoise.com

Robert J. Schuster (818) 706-6375
www.hodads.com

David Schwartz (310) 459-1419
FAX (310) 459-7448
www.davidschwartzmusic.com

Mike Semple (310) 651-6233
www.halfpipemusic.com

Kiran Shahani (310) 651-6233
www.halfpipemusic.com

Marc Shaiman (310) 572-4646
www.grooveaddicts.com

Michael Sherwood (310) 581-6500
www.eliasarts.com

Dan Silver (310) 437-4380
(Composer & Sound Designer) www.riptidemusic.com

Anna Sitko (323) 481-4581
www.audibleshift.com

Josh Sklair (310) 337-9727
www.bendymusic.com

Nathan Smith (213) 268-4226
FAX (323) 227-1498
www.nl3audio.com
(Re-Recording Mixer, Sound Designer & Supervising Sound Editor)

Steve Smith (310) 285-0303
www.marshbest.com

Andy Snavley (310) 337-9727
www.bendymusic.com
(Dialogue Editor, Re-Recording Mixer & Supervising Sound Editor)

Sneaker Pimps (310) 842-3891
www.musicfuzz.com

Craig Snider (310) 399-6900
www.emotomusic.com

Mark Snow (310) 572-4646
www.grooveaddicts.com

Bruce Somers (310) 568-3355
www.bluemusicla.com

SPARKS (310) 842-3891
www.musicfuzz.com

Squirrel Nut Zippers (310) 842-3891
www.musicfuzz.com

David Steinberg (323) 467-2529

Shepard Stern (310) 439-1903
www.sternworld.net

Bob Stewart (714) 973-3030
(Dialogue Editor & Music Editor) www.stewartsound.com

Chris Stills (310) 651-6233
www.halfpipemusic.com

Stoker (323) 656-0197
www.mosherandstoker.com

Andreas Straub (310) 392-9545
www.48windows.com

David Streefkerk (323) 466-4696
www.monadavis.com
(Sound Designer & Supervising Sound Editor)

Andy Sturmer (310) 651-6233
www.halfpipemusic.com

Tim Stutts (323) 445-8798
www.postdramatic.com
(Dialogue Editor, Re-Recording Mixer, Sound Designer & Supervising Sound Editor)

Michael Suby (310) 312-3329
www.s3mx.com

Jeff Sudakin (310) 410-1900
www.mesmerav.com

Summerfield Music, Inc./ Trailer Trash Music Library (818) 905-0400
(Reps for Composers) FAX (818) 905-0488
www.summerfieldmusic.com

Bobby Summerfield (818) 905-0400
www.summerfieldmusic.com

Jim Sutherland (310) 285-0303
www.marshbest.com

Stanislas Syrewicz (310) 285-0303
www.marshbest.com

Kathie Talbot (310) 651-6233
www.halfpipemusic.com

John Tartaglia (323) 666-6550

Danny Tate (310) 651-6233
www.halfpipemusic.com

Paca Thomas (818) 566-8555
www.advantageaudio.com
(Sound Designer & Supervising Sound Editor)

Scott Thomas (310) 651-6233
www.halfpipemusic.com

David Tobocman (310) 410-1900
www.mesmerav.com

Brandon Toh (310) 450-7070
www.room.tv

Ceiri Torjussen (323) 856-3000
www.thegelleragency.com

Rick Torres (310) 279-2388
www.ricktorres.com
(ADR Editor, Composer, Dialogue Editor, Music Editor, Music Supervisor, Re-Recording Mixer, Sound Designer, Sound Editor, Sound Effects Editor, Supervising Sound Editor & Voice Over Editor)

Franco Tortora (323) 466-4696
www.monadavis.com

Jeff Toyne (310) 285-0303
www.marshbest.com

dj True:129 (310) 651-6233
www.halfpipemusic.com

Neil Uchitel (323) 737-6995
www.audio.slappo.com
(Sound Editor, Sound Effects Editor & Supervising Sound Editor)

Kubilay Uner (323) 428-8429
(Composer) www.kubilayuner.com

Bill Ungerman (323) 222-1082
www.jhuck.com

Alexander Van Bubenheim (310) 450-7070
www.room.tv

Adrian Van Velsen (310) 285-0303
(Music Editor) www.marshbest.com

Scott Van Zen (818) 366-0330
www.citrusprods.com

Marta Victoria (562) 925-4514
www.icarusmusic.com

R. Walter Vincent (310) 410-1900
www.mesmerav.com

Bill Wadsworth (310) 396-4663
www.mindovereye.com

Chris Wagner (818) 505-8505
www.mattermusic.com

Shirley Walker (310) 572-4646
www.grooveaddicts.com

Michael Wandmacher (310) 478-8227
www.primalscreammusic.com

Adam Watkins (818) 505-8787
www.kingklong.com

Bruce Watson (310) 572-4646
www.grooveaddicts.com

Jim Watson (310) 828-5189
www.schtungmusic.com
(Re-Recording Mixer & Sound Designer)

Robert Wear (310) 572-4646
www.grooveaddicts.com

Billy White Acre (818) 909-9222
www.bigplanetmusic.com

Danny Wilde (323) 857-7299
www.blastmanagement.com

Ben Wilkins (310) 450-7070
(Re-Recording Mixer & Sound Editor) www.room.tv

Rob Winch (310) 828-5189
www.schtungmusic.com

Chaz Windus (310) 989-4814
www.blazinglazer.com

David Wingo (310) 652-8778
www.lspagency.net

Hal Winn (818) 708-7359
www.bulletswest.com

Chris Winston (310) 264-0407
www.onmusicandsound.com
(Music Editor, Re-Recording Mixer & Sound Editor)

Dave Wittman (310) 581-6500
www.eliasarts.com

Roger Wojahn (310) 829-6200
www.wojahn.com

Scott Wojahn (310) 829-6200
www.wojahn.com

Lindsay Wolfington (310) 285-0303
(Music Supervisor) www.marshbest.com

Patrick Woodland (949) 788-0103
(949) 788-0321
FAX (949) 788-0327
www.woodlandmusicproduction.com

Dan Wool (310) 842-3891
www.musicfuzz.com

Art Wright (310) 829-4765
www.thunder-sound.com
(Foley Artist, Sound Designer & Sound Editor)

Timothy Michael Wynn (310) 572-4646
(310) 578-9686
www.sonicfuel.net

Gabriel Yared (310) 572-4646
www.grooveaddicts.com

Christopher Young (310) 572-4646
www.grooveaddicts.com

John Zuker (818) 500-9288
www.johnzuker.com

11:11 MediaWorks (818) 780-4466
6611 Valjean Ave., Ste. 108 FAX **(818) 780-4467**
Van Nuys, CA 91406 **www.1111mediaworks.com**
(2D/3D and Stop-Motion Animation, Blue/Green Screen Compositing, Digital Matte Painting, Miniatures & Visual FX)

20twenty vfx (310) 395-2020
1419 Second St. FAX **(310) 393-2600**
Santa Monica, CA 90401 **www.20twentyvfx.com**
(2D/3D Animation, 3D Modeling, CGI, Visual FX & Visual FX Supervision)

3 Ring Circus (323) 466-5300
1040 N. Sycamore Ave. FAX **(323) 466-5310**
Hollywood, CA 90038 **www.3ringcircus.tv**
(Broadcast Design)

3dBob Productions (818) 559-9700
21601 Devonshire St., Ste. 112 FAX **(818) 559-9768**
Chatsworth, CA 91311 **www.3dbob.com**
(2D/3D Computer Animation, Digital FX & Motion Graphics)

A52 (310) 586-0650
2308 Broadway FAX **(310) 586-0651**
Santa Monica, CA 90404 **www.a52.com**
(2D/3D Computer Animation, Compositing, Digital and Visual FX & Matte Painting)
Executive Producer: Mark Tobin
VFX Artists: Kirk Balden, Tim Bird, Pat Murphy & Raul Ortego
3D Supervisor: Andrew Hall
Sales: Steven Monkarsh

ACME Digital Content (310) 217-0688
(310) 569-2263
2149 San Anseline Ave. **www.acmedc.com**
Long Beach, CA 90815
(3D Scanning, 3D Modeling, 3D Digitizing, CAD Conversion, Computer Animation & Rendering)

Acme Filmworks, Inc. (323) 464-7805
6525 Sunset Blvd., Ste. G-10 FAX **(323) 464-6614**
Hollywood, CA 90028 **www.acmefilmworks.com**
(2D/3D Animation, Character Cel Animation & Stop-Motion)
Executive Producers: Ron Diamond & David Schmier
Producer: Pernille D'Avolio
Directors: Gil Alkabetz, Garri Bardine, Jim Blashfield, Leslie Cabraga, Evert de Beijer, Paul and Menno De Nooijer, Michael Dudok De Wit, John Dilworth, Paul Driessen, Piotr Dumala, Stephen Flint-Muller, Daniel Guyonnet, Oliver Harrison, Anna Henckle-Donnersmarck, Chris Hinton, Greg Holfeld, Aleksandra Korejwo, Igor Kovalyov, Raimund Krumme, Chris Landreth, Christopher and Wolfgang Lauenstein, Caroline Leaf, Ashley Lenz, Susan Loughlin, Sean McBride, Frank and Caroline Mouris, Priit Parn, Luc Perez, Janet Perlman, Bill Plympton, Barry Purves, Joanna Quinn, Rosto, Erica Russell, Pam Stalker, Wendy Tilby/Amanda Forbis, Gianluigi Toccafondo, Miklos Varga, Solweig von Kleist, David Wasson, JC Wegman & Koji Yamamura
East Coast Sales Rep: David Schmier
Midwest Sales Rep: Tim Harwood
West Coast Sales Reps: Toni Saarinen & Jennifer Spencer

Acorn Entertainment (323) 238-4650
Hollywood Production Center
121 W. Lexington Dr., Ste. V100
Glendale, CA 91203 **www.acornentertainment.com**
(2D and 3D Animation, 3D Modeling, Animatics, Broadcast Design, Cel Animation, CGI, Character Animation and Design, Computer Animation, Graphic Design, Live Action Integration, Previsualizations, Rotoscoping & Storyboards)
Executive Producers: Evan Ricks & Thad Weinlein
Producer: Mary Wall
Broadcast Graphics: Bill Hastings
Client Services: Nikki Auckerman

ActiveQuest, Inc. (661) 295-3890
25655 Springbrook Ave., Bldg. 2A **www.activequest.com**
Santa Clarita, CA 91350
(2D Animation, 2D Paint, 3D Animation, 3D Digitizing, 3D Modeling, Animatics, Blue Screen Compositing, Broadcast Design, CGI, Character Animation, Character Design, Compositing, Computer Animation, Digital FX, Digital Ink, Digital Matte Painting, Digital Paint, Graphic Design, Green Screen Compositing, Illustrative Design, Live Action Integration, Matte Painting, Morphing, Motion Graphics, Photography, Pre-Production Planning, Previsualizations, Rotoscoping, Stop-Motion Animation, Time-Lapse Photography, Visual FX & Visual FX Supervision)

Aerocrane Rentals LLC (818) 252-7700
9824 Glen Oaks Blvd. FAX **(818) 252-7709**
Sun Valley, CA 91352 **www.aerocranerentals.com**
(Motion Capture, Portable Real Time Motion Control & Visual FX)
Technician: Craig Shumard

Alsup Digital FX (818) 512-8416
cgsupervisor.blogspot.com
(2D Animation, 3D Animation, 3D Modeling, Animatics, Blue Screen Compositing, Broadcast Design, CGI, Character Animation, Character Design, Compositing, Computer Animation, Digital FX, Digital Matte Painting, Digital Restoration, Graphic Design, Green Screen Compositing, Morphing, Motion Graphics, Pre-Production Planning, Previsualizations, Stereoscopic 3D, Storyboards, Visual FX & Visual FX Supervision)
Visual Effects & CG Supervisor: Isa A. Alsup

Altered Illusions (818) 471-0044
www.alteredillusions.com
(2D Animation, Broadcast Design, Compositing, Editorial, Motion Graphics & Visual FX)

Amalgamated Pixels, Inc. (818) 865-8423
2475 Townsgate Rd., Ste. 220 FAX **(818) 575-9032**
Westlake Village, CA 91361 **www.apixels.com**
(2D/3D Computer Animation, Compositing, Digital FX, Digital Matte Painting, Previsualizations & Rotoscoping)
Head of Production: Derry Frost
Executive Producer: Michael Morreale
Visual FX Supervisor: Phil Palousek
Director of Business: Paul Scott

Animal Logic (310) 664-8765
(310) 945-8765
2644 30th St. FAX **(310) 664-9355**
Santa Monica, CA 90405 **www.animallogic.com**
(3D Animation & Visual FX)
Executive Producer: Maury Strong
Head of Production: Nerissa Kavanagh

Animax Entertainment (818) 787-4444
6627 Valjean Ave. FAX **(818) 374-9140**
Van Nuys, CA 91406 **www.animaxentertainment.com**
(2D/3D Computer Animation, Character Design & Motion Graphics)

AniMill (818) 972-9116
(407) 654-4494
200 E. Angeleno Ave., Ste. 312 **www.animill.com**
Burbank, CA 91502
(2D Animation, 2D Paint, 3D Animation, 3D Modeling, Animatics, Blue/Green Screen Compositing, Broadcast Design, CGI, Character Animation, Compositing, Computer Animation, Digital FX, Digital Ink, Digital Paint, Graphic Design, Illustrative Design, Live Action Integration, Morphing, Motion Graphics, Photography, Pre-Production Planning, Previsualizations, Rotoscoping, Time-Lapse Photography, Visual FX & Visual FX Supervision)

Antifreeze Design (619) 795-2940
5241 Lewison Court **www.antifreezedesign.com**
San Diego, CA 92120
(Broadcast Design, Compositing & Rotoscoping)

Area 51 (626) 791-7151
1299 Boston St. **www.area51fx.com**
Altadena, CA 91001
(Animatics, CGI, Character Animation, Compositing & Digital Matte Painting)
Visual FX Supervisors: Glenn Campbell & Tim McHugh
Visual FX Co-Producer: Michelle Massie

Arsenal FX (310) 453-5400
1522A Cloverfield **www.arsenalfx.tv**
Santa Monica, CA 90404
(2D Animation, 2D Paint, 3D Animation, 3D Digitizing, 3D Modeling, Animatics, Blue Screen Compositing, Broadcast Design, CGI, Character Animation, Character Design, Compositing, Computer Animation, Digital FX, Digital Matte Painting, Digital Paint, Digital Restoration, Editorial, Graphic Design, Green Screen Compositing, Illustrative Design, Image Processing, Live Action Integration, Matte Painting, Morphing, Motion Control, Motion Graphics, Photography, Pre-Production Planning, Previsualizations, Real Time Motion Control, Rotoscoping, Scanning and Recording, Stop-Motion Animation, Ultimatte, Visual FX & Visual FX Supervision)

Associates & Yamashita (310) 664-9500
13600 Marina Pointe Dr., Ste. 1007 FAX **(310) 664-9977**
Marina del Rey, CA 90292 **www.aayamashita.com**
(3D Computer Animation, Cel Animation, Compositing & Live Action Integration)
President/Creative Director: Allen Yamashita

Asylum (310) 395-4975
631 Wilshire Blvd., Ste. 2A FAX **(310) 395-5625**
Santa Monica, CA 90401 **www.asylumfx.com**
(2D/3D Computer Animation, CGI, Compositing & Previsualization)
Executive Commercial Producer: Michael Pardee
Executive Feature Producer: Kathy Chasen-Hay

At The Post VFX (310) 452-4600
220 Main St., Ste. C FAX **(310) 733-1797**
Venice, CA 90291 **www.atthepost.net**
(2D Animation, 2D Paint, 3D Animation, 3D Modeling, Animatics, Blue Screen Compositing, Broadcast Design, CGI, Compositing, Computer Animation, Digital FX, Digital Matte Painting, Digital Paint, Editorial, Graphic Design, Green Screen Compositing, Image Processing, Live Action Integration, Matte Painting, Motion Graphics, Pre-Production Planning, Previsualizations, Rotoscoping, Visual FX & Visual FX Supervision)
Visual FX Supervisor: Wayne A. Shepherd

AvatarLabs (818) 728-6778
16838 Addison St. FAX **(818) 728-6782**
Encino, CA 91436 **www.avatarlabs.com**
(Motion Graphics)

Barbed Wire FX (310) 260-3111
1411 Fifth St., Ste. 503 FAX **(310) 260-3339**
Santa Monica, CA 90401 **www.barbedwirefx.com**
(2D/3D Computer Animation, Compositing, Matte Painting, Motion Graphics, Previsualizations, Storyboards & Visual FX Supervision)

Beau Studio (310) 857-6696
10355 Washington Blvd. FAX **(310) 861-5970**
Culver City, CA 90232 **www.beaustudio.com**
(2D Animation, 2D Paint, 3D Animation, 3D Modeling, Animatics, Blue Screen Compositing, CGI, Character Animation, Character Design, Compositing, Computer Animation, Digital FX, Digital Matte Painting, Digital Paint, Green Screen Compositing, Live Action Integration, Matte Painting, Morphing, Pre-Production Planning, Previsualizations, Rotoscoping, Time-Lapse Photography, Ultimatte, Visual FX & Visual FX Supervision)

Berkos & Associates (818) 788-8246
(2D and 3D Animation, Computer Animation, Blue and Green Screen Compositing, Stop-Motion & Time-Lapse Photography, Visual FX & Visual FX Supervision)
Producer/Director: Craig Berkos

Bill Melendez Productions, Inc. (818) 382-7382
13400 Riverside Dr., Ste. 201 **www.billmelendez.tv**
Sherman Oaks, CA 91463
(2D/3D & Character Animation)
Business Affairs: Joanna Coletta
Animation Supervisor: Larry Leichliter
Sales Rep: Jeff Arnold

Black Box Digital, LLC (310) 828-5832
409 Santa Monica Blvd., Ste. E FAX **(310) 828-8998**
Santa Monica, CA 90401 **www.blackboxdigital.com**
(2D/3D Computer Animation & Compositing)

Black Dragon Entertainment, Inc. (323) 874-8888
FAX **(323) 874-1058**
www.blackdragon.com

Blind (310) 314-1618
1702 Olympic Blvd. FAX **(310) 314-1718**
Santa Monica, CA 90404 **www.blind.com**
(2D/3D Computer Animation, Character Design & Digital and Visual FX)
Executive Producer: David Kleinman

Bling Imaging (323) 874-3003
1011 N. Fuller Ave., Ste. B **www.blingimaging.com**
West Hollywood, CA 90046
(2D Animation, 2D Paint, 3D Animation, 3D Digitizing, 3D Modeling, Animatics, Blue Screen Compositing, Broadcast Design, CGI, Character Animation, Character Design, Color Correction, Compositing, Computer Animation, Digital FX, Digital Ink, Digital Matte Painting, Digital Paint, Graphic Design, Green Screen Compositing, Illustrative Design, Image Processing, Live Action Integration, Matte Painting, Morphing, Motion Capture, Motion Graphics, Photography, Pre-Production Planning, Previsualizations, Rotoscoping, Storyboards, Time-Lapse Photography, Ultimatte, Visual FX & Visual FX Supervision)
VFX Supervisor: Paal Anand
VFX Producers: Kelle Holland & Fernando Zorrilla

Blissium (310) 453-7070
1630 Stewart St., Ste. B1 FAX **(310) 260-6111**
Santa Monica, CA 90404 **www.blissium.com**
(2D Animation, 3D Animation, 3D Modeling, Animatics, Blue Screen Compositing, Broadcast Design, Cel Animation, CGI, Character Design, Compositing, Computer Animation, Digital FX, Digital Matte Painting, Editorial, Graphic Design, Green Screen Compositing, Illustrative Design, Image Processing, Live Action Integration, Matte Painting, Morphing, Motion Capture, Motion Control, Motion Control Photography, Motion Graphics, Photography, Pre-Production Planning, Previsualizations, Real Time Motion Control, Rotoscoping, Stop-Motion Animation, Storyboards, Time-Lapse Photography, Ultimatte, Visual FX & Visual FX Supervision)

Blue Room (310) 727-2600
1600 Rosecrans Ave., Bldg. 5A FAX **(310) 727-2601**
Manhattan Beach, CA 90266 **www.blueroomfx.com**
(Blue/Green Screen Compositing, Broadcast Design, Compositing, Computer Animation, Digital FX, Digital Matte Painting, Digital Paint, Digital Restoration, Editorial, Graphic Design, Pre-Production Planning, Previsualizations, Rotoscoping, Visual FX & Visual FX Supervision)

BlueScreen, LLC/Bob Kertesz (323) 467-7572
www.bluescreen.com
(Blue/Green Screen, Graphics, Live Action Integration & Ultimatte)
Visual FX Supervisor: Bob Kertesz

Blur Studio, Inc. (310) 581-8848
589 Venice Blvd. FAX **(310) 581-8850**
Venice, CA 90291 **www.blur.com**
(2D/3D Computer Animation and Visual Effects)
President/Creative Director: Tim Miller

BrainForest Digital (818) 865-8333
5743 Corsa Ave., Ste. 220 FAX **(818) 865-9333**
Westlake Village, CA 91362 **www.brain4est.com**
(2D/3D Computer Animation, Animatics & Previsualizations)
Director: Joe Matamales
Production Coordinator: Merrilee Newman

Brickyard VFX (310) 453-5722
2054 Broadway FAX **(310) 453-5744**
Santa Monica, CA 90404 **www.brickyardvfx.com**
(3D Animation, FX and Modeling, Animatics, Compositing, Pre-Production Planning, Rotoscoping & Visual FX)

Buf, Inc. (323) 512-6000
(323) 791-8914
7720 W. Sunset Blvd., Ground Fl. FAX **(323) 512-6075**
Los Angeles, CA 90046 **www.buf.com**
President: Pierre Buffin
Producer: Vanessa Fourgeaud
General Manager: Giacun Caduff
Visual FX Supervisor: Olivier Dumont

Bully Bros. Post (310) 874-7000
1813 Centinela Ave. FAX **(310) 745-1645**
Santa Monica, CA 90404 **www.bullybrospost.com**

Caliban Filmworks (310) 385-9332
1262 Lago Vista Pl. FAX **(310) 385-1364**
Beverly Hills, CA 90210
(2D/3D Animation & Compositing)
President: Laurie Shearing

Camera Control, Inc. (310) 581-8343
3317 Ocean Park Blvd. FAX **(310) 581-8340**
Santa Monica, CA 90405 **www.cameracontrol.com**
(Portable Live Action and Miniature Motion Control Systems)
Head of Production: Jason Rau
Motion Control Operators: Tim Donlevy, George Hladky & Chris Toth

CBS Digital (323) 575-2310
7800 Beverly Blvd., Ste. 112A FAX **(323) 575-4450**
Los Angeles, CA 90036 **www.cbsdvfx.com**
(Animatics, Broadcast Design, CGI, Previsualizations, Rotoscoping & Ultimatte)

CCI Digital, Inc. (818) 562-6300
2921 W. Alameda Ave. FAX **(818) 562-8222**
Burbank, CA 91505 **www.ccidigital.com**
(Broadcast Design, Compositing & Digital Ink and Paint)

Charlie Company (310) 264-7100
1758 Berkeley St. FAX **(310) 264-7104**
Santa Monica, CA 90404 **www.charlieco.tv**

Chiodo Bros. Productions, Inc. (818) 842-5656
110 W. Providencia Ave. FAX **(818) 848-0891**
Burbank, CA 91502 **www.chiodobros.com**
(Miniature Photography & Stop Motion)
Producer: Edward Chiodo
Designer: Charles Chiodo
Director: Steven Chiodo

Christopher Nibley Cinematography (818) 509-0613
FAX **(818) 509-0625**
www.nibley.com
(Blue Screen Compositing, Green Screen Compositing, Miniatures, Previsualizations, Real Time Motion Control, Stereoscopic 3D & Visual FX)

Christov Effects & Design, Inc. (818) 842-0238
3805 W. Magnolia Blvd. **www.christovfx.com**
Burbank, CA 91505
(2D/3D Animation and FX, 3D Modeling, Animatics, Character Animation, Compositing, Digital Matte Painting & Visual FX)

Cinergy Creative (310) 455-2490
(818) 623-6558
www.cinergycreative.com
(2D/3D Computer Animation, Compositing, Digital and Visual FX & Live Action Integrating)
Creative Director: Leslie Allen
Producer: Elizabeth Lough

Cinesite (323) 462-6266
809 N. Cahuenga Blvd. **www.cinesite.com**
Hollywood, CA 90038
(2D/3D Computer Animation, Character Animation, Digital Matte Painting, Digital Film Mastering, Scanning and Recording & Digital Restoration)
Contact: Rita Cahill

Computer Café, Inc. (805) 922-9479
3130 Skyway Dr., Ste. 603 FAX **(805) 922-3225**
Santa Maria, CA 93455 **www.computercafe.com**
(3D Animation & Compositing)
Executive Producer: Jeff Barnes

Computer Café, Inc. (310) 395-9013
(805) 922-9479
1207 Fourth St., Ste. 200 FAX **(310) 395-9814**
Santa Monica, CA 90401 **www.computercafe.com**

Contraband (323) 933-1614
5820 Wilshire Blvd., Ste. 306 **www.contrabandusa.com**
Los Angeles, CA 90036
(2D/3D Computer Animation, Compositing, Live Action Integration & Visual FX)

CostFX (805) 455-7574
3039 Shasta FAX **(805) 965-6991**
Los Angeles, CA 90065 **www.costfx.com**
(2D Animation, 2D Paint, 3D Animation, 3D Digitizing, 3D Modeling, Animatics, Blue Screen Compositing, Broadcast Design, Cel Animation, CGI, Character Animation, Character Design, Clay Animation, Compositing, Computer Animation, Digital Film Mastering, Digital FX, Digital Ink, Digital Matte Painting, Digital Paint, Digital Restoration, Graphic Design, Green Screen Compositing, Illustrative Design, Image Processing, Live Action Integration, Matte Painting, Miniature Motion Control, Miniatures, Morphing, Motion Control Photography, Motion Graphics, Photography, Pre-Production Planning, Previsualizations, Rotoscoping, Scanning and Recording, Stop-Motion Animation, Storyboards, Time-Lapse Photography, Ultimatte, Visual FX & Visual FX Supervision)

Creative Character Engineering (818) 901-0507
16110 Hart St. FAX **(818) 901-8417**
Van Nuys, CA 91406 **www.creativecharacter.com**
(3D Animation, Character Animation & Compositing)
Creative Director: Andrew Clement

The Creative-Cartel (818) 752-3005
(818) 437-7149
4220 Lankershim Blvd., Second Fl. FAX **(818) 936-0708**
North Hollywood, CA 91602 **www.thecreative-cartel.com**
(2D Paint, 2D/3D Animation, 3D Modeling, Animatics, Blue/Green Screen Compositing, CGI, Character Animation, Compositing, Computer Animation, Digital Film Mastering, Digital FX, Digital Ink and Paint, Digital Restoration, Editorial, Live Action, Live Action Integration, Morphing, Pre-Production Planning, Previsualizations, Rotoscoping, Scanning and Recording, Visual FX & Visual FX Supervision)

A **Cutting Edge Productions, Inc.** (310) 326-4500
(818) 503-0400
22904 Lockness Ave. FAX **(310) 326-4715**
Torrance, CA 90501 **www.cuttingedgeproductions.tv**
(Blue/Green Screen, Broadcast Design & Visual FX)
Founder & Ceo: Bill Dedes

Daily Post (310) 417-4844
6701 Center Dr. West, Ste. 1111 FAX **(310) 410-1543**
Los Angeles, CA 90045 **www.dailypost.tv**

Digiscope (310) 315-6060
1447 Cloverfield Blvd. FAX **(310) 828-5856**
Santa Monica, CA 90404 **www.digiscope.com**
(3D Animation and Modeling, Compositing & Pre-Visualization)
Visual FX Executive Producer: Mary Stuart
Visual FX Supervisor: Dion Hatch

Digital Dimension (818) 344-3435
18425 Burbank Blvd. FAX **(818) 344-3451**
Tarzana, CA 91356 **www.digitaldimension.com**
(2D/3D Computer Animation, Animatics, Compositing, Digital Matte Painting, Live Action Integration, Motion Graphics, Previsualizations & Rotoscoping)

Digital Domain (310) 314-2800
300 Rose Ave. FAX **(310) 314-2888**
Venice, CA 90291 **www.digitaldomain.com**
(2D/3D Computer Animation, Compositing, Digital and Visual FX, Image Processing, Live Action Integration, Matte Painting & Miniature and Motion Control Photography)
VP/Head of Production: Ed Ulbrich

Digital Jungle Post Production (323) 962-0867
6363 Santa Monica Blvd. FAX **(323) 962-9960**
Los Angeles, CA 90038 **www.digijungle.com**

Doglight Studios, LLC (323) 222-1928
600 Moulton Ave., Ste. 302 FAX **(323) 222-8151**
Los Angeles, CA 90031 **www.doglight.com**
(2D/3D Computer Animation and Graphic Design)
Creative Director: Tony Honkawa

Dourmashkin Productions (818) 995-3997
3852 Camino de Solana FAX **(818) 784-0930**
Sherman Oaks, CA 91423
(Cel Animation)
Executive Producer/Director: Barbara Dourmashkin

Dreamscape Imagery, Inc. (323) 848-2066
2101 Kew Dr. FAX **(310) 496-0803**
Los Angeles, CA 90046 **www.dreamscapeimagery.com**
(3D Modeling and Animation, Character Animation, Compositing & Digital Matte Painting)

DUCK Studios, a.k.a. Duck Soup Studios (310) 478-0771
2205 Stoner Ave. FAX **(310) 478-0773**
Los Angeles, CA 90064 **www.duckstudios.com**
(2D/3D Computer Animation, Cel Animation, Character and Illustrative Design, Compositing, Digital Ink and Paint, Live Action Integration & Stop Motion)
Executive Producer: Mark Medernach
President/Director: Roger Chouinard
Directors: Gints Apsits, Richard Borge, Jamie Caliri, Richard Cullen, Delicatessen, Eric Deutschman, Barbara Di Pasquale, Docter Twins, Evil Cat Land, Faivre Brothers, Eric Goldberg, James Hackett, Chris Harding, Laura Heit, JL Design, Peter Kaboth, Piotr Karwas, Stephen Kirklys, Amica Kubo, Lane and Jan, Miwa Matreyek, Graham Morris, Yorico Murakami, Andy Murdock, The Mushroom Company, Takahiro Okubo, Ritxi Ostariz, Nina Paley, Hsin Ping Pan, Plankton Art Co., Corky Quakenbush, Chris Romano, Maureen Selwood, Kang Seong, Steve Sonnenleiter, Shy the Sun AKA The Blackheart Gang, Theodore Ushev, YELLOWSHED & Ryan Zunkley
Sales Representative: Andrew Halpern
Music Video Rep: Randi Wilens

Duncan Studio (626) 578-1587
87 N. Raymond Ave., Ste. 900 FAX **(626) 578-1327**
Pasadena, CA 91103 **www.duncanstudio.com**
(2D Animation, 2D Paint, 3D Animation, 3D Modeling, Animatics, Cel Animation, CGI, Character Animation, Character Design, Compositing, Computer Animation, Digital Ink, Digital Paint, Graphic Design, Compositing, Computer Animation, Digital Ink, Digital Paint, Graphic Design, Matte Painting, Pre-Visualizations & Storyboards)

Eden FX (323) 993-7050
1438 N. Gower St., Box 19, Bldg. 50 FAX **(323) 993-7051**
Los Angeles, CA 90028 **www.edenfx.com**
(2D/3D Animation, 3D Digitizing, 3D Modeling, Animatics, Blue/Green Screen Compositing, CGI, Character Animation, Character Design, Compositing, Computer Animation, Digital FX, Digital Matte Painting, Live Action Integration, Matte Painting, Pre-Production Planning, Previsualizations, Rotoscoping, Visual FX & Visual FX Supervision)
Creative Director/Co-President: John Gross
Executive Producer: Andrea D'Amico

Eight VFX (310) 828-9628
1712 Berkeley St. FAX **(310) 828-9631**
Santa Monica, CA 90404 **www.eightvfx.com**
(2D/3D Computer Animation, Compositing, Digital Matte Painting, Previsualization & Visual FX Supervisors)

Elektrashock, Inc. (310) 399-4985
1320 Main St. FAX **(310) 399-4972**
Venice, CA 90291 **www.elektrashock.com**
(3D Animation)

Encore Hollywood (323) 466-7663
6344 Fountain Ave. FAX **(323) 467-5539**
Hollywood, CA 90028 **www.encorehollywood.com**
(2D/3D Computer Animation and Modeling, Character Design, Compositing & Rotoscoping)
Visual FX Supervisor/Director: Tim Jacobsen

Engine Room (310) 860-9100
1040 N. Las Palmas, Bldg. 24 FAX **(310) 860-9111**
Los Angeles, CA 90038 **www.engineroomvfx.com**
(2D/3D Computer Animation & Compositing)
Executive Producer: Michael Caplan
Visual FX Supervisor: Dan Schmit

Entity FX (310) 899-9779
1437 Seventh St., Ste. 300 FAX **(310) 899-3113**
Santa Monica, CA 90401 **www.entityfx.com**
(2D/3D Animation and FX, 3D Modeling, Character Animation, Compositing, Digital Matte Painting, Live Action Integration, Model/Miniature Shoots, Morphing, Previsualizations, Rotoscoping, Visual FX & Visual FX Supervision)
President: Mat Beck
General Manager: Ellyn Lewis
Senior Producer: Trent Smith

EP Graphic Productions (818) 953-9375 (818) 953-4027
3921 W. Magnolia Blvd. FAX **(818) 953-2833**
Burbank, CA 91505 **www.ep-graphics.com**
(2D/3D Computer Animation and Graphics)
President/Creative Director: Eddie Pong

Eyestorm Productions (310) 582-3937
1559 Seventh St. FAX **(310) 582-3939**
Santa Monica, CA 90401 **www.eyestormproductions.com**
(2D Animation, 2D Paint, 3D Animation, 3D Modeling, Animatics, Blue/Green Screen Compositing, Broadcast Design, CGI, Character Animation, Character Design, Compositing, Computer Animation, Digital FX, Editorial, Graphic Design, Illustrative Design, Live Action Integration, Morphing, Motion Graphics, Previsualizations, Rotoscoping, Stop-Motion Animation, Storyboards, Time-Lapse Photography, Ultimatte & Visual FX)
Creative Directors: Michael Klima & Kyle Ruddick

Eyetronics (310) 371-6600 (800) 205-9808
3424 W. Carson St., Ste. 210 FAX **(310) 371-8700**
Torrance, CA 90503 **www.eyetronics.com**
(3D Digitizing, 3D Modeling, CGI, Character Animation, Computer Animation, Motion Capture & Visual FX)

Fantasy II Film Effects (818) 843-1413
12318 Branford FAX **(818) 252-5995**
Sun Valley, CA 91352
(Digital FX, Hi-Speed with Miniature Photography & Matte Painting)
Creative Director: Gene Warren Jr.

Filmworks/FX, Inc. (310) 577-3213
4121 Redwood Ave., Ste. 101 FAX **(310) 577-3215**
Los Angeles, CA 90066 **www.filmworksfx.com**
(2D/3D Computer Graphics, Compositing & Digital FX)
Contact: Sean Main

FISH EGGS (310) 452-8251
1261 Electric Ave. FAX **(310) 452-8364**
Venice, CA 90291 **www.fisheggs.tv**
(2D/3D Animation and FX, Broadcast Design, Compositing, Graphic Design, Green Screen Compositing, Motion Capture, Motion Graphics, Pre-Production Planning, Rotoscoping & Visual FX)

Framework Studio, LLC (310) 815-1245
3535 Hayden Ave., Ste. 300 FAX **(310) 815-9821**
Culver City, CA 90232 **www.frameworkla.com**
(2D Animation and Paint, 3D Animation, Digitizing and Modeling, Animatics, Blue/Green Screen Compositing, Broadcast Design, CGI, Compositing, Computer Animation, Digital FX, Digital Matte Painting, Graphic Design, Illustrative Design, Live Action Integration, Motion Graphics, Pre-Production Planning, Previsualizations, Rotoscoping, Stop-Motion Animation, Storyboards, Ultimatte, Visual FX & Visual FX Supervision)

Fred Wolf Films (818) 846-0611
4222 W. Burbank Blvd. FAX **(818) 846-0979**
Burbank, CA 91505 **www.fredwolffilms.com**
(Cel Animation)
President: Fred Wolf

Giant Studios (310) 839-1999
12615 Beatrice St. FAX **(310) 839-1991**
Los Angeles, CA 90066 **www.giantstudios.com**
(Motion Capture)

Giantsteps (310) 382-1523 (310) 415-6320
100 Market St., Third Fl. FAX **(310) 496-3228**
Venice, CA 90291 **www.giantsteps.us**

Gorilla Post (310) 394-7611
632-A Arizona Ave. FAX **(310) 394-7622**
Santa Monica, CA 90401 **www.gorillapost.net**
(2D Animation and FX, 2D Paint, 3D Animation and FX, Blue/Green Screen Facilities, Character Animation, Compositing, Digital Matte Painting, Model/Miniture Shoots, Morphing, Motion Capture, Pre-Production Planning, Rotoscoping, Ultimatte & Visual FX)

Gork Enterprises, Inc. (818) 837-7984
218 S. Brand Blvd., Second Fl. FAX (818) 365-1964
San Fernando, CA 91340 www.gork.com
(2D/3D Animation and FX, 3D Modeling, Animatics, Blue/Green Screen, Character Animation, Compositing, Digital Matte Painting, Morphing, Rotoscoping & Visual FX)

Gradient Effects (310) 821-3177
4120 Del Rey Ave. FAX (310) 821-0584
Marina del Rey, CA 90292 www.gradientfx.com
(2D Animation, 2D Paint, 3D Animation, 3D Digitizing, 3D Modeling, Animatics, Blue Screen Compositing, CGI, Character Animation, Character Design, Compositing, Computer Animation, Digital Film Mastering, Digital FX, Digital Matte Painting, Digital Paint, Editorial, Green Screen Compositing, Image Processing, Live Action Integration, Matte Painting, Morphing, Motion Capture, Pre-Production Planning, Previsualizations, Rotoscoping, Visual FX & Visual FX Supervision)

Hal (310) 659-4400
1022 Palm Ave. FAX (310) 659-4402
West Hollywood, CA 90069 www.hal.tv

Hammerhead Productions (818) 986-5535
FAX (818) 762-7311
www.hammerhead.com
(3D Modeling, Character Animation, Compositing & Digital Matte Painting)

Heaven - an Image Company, Ltd. (323) 791-9433
www.heavenanimage.com
(Broadcast Design, Graphic Design, Motion Graphics, Pre-Production Planning & Visual FX Supervision)

Hi-Ground Media (310) 845-9500
8500 Steller Dr., Ste. 4 FAX (310) 845-9559
Culver City, CA 90232 www.hi-ground.com
(2D/3D Animation, 2D Paint, 3D Modeling, Blue/Green Screen Compositing, Broadcast Design, CGI, Compositing, Computer Animation, Digital FX, Digital Matte Painting, Digital Paint, Graphic Design, Live Action Integration, Motion Graphics, Previsualization, Rotoscoping, Visual FX & Visual FX Supervision)

Hornet, Inc. (917) 351-0520
(310) 601-1355
3962 Ince Blvd., FAX (310) 641-2117
Culver City, CA 90232 www.hornetinc.com
(2D/3D Computer Animation & Digital and Visual FX)
CEO: Jon Slusser
President: Greg Harvey
Vice President: Greg Bedard
Executive Producer: Michael Feder

House of Moves, Inc. (310) 306-6131
5419 McConnell Ave. FAX (310) 437-4229
Los Angeles, CA 90066 www.moves.com
(Motion Capture)
CEO: Tom Tolles
Executive Producer: Scott Gagain
COO: Matt Lawrence

Adam Howard (310) 985-4448
www.howardgranitefilms.com
(2D/3D Computer Animation, Compositing & Visual FX)
Producer: Kelly Granite
Visual FX Supervisor/Director: Adam Howard

Humunculus (310) 827-1800
529 Victoria Ave. www.humunculus.com
Venice, CA 90291
(3D Animation & Broadcast Design)

[hy*drau'lx] (310) 319-2300
1447 Second St. FAX (310) 319-2305
Santa Monica, CA 90401 www.hydraulx.com
(2D/3D Animation and FX, 3D Modeling, Character Animation, Compositing, Digital Matte Painting, Morphing & Visual FX)
President: David Strause
Visual FX Supervisors: Colin Strause & Greg Strause
Executive Producer: Scott Michelson

I.E. Effects (310) 216-5678
(866) 540-3287
5811 Uplander Way, Ste. A FAX (310) 216-5616
Culver City, CA 90230 www.ieeffects.com
(3D Animation, 3D Modeling, CGI, Compositing, Digital Production, Editorial, Green Screen, Live Action Integration, Motion Graphics, Pre-Production Planning, Rotoscoping, Stereoscopic 3D Post Services, Visual FX & Visual FX Supervision)
Executive Producer: David Kenneth
VFX Supervisors: Aaron Kaminar & Dennis Michel
Executive In Charge of Production: Kris Murphy
Producer: Sarah M. Bavero

an ideal world (714) 953-9501
209 N. Bush St. FAX (714) 953-1195
Santa Ana, CA 92701 www.anidealworld.com
(2D/3D Animation, 3D Modeling, Animatics, Broadcast Design, Compositing, Blue Screen Compositing, CGI, Digital FX, Digital Restoration, Editorial, Graphic Design, Green Screen Compositing, Live Action Integration, Morphing, Motion Graphics, Pre-Production Planning, Previsualizations, Rotoscoping, Ultimatte, Visual FX & Visual FX Supervision)

Iguana Digital (818) 524-2600
(818) 620-3617
1020 N. Hollywood Way, Ste. 143 FAX (818) 508-3133
Burbank, CA 91505 www.iguanadigital.com

Image G/Ikonographics (818) 761-6644
10900 Ventura Blvd. www.imageg.com
Studio City, CA 91604
(Miniature Photography, Portable Real Time Motion Control, Stop Motion & Time-Lapse Photography)
Director: Thomas Barron

Imaginal Cells, Inc. (818) 785-0051
6314 Ethel Ave. FAX (818) 782-3756
Van Nuys, CA 91401 www.imaginalcellsinc.com
(2D Paint, 2D/3D Animation, 3D Modeling, Broadcast Design, Compositing, Computer Animation, Editorial, Graphic Design, Green Screen Compositing, Motion Graphics & Photography)

In-Sight Pix (310) 392-0999
(310) 399-5670
901 Abbot Kinney Blvd. FAX (310) 399-1334
Venice, CA 90291 www.insightpix.com
(3D Computer Animation & Visual FX)
Senior Producer: Melissa Davies

Infinity Filmworks (818) 881-3288
(Compositing, High Def Video & Live Action Integration)
Executive Producer/Director: Keith Melton

The Institution Post (818) 566-7801
423 N. Fairview St. www.the-institution.com
Burbank, CA 91505
(2D Animation, 2D Paint, 3D Animation, 3D Digitizing, 3D Modeling, Blue Screen Compositing, Broadcast Design, CGI, Compositing, Computer Animation, Digital Film Mastering, Digital FX, Digital Ink, Digital Matte Painting, Digital Paint, Digital Restoration, Editorial, Graphic Design, Green Screen Compositing, Illustrative Design, Image Processing, Live Action Integration, Matte Painting, Morphing, Motion Graphics, Pre-Production Planning, Previsualizations, Rotoscoping, Storyboards, Ultimatte, Visual FX & Visual FX Supervision)

July Sun Pictures (323) 461-0744
FAX (323) 461-4021
www.julysun.com
(2D/3D Animation/FX, 3D Modeling, Animatics, Blue/Green Screen Compositing, Digital Matte Painting, Motion Graphics, Pre-Production Planning, Rotoscoping & Scanning and Recording)

JV Media Design (714) 556-7468
(866) 909-4586
2300 Fairview Rd., Ste. O-103 FAX (714) 556-7468
Costa Mesa, CA 92626 www.jvmediadesign.com
(2D Animation, 3D Animation & Modeling, Character Animation and Design, Computer Animation, Graphic Design, Illustrative Design, Photography, Real Time Motion Control & Scanning and Recording)

ka-chew! (323) 468-3020
6353 Sunset Blvd. FAX (323) 468-3021
Los Angeles, CA 90028 www.kachew.com

Klasky Csupo, Inc. (323) 468-2600
1248 Highland Ave. FAX (323) 468-2675
Los Angeles, CA 90038 www.klaskycsupo.com
(Animation)

Kurtz & Friends (818) 841-8188
2312 W. Olive Ave. FAX (818) 841-6263
Burbank, CA 91506 www.kurtzandfriends.com
(2D/3D Computer Animation, Cel Animation, Character Design, Compositing, Digital Ink and Paint, Live Action Integration & Storyboards)
Producer: Boo Lopez
Director: Bob Kurtz

Lambo (310) 301-7700
4096 Glencoe Ave. FAX (949) 376-5593
Marina Del Rey, CA 90292 www.lambo.la

Lati2d (323) 852-1425
714 N. Laurel Ave. FAX (323) 852-1426
Los Angeles, CA 90046 www.lati2d.com
(2D/3D Computer Animation, Character Design, Digital and Visual FX, Live Action Integration, Logo with Type Design & Motion Graphics)
Creative Director: Water Kerner
Business Finances: Joanne Palmieri

Legacy Effects (818) 782-0870
340 Parkside Dr. FAX (818) 792-4322
San Fernando, CA 91340 www.sw-digital.com
(2D/3D Animation and FX, 2D Paint, 3D Modeling, Animatics, Blue/Green Screen Facilities, Character Animation, Compositing, Digital Matte Painting, Model/Miniature Shoots, Morphing, Motion Capture, Pre-Production Planning & Visual FX)
Executive Producer: Mike Pryor
CG Supervisor: Jabbar Raisani

Liquid Images (310) 392-8900
1635 12th St. FAX (310) 392-8930
Santa Monica, CA 90404 www.liquidimages.tv
(Compositing, Digital FX, Digital Matte Painting, Live Action Integration, Previsualization, Rotoscoping & Visual FX Supervision)

Liquid Light Studios (323) 851-5550
8039 Hemet Pl. FAX (323) 850-1060
Los Angeles, CA 90046 www.liquidlightstudios.com
(Computer Animation)
Executive Producer: Julie Pesusich

Liquid VFX (310) 392-1212
215 Rose Ave. FAX (310) 392-1222
Venice, CA 90291 www.laliquid.com
(Blue Screen Compositing, Compositing, Digital FX, Graphic Design, Green Screen Compositing, Morphing, Motion Graphics, Rotoscoping, Visual FX & Visual FX Supervision)
Visual FX Artists: James Bohn, Matthew Lydecker & Scott McNiel
Executive Producer: Romi Laine

Live Wire Productions & Visual FX (310) 831-6227
P.O. Box 245 www.livewirefilm.com
Palos Verdes Estates, CA 90274
(2D/3D Computer Animation, Blue Screen, Character Animation, Digital Compositing, Digital Intermediate, Miniature Photography & Visual FX)
Producer: Kristen Simmons
Visual FX Supervisor: Scott Simmons

Look! Effects, Inc. (323) 469-4230
6834 Hollywood Blvd., Ste. 200 FAX (323) 469-4931
Los Angeles, CA 90028 www.lookfx.com
(2D/3D Computer Animation, Compositing & Visual FX)
President/Visual FX Supervisor: Mark Driscoll
Art Director: Danny Kim
Visual FX Supervisors: Henrik Fett & Max Ivins

MacLeod Productions (310) 395-4739
502 10th St.
Santa Monica, CA 90402
(Computer Animation, Live Action Integration, Motion Control & Stereoscopic Visual FX)
Producer/Director: Sean MacLeod Phillips

Majikmaker Effects (818) 558-6400
www.majikmaker.com
(3D Animation, Animatics, Blue Screen Compositing, Broadcast Design, CGI, Compositing, Computer Animation, Digital FX, Green Screen Compositing, Live Action Integration, Pre-Production Planning, Previsualizations, Rotoscoping, Visual FX & Visual FX Supervision)

Mechnology (818) 840-9500
919 N. Victory Blvd. FAX (818) 840-9501
Burbank, CA 91502 www.mechnology.com

Method (310) 434-6500
730 Arizona Ave. FAX (310) 434-6501
Santa Monica, CA 90401 www.methodstudios.com
(2D/3D Computer Animation, Compositing, Digital Matte Painting, Previsualizations & Visual FX Supervision)
Executive Producer: Gabby Gourrier
Managing Director: Alex Frisch

MFX (323) 969-1011
3400 Barham Blvd. FAX (323) 969-1015
Los Angeles, CA 90068 www.mfxdesign.com
(2D/3D Computer Graphics & Compositing)
Visual FX Designer: Scott Milne

Michael Busch Digital Media/ TVart Inc. (213) 281-0264
8581 Santa Monica Blvd., Ste. 179 www.michaelbusch.com
West Hollywood, CA 90069
(2D Animation, 3D Animation, 3D Modeling, Broadcast Design, CGI, Character Animation, Compositing, Computer Animation, Digital FX, Editorial, Motion Graphics, Visual FX & Visual FX Supervision)
Visual FX Supervisor/Director: Michael Busch

Mind Over Eye, LLC (310) 396-4663 (310) 968-4259
1639 11th St., Ste. 117 FAX (310) 396-0663
Santa Monica, CA 90404 www.mindovereye.com
(2D/3D Animation and FX, 2D Paint, 3D Modeling, Animatics, Compositing, Morphing & Rotoscoping)

Mixin Pixls (310) 237-6438
www.mixinpixls.com
(2D/3D Computer Animation, Compositing, Digital FX & Visual FX)

Motion Analysis Studios (323) 461-3835
(Motion Capture) FAX (323) 461-3837
www.mastudios.com

Motion City Films (310) 434-1272
www.motioncity.com
(2D/3D Computer Animation, Blue/Green Screen Compositing, CGI, Compositing, Digital FX, Editorial, Motion Graphics & Visual FX)
Producer/Director: Jerry Witt

Motion Theory (310) 396-9433
321 Hampton Dr., Ste. 101 FAX (310) 396-7883
Venice, CA 90291 www.motiontheory.com
(2D/3D Animation and FX)

NBC Universal Artworks (212) 664-5972
30 Rockefeller Plaza, Ste. 1622W www.nbcartworks.com
New York, NY 10012

New Deal Studios, Inc. (310) 578-9929
4105 Redwood Ave. FAX (310) 578-7370
Los Angeles, CA 90066 www.newdealstudios.com
(3D Environments, Animation, Compositing, Matte Painting, Pre-Production Planning & Rotoscope Tracking)
Contact: David Sanger

Ntropic (310) 806-4950
2332 S. Centinela St., Ste.B FAX (310) 806-4959
Los Angeles, CA 90064 www.ntropic.com
(Animatics, Blue/Green Screen Compositing, Previsualizations & Rotoscoping)

Ocean Visual FX (714) 258-6678
8462 Gilford Circle **www.oceanvisualfx.com**
Huntington Beach, CA 92646
(3D Animation, 3D Modeling, Animatics, Blue/Green Screen Compositing, Broadcast Design, CGI, Character Animation, Character Design, Compositing, Computer Animation, Digital FX, Editorial, Graphic Design, Motion Capture, Motion Graphics, Pre-Production Planning, Previsualizations, Rotoscoping, Storyboards, Ultimatte, Visual FX & Visual FX Supervision)
Vice President/Technical Director: Rudy Sarzo
Head of 3D Character Animation: Jeff Clifton
President/VFX Supervisor: Robbie Robfogel

Opticam, Inc. (310) 452-0040
810 Navy St. FAX **(310) 452-0040**
Santa Monica, CA 90405
(Animation Camera, Cel Animation, Large Format Film, Motion Control, Motion Graphics & Rotoscoping)
Director: Annette Buehre-Nickerson

Pacific Motion Control, Inc. (818) 768-1573 (661) 644-1516
9812 Glenoaks Blvd. FAX **(818) 768-1575**
Sun Valley, CA 91352 **www.pacificmotion.net**
(Blue/Green Screen Facilities, Miniature Motion Control, Motion Control, Motion Control Photography, Real Time Motion Control, Stop-Motion Animation, Time-Lapse Photography & Visual FX)

Pacific Vision Productions, Inc. (626) 441-4869
210 Pasadena Ave. **www.pacificvision.com**
South Pasadena, CA 91030
(2D/3D Computer Animation, Compositing, Digital and Visual FX, Green Screen, Live Action Integration & Matte Painting)

PerformFX (818) 847-0030 (661) 609-4499
2301 Empire Ave. **www.performfx.com**
Burbank, CA 91504
(2D/3D Animation, Character Animation & Live Action Integration)

Perpetual Motion Pictures (661) 294-0788
26320 Diamond Pl., Ste 120 FAX **(661) 294-0786**
Santa Clarita, CA 91350
(2D/3D Computer Animation, Blue/Green Screen Compositing, Miniature Photography & Motion Control Photography)

Picture Mill (323) 465-8800
6422 Homewood Ave. FAX **(323) 465-8875**
Los Angeles, CA 90028 **www.picturemill.com**
(Broadcast Design)

Pixel Liberation Front (310) 396-9854
1285 Electric Ave. FAX **(310) 396-9874**
Venice, CA 90291 **www.thefront.com**
(2D/3D Computer Animation & Previsualization)
President: Colin Green
Head of Production: Sean Cushing

Pixel Magic (818) 760-0862
10635 Riverside Dr. FAX **(818) 760-4983**
Toluca Lake, CA 91602 **www.pixelmagicfx.com**
(2D/3D Computer Animation, Animatics, Compositing, Digital Matte Painting, Previsualization & Restoration)

Pixel Playground (818) 205-9910
FAX **(818) 501-0343**
www.pixelplaygroundinc.com
(2D/3D Animation and FX, 2D Paint, 3D Modeling, Character Animation, Compositing, Digital Matte Painting, Morphing, Rotoscoping, Ultimatte, Visual FX & Visual FX Supervision)

PixelMonger Inc./Scott Billups (818) 990-8993
15120 Hartsook St. **www.pixelmonger.com/esbindex.html**
Sherman Oaks, CA 91403
(2D Painting, 3D Modeling, Blue/Green Screen Compositing & Digital Matte Painting)

Pixerati (949) 681-8432 (909) 632-1740
14271 Albers Way FAX **(419) 593-4306**
Chino, CA 91710 **www.pixerati.com**
(3D Animation, 3D Modeling, Blue Screen Compositing, Broadcast Design, Character Animation, Character Design, Compositing, Computer Animation, Digital FX, Graphic Design, Green Screen Compositing, Image Processing, Live Action Integration, Morphing, Motion Capture, Motion Graphics, Pre-Production Planning, Previsualizations, Rotoscoping, Ultimatte, Visual FX & Visual FX Supervision)

Planet Blue (310) 899-3877
1250 Sixth St., Ste. 102 FAX **(310) 899-3787**
Santa Monica, CA 90401 **www.planetblue.com**
(2D/3D Computer Animation, Compositing & Image Processing)
President: Maury Rosenfeld
Executive Producer: Milt Alvarez

Playground Media Group (310) 315-3800
1813 Centinela Ave. FAX **(310) 315-3801**
Santa Monica, CA 90404 **www.playgroundla.com**
(2D/3D Computer Animation, Character Design & Compositing)

Point of Origin (818) 392-8735
www.pointoforiginmedia.com

The Post Group (323) 462-2300
6335 Homewood Ave. FAX **(323) 462-0836**
Hollywood, CA 90028 **www.postgroup.com**
(2D/3D Computer Animation & Compositing)
Contact: Ken Blaustein

Post Logic Studios (323) 461-7887
1800 N. Vine St., Ste. 100 FAX **(323) 461-7790**
Hollywood, CA 90028 **www.postlogic.com**
(2D/3D Computer Animation, Digital and Visual FX & Live Action Integration)

Prana Studios, Inc. (323) 645-6500
1145 N. McCadden Pl. **www.pranastudios.com**
Los Angeles, CA 90038

Praxis Films (323) 460-4393
c/o R. Sirott, 17324 Partheia St. FAX **(323) 460-4181**
Northridge, CA 91325
(3D Animation, Compositing, Miniature Photography & Motion Control)

Psychic Bunny (310) 862-4262
453 S. Spring St., Ste. 922 FAX **(213) 614-9046**
Los Angeles, CA 90013 **www.psychicbunny.com**

Public VFX (310) 450-6969
69 Market St. FAX **(310) 450-6999**
Venice, CA 90291
(2D Animation, 3D Computer Animation, Editorial & Visual FX)
Executive Producer: Sam Swisher

R.C. Gear (323) 465-3900 (800) 714-8099
6100 Melrose Ave. FAX **(323) 465-3600**
Los Angeles, CA 90038 **www.rc-gear.com**
(Broadcast Design, Graphic Design & Motion Graphics)

Radium (310) 264-6440
2115 Colorado Ave. **www.radium.com**
Santa Monica, CA 91404

Ratched Graphics (310) 696-4600
7920 Sunset Blvd., Ste. 200 FAX **(310) 696-4891**
Los Angeles, CA 90046 **www.asylument.com**

Reality Check Studios, Inc. (323) 465-3900 (323) 908-7000
6100 Melrose Ave. FAX **(323) 465-3600**
Los Angeles, CA 90038 **www.realityx.com**
(2D/3D Animation, 3D Modeling, Animatics, Blue/Green Screen Compositing, Broadcast Design, CGI, Character Animation and Design, Compositing, Computer Animation, Digital FX, Digital Matte Painting, Editorial, Graphic Design, Live Action Integration, Matte Painting, Motion Graphics, Previsualizations, Visual FX & Visual FX Supervision)
Contact: Andrew Heimbold

Red Magnet (310) 396-0100
215 Rose Ave. FAX **(310) 656-2801**
Venice, CA 90291 **www.redmagnetfx.com**
(2D/3D Animation, 3D Modeling, Animatics, Blue Screen Compositing, CGI, Character Animation, Compositing, Digital FX, Digital Matte Painting, Digital Restoration, Graphic Design, Live Action Integration, Matte Painting, Morphing, Motion Control, Motion Control Photography, Pre-Production Planning, Previsualizations, Rotoscoping, Ultimatte, Visual FX & Visual FX Supervision)
Executive Producer: Shira Boardman

RenderCore (866) 627-3149
(3D Animation and FX & Visual FX) FAX **(213) 623-3149**
www.rendercore.com

Renegade Animation, Inc. (818) 551-2351
116 N. Maryland Ave., Lower Level FAX **(818) 551-2350**
Glendale, CA 91206 **www.renegadeanimation.com**
(Cel Animation)
Producer: Ashley Postlewaite
Animation Director: Darrell Van Citters
Sales Rep: Andy Arkin

Rhythm + Hues Commercial Studios (310) 448-7900
5404 Jandy Pl. FAX **(310) 448-7601**
Los Angeles, CA 90066 **www.rhythm.com**
(2D Compositing, 3D Animation & Visual FX)
Executive Producer: Paul Babb
Head of Production, Commercial Digital: Lisa White
Animation/FX Directors: Clark Anderson, John-Mark Austin, Mark Dippé, EJ Foerster, Bill Kroyer, Pitof, Craig Talmy & James Wahlberg
Visual FX Supervisors: Eric DeHaven, John Heller, Tim Miller & Bill Westenhofer
East Coast Sales Rep: Carolyn Hill
Midwest/Detroit Sales Rep: Julie Ford, Kristina "KK" Kovacevic & Marci Miles
Western Region & Texas Sales Rep: Char Noonan
United Kingdom/Europe Sales Rep: Georgina Poushkine

Ring of Fire (310) 966-5055
1538 20th St. FAX **(310) 966-5056**
Santa Monica, CA 90404 **www.ringoffire.com**
(2D/3D Computer Animation, Compositing, HD Visual FX & Visual FX Supervision)
Executive Producer: John Myers
Creative Director: Jerry Spivack
Director of Sales: Amy Grgich

Rocket Films (213) 620-1476
2106 W. Glen Ave. FAX **(213) 625-1615**
Anaheim, CA 92801 **www.rocketfilms.com**
(Blue Screen, Miniature Photography, Motion Control, Rotoscoping & Stop Motion)
Executive Producer/Visual FX Supervisor: Jon Tucker

Rundell Filmworks (323) 817-4430
6363 Santa Monica Blvd., Ste. 207 FAX **(323) 817-4434**
Hollywood, CA 90038
Producer: Courtney Rundell
Editor: Matt Rundell

S4 Studios (323) 466-3910
1529 N. Cahuenga Blvd. FAX **(323) 466-3912**
Los Angeles, CA 90028 **www.s4studios.com**
(2D/3D Animation, 3D Modeling, Animatics, Blue/Green Screen Compositing, Broadcast Design, CGI, Character Animation and Design, Compositing, Computer Animation, Digital FX, Digital Matte Painting, Digital Restoration, Graphic Design, Illustrative Design, Matte Painting, Morphing, Motion Graphics, Previsualizations, Rotoscoping, Storyboards, Ultimatte & Visual FX)

Shelter Post (949) 809-2150
18500 Von Karman Ave., Ste. 140 FAX **(949) 809-2152**
Irvine, CA 92612 **www.shelterpost.com**

Shine (323) 937-7470
5410 Wilshire Blvd., Ste. 900 FAX **(323) 937-7420**
Los Angeles, CA 90036 **www.shinestudio.tv**

Sight Entertainment, Inc. (310) 392-2100
1639 11th St., Ste. 181 **www.sightus.com**
Santa Monica, CA 90404
(2D Animation, 2D Paint, 3D Animation, 3D Digitizing, 3D Modeling, Blue/Green Screen Compositing, Broadcast Design, Cel Animation, CGI, Character Animation, Character Design, Compositing, Computer Animation, Digital FX, Digital Matte Painting, Digital Paint, Digital Restoration, Editorial, Graphic Design, Illustrative Design, Image Processing, Live Action Integration, Miniature Motion Control, Morphing, Motion Graphics, Pre-Production Planning, Previsualizations, Rotoscoping, Storyboards, Time-Lapse Photography, Visual FX & Visual FX Supervision)

Sir Reel Pictures (818) 768-9778
(818) 415-7326
8036 Shadyglade Ave. **www.sirreelpictures.com**
North Hollywood, CA 91605
(Compositing & Matte Painting)

SoftMirage (714) 546-7030
(310) 560-8134
17993 Cowan St. FAX **(714) 546-3565**
Irvine, CA 92614 **www.softmirage.com**
(3D Animation and Modeling, Animatics, Graphic Design, Illustrative Design, Motion Graphics & Previsualizations)

Sony Pictures Imageworks (310) 840-8000
9050 W. Washington Blvd. FAX **(310) 840-8100**
Culver City, CA 90232 **www.imageworks.com**
(3D Character Animation & Visual FX)
Executive VP, Production Infrastructure/Executive Producer: Debbie Denise
Executive VP, Production/Executive Producer: Jenny Fulle

Special Blend (310) 909-7338
13020 Pacific Promenade, Ste. 107 FAX **(310) 909-7343**
Playa Vista, CA 90094 **www.specialblend.tv**

Standard (323) 224-3944
2020 N. Main St., Ste. 227 FAX **(323) 225-6226**
Los Angeles, CA 90031 **www.standardsite.com**
(3D Computer Graphics, Broadcast Design & Visual FX)

Stargate Digital (626) 403-8403
1001 El Centro St. FAX **(626) 403-8444**
South Pasadena, CA 91030 **www.stargatefilms.com**
(2D/3D Computer Animation, Blue Screen, Compositing, Laser Animation FX, Miniature Photography & Motion Control)

Steam (310) 636-4620
3021 Airport Ave., Ste. 201 FAX **(310) 636-4621**
Santa Monica, CA 90405 **www.steamshow.com**

STEELE Studios (310) 656-7770
5737 Mesmer Ave. FAX **(310) 656-7771**
Culver City, CA 90230 **www.steelevfx.com**
(2D Paint, 2D/3D Animation, 3D Modeling, Animatics, Blue Screen Compositing, Broadcast Design, CGI, Character Animation, Character Design, Compositing, Digital FX, Digital Matte Painting, Live Action Integration, Motion Capture, Motion Control, Motion Graphics, Pre-Production Planning, Previsualizations, Rotoscoping & Visual FX Supervision)
President/Creative Director: Jerry Steele
CEO/Sr. Executive Producer: Jo Steele

Stokes/Kohne Associates, Inc. (323) 468-2340
742 Cahuenga Blvd. FAX **(323) 468-2345**
Hollywood, CA 90038 **www.stokeskohne.com**
(2D Animation, Blue Screen Compositing, Broadcast Design, Cel Animation, Clay Animation, Compositing, Graphic Design, Green Screen Compositing, Miniature Motion Control, Miniatures, Motion Control, Motion Control Photography, Motion Graphics, Pre-Production Planning, Stop-Motion Animation, Time-Lapse Photography, Visual FX & Visual FX Supervision)
Visual FX Supervisor/Director: Dan Kohne

Storyheads Entertainment (323) 337-9062
8335 Sunset Blvd., Ste. 333 **www.storyheads.com**
West Hollywood, CA 90069
(2D/3D Animation and FX, Animatics, Cel Animation, Character Animation, Storyboards & Visual FX)
Founder/Creative Director: David Smith
Co-Founder/Executive Producer: Donna Smith

The Studio at New Wave Entertainment (818) 955-5276
(818) 295-8060
3003 W. Olive Ave. FAX **(818) 295-8061**
Burbank, CA 91505 **www.studio-nwe.com**
(3D Computer Animation & Visual FX)
Creative Director: Scott Williams
Director of Business Development: Richard Frank

Stuntless Productions (310) 918-8919
501 Santa Monica Blvd., Ste. 600 FAX **(310) 656-1300**
Santa Monica, CA 90401 **www.stuntless.com**

Subtext Studio (323) 533-0770
www.subtextstudio.com
(2D Animation, 3D Animation, 3D Modeling, Animatics, Blue Screen Compositing, Broadcast Design, CGI, Compositing, Computer Animation, Digital FX, Editorial, Graphic Design, Green Screen Compositing, Live Action Integration, Motion Graphics, Visual FX & Visual FX Supervision)
Executive Producer: Kirk Cameron

Super 78 (323) 464-7878
6900 Santa Monica Blvd. FAX (323) 464-7879
Hollywood, CA 90038 www.super78.com
(2D/3D Animation and FX, Character Animation, Compositing & Editorial)

Svengali FX (310) 310-8383
(310) 709-2836
228 Main St., Ste. 1 FAX (310) 943-1833
Venice, CA 90291 www.svengali-fx.com
(2D/3D Animation and FX, 3D Modeling, Animatics, Blue/Green Screen Facilities, Compositing, Digital Matte Painting, Model/Miature Shoots, Pre-Production Planning, Rotoscoping, Ultimatte & Visual FX)

Sway Studio (310) 844-7000
3535 Hayden Blvd., Fourth Fl. FAX (310) 844-7050
Culver City, CA 90232 www.swaystudio.com
(2D/3D Animation and FX, 3D Modeling, Animatics, Character Animation, Compositing, Digital Matte Painting, Rotoscoping & Visual FX)

Synthespian Studios (818) 753-1822
(413) 664-8176
5355 Cartwright Ave., Ste. 117 FAX (323) 576-5396
North Hollywood, CA 91601 www.synthespians.net
(2D Paint, CGI, Character Animation, Character Design, Compositing, Computer Animation, Digital FX, Green Screen Compositing, Live Action Integration, Morphing, Stereoscopic 3D, Visual FX & Visual FX Supervision)
President: Diana Walczak
General Manager: Michael Van Himbergen
Producers: Wendy Gipp & Amanda Roth
Directors: Jeff Kleiser & Diana Walczak

TeamWorks Digital (310) 991-5442
www.teamworksdigital.com
(2D/3D Animation and FX, 2D Paint, 3D Modeling, Animatics, Blue/Green Screen Facilities, Character Animation, Compositing, Morphing, Pre-Production Planning, Rotoscoping, Ultimatte & Visual FX)

Technicolor Creative Services - Hollywood (323) 817-6937
6040 Sunset Blvd. www.technicolor.com
Hollywood, CA 90028
(2D/3D Computer Animation, Compositing & Live Action Integration)
Contact: Jennifer Tellefsen

The Third Floor Previs Studios (323) 931-6633
5410 Wilshire Blvd., Ste. 1000 FAX (323) 931-9928
Los Angeles, CA 90036 www.thethirdfloorinc.com

Tigar Hare Studios (818) 907-6663
4485 Matilija Ave. FAX (818) 907-0693
Sherman Oaks, CA 91423 www.tigarhare.com
(3D Computer Animation, Broadcast Design, Character Animation, Compositing, Digital FX, Motion Capture, Previsualizations & Visual FX)
Executive Producer: Rhonda Cox
Creative Directors/Visual FX Supervisors: Dave Hare & Michael Tigar

Toon Makers, Inc. (818) 832-8666
17333 Ludlow St. www.toonmakers.com
Granada Hills, CA 91344
(Cel Animation, CGI & Character Design)
Producer: Rocky Solotoff

Trance (323) 651-1114
449 N. Edinburgh Ave. www.trancedesigns.com
Los Angeles, CA 90048

Trans FX, Inc. - TFX (805) 485-6110
(888) 876-7339
2361 Eastman Ave. FAX (805) 532-1645
Oxnard, CA 93030 www.transfx.com
(Scanning)

Transcontinuity Studios, Inc. (818) 980-8852
4710 W. Magnolia Blvd. FAX (818) 980-8974
Burbank, CA 91505 www.nealadamsentertainment.com
President/Creative Director: Neal Adams
VP/Executive Producer: Marilyn Adams
Head of Sales: Eric Knight

Ultimatte-Rentals.com (323) 512-1542
www.ultimatte-rentals.com
(Blue Screen Compositing, Compositing, Digital FX, Green Screen Compositing, Previsualizations, Ultimatte & Visual FX)

Uniconn Productions (818) 887-9108
8485 Valley Circle Blvd., Ste. 203 FAX (818) 348-6544
West Hills, CA 91304 www.uniconnproductions.com
(3D Computer, Clay Animation & Flash Animation)

Unsigned Records Multimedia (818) 377-4011
11684 Ventura Blvd., Ste. 717 www.unsigned-records.com
Studio City, CA 91604

Van Guard Animation (310) 360-8039
8703 W. Olympic Blvd. FAX (310) 360-8059
Los Angeles, CA 90035 www.vanguardanimation.com
(2D/3D Computer Animation, Compositing, Digital and Visual FX & Visual FX Supervision)

Velocity Visuals, Inc. (310) 376-7870
www.velocityfx.com
(2D Animation, 3D Animation, 3D Modeling, Animatics, Blue Screen Compositing, CGI, Character Animation, Character Design, Computer Animation, Digital FX, Digital Matte Painting, Green Screen Compositing, Live Action Integration, Matte Painting, Pre-Production Planning, Previsualizations, Rotoscoping, Visual FX & Visual FX Supervision)
Executive Producer/Creative Director: William Powloski
Computer Animation Director: Steward Burris

View Studio, Inc. (805) 745-8814
385 Toro Canyon Rd. www.viewstudio.com
Carpinteria, CA 93013
(2D/3D Computer Animation and Graphics, Compositing, Visual FX & Visual FX Supervision)
President/Creative Director: Bob Engelsiepen

Viewpoint, Inc. (310) 280-2000
10549 Jefferson Blvd. FAX (310) 845-9412
Culver City, CA 90232 www.viewpoint.com
(2D Paint, 2D/3D Animation, 3D Digitizing, 3D Modeling, Animatics, CGI, Computer Animation, Graphic Design, Motion Graphics, Photography, Previsualizations, Scanning and Recording & Storyboards)
Presidents: Bob Rice & Pat Vogt
Sales Rep: Vidette Schine

Virtualsets.com (323) 512-1542
www.virtualsets.com
(2D/3D Animation and FX, 3D Modeling, Blue/Green Screen Compositing, Broadcast Design, Digital Matte Painting, Motion Capture, Pre-Production Planning, Previsualizations, Rotoscoping, Ultimatte, Virtual Set Design & Visual FX)

Vital Distraction, LLC (805) 991-9866
(888) 339-4927
2045 Royal Ave., Ste. 234 FAX (805) 991-9866
Simi Valley, CA 93065 www.vitaldistraction.com
(2D/3D Animation, 3D Modeling, Animatics, CGI, Character Animation, Computer Animation, Digital FX, Digital Matte Painting, Live Action Integration, Pre-Production Planning, Previsualizations & Visual FX)

Whodoo EFX (310) 828-6060
FAX (310) 828-6066
www.whodooefx.com
(2D/3D Computer Animation & Digital and Visual FX)
Visual FX Supervisor: Helena Packer
Producer: Sarah Paul

Wicked Liquid FX (949) 250-8786
4120 Birch St., Ste. 122 FAX (949) 250-8701
Newport Beach, CA 92660 www.wickedliquidfx.com
(2D Paint, 2D/3D Animation and FX, 3D Modeling, Animatics, Character Animation, Compositing, Digital Matte Painting, Morphing, Motion Capture, Pre-Production Planning, Ultimatte & Visual FX)

Wut It Is **(323) 467-3300**
6121 Santa Monica Blvd., Ste. 201 FAX **(323) 467-7480**
Los Angeles, CA 90038 **www.wutitis.com**
(2D Animation, 2D Paint, 3D Animation, 3D Modeling, Blue Screen Compositing, Broadacst Design, Cel Animation, CGI, Character Animation, Character Design, Compositing, Computer Animation, Digital FX, Digital Ink, Digital Paint, Editorial, Graphic Design, Green Screen Compositing, Illustrative Design, Image Processing, Live Action Integration, Matte Painting, Morphing, Motion Graphics, Rotoscoping, Stop-Motion Animation, Ultimatte, Visual FX & Visual FX Supervision)

X 1 FX **(310) 836-9011**
5870 W. Jefferson Blvd., Ste. D FAX **(310) 836-9010**
Los Angeles, CA 90016 **www.x1fx.com**
Executive Producer: Edy Enriquez
Producer: Jon Jacobson
Scheduling: Edy Enriquez & Jon Jacobson
Flame Artist/Visual Effects Supervisor: Mark Larranaga
General Manager: Raena Singh

Xpletive **(818) 957-0100**
4910 Lauderdale Ave. **www.redgypsy.com**
Glendale, CA 91214
(2D/3D Computer Animation, Compositing, Motion Graphics & Visual Effects)

yU+co. **(323) 606-5050**
941 N. Mansfield Ave. FAX **(323) 606-5040**
Los Angeles, CA 90038 **www.yuco.com**
(2D/3D Computer Animation, Broadcast Design, Digital and Visual FX, Logo and Type Design & Motion Graphics)

Zak/Paperno **(323) 937-2517**
7000 Beverly Blvd.
Los Angeles, CA 90036
(Computer Graphics, FX Animation, Image Processing & Storyboards)
Executive Producer/Creative Director: Michael Zak
Creative Director: Lisa Paperno

Zoic, Inc. **(310) 838-0770**
3582 Eastham Dr. FAX **(310) 838-1169**
Culver City, CA 90232 **www.zoicstudios.com**
(2D/3D Animation and FX, 3D Modeling, Animatics, Character Animation, Compositing, Digital Matte Painting, Morphing, Pre-Production Planning, Rotoscoping & Visual FX)

Blue Room (310) 727-2600
1600 Rosecrans Ave., Bldg. 5A FAX **(310) 727-2601**
Manhattan Beach, CA 90266 **www.blueroomfx.com**

Chainsaw (323) 785-1550
(323) 785-1555
940 N. Orange Dr., Seond Fl. **www.chainsawedit.com**
Hollywood, CA 90038

The Digital Intermediate Group, LLC (310) 315-5720
40 N. Orange Dr., Ste. 121 FAX **(310) 315-5724**
Hollywood, CA 90038 **www.digroupusa.com**

Digital Jungle Post Production (323) 962-0867
6363 Santa Monica Blvd. FAX **(323) 962-9960**
Los Angeles, CA 90038 **www.digijungle.com**

Encore Hollywood (323) 466-7663
6344 Fountain Ave. FAX **(323) 467-5539**
Hollywood, CA 90028 **www.encorehollywood.com**

FotoKem (818) 846-3101
(818) 846-3102
2801 W. Alameda Ave. FAX **(818) 841-2130**
Burbank, CA 91505 **www.fotokem.com**

Gradient Effects (310) 821-3177
4120 Del Rey Ave. FAX **(310) 821-0584**
Marina del Rey, CA 90292 **www.gradientfx.com**

Hip Films (323) 467-2897
1622 Gower St. FAX **(323) 469-8251**
Hollywood, CA 90028 **www.hipfilms.com**

Hollywood-DI (323) 850-3550
1041 N. Formosa Ave. FAX **(323) 850-3551**
Fairbanks Bldg., Ste. 7 **www.hollywooddi.com**
West Hollywood, CA 90046

HTV - High Technology Video (323) 969-8822
(818) 760-7600
3575 Cahuenga Blvd. West, Fourth Fl. FAX **(323) 969-8860**
Los Angeles, CA 90068 **www.htvinc.net**

Illuminate – Arts, Media & Entertainment (323) 969-8822
3575 Cahuenga Blvd. West, Fourth Fl. FAX **(323) 969-8840**
Los Angeles, CA 90068 **www.illuminatehollywood.com**

iO Film (323) 822-4444
FAX **(323) 467-7300**
www.iofilm.net

iProbe Multilingual Solutions, Inc. (888) 489-6035
www.iprobesolutions.com

Laser Pacific Media Corporation (323) 462-6266
809 N. Cahuenga Blvd. FAX **(323) 464-3233**
Hollywood, CA 90038 **www.laserpacific.com**

Mechnology (818) 840-9500
919 N. Victory Blvd. FAX **(818) 840-9501**
Burbank, CA 91502 **www.mechnology.com**

Technicolor Creative Services - Hollywood (323) 817-6937
6040 Sunset Blvd. **www.technicolor.com**
Hollywood, CA 90028

Acutrack (888) 234-3472
FAX (925) 579-5001
www.acutrack.com

Affusion Media/ Visual Data Media Services Inc. (818) 558-3363
145 W. Magnolia Blvd. FAX (818) 845-2550
Burbank, CA 91505 www.visualdatainc.com
(All Formats & Standards Conversion)

AGF Media Services (818) 780-7400
(323) 467-1234
14932 Delano St. FAX (818) 904-9905
Van Nuys, CA 91411 www.agfmedia.com
(All Formats)

Antarctica Productions (310) 923-8505
(925) 899-8909
5027 Colfax Ave., Studio 5 www.antarcticaproductions.com
Valley Village, CA 91607

Archetype DVD (310) 613-6654
www.archetypedvd.com

Bitmax, LLC (323) 978-7878
6255 Sunset Blvd., Ste. 1515 FAX (323) 978-7879
Los Angeles, CA 90028 www.bitmax.net
(All Formats, DVD, DVDR & Standards Conversion)

Clonetown HD (323) 850-6608
(323) 851-0299
3131 Cahuenga Blvd. West FAX (323) 851-0277
Los Angeles, CA 90068 www.clonetownhd.com
(¾", 1", 8mm, Beta SP & SX, Betacam SP, CD-Audio, CD-ROM, Composer Dubs, D2, Digibeta, DV, DVCAM, DVC Pro, HDCAM, HDCAM SR, HDV, Hi-8mm, High Def, NTSC, Standards Conversions & VHS)

Complete Media Services (310) 306-5074
4127 Via Marina, Ste. 414 FAX (310) 306-5124
Marina del Rey, CA 90292
(All Formats, CD-ROM & DVD)

Copy Right Video (310) 315-4151
1554 18th St. FAX (310) 582-1554
Santa Monica, CA 90404 www.copyrightvideo.com
(All Formats)

Custom Video (310) 543-4901
707 Torrance Blvd., Ste. 105 www.customvideo.tv
Redondo Beach, CA 90277
(All Formats)

Deck Hand, Inc. (818) 557-8403
1905 Victory Blvd., Ste. 8 FAX (818) 557-8406
Glendale, CA 91201 www.deckhand.com
(Beta SP, Digital Betacam, DV, DV-5, DVCAM, DVCPRO, DVCPRO HD, DVD-R, HDCAM & HDV)

Disc Makers (800) 731-8009
(323) 876-1411
3445 Cahuenga Blvd. West FAX (323) 876-6724
Los Angeles, CA 90068 www.discmakers.com

Dub-It.com (323) 993-9570
(888) 993-8248
1110 N. Tamarind Ave. FAX (323) 962-3446
Hollywood, CA 90038 www.dub-it.com
(CD-ROM, DVD, DVD-R & VHS)

Dubscape, Inc. (818) 456-1051
7543 Loma Verde Ave. FAX (818) 456-1046
Canoga Park, CA 91303 www.dubscape.com
(1", 1/2", 3/4", Beta SP, Digibeta, Digital Betacam, D2, DV & DVCAM)

Duplitech Corporation (310) 781-1101
2637 Manhattan Beach Blvd. FAX (310) 781-1109
Redondo Beach, CA 90278 www.duplitech.com
(Blu Ray, CD, DVD & DVD-R)

The Edit Bay (714) 978-7878
571 N. Poplar St., Ste. I FAX (714) 978-7858
Orange, CA 92868 www.theeditbay.com
(3/4", 1", 8mm, Betacam SP, CD-ROM, Digital Betacam, DVD, Standards Conversion, S-VHS & VHS)

Filmcore Distribution/Vault Services (323) 769-8400
1010 N. Highland Ave. FAX (323) 769-8401
Los Angeles, CA 90038 www.filmcore.net
(1", 1/2", 3/4", Beta, Beta SP, D1, D2 & Digibeta)

Five Star Video/1555 TV (818) 558-1679
3400 W. Alameda Ave., Ste. A FAX (818) 558-4367
Burbank, CA 91505 www.1555.tv

Flow Motion Inc. (888) 818-3569
143 E. Gonzales Rd. FAX (888) 818-3569
Oxnard, CA 93036 www.flowmotioninc.com
(CD-Audio, CD-ROM, DVD, DVD-5, DVD-9, DVD-R, Blu Ray, DVCAM & DV)

Hellman Production, Inc. (323) 456-0446
6404 Wilshire Blvd., Ste. 700 www.hellmanproduction.com
Los Angeles, CA 90048

Home Run Software Services, Inc. (714) 901-0109
15562 Chemical Ln. FAX (714) 901-0102
Huntington Beach, CA 92649 www.home-run.com
(All Formats)

Imperial Media Services, Inc. (310) 396-2008
(800) 736-8273
3303 Pico Blvd., Ste. A FAX (310) 396-8894
Santa Monica, CA 90405 www.imperialmedia.com
(All Formats, Authoring, Duplication, DVD, DVDR, Replication, Standards Conversions, Transfers & VHS)

iProbe Multilingual Solutions, Inc. (888) 489-6035
www.iprobesolutions.com
(¾", ¾" SP, 1", Beta SP, Beta SX, Betacam SP, CD-Audio, CD-ROM, Composer Dubs, D1, D2, D3, D5, Digibeta, Digital Betacam, DV, DVC Pro, DVCAM, DVD, DVD-5, DVD-9, DVD-R, HD D5, HD Digibeta, HD DVC Pro, High Def, Laserdisc, NTSC, Standards Conversions, Super 8, S-VHS & VHS)

JR Media Services, Inc. (818) 557-0200
2501 W. Burbank Blvd., Ste. 200 FAX (818) 557-0201
Burbank, CA 91505 www.jrmediaservices.com

Level 3 Post (818) 840-7200
(818) 840-7889
2901 W. Alameda, Third Fl. www.level3post.com
Burbank, CA 91505

Lightning Media (818) 556-2777
3723 W. Olive Ave. FAX (818) 556-2770
Burbank, CA 91505 www.lightningmedia.com
(All Formats, High Def & Standards Conversion)

Lightning Media (323) 957-9255
1415 N. Cahuenga Blvd. FAX (323) 330-6217
Hollywood, CA 90028 www.lightningmedia.com
(All Formats, High Def & Standards Conversion)

New & Unique Videos (619) 644-3000
(800) 365-8433
7323 Rondel Court FAX (619) 644-3001
San Diego, CA 92119 www.newuniquevideos.com
(All Video Formats, CD-ROM & DVD)

OneWorld Language Solutions (323) 848-7993
FAX (323) 848-7995
www.oneworldlanguage.com

The Studios at Paramount (323) 956-3041
The Studios at Paramount FAX (323) 862-1181
Post Production Services www.thestudiosatparamount.com
5555 Melrose Ave.
Los Angeles, CA 90038
(All Formats)

Point360 (323) 957-5500
1147 Vine St. FAX (323) 466-7406
Hollywood, CA 90038 www.point360.com
(All Video Formats)

Point360 (IVC) (818) 569-4949
(866) 968-4336
2777 N.Ontario St. www.point360.com
Burbank, CA 91504
(All Video Formats)

Post and Beam (310) 828-1128
3025 Olympic Blvd., Ste. 112 FAX (310) 828-8211
Santa Monica, CA 90404 www.postandbeam.tv

Ⓐ **Post Digital Services** (323) 845-0812
1258 N. Highland Ave., Ste. 210 FAX (323) 845-0812
Hollywood, CA 90038 www.postdigitalservices.com
(¾", ¾" SP, 1", 2K, 4K, 8mm, 16mm, 35mm, All Formats, All Video Formats, Beta SP, Beta SX, Blu Ray, CD, Digibeta, DVD, HD D5, HD Digibeta, HD DVC Pro, Hi-8mm, High Def, Standards Conversions, Super 8, S-VHS, Tape Cloning & VHS)

Post Media Group, Inc. (310) 289-5959
337 S. Robertson Blvd. www.postmediagroup.tv
Beverly Hills, CA 90211

Post Modern Edit, LLC (949) 608-8700
2941 Alton Pkwy FAX (949) 608-8729
Irvine, CA 92606 www.postmodernedit.com
(All Video Formats, High Def & Standards Conversions)

Prime Digital Media Services (661) 964-0220
28111 Avenue Stanford FAX (661) 964-0550
Valencia, CA 91355 www.primedigital.com

Ⓐ **Santa Monica Video, Inc.** (310) 451-0333
(800) 843-3827
1505 11th St. FAX (310) 458-3350
Santa Monica, CA 90401 www.santamonicavideo.com
(All Formats)

Technicolor Creative Services - Glendale (818) 500-9090
1631 Gardena Ave. FAX (818) 500-4099
Glendale, CA 91204 www.technicolor.com
(1", 1/2", 3/4", 3/4" SP, Beta SP, Beta SX, CD-Audio, Composer Dubs, D1, D2, D3, D5, DVCAM, DVD, DVD-5, DVD-9, DVD-R, Digibeta/Digital Betacam, Motion Vector, Standards Versions, S-VHS & VHS)

TEDS (310) 237-6438
(All Formats & Standards Conversion) www.tedsla.com

Timecode Multimedia (310) 826-9199
12340 Santa Monica Blvd., Ste. 230
West Los Angeles, CA 90025
www.timecodemultimedia.com
(All Video Formats, Beta SP, Beta SX, CD-Audio, Composer Dubs, Digibeta, DV, DVC Pro, DVCAM, DVCPro, DVD, HD D5, High Def, NTSC, Standards Conversions, Tape Cloning & VHS)

Tylie Jones & Associates, Inc. (818) 955-7600
3620 W. Valhalla Dr. FAX (818) 955-8551
Burbank, CA 91505 www.tylie.com
(1", 1/2", 3/4", Beta, Beta SP, CD-Audio, CD-ROM, D1, D2, D3, D5, Digibeta, DVC Pro, DVD, HD D5, HD DVC Pro & High Def)

Victory Studios LA (818) 769-1776
10911 Riverside Dr., Ste. 100 FAX (818) 760-1280
North Hollywood, CA 91602 www.victorystudiosla.com
(3/4" SP, Betacam SP, CD-ROM, Digibeta, DV, DVC Pro, DVD, HD DVC Pro, Standards Conversions, S-VHS & VHS)

Westside Media Group (310) 979-3500
(818) 779-8600
12233 W. Olympic Blvd., Ste. 152 FAX (310) 979-3503
West Los Angeles, CA 90064
www.westsidemediagroup.com

World of Video & Audio (310) 659-5959
(866) 900-3827
8717 Wilshire Blvd. FAX (310) 659-8247
Beverly Hills, CA 90211 www.wova.com
(Digital Services, DVCPro HD, HDCam, Film, Most Tape Formats & Standards Conversions)

5th Wall Entertainment (323) 461-0600
6311 Romaine St., Ste. 7136
Hollywood, CA 90038 ww.5thwallentertainment.com

Acutrack (888) 234-3472
FAX (925) 579-5001
www.acutrack.com

Affusion Media/ Visual Data Media Services Inc. (818) 558-3363
145 W. Magnolia Blvd. FAX (818) 845-2550
Burbank, CA 91502 www.visualdatainc.com

Alter Ego Creative Entertainment (323) 937-3348
7280 Melrose Ave., Ste. 3 FAX (323) 661-2921
Los Angeles, CA 90046 www.alteregoce.com

AniMill (818) 972-9116
(407) 654-4494
200 E. Angeleno Ave., Ste. 312 www.animill.com
Burbank, CA 91502

Ascent Media DVD (818) 526-3000
2130 N. Hollywood Way www.ascentmedia.com
Burbank, CA 91505

Bitmax, LLC (323) 978-7878
6255 Sunset Blvd., Ste. 1515 FAX (323) 978-7879
Los Angeles, CA 90028 www.bitmax.net

BLINK Digital (818) 526-2800
2901 W. Alameda Ave., Fourth Fl. FAX (818) 526-2830
Burbank, CA 91505 www.blinkdigital.com

Chroma Titles, Inc. (310) 204-6852
(818) 988-9923
10718 McCune Ave. FAX (310) 204-6952
Los Angeles, CA 90034 www.chromatitles.com
(Authoring)

Cinevision Digital (213) 617-7200
424 Bamboo Ln. FAX (213) 617-7300
Los Angeles, CA 90012 www.cinevisiondigital.com

Clonetown HD (323) 850-6608
(323) 851-0299
3131 Cahuenga Blvd. West FAX (323) 851-0277
Los Angeles, CA 90068 www.clonetownhd.com

Cloud 19 (310) 839-5400
(310) 717-7819
3767 Overland Ave., Ste. 104 FAX (310) 839-5404
Los Angeles, CA 90034 www.cloud19.com

Coast Media Teleproductions, Inc. (949) 417-0300
17062 Murphy Ave., Bldg. B www.coastmedia.com
Irvine, CA 92614
(Authoring)

Complete Media Services (310) 306-5074
4127 Via Marina, Ste. 414 FAX (310) 306-5124
Marina del Rey, CA 90292
(Replication)

Copy Right Video (310) 315-4151
1554 18th St. FAX (310) 582-1554
Santa Monica, CA 90404 www.copyrightvideo.com

Crest National (323) 860-1300
(800) 961-8273
1000 Highland Ave. www.crestnational.com
Hollywood, CA 90038

Custom Video (310) 543-4901
707 Torrance Blvd., Ste. 105 www.customvideodubs.com
Redondo Beach, CA 90277

Directorsite DVD (310) 727-2770
Raleigh Manhattan Beach Studios FAX (310) 727-2601
1600 Rosecrans Ave., Bldg. 5A www.blueroomfx.com
Manhattan Beach, CA 90266

Disc Makers (800) 731-8009
(323) 876-1411
3445 Cahuenga Blvd. West FAX (323) 876-6724
Los Angeles, CA 90068 www.discmakers.com

Dogma Studios (310) 838-2973
4134 Del Rey Ave. FAX (310) 838-2975
Marina del Rey, CA 90292 www.dogmastudios.com

drotardesign.com (310) 753-6423
(310) 451-7106
914 Fourth St., Ste. 304 www.drotardesign.com
Santa Monica, CA 90403
(Authoring)

Dub-It.com (323) 993-9570
(888) 993-8248
1110 N. Tamarind Ave. FAX (323) 962-3446
Hollywood, CA 90038 www.dub-it.com
(Replication)

Duplitech Corporation (310) 781-1101
2637 Manhattan Beach Blvd. FAX (310) 781-1109
Redondo Beach, CA 90278 www.duplitech.com

DVDworx (213) 388-6220
523 S. Rampart St. FAX (213) 381-6223
Los Angeles, CA 90057 www.dvdworx.com
(Authoring)

Flow Motion Inc. (888) 818-3569
143 E. Gonzales Rd. FAX (888) 818-3569
Oxnard, CA 93036 www.flowmotioninc.com

FXF Productions, Inc. (310) 577-5009
1024 Harding Ave., Ste. 201 FAX (310) 577-1960
Venice, CA 90291 www.fxfproductions.com

Hellman Production, Inc. (323) 456-0446
6404 Wilshire Blvd., Ste. 700 www.hellmanproduction.com
Los Angeles, CA 90048

Illusion Factory (818) 598-8400
21800 Burbank Blvd., Ste. 225 www.illusionfactory.com
Woodland Hills, CA 91367

Imperial Media Services, Inc. (310) 396-2008
(800) 736-8273
3303 Pico Blvd., Ste. A FAX (310) 396-8894
Santa Monica, CA 90405 www.imperialmedia.com

JR Media Services, Inc. (818) 557-0200
2501 W. Burbank Blvd., Ste. 200 FAX (818) 557-0201
Burbank, CA 91505 www.jrmediaservices.com

Kappa Studios, Inc. (818) 843-3400
3619 W. Magnolia Blvd. FAX (818) 559-5684
Burbank, CA 91505 www.kappastudios.com

Lightning Media (323) 957-9255
1415 N. Cahuenga Blvd. FAX (323) 330-6217
Hollywood, CA 90028 www.lightningmedia.com

LightSoundImagination (323) 466-6655
(310) 497-9456
(Authoring) www.lightsoundimagination.com

Mind Over Eye, LLC (310) 396-4663
(310) 968-4259
1639 11th St., Ste. 117 FAX (310) 396-0663
Santa Monica, CA 90404 www.mindovereye.com

New & Unique Videos (619) 644-3000 (800) 365-8433
7323 Rondel Court FAX (619) 644-3001
San Diego, CA 92119 www.newuniquevideos.com

OneWorld Language Solutions (323) 848-7993
FAX (323) 848-7995
www.oneworldlanguage.com

The Studios at Paramount (323) 956-3041
The Studios at Paramount FAX (323) 862-2242
Post Production Services www.thestudiosatparamount.com
5555 Melrose Ave.
Los Angeles, CA 90038

Post and Beam (310) 828-1128
3025 Olympic Blvd., Ste. 112 FAX (310) 828-8211
Santa Monica, CA 90404 www.postandbeam.tv

Post Digital Services (323) 845-0812
1258 N. Highland Ave., Ste. 210 FAX (323) 845-0812
Hollywood, CA 90038 www.postdigitalservices.com
(Authoring, Blu-Ray & Replication)

Post Modern Digital, LLC (949) 608-8700
2941 Alton Pkwy FAX (949) 608-8760
Irvine, CA 92606 www.postmoderndigital.com
(Authoring & Replication)

Precision Productions + Post (310) 839-4600
10718 McCune Ave. FAX (310) 839-4601
Los Angeles, CA 90034 www.precisionpost.com

Prime Digital Media Services (661) 964-0220
28111 Avenue Stanford FAX (661) 964-0550
Valencia, CA 91355 www.primedigital.com

Santa Monica Video, Inc. (310) 451-0333
1505 11th St. FAX (310) 458-3350
Santa Monica, CA 90401 www.santamonicavideo.com

Station 22 Edit & Effects (310) 488-7726
3614 Overland Ave. www.station22.com
Los Angeles, CA 90034

Technicolor Creative Services (818) 260-1200
2233 N. Ontario St., Ste. 300 FAX (818) 260-1201
Burbank, CA 91504 www.technicolor.com
(Authoring)

Timecode Multimedia (310) 826-9199
12340 Santa Monica Blvd., Ste. 230
Santa Monica, CA 90025
(Authoring) www.timecodemultimedia.com

Transistor Studios (310) 613-3090
(Authoring) www.transistorstudios.com

Video Symphony (888) 871-2843 (818) 557-7200
266 E. Magnolia Blvd. FAX (818) 845-1951
Burbank, CA 91502 www.videosymphony.com
(Authoring)

Viking Video Cassettes, Inc. (626) 633-0883 (818) 262-8250
5620 Ayala Ave. FAX (626) 633-0884
Irwindale, CA 91706 www.myvikingvideo.com
(Replication)

World of Video & Audio (310) 659-5959 (866) 900-3827
8717 Wilshire Blvd. FAX (310) 659-8247
Beverly Hills, CA 90211 www.wova.com

Zoo Digital (310) 220-3939
2201 Park Pl., Ste. 100 FAX (310) 220-3958
El Segundo, CA 90245 www.zoodigital.com
(Authoring)

A Frame (818) 339-7390
www.aframepost.com
(24P Editing Systems, 35mm, Analog, Analog Decks, Avid Systems, Digibeta, Digital Decks, Digital Editing Systems, Digital Non-Linear, Editing Suites, Editing Supplies, Fiber, Film, Final Cut Pro Systems, Hard Drive Rentals, HD Decks, High Def, Linear Offline, Linear Online, Macintosh-Based Non-Linear Offline, Magnetic Hard Drives, Monitors, Non-Linear Hard Drives, Non-Linear Offline, Non-Linear Online, Video, Video Tape Monitors & Video Tape Recorders)

Aaron & Le Duc (310) 452-2034
2210 Third St., Ste. 316 www.leducdesign.com
Santa Monica, CA 90405
(High Def & Non-Linear Offline and Online)

Absolute Rentals (818) 842-2828
2633 N. San Fernando Blvd. FAX (818) 842-8815
Burbank, CA 91504 www.absoluterentals.com
(Digibeta, HD Video Decks & Non-Linear Offline)

Address One (310) 838-7783
(323) 465-4415
c/o Raleigh Studios FAX (323) 960-4961
662 N. Van Ness Ave., Ste. 301 www.addressone.tv
Los Angeles, CA 90004
(Avid Systems & Non-Linear Offline and Online)

Alternative Rentals (310) 204-3388
5805 W. Jefferson Blvd. FAX (310) 204-3384
Los Angeles, CA 90016 www.alternativerentals.com
(24P Editing Systems, AVID, Final Cut Pro & HD Online)

Artistic Resources Corporation (323) 965-5200
535 N. Brand Blvd., Ste. 235 FAX (323) 965-5209
Glendale, CA 91203 www.artisticresources.com

Atomic Post (310) 315-7245
3025 W. Olympic Blvd., Ste. 128 www.atomicpost.us
Santa Monica, CA 90404
(Avid & Final Cut Pro)

Audio Video Systems International (818) 888-7625
5101 Tendilla Ave. FAX (818) 730-5047
Woodland Hills, CA 91364 www.usedvideo.net
(Linear/Non-Linear Offline & Online Rentals)

Avid (818) 557-2520
(800) 949-2843
101 S. First St., Ste. 200 FAX (818) 557-2558
Burbank, CA 91502 www.avid.com
(Digital Non-Linear Offline and Online)

Ⓐ **B2 Services, Inc.** (818) 566-8769
3818 Burbank Blvd. FAX (818) 566-1378
Burbank, CA 91505 www.b2servicesinc.com
(24P Editing Systems, Analog Decks, Avid Systems, Digibeta, Digital Decks, Digital Editing Systems, Digital Non-Linear, Final Cut Pro Systems, Hard Drive Rentals, HD Decks, High Def, MacIntosh-Based Non-Linear Offline, Magnetic Hard Drive Monitors, Non-lInear Hard Drives, Non-Linear Offline and Online, Rentals Only & Video Tape Monitors and Recorders)

Big Time Picture Company, Inc. (310) 207-0921
12210½ Nebraska Ave. FAX (310) 826-0071
Los Angeles, CA 90025 www.bigtimepic.com
(Avid Systems, Digibeta, Digital Decks, Digital Editing Systems, Digital Non-Linear, Editing Suites, Final Cut Pro Systems, Hard Drive Rentals, High Def, Macintosh-Based Non-Linear Offline, Monitors & Non-Linear Offline)

Broadcast Store (818) 998-9100
9420 Lurline Ave., Ste. C FAX (818) 998-9106
Chatsworth, CA 91311 www.broadcaststore.com
(Video)

Ⓐ **Catalyst Post Services** (818) 841-4952
3029 W. Burbank Blvd. FAX (818) 566-4175
Burbank, CA 91505 www.catalystpost.com
(Avid Systems, Editing Suites & Non-Linear Offline and Online)

Christy's Editorial (818) 845-1755 / (800) 556-5706
3625 W. Pacific Ave. FAX (818) 845-1756
Burbank, CA 91505 www.christys.net
(Editing Supplies)

CRE - Computer & A/V Solutions (800) 427-2382 / (888) 444-1059
5732 Buckingham Pkwy FAX (877) 440-5252
Culver City, CA 90230
www.computerrentals.com/products/mac/mac_rentals_specialist.php
(Hard Drive Rentals, HD Decks, Monitors & Rentals Only)

D-Tech/Digital Storage Rentals (323) 876-8700 / (323) 850-8854
3575 Cahuenga Blvd., Ste. 125-1 FAX (323) 850-8865
Los Angeles, CA 90068 www.digirent.com

Ⓐ **Deck Hand, Inc.** (818) 557-8403
1905 Victory Blvd., Ste. 8 FAX (818) 557-8406
Glendale, CA 91201 www.deckhand.com
(HD and SD Video Tape Recorders & Monitors)

The Digital Difference (310) 581-8800
1201 Olympic Blvd. FAX (310) 581-8808
Santa Monica, CA 90404 www.digdif.com
(Avid, Editing Suites, Final Cut Pro, Non-Linear Offline and Online & Pro Tools)

Digital Symphony (818) 973-7600
1011 W. Alameda Ave., Ste. F FAX (818) 238-9600
Burbank, CA 91506 www.digitalsymphony.net
(24P Editing Systems, Avid Systems, Digibeta, Digital Cinema, Digital Decks, Digital Editing Systems, Digital Non-Linear, Editing Suites, Fiber, Film, Final Cut Pro Systems, Hard Drive Rentals, HD Dailies, HD Decks, Non-Linear Hard Drives, Non-Linear Offline, Non-Linear Online, Preview Systems, Video, Video Tape Monitors & Video Tape Recorders)

Digital Systems Media (949) 215-7151 / (877) 629-7810
17702 Mitchell North, Ste. 110 FAX (949) 215-6399
Irvine, CA 92614 www.digitalsystemsmedia.com
(Non-Linear Offline and Online)

Drive This! (310) 345-4304 / (800) 910-7646
FAX (626) 963-5706
www.drivethis.tv
(Hard Drive Rentals, HD and Fibre Rentals, Non-Linear Offline and Online & Video)

editSource (310) 572-7230
12044 Washington Blvd. FAX (310) 572-7238
Los Angeles, CA 90066 www.theeditsource.com
(Editing Suites & Non-Linear Offline)

Ⓐ **Electric Picture Solutions** (818) 766-5000
3753 Cahuenga Blvd. West FAX (818) 623-7547
Studio City, CA 91604 www.electricpicturesolutions.com
(Non-Linear Offline)

Entertainment Post (818) 846-0411
639 S. Glenwood Pl. FAX (818) 846-1542
Burbank, CA 91506 www.entpost.com
(Digibeta, Digital Non-Linear Offline and Online, Editing Suites, Hard Drive Rentals & Non-Linear Offline and Online)

Firestarter Rentals (310) 420-5146
880 W. First St., Ste. 513 FAX (866) 450-6716
Los Angeles, CA 90012
(D5 High Def Tape Deck Rentals)

Flaming Angel Films - The Edit Studio (323) 463-1996 / (323) 957-9177
1245 Vine St., Ste. 12 FAX (323) 469-9506
Los Angeles, CA 90038 www.flamingangelfilms.com
(Digital Editing Systems, Editing Suites, Final Cut Pro Systems, Macintosh-Based Non-Linear Offline & Non-Linear Offline)

Fotokem Nonlinear Services (818) 729-0007
900 W. Alameda Ave. FAX (818) 441-5199
Burbank, CA 91506 www.fotokem.com

Global Entertainment Partners/GEP (818) 380-8133
3747 Cahuenga Blvd. West FAX (818) 954-0211
Studio City, CA 91604 www.gepartners.com
(Non-Linear Offline)

Go Edit, Inc. (818) 284-6260
5614 Cahuenga Blvd. FAX (818) 985-6260
North Hollywood, CA 91601 www.goedit.tv

Ⓐ **Hula Post Production** (818) 954-0200
3747 Cahuenga Blvd. West FAX (818) 954-0211
Studio City, CA 91604 www.hulapost.com
(24P Editing Systems, Analog, Digital and HD Decks, Avid Systems, Digibeta, Digital Editing Systems, Digital Non-Linear, Editing Suites, Final Cut Pro, Hard Drive Rentals, High Def, Linear/Non-Linear Offline and Online, Monitors, Non-Linear Hard Drive Rentals & Video Tape Recorders & Monitors)

J/KAM Digital (818) 705-2986 / (818) 753-2923
FAX (818) 705-5475
www.jkamdigital.com
(24P Editing Systems, Avid Systems, Digibeta, Digital Editing Systems, Digital Non-Linear, Editing Suites, Final Cut Pro Systems, Hard Drive Rentals, HD Decks, High Def, Linear Offline, Non-Linear Offline, Non-Linear Online & Rentals Only)

Jurifilm Entertainment (310) 915-9559 / (877) 587-4345
4404 Westlawn Ave. FAX (310) 391-4217
Los Angeles, CA 90066 www.jurifilm.com
(Non-Linear Offline and Online)

HULA POST
PRODUCTION
HOLLYWOOD
F4
F5
F6
PREROLL
REC
HI-DEF POST PRODUCTION RENTALS
Decks – Drives – Editing Systems – Unity – Symphony – Nitris HD
HULA POST
PRODUCTION
LOS ANGELES NEW YORK
www.hulapost.com
LA ADDRESS: 3747 Cahuenga Blvd. West, Studio City, CA 91604 · 818-954-0200
VENICE ADDRESS: 228 Main Street · Suite 14, Venice, CA 90291 · 310-314-3101
NY ADDRESS: 20 West 22nd St. Suite 611, New York, NY 10010 · 212-367-7292

Kasdin Productions (310) 914-4847
www.kasdin.com
(Digibeta, Digital Non-Linear Offline and Online & Hard Drive Rentals)

Key Code Media, Inc. (818) 303-3900
11530 Ventura Blvd. FAX (818) 303-3901
Studio City, CA 91604 www.keycodemedia.com
(Non-Linear Offline and Online)

LA Digital Post, Inc. (310) 954-8650
(818) 487-5000
2260 Centinela Ave. FAX (310) 954-8686
West Los Angeles, CA 90064 www.ladigital.com
(Avid Systems, Digital Decks, Digital Editing Systems, Digital Non-Linear Offline and Online, Editing Suites, Final Cut Pro Systems, HD Decks, Linear/Non-Linear Offline and Online, Non-Linear Hard Drives)

LA Digital Post, Inc. (818) 487-5000
(310) 954-8650
11311 Camarillo St. FAX (818) 487-5015
Toluca Lake, CA 91602 www.ladigital.com
(Avid Systems, Digital Decks, Digital Editing Systems, Digital Non-Linear Offline and Online, Editing Suites, Final Cut Pro Systems, HD Decks, Linear/Non-Linear Offline and Online, Non-Linear Hard Drives)

Laurel Canyon Productions (818) 459-6630
(310) 738-4184
FAX (818) 450-0916
www.lcproductions.tv
(24P Editing Systems, Analog, Analog Decks, Avid Systems, Digibeta, Digital Decks, Digital Editing Systems, Digital Non-Linear, Editing Suites, Fiber, HD Decks, High Def, Non-Linear Offline, Non-Linear Online & Video Tape Recorders)

Les Sechler Specialty Products (310) 420-5146
32545-B Golden Lantern St., Ste. 114 FAX (615) 599-8020
Dana Point, CA 92629

M.G. Digital, Inc. (310) 558-3907
(310) 558-3424
8500 Steller Dr., Ste. 1 FAX (310) 559-7800
Culver City, CA 90232 www.mgdigital.us

Matchframe Video (818) 840-6800
610 N. Hollywood Way FAX (818) 840-2726
Burbank, CA 91505 www.matchframevideo.com
(24P Editing Systems, Analog Decks, Avid Systems, Digibeta, Digital Decks, Digital Non-Linear, Editing Suites, Editing Supplies, Fiber, Final Cut Pro Systems, High Def, Linear Offline, Linear Online, Macintosh-Based Non-Linear Offline, Monitors, Non-Linear Online & Video Tape Monitors)

Midtown Edit (323) 782-7900
(323) 801-2300
8489 W. Third St. FAX (323) 651-1240
Los Angeles, CA 90048 www.midtownedit.com
(Avid and Final Cut Pro, Decks, Editing Suites & Storage Rentals)

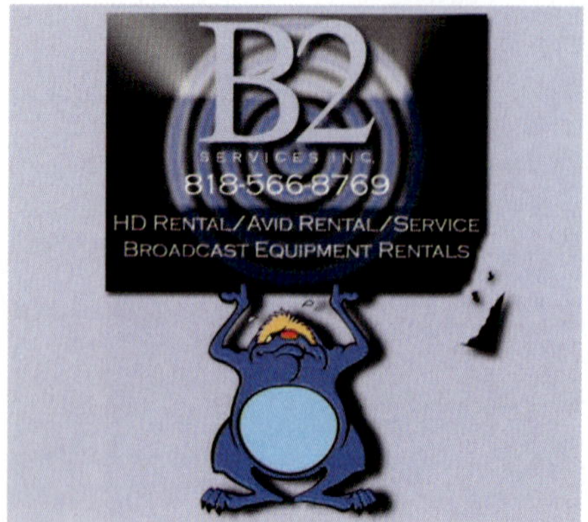

Monkey Works (310) 849-1640
12021 Wilshire Blvd., Ste. 605
Los Angeles, CA 90025
(Non-Linear Offline)

Moving Pictures & Sound (310) 236-5151
(Non-Linear Offline and Online) FAX (818) 474-7500
www.theavidguy.com

Moviola/J & R Film Company (323) 467-3107
(800) 468-3107
1135 N. Mansfield Ave. FAX (323) 464-1518
Hollywood, CA 90038 www.moviola.com

Orbit Digital (323) 298-2250
12233 W. Olympic Blvd., Ste 134 FAX (323) 850-3801
Los Angeles, CA 90064 www.orbitdigital.com
(Non-Linear Offline and Online & High Def)

Ⓐ **The Studios at Paramount** (323) 956-1445
The Studios at Paramount FAX (323) 862-2242
Post Production Services www.thestudiosatparamount.com
5555 Melrose Ave.
Los Angeles, CA 90038
(24P Editing Systems, 35mm, Analog, Analog Decks, Avid Systems, Digibeta, Digital Decks, Digital Editing Systems, Digital Non-Linear, Editing Suites, Fiber, Film, Linear/Non-Linear Offline and Online, Macintosh-Based Non-Linear Offline, Magnetic Hard Drives, Monitors, Non-Linear Hard Drives, Video Tape Monitors & Video Tape Recorders)

Pivotal Post (818) 760-6000
(818) 760-6007
4142 Lankershim Blvd. FAX (818) 760-6012
North Hollywood, CA 91602 www.pivotalpost.com

Planet Post (858) 573-9303
(619) 435-0888
(Non-Linear Online) www.planetpost.net

Post Media Group, Inc. (310) 289-5959
337 S. Robertson Blvd. www.postmediagroup.tv
Beverly Hills, CA 90211

Post-Op Video, Inc. (818) 840-9100
126 E. Alameda Ave. FAX (818) 840-1364
Burbank, CA 91502 www.postop.com
(Non-Linear Offline and Online)

Precision Productions + Post (310) 839-4600
10718 McCune Ave. FAX (310) 839-4601
Los Angeles, CA 90034 www.precisionpost.com
(Non-Linear Offline and Online)

Promax Systems, Inc. (949) 727-3977
(800) 977-6629
16 Technology Dr., Ste. 106 FAX (949) 727-3546
Irvine, CA 92618 www.promax.com

QSR Systems (323) 200-2155
FAX **(661) 257-6380**
www.qsrsystems.com
(Analog, Digital and HD Decks, Avid Systems, Digibeta, Digital Non-Linear, Final Cut Pro Systems, Hard Drive Rentals, Macintosh-Based Non-Linear Offline, Non-Linear Offline and Online, Non-Linear Hard Drives & Video)

Rave Enterprises, Inc. (323) 654-7283
2765 Carmar Dr. FAX **(323) 650-1874**
Los Angeles, CA 90046
(Non-Linear Hard Drive Rentals)

Runway, Inc. (310) 636-2000
(888) 297-2843
10575 Virginia Ave. FAX **(310) 636-2034**
Culver City, CA 90232 **www.runway.com**
(Non-Linear Offline and Online)

Sim Video Los Angeles (323) 978-9000
738 Cahuenga Blvd. FAX **(323) 978-9018**
Hollywood, CA 90038 **www.simvideola.com**
(Non-Linear Offline and Online)

Sonnet Technologies, Inc. (949) 587-3500
Eight Autry FAX **(949) 457-6351**
Irvine, CA 92618 **www.sonnettech.com**

TransAtlantic Post (818) 558-7500
2801 W. Olive Ave. FAX **(818) 558-7150**
Burbank, CA 91505 **www.transatlantic-post.com**

TV Magic, Inc. (818) 841-6886
107 W. Valencia Ave. **www.tvmagic.tv**
Burbank, CA 91502

TV Pro Gear (818) 246-7100
1630 Flower St. FAX **(818) 246-1945**
Glendale, CA 91201 **www.tvprogear.com**
(Non-Linear Offline and Online)

Universal Studios Editorial Facilities (818) 777-4728
100 Universal City Plaza FAX **(818) 733-4290**
Bldg. 2282, Ste. 154 **www.filmmakersdestination.com**
Universal City, CA 91608
(35mm, Avid Systems, Digital Editing Systems, Editing Suites, Final Cut Pro Systems, High Def, Macintosh-Based Non-Linear Offline & Non-Linear Offline)

Video Equipment Rentals (818) 956-1444
(800) 794-1407
912 Ruberta Ave. FAX **(818) 241-4519**
Glendale, CA 91201 **www.verrents.com**

Ⓐ **Visionary Forces Broadcast Rentals** (818) 562-1960
148 S. Victory Blvd. FAX **(818) 562-1270**
Burbank, CA 91502 **www.visionaryforces.com**
(Analog Decks, Digibeta, Digital Decks, HD Decks, Monitors, Rentals Only, Video Tape Monitors & Video Tape Recorders)

Westside Media Group (310) 979-3500
(818) 779-8600
12233 W. Olympic Blvd., Ste. 152 FAX **(310) 979-3503**
West Los Angeles, CA 90064 **www.wmgmedia.com**
(24P Editing Systems, Analog Decks, Avid Systems, Digibeta, Digital Decks, Digital Editing Systems, Digital Non-Linear, Editing Suites, Final Cut Pro Systems, Hard Drive Rentals, HD Decks, High Def, Video Tape Monitors & Video Tape Recorders)

Wexler Video (818) 846-9381
(800) 939-5371
1111 S. Victory Blvd. FAX **(818) 846-9399**
Burbank, CA 91502 **www.wexlervideo.com**
(Linear/Non-Linear Offline)

Roberto Abby (818) 468-7807
FAX (818) 244-4294
www.izonstudios.com/portfolio.html

Bruce Abrams (818) 343-2743
(818) 321-3710

Edward Abroms (818) 726-9128
(818) 769-6723
FAX (818) 450-0514
web.mac.com/eabroms/iweb

Anthony Adler (310) 288-8000
www.paradigmagency.com

Enrique Aguirre (310) 399-2040
www.kingcut.com

Nico Alba (310) 481-2200
www.unioneditorial.com

Ross Albert (310) 288-8000
www.paradigmagency.com

Jonathan Alberts (323) 468-2240
www.nyoffice.net

Michael Alberts (310) 202-6668
www.adeditor.com

Michel Aller (323) 856-3000
www.thegelleragency.com

Nick Allix (310) 319-9908
www.whitehousepost.com

Jon Alloway (323) 270-8854

Craig Alpert (310) 288-8000
www.paradigmagency.com

Javier Alvarez (310) 902-2876
FAX (509) 984-2876
www.baysevenedit.com

Timothy Alverson (310) 656-5151
www.innovativeartists.com

Justin Amore (310) 917-2761
www.optimus.com

Alison Amron (323) 468-2240
www.nyoffice.net

Peter Amundson (310) 288-8000
www.paradigmagency.com

Erik C. Andersen (818) 206-0144
www.allcrewagency.com

Kevin Anderson (310) 314-8110
www.rexedit.com

Lance E. Anderson (818) 284-6423
www.italentco.com

Tim Anderson (310) 399-2040
www.kingcut.com

Shira Ankori (310) 828-7500
www.redcar.com

Zack Arnold (818) 344-7944
www.fixitinpost.net

Sylvette Artinian (818) 717-9011
www.threepointlanding.com

George Artope (310) 393-7109
www.whynotcoco.com

Ken Assessor (818) 556-5700
www.point360.com

John Axelrad (310) 395-9550
www.skouras.com

Johnny Bachelier (310) 399-2040
www.kingcut.com

Stuart Baird (310) 282-9940
www.mirisch.com

Zene Baker (310) 656-5151
www.innovativeartists.com

Mark C. Baldwin (310) 282-9940
www.mirisch.com

Jason Ballantine (310) 273-6700
www.utaproduction.com

Sally Banta (310) 828-9555
www.thereelthinginc.com

Hernan Barangan (323) 468-2240
www.nyoffice.net

Phillip Bartell (323) 468-2240
www.nyoffice.net

Michael Bartoli (310) 828-7500
www.redcar.com

Roger Barton (310) 282-9940
www.mirisch.com

Will Barton (323) 468-2240
www.nyoffice.net

Daryl Baskin (818) 781-9233
www.orlandomanagement.com

Jonathan Baskin (323) 468-2240
www.nyoffice.net

Ned Bastille (310) 656-5151
www.innovativeartists.com

Sam Bauer (310) 274-6611
www.gershagency.com

David Baum (323) 467-8550
www.sunsetedit.com

Baxter (310) 288-8000
www.paradigmagency.com

Kirk Baxter (310) 586-0600
www.rockpaperscissors.com

Ben Bayan (323) 464-7800
www.baypost.com

Eric Beason (310) 288-8000
www.paradigmagency.com

Nicholas Beauman (310) 395-9550
www.skouras.com

Carsten Becker (310) 203-9990
(323) 440-6007

Megan Bee (310) 829-9333
www.butcheredit.com

David Beekman (310) 982-5982

Paul Belanger (310) 315-7245
www.atomicpost.us

Alan E. Bell (310) 395-9550
www.skouras.com

Rebecca Beluk (310) 576-6300
www.beast.tv

Brian Berdan (310) 395-9550
www.skouras.com

Peter Berger (310) 288-8000
www.paradigmagency.com

Debbie Berman (310) 282-9940
www.mirisch.com

Paul Bertino (310) 392-1577
(310) 314-8110
www.madriverpost.com

Jeff Betancourt (818) 284-6423
www.italentco.com

Todd Betts (310) 828-9555
www.thereelthinginc.com

Avril Beukes (310) 652-8778
www.lspagency.net

Kent Beyda (310) 273-6700
www.utaproduction.com

Heidi Black (310) 319-9908
www.whitehousepost.com

David Blackburn (818) 284-6423
(310) 576-6300
www.italentco.com

Ken Blackwell (310) 288-8000
www.paradigmagency.com

Sue Blainey (310) 656-5151
www.innovativeartists.com

Christopher Blakely (310) 450-1846
FAX (310) 399-9227
www.mainstreetmediainc.com

David Blanchard (818) 415-4978

Edie Bleiman (310) 282-9940
www.mirisch.com

Andy Blumenthal (323) 856-3000
www.thegelleragency.com

Micky Blythe (310) 288-8000
www.paradigmagency.com

Larry Bock (310) 656-5151
www.innovativeartists.com

Josh Bodnar (310) 319-9908
www.whitehousepost.com

Elisa Bonora (310) 450-7070
www.room.tv

Dan Bootzin (310) 305-5777
www.venicebeacheditorial.com

Charles Bornstein (310) 656-5151
www.innovativeartists.com

Michelle Botticelli (310) 656-5151
www.innovativeartists.com

George Bowers (310) 288-8000
www.paradigmagency.com

Scott Boyd (323) 856-3000
www.thegelleragency.com

Peter Boyle (310) 285-0303
www.marshbest.com

Robert Brakey (310) 288-8000
www.paradigmagency.com

Maryann Brandon (310) 273-6700
www.utaproduction.com

Derek G. Brechin (310) 282-9940
www.mirisch.com

Terri Breed (323) 663-2246

Wendy Greene Bricmont (310) 282-9940
www.mirisch.com

Brad Briggs (213) 458-3463
www.linkedin.com/in/bradleyjbriggs

Geraud Brisson (310) 652-8778
www.lspagency.net

David Brixton (310) 319-9908
www.whitehousepost.com

Don Brochu (310) 288-8000
www.paradigmagency.com

David Brodie (310) 586-0600
www.rockpaperscissors.com

Lisa Bromwell (310) 282-9940
www.mirisch.com

Tim Brooks (310) 576-6300
www.beast.tv

Christine Brown (310) 309-3780
www.cutters.com

Jeff Buchanan (310) 652-8778
www.lspagency.net

Jarred Buck (310) 264-5551
www.cakeshop.tv

Norman Buckley (310) 288-8000
www.paradigmagency.com

Sven Budelmann (310) 319-9908
www.whitehousepost.com

Conrad Buff (310) 282-9940
www.mirisch.com

Catherine Bull (310) 399-3350
www.spotwelders.com

Edgar Burcksen (310) 656-5151
www.innovativeartists.com

David Burghardt (310) 399-5959
www.luxedit.com

Anita Brandt Burgoyne (310) 282-9940
www.mirisch.com

Terence (Biff) Butler (310) 586-0600
www.rockpaperscissors.com

Peter Byck (323) 252-5272
www.ralphtheroadie.com

Shawna Callahan (323) 468-2240
www.nyoffice.net

Clay Cambern (310) 288-8000
www.paradigmagency.com

Malcolm Campbell (310) 652-8778
www.lspagency.net

Jeff W. Canavan (310) 656-5151
www.innovativeartists.com

Bruce Cannon (310) 288-8000
www.paradigmagency.com

Luis Carballar (310) 652-8778
www.lspagency.net

Ed Cardenas (323) 467-8550
www.sunsetedit.com

Gordon Carey (310) 576-6300
www.beast.tv

John Carter (310) 288-8000
www.paradigmagency.com

Matthew Cassel (310) 652-8778
www.lspagency.net

Jay Cassidy (310) 652-8778
www.lspagency.net

Angela Catanzaro (310) 288-8000
www.paradigmagency.com

David Checel (310) 450-1116
www.cutandrun.tv

Matt Chesse (310) 450-1116
www.cutandrun.tv

Bill Chessman (310) 305-5777
www.venicebeacheditorial.com

Scott Chestnut (310) 395-9550
www.skouras.com

Richard Chew (310) 395-9550
www.skouras.com

Debra Chiate (310) 652-8778
www.lspagency.net

John Chimples (323) 468-2240
www.nyoffice.net

Michael Choi (323) 468-2240
www.nyoffice.net

Pernille Bech Christensen (310) 395-9550
www.skouras.com

Lisa Zeno Churgin (310) 282-9940
www.mirisch.com

Chris Chynoweth (310) 576-6300
www.beast.tv

Chris Cibelli (310) 288-8000
www.paradigmagency.com

Julian Clarke (310) 288-8000
www.paradigmagency.com

Curtiss Clayton (323) 468-2240
www.nyoffice.com

Damion Clayton (310) 586-0600
www.rockpaperscissors.com

Anne V. Coates (310) 273-6700
www.utaproduction.com

James Coblentz (818) 284-6423
www.italentco.com

David Codron (310) 656-5151
www.innovativeartists.com

Steven Cohen (310) 285-0303
www.marshbest.com

Joseph Conarkov (818) 730-4905
www.editropolis.com

Dana Congdon (310) 288-8000
www.paradigmagency.com

John Coniglio (310) 288-8000
www.paradigmagency.com

Scott Conrad (818) 206-0144
www.allcrewagency.com

Mark Conte (310) 288-8000
www.paradigmagency.com

David Cook (310) 656-5151
www.innovativeartists.com

Tricia Cooke (310) 273-6700
www.utaproduction.com

Dany Cooper (310) 285-0303
www.marshbest.com

Maura Corey (310) 450-7070
www.room.tv

Jonathan Corn (310) 288-8000
www.paradigmagency.com

Hank Corwin (310) 395-9550
(310) 396-7272
www.skouras.com

Tom Costain (310) 656-5151
www.innovativeartists.com

Glenn Cote (818) 301-5651
FAX (818) 301-2681
www.glenncote.com

Cari Coughlin (323) 460-4767
www.jacobandkoleagency.com

David Coulson (310) 288-8000
www.paradigmagency.com

Olivier Bugge Coutte (310) 395-9550
www.skouras.com

Jacob Craycroft (646) 734-0765
(310) 652-8778

Douglas Crise (310) 652-8778
www.lspagency.net

Rye Dahlman (213) 361-1391
www.ryefilms.com

Robert Dalva (310) 288-8000
www.paradigmagency.com

Marc D'Andre (310) 450-1116
www.cutandrun.tv

Tanis Darling (310) 399-3350
www.spotwelders.com

Raul Davalos (310) 288-8000
www.paradigmagency.com

Annette Davey (310) 656-5151
www.innovativeartists.com

Freeman Davies (310) 288-8000
www.paradigmagency.com

Ian Davies (310) 319-9908
www.whitehousepost.com

Roderick Davis (310) 288-8000
www.paradigmagency.com

Tessa Davis (310) 828-6666
www.cosmostreet.com

Jennifer Dean (310) 396-7272
www.lostplanet.com

Keiko Deguchi (310) 288-8000
www.paradigmagency.com

Jose Delgado (310) 391-9181
www.wsrcreative.com

Jonathan Del Gatto (310) 576-6300
www.beast.tv

Todd Desrosiers (310) 288-8000
www.paradigmagency.com

Corky DeVault (310) 319-9908
www.whitehousepost.com

John Dingfield (310) 576-6300
www.beast.tv

Paul Dixon (310) 288-8000
www.paradigmagency.com

Jack Douglas (310) 829-9333
www.butcheredit.com

Tom Downs (323) 468-2240
www.nyoffice.net

Victor DuBois (310) 288-8000
www.paradigmagency.com

Robert Ducsay (310) 395-9550
www.skouras.com

Orlando Duenas (310) 288-8000
www.paradigmagency.com

Robert Duffy (310) 395-9550
(310) 399-3350
www.skouras.com

Carlos Duhaime (310) 450-7070
www.room.tv

Duwayne R. Dunham (323) 856-3000
www.thegelleragency.com

Michael Duthie (818) 284-6423
www.italentco.com

Frank Effron (310) 450-1116
www.cutandrun.tv

Peggy Eghbalian (310) 288-8000
www.paradigmagency.com

Einar (310) 481-2200
www.unioneditorial.com

Andrew Eisen (323) 856-3000
FAX (323) 856-3009
www.thegelleragency.com

Michael Elliot (310) 576-6300
www.beast.tv

Michael Ellis (310) 288-8000
www.paradigmagency.com

Suzy Elmiger (310) 285-0303
www.marshbest.com

Ken Eluto (323) 845-4144
www.montanartists.com

Nicholas Erasmus (310) 274-6611
www.gershagency.com

Bella Erikson (213) 908-5106
www.beamuniversal.com

Lucas Eskin (310) 392-1577
(310) 576-6300
www.madriverpost.com

Marta Evry (310) 288-8000
www.paradigmagency.com

Jennifer Fah (818) 588-8662
FAX (818) 908-8082
www.jennifermfah.com

Farah (323) 467-8550
www.sunsetedit.com

Gregg Featherman (818) 284-6423
www.italentco.com

Fritz Feick (323) 658-5700
www.editkings.com

Tim Fender (310) 576-6300
www.beast.tv

Chris Figler (323) 856-3000
www.thegelleragency.com

Kevin Filippini (323) 467-8550
www.sunsetedit.com

Vince Filippone (310) 282-9940
www.mirisch.com

David Finfer (310) 274-6611
www.gershagency.com

Sarah Flack (310) 395-9550
www.skouras.com

Peter Devaney Flanagan (323) 856-3000
www.thegelleragency.com

Seth Flaum (310) 288-8000
www.paradigmagency.com

Bill Flicker (310) 285-0303
www.marshbest.com

George Folsey (310) 288-8000
www.paradigmagency.com

Jeff Ford (310) 288-8000
www.paradigmagency.com

Fred Fouquet (310) 392-1577
www.madriverpost.com

Billy Fox (310) 288-8000
www.paradigmagency.com

David Frame (310) 968-1172
www.razoredits.com

Jo Francis (310) 652-8778
www.lspagency.net

Richard Francis-Bruce (310) 822-9113
www.murthaagency.com

Peter Frank (818) 284-6423
www.italentco.com

Patrick Fraser (323) 363-6125
www.editedbypatrick.com

Robert Frazen (310) 395-9550
www.skouras.com

Jeff Freeman (310) 288-8000
www.paradigmagency.com

Jay Friedkin (310) 481-2200
www.unioneditorial.com

Matt Friedman (310) 282-9940
www.mirisch.com

Lisa Fruchtman (310) 273-6700
www.utaproduction.com

Trish Fuller (310) 319-9908
www.whitehousepost.com

Patrick Gallagher (323) 460-4767
www.jacobandkoleagency.com

Nigel Galt (310) 652-8778
www.lspagency.net

Scott Gamzon (310) 288-8000
www.paradigmagency.com

John Ganem (310) 288-8000
www.paradigmagency.com

Michael Garber (323) 461-0600
www.5thwall.tv

Diego Del Sol Garcia (323) 468-2240
www.nyoffice.net

Kevin Garcia (310) 576-6300
www.beast.tv

Mitch Gardiner (310) 450-1116
www.cutandrun.tv

Glenn Garland (323) 856-3000
www.thegelleragency.com

Pablo Garrahan (310) 391-9181
(310) 391-9182
FAX (310) 391-9183
www.wsrcreative.com

Nicholas Gaster (310) 652-8778
www.lspagency.net

Christian Gazal (310) 395-9550
www.skouras.com

The Geller Agency (323) 856-3000
1547 Cassil Pl. FAX (323) 856-3009
Hollywood, CA 90028 www.thegelleragency.com
(Reps for Editors)

Chris Gendrin (714) 705-6099
www.postfactory.com

David George (213) 999-4003
FAX (213) 232-3333
homepage.mac.com/davidandlisala/Menu8.html

The Gersh Agency (310) 274-6611
(212) 997-1818
P.O. Box 5617 www.gershagency.com
Beverly Hills, CA 90210
(Reps for Editors)

John Gilbert (310) 395-9550
www.skouras.com

Chris Gill (310) 273-6700
www.utaproduction.com

Bob Gingg (310) 399-5959
www.luxedit.com

Adrienne Gits (310) 260-7910
www.rivaleditorial.com

Dana Glauberman (310) 395-9550
www.skouras.com

Mark Goldblatt (310) 282-9940
www.mirisch.com

William Goldenberg (310) 395-9550
www.skouras.com

Mollie Goldstein (323) 468-2240
www.nyoffice.net

Affonso Gonclaves (310) 288-8000
www.paradigmagency.com

Conrad Gonzalez (818) 284-6423
www.italentco.com

Dean Gonzalez (323) 467-8550
www.sunsetedit.com

Timothy A. Good (310) 656-5151
www.innovativeartists.com

Mike Goodman (310) 338-0580
www.alliancegroupllc.com

Margie Goodspeed (310) 282-9940
www.mirisch.com

Dick Gordon (310) 399-3350
www.spotwelders.com

Yana Gorskaya (310) 652-8778
www.lspagency.net

Tom Gould (818) 206-0144
www.allcrewagency.com

Anne Goursaud (310) 282-9940
www.mirisch.com

Dave Graack (760) 476-1783
www.jmdigitalworks.com

Elliot Graham (310) 288-8000
www.paradigmagency.com

Jeff Granzow (310) 288-8000
www.paradigmagency.com

Scott Gray (310) 274-6611
www.gershagency.com

Bruce Green (310) 273-6700
www.utaproduction.com

Jerry Greenberg (310) 273-6700
www.utaproduction.com

Kevin Greutert (310) 288-8000
www.paradigmagency.com

Jeff Grippe (310) 450-1116
www.cutandrun.tv

Jeff Groth (323) 468-2240
www.nyoffice.net

Jeff Gullo (818) 284-6423
www.italentco.com

Sam Gunn (310) 319-9908
www.whitehousepost.com

Lisa Gunning (310) 319-9908
(310) 273-6700
www.whitehousepost.com

Grant Gustafson (310) 319-9908
www.whitehousepost.com

Michael Hackett (310) 429-7640
www.hackettcuts.com

Tirsa Hackshaw (310) 288-8000
www.paradigmagency.com

Andrew Hafitz (310) 652-8778
www.lspagency.net

Celia Haining (818) 206-0144
www.allcrewagency.com

Alexander Hall (323) 468-2240
www.nyoffice.net

Haines Hall (310) 399-3350
www.spotwelders.com

Justine Halliday (323) 856-3000
www.thegelleragency.com

Richard Halsey (310) 656-5151
www.innovativeartists.com

Steve Hamilton (310) 319-9908
www.whitehousepost.com

Janice Hampton (818) 284-6423
www.italentco.com

Jim Hancock (949) 608-8700
www.postmoderncreative.com

Dan Hanley (310) 288-8000
www.paradigmagency.com

Paul Hardcastle (310) 319-9908
www.whitehousepost.com

Nicholas Wayman Harris (310) 481-2200
www.unioneditorial.com

Dahkil Hausif (310) 399-3350
www.spotwelders.com

Lee Haxall (310) 288-8000
www.paradigmagency.com

Greg Hayden (310) 285-0303
www.marshbest.com

James Haygood (310) 273-6700
www.utaproduction.com

Shon Hedges (310) 282-9940
www.mirisch.com

Alan Heim (310) 288-8000
www.paradigmagency.com

Michael Heldman (310) 399-3350
www.spotwelders.com

Max Heller (323) 468-2240
www.nyoffice.net

Dave Henegar (310) 829-9333
www.butcheredit.com

James Herbert (310) 282-9940
www.mirisch.com

Craig Herring (310) 288-8000
www.paradigmagency.com

Bruce Herrman (310) 396-7272
www.lostplanet.com

Emma E. Hickox (310) 273-6700
www.utaproduction.com

Dennis Hill (310) 288-8000
www.paradigmagency.com

Megan Hill (310) 395-9550
www.skouras.com

Michael Hill (310) 288-8000
www.paradigmagency.com

Paul Hirsch (310) 656-5151
www.innovativeartists.com

Joe Hobeck (310) 288-8000
www.paradigmagency.com

Tracy Hof (310) 210-6627

Robert Hoffman (818) 284-6423
www.italentco.com

Sabine Hoffman (310) 288-8000
www.paradigmagency.com

Todd Holmes (323) 468-2240
www.nyoffice.net

Chris Homel (310) 828-7500
www.redcar.com

Peter Honess (310) 822-9113
www.murthaagency.com

Hal Honigsberg (310) 264-9700
www.chrome.tv

Benjamin Hopkins (310) 717-9493
www.benhopkins.com

Chris Houghton (323) 468-2240
www.nyoffice.net

Maysie Hoy (310) 656-5151
www.innovativeartists.com

William Hoy (310) 288-8000
www.paradigmagency.com

Darin Hubbard (818) 207-3608
(818) 279-8308

Nate Hubbard (310) 345-1301
www.migranteditors.com

Sean Hubbert (323) 856-3000
www.thegelleragency.com

Ray Hubley (323) 468-2240
www.nyoffice.net

Martin Hunter (310) 288-8000
www.paradigmagency.com

Jack Hutchings (310) 319-9908
www.whitehousepost.com

Russell Icke (310) 319-9908
www.whitehousepost.com

Mark Imgrund (310) 592-8271
www.moxedit.com

Innovative Artists (310) 656-5151
1617 Broadway, Third Fl. FAX **(310) 656-5156**
Santa Monica, CA 90404 **www.innovativeartists.com**
(Reps for Editors)

International Creative Management - ICM (310) 550-4000
10250 Constellation Blvd. **www.icmtalent.com**
Los Angeles, CA 90067
(Reps for Editors)

iTalent Company (818) 284-6423
9701 Wilshire Blvd., 10th Fl. FAX **(866) 755-0708**
Beverly Hills, CA 90212 **www.italentco.com**
(Reps for Editors)

Robert Ivison (310) 652-8778
www.lspagency.net

Michael Jablow (310) 282-9940
www.mirisch.com

Mike Jackson (310) 288-8000
www.paradigmagency.com

Addison James (310) 309-3780
www.cutters.com

Bob Jenkins (310) 392-1577
www.madriverpost.com

Stephen Jess (310) 319-9908
www.whitehousepost.com

Allyson C. Johnson (310) 822-9113
www.murthaagency.com

Alaster Jordan (310) 319-9908
www.whitehousepost.com

Christjan Jordan (310) 828-6666
www.cosmostreet.com

Lawrence Jordan (310) 288-8000
www.paradigmagency.com

Gary Katz (310) 828-6666
www.cosmostreet.com

Robin Katz (323) 856-3000
www.thegelleragency.com

Virginia Katz (310) 282-9940
www.mirisch.com

Nina Kawasaki (310) 288-8000
www.paradigmagency.com

Andy Keir (310) 288-8000
www.paradigmagency.com

Paul Kelly (310) 576-6300
www.beast.tv

Melissa Kent (310) 288-8000
www.paradigmagency.com

Myron Kerstein (310) 273-6700
www.utaproduction.com

Jamie Kirkpatrick (310) 395-9550
www.skouras.com

Saar Klein (310) 395-9550
(310) 396-7272
www.skouras.com

Sloane Klevin (818) 284-6423
www.italentco.com

Elizabeth Kling (310) 822-9113
www.murthaagency.com

Lynzee Klingman (310) 273-6700
www.utaproduction.com

Joe Klotz (310) 652-8778
www.lspagency.net

Karen Knowles (310) 392-4848
www.kkeditorial.com

Michael N. Knue (310) 656-5151
www.innovativeartists.com

Robert Komatsu (310) 288-8000
www.paradigmagency.com

Igor Kovalik (310) 576-6300
www.beast.tv

Carole Kravetz (323) 460-4767
www.jacobandkoleagency.com

Bill Kruzykowski (818) 284-6423
www.italentco.com

Meg Kubicka (310) 319-9908
www.whitehousepost.com

Nadav Kurtz (310) 309-3780
www.cutters.com

Brian Lagerhausen (310) 576-6300
www.beast.tv

Frank Lagnese (310) 387-7773
www.allegropost.com

Robert K. Lambert (310) 273-6700
www.utaproduction.com

Marc Langley (310) 319-9908
www.whitehousepost.com

Sarah LaSpisa (310) 210-3141

Rick Lawley (310) 319-9908
www.whitehousepost.com

Richard Learoyd (310) 319-9908
www.whitehousepost.com

Greg Le Duc (310) 452-2034
www.leducdesign.com

Charlie Lee (310) 576-6300
www.beast.tv

Adriana Legay (310) 314-8110
www.rexedit.com

Robert Leighton (310) 395-9550
www.skouras.com

Lenny (323) 467-8550
www.sunsetedit.com

Ben Lester (310) 285-0303
www.marshbest.com

Martin Levenstein (323) 468-2240
www.nyoffice.net

Robert Levy (310) 393-7109
www.whynotcoco.com

Stuart Levy (310) 395-9550
www.skouras.com

Mary Lind-Horwitz (406) 961-5351
(818) 512 2794

Susan Littenberg (818) 284-6423
www.italentco.com

Carol Littleton (310) 273-6700
www.utaproduction.com

Mark Livolsi (818) 284-6423
www.italentco.com

Adam Lobel (310) 351-4764

Rick Lobo (310) 264-5551
(310) 309-3780
www.cakeshop.tv

Nick Lofting (310) 481-2200
www.unioneditorial.com

Tony Lombardo (310) 652-8778
www.lspagency.net

Gregg London (310) 395-9550
www.skouras.com

Melody London (323) 468-2240
www.nyoffice.net

Ben Longland (310) 828-6666
www.cosmostreet.com

Richard Lowe (323) 468-2240
www.nyoffice.net

Carlos Lowenstein (310) 319-9908
www.whitehousepost.com

Patrick Lussier (310) 288-8000
www.paradigmagency.com

Steve MacCorkle (310) 260-7910
www.rivaleditorial.com

Grant MacDowell (310) 917-2761
www.optimus.com

Stephen Mack (323) 468-2240
www.nyoffice.net

Andrew MacRitchie (310) 288-8000
www.paradigmagency.com

Lawrence Maddox (818) 284-6423
www.italentco.com

Filip Malasek (310) 319-9908
www.whitehousepost.com

Dan Maloney (310) 399-3350
www.spotwelders.com

Ethan Maniquis (310) 288-8000
www.paradigmagency.com

Jeff Marcello (323) 468-2240
www.nyoffice.net

Pamela March (310) 656-5151
www.innovativeartists.com

Andrew Marcus (310) 282-9940
www.mirisch.com

Mario Mares (310) 450-7070
www.room.tv

Stephen Mark (310) 656-5151
www.innovativeartists.com

Mary Jo Markey (310) 288-8000
www.paradigmagency.com

Richard Marks (310) 288-8000
www.paradigmagency.com

Bill Marmor (310) 314-8110
www.rexedit.com

Alex Marquez (310) 288-8000
www.paradigmagency.com

Marsh, Best & Associates (310) 285-0303
9150 Wilshire Blvd., Ste. 220
Beverly Hills, CA 90212
(Reps for Editors)
FAX (310) 285-0218
www.marshbest.com

Adam Marshall (310) 319-9908
www.whitehousepost.com

Nicholas Martin (323) 468-2240
www.nyoffice.net

Pam Martin (310) 399-3350
(310) 274-6611
www.spotwelders.com

Ed Marx (310) 288-8000
www.paradigmagency.com

Kelly Matsumoto (310) 288-8000
www.paradigmagency.com

Jim May (310) 395-9550
www.skouras.com

Frank Mazzola (310) 282-9940
www.mirisch.com

Tom McArdle (323) 856-3000
www.thegelleragency.com

Anne McCabe (310) 288-8000
www.paradigmagency.com

Kelly McClean (310) 399-2040
www.kingcut.com

Connor McDonald (310) 576-6300
www.beast.tv

Jeff McEvoy (310) 274-6611
www.gershagency.com

Gareth McEwen (310) 319-9908
www.whitehousepost.com

Ryan McGuire (310) 309-3780
www.cutters.com

Patrick McMahon (323) 856-3000
www.thegelleragency.com

Junior McRae (310) 450-7070
www.room.tv

Robert Mead (310) 395-9550
www.skouras.com

Rob Meltzer (818) 730-4905
www.editropolis.com

Sally Menke (310) 273-6700
www.utaproduction.com

Lenny Mesina (310) 309-3780
www.cutters.com

Richard Mettler (310) 309-3780
www.cutters.com

John Michel (818) 284-6423
www.italentco.com

Crandall Miller (310) 319-9908
www.whitehousepost.com

Michael R. Miller (310) 822-9113
www.murthaagency.com

Mike Miller (310) 587-3300

Todd E. Miller (310) 282-9940
www.mirisch.com

Paul Millspaugh (310) 656-5151
www.innovativeartists.com

Armen Minasian (310) 288-8000
www.paradigmagency.com

The Mirisch Agency (310) 282-9940
1925 Century Park East, Ste. 1070 FAX (310) 282-0702
Los Angeles, CA 90067 www.mirisch.com
(Reps for Editors)

Steve Mirkovich (310) 288-8000
www.paradigmagency.com

Timothy Mirkovich (310) 656-5151
www.innovativeartists.com

Tod Modisett (323) 856-3000
www.thegelleragency.com

Cindy Mollo (310) 652-8778
www.lspagency.net

Deborah Moran (310) 288-8000
www.paradigmagency.com

Jane Moran (310) 282-9940
www.mirisch.com

Amanda Moreau (310) 576-6300
www.beast.tv

Bob Mori (323) 855-4382
www.bobmori.com

Susan Morse (310) 273-6700
www.utaproduction.com

Ken Mowe (323) 467-8550
www.sunsetedit.com

Susan Munro (310) 828-7500
www.redcar.com

Walter Murch (310) 282-9940
www.mirisch.com

Michael S. Murphy (310) 656-5151
www.innovativeartists.com

The Murtha Agency (310) 822-9113
4240 Promenade Way, Ste. 232 FAX (310) 822-6662
Marina Del Rey, CA 90292 www.murthaagency.com
(Reps for Editors)

Grant Myers (323) 468-2240
www.nyoffice.net

Joel Negron (310) 395-9550
www.skouras.com

Aaron Neitz (310) 399-2040
www.kingcut.com

Jay Nelson (310) 450-1116
www.cutandrun.tv

New York Office (323) 468-2240
(212) 545-7895
6605 Hollywood Blvd., Ste. 200 FAX (323) 468-2244
Los Angeles, CA 90028 www.nyoffice.net
(Reps for Editors)

Martin Nicholson (310) 282-9940
www.mirisch.com

Aram Nigoghossian (310) 288-8000
www.paradigmagency.com

Marcelo Nonaca (949) 608-8700
www.postmoderncreative.com

Richard Nord (310) 288-8000
www.paradigmagency.com

Tom Nordberg (310) 288-8000
www.paradigmagency.com

Paul Norling (310) 576-6300
www.beast.tv

Dan Oberle (310) 319-9908
www.whitehousepost.com

Brendan O'Carroll (310) 458-9661
www.oasiseditorial.com

Jeremiah O'Driscoll (310) 395-9550
www.skouras.com

Juliette Olavarria (310) 820-5254
(310) 625-5254

Charles Olivier (323) 468-2240
www.nyoffice.net

Dave Oneal (818) 640-2941
www.popcultureentertainment.com

Dave Oneal (818) 640-2941
www.daveoneal.com

Conor O'Neill (310) 395-9550
www.skouras.com

Craig Ordelheide (818) 843-1553
(818) 429-0688
FAX (818) 843-1553

Valdis Oskarsdottir (310) 395-9550
www.skouras.com

Tina Pacheco (323) 468-2240
www.nyoffice.net

Daniel Padgett (323) 856-3000
www.thegelleragency.com

Jason Painter (310) 392-1577
www.madriverpost.com

Bill Pankow (310) 273-6700
www.utaproduction.com

Adam Parker (310) 264-9700
www.chrome.tv

Colby Parker Jr. (310) 319-9908
www.whitehousepost.com

Joel Pashby (323) 856-3000
www.thegelleragency.com

Igor Patalas (310) 314-8110
www.rexedit.com

Vikash Patel (818) 206-0144
www.allcrewagency.com

Rhonda Peacock (310) 587-3300

Jose Pedillo (310) 991-2464

Lance Pereira (310) 264-9700
www.chrome.tv

Cindia Perez (818) 729-0000
www.goschproductions.com

Greg Perler (310) 288-8000
www.paradigmagency.com

Michael Perlmutter (310) 313-4046
FAX (310) 313-4048
www.almostmidnight.com

Heather Persons (310) 288-8000
www.paradigmagency.com

Adam Pertofsky (310) 586-0600
www.rockpaperscissors.com

Jim Peterson (310) 452-2034
www.leducdesign.com

Alex Pitt (323) 665-4492
www.alexpittphotography.com

Bill Pollock (310) 450-7070
www.room.tv

Oliver Power (310) 264-8498
www.60-hz.com

Steve Prestemon (310) 319-9908
www.whitehousepost.com

Peck Prior (310) 288-8000
www.paradigmagency.com

Jamie Proctor (310) 394-1048

Monique Prudhomme (310) 656-5151
www.innovativeartists.com

Dallas Puett (310) 282-9940
www.mirisch.com

Jake Pushinsky (310) 656-5151
www.innovativeartists.com

Jeremy Quayhackx (310) 391-2891
(213) 840-0811
www.q-edit.com

Julius Ramsay (323) 876-4770

Matt Ramsey (310) 656-5151
www.innovativeartists.com

John Rantz (310) 391-9181
www.wsrcreative.com

Gary Ras (626) 437-5346
www.garyras.com

Fred Raskin (310) 395-9550
www.skouras.com

David Ray (310) 288-8000
www.paradigmagency.com

Irit Raz (818) 206-0144
www.allcrewagency.com

Anthony Redman (310) 288-8000
www.paradigmagency.com

Jim Reed (949) 608-8700
www.postmoderncreative.com

Mark Rees (310) 829-9333
www.butcheredit.com

Steve Rees (323) 467-8550
www.sunsetedit.com

David Rennie (323) 856-3000
www.thegelleragency.com

Jimmie Rhee (818) 729-0000
www.goschproductions.com

Nancy Richardson (310) 285-0303
www.marshbest.com

Geoff Richman (310) 395-9550
www.skouras.com

Scott Richter (323) 856-3000
www.thegelleragency.com

Tatiana S. Riegel (310) 656-5151
www.innovativeartists.com

Josh Rifkin (323) 468-2240
www.nyoffice.net

David Riggs (310) 463-0115
FAX (818) 766-5365

Stephen Rivkin (310) 288-8000
www.paradigmagency.com

Stuart Robertson (213) 908-5106
www.beamuniversal.com

Adam Robinson (310) 319-9908
www.whitehousepost.com

Alex Rodriguez (323) 460-4767
(310) 319-9908
www.jacobandkoleagency.com

Jay Rogers (310) 264-5551
www.cakeshop.tv

Julie Rogers (310) 652-8778
www.lspagency.net

Tom Rolf (310) 288-8000
www.paradigmagency.com

Mario Roman (213) 842-1009
FAX (310) 854-6590
sketchtv.com/pp/mario_roman_avid_editor.htm

Ron Roose (310) 288-8000
www.paradigmagency.com

David Rosenbloom (310) 288-8000
www.paradigmagency.com

Steven Rosenblum (310) 395-9550
www.skouras.com

Harvey Rosenstock (310) 288-8000
www.paradigmagency.com

Kevin D. Ross (310) 288-8000
www.paradigmagency.com

Roger Roth (818) 901-1178
(310) 963-4812
FAX (818) 901-1179

Maynard Rothchild (213) 434-1800

Steve Rotter (310) 288-8000
www.paradigmagency.com

Christopher Rouse (310) 656-5151
www.innovativeartists.com

Kiran Rouzie (310) 394-1048

Geoffrey Rowland (310) 282-9940
www.mirisch.com

Luis Ruiz (310) 399-5959
www.luxedit.com

Matt Rundell (323) 817-4430

Michael Ruscio (310) 656-5151
www.innovativeartists.com

Billy Sacdalan (310) 305-5777
www.venicebeacheditorial.com

Michael L. Sale (310) 282-9940
www.mirisch.com

Keith Salmon (310) 394-1048

Livio Sanchez (310) 576-6300
www.beast.tv

Mark Sanders (310) 264-5551
www.cakeshop.tv

Nat Sanders (310) 652-8778
www.lspagency.net

Ronald Sanders (310) 822-9113
www.murthaagency.com

Danny Saphire (310) 288-8000
www.paradigmagency.com

Lara Sarkissian (323) 660-7710
FAX (323) 660-7715
www.aleraenterprises.com

Pietro Scalia (310) 395-9550
www.skouras.com

Scot Scalise (310) 288-8000
www.paradigmagency.com

Glen Scantlebury (310) 273-6700
www.utaproduction.com

Lauren Schaffer (310) 656-5151
www.innovativeartists.com

William Scharf (323) 460-4767
www.jacobandkoleagency.com

Ian Schiff (310) 702-6374
FAX (801) 720-2090

Hervé Schneid (310) 273-6700
www.utaproduction.com

Adam Schwartz (310) 576-6300
www.beast.tv

John Scott (310) 285-0303
www.marshbest.com

Eric Sears (310) 282-9940
www.mirisch.com

Sam Seig (310) 652-8778
www.lspagency.net

Jeff Selis (310) 450-7070
www.room.tv

Sam Selis (310) 576-6300
www.beast.tv

Stephen Semel (323) 460-4767
www.jacobandkoleagency.com

Nick Senser (310) 399-5959
www.luxedit.com

Jim Settlemoir (818) 953-8919
www.burbankpost.tv

Robert Shafer (818) 556-5700
www.point360.com

Rick Shaine (310) 285-0303
www.marshbest.com

Rick Shambaugh (310) 305-5777
www.venicebeacheditorial.com

Jonathan Shaw (323) 856-3000
www.thegelleragency.com

Stewart Shevin (310) 576-6300
www.beast.tv

Trudy Ship (310) 282-9940
www.mirisch.com

Mark Shockley (310) 567-9191
(310) 770-3860
www.evolutionla.com

Terilyn Shropshire (323) 460-4767
www.jacobandkoleagency.com

Wendy Shuey (213) 989-6884
www.wendyshuey.com

Tim Silano (818) 648-6699
www.schradersexorcism.com

Steve Silkensen (323) 468-2240
www.nyoffice.net

Jonathan Silver (310) 450-7070
www.room.tv

Cara Silverman (310) 656-5151
www.innovativeartists.com

Conrad Smart (323) 856-3000
www.thegelleragency.com

Alec Smight (310) 282-9940
www.mirisch.com

Bud Smith (310) 282-9940
www.mirisch.com

Byron Smith (310) 395-9550
www.skouras.com

Howard E. Smith (310) 273-6700
www.utaproduction.com

John Smith (310) 319-9908
www.whitehousepost.com

Lee Smith (310) 274-6611
www.gershagency.com

Paul Martin Smith (310) 282-9940
www.mirisch.com

Peter Smith (310) 305-5777
www.venicebeacheditorial.com

Richard Smith (310) 576-6300
www.beast.tv

Scott Smith (310) 282-9940
www.mirisch.com

Wendy Smith (310) 288-8000
www.paradigmagency.com

Greg Snider (310) 319-9908
www.whitehousepost.com

Paul Snyder (310) 396-7272
www.lostplanet.com

Sandy Solowitz (310) 288-8000
www.paradigmagency.com

Suzanne Spangler (323) 468-2240
www.nyoffice.net

Lucas Spaulding (310) 399-3350
www.spotwelders.com

Tim Squyres (310) 273-6700
www.utaproduction.com

Zach Staenberg (310) 395-9550
www.skouras.com

Jim Staskauskas (310) 917-2761
www.optimus.com

Jon Stefansson (310) 399-3350
www.spotwelders.com

Laura Steiger (310) 288-8000
www.paradigmagency.com

Paula Stein (310) 430-9642
www.paulastein.net

William Steinkamp (310) 652-8778
www.lspagency.net

Ben Stephens (310) 319-9908
www.whitehousepost.com

Mark Stevens (310) 288-8000
www.paradigmagency.com

Jason Stewart (323) 856-3000
www.thegelleragency.com

Kevin Stitt (310) 282-9940
www.mirisch.com

Eric Strand (310) 282-9940
www.mirisch.com

Tim Streeto (310) 282-9940
www.mirisch.com

Christina Stumpf (310) 319-9908
www.whitehousepost.com

Robb Sullivan (310) 395-9550
www.skouras.com

Suzanna Camejo & Associates/
Artists For The Environment (310) 479-4470
(Reps for Editors)

Adam Svatek (310) 576-6300
www.beast.tv

Derek Swanson (310) 576-6300
www.beast.tv

Steve Swersky (310) 202-6668
www.adeditor.com

Craig Tanner (310) 288-8000
www.paradigmagency.com

Peter Tartar (310) 399-5959
www.luxedit.com

TDN Artists (818) 906-0006
3685 Motor Ave., Ste. 220 FAX (818) 301-2224
Los Angeles, CA 90034 www.tdnartists.com
(Reps for Editors)

David Tedeschi (310) 656-5151
www.innovativeartists.com

David Teixeira (619) 291-2403
www.visualconcepts.tv

Chris Tellefsen (310) 285-0303
www.marshbest.com

Kevin Tent (323) 856-3000
www.thegelleragency.com

Scott Tetti (323) 658-5700
www.editkings.com

Dinh Long Thai (626) 688-5818
www.chopstickninja.com

Andy Thomas (323) 468-2240
www.nyoffice.net

James Thomas (310) 273-6700
www.unitedtalent.com

Drew Thompson (310) 314-8110
www.rexedit.com

Val Thrasher (310) 392-1577
(310) 576-6300
www.madriverpost.com

Dylan Tichenor (310) 273-6700
www.utaproduction.com

Jennifer Tiexiera (323) 468-2240
www.nyoffice.net

Greg Tillman (323) 856-3000
www.thegelleragency.com

Camilla Toniolo (310) 285-0303
www.marshbest.com

Neil Travis (310) 273-6700
www.utaproduction.com

Scott Trembley (310) 481-2200
www.unioneditorial.com

Michael Trent (310) 288-8000
www.paradigmagency.com

Leo Trombetta (310) 652-8778
www.lspagency.net

Ann Trulove (323) 468-2240
www.nyoffice.net

Plummy Tucker (310) 285-0303
www.marshbest.com

Barbara Tulliver (310) 282-9940
www.mirisch.com

Jim Ulbrich (310) 576-6300
www.beast.tv

Frank J. Urioste (310) 282-9940
www.mirisch.com

Jaime Valdueza (310) 396-7272
www.lostplanet.com

Angelo Valencia (310) 576-6300
www.beast.tv

John Valerio (310) 656-5151
www.innovativeartists.com

Henk Van Eeghen (310) 288-8000
www.paradigmagency.com

Randy Vandegrift (310) 447-8575
www.randyvandegrift.com

Nikki Vapensky (310) 319-9908
www.whitehousepost.com

Tara Veneruso (323) 463-1996
(323) 957-9177
FAX (323) 469-9506
www.flamingangelfilms.com

Fernando Villena (310) 288-8000
www.paradigmagency.com

Christian Wagner (310) 288-8000
www.paradigmagency.com

Wayne Wahrman (310) 288-8000
www.paradigmagency.com

Doug Walker (310) 576-6300
www.beast.tv

Jonah Walker (323) 791-3153
www.whaleofatale.net

Lesley Walker (310) 285-0303
www.marshbest.com

Angus Wall (310) 586-0600
www.rockpaperscissors.com

Matt Walsh (310) 319-9908
www.whitehousepost.com

Chris Walter (310) 930-8118
FAX (310) 496-0776
www.chriswalteredits.com

Edward A. Warschilka (310) 282-9940
www.mirisch.com

Brad Waskewich (310) 399-3350
www.spotwelders.com

Rob Watzke (310) 576-6300
(310) 828-7500
www.beast.tv

Steven Weisberg (310) 282-9940
www.mirisch.com

Adam Weiss (310) 288-8000
www.paradigmagency.com

Steve Welch (310) 395-9550
www.skouras.com

Juliette Welfling (310) 652-8778
www.lspagency.net

Ethan Wells (310) 305-5777
www.venicebeacheditorial.com

Doug Werby (310) 399-5959
www.luxedit.com

Jeff Werner (310) 288-8000
www.paradigmagency.com

Dirk Westervelt (818) 284-6423
www.italentco.com

Chris Whiffen (310) 450-7070
www.room.tv

Christophe Williams (310) 319-9908
www.whitehousepost.com

Kelix Williams (310) 450-7070
www.room.tv

Kelly Williams (310) 450-7070
www.room.tv

Chris Willingham (310) 288-8000
www.paradigmagency.com

Scott Wilson (310) 450-7070
www.room.tv

Scott C. Wilson (310) 490-9346
www.metalogicmusic.com/resume.htm

Dave Winter (310) 991-2464

Jeff Wishengrad (310) 587-3300
(818) 284-6423
www.italentco.com

Jeffrey Wolf (310) 288-8000
www.paradigmagency.com

Michael Wolf (310) 357-7211
www.wildpictures.com

Julia Wong (310) 288-8000
www.paradigmagency.com

Craig Wood (310) 288-8000
www.paradigmagency.com

Matthew Wood (310) 319-9908
www.whitehousepost.com

Chris Wright (323) 467-8550
www.sunsetedit.com

John Wright (310) 288-8000
www.paradigmagency.com

Justine Wright (310) 273-6700
www.utaproduction.com

Miklos Wright (310) 652-8778
www.lspagency.net

Gabriel Wrye (310) 285-0303
www.marshbest.com

Steve Wystrach (213) 369-6903

Bill Yahruas (310) 282-9940
www.mirisch.com

Toby Yates (310) 656-5151
www.innovativeartists.com

William Yeh (310) 656-5151
www.innovativeartists.com

Greg Young (310) 305-5777
www.venicebeacheditorial.com

Gary Youngman (310) 477-9668

David Zieff (323) 468-2240
www.nyoffice.net

Dan Zimmerman (310) 273-6700
www.utaproduction.com

Dean Zimmerman (310) 273-6700
www.unitedtalent.com

Don Zimmerman (310) 273-6700
www.utaproduction.com

Kevin Zimmerman (310) 319-9908
www.whitehousepost.com

Paul Zucker (310) 652-8778
www.lspagency.net

Karen Knowles Zuniga (310) 260-7910
www.rivaleditorial.com

Bonded Services, Inc. (818) 848-9766
3205 Burton Ave. FAX (818) 848-9849
Burbank, CA 91504 www.bonded.com

FilmCore Distribution/ Vault Services (323) 464-8600
1010 N. Highland Ave. FAX (323) 464-3067
Los Angeles, CA 90038 www.filmcore.net

Ⓐ **Hollywood Vaults, Inc.** (323) 461-6464
(800) 569-5336
742 Seward St. FAX (323) 461-6479
Los Angeles, CA 90038 www.hollywoodvaults.com

Iron Mountain Film & Sound Archives (323) 466-9287
(800) 899-4766
1025 N. Highland Ave. FAX (323) 467-8068
Hollywood, CA 90038 www.ironmountain.com

KISS Media Vaults & Self Storage (818) 769-5477
(818) 769-2080
4444 Vineland Ave. FAX (818) 769-1639
Toluca Lake, CA 91602 www.kissvaults.com

Los Angeles Fine Arts & Wine Storage Company (310) 447-7700
2290 Centinela Ave. www.lafinearts&wine.com
West Los Angeles, CA 90064

Pacific Title Archives (818) 239-1960
3520 Valhalla Dr. FAX (818) 972-9724
Burbank, CA 91505 www.pacifictitlearchives.com

Pacific Title Archives (323) 938-3711
4800 W. San Vicente FAX (323) 938-6364
Los Angeles, CA 90019 www.pacifictitlearchives.com

Pacific Title Archives (818) 760-4223
10717 Vanowen St. FAX (818) 760-1704
North Hollywood, CA 91605
www.pacifictitlearchives.com

Seward Film & Tape Vaults (323) 653-4390
(818) 209-0516
1010 N. Seward St. FAX (818) 508-7958
Los Angeles, CA 90038

Williams Data and Film Protection Services (323)-234-3453
1925 E. Vernon Ave www.williamsrecords.com
Los Angeles, CA 90058

Cinetech (661) 222-9073
27200 Tourney Rd., Ste. 100
Valencia, CA 91355
FAX (661) 253-3637

Deluxe Laboratories (323) 960-8622 / (323) 960-3600
5433 Fernwood Ave.
Hollywood, CA 90027
FAX (323) 960-7016
www.bydeluxe.com
(35mm Black/White & Color)
Cutoffs: 10pm Fri & 4am Sun–Thurs

Filmworks/FX, Inc. (310) 577-3213
4121 Redwood Ave., Ste. 101
Los Angeles, CA 90066
FAX (310) 577-3215
www.filmworksfx.com
(16mm, 35mm & Super 16)
Contact: Sean Main

FotoKem (818) 846-3101 / (818) 846-3102
2801 W. Alameda Ave.
Burbank, CA 91505
FAX (818) 841-2130
www.fotokem.com
Hours: 24 Hours Mon–Fri

Hollywood Film & Video, Inc. (323) 464-2181 / (949) 306-2107
6060 Sunset Blvd.
Los Angeles, CA 90028
FAX (323) 464-0893
www.hfv.com
Cutoffs: 16mm Black/White 9am, 35mm/16mm Color 2am & Color Reversal 10am Mon–Thurs

Intellikey Labs (818) 241-7373
1265 Los Angeles St., Ste. 200
Glendale, CA 91204
FAX (818) 241-7371
www.intellikeylabs.com
(Optical Media Quality Assurance)

Laser Pacific Media Corporation (323) 462-6266
809 N. Cahuenga Blvd.
Hollywood, CA 90038
FAX (323) 464-3233
www.laserpacific.com
Cutoffs: 2am Mon–Fri & Midnight Sun
Contact: Peter McEvoy

NT Audio Video Film Labs (310) 828-1098
1833 Centinela Ave.
Santa Monica, CA 90404
www.ntaudio.com
(Film Preservation & Restoration)

Pro8mm (818) 848-5522
2805 W. Magnolia Blvd.
Burbank, CA 91505
FAX (818) 848-5956
www.pro8mm.com
(16mm, Super 8 & Super 16)

Spectra Film & Video (818) 762-4545
5626 Vineland Ave.
North Hollywood, CA 91601
FAX (818) 762-5454
www.spectrafilmandvideo.com
(16mm, 35mm, Super 8 & Telecine)
Cut Off: 10:30am Mon–Fri

SplitReel, Inc. (323) 528-1832

Technicolor, Inc. (818) 769-8500
4050 Lankershim Blvd.
Universal City, CA 91604
FAX (818) 761-4835
www.technicolor.com
Cutoffs: 3am Sun–Thurs (By Appointment)
Contact: Tim Knapp

Technicolor, Inc./CFI (818) 505-2821 / (818) 754-5054
4050 Lankershim Blvd.
North Hollywood, CA 91604
FAX (818) 761-4835
www.technicolor.com
(35mm & 65/70mm)
Cutoffs: 3am Sun–Thurs, 10pm Fri (Develop and Print) & Midnight Fri (Develop & Prep)
Contact: Mike Munson

30 Min Foto (323) 463-1678
5834 Santa Moncia Blvd.
Hollywood, CA 90038
(Full Service Processing)

A & I Hollywood (323) 856-5280 (800) 883-9088
933 N. Highland Ave. FAX (323) 856-5110
Los Angeles, CA 90038 www.aandi.com
(Black/White and Color Processing, Digital Imaging, Film Output, Printing, Quantity Duplication, Restoration, Retouching & Scanning)

A & I Santa Monica (310) 264-2622
1550 17th St. FAX (310) 453-8463
Santa Monica, CA 90404 www.aandi.com
(Black and White, Color, Digital Imaging, Film Output, Full Service Processing, Printing, Quantity Duplication, Retouching & Scanning)

Cinetech (661) 222-9073
27200 Tourney Rd., Ste. 100 FAX (661) 253-3637
Valencia, CA 91355

Foto First Digital Imaging (310) 657-2711
100 N. La Cienega Blvd., Ste. 110 FAX (310) 657-2835
Los Angeles, CA 90048 www.fotofirstla.com
(Digital Imaging and Printing, Film Output, Processing & Scanning)

Goldencolor Photo Lab (310) 274-3445 (800) 444-2551
9020 W. Olympic Blvd. FAX (310) 274-6260
Beverly Hills, CA 90211 www.goldencolor.com

GP Color (818) 504-1200
8211 Lankershim Blvd. FAX (818) 504-1220
North Hollywood, CA 91605 www.gpcolor.com
(Digital Imaging, Mural Prints, Processing, Restoration & Retouching)

Imagexperts (323) 460-7070 (888) 846-2439
6630 W. Sunset Blvd. FAX (323) 460-2010
Hollywood, CA 90028 www.imagexperts.com
(Full Service Processing, Large Format Prints, Mural Prints, Quantity Duplication & Scanning)

Isgo Hollywood (323) 876-8085
933 N. Highland Ave. (inside A&I) www.isgophoto.com
Hollywood, CA 90038
(Black and White, Color, Digital Imaging, Film Output, Full Service Processing, Printing, Quantity Duplication, Retouching & Scanning)

Lightbox (323) 933-2080
7122 Beverly Blvd. FAX (323) 933-5992
Los Angeles, CA 90036 www.lightboxstudio.com
(Black and White, Color, Digital Imaging, Processing & Retouching)

Nardulli (323) 882-8331
1315 Pleasant Ave. FAX (323) 882-8077
Los Angeles, CA 90033 www.nardulli.com
(Black/White Processing, Mural Prints & Quantity Duplication)

One Hour Photo Center (818) 501-1234
14535 Ventura Blvd. www.1hrphotoctr.com
Sherman Oaks, CA 91403

The Studios at Paramount (323) 956-8380
The Studios at Paramount
Still Photo Lab www.thestudiosatparamount.com
5555 Melrose Ave.
Hollywood, CA 90038

Paris Photo Lab Imaging (310) 204-0500 (323) 939-8893
8016 Melrose Ave. FAX (310) 837-7017
Los Angeles, CA 90046 www.parisphoto.com
(Digital Imaging, Processing, Restoration & Retouching)

Photomax Lab Corp. (323) 850-0200
7190 Sunset Blvd. FAX (323) 850-0206
Los Angeles, CA 90046 www.photomaxlab.net
(Digital Imaging, Full Service Processing, One Hour Processing, Quantity Duplication, Restoration & Retouching)

Prints of the City (310) 477-1533 (310) 613-1234
3124 S. Sepulveda Blvd. FAX (310) 477-0601
Los Angeles, CA 90034 www.printsphoto.com/la411.html

Pro One, Los Angeles (323) 468-1811
6613 Sunset Blvd. FAX (323) 468-1825
Hollywood, CA 90028 www.proonela.com

Prolab Digital Imaging (310) 625-4411
5441 W. 104th St. FAX (310) 204-6939
Los Angeles, CA 90045 www.prolabdigital.com
(Digital Imaging, Mural Prints, Processing, Quantity Duplication, Restoration & Retouching)

Quick Photo Print (818) 761-7130
10055 Riverside Dr. FAX (818) 509-1410
Toluca Lake, CA 91602 www.quickphotoprint.org
(Full Service Processing & Quantity Duplication)

SuperColor (323) 874-2188 (323) 874-2648
979 N. La Brea Ave. FAX (323) 874-7902
Los Angeles, CA 90038 www.supercolorimaging.com

Warner Bros. Studio Facilities - Photo Lab (818) 954-7118
4000 Warner Blvd., Bldg. 44LL FAX (818) 954-6732
Burbank, CA 91522 www.wbsf.com
(Digital Imaging & Full Service Processing)

The Andrita Media Center (323) 344-4500
3030 Andrita St.
Los Angeles, CA 90065
FAX **(323) 344-4800**
www.andritastudios.com

Cinesat, Inc. (213) 596-5180
(818) 802-7719
c/o Los Angeles Center Studios
1201 W. Fifth St., Ste. FF
Los Angeles, CA 90017
FAX **(213) 596-5181**
www.cinesat.net

Coastal Media Group (818) 880-9800
26660 Agoura Rd.
Calabasas, CA 91302
FAX **(818) 579-9026**
www.coastalmediagroup.com

Envision Studios (310) 451-1515
1528 Sixth St., Ste. 100
Santa Monica, CA 90401
FAX **(310) 393-2697**
www.envisionstudios.tv

Fastlane Broadcast Studio (818) 841-3888
(562) 335-7400
3062 N. Lima St.
Burbank, CA 91504
FAX **(818) 841-3188**
www.fastlanebroadcast.com

Pacific Television Center (310) 287-3823
3440 Motor Ave., Circular Bldg.
Los Angeles, CA 90034
(Satellite Uplink)
FAX **(310) 287-3808**
www.pactv.com

Post Modern Broadcast Studios, LLC (949) 608-8700
2941 Alton Pkwy
Irvine, CA 92606
FAX **(949) 608-8729**
www.postmodernstudios.com
(Domestic Satellite Uplink, Fiber Optic Network, International Satellite Uplink & Video Transmission Coordination)

Prime Digital Media Services (661) 964-0220
28111 Avenue Stanford
Valencia, CA 91355
FAX **(661) 964-0550**
www.primedigital.com
(Domestic/International Satellite Uplink & Fiber Optic Network)

Selak Entertainment, Inc. (818) 842-5800
P.O. Box 1475
Burbank, CA 91507
www.selakentertainment.com
(Domestic Satellite Uplink, Fiber Optic Network, International Satellite Uplink, Satellite Uplink & Video Transmission Coordination)

Strategic Television, Inc. (805) 379-3663
15315 Magnolia Blvd., Ste. 423
Sherman Oaks, CA 91403
FAX **(805) 379-3645**
www.strategictv.com
(Domestic/International Video Transmission Coordination)

Video Production Specialists (VPS) (866) 447-3877
FAX **(310) 577-0850**
www.videoproductionspecialists.com
(Domestic/International Video Transmission Coordination)

5 Alarm Music (626) 304-1698
FAX (626) 795-2058
www.5alarmmusic.com
(Acoustic, Backgrounds, Clearance, Contemporary, Ethnic, Holiday Music, Licensing, Music Library & Vintage)

615 Music (818) 846-1615
www.615music.com
(Acoustic, Contemporary, Ethnic, Holiday Music & Music Library)

7-Out-Music (323) 650-0767
2355 Westwood Blvd., Ste. 190 FAX (323) 650-2906
Los Angeles, CA 90064 www.7outmusic.com

AE Music Publishing (310) 696-4600
7920 Sunset Blvd., Ste. 200 FAX (310) 696-4891
Los Angeles, CA 90046 www.asylument.com
(Music Library)

Associated Production Music (323) 461-3211
(800) 543-4276
6255 Sunset Blvd., Ste. 820 FAX (323) 461-9102
Hollywood, CA 90028 www.apmmusic.com

AudioMicro (818) 574-6294
(404) 759-3838
4550 Fulton Ave., Ste. 107 FAX (320) 451-3838
Sherman Oaks, CA 91423 www.audiomicro.com

Beyond (323) 856-7073
1545 N. Wilcox Ave., Ste. 222 FAX (323) 856-5917
Hollywood, CA 90028 www.musicbeyond.com

Big Planet Music, Inc. (818) 909-9222
www.bigplanetmusic.com
(Acoustic, Backgrounds, Contemporary, Licensing & Music Library)

Brand X Music (323) 651-2816
(Music Library, Licensing & Sound FX) FAX (323) 651-2946
www.brandxmusic.net

Bug Music Publishing (323) 466-4352
1645 N. Vine St., PH FAX (323) 466-2366
Los Angeles, CA 90028 www.bugmusic.com

Cherry Lane Music Publishing (212) 561-3000
Six E. 32nd St., 11th Fl. www.cherrylane.com
New York, NY 10016

Christmas and Holiday Music (949) 859-1615
26642 Via Noveno www.christmassongs.com
Mission Viejo, CA 92691
(Holiday Music)

Cinetrax (323) 874-9590
8033 Sunset Blvd., Ste. 400 FAX (323) 874-9592
Los Angeles, CA 90046 www.cinetrax.com

CSS Music/Dawn Music (323) 666-7968
(800) 468-6874
1948 Riverside Dr. www.cssmusic.com
Los Angeles, CA 90039
(Music & Sound FX)

Diamond E Music (805) 491-0330
16030 Ventura Blvd., Ste. 300 www.diamondemusic.com
Encino, CA 91436

EMI Music Publishing - Film Soundtrack Div. (310) 586-2740
2700 Colorado Ave., Ste. 100 FAX (310) 586-2795
Santa Monica, CA 90404 www.emimusicpub.com

Evolution Music Partners, LLC (310) 623-3388
9100 Wilshire Blvd. FAX (310) 623-1897
East Tower, Ste. 201 www.evolutionmusicpartners.com
Beverly Hills, CA 90212

Extreme Production Music (310) 395-0408
(800) 542-9494
1531 14th St. FAX (310) 395-0409
Santa Monica, CA 90404 www.extrememusic.com

FirstCom Music (310) 358-4915
(800) 858-8880
8750 Wilshire Blvd., Second Fl. FAX (310) 385-4314
Beverly Hills, CA 90211 www.firstcom.com

Gefen, Inc. (818) 772-9100
20600 Nordoff St. FAX (818) 772-9120
Chatsworth, CA 91311 www.gefen.com
(Backgrounds & Sound FX)

Groove Addicts Production Music Catalog (310) 572-4646
(800) 400-6767
(Acoustic & Contemporary) FAX (310) 572-4647
www.grooveaddicts.com

The Hit House (310) 378-8633
2621 Mathews Ave. FAX (310) 793-2625
Redondo Beach, CA 90278 ww.thehithouse.com

The Hollywood Edge (323) 603-3252
(800) 292-3755
7080 Hollywood Blvd., Ste. 519 FAX (323) 603-3298
Los Angeles, CA 90028 www.hollywoodedge.com

Hum (310) 260-4949
1547 Ninth St. FAX (310) 260-4944
Santa Monica, CA 90401 www.humit.com

JED (949) 290-2157
FAX (949) 290-2157

JRT Music (888) 578-6874
(888) 578-6874
143 28th St. FAX (718) 499-0470
Brooklyn, NY 11232 www.jrtmusic.com
(Acoustic, Backgrounds, Clearance, Licensing & Music Library)

Killer Tracks (310) 865-4455
9255 W. Sunset Blvd., Ste. 200 FAX (800) 865-4470
Los Angeles, CA 90069 www.killertracks.com
(Contemporary)

Latin Music Specialists (818) 774-1441
P.O. Box 571480 FAX (818) 774-9172
Tarzana, CA 91357

Leiber & Stoller Music Publishing (310) 273-6401
9000 Sunset Blvd., Ste. 1107 FAX (310) 273-1591
Los Angeles, CA 90069
(1950s, 1960s & Vintage)

Like Dat Music (858) 254-6779
P.O. Box 9476 FAX (858) 225-0864
Rancho Santa Fe, CA 92067 www.tjknowles.com

Los Angeles Post Music, Inc. (818) 501-8329
165 Culver Blvd., Ste. D FAX (818) 990-7661
Playa Del Rey, CA 90293 www.lapostmusic.com

Mamalahoa Publishing (310) 472-7775
330 S. Barrington Ave., Ste. 305 FAX (310) 472-7775
Los Angeles, CA 90049 www.mamalahoapublishing.com
(Acoustic, Backgrounds, Clearance, Contemporary, Ethnic, Holiday Music, Licensing, Music Library & Vintage)

Megatrax Production Music (818) 255-7100
(888) 634-2555
7629 Fulton Ave. FAX (818) 255-7199
North Hollywood, CA 91605 www.megatrax.com

MGM Music (310) 586-8905
10250 Constellation Blvd. www.mgm.com
Los Angeles, CA 90067

Mophonics (310) 452-0331
200 Westminister Ave. FAX **(310) 452-0356**
Venice, CA 90291 **www.mophonics.com**
(Acoustic, Backgrounds, Clearance, Contemporary, Ethnic, Holiday Music, Licensing, Music Library, Sound FX & Vintage)

Music For The Masses (323) 874-1170
7510 Sunset Blvd., Ste. 1022 FAX **(323) 874-5570**
Los Angeles, CA 90046

Non-Stop Music Library (818) 752-1898
4605 Lankershim Blvd., Ste. 305 FAX **(818) 752-1899**
North Hollywood, CA 91602 **www.nonstopmusic.com**

OGM Music, a Division of OGM, Inc. (323) 461-2701
(800) 421-4163
6464 Sunset Blvd, Ste. 790 FAX **(323) 461-1543**
Hollywood, CA 90028 **www.ogmmusic.com**

Opus 1
Music Production Library, LLC (818) 508-2040
(888) 757-6787
12711 Ventura Blvd., Ste. 170 FAX **(818) 508-2044**
Studio City, CA 91604 **www.opus1musiclibrary.com**

Premier Tracks (760) 416-0805
(866) 777-0805
1775 E. Palm Canyon Dr., Ste. H239 FAX **(760) 416-1855**
Palm Springs, CA 92264 **www.premiertracks.com**

Quincy Jones Music Publishing (323) 957-6601
6671 Sunset Blvd., Ste. 1574A FAX **(323) 962-5231**
Los Angeles, CA 90028 **www.quincyjonesmusic.com**

Riptide Music, Inc. (310) 437-4380
(310) 422-1768
4121 Redwood Ave., Ste. 202 FAX **(310) 437-4384**
Los Angeles, CA 90066 **www.riptidemusic.com**

S3 Music + Sound (310) 312-3329
11681 Gateway Blvd. FAX **(310) 312-8827**
Los Angeles, CA 90064 **www.s3mx.com**

ScreenMusic International (818) 789-2954
18034 Ventura Blvd., Ste. 450 FAX **(818) 789-5801**
Encino, CA 91316 **www.screenmusic.com**
(Music Clearance, Library and Licensing)

Serafine Inc. (310) 399-9279
(805) 579-8525
P.O. Box 1798 **www.serafinecollective.com**
Simi Valley, CA 93062

Songs To Your Eyes, Ltd. (323) 988-9725
22040 Del Valle St. FAX **(323) 201-2045**
Woodland Hills, CA 91364 **www.songstoyoureyes.com**

Sonic Safari Music (818) 247-6219
663 W. California Ave. FAX **(818) 241-1333**
Glendale, CA 91203 **www.sonicsafarimusic.com**
(Ethnic & Tribal)

Soundtrack Marketing (323) 274-3800
1641 Riverside Dr. FAX **(818) 500-7390**
Glendale, CA 91201 **www.soundtrackmarketing.com**

Southern Library of Recorded Music (760) 202-2327
39 Via San Marco FAX **(760) 202-2327**
Rancho Mirage, CA 92270

Summerfield Music, Inc./
Trailer Trash Music Library (818) 905-0400
14024 Roblar Rd. FAX **(818) 905-0488**
Sherman Oaks, CA 91423 **www.summerfieldmusic.com**

Two Steps From Hell (310) 963-0659
(310) 985-1126
P.O. Box 2546 **www.twostepsfromhell.com**
Venice, CA 90294

Uncommon Trax (312) 266-3611
610 N. Fairbanks Court, Third Fl. FAX **(312) 640-2860**
Chicago, IL 60611 **www.uncommontrax.com**
(Acoustic, Backgrounds, Contemporary, Licensing & Sound FX)

Urban Style Music (310) 435-9499
(323) 327-2703
www.urbanstylemusic.com

Windswept Pacific Music Publishing (310) 550-1500
9320 Wilshire Blvd., Ste. 200 FAX **(310) 247-0195**
Beverly Hills, CA 90212 **www.windsweptpacific.com**

Zoo Street Music (818) 955-5268
2701 W. Willow St. FAX **(818) 295-5001**
Burbank, CA 91505 **www.zoostreet.com**

48 Windows Music and Mix (310) 392-9545
1661 Lincoln Blvd., Ste. 220 FAX (310) 392-9445
Santa Monica, CA 90404 www.48windows.com
Contact: Eric Garcia
Sound Designers: Sonia Castro & Michael Chandler
Composers: Eric Garcia & Andreas Straub

740 Sound Design (310) 574-0740
12509 Beatrice St. FAX (310) 306-0744
Los Angeles, CA 90066 www.740sounddesign.com

A B Audio Visual Ent., Inc. (562) 429-1042
3765 Marwick Ave. FAX (562) 429-2401
Long Beach, CA 90808 www.abaudio.com
Creative Director: Linda Rippee
Executive Producer/Composer: Arlan H. Boll

Advantage Audio/Jim Hodson (818) 566-8555
1026 N. Hollywood Way FAX (818) 566-8963
Burbank, CA 91505 www.advantageaudio.com
President/Sound Designer: Jim Hodson
Sound Designers: Heather Holbrook, Bob Poole & Paca Thomas

Alan Audio Works (310) 753-1564
(323) 906-8700
4222 Santa Monica Blvd. FAX (562) 408-6822
Los Angeles, CA 90029 www.alanaudioworks.com

Alan Ett Music Group (818) 508-3303
12711 Ventura Blvd., Ste. 110 FAX (818) 508-3314
Studio City, CA 91604 www.aemg.com
Composers: Alan Ett & Scott Liggett

AMI Music Group (310) 654-4060
Composer: Norman Arnold FAX (323) 654-4061
www.amimusicgroup.com

Audible Shift (323) 481-4581
Raleigh Studios www.audibleshift.com
662 N. Van Ness Ave., Ste. 200
Los Angeles, CA 90004
Creative Director/Sound Designer: Kadet Kuhne
Composers: Brad Breeck, Raja Das, Steve McClure & Anna Sitko

Bad Ass Music, Inc. (818) 342-5969
P.O. Box 18315 FAX (818) 206-0302
Encino, CA 91416 www.badassmusic.net

Barbara Marshall Music (831) 622-7778
(831) 320-7778
FAX (831) 622-7733
Contacts: Barbara Marshall & Susan McGonigle

barton:holt (310) 478-2120
11836 W. Pico Blvd. FAX (310) 478-2130
Los Angeles, CA 90064 www.bartonholt.com

bbm/bill bodine music (310) 459-6500
921 Iliff St. FAX (310) 459-4572
Pacific Palisades, CA 90272 www.billbodinemusic.com
Composer/Sound Designer: Bill Bodine

A **Bell Sound Studios** (323) 461-3036
916 N. Citrus Ave. FAX (323) 461-8764
Hollywood, CA 90038 www.bellsound.com
Contact: John Osiecki

Bendy (310) 337-9727
(310) 753-9702
FAX (310) 645-2708
Executive Producer: Bob Gannon www.bendymusic.com
Composers/Sound Designers: Dean Menta & Andy Snavley
Composer: Josh Sklair

betafish music (310) 881-6307
1537 14th St. FAX (973) 796-2892
Santa Monica, CA 90404 www.betafish.net

BIG EARS sound design + music (310) 597-3600
3435 Ocean Park Blvd., Ste. 107 FAX (760) 529-5058
Santa Monica, CA 90405 www.bigears.com
Executive Producer: Wendy Fraser
Creative Director/Sound Designer: Marc Levisohn
Manager: Felicia Lee
Composers: Mike Freedman & Marc Levisohn

Big Planet Music, Inc. (818) 909-9222
www.bigplanetmusic.com
Creative Director & Chief Composer: Billy White Acre
Producer: Kharin Gilbert

Blast! Music Management (323) 857-7299
427 N. Citrus Ave. FAX (323) 937-9403
Los Angeles, CA 90036 www.blastmanagement.com
Executive Producer: Aaron Jacoves
Composers: Scott Bennett, Rick Boston, Cadesky/Dyer, Bruno Coon, dj Chris Paul, Daniel Kolton, Latin Music Artist Alliance, Wendy MaHarry, Jeff Martin/Idaho, Monster Music, John Paesano, Popular Beat Combo, Luis Resto, & Danny Wilde
Producers: Duro, Ed Rose, Phil Tan & Paul Williams

Blue Music & Sound Design (310) 568-3355
5839 Green Valley Circle, Ste. 200 FAX (310) 568-0033
Culver City, CA 90230 www.bluemusicla.com
Executive Producer/Creative Director: Paul Hoffman
Composers: Hal Cragin, Mitchell Forman, Adam Giorgoni, Steve Love, Guy Moon & David Rolfe
Composer/Sound Designers: Paul Hoffman & Bruce Somers

Blue Tango Productions (949) 813-2450
668 N. Coast Hwy, Ste. 226
Laguna Beach, CA 92651
www.bluetangoproductions.com
Music & Sound Producer: Marla Friedler

Braincloud (323) 935-2032
FAX (323) 935-2032
www.braincloudsound.com

Bullets (818) 708-7359
4520 Callada Pl. FAX (818) 708-9648
Tarzana, CA 91356 www.bulletswest.com
Composers: Mark Mercury & Hal Winn

Cashman Commercials (661) 222-9300
(800) 789-7234
26136 N. Twain Pl. FAX (661) 222-9355
Stevenson Ranch, CA 91381
www.cashmancommercials.com
Composer: Marc Cashman

Chace (818) 842-8346
(800) 842-8346
201 S. Victory Blvd. FAX (818) 842-8353
Burbank, CA 91502 www.chace.com
Contact: James Eccles

Chris Bell Music and Sound Design (707) 363-1000
www.chrisbellmusicandsounddesign.com

Circle Moon Music (323) 852-9991
www.seanmorris.com

Citrus Productions (818) 366-0330
17049 Lisette St. www.citrusprods.com
Granada Hills, CA 91344
Composer: Scott Van Zen

Cloud 19 (310) 839-5400
(310) 717-7819
3767 Overland Ave., Ste. 104 FAX (310) 839-5404
Los Angeles, CA 90034 www.cloud19.com

Confidence Head (310) 393-7577
1316 Third Street Promenade, Ste.109 FAX (310) 584-1534
Santa Monica, CA 90401 www.confidencehead.com
Contact: Michael Coulter
Composers: Michael Coulter & Tobias Johnston

Craig Harris Music (323) 851-8510
P.O. Box 1508 **www.craigharrismusic.com**
Los Angeles, CA 90078
Composer/Sound Designer: Craig Harris

Decibel Architects (310) 670-4999
3780 Selby Ave. FAX (978) 683-7897
Los Angeles, CA 90034 **www.dasoundmusic.com**
Executive Producer: Renée
Composer: Tom Page

DeepMix (323) 769-3500
6255 Sunset Blvd., Ste. 1024 FAX (323) 417-5134
Hollywood, CA 90028 **www.deepmix.com**
Partner/Executive Producer: Brad Colerick
Managing Partner/Creative Director: Dave Curtin
Producer/NY: Marc Morris
Production Manager: Nate Fisher-Shaffer
Assistant Producer: Bobbi Hamilton
Accountant: Takayo Horikoshi

Diblasi Music Prod. (818) 884-7895
www.diblasimusic.com

Druz Music (323) 466-6446
6446 Rodgerton Dr. FAX (323) 463-6446
Los Angeles, CA 90068
Contact: Jacqueline Druz

E-Records (310) 279-2388
c/o Rick Torres, P.O. Box 352065 **www.ricktorres.com**
Los Angeles, CA 90035

Ear to Ear Music & Sound Design (310) 581-1660
1660 Ninth St. FAX (310) 581-1661
Santa Monica, CA 90404 **www.eartoear.com**
Contact: Amy Lyngos
Composer/Sound Designer: Brian Banks

Earshot Music Productions (323) 467-2529
FAX (323) 467-7650
Composer/Sound Designer: David Steinberg

Elias Arts LA (310) 581-6500
2219 Main St. FAX (310) 581-4800
Santa Monica, CA 90405 **www.eliasarts.com**
Executive VP & General Manager: Ann Haugen
Creative Director: Dave Gold
Composers: Chris Campanaro, Jimmy Haun, Chip Jenkins, Christopher Kemp, Michael Sherwood & Dave Wittman
Director of Sound: Dean Hovey
Sr. VP of Sales and Business Development: Scott Cymbala
Producer: Kala Sherman

EMOTO (310) 399-6900
1615 16th St. FAX (310) 399-5333
Santa Monica, CA 90404 **www.emotomusic.com**
Executive Producer: Paul Schultz
Composers: John Adair, Paul Bessenbacher, Ryan Elder, Steve Hampton, Tony Morales & Craig Snider
Sound Designer: 740 Sound Design

Endless Noise (310) 566-1463
1453 Third St. Promenade, Ste. 320 FAX (310) 566-1469
Santa Monica, CA 90401 **www.endlessnoise.com**
Producer: Mary Catherine Finney
Creative Director/Composer: Jeff Elmassian
Composers: Chris Guardino & Andy Rehfeldt
Sound Designers: Scott Friedman, Hao Lam & Erik Schuiten

Finger Music (310) 393-5340
618 Venezia Ave. FAX (310) 399-5398
Venice, CA 90291 **www.fingermusic.tv**
Executive Producer: Tania Thiele
Creative Directors: Dave Hodge & Hein Hoven
Composers: Rick Boston, James DiSalvio, Dom and Ant, Dave Hodge, Daniel Lenz, David A. Logan, Photek, Spookey Ruben & Joey Rubenstien
Sound Designers: Onnalee Blank, Richard Devine, Dave Hodge & Hein Hoven

Fuel Music (310) 640-3435
www.ifuelmusic.com
Composer/Sound Designer: Brad Chiet

Full Score Productions (310) 889-9827
15551 Belcanto Dr. FAX (310) 889-9827
Los Angeles, CA 90077 **www.fullscore.com**
Contact: Amy Ferguson
Production Supervisor: Saralee Gleckler

Gary Myrick Music (818) 382-4792
www.garymyrick.com
Composers: Gina Felicetta & Gary Myrick

Geoff Levin Music (818) 841-6607
719 S. Main St. FAX (818) 841-2520
Burbank, CA 91506 **www.geofflevin.com**
Composer: Geoff Levin

David George (213) 999-4003
(323) 936-3006
FAX (213) 627-5566
homepage.mac.com/davidandlisala/menu8.html

Glaser Musicworks (310) 204-6111
(800) 972-6694
1941 Livonia Ave. FAX (310) 204-6222
Los Angeles, CA 90034 **www.samglaser.com**
Contacts: Marcia Baron
Executive Producer/Composer: Sam Glaser

Grind Music & Sound (818) 565-5565
4804 Laurel Canyon Blvd., Ste. 716 **www.grindinc.com**
Valley Village, CA 91607
Composer/Sound Designer: Michelle Garuik

Groove Addicts (310) 572-4646
FAX (310) 572-4647
Contact: Julie Ward **www.grooveaddicts.com**
Executive Producer/Composer: Dain Blair
Composers: Tori Amos, Craig Armstrong, David Arnold, Angelo Badalamenti, Luis Balcov, John Barry, Steve Bartek, Tyler Bates, Christophe Beck, Byron Brizuela, Jon Brion, BT, Al Capps, Teddy Castellucci, Stanley Clarke, George Clinton, Harry Cody, Stewart Copeland, Don Davis, John Debney, Ann Dudley, Rob Dougan, The Dust Brothers, Cliff Eidelman, Danny Elfman, Nick Glenne-Smith, Joel Goldsmith, Paul Haslinger, Mark Isham, Alexander Janko, Maurice Jarre, Rolfe Kent, Wojciech Kilar, Chris Lennertz, Joel McNeely, Jonathan Miller, Paul Mirkovich, David Newman, John Ottman, Howard Pfeifer, Tony Phillips, Nicholas Pike, Nicola Piovani, Basil Poledouris, Rachel Portman, John Powell, Trevor Rabin, Graeme Revell, Stan Ridgeway, Lalo Schifrin, Marc Shaiman, Mark Snow, Shirley Walker, Bruce Watson, Timothy Michael Wynn, Phil-X, Gabriel Yared & Christopher Young
Sound Designers: Kim B. Christensen, Jonathan Miller & Robert Wear

Halfpipe Music (310) 651-6233
P.O. Box 10534 FAX (323) 851-9648
Beverly Hills, CA 90213 **www.halfpipemusic.com**
Composers: Shane August, Scott Bennett, Rick Boston, Meredith Chinn, dj JUN, dj True: 129, Christopher Faizi, Sean Hennessy, Kent Karlsson, Daniel Kolton, Jeff Martin, Stephen McCarthy, The Newton Brothers, John O, Joey Peters, Mike Semple, Kiran Shahani, Chris Stills, Andy Sturmer, Kathie Talbot, Danny Tate, Scott Thomas & Rick Torres

The Hit House (310) 378-8633
2621 Mathews Ave. FAX (310) 793-2625
Redondo Beach, CA 90278 **www.thehithouse.com**
Executive Producer: Sally House
Creative Director/Composer: Scott Miller
Music Supervisor/Producer: Gabriele Corcos
Engineer/Mixer: Jeff Kanan

Horrible Music, LLC (310) 260-9939
13101 Addison St. **www.horriblemusic.net**
Sherman Oaks, CA 91423
Composer/Sound Designer: Jud Haskins

Howling Music (818) 707-8263
12439 Magnolia Blvd., Ste. 240 FAX (818) 991-4881
North Hollywood, CA 91607 **www.howlingmusic.com**
Executive Producer: Kim Pawlik
Creative Director: David Grow
Producers: Kimberly Lambert & Thomas C. Mayer

HUM Music + Sound Design (310) 260-4949
1547 Ninth St. FAX (310) 260-4944
Santa Monica, CA 90401 www.humit.com
Executive Producer: Debbi Landon
Producer: Chanel Scott
Associate Producer: Kristina Iwankiw
Creative Director: Jeff Koz
Associate Creative Director: Alex Kemp
Composers: Scott Glenn, Robert Lopez & Hirotaka Matsuoka
Sound Designer: Dan Hart
West Coast Sales Rep: Reber/Covington
Midwest Sales Rep: Nikki Weiss
Texas and East Coast Sales Rep: Unique Koz

Icarus Music (562) 925-4514
4954 Briercrest Ave. www.icarusmusic.com
Lakewood, CA 90713
Composers: Eddie Freeman & Marta Victoria

IM Sound and Music (323) 573-2896
P.O. Box 931493 www.johnmassari.com
Los Angeles, CA 90093
Composer: John Massari

James O'Brien Music (310) 396-6731
Composer: James O'Brien FAX (909) 337-5694
Executive Producer: Jen Earle www.jamesobrienmusic.com
Sound Designer: Joseph Ma
Music Producer: Chris Garcia

Jet Stream Sound (323) 883-0123
3610 W. Magnolia Blvd. FAX (818) 531-0401
Burbank, CA 91505 www.jetstreamsound.com

Jill Fraser Music (818) 908-9083
www.jillfrasermusic.com
Composer/Sound Designer: Jill Fraser

The Jingle Factory (818) 789-0226
(818) 943-2668
13964 La Maida St. FAX (818) 789-0250
Sherman Oaks, CA 91423 www.jinglefactory.com
Composer: Dan McNamara

Jingle Jangle Music (818) 706-6375
(818) 489-5585
5522 Modena Pl. FAX (818) 706-0046
Agoura Hills, CA 91301 www.hodads.com
Composer/Sound Designer: Robert J. Schuster

John Zuker Music (818) 500-9288
1615 Virginia Ave. FAX (818) 500-0558
Glendale, CA 91202 www.johnzuker.com
Composer/Sound Designer: John Zuker

Jon Huck Music & Sound Design (323) 222-1082
Composer/Sound Designer: Jon Huck www.jhuck.com
Composers: Joe Berardi, Roddy Bottum, Dan Crane, Carey Fosse, Dino Herrmann, The Millionaire & Bill Ungerman

The King Klong Music Group (818) 505-8787
(888) 766-4792
FAX (801) 365-5152
Creative Director: Steve Klong www.mixinpixls.com
Producers/Composers: Laura B., Garret Bever, Manoj Gopinath, Howard Pfeifer & Adam Watkins

L.A. Entertainment, Inc. (800) 579-9157
7095 Hollywood Blvd., Ste. 826 FAX (323) 924-1095
Hollywood, CA 90028 www.warriorrecords.com
Composer/Sound Designer: Jim Ervin

Latin Music Specialists (818) 774-1441
P.O. Box 571480 FAX (818) 774-9172
Tarzana, CA 91357
Contact: Sara Traina

Les Hooper Music (818) 501-2727
4526 Rubio Ave. FAX (818) 995-6773
Encino, CA 91436
Composer/Sound Designer: Les Hooper

Like Dat Music (858) 254-6779
P.O. Box 9476 FAX (858) 225-0864
Rancho Santa Fe, CA 92067 www.tjknowles.com
Executive Producer/Creative Director: T.J. Knowles
Composer/Sound Designer: Bobby Crew
Producer: Jay Knowles

Lyon Studios (949) 675-4790
(323) 962-6117
222 21st St. FAX (949) 675-2139
Newport Beach, CA 92663 www.lyonstudios.com
Contact: Curt Lyon

Machine Head (310) 392-8393
1641 20th St. FAX (310) 392-9676
Santa Monica, CA 90404 www.machinehead.com
Head of Production: Vicki Ordeshook
Creative Director/Sound Designer: Stephen Dewey
Composer: Adam Schiff
Music Supervisor: Jason Bentley
Composer/Sound Designer: Johannes Hammers
Sound Designer: Dustin Camilleri
Engineer: Kip Smedley

malleryscores (323) 462-4862
6119 Glen Alder FAX (323) 462-6842
Hollywood, CA 90068 www.malleryscores.com
Creative Director: Billy Mallery
Producer: Wanda Chan
Music Supervisor: Tracy Talley

Margarita Mix de Santa Mónica (310) 396-3333
1661 Lincoln Blvd., Ste. 101 FAX (310) 396-9633
Santa Monica, CA 90404 www.lastudios.com
Contacts: Michele Millard & Whitney Warren
Mixers: Jack Aurora, Jimmy Hite, Jeff Levy & Jonathan Whitehead

Margarita Mix Hollywood (323) 962-6565
6838 Romaine St. FAX (323) 962-8662
Hollywood, CA 90038 www.lastudios.com
Contact: Veneta Butler

Matter Music (818) 505-8505
FAX (818) 505-9241
www.mattermusic.com
Composers: Ric Markmann, Dan Pinella & Chris Wagner

Mental Music Productions (213) 713-8868
P.O. Box 97311 www.mental-music.com
Sherman Oaks, CA 91413

Mesmer, Inc. (310) 410-1900
6080 Center Dr., Ste. 210 FAX (310) 410-1901
Los Angeles, CA 90045 www.mesmerav.com
Composer/Sound Designers: David S. Blau, Lee Curreri, Lucas Eskin, Brian Miller, Alan Porzio, Jeff Sudakin, David Tobocman, Kubilay Uner & R. Walter Vincent

Mind Over Eye, LLC (310) 396-4663
(310) 968-4259
1639 11th St., Ste. 117 FAX (310) 396-0663
Santa Monica, CA 90404 www.mindovereye.com
Composer: Bill Wadsworth

The Mix (310) 260-9838
1548 Ninth St. FAX (310) 260-3978
Santa Monica, CA 90401 www.themixsantamonica.com
Sound Designers/Mixers: Steve Davis, Josh Eichenbaum, Ted Lobinger & Nick Michaud

Mona Davis Music, Inc. (323) 270-270
2633 Lincoln Blvd., Ste. 602 www.monadavis.com
Santa Monica, CA 90405
Contact: Barbara Richter
Producers: Dany Crusius & Alex Menck
Sound Designer: David Streefkerk
Composers: Tom Batoy, Alex Menck & Franco Tortora

Mophonics (310) 452-0331
(212) 260-8183
200 Westminster Ave. www.mophonics.com
Venice, CA 90291
Partner/Head of Production: Shelley Altman
Partner/Composer/Creative Director: Stephan Altman
Producer: Jean Scofield
Music Supervisor/Producer: Josh Marcy

Mosher Music (323) 656-0197 / (323) 578-3868
Composers: Tim Mosher & Stoker FAX (323) 656-0197
www.mosherandstoker.com

Music Forever (323) 461-4646
1606 N. Highland Ave. FAX (323) 461-1904
Los Angeles, CA 90028 www.musicforever.com
Executive Producer: David Streja
Composer: Anthony Marinelli
Head Engineer: Clint Bennett

The Music Kitchen, Inc. (661) 338-4749
12400 Connery Way www.themusickitchen.com
Bakersfield, CA 93312
Composer/Sound Designer: Michael Benghiat

Musikvergnuegen (323) 856-5900
1545 N. Wilcox Ave., Ste. 202 FAX (323) 856-5917
Hollywood, CA 90028 www.musikvergnuegen.com
Executive Producer: Pat Weaver
West Coast Head of Sales: Andria Ellis
Mid West Head of Sales: Mary Ida Bonadio
East Coast Head of Sales: Carl Forsberg

Mutato Muzika (310) 360-0561 / (310) 994-2407
8760 Sunset Blvd. FAX (310) 360-0837
West Hollywood, CA 90069 www.mutato.com
Composer/Sound Designer: Mark Mothersbaugh
Contact: Robert Miltenberg

ON Music and Sound (310) 264-0407
2042-A Broadway FAX (310) 264-0381
Santa Monica, CA 90404 www.onmusicandsound.com
Composer: Chris Winston
Sound Designer: Mark Jasper

Orange Dog Music (818) 448-9262
6434 Whitman Ave. www.orangedogmusic.com
Lake Balboa, CA 91406
Composer/Sound Designer: Wes Hambright

Pacific Coast Presentations, Inc. (949) 548-9432
6100 West Coast Hwy, Ste. C FAX (949) 548-1622
Newport Beach, CA 92663 www.pcpmusic.com
Contact: Edo Guidotti

Portis Music (818) 216-2841
4300 Shadyglade Ave.
Studio City, CA 91604
Composer/Sound Designer: Michael Portis

Primal Scream/Rubberband (310) 478-8227
1616 Buitler Ave. www.primalscreammusic.com
West Los Angeles, CA 90025
Creative Director: Nicole Dionne
Producer: Christopher Garcia
Assistant Producer: Hans Hitner
Music Supervisors: Lisa Brown & Happy Walters
Composers/Sound Designers: Klaus Badelt, Scott Burton, Ramin Djuadi, The Engine Room, Christopher Garcia, Godhead, Peter Himmelman & Michael Wandmacher

Prison Diet (310) 497-5259 / (310) 722-9244
1654 Golden Gate www.prisondiet.tv
Los Angeles, CA 90026

Rad Music (310) 440-0055
501 Hanley Pl. FAX (310) 476-5106
Los Angeles, CA 90049
Composer/Sound Designer: Dan Radlauer

Radius360 (818) 926-6704
13547 Ventura Blvd., Ste. 612 www.radius360.com
Sherman Oaks, CA 91423
Owner/Sound Supervisor: Bo Bennike
Accounting: Shania Warren-Bennike

Riptide Music, Inc. (310) 437-4380 / (310) 422-1768
4121 Redwood Ave., Ste. 202 FAX (310) 437-4384
Los Angeles, CA 90066 www.riptidemusic.com
Executive Producer: Bob Kaminsky
Executive Producer/Composer: Rich Goldman
Composer: Dan Silver

Room (310) 450-7070
1426 Main St. FAX (310) 450-5010
Venice, CA 90291 www.room.tv
Contacts: Jason Barager, Victor Ginzburg, Christine Havercroft & Robin Nixon
Sound Designers: Barry Jamieson, Vincenzo Lorusso, Elad Marish, Brandon Toh & Ben Wilkins
Composers: Barry Jamieson, Elad Marish, Naughty G, Brandon Toh & Alexander Van Bubenheim

S3 Music + Sound (310) 312-3329
11681 Gateway Blvd. FAX (310) 312-8827
Los Angeles, CA 90064 www.s3mx.com
Composers: Adam Sanborne & Michael Suby
Producer: Steve Schemerhorn

Saparoff Music (310) 455-1950
19709 Horseshoe Dr. FAX (310) 455-0827
Topanga, CA 90290 www.saparoffmusic.com
Owner/Composer/Sound Designer: Andrea Saparoff

Schtung Music (310) 828-5189
1825 Stanford St. FAX (310) 828-4189
Santa Monica, CA 90404 www.schtungmusic.com
Contact: Susanna Kalliomaki
Composers: Andrew Hagen, Eddie Reyes, Jim Watson & Rob Winch (Plus World Group)
Sound Designer: Andrew Hagen
Chief Engineer: Jim Watson
Producer: Andrew Hagen

Scott Rea Music (866) 630-6372
P.O. Box 691522 www.scottreamusic.com
West Hollywood, CA 90069
Composer/Sound Designer: Scott Rea

ScreenMusic International (818) 789-2954
18034 Ventura Blvd., Ste. 450 FAX (818) 789-5801
Encino, CA 91316 www.screenmusic.com
Contact: Melissa Bree

Sensory Overload Music (818) 985-3300
2461 Santa Monica Blvd., Ste. 452 FAX (818) 761-3934
Santa Monica, CA 90404 www.sensory-overload.com
Composer: Bryan E. Miller

Serafine Inc. (310) 399-9279
P.O. Box 1798 www.serafinecollective.com
Simi Valley, CA 93065
Contact: Frank Serafine

Slappo Music & Sound Design (323) 737-6995
2554 Lincoln Blvd., Ste. 1086 FAX (323) 737-6990
Venice, CA 90291 www.audio.slappo.com
Senior Composer/Sound Designer: Neil Uchitel

Sonic Fuel (310) 578-9686
Composers: Chris Lennertz & Tim Wynn FAX (310) 578-0442
www.sonicfuel.net

Sonicfruit (310) 291-1122 / (323) 469-1222
FAX (323) 469-1222
www.sonicfruit.com
Composer/Sound Designer: Kathryn Korniloff

Soundbath Music & Sound (310) 392-0369 / (310) 990-0202
675A Rose Ave. FAX (310) 392-0359
Venice, CA 90291 www.soundbath.com
Composer: Garron Chang

Soundelux Design Music Group (323) 603-3203
7080 Hollywood Blvd., Ste. 100 FAX (323) 603-3287
Hollywood, CA 90028 www.soundeluxdmg.com
Creative Director: Scott Martin Gershin
Contact: Becky Allen

Soundmine (818) 767-4226
8457 Petaluma Dr. www.soundmine.com
Sun Valley, CA 91352

SoundTrack Studio (310) 477-7195
www.soundtrackstudio.com
Composer: Garron R. Larcombe

Sternworld Productions, Inc. (310) 439-1903
923 Marco Pl. www.sternworld.net
Venice, CA 90291
Composer/Producer: Shepard Stern

Stewart Sound Factory (714) 973-3030
204 N. Broadway, Ste. N FAX (714) 973-2530
Santa Ana, CA 92701 www.stewartsound.com
Contact: Suzi Alderson
Composer: Bob Stewart

Stimmung (310) 460-0123
2052 Broadway FAX (310) 460-0122
Santa Monica, CA 90404 www.stimmung.tv
Executive Producer: Ceinwyn Clark
Producer: Kelly Fuller
Sound Designers: Michael Anastasi, Reinhard Denke & Gus Koven
Composers: Jason Johnson & Spookey Ruben
Music Supervisor: Liza Richardson
Contact: Kathleen Lee

Summerfield Music, Inc./
Trailer Trash Music Library (818) 905-0400
14024 Roblar Rd. FAX (818) 905-0488
Sherman Oaks, CA 91423 www.summerfieldmusic.com
Composer: Bobby Summerfield

Tartaglia Music Productions (323) 666-6550
3854 Shannon Rd. FAX (323) 666-6599
Los Angeles, CA 90027
Composer/Sound Designer: John Tartaglia
Production Coordinator: Odile Ledoux

Technicolor Creative Services - Hollywood (323) 860-7600 (323) 860-7816
1438 N. Gower St., Box 50, Bldg. 48 FAX (323) 860-7801
Hollywood, CA 90028 www.technicolor.com

Thunder Music + Sound Design (310) 829-4765
3211 Olympic Blvd. FAX (310) 315-6399
Santa Monica, CA 90404 www.thunder-sound.com
Composer/Sound Designer: Art Wright

Timeless Entertainment Corporation (949) 756-1600
15 Alicante Aisle FAX (949) 756-1661
Irvine, CA 92614 www.timelessentertainment.com
Contact: Fred Bailin

TommyMusic (310) 397-3115 (310) 902-4784
4028 Albright Ave.
Los Angeles, CA 90066
Executive Producer/Composer: Tommy O'Brien

Trivers/Myers Music, Inc. (310) 640-9166
550 N. Continental, Ste. 100 FAX (310) 647-5869
El Segundo, CA 90245 www.triversmyersmusic.com

The V Group (310) 395-0252
359 21st St. FAX (310) 319-2030
Santa Monica, CA 90402 www.thevgroup.net

Volume (310) 578-8277
624 Milwood Ave.
Venice, CA 90291
Music Supervisor: Maureen Thompson

Walt Disney Studios (818) 560-2731
500 S. Buena Vista St. FAX (818) 562-3262
Burbank, CA 91521 www.buenavistapost.com

Warner Bros. Studio Facilities - Post Production Services (818) 954-1625 (818) 954-2515
4000 Warner Blvd. FAX (818) 954-4138
Burbank, CA 91522 www.wbpostproduction.com

Warren Dewey Sound Design (310) 392-6392
2114 Pico Blvd. FAX (310) 392-2346
Santa Monica, CA 90405
Sound Designer: Warren Dewey

Wojahn Bros. Music (310) 829-6200
1524-D Cloverfield Blvd. FAX (310) 829-6222
Santa Monica, CA 90404 www.wojahn.com
Composers: Roger Wojahn & Scott Wojahn

Zoo Street Music (818) 955-5268
FAX (818) 295-5001
www.zoostreet.com
Music Supervisors: Omar Herrera & Yosuke Kitazawa

BloomFilm (323) 850-5575
FAX (323) 850-7304

Buena Vista Imaging (818) 560-5284
(818) 560-5542
500 S. Buena Vista St., Camera Bldg. FAX (818) 563-4735
Burbank, CA 91521 www.studioservices.go.com

Fuel (310) 558-8755
1040 N. Sycamore Ave. www.fueldesign.com
Hollywood, CA 90038

Hollywood Title (310) 394-3300
1526 14th St., Ste. 106 FAX (310) 394-3304
Santa Monica, CA 90404 www.hollywoodtitle.com

Stewart Motion Picture Services (818) 845-6610
725 S. San Fernando Blvd. FAX (818) 845-6667
Burbank, CA 91502 www.stewartmps.com

Visions Optical Effects (323) 854-0399
3257 N. Knoll Dr. FAX (323) 850-8138
Los Angeles, CA 90068 www.visions-optical-effects.com

20twenty vfx (310) 395-2020
1419 Second St. FAX **(310) 393-2600**
Santa Monica, CA 90401 **www.20twentyvfx.com**

30 Second Films (310) 315-1750
3019 Pico Blvd. FAX **(310) 315-1757**
Santa Monica, CA 90405 **www.30secondfilms.com**
(Computer Graphics & Non-Linear Offline and Online)
Contact: Alan J. Stamm

303 Post (818) 783-3212
(818) 231-8132
4528 Murietta Ave., Ste. 2 **www.303post.com**
Sherman Oaks, CA 91423
(Avid Systems, Editing, Film Editing, Finishing, HD Editing, HD Finishing & Non-Linear Offline and Online)

310 Studios (818) 566-3083
419 S. Flower St. FAX **(818) 747-7637**
Burbank, CA 91502 **www.310studios.com**
(All Formats)

60Hz, Inc. (310) 264-8498
1660 Stanford St. FAX **(310) 264-8497**
Santa Monica, CA 90404 **www.60-hz.com**

Aaron & Le Duc (310) 452-2034
2210 Third St., Ste. 316 **www.leducdesign.com**
Santa Monica, CA 90405
(Computer Graphics, Digital Online, Duplication, High Def & Linear/Non-Linear Offline and Online)
Contact: Greg Le Duc

Absolute Films (626) 442-6454
(323) 692-1010
1441 Huntington Dr., Bldg. 301 FAX **(626) 448-1930**
South Pasadena, CA 91030 **www.absolutefilms.net**
(Duplication, HD Editing, Non-Linear Offline and Online & Standards Conversion)

Absolute Post (818) 842-7966
2633 N. San Fernando Blvd. FAX **(818) 842-8815**
Burbank, CA 91504 **www.absolutepost.tv**
Contact: Misty Tamburelli

Address One (310) 838-7783
(323) 465-4415
c/o Raleigh Studios FAX **(323) 960-4961**
662 N. Van Ness Ave., Ste. 301 **www.addressone.tv**
Los Angeles, CA 90004
(Avid Systems, Color Correction, Compositing, Computer Animation, Computer Graphics, Digital Editing Systems, Digital Online, DVD Design, DVD Menus, Final Cut Pro Systems, Finishing, Graphic Design, Graphics, HD Editing, HD Finishing, HD Online, Motion Graphics, Non-Linear Offline and Online, Post Supervision, Pre-Visualization & Subtitles)
Contact: Tess Thompson

Advanced Video, Inc. (323) 469-0707
723 N. Cahuenga Blvd.
Hollywood, CA 90038
(Duplication, Non-Linear Offline, Standards Conversion & Telecine)

Aftershock Digital (323) 658-5700
8222 Melrose Ave., Ste. 304 FAX **(323) 658-5200**
Los Angeles, CA 90046 **www.editkings.com**
(High Def & Non-Linear Offline and Online)
Contact: Fritz Feick

Alera Enterprises, Inc. (323) 660-7710
3179 Casitas Ave., Ste. 121 FAX **(323) 660-7715**
Los Angeles, CA 90039 **www.aleraenterprises.com**
(Authoring, HD Editing, HD Finishing, HD Online, Non-Linear Offline and Online & Post Supervision)

AlphaDogs, Inc. (818) 729-9262
1612 W. Olive Ave., Ste. 200 FAX **(818) 729-8537**
Burbank, CA 91506 **www.alphadogs.tv**
(Avid Systems, Color Correction, Compositing, Digital Media Transfers, Duplication, DVD Design, DVD Menus, Final Cut Pro Systems, Finishing, Graphic Design, Graphics, HD Editing, HD Finishing, HD Online, Motion Graphics, Non-Linear Offline & Non-Linear Online)

Alter Ego Creative Entertainment (323) 937-3348
7280 Melrose Ave., Ste. 3 FAX **(323) 937-3334**
Los Angeles, CA 90046 **www.alteregoce.com**
(Computer Animation and Graphics & Non-Linear Offline and Online)

American Video Group (310) 477-1535
2542 Aiken Ave. **www.americanvideogroup.com**
Los Angeles, CA 90064
(Digital Non-Linear Offline and Online)
Contacts: John Berzner & Alison Kearney

Arsenal FX (310) 453-5400
1522A Cloverfield **www.arsenalfx.tv**
Santa Monica, CA 90404
(All Formats, Color Correction, Compositing, Computer Animation, Computer Graphics, Digital Colorization, Digital Editing Systems, Digital Film Mastering, Digital Media Transfers, Digital Online, DVD Design, DVD Menus, Edge Coding, Final Cut Pro Systems, Finishing, Graphic Design, Graphics, HD Editing, HD Finishing, HD Online, HD Remastering, HD Telecine, Mastering, Motion Graphics, Non-Linear Offline, Non-Linear Online, Post Supervision, Pre-Visualization, Tape to Tape Color Correction, Tape to Tape Film, Simulation, Tape to Tape Transfers & Video to Still Transfers)

Ascent Media - Creative Services (310) 434-7000
520 Broadway, Fifth Fl. **www.ascentmedia.com**
Santa Monica, CA 90401

Atomic Post (310) 315-7245
3025 W. Olympic Blvd., Ste. 124 **www.atomicpost.us**
Santa Monica, CA 90404
(All Formats, Avid and Final Cut Pro Systems, DVD Design, Editing, Graphic Design, Graphics, High Def, HD Editing & Linear and Non-Linear Online)

Autonomy, Inc. (323) 662-7048
www.autonomy.tv
(Computer Graphics & Digital Non-Linear Offline and Online)

Avenue Digital, LLC (818) 559-6553
4403 W. Magnolia Blvd. **www.avenuedigital.net**
Burbank, CA 91505

Big Time Picture Company, Inc. (310) 207-0921
12210½ Nebraska Ave. FAX **(310) 826-0071**
Los Angeles, CA 90025 **www.bigtimepic.com**
(Avid and Final Cut Pro Systems, Film Editing & Non-Linear Offline and Online)

Bitmax, LLC (323) 978-7878
6255 Sunset Blvd., Ste. 1515 FAX **(323) 978-7879**
Los Angeles, CA 90028 **www.bitmax.net**
(DVD Duplication)

Black Dragon Entertainment, Inc. (323) 874-8888
FAX **(323) 874-1058**
www.blackdragon.com
(Computer Graphics, Non-Linear Offline and Online & Tape to Tape Color Correction)

Blue Room (310) 727-2600
1600 Rosecrans Ave., Bldg. 5A FAX **(310) 727-2601**
Manhattan Beach, CA 90266 **www.blueroomfx.com**
(Authoring, Captions, Compositing, Computer Graphics, Digital, Digital Editing Systems, Digital Intermediate Services, Digital Online, Duplication, DVD Design, DVD Menus, Editing, Final Cut Pro Systems, Finishing, High Def, HD Editing, HD Finishing, HD Remastering, HD Online, New Media Encoding, Non-Linear Offline and Online, Non-Linear Editing, Offline, Online, Post Supervision, Pre-Visualization, Standards Conversions, Subtitles & Tape to Tape Color Correction)

Bobine Telecine Post (310) 582-1240
1447 Cloverfield Blvd., Ste. 101 FAX **(310) 582-1245**
Santa Monica, CA 90404 **www.bobinetelecine.com**
(Color Correction, Duplication, Film to Tape Transfers, Tape to Tape Correction & Telecine)
Contacts: Julie Airale & Jais Lamaire

Brickyard VFX (310) 453-5722
2054 Broadway FAX **(310) 453-5744**
Santa Monica, CA 90404 **www.brickyardvfx.com**
(Computer Graphics & Non-Linear Online)

Burbank Post (818) 953-8919
3619 W. Magnolia Blvd. **www.burbankpost.tv**
Burbank, CA 91505
(Authoring, HD Finishing & Non-Linear Offline and Online)
Contact: Chris Settlemoir & Jim Settlemoir

Caliban Filmworks (310) 385-9332
1262 Lago Vista Pl. FAX **(310) 385-1364**
Beverly Hills, CA 90210
(Computer Graphics & Non-Linear Offline)

Castle Creek Productions (310) 979-7170
12233 W. Olympic Blvd., Ste. 314 FAX **(310) 979-7173**
Los Angeles, CA 90064 **www.castlecreekproductions.com**
(Offline & Online)

CCI Digital, Inc. (818) 562-6300
2921 W. Alameda Ave. FAX **(818) 562-8222**
Burbank, CA 91505 **www.ccidigital.com**
(Compositing, Computer Graphics, Digital Online, Duplication, High Def, Non-Linear Offline & Telecine)
Contact: Craig Barnes

Cerulean FX (310) 854-2114
1558 10th St., Ste. D www.ceruleanfx.com
Santa Monica, CA 90401
(Color Correction, Colorizations, Compositing & Digital Colorization)

Chainsaw (323) 785-1550
(323) 785-1555
940 N. Orange Dr., 2nd Fl. www.chainsawedit.com
Hollywood, CA 90038
(All Formats, Authoring, Avid Systems, Color Correction, Colorizations, Compositing, Digital Colorization, Digital Editing Systems, Digital Intermediate Services, Digital Online, Duplication, Finishing, HD Editing, HD Finishing, HD Online, Mastering, Mobile Facility, New Media Encoding, Non-Linear Offline and Online, Post Supervision, Standards Conversions & Tape to Tape Transfers)

Christopher Gray Post Production Services (310) 395-9845
(310) 395-9845
1322 Second St., Ste. 28 FAX (310) 451-1541
Santa Monica, CA 90401 www.cgpost.com
(Duplication & Non-Linear Offline and Online)

Christy's Editorial (818) 845-1755
(800) 556-5706
3625 W. Pacific Ave. FAX (818) 845-1756
Burbank, CA 91505 www.christys.net
(Film Editing & Non-Linear Offline and Online)

Cinema Libre Studio (818) 349-8822
8328 DeSoto Ave. FAX (818) 349-9922
Canoga Park, CA 91304 www.cinemalibrestudio.com
(Computer Graphics, Linear Online, Non-Linear Offline and Online, Subtitles & Tape to Film Transfers)

Cinesite (323) 462-6266
809 N. Cahuenga Blvd. www.cinesite.com
Hollywood, CA 90038
(Digital Film Mastering, Recording & Scanning)
Contact: Rita Cahill

Clonetown HD (323) 850-6608
(323) 851-0299
3131 Cahuenga Blvd. West FAX (323) 851-0277
Los Angeles, CA 90068 www.clonetownhd.com
(All Formats, Authoring, Avid Systems, Captions, Digital Editing Systems, Digital Media Transfers, Duplication, Final Cut Pro Systems, HD Editing, HD Finishing, HD Online, New Media Encoding, Non-Linear Offline and Online, Non-Linear Editing, Recording, Standards Conversions & Tape to Tape Transfers)

Cloud 19 (310) 839-5400
(310) 717-7819
3767 Overland Ave., Ste. 104 FAX (310) 839-5404
Los Angeles, CA 90034 www.cloud19.com

Coast Media Teleproductions, Inc. (949) 417-0300
17062 Murphy Ave., Bldg. B www.coastmedia.com
Irvine, CA 92614
(Computer Graphics & Digital Linear/Non-Linear Offline and Online)
Contact: Joyce Smith

Company 3 LA (310) 255-6600
1661 Lincoln Blvd., Ste. 400 FAX (310) 255-6602
Santa Monica, CA 90404 www.company3.com
(Compositing, DI Services, Film Scanning and Recording, HD and SD Tape to Tape Correction & Telecine)

The Complex Studios (310) 477-1938
2323 Corinth Ave. FAX (310) 607-9631
West Los Angeles, CA 90064 www.thecomplexstudios.com

Crest National Optical Disc (323) 860-1300 (800) 961-8273
1000 Highland Ave. FAX (323) 466-7128
Hollywood, CA 90038 www.crestnational.com
(Analog/Digital Online, Computer Graphics, Duplication, Edge Coding, Standards Conversion & Telecine)
Contact: John M. Walker

Daily Post (310) 417-4844
6701 Center Dr. West, Ste. 1111 FAX (310) 410-1543
Los Angeles, CA 90045 www.dailypost.tv

Defy Agency (310) 204-2340
5883 Blackwelder St., Ste. B FAX (310) 204-2341
Culver City, CA 90232 www.defyagency.com

Different by Design (310) 689-2470 (310) 569-8038
12233 W. Olympic Blvd., Ste. 120 FAX (310) 689-2471
Los Angeles, CA 90064 www.dxdproductions.com
(Duplication & HD and SD Non-Linear Online)

Digiscope (310) 315-6060
1447 Cloverfield Blvd. FAX (310) 828-5856
Santa Monica, CA 90404 www.digiscope.com
(Compositing, Editing & Pre-Visualization)

The Digital Intermediate Group, LLC (310) 315-5720
40 N. Orange Dr., Ste. 121 FAX (310) 315-5724
Hollywood, CA 90038 www.digroupusa.com
(All Formats, Avid Systems, Color Correction, Compositing, Computer Graphics, Computer/Motion Graphics, Digital, Digital Colorization, Digital Editing Systems, Digital Film Mastering, Digital Online, Film Restoration and Preservation, Film Scanning and Recording, Film to Tape Transfers, Finishing, High Def, HD Finishing, HD Remastering, Mastering, Post Supervision, Recording, Scanning, Standards Conversion, Subtitles, Tape to Tape Color Correction, Tape to Tape Film Simulation & Video to Still Transfers)

A **Digital Jungle Post Production** (323) 962-0867
6363 Santa Monica Blvd. FAX (323) 962-9960
Hollywood, CA 90038 www.digijungle.com
(Digital Intermediate & Post Production Services)

Dogma Studios (310) 838-2973
4134 Del Rey Ave. FAX (310) 838-2975
Marina del Rey, CA 90292 www.dogmastudios.com
(Encoding & New Media)

The Dreaming Tree (818) 845-3230
2817 W. Magnolia Blvd., Ste. A FAX (818) 688-8180
Burbank, CA 91505 www.dreamingtreeproductions.com

DVS Intelestream (310) 447-1111 (818) 841-6750
2133 S. Bundy Dr. FAX (310) 447-1050
Los Angeles, CA 90064 www.dvs.tv
(Duplication, Telecine & Standards Conversion)

editSource (310) 572-7230 (310) 466-3624
12044 Washington Blvd. FAX (310) 325-4387
Los Angeles, CA 90066 www.theeditsource.com

Encore Hollywood (323) 466-7663
6344 Fountain Ave. FAX (323) 467-5539
Hollywood, CA 90028 www.encorehollywood.com
(Compositing, Computer Graphics, Digital Intermediate Services, Digital Online, Digital Telecine, Duplication, HD Online and Telecine, Standards Conversion & Tape to Tape Color Correction)
Contact: Barry Goldscher

Entertainment Post (818) 846-0411
639 S. Glenwood Pl. FAX (818) 846-1542
Burbank, CA 91506 www.entpost.com

Eric Blum Productions, Inc. (818) 707-4524 (818) 707-4526
31139 Via Colinas, Ste. 210 FAX (818) 707-0071
Thousand Oaks, CA 91362 www.ebproductions.com
(Compositing, Computer Graphics, Duplication & Linear/Non-Linear Online)

Film Technology Company, Inc. (323) 464-3456
726 N. Cole Ave. FAX (323) 464-7439
Hollywood, CA 90038 www.filmtech.com/
(Duplication, Tape to Tape Color Correction & Telecine)
Contact: Alan Stark

FILMLOOK Media and Post/ FILMLOOK Inc. (818) 845-9200
2917 W. Olive Ave. FAX (818) 845-9238
Burbank, CA 91505 www.filmlook.com
(Authoring, Captions, Color Correction, Computer Graphics, Digital Editing Systems, Duplication, DVD Design, DVD Menus, Final Cut Pro Systems, Finishing, Graphic Design, Graphics, HD Editing, HD Finishing, HD Online, HD Remastering, Linear Offline, Linear Online, Mastering, Motion Graphics, New Media Encoding, Non-Linear Offline, Non-Linear Online & Tape to Tape Film Simulation)
Contacts: Anna Cordova & Robert Faber

Findley Productions (310) 559-5680
8522 National Blvd., Ste. 106 FAX (310) 454-7503
Culver City, CA 90232 www.findleyproductions.com
(Non-Linear Offline and Online)
Contact: Sean Findley

Fortitude Editorial, Inc (323) 337-1175
940 N. Orange Dr., Ste. 150 FAX (323) 337-1439
Los Angeles, CA 90038 www.fortitudeeditorial.com
(Avid Systems, Captions, Color Correction, Colorizations, Compositing, Computer Graphics, Digital Editing Systems, Final Cut Pro Systems, Finishing, Graphic Design, Graphics Submitted, HD Editing, HD Finishing, Linear/Non-Linear Offline and Online, Post Supervision, Tape to Tape Color Correction & Tape to Tape Transfers)

FotoKem (818) 846-3101 (818) 846-3102
2801 W. Alameda Ave. FAX (818) 841-2130
Burbank, CA 91505 www.fotokem.com
(All Formats, Digital Intermediate Services, Digital Telecine, Duplication, DVD, Online & Standards Conversion)

Fox Studios (310) 369-7678 (310) 369-4636
10201 W. Pico Blvd. FAX (310) 369-4407
Los Angeles, CA 90035 www.foxpost.com

Framework Post (310) 696-4600
7920 Sunset Blvd., Ste. 200 FAX (310) 696-4891
Los Angeles, CA 90046 www.asylument.com
(Avid Systems, Color Correction, Compositing, Computer Animation, Computer Graphics, Digital Editing Systems, Digital Online, Duplication, DVD Design, DVD Menus, Graphic Design, Graphics, HD Editing, HD Finishing, HD Online, Motion Graphics, Non-Linear Offline and Online, Post Supervision, Recording, Scanning, Tape to Tape Transfers & Video to Still Transfers)

Full Moon & High Tide Studios (310) 647-1958
424 Main St. FAX (310) 647-1960
El Segundo, CA 90245 www.fmht.net
(Duplication & Non-Linear Offline and Online)

FXF Productions, Inc. (310) 577-5009
1024 Harding Ave., Ste. 201 FAX (310) 577-1960
Venice, CA 90291 www.fxfproductions.com
(Computer Graphics, Non-Linear Offline and Online & Subtitles)

Gorilla Post (310) 394-7611
632-A Arizona Ave. FAX (310) 394-7622
Santa Monica, CA 90401 www.gorillapost.net
(Color Correction, Computer Graphics & Non-Linear Online)

A Gosch Production (818) 729-0000
2227 W. Olive Ave. www.goschproductions.com
Burbank, CA 91506
(Non-Linear Offline and Online)

Happy Pixel Post (310) 392-8047
1826 14th St. www.happypixelstudios.com
Santa Monica, CA 90404
(Color Correction, Compositing, Computer/Motion Graphics, DVD, Editing, Final Cut Pro Systems, High Def, HD Editing, HD Finishing, HD Online, Non-Linear Offline and Online & Post Supervision)

HD Pictures & Post, Inc. (310) 264-2575
12233 W. Olympic Blvd., Ste.120 FAX **(310) 689-2471**
Los Angeles, CA 90064 **www.hdpicturesandpost.com**

Hip Films (323) 467-2897
1622 Gower St. FAX **(323) 469-8251**
Hollywood, CA 90028 **www.hipfilms.com**
(Avid Systems, Color Correction, Computer Animation, Computer Graphics, Digital Film Mastering, Digital Intermediate Services, Digital Online, Digital Telecine, DVD Designs and Menus, Editing, Film to Tape Transfers, Final Cut Pro Systems, Finishing, High Def, HD Editing, HD Finishing, HD Remastering, HD Telecine, HD Online, Mastering, Mobile Facility & Motion Graphics)

Home Planet Post, Inc. (805) 201-2618
FAX **(805) 965-2329**
www.homeplanetproductions.com

HTV - High Technology Video (323) 969-8822 (818) 760-7600
3575 Cahuenga Blvd. West, Fourth Fl. FAX **(323) 969-8860**
Los Angeles, CA 90068 **www.htvinc.net**
(Computer Graphics, Digital Intermediate Services, Digital Offline and Online, Duplication, HD Online and Telecine & Standards Conversion)
Contacts: Jim Hardy, Mark Shore & Steve Tannen

an ideal world (714) 953-9501
209 N. Bush St. FAX **(714) 953-1195**
Santa Ana, CA 92701 **www.anidealworld.com**
(Color Correction, Compositing, Computer Animation, Computer Graphics, Digital Editing Systems, Digital Online, Film Restoration, Final Cut Pro Systems, Finishing, Graphic Design, Graphics, HD Editing, HD Finishing, HD Online, Motion Graphics, Non-Linear Offline, Non-Linear Online, Post Supervision, Pre-Visualization, Tape to Tape Color Correction & Tape to Tape Film Simulation)

Illuminate – Arts, Media & Entertainment (323) 969-8822
3575 Cahuenga Blvd. West, Fourth Fl. FAX **(323) 969-8840**
Los Angeles, CA 90068 **www.illuminatehollywood.com**
(All Formats, Authoring, Avid Systems, Captions, Color Correction, Colorizations, Compositing, Computer Animation, Computer Graphics, Digital Colorization, Digital Editing Systems, Digital Film Mastering, Digital Intermediate Services, Digital Online, Digital Telecine, Duplication, DVD Design, DVD Menus, Edge Coding, Film Editing, Film Preservation and Restoration, Film Recording, Final Cut Pro Systems, Finishing, Graphic Design, Graphics, HD Editing, HD Finishing, HD Remastering, HD Telecine, HD Online, Linear Offline and Online, Mastering, Mobile Facility, Motion Graphics, Negative Cutting, New Media Encoding, Non-Linear Offline and Online, Post Supervision, Pre-Visualization, Recording, Scanning, Standards Conversions, Subtitles, Tape to Tape Color Correction, Tape to Tape Film Simulation, Tape to Tape and Film to Tape Transfers, Telecine, Training for Computer Graphics & Video to Still Transfers)
Contacts: Eric Geisler, James Hardy, Patricia Sullivan & AJ Ullman

The Institution Post (818) 566-7801
423 N. Fairview St. **www.the-institution.com**
Burbank, CA 91505
(All Formats, Authoring, Avid Systems, Color Correction, Compositing, Computer Animation, Computer Graphics, Digital Editing Systems, Digital Film Mastering, Digital Intermediate Services, Digital Media Transfers, Digital Online, DVD Design, DVD Menus, Film Editing, Final Cut Pro Systems, Finishing, Graphic Design, Graphics, HD Editing, HD Finishing, HD Online, HD Remastering, Linear Offline, Linear Online, Mastering, Motion Graphics, New Media Encoding, Non-Linear Offline, Non-Linear Online, Post Supervision & Pre-Visualization)

Inter Video (818) 843-3624
2211 N. Hollywood Way FAX **(818) 843-6884**
Burbank, CA 91505 **www.intervideo24.com**
(Computer Graphics & Standards Conversion)
Contact: Richard Clark

iO Film (323) 822-4444
1415 Cahuenga Blvd. FAX **(323) 467-7300**
Hollywood, CA 90028 **www.iofilm.net**
(Digital Intermediate Services, Film Scanning and Recording & HD Finishing)

iProbe Multilingual Solutions, Inc. (888) 489-6035
www.iprobesolutions.com
(All Formats, Authoring, Avid Systems, Captions, Color Correction, Colorizations, Compositing, Computer Animation, Computer Graphics, Digital Colorization, Digital Editing Systems, Digital Film Mastering, Digital Intermediate Services, Digital Online, Digital Telecine, Duplication, DVD Design, DVD Menus, Edge Coding, Film Editing, Film to Tape Transfers, Final Cut Pro Systems, Finishing, Graphic Design, Graphics, HD Editing, HD Finishing, HD Remastering, HD Telecine, HD Online, Linear/Non-Linear Offline and Online, Mastering, Motion Graphics, Negative Cutting, New Media Encoding, Post Supervision, Pre-Visualization, Recording, Scanning, Standards Conversions, Subtitles, Tape to Tape Color Correction, Tape to Tape Film Simulation, Tape to Tape Transfers, Telecine, Training for Computer Graphics & Video to Still Transfers)

Izon Studios (818) 244-4294
445 South Central Ave., Ste. 401 FAX **(818) 244-1202**
Glendale, CA 91204 **www.izonstudios.com/portfolio.html**

Jetty Studios, Inc. (818) 260-9261
1612 W. Olive Ave., Ste. 304 FAX **(818) 260-9701**
Burbank, CA 91506 **www.jettystudios.com**
(Captions, Color Correction, Computer Graphics, Duplication & Non-Linear Offline)

JM Digital Works (760) 476-1783
2460 Impala Dr. FAX **(760) 476-1788**
Carlsbad, CA 92008 **www.jmdigitalworks.com**
(Digital Online, Duplication & Offline)
Contact: Ken Kebow

Kappa Studios, Inc. (818) 843-3400
3619 W. Magnolia Blvd. FAX **(818) 559-5684**
Burbank, CA 91505 **www.kappastudios.com**
(Duplication & Non-Linear Offline and Online)
Contact: Paul Long

Kinetic Imageworks, Inc. (323) 874-4000
3575 Cahuenga Blvd. West, Ste. 640 FAX **(323) 874-4555**
Los Angeles, CA 90068 **www.kineticimageworks.com**
(Offline & Online)

LA Digital Post, Inc. (310) 954-8650 (818) 487-5000
2260 Centinela Ave. FAX **(310) 954-8686**
West Los Angeles, CA 90064 **www.ladigital.com**
(Avid Systems, Color Correction, Compositing, Duplication, Final Cut Pro Systems, Graphics, HD Editing, HD Online, HD/SD Finishing, Offline, Standards Conversions & Visual FX)

LA Digital Post, Inc. (818) 487-5000 (310) 954-8650
11311 Camarillo St. FAX **(818) 487-5015**
Toluca Lake, CA 91602 **www.ladigital.com**
(Avid Systems, Color Correction, Compositing, Duplication, Final Cut Pro Systems, Graphics, HD Editing, HD Online, HD/SD Finishing, Offline, Standards Conversions & Visual FX)

LandShark Post, Inc. (818) 843-0045
2917 W. Olive Ave. FAX **(818) 843-0074**
Burbank, CA 91505 **www.landsharkpost.com**
(All Formats, Authoring, Color Correction, Compositing, Computer Animation, Computer Graphics, Digital Colorization, Digital Editing Systems, Digital Online, DVD Design, DVD Menus, Final Cut Pro Systems, Finishing, Graphic Design, Graphics, HD Editing, HD Finishing, HD Online, Motion Graphics, Non-Linear Offline, Non-Linear Online & Post Supervision)

Laser Pacific Media Corporation (323) 462-6266
809 N. Cahuenga Blvd. FAX **(323) 464-3233**
Hollywood, CA 90038 **www.laserpacific.com**
(Digital Intermediate Services, High Def, Online & Telecine)
Contact: Hawk Hamilton

Laurel Canyon Productions (818) 459-6630 / (310) 738-4184
1101 S. Flower Ave. FAX **(818) 450-0916**
Burbank, CA 91502 **www.lcproductions.tv**
(All Formats, Avid Systems, Color Correction, Colorizations, Computer Graphics, Digital Editing Systems, Digital Intermediate Services, Digital Media Transfers, Digital Online, Duplication, Film Editing, Finishing, Graphics, HD Editing, HD Finishing, HD Online, Motion Graphics, Non-Linear Offline, Non-Linear Online, Post Supervision & Tape to Tape Transfers)

Level 3 Post (818) 840-7200 / (818) 840-7889
2901 W. Alameda, Third Fl. **www.level3post.com**
Burbank, CA 91505
(Digital Online and Telecine, Duplication, HD Online and Telecine, Standards Conversion & Tape to Tape Color Correction)

Lightning Media (818) 556-2777
3723 W. Olive Ave. FAX **(818) 556-2770**
Burbank, CA 91505 **www.lightningmedia.com**
(All Formats, High Def & Standards Conversion)

Lightning Media (323) 957-9255
1413 Cole Pl. FAX **(323) 330-6217**
Hollywood, CA 90028 **www.lightningmedia.com**

Liquid VFX (310) 392-1212
215 Rose Ave. FAX **(310) 392-1222**
Venice, CA 90291 **www.laliquid.com**
(All Formats, Color Correction, Compositing, Computer Graphics, Digital Online, Duplication, Finishing, Graphics, HD Finishing, HD Online, Motion Graphics, Post Supervision & Standards Conversions)

A **Los Feliz Post** (323) 512-7678
6767 Forest Lawn Dr., Ste. 115 FAX **(323) 845-9998**
Los Angeles, CA 90068 **www.lfpost.com**
(Color Correction, Duplication, High Def, Non-Linear Offline and Online, Standards Conversion, Subtitles & Tape to Tape Correction)

Madrik Multimedia, LLC (213) 596-5180 / (818) 802-7719
1201 W. Fifth St. FAX **(213) 596-5181**
Los Angeles, CA 90017 **www.madrik.com**
(All Formats, Avid and Final Cut Pro Systems, Computer/Motion Graphics, Editing & High Def Editing)

Master Communication (310) 832-3303
445 W. Seventh St. FAX **(310) 832-0296**
San Pedro, CA 90731 **www.bestmedia.com**
(Non-Linear Offline and Online)
Contact: Mary Jo Masters

Matchframe Video (818) 840-6800
610 N. Hollywood Way FAX **(818) 840-2726**
Burbank, CA 91505 **www.matchframevideo.com**
(All Formats, Authoring, Avid Systems, Color Correction, Compositing, Digital Editing Systems, Digital Film Mastering, Digital Media Transfers, Duplication, DVD Design, DVD Menus, Film Editing, Film Preservation, Film Recording, Film to Tape Transfers, Final Cut Pro Systems, Finishing, Graphic Design, Graphics, HD Editing, HD Finishing, HD Online, HD Remastering, HD Telecine, Linear Offline, Linear Online, Mastering, New Media Encoding, Non-Linear Offline, Non-Linear Online, Post Supervision, Recording, Standards Conversions, Tape to Tape Color Correction, Tape to Tape Transfers, Telecine & Video to Still Transfers)

Mechnology (818) 840-9500
919 N. Victory Blvd. FAX **(818) 840-9501**
Burbank, CA 91502 **www.mechnology.com**

Media Fishtank (818) 883-6092
22738 Roscoe Blvd. FAX **(818) 883-6013**
West Hills, CA 91304 **www.mediafishtank.com**
(Authoring, Avid Systems, Color Correction, Colorizations, Compositing, Computer Graphics, Digital Editing Systems, Digital Media Transfers, Duplication, DVD Design, DVD Menus, Graphics, HD Editing, Non-Linear Offline and Online, Subtitles, Tape To Tape Color Correction & Video to Still Transfers)

Media International (805) 658-3339 / (800) 477-7575
5740 Ralston St., Ste. 304 FAX **(805) 658-3331**
Ventura, CA 93003 **www.mediainternational.com**
(Duplication & Offline and Online Editing)
Contacts: John Hasbrouck & Jolene Jackson

Mega Mace Creative (323) 730-0175
www.megamace.com

Metro Encoding (818) 558-7800
4425 W. Riverside Dr., Ste. 202 **www.metroencoding.com**
Burbank, CA 91505
(Authoring, Digital Media Transfers, Digital Online, HD Online, New Media Encoding, Training for Computer Graphics & Video to Still Transfers)

Midtown Edit (323) 782-7900 / (323) 801-2300
8489 W. Third St. FAX **(323) 651-1240**
Los Angeles, CA 90048 **www.midtownedit.com**
(Avid and Final Cut Pro, Decks, Editing Suites & Storage Rentals)

Mind Over Eye, LLC (310) 396-4663 / (310) 968-4259
1639 11th St., Ste. 117 FAX **(310) 396-0663**
Santa Monica, CA 90404 **www.mindovereye.com**
(HD and SD Offline and Online)

Mixin Pixls (310) 237-6438
www.mixinpixls.com
(Captions, Final Cut Pro Systems, Non-Linear Online, Recording & Subtitles)

Motion City Films (310) 434-1272
www.motioncity.com
(Computer Animation, Computer/Motion Graphics, Editing & Non-Linear Offline and Online)

Moving Media (310) 453-1686
3017 Nebraska Ave. FAX **(310) 453-1715**
Santa Monica, CA 90404 **www.movingmedia.tv**
(Video Encoding)

NBC Universal Artworks (212) 664-5972
30 Rockefeller Plaza, Ste. 1622W **www.nbcartworks.com**
New York, NY 10012
(Computer Graphics, Graphic Design, Graphics, Motion Graphics & New Media Encoding)

Ntropic (310) 806-4950
2332 South Centinela St., Ste. B FAX **(310) 806-4959**
Los Angeles, CA 90064 **www.ntropic.com**

Oracle Post (818) 752-2800
4720 W. Magnolia Blvd. FAX **(818) 769-2624**
Burbank, CA 91505 **www.oraclepost.com**
(Non-Linear Offline and Online)
Contacts: James Lifton & Paulette Lifton

Oracle Post (310) 449-5550
3232 Nebraska Ave. FAX **(310) 449-5554**
Santa Monica, CA 90404 **www.oraclepost.com**
(Non-Linear Offline and Online)
Contacts: James Lifton & Paulette Lifton

Outpost Digital (310) 752-2300
1620 Euclid St. FAX **(310) 752-2299**
Santa Monica, CA 90404 **www.outpostdigital.com**
(Color Correction, Design, High Def & Non-Linear Offline and Online)
Contacts: Brody McHugh & Evan Schechtman

Padded Cell Productions (310) 729-3063
520 Washington Blvd., Ste. 494
Marina del Rey, CA 90292
(Digital Non-Linear Offline and Online)
Contact: Rich Lewis

The Studios at Paramount (323) 956-1445
The Studios at Paramount FAX **(323) 862-2242**
Post Production Services **www.thestudiosatparamount.com**
5555 Melrose Ave.
Los Angeles, CA 90038
(All Formats, Avid Systems, Captions, Color Correction, Colorizations, Compositing, Computer Graphics, Digital Editing Systems, Digital Film Mastering, Digital Online, Duplication, DVD Design, DVD Menus, Edge Coding, Film Editing, Film Recording, Finishing, Graphic Design, Graphics, HD Editing, HD Finishing, HD Online, Linear/Non-Linear Offline and Online, Mastering, Mobile Facility, Motion Graphics, Negative Cutting, New Media Encoding, Standards Conversions, Tape to Tape Color Correction, Tape to Tape Film Simulation & Tape to Tape Transfers)

Pixel Blues, Inc. (818) 766-4600
411 W. Alameda Blvd., Ste. 401 FAX **(818) 766-4601**
North Hollywood, CA 91602 **www.pixelblues.com**
(Computer Graphics & Online Editing)

Pixel Plantation (818) 566-7777
4111 W. Alameda Ave., Ste. 301 **www.pixelplantation.com**
Burbank, CA 91505
(All Formats, Avid Systems, Color Correction, Compositing, Digital Online, Duplication, Finishing, Graphics, HD Editing, HD Finishing, HD Online, Non-Linear Offline & Non-Linear Online)

PlasterCITY Digital Post Facility (323) 469-9800
6500 Sunset Blvd. FAX **(323) 462-4620**
Los Angeles, CA 90028 **www.plastercitypost.com**
(Color Correction, Colorization, Digital Online, Final Cut Pro Systems, High Def, HD Editing, HD Finishing, HD Online, Linear/Non-Linear Offline and Online, Online & Post Supervision)

Point360 (818) 569-4949
(866) 968-4336
1133 N. Hollywood Way FAX **(818) 556-5753**
Burbank, CA 91505 **www.point360.com**
(Avid Systems, Captions, Color Correction, Digital Film Mastering, Digital Intermediate Services, Digital Media Transfers, Digital Online, Digital Telecine, Duplication, Film Recording, Film Restoration, Film Scanning, Film to Tape Transfers, Final Cut Pro Systems, Finishing, HD Editing, HD Finishing, HD Online, HD Remastering, HD Telecine, Linear Online, Mastering, New Media Encoding, Standards Conversions, Subtitles, Tape to Tape Color Correction, Tape to Tape Transfers & Telecine)

Point360 (323) 957-5500
1147 Vine St. FAX **(323) 466-7406**
Hollywood, CA 90038 **www.point360.com**
(Captions, Digital Editing Systems, Digital Film Mastering, Digital Online, Digital Telecine, Duplication, Finishing, HD Editing, HD Finishing, HD Online, HD Remastering, HD Telecine, New Media Encoding & Standards Conversions)
Contact: Shellie L. Yaseen

Point360 (310) 481-7000
12421 W. Olympic Blvd. FAX **(310) 207-8404**
Los Angeles, CA 90064 **www.point360.com**
(Avid Systems, Color Correction, Compositing, Computer Animation, Final Cut Pro Systems, HD Editing, HD Online, HD Remastering, Non-Linear Offline, Non-Linear Online & Post Supervision)

Post and Beam (310) 828-1128
3025 Olympic Blvd., Ste. 112 FAX **(310) 828-8211**
Santa Monica, CA 90404 **www.postandbeam.tv**

A **Post Digital Services** (323) 845-0812
1258 N. Highland Ave., Ste. 210 FAX **(323) 845-0812**
Hollywood, CA 90038 **www.postdigitalservices.com**
(All Formats, Authoring, Avid Systems, Blu-Ray, Captions, CGI, Color Correction, Compositing, Computer Animation, Computer Graphics, Digital Colorization, Digital Editing Systems, Digital Film Mastering, Digital Intermediate Services, Digital Media Transfers, Digital Online, Duplication, DVD Design, DVD Menus, Film Editing, Film Preservation, Film Recording, Film Restoration, Film Scanning, Film to Tape Transfers, Final Cut Pro Systems, Finishing, Graphic Design, Graphics, HD Editing, HD Finishing, HD Online, HD Remastering, Linear Offline, Mastering, Motion Graphics, New Media Encoding, Non-Linear Offline, Non-Linear Online, Post Supervision, Pre-Visualization, Recording, Scanning, Standards Conversions, Subtitles, Tape to Tape Color Correction, Tape to Tape Film Simulation, Tape to Tape Transfers & Video to Still Transfers)

The Post Group (323) 462-2300
6335 Homewood Ave. FAX **(323) 462-0836**
Hollywood, CA 90028 **www.postgroup.com**
(Compositing, Digital Online, Duplication, HD Telecine, Standards Conversion, Tape to Tape Color Correction & Telecine)

Post Logic Studios (323) 461-7887
1800 N. Vine St., Ste. 100 FAX **(323) 461-7790**
Los Angeles, CA 90028 **www.postlogic.com**
(Computer Graphics, Digital Online, Duplication, Film Transfers & Standards Conversion)

Post Media Group, Inc. (310) 289-5959
337 S. Robertson Blvd. **www.postmediagroup.tv**
Beverly Hills, CA 90211

Post Modern Edit, LLC (949) 608-8700
2941 Alton Pkwy FAX **(949) 608-8729**
Irvine, CA 92606 **www.postmodernedit.com**
(Authoring, Captions, Color Correction, Compositing, Computer Animation, Computer Graphics, Digital Editing Systems, Digital Media Transfers, Digital Online, Duplication, DVD Design, DVD Menus, Final Cut Pro Systems, Finishing, Graphic Design, HD Editing, HD Finishing, HD Online, Linear Online, Mastering, Motion Graphics, New Media Encoding, Non-Linear Online, Post Supervision, Standards Conversion, Subtitles & Tape to Tape Transfers)
Contacts: Kelli Alvarado, Michael Boyd, Rich O'Neill, Mike Pearce & Jason Szymanski

Precision Productions + Post (310) 839-4600
10718 McCune Ave. FAX **(310) 839-4601**
Los Angeles, CA 90034 **www.precisionpost.com**

Prime Digital Media Services (661) 964-0220
(323) 864-8331
28111 Avenue Stanford FAX **(661) 964-0550**
Valencia, CA 91355 **www.primedigital.com**
(Color Correction, Duplication, HD Online, Non-Linear Offline, Standards Conversion, Telecine & Transmission Services)
Contact: Brigitte Prouty

Qube Cinema, Inc. (818) 392-8155
4640 Lankershim Blvd., Ste. 601 FAX **(818) 301-0401**
North Hollywood, CA 91602 **www.qubecinema.com**
(Digital Cinema Servers and Software & Digital Film Mastering)

Quest Pictures (213) 534-3620
1201 W. Fifth St., Ste. T-230 **www.questpictures.com**
Los Angeles, CA 90017
(All Formats, Authoring, Color Correction, Colorizations, Compositing, Computer Graphics, Digital Colorization, Digital Editing Systems, Digital Film Mastering, Duplication, DVD Design, DVD Menus, Film Editing, Final Cut Pro Systems, Graphic Design, Graphics, HD Editing, HD Online, Mastering, Motion Graphics, Non-Linear Offline and Online, Post Supervision, Pre-Visualization, Recording & Video to Still Transfers)

Raleigh Studios - Post Production (323) 871-5649
5300 Melrose Ave. FAX **(323) 871-5629**
Hollywood, CA 90038 **www.raleighstudios.com**
(Digital Non-Linear Offline & Film Editing)
Contact: Mike Donahue

Raycom Post (818) 846-0101
4450 Lakeside Dr., Ste. 300 FAX **(818) 846-0277**
Burbank, CA 91505 **www.raycompost.com**
(Avid Systems, Captions, Color Correction, Downconversions, Duplication, Graphics, HD Editing, High Def, Non-Linear Online & Standards Conversion)

Red Dog Post & Design (310) 237-6438
www.reddogpost.com
(Authoring, Avid Systems, Captions, Color Correction, Compositing, Computer Animation, Digital Editing Systems, Digital Intermediate Services, Final Cut Pro Systems, Offline, Online, Recording & Subtitles)
Contact: Jeff Miller

Red Magnet (310) 396-0100
215 Rose Ave. FAX **(310) 656-2801**
Venice, CA 90291 **www.redmagnetfx.com**
(Compositing, Digital Online, HD Finishing, HD Online, Linear and Non-Linear Online, Online, Post Supervision & Previsualizations)
Contact: Shira Boardman

rednavel fLmworx (323) 467-7778
1670 Beverly Blvd., Ste. 10 **www.rednavel.com**
Los Angeles, CA 90038
(Negative Cutting & Telecine)

RentHD.com/Lightpost Productions (818) 955-7678
1701 W. Burbank Blvd., Ste. 201 FAX **(818) 955-5181**
Burbank, CA 91506 **www.renthd.com**
(Authoring, Color Correction, Film Restoration, Film to Tape Transfers, Final Cut Pro Systems, HD Online & Mastering)

Richard Flores Negative Cutting (818) 563-4824
217 W. Alameda Ave., Ste. 101 FAX **(818) 563-4813**
Burbank, CA 91502 **www.gotneg.com**

Ring of Fire (310) 966-5055
1538 20th St. FAX **(310) 966-5056**
Santa Monica, CA 90404 **www.ringoffire.com**
(High Def & Non-Linear Online)

Rocket Dailies (310) 701-5999
(Color Correction, Film To Tape Transfers & Telecine)

Roush Media (818) 559-8648
84 E. Santa Anita Ave. **www.roush-media.com**
Burbank, CA 91502
(Color Correction, Digital Intermediate Services, Digital Media Transfers, Duplication, Final Cut Pro Systems, Hard Drive to Tape Transfers, HD Editing, HD Finishing, HD Online, Mastering, New Media Encoding & Tape to Tape Color Correction)

Rundell Filmworks (323) 817-4430
6363 Santa Monica Blvd., Ste. 207 FAX **(323) 817-4434**
Hollywood, CA 90038

Runway, Inc. (310) 636-2000
10575 Virginia Ave. FAX **(310) 636-2034**
Culver City, CA 90232 **www.runway.com**
(Avid Systems, Digital Editing Systems, Final Cut Pro Systems, HD Editing, HD Finishing, HD Online & Non-Linear Offline and Online)
Contacts: Daniel Bernato, Howard Brock & Nancy Jundi

Rushes (323) 954-9494
7819 Beverly Blvd. FAX **(323) 937-9239**
Los Angeles, CA 90036 **www.rushes.tv**
(Color Correction, Duplication, Film Scanning and Recording, Film to Tape Transfers, Standards Conversion, Tape to Tape Color Correction & Telecine)
Contacts: Lisa Boolootian & Steve Shere

Santa Monica Video, Inc. (310) 451-0333 (800) 843-3827
1505 11th St. FAX **(310) 458-3350**
Santa Monica, CA 90401 **www.santamonicavideo.com**
(Duplication)

Screen Door Entertainment, Inc. (818) 781-5600
15223 Burbank Blvd. FAX **(818) 781-5601**
Sherman Oaks, CA 91411 **www.sdetv.com**

Secret Headquarters, Inc. (323) 677-2092
5767 W. Adams Blvd. FAX **(323) 677-2096**
Los Angeles, CA 90016 **www.secrethq.com**
(All Formats, Authoring, Avid Systems, Color Correction, Digital Film Mastering, Digital Media Transfers, Duplication, DVD Menus, Final Cut Pro Systems, Finishing, HD Editing, HD Finishing, HD Online, Mastering, Offline & Online)
Contacts: Kristin Anderson, Dave Bogosian, Greg Huson, Lance Mueller & Chris Ogden

Shapeshifter (323) 876-3444
3405 Cahuenga Blvd. West FAX **(323) 876-1444**
Los Angeles, CA 90068 **www.shapeshifter.biz**
(HD Avid, Nitris and Final Cut Pro Systems & Standard and HD Offline and Online)
Contact: Russo Anastasio

Shelter Post (949) 809-2150
18500 Von Karman Ave., Ste. 140 FAX **(949) 809-2152**
Irvine, CA 92612 **www.shelterpost.com**

Solventdreams (323) 906-9700
4222 Santa Monica Blvd. FAX **(323) 906-9711**
Los Angeles, CA 90029 **www.solventdreams.com**
(Computer Graphics, HD and Online Editing)

Sonic Pool (323) 460-4649
6860 Lexington Ave. FAX **(323) 460-6063**
Los Angeles, CA 90038 **www.sonicpool.com**
(Duplication & Non-Linear Offline and Online)

Sony Pictures Studios (310) 244-5722
10202 W. Washington Blvd. FAX **(310) 244-2303**
Culver City, CA 90232 **www.sonypicturesstudios.com**
(Telecine & Video Transfers)
Contact: Tom McCarthy

SSI/Advanced Post Services (323) 969-9333
7165 Sunset Blvd. FAX **(323) 969-8333**
Los Angeles, CA 90046 **www.ssipost.com**

SSI/Advanced Post Services (323) 874-9344
7155 Santa Monica Blvd. FAX **(323) 850-7189**
Los Angeles, CA 90046 **www.ssipost.com**
(Duplication, Offline, Online & Telecine)
Contact: Stuart Bartell

Stampede Post Productions (323) 463-8000
931 N. Citrus Ave. FAX **(323) 463-8010**
Hollywood, CA 91104 **www.stampedepost.com**
(Editing, Graphics, High Def, Online & Standards Conversion)

Standard (323) 224-3944
2020 N. Main St., Ste. 227 **www.standardsite.com**
Los Angeles, CA 90031
(Color Correction, Colorizations, Compositing, Computer Animation, Computer Graphics, Computer/Motion Graphics, Digital, Digital Colorization, Digital Editing Systems, Digital Film Mastering, Digital Online, DVD, DVD Menus and Design, Editing, Final Cut Pro Systems, Finishing, Graphic Design, Graphics, High Def, HD Editing, HD Finishing, HD Online, Non-Linear Offline and Online, Online & Post Supervision)

Stargate Digital (626) 403-8403
1001 El Centro St. FAX **(626) 403-8444**
South Pasadena, CA 91030 **www.stargatefilms.com**
(Compositing, Digital Online & Non-Linear Offline)
Contact: Darren Frankel

Station 22 Edit & Effects (310) 488-7726
3614 Overland Ave. **www.station22.com**
Los Angeles, CA 90034
(Authoring, Color Correction, Compositing, Computer Animation, Computer Graphics, Digital Editing Systems, Digital Online, Duplication, DVD Design, DVD Menus, Film Editing, Final Cut Pro Systems, Graphic Design, Graphics, HD Editing, HD Online, Motion Graphics, New Media Encoding & Non-Linear Offline and Online)
Contacts: Noah Clark, Michael Degnan, Paul McConville & Gregg Orenstein

STEELE Studios (310) 656-7770
5737 Mesmer Ave. FAX **(310) 656-7771**
Culver City, CA 90230 **www.steelevfx.com**
(Color Correction, Compositing, Computer Animation, Computer Graphics, Computer/Motion Graphics, Digital Colorization, Digital Editing Systems, Digital Intermediate Services, Digital Online, Duplication, Film Editing, Finishing, HD Editing, HD Finishing, HD Online, HD Remastering, Linear, Linear/Non-Linear Offline and Online, Post Supervision, Pre-Visualization, Tape to Tape Color Correction & Tape to Tape Transfers)

Sunset Edit (323) 467-8550 (818) 679-4014
849 N. Seward St. FAX **(323) 467-8545**
Los Angeles, CA 90038 **www.sunsetedit.com**

SuperDailies, Inc. (310) 306-0228 (800) 224-1130
2627 Naples Ave. FAX **(310) 306-0248**
Venice, CA 90291 **www.superdailies.com**
(DP Supervised Telecine)
Contact: Ed Colman

Switch Studios (310) 301-1800
316 S. Venice Blvd. FAX **(310) 496-1964**
Venice, CA 90291 **www.switch-studios.com**
(Color Correction, Computer Graphics, DVD Design, Editing, HD Finishing, Mastering, New Media Encoding, Non-Linear Offline and Online & Post Supervision)

The Syndicate (310) 260-2320
1207 Fourth St., Ste. 200 FAX **(310) 260-2420**
Santa Monica, CA 90401 **www.syndicate.tv**
(Color Correction, Colorization, Computer Graphics, Duplication, Film to Tape Transfers, Nonlinear Online, Standards Conversion, Subtitles, Tape to Tape Color Correction, Telecine & Visual Effects)

Technicolor Creative Services - Hollywood (323) 817-6937
6040 Sunset Blvd. **www.technicolor.com**
Hollywood, CA 90028
(Color Correction, Digital Intermediate Services, Film Restoration and Preservation & Telecine)
Contact: Jennifer Tellefsen

TEDS (310) 237-6438
www.tedsla.com
(All Formats, Avid Systems, Captions, Compositing, Computer Animation, Final Cut Pro Systems & Subtitles)

Threshold Sound + Vision (310) 571-0500
2114 Pico Blvd. FAX **(310) 571-0505**
Santa Monica, CA 90405 **www.thresholdsound.com**
(Duplication & Linear/Non-Linear Offline and Online)
Contact: Peter Barker

Timecode Multimedia (310) 826-9199
12340 Santa Monica Blvd., Ste. 230
West Los Angeles, CA 90025
www.timecodemultimedia.com
(Authoring, Captions, Color Correction, Colorizations, Computer Graphics, Digital Colorization, Digital Online, Duplication, DVD Design, DVD Menus, Final Cut Pro Systems, Finishing, Graphics, HD Editing, HD Finishing, HD Online, HD Remastering, Linear Online, Mastering, Motion Graphics, Non-Linear Offline, Non-Linear Online, Post Supervision, Standards Conversions, Tape to Tape Transfers & Video to Still Transfers)
Contacts: Marc Cabaniss & Stuart Ferreyra

Tree Falls Post (323) 851-0299
3131 Cahuenga Blvd. West FAX **(323) 851-0277**
Los Angeles, CA 90068 **www.tfpost.com**
(All Formats, Authoring, Avid Systems, Captions, Color Correction, Digital Editing Systems, Digital Online, Duplication, Final Cut Pro Systems, Finishing, HD Editing, HD Finishing, HD Online, Mastering, New Media Encoding, Standards Conversions, Subtitles & Tape to Tape Transfers)

Tunnel Post (310) 260-1208
409 Santa Monica Blvd., Ste. 2E FAX **(310) 260-1209**
Santa Monica, CA 90401 **www.tunnelpost.com**

Universal Studios Digital Services (818) 777-1111
100 Universal City Plaza, Bldg. 3153 FAX **(818) 866-5258**
Universal City, CA 91608 **www.filmmakersdestination.com**
(Color Correction, Duplication, Editing, Encoding & Telecine)
Contact: Ron Silveira

US Computamatch, Inc. (310) 396-0987
(310) 722-9800
1661 Lincoln Blvd., Ste. 200 FAX **(310) 396-0986**
Santa Monica, CA 90404 **www.uscomputamatch.com**
(Digital Intermediate Services, Film Data Management, Film Scanning, Film to Tape Transfers & Negative Cutting)
Contact: Marilyn Sommer

Vendetta Post (310) 587-9100
225 Santa Monica Blvd., Ninth Fl. FAX **(310) 587-9299**
Santa Monica, CA 90401 **www.vendettapost.com**
(Computer Graphics & Non-Linear Online)

Victory Studios LA (818) 769-1776
10911 Riverside Dr., Ste. 100 FAX **(818) 760-1280**
North Hollywood, CA 91602 **www.victorystudiosla.com**
(Avid Systems, Color Correction, Digital Editing Systems, Duplication, Final Cut Pro Systems, Graphics, HD Editing, HD Online, Non-Linear Offline, Non-Linear Online & Standards Conversions)

The Video Agency, Inc./ TVA Productions (818) 505-8300
(888) 322-4296
3950 Vantage Ave. FAX **(818) 505-8370**
Studio City, CA 91604 **www.tvaproductions.com**
(Computer Graphics, Duplication & Linear/Non-Linear Offline and Online)
Contact: Jeffery Goddard

Video Symphony (888) 871-2843
(818) 557-7200
266 E. Magnolia Blvd. FAX **(818) 845-1951**
Burbank, CA 91502 **www.videosymphony.com**
(Digital Online, Linear/Non-Linear Offline & Training For Computer Graphics)
Contact: Mike Flanagan

View Studio, Inc. (805) 745-8814
385 Toro Canyon Rd. **www.viewstudio.com**
Carpinteria, CA 93013

Visual Data Media Services, Inc. (818) 558-3363
(888) 418-4782
145 W. Magnolia Blvd. FAX **(818) 558-3368**
Burbank, CA 91502 **www.visualdatainc.com**
(Authoring, Captions, Duplication, DVD Design, DVD Menus, HD Editing, Non-Linear Offline, Non-Linear Online, Standards Conversions, Subtitles & Tape to Tape Color Correction)

Visual Image (323) 962-2233
1015 N. Cahuenga Blvd., Ste. 4200
Hollywood, CA 90038 **www.visualimagehollywood.com**
(Digital Non-Linear Online and Offline, Duplication, Graphics & New Media Encoding)
Contact: Steve Goodwin

Vitello Productions (818) 955-9930
1150 W. Olive Ave. FAX **(818) 955-9926**
Burbank, CA 91506 **www.vitello.com**
(Color Correction, Computer Graphics, Non-Linear Offline and Online & Standards Conversion)

Warner Bros. Studio Facilities - Post Production Services (818) 954-1625
(818) 954-2515
4000 Warner Blvd. FAX **(818) 954-4138**
Burbank, CA 91522 **www.wbpostproduction.com**

West Post Digital (310) 857-5000
1703 Stewart St. FAX **(310) 857-5060**
Santa Monica, CA 90404 **www.westpostdigital.com**
(Authoring, Color Correction, Duplication, DVD Design & Finishing)
Contacts: Todd Brown & Kenny Fields

Westside Media Group (310) 979-3500
(818) 779-8600
12233 W. Olympic Blvd., Ste. 152 FAX **(310) 979-3503**
West Los Angeles, CA 90064
www.westsidemediagroup.com
(Authoring, Avid Systems, Captions, Color Correction, Duplication, DVD Authoring, DVD Design, DVD Menus, Film Transfers, Final Cut Pro Systems, Finishing, HD Editing, HD Finishing, HD Online, Post Supervision, Standards Conversions, Subtitles & Video to Still Transfers)
Contacts: Scott Ellison, Lewis Lipstone & Shirley Lipstone

Wild Pictures (310) 526-7225
100 Market St., Third Fl. **www.wildpictures.com**
Venice, CA 90291
(Avid Systems, Color Correction, Compositing, Computer Animation, Computer Graphics, Digital Editing Systems, Digital Online, Duplication, Film Editing, Final Cut Pro Systems, Finishing, Graphic Design, HD Editing, HD Finishing, HD Online, Motion Graphics, New Media Encoding, Non-Linear Offline, Non-Linear Online & Post Supervision)

Windowseat Pictures **(310) 535-3650**
121 Sheldon St. **www.windowseatpictures.com**
El Segundo, CA 90245
(All Formats, Authoring, Avid Systems, Color Correction, Colorizations, Compositing, Computer Animation, Computer Graphics, Digital Colorization, Digital Editing Systems, Digital Film Mastering, Digital Intermediate Services, Digital Media Transfers, Digital Online, Duplication, DVD Design, DVD Menus, Film Editing, Film to Tape Transfers, Final Cut Pro Systems, Finishing, Graphic Design, Graphics, HD Editing, HD Finishing, HD Online, HD Remastering, Mastering, Mobile Facility, Motion Graphics, New Media Encoding, Non-Linear Offline, Non-Linear Online, Post Supervision, Pre-Visualization, Recording, Scanning, Standards Conversions, Subtitles, Tape to Tape Color Correction, Tape to Tape Film Simulation, Tape to Tape Transfers, Telecine & Video to Still Transfers)

World of Video & Audio **(310) 659-5959** **(866) 900-3827**
8717 Wilshire Blvd. FAX **(310) 659-8247**
Beverly Hills, CA 90211 **www.wova.com**
(Duplication, DVCPro, HDCam and HDV Downconversions, Linear and Non-Linear Editing & Standards Conversions)

World Television Productions **(323) 469-5638**
5757 Wilshire Blvd., Ste. 470 FAX **(323) 469-2193**
Los Angeles, CA 90036
(Duplication & Linear/Non-Linear Offline and Online)
Contact: Hugo Morales

Yada/Levine Video Productions **(323) 461-1616**
1253 Vine St., Ste. 21A FAX **(323) 461-2288**
Hollywood, CA 90038 **www.yadalevine.com**
(Computer Graphics & Non-Linear Offline)
Contact: Michael Yada

Zona Productions, Inc. **(323) 876-0132**
(Non-Linear Offline and Online)
Contacts: Timothy Kitz & Daniel Zimbaldi

Terra Abroms (818) 426-0019
FAX (818) 450-0514

Ada Anderson (310) 270-7121

Brad Arensman (818) 445-3536
(661) 257-2020
FAX (661) 257-4018

Bryan Barker (310) 869-9765
web.mac.com/bbarker/

Scott Carrey (310) 765-4967
(310) 985-1303
FAX (310) 765-4967
www.scarrey.com

Ed Chapman (213) 200-9952
FAX (818) 980-9788
www.edchapman.com

Ellen Doskey (831) 899-1894

Monette Dubin (310) 994-4079
www.imdb.com/name/nm1582167

Shawn Dury (310) 200-7593
(213) 501-1499

Edy H. Enriquez (310) 836-9011
(323) 252-0904
FAX (310) 836-9010
www.x1fx.com

John Frost (323) 481-5045

Bob Hackl (818) 990-2617
(818) 207-1753

Lauren E. Jackson (818) 300-3414

Peter Lauritson (310) 374-3980
(310) 729-3763
FAX (310) 937-0974

David McCann (310) 282-9940
www.mirisch.com

David Persoff (323) 791-3840

Eliza Pelham Randall (310) 962-9463
(323) 525-1225
www.queenofspades.com

Jason Reeves (310) 417-4838
(310) 428-0575
www.triageinc.com

Jim Sterling (310) 503-5590
www.postwise.com

Bradley Van Herbst (213) 700-2664
www.vanimages.com

Susan Vogelfang (310) 306-2648

Marc Wielage (818) 486-7747
www.cinesound.tv

100% QC Central (323) 316-8298
www.qccentral.com

Ascent Media - Creative Services (310) 434-7000
520 Broadway, Fifth Fl.
Santa Monica, CA 90401
www.ascentmedia.com

CCI Digital, Inc. (818) 562-6300
FAX (818) 562-8222
www.ccidigital.com

The Post Group (323) 462-2300
6335 Homewood Ave.
Hollywood, CA 90028
FAX (323) 462-0836
www.postgroup.com

Post Logic Studios (323) 461-7887
1800 N. Vine St., Ste. 100
Los Angeles, CA 90028
FAX (323) 461-7790
www.postlogic.com

Santa Monica Video, Inc. (310) 451-0333
(800) 843-3827
1505 11th St.
Santa Monica, CA 90401
FAX (310) 458-3350
www.santamonicavideo.com

Alternative Rentals (310) 204-3388
FAX (310) 204-3384
www.alternativerentals.com

American Film Institute (AFI) (323) 856-7600
2021 N. Western Ave. FAX (323) 467-4578
Los Angeles, CA 90027 www.afi.com
(16mm, 35mm, 70mm, Dolby SR Stereo & Video Projection)

American Hi Definition, Inc. (818) 222-0022
7635 Airport Business Pkwy FAX (818) 222-0818
Van Nuys, CA 91406 www.hi-def.com

Arenas (323) 785-5535
3375 Barham Blvd. FAX (323) 785-5560
Los Angeles, CA 90068
www.arenasgroup.com/info-screen.html

Big Red Productions, Inc. (714) 842-4338
(714) 402-2291
FAX (718) 842-4798
www.bigredprod.com

Big Time Picture Company, Inc. (310) 207-0921
12210½ Nebraska Ave. FAX (310) 826-0071
Los Angeles, CA 90025 www.bigtimepic.com
(3/4", 35mm, Beta SP, Digibeta, Dolby A and A/SR Stereo, DVCAM, DVD, High Def, VHS & Video Projection)

The Charles Aidikoff Screening Room (310) 274-0866
150 S. Rodeo Dr., Ste. 140 FAX (310) 550-1794
Beverly Hills, CA 90212 www.aidikoff.tv
(35mm, Dolby A/SR/SRD, DTS, Satellite Teleconferencing & Video Projection)

Cinespace (323) 817-3456
6356 Hollywood Blvd., Second Fl. FAX (323) 860-9794
Hollywood, CA 90028 www.cinespace.info
(Beta, DVD, High Def, Mini DV & VHS)

The Clip Joint for Film (818) 842-2525
833-B N. Hollywood Way FAX (818) 842-2644
Burbank, CA 91505

The Culver Studios (310) 202-1234
9336 W. Washington Blvd. FAX (310) 202-3536
Culver City, CA 90232 www.theculverstudios.com
(Film and D-Cinema Video Projection)

Dalsa (818) 884-7000
6160 Variel Ave. FAX (818) 884-7022
Woodland Hills, CA 91367 www.dalsa.com/dc
(1/2", 3/4", 5.1, Beta, D-Cinema, Digibeta, Digital Projection, DLP, DV CAM, DVD, High Def, HDCAM, Mini DV, SRW-5000, THX Sound and Video Facilities, VHS, Video Facilities & Video Projection)

Delicate Productions, Inc. (805) 388-1800
874 Verdulera St. FAX (805) 388-1037
Camarillo, CA 93010 www.delicate.com

Dick Clark Screening Room (310) 255-4699
2900 Olympic Blvd., First Fl.
Santa Monica, CA 90404
www.dickclarkproductionstheatre.com

Fine Arts Theatre (310) 701-8925
(310) 659-3875
8556 Wilshire Blvd. FAX (310) 861-9005
Beverly Hills, CA 90211 www.studioscreenings.com
(35mm, 5.1, Anamorphic/3D Projection, Beta, D-Cinema, Digibeta, Digital Projection, DLP, Dolby, Dolby A/SR/SRD, Dolby SR Digital Stereo, Dolby SR Stereo, DV CAM, DVD, Facilities, Film, High Def, HD CAM, Mini DV, Multitrack Printmasters, SR, SRD, VHS, Video Facilities & Video Projection)

Fox Studios (310) 369-2406
(310) 369-4636
10201 W. Pico Blvd. FAX (310) 369-0503
Los Angeles, CA 90035 www.foxpost.com
(16mm, 35mm, 70mm, Digibeta 3/4" and 1/2", DLP Video Projection, Dolby A/SR/SRD, DTS, DVCAM, DVD, HDCAM, MMR8 Hard Drives, QC Software All Formats, SDDS, SRW-5000 & THX Sound and Video Facilities)

Goethe-Institut (323) 525-3388
5750 Wilshire Blvd., Ste. 100 FAX (323) 934-3597
Los Angeles, CA 90036 www.goethe.de/losangeles

Hollywood-DI (323) 850-3550
1041 Formosa Ave. FAX (323) 850-3551
Fairbanks Bldg., Ste. 7 www.hollywooddi.com
West Hollywood, CA 90046
(35mm, 5.1, D-Cinema, Digibeta, Digital Projection, DLP, Dolby, DVD, Final Cut Pro, HDCAM SR & QT and DPX Playback & SRW-5000)

The Jim Henson Company (323) 802-1500
1416 N. La Brea Ave. FAX (323) 802-1825
Hollywood, CA 90028 leasing.henson.com/events.html

LACMA (The Los Angeles County Museum Of Art) (323) 857-6039
(323) 857-4768
5905 Wilshire Blvd. FAX (323) 857-6021
Los Angeles, CA 90036 www.lacma.org
(35mm, 70mm, DTS, SDDS & Video Projection)

Los Angeles Center Studios (213) 534-3000
1201 W. Fifth St., Ste. T-110 FAX (213) 534-3001
Los Angeles, CA 90017 www.lacenterstudios.com
(35mm, Digital Projection, Satellite Teleconferencing, VHS & Video Projection)

Los Angeles Film School Theater (323) 860-0789
6363 Sunset Blvd., Ste. 500 www.lafilm.edu
Los Angeles, CA 90028

New Deal Studios, Inc. (310) 578-9929
4121 Redwood Ave. FAX (310) 578-7370
Los Angeles, CA 90066 www.newdealstudios.com
(35mm, 70mm, Anamorphic/3D Projection, Digital Video & VistaVision)

Pacific Design Center/ SilverScreen Theater (310) 657-0800
8687 Melrose Ave. FAX (310) 652-8576
West Hollywood, CA 90069 www.pacificdesigncenter.com
(35mm & High Def)

The Studios at Paramount (323) 956-5520
The Studios at Paramount
Post Production Services
5555 Melrose Ave. www.thestudiosatparamount.com
Los Angeles, CA 90038
(¾", 35mm, 5.1, 70mm, Anamorphic/3D Projection, Beta, Blu-ray, D-Cinema, Digibeta, Digital Projection, DLP, Dolby, Dolby A, Dolby SR and SRD, DTS, DV CAM, DVD, Film, HDCAM, High Def, Mini DV, Multi-Media Presentations, Satellite Teleconferencing, SDDS, SR, SRD, SRW-5000, THX, Video Projection & VistaVision)

PlasterCITY Digital Post Facility (323) 469-9800
6500 Sunset Blvd. FAX (323) 462-4620
Los Angeles, CA 90028 www.plastercitypost.com
(Beta, D-Cinema, Digibeta, Digital Projection, DV CAM, DVD, High Def, HDCAM, SRW-5000 & Video Projection)

Raleigh Studios (323) 960-3456
5300 Melrose Ave. FAX (323) 871-5600
Hollywood, CA 90038 www.raleighstudios.com
(16mm, 35mm, Dolby SR Digital Stereo, HD Projection, Multitrack Printmasters & Video Projection)

Renberg Theatre (323) 860-7336
The Village at Ed Gould Plaza FAX (323) 308-4103
1125 N. McCadden Pl. www.lagaycenter.org
Los Angeles, CA 90038
(16mm, 35mm, Dolby Surround, DVD & VHS)

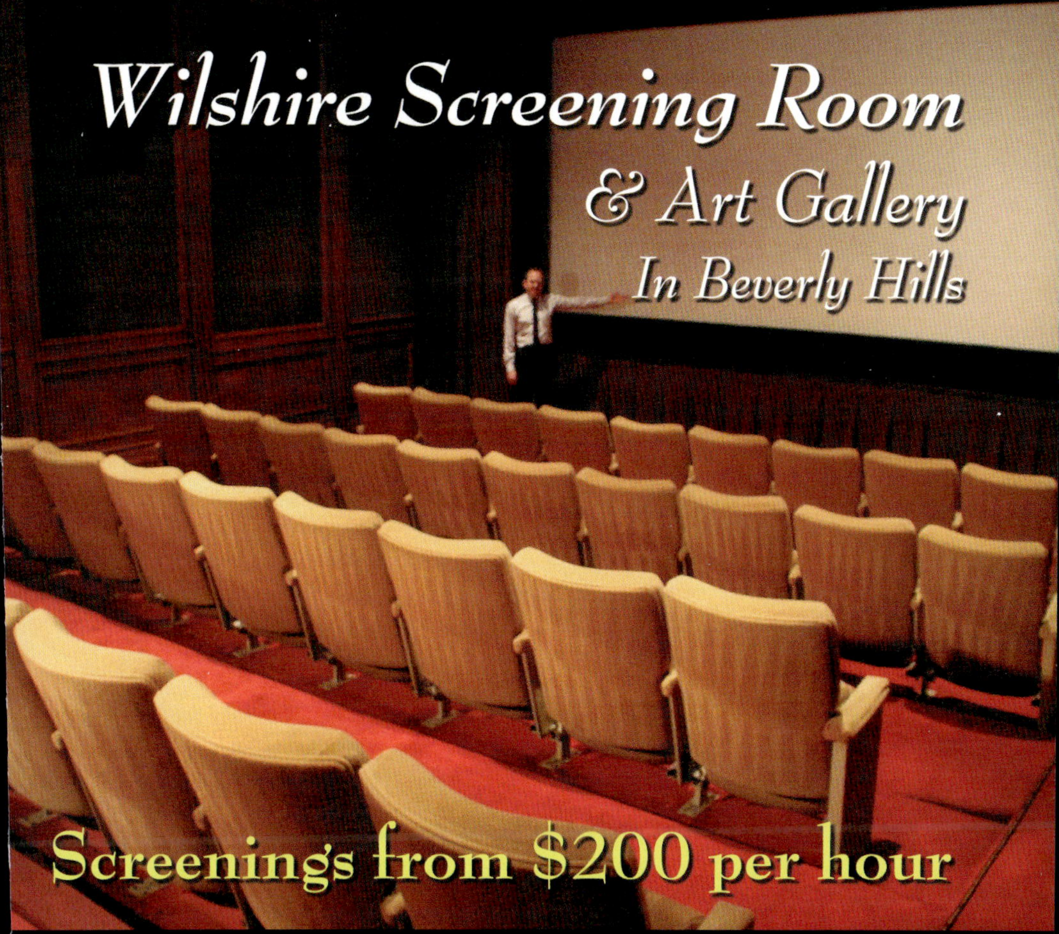

Santa Monica Screening (310) 393-8306
1526 14th St., Ste. 102 **www.smscreening.com**
Santa Monica, CA 90404

Sony Pictures Studios (310) 244-5721
10202 W. Washington Blvd.
Culver City, CA 90232 **www.sonypicturesstudios.com**
(16mm, 35mm, 70mm, DTS, Dolby A/SR Stereo, SDDS, SRD & Video Facilities)

Spartan Mobile Suites, Inc. (310) 587-3377
3727 W. Magnolia Blvd., Ste. 156 FAX **(661) 702-0550**
Burbank, CA 91505
(35mm Mobile Facilities)

Sunset Bronson Studios (323) 460-5858
5800 W. Sunset Blvd. FAX **(323) 460-3844**
Los Angeles, CA 90028 **www.sgsandsbs.com**

Sunset Gower Studios (323) 467-1001
1438 N. Gower St. **www.sgsandsbs.com**
Los Angeles, CA 90028

Sunset Screening Rooms (310) 652-1933
2212 W. Magnolia Blvd. FAX **(310) 652-3828**
Burbank, CA 91506
(3D, 16mm, 35mm, 70mm, Dolby SRD, DTS & Video Facilities)

Sunset Screening Rooms (310) 652-1933
8730 Sunset Blvd. FAX **(310) 652-3828**
West Hollywood, CA 90069

Switch Studios (310) 301-1800
316 S. Venice Blvd. FAX **(310) 496-1964**
Venice, CA 90291 **www.switch-studios.com**
(Digital Projection & HD Video Projection)

Theatrical Concepts, Inc. (818) 597-1100
3030 Triunfo Canyon Rd. FAX **(818) 597-0202**
Agoura Hills, CA 91301 **www.theatrical.com**
(5.1, Dolby & HD Mobile Facilities)

Warner Bros. Studio Facilities - Projection (818) 954-2144
4000 Warner Blvd. FAX **(818) 954-7915**
Burbank, CA 91522 **www.wbpostproduction.com**
(16mm, 35mm, 70mm, Dolby A/SR/SRD, Stereo & Video Facilities)

Ⓐ **Wilshire Screening Room** (310) 701-8925
(310) 659-3875
8670 Wilshire Blvd., Ste. 112 FAX **(310) 861-9005**
Beverly Hills, CA 90211 **www.studioscreenings.com**

LA 411

Stock Footage & Photos

LA 411

ABCNews VideoSource (212) 456-5421 / (800) 789-1250
125 West End Ave. FAX (212) 456-5428
New York, NY 10023 www.abcnewsvsource.com
Footage: ABC News 1963–Present

Ⓐ Action Footage/ Warren Miller Entertainment (800) 729-3456
www.wmefootage.com
Footage: Comedy, Extreme/Adventure Sports, Scenics, Time-Lapse & Vintage

Action Sports Adventure (212) 375-7622 / (866) 473-5264
902 Broadway FAX (212) 807-0221
New York, NY 10010 www.corbismotion.com
Footage: Sports

Action Sports/Scott Dittrich Films (310) 459-2526 / (212) 681-6565
P.O. Box 301 FAX (310) 456-1743
Malibu, CA 90265 www.sdfilms.com
Footage: Aerials, Animals, Cities, Clouds, Natural Disasters, People, Pollution, Professional and Extreme Sports, Scenics, Sunsets, Time-Lapse & Waves

AeronauticPictures.com (805) 985-2320
P.O. Box 1748 www.aeronauticpictures.com/
Ojai, CA 93024 royalty-free-stock-footage/
Footage: Film, High Def and Video: Aerial & Location

Alan Benoit Photography (480) 967-2241 / (602) 526-1800
1101 E. Mesquite St. FAX (480) 926-8888
Gilbert, AZ 85296
Photos: All Subjects

All-Stock (310) 317-9996 / (800) 323-0079
P.O. Box 1705 www.all-stock.com
Pacific Palisades, CA 90272
Footage: All Subjects

AM Stock-Cameo Film Library (818) 762-7865
10513 Burbank Blvd. FAX (818) 762-6480
North Hollywood, CA 91601
Footage: 35mm and HD, Aerials, Buildings, Cities, Nature & Skylines

Ambient Images (310) 312-6640 / (800) 627-8057
11600 Rochester Ave., Ste. 11 FAX (310) 312-5590
Los Angeles, CA 90025 www.ambientimages.com
Photos: Aerials, Agriculture, Beaches, California Cityscapes, City, National and State Parks, Landscapes, Museums, Neighborhoods, New York Panoramics, Rural Scenes & Sports and Recreation

America by Air Stock Footage Library (800) 488-6359
154 Euclid Blvd. FAX (413) 235-1462
Lantana, FL 33462 www.americabyair.com
Footage: 35mm and High Def, Aerials, Contemporary & International

American Playback Images (818) 954-9870
27748 Caraway Ln., Ste. 1 FAX (818) 955-5112
Santa Clarita, CA 91350 www.americanplayback.com
Footage: Americana, Cartoons, Commercials, Historical, Movie Clips, News & Playback

Anchor Archives (213) 369-6903
Footage: 1950s Americana, Celebrities, Nautical, Travelogue & Vintage

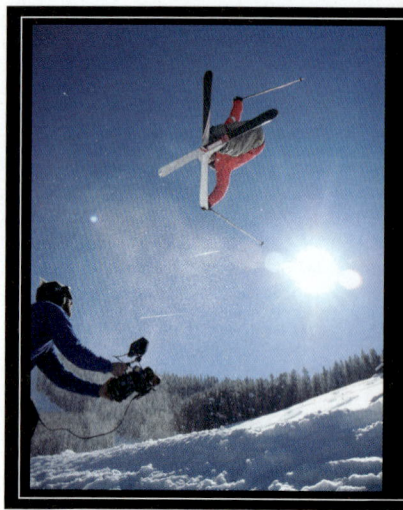

Animation Trip (858) 793-1900
3830 Valley Center Dr., Ste. 705-833 FAX **(858) 793-1942**
San Diego, CA 92130 **www.animationtrip.com/licensing**
Footage and Photos: Computer Animation and Illustrations, High-Tech Imagery & Special FX

A **Apex Stock** (323) 443-2580 (888) 250-2739
6725 W. Sunset Blvd., Ste. 490 FAX **(323) 443-2579**
Hollywood, CA 90028 **www.apexstock.com**

ARC Science Simulations (970) 667-1168 (800) 759-1642
P.O. Box 1955 FAX **(970) 667-1105**
Loveland, CO 80539 **www.arcscience.com**
Footage: High Resolution 2D and 3D Earth-From-Space AnimationPhotos: Earth Textures, Earth-From-Space & High Resolution Cloud Layers

Archive Films by Getty Images (800) 462-4379
6300 Wilshire Blvd., 16th Fl. **www.gettyimages.com**
Los Angeles, CA 90048
Footage: Americana, Business/Industry, Cartoons, Celebrities, Destinations, Educational, Events, Film Genres, Home Movies, Lifestyle, News, Newsreels, Political, Sports & Travel

Artbeats (541) 863-4429 (800) 444-9392
1405 N. Myrtle Rd. FAX **(541) 863-4547**
Myrtle Creek, OR 97457 **www.artbeats.com**
Footage: Aerials, Animals, Archival, Backgrounds, Lifestyles & Nature

Battlegrounds (502) 339-7934
9801 Somerford Rd. FAX **(502) 339-7934**
Louisville, KY 40242 **www.battlegroundsvideo.com**
Footage: Military and Generic

BBC Motion Gallery, Los Angeles (818) 299-9720
4144 Lankershim Blvd., Ste. 200 FAX **(818) 299-9763**
North Hollywood, CA 91602 **www.bbcmotiongallery.com**
Footage: Arts, Bloopers, Communications, Current Events, Destinations, Entertainment, Historical, Leisure, Lifestyles, Medicine, Music, Natural History, News, Politics, Reality, Science, Stock, Technology, Travel and Locations, Universal Newsreels & Wildlife

BBC Motion Gallery, New York (212) 705-9399
747 Third Ave., Sixth Fl. FAX **(212) 705-9342**
New York, NY 10017 **www.bbcmotiongallery.com**
Footage: Arts, Bloopers, Communications, Current Events, Destinations, Entertainment, Historical, Leisure, Lifestyles, Medicine, Music, Natural History, News, Politics, Reality, Science, Stock, Technology, Travel and Locations, Universal Newsreels & Wildlife

BBC Motion Gallery, Toronto (416) 362-3223
130 Spadina Ave., Ste. 401 FAX **(416) 362-3553**
Toronto, ON M5V 2L4 Canada **www.bbcmotiongallery.com**
Footage: Arts, Bloopers, Communications, Current Events, Destinations, Entertainment, Historical, Leisure, Lifestyles, Medicine, Music, Natural History, News, Politics, Reality, Science, Stock, Technology, Travel and Locations, Universal Newsreels & Wildlife

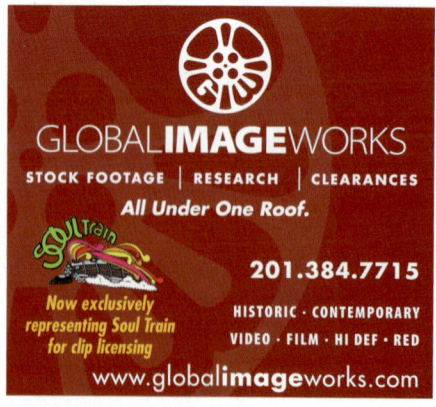

Bill Bachmann Studios (407) 333-9988
FAX (407) 333-2130
www.billbachmann.com
Photos: Abstracts, Beaches, Business, Caribbean, Lifestyle, Medical, Minorities, Sports & World Travel

BlackLight Films (323) 436-7070
(323) 436-2229
3371 Cahuenga Blvd. West FAX (323) 436-2230
Hollywood, CA 90068 www.blacklightfilms.com
Footage: Aerials, Agriculture, Americana, Animals, Architecture, Cityscapes, Clouds, Contemporary, Cultures, Deserts, Flowers, Historical Landmarks, International People and Scenery, Landscapes, Lifestyles, Moons, Mountains, Nature, Oceans, Rivers, Rural, Scenic, Seasons, Skies, Storms, Suns, Sunsets, Time-Lapse, Transportation, Travel & Wildlife

Blue Fier Photography/Blue Fier (818) 344-5527
(818) 726-5527
7450 Beckford Ave. FAX (818) 344-5556
Reseda, CA 91335 www.bluefier.com
Photos: Clouds, Deserts, Forests, Landscapes, Mountains, Panoramics, Roads, Scenics, Skies, Skylines, Sunsets & Water

Blue Sky Stock Footage/ Bill Mitchell (310) 305-8384
(877) 992-5477
FAX (310) 305-8985
www.blueskyfootage.com
Footage: 35mm, High Def and Super 16mm Time-Lapse and Real-Time, Aerials, Agriculture, Airplanes, Americana, Animals, Architecture, Cityscapes, Clouds, Deserts, Driving Shots, Eclipses, Experimental, Flowers, Fires, Forests, Highways, Historical Landmarks, International People and Scenery, Landscapes, Lighting, Motion Control, Mountains, Nature, Oceans, Rivers, Rural, Seasons, Space, Skies, Stars/ Comets/Planets, Storms, Suns and Moons, Traffic, Trains, Transportation & Underwater

Boeing Image Licensing (206) 662-1551
P.O. Box 3707, M/C 14-84 FAX (206) 655-1320
Seattle, WA 98124 www.boeingimages.com
Footage: Aerials, Aerospace, Airplanes, Archival, Cityscapes, Computer Graphics, Contemporary, Deserts, Experimental, Helicopters, Historical Landmarks, Jets, Landscapes, Manufacturing, Military, Missiles, Mountains, Oceans, Rockets, Satellites, Skies, Space, Suns and Moons, Technology, Transportation, Travel & Weapons

The Bridgeman Art Library (212) 828-1238
65 E. 93rd St. FAX (212) 828-1255
New York, NY 10128 www.bridgemanart.com
Photos: Fine Art and History

Budget Films, Inc. (323) 660-0187
(323) 660-0800
4427 Santa Monica Blvd. FAX (323) 660-5571
Los Angeles, CA 90029 www.budgetfilms.com
Footage: Beauty, Current Events, Technology & Vintage Black/ White and Color

Camera One (206) 523-3456
8523 15th Ave. NE FAX (206) 523-3668
Seattle, WA 98115 www.cameraone.us
Footage: Aerials, Archeology, Caribbean, Cities, Clouds, Eclipse, Europe, Landscapes, Lightning, Moons, National Parks, Nature, Natural and Traffic/Urban Time-Lapse, Northwest, Outdoor Sports, Scenics, Southwest, Storms, Sunrises and Sunsets, Underwater, Whitewater & Wildlife

Carl Barth Images (805) 969-2346
(805) 637-0881
P.O. Box 5325
Santa Barbara, CA 93150
Footage: Aerials, Contemporary Establishing Shots, Scenics & Skylines

Carter Productions (303) 499-9430
(303) 589-8881
P.O. Box 3537 FAX (303) 499-6130
Boulder, CO 80307
Footage: Cityscapes, Hawaii, North American Wildlife & Rocky Mountain Scenery

CBS News Archives/ BBC Motion Gallery (818) 299-9720
4144 Lankershim Blvd., Ste. 200
North Hollywood, CA 91602 www.bbcmotiongallery.com
Footage: CBS News 1954–Present

CelebrityFootage (310) 360-9600
320 S. Almont Dr. www.celebrityfootage.com
Beverly Hills, CA 90211
Footage: Award Ceremonies, Celebrities, Entertainment, Events, High Def, Hollywood, Movie Premieres, People, Red Carpet Arrivals & Stars

Channel Sea Television (949) 489-9949
(714) 299-9309
28462 Calle Pinata
San Juan Capistrano, CA 92675
Footage: Sailing & Yacht Racing

Chicagoland News Footage (312) 455-1212
1613 W. Huron St. www.redwagonproductions.tv
Chicago, IL 60622
Footage: Chicagoland Rescues, Crimes, Fires, Gangs, Medical Emergencies & Natural Disasters

Cinegraph (312) 939-1300
47 W. Polk St., Ste. 100-113 FAX (312) 341-1709
Chicago, IL 60605 www.cinegraph.com

Classic Images (310) 277-0400
(800) 949-2547
469 S. Bedford Dr. FAX (310) 277-0412
Beverly Hills, CA 90212 www.classicimg.com
Footage: 16mm, 35mm, 1890s–Present, Aerials, Americana, Archival, Cartoons, Cityscapes, Commercials, Educational, High Def, Historical, Hollywood, Industry, Music, Nature, Newsreel, Sports, Technology, Time-Lapse, Travel, Underwater, Vintage TV and Film & Wildlife

Clay Lacy Aviation, Inc. (818) 989-2900
(800) 423-2904
7435 Valjean Ave. FAX (818) 909-9537
Van Nuys, CA 91406 www.claylacy.com
Footage: Aerials

The Clip Joint for Film (818) 842-2525
833-B N. Hollywood Way FAX (818) 842-2644
Burbank, CA 91505
Footage: All Subjects

CNN ImageSource (404) 827-3326
One CNN Center www.cnnimagesource.com
Atlanta, GA 30303
Footage: 1980–Present Current Events

Collegiate Images (954) 343-8000
(818) 625-1606
13450 Sunrise Blvd., Ste. 70 FAX (954) 343-8001
Sunrise, FL 33323
Footage: College Sports

The Communications Group, Inc. (919) 828-4086
(888) 479-3456
P.O. Box 50157 FAX (919) 832-7797
Raleigh, NC 27650 www.cgfilm.com
Footage: Aerials, Boston, High Def, North Carolina Cities, Farms and Landscapes & The Big Dig

Compro Productions, Inc. (770) 918-8163
2055 Boar Tusk Rd. NE www.compro-atl.com
Conyers, GA 30012
Footage: Cities, European and Asian Landscapes, Landmarks & People

Corbis (323) 602-5700
3455 S. La Cienega Blvd. FAX (323) 602-5701
Los Angeles, CA 90016 www.corbis.com
Photos: Backgrounds, Classic Illustrations, Computer Graphics, Maps, People, Textures & Worldwide Locations

Corbis (212) 777-6200 / (800) 999-0800
902 Broadway, Third Fl. FAX (212) 533-4034
New York, NY 10010 www.corbis.com
Photos: All Subjects

Corbis Motion (212) 375-7622 / (866) 473-5264
902 Broadway FAX (212) 807-0221
New York, NY 10010 www.corbismotion.com
Footage: All Subjects

CTV Television, Inc. (416) 332-7389 / (800) 628-7780
Nine Channel 9 Court FAX (416) 332-7384
Toronto, ON M1S 4B5 Canada www.archivesales.ctv.ca
Footage: Classic News, Documentary and Sports

Custom Medical Stock Photo, Inc. (773) 267-3100 / (800) 373-2677
3660 W. Irving Park Rd. FAX (773) 267-6071
Chicago, IL 60618 www.cmsp.com
Footage & Photos: Medical & Science

dick clark productions Media Archives (310) 786-8971
9200 Sunset Blvd. www.dickclarkproductions.com
West Hollywood, CA 90069
Footage: 1950s–1900s Pop/Rock Music Performances

Documentary Educational Resources (617) 926-0491 / (800) 569-6621
101 Morse St. FAX (617) 926-9519
Watertown, MA 02472 www.der.org
Footage: Anthropology, Cultures & People

Doubletime Productions (516) 869-1170 / (866) 226-4474
162 Pond View Dr. FAX (516) 869-1171
Port Washington, NY 11050
www.doubletimeproductions.com
Footage: AMTRAK Official Licensing, Animals, Beaches and Sunsets, Chicago, Cityscapes, Deserts, Florida, Landscapes, Lifestyles, Mountains, New York Panoramic and Rural Scenes, North American Wildlife, Northwest, Rocky Mountain Scenery, Scenics, Southwest, Traffic, Trains, Transportation & Travel

Dynasty Films (310) 913-7700 / (818) 823-6088
(Time-Lapse) www.dynastyfilms.com

eFootage, LLC (626) 395-9593
87 N. Raymond, Ste. 850 FAX (626) 792-5394
Pasadena, CA 91103 www.efootage.com
Footage: All Subjects

Establishing Shots of Chicago (847) 816-9020
P.O. Box 7160 www.nedmiller.com
Libertyville, IL 60048
Footage: Chicago

eVox Productions, LLC (310) 605-1400
2363 E. Pacifica Pl. FAX (310) 605-1429
Rancho Dominguez, CA 90220 www.evox.com
Footage: Cars

Excavated Film Research (213) 369-6903
(Archival Consulting)

Film & Video Stock Shots, Inc. (818) 760-2098 / (888) 436-6824
10442 Burbank Blvd. FAX (818) 760-3294
North Hollywood, CA 91601 www.stockshots.com
Footage: Aerials, Animals, Archival, Cartoons, Current Images, Lifestyles, Manufacturing, Medical, Microscopy, Nature, News, Slapstick, Space, Sports, Time-Lapse, Underwater & Worldwide Locations

FILM Archives, Inc. (310) 822-9164 / (212) 696-2616
4337 Marina City Dr., Ste. 939 FAX (310) 822-9164
Marina del Rey, CA 90292 www.filmarchivesonline.com
Footage: 1890s–Present, Contemporary, Educational, Feature Films, People, Sports, Travel & Vintage

Film Bank, Inc./Corbis Motion (866) 473-5264 / (323) 602-5750
3455 S. La Cienega Blvd. FAX (323) 602-5837
Los Angeles, CA 90016 www.corbismotion.com
Footage: Aerials, Animals, Archival and Contemporary Sports, Medical, Nature, News, People, Science, Special FX, Technology, Time-Lapse, Underwater & Worldwide Locations

Fish Films Footage World (818) 905-1071
4548 Van Noord Ave. FAX (818) 905-0301
Studio City, CA 91604 www.footageworld.com
Footage: Aerials, Americana, Archival, Cartoons, Cities, Classic TV, Commericals, Computer Graphics, Contemporary, Cultures, Educational, Extreme Sports, High Def, Historical, Landmarks, Lifestyles, Nature, Newsreels, Oddities, Scenics, Time-Lapse, Travel, Underwater, Wildlife & Worldwide Locations

FoodPix (323) 257-4400
99 Pasadena Ave. FAX (323) 257-3122
South Pasadena, CA 91030 www.foodpix.com
Photos: Food

Footage Hollywood (818) 760-1500
10520 Magnolia Blvd. FAX (818) 760-1532
North Hollywood, CA 91601 www.footagehollywood.com
Footage: Celebrity Newsreel, Interviews & Vintage–Present Film Trailers

The Footage Store (818) 556-6080
2121 Scott Rd., Ste. 201 FAX (818) 556-6080
Burbank, CA 91504 www.footagestore.com
Footage: All Subjects

Footage-Now (310) 951-5266
3007 Washington Blvd., Ste. 220
Marina Del Rey, CA 90292
Footage: 35mm Motion Picture Images, Aerials, Backgrounds, Beaches, Cityscapes, Clouds, Contemporary, Kids, Landmarks, Scenics & Suns

FootageBank HD/ footagehead Royalty Free (310) 822-1400 / (888) 653-1400
1733 Abbot Kinney Blvd., Ste. C FAX (310) 822-4100
Venice, CA 90291 www.footagebank.com
Footage: 35mm and High Def, Aerials, Animals, Archival, Landscapes, Space, Technology, Time-Lapse, Travel, Underwater & Worldwide Locations

FootageFinder (775) 323-0965 / (800) 852-2330
940 Matley Ln., Ste. 1 FAX (775) 323-1055
Reno, NV 89502 www.footagefinder.com
Footage: Fighter Jets, Ghost Towns, Las Vegas and Reno Nevada, Outdoor Activities, Steam Locomotives, Western States & WWII Aircraft

Four Palms Royalty Free Digital Video (703) 834-0200 / (800) 747-2567
11260 Roger Bacon Dr., Ste. 502 FAX (703) 834-0219
Reston, VA 20190 www.fourpalms.com
Footage: Aerials, American and European Scenes, Animals, Animation, Insects, Nature, People, Professions, Space, Sports, Time-Lapse & Transportation

Framepool Inc. (310) 402-4626 / (800) 331-1314
10905 Ohio Ave., Ste. 116 FAX (866) 928-6637
Los Angeles, CA 90024 www.framepool.com
Footage: Aerials, Aerospace, Agriculture, Animals, Cityscapes, Clouds, Commercials, Contemporary, Cultures, Deserts, Flowers, International People and Scenery, Landscapes, Lightning, Lifestyles, Mountains, Nature, Scenics, Seasons, Space, Stars/Comets/Planets, Storms, Time-Lapse, Traffic, Transportation, Underwater & Wildlife

Framepool Inc. (305) 401-8597 / (800) 331-1314
3033 Silver Palm Dr. FAX (866) 928-6637
Edgewater, FL 32141 www.framepool.com
Footage: Aerials, Aerospace, Agriculture, Animals, Cityscapes, Clouds, Commercials, Contemporary, Cultures, Deserts, Flowers, International People and Scenery, Landscapes, Lightning, Lifestyles, Mountains, Nature, Scenic, Seasons, Space, Stars/Comets/Planets, Storms, Time-Lapse, Traffic, Transportation, Underwater & Wildlife

Freewheelin' Films Stock Footage (970) 925-2640 (888) 740-0360
44895 Hwy 82 FAX **(970) 925-9369**
Aspen, CO 81611 **www.fwf.com**
Footage: Aerials, Cityscapes, Motor Sports, Scenics, Sports & Travelogues

Getty Images (323) 202-4200 (800) 462-4379
6300 Wilshire Blvd., 16th Fl. **www.gettyimages.com**
Los Angeles, CA 90048
Photos: All Subjects, Illustration & Film

A **Global ImageWorks, LLC** (201) 384-7715
65 Beacon St. FAX **(201) 501-8971**
Haworth, NJ 07641 **www.globalimageworks.com**
Footage: 9/11, Aerials, Cityscapes, Contemporary, Entertainment, Global Conflict, Historic, Interviews, Lifestyles, Music, Nature, Politics, Pop Culture, Science, Technology, Terrorism, Time Lapse, Underwater & World locations

Great Waves/Delaney Films (805) 653-2699
473 Mariposa Dr. FAX **(805) 653-2699**
Ventura, CA 93001
Footage: Ocean Scenes & Surfing

Greg Hensley Productions (970) 984-3158
www.greghensley.com
Footage: High Def, Time-Lapse & Wildlife

HBO Archives (212) 512-7171 (877) 426-1121
1100 Avenue of the Americas FAX **(212) 512-5225**
New York, NY 10036 **www.hboarchives.com**
Footage: Entertainment News Collection, Contemporary Stock From HBO Films, High Def, Iconic Sports, Newsreels & Royalty-Free Wildlife Footage

Historic Films (631) 477-9700 (800) 249-1940
211 Third St. FAX **(631) 477-9800**
Greenport, NY 11944 **www.historicfilms.com**
Footage: 1895–Present, All Subjects, Historical, Hollywood, Musical Performances & Newsreels

The Hollywood Film Registry (310) 456-8184
5473 Santa Monica Blvd., Ste. 408 FAX **(323) 957-2159**
Los Angeles, CA 90029
Footage: Current & Historical

Hollywood Licensing, LLC (310) 442-5685
12233 W. Olympic Blvd., Ste. 170 FAX **(310) 442-5683**
Los Angeles, CA 90064 **www.hollywoodlicensing.com**
Footage: All Subjects, America's Funniest Home Videos & Red Bull Extreme Sports

Hot Shots/Corbis Motion (212) 375-7622 (866) 473-5264
902 Broadway FAX **(212) 807-0221**
New York, NY 10010 **www.corbismotion.com**
Footage: Aerials, Archival, Contemporary, Culture, Landmarks, Lifestyles, Newsreels, Scenics, Time-Lapse & Worldwide Locations

Image Bank Films and Archive Films by Getty Images (800) 462-4379
6300 Wilshire Blvd., 16th Floor FAX **(323) 202-4207**
Los Angeles, CA 90048 **www.gettyimages.com**
Footage: Archival & Contemporary

Inter Video (818) 843-3624
2211 N. Hollywood Way FAX **(818) 843-6884**
Burbank, CA 91505 **www.intervideo24.com**
Footage: Aviation, Computer Graphics, Medical, News, Space, Sports, Travel & Weather

International Travel Films (323) 461-9994
224 N. Rossmore Ave. FAX **(323) 461-9996**
Los Angeles, CA 90004 **www.itfstock.com**
Footage: People, Ships, Trains & Worldwide Locations

ITN Source (818) 953-4115
3500 W. Olive Ave., Ste. 1490 FAX **(818) 953-4137**
Burbank, CA 91505 **www.itnsource.com**
Footage: News

Joan Kramer & Associates, Inc. (310) 446-1866
10490 Wilshire Blvd., Ste. 1701 FAX **(310) 446-1856**
Los Angeles, CA 90024 **www.erwinkramer.com**
Photos: Corporate, Glamour, Industry, Leisure, People, Scenics, Underwater & World Travel

John Sandy Productions, Inc. (303) 721-6121
P.O. Box 5104 FAX **(303) 721-0466**
Englewood, CO 80155 **www.jsptv.com**
Footage: Business, Extreme Sports, Medical, Mountain Biking, Outdoor Sports & Skiing

Kesser Post Production/ Kesser Image Library (305) 663-4443
4601 Ponce De Leon Blvd. FAX **(305) 663-4446**
Coral Gables, FL 33146 **www.kesser.com**
Footage: All Subjects

LA News Service (310) 345-1437
713 Hamden Pl. FAX **(310) 230-0817**
Pacific Palisades, CA 90342 **www.highdefinition.net**
Footage & Photos: 1982–1997 Los Angeles Accidents, Earthquakes, Fires, Police Pursuits & Storms
High Def Footage: Amsterdam, Berlin, Hawaii, LA, London, National Parks, San Francisco, Scenic & Views

Larry Dorn Associates/ World Backgrounds (323) 935-6266
5919 W. Third St., Ste. 1D FAX **(323) 935-9523**
Los Angeles, CA 90036 **www.worldbackgrounds.com**
Footage: American/International Locations, Jets, Scenics, Small Aircraft, Sports, Transportation, Underwater & World War II

The Library of Moving Images (323) 469-7499
6671 Sunset Blvd., Ste. 1581 FAX **(323) 469-7559**
Hollywood, CA 90028 **www.libraryofmovingimages.com**
Footage: 1890s–Present Historical Hollywood & 20th Century Images and Events

LifeStockPhotos.com (951) 609-8020 (909) 244-8498
31882 Birchwood Dr. **www.lifestockphotos.com**
Lake Elsinore, CA 92532
Footage & Photos: All Subjects

Linear Cycle Productions (818) 347-9880
P.O. Box 2608 FAX **(818) 347-9880**
North Hills, CA 91393 **www.linearcycleproductions.com**
Footage: People & Vintage–1990

Louis Wolfson II Florida Moving Image Archive (305) 375-1505
101 W. Flagler St. FAX **(305) 375-4436**
Miami, FL 33130 **www.fmia.org**
Footage: The Caribbean, Cuba, Florida, Miami & Space Program

Jay Maisel (212) 431-5013
190 Bowery FAX **(212) 925-6092**
New York, NY 10012 **www.jaymaisel.com**
Photos: Africa, Europe, Landscapes, People, Travel & U.S.

March of Time Newsreels and Documentaries (212) 512-7171 (212) 512-5664
1100 Avenue of the Americas FAX **(212) 512-7040**
New York, NY 10036 **www.themarchoftime.net**

Maxx Images, Inc. (604) 985-2560 (888) 511-3939
711 W. 15th St. FAX **(604) 985-2590**
N. Vancouver, BC V7M 1T2 Canada
www.maxximages.com
Footage: Aerials, British Columbia, Killer Whales, Mountains, Oceans, Underwater & Wildlife

Media Bakery, LLC (888) 899-6809
Footage & Photos: All Subjects FAX **(805) 682-9327**
www.mediabakery.com

Michael Ochs Archives (310) 306-6111
524 Victoria Ave. FAX **(310) 821-4908**
Venice, CA 90291 **www.michaelochs.com**
Photos: Celebrities, Music & Photo Journalism

Military Combat Stock Library (503) 597-7030
5801 N.W. Cornelius Pass Rd. FAX **(503) 597-7037**
Hillsboro, OR 97124 **www.militarylibrary.net**

Moe DiSesso Film Library (661) 255-7969
24233 Old Rd. FAX (661) 255-8179
Santa Clarita, CA 91321
Footage: Animals

National Geographic Digital Motion (310) 734-5302 / (877) 730-2022
9100 Wilshire Blvd., Ste. 401E FAX (310) 858-5801
Beverly Hills, CA 90212 www.ngdigitalmotion.com
Footage: Archeology, Architecture, Ceremonies, Cities, Landmarks, Natural Disasters, Natural History, People, Wildlife & World Scenes

NBC News Archives (818) 840-4249 / (212) 664-3797
3000 W. Alameda Ave., Ste. 3352 FAX (818) 840-4388
Burbank, CA 91523 www.nbcnewsarchives.com
Footage: NBC News from 1940s–Present

New & Unique Videos (619) 644-3000 / (800) 365-8433
7323 Rondel Court FAX (619) 644-3001
San Diego, CA 92119 www.newuniquevideos.com
Footage: Aerials, Animals, Archival Film, Beaches and Sunsets, Bloopers, Cities, Contemporary, Corporate/Industrial, Current Events, High Def and Betacom SP, International, Lifestyles, Medical, Military, People, Scenics, Sports, Travel and Locations, Technological, Underwater & Wildlife

NHL Hockey Archive (201) 750-5860 / (201) 750-5800
240 Pegasus Ave. FAX (201) 750-5850
Northvale, NJ 07647 www.nhlhockeyarchive.com
Footage: NHL Hockey 1920s–Present

Oddball Film + Video (415) 558-8112 / (415) 558-8122
275 Capp St. FAX (415) 558-8116
San Francisco, CA 94110 www.oddballfilm.com
Footage: Archival, Contemporary & Offbeat

Odyssey Productions, Inc. (503) 223-3480
2800 NW Thurman St. FAX (503) 223-3493
Portland, OR 97210 www.odysseypro.com
Footage: All Subjects

Omega Media Group, Inc. (770) 449-8870
3100 Medlock Bridge Rd., Ste. 100 FAX (770) 449-5463
Norcross, GA 30071 www.omegamediagroup.com
Footage: All Subjects

Pan American Video (707) 822-3800 / (800) 726-2634
Footage: All Subjects 1900s–1970s FAX (707) 822-0800
www.panamvideo.com

Paramount Pictures - Stock Footage Library (323) 956-8582
5555 Melrose Ave.
Hollywood, CA 90038
Footage: 1920s–Present Paramount Features and Television

Photodisc by Getty Images (323) 202-4200 / (800) 462-4379
6300 Wilshire Blvd., 16th Fl. www.gettyimages.com
Los Angeles, CA 90048
Footage: All Subjects; Royalty-Free

Photovault (415) 552-9682
1045 17th St. www.photovault.com
San Francisco, CA 94107
Footage & Photos: All Subjects

PicturesNow.com (415) 435-1076
Digital Photos: Historic Photo Library FAX (415) 435-5027
www.picturesnow.com

Producers Library (818) 752-9097 / (800) 944-2135
10832 Chandler Blvd. FAX (818) 752-9196
North Hollywood, CA 91601 www.producerslibrary.com
Footage: 35mm and High Def: Cities, Feature Film Outtakes, Historic, Hollywood, Locations, Newsreels & Scenics

Pyramid Media (310) 828-7577 / (800) 421-2304
P.O. Box 1048 FAX (310) 453-9083
Santa Monica, CA 90406 www.pyramidmedia.com
Footage: Animals, Geography, Medical, Nature, Safety, Science, Sports & Vintage Educational

Questar, Inc. (312) 266-9400 / (800) 544-8422
307 N. Michigan Ave., Ste 500 FAX (312) 266-9523
Chicago, IL 60601 www.questar1.com
Footage: Travel

Reel Orange (949) 548-4524
316 La Jolla Dr. FAX (949) 548-0749
Newport Beach, CA 92663 www.reelorange.com
Footage: Aerials, Environmental & Grand Canyon

Robertstock/ClassicStock (800) 786-6300
4203 Locust St. FAX (800) 786-1920
Philadelphia, PA 19104 www.classicstock.com
Photos: 1920s-1990s Lifestyles

Rocky Mountain Motion Pictures (323) 461-9900 / (435) 649-1030
937 N. Citrus Ave. FAX (323) 461-0100
Los Angeles, CA 90038 www.rmmp.com
Footage: All Subjects

Royaltyfreestore.com (503) 521-9004
13500 SW Pacific Hwy, Ste. 144 FAX (503) 521-9004
Tigard, OR 97224 www.royaltyfreestore.com

SF.V International (813) 884-5963
11219 Bloomington Dr. FAX (813) 888-6713
Tampa, FL 33635 www.stockfilmvideo.com
Footage: Archival & Contemporary

Shooting Star International (323) 469-2020
1441 N. McCadden Pl. FAX (323) 464-0880
Los Angeles, CA 90028 www.shootingstaragency.com
Photos: Celebrities, Entertainment, Geography, Glamour, Historical, Human Interest, Movie Stills & News

Silverman Stock Footage (917) 470-9104
210 Douglass St. www.silvermanstockfootage.com
Brooklyn, NY 11217
Footage: Aerials, Airplanes, Americana, Animals, Architecture, Archival, Cityscapes, Clouds, Contemporary, Cultures, Deserts, Extreme Sports, Flowers, International People, Landscapes, Lifestyles, Nature, Oceans, Scenics, Space, Storms, Suns and Moons, Time-Lapse, Traffic & Underwater

Sony Pictures Stock Footage (310) 244-3704 / (323) 857-8180
10202 W. Washington Blvd.
Turner Bldg., Ste. 4314
Culver City, CA 90232
www.sonypicturesstockfootage.com
Footage: Action, Aerials, Aerospace, Airplanes, Americana, Animals, Architecture, Cityscapes, Clouds, Contemporary, Cultures, Deserts, Driving Shots, Explosions, Fires, Forests, Futuristic, Highways, Historical Landmarks, International People and Scenery, Landscapes, Lightning, Mountains, Nature, Oceans, Rivers, Rural, Scenic, Seasons, Skies, Space, Stars/Comets/Planets, Storms, Suns and Moons, Traffic, Trains, Transportation, Travel, Underwater & Wildlife

The Source Stock Footage Library, Inc. (520) 298-4810
140 S. Camino Seco, Ste. 308 FAX (520) 290-8831
Tucson, AZ 85710 www.sourcefootage.com
Footage: Aerials, Business, Clouds, Destinations, Lifestyles, Sports, Technology, Time-Lapse & Underwater

Spalla Video (212) 765-4646 / (914) 476-4880
99 Buena Vista Ave., First Fl.
Yonkers, NY 10701
Footage: Celebrities & Historic Events

Sports Cinematography Group (310) 785-9100 (212) 744-5333
73 Market St. FAX **(310) 564-7500**
Venice, CA 90291 **www.sportscinematographygroup.com**
Footage: Extreme Sports, Motor Racing, Nature, Sports & Wildlife

The Stock Shop/Medichrome/ Anatomy Works (212) 453-3426 (800) 493-4305
116 E. 27th St., Fifth Fl. FAX **(212) 447-9732**
New York, NY 10016 **www.blackstar.com**
Photos: Medical & Medical Illustrations

Storm Video (262) 443-0352
P.O. Box 161 **www.stormvideo.com**
Cross Plains, WI 53528
Footage: Blizzard, Clouds, Hurricanes, Lightning, Storm Chasing, Supercells & Tornadoes

StormStock (817) 276-9500
P.O. Box 122020 FAX **(817) 795-1132**
Arlington, TX 76012 **www.stormstock.com**
Footage: 16mm, 35mm, Blizzards, Beaches, Caribbean, Clouds, Disasters, Environmental, Fires, Flash Floods, Hail, High Def, High Resolution, Hurricane Katrina, Hurricanes, Landscapes, Lightning, Microbursts, Natural Disasters, Natural History, Nature, Oceans, Radar, Science, Seasons, Skies, Storm Clouds, Storms, Sunrises, Sunsets, Time-Lapse, Tornadoes, Traffic & Waves

Third Millennium Films (212) 675-8500
89 Fifth Ave., Ste. 1002 FAX **(212) 675-6042**
New York, NY 10003 **www.thirdmillenniumfilms.net**
Footage: Archival, Animals, Lifestyles, New York City Aerials, Time-Lapse, Vintage & World Locations

Thought Equity Motion (866) 815-6599
4130 Cahuenga Blvd., Ste. 315 **www.thoughtequity.com**
Universal City, CA 91602
Footage: Aerials, Aerospace, Americana, Animals, Architecture, Archival, Cityscapes, Commercials, Computer Graphics, Cultures, Extreme Sports, Flowers, Historical Landmarks, International People and Scenery, Landscapes, Lifestyles, Nature, Newsreels, Rural, Scenic, Seasons, Sports, Time-Lapse, Travel & Wildlife

Tim Allen & Associates (850) 763-5795
1118 Jenks Ave. FAX **(850) 785-3508**
Panama City, FL 32401 **www.timallenphotography.com**
Photos: All Subjects

UCLA Film and Television Archive (323) 466-8559
1015 N. Cahuenga Blvd. FAX **(323) 461-6317**
Hollywood, CA 90038
Footage: 1900s–1980s Newsreels

Universal Studios Stock Footage Library (818) 777-1695
100 Universal Plaza FAX **(818) 866-0763**
Bldg. 2313A, Lower Level **www.filmmakersdestination.com**
Universal City, CA 91608
Footage: All Subjects

US Air Force Motion Picture Office (310) 235-7522 (310) 235-7511
10880 Wilshire Blvd., Ste. 1240 FAX **(310) 235-7500**
Los Angeles, CA 90024
Footage: Air Force

US Army Office of Public Affairs (310) 235-7621 (310) 235-7622
10880 Wilshire Blvd., Ste. 1250 FAX **(310) 235-6075**
Los Angeles, CA 90024
www.defenselink.mil/faq/pis/PC12FILM.html
Footage: U.S. Army

Video Tape Library, Inc./VTL (323) 656-4330
1525 N. Crescent Heights Blvd., Ste. 2 FAX **(323) 656-8746**
Los Angeles, CA 90046 **www.videotapelibrary.com**
Footage: Aerials, Americana, Animals, Archival, Bloopers, Cities, Cultures, Downloadable Comps, Extreme and Recreational Sports, HD Footage, Historical, Landmarks, Landscapes, Lifestyles, News, People, Professionals, Time-Lapse, Travel Locations & Underwater

WGBH Stock Sales (617) 300-3901
One Guest St. FAX **(617) 300-1056**
Brighton, MA 02135 **www.wgbhstocksales.org**
Footage: American Experience, Antiques Roadshow, Frontline, Julia Child & NOVA

White Rain Films, Ltd. (206) 682-5417 (800) 816-5244
2009 Dexter Ave. North FAX **(206) 682-3038**
Seattle, WA 98109 **www.whiterainfilms.com**
Footage: Aerials, Icons, People, Time-Lapse, Travel & Wildlife

Wings Wildlife Production, Inc. (949) 830-7845
Two McLaren, Ste. A FAX **(949) 830-5116**
Irvine, CA 92618 **www.wildlifelibrary.com**
Footage: 35mm African and North American Wildlife

Wish You Were Here Film & Video, Inc. (866) 347-8625 (818) 371-9649
www.wywhstock.com
Footage: 35mm and High Def, Aerials, Destinations, Landmarks, Scenics, Time-Lapse & Wildlife

WPA Film Library (800) 777-2223 (708) 460-0555
16101 S. 108th Ave. FAX **(708) 460-0187**
Orland Park, IL 60467 **www.wpafilmlibrary.com**
Footage: 1895-21st Century, Americana, Classic Commercials and Industrial Films, High Def, Historic, Music, Politics & UFO Collection

WTTW Digital Archives (773) 509-5412
5400 N. St. Louis Ave. FAX **(773) 509-5307**
Chicago, IL 60625 **www.wttwdigitalarchives.com**
Footage: Aerials, Airplanes, Americana, Architecture, Archival, Cityscapes, Contemporary, Cultures, Deserts, Flowers, Historical Landmarks, International People and Scenery, Landscapes, Lifestyles, Mountains, Nature, Oddities, Rural, Scenic, Seasons, Sports, Trains & Transportation

11:11 MediaWorks (818) 780-4466
6611 Valjean Ave., Ste. 108 FAX **(818) 780-4467**
Van Nuys, CA 91406 **www.1111mediaworks.com**
(Feature Film Titles, Logos, Station ID Packages, TV Network/Cable ID's and Packages & TV Show Titles and Opens)

3 Ring Circus (323) 466-5300
1040 N. Sycamore Ave. FAX **(323) 466-5310**
Los Angeles, CA 90038 **www.3ringcircus.tv**
(Animated Logos, Cable ID's, Cable Packages, Feature Film, ID's, Logos, Opens, Station ID Packages, TV Network ID's, TV Network Packages & TV Show)

60Hz, Inc. (310) 264-8498
1660 Stanford St. FAX **(310) 264-8497**
Santa Monica, CA 90404 **www.60-hz.com**

A52 (310) 586-0650
2308 Broadway FAX **(310) 586-0651**
Santa Monica, CA 90404 **www.a52.com**
(Feature Film Titles, Logos, Station ID Packages, TV Network/Cable ID's and Packages & TV Show Titles and Opens)

Aberdeen Captioning, Inc. (949) 858-4463 (800) 688-6621
22362 Gilberto, Ste. 120 FAX **(949) 858-4405**
Rancho Santo Margarita, CA 92688 **www.abercap.com**
(Closed Captioning, DVD Subtitles, Foreign, Real Time Captioning & Subtitles)

Acme Filmworks, Inc. (323) 464-7805
6525 Sunset Blvd., Ste. G-10 FAX **(323) 464-6614**
Hollywood, CA 90028 **www.acmefilmworks.com**
(Captions, Feature Film Titles, Logos, Station ID Packages, Subtitles, TV Network/Cable ID's and Packages & TV Show Titles and Opens)

Acorn Entertainment (310) 568-0781
5777 W. Century Blvd., 10th Fl.
Los Angeles, CA 90045 **www.acornentertainment.com**
(Feature Film Titles, Logos, Station ID Packages, TV Network/Cable ID's and Packages & TV Show Titles and Opens)

Altered Illusions (818) 471-004
www.alteredillusions.com
(Feature Film Titles, Logos, Station ID Packages, TV Network/Cable ID's and Packages & TV Show Titles and Opens)

Animax Entertainment (818) 787-4444
6627 Valjean Ave. FAX **(818) 374-9140**
Van Nuys, CA 91406 **www.animaxent.com**
(Feature Film Titles, Logos, Station ID Packages, TV Network/Cable ID's and Packages & TV Show Titles and Opens)

AniMill (818) 972-9116 (407) 654-4494
200 E. Angeleno Ave., Ste. 312 **www.animill.com**
Burbank, CA 91502
(Animated Logos, Cable ID's, Cable Packages, Feature Film, ID's, Logos, Opens, Packages, Station ID Packages, Titles, TV Show, Visual Description, TV Network ID's & TV Network Packages)

Antifreeze Design (619) 795-2940
5241 Lewison Court **www.antifreezemotiongraphics.com**
San Diego, CA 92120
(Feature Film Titles, Logos, Station ID Packages, TV Network/Cable ID's and Packages & TV Show Titles and Opens)

Associates & Yamashita (310) 664-9500
13600 Marina Pointe Dr., Ste. 1007 FAX **(310) 664-9977**
Marina del Rey, CA 90292 **www.aayamashita.com**
(Feature Film Titles, Logos, Station ID Packages, TV Network/Cable ID's and Packages & TV Show Titles and Opens)

Autonomy, Inc. (323) 662-7048
www.autonomy.tv
(Logos, Station ID Packages, TV Network/Cable ID's and Packages & TV Show Titles and Opens)

AvatarLabs (818) 728-6778
16838 Addison St. FAX **(818) 728-6782**
Encino, CA 91436 **www.avatarlabs.com**
(Feature Film Titles, Logos, Station ID Packages, TV Network/Cable ID's and Packages & TV Show Titles and Opens)

Belief, LLC (310) 998-0099
1832 Franklin St. FAX **(310) 998-0066**
Santa Monica, CA 90404 **www.belief.com**
(Captions, Feature Film Titles, Logos, Station ID Packages, TV Network/Cable ID's and Packages & TV Show Titles and Opens)

Berkos & Associates (818) 788-8246
(Feature Film Titles, Logos, Station ID Packages, TV Network/Cable ID's and Packages & TV Titles and Opens)

Big Machine Design (818) 841-2226
201 N. Hollywood Way FAX **(323) 372-3926**
Burbank, CA 91505 **www.bigmachine.net**

Black Box Digital, LLC (310) 828-5832
409 Santa Monica Blvd., Ste. E FAX **(310) 828-8998**
Santa Monica, CA 90401 **www.blackboxdigital.com**
(Feature Film Titles, Logos, Station ID Packages, TV Network/Cable ID's and Packages & TV Show Titles and Opens)

Blind (310) 314-1618
1702 Olympic Blvd. FAX **(310) 314-1718**
Santa Monica, CA 90404 **www.blind.com**
(Feature Film Titles, Logos, Station ID Packages, TV Network/Cable ID's and Packages & TV Show Titles and Opens)

Bling Imaging (323) 874-3003
1011 N. Fuller Ave., Ste. B **www.blingimaging.com**
West Hollywood, CA 90046
(Animated Logos, AVI Subtitles, Cable ID's, Cable Packages, Domestic, DVD Subtitles, Feature Film, Foreign, ID's, Logos, Opens, Station ID Packages, Subtitles, Titles, TV Network ID's, TV Network Packages, TV Show, Video Subtitles & Visual Description)

Blue 105 (818) 563-4335
2600 W. Olive Ave., Fifth Fl. FAX **(818) 563-4223**
Burbank, CA 91505 **www.blue105.com**
(Domestic and Foreign Language Captions and Subtitles)

Blur Studio, Inc. (310) 581-8848
589 Venice Blvd. FAX **(310) 581-8850**
Venice, CA 90291 **www.blur.com**
(Feature Film Titles, Logos, Station ID Packages, TV Network/Cable ID's and Packages & TV Show Titles and Opens)

Brand New School (310) 315-9959
2415 Michigan Ave., Bldg. H, Ste. 100 FAX **(310) 315-9939**
Santa Monica, CA 90404 **www.brandnewschool.com**
(Feature Film Titles, Logos, Station ID Packages, TV Network/Cable ID's and Packages & TV Show Titles and Opens)

Buck (213) 623-0111
515 W. Seventh St., Fourth Fl. FAX **(213) 623-0117**
Los Angeles, CA 90014 **www.buck.tv**

Buena Vista Imaging (818) 560-5284
500 S. Buena Vista St., Camera Bldg. FAX **(818) 563-4735**
Burbank, CA 91521 **www.disney.com**
(Feature Film Titles & Subtitles)

Bully Bros. Post (310) 874-7000
1813 Centinela Ave. FAX **(310) 745-1645**
Santa Monica, CA 90404 **www.bullybrospost.com**

CaptionMax (818) 295-2500 (612) 341-3566
441 N. Varney St. FAX **(818) 295-2509**
Burbank, CA 91502 **www.captionmax.com**
(Audio Description, Closed Captioning, Domestic, DVD Subtitles, Foreign, Real Time Captioning, Subtitles & Video Subtitles)

Captions, Inc. (818) 260-2700 (800) 227-8466
640 S. Glenwood Pl. FAX **(818) 260-2850**
Burbank, CA 91506 **www.captionsinc.com**
(Captions & Subtitles)

Charles Lecoanet Design (310) 839-4716 (310) 621-1148
10767 Woodbine St., Ste. 212 **www.charleslecoanet.com**
Los Angeles, CA 90034
(Feature Film, ID Packages, Logos, Opens, Titles & TV Shows)

Charlie Company (310) 264-7100
1758 Berkeley St. FAX **(310) 264-7104**
Santa Monica, CA 90404 **www.charlieco.tv**

Cinergy Creative (310) 455-2490 (818) 623-6558
www.cinergycreative.com
(Feature Film Titles, Logos, Station ID Packages, TV Network/Cable ID's and Packages & TV Show Titles and Opens)

Cinetyp, Inc. (323) 463-8569
843 Seward St. FAX **(323) 463-4129**
Hollywood, CA 90038 **www.cinetyp.com**
(Captions & Subtitles)

Closed Captioning Services, Inc. (818) 848-8826
4450 Lakeside Dr., Ste. 350 FAX **(818) 848-2023**
Burbank, CA 91505
(Captions, Feature Film Titles, Subtitles & Video Description)

CTS LanguageLink (800) 208-2620
9920 Jordan Circle, Ste. A FAX **(360) 693-9292**
Santa Fe Springs, CA 90670 **www.ctslanguagelink.com**
(Captions & Subtitles)

Daily Post/Transcripts (310) 417-4844
6701 Center Dr. West, Ste. 1111 FAX **(310) 410-1543**
Los Angeles, CA 90045 **www.dailypost.tv**

Deborah Ross Film Design (310) 559-5600
10536 Culver Blvd., Ste. A FAX **(310) 559-5602**
Culver City, CA 90232 **www.drfilmdesign.com**
(Feature Film Titles, Logos & TV Show Titles and Opens)

Design & Direction, Inc. (310) 395-6730
437 San Vicente Blvd., Ste. C FAX **(310) 395-0520**
Santa Monica, CA 90402 **www.ddi.ms**
(Feature Film Titles, Logos, Station ID Packages, TV Network/Cable ID's and Packages & TV Show Titles and Opens)

Digiscope (310) 315-6060
1447 Cloverfield Blvd. FAX **(310) 828-5856**
Santa Monica, CA 90404 **www.digiscope.com**
(Captions, Feature Film Titles, Logos & Subtitles)

Digital Dimension (818) 344-3435
18425 Burbank Blvd. FAX **(818) 344-3451**
Tarzana, CA 91356 **www.digitaldimension.com**
(Captions, Feature Film Titles, Logos, Station ID Packages, TV Network/Cable ID's and Packages & TV Show Titles and Opens)

Digital Jungle Post Production (323) 962-0867
6363 Santa Monica Blvd. FAX **(323) 962-9960**
Hollywood, CA 90038 **www.digijungle.com**
(Animated Logos, Cable ID's, Cable Packages, DVD Subtitles, Feature Film, ID's, Logos, Opens, Station ID Packages, Subtitles, Titles, TV Network ID's, TV Network Packages, TV Show & Video Subtitles)

Doglight Studios, LLC (323) 222-1928
600 Moulton Ave., Ste. 302 FAX **(323) 222-8151**
Los Angeles, CA 90031 **www.doglight.com**
(Logos & TV Show Titles and Opens)

Dubscape, Inc. (818) 456-1051
7543 Loma Verde Ave. FAX **(818) 456-1046**
Canoga Park, CA 91303 **www.dubscape.com**
(Captions)

DUCK Studios, a.k.a. Duck Soup Studios (310) 478-0771
2205 Stoner Ave. FAX **(310) 478-0773**
Los Angeles, CA 90064 **www.duckstudios.com**
(Feature Film Titles, Logos, Station ID Packages & TV Show Titles and Opens)

Elektrashock, Inc. (310) 399-4985
1320 Main St. FAX **(310) 399-4972**
Venice, CA 90291 **www.elektrashock.com**
(Feature Film Titles, Logos, Station ID Packages, TV Network/Cable ID's and Packages & Show Titles and Opens)

European Captioning Institute (ECI) (818) 238-4231
303 N. Glenoaks Blvd., Ste. 200 FAX **(818) 238-4266**
Burbank, CA 91502 **www.ecisubtitling.com**
(Audio Description, Closed Captioning, Domestic, DVD Subtitles, Feature Film, Foreign, Real Time Captioning, TV Show & Video Subtitles)

Filmworks/FX, Inc. (310) 577-3213
4121 Redwood Ave., Ste. 101 FAX **(310) 577-3215**
Los Angeles, CA 90066 **www.filmworksfx.com**
(Feature Film Titles & TV Show Titles and Opens)

FISH EGGS (310) 452-8251
1261 Electric Ave. FAX **(310) 452-8364**
Venice, CA 90291 **www.fisheggs.tv**
(Captions, Feature Film Titles, Logos, Station ID Packages, Subtitles, TV Network/Cable ID's and Packages & TV Show Opens and Titles)

Framework Studio, LLC (310) 815-1245
3535 Hayden Ave., Ste. 300 FAX **(310) 815-9821**
Culver City, CA 90232 **www.frameworkla.com**
(Animated Logos, Cable ID's and Packages, Domestic, Feature Film, ID's, Logos, Opens, Station ID Packages, Titles, TV Show & TV Network ID's and Packages)

Fuel (310) 558-8755
1040 N. Sycamore Ave. **www.fueldesign.com**
Hollywood, CA 90038
(Captions, Feature Film Titles, Logos, Station ID Packages, Subtitles, TV Network/Cable ID's and Packages & TV Show Titles and Opens)

FutureCircus (310) 592-8948
FAX **(310) 392-5140**
www.futurecircus.com
(Feature Film Titles, Logos, Station ID Packages, TV Network/Cable ID's and Packages & TV Show Titles and Opens)

Hollywood Title (310) 394-3300
1526 14th St., Ste. 106 FAX **(310) 394-3304**
Santa Monica, CA 90404 **www.hollywoodtitle.com**
(Feature Film Titles, Logos, Subtitles & TV Show Titles and Opens)

Hornet, Inc. (917) 351-0520 (310) 601-1355
3962 Ince Blvd. FAX **(310) 641-2117**
Culver City, CA 90232 **www.hornetinc.com**
(Feature Film Titles, Logos, Station ID Packages, TV Network/Cable ID's and Packages & TV Show Titles and Opens)

Humunculus (310) 827-1800
529 Victoria Ave. **www.humunculus.com**
Venice, CA 90291
(Feature Film Titles, Logos, Station ID Packages, TV Network/Cable ID's and Packages & TV Show Titles and Opens)

Imaginary Forces (323) 957-6868
6526 Sunset Blvd. FAX **(323) 957-9577**
Los Angeles, CA 90028 **www.imaginaryforces.com**
(Feature Film Titles, Logos, Station ID Packages, TV Network/Cable ID's and Packages & TV Show Titles and Opens)

iProbe Multilingual Solutions, Inc. (888) 489-6035
www.iprobesolutions.com
(Animated Logos, Audio Description, AVI Subtitles, Cable ID's, Cable Packages, Closed Captioning, Domestic, DVD Subtitles, Feature Film, Foreign, ID's, Logos, Opens, Real Time Captioning, Station ID Packages, Subtitles, Titles, TV Show, Visual Description, Video Subtitles, TV Network ID's & TV Network Packages)

JBI Studios (818) 592-0056
21432 Wyandotte FAX **(818) 592-6994**
Canoga Park, CA 91303 **www.jbistudios.com**
(Captions & Subtitles)

JR Media Services, Inc. (818) 557-0200
2501 W. Burbank Blvd., Ste. 200 FAX **(818) 557-0201**
Burbank, CA 91505 **www.jrmediaservices.com**
(Audio Description, AVI Subtitles, Closed Captioning, Domestic, DVD Subtitles, Feature Film, Foreign, Subtitles, Titles, TV Network Packages, TV Show, Video Subtitles & Visual Description)

ka-chew! (323) 468-3020
6353 Sunset Blvd. FAX **(323) 468-3021**
Los Angeles, CA 90028 **www.kachew.com**
(Feature Film Titles, Logos, Station ID Packages, TV Network/Cable ID's and Packages & TV Show Titles and Opens)

The Kitchen, a TM Systems Company (818) 306-5300
12711 Ventura Blvd., Ste. 217 **www.thekitchen.tv**
Studio City, CA 91604
(Closed Captioning & Subtitles)

Kurtz & Friends (818) 841-8188
2312 W. Olive Ave. FAX **(818) 841-6263**
Burbank, CA 91506 **www.kurtzandfriends.com**
(Feature Film Titles, Logos & TV Show Titles and Opens)

Lati2d (323) 852-1425
714 N. Laurel Ave. FAX **(323) 852-1426**
Los Angeles, CA 90046 **www.lati2d.com**
(Feature Film Titles, Logos, Menus and DVD Design, Station ID Packages, TV Network/Cable ID's and Packages & TV Show Titles and Opens)

Lava Creative, Inc. (310) 829-5282
953 Fourth St., Ste. 304 FAX **(310) 496-1295**
Santa Monica, CA 90403 **www.lavacreative.tv**
(Animated Logos, Cable ID's, Cable Packages, ID's, Logos, Opens, Packages, Titles, TV Show, TV Network ID's & TV Network Packages)

Level 3 Post (818) 840-7200 (818) 840-7889
2901 W. Alameda, Third Fl. **www.level3post.com**
Burbank, CA 91505

Live Wire Productions & Visual FX (310) 831-6227
P.O. Box 245 **www.livewirefilm.com**
Palos Verdes Estates, CA 90274
(Feature Film Titles, Logos, Station ID Packages, TV Network/Cable ID's and Packages & TV Show Titles and Opens)

Marcland International Communications (818) 557-6677
www.marcland.com
(Domestic and Foreign DVD and Video Subtitles)

Media Access at Group WGBH/ The Caption Center (818) 562-3344
300 E. Magnolia Blvd., Second Fl. FAX **(818) 562-3388**
Burbank, CA 91502 **www.wgbh.org/caption**
(Captions & Subtitles)

Melliott Title Design (818) 345-3099
FAX **(818) 705-6432**
(Feature Film Titles, Subtitles & TV Show Titles)

MFX (323) 969-1011
3400 Barham Blvd. FAX **(323) 969-1015**
Los Angeles, CA 90068 **www.mfxdesign.com**
(Feature Film Titles, Logos, Station ID Packages, TV Network/Cable ID's and Packages & TV Show Titles and Opens)

Michael Kelley Motion Graphics (310) 450-4594
1223 Wilshire Blvd., Ste. 577 FAX **(310) 450-3594**
Santa Monica, CA 90403 **www.michael-kelley.com**
(Feature Film Titles, Logos, Station ID Packages, TV Network/Cable ID's and Packages & TV Show Titles and Opens)

Mind Over Eye, LLC (310) 396-4663 (310) 968-4259
1639 11th St., Ste. 117 FAX **(310) 396-0663**
Santa Monica, CA 90404 **www.mindovereye.com**
(Captions, Feature Film Titles, Logos, Station ID Packages, TV Network/Cable ID's and Packages & TV Show Titles and Opens)

Mixin Pixls (310) 237-6438
www.mixinpixls.com
(Audio Description, AVI Subtitles, Closed Captioning, DVD Subtitles, Feature Film, Foreign, Real Time Captioning, Subtitles, Video Subtitles & Visual Description)

mOcean (310) 481-0808
2440 S. Sepulveda Blvd., Ste. 150 FAX **(310) 481-0807**
Los Angeles, CA 90064 **www.moceanla.com**
(Feature Film Titles, Logos, Station ID Packages, TV Network/Cable ID's and Packages & TV Show Titles and Opens)

Montgomery & Co. Creative (310) 558-4914
8611 Washington Blvd. FAX **(310) 558-4915**
Culver City, CA 90232 **www.montgomerycreative.com**
(Captions, Feature Film Titles, Logos, Station ID Packages, Subtitles, TV Network/Cable ID's and Packages & TV Show Titles and Opens)

Moving Pixels (310) 581-1377
1558 10th St., Ste. D FAX **(310) 496-2072**
Santa Monica, CA 90401 **www.movingpixels.com**
(Logos & TV Show Titles and Opens)

National Captioning Institute (818) 238-0068
303 N. Glenoaks Blvd., Ste. 200
Burbank, CA 91502
(Audio Description, Closed Captioning, DVD Subtitles, Real Time Captioning & Subtitles)

NBC Universal Artworks (212) 664-5972
30 Rockefeller Plaza, Ste. 1622W **www.nbcartworks.com**
New York, NY 10012

OneWorld Language Solutions (323) 848-7993
(Captions & Subtitles) FAX **(323) 848-7995**
www.oneworldlanguage.com

Opticam, Inc. (310) 452-0040
810 Navy St. FAX **(310) 452-0040**
Santa Monica, CA 90405
(Feature Film Titles, Logos, Subtitles & TV Show Titles and Opens)

Pacific Vision Productions, Inc. (626) 441-4869
210 Pasadena Ave. **www.pacificvision.com**
South Pasadena, CA 91030
(Feature Film Titles, Logos & TV Show Titles and Opens)

Dan Perri/Movie Titles (323) 259-1800
1472 Silverwood Dr. FAX **(323) 550-8884**
Los Angeles, CA 90041
(Feature Film Titles, Logos & TV Show Titles and Opens)

Picture Mill (323) 465-8800
6422 Homewood Ave. FAX **(323) 465-8875**
Los Angeles, CA 90028 **www.picturemill.com**
(Feature Film Titles, Logos, Station ID Packages, TV Network/Cable and Packages & TV Show Titles and Opens)

PixelMonger Inc./Scott Billups (818) 990-8993
15120 Hartsook St. **www.pixelmonger.com/esbindex.html**
Sherman Oaks, CA 91403
(Feature Film Titles, Logos, Station ID Packages, TV Network/Cable ID's and Packages & TV Show Titles and Opens)

Planet Blue (310) 899-3877
1250 Sixth St., Ste. 102 FAX **(310) 899-3787**
Santa Monica, CA 90401 **www.planetblue.com**
(Feature Film Titles, Logos, Station ID Packages, TV Network/Cable ID's and Packages & TV Show Titles and Opens)

PlasterCITY Digital Post Facility (323) 469-9800
6500 Sunset Blvd. FAX **(323) 462-4620**
Los Angeles, CA 90028 **www.plastercitypost.com**
(Feature Film, Opens & TV Show)

Point of Origin (818) 392-8735
www.pointoforiginmedia.com

The Post Group (323) 462-2300
6335 Homewood Ave. FAX **(323) 822-7370**
Hollywood, CA 90028 **www.postgroup.com**
(Captions, Feature Film Titles, Station ID Packages, Subtitles, TV Network/Cable ID's and Packages & TV Show Titles and Opens)

Post Logic Studios (323) 461-7887
1800 N. Vine St., Ste. 100 FAX **(323) 461-7790**
Los Angeles, CA 90028 **www.postlogic.com**
(Captions, Feature Film Titles, Logos, Station ID Packages, Subtitles, TV Network/Cable ID's and Packages & TV Show Titles and Opens)

Post Modern Edit, LLC (949) 608-8700
2941 Alton Pkwy FAX **(949) 608-8729**
Irvine, CA 92606 **www.postmodernedit.com**
(Animated Logos, Cable ID's, Closed Captioning, Domestic, DVD Subtitles, Feature Film, Foreign Language, Logos, Station ID Packages, TV Show & Video Subtitles)

Prime Digital Media Services (661) 964-0220
28111 Avenue Stanford FAX **(661) 964-0550**
Valencia, CA 91355 **www.primedigital.com**

PRoGRESS bureau of design (310) 471-7014
12436 Deerbrook **www.progressdesign.com**
Los Angeles, CA 90049
(Logos, Station ID Packages, TV Network/Cable ID's and Packages & TV Show Titles and Opens)

Psychic Bunny (310) 862-4262
453 S. Spring St., Ste. 922 FAX **(213) 614-9046**
Los Angeles, CA 90013 **www.psychicbunny.com**

Radium (310) 264-6440
2115 Colorado Ave. **www.radium.com**
Santa Monica, CA 91404
(Captions, Feature Film Titles, Logos, Station ID Packages, Subtitles, TV Network/Cable ID's and Packages & TV Show Titles and Opens)

Reality Check Studios, Inc. (323) 465-3900 (323) 908-7000
6100 Melrose Ave. FAX **(323) 465-3600**
Los Angeles, CA 90038 **www.realityx.com**
(Feature Film, Foreign and Domestic, ID's, Logos, Opens, Packages, Station ID Packages, Titles, TV Network/Cable & TV Show)

Renegade Animation, Inc. (818) 551-2351
116 N. Maryland Ave., Lower Level FAX **(818) 551-2350**
Glendale, CA 91206 **www.renegadeanimation.com**
(Feature Film Titles, Logos, TV Network/Cable ID's and Packages & TV Show Titles and Opens)

Ring of Fire (310) 966-5055
1538 20th St. FAX **(310) 966-5056**
Santa Monica, CA 90404 **www.ringoffire.com**
(Feature Film Titles, Logos, Station ID Packages, TV Network/Cable ID's and Packages & TV Show Titles and Opens)

Scratch Films (323) 664-9509
www.scratchfilms.net

Shine (323) 937-7470
5410 Wilshire Blvd., Ste. 900 FAX **(323) 937-7420**
Los Angeles, CA 90036 **www.shinestudio.tv**

Sir Reel Pictures (818) 768-9778 (818) 415-7326
8036 Shadyglade Ave. **www.sirreelpictures.com**
North Hollywood, CA 91605
(Feature Film Titles, Logos, Station ID Packages, TV Network/Cable ID's and Packages & TV Show Titles and Opens)

Paul Soady (323) 939-8785
(Captions, Feature Film Titles, Logos, Station ID Packages, Subtitles & TV Network/Cable ID's and Packages)

Sony Pictures Imageworks (310) 840-8000
9050 W. Washington Blvd. FAX **(310) 840-8100**
Culver City, CA 90232 **www.imageworks.com**
(Feature Film Titles & Logos)

Squelch Closed Captioning (310) 702-8985 (310) 702-2662
2121 Cloverfield Blvd., Ste. 202 **www.squelch.cc**
Santa Monica, CA 90404
(Closed Captioning, Domestic, DVD Subtitles, Feature Films, Foreign, Opens, Real Time Captioning, Subtitles, Titles, TV Show, Visual Description & Video Subtitles)

Standard (323) 224-3944
2020 N. Main St., Ste. 227 FAX **(323) 225-6226**
Los Angeles, CA 90031 **www.standardsite.com**
(Captions, Feature Film Titles, Logos, Station ID Packages, Subtitles, TV Network/Cable ID's and Packages & TV Show Titles and Opens)

Stardust Studios (310) 399-6047
1920 Main St., Ste. A FAX **(310) 399-7486**
Santa Monica, CA 90405 **www.stardust.tv**
(Captions, Feature Films Titles, Logos, Station ID Packages, TV Network/Cable ID's and Packages & TV Show Opens and Titles)

Stargate Digital (626) 403-8403
1001 El Centro St. FAX **(626) 403-8444**
South Pasadena, CA 91030 **www.stargatefilms.com**
(Feature Film Titles, Logos & TV Show Titles and Opens)

STEELE Studios (310) 656-7770
5737 Mesmer Ave. FAX **(310) 656-7771**
Culver City, CA 90230 **www.steelevfx.com**
(Logos & TV Show Titles and Opens)

Stokes/Kohne Associates, Inc. (323) 468-2340
742 Cahuenga Blvd. FAX **(323) 468-2345**
Hollywood, CA 90038 **www.stokeskohne.com**
(Animated Logos, Cable ID's, Cable Packages, Feature Film, ID's, Logos, Opens, TV Network ID's & TV Show)

STS Foreign Language Services/ a division of STS Media Services, Inc. (818) 563-3004
P.O. Box 10213 **www.stsforeignlanguage.com**
Burbank, CA 91510
(Closed Captioning, DVD Subtitles, Feature Film Titles, Foreign, Logos, Subtitles, TV Show Titles and Opens & Video Subtitles)

The Studio at New Wave Entertainment (818) 955-5276 (818) 295-8060
3003 W. Olive Ave. FAX **(818) 295-8061**
Burbank, CA 91505 **www.nwe.com**
(Feature Film Titles, Logos, Station ID Packages, TV Network/Cable ID's and Packages & TV Show Titles and Opens)

Subtext Studio/Subtext Semantics (323) 533-0770
www.subtextstudio.com
(Animated Logos, Cable ID's, Cable Packages, Feature Film, ID's, Logos, Opens, Station ID Packages, Titles, TV Network ID's, TV Network Packages & TV Show)

TeamWorks Digital (310) 991-5442
www.teamworksdigital.com
(Feature Film Titles, Logos, Station ID Packages, TV Show Titles and Opens & TV Network/Cable ID's and Packages)

Technicolor Creative Services - Burbank (818) 480-5100 (310) 801-7300
www.technicolor.com

The Thomas Cobb Group (310) 822-1515
4051 Glencoe Ave., Studio 1 FAX **(310) 822-5015**
Venice, CA 90292 **www.tcgstudio.com**
(Feature Film Titles, Logos, Station ID Packages, TV Network/Cable ID's and Packages & TV Show Titles and Opens)

Tigar Hare Studios (818) 907-6663
4485 Matilija Ave. FAX **(818) 907-0693**
Sherman Oaks, CA 91423 **www.tigarhare.com**
(Feature Film Titles, Station ID Packages, TV Network/Cable ID's and Packages & TV Show Titles and Opens)

Titra California, Inc. (818) 244-3663
733 Salem St. FAX **(818) 244-6205**
Glendale, CA 91203 **www.titra.com**
(Captions & Subtitles)

Toon Makers, Inc. (818) 832-8666
17333 Ludlow St. **www.toonmakers.com**
Granada Hills, CA 91344
(Feature Film Titles, Logos, Station ID Packages, TV Network/Cable ID's and Packages & TV Show Titles and Opens)

Trance (323) 651-1114
449 N. Edinburgh Ave. **www.trancedesigns.com**
Los Angeles, CA 90048
(Logos & TV Show Titles and Opens)

Velocity Visuals, Inc. (310) 376-7870
www.velocityfx.com

View Studio, Inc. (805) 745-8814
385 Toro Canyon Rd. www.viewstudio.com
Carpinteria, CA 93013
(Feature Film Titles, Logos, Station ID Packages, TV Network/Cable ID's and Packages & TV Show Titles and Opens)

Visiontext (818) 526-3000
2130 N. Hollywood Way FAX (818) 526-2917
Burbank, CA 91505 www.visiontext.com
(Captions & Subtitles)

Visual Data Media Services, Inc. (818) 558-3363
(888) 418-4782
145 W. Magnolia Blvd. FAX (818) 558-3368
Burbank, CA 91502 www.visualdatainc.com

VITAC (818) 755-0410
(800) 278-4822
4605 Lankershim Blvd., Ste. 250 FAX (818) 755-0411
North Hollywood, CA 91602 www.vitac.com
(Audio Description, Captions, Closed Captioning, DVD Subtitles, Real Time Captioning, Subtitles, Video Subtitles & Visual Description)

Viva Broadcast Design & Production (805) 969-9933
701 Coyote Rd. FAX (805) 969-4482
Santa Barbara, CA 93108 www.vivadesign.com
(Logos, Station ID Packages, TV Network/Cable ID's and Packages & TV Show Titles and Opens)

West Coast Title (818) 953-7102
116 S. Buena Vista St. www.titlesandopticals.com
Burbank, CA 91505
(Feature Film Titles, Logos & TV Show Titles and Opens)

Wicked Liquid FX (949) 250-8786
4120 Birch St., Ste. 122 FAX (949) 250-8701
Newport Beach, CA 92660 www.wickedliquidfx.com
(Captions, Feature Film Titles, Logos, Station ID Packages, Subtitles, TV Network/Cable ID's and Packages & TV Show Titles and Opens)

Wut It Is (323) 467-3300
6121 Santa Monica Blvd., Ste. 201 FAX (323) 467-7480
Los Angeles, CA 90038 www.wutitis.com
(Animated Logos, Cable ID's, Cable Packages, Domestic, Feature Film, Foreign, Logos, Opens, Station ID Packages, Titles, TV Network ID's, TV Network Packages, TV Show & Visual Description)

yU+co. (323) 606-5050
941 N. Mansfield Ave. FAX (323) 606-5040
Los Angeles, CA 90038 www.yuco.com
(Feature Film Titles, Logos, Station ID Packages, TV Network/Cable ID's and Packages & TV Show Titles and Opens)

Zak/Paperno (323) 937-2517
7000 Beverly Blvd.
Los Angeles, CA 90036
(Feature Film Titles, Logos, Station ID Packages, TV Network/Cable ID's and Packages & TV Show Titles and Opens)

Zoic, Inc. (310) 838-0770
3582 Eastham Dr. FAX (310) 838-1169
Culver City, CA 90232 www.zoicstudios.com
(Feature Film Titles)

Oliver Arnold (310) 788-3918
(3D) www.d-a-a.com

Kirk Balden (310) 586-0650
www.a52.com

Anthony Barcelo (310) 788-3918
www.d-a-a.com

Dominik Bauch (310) 788-3918
www.d-a-a.com

Brian Begun (310) 788-3918
www.d-a-a.com

Javier Bello (310) 788-3918
(3D) www.d-a-a.com

Vlad Bina (310) 788-3918
www.d-a-a.com

Tim Bird (310) 586-0650
www.a52.com

James Bohn (310) 392-1212
www.laliquid.com

Thomas Briggs (310) 788-3918
(3D) www.d-a-a.com

Ronn Brown (310) 788-3918
www.d-a-a.com

Steven Browning (310) 788-3918
www.d-a-a.com

Kevin Cahill (310) 450-3448
FAX (310) 450-3448
www.luminetik.com

Kevin Carr (310) 788-3918
www.d-a-a.com

R. Kevin Clarke (310) 788-3918
(3D) www.d-a-a.com

Matt Collorafice (310) 788-3918
www.d-a-a.com

David Crawford (310) 788-3918
(2D) www.d-a-a.com

Brandon Davis (310) 788-3918
(3D) www.d-a-a.com

Andrew Edwards (310) 788-3918
(2D) www.d-a-a.com

Jim Gorman (310) 788-3918
www.d-a-a.com

Robin Graham (310) 788-3918
(2D) www.d-a-a.com

Don Greenberg (310) 788-3918
www.d-a-a.com

Sarah Grossmann (310) 788-3918
(2D) www.d-a-a.com

Christophe Gwynne (310) 788-3918
(3D) www.d-a-a.com

Brad Hayes (310) 788-3918
(3D) www.d-a-a.com

Tim Hedegaard (323) 512-1542
(3D) www.ultimatte-rentals.com

Jeff Heusser (310) 788-3918
(2D) www.d-a-a.com

Yoshiko Hirata (310) 788-3918
(2D) www.d-a-a.com

Philip Ineno (310) 399-2040
www.kingcut.com

Josh Kirschenbaum (310) 399-5959
www.luxedit.com

Joshua LaCross (310) 788-3918
(2D) www.d-a-a.com

Giancarlo Lari (310) 788-3918
(3D) www.d-a-a.com

Chris Ledoux (310) 788-3918
(2D) www.d-a-a.com

Gerta Linn (310) 828-6060
www.whodooefx.com

Ken Littleton (310) 788-3918
(2D) www.d-a-a.com

Lawrence Littleton (310) 788-3918
(2D) www.d-a-a.com

Daniel Loeb (310) 788-3918
(3D) www.d-a-a.com

David Lombardi (310) 788-3918
(3D) www.d-a-a.com

Matthew Lydecker (310) 392-1212
www.laliquid.com

Scott McNiel (310) 392-1212
www.laliquid.com

Daniel Mellitz (310) 788-3918
www.d-a-a.com

Scott Milne (323) 969-1011
www.mfxdesign.com

Pat Murphy (310) 586-0650
www.a52.com

Alessandro Nardini (310) 788-3918
(3D) www.d-a-a.com

Raul Ortego (310) 586-0650
www.a52.com

Helena Packer (310) 828-6060
(310) 285-0303
www.whodooefx.com

Todd Sheridan Perry (310) 788-3918
(3D) www.d-a-a.com

Scott Rader (310) 788-3918
(2D) www.d-a-a.com

D. Ryan Reeb (310) 420-0970
www.ryanreeb.com

Rick Rische (310) 788-3918
(Digital Matte Painting) www.d-a-a.com

Mike Saz (310) 788-3918
(2D) www.d-a-a.com

David Schoneveld (310) 788-3918
(3D) www.d-a-a.com

Brad Scott (310) 788-3918
www.d-a-a.com

Greg Scribner (310) 788-3918
(2D) www.d-a-a.com

Howard Shur (323) 467-8550
www.sunsetedit.com

Alan Sonneman (310) 788-3918
(Digital Matte Painting) www.d-a-a.com

TellAVision (310) 230-5303
1060 20th St., Ste. 8 FAX (310) 388-5550
Santa Monica, CA 90403 www.tellavisionagency.com
(Reps for 3D Artists)

Adam Watkins (310) 788-3918
(818) 505-8787
(3D) www.d-a-a.com

John Willette (310) 788-3918
(3D) www.d-a-a.com

Mark Wurts (310) 788-3918
(3D) www.d-a-a.com

John Allison (818) 259-9503
www.allisonfx.com

Isa A. Alsup (818) 512-8416
www.acefx.com

Paal Anand (323) 874-3003
www.blingimaging.com

Peter Anderson (818) 951-6066
(Visual FX Supervisor/Producer)

Scott E. Anderson (310) 550-4474
(213) 399-1600
FAX (310) 591-8830
(2D, 3D, Visual FX Consultant & Visual FX Supervisor)

Wenden K. Baldwin (213) 713-1381
(Visual FX Producer) www.wendenbaldwin.com

James Balsam (323) 660-5580
(Motion Control and VFX Camera Operator)

Angela Barson (310) 285-0303
www.marshbest.com

Ash Beck (310) 788-3918
(Visual FX Supervisor) www.d-a-a.com

Mat Beck (310) 899-9779
FAX (310) 899-3113
www.entityfx.com

John Berton (310) 285-0303
www.marshbest.com

Angus Bickerton (310) 285-0303
www.marshbest.com

Scott Billups (818) 990-8993
www.ambitiousent.com

R. Edward Black (818) 640-6814
(Visual FX Supervisor)

Nick Brooks (310) 788-3918
www.d-a-a.com

David Burton (310) 788-3918
(3D) www.d-a-a.com

André Bustanoby (310) 788-3918
(Visual FX Supervisor) www.d-a-a.com

Glenn Campbell (818) 238-9660
www.area51fx.com

Mike Chambers (310) 488-6270
(Visual FX Producer/Supervisor) www.mrcvfx.com

Ed Chapman (213) 200-9952
FAX (818) 980-9788
www.edchapman.com

Peter Conlon (323) 467-3300
www.wutitis.com
(2D, 3D, Virtual Set Designer, Visual FX Consultant & Visual FX Supervisor)

Joyce Cox (323) 664-7294
(323) 377-5806
FAX (323) 906-9475

Joshua Cushner (323) 650-8750
(Motion Control Operator & Visual FX Consultant)

Nick Davis (310) 285-0303
www.marshbest.com

Michael J. DeCourcey (310) 480-4031
www.decourcey.com

Eric DeHaven (310) 448-7900
www.rhythm.com

Stevan del George (818) 512-8416
www.acefx.com

Jean-Marc Demmer (310) 828-9628
www.eightvfx.com

Digital Artists Agency/DAA (310) 788-3918
13323 Washington Blvd., Ste. 304 FAX (310) 788-3415
Los Angeles, CA 90066 www.d-a-a.com
(Reps for Visual FX Artists)

Mark Driscoll (323) 469-4230
www.lookfx.com

Olivier Dumont (323) 512-6000
www.buf.com

Art Durinski (310) 440-3896
(310) 665-6982
FAX (310) 440-3896
(2D, 3D, Visual FX Consultant, Visual FX Producer & Visual FX Supervisor)

Shawn Dury (310) 200-7593
(213) 501-1499

Richard Edlund (310) 282-9940
www.mirisch.com

Chris Edwards (323) 931-6633
FAX (323) 931-9928
www.thethirdfloorinc.com

Harrison Ellenshaw (323) 804-0475
(Visual FX Supervisor/Producer)

Volker Engel (310) 788-3918
(Visual FX Supervisor) www.d-a-a.com

Edy H. Enriquez (310) 836-9011
(323) 252-0904
FAX (310) 836-9010
www.x1fx.com

Jonathan Erland (323) 257-1163
(323) 243-8999
(Composite Photography Consultant) FAX (323) 257-0604
www.digitalgreenscreen.com

Henrik Fett (323) 469-4230
www.lookfx.com

Michael Fink (310) 200-8418
FAX (310) 459-7525
www.utaproduction.com

Brenton Fletcher (323) 251-6495

Mark Forker (310) 788-3918
www.d-a-a.com

Scott Friedman (310) 566-1463
www.endlessnoise.com

Sari Gennis (323) 965-9555
FAX (323) 965-1133

Charlie Gibson (310) 273-6700
www.utaproduction.com

Karen Goulekas (310) 273-6700
www.unitedtalent.com

Kelly Granite (415) 373-7488
(Visual FX Producer) www.howardgranitefilms.com

Robert Grasmere (310) 285-0303
www.marshbest.com

Matthew Gratzner (310) 578-9929
FAX (310) 578-7370
www.newdealstudios.com

John Gross (323) 993-7050
FAX (323) 993-7051
www.edenfx.com

Ben Grossman (310) 788-3918
(2D) www.d-a-a.com

Joachim Grueninger (310) 285-0303
www.marshbest.com

Chris Guardino (310) 566-1463
www.endlessnoise.com

Shari Hanson (562) 433-8502
(Visual FX Producer)

David Hare (818) 907-6663
www.tigarhare.com

Robb Hart (714) 953-9501
(Visual FX Supervisor) www.anidealworld.com

Dion Hatch (310) 315-6060
www.digiscope.com

John Heller (310) 448-7900
www.rhythm.com

Kelle Holland (323) 874-3003
www.blingimaging.com

Adam Howard (310) 985-4448

Edward Irastorza (310) 788-3918
(3D) www.d-a-a.com

Max Ivins (323) 469-4230
www.lookfx.com

Evan Jacobs (310) 282-9940
(310) 613-6164
(Visual FX Supervisor) www.mirisch.com

Tim Jacobsen (323) 466-7663
www.encorehollywood.com

Joni Jacobson (310) 497-7225

Chas Jarrett (310) 285-0303
www.marshbest.com

Aaron Kaminar (310) 216-5678
www.ieeffects.com

Michael Karp (818) 515-8917
members.aol.com/mckarp
(Matchmove Supervisor & Motion Control Operator)

Tamara Watts Kent (818) 363-6149
(Visual FX Producer) FAX (818) 363-2449
www.stormcloudvfx.com

Richard Kerrigan (310) 268-8324
(310) 351-7379
(Visual FX Supervisor/Consultant)

Bob Kertesz (323) 467-7572
www.bluescreen.com
(Visual FX Consultant & Visual FX Supervisor)

John Kilkenny (310) 369-5880
(Visual FX Producer/Supervisor)

Marc Kolbe (310) 285-0303
www.marshbest.com

Neil Krepela (310) 452-2488

Tim Landry (818) 768-9778
www.timlandry.com

Rick Lieberman (310) 709-4832
(305) 321-3556

Keegan Martin (818) 990-8993
www.ambitiousent.com

Michelle Massie (818) 238-9660
www.area51fx.com

Tim McGovern (310) 788-3918
(Visual FX Supervisor) www.d-a-a.com

Tim McHugh (818) 238-9660
www.area51fx.com

Gregory L. McMurry (310) 273-6700
www.utaproduction.com

Dennis Michel (310) 216-5678
www.ieeffects.com

Tim Miller (310) 448-7900
www.rhythm.com

Jeb Milne (310) 788-3918
(Visual FX Producer) www.d-a-a.com

The Mirisch Agency (310) 282-9940
1925 Century Park East, Ste. 1070 FAX (310) 282-0702
Los Angeles, CA 90067 www.mirisch.com
(Reps for Visual FX Supervisors)

Roger Nall (818) 780-4466
FAX (818) 780-4467
www.1111mediaworks.com

Gary Nolin (661) 255-8486

Jeffrey A. Okun (310) 282-9940
www.mirisch.com

Phil Palousek (818) 865-8423
www.apixels.com

William Powloski (310) 376-7870
www.velocityfx.com
(Visual FX Consultant, Producer and Supervisor)

Ted Rae (310) 788-3918
(Visual FX Supervisor) www.d-a-a.com

Fred Raimondi (818) 990-8993
www.ambitiousent.com

Eliza Pelham Randall (310) 962-9463
(323) 525-1225
www.queenofspades.com
(Visual FX Consultant, Visual FX Producer & Visual FX Supervisor)

Kelley R. Ray (323) 934-4210
(323) 371-6745
www.kelleyray.com

John Richardson (310) 474-4047

Eric J. Robertson (310) 282-9940
www.mirisch.com

Robbie Robfogel (714) 258-6678
www.oceanvisualfx.com

Mark Russell (310) 273-6700
www.utaproduction.com

Robert Scopinich (310) 592-9362
(2D, 3D, Reps for Visual FX Producers, Virtual Set Designer, Visual FX Consultant, Visual FX Producer & Visual FX Supervisor)

Wayne A. Shepherd (310) 452-4600
www.atthepost.net

Boyd Shermis (818) 347-2515
(Visual FX Designer/Supervisor) FAX (818) 347-2529
www.fxtc.com

Janette Shew (323) 692-0115
(323) 791-6318
(Digital FX Producer)

Kathy Siegel (323) 644-8814
(323) 578-1591
(Animation and Visual FX Supervisor) www.fxgal.com

Scott Simmons (310) 831-6227
www.livewireprod.com

Elan Soltes (323) 533-6226
(Visual FX Consultant, Producer & Supervisor)

Ellen Somers (661) 644-5848

Jerry Steele (310) 656-7770
FAX (310) 656-7771
www.steelevfx.com

Mark Stetson (310) 377-7239

Colin Strause (310) 319-2300
www.hydraulx.com

Greg Strause (310) 319-2300
www.hydraulx.com

Jacques Stroweis (310) 770-3235
FAX (323) 650-4632

Mary Stuart (818) 284-6423
(310) 315-6060
www.italentco.com

David G. Stump (323) 650-5662
FAX (323) 650-5663
(Blue/Green Screen, CGI & Matte Photography Technician)

Eric Swenson (888) 965-4321
FAX (888) 965-4321
www.ericvfx.com
(Visual FX Consultant & Visual FX Supervisor)

Bill Taylor (310) 282-9940
www.mirisch.com

Michael Tigar (818) 907-6663
www.tigarhare.com

Marc Weigert (310) 788-3918
(Visual FX Producer) www.d-a-a.com

Phyllis Weisband-Fibus (818) 726-2611
(Visual FX Producer/Supervisor) FAX (818) 760-8112

Bill Westenhofer (310) 448-7900
www.rhythm.com

Terry Whiteside (323) 882-8322
(323) 646-5235
(Visual FX Producer)

Steffan Wild (310) 788-3918
www.d-a-a.com

Brian Yarnell (323) 467-3300
www.wutitis.com
(2D, 3D, Virtual Set Designer, Visual FX Consultant & Visual FX Supervisor)

Fernando Zorrilla (323) 874-3003
www.blingimaging.com

Susan Zwerman (818) 760-4242
(Visual FX Producer) www.crystalrain.biz

CLASSIC LOS ANGELES FILM LOCATIONS

THE BILTMORE HOTEL

GHOSTBUSTERS

INT. NEW YORK HOTEL - BALLROOM - NIGHT

Venkman (Bill Murray), Ray (Dan Aykroyd) & Egon (Harold Ramis) cautiously enter.

RAY

You know, it just occurred to me that we really haven't had a successful test of this equipment.

EGON

I blame myself.

VENKMAN

So do I.

RAY

Well, no sense in worrying about it now.

VENKMAN

Why worry? Each one of us is carrying an un-licensed nuclear accelerator on his back.

Venkman, Ray & Egon desperately try to nail Slimer with their laser guns, resulting in massive destruction to the ballroom. They turn off the laser streams.

EGON

There's something very important that I forgot to tell you.

VENKMAN

What?

EGON

Don't cross the streams.

VENKMAN

Why?

EGON

It would be bad.

VENKMAN

I'm fuzzy on the whole good/bad thing.
What do you mean by bad?

EGON

Try to imagine all life as you know it stopping instantaneously and every molecule in your body exploding at the speed of light.

RAY

Total protonic reversal.

VENKMAN

Right. That's bad. Okay. All right.
Important safety tip. Thanks, Egon.

SCREENPLAY BY:

Dan Aykroyd & Harold Ramis

ALSO FILMED AT THE MILENIUM BILTMORE HOTEL:

Beverly Hills Cop, Bugsy, Wedding Crashers, Vertigo

LA 411

www.LA411.com

■ PICTURED:
Millennium Biltmore

■ LOCATION:
Downtown Los Angeles

■ PHOTOGRAPHER:
Michael Rueter
Michael Rueter Photography/L.A.-N.Y.
www.michaelrueter.com

Supporting production in Southern California for 31 years

Sets & Stages

BenKitayStudios

FILM & VIDEO STAGE RENTALS

6309 Eleanor Ave Hollywood CA 90038
(323)466-9015 (323)466-4421 FAX
INFO@BENKITAY.COM

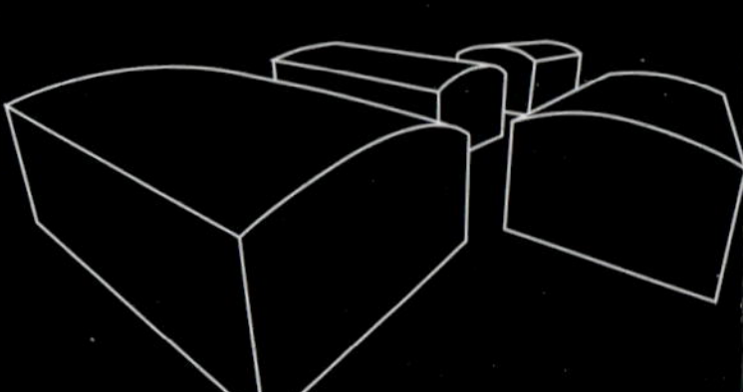

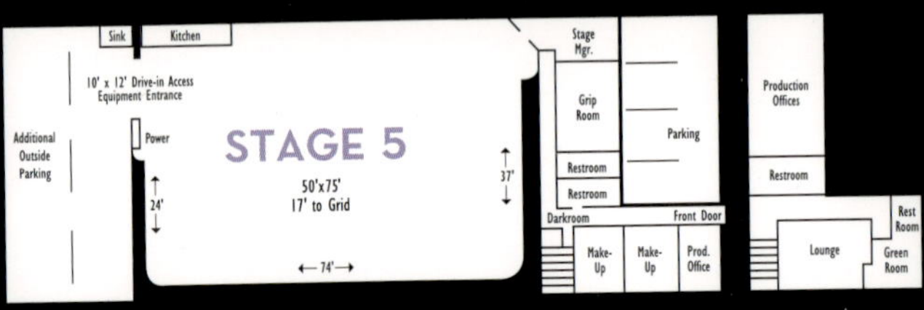

- COMPLETE LIGHTING & GRIP PACKAGES
- WI-FI EQUIPPED PRODUCTION OFFICES
- SILENT AIR CONDITIONING
- MULTIPLE MAKE-UP & WARDROBE ROOMS
- SEPARATE CELEBRITY ACCESS
- STAGE 20 AUDIENCE RATED
- AMPLE SECURE PARKING
- STAR DRESSING ROOMS
- EXPENDABLE SUPPLIES
- DRIVE-IN ACCESS
- 24 HR SECURITY
- PREP KITCHENS
- 24/7 ACCESS

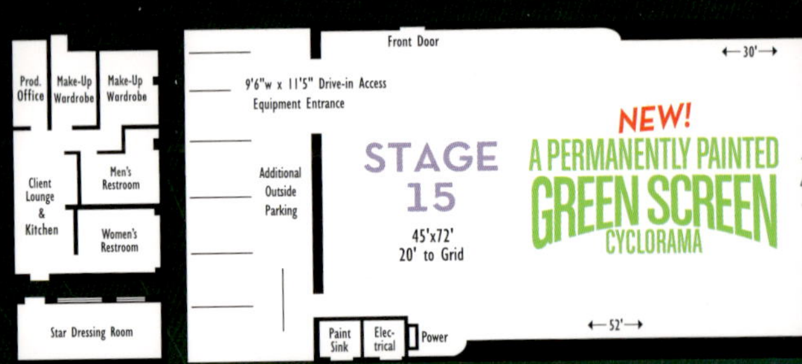

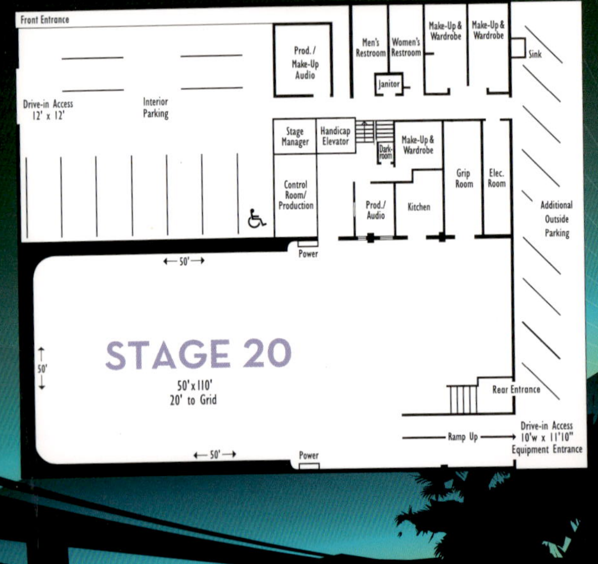

HOLLYWOOD

benkitay.com

SEE OUR DOUBLE PAGE AD IN THIS SECTION!

Ⓐ ADVERTISER SYMBOL

Refer to the General Index for cross-referencing items in this section.

Alp Altiner (310) 568-2733
www.411creatives.com

Art Pic (818) 503-5999
6826 Troost Ave. FAX (818) 503-5995
North Hollywood, CA 91605 www.artpic2000.com
(Faux Finishes & Murals)

Brainworks, Inc. (323) 782-1425
www.brainworksart.com
(Backdrops, Faux Finishes & Murals)

Castex Rentals (323) 462-1468
1044 Cole Ave. FAX (323) 462-3719
Hollywood, CA 90038 www.castexrentals.com
(Backings, Blue Screens, Chroma Key Drops, Green Screens, Muslin, Rigging & Scrims)

Cinnabar (818) 842-8190
4571 Electronics Pl. FAX (818) 842-0563
Los Angeles, CA 90039 www.cinnabar.com
(Backings, Decorative Painting, Faux Finishes, Murals, Painted Backings, Scenic Artist, Textured & Trompe L'Oeil)

Ⓐ **Composite Components Company** (323) 257-1163 (323) 243-8999
134 N. Avenue 61, Ste. 102/3 FAX (323) 257-0604
Los Angeles, CA 90042 www.digitalgreenscreen.com
(Blue, Green and Red Screens & Paint)

Continental Scenery, Inc. (818) 768-8075
7802 Clybourn Ave. FAX (818) 768-6939
Sun Valley, CA 91352 www.continentalscenery.com

DammannART Scenic Backdrops (310) 214-3903 (888) 957-0320
FAX (310) 783-0275
www.backdrops.net

Dapper Cadaver (818) 771-0818
www.bjwinslow.com

Dazian Fabrics (818) 287-3800 (877) 432-9426
7120 Case Ave. FAX (818) 287-3810
North Hollywood, CA 91605 www.dazian.com

Demar Feldman Studios, Inc. (323) 938-5826 (213) 760-0271
241 S. Norton Ave. FAX (323) 938-4368
Los Angeles, CA 90004
(Custom Backings, Decorative Painting, Faux Finishes & Trompe L'Oeil)

Bridget Duffy (310) 675-2715 (310) 422-2910
FAX (310) 675-2400
www.duffyart.com
(Airbrushing, Custom Backings, Faux Finishes, Murals, Painted Backings, Scenic Artist & Trompe L'Oeil)

Sean Falkner (310) 717-9034 (562) 799-1514
mysite.verizon.net/resv3n82/
(Backdrops, Backings, Chroma Key Drops, Decorative Painting, Faux Finishes, Murals, Paint, Painted Backings, Scenic Artist, Textured & Trompe L'Oeil)

Fauve Creations (818) 481-2019
6553 Randi Ave. www.fauveassociates.com
Woodland Hills, CA 91303
(Airbrushing, Backdrops, Backings, Custom, Decorative Painting, Faux Finishes, Murals, Paint, Painted Backings, Patinas, Scenic Artist, Scrims & Trompe L'Oeil)

Ⓐ **Fore-Peak** (323) 460-4192 (407) 649-9937
1040 N. Las Palmas Ave. FAX (323) 871-8141
Los Angeles, CA 90038 home.earthlink.net/~forepeak

Franklymade Inc. (888) 278-3289
1413 Thayer Ave. FAX (310) 427-6160
Los Angeles, CA 90024 www.franklymade.com

Grosh Scenic Rentals (323) 662-1134 (877) 363-7998
4114 Sunset Blvd. FAX (323) 664-7526
Los Angeles, CA 90029 **www.grosh.com**

Hollywood Rentals/ESS/Olesen (818) 407-7800
12800 Foothill Blvd. FAX (818) 407-7875
Sylmar, CA 91342 **www.hollywoodrentals.com**
(Gauze, Muslin, Nets, Screens & Scrims)

Ⓐ **JC Backings Corporation** (310) 244-5830
5905 Smiley Dr. FAX (310) 244-7949
Culver City, CA 90232 **www.jcbackings.com**
(Backdrops, Backings, Custom, Digital Imaging, Digital Print, Painted and Photo Backings & Rentals)

Thomas Lenz (772) 285-4368
8650 Hervey Ave. **www.hometown.aol.com/lenzart/homepage.html**
Los Angeles, CA 90034

Ed Lister (805) 963-1089
(Custom Backings & Murals) www.edlisterscenic.com

Los Angeles Rag House (818) 276-1130
100 E. Santa Anita Ave. FAX (818) 842-2150
Burbank, CA 91502 www.laraghouse.com

Lund Background Pictures (818) 994-6693
(818) 231-5863
www.lundpix.com
(Backdrops, Backings, Custom, Cycloramas, Digital Imaging, Murals, Muslin, Photo Backings, Rentals, Scrims, Video Backdrops & Virtual Sets)

Pacific Imaging (818) 764-8500
12712 Saticoy St. FAX (818) 764-8505
North Hollywood , CA 91605
(Custom Murals, Digital Imaging & Photo Backings)

photowow.com (310) 820-3197
11950 Wilshire Blvd. FAX (310) 820-3175
Los Angeles, CA 90025 www.photowow.com
(Digital Imaging & Mural Prints)

Prolab Digital Imaging (310) 625-4411
5441 W. 104th St. FAX (310) 204-6939
Los Angeles, CA 90045 www.prolabdigital.com

The Rag Place, Inc. (818) 765-3338
13160 Raymer St. FAX (818) 765-3860
North Hollywood, CA 91605 www.theragplace.com
(Material Backings)

Ragtime Rentals, Inc. (323) 769-0650
6011 Waring Ave. FAX (323) 461-8065
Hollywood, CA 90038 www.ragtimerentals.com
(Backings, Blue and Green Screens & Rigging)

A **Really Fake Digital** (323) 221-6995
696 Moulton Ave., Ste. B FAX (323) 227-9033
Los Angeles, CA 90031 www.reallyfake.com
(Backdrops, Backings, Custom, Digital Imaging, Murals, Photo Backings & Printed Scrims and Fabrics)

Rosco Backdrops (818) 543-6700
(626) 252-4162
1265 Los Angeles St. FAX (818) 662-9470
Glendale, CA 91204 www.roscodigital.com

Rose Brand (818) 505-6290
(800) 360-5056
10616 Lanark St. FAX (818) 505-6293
Sun Valley, CA 91352 www.rosebrand.com
(Chroma Key Drops, Custom Backings, Muslin, Scenery Paint & Scrims)

Scenic Express, Inc. (323) 254-4351
3019 Andrita St. FAX (323) 254-4411
Los Angeles, CA 90065 www.scenicexpress.net

Schmidli Backdrops (323) 938-2098
5830 W. Adams Blvd. FAX (323) 938-2486
Culver City, CA 90232 www.schmidli.com
(Digital, Scenic and Textured Backdrops)

Sew What? Inc. (310) 639-6000
1978 Gladwick St. FAX (310) 639-6036
Rancho Dominguez, CA 90220 www.sewwhatinc.com

Sky Drops Inc. (818) 633-2639
999 N. Mission Rd. www.skydrops.com
Los Angeles, CA 90033
(Airbrushing, Backdrops, Backings, Chroma Key Drops, Custom, Decorative Painting, Faux Finishes, Flameproofing, Green Screens, Murals, Paint, Painted Backings, Patinas, Photo Backings, Rentals, Scenic Artist, Scrims, Textured, Trompe L'Oeil & Video Backdrops)

Solbrook Display Corporation (818) 761-3297
10620 Magnolia Blvd. FAX (818) 761-7697
North Hollywood, CA 91601 www.solbrook.com

Studio Dynamics (562) 531-6700
(800) 595-4273
7703 Alondra Blvd. FAX (562) 531-6769
Paramount, CA 90723 www.studiodynamics.com
(Backdrops, Backings, Blue Screens, Chroma Key Drops, Green Screens, Painted Backings, Rentals & Textured)

Theatrical Concepts, Inc. (818) 597-1100
3030 Triunfo Canyon Rd. FAX (818) 597-0202
Agoura Hills, CA 91301 www.theatrical.com
(Video Backgrounds & Virtual Sets)

Triangle Scenery (323) 662-8129
1215 Bates Ave. FAX (323) 662-8120
Los Angeles, CA 90029 www.tridrape.com
(Stage & Studio Drapes)

UVFX Scenic Productions (310) 821-2657
171 Pier Ave. FAX (310) 392-6817
Santa Monica, CA 90405 www.uvfx.com
(Airbrushing, Backdrops, Backings, Custom, Decorative Painting, Murals, Painted Backings & Scenic Artist)

Virtualsets.com (323) 512-1542
www.virtualsets.com
(Blue Screens, Chroma Key Drops, Cycloramas, Digital Imaging, Green Screens, Red Screens, Rentals, Video Backdrops & Virtual Sets)

Warner Bros. Studio Facilities - Scenic Art (818) 954-2032
4000 Warner Blvd. FAX (818) 954-4472
Burbank, CA 91522 www.wbsf.com

West Coast Backings (818) 772-0069
8579 Canoga Ave. FAX (818) 772-0097
Canoga Park, CA 91303 www.westcoastbackings.com

Zing Graphics (562) 946-0304
12309 Telegraph Rd. FAX (562) 946-0303
Santa Fe Springs, CA 90670 www.zinggraphics.com
(Backdrops, Backings, Custom, Digital Imaging, Rentals, Scrims & Stage/Studio Drapes)

AMP Studios (805) 955-7742 (805) 955-7770
101 W. Cochran St. FAX (805) 955-7705
Simi Valley, CA 93065 www.ampstudios.com

Area 101 Studios (323) 868-6183
1051 Cole Ave. www.area101studio.com
Hollywood, CA 90038

The Artists Consortium, LLC (310) 613-8094 (310) 770-9250
155 W. Washington Blvd., Ste. 840
Los Angeles, CA 90015 www.theartistsconsortium.com

Basso Design Scenery and Props (818) 759-5536
11478 Hart St. www.bassodesign.com
North Hollywood, CA 91605

BPS - Burbank Production Studios (818) 567-0088
505 S. Flower St. FAX (818) 567-4796
Burbank, CA 91502 www.bps.tv

Composite Components Co. (323) 257-1163 (323) 243-8999
134 N. Avenue 61, Ste. 102/3 FAX (323) 257-0604
Los Angeles, CA 90042 www.digitalgreenscreen.com

Costa Mesa Studios (949) 515-9942
711 W. 17th St., Ste. D10 FAX (949) 515-4230
Costa Mesa, CA 92627 www.costamesastudios.com

A **Cutting Edge Productions, Inc.** (310) 326-4500 (818) 503-0400
22904 Lockness Ave. FAX (310) 326-4715
Torrance, CA 90501 www.cuttingedgeproductions.tv

Digital Film Studios (818) 771-0019
11800 Sheldon St., Ste. C-D FAX (818) 771-0575
Sun Valley, CA 91352 www.digitalfilmstudios.com

Epiphany Media (323) 819-1001
5300 Melrose Ave. www.epiphanymedia.com
Hollywood, CA 90038

HD Vision Broadcast Center (818) 769-4500
10900 Ventura Blvd. FAX (818) 769-7150
Studio City, CA 91604 www.hdvisionbc.com

Hip Studios (323) 467-2897 (323) 833-5920
6121 Sunset Blvd. FAX (323) 469-8251
Hollywood, CA 90028 www.hipfilms.com

Laurel Canyon Stages (818) 768-8935
9337 Laurel Canyon Blvd. FAX (818) 768-6852
Arleta, CA 91331 www.lcstages.com

Mack Sennett Stage/Triangle (323) 660-8466
1215 Bates Ave. www.macksennettstage.com
Los Angeles, CA 90029

The Mods (818) 558-1290
437 N. Varney St. FAX (818) 558-1812
Burbank, CA 91502 www.themods.tv

mun2 (818) 622-4033 (818) 622-4044
100 Universal City Plaza FAX (818) 622-4132
Universal City, CA 91608 www.holamun2.com/images/misc/mun2-studio.pdf

Occidental Studios, Inc. (213) 384-3331
201 N. Occidental Blvd. FAX (213) 384-2684
Los Angeles, CA 90026 www.occidentalstudios.com

Pacific Motion Control, Inc. (818) 768-1573 (661) 644-1516
9812 Glenoaks Blvd. FAX (818) 768-1575
Sun Valley, CA 91352 www.pacificmotion.net

Pro HD Rentals, Inc. (310) 453-3301
FAX (310) 453-3310
www.prohdrentals.com

The Production Group Studios (323) 469-8111
1330 N. Vine St. FAX (323) 962-2182
Los Angeles, CA 90028 www.productiongroup.tv

Prospect Studios (818) 560-7450
4151 Prospect Ave. FAX (818) 841-8328
Los Angeles, CA 90027 www.disneystudios.com

Quixote Studios (323) 960-9191
1000 N. Cahuenga Blvd. FAX (323) 960-3366
Los Angeles, CA 90038 www.quixote.com

ShowBiz Studios (818) 989-7007
15541 Lanark St. FAX (818) 989-8272
Van Nuys, CA 91406 www.showbizstudios.com

Siren Studios (323) 467-3559 (323) 960-9045
6063 W. Sunset Blvd. FAX (323) 461-6744
Hollywood, CA 90028 www.sirenstudios.com

Solar Studios (818) 240-1893 (310) 489-7801
1601 S. Central Ave. FAX (818) 242-1691
Glendale, CA 91204 www.solarstudios.com

Sound Matrix Studios (714) 437-9595 (714) 402-7450
18060 Newhope St. www.soundmatrixstudios.com
Orange County, CA 92708

Source Film Studio (323) 463-5555
1111 N. Beachwood Dr. FAX (323) 463-5556
Los Angeles, CA 90038 www.sourcefilmstudio.com

Standard (323) 224-3944
2020 N. Main St., Ste. 227 FAX (323) 225-6226
Los Angeles, CA 90031 www.standardsite.com

Stargate Stage (626) 403-8403
6827 Valjean Ave. FAX (626) 403-8444
Van Nuys, CA 91406 www.stargatefilms.com

studio/stage (323) 463-3900
520 N. Western Ave. FAX (323) 463-3933
Los Angeles, CA 90004 www.studio-stage.com

Warner Bros. Studio Facilities - Operations (818) 954-2577
4000 Warner Blvd. FAX (818) 954-4467
Burbank, CA 91522 www.wbsf.com

Westside Media Center Studios (323) 692-5360 (323) 697-0951
12312 W. Olympic Blvd.
Los Angeles, CA 90064
www.westsidemediastudios.weebly.com

16 Penny Scenery & Props, Inc. (818) 623-1122
5723 Auckland Ave. FAX (818) 623-1120
North Hollywood, CA 91601 www.16pennyinc.com

360 Designworks/ 360 Propworks Inc. (310) 323-3326
1441 W. 132nd St. FAX (310) 323-3352
Los Angeles, CA 90249 www.360designworks.com
(Custom Fabrication, High-Tech Sets, Landscapes, Set Construction, Steel Fabrication, Turnkey Art & Welding)

41 Sets (323) 860-2442
1040 N. Las Palmas Ave., Bldg. 42 FAX (323) 860-2442
Los Angeles, CA 90038 www.41sets.com
(Custom Fabrication, Foam Sculpting, Grading, High-Tech Sets, Landscapes, Ramps, Recycled Sets, Set Construction, Steel Fabrication, Turnkey Art & Welding)

Accurate Staging (310) 324-1040
(310) 327-5049
1820 W. 135th St. FAX (310) 324-1017
Gardena, CA 90249 www.accuratestaging.com

Acme Design Group (818) 767-8888
11001 Fleetwood St. www.acme-designgroup.com
Sun Valley, CA 91352

Ⓐ **Action Sets and Props/ WonderWorks** (818) 992-8811
7231 Remmet Ave. FAX (818) 347-4330
Canoga Park, CA 91303 www.wonderworksweb.com
(Hi-Tech Sets & Space Shuttle Cockpit)

Air Hollywood (818) 890-6801
(877) 466-2587
13240 Weidner St. FAX (818) 890-7041
Pacoima, CA 91331 www.airhollywood.com

All Access Staging & Productions (310) 784-2464
1320 Storm Pkwy FAX (310) 517-0899
Torrance, CA 90501 www.allaccessinc.com

All Sets (310) 430-0971
(310) 430-0970
2529 N. San Fernando Rd. FAX (323) 221-9600
Los Angeles, CA 90065 www.allsets.com

B and R Scenery, Inc. (805) 388-8555
486 Constitution Ave. FAX (805) 388-9996
Camarillo, CA 93012 www.bandrscenery.com

Barndog Productions (310) 899-9815
FAX (310) 828-4278

Basso Design Scenery and Props (818) 759-5536
11478 Hart St. www.bassodesign.com
North Hollywood, CA 91605

Beachwood Services, Inc. (310) 202-3566
9336 W. Washington Blvd. FAX (310) 202-3295
Bldg. B, Ste. 200 www.beachwoodservices.com
Culver City, CA 90232

Benchmark Scenery, Inc. (818) 507-1351
1757 Standard Ave. FAX (818) 507-1354
Glendale, CA 91201

California Paving & Grading (323) 255-1144
(818) 956-5939
3253 Verdugo Rd. FAX (323) 255-3473
Los Angeles, CA 90065 www.calpave.com
(Grading & Paving)

Carthay Set Services (818) 762-3566
5539 Riverton Ave. FAX (818) 762-3707
North Hollywood, CA 91601 www.carthay.com

Century Studio Corporation (310) 287-3600
(888) 878-2437
8660 Hayden Pl., Ste. 100 FAX (310) 287-3608
Culver City, CA 90232 www.centurystudio.com

Cinnabar (818) 842-8190
4571 Electronics Pl. FAX (818) 842-0563
Los Angeles, CA 90039 www.cinnabar.com
(Custom Fabrication, Set Construction, Steel Fabrication & Welding)

Company Inc. Sets (818) 679-2401
5934 Noble Ave. FAX (818) 988-8440
Van Nuys, CA 91411 www.companyincsets.com

Concept Design (626) 932-0082 (800) 846-0717
718 Primrose Ave. FAX (626) 932-0072
Monrovia, CA 91016 www.conceptdesigninc.com

Continental Scenery, Inc. (818) 768-8075
7802 Clybourn Ave. FAX (818) 768-6939
Sun Valley, CA 91352 www.continentalscenery.com

The Culver Studios (310) 202-3338
8601 Hayden Pl. FAX (310) 202-3538
Culver City, CA 90232 www.culversets.com

David Weller Design (310) 398-1982
601 Coeur D Alene Ave., Ste. 2 www.wellerdesign.com
Venice, CA 90291

Elden Sets, Props and Backdrops (323) 550-8922
2767 W. Broadway www.eldenworks.com/rickelden
Eagle Rock, CA 90041

Executive Set (310) 456-8833
3951 Ridgemont Dr. FAX (310) 456-5692
Malibu, CA 90265

Festival Artists, Inc. (626) 334-9388 (626) 303-6042
120 N. Aspan Ave. FAX (626) 969-8595
Azusa, CA 91702 www.festivalartists.org
(Foam Sculpting)

Fox Studios (310) 369-2712 (310) 369-4636
Staff Shop, 10201 W. Pico Blvd. FAX (310) 969-1006
Los Angeles, CA 90035 www.foxstudios.com
(Custom Fabrication)

Global Entertainment Industries (818) 567-0000
2948 N. Ontario St. FAX (818) 567-0007
Burbank, CA 91504 www.globalentind.com

Goathouse and TTS Studios (818) 982-9872
7303 Ethel Ave. FAX (818) 982-9199
North Hollywood, CA 91605 www.ttsloft.com

Good Sets, Inc. (323) 665-9983
2012 Hyperion Ave. FAX (323) 665-9984
Los Angeles, CA 90027

Gothic Moon Productions, Inc. (714) 453-0970 (714) 210-5840
535 W. Palm Ave. FAX (714) 210-5841
Orange, CA 92868 www.gothicmoon.com

Hollywood Flats & Risers (323) 660-8466
1215 Bates Ave. www.macksennettstage.com
Los Angeles, CA 90029

I.D.F. Studio Scenery (818) 982-7433
6844 Lankershim Blvd. FAX (818) 982-7435
North Hollywood, CA 91605 www.idfstudioscenery.com

Industrial Artists (626) 355-1913
803 Woodland Dr.
Sierra Madre, CA 91024

Ironwood (818) 265-2055
1514 Flower St. FAX (818) 265-1680
Glendale, CA 91201 ironwoodscenic.com

Isolated Ground (818) 551-1399
918 Justin Ave. FAX (818) 551-1018
Glendale, CA 91201 www.isolatedground.com

Jet Sets (818) 764-5644 (800) 717-7387
6910 Farmdale Ave. FAX (818) 764-6655
North Hollywood, CA 91605 www.jetsets.com

KCW Studios (626) 698-0029
318 S. Date Ave. FAX (626) 943-0190
Alhambra, CA 91803 www.kcwstudios.com
(Custom Fabrication, Foam Sculpting, High-Tech Sets, Landscapes, Ramps, Recycled Sets, Set Construction, Steel Fabrication, Turnkey Art & Welding)

Kinderspiel (323) 876-6549
(323) 216-0403
3103 Lincoln Park Ave. www.kinder-spiel.net
Los Angeles, CA 90031
(Steel Fabrication)

L.A. Propoint, Inc. (818) 767-6800
10870 La Tuna Canyon FAX (818) 767-3900
Sun Valley, CA 91352 www.lapropoint.com
(Custom Fabrication, High-Tech Sets, Set Construction, Steel Fabrication & Welding)

Laser Edge, Inc. (310) 450-5200
2401 Lincoln Blvd. FAX (310) 450-5288
Santa Monica, CA 90405 www.laseredge.net
(CNC Routing, Laser and Vinyl Cutting & Vacu-Forming)

Lexington Design & Fabrication (818) 768-5768
12660 Branford St. FAX (818) 768-4217
Arleta, CA 91331 www.lex-usa.com
(Action Sports Ramps and Sets, CNC Renting, Custom Fabrication, High-Tech Sets, Landscapes, Set Construction, Space Shuttle Cockpit & Steel Fabrication)

Max's Flats & Props (562) 531-3056
(323) 401-2746
6833 E. Rosecrans Ave., Ste. C
Paramount, CA 90723
(Custom Fabrication, Foam Sculpting, High-Tech Sets, Recycled Sets, Set Construction, Steel Fabrication & Welding)

NBC Universal Moulding Shop (818) 777-5551
100 Universal City Plaza, Stage 747 FAX (818) 733-2305
Universal City, CA 91608 www.filmmakersdestination.com

NBC Universal Stock Units (818) 777-1126
100 Universal City Plaza, Bldg. 3156 FAX (818) 866-1363
Universal City, CA 91608 www.filmmakersdestination.com

A **The Studios at Paramount** (323) 956-4242
The Studios at Paramount
Wood Moulding/Millwork
5555 Melrose Ave. www.thestudiosatparamount.com
Hollywood, CA 90038

Powerhouse Entertainment (818) 765-1200
11461-A Hart St. FAX (818) 765-1209
North Hollywood, CA 91605 www.powerhousesets.com

Pro Sets West (866) 776-7381
(818) 563-1800
1205 S. Flower St. FAX (818) 303-0240
Burbank, CA 91502 www.prosetswest.net

Prop Masters, Inc. (818) 846-3915
2721 W. Empire Ave. FAX (818) 846-1278
Burbank, CA 91504 www.propmastersinc.com
(Set Construction)

Rain For Rent (805) 525-3306
(805) 331-0175
333 S. 12th St. FAX (805) 525-7663
Santa Paula, CA 93061 www.rainforrent.com
(Filtration Systems, Pipes, Pumps & Tanks)

Reel Orange (949) 548-4524
316 La Jolla Dr. FAX (949) 548-0749
Newport Beach, CA 92663 www.reelorange.com

Renmark Entertainment Engineering (310) 457-2148
327 E. Harry Bridges Blvd.
Wilmington, CA 90744
www.renmarkentertainmentengineering.com

Alan Roderick-Jones (310) 457-3029
(310) 985-4265
29630 Cuthbert Rd. www.alanrjstudios.com
Malibu, CA 90265

Safe Sets Recycling Corp. (310) 359-0754
2118 Wilshire Blvd., Ste. 314 FAX (310) 828-6477
Santa Monica, CA 90403 www.safesetsrecycling.org
(Recycled Sets)

Scenario Design, Inc. (323) 278-3860
5340 Harbor St. FAX (323) 278-3870
Los Angeles, CA 90040 www.scenariodesign.com

Scenery West (818) 765-8661
11461 Hart St. FAX (818) 765-5495
North Hollywood, CA 91605 www.scenerywest.com

Scenic Design Works, Inc. (310) 367-9571
(310) 216-1561
6020 W. 76th St.
Los Angeles, CA 90045

Scenic Express, Inc. (323) 254-4351
3019 Andrita St. FAX (323) 254-4411
Los Angeles, CA 90065 www.scenicexpress.net

Scenic Highlights, Inc. (818) 252-7760
11759 Sheldon St. FAX (818) 252-7766
Sun Valley, CA 91352

The Scenic Route, Inc. (818) 896-6006
(818) 381-7529
13516 Desmond St. FAX (818) 896-6709
Pacoima, CA 91331 www.the-scenic-route.com
(Custom Fabrication, Foam Sculpting, High-Tech Sets, Set Construction, Steel Fabrication & Welding)

Sculptors Pride Design Studios (626) 256-4779
902 S. Primrose Ave.
Monrovia, CA 91016
(Landscapes)

Set Logic (310) 450-4018
P.O. Box 755 FAX (310) 450-4018
Venice, CA 90291
(Set Construction)

Set Masters (818) 982-1506
(818) 238-0868
11650 Hart St. FAX (818) 982-1508
North Hollywood, CA 91605 www.setmasters.com
(Set Construction)

The Set Shop (213) 680-1668
(310) 486-1741
428 Colyton St. FAX (213) 680-4269
Los Angeles, CA 90013 www.thesetshop.tv

Sew What? Inc. (310) 639-6000
1978 Gladwick St. FAX (310) 639-6036
Rancho Dominguez, CA 90220 www.sewwhatinc.com

Snow Park Technologies (530) 550-2623
(530) 550-2600
FAX (530) 550-2621
www.snowparktech.com
(Custom Fabrication, Grading, Landscapes, Set Construction, Snow Settings & Welding)

So Cal Production Source (310) 699-2787
FAX (310) 618-0129
www.scpsunlimited.com
(Custom Fabrication, Foam Sculpting, Grading, High-Tech Sets, Landscapes, Paving, Ramps, Recycled Sets, Set Construction, Steel Fabrication, Turnkey Art & Welding)

Sony Pictures Studios (310) 244-5541
10202 W. Washington Blvd. www.sonypicturesstudios.com
Culver City, CA 90232

Spohn Ranch, Inc. (877) 489-3539
15131 Clark Ave., Ste. B FAX (626) 330-5503
City of Industry, CA 91745 www.spohnranch.com
(Action Sports Ramps and Sets)

Steeldeck, Inc. (323) 290-2100
(800) 507-8243
3339 Exposition Pl. FAX (323) 290-9600
Los Angeles, CA 90018 www.steeldeck.com

Storyland Studios/Foam Works (951) 674-0998
(800) 218-1932
590 Crane St. FAX (951) 674-0245
Lake Elsinore, CA 92530 www.foamworks.com

A **Tractor Vision** (323) 235-2885
340 E. Jefferson Blvd. www.tractorvision.com
Los Angeles, CA 90011

Tribal Scenery (818) 558-4045
3216 Vanowen St. FAX (818) 558-4356
Burbank, CA 91505 www.tribalscenery.com

Turntable Works (714) 688-2555
(800) 773-9442
1400 N. Jefferson Ave., Ste. A FAX (714) 688-2553
Anaheim, CA 92807 www.turntable-works.com
(Custom Fabrication, Ramps, Set Construction, Steel Fabrication & Welding)

United Pacific Studios (213) 489-2001
729 E. Temple St. FAX (213) 489-2098
Los Angeles, CA 90012 www.unitedpacificstudios.com

A **Vision Scenery Corporation** (818) 567-2818
26 E. Providencia Ave. FAX (818) 567-2839
Burbank, CA 91502 www.visionscenery.com

The Walt Disney Studios - Set Construction (818) 560-6560
(818) 560-5349
500 S. Buena Vista St. FAX (818) 506-8518
Burbank, CA 91521

Warner Bros. Studio Facilities - Construction Services (818) 954-7820
4000 Warner Blvd., Bldg. 44 FAX (818) 954-4635
Burbank, CA 91522 www.wbsf.com

Action Artists Agency (323) 337-4666
1444¼ Glendale Blvd. FAX (323) 395-5663
Los Angeles, CA 90026 www.action-artists.com
(Reps for Set Sketchers)

Daniel Alvarado (626) 798-9039

Artistfoundry (323) 309-0868
7440 Cuvier St. www.artistfoundry.net
San Diego, CA 92037

Ted Baumgart (818) 957-1071

Concept Design (626) 932-0082
(800) 846-0717
718 Primrose Ave. FAX (626) 932-0072
Monrovia, CA 91016 www.conceptdesigninc.com

Cameron Crockett (310) 567-2777
FAX (562) 997-0971
www.ultra-unit.com

Thomas Drotar (310) 399-5700
236 Main St. www.thomasdrotar.com
Venice, CA 90291

Bob Einfrank (310) 893-4241
(310) 876-2024

John Hansen (323) 851-2245
(917) 855-1188
FAX (323) 851-2249

Robert Hunt/Studio E Design (310) 641-9319
(310) 500-9619
FAX (310) 641-3926
www.setsketch.com

Brian Johnson/Live Brain Studio (323) 574-8088
(310) 823-6110
6204 Vista Del Mar, Ste. 180 www.livebrainstudio.com
Playa del Rey, CA 90293

Jacqui Masson (213) 483-4400
(213) 220-3530
FAX (213) 483-4400

Peter Davidson Design/ Previsuals & Design (310) 581-9335
2801 Ocean Park Blvd., Ste. 236 FAX (310) 581-9385
Santa Monica, CA 90405 www.pdavidsondesign.com

Reinman Illustration/Design (805) 640-7393
4612 Thacher Rd.
Ojai, CA 93023

Gerry Schelly (213) 687-3720
www.geocities.com/gerryschelly

Storyboards, Inc. (310) 581-4050
(800) 289-0109
100 Market St., Ste. E FAX (310) 581-4060
Venice, CA 90291 www.storyboardsinc.com

James Vaughn (323) 376-2075
www.greatbigspots.com

1020 Studios (323) 883-0262
1020 N. Sycamore Ave. FAX (323) 874-6330
Los Angeles, CA 90038 www.1020studios.com
(Insert Stage)

1140 The Notion Studio (213) 745-7111
(310) 384-4356
1140 S. Hope St. www.thenotionstudio.com
Los Angeles, CA 90015

The 1st Stage of Fear (818) 633-9594
21512 Nordhoff St. FAX (702) 554-7989
Chatsworth, CA 91311 www.the1ststage.com

30th Street Garage (619) 234-4325
3335 30th St. FAX (619) 234-2055
San Diego, CA 92104 www.30thstreetgarage.com

360 Designworks/
360 Propworks Inc. (310) 323-3326
1441 W. 132nd St. FAX (310) 323-3352
Los Angeles, CA 90249
www.360designworks.com/shoot.htm
Contacts: Kevin Boyle, Peter McKinney & Randy Young

A 5th & Sunset Los Angeles (310) 979-0212
12322 Exposition Blvd. FAX (310) 979-0214
Los Angeles, CA 90064 www.5thandsunsetla.com
Contact: Molly Lynch

ABC 7 Broadcast Center (818) 560-7450
500 Circle Seven Dr. FAX (818) 841-8328
Glendale, CA 91201 www.disneystudios.com

WARNER BROS. STUDIO FACILITIES

STAGES & SETS

35 SOUND STAGES

ASHLEY BLVD.
(BROWNSTONE STREET)

EMBASSY COURTYARD

FRENCH STREET

JUNGLE/LAGOON

MIDWEST STREET

NEW YORK
STREET/PARK

PARK PLACE

WARNER VILLAGE

BLONDIE STREET

PARK BLVD.

PRODUCTION SERVICES

Set Construction • Sign • Scenic • Digital Backings
Metal • Staff Shop • Paint • Hardware Rentals
Property/Set Dressing • Drapery • Upholstery
Hand Props • Designer Collection
Furniture Repair & Refining • Costumes
Set Lighting • Grip • Canvas Room • Special FX
Production Sound & Video Services
Expendable Store • Lumberyard • Transportation
Production Catering • Post Production Services...
and more!

4000 Warner Boulevard
Burbank, CA 91522
818.954.3000
www.wbsf.com

RALEIGH

Raleigh Studios Hollywood

5300 Melrose Ave, Hollywood, CA, 90038

STAGE 1	125' L x 115' W x 35' H	14,375
STAGE 2	148' L x 65' W x 25' H	9,620
STAGE 3	148' L x 58' W x 28' H	8,584
STAGE 5	148' L x 90' W x 35' H	13,320
STAGE 6	62' L x 33' W x 18' H	3,800
STAGE 7	90' L x 75' W x 20' H	6,750
STAGE 8	100' L x 60' W x 20' H	6,000
STAGE 9	100' L x 50' W x 20' H	5,000
STAGE 10	77' L x 49' W x 20' H	6,083
STAGE 11	136'L x 120' W x 45' H	16,320
STAGE 12	136'L x 120' W x 45' H	16,320
STAGE 14	130' L x 110' W x 30'H	14,300

Raleigh Studios Playa Vista

5600 Campus Center Dr, CA, 90094

STAGE 29	200' L x 49' W x 31' H	9,800
STAGE 30	220' L x 49' W x 31' H	10,780
STAGE 31	741' L x 102 W x 72' H	75,582
STAGE 32	741' L x 102 W x 72' H	75,582
STAGE 33	126' L x 84' W x 22' H	10,584
STAGE 34	126' L x 84' W x 22' H	13,104

Raleigh Studios Manhattan Beach

1600 Rosecrans Ave, Manhattan Beach, CA, 90266

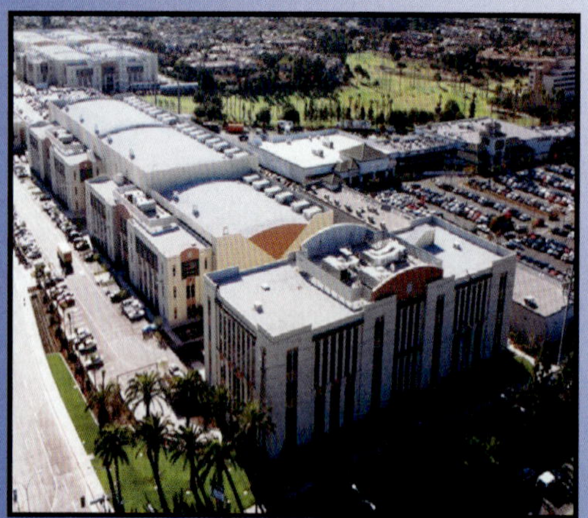

STAGE 15	150' L x 120' W x 35' H	18,000
STAGE 16	150' L x 120' W x 35' H	18,000
STAGE 17	150' L x 120' W x 35' H	18,000
STAGE 18	150' L x 120' W x 35' H	18,000
STAGE 19	150' L x 120' W x 35' H	18,000
STAGE 20	150' L x 120' W x 35' H	18,000
STAGE 21	150' L x 120' W x 35' H	18,000
STAGE 22	195' L x 130' W x 45' H	18,000
STAGE 23	195' L x 130' W x 45' H	25,350
STAGE 24	195' L x 130' W x 45' H	25,350
STAGE 25	195' L x 130' W x 45' H	25,350
STAGE 26	195' L x 130' W x 45' H	25,350
STAGE 27	195' L x 130' W x 45' H	25,350
STAGE 28	150' L x 120' W x 35' H	18,000

New York Street Backlot

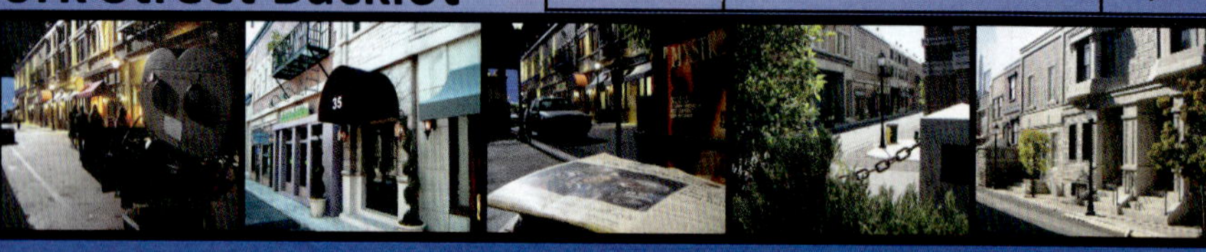

STUDIOS

Raleigh Studios Baton Rouge

at the Celtic Media Centre
10000 Celtic Ave., Baton Rouge, LA, 70809

77' L x 52' W x 17' H	STAGE 1
104' L x 63' W x 28' H	STAGE 2
206' L x 134' W x 45'S 70'C	STAGE 5
220' L x 140' W x 40'S 70'C	STAGE 6
252' L x 127' W x 40'F 30'R	STAGE 8

Raleigh Studios Budapest

Felsokert Utca, Budapest, Hungary

148' L x 132' W x 41' H	STAGE 1
148' L x 132' W x 41' H	STAGE 2
180' L x 148' W x 47' H	STAGE 3
180' L x 148' W x 47' H	STAGE 4
148' L x 132' W x 35' H	STAGE 5
303 L x 148' W x 65' H	STAGE 6
115' L x 98' W x 35' H	STAGE 7
115' L x 98' W x 35' H	STAGE 8
53' L x 43' W x 13' H	STAGE 9 Visual EFX Stage

Raleigh Film, Budapest

Felsokert Utca, Budapest, Hungary

Full Motion Picture Production Services
The Best Of Local Crews & Crafts
Experienced Local Production Managers
Professional Production Estimating
ccess to the Best Equipment And Facilities
Hassle-Free Tax Incentive Recovery
English Speaking Keys
Western Production Sensibilities
Expert Location Managers
4-Hour Contact in Los Angeles & Budapest

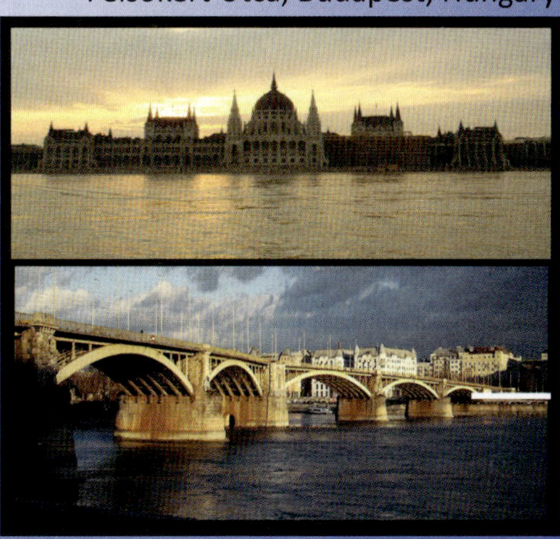

Albuerne, Inc. (323) 665-1307
(213) 926-0444
2990 Allesandro St. FAX (323) 665-7034
Los Angeles, CA 90039 www.albuerneinc.com

Albuquerque Studios (505) 227-2000
5650 University Blvd. SE FAX (505) 227-2001
Albuquerque, NM 87106 www.abqstudios.com

Alley Kat Studio (323) 462-1755
(323) 462-4546
1455 N. Gordon St. FAX (323) 962-3693
Hollywood, CA 90028 www.alleykatstudios.com
Contacts: June Brown & Rayna Vonk

Alva's Dance Studio (310) 519-1314
(800) 403-3447
1417 W. Eighth St. FAX (310) 831-6110
San Pedro, CA 90732
www.alvas.com/performance_gallery
(Dance and Rehearsal Studio)
Contact: Matt Lincir

AMP Studios (805) 955-7742
(805) 955-7770
101 W. Cochran St. FAX (805) 955-7705
Simi Valley, CA 93065 www.ampstudios.com

The Andrita Media Center (323) 344-4500
3030 Andrita St. FAX (323) 344-4800
Los Angeles, CA 90065 www.andritastudios.com

Apache Rental Group (818) 842-9944
(323) 440-7799
FAX (818) 842-9269
www.apacherentalgroup.com

Area 101 Studios (323) 868-6183
1051 Cole Ave. www.area101studio.com
Hollywood, CA 90038

The Artists Consortium, LLC (310) 613-8094
(310) 770-9250
155 W. Washington Blvd., Ste. 840
Los Angeles, CA 90015 www.theartistsconsortium.com
Contact: Coby Shammash

Aspic Studios (310) 740-7896
1213 N. Main St. www.aspicstudios.com
Los Angeles, CA 90012

Avenue Six Studios (818) 781-6600
(818) 933-0818
7900 Haskell Ave. FAX (818) 781-6611
Van Nuys, CA 91406 www.avenuesixstudios.com

The Barker Hangar/ Santa Monica Air Center (310) 390-9071
(310) 390-8751
3021 Airport Ave., Ste. 203 FAX (310) 391-8824
Santa Monica, CA 90405 www.barkerhangar.com
Contacts: Judi Barker & Joe Loving

Bellevarado Studios (213) 413-9611
2107 Bellevue Ave. FAX **(213) 413-9601**
Los Angeles, CA 90026 **www.bellevaradostudios.com**

Ⓐ **Ben Kitay Studios** (323) 466-9015
1015 N. Cahuenga Blvd. FAX **(323) 466-4421**
Hollywood, CA 90038 **www.benkitay.com**
Contact: Ben Kitay

Big Picture Soundstage (818) 842-6060
3050 Lima St. FAX **(818) 842-6066**
Burbank, CA 91504 **www.bigpicturesoundstage.com**

Big Vision Studios (818) 841-4008
(702) 493-9292
FAX **(323) 372-3937**
www.bigvision.com

BPS - Burbank Production Studios (818) 567-0088
505 S. Flower St. FAX **(818) 567-4796**
Burbank, CA 91502 **www.bps.tv**
Contacts: I-Li Chen & Carolyn Collins

California City Studios, Inc. (213) 628-8801
(866) 966-3456
1610 Pesch Dr. FAX **(760) 373-8565**
Mojave, CA 93501 **www.californiacitystudios.com**
Contact: Russell Michael

Casablanca Studios, Inc. (760) 251-9980
(866) 746-6843
66321 Pierson Blvd. FAX **(760) 251-9878**
Desert Hot Springs, CA 92240
www.casablancastudios.com

CBS Studio Center (818) 655-5665
(818) 655-5000
4024 Radford Ave. FAX **(818) 655-8000**
Studio City, CA 91604 **www.cbssc.com**
Contact: Al Ellena

Centinela Studios (310) 396-3688
3401 Exposition Blvd. FAX **(310) 396-1984**
Santa Monica, CA 90401 **www.centinelastudios.com**
Contacts: Roger Webster & Bernard Perloff

Ⓐ **Century Studio Corporation** (310) 287-3600
(888) 878-2437
8660 Hayden Pl., Ste. 100 FAX **(310) 287-3608**
Culver City, CA 90232 **www.centurystudio.com**
Contact: Trish Benson

Ⓐ **Chandler Valley Center Studios, Inc.** (818) 763-3650
(818) 424-4551
13927 Saticoy St. FAX **(818) 990-4755**
Van Nuys, CA 91402 **www.cvcstudios.com**
Contact: Claudette Fillet

Cheyenne Studios (661) 257-8600
27567 Fantastic Ln. FAX **(661) 257-8664**
Castaic, CA 91384 **www.cheyennestudios.com**
Contact: Ray Izad-Mehr

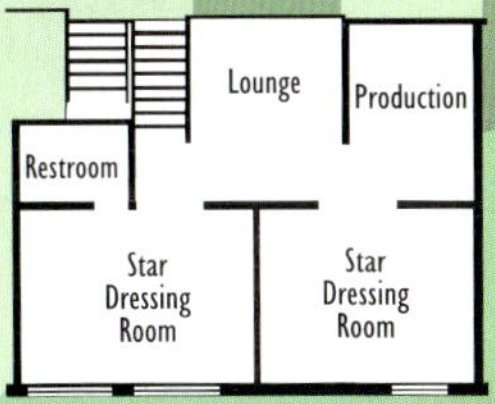

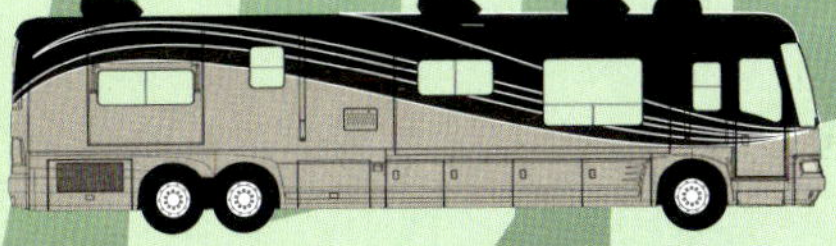

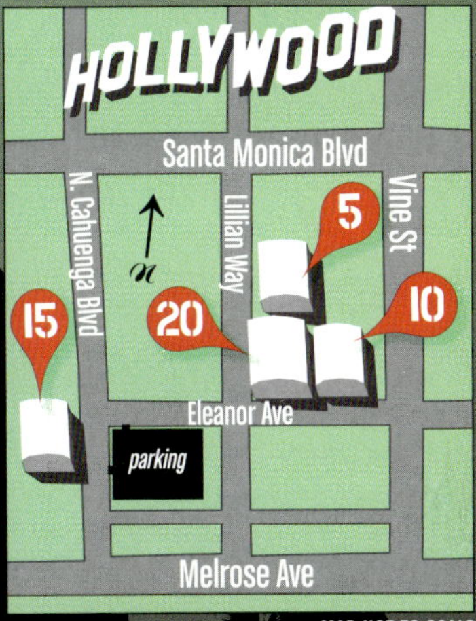

Coast Media Teleproductions, Inc. (949) 417-0300
17062 Murphy Ave., Bldg. B **www.coastmedia.com**
Irvine, CA 92614
Contact: Joyce Smith

Coastal Media Group (818) 880-9800
26660 Agoura Rd. FAX **(818) 579-9026**
Calabasas, CA 91302 **www.coastalmediagroup.com**

Complete Actors Place/CAP (818) 990-2001
13752 Ventura Blvd. **www.completeactorsplace.com**
Sherman Oaks, CA 91423

Costa Mesa Studios (949) 515-9942
711 W. 17th St., Ste. D10 FAX **(949) 515-4230**
Costa Mesa, CA 92627 **www.costamesastudios.com**

Ⓐ **The Culver Studios** (310) 202-1234
9336 W. Washington Blvd. FAX **(310) 202-3201**
Culver City, CA 90232 **www.theculverstudios.com**
Contacts: Laural Ayala & Rob Vaupel

Ⓐ **Cutting Edge Productions, Inc.** (310) 326-4500 (818) 503-0400
22904 Lockness Ave. FAX **(310) 326-4715**
Torrance, CA 90501 **www.cuttingedgeproductions.tv**
Contact: Bill Dedes

Ⓐ **D.C. Stages & Sets** (213) 629-5434 (310) 804-5712
1360 E. Sixth St. FAX **(213) 627-5950**
Los Angeles, CA 90021 **www.dcstages.com**
Contact: Diane Markoff

Ⓐ **Delfino Studios** (818) 361-2421 (877) 512-0400
12501 Gladstone Ave. FAX **(818) 361-5891**
Sylmar, CA 91342 **www.delfinostudios.com**
Contact: Linda Masino

Digital Film Studios (818) 771-0019
11800 Sheldon St., Ste. C-D FAX **(818) 771-0575**
Sun Valley, CA 91352 **www.digitalfilmstudios.com**

Dirt Cheap Sound Stage (310) 401-3171 (909) 856-4939
3019 Olympic Blvd., Stage B FAX **(310) 496-0530**
Santa Monica, CA 90404 **www.dirtcheapsoundstage.com**

Downey Studios (562) 922-8003 (562) 228-8812
12214 Lakewood Blvd. FAX **(562) 922-8010**
Downey, CA 90242 **www.downeystudios.com**

Epiphany Media (323) 819-1001
5300 Melrose Ave. **www.epiphanymedia.com**
Hollywood, CA 90038

Evolution Studios (818) 754-1760
4200 Lankershim Blvd. FAX **(818) 754-1781**
Universal City, CA 91602 **www.evolutiondancestudios.com**
(Dance and Rehearsal Studio)

Eyeboogie (323) 315-5750
6425 Hollywood Blvd., Ste. 315 FAX **(323) 315-5160**
Hollywood, CA 90028 **www.eyeboogie.com**

Fastlane Broadcast Studio (818) 841-3888 / (562) 335-7400
3062 N. Lima St. FAX (818) 841-3188
Burbank, CA 91504 www.fastlanebroadcast.com

The Focus Studio (310) 399-9400
Four Rose Ave. FAX (310) 399-1180
Venice, CA 90291 www.thefocusstudio.com

A **Fox Studios** (310) 369-2786 / (310) 369-4636
10201 W. Pico Blvd. FAX (310) 369-8858
Los Angeles, CA 90035 www.foxstudios.com
Contact: Kimberly Fine

Future Lighting (310) 312-9772 / (310) 346-1649
626 Oxnard Blvd. www.futurelighting.net
Oxnard, CA 93030

Glaxa DT (323) 663-5295
3719 Sunset Blvd.
Los Angeles, CA 90026

Glendale Studios (818) 550-6000
1239 S. Glendale Ave. FAX (818) 550-6111
Glendale, CA 91205 www.glendalestudios.com
Contact: Steve Makhanian

GMT Studios (310) 649-3733
5751 Buckingham Pkwy FAX (310) 216-0056
Culver City, CA 90230 www.gmtstudios.com
Contacts: Morgan Denton & Gina DiPietro

Gothic Moon Productions, Inc. (714) 453-0970 / (714) 210-5840
535 W. Palm Ave. FAX (714) 210-5841
Orange, CA 92868 www.gothicmoonstudio.com

GoTV Studios, Inc. (818) 933-2100 / (818) 933-2122
14144 Ventura Blvd., Ste. 300 FAX (818) 704-9386
Sherman Oaks, CA 91423
studiorentals.gotvnetworks.com

Grant McCune Design, Inc. (818) 779-1920
6836 Valjean Ave. FAX (818) 781-9108
Van Nuys, CA 91406 www.gmdfx.com
Contacts: Monty Shook & Michael Yost

HALA Studios (818) 883-4771 / (818) 288-6004
15844 Strathern St. FAX (818) 883-4871
Van Nuys, CA 91406 www.halastudios.com

The Hayden Studios (310) 430-7550 / (310) 314-9447
3555 Hayden Ave. FAX (310) 314-9433
Culver City, CA 90232 www.3555hayden.com

Hayvenhurst & Saticoy Stages
Hollywood Mobile Systems, Inc. (818) 909-6999
7021 Hayvenhurst Ave. FAX (818) 782-0635
Van Nuys, CA 91406 www.hmsstages.com
Contacts: Judy or Gladys

CHANDLER VALLEY CENTER

America's premiere hi-tech studios, Chandler Valley Center Studios are centrally located with easy access from Interstate 405 and the 170 and 101 Freeways, just minutes from CBS, NBC, Universal, Warner Bros and Disney Studios. Designed to produce the finest commercials, sitcoms and movies, we offer two studios, one with over 20,000 square feet of space, and the other featuring over 18,000 square feet of space. Both studios feature state of the art Cyclorama's and 33 to 35 foot ceilings for maximum production space. With over 4800 Amps of power at your disposal, you will have power to spare. Our state of the art studios are just 5 years old and we will provide you with maximum comfort while filming with over 175 tons of air conditioning. Our complex also features the convenience of parking for over 300 vehicles to accommodate your needs. Chandler Valley Center Studios awaits your production call!

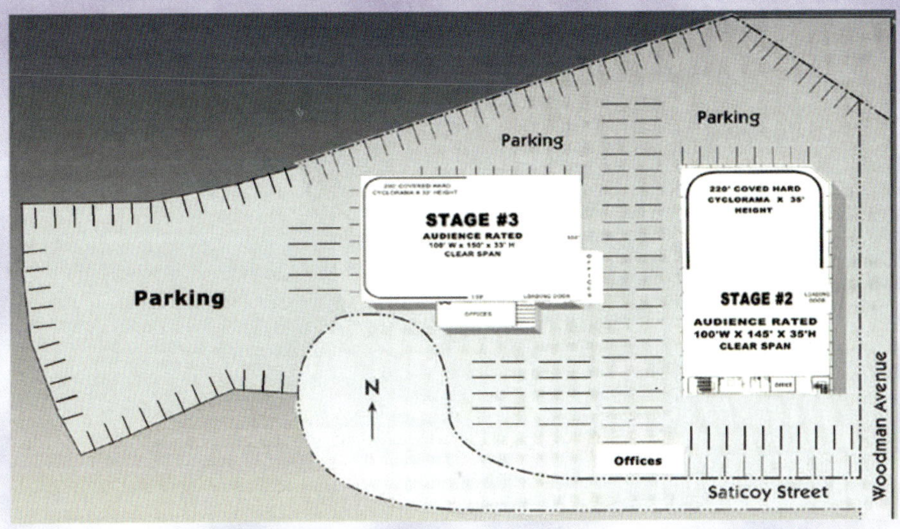

NBC UNIVERSAL

The Filmmakers Destination

UNIVERSAL STUDIOS STAGES

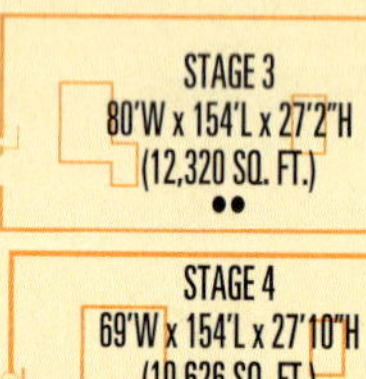

STAGE 5
64'W x 139'L x 23'4"H
(8,896 SQ. FT.)

STAGE 6
63'W x 139'L x 19'10"H
(8,757 SQ. FT.)
••

STAGE 16
80'W x 144'L x 28'8"H
(11,520 SQ. FT.)
••

STAGE 17
70'W x 144'L x 28'10"H
(10,080 SQ. FT.)
••

STAGE 18
74'W x 144'L x 29'1"H
(10,656 SQ. FT.)
••

STAGE 19*
74'W x 144'L x 27'10"H
(9,934 SQ. FT.)

STAGE 20
74'W x 144'L x 27'1"H
(10,656 SQ. FT.)

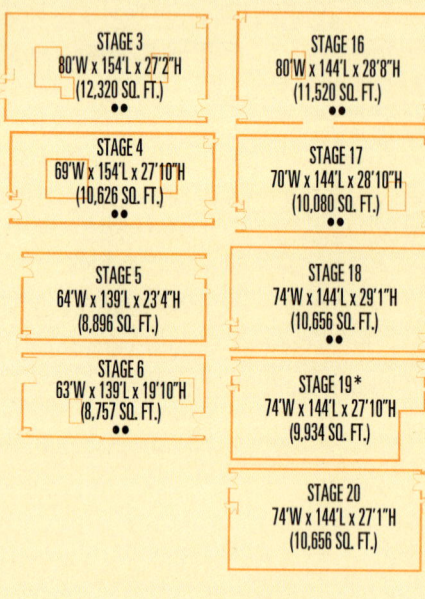

STAGE 22
74'W x 157'L x 27'H
(11,618 SQ. FT.)
••

STAGE 23
76'W x 157'L x 28'1"H
(11,932 SQ. FT.)
••

STAGE 24
112'W x 157'L x 33'4"H
(17,584 SQ. FT.)
••

STAGE 25
112'W x 157'L x 33'4"H
(17,584 SQ. FT.)

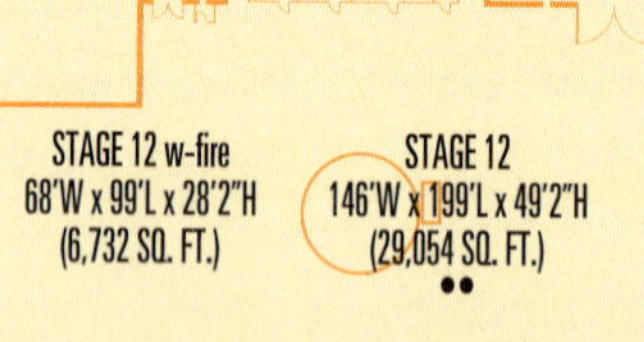

* actual usable floor space
•• stages with pits
••• silent air stages

Featuring:

NBC Universal Production Services
- Stages & Backlot Locations
- Green Screen Cyc
- Property & Drapery
- Costume
- Transportation
- Lighting & Grip
- Staff & Moulding Shops
- Graphic Design & Sign Shop
- Production Office Services

Universal Studios Sound
- Sound Mixing
- Sound Editorial & Design
- Digital Mastering
- Screening & Projection
- ADR
- Audio Preservation & Restoration
- In-house Remote Feature DI Facility

Universal Studios Digital Services
- Color Correction
- Editing
- Encoding
- Digital Theater
- Duplication
- Telecine

Studio Special Events

Editorial Facilities

Stock Footage Library

Additional services at NBC New York:
- Global Media Insert Studios
- ArtWorks Motion Graphics and Title Design
- Special Effects Make-up
- Prosthetics Shop

800.892.1979

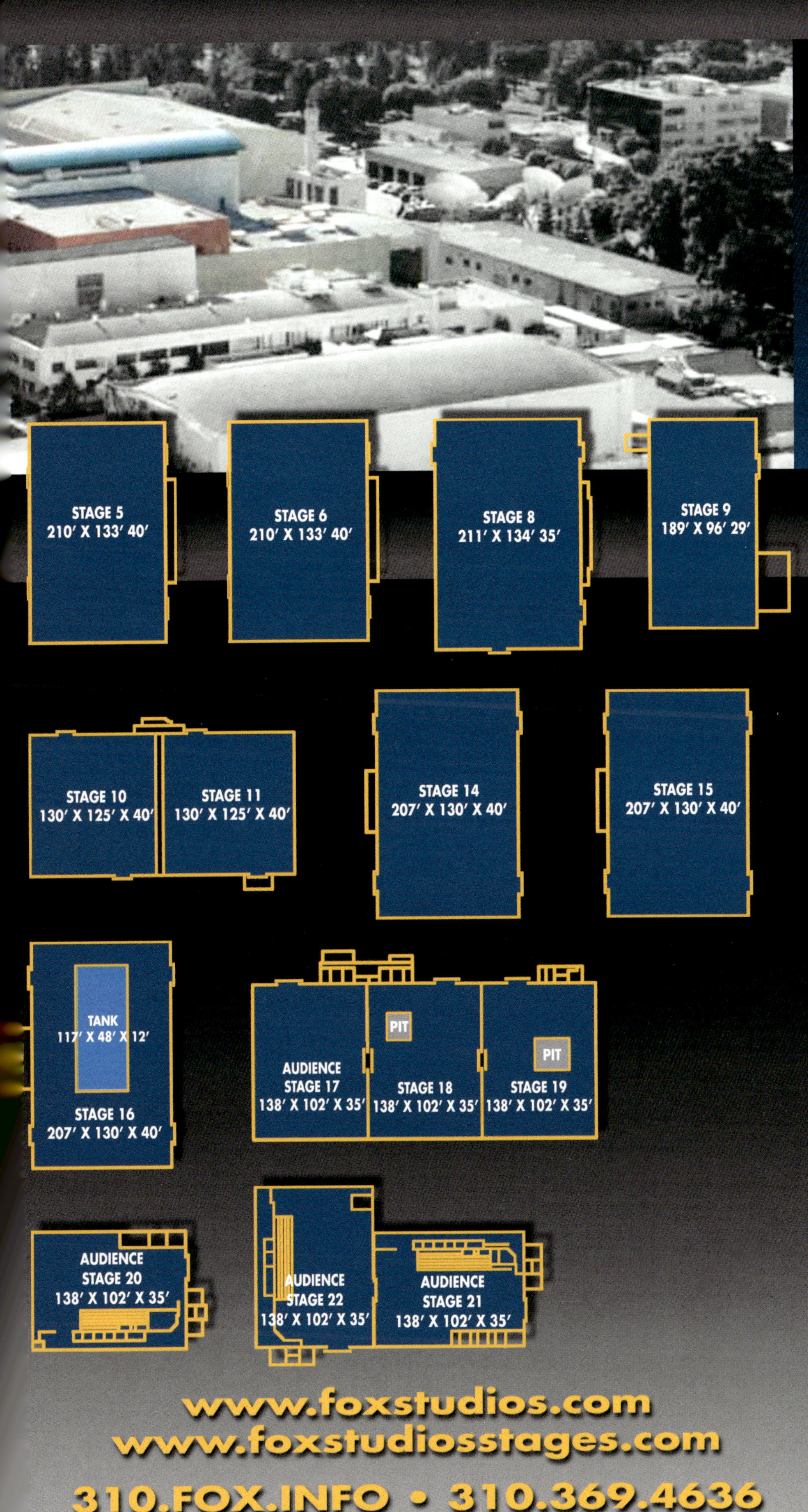

www.foxstudios.com
www.foxstudiosstages.com

310.FOX.INFO • 310.369.4636

Hollywood Center Studios

We have the stage for you.

With 11 soundstages in a wide range of sizes, Hollywood Center Studios will work with you to select the ideal stage for your production.

- Eleven full-service soundstages—silent air, audience-rated.
- New Virtual Set stage for webcasts and other live programming.
- Three hard cove cyc stages (4,400, 10,700 and 14,400 sq. ft.).
- Convenient, well-appointed dressing rooms and other support facilities.
- Onsite lighting and grip rentals. Expendables sales.
- Five all-digital TV control rooms—three upgraded to HDTV.
- Prompt, responsive technical and facility support staff.
- Production offices, editing rooms, scenery storage and shop space.
- 24-hour security. Ample parking for more than 1000 vehicles.

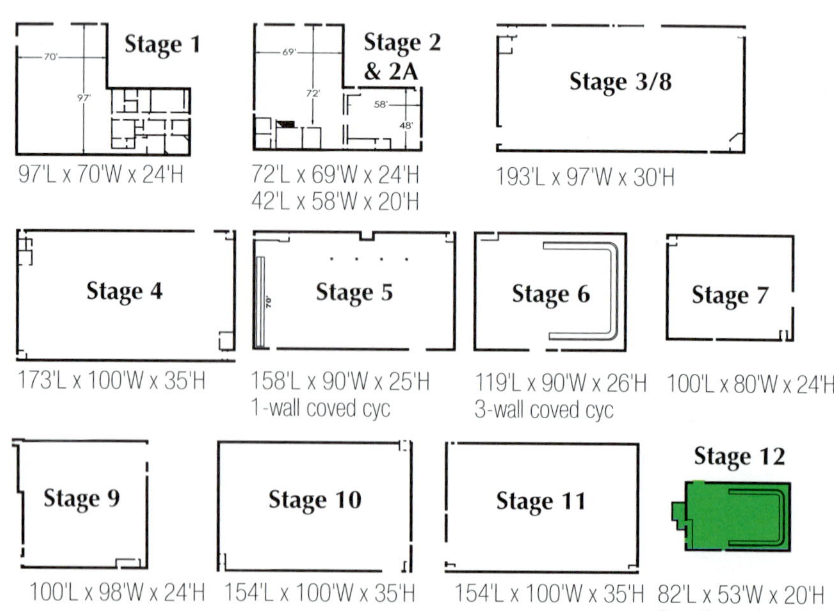

Hollywood Center Studios (323) 860.0000
1040 North Las Palmas Avenue, Los Angeles 90038
info@hollywoodcenter.com www.hollywoodcenter.com

Shoot on green. Effortlessly.

You asked. We listened. Hollywood Center Studio's new Green Screen stage measures 80'L X 50'W with 20 feet to the grid. Its three-wall hard cove cyc is painted with industry-standard Rosco Chroma Key Green video paint. It's also pre-lit with twelve 6K space lights. Shooting green screen has never been simpler or more economical.

Stage 12

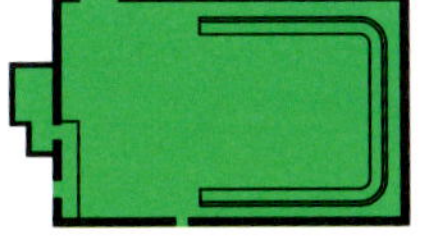

82'L x 53'W x 20'H
3-wall coved cyc

We can do it all. Virtually.

Now there's a new way to produce broadcast quality content for television, the web, private networks and other delivery platforms. Our Virtual Set stage allows you to place talent inside a 3-dimensional virtual set that has the look and feel of a real environment. Choose from dozens of pre-rendered sets, or have one custom built. Professional grade lighting and HD cameras are included. This all-in-one solution is an ideal way to produce great looking content quickly, while keeping costs low.

Virtual Set Stage

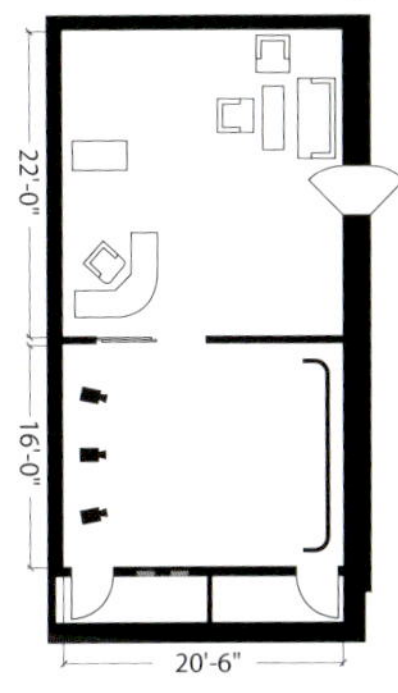

22'L x 20'6"W &
16'L x 20'6"

Hollywood Center Studios

Hollywood Center Studios (323) 860.0000
1040 North Las Palmas Avenue, Los Angeles 90038
info@hollywoodcenter.com www.hollywoodcenter.com

HD Vision Broadcast Center (818) 769-4500
FAX (818) 769-7150
www.hdvisionbc.com

The Henson Soundstage (323) 802-1587
1416 N. La Brea Ave. FAX (323) 802-1825
Hollywood, CA 90028 leasing.henson.com
Contact: Howard Sharp

Hip Studios (323) 467-2897
(323) 833-5920
6121 Sunset Blvd. FAX (323) 469-8251
Hollywood, CA 90028 www.hipfilms.com

Hollywood Camera, Inc. (818) 972-5000
3100 N. Damon Way FAX (818) 972-5010
Burbank, CA 91505 www.hollywoodcamera.com
Contact: Serge

A **Hollywood Center Studios** (323) 860-0000
1040 N. Las Palmas Ave. FAX (323) 860-8105
Hollywood, CA 90038 www.hollywoodcenter.com
Contact: Richard Schnyder

Hollywood Dance Center (323) 467-0825
817 N. Highland Ave. FAX (323) 467-1525
Hollywood, CA 90038 www.hollywooddancecenter.com
(Dance Rehearsal Studios)
Contact: Pamela Phillips

Hollywood Locations (213) 534-3456
1201 W. Fifth St., Ste. F-170 www.hollywoodlocations.com
Los Angeles, CA 90017

Hollywood Loft (323) 957-9398
6161 Santa Monica Blvd., Ste. 400 www.hollywoodloft.com
Hollywood, CA 90038
Contact: Michael Lohr

Huron SubStation (323) 225-8909
2640 Huron St. FAX (323) 225-8909
Los Angeles, CA 90065 www.huronsubstation.com

Illuminate Broadcast Center (818) 769-4500
(323) 595-0234
10900 Ventura Blvd. FAX (818) 769-7150
Studio City, CA 91604 www.illuminatehollywood.com

Image G (818) 761-6644
10900 Ventura Blvd. www.imageg.com
Studio City, CA 91604

Impact Studios (323) 932-8864
(323) 932-9888
1150 S. La Brea Ave. FAX (323) 932-8895
Los Angeles, CA 90019 www.impactstunts.com

The Jim Henson Company (323) 802-1500
1416 N. La Brea Ave. FAX (323) 802-1825
Hollywood, CA 90028 leasing.henson.com/events.html

Kappa Studios, Inc. (818) 843-3400
3619 W. Magnolia Blvd. FAX **(818) 559-5684**
Burbank, CA 91505 **www.kappastudios.com**
Contact: Paul Long

KCET Studios (323) 953-5258
(818) 692-5766
4401 Sunset Blvd. FAX **(323) 953-5496**
Los Angeles, CA 90027 **www.kcetstudios.com**
Contact: Joe Keaney

KCW Studios (626) 698-0029
318 S. Date Ave. FAX **(626) 943-0190**
Alhambra, CA 91803 **www.kcwstudios.com**

KSCI TV (310) 442-2340
(310) 430-5200
1990 S. Bundy Dr., Ste. 850 FAX **(310) 479-8118**
Los Angeles, CA 90025 **www.la18.tv**

The LA Lofts (323) 462-5880
6442 Santa Monica Blvd. FAX **(323) 462-7858**
Hollywood, CA 90038 **www.thelalofts.com**
Contact: Wendy

Lacy Street Production Center (323) 222-8872
2630 Lacy St. FAX **(323) 222-1258**
Los Angeles, CA 90031 **www.lacystreet.com**
Contacts: Austin Lander & Don Randles

Laurel Canyon Stages (818) 768-8935
9337 Laurel Canyon Blvd. FAX **(818) 768-6852**
Arleta, CA 91331 **www.lcstages.com**
Contact: Mary Claypool

Lightbox (323) 933-2080
7122 Beverly Blvd. FAX **(323) 933-5992**
Los Angeles, CA 90036 **www.lightboxstudio.com**

Line 204 Studios (323) 960-0113
1034 N. Seward St. FAX **(323) 960-8509**
Hollywood, CA 90038 **www.line204.com**
Contact: Alton Butler

Lone Star Studios (310) 344-4465
Contact: Marty Halfon FAX **(310) 277-7796**
www.lonestarstudio.com

A **Los Angeles Center Studios** (213) 534-3000
1201 W. Fifth St., Ste. T-110 FAX **(213) 534-3001**
Los Angeles, CA 90017 **www.lacenterstudios.com**
Contact: Ken Johnson

Lot 613 (323) 934-7777
613 N. Imperial St. FAX **(323) 934-6582**
Los Angeles, CA 90021 **www.lot613.com**

A **The Lot** (323) 850-3180
(323) 850-2832
1041 N. Formosa Ave. **www.skyepartners.com**
West Hollywood, CA 90046
Contact: Tricia Bodak-Smith

Mack Sennett Stage/Triangle (323) 660-8466
1215 Bates Ave. **www.macksennettstage.com**
Los Angeles, CA 90029
Contact: Stephen Collins

McNulty Nielsen, Inc. (310) 704-1713
6930¼ Tujunga Ave. FAX **(323) 372-3768**
North Hollywood, CA 91605 **www.mcnultynielsen.com**

Miauhaus Studios (323) 933-6180
1201 S. La Brea Ave. FAX **(323) 933-6279**
Los Angeles, CA 90019 **www.miauhaus.com**
Contact: Rinat Greenberg

Modern Art Pictures (818) 484-7500
326 Mira Loma Ave. FAX **(818) 484-7502**
Glendale, CA 91204 **www.modernartpictures.com**

The Mods (818) 558-1290
437 N. Varney St. FAX **(818) 558-1812**
Burbank, CA 91502 **www.themods.tv**
Contact: Simon Reeves

mun2 (818) 622-4033
(818) 622-4044
100 Universal City Plaza FAX **(818) 622-4132**
Universal City, CA 91608 **www.holamun2.com/images/misc/mun2-studio.pdf**

NBC Burbank (818) 840-3223
3000 W. Alameda Ave. FAX **(818) 840-3472**
Burbank, CA 91523 **www.filmmakersdestination.com**
Contact: Carl Geller

Ⓐ **NBC Universal Stages** (818) 777-3000
100 Universal City Plaza FAX **(818) 866-0293**
Bldg. 4250-3 **www.filmmakersdestination.com**
Universal City, CA 91608
Contact: Jeff Berry

Ⓐ **New Deal Studios, Inc.** (310) 578-9929
4105 Redwood Ave. FAX **(310) 578-7370**
Los Angeles, CA 90066 **www.newdealstudios.com**
Contact: David Sanger

North Field Properties/Hangar 8 (310) 392-8844
3100 Donald Douglas Loop North FAX **(310) 392-9105**
Santa Monica, CA 90405 **www.hangar8.net**
Contacts: Jay Becker & Kurt Sebesta

Ⓐ **Occidental Studios, Inc.** (213) 384-3331
7333 Radford Ave. FAX **(213) 384-2684**
North Hollywood, CA 91605 **www.occidentalstudios.com**

Occidental Studios, Inc. (213) 384-3331
940 N. Orange Dr. FAX **(213) 384-2684**
Los Angeles, CA 90038 **www.occidentalstudios.com**
Contact: Ricky Stoutland

Occidental Studios, Inc. (213) 384-3331
201 N. Occidental Blvd. FAX **(213) 384-2684**
Los Angeles, CA 90026 **www.occidentalstudios.com**
Contact: Ricky Stoutland

OneTake Studio (213) 627-1866
821 Mateo St. FAX **(213) 244-9957**
Los Angeles, CA 90021 **www.onetakestudio.com**

6th and
Sunset
LOS ANGELES
Versatile, contemporary
studio spaces
Supported by first-class production services
12322 Exposition Blvd.
W. Los Angeles, CA 90064
310-979-0212
www.5thandsunsetla.com

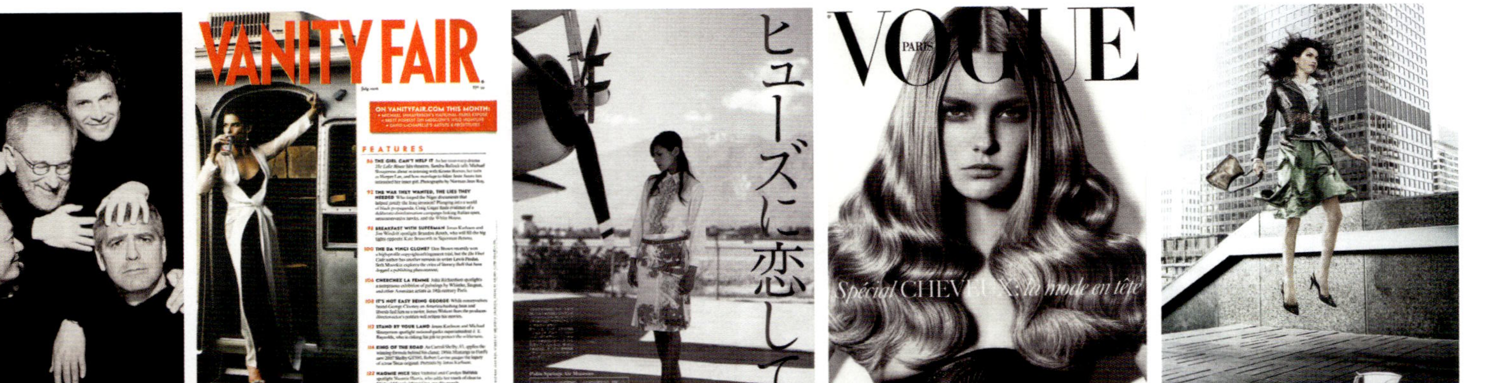
Production Services • Casting • Equipment • Digital • Catering
VANITY FAIR
ヒューズに恋して
VOGUE
PARIS
Spécial CHEVEUX la mode en tête
Feel what better water does for you.
BRITA

Orange County Studio (323) 965-8881
14450 Hoover St. FAX **(323) 965-8882**
Los Angeles, CA 90004 **www.orangecountystudio.com**

Pacific Motion Control, Inc. (818) 768-1573
(661) 644-1516
9812 Glenoaks Blvd. FAX **(818) 768-1575**
Sun Valley, CA 91352 **www.pacificmotion.net**

Paladin Stage (323) 851-8222
(323) 851-0900
1001 N. Poinsettia Pl. FAX **(323) 851-7328**
Los Angeles, CA 90046
Contact: Darrin Scane

Panavision (818) 316-1000
Corporate Headquarters FAX **(818) 316-1111**
6219 DeSoto Ave. **www.panavision.com**
Woodland Hills, CA 91367
Contact: Heather Mayer

A **The Studios at Paramount** (323) 956-8811
The Studios at Paramount
Client Services **www.thestudiosatparamount.com**
5555 Melrose Ave.
Hollywood, CA 90038

Pasadena Production Studios (626) 584-4090
39 E. Walnut St. FAX **(626) 584-4099**
Pasadena, CA 91103 **www.danwolfe.com**
Contact: Richard Ivler

Pier 59 Studios West (310) 829-5959
2415 Michigan Ave. FAX **(310) 829-9550**
Santa Monica, CA 90404 **www.pier59studioswest.com**

Pointe Studios (310) 675-7870
(310) 675-1785
3501 Jack Northrup Ave. FAX **(310) 675-7872**
Hawthorne, CA 90250 **www.pointestudios.com**

Post Modern
Broadcast Studios, LLC (949) 608-8700
2941 Alton Pkwy FAX **(949) 608-8729**
Irvine, CA 92606 **www.postmodernstudios.com**
Contacts: Jay Antonos & John Reynolds

Prefix Studios (310) 815-1951
(800) 801-7484
8735 W. Washington Blvd. FAX **(310) 815-1935**
Culver City, CA 90232 **www.petemcarthur.com**
(Still Photography)

SOUND STAGES
LIGHTING AND GRIP RENTAL
PRODUCTION OFFICE SPACE
EDITORIAL SUITES
EXPENDABLES AND OFFICE SUPPLIES
HIGH SPEED DATA AND VOICE CONNECTIVITY
MILL AND STORAGE SPACE
SCREENING ROOMS
GLOBAL CUISINE BY GARY ARABIA, RESTAURANT
CATERING AND EVENT PRODUCTION
PARKING STRUCTURE W/BASECAMP
3 WALL CYCLORAMA 50' X 100' 50' X 25'H

STAGE SPECS:

STAGE 1 127' x 105' x 35' *(13,335 Sq.Ft.)*
STAGE 2 127' x 105' x 35' *(13,335 Sq.Ft.)*
STAGE 3 127' x 105' x 35' *(13,335 Sq.Ft.)*
STAGE 4 127' x 105' x 35' *(13,335 Sq.Ft.)*
STAGE 3/4 254' X 105' X 35' *(26,670 sq.ft.)*
STAGE 5 112' x 92'6" x 35' *(10,360 sq.ft.)*
STAGE 6 98' x 92'6" x 35' *(9,065 sq.ft.)*
STAGE 7 112' x 72'6" x 27'*(8,120 sq.ft.)*, 3 wall cyc
MILL *(19,110 sq.ft.)*

www.skyepartners.com

TEL 323.850.3180 / **FAX** 323.850.3190
THE LOT 1041 N. Formosa Ave. West Hollywood, Ca 90046

Pro HD Rentals, Inc. (310) 453-3301
1448 19th St. FAX **(310) 453-3310**
Santa Monica, CA 90404 **www.prohdrentals.com**

The Production Group Studios (323) 469-8111
1330 N. Vine St. FAX **(323) 962-2182**
Los Angeles, CA 90028 **www.productiongroup.tv**
Contact: Carol Noorigian

Prospect Studios (818) 560-7450
4151 Prospect Ave. FAX **(818) 841-8328**
Los Angeles, CA 90027 **www.disneystudios.com**

Quixote Studios (323) 851-5030
1011 N. Fuller Ave. FAX **(323) 851-5029**
West Hollywood, CA 90046 **www.quixote.com**

Quixote Studios - Griffith Park (323) 957-9933
4585 Electronics Pl. FAX **(323) 957-9944**
Los Angeles, CA 90039 **www.quixote.com**

A **Raleigh Studios** (323) 960-3456
5300 Melrose Ave. FAX **(323) 960-4712**
Hollywood, CA 90038 **www.raleighstudios.com**
Contacts: Dana Bromley, Yolanda Montellano, Kevin Murphy, Michael Newport & Willi Schmidt

Raleigh Studios - Manhattan Beach (310) 727-2700
1600 Rosecrans Ave. FAX **(310) 727-2710**
Manhattan Beach, CA 90266 **www.raleighstudios.com**
Contact: Dana Bromley

Ready Set Studio (310) 213-9431
(626) 644-5968
10949 Pendleton St. **www.readysetstudio.com**
Sun Valley, CA 91352

RecCenter Studio (213) 413-9300
(323) 868-4226
1161 Logan St. FAX **(213) 413-9301**
Los Angeles, CA 90026 **www.reccenterstudio.com**

Redemption Stages (818) 238-0012
(818) 590-0042
2980 & 2982 N. Ontario St. FAX **(818) 238-0095**
Burbank, CA 91504 **www.redemptionstages.com**

Ren-Mar Studios (323) 463-0808
846 N. Cahuenga Blvd. FAX **(323) 465-8173**
Hollywood, CA 90038 **www.renmarstudios.com**
Contact: Carol Cassella

Ringleader Productions (310) 295-4660
11155 Massachusetts Ave. FAX **(310) 945-5912**
Los Angeles, CA 90025 **www.ringleaderstages.com**

S.I.R. Rehearsal Studios (323) 957-5460
6465 Sunset Blvd. FAX **(323) 957-5472**
Hollywood, CA 90028 **www.sir-usa.com**
(Music Performance Stages)
Contact: Rich Samore

Sanders Studio (714) 444-3000
211 E. Columbine Ave., Ste. A FAX **(714) 444-3001**
Santa Ana, CA 92707 **www.sandersstudio.tv**

Santa Clarita Studios (661) 294-2000
25135 Anza Dr., Ste. C FAX **(661) 294-2020**
Santa Clarita, CA 91355 **www.sc-studios.com**

Screenland Studios (818) 508-2288
10501 Burbank Blvd. **www.screenlandstudios.com**
North Hollywood, CA 91601
Contacts: Karen Apostolina & Steve Apostolina

Sessions West Studios, Inc. (310) 450-9228
2601 Ocean Park Blvd., Ste. 120 FAX **(310) 450-7794**
Santa Monica, CA 90405 **www.sessionsweststudios.com**
(Insert Stage)

ShowBiz Studios (818) 989-7007
15521 Lanark St. FAX **(818) 989-8272**
Van Nuys, CA 91406 **www.showbizstudios.com**
Contact: Scott Webley

Silver Dream Factory, Inc. (714) 836-1853
(714) 225-3708
26075 Getty Dr. FAX **(949) 582-1147**
Laguna Niguel, CA 92677 **www.standingsets.com**

Siren Studios (323) 467-3559
(323) 960-9045
6063 W. Sunset Blvd. FAX **(323) 461-6744**
Hollywood, CA 90028 **www.sirenstudios.com**
Contact: Monica Macdonald

A Small Stage (310) 488-7726
3614 Overland Ave. **www.asmallstage.com**
Los Angeles, CA 90034

SmashBox Studios (310) 558-7660
8549 Higuera St. FAX **(310) 815-8632**
Culver City, CA 90232 **www.smashboxstudios.com**
Contact: Anthony Tamayo

Solar Studios (818) 240-1893
(310) 489-7801
1601 S. Central Ave. FAX **(818) 242-1691**
Glendale, CA 91204 **www.solarstudios.com**
Contact: Peter Cohn

A **Sony Pictures Studios** (310) 244-6926
10202 W. Washington Blvd. FAX **(310) 244-8090**
Culver City, CA 90232 **www.sonypicturesstudios.com**

Sound City Center Stage (818) 304-0573
15464 Cabrito Rd. FAX **(818) 304-0578**
Van Nuys, CA 91406 **www.soundcitycenterstage.com**

Sound Matrix Studios (714) 437-9595 / (714) 402-7450
18060 Newhope St. **www.soundmatrixstudios.com**
Orange County, CA 92708

Source Film Studio (323) 463-5555
1111 N. Beachwood Dr. FAX **(323) 463-5556**
Los Angeles, CA 90038 **www.sourcefilmstudio.com**
Contact: Bobby Naidu

South Bay Studios (310) 762-1360
20434 S. Santa Fe Ave. FAX **(310) 639-2055**
Long Beach, CA 90810 **www.southbaystudios.com**
Contact: Ron Kusumi

Stargate Stage (626) 403-8403
6827 Valjean Ave. FAX **(626) 403-8444**
Van Nuys, CA 91406 **www.stargatefilms.com**

Stu Segall Productions (858) 974-8988
4705 Ruffin Rd. FAX **(858) 974-8978**
San Diego, CA 92123 **www.stusegall.com**

Studio 12000 (562) 696-7175
12000 E. Washington Blvd. FAX **(562) 945-2067**
Whittier, CA 90606 **www.studio12000.com**
Contacts: Joseph S. Ball & Victoria Minyard

Studio 34 (323) 223-1234
141 W. Ave. 34 **www.studio34.com**
Los Angeles, CA 90031
Contact: Eric Ortiz

Studio C2 (626) 799-3430 / (310) 761-1767
1605 Mahalo Pl. FAX **(626) 799-3506**
Rancho Dominguez, CA 90220 **www.studio-c2.com**

studio/stage (323) 463-3900
520 N. Western Ave. FAX **(323) 463-3933**
Los Angeles, CA 90004 **www.studio-stage.com**

Sunset Bronson Studios (323) 460-5858
5800 W. Sunset Blvd. FAX **(323) 460-3844**
Los Angeles, CA 90028 **www.sgsandsbs.com**
Contacts: Terri Melkonian & Beth Talbert

Sunset Gower Studios (323) 467-1001
1438 N. Gower St. FAX **(323) 467-2717**
Hollywood, CA 90028 **www.sgsandsbs.com**
Contact: Terri Melkonian

Syncro Aviation, Inc./Hanger 902 (818) 901-9878
7701 Woodley Ave. FAX **(818) 901-9561**
Van Nuys, CA 91406

TAN Broadcast Center (323) 465-0411
6430 Sunset Blvd., Ste. 1200 FAX **(323) 957-6583**
Los Angeles, CA 90028 **www.tantvstudio.com**
Contact: Matthew Jackels

Total Digital Productions, Inc. (818) 241-9792
1550 Flower St. FAX **(661) 298-1836**
Glendale, CA 91201

Towards 2000, Inc. (818) 557-0903
215 W. Palm Ave., Ste. 204 FAX **(818) 557-0596**
Burbank, CA 91502 **www.t2k.com**
Contact: Mark Rowlands

True Sound & Studio Rentals (323) 839-7705
www.ssrrentals.com

UCLA Dept. of Film & TV (310) 825-2503
225 E. Melnitz Hall, Box 951622 FAX **(310) 206-1686**
Los Angeles, CA 90095 **www.tft.ucla.edu**

UFO-The Poodle Parlor (213) 694-0556
2476 Hunter St. **www.ufo-thepoodleparlor.com**
Los Angeles, CA 90021
Contact: Joel Unangst

The Walt Disney Studios (818) 560-7450
500 S. Buena Vista St. FAX **(818) 841-8328**
Burbank, CA 91521
Contact: Tim Schmidt

Ⓐ **Warner Bros. Studio Facilities - Operations** (818) 954-2577
4000 Warner Blvd. FAX **(818) 954-4467**
Burbank, CA 91522 **www.wbsf.com**
Contact: Perry Husman

Ⓐ **Westside Media Center Studios** (323) 692-5360 (323) 697-0951
12312 W. Olympic Blvd.
Los Angeles, CA 90064
www.westsidemediastudios.weebly.com
Contacts: Lauren Bowes, Kenneth Falcon & Tammy McCann

Wild West Media (949) 260-3860
2192 Martin, Ste. 270 FAX **(949) 260-3869**
Irvine, CA 92612 **www.wildwestmedia.com**
Contact: Kareem Marashi & Brian Turner

World Television Productions (323) 469-5638
5757 Wilshire Blvd., Ste. 470 FAX **(323) 469-2193**
Los Angeles, CA 90036
Contact: Hugo Morales

Sound Stages • Lighting & Grip • Expendables

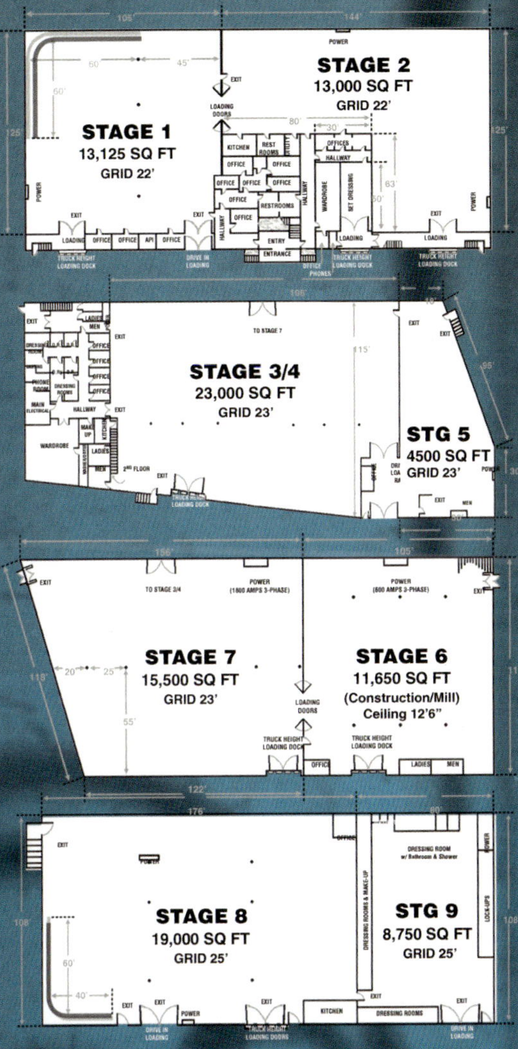

- Lighting & Grip Equipment
- Hardwall Cycloramas
- Lighting/Rigging Grids
- Dimmers & Distribution
- Air Conditioning
- Expendables
- Drive-in & Truck Height Doors
- Dressing/Make-up/Wardrobe
- Production Offices w/Phones
- High-Speed Internet Access
- Copy & Fax Machines
- On-Site Parking

• WWW.CENTURYSTUDIO.COM •

tel: 310.287.3600 • 888.8STAGES • *fax:* 310.287.3608

8660 Hayden Place, Ste. #100, Culver City, CA 90232

Accurate Staging (310) 324-1040 / (310) 327-5049
1820 W. 135th St. FAX (310) 324-1017
Gardena, CA 90249 www.accuratestaging.com
(Platforms, Portable Stages & Rolling Risers)

A **All Access Staging & Productions** (310) 784-2464
1320 Storm Pkwy FAX (310) 517-0899
Torrance, CA 90501 www.allaccessinc.com
(Platforms, Portable Stages & Risers)

B and R Scenery, Inc. (805) 388-8555
486 Constitution Ave. FAX (805) 388-9996
Camarillo, CA 93012 www.bandrscenery.com
(Chair and Choir Risers, Flats, Platforms, Portable Stages, Ramps, Rolling Risers, Steel Risers & Wood Risers)

Bartle International Group (818) 252-5806 / (818) 266-5272
FAX (818) 252-5807
www.bigprod.com

Beckman Rigging/BRS Rigging (310) 532-3933 / (661) 510-2518
13516 S. Mariposa Ave. FAX (310) 532-3993
Gardena, CA 90247 www.brsrigging.com
(Disabled Persons' Lifts and Ramps, Platforms, Portable Stages, Ramps & Step Units)

A **Bill Ferrell Co.** (818) 994-1952 / (866) 994-1952
14744 Oxnard St. FAX (818) 994-9670
Van Nuys, CA 91411 www.billferrell.com
(Ferrellels, Portable Stages & Steeldeck)

Brown-United Grandstands & Staging (800) 442-7696 / (626) 357-1161
P.O. Box 362 FAX (626) 358-3064
Monrovia, CA 91017 www.brownunited.com
(Bleachers, Disabled Persons Lifts and Ramps, Platforms, Portable Stages, Risers & Theater Seats)

Fuller Street Productions (877) 637-8733
10702 Hathaway Dr., Ste. 2 FAX (877) 637-8733
Santa Fe Springs, CA 90670 www.fullerstreet.com
(Bleachers, Disabled Persons' Lifts and Ramps, Flats, Getaway Stairs, Platforms, Portable Stages, Ramps, Risers, Rolling Risers, Step Units, Theater Seats & Wagons)

Hollywood Flats & Risers (323) 660-8466
1215 Bates Ave. www.macksennettstage.com
Los Angeles, CA 90029
(Flats and Risers Only)

HSG, Inc. (323) 733-8552
4845 Exposition Blvd. FAX (323) 733-3306
Los Angeles, CA 90016 www.hsg-inc.com
(Platforms & Swing Stages)

A **Merrill Carson Entertainment** (818) 780-1735 / (818) 782-5758
7905 Lloyd Ave. FAX (818) 780-7738
North Hollywood, CA 91605 www.merrillcarson.com
(Bleachers, Chair and Choir Risers & Portable Stages)

Mike Brown Grandstands, Inc. (909) 593-1444 / (800) 266-2659
(Bleachers, Platforms & Portable Stages) FAX (909) 593-1745
www.mbgs.com

Merrill Carson
ENTERTAINMENT
Call 1-818-780-1735
North Hollywood, CA
Gymnasium-style, natural wood bleachers also available.
Countless configurations are possible to meet your specific space requirements.
Bleachers
Available from 1–17 rows high and in units of 8′ and 16′ wide.
Stage Platforms
Panels are 4′ x 8′ and are available in heights of 1′, 2′, 3′, and 4′.
Choir Risers
Available in straight or curved 8′ wide units—either 3, 6 or 9 rows high.
Chair Risers
Available in 8′ wide units—either 3, 5 or 8 rows high.
View our online photo gallery at www.merrillcarson.com

NBC Burbank (818) 840-3223
3000 W. Alameda Ave. FAX **(818) 840-3472**
Burbank, CA 91523 **www.filmmakersdestination.com**

NBC Universal Stages (818) 777-3000
100 Universal City Plaza, Bldg. 4250-3 FAX **(818) 866-0293**
Universal City, CA 91608 **www.filmmakersdestination.com**

The Photobubble Company (323) 993-8750
(310) 467-5131
1641 N. Ivar Ave. **www.photobubblecompany.com**
Los Angeles, CA 90028

Precision Turntable Services (661) 252-8444
28155 La Veda Ave. **www.precisionturntables.com**
Santa Clarita, CA 91387
(Turntables)

UPSTAGE PARALLELS
STEELDECK™
FOLDING PARALLEL
GETAWAY
STEP UNIT
WE OFFER A LARGE VARIETY OF PLATFORMING, WAGONS, TRIANGLES & ROLLING BAND RISERS. DELIVERY & SET-UP AVAILABLE.
www.upstagerentals.com
4000 CHEVY CHASE DRIVE
LOS ANGELES, CA 90039
PHONE: (818) 247-1149

Premier Lighting & Production Co. (818) 762-0884
(800) 770-0884
12023 Victory Blvd. FAX **(818) 762-0896**
North Hollywood, CA 91606 **www.premier-lighting.com**

Scenic Express, Inc. (323) 254-4351
3019 Andrita St. FAX **(323) 254-4411**
Los Angeles, CA 90065 **www.scenicexpress.net**
(Platforms & Portable Stages)

ShowBiz Enterprises, Inc. (818) 989-7007
15541 Lanark St. FAX **(818) 989-8272**
Van Nuys, CA 91406 **www.showbizenterprises.com**

Stage Systems (909) 944-8521
(909) 713-9115
1667 La Paz Ave. FAX **(909) 944-0720**
Ontario, CA 91764 **www.stagelinestagesystems.com**
(Portable Stages, Ramps & Risers)

Stage Tech (562) 407-1133
14523 Marquardt Ave. FAX **(562) 407-1306**
Santa Fe Springs, CA 90630 **www.stage-tech.com**

Ⓐ **Steeldeck, Inc.** (323) 290-2100
(800) 507-8243
3339 Exposition Pl. FAX **(323) 290-9600**
Los Angeles, CA 90018 **www.steeldeck.com**
(Platforms, Portable Stages & Risers)

Studio City Rentals (818) 543-0300
900 Grand Central Ave. FAX **(818) 543-0310**
Glendale, CA 91201 **www.studiocityrental.com**

Ⓐ **Upstage Parallels, Inc.** (818) 247-1149
(866) 387-7824
4000 Chevy Chase Dr. FAX **(818) 244-4835**
Los Angeles, CA 90039 **www.upstageparallels.com**
(Getaway Stairs, Risers & Wagons)

Ⓐ Aero Mock-Ups, Inc. (818) 982-7327 / (888) 662-5877
13126 Saticoy St. FAX (818) 982-0122
North Hollywood, CA 91605 www.aeromockups.com
(Airplane Mock-Ups & Airport Terminals)

Ⓐ Air Hollywood (818) 890-6801 / (877) 466-2587
13240 Weidner St. FAX (818) 890-7041
Pacoima, CA 91331 www.airhollywood.com
(Airplane Mock-Ups, Airport Terminals, Bar, Cockpit, Interrogation Room & Office)

Art Scholl Aviation (909) 874-5800
1700 W. Miro Way FAX (909) 829-7695
Rialto, CA 92376 www.artschollaviation.com
(Airplane Mock-Ups)

Avenue Six Studios (818) 781-6600
7900 Haskell Ave. FAX (818) 781-6611
Van Nuys, CA 91406 www.avenuesixstudios.com
(Meeting/Conference Room, Office, Parking Lot & Warehouse)

Aviation Warehouse (760) 388-4215
20020 El Mirage Airport Rd. FAX (760) 388-4236
El Mirage, CA 92301 www.aviationwarehouse.net

California City Studios, Inc. (760) 373-4966 / (866) 966-3456
1610 Pesch St. FAX (760) 373-8565
Mojave, CA 93501 www.californiacitystudios.com
(Courtyards, Deserts, Diner, Farm House, Gas Station, Iraqi Village, Mexican Village, Resturant, Water Tanks & Western Town)

Club Ed (661) 946-1515
42848 150th St. East FAX (661) 946-0454
Lancaster, CA 93535 www.avlocations.com
(Bar, Diner, Gas Station, Market & Motel)

D.C. Stages & Sets (213) 629-5434 / (310) 804-5712
1360 E. Sixth St. FAX (213) 627-5950
Los Angeles, CA 90021 www.dcstages.com
(City Hall/Rotunda, Courtrooms/Superior and Municipal, D.A.'s Office, Detective's Office, Doctor's Office, Drunk Tank, Elevators, Emergency Room, FBI Headquarters, Hospital, Hotel Suite, Interrogation Rooms, Jail, Judge's Chambers, Law Library/Mezzanine, Line-up Rooms, Lobby, Mayor's Office, Meeting/Conference Room, Modern Home and Cottage, New York House, Parking Lots/Alleys, Patient Exam Room/Lab, Police Precinct/Booking Room, Restaurant/Bar & Warehouse/Dock Offices)
Contact: Diane Markoff

Family Amusement Corporation (323) 660-8180 / (800) 262-6467
876 N. Vermont Ave. FAX (323) 660-8976
Los Angeles, CA 90029 www.familyamusement.com
(Video Game Arcade)

Four Aces (310) 396-2211
14499 E. Avenue Q FAX (310) 396-5993
Palmdale, CA 93591 www.4-aces.com
(Diner/Bar, Gas Station and Motel Interiors and Exteriors)

Glaxa DT (323) 663-5295
3719 Sunset Blvd.
Los Angeles, CA 90026
(Bar, Diner & Nightclub)

GMT Studios (310) 649-3733
5751 Buckingham Pkwy FAX (310) 216-0056
Culver City, CA 90230 www.gmtstudios.com
(Courtroom, Detective Office, Interrogation Room & Prison)
Contact: Gina DiPietro

Hip Films (323) 467-2897
1622 Gower St. FAX (323) 469-8251
Hollywood, CA 90028 www.hipfilms.com
(Bar & Restaurant)

Hollywood Production Center (818) 480-3100
121 W. Lexington Dr. FAX **(818) 480-3199**
Glendale, CA 91203 **www.hollywoodpc.com**
(D.A.'s Office, Detective's Office, Doctor's Office, Elevator Lobby, Elevators, FBI Headquarters, Interrogation Room, Judge's Chambers, Line-up Rooms, Lobby, Mayor's Office, Meeting/Conference Room, Office & Parking Lot)

Jets & Props (818) 505-0199 / (818) 324-0884
(Airplane Mock-Ups) FAX **(818) 505-0199**
www.jetsandprops.com

Jon S. Clark Private Rail Cars (323) 497-1830
P.O. Box 3613
Cerritos, CA 90703
(Railroads, Streamlined Railroad Passenger Cars & Trains)

Kevin Mcateer Locations (805) 241-0992 / (818) 970-0469
(Diner)

Lacy Street Production Center (323) 222-8872
2630 Lacy St. FAX **(323) 222-1258**
Los Angeles, CA 90031 **www.lacystreet.com**
(Apartment, Church, Courtroom, Diner, Hotel, House, Interrogation Room, Jail Cell, Mechanic's Shop, Nightclub & Police Station)
Contacts: Austin Lander & Don Randles

Laurel Canyon Stages (818) 768-8935
9337 Laurel Canyon Blvd. FAX **(818) 768-6852**
Arleta, CA 91331 **www.lcstages.com**
(Spaceship Interior)
Contact: Mary Claypool

Los Angeles Center Studios (213) 534-3000
FAX **(213) 534-3001**
www.lacenterstudios.com
(Bar, City Street Facades, Courtroom, Diner, Elevator Lobby, Elevators, Interrogation Room, Lobby, Morgue, Office, Parking Lot, Police Station, Prison, Restaurant & Warehouse)

Melody Ranch Studio (661) 259-9669 / (661) 259-7788
P.O. Box 220597 FAX **(661) 259-3788**
Newhall, CA 91322 **www.melodyranchstudio.com**
(Western Town)

Monad Railway Equipment Co. (562) 404-8641 / (562) 522-7894
15220 Valley View Ave. FAX **(562) 404-8541**
La Mirada, CA 90638 **www.monadrailway.com**
(Locomotives, Passenger Rail Cars & Train Mock-Ups)
Contact: Lon Orlenko

NBC Universal Stages (818) 777-3000
100 Universal City Plaza FAX **(818) 866-0293**
Bldg. 4250-3 **www.filmmakersdestination.com**
Universal City, CA 91608
(City Street Facades, Gas Station, House, Parking Lot, Passenger Rail Cars, Warehouse & Western Town)
Contact: Jeff Berry

The Studios at Paramount (323) 956-5783
The Studios at Paramount
New York Streets **www.thestudiosatparamount.com**
5555 Melrose Ave.
Hollywood, CA 90038

Producers Air Force (818) 845-5970 / (818) 795-7463
One Orange Grove Terrace FAX **(818) 845-4033**
Burbank, CA 91501 **www.producersairforce.com**
(Airplane Mock-Ups & Cockpit)

Ready Set Studio (310) 213-9431 / (626) 644-5968
10949 Pendleton St. **www.readysetstudio.com**
Sun Valley, CA 91352

Ⓐ **Riverfront Stages, Inc.** (818) 364-7250
13100 Telfair Ave. FAX **(818) 364-7251**
Sylmar, CA 91342 **www.riverfrontstages.com**
(Apartment, Bar/Restaurant, Conference Room, Courtroom, Diner, Elevator, Elevator Lobby, Hospital, Hotel, House, Interrogation Room, Jail Cell, Judge's Chambers, Office & Police Station)
Contact: Christine Johnson

Sets In The City (310) 575-5666
25655 Springbrook Ave. **www.setsinthecity.net**
Saugus, CA 91350

Silver Dream Factory, Inc. (714) 836-1853 / (714) 225-3708
26075 Getty Dr. FAX **(949) 582-1147**
Laguna Niguel, CA 92677 **www.standingsets.com**
(Airplane Mock-Ups, Bedroom, Detective's Office, Hospital, Interrogation Room, Medical Facility, Morgue, Office, Police Station & Prison)

Solar Studios (818) 240-1893 / (310) 489-7801
1601 S. Central Ave. FAX **(818) 242-1691**
Glendale, CA 91204 **www.solarstudios.com**

Syncro Aviation, Inc./Hanger 902 (818) 901-9878
7701 Woodley Ave. FAX **(818) 901-9561**
Van Nuys, CA 91406
(Airplane & Ramp)

United Pacific Studios (213) 489-2001
729 E. Temple St. FAX **(213) 489-2098**
Los Angeles, CA 90012 **www.unitedpacificstudios.com**
(Bar, Detective's Office, Diner, Doctor's Office, Elevator, Hospital, Hotel Room, House, Interrogation Room, Lawyer's Office, Line-up Room, Lobby, Meeting/Conference Room, Modern Home, Motel, Nightclub, Office, Parking Lots/Alleys, Patient Exam Room, Prison/Jail Cells, Restaurant/Bar & Warehouse)

Veluzat Motion Picture Ranch (661) 259-9669
P.O. Box 220597 FAX **(661) 259-3788**
Newhall, CA 91322 **www.melodyranchstudio.com**
(Bar, Church, Diner & Gas Station)

Willow Studios (213) 625-5771 / (310) 849-5452
1333-1335 Willow St. FAX **(213) 625-0101**
Los Angeles, CA 90013 **www.willowstudios.net**
(Alley, Bar, Bedroom, City Street Facades, D.A.'s Office, Detective's Office, Diner, Doctor's Office, Elevators, Emergency Room, FBI Headquarters, Hotel Suite, House, Interrogation Room, Judge's Chambers, Line-up Rooms, Mayor's Office, Mechanic's Shop, Meeting/Conference Room, Morgue, Motel, Nightclub, Office, Parking Lot, Police Station, Prison, Restaurant & Warehouse)

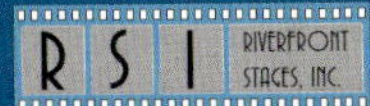

RIVERFRONT STAGES

RSI: TELFAIR

13100 Telfair Avenue, Sylmar, CA 91342
818 364-7250 www.riverfrontstages.com

50,000 square foot modern facility / ample parking / minutes north of Hollywood / air conditioning / stage power / contemporary and period office interiors / set dressing available

RSI: TREADWELL

3061 Treadwell Street, Los Angeles, CA 90065
818 364-7250 www.riverfrontstages.com

fully air conditioned / 3,500 sq. ft. mill space / 3,600 amps stage power / 4,600 sq ft of office space/close to downtown LA / on-site basecamp parking

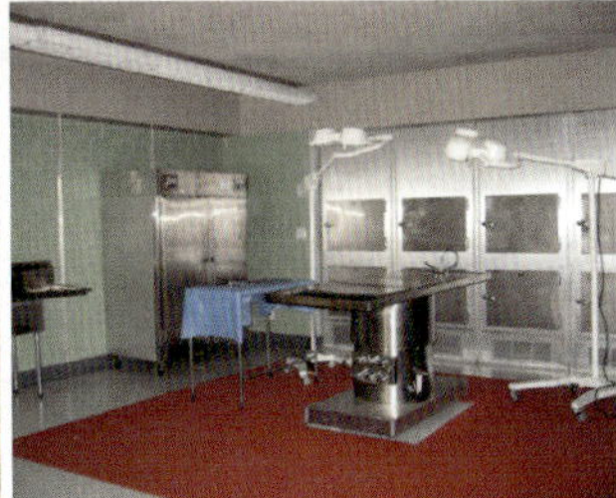

RSI: TREADWELL

40,000 sq. ft. facility with office space for short-term or long-term Production needs. Fully air-conditioned, 3,500 sq. ft. mill space, 4,600 sq. ft. fenced parking, 20'-30' high ceilings and close to downtown Los Angeles

classic courtroom with stairway, elevators, witness room and judge's chambers / police precinct with bullpen, offices, interrogation room and elevator / East Coast bar/ pub with restaurant and patio / modern apartment / Colonial style home with foyer, living room, dining room and large kitchen / jail cells

RSI: TELFAIR

Albuerne, Inc.
2990 Allesandro St.
Los Angeles, CA 90039
(323) 665-1307
(213) 926-0444
FAX (323) 665-7034
www.albuerneinc.com

AMP Studios
101 W. Cochran St.
Simi Valley, CA 93065
(805) 955-7742
(805) 955-7770
FAX (805) 955-7705
www.ampstudios.com

The Andrita Media Center
3030 Andrita St.
Los Angeles, CA 90065
(323) 344-4500
FAX (323) 344-4800
www.andritastudios.com

A **Ben Kitay Studios**
1015 N. Cahuenga Blvd.
Hollywood, CA 90038
(323) 466-9015
FAX (323) 466-4421
www.benkitay.com

Century Studio Corporation
8660 Hayden Pl., Ste. 1
Culver City, CA 90232
(310) 287-3600
(888) 878-2437
FAX (310) 287-3608
www.centurystudio.com

Chandler Valley Center Studios, Inc.
13927 Saticoy St.
Van Nuys, CA 91402
(818) 763-3650
(818) 424-4551
FAX (818) 990-4755
www.cvcstudios.com

Coastal Media Group
26660 Agoura Rd.
Calabasas, CA 91302
(818) 880-9800
FAX (818) 579-9026
www.coastalmediagroup.com

Costa Mesa Studios
711 W. 17th St., Ste. D10
Costa Mesa, CA 92627
(949) 515-9942
FAX (949) 515-4230
www.costamesastudios.com

Fastlane Broadcast Studio
3062 N. Lima St.
Burbank, CA 91504
(818) 841-3888
(562) 335-7400
FAX (818) 841-3188
www.fastlanebroadcast.com

Fox Studios
10201 W. Pico Blvd.
Los Angeles, CA 90035
(310) 369-2786
(310) 369-4636
FAX (310) 369-8858
www.foxstudios.com

GoTV Networks, Inc.
14144 Ventura Blvd., Ste. 300
Sherman Oaks, CA 91423
(818) 933-2100
(818) 933-2122
studiorentals.gotvnetworks.com

The Hayden Studios
3555 Hayden Ave.
Culver City, CA 90232
(310) 430-7550
(310) 314-9447
FAX (310) 314-9433
www.3555hayden.com

Hollywood Center Studios
1040 N. Las Palmas Ave.
Hollywood, CA 90038
(323) 860-0000
FAX (323) 860-8105
www.hollywoodcenter.com

KCET Studios
4401 Sunset Blvd.
Los Angeles, CA 90027
(323) 953-5258
(818) 692-5766
FAX (323) 953-5496
www.kcetstudios.com

Lacy Street Production Center
2630 Lacy St.
Los Angeles, CA 90031
(323) 222-8872
FAX (323) 222-1258
www.lacystreet.com

Los Angeles Center Studios
1201 W. Fifth St., Ste. T-110
Los Angeles, CA 90017
(213) 534-3000
FAX (213) 534-3001
www.lacenterstudios.com

The Lot
1041 N. Formosa Ave.
West Hollywood, CA 90046
(323) 850-3180
(323) 850-2832
www.skyepartners.com

mun2
100 Universal City Plaza
Universal City, CA 91608
(818) 622-4033
(818) 622-4044
FAX (818) 622-4132
www.holamun2.com/images/misc/mun2-studio.pdf

NBC Burbank
3000 W. Alameda Ave.
Burbank, CA 91523
(818) 840-3223
FAX (818) 840-3472
www.filmmakersdestination.com

The Studios at Paramount
The Studios at Paramount
Client Services
5555 Melrose Ave.
Hollywood, CA 90038
(323) 956-8811
www.thestudiosatparamount.com

The Production Group Studios
1330 N. Vine St.
Hollywood, CA 90028
(323) 469-8111
FAX (323) 962-2182
www.productiongroup.tv

Raleigh Studios - Manhattan Beach
1600 Rosecrans Ave.
Manhattan Beach, CA 90266
(310) 727-2700
FAX (310) 727-2710
www.raleighstudios.com

Redemption Stages
2980 & 2982 N. Ontario St.
Burbank, CA 91504
(818) 238-0012
(818) 590-0042
FAX (818) 238-0095
www.redemptionstages.com

Ren-Mar Studios
846 N. Cahuenga Blvd.
Hollywood, CA 90038
(323) 463-0808
FAX (323) 465-8173
www.renmarstudios.com

South Bay Studios
20434 S. Santa Fe Ave.
Long Beach, CA 90810
(310) 762-1360
FAX (310) 639-2055
www.southbaystudios.com

Sunset Bronson Studios
5800 W. Sunset Blvd.
Los Angeles, CA 90028
(323) 460-5858
FAX (323) 460-3844
www.sgsandsbs.com
Contacts: Terri Melkonian & Beth Talbert

Sunset Gower Studios
1438 N. Gower St.
Los Angeles, CA 90028
(323) 467-1001
FAX (323) 467-2717
www.sgsandsbs.com
Contact: Terri Melkonian

Warner Bros. Studio Facilities - Operations
4000 Warner Blvd.
Burbank, CA 91522
(818) 954-2577
FAX (818) 954-4467
www.wbsf.com

Westside Media Center Studios
12312 W. Olympic Blvd.
Los Angeles, CA 90064
(323) 692-5360
(323) 697-0951
www.westsidemediastudios.weebly.com

STANDING SETS	Aero Mock-Ups, Inc.	Air Hollywood	Art Scholl Aviation	Club Ed	D.C.Stages & Sets	Downey Studios	Four Aces	Glaxa DT	GMT Studios	Hip Films	Jets & Props	Jon S. Clark Private Rail Cars	Kevin Mcateer Locations	Lacy Street Production Center	Laurel Canyon Stages	Los Angeles Center Studios	Melody Ranch	Monad Railway Equipment Co.	NBC Universal Stages	Paramount Studios Backlot Operations	Producers Air Force	Ready Set Studio	Riverfront Stages, Inc.	Silver Dream Factory	Syncro Aviation/Hanger 902	United Pacific Studios	Veluzat Motion Picture Ranch	Willow Studios
AIRPLANE	•	•	•								•										•				•			
AIRPORT TERMINAL	•	•																				•			•			
APARTMENT														•						•		•	•					
ARMY CAMP																												
BAR/RESTAURANT	•	•		•	•		•	•		•						•				•			•			•	•	•
CELL BLOCK									•							•												
CHURCH														•													•	
CITY HALL					•																							
CITY STREET FACADES																•				•								•
CLASSROOM																						•			•			
CONFERENCE ROOM					•	•										•							•		•	•		•
COURTROOM					•				•					•		•							•					
D.A.'S OFFICE					•																	•	•			•		•
DETECTIVE'S OFFICE					•				•														•			•		•
DINER				•			•	•					•	•		•							•	•		•	•	•
DINING RAIL CAR																		•										
DOCTOR'S OFFICE					•																		•	•		•		•
DRUNK TANK					•											•							•					
ELEVATOR					•											•			•			•	•			•		•
ELEVATOR LOBBY					•	•										•			•			•	•					
EMERGENCY ROOM					•																		•					•
EXAM ROOM/LAB					•											•							•			•		•
FARMHOUSE																												
FBI HEADQUARTERS						•																						•
GAS STATION				•			•												•								•	
HELICOPTER																									•			
HOSPITAL					•																		•			•		
HOTEL					•									•					•				•			•		•
HOUSE					•	•								•					•			•	•			•		•
INTERROGATION ROOM	•	•			•				•					•		•							•			•		•
JAIL					•											•										•		•
JAIL CELL					•									•		•							•			•		•
JET FIGHTER																					•				•			
JUDGE'S CHAMBERS					•																	•	•					•
LIBRARY					•																							
LINE-UP ROOM					•																					•		•
LOBBY					•	•										•			•						•	•		
LOCOMOTIVE																		•										
MARKET				•																								
MAYOR'S OFFICE					•																	•	•					•
MECHANICS SHOP														•											•			•
MILITARY AIRCRAFT																									•			
MILITARY BARRACKS																												
MORGUE																•												•
MOTEL				•			•															•				•		•
NIGHTCLUB								•						•												•		•
OFFICE	•	•			•	•										•						•	•	•	•	•		•
OCTAGONAL OFFICE					•																							
PARKING LOT					•	•										•			•	•			•		•	•		•
PASSENGER RAIL CAR												•						•	•									
POLICE STATION					•				•					•		•							•	•				•
PRISON					•				•					•		•										•		•
SCI FI INTERIOR					•										•													
WAREHOUSE					•	•													•			•			•	•		•
WESTERN TOWN					•												•		•									

STAGE NAME	PHONE	STAGE NUMBER	LENGTH	WIDTH	HEIGHT	AREA SQUARE FEET	SOUND STAGE	INSERT	POWER/AMPS	CYCLORAMAS
Raleigh Studios - Playa Vista	323-960-FILM	31	741	102	72	75582	•		24000 amps	
Raleigh Studios - Playa Vista	323-960-FILM	32	741	102	72	75582	•		24000 amps	
Downey Studios	562-922-8000	2	365	200	22	73000	•		1600 amps	
Downey Studios	562-922-8000	290	500	110	63	55000			4800ac	
Sony Pictures Studios	310-224-6926	15	311	135	40	41985	•		9000 amps	
Downey Studios	562-922-8000	11	200	200	22	40000	•		1600 amps	
Quixote Studios Griffith Park	323-957-9933	8	220	180	42	39600	•		2400 amps	3 wall hard
Barker Hangar/Santa Monica Air Ctr	310-390-9071	A	234	150	45	35100			Unlimited	
Occidental Studios, Inc.	213-384-3331	5	180	180	16	32400	•		4600 amps	
Warner Bros. Studio Facilities	818-954-2577	16	238	135	65	32130	•		Unlimited	
Hollywood Locations	213-534-3456	2	177	180	30	31860	•		1000 amps	
Sony Pictures Studios	310-244-6926	27	237	134	80	31758	•		9600 amps	
The Walt Disney Studios	818-560-7450	2	240	130	40	31200	•		Unlimited	
Sony Pictures Studios	310-244-6926	30	236	132	50	31152	•		9600 amps	
Centinela Studios	310-396-3688	a	200	150	22	30000			600ac/320dc	
NBC Universal	818-777-3000	12	199	146	49' 2	29054	•		Unlimited	
Fox Studios	310-369-2786	6	210	134	40	28140	•		9600ac/dc avail.	
Fox Studios	310-369-2786	8	211	133	35	28063	•		9600ac/dc avail.	
Fox Studios	310-369-2786	5	210	133	40	27930	•		9600ac/dc avail.	
Lone Star Studios	818-837-6002	1	180	152	24	27360	•		1200ac	
Fox Studios	310-369-2786	14&15	207	130	40	26910	•		9600ac/dc avail.	
Fox Studios	310-369-2786	16	207	129	40	26703	•		9600ac/dc avail.	
The Lot	323-850-3184	3/4	254	105	35	26670	•		4800 amps	
The Culver Studios	310-202-3400	3	219	119	35	26061	•		7200ac	
Raleigh Studios - Manhattan Beach	323-960-FILM	23	195	130	45	25350	•		7200 amps	
Raleigh Studios - Manhattan Beach	323-960-FILM	24	195	130	45	25350	•		7200 amps	
Raleigh Studios - Manhattan Beach	323-960-FILM	25	195	130	45	25350	•		7200 amps	
Raleigh Studios - Manhattan Beach	323-960-FILM	26	195	130	45	25350	•		7200 amps	
Raleigh Studios - Manhattan Beach	323-960-FILM	27	195	130	45	25350	•		7200 amps	
Warner Bros. Studio Facilities	818-954-2577	29	182	138	45	25116	•		Unlimited	
Ren-Mar Studios	323-463-0808	8/9	215	117	38	25155	•		9000 amps	
CBS Studio Center	818-655-5664	21	190	130	45	24700	•		7200ac	
CBS Studio Center	818-655-5664	B21	190	130	19	24700	•		6000ac	
D.C. Stages & Sets	213-629-5434	III	360	68	19' 6	24480	•	•	500 amps	
CBS Studio Center	818-655-5664	3	200	120	41	24000	•		1000ac/12800dc	
Albuquerque Studios	505-227-2000	3	178	134	55	23852	•		6400 amps	
Albuquerque Studios	505-227-2000	4	178	134	55	23852	•		6400 amps	
Albuquerque Studios	505-227-2000	7	178	134	55	23852	•		6400 amps	
Albuquerque Studios	505-227-2000	8	178	134	55	23852	•		6400 amps	
Sony Pictures Studios	310-244-6926	29	197	118	40	23246	•		9600 amps	
Sony Pictures Studios	310-244-6926	28	197	117	40	23049	•		9600 amps	
Sony Pictures Studios	310-244-6926	26	196	117	40	22932	•		9600 amps	

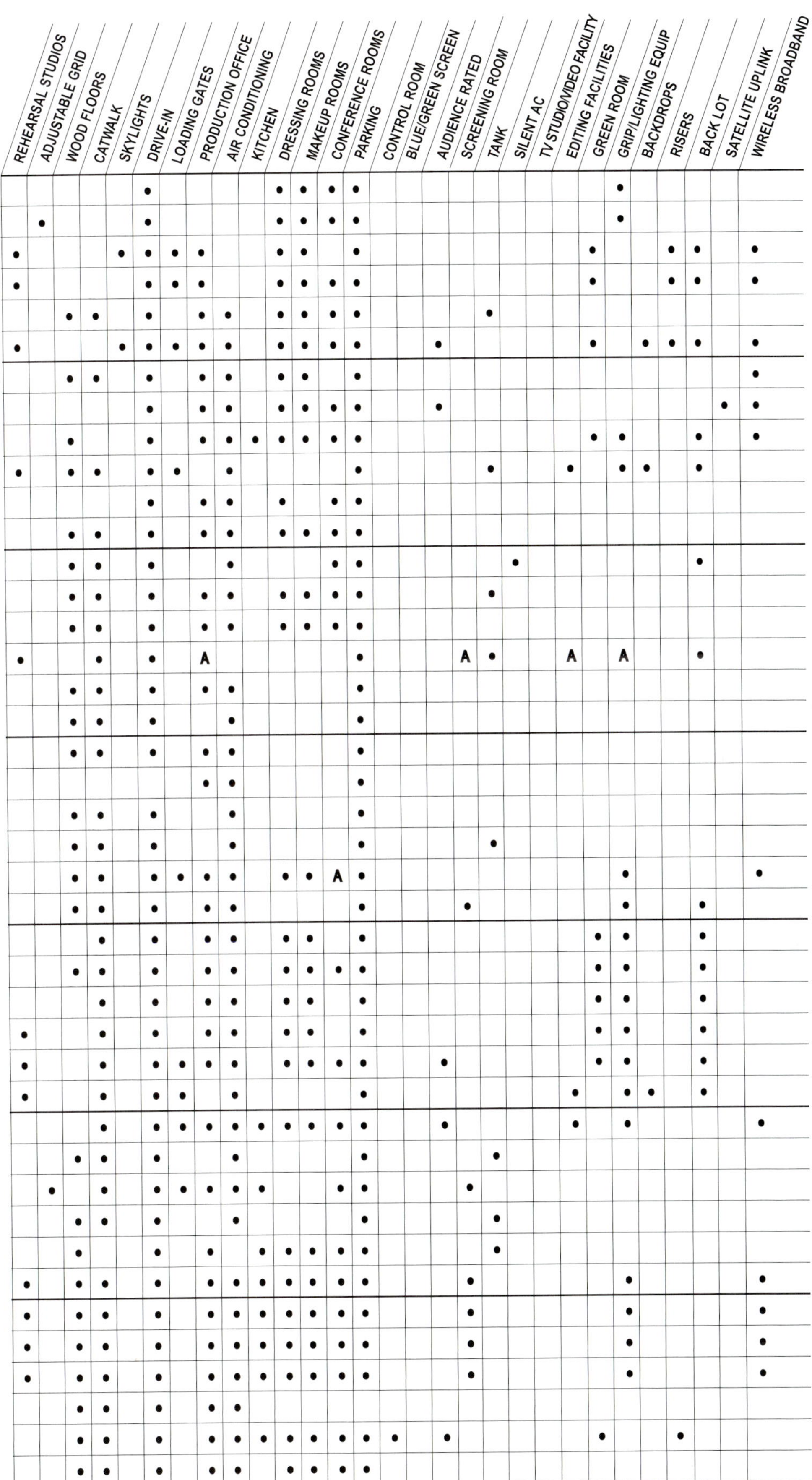

REHEARSAL STUDIOS	ADJUSTABLE GRID	WOOD FLOORS	CATWALK	SKYLIGHTS	DRIVE-IN	LOADING GATES	PRODUCTION OFFICE	AIR CONDITIONING	KITCHEN	DRESSING ROOMS	MAKEUP ROOMS	CONFERENCE ROOMS	PARKING	CONTROL ROOM	BLUE/GREEN SCREEN	AUDIENCE RATED	SCREENING ROOM	TANK	SILENT AC	TV STUDIO/VIDEO FACILITY	EDITING FACILITIES	GREEN ROOM	GRIP/LIGHTING EQUIP	BACKDROPS	RISERS	BACK LOT	SATELLITE UPLINK	WIRELESS BROADBAND
					•					•	•	•	•										•					
	•				•					•	•	•	•										•					
•				•	•	•	•			•	•		•									•			•	•		•
•					•	•	•			•	•	•	•									•			•	•		•
		•	•		•		•	•		•	•	•	•					•										
•				•	•	•	•	•		•	•	•	•			•						•		•	•	•		•
		•	•		•		•	•		•	•		•															•
					•		•	•		•	•	•	•			•											•	•
		•			•		•	•	•	•	•	•	•									•	•			•		•
•		•	•		•	•		•					•					•			•		•	•		•		
					•		•	•		•		•	•															
		•	•		•		•	•		•	•	•	•															
		•	•		•			•				•	•						•							•		
		•	•		•		•	•		•	•	•	•					•										
		•	•		•		•	•		•	•	•	•															
•			•		•		A						•				A	•			A		A			•		
		•	•		•		•	•					•															
		•	•		•			•					•															
		•	•		•		•	•					•															
							•	•					•															
		•	•		•			•					•															
		•	•		•			•					•					•										
		•	•		•	•	•	•		•	•	A	•										•					•
		•	•		•		•	•					•				•						•			•		
			•		•		•	•		•	•		•									•	•			•		
		•	•		•		•	•		•	•	•	•									•	•			•		
			•		•		•	•		•	•		•									•	•			•		
•			•		•		•	•		•	•		•									•	•			•		
•			•		•	•	•	•		•	•	•	•			•						•	•			•		
•			•		•	•		•					•								•		•	•		•		
			•		•	•	•	•	•	•	•	•	•			•					•		•					•
		•	•		•			•					•					•										
	•		•		•	•	•	•	•			•	•				•											
		•	•		•			•					•					•										
		•			•		•		•	•	•	•	•					•										
•		•	•		•		•	•	•	•	•	•	•				•						•					•
•		•	•		•		•	•	•	•	•	•	•				•						•					•
•		•	•		•		•	•	•	•	•	•	•				•						•					•
•		•	•		•		•	•	•	•	•	•	•				•						•					•
		•	•		•		•	•																				
		•	•		•		•	•	•	•	•	•	•	•		•						•			•			
		•	•		•		•	•		•	•	•	•															

A = Available to Rent

STAGE NAME	PHONE	STAGE NUMBER	LENGTH	WIDTH	HEIGHT	AREA SQUARE FEET	SOUND STAGE	INSERT	POWER/AMPS	CYCLORAMAS
Century Studio Corporation	888-878-2437	3/4	198	115	23	22775	•	•	1800ac	
Sony Pictures Studios	310-244-6926	25	194	117	40	22698	•		9600 amps	
Warner Bros. Studio Facilities	818-954-2577	15	206	110	35	22660	•		Unlimited	
CBS Studio Center	818-655-5664	2	200	110	33	22000	•		9000ac/9000dc	
CBS Studio Center	818-655-5664	9	200	110	31	22000	•		5000ac/8000dc	
CBS Studio Center	818-655-5664	10	200	110	31	22000	•		8000ac/11200dc	
Warner Bros. Studio Facilities	818-954-2577	19	160	135	35	21600	•		Unlimited	
Warner Bros. Studio Facilities	818-954-2577	20	160	135	35	21600	•		Unlimited	
Warner Bros. Studio Facilities	818-954-2577	21	160	135	35	21600	•		Unlimited	
Warner Bros. Studio Facilities	818-954-2577	22	160	135	35	21600	•		Unlimited	
Warner Bros. Studio Facilities	818-954-2577	23	160	135	45	21600	•		Unlimited	
Warner Bros. Studio Facilities	818-954-2577	24	160	135	35	21600	•		Unlimited	
Warner Bros. Studio Facilities	818-954-2577	25	160	135	35	21600	•		Unlimited	
Warner Bros. Studio Facilities	818-954-2577	26	160	135	35	21600	•		Unlimited	
Sunset Bronson Studios	323-315-9417	9	247	87	29	21489	•		7200 amps	
Prospect Studios	818-560-7450	4	216	97	40	20952	•	•	Unlimited	
Sony Pictures Studios	310-244-6926	11	201	103	31	20703	•		7200 amps	
NBC Universal	818-777-3000	27	199	99	39' 10	19701	•		Unlimited	
Hollywood Center Studios	323-860-0000	3&8	194	100	30	19400	•		3200ac/2400dc	
The Andrita Media Center	323-344-4500	1	160	120	18	19200	•			
Delfino Studios	818-361-2421	3	213	90	34' 8	19170	•		1800ac	
Century Studio Corporation	888-878-2437	8	176	108	25	19000	•	•	1200ac	2 wall hard
The Walt Disney Studios	818-560-7450	3	190	100	39	19000	•		Unlimited	
Paramount Pictures	323-956-8811	5	247	76	34	18772			120-208v / 3840a	
Sony Pictures Studios	310-244-6926	12	179	104	37	18616	•		7200 amps	
Paramount Pictures	323-956-8811	18	185	99	40	18315			120-208v / 4800a	
Prospect Studios	818-560-7450	6w	144	127	19	18288	•	•	Unlimited	
Fox Studios	310-369-2786	9	189	96	29	18144	•		9600ac/dc avail	
NBC Burbank	818-840-3223	11	179	101	30	18079	•		Unlimited	3 wall soft
Paramount Pictures	323-956-8811	15	164	110	56	18040			120-208v / 9600a	
CBS Studio Center	818-655-5664	22–23	150	120	35	18000	•		6000ac	
CBS Studio Center	818-655-5664	B22	150	120	19	18000	•		6000ac	
CBS Studio Center	818-655-5664	B23	150	120	19	18000	•		6000ac	
Los Angeles Center Studios	213-534-3000	1	150	120	43	18000	•		Unlimited	
Los Angeles Center Studios	213-534-3000	2	150	120	43	18000	•		Unlimited	
Los Angeles Center Studios	213-534-3000	3	150	120	35	18000	•		Unlimited	
Los Angeles Center Studios	213-534-3000	4	150	120	35	18000	•		Unlimited	
Los Angeles Center Studios	213-534-3000	5	150	120	35	18000	•		Unlimited	
Los Angeles Center Studios	213-534-3000	6	150	120	35	18000	•		Unlimited	
Raleigh Studios - Manhattan Beach	323-960-FILM	15	150	120	35	18000	•		7200 amps	
Raleigh Studios - Manhattan Beach	323-960-FILM	16	150	120	35	18000	•		7200 amps	2 wall hard
Raleigh Studios - Manhattan Beach	323-960-FILM	17	150	120	35	18000	•		7200 amps	

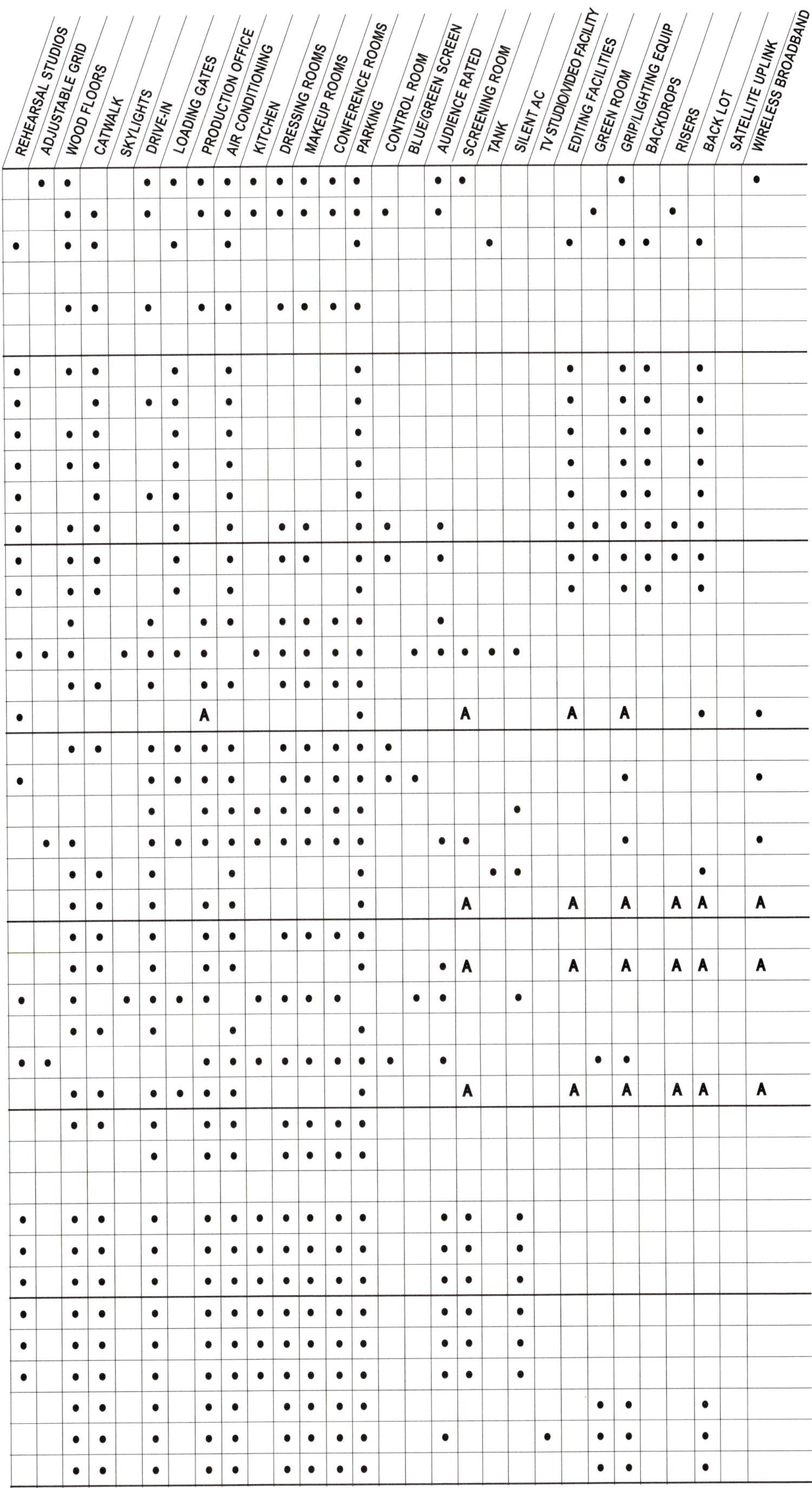

REHEARSAL STUDIOS	ADJUSTABLE GRID	WOOD FLOORS	CATWALK	SKYLIGHTS	DRIVE-IN	LOADING GATES	PRODUCTION OFFICE	AIR CONDITIONING	KITCHEN	DRESSING ROOMS	MAKEUP ROOMS	CONFERENCE ROOMS	PARKING	CONTROL ROOM	BLUE/GREEN SCREEN	AUDIENCE RATED	SCREENING ROOM	TANK	SILENT AC	TV STUDIO/VIDEO FACILITY	EDITING FACILITIES	GREEN ROOM	GRIP/LIGHTING EQUIP	BACKDROPS	RISERS	BACK LOT	SATELLITE UPLINK	WIRELESS BROADBAND
	•	•			•	•	•	•	•	•	•	•	•			•	•						•					•
		•	•		•		•	•	•	•	•	•	•	•		•						•			•			
•		•	•			•		•					•					•			•		•	•		•		
		•	•		•		•	•		•	•	•	•															
•		•	•			•		•					•								•		•	•		•		
•			•		•	•		•					•								•		•	•		•		
•		•	•			•		•					•								•		•	•		•		
•		•	•			•		•					•								•		•	•		•		
•			•		•	•		•					•								•		•	•		•		
•		•	•			•		•		•	•		•	•		•					•	•	•	•	•	•		
•		•	•			•		•		•	•		•	•		•					•	•	•	•	•	•		
•		•	•			•		•					•								•		•	•		•		
		•			•		•	•		•	•	•	•			•												
•	•	•		•	•	•	•		•	•	•	•	•		•	•	•	•	•									
		•	•		•		•	•		•	•	•	•															
•							A						•				A				A		A			•		•
		•	•		•	•	•	•		•	•	•	•	•														
•					•	•	•	•		•	•	•	•	•	•								•					•
					•		•	•	•	•	•	•	•						•									
	•	•			•	•	•	•	•	•	•	•	•			•	•						•					•
		•	•		•			•					•					•	•							•		
		•	•		•		•	•					•				A				A		A	A		A		A
		•	•		•		•	•		•	•	•	•															
		•	•		•		•	•					•			•	A				A		A	A		A		A
•		•		•	•	•	•		•	•	•	•			•	•			•									
		•	•		•			•					•															
•	•						•	•	•	•	•	•	•	•		•						•	•					
		•	•		•	•	•	•					•				A				A		A	A		A		A
		•	•		•		•	•		•	•	•	•															
					•		•	•		•	•	•	•															
•		•	•		•		•	•	•	•	•	•	•			•	•		•									
•		•	•		•		•	•	•	•	•	•	•			•	•		•									
•		•	•		•		•	•	•	•	•	•	•			•	•		•									
•		•	•		•		•	•	•	•	•	•	•			•	•		•									
•		•	•		•		•	•	•	•	•	•	•			•	•		•									
•		•	•		•		•	•	•	•	•	•	•			•	•		•									
		•	•		•		•	•		•	•	•	•									•	•			•		
		•	•		•		•	•		•	•	•	•			•				•		•	•			•		
		•	•		•		•	•		•	•	•	•									•	•			•		

A = Available to Rent

STAGE NAME	PHONE	STAGE NUMBER	LENGTH	WIDTH	HEIGHT	AREA SQUARE FEET	SOUND STAGE	INSERT	POWER/AMPS	CYCLORAMAS
Raleigh Studios - Manhattan Beach	323-960-FILM	18	150	120	35	18000	•		7200 amps	
Raleigh Studios - Manhattan Beach	323-960-FILM	19	150	120	35	18000	•		7200 amps	
Raleigh Studios - Manhattan Beach	323-960-FILM	20	150	120	35	18000	•		7200 amps	
Raleigh Studios - Manhattan Beach	323-960-FILM	21	150	120	35	18000	•		7200 amps	
Raleigh Studios - Manhattan Beach	323-960-FILM	22	150	120	35	18000	•		7200 amps	
Raleigh Studios - Manhattan Beach	323-960-FILM	28	150	120	35	18000	•		7200 amps	
Ren-Mar Studios	323-463-0808	4	100	180	30	18000	•		6500 amps	
Ren-Mar Studios	323-463-0808	5	100	180	30	18000	•		6500 amps	
Paramount Pictures	323-956-8811	16	170	105	40	17850			120-208v / 9600a	
Albuquerque Studios	505-227-2000	5	149	119	35	17731	•		2400 amps	
Albuquerque Studios	505-227-2000	6	149	119	35	17731	•		2400 amps	
Albuquerque Studios	505-227-2000	1	148	119	45	17612	•		4000 amps	
Albuquerque Studios	505-227-2000	2	148	119	45	17612	•		4000 amps	
NBC Universal	818-777-3000	24	157	112	33' 4	17584	•		Unlimited	
NBC Universal	818-777-3000	25	157	112	33' 4	17584	•		Unlimited	
Hollywood Center Studios	323-860-0000	4	174	100	35	17400	•		1600ac / 2400dc	
Paramount Pictures	323-956-8811	14	217	95/64	38	17328			120-208v / 9600a	
The Culver Studios	310-202-3400	15	132	129	43	17028	•		7200ac	
The Culver Studios	310-202-3400	16	131	129	46	16899	•		3200ac	
Warner Bros. Studio Facilities	818-954-2577	8	125	135	35	16875	•		Unlimited	
Warner Bros. Studio Facilities	818-954-2577	9	125	135	35	16875	•		Unlimited	
Warner Bros. Studio Facilities	818-954-2577	10	125	135	35	16875	•		Unlimited	
Warner Bros. Studio Facilities	818-954-2577	12	125	135	35	16875	•		Unlimited	
Sunset-Gower Studios	323-467-1001	14	128	131	35	16768	•		4800 amps	
Warner Bros. Studio Facilities	818-954-2577	4	124	135	35	16740	•		Unlimited	
Warner Bros. Studio Facilities	818-954-2577	17	124	135	35	16740	•		Unlimited	
Paramount Pictures	323-956-8811	8	147	113	30	16611			120-208v / 13200a	
Paramount Pictures	323-956-8811	9	147	113	30	16611			120-208v / 13200a	
Sunset-Gower Studios	323-467-1001	12	128	129	35	16512	•		4800 amps	
Raleigh Studios - Hollywood	323-960-FILM	11	136	120	45	16320	•		6000 amps	
Raleigh Studios - Hollywood	323-960-FILM	12	136	120	45	16320	•		8000 amps	
Fox Studios	310-369-2786	10&11	125	130	40	16250	•		7200ac/dc avail.	
Sony Pictures Studios	310-244-6926	23	157	102	35	16014	•		7200 amps	
Sony Pictures Studios	310-244-6926	24	157	102	35	16014	•		7200 amps	
South Bay Studios	310-762-1360	3	160	100	25	16000		•	Unlimited	3 wall hard
Sunset-Gower Studios	323-467-1001	7	143	107	29	15943	•		4800 amps	
Sunset-Gower Studios	323-467-1001	9	149	107	35	15943	•		7200 amps	
D.C. Stages & Sets	213-629-5434	II	232	68	19' 6	15776	•	•	500 amps	
Sunset Bronson Studios	323-315-9417	6	132	119	30	15708	•		2400 amps	
Paramount Pictures	323-956-8811	32	144	109	46	15696			120-208v / 7200a	
Paramount Pictures	323-956-8811	29	145	108	35	15660			120-208v / 9600a	
Sony Pictures Studios	310-244-6926	14	88	177	34	15576	•		9600 amps	

LA 411 Stage Chart: 18,000—15,576 Sq. Ft. LA 411

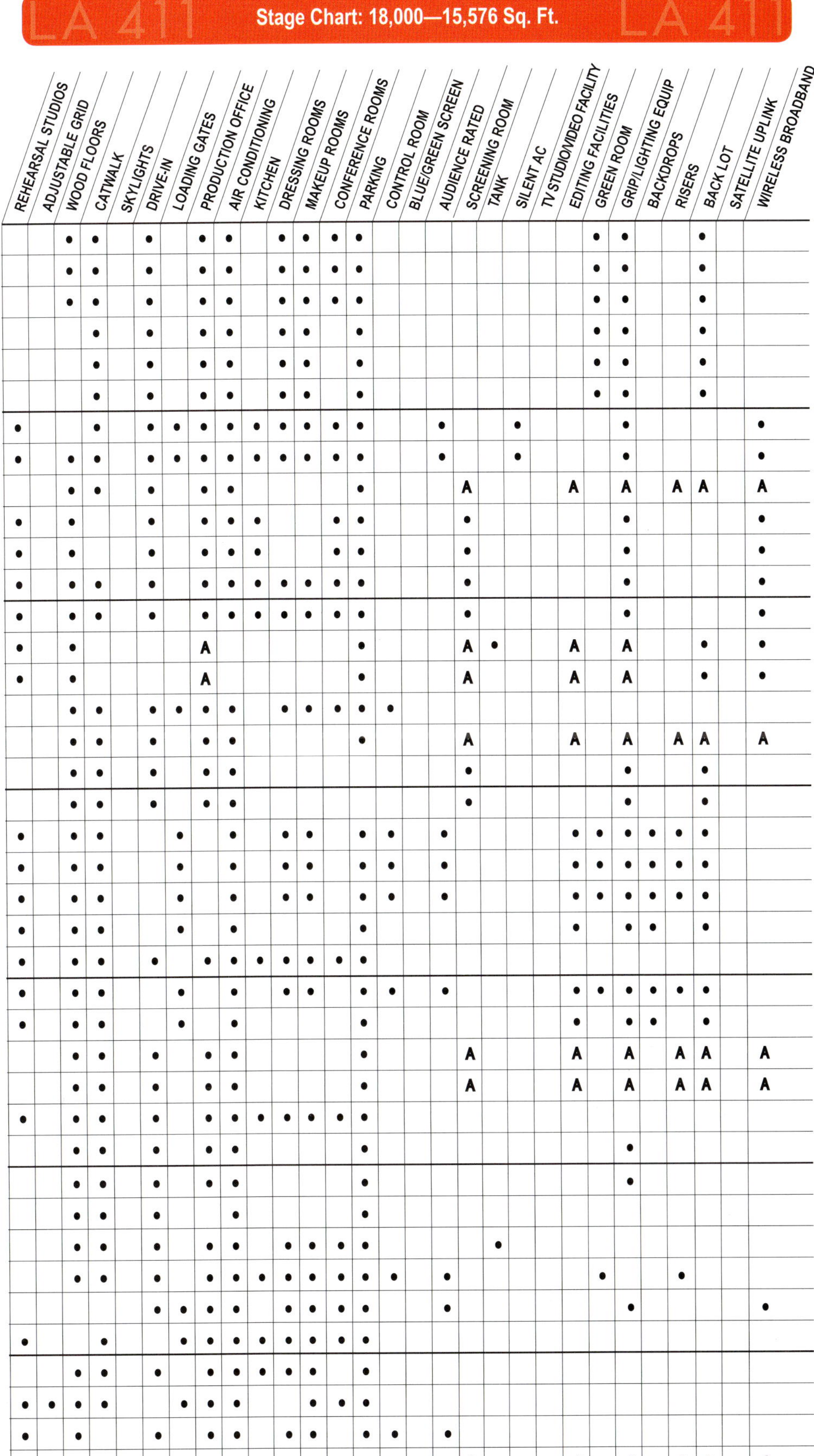

REHEARSAL STUDIOS	ADJUSTABLE GRID	WOOD FLOORS	CATWALK	SKYLIGHTS	DRIVE-IN	LOADING GATES	PRODUCTION OFFICE	AIR CONDITIONING	KITCHEN	DRESSING ROOMS	MAKEUP ROOMS	CONFERENCE ROOMS	PARKING	CONTROL ROOM	BLUE/GREEN SCREEN	AUDIENCE RATED	SCREENING ROOM	TANK	SILENT AC	TV STUDIO/VIDEO FACILITY	EDITING FACILITIES	GREEN ROOM	GRIP/LIGHTING EQUIP	BACKDROPS	RISERS	BACK LOT	SATELLITE UPLINK	WIRELESS BROADBAND
		•	•		•		•	•		•	•	•	•									•	•			•		
		•	•		•		•	•		•	•	•	•									•	•			•		
		•	•		•		•	•		•	•	•	•									•	•			•		
			•		•		•	•		•	•		•									•	•			•		
			•		•		•	•		•	•		•									•	•			•		
			•		•		•	•		•	•		•									•	•			•		
•			•		•	•	•	•	•	•	•	•	•			•			•				•					•
•		•	•		•	•	•	•	•	•	•	•	•			•			•				•					•
		•	•		•		•	•					•				A				A		A		A	A		A
•		•			•		•	•	•			•	•				•						•					•
•		•			•		•	•	•			•	•				•						•					•
•		•	•		•		•	•	•	•	•	•	•				•						•					•
•		•	•		•		•	•	•	•	•	•	•				•						•					•
•		•					A						•				A	•			A		A			•		•
•		•					A						•				A				A		A			•		•
		•	•		•	•	•	•		•	•	•	•	•														
		•	•		•		•	•					•				A				A		A		A	A		A
		•	•		•		•	•									•						•			•		
		•	•		•		•	•									•						•			•		
•		•	•			•		•		•	•		•	•		•					•	•	•	•	•	•		
•		•	•			•		•		•	•		•	•		•					•	•	•	•	•	•		
•		•	•			•		•		•	•		•	•		•					•	•	•	•	•	•		
•		•	•			•		•					•								•		•	•		•		
•		•	•		•		•	•	•	•	•	•	•															
•		•	•			•		•		•	•		•	•		•					•	•	•	•	•	•		
•		•	•			•		•					•								•		•	•		•		
		•	•		•		•	•					•				A				A		A		A	A		A
		•	•		•		•	•					•				A				A		A		A	A		A
•		•	•		•		•	•	•	•	•	•	•															
		•	•		•		•	•					•										•					
		•	•		•		•	•					•										•					
		•	•		•			•					•															
		•	•		•		•	•		•	•	•	•					•										
		•	•		•		•	•	•	•	•	•	•	•		•						•			•			
					•	•	•	•		•	•	•	•			•							•					•
•			•			•	•	•	•	•	•	•	•															
		•	•		•		•	•	•	•	•		•															
•	•	•	•			•	•	•			•	•	•															
•		•			•		•	•		•	•		•	•		•												
		•	•		•		•	•		•	•		•	•		•	A				A		A		A	A		A
		•	•		•		•	•		•	•		•	•			A			•	A	•	A		A	A		A
		•	•		•		•	•		•	•	•	•					•										

A = Available to Rent

STAGE NAME	PHONE	STAGE NUMBER	LENGTH	WIDTH	HEIGHT	AREA SQUARE FEET	SOUND STAGE	INSERT	POWER/AMPS	CYCLORAMAS
Hollywood Center Studios	323-860-0000	10	154	101	35	15554	•		7200 amps	
Hollywood Center Studios	323-860-0000	11	154	101	35	15554	•		7200 amps	
Paramount Pictures	323-956-8811	31	145	107	35	15515			120-208v / 4,800a	
Sony Pictures Studios	310-244-6926	21	152	102	28	15504	•		7200 amps	
Sony Pictures Studios	310-244-6926	22	152	102	28	15504	•		7200 amps	
Century Studio Corporation	888-878-2437	7	111	156	23	15500	•	•	1800ac	
Paramount Pictures	323-956-8811	20	153	99	35	15147			120-208v / 9600a	
Chandler Valley Center Studios, Inc.	818-763-3650	3	150	100	33	15000	•		4800ac	3 wall hard
North Field Properties/Hangar 8	310-392-8844	Hgr 8	100	150	30	15000			3PH/208v	
Prospect Studios	818-560-7450	7	150	100	42	15000	•	•	Unlimited	
Prospect Studios	818-560-7450	9	150	100	42	15000	•	•	Unlimited	
Stu Segall Productions	858-974-8988	3	100	150	20	15000	•	•	400ac	
The Walt Disney Studios	818-560-7450	6	150	100	40	15000	•		Unlimited	
The Walt Disney Studios	818-560-7450	7	150	100	40	15000	•		Unlimited	
Paramount Pictures	323-956-8811	19	153	98	35	14,994			120-208v / 7200a	
Warner Bros. Studio Facilities	818-954-2577	6	110	135	35	14850	•		Unlimited	
Warner Bros. Studio Facilities	818-954-2577	14	110	135	35	14850	•		Unlimited	
Warner Bros. Studio Facilities	818-954-2577	7	109	135	35	14715	•		Unlimited	
Warner Bros. Studio Facilities	818-954-2577	11	109	135	35	14715	•		Unlimited	
Warner Bros. Studio Facilities	818-954-2577	18	109	135	35	14715	•		Unlimited	
Warner Bros. Studio Facilities	818-954-2577	5	108	135	35	14580	•		Unlimited	
Chandler Valley Center Studios, Inc.	818-763-3650	2	145	100	35	14500	•		4800ac	3 wall hard
The Culver Studios	310-202-3400	6	142	102	30	14484	•		7200ac	
Hollywood Center Studios	323-860-0000	5	160	90	25	14400	•		9600ac/1600dc	1 wall hard
Occidental Studios, Inc.	213-384-3331	12	120	120	45	14400	•		12000 amps	
Quixote Studios Griffith Park	323-957-9933	7	120	120	42	14400			2400 amps	
Raleigh Studios - Hollywood	323-960-FILM	1	125	115	35	14375	•		5600 amps	
CBS Studio Center	818-655-5664	12	130	110	29	14300	•		6000ac/4800dc	
Raleigh Studios - Hollywood	323-960-FILM	14	130	110	30	14300	•		8000 amps	
NBC Universal	818-777-3000	41	140	102	30' 1	14280	•		Unlimited	
NBC Universal	818-777-3000	42	140	102	30	14280	•		Unlimited	
NBC Universal	818-777-3000	43	140	102	30' 3	14280	•		Unlimited	
NBC Universal	818-777-3000	44	140	102	30	14280	•		Unlimited	
Sunset-Gower Studios	323-467-1001	1	152	93.5	22	14212	•		4800 amps	
Santa Clarita Studios	661-294-2000	7	94	150	35	14100	•		3600 amps	
Santa Clarita Studios	661-294-2000	8	94	150	35	14100	•		3600 amps	
Fox Studios	310-369-2786	18	138	102	35	14076	•		7200ac/dc avail.	
Fox Studios	310-369-2786	17&19	138	102	35	14076	•		9600ac/dc avail.	
Fox Studios	310-369-2786	20	138	102	35	14076	•		4800ac/dc avail.	
Fox Studios	310-369-2786	21	138	102	35	14076	•		4800ac/dcavail.	
Fox Studios	310-369-2786	22	138	102	35	14076	•		4800ac/dc avail.	
Sunset-Gower Studios	323-467-1001	16	138	102	35	14000	•		4800 amps	

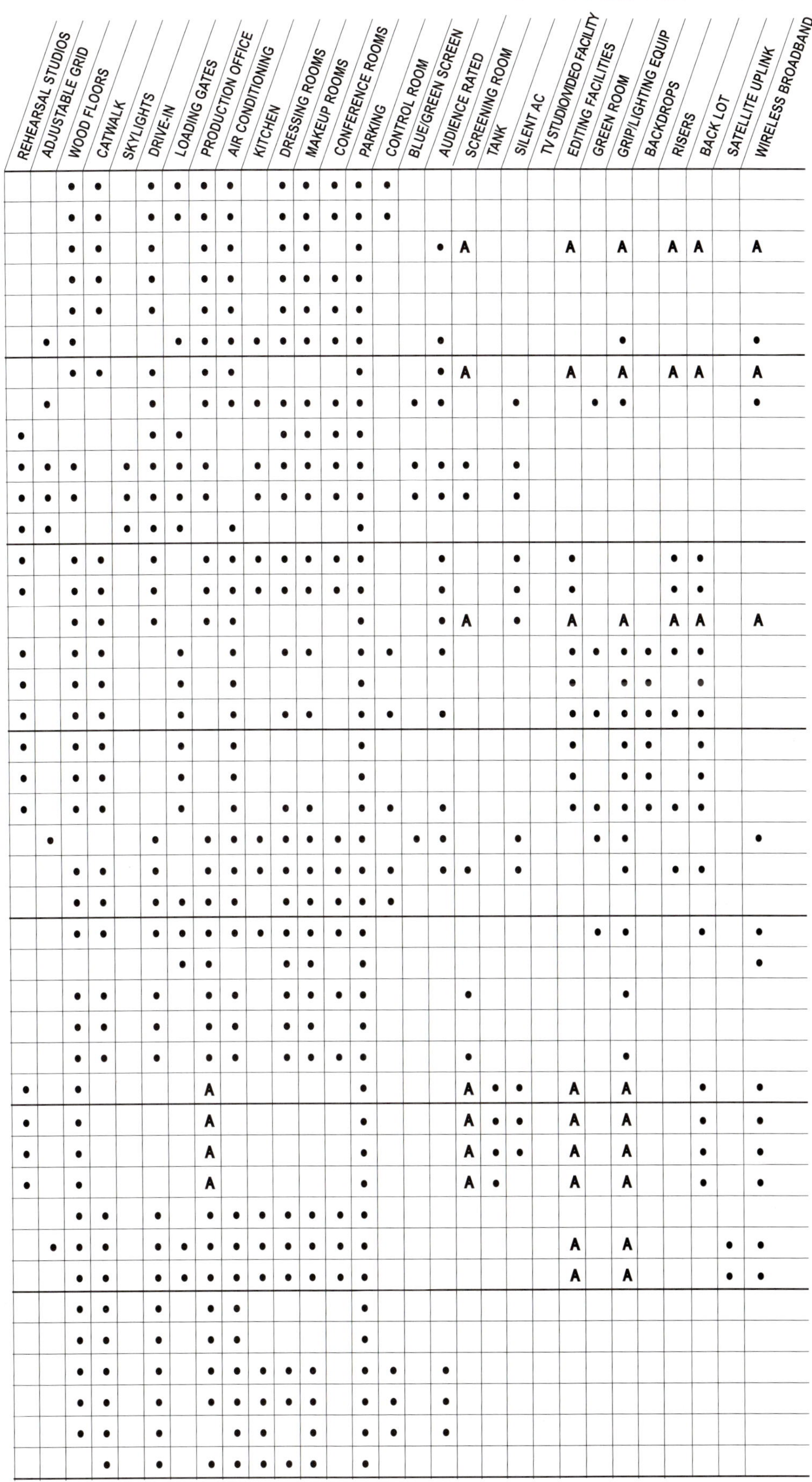

REHEARSAL STUDIOS	ADJUSTABLE GRID	WOOD FLOORS	CATWALK	SKYLIGHTS	DRIVE-IN	LOADING GATES	PRODUCTION OFFICE	AIR CONDITIONING	KITCHEN	DRESSING ROOMS	MAKEUP ROOMS	CONFERENCE ROOMS	PARKING	CONTROL ROOM	BLUE/GREEN SCREEN	AUDIENCE RATED	SCREENING ROOM	TANK	SILENT AC	TV STUDIO/VIDEO FACILITY	EDITING FACILITIES	GREEN ROOM	GRIP/LIGHTING EQUIP	BACKDROPS	RISERS	BACK LOT	SATELLITE UPLINK	WIRELESS BROADBAND
		•	•		•	•	•	•		•	•	•	•	•														
		•	•		•	•	•	•		•	•	•	•	•														
		•	•		•		•	•		•	•		•			•	A				A		A		A	A		A
		•	•		•		•	•		•	•	•	•															
		•	•		•		•	•		•	•	•	•															
	•	•				•	•	•	•	•	•	•	•			•							•					•
		•	•		•		•	•					•			•	A				A		A		A	A		A
	•				•		•	•	•	•	•	•	•		•	•			•			•	•					•
•					•	•				•	•	•	•															
•	•	•		•	•	•	•		•	•	•	•	•		•	•	•		•									
•	•	•		•	•	•	•		•	•	•	•	•		•	•	•		•									
•	•			•	•	•		•					•															
•		•	•		•		•	•	•	•	•	•	•			•			•		•				•	•		
•		•	•		•		•	•	•	•	•	•	•			•			•		•				•	•		
		•	•		•		•	•					•			•	A		•		A		A		A	A		A
•		•	•			•		•		•	•		•	•		•					•	•	•	•	•	•		
•		•	•			•		•					•								•		•	•		•		
•		•	•			•		•		•	•		•	•		•					•	•	•	•	•	•		
•		•	•			•		•					•								•		•	•		•		
•		•	•			•		•					•								•		•	•		•		
•		•	•			•		•		•	•		•	•		•					•	•	•	•	•	•		
	•				•		•	•	•	•	•	•	•		•	•			•			•	•					•
		•	•		•		•	•	•	•	•	•	•	•		•	•		•				•		•	•		
		•	•		•	•	•	•		•	•	•	•	•														
		•	•		•	•	•	•	•	•	•	•	•									•	•			•		•
						•	•			•	•		•															•
		•	•		•		•	•		•	•	•	•				•						•					
		•	•		•		•	•		•	•		•															
		•	•		•		•	•		•	•	•	•				•						•					
•		•					A						•				A	•	•		A		A			•		•
•		•					A						•				A	•	•		A		A			•		•
•		•					A						•				A	•	•		A		A			•		•
•		•					A						•				A	•			A		A			•		•
		•	•		•		•	•	•	•	•	•	•															
	•	•	•		•	•	•	•	•	•	•	•	•								A		A				•	•
		•	•		•	•	•	•	•	•	•	•	•								A		A				•	•
		•	•		•		•	•					•															
		•	•		•		•	•					•															
		•	•		•		•	•	•	•	•		•	•		•												
		•	•		•		•	•	•	•	•		•	•		•												
		•	•		•			•	•		•		•	•		•												
			•		•		•	•	•	•	•		•															

A = Available to Rent

STAGE NAME	PHONE	STAGE NUMBER	LENGTH	WIDTH	HEIGHT	AREA SQUARE FEET	SOUND STAGE	INSERT	POWER/AMPS	CYCLORAMAS
CBS Studio Center	818-655-5664	14–17	140	100	35	14000	•		5000ac/4800dc	
CBS Studio Center	818-655-5664	18–20	140	100	24	14000	•		3600ac/3200dc	
NBC Universal	818-777-3000	37	140	100	30	14000	•		Unlimited	
Warner Bros. Ranch	818-954-2577	30	100	138	35	13800	•		Unlimited	
NBC Universal	818-777-3000	28	142	98	43' 11	13916	•		Unlimited	
Paramount Pictures	323-956-8811	4	195	71	26	13845			120-208v / 4800a	
Lone Star Studios	818-837-6002	2&3	152	91	24	13832	•		1200ac	
Studio 34	323-223-1234	2	192	72	20	13824	•		8600ac	
The Culver Studios	310-202-3400	14	136	101	39	13736	•		7200ac	
NBC Universal	818-777-3000	29	141	97	27	13677	•		Unlimited	
NBC Universal	818-777-3000	31	141	97	27	13677	•		Unlimited	
Sunset-Gower Studios	323-467-1001	15	138	99	35	13662	•		4800 amps	
The Culver Studios	310-202-3400	12	136	99	40	13464	•		120/208v	
The Culver Studios	310-202-3400	5	131	102	30	13362	•		7200ac	
The Lot	323-850-3184	1	127	105	35	13335	•		4800 amps	
The Lot	323-850-3184	2	127	105	35	13335	•		4800 amps	
The Lot	323-850-3184	3	127	105	35	13335	•		4800 amps	
The Lot	323-850-3184	4	127	105	35	13335	•		4800 amps	
The Culver Studios	310-202-3400	11	136	98	40	13328	•		7200ac	2 wall hard w/cove
Raleigh Studios - Hollywood	323-960-FILM	5	148	90	35	13320	•		5000 amps	3 wall hard
Century Studio Corporation	888-878-2437	1	125	105	22	13125	•	•	1800ac	2 wall hard
Raleigh Studios - Playa Vista	323-960-FILM	34	156	84	22	13104	•		3600 amps	
Century Studio Corporation	888-878-2437	2	125	144	22	13,000	•	•	1200ac	
Saticoy Stage	818-909-6999	3	115'6	112'6	36	12994			12000ac	
Paramount Pictures	323-956-8811	23	170	75	28	12750			120-208v / 4800a	
Paramount Pictures	323-956-8811	24	170	75	28	12750			120-208v / 7200a	
Paramount Pictures	323-956-8811	25	169	75	28	12675			120-208v / 9600a	
Paramount Pictures	323-956-8811	17	186	68	36	12648			120-208v / 7200a	
Sony Pictures Studios	310-244-6926	10	144	86	29	12384	•		4800 amps	
NBC Burbank	818-840-3223	2	139	89	42	12371	•		Unlimited	4 wall hard
NBC Burbank	818-840-3223	4	139	89	42	12371	•		Unlimited	4 wall soft
Warner Bros. Ranch	818-954-2577	31	78	158	35	12324	•		Unlimited	
NBC Universal	818-777-3000	3	154	80	27' 2	12320	•		Unlimited	
Sunset-Gower Studios	323-467-1001	2	138	89	24	12282	•		4800 amps	
The Walt Disney Studios	818-560-7450	5	128	95	40	12200	•		Unlimited	
Lone Star Studios	818-837-6002	4	152	80	24	12160	•		1200ac	
CBS Studio Center	818-655-5664	4	120	100	26	12000	•		5000ac/11200dc	
CBS Studio Center	818-655-5664	5	120	100	26	12000	•		5000ac/9600dc	
NBC Universal	818-777-3000	23	157	76	28	11932	•		Unlimited	
Stu Segall Productions	858-974-8988	4	110	108	20	11880	•	•	400ac	
NBC Burbank	818-840-3223	9	149	79	19	11745	•		Unlimited	3 wall soft
Sunset Bronson Studios	323-315-9417	9B	135	87	29	11745	•			

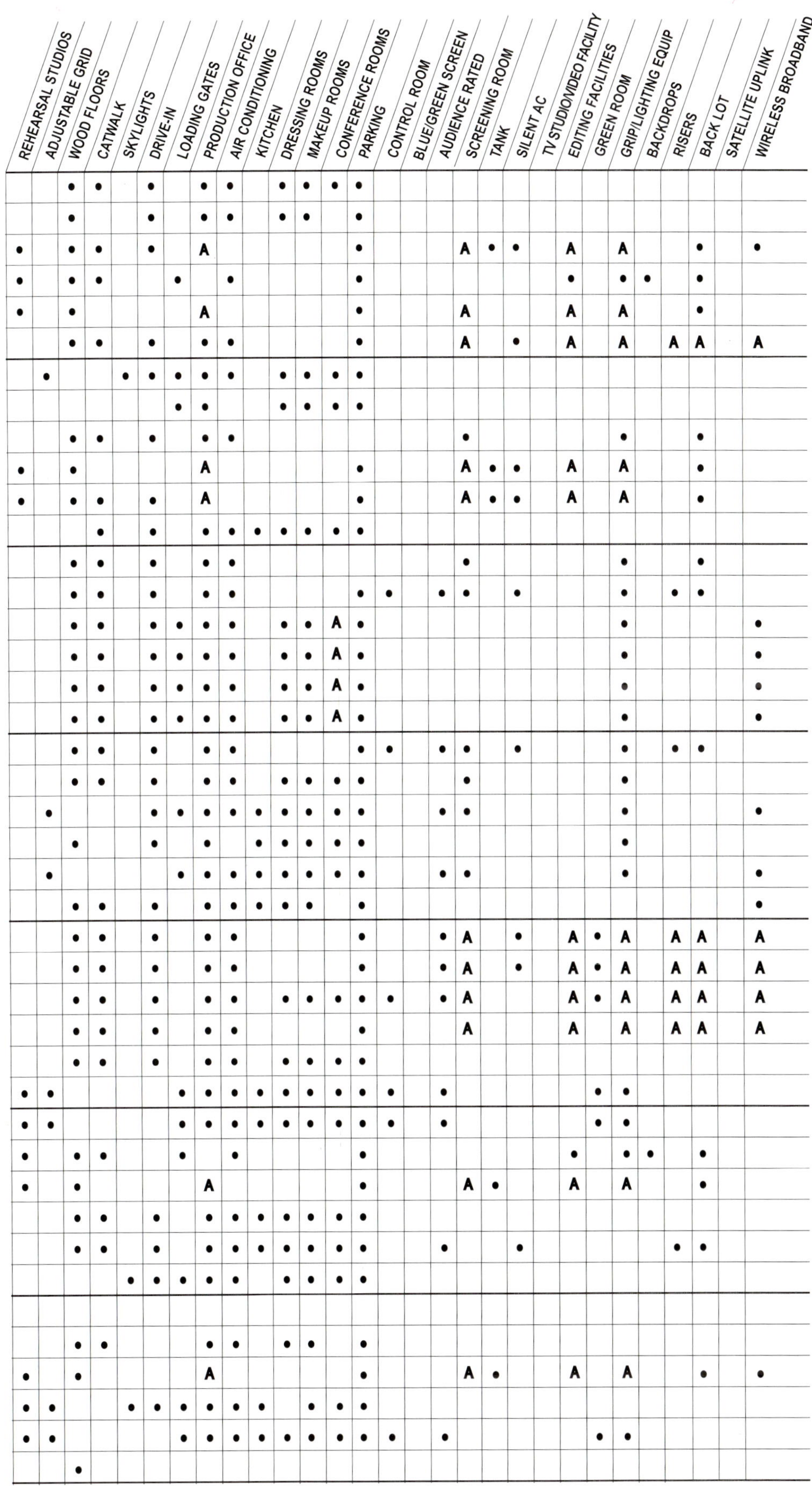

REHEARSAL STUDIOS	ADJUSTABLE GRID	WOOD FLOORS	CATWALK	SKYLIGHTS	DRIVE-IN	LOADING GATES	PRODUCTION OFFICE	AIR CONDITIONING	KITCHEN	DRESSING ROOMS	MAKEUP ROOMS	CONFERENCE ROOMS	PARKING	CONTROL ROOM	BLUE/GREEN SCREEN	AUDIENCE RATED	SCREENING ROOM	TANK	SILENT AC	TV STUDIO/VIDEO FACILITY	EDITING FACILITIES	GREEN ROOM	GRIP/LIGHTING EQUIP	BACKDROPS	RISERS	BACK LOT	SATELLITE UPLINK	WIRELESS BROADBAND
		•	•		•		•	•		•	•	•	•															
		•			•		•	•		•	•		•															
•		•	•		•		A						•				A	•	•		A		A			•		•
•		•	•			•		•					•								•		•	•		•		
•		•					A						•				A				A		A			•		
		•	•		•		•	•					•				A		•		A		A		A	A		A
	•			•	•	•	•	•		•	•	•	•															
						•	•			•	•	•	•															
		•	•		•		•	•									•						•			•		
•		•					A						•				A	•	•		A		A			•		
•		•	•		•		A						•				A	•	•		A		A			•		
			•		•		•	•	•	•	•	•	•															
		•	•		•		•	•									•						•			•		
		•	•		•		•	•					•	•		•	•		•				•		•	•		
		•	•		•	•	•	•		•	•	A	•										•					•
		•	•		•	•	•	•		•	•	A	•										•					•
		•	•		•	•	•	•		•	•	A	•										•					•
		•	•		•	•	•	•		•	•	A	•										•					•
		•	•		•		•	•					•	•		•	•		•				•		•	•		
		•	•		•		•	•		•	•	•	•				•						•					
	•				•	•	•	•	•	•	•	•	•			•	•						•					•
		•			•		•		•	•	•	•	•										•					
	•					•	•	•	•	•	•	•	•			•	•						•					•
		•	•		•		•	•	•	•			•															•
		•	•		•		•	•					•			•	A		•		A	•	A		A	A		A
		•	•		•		•	•					•			•	A		•		A	•	A		A	A		A
		•	•		•		•	•		•	•	•	•	•		•	A				A	•	A		A	A		A
		•	•		•		•	•					•				A				A		A		A	A		A
		•	•		•		•	•		•	•	•	•															
•	•					•	•	•	•	•	•	•	•	•		•						•	•					
•	•					•	•	•	•	•	•	•	•	•		•						•	•					
•		•	•			•		•					•								•		•	•		•		
•		•					A						•				A	•			A		A			•		
		•	•		•		•	•	•	•	•	•	•															
		•	•		•		•	•	•	•	•	•	•			•			•						•	•		
				•	•	•	•	•		•	•	•	•															
		•	•				•	•		•	•		•															
•		•					A						•				A	•			A		A			•		•
•	•			•	•	•	•	•	•		•	•	•															
•	•					•	•	•	•	•	•	•	•	•		•						•	•					
		•																										

A = Available to Rent

STAGE NAME	PHONE	STAGE NUMBER	LENGTH	WIDTH	HEIGHT	AREA SQUARE FEET	SOUND STAGE	INSERT	POWER/AMPS	CYCLORAMAS
Delfino Studios	818-361-2421	4	163	72	14	11736	•		Generator Req.	
Century Studio Corporation	888-878-2437	6	111	105	13	11650	•	•	600ac	
NBC Universal	818-777-3000	22	157	74	27	11618	•		Unlimited	
Sunset-Gower Studios	323-467-1001	4	158	73	23	11534	•		4800 amps	
Paramount Pictures	323-956-8811	7	167	69	23/65	11523			120-208v / 7200a	
NBC Universal	818-777-3000	16	144	80	28' 8	11520	•		Unlimited	
Santa Clarita Studios	661-294-2000	1	90	128	24	11520	•		3600 amps	
Santa Clarita Studios	661-294-2000	2	90	128	24	11520	•		3600 amps	2 wall hard
Santa Clarita Studios	661-294-2000	3	90	128	24	11520	•		3600 amps	
Santa Clarita Studios	661-294-2000	4	90	128	24	11520	•		4800 amps	
Santa Clarita Studios	661-294-2000	5	90	128	24	11520	•		3600 amps	
Santa Clarita Studios	661-294-2000	6	90	128	24	11520	•		3600 amps	
Sunset-Gower Studios	323-467-1001	3	157	72	24	11304	•		4800 amps	
Sony Pictures Studios	310-244-6926	9	152	74	32	11248	•		7200 amps	3 wall hard
Ren-Mar Studios	323-463-0808	6	70	160	30	11200	•		6500 amps	
Stu Segall Productions	858-974-8988	6	80	140	20	11200	•	•	400ac	
GMT Studios	310-649-3733	7	116	96	25	11136	•		3600ac	
The Walt Disney Studios	818-560-7450	4	128	87	40	11100	•		Unlimited	
South Bay Studios	310-762-1360	14	110	100	25	11000		•	Unlimited	3 wall hard
The Andrita Media Center	323-344-4500	2	110	100	18	11000	•			
The Walt Disney Studios	818-560-7450	1	154	71	40	10934	•		Unlimited	
Delfino Studios	818-361-2421	1	120	90	23	10800	•		1800ac	2 wall hard
Hollywood Center Studios	323-860-0000	6	120	90	26	10800	•		1600ac/2400dc	3 wall hard
Warner Bros. Studio Facilities	818-954-2577	1	109	99	35	10791	•		Unlimited	
Warner Bros. Studio Facilities	818-954-2577	3	109	99	35	10791	•		Unlimited	
Raleigh Studios - Playa Vista	323-960-FILM	30	220	49	31	10780	•		2400 amps	
Warner Bros. Studio Facilities	818-954-2577	2	109	98	35	10682	•		Unlimited	
Paramount Pictures	323-956-8811	27	127	84	32	10668			120-208v / 9600a	
Warner Bros. Studio Facilities	818-954-2577	27	79	135	35	10665	•		Unlimited	
Warner Bros. Studio Facilities	818-954-2577	27A	79	135	35	10665	•		Unlimited	
Warner Bros. Studio Facilities	818-954-2577	28	79	135	35	10665	•		Unlimited	
Warner Bros. Studio Facilities	818-954-2577	28A	79	135	35	10665	•		Unlimited	
Paramount Pictures	323-956-8811	1	146	73	25	10,658			120-208v / 7200a	
NBC Universal	818-777-3000	18	144	74	29' 1	10656	•		Unlimited	
NBC Universal	818-777-3000	20	144	74	27' 1	10656	•		Unlimited	
NBC Universal	818-777-3000	4	154	69	27' 10	10626	•		Unlimited	
NBC Burbank	818-840-3223	1	119	89	42	10591	•		Unlimited	3 wall soft
Raleigh Studios - Playa Vista	323-960-FILM	33	126	84	22	10584	•		3000 amps	
Prospect Studios	818-560-7450	5	87	121	56	10527	•	•	Unlimited	
NBC Burbank	818-840-3223	3	118	89	42	10502	•		Unlimited	3 wall soft
Sunset-Gower Studios	323-467-1001	8	126.5	83	35	10500	•		7200 amps	
The Lot	323-850-3184	5	112	92.5	35	10360	•		4800 amps	

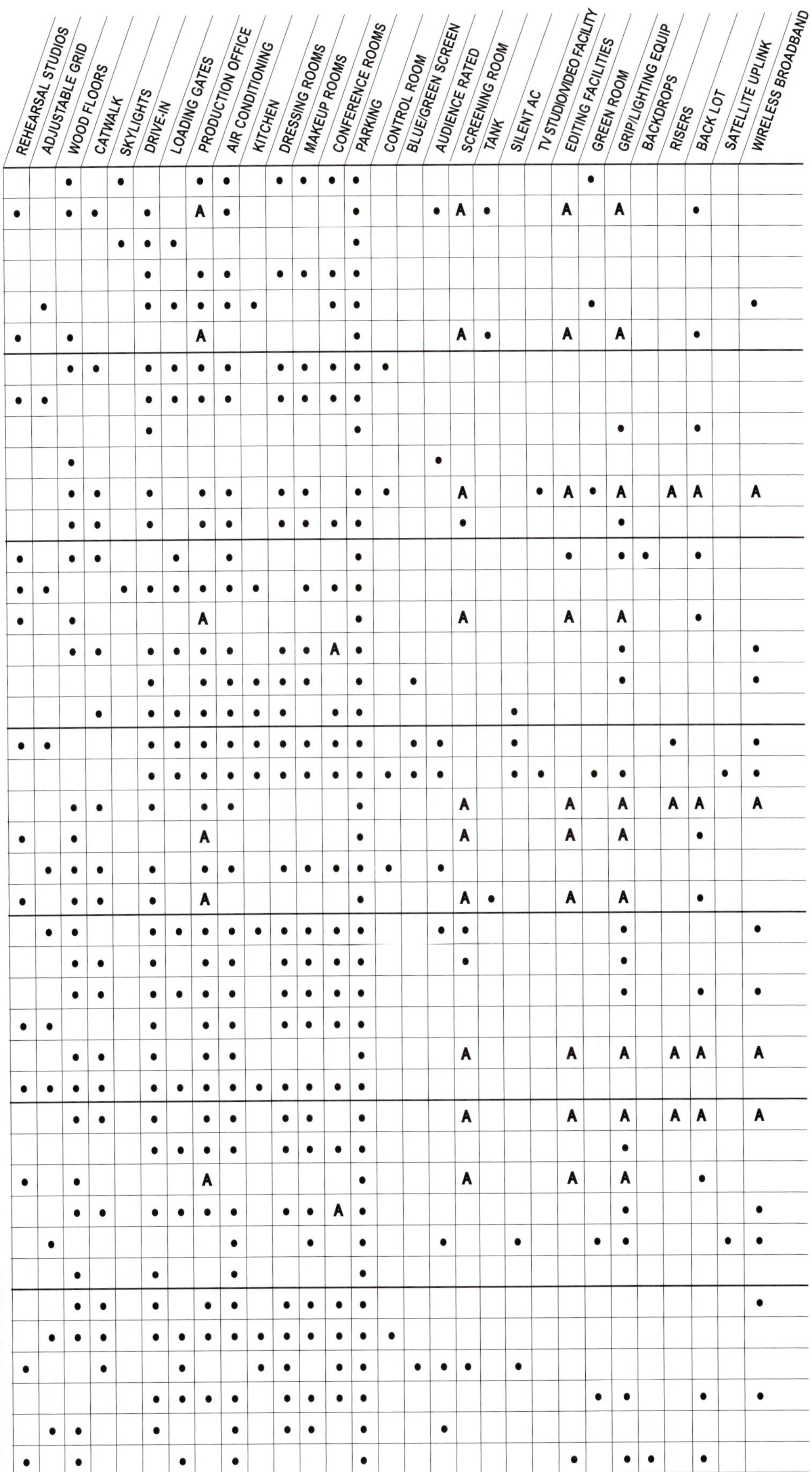

REHEARSAL STUDIOS	ADJUSTABLE GRID	WOOD FLOORS	CATWALK	SKYLIGHTS	DRIVE-IN	LOADING GATES	PRODUCTION OFFICE	AIR CONDITIONING	KITCHEN	DRESSING ROOMS	MAKEUP ROOMS	CONFERENCE ROOMS	PARKING	CONTROL ROOM	BLUE/GREEN SCREEN	AUDIENCE RATED	SCREENING ROOM	TANK	SILENT AC	TV STUDIO/VIDEO FACILITY	EDITING FACILITIES	GREEN ROOM	GRIP/LIGHTING EQUIP	BACKDROPS	RISERS	BACK LOT	SATELLITE UPLINK	WIRELESS BROADBAND
		•		•			•	•		•	•	•	•									•						
•		•	•		•		A	•					•			•	A	•			A		A			•		
				•	•	•							•															
					•		•	•		•	•	•	•															
	•				•	•	•	•	•			•	•									•						•
•		•					A						•				A	•			A		A			•		
		•	•		•	•	•	•		•	•	•	•	•														
•	•				•	•	•	•		•	•	•	•															
					•								•										•			•		
		•														•												
		•	•		•		•	•		•	•		•	•			A			•	A	•	A		A	A		A
		•	•		•		•	•		•	•	•	•				•						•					
•		•	•			•		•					•								•		•	•		•		
•	•			•	•	•	•	•	•		•	•	•															
•		•					A						•				A				A		A			•		
		•	•		•	•	•	•		•	•	A	•										•					•
					•		•	•	•	•	•		•		•								•					•
			•		•	•	•	•	•	•		•	•						•									
•	•				•	•	•	•	•	•	•	•	•		•	•			•						•			•
					•	•	•	•	•	•	•	•	•	•	•	•			•	•		•	•				•	•
		•	•		•		•	•					•				A				A		A		A	A		A
•		•					A						•				A				A		A			•		
	•	•	•		•		•	•		•	•	•	•	•		•												
•		•	•		•		A						•				A	•			A		A			•		
	•	•			•	•	•	•	•	•	•	•	•			•	•						•					•
		•	•		•		•	•		•	•	•	•				•						•					
		•	•		•	•	•	•		•	•	•	•										•			•		•
•	•				•		•	•		•	•	•	•															
		•	•		•		•	•					•				A				A		A		A	A		A
•	•	•	•		•	•	•	•	•	•	•	•	•															
		•	•		•		•	•		•	•		•				A				A		A		A	A		A
					•	•	•	•		•	•	•	•										•					
•		•					A						•				A				A		A			•		
		•	•		•	•	•	•		•	•	A	•										•					•
	•							•			•		•			•			•			•	•				•	•
		•			•			•					•															
		•	•		•		•	•		•	•	•	•															•
	•	•	•		•	•	•	•	•	•	•	•	•	•														
•			•			•			•	•		•	•		•	•	•		•									
					•	•	•	•		•	•	•	•									•	•			•		•
	•	•			•			•		•	•		•			•												
•		•				•		•					•								•		•	•		•		

A = Available to Rent

STAGE NAME	PHONE	STAGE NUMBER	LENGTH	WIDTH	HEIGHT	AREA SQUARE FEET	SOUND STAGE	INSERT	POWER/AMPS	CYCLORAMAS
KCET Studios	323-953-5258	2	110	70	25' 6	7700	•		1200ac	180 white/black
Sunset Bronson Studios	323-315-9417	3	100	76	30	7600	•		9600 amps	
Sunset Bronson Studios	323-315-9417	5	101	75	30	7575	•		9600 amps	
Paramount Pictures	323-956-8811	6	109	69	30	7521			120-208v / 9600a	
The Henson Soundstage	323-856-2682	1	100	75	26	7500	•	•	1200 amps	3 wall hard
Quixote Studios Griffith Park	323-957-9933	6	120	60	24	7200	•		2400 amps	3 wall hard
South Bay Studios	310-762-1360	1	120	60	19	7200	•	•	Unlimited	3 wall hard
CBS Studio Center	818-655-5664	11	110	65	27	7150	•		3600ac/4800dc	
Solar Studios	818-240-1893	1	110	65	14-22	7150	•	•	1200 amps	2 wall hard
Sunset Bronson Studios	323-315-9417	2	94	75.5	30	7097	•		9600 amps	
Redemption Stages	818-238-0012	2	110	64	18	7040	•		2400	2 wall
ShowBiz Studios	818-989-7007	4	105	67	30	7035	•		4800	2 wall
Line 204 Studios	323-960-0113	B/West	100	70	27	7000	•		1200ac	
South Bay Studios	310-762-1360	2	140	50	25	7000		•	Unlimited	3 wall hard
UFO - The Poodle Parlor	213-694-0556	1	88	78	15	6864			400ac	
NBC Universal	818-777-3000	33	99	69	25	6831	•		Unlimited	
NBC Universal	818-777-3000	34	99	69	25	6831	•		Unlimited	
NBC Universal	818-777-3000	35	99	69	25	6831	•		Unlimited	
NBC Universal	818-777-3000	36	99	69	24' 11	6831	•		Unlimited	
Occidental Studios, Inc.	213-384-3331	11	100	68	18	6800	•		3600 amps	3 wall hard
Paramount Pictures	323-956-8811	26	100	68	28	6,800			120-208v / 9600a	
Hollywood Center Studios	323-860-0000	1	97	70	24	6790	•		800ac/1200dc	
Hollywood Center Studios	323-860-0000	2	97	70	24	6790	•		800ac/1200dc	
D.C. Stages & Sets	213-629-5434	MILL	169	40	19' 6	6760	•	•	500 amps	
Raleigh Studios - Hollywood	323-960-FILM	7	90	75	20	6750	•		2000 amps	2 wall hard
KCET Studios	323-953-5258	1	92	70	25' 6	6440	•		1200ac	180 white/black
The Culver Studios	310-202-3400	2	54	119	40	6426	•		120/208v	
Apache Studios	818-842-9944	1	70	90	21	6300	•	•	2400 amps	
Burbank Valcom Studios	818-848-5800	2	90	70	17	6300	•	•	2000ac	3 wall soft
Gothic Moon Studio	714-453-0970	1	90	70	14	6300	•		800 amps	2 wall hard
Line 204 Studios	323-960-0113	A/East	90	70	25	6300	•		1200ac	2 wall hard
Studio C2	310-761-1767	1	105	60	24	6300			1200ac	3 wall hard
Laurel Canyon Stages	818-768-8935	B	93	67	18	6231			600-1200ac	
Paramount Pictures	323-956-8811	12	95	65	38	6175		•	120-208v / 2400a	
Warner Bros. Ranch	818-954-2577	33	78	78	20	6084	•	•	Unlimited	
Raleigh Studios - Hollywood	323-960-FILM	10	79	77	20	6083	•		3600 amps	
Paramount Pictures	323-956-8811	11	95	64	38	6080		•	120-208v / 2400a	
Sunset Bronson Studios	323-315-9417	10	81	75	29	6075	•		2400 amps	
Raleigh Studios - Hollywood	323-960-FILM	8	100	60	20	6000	•		1200 amps	
AMP Studios	805-955-7742	A	85	68	26	5780	•		5640 amps	3 wall soft
New Deal Studios, Inc.	310-578-9929	1	78	73	25	5694		•	1800ac	
The Culver Studios	310-202-3400	7	80	70	30	5600	•		7200ac	

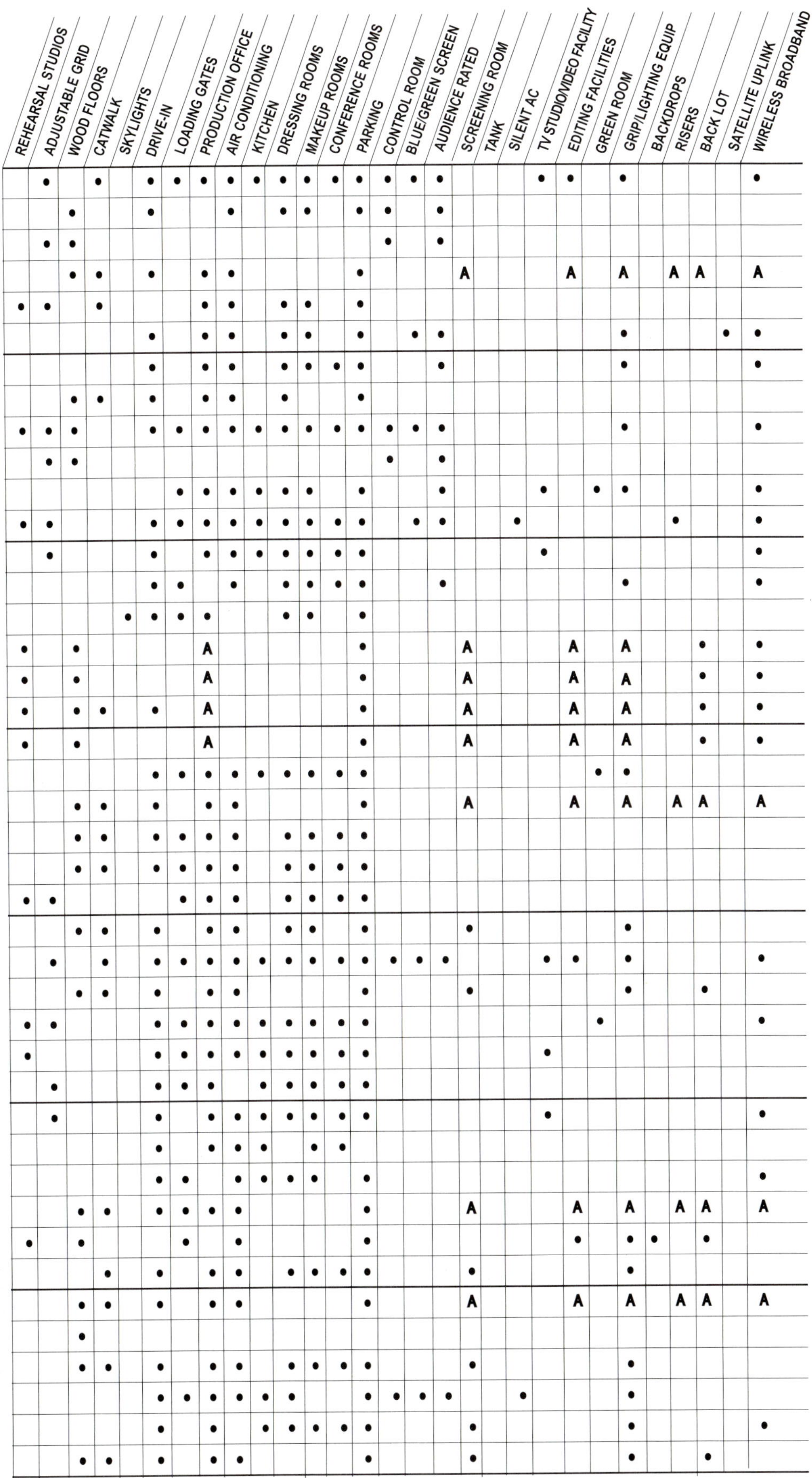

REHEARSAL STUDIOS	ADJUSTABLE GRID	WOOD FLOORS	CATWALK	SKYLIGHTS	DRIVE-IN	LOADING GATES	PRODUCTION OFFICE	AIR CONDITIONING	KITCHEN	DRESSING ROOMS	MAKEUP ROOMS	CONFERENCE ROOMS	PARKING	CONTROL ROOM	BLUE/GREEN SCREEN	AUDIENCE RATED	SCREENING ROOM	TANK	SILENT AC	TV STUDIO/VIDEO FACILITY	EDITING FACILITIES	GREEN ROOM	GRIP/LIGHTING EQUIP	BACKDROPS	RISERS	BACK LOT	SATELLITE UPLINK	WIRELESS BROADBAND
	•		•		•	•	•	•	•	•	•	•	•	•	•	•				•	•		•					•
		•			•			•		•	•		•	•		•												
	•	•												•		•												
		•	•		•		•	•					•				A				A		A		A	A		A
•	•		•				•	•		•	•		•															
					•		•	•		•	•		•		•	•							•				•	•
					•		•	•		•	•	•	•			•							•					•
		•	•		•		•	•		•			•															
•	•	•			•	•	•	•	•	•	•	•	•	•	•	•							•					•
	•	•												•		•												
						•	•	•	•	•	•		•			•				•		•	•					•
•	•				•	•	•	•	•	•	•	•	•		•	•			•						•			•
	•				•		•	•	•	•	•	•	•							•								•
					•	•		•		•	•	•	•			•							•					•
				•	•	•	•			•	•		•															
•		•					A						•				A				A		A			•		•
•		•					A						•				A				A		A			•		•
•		•	•		•		A						•				A				A		A			•		•
•		•					A						•				A				A		A			•		•
					•	•	•	•	•	•	•	•	•									•	•					
		•	•		•		•	•					•				A				A		A		A	A		A
		•	•		•	•	•	•		•	•	•	•															
		•	•		•	•	•	•		•	•	•	•															
•	•					•	•	•		•	•	•	•															
		•	•		•		•	•		•	•		•				•						•					
	•		•		•	•	•	•	•	•	•	•	•	•	•	•				•	•		•					•
		•	•		•		•	•					•				•						•			•		
•	•				•	•	•	•	•	•	•	•	•									•						•
•					•	•	•	•	•	•	•	•	•							•								
	•				•	•	•		•	•	•	•	•															
	•				•		•	•	•	•	•	•	•							•								•
					•		•	•	•		•	•																
					•	•		•	•	•	•		•															•
		•	•		•	•	•	•					•				A				A		A		A	A		A
•		•				•		•					•								•		•	•		•		
			•		•		•	•		•	•	•	•				•						•					
		•	•		•		•	•					•				A				A		A		A	A		A
		•																										
		•	•		•		•	•		•	•	•	•				•						•					
					•	•	•	•	•	•			•	•	•	•			•				•					
					•		•		•	•	•	•	•				•						•					•
		•	•		•		•	•					•				•						•			•		

A = Available to Rent

STAGE NAME	PHONE	STAGE NUMBER	LENGTH	WIDTH	HEIGHT	AREA SQUARE FEET	SOUND STAGE	INSERT	POWER/AMPS	CYCLORAMAS
The Culver Studios	310-202-3400	8	80	70	29	5600	•		7200ac	
The Culver Studios	310-202-3400	9	80	70	30	5600	•		7200ac	
Paramount Pictures	323-956-8811	3	94	59	37	5546		•	120-208v / 7200a	
Ben Kitay Studios	323-466-9015	20	110	50	20	5500	•	•	2400ac	3 wall hard
Mack Sennett Stage/Triangle	323-660-8466	1	100	55	23	5500	•		2000ac	3 wall hard
Stu Segall Productions	858-974-8988	1	55	100	20	5500	•	•	400ac	
Sunset-Gower Studios	323-467-1001	5	86	60	19	5160	•		4800 amps	2 wall hard
Prospect Studios	818-560-7450	1	74	68	35	5032	•	•	Unlimited	
Raleigh Studios - Hollywood	323-960-FILM	9	100	50	20	5000	•		3300 amps	3 wall hard
South Bay Studios	310-762-1360	10–12	100	50	25	5000		•	Unlimited	2 & 3 wall hard
GMT Studios	310-649-3733	4	70	70	24	4900	•	•	1200ac	2 wall hard
Grant McCune Design, Inc.	818-779-1920	3	100	49	16	4900			600ac	
Paladin Stage	323-851-8222	1	80	60	24	4800	•	•	1600ac	2 wall hard
Quixote Studios	323-851-5030	4	80	60	20	4800			1600 amps	2 wall hard
South Bay Studios	310-762-1360	5	80	60	19	4800	•	•	Unlimited	3 wall hard
Ben Kitay Studios	323-466-9015	10	80	59	17	4720	•	•	1200ac	3 wall hard
Siren Studios	323-467-3559	2	55	85	16	4675	•		1400 amps	4 wall soft
Orange County Studio	323-965.8881		70	66		4620	•	•		
Ren-Mar Studios	323-463-0808	7	66	70	38	4620	•	•	4000 amps	3 wall hard
Occidental Studios, Inc.	213-384-3331	6	74	62	20	4588	•		2400 amps	2 wall hard
BelleVarado Studios	213-413-9611	22	40	40	18	4500	•		200/200 amps	3 wall
Glaxa DT	323-663-5295	1	75	60	18	4500	•	•	400ac	2 wall hard
Hip Studios	323-467-2897	B	90	50	17	4500	•		400amps	2 wall hard
Century Studio Corporation	888-878-2437	5	114	50	23	4400	•	•	1800ac	
Glendale Studios	818-550-6000	2	80	55	18	4400	•	•	5000ac	4 wall soft
Occidental Studios, Inc.	213-384-3331	10	80	55	17	4400	•		1600 amps	2 wall soft
Occidental Studios, Inc.	213-384-3331	4	75	55	16	4125	•		2400 amps	2 wall hard
Studio 34	323-223-1234	1	84	48	19	4032	•		8600ac	
Big Vision Studios	818-841-4008	1	80	50	24	4000	•	•	400ac	
Cutting Edge Productions	310-326-4500	1	80	50	17	4000	•	•	2500ac	2- wall hard
GMT Studios	310-649-3733	2	80	50	17	4000	•	•	600ac	3 wall hard
Hollywood Center Studios	323-860-0000	12 GS	80	50	20	4000	•		2800 amps	3 wall green
Stargate Stage	626-403-8403	1	80	50	25	4000		•		1 wall hard
Stu Segall Productions	858-974-8988	2	80	50	20	4000	•	•	400ac	
Studio C2	310-761-1767	2	80	50	24	4000			1200ac	
Westside Media Center Studios	323-692-5360	3	58	67	18	3950	•		800 amps	
SmashBox Studios	310-558-7660	STG	80	49	22	3920	•	•	1200ac	2 wall hard
Sunset Bronson Studios	323-315-9417	7	80	49	21	3920	•		12400 amps	
Quixote Studios	323-851-5030	2	90	42	19	3780			1200 amps	2 wall hard
Ben Kitay Studios	323-466-9015	5	75	50	17	3750	•	•	1200ac	3 wall hard
Burbank Valcom Studios	818-848-5800	1	75	50	16	3750	•	•	1300ac	3 wall hard/soft
Apache Studios	818-842-9944	2	90	40	15	3600	•	•	2400 amps	

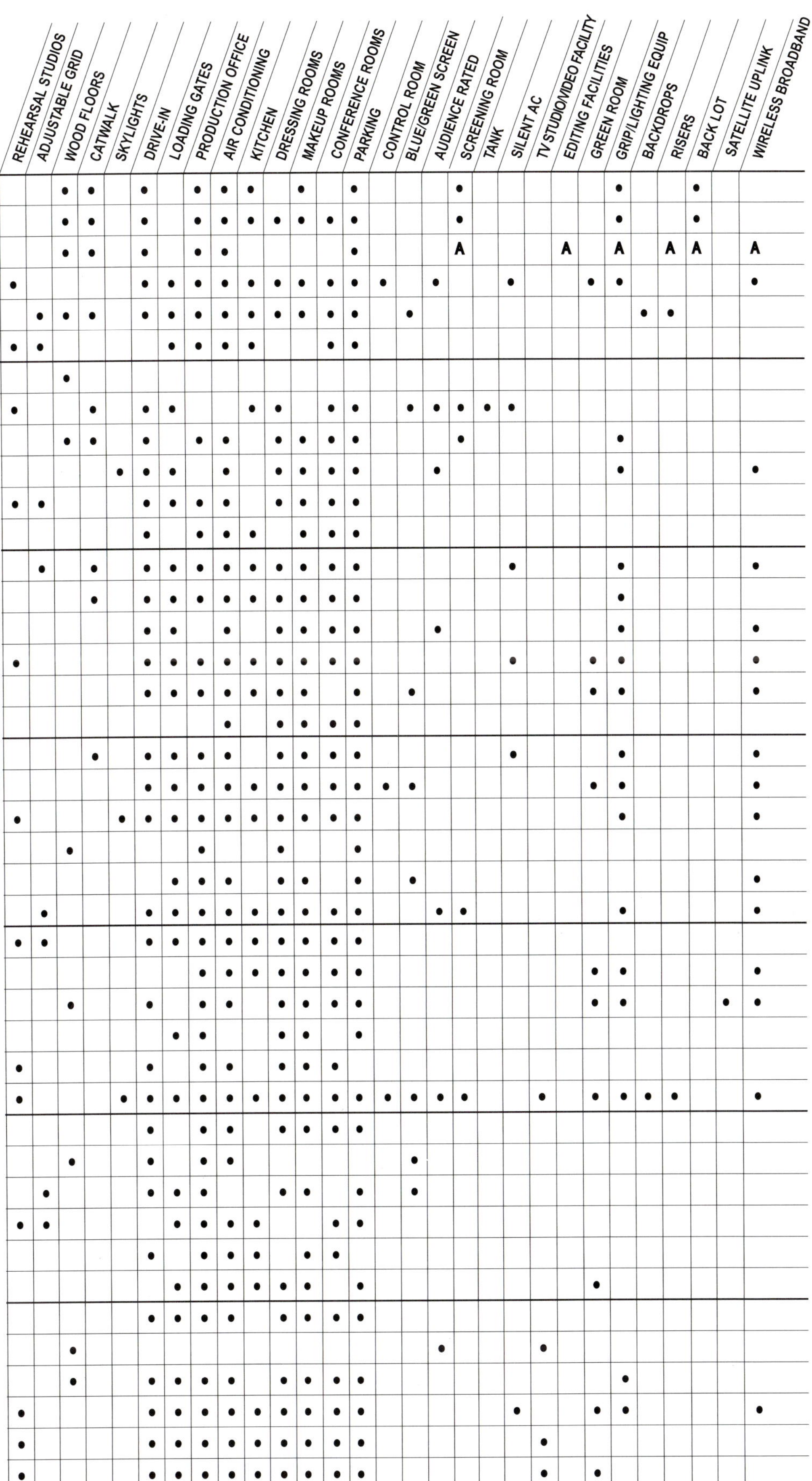

REHEARSAL STUDIOS	ADJUSTABLE GRID	WOOD FLOORS	CATWALK	SKYLIGHTS	DRIVE-IN	LOADING GATES	PRODUCTION OFFICE	AIR CONDITIONING	KITCHEN	DRESSING ROOMS	MAKEUP ROOMS	CONFERENCE ROOMS	PARKING	CONTROL ROOM	BLUE/GREEN SCREEN	AUDIENCE RATED	SCREENING ROOM	TANK	SILENT AC	TV STUDIO/VIDEO FACILITY	EDITING FACILITIES	GREEN ROOM	GRIP/LIGHTING EQUIP	BACKDROPS	RISERS	BACK LOT	SATELLITE UPLINK	WIRELESS BROADBAND
		•	•		•		•	•	•		•		•				•						•			•		
		•	•		•		•	•	•	•	•	•	•				•						•			•		
		•	•		•		•	•					•				A				A		A		A	A		A
•					•	•	•	•	•	•	•	•	•	•		•			•			•	•					•
	•	•	•		•	•	•	•	•	•	•	•	•		•									•	•			
•	•					•	•	•	•			•	•															
		•																										
•			•		•	•			•	•		•	•		•	•	•	•	•									
		•	•		•		•	•		•	•	•	•				•						•					
				•	•	•		•		•	•	•	•			•							•					•
•	•				•	•	•	•		•	•	•	•															
					•		•	•	•		•	•	•															
	•		•		•	•	•	•	•	•	•	•	•						•				•					•
			•		•	•	•	•	•	•	•	•	•										•					
					•	•		•		•	•	•	•			•							•					•
•					•	•	•	•	•	•	•	•	•						•			•	•					•
					•	•	•	•	•	•	•		•		•							•	•					•
								•		•	•	•	•															
			•		•	•	•	•		•	•	•	•						•				•					•
					•	•	•	•	•	•	•	•	•	•	•							•	•					•
•				•	•	•	•	•	•	•	•	•	•										•					•
		•					•			•			•															
						•	•	•		•	•		•		•													•
	•				•	•	•	•	•	•	•	•	•			•	•						•					•
•	•				•	•	•	•	•	•	•	•	•															
							•	•	•	•	•	•	•									•	•					•
		•			•		•	•		•	•	•	•									•	•				•	•
						•	•			•	•		•															
•					•		•	•		•	•	•																
•				•	•	•	•	•	•	•	•	•	•	•	•	•	•			•		•	•	•	•			•
					•		•	•		•	•	•	•															
		•			•		•	•							•													
	•				•	•	•			•	•		•		•													
•	•					•	•	•	•			•	•															
					•		•	•	•		•	•																
						•	•	•	•	•	•		•									•						
					•	•	•	•		•	•	•	•															
		•														•				•								
		•			•	•	•	•		•	•	•	•										•					
•					•	•	•	•	•	•	•	•	•						•			•	•					•
•					•	•	•	•	•	•	•	•	•							•								
•					•	•	•	•	•	•	•	•	•							•		•						

A = Available to Rent

STAGE NAME	PHONE	STAGE NUMBER	LENGTH	WIDTH	HEIGHT	AREA SQUARE FEET	SOUND STAGE	INSERT	POWER/AMPS	CYCLORAMAS
HD Vision Broadcast Center	818-769-4500	A	60	60	16	3600	•	•	400 amps	
The MODS	818-558-1290	1	45	80	18	3600			2400 amps	70'
Los Angeles Center Studios	213-534-3000	O.M.				3500	•		Unlimited	hard wall
Impact Studios	323-932-8864	1	74	47	21	3478	•			1 wall hard
Source Film Studio	323-463-5555	2	71	46	27	3266	•	•	2000 amps	3 wall
5th & Sunset Los angeles	310-979-0212	XXL	50	65	13	3250			900ac	2 wall hard
Ben Kitay Studios	323-466-9015	15	72	45	20	3240	•	•	1800ac	3 wall hard
Sanders Studio	714-444-3000	1	30	24	12	3200			300	8 corners
Panavision	818.316.1080	1	60	53	16	3180	•	•	2400ac	2 wall hard
The Culver Studios	310-202-3400	10	79	39	20	3081	•		7200ac	
Dirt Cheap Sound Stage	310-401-3171		60	50	22	3000	•	•		2 wall soft
Miauhaus Studios	323-933-6180	1	75	40	24	3000			400ac	3 wall
Solar Studios	818-240-1893	2	75	40	19	3000		•	600 amps	3 wall hard
The L.A. Lofts	323-462-5880	2	70	30	12	3000			200 amps	
UFO - The Poodle Parlor	213-694-0556	2	99	29	12	2871			400ac	
AMP Studios	805-955-7742	B	60	45	22	2700	•		4300 amps	3 wall soft
SmashBox Studios	310-558-7660	SB	55	48	22	2640			200ac	1 wall hard
Impact Studios	323-932-8864	3	48	54	24	2592	•			1 wall hard
The Production Group Studios	323-469-8111	2	60	43	18	2580	•		400ac	3 wall soft,hard
The L.A. Lofts	323-462-5880	1	50	30	12	2500			200 amps	
The L.A. Lofts	323-462-5880	4	30	45	12	2500		•	200 amps	1 wall
5th & Sunset Los Angeles	310-979-0212	XL	40	60	12	2400			300ac	1 wall
Epiphany Media	323-960-4000	6	60	40	15	2400	•	•	2000ac	3 wall
SmashBox Studios	310-558-7660	LB	75	32	18	2400			200ac	
Burbank Production Studios	818-567-0088	1	50	45	15	2250	•		600ac	3 wall hard white
5th & Sunset Los Angeles	310-979-0212	L	42	53	15	2226			600ac	1 wall
Mack Sennett Stage/Triangle	323-660-8466	2	60	35	23	2100	•	•	800ac	
Occidental Studios, Inc.	213-384-3331	7	70	30	16	2100			600 amps	2 wall hard
Screenland Studios	818-508-2288	D	70	30	14' 6	2100			220ac	
Raleigh Studios - Hollywood	323-960-FILM	6	62	33	18	2046	•	•	2800 amps	3 wall hard
Area 101	323-464-4467	B	50	40	12	2000			160 amps	
Siren Studios	323-467-3559	1	50	40	25	2000			1400 amps	4 wall hard
Miauhaus Studios	323-933-6180	2	52	38	24	1976			400ac	2 wall
5th & Sunset Los Angeles	310-979-0212	M	36	54	15	1944			300ac	1 wall
Westside Media Center Studios	323-692-5360	2	51	38	18	1938	•		400 amps	
Digital Film Studios	818-771-0019	1	55	35	15.5	1925		•	600 amps	3 Wall
Miauhaus Studios	323-933-6180	3	50	38	24	1900			400ac	2 wall
SmashBox Studios	310-558-7660	BB	48	38	22	1824			200ac	2 wall hard
Quixote Studios	323-851-5030	3	60	30	12	1800		•	800 amps	Eggshell
Sound Matrix Studios	714-437-9696	A	38	47	18	1786	•		450 amps	2 hard w/catwalk
Sound Matrix Studios	714-437-9696	B	38	44	18	1672	•		450 amps	
The Andrita Media Center	323-344-4500	3	36	44	11	1584	•			

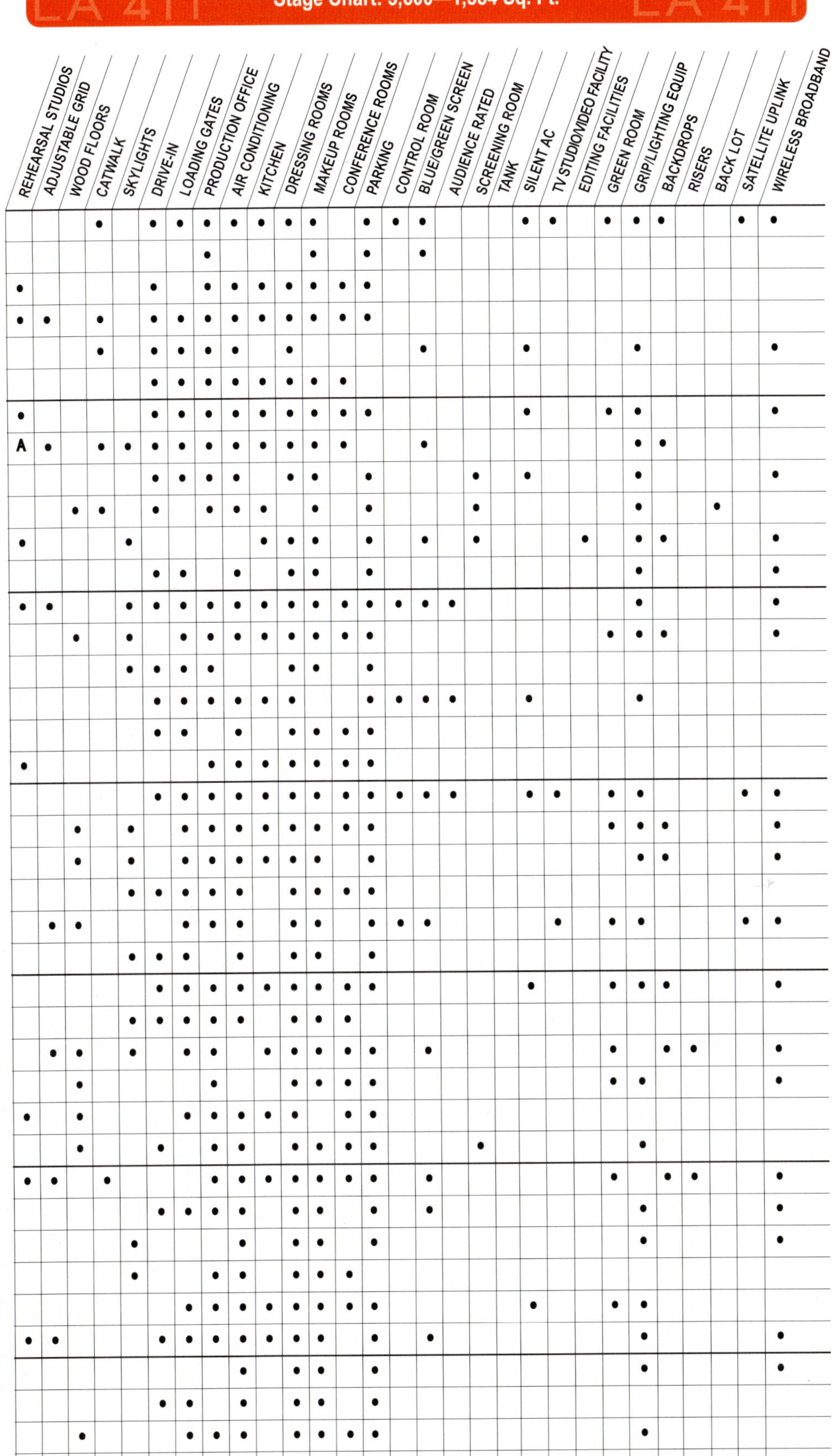

REHEARSAL STUDIOS	ADJUSTABLE GRID	WOOD FLOORS	CATWALK	SKYLIGHTS	DRIVE-IN	LOADING GATES	PRODUCTION OFFICE	AIR CONDITIONING	KITCHEN	DRESSING ROOMS	MAKEUP ROOMS	CONFERENCE ROOMS	PARKING	CONTROL ROOM	BLUE/GREEN SCREEN	AUDIENCE RATED	SCREENING ROOM	TANK	SILENT AC	TV STUDIO/VIDEO FACILITY	EDITING FACILITIES	GREEN ROOM	GRIP/LIGHTING EQUIP	BACKDROPS	RISERS	BACK LOT	SATELLITE UPLINK	WIRELESS BROADBAND
			•		•	•	•	•	•	•	•		•	•	•				•	•		•	•	•			•	•
							•				•		•		•													
•					•		•	•	•	•	•	•	•															
•	•		•		•	•	•	•	•	•	•	•	•															
			•		•	•	•	•		•					•				•				•					•
					•	•	•	•	•	•	•	•																
•					•	•	•	•	•	•	•	•	•						•			•	•					•
A	•		•	•	•	•	•	•	•	•	•	•			•								•	•				
					•	•	•	•		•	•		•				•		•				•					•
		•	•		•		•	•	•		•		•				•						•			•		
•				•					•	•	•		•		•		•				•		•	•				•
					•	•		•		•	•		•										•					•
•	•			•	•	•	•	•	•	•	•	•	•	•	•	•							•					•
		•		•		•	•	•	•	•	•	•	•									•	•	•				•
				•	•	•	•			•	•		•															
					•	•	•	•	•	•			•	•	•	•			•				•					
					•	•		•		•	•	•	•															
•							•	•	•	•	•	•	•															
					•	•	•	•	•	•	•	•	•	•	•	•			•	•		•	•				•	•
		•		•		•	•	•	•	•	•	•	•									•	•	•				•
		•		•		•	•	•	•	•	•		•										•	•				•
				•	•	•	•	•		•	•	•	•															
	•	•				•	•	•		•	•		•	•	•					•		•	•				•	•
				•	•	•		•		•	•		•															
					•	•	•	•	•	•	•	•	•						•			•	•	•				•
				•	•	•	•	•		•	•	•																
	•	•		•		•	•		•	•	•	•	•		•							•		•	•			•
		•					•			•	•	•	•									•	•					•
•		•				•	•	•	•	•		•	•															
		•			•		•	•		•	•	•	•				•						•					
•	•		•				•	•	•	•	•	•	•		•							•		•	•			•
					•	•	•	•		•	•		•		•								•					•
				•				•		•	•		•										•					•
				•			•	•		•	•	•																
						•	•	•	•	•	•	•	•						•			•	•					
•	•				•	•	•	•	•	•	•		•		•								•					•
								•		•	•		•										•					•
					•	•		•		•	•		•															
		•				•	•	•		•	•	•	•										•					
•	•		•		•	•	•	•	•	•	•	•	•		•				•			•	•	•				•
•		•					•	•	•	•	•	•	•		•							•	•	•				•
						•	•	•		•	•	•	•	•	•													•

A = Available to Rent

STAGE NAME	PHONE	STAGE NUMBER	LENGTH	WIDTH	HEIGHT	AREA SQUARE FEET	SOUND STAGE	INSERT	POWER/AMPS	CYCLORAMAS
Silver Dream Factory	714-836-1853	2	45	35	16	1575	•	•	400ac	
Huron Substation	323-225-8909		46	32	45	1472			200ac	
UFO - The Poodle Parlor	213-694-0556	3	49	29	18	1421			400ac	
5th & Sunset Los Angeles	310-979-0212	S	35	40	18	1400			300ac	1 wall
Coast Media Teleproductions, Inc.	949-417-0300	1	35	40	18	1400	•		1200 amps	2 wall hard
The L.A. Lofts	323-462-5880	3	28	30	12	1400			120 amps	
Westside Media Center Studios	323-692-5360	1	51	27	18	1375	•		225 amps	2 wall hard
SmashBox Studios	310-558-7660	Sky	35	39	13	1365			200ac	
SmashBox Studios	310-558-7660	SM	42	32	14	1344			200ac	1 wall hard
Redemption Stages	818-238-0012	1	20	64	18	1280	•		2400	
South Bay Studios	310-762-1360	6–9	40	32	27	1280		•	Unlimited	
Occidental Studios, Inc.	213-384-3331	8	35	35	16	1225	•		600 amps	2 wall hard
Apache Studios	818-842-9944	3	30	40	20	1200	•	•		
The Production Group Studios	323-469-8111	3	40	30	13	1200	•		800ac	3 wall hard
Source Film Studio	323-463-5555	1	45	25	15	1125	•	•	300 amps	4 wall
Hollywood Loft	323-957-9398	1	35	32	15	1120	•	•	200ac	1 wall hard
Occidental Studios, Inc.	213-384-3331	3	36	31	14	1116	•	•	1200 amps	
Albuerne, Inc.	323-665-1307	1	35	30	12	1050	•	•	600 amps	2 wall covered
Hollywood Camera, Inc.	818-972-5000	1	30	35	16	1050	•	•	600ac	
Occidental Studios, Inc.	213-384-3331	9	32	32	17	1024	•	•	400 amps	2 wall hard
Silver Dream Factory	714-836-1853	1	40	25	16	1000	•	•	240ac	1 wall
Pacific Motion Control, Inc.	818-768-1573	1	25	39	16	975		•	200 amps	
RecCenter Studio	213-413-9300	1	38	24	19	912				
Digital Film Studios	818-771-0019	2	35	24	15	840		•	200-400 amps	1 Wall
The Artists Consortium	310-613-8094	1	30	25	10	750			100 amps	3 wall soft
CAP, Complete Actors Place	818-990-2001		30	24	18	720				
Screenland Studios	818-508-2288	E	35	20	10	700			220ac	
studio/stage	323-463-3900	1	29	22	14	638	•	•	400 amps	3 wall hard
Costa Mesa Studios	949-515-4230	1	34	18	25	612	•		5K(6)/20 amps	
Burbank Production Studios	818-567-0088	2	35	16	13	560	•		120ac	3 wall hard green
True Sound and Studio Rental	323-839-7705	Main	34	16	13' 6	544	•		60 amps	
Impact Studios	323-932-8864	2	20	20	21	400		•		1 wall hard
Hollywood Center Studios	323-860-0000	Virtual	20	16	10	320	•		300 amps	3 wall soft

Stage Chart: 1,575—320 Sq. Ft.

LA 411

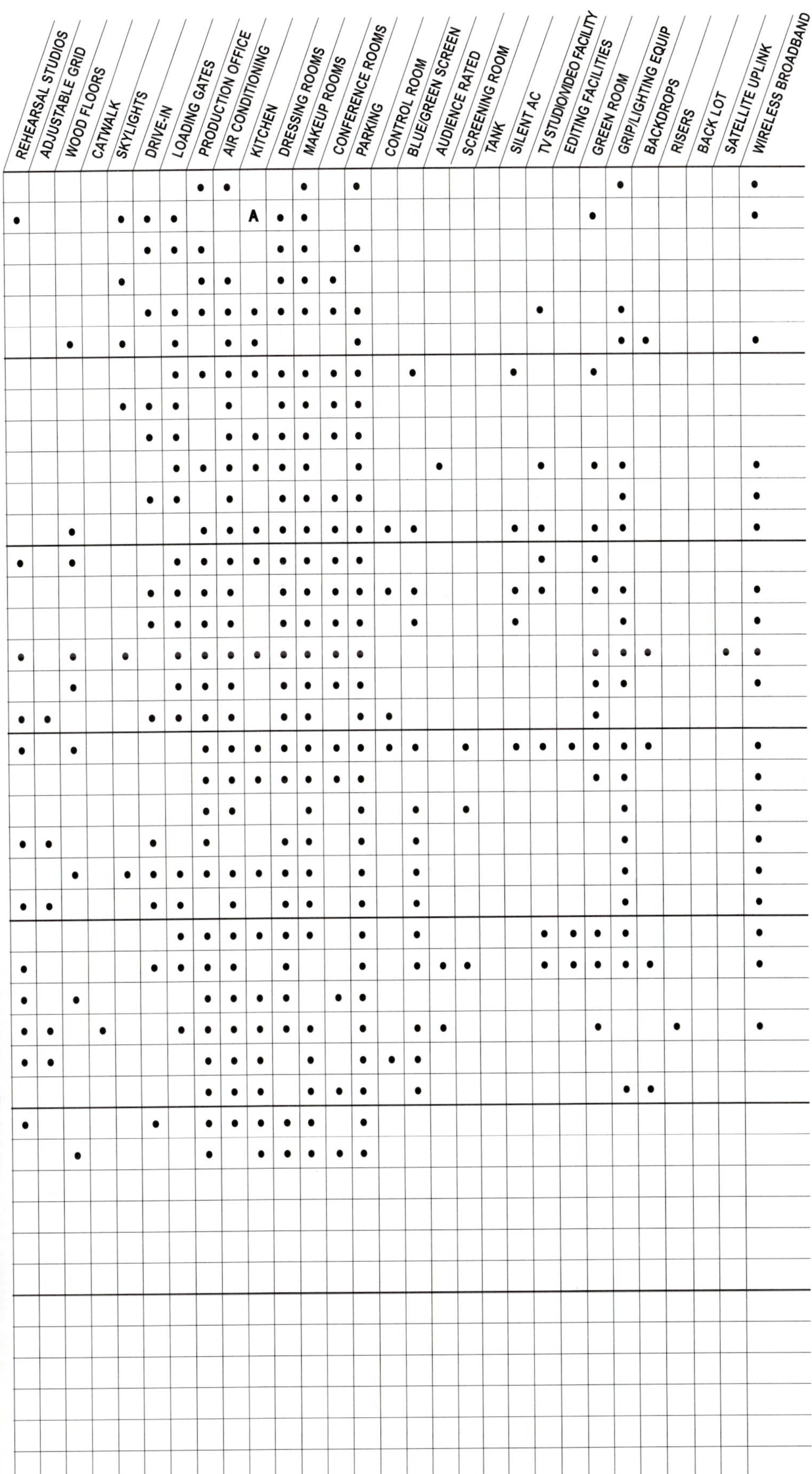

Rehearsal Studios	Adjustable Grid	Wood Floors	Catwalk	Skylights	Drive-In	Loading Gates	Production Office	Air Conditioning	Kitchen	Dressing Rooms	Makeup Rooms	Conference Rooms	Parking	Control Room	Blue/Green Screen	Audience Rated	Screening Room	Tank	Silent AC	TV Studio/Video Facility	Editing Facilities	Green Room	Grip/Lighting Equip	Backdrops	Risers	Back Lot	Satellite Uplink	Wireless Broadband
							•	•			•		•										•					•
•				•	•	•			A	•	•											•						•
					•	•	•			•	•		•															
				•			•	•		•	•	•																
					•	•	•	•	•	•	•	•	•							•			•					
		•		•		•		•	•				•										•	•				•
						•	•	•	•	•	•	•	•		•				•			•						
				•	•	•		•		•	•	•	•															
					•	•		•	•	•	•	•	•															
						•	•	•	•	•	•		•			•				•		•	•					•
					•	•		•		•	•	•	•										•					•
		•					•	•	•	•	•	•	•	•	•				•	•		•	•					•
•		•				•	•	•	•	•	•	•	•							•		•						
					•	•	•	•		•	•	•	•	•	•				•	•		•	•					•
					•	•	•	•		•	•	•	•		•				•				•					•
•		•		•		•	•	•	•	•	•	•	•									•	•	•			•	•
		•				•	•	•		•	•	•	•									•	•					•
•	•				•	•	•	•		•	•		•	•								•						
•		•					•	•	•	•	•	•	•	•	•		•		•	•	•	•	•	•				•
							•	•	•	•	•	•	•									•	•					•
							•	•			•		•		•		•						•					•
•	•				•		•			•	•		•		•								•					•
		•		•	•	•	•	•	•	•	•		•		•								•					•
•	•				•	•		•		•	•		•		•								•					•
						•	•	•	•	•	•		•		•					•	•	•	•					•
•					•	•	•	•		•			•		•	•	•			•	•	•	•	•				•
•		•					•	•	•	•		•	•															
•	•		•			•	•	•	•	•	•		•		•	•						•			•			•
•	•						•	•	•		•		•	•	•													
							•	•	•		•	•	•		•								•	•				
•					•		•	•	•	•	•		•															
		•					•		•	•	•	•	•															

A = Available to Rent

20TH CENTURY FOX BLDG.

CENTURY CITY

DIE HARD

INT. HANS' OFFICE - NIGHT

Suddenly Hans' (Alan Rickman) CB crackles to life.

HANS
(picking it up)
I told all of you...I want radio silence until further --

INT. 34th FLOOR - ON MCCLANE - INTERCUT

Mcclane (Bruce Willis) is on a CB.

MCCLANE
Gee, I'm sorry, Hans, nobody gave me the message. You shoulda put it on the bulletin board. Anyway, I thought you and Franco and Karl and the other boys might be lonely, now that I waxed Tony and Marco and their buddy. So I invited some of the guys from my card game.

HANS
I assume you are our mysterious party crasher. You are most troublesome for a...security guard?

MCCLANE
(into CB)
BZZZ! Sorry, Hans, wrong guess. Would you like to go for Double Jeopardy, where the stakes are double and the scores really change?

After a long pause.

HANS
Mr. Mystery Guest. Are you still there?

MCCLANE
I wouldn't think of leaving, Hans. Unless you want to open the front door...?

HANS
I'm afraid not. But you have me at a loss -- you know my name, but who are you?
(scornfully)
Just another American who saw too many movies as a child. Another orphan of a bankrupt culture who thinks he's John Wayne...Rambo... Marshal Dillion.

MCCLANE
Actually, I was always partial to Roy Rogers. I really dug those sequined shirts.

HANS
Do you really think you have a chance against us, Mr. Cowboy?

A LIGHT blinks on the elevator.

MCCLANE
Yipee-yi-yea...mother-f@%ker.

SCREENPLAY BY:
Jeb Stuart & Steven E. de Sauza, based on a novel by Roderick Thorp

LA 411

www.LA411.com

■ PICTURED:
20th Century Fox Building

■ LOCATION:
Century City

■ PHOTOGRAPHER:
Michael Rueter
Michael Rueter Photography/L.A.-N.Y.
www.michaelrueter.com

Supporting production in Southern California for 31 years

Ⓐ ADVERTISER SYMBOL

Refer to the General Index for cross-referencing items in this section.

Action Air Express (310) 390-8802 (866) 390-8802
2701 Airport Ave. FAX (310) 390-8831
Santa Monica, CA 90405 www.actionairexpress.com

Air Charter Guru (866) 501-4878
FAX (972) 931-4878
www.aircharterguru.com

Air One Charter (310) 743-0103 (877) 247-1359
6101 W. Centinela Ave., Ste. 375 FAX (310) 743-0140
Culver City, CA 90230 www.aironecharter.com
(24-Hour Service)

Air Royale International (310) 289-9800 (800) 776-9253
9100 Wilshire Blvd. FAX (310) 289-9804
Ste. 420, West Tower www.airroyale.com
Beverly Hills, CA 90212
(24-Hour Service)

Altitude Aviation (310) 379-4448 (310) 489-8938
2309 Pacific Coast Hwy, Ste. 204 FAX (310) 937-7112
Hermosa Beach, CA 90254 www.altitudeaviation.com
(24-Hour Service)

Behind the Scenes (818) 344-9287 (888) 287-3456
5931 Vanalden Ave. FAX (818) 344-9284
Tarzana, CA 91356 www.btsfreight.com

Briles Wing & Helicopter, Inc. (818) 994-1445
16303 Waterman Dr. FAX (818) 994-1447
Van Nuys, CA 91406 www.toflyla.com

Celebrity Helicopters (877) 999-2099
961 W. Alondra Blvd. FAX (877) 999-2099
Compton, CA 90220 www.celebheli.com

Championship Aviation, Inc. (866) 359-2538 (909) 614-1933
7000 Merrill Ave., Hangar 385 & 390 FAX (909) 993-5143
Chino, CA 91710 www.championshipaviation.com

Charter Services/ CSI Aviation Services, Inc. (800) 765-9464 (505) 761-9000
(24-Hour Service) FAX (505) 342-7377
www.airchartertravel.com

Chrysler Aviation, Inc. (818) 989-7900
7120 Hayvenhurst Ave., Ste. 309 FAX (818) 989-0116
Van Nuys, CA 91406 www.chrysleraviation.com

Clay Lacy Aviation, Inc. (818) 989-2900 (800) 423-2904
7435 Valjean Ave. FAX (818) 909-9537
Van Nuys, CA 91406 www.claylacy.com

Elite Aviation, Inc. (818) 988-5387
7501 Hayvenhurst Pl. FAX (818) 988-2111
Van Nuys, CA 91406 www.eliteaviation.com

Global Exec Aviation (562) 424-0663 (888) 878-0788
3250 Airflite Way FAX (562) 424-1144
Long Beach, CA 90807 www.globalexecaviation.com

Hangar 1 Productions (213) 483-6898
1910 W. Sunset Blvd., Ste. 900 FAX (213) 483-4185
Los Angeles, CA 90026 www.hangar1project.com

Heli-USA (818) 994-1445 (877) 863-5952
16303 Waterman Dr. FAX (818) 994-1447
Van Nuys, CA 91406 www.toflyla.com

Helinet Aviation Services (818) 902-0229 (800) 221-8389
16644 Roscoe Blvd. FAX (818) 902-9278
Van Nuys, CA 91406 www.helinet.com

Hosking Aviation (661) 251-5151
FAX (435) 649-9904

Island Express Helicopter (310) 510-2525 (800) 228-2566
1175 Queens Hwy South FAX (310) 510-9671
Long Beach, CA 90802 www.islandexpress.com

A **Jet Productions** (818) 781-4742 (877) 895-1790
7240 Hayvenhurst Ave., Ste. 148 FAX (818) 781-4743
Van Nuys, CA 91406 www.jetproductions.net

Jet Set Private Air Service (310) 301-9609 (310) 430-8161
26 Washington Blvd. FAX (310) 301-9468
PH, Freeman Towers www.iflyjetset.com
Los Angeles, CA 90292
(24-Hour Service)

Exclusively to the entertainment industry ...
Private Jet Charters,
Production Travel,
Jet Rentals for
Film, Video and
Commercial Shoots.
JET PRODUCTIONS
WORLDWIDE PRIVATE JET CHARTER
Van Nuys Airport 818-781-4742
toll free 877-895-1790
www.jetproductions.net e-mail: info@jetproductions.net

Jets.com
(800) 370-7719
(617) 471-5531
FAX (617) 472-0850
www.jets.com

JetStream International
(800) 891-0456
(786) 202-8884
FAX (305) 447-1919
www.jetstreamintl.com

Le Bas International
3440 Empresa Dr., Ste. B
San Luis Obispo, CA 93401
(805) 593-0510
(800) 331-5466
FAX (805) 593-0509
www.lebas.com

Maguire Aviation
7155 Valjean Ave.
Van Nuys, CA 91406
(818) 989-2300
(800) 451-7270
FAX (818) 902-9386

MC Aviation
7150 Hayvenhurst Ave.
Van Nuys, CA 91406
(818) 904-9860
FAX (818) 904-0324
www.mcaviation.aero

Metro-Jet, LLC
12101 S. Crenshaw Blvd., Ste. 1
Hawthorne, CA 90250
(562) 869-4128
(888) 682-6227
FAX (562) 923-7181

Orbic Helicopters, Inc.
16700 Roscoe Blvd.
Van Nuys, CA 91406
(818) 988-6532
(818) 989-9986
FAX (818) 988-2014
www.orbichelicopters.com

Rock-It Air Charter, Inc.
LA International Airport
6201 W. Imperial Hwy
Los Angeles, CA 90045
(310) 568-3781
(310) 702-6770
FAX (310) 568-3785
www.rockitair.com

Rotor Aviation
3250 Airflite Way
Long Beach, CA 90807
(562) 595-6867
FAX (562) 595-5323
www.rotoraviation.com

Studio Jet
(24-Hour Service)
(818) 769-3535
FAX (818) 301-2536
www.studiojet.com

Style Aviation Services, Inc.
7415 Hayvenhurst Pl.
Van Nuys, CA 91406
(818) 988-2931
FAX (818) 988-2953
www.styleair.com

Sun Air Jets
Camarillo Airport, 855 Aviation Dr.
Camarillo, CA 93010
(805) 389-9339
FAX (805) 987-4720
www.sunairjets.com

Sun Quest
7415 Hayvenhurst Pl.
Van Nuys, CA 91406
(818) 778-6520
(800) 529-7595
FAX (818) 778-6526
www.sunquestexec.com

SwishAir, LLC
5702 Colfax Ave.
North Hollywood, CA 91601
(818) 985-1345
www.swish-air.com

TwinAir
7552 Hayvenhurst Pl.
Van Nuys, CA 91406
(818) 988-7573
FAX (818) 988-7578
www.twinair.net

West Airways, Inc.
22636 Airport Way
Terminal Bldg., Ste. 1
California City, CA 93505
(760) 373-1468
(877) 247-6684
FAX (760) 373-0078
www.westairways.com

Xpeditious Unlimited
12911 Simms Ave., Ste. E
Hawthorne, CA 90250
(310) 644-1286
(310) 227-5106
FAX (310) 644-4636
www.xpeditiousunlimited.com

Advanced Express, Inc. (310) 640-8400
(800) 767-2326
FAX (310) 640-9413
www.advancedexpress.com

Air Charter Guru (866) 501-4878
FAX (972) 931-4878
www.aircharterguru.com

Air France Cargo (310) 646-3621
FAX (310) 646-1002
www.airfrancecargo.com

Air Ground Shippers, Inc. (323) 285-6634
(24-Hour Service) www.airgroundshippers.com

Airways Freight (310) 372-1175
1122 Ardmore Ave. FAX (310) 372-2623
Hermosa Beach, CA 90254 www.airwaysfreight.com

Alliance Air Freight, Inc. (818) 982-3800
(800) 684-6359
13345 Saticoy St. FAX (818) 982-4337
North Hollywood, CA 91605 www.shipalliance.com

Anchor News Courier (800) 747-6397
P.O. Box 7083 FAX (818) 841-3809
Burbank, CA 91510

Art Pack, Inc. (310) 324-5553
225 W. 134th St. FAX (310) 324-6633
Los Angeles, CA 90061 www.artpack.us

Atlant USA, Inc. (310) 649-6495
FAX (310) 631-1830
www.atlant.com

Atlas Worldwide Transportation (310) 968-2090
(310) 798-9467
505 Earle Ln. FAX (310) 318-6497
Redondo Beach, CA 90278 www.atlasworldwidetrans.com

Behind the Scenes (818) 344-9287
(888) 287-3456
5931 Vanalden Ave. FAX (818) 344-9284
Tarzana, CA 91356 www.btsfreight.com

Bellair Express (310) 216-9200
(800) 888-7785
5140 W. 106th St., Stes. J & K FAX (310) 216-7124
Inglewood, CA 90304 www.bellairlax.com
(24-Hour Service)

Bluebird Express, LLC (310) 645-0300
5261B W. Imperial Hwy www.bluebird-courier.com
Los Angeles, CA 90045

Bonded Services, Inc. (310) 680-6830
441 N. Oak St. FAX (310) 680-9099
Inglewood, CA 90302 www.bonded.com

British Airways World Cargo (310) 646-7826
FAX (310) 670-0631
www.baworldcargo.com

DB Schenker (323) 908-4800
(800) 541-6261
2815 W. El Segundo Blvd. FAX (323) 908-4874
Hawthorne, CA 90250 www.dbschenkerusa.com

Delta Air Logistics (800) 352-2746

Delta Dash (800) 352-2746
(Small Package Express) www.deltacargo.com

DHL Gloabl Forwarding (310) 297-4400
(800) 354-1743
FAX (310) 417-8057

DHL Worldwide Express (800) 225-5345
FAX (310) 331-4598
www.dhl-usa.com

Distribution by Air, Inc. (DBA) (323) 779-6900
(800) 553-1449
2701 El Segundo Blvd. FAX (323) 779-6958
Hawthorne, CA 90250 www.dbaco.com

Efficient Delivery Service (818) 817-2700
7065 Hayvenhurst Ave., Ste. 7 FAX (818) 205-9883
Van Nuys, CA 91406
www2.efficientdeliveryservice.com/entrack/index.asp

ETC International Freight System (310) 632-2555
(800) 383-3157
2450 S. Sequoia Dr. FAX (310) 632-3044
Compton, CA 90220 www.etcinternational.com

Excalibur International Couriers (310) 568-1000
235 S. Glasgow Ave. FAX (310) 568-1604
Inglewood, CA 90301 www.excaliburintl.com

Federal Express (800) 463-3339
www.fedex.com

FedEx Custom Critical (800) 762-3787
(800) 255-2421
(24-Hour Service) FAX (234) 310-4172
www.fedexcustomcritical.com

Graf Air Freight (424) 205-1000
FAX (424) 205-1006
www.grafairfreight.com

JM-SA Logistics Consultants, Inc. (310) 827-6597
(310) 663-4464
5230 Pacific Concourse Dr., Ste. 200A FAX (310) 643-4516
Los Angeles, CA 90045 www.jmsalogistics.com

Karmel Courier & Messenger Service (714) 526-8382
(888) 995-7433
FAX (714) 670-3496
www.karmel.com

KLS Transportation (310) 327-3309
FAX (310) 327-3305

Lufthansa Cargo (800) 542-2746
FAX (877) 543-2948
www.lhcargo.com

Marken Worldwide Express (310) 641-8393
(800) 627-5361
FAX (310) 641-8396
www.marken.com

Midnite Express (310) 330-2300
(800) 643-6483
FAX (310) 330-2358
www.mnx.com

Moving Pictures Anywhere Company (310) 590-1660
(866) 744-7672
8901 S. La Cienega Blvd., Ste. 105 FAX (310) 590-1688
Inglewood, CA 90301 www.movingpicturesanywhere.com

Norman Kreiger, Inc. (310) 215-0071
(310) 668-5700
921 W. Artesia Blvd. FAX (310) 668-5800
Rancho Dominguez, CA 90220 www.nkinc.com

Pacific Express (800) 322-9521
FAX (714) 992-1026

Pack Air (310) 337-0529
FAX (310) 337-0669

Paramount Courier Inc. (310) 693-0503
601 Hindry Ave. FAX (310) 670-4640
Inglewood, CA 90301 www.paramountcourier.com

ProCourier, Inc. (800) 834-7579
(949) 251-1777
www.procourier.com

Qantas Cargo, Ltd. (800) 227-0290
FAX (310) 665-2201

Quick International Courier (310) 414-9211
(800) 788-4529
FAX (310) 414-0659
www.quickintl.com

Reels On Wheels Unlimited (877) 576-6300
(213) 620-9787
FAX (914) 633-6932
www.reelsonwheels.com

Rock-It Cargo USA, Inc. (310) 410-0935
(516) 825-7356
FAX (310) 410-0628
www.rockitcargo.com

Saturn Freight Systems (323) 779-1230
12333 S. Van Ness Ave. FAX (323) 779-1277
Hawthorne, CA 90250 www.saturnfreight.com

Security Couriers, Inc. (818) 789-3999
(888) 863-7736
13351-D Riverside Dr., Ste. 671 FAX (818) 789-3888
Sherman Oaks, CA 91423 www.securitycouriers.com

Sky Courier (800) 759-0499
FAX (310) 680-0699

SOS Global Express, Inc. (310) 817-1162
(800) 628-6363
17236 S. Main St. www.sosglobal.com
Gardena, CA 90248

TBI/Truck Brokers, Inc. (800) 900-3572
FAX (407) 876-8691
www.truckbrokersinc.com

Time Machine Courier (213) 975-9850
(800) 734-8463
FAX (213) 975-9858
www.timemachinenetwork.com

Total Transportation Concept, Inc. (310) 337-0515
(800) 582-7110
8728 Aviation Blvd. FAX (310) 337-7901
Inglewood, CA 90301 www.totaltrans.com

U.S. Postal Service Express Mail (LAX) (800) 275-8777
(310) 649-7400
FAX (323) 586-1498

United Airlines Cargo (800) 631-1500
(310) 342-8391
FAX (310) 342-8361

UPS Logistics (800) 528-6070
www.upslogistics.com

USAir Cargo (888) 300-0099

Westside Express, Inc./ Nationwide Express (310) 470-4470
(800) 207-2222
FAX (310) 470-2557

World Courier (310) 410-7230
(800) 221-6600
FAX (310) 410-7247
www.worldcourier.com

Xpeditious Unlimited (310) 644-1286
(310) 227-5106
12911 Simms Ave., Ste. E FAX (310) 644-4636
Hawthorne, CA 90250 www.xpeditiousunlimited.com

Aerolineas Argentinas (800) 333-0276
www.aeroargentinas.com

Aeromexico (800) 237-6639
www.aeromexico.com

Air Canada (888) 247-2262
FAX (888) 422-7533
www.aircanada.ca

Air France (800) 237-2747
www.airfrance.com

Air Jamaica (800) 523-5585
www.airjamaica.com

Air New Zealand (800) 262-1234
(866) 629-4919
www.airnz.com

Alaska Airlines (800) 426-0333
www.alaskaair.com

Alitalia (800) 223-5730
www.alitaliausa.com

American Airlines (800) 433-7300
www.aa.com

ANA All Nippon Airways (800) 235-9262
www.anaskyweb.com

Asiana Airlines (800) 227-4262
(213) 365-4500
www.flyasiana.com

Avianca (800) 284-2622
www.avianca.com

British Airways (800) 247-9297
www.britishairways.com

Cathay Pacific (310) 615-1113
(800) 233-2742
www.cathaypacific.com

China Airlines (800) 227-5118
www.china-airlines.com

Continental Airlines (800) 525-0280
www.continental.com

Delta Airlines (800) 241-4141
www.delta.com

Egypt Air (800) 334-6787
www.egyptair.com

El Al Israel Airlines (800) 223-6700
www.elal.com

Finnair (800) 950-5000
www.finnair.com

Garuda-Indonesia (800) 342-7832
www.garuda-indonesia.com

Grupo Taca (800) 327-9832
(800) 225-2272
www.taca.com

Hawaiian Airlines (800) 367-5320
www.hawaiianair.com

Iberia Airlines (800) 772-4642
www.iberia.com

Japan Airlines (800) 525-3663
www.jal.com

Korean Air (310) 646-4866
(800) 438-5000
www.koreanair.com

Lan Airlines (310) 416-9061
(866) 435-9526

LOT Polish Airlines (212) 789-0970
www.lot.com

LTU (866) 266-5588
FAX (407) 831-2470
www.airberlin.com

Malaysia Airlines (800) 552-9264
www.malaysiaairlines.com.my

Martinair-Holland (800) 627-8462
FAX (561) 391-2188
www.martinairusa.com

Mexicana Airlines (800) 531-7921
www.mexicana.com

Midwest Airlines (800) 452-2022
www.midwestairlines.com

Northwest Airlines (800) 225-2525
(800) 447-4747

Philippine Airlines (800) 435-9725
www.phillippineair.com

Qantas (800) 227-4500
www.qantas.com.au

SAS Scandinavian Airlines (800) 221-2350
www.flysas.com

Singapore Airlines (800) 742-3333
www.singaporeair.com/americas

Southwest (800) 435-9792
www.iflyswa.com

Swiss (877) 359-7947
www.swiss.com

Taca International (800) 535-8780
www.taca.com

Thai Airways International (800) 426-5204
www.thaiair.com

United Airlines/United Express (800) 241-6522
www.ual.com

US Airways (800) 428-4322
www.usairways.com

USAirways/USAirways Express (800) 428-4322
www.usairways.com

Varig Brazilian Airlines (800) 468-2744
www.varig.com.br

Virgin Atlantic Airways (800) 862-8621
www.virgin-atlantic.com

1800Fly1800
(310) 330-7500
(800) 359-1800
FAX (310) 419-8129
www.1800fly1800.com

Amour Way Limousine and Travel Service
(310) 591-8690
(866) 261-6651
P.O. Box 661749
Los Angeles, CA 90066
FAX (310) 390-9315
www.amourway.com

Emerald Limousine Service
(310) 591-6060
P.O. Box 83669
Los Angeles, CA 90083
FAX (310) 750-9154
www.limobyemerald.com

Express Shuttle/Limousine
(800) 427-7483
(800) 310-8267
FAX (310) 323-8222
www.expressshuttle.com

Limos At Your Service
(323) 646-1135
4858 W. Century Blvd.
Los Angeles, CA 90045
FAX (310) 645-9305
www.limosatyourservice.net

Prime Time Airport Shuttle
(800) 733-8267
www.primetimeshuttle.com

Shuttle 2000
(800) 977-7872
www.shuttle2000.com

Shuttle One
(310) 670-6666
FAX (310) 670-7883

Southern California Coach
(800) 232-6224
www.karmel.com

SuperShuttle
(800) 258-3826
www.supershuttle.com

Van Nuys Fly-Away Bus Service
(866) 435-9529
7610 Woodley Ave.
Van Nuys, CA 91406
www.lawa.org/vny

Agua Dulce Airport (661) 268-8835
33638 Agua Dulce Canyon Rd. FAX (661) 268-7662
Agua Dulce, CA 91390

Bob Hope Airport (818) 840-8840
2627 Hollywood Way FAX (818) 848-1173
Burbank, CA 91505 www.bobhopeairport.com
(No Filming at Airport)

Brackett Field Airport (909) 593-1395
1615 McKinley Ave. FAX (909) 593-5224
La Verne, CA 91750 www.americanairports.net
Contact: Jared Fox-Tuck

California City Municipal Airport (760) 373-4867 (760) 559-5629
22636 Airport Way, Box 8 FAX (760) 373-4869
California City, CA 93505 www.calcityairport.com
Contact: Tom Weil

Camarillo Airport (805) 388-4272
555 Airport Way, Ste. B FAX (805) 388-4366
Camarillo, CA 93010
Contact: Tad Dougherty

Chino Airport (909) 597-3910
7000 Merrill Ave., Box 1 FAX (909) 597-0274
Chino, CA 91710
Contact: James Jenkins

Compton Airport (310) 631-8140
901 W. Alondra Blvd. FAX (310) 762-9801
Compton, CA 90220 www.americanairports.net
Contact: Luis Rosales

El Monte Airport (626) 448-6129
Contact: Richard Smith FAX (626) 448-6179
www.americanairports.net

Fox Airfield (661) 940-1709
Contact: Steve Irving FAX (661) 942-6754

Fullerton Municipal Airport (714) 738-6323
Contact: Rod Propst FAX (714) 738-3112
www.ci.fullerton.ca.us

Hawthorne Municipal Airport (310) 349-1637
12101 S. Crenshaw Blvd., Ste. 3 FAX (310) 978-9144
Hawthorne, CA 90250
Contact: Don Knechtel

Inyokern Airport (760) 377-5844
Contact: Scott Seymour FAX (760) 377-4194
www.inyokernairport.com

John Wayne Airport - Orange County (949) 252-5171 (949) 252-5182
3160 Airway Ave. FAX (949) 252-5178
Costa Mesa, CA 92626 www.ocair.com
Contact: Ann McCarley

LA County Whiteman Airport (818) 896-5271
12653 Osborne St. FAX (818) 897-2654
Pacoima, CA 91331
Contact: John Frymyer

LAX - Airfield Operations Bureau/ Film Office (310) 417-0475
7333 World Way West, Ste. 311 FAX (310) 641-8949
Los Angeles, CA 90045

Long Beach Airport (562) 570-2600 (562) 570-2619
4100 Donald Douglas Dr. FAX (562) 570-2601
Long Beach, CA 90808 www.lgb.org

McClellan-Palomar Airport (760) 431-4646
2198 Palomar Airport Rd. FAX (760) 931-5713
Carlsbad, CA 92008
Contact: Floyd Best

Mojave Airport (661) 824-2433 (661) 824-2434
1434 Flightline, Bldg. 58 FAX (661) 824-2914
Mojave, CA 93501 www.mojaveairport.com
Contact: Debbie Roth

Montgomery Field (858) 573-1440 (858) 573-1441
FAX (858) 279-0536

Ontario International Airport (909) 975-5344 (909) 975-5340
Operations Center FAX (909) 937-2800
1940 E. Moore Way www.lawa.org
Ontario, CA 91761
Contact: Kim Ellis

Oxnard Airport (805) 382-3022 (805) 382-3024
Contact: Chris Hastert FAX (805) 382-9845

Palm Springs International Airport (760) 318-3800
3400 E. Tahquitz Canyon Way FAX (760) 318-3815
Palm Springs, CA 92262 www.palmspringairport.com

Palmdale Airport (661) 266-7602 (818) 908-5950
41000 20th St. East FAX (661) 266-7604
Palmdale, CA 93550 www.lawa.org
Contact: Sgt. Curtis Thompson

Perris Valley Airport (951) 657-3904
2091 Goetz Rd. FAX (951) 657-6178
Perris, CA 92570 www.skydiveperris.com
Contacts: Patrick Conaster & Melanie Conaster

Riverside Municipal Airport (951) 351-6113
6951 Flight Rd. FAX (951) 359-3570
Riverside, CA 92504 www.riversideca.gov/airport
Contacts: Mark Kranenburg & Barbara McIlwaine

San Diego International Airport - Lindberg Field (619) 400-2400
Contact: Bryan Enarson FAX (619) 400-2549
www.san.org

Santa Monica Airport (310) 458-8591
3223 Donald Douglas Loop South, Ste. 3 FAX (310) 572-4495
Santa Monica, CA 90405 www.santamonicaairport.org
Contact: Bob Trimborn

Santa Ynez Valley Airport (805) 688-8390
900 Airport Rd. FAX (805) 688-6105
Santa Ynez, CA 93460 www.santaynezairport.com
Contact: Kim Joos

Southern California Logistics Airport (760) 243-1900
18374 Phantom FAX (760) 243-1929
Victorville, CA 92394 www.globalaccessvcv.com
Contact: Mary Morgan

Torrance Municipal Airport (310) 784-7900
FAX (310) 784-7930

Van Nuys Airport (818) 785-8838 (818) 908-5950
www.lawa.org

Avalon Transportation, Inc.
(310) 391-6161
(800) 528-2566
5239 Sepulveda Blvd.
Culver City, CA 90230
FAX (310) 391-8017
www.avalontrans.com

Cantos Collection
(310) 780-6002
(213) 303-2228
P.O. Box 34813
Los Angeles, CA 90034
FAX (213) 558-3745
www.cantoscollection.com

Coach America
(562) 634-7969
(800) 642-3287
FAX (562) 634-5818
www.coachusa.com

Coach Engineering/Dave Weiner
(818) 563-2399
(818) 406-5130
FAX (818) 563-1399
www.coachengineering.com

Coast to Coast Coach
(661) 268-0404
FAX (661) 268-0666
www.coasttocoastcoach.com

Fast Deer Bus Charters
(323) 266-6388
(888) 378-3337
FAX (323) 266-6387
www.fastdeerbus.com

Fleetwood Limousine
(310) 645-6092
(800) 283-5893
FAX (310) 645-1245

Greyhound Bus Lines
(213) 629-8401
(214) 849-8966
www.greyhound.com

KLS Limousine Service Inc.
(310) 247-0804
(877) 936-5466
9663 Santa Monica Blvd., Ste. 773
Beverly Hills, CA 90210
FAX (310) 247-0805
www.klsla.com

Silverado Coach Company, Inc.
(818) 251-9700
(800) 544-7999
FAX (818) 884-4997
www.silveradocoach.com

Special Events Services, SES Inc.
(310) 831-1761
(800) 738-6739
1891 N. Gaffey St., Ste. M
Los Angeles, CA 90731
FAX (310) 831-2528
www.specialeventsservices.com

Starline
(323) 463-3333
(800) 959-3131
www.starlinetours.com

Sunrize Plaza Transportation Co./SPT
(310) 406-3115
(800) 564-5806
FAX (310) 406-3119

Tourcoach Charter Service
(323) 262-1114
(323) 463-3131
FAX (323) 262-1414
www.tourcoach.com

Transportation Charter Services, Inc.
(714) 637-4300
(800) 833-5773
FAX (714) 637-4377
www.tcsbus.com

Audi of Downtown LA (213) 745-7200
1900 S. Figueroa St. FAX (213) 222-1263
Los Angeles, CA 90007 www.audiofdtla.com
(Audi)

Bauer Jaguar (714) 953-4800
1455 S. Auto Mall Dr. FAX (714) 953-4863
Santa Ana, CA 92705 www.bauerjaguar.com
(Jaguar)

Beverly Hills BMW (310) 358-7800
8825 Wilshire Blvd. FAX (310) 358-7882
Beverly Hills, CA 90211 www.beverlyhillsbmw.com
(BMW)

Browning Auto Group (562) 356-6522
FAX (562) 653-9305
www.browningautogroup.com
(Acura, Chevrolet, Dodge, Honda, Kia, Mazda, Mitsubishi, Oldsmobile & Toyota)

Calstar Motors (866) 738-0000
700 S. Brand Blvd. FAX (818) 240-5340
Glendale, CA 91204 www.calstarmercedes.com
(Mercedes-Benz)

Cerritos Auto Square (888) 364-2288
10901 Auto Square Dr. www.cerritosautosquare.com
Cerritos, CA 90703
(Acura, Buick, Chevrolet, Chrysler, Dodge, Ford, GMC, Honda, Hummer, Hyundai, Infinity, Isuzu, Kia, Lexus, Lincoln, Mazda, Mercury, Mitsubishi, Nissan, Pontiac, Saturn, Suzuki, Toyota & Volvo)

Circle Imports (562) 597-3663
(800) 675-2472
(Audi, Porsche & Volkswagen) www.circleimports.com

Downtown LA Motors (213) 748-8951
1801 S. Figueroa St. www.dtlamotors.com
Los Angeles, CA 90015
(Audi, Buick, Chevrolet, Mercedes-Benz, Nissan, Porsche & Volkswagen)

Environmental Motors (818) 244-6938
109 Franklin Court FAX (818) 244-8463
Glendale, CA 91024 www.environmentalmotors.com
(Eco-Friendly Automobiles)

Felix Chevrolet (213) 748-6141
3330 S. Figueroa St. www.felixautos.com
Los Angeles, CA 90007
(Chevrolet)

Galpin Ford (800) 564-2458
15505 Roscoe Blvd. www.galpinford.com
North Hills, CA 91343
(Aston Martin, Ford, Jaguar, Lincoln, Mazda, Mercury, Saturn & Volvo)

Honda of Hollywood (323) 466-7191
(800) 371-3718
6525 Santa Monica Blvd. FAX (323) 372-3200
Hollywood, CA 90038 www.hondaofhollywood.com
(Honda)

Huntington Beach Dodge (714) 847-5515
(888) 895-7193
16555 Beach Blvd. www.hbdodge.com
Huntington Beach, CA 92647
(Dodge)

Jessup Auto Plaza (760) 328-9999
(800) 900-5277
68-111 E. Palm Canyon www.jessupautoplaza.com
Cathedral City, CA 92234
(Buick, Cadillac, GMC, Hummer, Pontiac & Saab)

Jim Falk Lexus of Beverly Hills (310) 274-5200
(888) 860-7618
9230 Wilshire Blvd. FAX (310) 275-3248
Beverly Hills, CA 90210 www.beverlyhillslexus.com
(Lexus)

Keyes Automotive Group (818) 782-0122
www.keyescars.com
(Acura, Audi, Lexus, Mercedes-Benz, Scion & Toyota)

Kirby Auto (805) 644-2241
6424 Leland St. www.kirbyauto.com
Ventura, CA 93003
(Jeep, Oldsmobile & Suzuki)

Land Rover South Bay (310) 798-0550
(877) 276-0441
900 N. Pacific Coast Hwy FAX (310) 798-6845
Redondo Beach, CA 90277 www.landroversouthbay.com
(Land Rover)

Mark Christopher Auto Center (909) 390-2900
2131 Convention Center Way FAX (909) 390-8174
Ontario, CA 91764 www.markchristopher.com
(Cadillac, Chevrolet, Hummer & Oldsmobile)

Martin Automotive Group (800) 601-5063
12101 W. Olympic Blvd. FAX (310) 826-3717
Los Angeles, CA 90064 www.martinautogroup.com
(Cadillac, GMC, Isuzu & Pontiac)

Miller Automotive (818) 787-8400
www.millerautomotive.com
(Honda, Infinity, Mitsubishi, Nissan & Toyota)

Newport Beach Auto Center (949) 673-0900
445 E. Pacific Coast Hwy FAX (949) 675-3082
Newport Beach, CA 92660 www.powerdirect.com
(Audi, Bentley & Porsche)

Norm Reeves Honda Superstore (888) 829-9978
18500 Studebaker Rd. FAX (562) 402-4584
Cerritos, CA 90703 www.normreeveshondacerritos.com

Penske Automotive Group (626) 580-6000
3534 N. Peck Rd. FAX (626) 580-6158
El Monte, CA 91731 www.penskeautomotive.com
(Audi, Honda, Lexus, Maybach, Merecedes-Benz & Toyota)

Phillips Auto of Newport Beach (949) 574-7777
1220 W. Coast Hwy FAX (949) 631-2192
Newport Beach, CA 92663 www.phillipsauto.com
(Aston Martin, BMW, Chevrolet, Dodge, Ferrari & Ford)

Sierra Autocars, Inc. (800) 404-2886
1450 S. Shamrock Ave. www.sierraauto.com
Monrovia, CA 91016
(Acura, Buick, Chevrolet, Honda, Isuzu, Saturn & Subaru)

Silver Star Auto Group (805) 371-5400
(800) 496-6446
3905 Auto Mall Dr. FAX (805) 494-9688
Thousand Oaks, CA 91362 www.silverstarauto.com
(Buick, Cadillac, GMC, Honda, Hummer, Jaguar, Land Rover, Lexus, Lotus, Mazda, Mercedes-Benz, Mitsubishi, Nissan, Saab & Subaru)

Team Automotive Group (626) 449-3333
(800) 809-9420
3003 E. Colorado Blvd. www.teamchevyolds.com
Pasadena, CA 91107
(Chevrolet, Hummer, Hyundai & Oldsmobile)

Toyota of Hollywood (866) 286-3721
(Lincoln, Mercury, Scion & Toyota) FAX (323) 860-5628
www.hollywoodtoyota.com

Tustin Auto Center (888) 449-6414
www.tustinautocenter.com
(Acura, Buick, Cadillac, Chevrolet, Chrysler, Dodge, Ford, GMC, Infinity, Jeep, Lexus, Lincoln, Mazda, Mercury, Mitsubishi, Nissan, Pontiac & Toyota)

Universal City Nissan (866) 301-1111
(866) 245-8623
3550 Cahuenga Blvd. West FAX **(818) 755-7380**
Los Angeles, CA 90068 **www.universalcitynissan.com**
(Nissan)

Volkswagen Santa Monica (310) 829-1888
(866) 469-6576
2440 Santa Monica Blvd. FAX **(310) 829-5878**
Santa Monica, CA 90404 **www.vw-sm.com**
(Volkswagen)

Westside Volvo (310) 391-0445
11201 Washington Blvd. FAX **(310) 398-2814**
Culver City, CA 90230 **www.westsidevolvo.com**
(Volvo)

1800Fly1800
(310) 330-7500
(800) 359-1800
FAX (310) 419-8129
www.1800fly1800.com

(213) Limousine
7336 Santa Monica Blvd., Ste. 444
Los Angeles, CA 90046
(888) 213-5466
FAX (888) 213-5466
www.213limo.com

21st Century Limousine
3188 Airway Ave., Ste. G
Costa Mesa, CA 92626
(310) 214-5466
(877) 214-5466
www.21stcenturylimo.com

310 Picture Cars
6709 La Tijera Blvd., Ste. 247
Los Angeles, CA 90045
(310) 678-8007
www.picturecardiv.com

A.L.S. Limousine, Inc.
2118 Wilshire Blvd., Ste. 251
Santa Monica, CA 90403
(310) 338-0000
(877) 310-5466
FAX (310) 568-0766
www.alslimo.com

AAA Limousine Service
(818) 704-4746
(800) 232-4133
FAX (818) 888-1280
www.aaalimo.net

Absolute Transportation Service
(310) 270-5253
(877) 801-2345
www.americanlimousine.us

Affordable West, Inc.
1040 N. La Brea Ave.
Hollywood, CA 90038
(323) 467-7182
FAX (323) 467-6520

Alamo
9020 Aviation Blvd.
Inglewood, CA 90301
(See Web Site for Additional Locations)
(800) 327-9633
(310) 649-2242
www.alamo.com

Aloha Limousine
P.O. Box 352
Hawthorne, CA 90251
(310) 641-1811
(323) 464-2456
FAX (310) 978-6366

Avalon Transportation, Inc.
5239 Sepulveda Blvd.
Culver City, CA 90230
(310) 391-6161
(800) 528-2566
FAX (310) 391-8017
www.avalontrans.com

Avis
4904 N. Van Nuys Blvd.
Sherman Oaks, CA 91403
(See Web Site for Additional Locations)
(818) 382-7755
(818) 385-1927
www.avis.com

Avon Studio Transportation
7080 Santa Monica Blvd.
Los Angeles, CA 90038
(323) 850-0826
(800) 432-2866
FAX (323) 467-4239
www.avonrents.com

Beverly Hills Rent-A-Car
11647 Ventura Blvd.
Studio City, CA 91604
(818) 623-6700
(310) 901-0135
FAX (818) 623-0400
www.bhrentacar.com

Black & White Car and Limousine Service
(818) 781-1555
(800) 924-1624
FAX (818) 995-4188
www.blackwhitecarservice.com

Blue Moon Limousine & Sedan
(714) 546-6737
(800) 726-1837
FAX (714) 546-7048

Budget
(800) 527-7000
(310) 642-4500
www.budget.com

Ⓐ **Budget of Beverly Hills**
9815 Wilshire Blvd.
Beverly Hills, CA 90212
(310) 966-0642
FAX (310) 578-1068
www.budgetbeverlyhills.com

Ⓐ **California Rent-A-Car**
11725 Santa Monica Blvd.
Los Angeles, CA 90025
(310) 477-2727
FAX (310) 477-9176
www.productioncarrental.com

Celebrity Executive Car
(310) 398-8779
(323) 850-8000
FAX (310) 398-6730

Classic Car Rental Connection
17514 Ventura Blvd.
Encino, CA 91316
(818) 728-0607
FAX (818) 728-0684
www.101classiccarrental.com

CLS Transportation
(800) 266-2577
FAX (310) 414-8126
www.clslimo.com

Crown Limousine L.A.
(310) 737-0888
(800) 933-5466
FAX (310) 737-0890
www.crownlimola.com

Dollar
(See Web Site for Locations)
(800) 800-4000
(866) 434-2226
www.dollar.com

Dream One
(800) 538-8799
(310) 670-5466
FAX (310) 670-0558
www.dreamonesedans.com

ELS Transportation
4720 171st St.
Lawndale, CA 90260
(310) 410-8100
FAX (310) 542-4108
www.elstransportation.com

Enterprise
(See Web Site for Locations)
(800) 261-7331
www.enterprise.com

Exclusive Sedan Service
12580 Saticoy St.
North Hollywood, CA 91605
(818) 765-7311
(800) 400-7332
FAX (818) 765-0183
www.exclusivesedan.com

Executive Productions
3951 Ridgemont Dr.
Malibu, CA 90265
(310) 456-8833
FAX (310) 456-5692

Executive Transit, Inc.
(626) 568-4110
(800) 468-6529
FAX (626) 685-2626

Exquisite Limo and Sedan Service
10834 S. Freeman Ave.
Inglewood, CA 90304
(310) 674-3326
(310) 420-0277
FAX (310) 674-4447
www.exquisitelimoandsedanservice.com

Fleetwood Limousine
(310) 645-6092
(800) 283-5893
FAX (310) 645-1245

Ⓐ **Galpin Studio Rentals**
1763 N. Ivar Ave.
Hollywood, CA 90028
(323) 957-3333
(800) 256-6219
FAX (323) 856-6790
www.galpinstudiorentals.com

Galpin Studio Rentals
8353 Sepulveda Blvd.
North Hills, CA 91343
(818) 891-1752
(800) 256-6219
FAX (818) 778-3027
www.galpinstudiorentals.com

Gemstar Limousine Service
(310) 457-7307
(800) 922-5466
FAX (310) 457-6307
www.gemstarlimo.com

Hertz
9000 Airport Blvd.
Los Angeles, CA 90045
(See Web Site for Additional Locations)
(818) 268-5779
(818) 847-8008
FAX (310) 568-3461
www.hertz.com

Integrated Transportation Services
3047 S. Robertson Blvd.
Los Angeles, CA 90034
(310) 845-1234
(800) 487-4255
FAX (310) 558-0748
www.itslimo.com

Jack's Heaven
(213) 819-5466
(213) 500-0077

Marathon
12903 Washington Blvd.
Los Angeles, CA 90066
(800) 586-4004
(310) 827-5600
FAX (310) 823-6526
www.marathonrentacar.com

Midway Car Rentals
1800 S. Sepulveda Blvd.
West Los Angeles, CA 90025
(310) 445-4355
(800) 824-5260
FAX (310) 445-4368
www.midwaycarrental.com

National
(See Web Site for Locations)
(800) 227-7368
(310) 338-8200
www.nationalcar.com

Olympic Rent A Car (310) 751-6501
(818) 262-5355
9230 W. Olympic Blvd., Ste. 200 FAX (310) 274-1271
Beverly Hills, CA 90212 **www.olympicrentacar.com**

Red Carpet Limousine Service, Inc. (310) 398-9700
FAX (310) 398-9750
www.rcllimo.com

Rent-A-Wreck (310) 826-7555
(800) 995-0994
12333 W. Pico Blvd. FAX (310) 207-0681
West Los Angeles, CA 90064 **www.rentawreck.com**
(See Web Site for Additional Locations)

Secure Transportation (562) 941-0107
(800) 856-9994
13111 Meyer Rd. FAX (562) 906-2947
Whittier, CA 90605 **www.securetransportation.com**

Silverado Coach Company, Inc. (818) 251-9700
(800) 544-7999
FAX (818) 884-4997
www.silveradocoach.com

Thrifty (800) 367-2277
(310) 645-1881
5440 W. Century Blvd. **www.thrifty.com**
Los Angeles, CA 90045
(See Web Site for Additional Locations)

24 Hr. Production Catering
(818) 321-7403
(818) 884-2290
FAX (818) 704-1992
www.productioncatering.com

4 Seasons Catering
(818) 347-1105
(818) 314-4229
(Breakfast, Lunch & Second Meals) FAX (818) 992-1468
www.4seasonscaterers.com

5 Star Catering (800) 575-1710
3802 N. Earle Ave. FAX (626) 307-9100
Rosemead, CA 91770 www.5starmotorhomes.com

A & M Catering
(818) 709-5385
(818) 535-9411
19201 Halstead St. FAX (818) 709-5385
Northridge, CA 91324 www.aandmcatering.net
(Mobile Kitchen Facilities)

Abbey Road Catering (310) 649-4040
www.abbeyroadfilmcatering.com

About Thyme Location Catering
(818) 252-7378
(818) 679-7609
2911 N. Brighton St. FAX (818) 252-7378
Burbank, CA 91504

Above & Beyond The Culinary Experience (310) 991-9353
4071 Liberty Canyon Rd. www.aandbcatering.com
Agoura Hills, CA 91301

ACME Location Catering (818) 601-2963
FAX (818) 346-1436
(Breakfast, Lunch & Mobile Kitchen Facilities)

Aki Specialty Cuisine Services
(818) 266-9912
(818) 895-6641
FAX (818) 895-6678
www.classiccateringshowroom.com
(Dim-Sum, Second Meals, Sushi & Tempura)

Alex's Gourmet Catering
(818) 775-0590
(818) 355-8218
20928 Itasca FAX (818) 775-0591
Chatsworth, CA 91311

All American Softy & Coffee (818) 881-8890
(24-Hour Service) www.allamericansofty.com

Allstar Catering L.L.C. (818) 262-6197
(Mobile Kitchen Facilities) www.allstarexpress.com

Ammo Catering & Cafe
(323) 871-2666
(323) 467-3293
1155 N. Highland Ave. www.ammocafe.com
Hollywood, CA 90038

Ann & Mario Catering
(818) 262-1750
(818) 262-2727
FAX (818) 353-7953
www.annandmariocatering.com

Apple Spice Junction (818) 994-7400
16760 Stagg St., Ste. 202 FAX (818) 994-7014
Van Nuys, CA 91406 www.applespice.com
(Drop-Off Lunches and On-Site Catering)

Auntie Em's Kitchen (323) 255-0800
4616 Eagle Rock Blvd.
Los Angeles, CA 90041

Austro Catering Services, Inc.
(310) 505-1799
(661) 253-1486
(Mobile Kitchen Facilities) FAX (661) 253-4558
www.austrocatering.com

Avant-Garde Catering
(805) 382-4515
(805) 443-0796
(Mobile Kitchen Facilities) FAX (805) 815-3685

Backlot Bistro
(818) 843-6603
(818) 731-6924
2009 W. Burbank Blvd. FAX (818) 843-0551
Burbank, CA 91506
(Mobile Kitchen Facilities)

Bella Luna Cuisine
(310) 871-7601
(310) 413-9823

Best Boy espresso (323) 665-2378
www.myspace.com/bestboy
(24 Hour Service, Mobile Cappuccino, Coffee & Smoothie Service)

Big Picture Catering (818) 768-8220

Big Screen Cuisine Catering
(818) 526-0009
(310) 367-3332
2618 W. Magnolia Blvd. www.bigscreencuisine.com
Burbank, CA 91505
(Mobile Kitchen Facilities)

Black Tie Catering and Events/ BT Daily (310) 337-9900
5741 Buckingham Pkwy, Ste. D FAX (310) 337-9916
Culver City, CA 90230 www.blacktieevent.com
(Mobile Kitchen Facilities)

Blended Drink Catering/ California Brain Chill
(818) 635-2262
(888) 525-8423
(Blended Drinks, Smoothies & Sundae Bar) FAX (818) 972-3952
www.californiabrainchill.com

Bobby Weisman Caterers (818) 843-9999
736 S. Glenwood Pl. FAX (818) 843-9995
Burbank, CA 91506 www.bobbyweisman.com
(Mobile Kitchen Facilities)

Creative Catering For The Entertainment Industry
FEDERICO BARBIER
(323) 733-5544
(323) 733-5545 Fax
toucancatering.com
TOUCAN

Bonne Bouffe Catering (310) 629-7423 / (310) 397-1660
1521 Venice Blvd.
Venice, CA 90291

Bourbon Street Catering (818) 361-7494 / (818) 674-8144
(Mobile Kitchen Facilities) FAX (818) 361-7494
www.bourbonstreetcatering.com

Boyz In The Kitchen (818) 762-2336 / (818) 636-2137
FAX (818) 762-2331
www.boyzinthekitchencatering.com

Bread & Wine (323) 939-8725 / (323) 896-1558
4523 W. 16th Pl.
Los Angeles, CA 90019
www.bread-wine.com

Breakfast Brothers (310) 880-0406

Breakfast Rendezvous (818) 787-5502 / (818) 349-5211
(24-Hour Service)

Ⓐ **Breakfast! Rise & Shine/ Rise & Shine Lunch Catering** (310) 649-0906
7401 W. 88th Pl. FAX (310) 649-0264
Los Angeles, CA 90045 www.riseandshinecatering.com
(Breakfasts & Mobile Kitchen Facilities)

Brick House Kitchen Catering (310) 670-0889
7929 Emerson Ave. www.brickhousecatering.com
Los Angeles, CA 90045

Bruce's Gourmet Catering, Inc. (818) 376-1288
13631 Saticoy St. FAX (818) 376-1505
Panorama City, CA 91402
(Mobile Kitchen Facilities)

Café on Location, Inc. (818) 758-9858
19451 Ventura Blvd. FAX (818) 758-9754
Tarzana, CA 91356
(Mobile Kitchen Facilities)

California Catering (323) 216-6210
(Mobile Kitchen Facilities)

Camille's (626) 202-5214 / (626) 791-4081
FAX (866) 222-7760
www.camilleskitchen.com

Cappuccino Connection (800) 270-0188 / (800) 270-0188
FAX (805) 969-7295
www.capbar.com

Cappuccino On Call (323) 481-6575
(Cappuccino & Espresso) FAX (323) 463-8377
www.cappuccinooncall.com

Cappuccino? (818) 731-5285 / (866) 955-5282
(Mobile Espresso Service) FAX (866) 451-3752
www.gotcappuccino.com

The Cast Supper, Inc. (818) 908-0069
(Mobile Kitchen Facilities) FAX (818) 908-9737
www.thecastsupper.com

Catered Occasions (310) 568-1004
6517 S. Sepulveda Blvd. FAX (310) 568-1069
Los Angeles, CA 90045
www.cateredoccasionsevents.com

Catering by Michael (310) 999-1638
FAX (310) 793-8472
www.cateringbymichael.net

CateringUnlimited.com (805) 782-8070 / (805) 544-5777
2990 Dairy Creek Rd. FAX (805) 782-8071
San Luis Obispo, CA 93405 www.cateringunlimited.com

Celebrity A La Carte (323) 848-2300
www.celebrityalacarte.com

Chef 2 Go (805) 698-0465
www.chef2go.us

Chef Robért Motion Picture Catering (818) 686-6449 / (323) 864-6605
7336 Santa Monica Blvd., Ste. 692 FAX (818) 686-6602
West Hollywood, CA 90046 www.chefrobertcatering.com

Ⓐ **Chefs on Location** (626) 309-9042 / (626) 437-9153
(Mobile Kitchen Facilities) FAX (626) 448-4379
www.chefsonlocation.net

The Crepe Lady (714) 686-0065
FAX (562) 342-6212
www.thecrepelady.com

Crepes of Paris (323) 679-4973
118 S. Wetherly Dr., Ste. 101 www.crepesofparis.com
Los Angeles, CA 90048

Cross Culture Cuisine (661) 713-5392
43941 Blue Sky Court FAX (661) 723-6925
Lancaster, CA 93536

chefs on location catering, inc.

www.chefsonlocation.com

- a complete catering service
- short notice
- 24 hour service
- vegetarian menu
- entrees include a full salad bar, desserts & drinks
- truck rental
- table & chairs
- breakfast, lunch & second meal
- linen/silverware
- **WE DO BBQ!**

- 626-442-7331 OFFICE
- 626-309-9042
- 626-448-4379 FAX
- 626-437-9153 CELL

Curbside Café (818) 901-8041 / (818) 744-4742
15410 Runnymede St.
Van Nuys, CA 91406
www.thecurbsidecafe.com
(24-Hour Mobile Espresso Service & Smoothie Bar)

de ja Food Catering (661) 254-4115
24811 N. San Fernando Rd., Unit B-C
Santa Clarita, CA 91321
FAX (661) 254-2115
www.dejafood.com

Dean's Catering (818) 625-5850 / (818) 999-5850
FAX (818) 999-5851

Debbie's Dinners (323) 936-4545
6031 Venice Blvd.
Los Angeles, CA 90034
FAX (323) 936-4358
www.debbiesdinners.com

Delizia (310) 399-9400
FAX (310) 399-1180
www.thefocusstudio.com

Deluxe Catering, Inc. (818) 985-9069 / (818) 590-9069
(Mobile Kitchen Facilities)
FAX (818) 985-1298

Desert Rose Grill (818) 482-9198 / (818) 785-7574
FAX (661) 288-1958
www.desertrosegrill.com

El Cholo Catering (323) 737-7718
1121 S. Western Ave.
Los Angeles, CA 90006
FAX (323) 737-1873
(24-Hour Service & Mobile Kitchen Facilities)

Encore Catering (818) 222-6679 / (800) 362-6738
P.O. Box 8686
Calabasas, CA 91372
FAX (818) 222-3834
www.encorecatering.net

Entertainment Catering (626) 575-1430 / (562) 773-0402
1500 Chico Ave., Ste. F — FAX (626) 575-1429
South El Monte, CA 91733

Espresso Express (310) 200-7274
10600 Culver Blvd. — www.eemobile.com
Culver City, CA 90232
(24-Hour Moble Cappuccino Coffee Bar)

Eva Parkinson Catering, Inc. (310) 398-7664
12809 Venice Blvd. — FAX (310) 390-4256
Los Angeles, CA 90066

Famous Dave's BBQ (866) 408-7427
FAX (949) 421-5110
www.famousdaves.com

Final Cut Catering (818) 704-6219 / (818) 516-8956
5223 Alhama Dr. — FAX (818) 887-9046
Woodland Hills, CA 91364
(Mobile Kitchen Facilities)

First Take Catering Services (805) 577-1554 / (800) 318-7797
950 Enchanted Way, Ste. 101 — FAX (805) 584-5147
Simi Valley, CA 93065
(Mobile Kitchen Facilities)

Flatbush & J Gourmet Company, Inc. (310) 312-3632 / (310) 283-3043
11058 Santa Monica Blvd. — FAX (310) 312-3679
Los Angeles, CA 90025 — www.flatbushandj.com

Flava Catering (310) 839-7106 / (323) 293-5282
(Caribbean Creole Cuisine) — www.flavalady.com

Flavors with Love (323) 382-0550 / (818) 335-0548
6335 Homewood Ave. — FAX (323) 382-0551
Hollywood, CA 90028 — www.flavorswithlove.com

Food Fetish (818) 762-7850
(24-Hour Service) — FAX (818) 762-8470
www.foodfetishcatering.com

Food Lab Catering, LLC (323) 980-0833 / (323) 851-7120
7253 Santa Monica Blvd. — FAX (323) 461-7837
West Hollywood, CA 90046 — www.foodlabcatering.com

For Stars Express Catering (310) 322-1972
www.forstarscatering.com

Gala Catering, Inc. (818) 833-8350
FAX (818) 833-8356

George Studio Catering (661) 309-9034 / (310) 505-6676
17789 Sierra Hwy — FAX (661) 309-9034
Santa Clarita, CA 91351 — www.georgestudiocatering.com

The Gourmet Chabar (818) 341-8682
9525 Cozycroft Ave., Ste. M — FAX (818) 341-8696
Chatsworth, CA 91311

Gourmet on Location (818) 255-2085 / (818) 314-9696
13351-D Riverside Dr., Ste. 421 — FAX (818) 901-9022
Sherman Oaks, CA 91423
(Mobile Kitchen Facilities)

Hat Trick Catering (818) 897-2393 / (818) 968-4403
10953 San Fernando Rd. — FAX (818) 897-8082
Pacoima, CA 91331
(Mobile Kitchen Facilities)

Hollywood Caterers (818) 345-6718
7527 Reseda Blvd., Ste. B — FAX (818) 345-6719
Reseda, CA 91335 — www.hollywood-caterers.com
(Mobile Kitchen Facilities)

Il Bella Events (323) 436-0082 / (213) 785-4455
12824 E. Hadley St., Stes. 105 & 106 — FAX (866) 399-0417
Whittier, CA 90601 — www.ilbellaevents.com
(24-Hour Service)

In Good Taste L.A. (323) 630-2359 / (323) 424-4436
FAX (323) 424-4436
www.ingoodtastela.com

J.R.'s Gourmet Catering (805) 688-0086
1210 Mission Dr., Ste. H — FAX (805) 688-5396
Solvang, CA 93463 — www.jrscatering.net

Jacopo's Catering (310) 454-8494
15415 Sunset Blvd. — www.jacopos.com
Los Angeles, CA 90046

Java The Truck - Entertainment Coffee Service (310) 717-6967
8180 Manitoba St., Ste. 333 — FAX (818) 994-4228
Playa Del Rey, CA 90293 — www.javathetruck.com

Jennie Cook Catering (323) 982-0052
3048 Fletcher Dr. — FAX (323) 982-9180
Los Angeles, CA 90065 — www.jenniecooks.com

Joe's Studio Services (818) 469-9047 / (866) 671-5637
FAX (661) 729-9323
www.joesstudioservices.com

Johnny Pacific Fine Rustic Cuisine (818) 640-3920 / (818) 640-4562
FAX (818) 255-9930
www.johnnypacificcatering.com

Jolly Brothers Catering (805) 687-2023 / (805) 969-5656
423 W. Victoria St. — FAX (805) 969-5656
Santa Barbara, CA 93101

Karen's Espresso (818) 342-8400 / (818) 770-8826
www.karensespresso.com
(24-Hour Mobile Espresso and Smoothie Service)

Karma Kappuccino, Inc. (818) 787-8729
5632 Halbrent Ave. — FAX (818) 787-8729
Van Nuys, CA 91411
(24-Hour Mobile Espresso Service & Smoothie Bar)

Leave It To Linda Catering (310) 848-4197
1174 Amherst Ave., Ste. 306 — www.leaveittolinda.com
Los Angeles, CA 90049

Let's Have A Cart Party (310) 246-1230
FAX (310) 786-1719
www.letshaveacartparty.com

Life In The Food Chain/Patty Domay (661) 255-3625 / (661) 222-8334
(Breakfasts)

Little Next Door (323) 951-1010
8142 W. Third St. — FAX (323) 951-0487
Los Angeles, CA 90048 — www.thelittledoor.com

Lori's Kitchen (310) 473-5783
FAX (818) 787-5066

Luigi's Kitchen Catering & Tray Service (818) 702-0575 / (818) 523-2151
6181 N. Figueroa St. — FAX (818) 702-0575
Los Angeles, CA 90042 — www.luigiskitchen.com
(24-Hour Service)

M.B.'s Food/Mary Beth Pape (310) 398-3653
(Breakfasts) — FAX (310) 398-3653

Mario Guzman Catering (818) 997-7478 / (818) 421-1876
14053 Lanark St. — FAX (818) 997-7478
Panorama, CA 91402

Matt's Coffee Express (805) 388-5035 / (805) 377-3630
P.O. Box 675 FAX (805) 388-5035
Somis, CA 93066
(24-Hour Mobile Coffee Service)

Michael's Epicurean, Inc. (818) 360-7626 / (818) 262-5702
P.O. Box 33965 www.michaelsepicurean.com
Granada Hills, CA 91394
(24-Hour Service)

Neil Richardson's Premier Breakfast (310) 248-2309 / (310) 849-6463
P.O. Box 36745
Los Angeles, CA 90036

New Frontier Espresso Bar Catering (310) 839-3423 / (800) 949-5282
12021 Wilshire Blvd., Ste. 352 FAX (310) 839-3453
Los Angeles, CA 90025 www.nfcoffee.com
(Mobile Espresso Bar)

Off The Shelf Catering (310) 440-0794 / (310) 936-5665
9854 National Blvd., Ste. 234 FAX (310) 494-0794
Los Angeles, CA 90034
(Mobile Kitchen Facilities)

Oranges/Sardines (323) 244-4427 / (323) 256-6172
(Breakfast) www.orangessardines.com/Breakfast

Panini Di Ambra, I (323) 463.1200 / (323) 459-1541
5633 Hollywood Blvd. FAX (323) 465-9388
Los Angeles, CA 90028 www.thepaninilady.com
(24-Hour Service, Lunches & Second Meals)

Patrick's Location Catering (805) 388-5544
FAX (805) 388-5544
(24-Hour Service & Mobile Kitchen Facilities)

Piknic (310) 975-9108 / (310) 601-0351
13020 Pacific Promenade, Ste. 1 FAX (310) 862-5762
Playa Vista, CA 90094 www.piknic.us
(24-Hour Service)

Reel Chefs Catering (310) 613-6986 / (310) 397-5405
FAX (310) 388-0717
www.reelchefscatering.com

Richard Friedman Catering (310) 450-4377
1326 Pico Blvd. FAX (323) 932-1499
Santa Monica, CA 90405

Ruisseau Espresso (213) 663-9455
819 N. Florence St. www.ruisseau.biz
Burbank, CA 91506
(Cappuccino Bar)

Sam's Mobile Espresso Bar (310) 582-0627 / (415) 455-6005
(Espresso Bar) FAX (415) 488-1206
www.samsmobileespresso.com

Sandmarsh Coffee Lady (310) 429-4633
720 Angelus Pl.
Venice, CA 90291
(Coffee Service, Smoothies & Teas)

Charlie Scola aka PartyCharlie (310) 214-9158
www.charliescola.com

Silver Grill Catering (818) 255-2085 / (818) 314-9696
FAX (818) 255-2084

Smoky Mountain B-B-Q (951) 461-9299
26371 Beckman Court, Ste. G
Murrieta, CA 92562 www.smokymountainbbq.com

A **Some Like It Hot Catering** (818) 765-5663 / (323) 461-0706
FAX (818) 765-5338
www.somelikeithotcatering.com

Studio Café & Catering at Raleigh Studios (323) 466-3111 / (323) 960-4799
5300 Melrose Ave. FAX (323) 871-5600
Hollywood, CA 90038 www.raleighstudios.com

Taco-Man! LLC (310) 784-1399 / (310) 951-3248
P.O. Box 1483 FAX (310) 784-1396
Torrance, CA 90505 www.taco-man.com

Taste Catering, Inc. (949) 215-7373
FAX (949) 215-7494
www.tastecateringcafe.com
(24-Hour Service & Mobile Kitchen Facilities)

Taylor Made Production Catering, Inc. (818) 404-0564
(Mobile Kitchen Facilities)

TomKats, Inc. (800) 670-2248
FAX (615) 256-5055
www.tomkats.com

Too Tasty Catering (818) 241-8190 / (818) 355-5431
329 Winchester Ave. FAX (818) 549-0848
Glendale, CA 91201 www.tootasty-catering.com

A **Toucan Catering, Inc.** (323) 733-5544
(24-Hour Service) FAX (323) 733-5545

Village Catering (323) 939-2154
214 S. McCadden Pl. FAX (323) 931-8538
Los Angeles, CA 90004

What's Cooking Good Looking Caterers (818) 349-0926
FAX (818) 349-1492

Wild Wild West Catering (818) 317-3015
6552 Greenbush Ave. FAX (818) 989-5890
Valley Glen, CA 91401

Wolfgang Puck Catering (323) 491-1250
6801 Hollywood Blvd., Ste. 501 www.wolfgangpuck.com
Los Angeles, CA 90028

AAA Communications (626) 813-7580 (888) 925-5437
16025 Arroyo Hwy, Ste. H FAX (626) 813-7460
Irwindale, CA 91706 www.aaacomm.com
(Cellular Phones, Multi-Line Phone Systems, Pagers & Walkie Talkies)

AAAAAA-You! Walkie Rentals (310) 383-6572
(Walkie Talkies)

A Airwaves Cellular (818) 501-8200 (800) 400-9929
13400 Riverside Dr., Ste. 103 FAX (818) 528-7686
Sherman Oaks, CA 91423
(Cellular Phones, Nextels, Walkie Talkies & Wireless Internet)

American Radio (619) 239-5020 (877) 247-8866
6310 Riverdale St. FAX (619) 239-5925
San Diego, CA 92120 www.americanradio.us
(Base Stations, Cellular Phones, Repeaters & Walkie Talkies)

American Radio (714) 636-8101 (877) 247-8866
11570 Trask Ave. FAX (714) 636-8267
Garden Grove, CA 92843 www.americanradio.us
(Base Stations, Cellular Phones, Repeaters & Walkie Talkies)

Anytime Production Rentals (323) 461-8483
755 N. Lillian Way FAX (323) 461-2338
Hollywood, CA 90038 www.anytime-rentals.com
(Bullhorns, Helicopter Headsets & Walkie Talkies)

Apache Rental Group (818) 842-9944 (818) 842-9875
3910 W. Magnolia Blvd. FAX (818) 842-9269
Burbank, CA 91505 www.apacherentalgroup.com
(Base Stations, Bullhorns, Cellular Phones, Pagers, Repeaters & Walkie Talkies)

Atomic Production Supplies (818) 566-8811
2621 N. Ontario St. FAX (818) 566-8311
Burbank, CA 91504 www.atomicproductionsupplies.com
(Cellular Phones, Nextels & Walkie Talkies)

Attack, Inc. (949) 650-4454 (949) 650-4414
P.O. Box 790 FAX (949) 650-4674
Newport Beach, CA 92661 www.attack.ac
(Digital Phone Systems)

AVS (818) 954-8842
712 S. Main St. FAX (818) 954-9122
Burbank, CA 91506 www.aerialvideo.com
(Miniature Talent Cueing Systems, Repeaters, Walkie Talkies & Wired/Wireless Intercom Systems)

The Beacon Group/ Verizon Wireless and Wireline (323) 253-0803
FAX (323) 466-4550
www.thebeacongroup.com

C3 Communications Cabling Consulting (818) 787-6700 (818) 231-3079
7751 Densmore Ave. FAX (818) 787-6701
Van Nuys, CA 91406 www.c-3usa.com
(Fax Installation, Internet Connection, Office Phones, Rental Phones, Telephone Systems, Temporary Land Lines & Voice/ Data Cabling)

Call Box, Inc. (818) 517-1034
20660 Celtic St. FAX (818) 772-1035
Chatsworth, CA 91311
(Walkie Talkies)

Cellular Abroad (310) 862-7100 (800) 287-5072
425 Culver Blvd. FAX (310) 919-2820
Playa del Rey, CA 90293 www.cellularabroad.com
(Cellular Phones)

Cinesat, Inc. (213) 596-5180 (818) 802-7719
c/o Los Angeles Center Studios FAX (213) 596-5181
1201 W. Fifth St., Ste. FF www.cinesat.net
Los Angeles, CA 90017
(Satellite Internet Connections)

Coffey Sound & Communications, Inc. (323) 876-7525 / (888) 293-3030
3325 Cahuenga Blvd. West FAX (323) 876-4775
Hollywood, CA 90068 www.coffeysound.com
(Bullhorns, Cellular Phones, Fax Machines, Repeaters & Walkie Talkies)

CP Communications, Inc. (800) 385-3331 / (818) 954-9970
2521 N. Ontario St. FAX (818) 954-9969
Burbank, CA 91504 www.cpcomms.com
(2-Ways, Cellular Phones, Helicopter Headsets, Intercom Systems, Mobile Services, Repeaters, Telephone Systems, Walkie Talkies & Wireless Mics)

Day Wireless Systems (818) 557-7390 / (800) 235-7011
2211 N. San Fernando Blvd. FAX (818) 557-0254
Burbank, CA 91504 www.daywireless.com
(Base Stations, Cellular Phone/Fax Equipment, Nextels, Pagers, Repeaters, Walkie Talkies & Wireless Systems)

A **Exchange Communications** (888) 679-6111 / (505) 501-1029
8217 Lankershim Blvd., Ste. 43 FAX (888) 694-8111
North Hollywood, CA 91605 www.exchangecom.net
(Internet Connectivity, Office Phone Systems, Satellite Internet Connection, Temporary Land Lines & Wireless Internet)

Heavy Artillery Production Rentals (310) 295-1202
3200 S. La Cienega Blvd. FAX (310) 295-1202
Los Angeles, CA 90016 www.heavyartilleryrentals.com
(Base Stations, Bullhorns, Mobile Services & Walkie Talkies)

Hollywood Telephone/ Will Communications (310) 536-9777
2627 Manhattan Beach Blvd., Ste. 211 FAX (310) 536-9276
Redondo Beach, CA 90278 www.willcommunications.com
(Rental Phone Systems and Installation)

J & R Productions (818) 845-6440 / (800) 818-7234
201 N. Hollywood Way, Ste. 102 FAX (818) 557-0270
Burbank, CA 91505
(Bullhorns, Cellular Phones, Pagers & Walkie Talkies)

J. Dolan Communications (818) 487-7203
11331 Ventura Blvd., Ste. 1A FAX (818) 487-7208
Studio City, CA 91604 www.dolancommunications.com
(2-Ways, Base Stations, Bullhorns, Helicopter Headsets, Intercom Systems, Internet Connectivity, Radios, Repair, Repeaters, Walkie Talkies, Wired/Wireless Intercom Systems & Wireless Internet)

JLH Communications (310) 398-7430
12549 Everglade St. FAX (310) 398-7430
Los Angeles, CA 90066
(Office Phone Systems and Installation)

Jun's Electronics (310) 390-8003
5563 Sepulveda Blvd., Ste. D FAX (310) 390-4393
Culver City, CA 90230 www.hamcity.com
(Radios, Rentals, Repeaters & Walkie Talkies)

LCS (310) 476-8380
2554 Lincoln Blvd., Ste. 421 FAX (818) 789-6435
Venice, CA 90291
(Acoustic Coupler Systems, Base Stations, Bullhorns, Cellular Data Interfaces and Phone/Fax Equipment, Nextels, Office Phone Systems, Pagers, Repeaters, Satellite Systems & Walkie Talkies)

LCS (310) 476-8380
15445 Ventura Blvd., Ste. 3312 FAX (818) 789-6435
Sherman Oaks, CA 91403

Line 204 (323) 960-0113
1034 N. Seward St. FAX (323) 960-0163
Los Angeles, CA 90038 www.line204.com
(Base Stations, Cellular Phones, Repeaters & Walkie Talkies)

Location Connect (800) 818-8324 (626) 792-0000
200 E. Del Mar Blvd., Ste. 300 FAX (626) 844-1001
Pasadena, CA 91105 **www.locationconnect.com**
(Digital Phone Systems, Fax Equipment, Installation, Intercom Systems, Internet Connectivity, Mobile Services, Rentals, Repeaters, Satellite Internet Connection, Satellite Phones, Satellite-Based Service, Telephone Systems, Temporary Land Lines, Wired/Wireless Intercom Systems & Wireless Internet)

Location Sound Corporation (818) 980-9891 (800) 228-4429
10639 Riverside Dr. FAX (818) 980-9911
North Hollywood, CA 91602 **www.locationsound.com**
(2-Way Radios, Base Stations, Bullhorns, Intercom Systems, Radios, Rentals, Repair, Repeaters, Walkie Talkies, Wired/Wireless Intercom Systems & Wireless Mics)

Los Angeles Telemedia Associates, Inc. (818) 386-2013
3609 Meadville Dr. **www.losangelestelemedia.com**
Sherman Oaks, CA 91403
(Installation, Internet Connectivity, Rental Phone Systems & Telephone Systems)

Loud and Clear Communications (310) 350-1717
2118 Wilshire Blvd., Ste. 164 FAX (310) 496-3247
Santa Monica, CA 90403
(2-Ways, Bullhorns, Cellular Phones, Helicopter Headsets, Radios, Rentals, Repeaters & Walkie Talkies)

MDT Communications (323) 934-6300
5818 W. Third St. FAX (323) 934-4947
Los Angeles, CA 90036 **www.mdtcom.com**
(Cellular Phones & Nextels)

Miller Production Services (310) 287-0466
3520 Helms Ave. FAX (310) 287-0467
Culver City, CA 90232
(Base Stations, Bullhorns, Cellular Fax Equipment, Cellular/Satellite Phones, Helicopter Headsets, Pagers, Repeaters & Walkie Talkies)

The Neighborhood Phone Co. (323) 254-7466 (323) 376-4232
5260 Dahlia Dr. FAX (323) 258-7646
Los Angeles, CA 90041
(Digital Phone Systems, Installation, Telephone Systems & Temporary Land Lines)

On Set Communications, Inc. (818) 512-1918
(Walkie-Talkies) FAX (818) 260-0225
www.onsetcommunications.net

Out of Frame Communications (323) 462-1898
1126 N. Citrus Ave. FAX (323) 462-1897
Hollywood, CA 90038 **www.outofframela.com**
(Base Stations, Cell Phones & Walkie Talkies)

The Production Truck, Inc. (818) 459-0425
711 Ruberta Ave. FAX (818) 459-0427
Glendale, CA 91201 **www.theproductiontruck.com**
(Walkie Talkies)

Protocol (818) 782-5705 (800) 400-5705
15635 Saticoy St., Ste. A FAX (818) 782-5817
Van Nuys, CA 91406 **www.walkietalkie.com**
(2-Ways, Base Stations, Bullhorns, Radios, Rentals, Repeaters & Walkie Talkies)

Quixote Studios (323) 960-9191
1000 N. Cahuenga Blvd. FAX (323) 960-3366
Los Angeles, CA 90038 **www.quixote.com**

Reliable Telephone & Data, Inc. (818) 455-8300 (800) 942-7200
15802-A Arminta St. FAX (818) 920-1202
Van Nuys, CA 91406 **www.latelephone.com**
(Digital Phone Systems & Telephone Systems)

Rock Bottom Rentals (310) 315-2600 (800) 794-5444
1310 Westwood Blvd. FAX (310) 582-1178
Los Angeles, CA 90024 **www.rockbottomrentals.com**
(Base Stations, Bullhorns, Cellular Phone/Fax Equipment, Nextels, Pagers, Repeaters, Satellite Phones & Walkie Talkies)

Rocket Internet (877) 447-6253 | (310) 532-9216
200 Oceangate, Eighth Fl. FAX **(562) 432-6096**
Long Beach, CA 90802 **www.rocketinternet.net**
(Internet Connectivity)

Rockstar Communications, Inc (818) 645-3390 | (323) 578-6088
1954 N. Hillhurst Ave., Ste. 108 FAX **(323) 662-3233**
Los Angeles, CA 90027
(Base Stations, Bullhorns, Cellular Phones, Internet Connectivity, Rentals, Repeaters, Walkie Talkies & Wireless Internet)

S&W Communications, Inc. (818) 786-7050
14714 Lull St. FAX **(818) 786-3289**
Van Nuys, CA 91405 **www.swphonedata.com**
(Phone Installation and Systems)

Samy's Camera (323) 938-2420 | (800) 321-4726
431 S. Fairfax Ave. FAX **(323) 937-2919**
Los Angeles, CA 90036 **www.samys.com**
(Walkie Talkies)

Samy's Camera (310) 450-4551
585 Venice Blvd. FAX **(310) 450-8590**
Venice, CA 90291 **www.samys.com**

Selak Entertainment, Inc. (818) 842-5800
P.O. Box 1475 **www.selakentertainment.com**
Burbank, CA 91507
(Internet Connectivity, Satellite-Based Service, Satellite Internet Connection, Satellite Phones, Temporary Land Lines & Wireless Internet)

Set Stuff, Inc. (323) 993-9500
1105 N. Sycamore Ave. FAX **(323) 993-9506**
Hollywood, CA 90038 **www.setstuffrentals.com**
(40-Watt Base Stations, Cellular Phones, Helicopter Headsets, Nextels, Pagers, Repeaters & Walkie Talkies)

SJM Industrial Radio (310) 640-2700 | (800) 688-1653
1212 E. Imperial Ave. FAX **(310) 640-9635**
El Segundo, CA 90245 **www.sjmradio.com**
(Authorized Motorola Dealer, Base Stations, Bullhorns, Cellular Phones, Installation, Radios, Repeaters, Repair, Satellite Phones & Walkie Talkies)

Skye Rentals (323) 462-5934
920 N. Citrus Ave. FAX **(323) 462-5935**
Hollywood, CA 90038 **www.skyerentals.com**
(2-Ways, Base Stations, Bullhorns, Helicopter Headsets, Internet Connectivity, Radios, Rentals, Repeaters, Satellite Phones, Walkie Talkies & Wireless Internet)

Star Communications, Inc. (310) 659-3232
9107 Wilshire Blvd., Ste. 500 FAX **(310) 659-3377**
Beverly Hills, CA 90210 **www.starcommunicationsinc.net**
(Cellular Phones)

TCH/The Camera House (818) 997-3802
7351 Fulton Ave. FAX **(818) 997-3885**
North Hollywood, CA 91605 **www.thecamerahouse.com**

Theatrical Concepts, Inc. (818) 597-1100
3030 Triunfo Canyon Rd. FAX **(818) 597-0202**
Agoura Hills, CA 91301 **www.theatrical.com**
(Walkie Talkies)

Warner Bros. Studio Facilities - Production Sound & Video (818) 954-2511
4000 Warner Blvd., Bldg. 28 FAX **(818) 954-2491**
Burbank, CA 91522 **www.wbsf.com**

Wilcox Sound and Communications (818) 557-3377
4545 Chermak St. FAX **(818) 557-3367**
Burbank, CA 91505

Wired Accessories, Inc. (818) 344-9998 | (877) 947-3352
9601 Owensmouth Ave., Ste. 1 FAX **(818) 344-9991**
Chatsworth, CA 91311 **www.wiredaccessories.com**
(Cellular Phones, Nextels & Walkie Talkies)

Wright Communications (818) 340-5481 | (818) 307-7224
4558 Don Pio Dr. **www.themobilehotspot.com**
Woodland Hills, CA 91364
(Cellular Phones, Internet Connectivity, Portable Faxing, Rentals, Sales & Wireless Internet)

Argentina Consulate General (323) 954-9155
FAX (323) 934-9076
www.usargentina.com

Australian Consulate General (310) 229-4800
2049 Century Park East, 19th Fl. FAX (310) 277-2258
Los Angeles, CA 90067

Austrian Consulate General (310) 444-9310
FAX (310) 477-9897
www.austria-la.org

Barbados Consulate General (213) 380-2198
(800) 221-9831
FAX (213) 384-2763
www.barbados.org

Belgian Consulate General (323) 857-1244
FAX (323) 936-2564

Brazilian Consulate General (323) 651-2664
8484 Wilshire Blvd., Ste. 711 FAX (323) 651-1274
Beverly Hills, CA 90211 www.brazilian_consulate.org

Canadian Consulate General (213) 346-2700
FAX (213) 620-8827
www.losangeles.gc.ca

Chile Consulate General (323) 933-3697
FAX (323) 933-3842

China Consulate General (213) 807-8088
FAX (213) 380-1961
www.chinaconsulatela.org

Costa Rica Consulate General (213) 380-7915
(800) 343-6332
FAX (213) 380-5639
www.costarica-embassy.org

Finland Consulate General (310) 203-9903
1801 Century Park East, Ste. 2100 FAX (310) 203-9186
Los Angeles, CA 90067 www.finland.org

French Consulate General (310) 235-3200
FAX (310) 312-0704
www.info-france-usa.org

German Consulate General (323) 930-2703
FAX (323) 930-2805
www.germany.info/losangeles.org

Great Britain Consulate General (310) 481-0031
FAX (310) 481-2960
www.britainusa.com

Greek Consulate General (310) 826-5555
12424 Wilshire Blvd., Ste. 800 FAX (310) 826-8670
Los Angeles, CA 90025
www.greekembassy.org/losangeles/

Guatemala Consulate General (213) 365-9251
1625 W. Olympic Blvd., Ste. 422 FAX (213) 365-9245
Los Angeles, CA 90015

Honduras Consulate General (213) 383-9244
3550 Wilshire Blvd., Ste. 410 FAX (213) 383-9306
Los Angeles, CA 90010 www.hondurasemb.org

Israeli Consulate General (323) 852-5500
FAX (323) 852-5555
www.israeliconsulatela.org

Italy Consulate General (310) 820-0622
12400 Wilshire Blvd., Ste. 300 FAX (310) 820-0727
Los Angeles, CA 90025 sedi.esteri.it/losangeles/

Japanese Consulate General (213) 617-6700
3650 Watseka Ave., Ste.15 FAX (213) 617-6727
Los Angeles, CA 90034 www.la.us.emb-japan.go.jp

Malaysia Consulate General (213) 892-1238
550 S. Hope St., Ste. 400 FAX (213) 892-9031
Los Angeles, CA 90071

Mexico Consulate General (213) 351-6800

The Netherlands Consulate General (310) 268-1598
(877) 388-2443
11766 Wilshire Blvd., Ste. 1150 FAX (310) 312-0989
Los Angeles, CA 90025 www.ncla.org

New Zealand Consulate General (310) 566-6555
2425 Olympic Blvd., Ste. 600E FAX (310) 566-6556
Santa Monica, CA 90404 www.nzcgla.com

Nicaragua Consulate General (213) 252-1170
3550 Wilshire Blvd., Ste. 200 FAX (213) 252-1177
Los Angeles, CA 90010
www.consuladodenicaragua.com

Peruvian Consulate General (213) 252-5910
3450 Wilshire Blvd., Ste. 800 FAX (213) 252-8130
Los Angeles, CA 90010

Philippines Consulate General (213) 639-0980
3600 Wilshire Blvd., Ste. 500 FAX (213) 639-0990
Los Angeles, CA 90010 www.philippineconsulatela.org

Saudi Arabia Consulate General (310) 479-6000
2045 Sawtelle Blvd. FAX (310) 479-2752
West Los Angeles, CA 90025

South African Consulate General (323) 651-0902
6300 Wilshire Blvd., Ste. 600 FAX (323) 651-5969
Los Angeles, CA 90048 www.link2southafrica.com

South Korea Consulate General (213) 385-9300
FAX (213) 385-1849
www.koreanconsulatela.org

Spanish Consulate General (323) 938-0158
FAX (323) 938-2502

Sweden Consulate General (619) 233-1106
750 B St., 1020 Symphony Towers FAX (619) 233-9890
San Diego, CA 92101

Switzerland Consulate General (310) 575-1145
11766 Wilshire Blvd., Ste. 1400 FAX (310) 575-1982
Los Angeles, CA 90025 www.swissemb.org/la/

Thailand Consulate General (323) 962-9574
611 N. Larchmont Blvd., Second Fl. FAX (323) 962-2128
Los Angeles, CA 90004 www.thai-la.net

Turkey Consulate General (323) 655-8832
6300 Wilshire Blvd., Ste. 2010 FAX (323) 655-8681
Los Angeles, CA 90048 www.turkiye.net/lacg

Uruguay Consulate General (310) 394-5777
429 Santa Monica Blvd., Ste. 400 FAX (310) 394-5140
Santa Monica, CA 90401

Crating & Packing

Art Pack, Inc.
225 W. 134th St.
Los Angeles, CA 90061
(310) 324-5553
FAX **(310) 324-6633**
www.artpack.us

Banner Packing
(310) 276-0804
FAX **(310) 659-9887**

Beverly Packing, Inc.
645 N. Fairfax Ave.
Los Angeles, CA 90036
(323) 658-8365
FAX **(323) 658-5815**
www.beverlypacking.com

Box Brothers
(310) 478-4008
(800) 842-6937
FAX **(310) 478-0667**
www.boxbros.com

Cooke's Crating
(323) 268-5101
FAX **(323) 262-2001**
www.cookescrating.com

Dynamic L.A., Inc.
11755 Sheldon St.
Sun Valley, CA 91352
(818) 771-1111
FAX **(818) 771-1159**
www.dynamicla.com

ETC International Freight System
2450 S. Sequoia Dr.
Compton, CA 90220
(24-Hour Service)
(800) 383-3157
(310) 632-2555
FAX **(310) 632-3044**
www.etcinternational.com

Fine Art Shipping
404 N. Oak St.
Inglewood, CA 90302
(310) 677-0011
(800) 421-7464
FAX **(310) 677-8586**
www.fineartship.com

Global Pack & Mail
1020 N. Hollywood Way
Burbank, CA 91505
(818) 556-3553
FAX **(818) 556-3773**
www.globalpackandmail.com

LA Packing, Crating & Transport
5722 W. Jefferson Blvd.
Los Angeles, CA 90016
(323) 937-2669
(800) 852-9836
FAX **(323) 937-9012**
www.lapacking.com

Packaging Store
4525 San Fernando Rd.
Glendale, CA 91204
(818) 956-1137
FAX **(818) 763-2050**
www.gopackagingstore.com

Packaging Store
10218 Riverside Dr.
Toluca Lake, CA 91602
(818) 763-1808
FAX **(818) 763-2050**
www.gopackagingstore.com

UsedCardboardboxes.com
4032 Wilshire Blvd., Ste. 402
Los Angeles, CA 90010
(24-Hour Service, New, Surplus and Used Boxes)
(888) 269-3788
(323) 724-2500
FAX **(323) 315-4194**
www.usedcardboardboxes.com

Customs Brokers & Carnets

Atlant USA, Inc.
(310) 649-6495
FAX **(310) 631-1830**
www.atlant.com

DB Schenker
2815 W. El Segundo Blvd.
Hawthorne, CA 90250
(323) 908-4800
(800) 541-6261
FAX **(323) 908-4874**
www.dbschenkerusa.com

ETC International Freight System
2450 S. Sequoia Dr.
Compton, CA 90220
(24-Hour Service)
(800) 383-3157
(310) 632-2555
FAX **(310) 632-3044**
www.etcinternational.com

Hahn International
(24-Hour Service)
(310) 216-6691
FAX **(310) 216-1681**

Moving Pictures Anywhere Company
8901 S. La Cienega Blvd., Ste. 105
Inglewood, CA 90301
(24-Hour Service)
(310) 590-1660
(866) 744-7672
FAX **(310) 590-1688**
www.movingpicturesanywhere.com

Rock-It Cargo USA, Inc.
(310) 410-0935
(516) 825-7356
FAX **(310) 410-0628**
www.rockitcargo.com

Schick International Forwarding
11099 S. La Cienega Blvd., Ste. 240
Los Angeles, CA 90045
(24-Hour Service)
(310) 215-1004
(800) 590-6050
FAX **(310) 215-1197**
www.schickintl.com

Total Transportation Concept, Inc.
8728 Aviation Blvd.
Inglewood, CA 90301
(310) 337-0515
(800) 582-7110
FAX **(310) 337-7901**
www.totaltrans.com

LA 411 Film Commissions & Permit Offices—California LA 411

Alhambra (626) 570-5021
111 S. First St. FAX **(626) 308-4868**
Alhambra, CA 91801 **www.cityofalhamba.org**
(Issues Permits)
Contact: Kim Johnson

Anaheim (714) 765-5183
Traffic Engineering Division FAX **(714) 765-4667**
200 S. Anaheim Blvd.
Anaheim, CA 92805
(Issues Permits)
Contact: Cyndee Blake

Antelope Valley (661) 723-6090
(661) 510-4231
44933 Fern Ave. FAX **(661) 723-5914**
Lancaster, CA 93534 **www.avfilm.com**

Arcadia (626) 574-5430
P.O. Box 60021 FAX **(626) 447-9173**
Arcadia, CA 91066 **www.ci.arcadia.ca.us**
(Issues Permits)
Contact: Silva Vergel

Avalon (310) 510-7646
125 Metropole Ave., Ste. 103 FAX **(310) 510-1646**
Avalon, CA 90704 **www.catalina.com**
(Issues Permits)
Contact: Shirley Davy

Bell (323) 588-6211
6330 Pine Ave. FAX **(323) 771-9473**
Bell, CA 90201
(Issues Permits)

Bell Gardens (562) 806-7700
(562) 806-7740
7100 Garfield Ave. FAX **(562) 806-7720**
Bell Gardens, CA 90201 **www.bellgardens.org**
(Issues Permits)
Contact: Carmen Morales

Bellflower (562) 804-1424
16600 Civic Center Dr. FAX **(562) 925-8660**
Bellflower, CA 90706 **www.bellflowerbusiness.com**
(Issues Permits)
Contact: Community Development

Berkeley (510) 549-7040
(800) 847-4823
2015 Center St. FAX **(510) 644-2052**
Berkeley, CA 94704 **www.visitberkeley.com**
(Issues Permits)

Beverly Hills (310) 285-2408
455 N. Rexford Dr., Ste. G10 FAX **(310) 273-0972**
Beverly Hills, CA 90210 **www.beverlyhills.org**
(Issues Permits)
Contact: Benita Miller

Bradbury (626) 358-3218
600 Winston Ave. FAX **(626) 303-5154**
Bradbury, CA 91010 **www.cityofbradbury.org**
(Issues Permits)
Contacts: Claudia Saldana & Jennifer Vasquez

Burbank (818) 238-3105
200 N. Third St. FAX **(818) 238-3109**
Burbank, CA 91502 **www.ci.burbank.ca.us/police/filmpermits.html**
(Issues Permits)
Contact: Norma Brolsma

Bureau of Land Management (760) 252-6000
(951) 779-6700
2601 Barstow Rd. FAX **(951) 779-0294**
Barstow, CA 92311 **www.filminlandempire.com**
(Issues Permits)
Contacts: Sheri Davis & Dan Taylor

Calabasas (805) 495-7521
Calabasas Film Office FAX **(805) 495-7621**
25 W. Rolling Oaks Dr., Ste. 201 **www.cityofcalabasas.com**
Thousand Oaks, CA 91361
(Issues Permits)

Calaveras County (800) 225-3764
(209) 736-0049
P.O. Box 637, 1192 S. Main St. FAX (209) 736-9124
Angels Camp, CA 95222 www.filmcalaveras.org
Contact: Lisa Reynolds

Carson (310) 952-1748
701 E. Carson St. FAX (310) 518-2874
Carson, CA 90745 ci.carson.ca.us
(Issues Permits)
Contact: Yuko Dunham

Catalina Island (310) 510-7645
P.O. Box 217 FAX (310) 510-7606
Avalon, CA 90704
(Issues Permits)

Cerritos (562) 916-1236
18125 S. Bloomfield Ave. FAX (562) 916-1237
Cerritos, CA 90703 www.ci.cerritos.ca.us
(Issues Permits)
Contact: Arcy Hinojosa

Claremont (909) 399-5497
207 Harvard Ave. FAX (909) 399-5492
Claremont, CA 91711
(Issues Permits)
Contact: Aileen Flores

Clovis (559) 299-7273
(559) 299-7363
325 Pollasky Ave. FAX (559) 299-2969
Clovis, CA 93612 www.clovischamber.com
(Issues Permits)

Covina (626) 384-5503
(626) 384-5400
City of Covina, 125 E. College St. www.ci.covina.ca.us
Covina, CA 91723
(Issues Permits)
Contact: Kathy Cordova

Culver City (310) 837-1221
Culver City Police Dept.
4040 Duquesne Ave.
Culver City, CA 90232
(Issues Permits)
Contact: Lt. Danjou

Diamond Bar/EIDC (213) 977-8600
1201 W. Fifth St., Ste. T-800 FAX (213) 977-8610
Los Angeles, CA 90017 www.eidc.com
(Issues Permits)
Contact: Mike Bobenko

Downey (562) 904-7251
(562) 904-7246
11111 Brookshire Ave. FAX (562) 904-7270
Downey, CA 90241
(Issues Permits)
Contact: Louretta Horton

Duarte (626) 357-7931
1600 E. Huntington Dr. www.accessduarte.com
Duarte, CA 91010
(Issues Permits)
Contact: Pat Razavi

El Dorado County Lake Tahoe (530) 626-4400
(800) 457-6279
542 Main St. FAX (530) 626-8850
Placerville, CA 95667 www.filmtahoe.com
(Issues Permits)
Contact: Kathleen Dodge

El Monte (626) 580-2131
(Issues Permits) FAX (626) 454-3220
Contact: Mark Sullivan

A **Fresno** (559) 621-8358
(559) 908-0539
Fresno Film & Entertainment FAX (559) 457-1505
Commission www.fresnofilm.com
2600 Fresno St., Ste. 2156-02
Fresno, CA 93721
(Issues Permits)
Contact: Ray Arthur

Fresno County (559) 262-4271
2220 Tulare St., Ste. 800 FAX (559) 442-6969
Fresno, CA 93721 www.filmfresno.com
Contacts: Gigi Gibbs & Kristie Johnson

Glendale (818) 548-2090
(818) 548-4000
613 E. Broadway, Ste. 110 FAX (818) 241-5386
Glendale, CA 91206 www.ci.glendale.ca.us
(Issues Permits)
Contact: Judy Herwig

Glendora (626) 914-8244
116 E. Foothill Blvd. FAX (626) 852-9650
Glendora, CA 91741 www.ci.glendora.ca.us
(Issues Permits)
Contact: Kay Dudley

Hawthorne (310) 349-2935
4455 W. 126th St. FAX (310) 978-9858
Hawthorne, CA 90250 www.cityofhawthorne.com
(Issues Permits)

Hermosa Beach (310) 318-0239
(310) 318-0280
1315 Valley Dr. FAX (310) 372-4333
Hermosa Beach, CA 90254 www.hermosabch.org
(Issues Permits)
Contact: Shaunna Miller Donahue

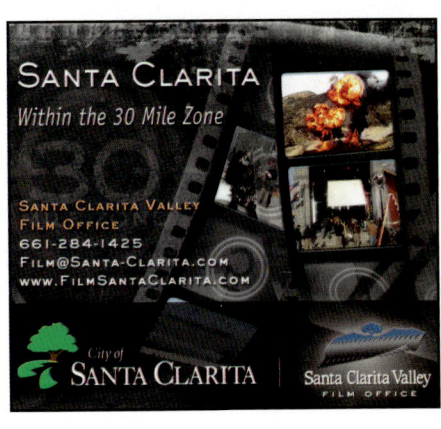

Humboldt County (707) 444-6633
(800) 338-7352
520 E St. FAX (707) 443-5115
Eureka, CA 95501 www.filmhumboldt.org
(Issues Permits)
Contact: Mary Cruse

Huntington Beach (714) 536-5434 / (714) 536-5496
2000 Main St. FAX (714) 374-1654
Huntington Beach, CA 92648
(Issues Permits)
Contacts: Barbara Gray & Janeen Laudenback

Inglewood (310) 412-5500 / (310) 412-5257
One Manchester Blvd. FAX (310) 330-5735
Inglewood, CA 90301 www.cityofinglewood.org
(Issues Permits)

Inland Empire (951) 779-6700
Inland Empire Film Commission FAX (951) 779-0294
1201 Research Park Dr., Ste. 100
Riverside, CA 92507 www.filminlandempire.com
(Issues Permits)
Contacts: Sheri Davis & Dan Taylor

Kern County (661) 868-5376 / (800) 500-5376
2101 Oak St. FAX (661) 861-2017
Bakersfield, CA 93301 www.filmkern.com
(Issues Permits)
Contacts: Rick Davis & Dave Hook

La Cañada Flintridge (818) 790-8880
1327 Foothill Blvd. FAX (818) 790-7536
La Cañada Flintridge, CA 91011 www.lcf.ca.gov
(Issues Permits)
Contact: Gil Meyer

La Habra Heights (562) 694-6302
1245 N. Hacienda Rd. FAX (562) 694-4410
La Habra Heights, CA 90631
(Issues Permits)
Contact: Amy Smith-Parker

La Mirada (562) 943-0131
13700 La Mirada Blvd. FAX (562) 943-3666
La Mirada, CA 90638 www.cityoflamirada.org
(Issues Permits)
Contact: Karen Bufkin

Lake County (707) 263-2277
255 N. Forbes St. FAX (707) 263-1012
Lakeport, CA 95453 www.lakecounty.com
(Issues Permits)
Contact: Debra Sommerfield

Lake Tahoe (South) (530) 542-6004
1052 Tata Ln. www.ci.south-lake-tahoe.ca.us/
South Lake Tahoe, CA 96150
(Issues Permits)
Contact: Angela Peterson

Lakewood (562) 866-9771
5050 Clark Ave. FAX (562) 866-0505
Lakewood, CA 90712 www.lakewoodcity.org
(Issues Permits)
Contact: Doug Butler

Livermore Valley (925) 447-1606
Livermore Valley Film Commission FAX (925) 447-1641
2157 First St. www.livermorechamber.org
Livermore, CA 94550
(Issues Permits)

Lomita (310) 325-7110
24300 Narbonne Ave. FAX (310) 325-4024
Lomita, CA 90717 www.lomita.com/cityhall
(Issues Permits)
Contact: Pat Negrete

Long Beach (562) 570-5399 / (562) 570-5333
Long Beach City Hall FAX (562) 570-5335
One World Trade Center, Ste. 300 www.filmlongbeach.com
Long Beach, CA 90831
(Issues Permits)
Contacts: Tasha Day & Andy Witherspoon

Los Angeles City & County - Film L.A., Inc. (213) 977-8600
1201 W. Fifth St., Ste. T800 FAX (213) 977-8610
Los Angeles, CA 90017 www.filmlainc.com
(Issues Permits)

Los Angeles County Department of Parks & Recreation (213) 738-2961
433 S. Vermont Ave. FAX (213) 738-6444
Los Angeles, CA 90020
(Issues Permits)
Contacts: Sheila Ortega & Rosanna Franco

Los Padres National Forest - Monterey (831) 385-5434
406 S. Mildred FAX (831) 385-0628
King City, CA 93930 www.fs.fed.us/r5/lospadres
Contact: Manny Madrigal

Los Padres National Forest - Mt. Pinos (661) 245-3731
34580 Lockwood Valley Rd. FAX (661) 245-1526
Frazier Park, CA 93225 www.fs.fed.us/r5/lospadres
Contact: Loreigh Brannan

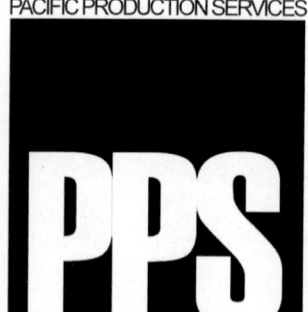

Los Padres National Forest - Ojai (805) 646-4348
1190 E. Ojai Ave. FAX (805) 646-0484
Ojai, CA 93023 www.fs.fed.us/r5/lospadres
Contact: Al Hess

Los Padres National Forest - Santa Barbara (805) 967-3481
3505 Paradise Rd. FAX (805) 967-7312
Santa Barbara, CA 93105 www.fs.fed.us/r5/lospadres
Contact: Tony Martinez

Los Padres National Forest - Santa Lucia (805) 925-9538
1616 N. Carlotti Dr. FAX (805) 961-5781
Santa Maria, CA 93454 www.fs.fed.us/r5/lospadres
Contacts: Jill Evans & Michael Crain

Malibu (805) 495-7521
23815 Stuart Ranch Rd. FAX (805) 495-7621
Malibu, CA 90265 www.ci.malibu.ca.us
(Issues Permits)

Mammoth Lakes & Mono County (760) 934-0628 (760) 914-0405
P.O. Box 24 FAX (760) 934-0700
Mammoth Lakes, CA 93546
(Issues Permits) www.mammothfilmlocations.com
Contact: James Vanko

Manhattan Beach (310) 802-5558
1400 Highland Ave. FAX (310) 802-5001
Manhattan Beach, CA 90266 www.citymb.info
(Issues Permits)
Contacts: Steve Charelian & Colette Bellavance

Mendocino County (Film Office) (707) 961-6300
332 N. Main St. FAX (707) 964-2056
Fort Bragg, CA 95437 www.filmmendocino.com
Contact: Debra DeGraw

Mendocino County (Permit Office) (707) 463-4441
501 Low Gap Rd., Ste. 1010 FAX (707) 463-5649
Ukiah, CA 95482 www.mendocinocoast.com/filmoffice/
(Issues Permits)
Contact: Denice Brown

Modesto (209) 526-5588 (888) 640-8467
1150 Ninth St., Ste. C FAX (209) 526-5586
Modesto, CA 95354 www.visitmodesto.com
(Issues Permits)

Modoc County (530) 233-6406
203 W. Fourth St. FAX (530) 233-6420
Alturas, CA 96101
(Issues Permits)
Contact: Scott Kessler

Monrovia (626) 932-5586 (626) 932-5550
415 S. Ivy Ave. FAX (626) 932-5569
Monrovia, CA 91016
(Issues Permits)
Contact: Sheila Spicer-Batice

Montebello (323) 887-1490
1600 W. Beverly Blvd. FAX (323) 887-1488
Montebello, CA 90640
(Issues Permits)
Contact: Lynda Carter

Monterey (Permit Office) (831) 646-3805 (831) 646-3830
Monterey Police Dept. FAX (831) 646-3802
351 Madison Ave.
Monterey, CA 93940
(Issues Permits)
Contact: Capt. Tim Shelby

Monterey County (831) 646-0910
801 Lighthouse Ave., Ste. 104 FAX (831) 655-9250
Monterey, CA 93940 www.filmmonterey.org
Contact: Karen Nordstrand

Monterey Park (626) 307-1338 (626) 307-1371
320 W. Newmark Ave. FAX (626) 307-0753
Monterey Park, CA 91754
(Issues Permits)
Contact: Film Liaison

Napa County Public Works (707) 253-4351
1195 Third St., Ste. 201 FAX (707) 279-2979
Napa, CA 94559 www.co.napa.ca.us
(Issues Permits)

Newport Beach (949) 675-8888 (714) 801-5553
1624 W. Oceanfront Walk FAX (949) 644-3073
Newport Beach, CA 92663
(Issues Permits)
Contact: Joseph Cleary

Norwalk (562) 929-5713
12700 Norwalk Blvd. FAX (562) 929-5966
Norwalk, CA 90650 www.ci.norwalk.ca.us
(Issues Permits)
Contact: Finance Department - Business License Section

Oakland (510) 238-4734 (510) 238-3456
150 Frank H. Ogawa Plaza, Ste. 8215 FAX (510) 238-6149
Oakland, CA 94612 www.filmoakland.com
(Issues Permits)

Orange County (714) 278-7569
CSUF, P.O. Box 6850 FAX (714) 278-7521
Fullerton, CA 92834 www.filmorangecounty.org

Orange County - Unincorporated Area (Permit Office) (714) 834-5238 (714) 834-5738
300 N. Flower St. FAX (714) 835-7425
Santa Ana, CA 92703 www.ocpermits.com
(Issues Permits)
Contact: Carolyn Uribe

Oxnard (805) 385-7444 (800) 422-6332
400 E. Esplanade Dr., Ste. 301 FAX (805) 385-7452
Oxnard, CA 93036 www.filmventuracounty.com
(Issues Permits)
Contact: Mary Hernandez

Pacific Palms (626) 810-4455 (800) 524-4557
One Industry Hills Pkwy www.pacificpalmsresort.com
City of Industry, CA 91744
(Issues Permits)
Contact: Michael Swyney

Palm Springs (760) 323-8265
401 S. Pavilion Way FAX (760) 323-8279
Palm Springs, CA 92262
(Issues Permits)
Contact: Lois Ware

Palm Springs/Coachella Valley (951) 779-6700 (760) 864-1313
1201 Research Park Dr., Ste. 100 FAX (951) 779-0294
Riverside, CA 92507 www.filminlandempire.com

Palmdale (661) 267-5115 (888) 434-5628
38300 Sierra Hwy, Ste. A FAX (661) 267-5122
Palmdale, CA 93550 www.cityofpalmdale.org
(Issues Permits)
Contact: Barbara Vilardo

Palos Verdes Estates (310) 378-0383
340 Palos Verdes Dr. West FAX (310) 378-7820
Palos Verdes Estates, CA 90274
(Issues Permits) www.palosverdes.com/pve
Contact: Vickie Kroneberger

Paramount (562) 220-2048 (562) 220-2000
16400 Colorado Ave. FAX (562) 220-2051
Paramount, CA 90723 www.paramountcity.com
(Issues Permits)
Contact: John Carver

Pasadena (626) 744-3964
175 N. Garfield Ave. FAX (626) 744-4785
Pasadena, CA 91101 www.filmpasadena.com
(Issues Permits)
Contact: Kristin Dewey

Placer-Lake Tahoe (530) 889-4091
(877) 228-3456
175 Fulweiler Ave. FAX (530) 889-4095
Auburn, CA 95603 www.placer.ca.gov/films
(Issues Permits)
Contact: Beverly Lewis

Pomona (909) 620-2051
505 S. Garey Ave. www.ci.pomona.ca.us
Pomona, CA 91766
(Issues Permits)
Contact: Tracy Radcliffe

Rancho Palos Verdes (310) 544-5205
30940 Hawthorne Blvd. FAX (310) 544-5291
Rancho Palos Verdes, CA 90275
(Issues Permits) www.palosverdes.com/rpv
Contact: Toni Harris

Redding/Shasta County (530) 225-4105
(800) 874-7562
777 Auditorium Dr. FAX (530) 225-4354
Redding, CA 96001 www.visitredding.org
(Issues Permits)
Contact: Sherry Ferguson

Redondo Beach (310) 318-0603
(310) 372-1171
415 Diamond St., Ste. C FAX (310) 937-6666
Redondo Beach, CA 90277 www.redondo.org
(Issues Permits)
Contact: Ron Brown

Ridgecrest (760) 375-8202
(800) 847-4830
139 Balsam St., Ste. 1700 FAX (760) 375-9850
Ridgecrest, CA 93555 www.filmdeserts.com
(Issues Permits)

Riverside (877) 748-7433
3900 Main St. FAX (951) 826-5744
Riverside, CA 92522 www.riversideca.gov
(Issues Permits)
Contacts: Simone McFarland & Sherry Shimshock

Riverside County (951) 779-6700
1201 Research Park Dr., Ste. 100 FAX (951) 779-0294
Riverside, CA 92507 www.filminlandempire.com
(Issues Permits)

Rolling Hills Estates (310) 377-1577
4045 Palos Verdes Dr. North FAX (310) 377-4468
Rolling Hills Estates, CA 90274
(Issues Permits)
Contact: Kelley Thom

Rosemead (626) 569-2100
8838 E. Valley Blvd. FAX (626) 307-9218
Rosemead, CA 91770 www.cityofrosemead.org
(Issues Permits)
Contacts: Bill Crowe & Don Wagner

Sacramento (916) 808-7777
(916) 808-5553
1608 I St. FAX (916) 808-7788
Sacramento, CA 95814 www.filmsacramento.com
Contact: Lucy Steffens

San Bernardino County (951) 779-6700
1201 Research Park Dr., Ste. 100 FAX (951) 779-0294
Riverside, CA 92507 www.filminlandempire.com
(Issues Permits)
Contact: Sheri Davis

San Diego (619) 234-3456
1010 Second Ave., Ste. 1500 FAX (619) 234-4631
San Diego, CA 92101 www.sdfilm.com
(Issues Permits)
Contacts: Cathy Anderson & Kathy McCurdy

San Fernando (818) 898-1211
117 Macneil St. FAX (818) 365-8090
San Fernando, CA 91340 www.ci.san-fernando.ca.us
(Issues Permits)
Contact: Sandra Huicochea

San Francisco (415) 554-6241
San Francisco Film Commission FAX (415) 554-6503
One Dr. Carlton B. Goodlett Pl., Ste. 473 www.filmsf.org
San Francisco, CA 94102
(Issues Permits)
Contacts: Laurel Barsotti, Stefanie Coyote & Christine Munday

San Jose (408) 792-4111
(800) 726-5673
408 Almaden Blvd. FAX (408) 295-3937
San Jose, CA 95110 www.sanjose.org/film
Contact: Kate Manley

San Luis Obispo (805) 541-8000
(800) 634-1414
811 El Capitan, Ste. 200 FAX (805) 543-9498
San Luis Obispo, CA 93401 www.sanluisobispocounty.com
Contacts: Jonni Biaggini & Dave Kastner

San Marino (626) 300-0718
(626) 300-0700
2200 Huntington Dr. FAX (626) 300-0709
San Marino, CA 91108
(Issues Permits)
Contacts: Rob Wishner & Matthew Ballantyne

San Mateo County (650) 348-7600
(800) 288-4748
San Mateo County Film Commission FAX (650) 348-7687
111 Anza Blvd., Ste. 410 www.filmsanmateocounty.com
Burlingame, CA 94010
(Issues Permits)

Santa Barbara City (Permit Office) (805) 897-2300
Santa Barbara Police Dept. FAX (805) 897-3744
215 E. Figueroa St. www.filmsantabarbara.com
Santa Barbara, CA 93101
(Issues Permits)
Contact: Leo Gomez

Santa Barbara County (805) 966-9222
(805) 570-7179
Santa Barbara County Film Commission FAX (805) 966-1728
1601 Anacapa St. www.filmsantabarbara.com
Santa Barbara, CA 93101
Contact: Martine White

Santa Barbara County (Permit Office) (805) 568-3074
(805) 568-3030
123 E. Anapamu St. FAX (805) 568-3103
Santa Barbara, CA 93101 www.filmsantabarbara.com
(Issues Permits)
Contact: Jim Norris

Ⓐ **Santa Clarita** (661) 284-1425
23920 Valencia Blvd., Ste. 235 FAX (661) 286-4001
Santa Clarita, CA 91355 www.filmsantaclarita.com
(Issues Permits)

Santa Cruz County (831) 425-1234
(800) 833-3494
1211 Ocean St. FAX (831) 425-1260
Santa Cruz, CA 95060 www.santacruz.org
(Issues Permits)
Contact: Christina Glynn

Santa Fe Springs (562) 868-0511
11710 E. Telegraph Rd. FAX (562) 868-7112
Santa Fe Springs, CA 90670 www.santafesprings.org
(Issues Permits)
Contact: Julie Herrera

Santa Monica (310) 458-8737
P.O. Box 2200 FAX (310) 576-3598
Santa Monica, CA 90407 www.santa-monica.org/epwm
(Issues Permits)
Contacts: Kathy Ruff & Vee Gomez

Santa Monica Mountains (805) 370-2308
401 W. Hillcrest Dr. FAX (805) 370-1851
Thousand Oaks, CA 91360 www.nps.gov/samo/
(Issues Permits)
Contact: Alice Allen

Shasta County (800) 874-7562 / (530) 225-4105
777 Auditorium Dr. FAX **(530) 225-4354**
Redding, CA 96001 **www.visitredding.org**

Sonoma County (707) 565-7170
Sonoma County Film Program FAX **(707) 565-7231**
401 College Ave., Ste. D **www.sonomacountyfilm.com**
Santa Rosa, CA 95401
(Issues Permits)
Contact: Colette Thomas

South Gate (323) 563-9500
8650 California Ave. FAX **(323) 357-5818**
South Gate, CA 90280 **www.cityofsouthgate.org**
(Issues Permits)
Contact: Diane Warden

South Pasadena (626) 403-7263
1414 Mission St. **www.ci.south-pasadena.ca.us**
South Pasadena, CA 91030

Temple City (626) 285-2171
9701 Las Tunas Dr. FAX **(626) 285-8192**
Temple City, CA 91780 **www.templecity.us**
(Issues Permits)
Contact: Mary Flandrick

Torrance (310) 618-5828
Business License Office FAX **(310) 618-5832**
3031 Torrance Blvd. **www.torrnet.com**
Torrance, CA 90503
(Issues Permits)
Contact: Jill Weldin

Tulare County (559) 624-7072 / (559) 624-7000
5961 S. Mooney Blvd. FAX **(559) 730-2591**
Visalia, CA 93277 **www.co.tulare.ca.us**
Contact: Loretta Feldstein

Tuolumne County (209) 533-6911
Two S. Green St. FAX **(209) 532-2502**
Sonora, CA 95370 **www.tcfilm.org**
(Issues Permits)
Contact: Jerry Day

Two Harbors (310) 510-4249
P.O. Box 5086 FAX **(310) 510-3549**
Avalon, CA 90704
(Issues Permits)
Contact: Gina Long

Vallejo/Solano County (707) 642-3653 / (800) 482-5535
289 Mare Island Way FAX **(707) 644-2206**
Vallejo, CA 94590 **www.visitvallejo.com/film**

Ventura County (Film Office) (805) 384-1800
1601 Carmen Dr., Ste. 215 FAX **(805) 384-1805**
Camarillo, CA 93010 **www.filmventuracounty.com**

Ventura County (Permit Office) (805) 654-2406
Attn: Film Permits FAX **(805) 477-7168**
800 S. Victoria Ave., L-1740 **www.ventura.org**
Ventura, CA 93009
(Issues Permits)
Contacts: Dan Price & Pat Richards

Vernon Fire Dept. (323) 583-8811 / (323) 583-4821
4305 Santa Fe Ave. FAX **(323) 826-1407**
Vernon, CA 90058 **www.cityofvernon.org**
(Issues Permits)
Contact: Capt. Dan Armellini

Walnut (909) 595-7543
21201 La Puente Rd. FAX **(909) 595-6095**
Walnut, CA 91789 **www.ci.walnut.ca.us**
(Issues Permits)
Contacts: Tony Ramos & Bevin Handel

West Covina (626) 939-8503
1444 W. Garvey Ave.
West Covina, CA 91790
(Issues Permits)
Contact: Cmdr Myrick

West Hollywood (323) 848-6489
8300 Santa Monica Blvd., Third Fl. FAX **(323) 848-6561**
West Hollywood, CA 90069 **www.weho.org**
(Issues Permits)
Contact: Terry House

Westlake Village (818) 706-1613
31200 Oak Crest Dr. FAX **(818) 706-1391**
Westlake Village, CA 91361 **www.wlv.org**
(Issues Permits)
Contact: Kerry Kallman

Whittier (562) 945-8282
13230 E. Penn St. FAX **(562) 945-8247**
Whittier, CA 90602 **www.whittierpd.org**
(Issues Permits)
Contact: Aviv Bar

Yosemite/Madera County (559) 760-1143
Yosemite/Madera County FAX **(559) 658-2851**
Film Commission, Box 3690 **www.yosemitefilm.com**
Oakhurst, CA 93644

Yreka (530) 841-2386 / (530) 841-2321
701 Fourth St. FAX **(530) 842-4836**
Yreka, CA 96097
(Issues Permits)
Contacts: Pam Hayden & Brian W. Meek

Alabama (334) 242-4195
Alabama Film Office FAX **(334) 242-2077**
401 Adams Ave., Ste. 616 **www.alabamafilm.org**
Montgomery, AL 36104
Contact: Linda Swann

Alabama-Mobile (251) 438-7100
Mobile Film Office FAX **(251) 438-7104**
164 Saint Emanuel St. **www.mobilefilmoffice.com**
Mobile, AL 36602

Alaska (907) 269-8491
Alaska Film Office **www.film.alaska.gov**
550 W Seventh Ave., 17th Fl.
Anchorage, AK 99501
Contact: Dave Worrell

Alaska Film Group (907) 561-6445
P.O. Box 92008 FAX **(907) 783-2625**
Anchorage, AK 99509 **www.alaskafilmgroup.org**

Arizona (602) 771-1193 (800) 523-6695
Arizona Film Office FAX **(602) 771-1211**
1700 W. Washington St. Ste. 220
Phoenix, AZ 85007 **www.azcommerce.com/film**
Contact: Harry Tate

Arizona-Cochise County (520) 432-9200 (520) 432-9215
Cochise County Film Office FAX **(520) 432-5016**
1415 Melody Ln., Bldg. G **www.explorecochise.com**
Bisbee, AZ 85603

Arizona-Cottonwood (928) 634-7593 (928) 649-0509
Cottonwood Film Office FAX **(928) 634-7594**
1010 S. Main St. **www.cottonwood.verdevalley.com**
Cottonwood, AZ 86326

Arizona-Globe (928) 425-4495 (800) 804-5623
The Globe-Miami Regional Film Office FAX **(928) 425-3410**
1360 N. Broad St. **www.globemiamichamber.com**
Globe, AZ 85501

Arizona-Page-Lake Powell (928) 645-2741 (888) 261-7243
Page-Lake Powell Film Office FAX **(928) 645-3181**
P.O. Box 727 **www.pagechamber.com**
Page, AZ 86040

Arizona-Phoenix (602) 262-4850
Phoenix Film Office FAX **(602) 534-2295**
200 W. Washington St. **www.filmphoenix.com**
Phoenix, AZ 85003

Arizona-Prescott (928) 777-1275 (866) 878-2489
Prescott Film Office, P.O. Box 2059 FAX **(928) 777-1255**
Prescott, AZ 86302 **www.cityofprescott.net/business/film/**

Arizona-Sedona (928) 204-1123
Sedona Film Office, P.O. Box 478 FAX **(928) 204-1064**
Sedona, AZ 86339 **www.sedonafilmoffice.com**
Contact: Lori Reinhart

Arizona-Tucson (520) 770-2151 (877) 311-2489
Tucson Film Office FAX **(520) 884-7804**
100 S. Church Ave. **www.filmtucson.com**
Tucson, AZ 85701

Arizona-Wickenburg (928) 684-5479 (928) 684-0977
Wickenburg Film Office FAX **(928) 684-5470**
216 N. Frontier St. **www.wickenburgchamber.com**
Wickenburg, AZ 85390

Arizona-Yuma (928) 314-9247
Yuma Film Commission, P.O. Box 172 FAX **(928) 314-2280**
Yuma, AZ 85366 **www.filmyuma.com**
Contacts: Yvonne Taylor

Arkansas (501) 682-7676 / (501) 682-7326
Arkansas Film Office FAX **(501) 682-3456**
One State Capitol Mall, Fourth Fl. **www.arkansasedc.com**
Little Rock, AR 72201
Contact: Christopher Crane

Association of Film Commissioners International **(406) 495-8040**
314 N. Main, Ste. 307 FAX **(406) 495-8039**
Helena, MT 59601 **www.afci.org**

Bahamas **(242) 322-4373**
Bahamas Film Commission FAX **(242) 356-5904**
P.O. Box N-3701 **www.bahamasfilm.com**
The Nassau Bahamas
Contact: Grace Caron

British Virgin Islands **(284) 494-4119**
British Virgin Islands Film Commission FAX **(284) 494-3866**
P.O. Box 134
Road Town, Tortola Virgin Islands (British)

Ⓐ **California** **(323) 860-2960** / **(800) 858-4749**
California Film Commission FAX **(323) 860-2972**
7080 Hollywood Blvd., Ste. 900 **www.film.ca.gov**
Los Angeles, CA 90028
Contact: Amy Lemisch

Canada-Alberta **(780) 422-8584**
Alberta Film Commission, Fifth Fl. FAX **(780) 422-8582**
Commerce Pl. 10155-102 St. **www.albertafilm.ca**
Edmonton, AB T5J 4L6 Canada
Contact: Dan Chugg

Canada-Argenteuil Laurentians (450) 562-2446
Argenteuil-Laurentians Film Commission FAX (450) 562-1911
430 Grace St. www.filmlaurentides.ca
Lachute, QC J8H 1M6 Canada

Canada-British Columbia (604) 660-2732
BC Film Commission FAX (604) 660-4790
201-865 Hornby St. www.bcfilmcommission.com
Vancouver, BC V6Z 2G3 Canada

Canada-Calgary (403) 221-7829
(403) 221-7868
Calgary Film Commission FAX (403) 221-7828
731 First St. SE
Calgary, AB T2G 2G9 Canada
Contact: Beth Thompson

Canada-Cariboo Chilcotin (250) 392-1764
Cariboo Chilcotin Film Commission FAX (250) 392-4408
450 Mart St. www.ccfilmcommission.com
Williams Lake, BC V2G 1N3 Canada

Canada-Columbia Shuswap (250) 832-8194
Columbia Shuswap Film Commission FAX (250) 832-3375
P.O. Box 978 www.filmcolumbiashuswap.com
Salmon Arm, BC V1E 4P1 Canada

Canada-Edmonton (780) 917-7627
(800) 463-4667
Edmonton Film Commission www.filminedmonton.com
World Trade Center
9990 Jasper Ave., Fifth Fl.
Edmonton, AB T5J 1P7 Canada
Contact: Patti Tucker

Canada-Manitoba (204) 947-2040
Manitoba Film & Sound FAX (204) 956-5261
410-93 Lombard Ave. www.mbfilmsound.ca
Winnipeg, MB R3B 3B1 Canada
Contact: Carole Vivier

Canada-Montreal (514) 872-2883
Montreal Film & TV Commission FAX (514) 872-3409
303 Notre Dame St. East, Sixth Fl. www.montrealfilm.com
Montreal, QC H2Y 3Y8 Canada
Contact: Andre LaFord

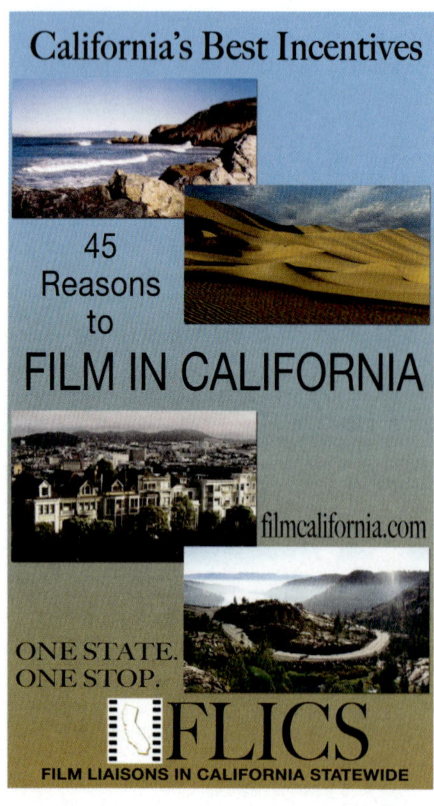

Canada-Nanaimo (250) 386-3976
(888) 537-3456
Greater Victoria Film Commission FAX (250) 386-3967
P.O. Box 34, 794 Fort St. www.filmvictoria.com
Victoria, BC V8W 1H2 Canada
Contact: Beverley Dondale

Canada-New Brunswick (506) 869-6868
New Brunswick Film, P.O. Box 5001 FAX (506) 869-6840
Moncton, NB E1C 8R3 Canada www.nbfilm.com
Contact: Roger Cyr

Canada-Newfoundland (709) 738-3456
Newfoundland & Labrador Film FAX (709) 739-1680
12 King's Bridge Rd. www.nlfdc.ca
St. John's, NF A1C 3K3 Canada
Contact: Chris Bonnell

A **Canada-Northwest Territories** (867) 920-8793
NWT Film Commission, P.O. Box 1320 FAX (867) 873-0101
Yellowknife, NT X1A 2L9 Canada
www.iti.gov.nt.ca/artscrafts/filmcommission.shtml
Contact: Carla Wallis

Canada-Nova Scotia (902) 424-7177
Collins Bank Building, Third Fl. FAX (902) 424-0617
1869 Upper Water St. www.filmnovascotia.com
Halifax, NS B3J 1S9 Canada
Contact: Ann MacKenzie

Canada-Okanagan (250) 717-0087
Okanagan Film Commission FAX (250) 868-0512
1450 KLO Rd. www.okanaganfilm.com
Kelowna, BC V1W 3Z4 Canada

Canada-Ontario (416) 314-6858
Ontario Media Development FAX (416) 314-6876
175 Bloor St. East, South Tower, Ste. 501 www.omdc.on.ca
Toronto, ON M4W 3R8 Canada
Contact: Gail Thomson

Canada-Prince Edward Island (902) 368-6300
(800) 563-3734
PEI Film Commission, P.O. Box 340 FAX (902) 368-6301
Charlottetown, PE C1A 7K7 Canada www.techpei.com
Contact: Nancy Roberts

Canada-Quebec City (418) 641-6766
Quebec City Film & TV Commission FAX **(418) 691-5777**
43, Buade St., Third Fl., Ste. 310 **www.filmquebec.com**
Quebec G1R 4A2 Canada
Contacts: Lorraine Boily, Geneviève Doré & Karine Latulippe

Canada-Saskatchewan (306) 798-9800
Sask Film, 1831 College Ave. FAX **(306) 798-7768**
Regina, SK S4P 3V5 Canada **www.saskfilm.com**
Contact: Susanne Bell

Canada-Thompson-Nicola (250) 377-8673
Thompson-Nicola Film Commission FAX **(250) 372-5048**
300-465 Victoria St. **www.tnrdfilm.com**
Kamloops, BC V2C 2A9 Canada
Contact: Victoria Weller

Canada-Toronto (416) 338-3456
Toronto Film & TV Office, City Hall FAX **(416) 392-0675**
Rotunda North, 100 Queen St. West **www.toronto.ca/tfto**
Toronto, ON M5H 2N2 Canada
Contact: Rhonda Silverstone

Canada-Yukon (867) 667-5400
Yukon Film & Sound Commission FAX **(867) 393-7040**
P.O. Box 2703 **www.reelyukon.com**
Whitehorse, YT Y1A 2C6 Canada
Contact: Iris Merritt

Colorado (303) 592-4075 (800) 726-8887
Colorado Office of Film **www.coloradofilm.org**
Television & Media, 1625 Broadway, Ste. 2700
Denver, CO 80202
Contact: Kevin Shand

Colorado-Boulder (303) 442-2911 (303) 938-2066
Boulder Film Commission FAX **(303) 938-2098**
2440 Pearl St. **www.bouldercoloradousa.com/film**
Boulder, CO 80302

Colorado-Clear Creek County (303) 567-4660 (800) 882-5278
Chamber & Tourism Bureau FAX **(303) 567-0967**
of Clear Creek County **www.clearcreekcounty.org**
2060 Miner St., P.O. Box 100
Idaho Springs, CO 80452

Colorado-Colorado Springs (719) 685-7635 (800) 888-4748
Colorado Springs Film Commission FAX **(719) 635-4968**
515 S. Cascade Ave. **www.filmcoloradosprings.com**
Colorado Springs, CO 80903
Contact: Ms. Floy Kennedy

Colorado-Fremont/Custer County (719) 275-2331
Fremont/Custer County Film Office FAX **(719) 275-2332**
403 Royal Gorge Blvd.
Canon City, CO 81212

Colorado-Southwest (970) 247-0312
Southwest Colorado Travel Region FAX **(970) 385-7884**
295-A Girard **www.swcolotravel.org**
Durango, CO 81303

Colorado-Telluride (310) 994-9753
Telluride Film Commission FAX **(970) 728-4720**
P.O. Box 182 **www.filmtelluride.com**
Telluride, CO 81435

Connecticut (860) 256-2800
CT Commission on Culture and Tourism FAX **(860) 256-2763**
One Constitution Plaza **www.ctfilm.com**
Hartford, CT 06103
Contacts: Ellen Woolf & Mark Dixon

Delaware (866) 284-7483
Delaware Tourism Office **www.visitdelaware.com**
99 Kings Hwy
Dover, DE 19901
Contact: Nikki Boone

District of Columbia (202) 727-6608
DC Film & TV, 441 Fourth St. FAX **(202) 727-3246**
NW Ste. 760N **www.film.dc.gov**
Washington, DC 20001
Contact: Crystal Palmer

Dominican Republic (809) 694-2291 (809) 330-2234
Santo Domingo Film, Serie 23 FAX **(305) 946-8531**
San Pedro de Macoris 22007 **www.santodomingofilm.com**
Dominican Republic
Contact: Tracey Cuesta

Florida (818) 508-7772 / (877) 352-3456
Governor's Office of Film & Entertainment FAX (818) 508-7747
5426 Simpson Ave. www.filminflorida.com
North Hollywood, CA 91607
Contact: Paul Sirmons

Florida-Cape Canaveral (877) 572-3224
Space Coast Film Commission FAX (321) 433-4476
430 Brevard Ave., Ste. 150 www.space-coast.com
Cocoa Village, FL 32922

Florida-Central Florida (863) 534-2507 / (800) 828-7655
Central Florida Motion Picture/TV FAX (863) 534-0886
600 N. Broadway, Ste. 300 www.filmcentralflorida.com
Bartow, FL 33830

Florida-Collier County (239) 659-3456
Collier County Film Commission FAX (239) 213-3053
755 Eighth Ave. South
Naples, FL 34102

Florida-Emerald Coast (850) 651-7644 / (800) 322-3319
Emerald Coast TDC Film Commission FAX (850) 651-7149
1540 Miracle Strip Pkwy www.destin-fwb.com/film
Fort Walton Beach, FL 32548

Florida-Fort Lauderdale (954) 627-0128 / (800) 741-1420
The Broward Alliance Film Commission FAX (954) 524-3167
110 E. Broward Blvd., Ste. 1990 www.filmbroward.com
Fort Lauderdale, FL 33301

Florida-Jacksonville (904) 630-7247
Jacksonville Film & TV Office FAX (904) 630-2919
One W. Adams St., Ste. 200 www.filmjax.com
Jacksonville, FL 32202

Florida-Key West (305) 293-1800 / (800) 345-6539
Florida Keys & Key West FAX (305) 296-0788
Film Commission www.filmkeys.com
1201 White St., Ste. 102
Key West, FL 33040

Florida-Miami Beach (305) 673-7070
Miami Beach Film Commission FAX (305) 673-7063
1700 Convention Center Dr. www.miamibeachfl.gov
Miami, FL 33139

Florida-Miami-Dade (305) 375-3288
Miami-Dade Mayor's Office FAX (305) 375-3266
of Film & Entertainment www.filmiami.org
111 NW First St., Ste. 2540
Miami, FL 33128

Florida-Orlando (407) 422-7159
Metro Orlando Film & FAX (407) 841-9069
Entertainment Commission www.filmorlando.com
301 E. Pine St., Ste. 900
Orlando, FL 32801

Florida-Palm Beach County (561) 233-1000 / (800) 745-3456
Palm Beach County Film & FAX (561) 233-3113
Television Commission www.pbfilm.com
1555 Palm Beach Lakes Blvd., Ste. 900
West Palm Beach, FL 33401

Florida-Tampa Bay (813) 342-4088 / (800) 826-8358
Tampa Bay Film Commission FAX (813) 223-0083
401 E. Jackson St., Ste. 2100 www.filmtampabay.com
Tampa, FL 33602
Contact: Lindsey Norris

Georgia (404) 962-4052
Georgia Film, Video & Music Office FAX (404) 962-4053
75 Fifth St., Ste. 1200 www.georgia.org
Atlanta, GA 30308

Georgia-Savannah (912) 651-3696 / (912) 651-2360
Savannah Film Commission FAX (912) 651-0982
P.O. Box 1027 www.savannahfilm.org
Savannah, GA 31402

Hawaii (808) 586-2570
Hawaii Film Office, P.O. Box 2359 FAX (808) 586-2572
Honolulu, HI 96804 www.hawaiifilmoffice.com
Contact: Donne Dawson

Hawaii-Big Island (808) 327-3663 / (808) 961-8366
Big Island Film Office FAX (808) 327-3667
25 Aupuni St., Ste. 109 www.filmbigisland.com
Hilo, HI 96720
Contact: Marilyn Killeri

Hawaii-Honolulu (808) 527-6108
Honolulu Film Office FAX (808) 527-6102
530 S. King St., Ste. 306 www.filmhonolulu.com
Honolulu, HI 96813

Hawaii-Kauai (808) 241-6390
Kauai Film Commission FAX (808) 241-6399
4444 Rice St., Ste. 200 www.filmkauai.com
Lihue, HI 96766
Contact: Tiffani Lizama

Hawaii-Maui (808) 270-7415 / (808) 270-7710
Maui County Film Office FAX (808) 270-7995
One Main Plaza www.filmmaui.com
2200 Main St., Ste. 305
Wailuku, HI 96793
Contact: Benita Brazier

A **Idaho** (208) 334-2470 / (800) 942-8338
Idaho Film Office FAX (208) 334-2631
700 W. State St., Box 83720 www.filmidaho.com
Boise, ID 83720
Contacts: Kat Haase & Peg Owens

Illinois (312) 814-3600
Illinois Film Office FAX (312) 814-8874
100 W. Randolph St., Third Fl. www.illinoisfim.biz
Chicago, IL 60601
Contact: Betsy Steinberg

Illinois-Chicago (312) 744-6415
Chicago Film Office FAX (312) 744-1378
121 N. LaSalle St., Ste. 806 egov.cityofchicago.org
Chicago, IL 60602

Indiana (317) 232-8888
Film Indiana FAX (317) 232-4146
One N. Capitol Ave., Ste. 700 www.filmindiana.com
Indianapolis, IN 46204
Contact: Erin Newell

Iowa-Cedar Rapids (319) 398-5009 / (800) 735-5557
Cedar Rapids Convention & FAX (319) 398-5089
Visitors Bureau www.cedar-rapids.com
119 First Ave. SE
Cedar Rapids, IA 52406

Iowa-Des Moines (515) 242-4726
Iowa Film Office, 200 E. Grand Ave. FAX (515) 242-4718
Des Moines, IA 50309 www.traveliowa.com/film/
Contact: Steven Schott

Jamaica-Kingston (876) 978-7755 / (888) 468-3785
Jamaica Film Commission FAX (876) 978-0140
18 Trafalgar Rd. www.filmjamaica.com
Kingston 10 Jamaica
Contact: Del Crooks

Kansas (785) 296-4927 / (888) 701-3456
Kansas Film Commission FAX (785) 296-3490
1000 SW Jackson St., Ste. 100 www.filmkansas.com
Topeka, KS 66612
Contact: Peter Jasso

Kansas-Wichita (316) 660-6308
Greater Wichita Convention & Visitors Bureau/ Wichita Film Commission
100 S. Main St., Ste. 100
Wichita, KS 67202
FAX (316) 265-0162
www.visitwichita.com

Kentucky (502) 564-3456 (800) 345-6591
Kentucky Film Office
500 Mero St.
2200 Capital Plaza Tower
Frankfort, KY 40601
FAX (502) 564-7588
www.kyfilmoffice.com

Louisiana (225) 342-5403 (888) 655-0447
Governor's Office of Film & TV
800 Distributors Row, Ste. 101
Harahan, LA 70123
Contact: Alex Schott
FAX (504) 736-7287
www.lafilm.org

Louisiana-New Orleans (504) 658-0912
FAX (504) 658-0934
www.cityofno.com/portal.aspx

Louisiana-Northeast (800) 843-1872
Northeast Louisiana Film Commission
400 Lea Joyner Memorial Expressway
P.O. Box 14092
Monroe, LA 71201
Contact: C.J. Sartor
www.nelafilm.org

Louisiana-Shreveport (318) 673-7515
505 Travis St., Ste. 200
Shreveport, LA 71101
FAX (318) 673-5085
www.shreveport-bossierfilm.com

Maine (207) 624-7631 (207) 624-7631
Maine Film Office
59 State House Station
Augusta, ME 04333
Contact: Lea Girardin
FAX (207) 287-8070
www.filminmaine.com

Maryland (410) 767-6340 (800) 333-6632
Maryland Film Office
217 E. Redwood St., Ninth Fl.
Baltimore, MD 21202
Contact: Jack Gerbes
FAX (410) 333-0044
www.marylandfilm.org

Massachusetts (617) 635-4455 (617) 635-3911
Mayor's Office of Special Events & Film
City Hall, Ste. 802
Boston, MA 02201
FAX (617) 635-4428

Massachusetts-Boston (617) 635-3911 (617) 635-4455
City of Boston Film Bureau
City Hall, Ste. 202
Boston, MA 02201
FAX (617) 635-4428
www.cityofboston.gov/film

Mexico (52 55) 5688 7813 (52 55) 5688 0970
National Film Commission - Mexico
Av. Division Del Norte 2462
Quinto Piso
Col. Portales C.P. 03300 Mexico
Contact: Jorge Santoyo
FAX (52 55) 5688 7027
www.conafilm.org.mx

A **Mexico-Baja California** (52) 664 682 3367
P.O. Box 2448
Chula Vista, CA 91912
FAX (52) 664 682 3331
www.bajafilm.com

Michigan (517) 373-0638 (800) 477-3456
Michigan Film Office
702 W. Kalamazoo, P.O. Box 30739
Lansing, MI 48909
Contact: Janet Lockwood
FAX (517) 241-2930
www.michigan.gov/filmoffice

Minnesota (651) 645-3600
Minnesota Film & TV Board
2446 University Ave. West, Ste. 100
St. Paul, MN 55114
Contact: Lucinda Winter
FAX (651) 645-7373
www.mnfilmandtv.org

Mississippi (601) 359-3297 (601) 359-3422
Mississippi Film Office, P.O. Box 849
Jackson, MS 39205
FAX (601) 359-5048
www.visitmississippi.org/film

Mississippi-Greenwood (662) 453-9197 (800) 748-9064
Greenwood Film Office
P.O. Drawer 739
Greenwood, MS 38935
FAX (662) 453-5526
www.greenwoodms.org

Mississippi-Natchez (601) 446-6345 (800) 647-6724
Natchez Film Commission
640 S. Canal St., Box C
Natchez, MS 39120
FAX (601) 442-0814
www.cityofnatchez.com

Mississippi-Tupelo (662) 841-6521 (800) 533-0611
Tupelo Film Commission
P.O. Box 47
Tupelo, MS 38802
FAX (662) 841-6558
www.tupelo.net

Mississippi-Vicksburg (601) 636-9421
Vicksburg Convention & Visitors Bureau
P.O. Box 110
Vicksburg, MS 39181
FAX (601) 636-9475
www.visitvicksburg.com

Missouri-Kansas City (816) 471-2215
Film Commission of Greater Kansas City
1906 Wyandotte
Kansas City, MO 64108
FAX (816) 471-6500
www.kcfilm.com

Montana (406) 841-2876 (800) 553-4563
Montana Film Office
301 S. Park Ave.
Helena, MT 59620
Contacts: John Ansotegui & Sten Iversen
FAX (406) 841-2877
www.montanafilm.com

Montana-Southcentral (406) 222-0438
Montana Film Center, P.O. Box 253
Livingston, MT 59047

Navajo Nation (505) 863-0404
Navajo Nation Film Office, 105 W. Aztec
Gallup, NM 87301
Contact: Kee Long
FAX (505) 863-0406
www.cia-g.com/~navflmof

Nebraska (402) 471-3746 (800) 228-4307
Nebraska Film Office
P.O. Box 98907
Lincoln, NE 68509
FAX (402) 471-3365
www.filmnebraska.org

Nebraska-Omaha (402) 444-7737
Omaha Film Office
1001 Farnam St. Ste. 200
Omaha, NE 68102
FAX (402) 444-4511
www.visitomaha.com

A **Nevada** (702) 486-2711 (877) 638-3456
Nevada Film Office Las Vegas
555 E. Washington Ave., Ste. 5400
Las Vegas, NV 89101
Contact: Charles Geocaris
FAX (702) 486-2712
www.nevadafilm.com

Nevada-Reno-Tahoe (775) 687-1814 (800) 336-1600
Nevada Film Office Reno/Tahoe
108 E. Proctor
Carson City, NV 89701
FAX (775) 687-4497
www.nevadafilm.com

New Hampshire (603) 271-2220
New Hampshire Film & TV Office
20 Park St.
Concord, NH 03301
Contact: Matthew Newton
FAX (603) 271-6826
www.nh.gov/film

New Jersey (973) 648-6279
New Jersey Motion Picture Commission
153 Halsey St. P.O. Box 47023
Newark, NJ 07101
Contact: Joseph Friedman
FAX (973) 648-7350
www.njfilm.org

New Jersey-Fort Lee (201) 592-3663 (201) 693-2763
Fort Lee Film Commission FAX (201) 585-7222
309 Main St. www.fortleefilm.org
Fort Lee, NJ 07024

New Mexico (505) 827-9810 (800) 545-9871
New Mexico Film Office FAX (505) 827-9799
P.O. Box 20003 www.nmfilm.com
Santa Fe, NM 87504
Contact: Lisa Stroot

New Mexico-Albuquerque (505) 768-3283
Albuquerque Film Office FAX (505) 768-3280
P.O. Box 1293 www.filmabq.com
Albuquerque, NM 87103

New Mexico-Rio Rancho (505) 891-7258 (888) 746-7262
Rio Rancho Convention & Visitors Bureau FAX (505) 892-8328
P.O. Box 15550 www.rioranchonm.org/film.php
Rio Rancho, NM 87174
Contact: Judi Snow

New York State (212) 803-2330
Governor's Office for Motion Picture & Television Development FAX (212) 803-2339
633 Third Ave. 33rd Fl. www.nylovesfilm.com/index.asp
New York, NY 10017
Contact: Pat Swinney Kaufman

New York-Nassau County (516) 572-0012
Nassau County Film Office FAX (516) 572-0260
Eisenhower Park, Administration Bldg. www.longislandfilm.com
1899 Hempstead Tpke
East Meadow, NY 11554

New York-New York City (212) 489-6710
NYC Mayor's Office of Film, Theatre & Broadcasting FAX (212) 307-6237
www.nyc.gov/film
1697 Broadway
New York, NY 10019

New York-Rochester (585) 279-8308
Rochester/Finger Lakes Film Office FAX (585) 232-4822
45 East Ave., Ste. 400 www.filmrochester.org
Rochester, NY 14604

New York-Suffolk County (631) 853-4800
Suffolk County Film Office FAX (631) 853-4888
H. Lee Dennison Bldg., Second Fl.
100 Veterans Hwy
Hauppauge, NY 11788
www.suffolkcountyfilmcommission.com

New York-Upstate (518) 584-3255 (800) 526-8970
Capital-Saratoga Film Commission FAX (518) 587-0318
28 Clinton St. www.capital-saratogafilm.com
Saratoga Springs, NY 12866

North Carolina (919) 733-9900 (866) 468-2273
North Carolina Film Office FAX (919) 715-0151
4324 Mail Service Center www.ncfilm.com
Raleigh, NC 27699
Contact: Aaron Syrett

North Carolina-Charlotte (704) 347-8942 (800) 554-4373
Charlotte Regional Film Commission FAX (704) 347-8981
550 South Caldwell St., Ste. 760 www.charlotteusa.com
Charlotte, NC 28202

North Carolina-Durham (919) 680-8313
Durham Film Office, 101 E. Morgan St. FAX (919) 683-8353
Durham, NC 27701 www.durham-nc.com

North Carolina-Greensboro (336) 393-0001
Piedmont Triad Film Commission FAX (336) 668-3749
7025 Albert Pick Rd., Ste. 303 www.piedmontfilm.com
Greensboro, NC 27409

North Carolina-Northeast (252) 482-4333 (888) 872-8562
Northeast Partnership Film Office FAX (252) 482-3366
119 W. Water St. www.ncnortheast.com
Edenton, NC 27932

North Carolina-Western North Carolina (828) 687-7234
Western North Carolina Film Commission FAX (828) 687-7552
134 Wright Brothers Way www.wncfilm.com
Fletcher, NC 28732

North Carolina-Wilmington (910) 343-3456
Wilmington Regional Film Commission, Inc. FAX (910) 343-3457
www.wilmingtonfilm.com
1223 N. 23rd St.
Wilmington, NC 28405

North Dakota (701) 328-2509 (800) 435-5663
North Dakota Film Commission FAX (701) 328-4878
1600 E. Century Ave., Ste. 2 www.ndtourism.com
Bismarck, ND 58502
Contact: Tourism Director

Ohio-Cincinnati (513) 784-1744
Cincinnati & Northern Kentucky Film Commission FAX (513) 768-8963
www.film-cincinnati.org
602 Main St., Ste. 712
Cincinnati, OH 45202

Ohio-Cleveland (216) 623-3910
Greater Cleveland Film Commission FAX (216) 623-0876
1301 E. Ninth St., Ste. 120 www.clevelandfilm.com
Cleveland, OH 44113
Contacts: Sara Dering, Kammeron Hughes, Erin Kaminski & Ivan Schwarz

Ohio-Columbus (614) 264-2324
Greater Columbus Film Commission
P.O. Box 12735 www.columbusfilmcommission.com
Columbus, OH 43212
Contact: Steve Cover

Ohio-Dayton (800) 221-8235
One Chamber Plaza, Ste. A www.daytoncvb.com
Dayton, OH 45402

Oklahoma (405) 230-8440 (800) 766-3456
Oklahoma Film & Music Office FAX (405) 230-8640
120 N. Robinson, Sixth Fl. www.oklahomafilm.org
Oklahoma City, OK 73102
Contact: Jill Simpson

Oregon (503) 229-5832
Oregon Film & Video Office FAX (503) 229-6869
121 SW Salmon St., Ste. 1205 www.oregonfilm.org
Portland, OR 97204

Pennsylvania (717) 783-3456
Pennsylvania Film Office FAX (717) 787-0687
Commonwealth Keystone Bldg. www.filminpa.com
400 North St., Fourth Fl.
Harrisburg, PA 17120
Contact: Jane Shecter

Pennsylvania-Philadelphia (215) 686-2668
Greater Philadelphia Film Office FAX (215) 686-3659
100 S. Broad St., Ste. 600 www.film.org
Philadelphia, PA 19110

Pennsylvania-Pittsburgh (412) 261-2744 (888) 744-3456
Pittsburgh Film Office FAX (412) 471-7317
130 Seventh St., Ste. 1000 www.pghfilm.org
Pittsburgh, PA 15222

Puerto Rico (787) 758-4747
Puerto Rico Film Commission FAX (787) 756-5706
355 F.D. Roosevelt Ave., Ste. 106 www.puertoricofilm.com
P.O. Box 362350
Hato Rey 00918 Puerto Rico
Contacts: Cristina Caraballo & Luis Rief Kohl

Rhode Island (401) 222-3456 / (401) 222-6666
Rhode Island Film & TV Office FAX **(401) 222-3018**
One Capitol Hill, Third Fl. **www.film.ri.gov**
Providence, RI 02908
Contact: Steven Feinberg

Rhode Island-Providence (401) 222-3456 / (401) 222-6666
Department of Art, Culture & Tourism FAX **(401) 222-3018**
25 Dorrance St. **www.providenceri.com/film**
Providence, RI 02903

South Carolina (803) 737-0490
South Carolina Film Commission FAX **(803) 737-3104**
1205 Pendleton St., Ste. 529 **www.filmsc.com**
Columbia, SC 29201
Contact: Jeff Monks

South Dakota (605) 773-3301 / (800) 952-3625
South Dakota Film Office FAX **(605) 773-3256**
711 E. Wells Ave. **www.filmsd.com**
Pierre, SD 57501
Contact: Emily Currey

Tennessee (615) 741-3456 / (877) 818-3456
Tennessee Film, Entertainment and FAX **(615) 741-5554**
Music Commission **www.filmtennessee.com**
312 Eighth Ave. North, Ninth Fl.
Nashville, TN 37243

Tennessee-Knoxville (865) 246-2629
East Tennessee Television & FAX **(865) 523-2071**
Film Commission 17 Market Square, Ste. 201
Knoxville, TN 37902 **www.ettfc.com**

Tennessee-Memphis (901) 527-8300
Memphis & Shelby County FAX **(901) 527-8326**
Film Commission **www.memphisfilmcomm.org**
50 Peabody Pl., Ste. 250
Memphis, TN 38103

Tennessee-Nashville (615) 880-1827 / (615) 862-4700
Mayor's Office of Film FAX **(615) 862-6025**
222 Second Ave. North, Ste. 418 **www.filmnashville.com**
Nashville, TN 37201

Texas (512) 463-9200
Texas Film Commission, P.O. Box 13246 FAX **(512) 463-4114**
Austin, TX 78711 **www.texasfilmcommission.com**
Contact: Bob Hudgins

Texas-Austin (512) 583-7229 / (512) 583-7230
Austin Film Commission FAX **(512) 583-7281**
301 Congress Ave., Ste. 200 **www.austintexas.org**
Austin, TX 78701

Texas-Dallas/Fort Worth (214) 571-1050
Dallas Film Commission FAX **(214) 665-2907**
325 N. St. Paul St., Ste. 700
Dallas, TX 75201 **www.dallasfilmcommission.com**

Texas-El Paso (915) 534-0698 / (800) 351-6024
El Paso Film Commission FAX **(915) 532-2963**
One Civic Center Plaza **www.visitelpaso.com/film**
El Paso, TX 79901

Texas-Houston (713) 437-5251 / (713) 227-1407
Houston Film Commission FAX **(713) 223-3816**
901 Bagby, Ste. 100 **www.filmhouston.texaswebhost.com**
Houston, TX 77002

A **Texas-San Antonio** (210) 207-6730 / (800) 447-3372
San Antonio Film Commission FAX **(210) 207-9731**
203 S. St. Mary's St., Second Fl. **www.filmsanantonio.com**
San Antonio, TX 78205

Texas-South Padre Island (956) 761-3005 / (800) 657-2373
South Padre Island Film Commission **www.sopadre.com**
7355 Padre Blvd.
Port Isabel, TX 78597

U.S. Virgin Islands (340) 775-1444 / (340) 774-8784
U.S. Virgin Island Film Promotion Office FAX **(340) 774-4390**
P.O. Box 6400 **www.filmusvi.com**
St. Thomas 00804 Virgin Islands (US)
Contact: Caroline Simon

Utah (801) 538-8740 / (800) 453-8824
Utah Film Commission FAX **(801) 538-1397**
Council Hall/Capitol Hill, 300 N. State St. **www.film.utah.gov**
Salt Lake City, UT 84114
Contact: Marshall Moore

Utah-Kane County (435) 644-5033 / (800) 733-5263
Kane County Film Commission FAX **(435) 644-5923**
78 South 100 East **www.kaneutah.com**
Kanab, UT 84741

Utah-Moab (435) 259-4341
Moab to Monument Valley FAX **(435) 259-4135**
Film Commission, 217 E. Center St. **www.filmmoab.com**
Moab, UT 84532

Utah-Park City (435) 649-6100 / (800) 453-1360
Park City Film Commission FAX **(435) 649-4132**
1910 Prospector Ave., Ste. 103 **www.parkcityinfo.com**
Park City, UT 84060

Ute Mountain Ute Tribe (970) 564-5725
Ute Mountain Ute Tribe Film Office FAX **(970) 564-5401**
110 Mike Wash Rd., P.O. Box 248 **www.utemountain.org**
Towaoc, CO 81334
Contact: Lynn Hartman

Vermont (802) 828-3618
Vermont Film Commission FAX **(802) 828-0607**
10 Baldwin St. **www.vermontfilm.com**
Montpelier, VT 05633
Contacts: Joe Bookchin & Perry Schafer

Virginia (804) 545-5530 / (800) 854-6233
Virginia Film Office FAX **(804) 545-5531**
901 E. Byrd St., West Tower, 19th Fl. **www.film.virginia.org**
Richmond, VA 23219

Virginia-Central Virginia (804) 216-2772
Central Virginia Film Office FAX **(804) 862-1200**
One New Millennium Dr. **www.cvfo.org**
Petersburg, VA 23805

Washington (206) 256-6151
Washington State Film Office FAX **(206) 256-6154**
2001 Sixth Ave., Ste. 2600 **www.filmwashington.com**
Seattle, WA 98121

Washington-Seattle (206) 684-0903 / (206) 684-5030
Seattle Film & Music Office FAX **(206) 684-0379**
700 Fifth Ave., Ste. 5752 **www.seattle.gov/filmandmusic**
P.O. Box 94708
Seattle, WA 98124

West Virginia (866) 698-3456 / (304) 550-1871
West Virginia Film Office FAX **(304) 558-1662**
90 MacCorkle Ave. SW **www.wvfilm.com**
S. Charleston, WV 25303
Contact: Pamela Haynes

Wisconsin (414) 287-6235
Wisconsin Film Office **www.filmwisconsin.net**
648 N. Plankinton Ave., Ste. 425
Milwaukee, WI 53203
Contact: Melissa Musante

Wyoming (307) 777-3400 / (800) 458-6657
Wyoming Film Office FAX **(307) 777-2877**
I-25 at College Dr. **www.filmwyoming.com**
Cheyenne, WY 82002
Contact: Michell Howard

Australia-Melbourne 61 3 9660 3240 / 61 3 9660 3200
Melbourne Film Office/Film Victoria FAX 61 3 9660 3201
Level 7, 189 Flinders Ln. www.film.vic.gov.au
Melbourne, Victoria 3000 Australia

Australia-New South Wales 61 2 9264 6400
Level 13, 227 Elizabeth St. FAX 61 2 9264 4388
Sydney, NSW 2000 Australia www.fto.nsw.gov.au

Australia-Queensland 61 7 3224 4114 / 61 7 3225 1486
Level 15, 111 George St., Brisbane FAX 61 7 3224 6717
Queensland 4000 Australia www.pftc.com.au

Austria 43 1 58858 0
Opernring 3/2 FAX 43 1 586 8659
1010 Vienna, Austria www.location-austria.at

France 33 1 53 83 98 98
33, rue des Jeûneurs FAX 33 1 53 83 98 99
75002, Paris, France www.filmfrance.net

Germany-Bavaria 49 89 544 60 216 / 49 89 544 60 217
Sonnenstraße 21 FAX 49 89 544 60 223
Munich, Bavaria 80331 www.location-bayern.com
Germany

Germany-Berlin 49 331 743 8730 / 49 331 743 8731
Berlin Brandenburg Film Commission FAX 49 331 743 8799
August-Bebel-Straße 26-53 www.bbfc.de
14482 Postdam-Babelsberg
Germany

Ireland 353 91 561 398
Location Services FAX 353 91 561 405
Rockford House St. Augustine St. www.irishfilmboard.ie
Galway, Ireland

Italy-Campania 39 81 509 1533 / 39 338 696 9028
Via Lago Patria 200 FAX 39 81 509 8470
Giugliano in Campania 80014 Italy
www.campaniafilmcommission.org

Netherlands-Rotterdam 31 10 436 0747
Rouchussenstraat 3C FAX 31 10 436 0553
Rotterdam 3015 EA Netherlands www.rff.rotterdam.nl

New Zealand 64 4 385 0766
23 Frederick St. FAX 64 4 384 5840
Wellington New Zealand www.filmnz.com

Northern Ireland 44 28 9023 2444
21 Alfred St. FAX 44 28 9023 9918
Belfast BT2 8ED Ireland www.niftc.co.uk

Norway 47 55 56 4343
Georgernes Verft 12 FAX 47 90 88 7385
Bergen N-5011 Norway www.norwegianfilm.com

Peru Film Commission (310) 954-6407
P.O. Box 661266 www.filmperu.com
Los Angeles, CA 90066

Portugal 351 213 230 800
Rua S. Pedro de Alcantara, 45-1 FAX 351 213 343 1952
Lisboa 1269-138 Portugal www.icam.pt

Scotland-Edinburgh 44 131 622 7337
63 George St. FAX 44 131 622 7338
Edinburgh EH2 2JG United Kingdom www.edinfilm.com

Scotland-Glasgow 0141 302 1700
Scottish Screen FAX 0141 302 1778
Second Fl. 249 W. George St. www.scottishscreen.com
Glasgow G2 4QE United Kingdom

Scotland-Highlands & Islands 44 1463 710221
Inverness Castle FAX 44 1463 710848
Inverness IV2 3EG United Kingdom www.scotfilm.org

Spain-Barcelona 34 93 454 8066
Barcelona Plató Film Commission FAX 34 93 323 8048
C/ Mallorca, 209, Principal-1 www.barcelonafilm.com
Barcelona 08036 Spain
Contact: Júlia Goytisolo

Spain-Canary Islands 34 922 237871
Tenerife Film, C/Áurea Diaz Flores, s/n. FAX 34 922 237872
38005 Santa Cruz de Tenerife www.tenerifefilm.com
Islas Canarias Spain

Sweden 46 8 55 60 61 00
P.O. Box 27183 FAX 46 8 55 60 61 05
Stockholm, Sweden S-10252 Sweden
www.swedenfilmcommission.com

UK 44 20 7861 7861
UK Film Council, 10 Little Portland St. FAX 44 20 7861 7862
London WIW 7JG United Kingdom
www.ukfilmcouncil.org.uk

UK-East Midlands 44 115 934 9090
35-37 St. Mary's Gate FAX 44 115 950 0988
Nottingham NG1 1PU United Kingdom
www.em-media.org.uk

UK-Isle of Main 44 1624 687173
First Fl., Hamilton House, Peel Rd. FAX 44 1624 687171
Douglas IMI 5EP United Kingdom www.gov.im/dti/iomfilm

UK-Liverpool 0151 233 6380
P.O. Box 2008 www.liverpool.gov.uk
Municipal Bldgs., Dale St.
Liverpool L22DH United Kingdom

UK-London 44 207 613 7676
Film London, Ste. 6.10 FAX 44 207 613 7677
The Tea Bldg., 56 Shoreditch High St.
London E1 6JJ United Kingdom www.filmlondon.org.uk

UK-South West Screen 44 117 952 9977
St. Bartholomews Court, Lewins Mead FAX 44 117 952 9988
Bristol BS1 5BT United Kingdom www.swscreen.co.uk

UK-Yorkshire 44 (0) 113 294 4410
Studio 22, 46 The Calls FAX 44 (0) 113 294 4989
Leeds LS2 7EY United Kingdom
www.screenyorkshire.co.uk

1st Wave Productions (310) 474-2439
2017 Pacific Ave. FAX (310) 474-5282
Venice, CA 90291 www.1stwaveproductions.com
(Short-Term Housing)

Airtel Plaza Hotel & Conference Center (818) 997-7676
(800) 224-7835
7277 Valjean Ave. FAX (818) 785-8864
Van Nuys, CA 91406 www.airtelplaza.com
(Monthly Rates)

The Anabelle Hotel (818) 845-7800
2011 W. Olive Ave. FAX (818) 845-0054
Burbank, CA 91506 www.coastanabelle.com

The Argyle Hotel (323) 848-6658
8358 W. Sunset Blvd. FAX (323) 654-1004
West Hollywood, CA 90069 www.argylehotel.com

Bamboo Retreats (323) 962-0270
www.bambooretreats.com

Bel-Air Hotel (310) 472-1211
(800) 648-4097
FAX (310) 476-5890
www.hotelbelair.com

The Belamar Hotel (310) 750-0300
3501 Sepulveda Blvd. FAX (310) 750-0307
Manhattan Beach, CA 90266 www.thebelamar.com

Best Rest Inn (661) 248-2700
51541 N. Peace Valley Rd. FAX (661) 248-2720
Lebec, CA 93243 www.bestrestinn.com

Best Western (310) 677-7733
(800) 424-5005
(See Web Site for Locations) FAX (310) 671-7722
www.bestwestern.com

Best Western Heritage Inn (909) 466-1111
8179 Spruce Ave. FAX (908) 466-3876
Rancho Cucamonga, CA 91730
www.bestwestern.com/heritageinnranchocucamonga

Beverly Garland's Holiday Inn Universal Studios Hollywood (818) 980-8000
(800) 238-3759
4222 Vineland Ave. FAX (818) 766-5230
North Hollywood, CA 91602 www.beverlygarland.com

Beverly Hills Hotel (310) 276-2251
(800) 283-8885
9641 Sunset Blvd. FAX (310) 887-2887
Beverly Hills, CA 90210 www.beverlyhillshotel.com

Beverly Hills Plaza Hotel (310) 275-5575
FAX (310) 278-3325
www.beverlyhillsplazahotel.com

Breeze Suites (310) 656-0311
609 Broadway FAX (310) 656-0360
Santa Monica, CA 90401 www.breezesuites.com
(Monthly Rates)

Broadcast Center (AIMCO) (323) 965-5516
(877) 291-5814
7660 Beverly Blvd. FAX (323) 965-5520
Los Angeles, CA 90036 www.broadcastcenterapts.com
(Short-Term Housing)

Burbank Marriott (818) 843-6000
2500 Hollywood Way FAX (818) 842-9720
Burbank, CA 91505
(See Web Site for Additional Locations)

Canary Hotel (805) 884-0300
(805) 879-9142
31 W. Carrillo St. FAX (805) 879-9145
Santa Barbara, CA 93101 www.canarysantabarbara.com

The Carlyle Inn (310) 275-4445
(800) 322-7595
FAX (310) 859-0496
www.carlyle-inn.com

Carriage Inn (760) 446-7910
901 N. China Lake Blvd. FAX (760) 446-6408
Ridgecrest, CA 93555 www.carriageinn.biz

Century Wilshire Hotel (310) 474-4506
(800) 421-7223
10776 Wilshire Blvd. FAX (310) 474-2535
Los Angeles, CA 90024 www.centurywilshirehotel.com

Chamberlain Hotel (310) 657-7400
(800) 210-9693
1000 Westmount Dr. FAX (310) 854-6744
West Hollywood, CA 90069 www.korhotelgroup.com

Channel Road Inn (310) 459-1920
219 W. Channel Rd. FAX (310) 454-9920
Santa Monica, CA 90402 www.channelroadinn.com

Chateau Marmont Hotel (323) 656-1010
8221 Sunset Blvd. FAX (323) 655-5311
Hollywood, CA 90046 www.chateaumarmont.com

Cinema Suites Bed & Breakfast (323) 272-3160
925 S. Fairfax Ave. FAX (323) 272-3162
Los Angeles, CA 90036 www.cinemasuites.biz
(Extended Stay, Monthly Rates, Pet Friendly & Short-Term Housing)

Citrus Suites, LLC (310) 943-7200
(888) 457-6390
1915 Ocean Way www.citrussuites.com
Santa Monica, CA 90405
(Short-Term Housing)

The Country Inn and Suites by Carlson (818) 222-5300
(800) 456-4000
(See Web Site for Locations) FAX (818) 591-0870
www.countryinns.com

Courtyard by Marriott Los Angeles Westside (310) 484-7000
(800) 736-2593
6333 Bristol Pkwy FAX (310) 590-2593
Culver City, CA 90230 www.marriott.com/laxcv

the Crescent (310) 247-0505
403 N. Crescent Dr. FAX (310) 247-9053
Beverly Hills, CA 90210 www.crescentbh.com

Crowne Plaza of Beverly Hills (310) 553-6561
1150 S. Beverly Dr. FAX (310) 277-4469
Los Angeles, CA 90035 www.ichotelsgroup.com
(See Web Site for Additional Locations)

Custom Hotel Los Angeles (310) 645-0400
8639 Lincoln Blvd. FAX (310) 258-5738
Los Angeles, CA 90045 www.customhotel.com

Days Inn (661) 824-2421
16100 Sierra Hwy FAX (661) 824-2345
Mojave, CA 93501 www.the.daysinn.com/mojave19743

Disneyland Hotel (714) 778-6600
FAX (714) 956-6597
www.disneyland.com

Doubletree Hotels & Guest Suites (310) 395-3332
(See Web Site for Locations) www.doubletree.com

Élan Hotel (323) 658-6663
(888) 611-0398
8435 Beverly Blvd. FAX (323) 658-6640
Los Angeles, CA 90048 www.elanhotel.com

Empress Hotel of La Jolla (858) 454-3001
(888) 369-9900
FAX (858) 454-6387
www.empress-hotel.com

Fairmont Miramar Hotel (310) 576-7777
101 Wilshire Blvd. FAX (310) 458-7912
Santa Monica, CA 90401 www.fairmont.com

Farmer's Daughter (323) 937-3930
(800) 334-1658
115 S. Fairfax Ave. FAX (323) 932-1608
Los Angeles, CA 90036 www.farmersdaughterhotel.com

Figueroa Hotel (213) 627-8971
(800) 421-9092
939 S. Figueroa St. FAX (213) 689-0305
Los Angeles, CA 90015 www.figueroahotel.com

The Four Seasons (310) 273-2222
(800) 332-3442
300 S. Doheny Dr. FAX (310) 859-3824
Los Angeles, CA 90048 www.fourseasons.com
(See Web Site for Additional Locations)

The Four Seasons (805) 969-2261
(800) 332-3442
The Four Seasons Biltmore FAX (805) 565-8323
1260 Channel Dr. www.fourseasons.com
Santa Barbara, CA 93108
(See Web Site for Additional Locations)

The Four Seasons (310) 275-5200
(800) 545-4000
9500 Wilshire Blvd. FAX (310) 274-2851
Beverly Hills, CA 90212 www.fourseasons.com

The Georgian (310) 395-9945
(800) 538-8147
1415 Ocean Ave. FAX (310) 656-0904
Santa Monica, CA 90401 www.georgianhotel.com

The Grafton on Sunset (323) 654-4600
(800) 821-3660
8462 Sunset Blvd. FAX (323) 654-5918
West Hollywood, CA 90069 www.graftononsunset.com

Hilton Hotels (213) 624-0000
Hilton Checkers, 535 S. Grand Ave. FAX (213) 626-9906
Los Angeles, CA 90071 www.hilton.com
(See Web Site for Additional Locations)

Hilton Hotels (310) 410-6039
(310) 410-4000
5711 W. Century Blvd. FAX (310) 410-6177
Los Angeles, CA 90045 www.losangelesairport.hilton.com
(Extended Stay, Monthly Rates, Pet Friendly; See Web Site for Additional Locations)

Hilton Hotels (714) 750-4321
(800) 445-8667
Anaheim Hilton, 777 Convention Way FAX (714) 740-4460
Anaheim, CA 92802 www.hilton.com
(See Web Site for Additional Locations)

Hilton Hotels (310) 274-7777
Beverly Hilton, 9876 Wilshire Blvd. FAX (310) 285-1313
Beverly Hills, CA 90210 www.hilton.com
(See Web Site for Additional Locations)

Holiday Inn (310) 649-5151
(800) 972-2576
9901 La Cienega Blvd. FAX (310) 670-3619
Los Angeles, CA 90045 www.holiday-inn.com
(See Web Site for Additional Locations)

Holiday Inn Express Century City (310) 553-1000
(See Web Site for Additional Locations) FAX (310) 277-1633
www.ihg.com

Hollywood Roosevelt (323) 466-7000
(800) 950-7667
7000 Hollywood Blvd. FAX (323) 462-8056
Hollywood, CA 90028 www.hollywoodroosevelt.com

Home In Venice Beach (310) 489-9908
(Short-Term Housing) www.homeinvenicebeach.com

The Horizon Hotel (800) 377-7855
(760) 409-6199
1050 E. Palm Canyon Dr. www.thehorizonhotel.com
Palm Springs, CA 92264

Hotel Bel-Air (310) 472-1211
(800) 648-4097
www.hotelbelair.com

Hotel Casa Del Mar (310) 581-5533
(800) 898-6999
1910 Ocean Way FAX (310) 581-5503
Santa Monica, CA 90405 www.hotelcasadelmar.com

Hotel Oceana (310) 393-0486
(800) 777-0758
849 Ocean Ave. FAX (310) 458-1182
Santa Monica, CA 90403 www.hoteloceana.com

Hotel Sofitel Los Angeles (310) 278-5444
8555 Beverly Blvd. FAX (310) 657-2816
Los Angeles, CA 90048 www.sofitel.com

Housing Solutions (323) 665-2927
(Short-Term Housing) FAX (323) 665-3007
www.villawest.com

Hyatt (310) 277-1234
(800) 233-1234
The Park Hyatt Hotel FAX (310) 785-9240
2151 Avenue of The Stars www.hyatt.com
Century City, CA 90067
(See Web Site for Additional Locations)

ITT Sheraton Hotels (818) 980-1212
(800) 325-3535
Sheraton Universal Hotel FAX (818) 985-4980
333 Universal Hollywood Dr. www.sheraton.com
Universal City, CA 91608
(See Web Site for Additional Locations)

Jamaica Bay Inn (310) 823-5333
(888) 823-5333
4175 Admiralty Way FAX (310) 823-1325
Marina del Rey, CA 90292
www.bestwestern-jamaicabay.com

Kyoto Grand Hotel & Gardens (213) 629-1200
120 S. Los Angeles St. FAX (213) 622-0980
Los Angeles, CA 90012 www.kyotograndhotel.com

L.A. Residence (323) 650-5565
1416 Havenhurst Dr. FAX (323) 617-4546
West Hollywood, CA 90046 www.laresidence.ws
(Short-Term Housing)

LA Furnished Apartments (323) 788-4483
(877) 523-8764
FAX (323) 965-9963
www.furnapt.com

La Jolla Village Lodge (858) 551-2001
(877) 551-2001
1141 Silverado St. FAX (858) 551-3277
La Jolla, CA 92037 www.lajollavillagelodge.com

LAluxeRE (310) 734-8126
11041 Santa Monica Blvd., Ste. 517 www.laluxere.com
Los Angeles, CA 90025
(Extended Stay, Monthly Rates, Pet Friendly & Short-Term Housing)

Le Meridien at Beverly Hills (310) 247-0400
(800) 543-4300
465 S. La Cienega Blvd. FAX (310) 247-0315
Los Angeles, CA 90048 www.lemeridien.com

Le Merigot (310) 395-9700
1740 Ocean Ave. FAX (310) 395-9200
Santa Monica, CA 90401 www.lemerigothotel.com

Le Montrose Suite Hotel (310) 855-1115 / (800) 776-0666
900 Hammond St. FAX (310) 657-9192
West Hollywood, CA 90069 www.lemontrose.com

Le Parc (310) 855-8888 / (800) 578-4837
733 N. West Knoll Dr. FAX (310) 659-7812
West Hollywood, CA 90069 www.leparcsuites.com

Loews Santa Monica Beach Hotel (310) 458-6700 / (800) 235-6397
1700 Ocean Ave. FAX (310) 458-6761
Santa Monica, CA 90401 www.loewshotels.com

The London West Hollywood (310) 854-1111
1020 N. San Vicente Blvd.
West Hollywood, CA 90069
www.thelondonwesthollywood.com
(See Web Site for Additional Locations)

Los Angeles Marriott-Downtown (213) 617-1133
333 S. Figueroa St. FAX (213) 613-0291
Los Angeles, CA 90071 www.marriott.com
(See Web Site for Additional Locations)

Los Feliz Lodge (323) 913-1443 / (323) 313-5780
1507 N. Hoover St. FAX (323) 660-0447
Los Angeles, CA 90027 www.losfelizlodge.com

Luxe Hotel Rodeo Drive (310) 273-0300 / (800) 589-3711
360 N. Rodeo Dr. FAX (310) 859-8730
Beverly Hills, CA 90210 www.luxehotels.com
(See Web Site for Additional Locations)

Maison 140 Hotel (310) 281-4000 / (800) 670-6182
140 S. Lasky Dr. FAX (310) 281-4001
Beverly Hills, CA 90212 www.maison140.com

Marriott (310) 546-7511
Manhattan Beach Marriott FAX (310) 939-1486
1400 Parkview Ave. www.marriott.com
Manhattan Beach, CA 90266

Marriott (310) 421-3100 / (310) 421-3102
Marriott Residence Inn www.marriott.com
1700 N. Sepulveda Blvd.
Manhattan Beach, CA 90266

Marriott (310) 641-5700 / (800) 228-9290
LAX Marriott, 5855 W. Century Blvd. FAX (310) 337-5358
Los Angeles, CA 90045 www.marriott.com
(See Web Site for Additional Locations)

Marriott (310) 301-3000
Marina Beach Marriott FAX (310) 448-4870
4100 Admiralty Way www.marriott.com
Marina del Rey, CA 90292

Marriott (760) 341-2211 / (800) 331-3112
Desert Springs Resort & Spa FAX (760) 341-1872
74855 Country Club Dr. www.marriott.com
Palm Desert, CA 92260

Marriott (310) 556-2777
Courtyard by Marriott FAX (310) 203-0563
10320 W. Olympic Blvd. www.marriott.com
West Los Angeles, CA 90064

Millennium Biltmore Hotel (213) 624-1011 / (800) 245-8673
506 S. Grand Ave. FAX (213) 612-1545
Los Angeles, CA 90071 www.thebiltmore.com

Mondrian (323) 650-8999 / (800) 606-6090
8440 W. Sunset Blvd. FAX (323) 650-5215
West Hollywood, CA 90069 www.mondrianhotel.com

Motel 6 (323) 464-6006
(See Web Site for Locations) FAX (323) 464-4645
www.motel6.com

Oakwood Temporary Housing (888) 745-3429
3600 Barham Blvd. www.oakwood.com/production
Los Angeles, CA 90068
(See Web Site for Additional Locations)

Omni Hotel (213) 617-3300 / (800) 843-6664
FAX (213) 617-3399
www.omnihotels.com

The Orlando (323) 658-6600 / (800) 624-6835
8384 W. Third St. FAX (323) 653-3464
Los Angeles, CA 90048 www.theorlando.com

The Palmdale Hotel (661) 273-1200 / (800) 272-6232
(See Web Site for Additional Locations) FAX (661) 947-9593
www.ramada.com

Peninsula Beverly Hills Hotel (310) 551-2888 / (800) 462-7899
9882 S. Santa Monica Blvd. FAX (310) 788-2319
Beverly Hills, CA 90212 www.peninsula.com

Queen Mary Hotel (562) 435-3511 / (800) 437-2934
1126 Queen's Hwy FAX (562) 437-4531
Long Beach, CA 90802 www.queenmary.com

Radisson Hotels (818) 709-7054 / (818) 822-4019
9777 Topanga Canyon Blvd. FAX (818) 988-3573
Chatsworth, CA 91311 www.radisson.com

Radisson Hotels (310) 348-4550 / (310) 649-1776
6161 W. Centinela Ave. FAX (310) 649-6566
Culver City, CA 90230 www.radisson.com/culvercityca

Radisson Hotels (310) 670-9000
6225 W. Century Blvd. www.radisson.com
Los Angeles, CA 90045
(See Web Site for Additional Locations)

Radisson Hotels International (310) 348-4550 / (800) 333-3333
6161 Centinela Ave. FAX (310) 649-4411
Culver City, CA 90230 www.radisson.com/culvercityca
(See Web Site for Additional Locations)

Ramada (310) 419-1011
(See Web Site for Additional Locations) FAX (310) 412-1294
www.ramada.com

Renaissance Hotels (323) 856-1200 / (800) 468-3571
1755 N. Highland Ave. FAX (323) 856-1205
Hollywood, CA 90028 www.renaissancehotels.com
(See Web Site for Additional Locations)

The Ritz-Carlton - Laguna Nigel (949) 240-2000 / (800) 241-3333
One Ritz-Carlton Dr. FAX (949) 240-1061
Dana Point, CA 92629 www.ritzcarlton.com
(See Web Site for Additional Locations)

The Ritz-Carlton - Marina del Rey (310) 823-1700 / (800) 241-3333
4375 Admiralty Way FAX (310) 823-2403
Marina del Rey, CA 90292 www.ritzcarlton.com
(See Web Site for Additional Locations)

The Ritz-Carlton - Pasadena (626) 568-3900
1401 S. Oak Knoll Ave. FAX (626) 568-3700
Pasadena, CA 91106 www.ritzcarlton.com
(See Web Site for Additional Locations)

Royal Equestrian (818) 843-2441
1200 Riverside Dr. FAX (818) 843-0948
Burbank, CA 91506
(Short-Term Housing)

Royal Palace Westwood (310) 208-6677
(800) 631-0100
FAX (310) 824-3732
www.royalpalacewestwood.com

Royal Scandinavian Inn (805) 688-8000
(800) 624-5572
400 Alisal Rd. FAX (805) 688-0761
Solvang, CA 93463 www.royalscandinavianinn.com

San Ysidro Ranch (805) 969-5046
(800) 368-6788
900 San Ysidro Ln. FAX (805) 565-1995
Santa Barbara, CA 93108 www.sanysidroranch.com

SeaCastle (310) 917-1998
(800) 295-0022
1725 Ocean Front Walk FAX (310) 917-1178
Santa Monica, CA 90401 www.theseacastle.com
(Extended Stay)

Shangri-La (310) 394-2791
1301 Ocean Ave. FAX (310) 451-3351
Santa Monica, CA 90401 www.shangrila-hotel.com

Sheraton Delfina (310) 399-9344
(888) 627-8532
530 W. Pico Blvd. FAX (310) 399-3322
Santa Monica, CA 90405 www.sheratonsantamonica.com

Shutters on the Beach (310) 458-0030
(800) 334-9000
One Pico Blvd. FAX (310) 458-4589
Santa Monica, CA 90405 www.shuttersonthebeach.com

Sportsmen's Lodge Hotel (818) 769-4700
(800) 821-8511
12825 Ventura Blvd. FAX (818) 769-4798
Studio City, CA 91604 www.slhotel.com

The Standard (323) 650-9090
8300 Sunset Blvd. FAX (323) 650-2820
West Hollywood, CA 90069 www.standardhotel.com

Sunset Marquis Hotel (310) 657-1333
(800) 858-9758
1200 N. Alta Loma Rd. FAX (310) 652-5300
West Hollywood, CA 90069 www.sunsetmarquishotel.com

TENTEN Wilshire, LLC (877) 338-1010
1010 Wilshire Blvd. FAX (213) 482-4722
Los Angeles, CA 90017 www.1010wilshire.com
(Short-Term Housing)

Town House Motel (661) 942-1195
(661) 496-6607
44125 N. Sierra Hwy FAX (661) 945-2084
Lancaster, CA 93534 www.townhouselancaster.com

Trump International Hotel Las Vegas (702) 476-7208
2000 Fashion Show Dr. FAX (702) 476-7220
Las Vegas, NV 89109 www.trumplasvegashotel.com

Viceroy Hotel (310) 260-7500
(800) 670-6185
1819 Ocean Ave. FAX (310) 260-7515
Santa Monica, CA 90401 www.viceroysantamonica.com

The W Hotel (310) 208-8765
FAX (310) 824-0355
www.whotels.com

WEbster8 (323) 556-8050
116 N. Sycamore Ave. FAX (323) 556-8010
Los Angeles, CA 90036 www.webster8.com
(Monthly Rates)

The Westin Bonaventure (213) 624-1000
(See Web Site for Locations) FAX (213) 612-4800
www.westin.com

Wilshire Grand Hotel & Centre (213) 688-7777
930 Wilshire Blvd. FAX (213) 612-3989
Los Angeles, CA 90017 www.wilshiregrand.com

1800Fly1800
(310) 330-7500
(800) 359-1800
FAX (310) 419-8129
www.1800fly1800.com

(213) Limousine (888) 213-5466
7336 Santa Monica Blvd., Ste. 444
Los Angeles, CA 90046
FAX (888) 213-5466
www.213limo.com

21st Century Limousine
(310) 214-5466
(877) 214-5466
3188 Airway Ave., Ste. G
Costa Mesa, CA 92626
www.21stcenturylimo.com

310 Picture Cars (310) 678-8007
6709 La Tijera Blvd., Ste. 247
Los Angeles, CA 90045

A.L.S. Limousine, Inc.
(310) 338-0000
(877) 310-5466
2118 Wilshire Blvd., Ste. 251
Santa Monica, CA 90403
FAX (310) 568-0766
www.alslimo.com

AAA Limousine Service
(818) 704-4746
(800) 232-4133
FAX (818) 888-1280
www.aaalimo.net

Absolute Transportation Service
(310) 270-5253
(877) 801-2345
www.americanlimousine.us

Ace Limousine (310) 459-0465
P.O. Box 5431
Santa Monica, CA 90409
www.ace-limo.com

Affordable West, Inc. (323) 467-7182
1040 N. La Brea Ave.
Hollywood, CA 90038
FAX (323) 467-6520

Allways Chauffeurs & Bodyguards (310) 385-9088
FAX (310) 385-9038
www.allwaysdrivers.com

Aloha Limousine
(310) 641-1811
(323) 464-2456
P.O. Box 352
Hawthorne, CA 90251
FAX (310) 978-6366

AM-PM Limousine Service
(323) 876-2676
(800) 995-2676
FAX (323) 876-1507

Amour Way Limousine and Travel Service
(310) 591-8690
(866) 261-6651
P.O. Box 661749
Los Angeles, CA 90066
FAX (310) 390-9315
www.amourway.com

AMS/Pacific Limousine & Transportation, Inc.
(310) 649-5466
(310) 838-4727
2006 S. La Cienega
Los Angeles, CA 90034
FAX (310) 838-9208
www.amspacific.com

Anytime Limousine Service
(818) 764-9116
(800) 760-5466
6844 Bellaire Ave.
North Hollywood, CA 91605
FAX (818) 765-4756
www.anytimelimousines.com

Avalon Transportation, Inc.
(310) 391-6161
(800) 528-2566
5239 Sepulveda Blvd.
Culver City, CA 90230
FAX (310) 391-8017
www.avalontrans.com

Avectra Global Transportation (818) 752-1600 (888) 928-3287
10945 Bluffside Dr., Ste. 236 FAX (818) 232-0352
Studio City, CA 91604 www.avectralimo.com

Avenue LS Inc. (818) 335-3303 (877) 283-6835
14249 Kittridge St. FAX (818) 786-0792
Venice, CA 91405 www.lalimousin.com

Avon Studio Transportation (323) 850-0826 (800) 432-2866
7080 Santa Monica Blvd. FAX (323) 467-4239
Los Angeles, CA 90038 www.avonrents.com

Baron Limousine (866) 759-6929 (818) 774-1038
FAX (818) 774-1333
www.labaronlimo.com

Beverly Hills Rent-A-Car (323) 464-5900 (310) 901-0135
800 N. La Brea FAX (323) 464-2506
Los Angeles, CA 90038 www.bhrentacar.com

Black & White Car and Limousine Service (818) 781-1555 (800) 924-1624
FAX (818) 995-4188
www.blackwhitecarservice.com

Blue Moon Limousine & Sedan (714) 546-6737 (800) 726-1837
FAX (714) 546-7048

Budget (800) 527-7000 (310) 642-4500
(See Web Site for Locations) www.budget.com

California Rent-A-Car (310) 477-2727
11725 Santa Monica Blvd. FAX (310) 477-9176
Los Angeles, CA 90025 www.productioncarrental.com

Carey Limousine Service (310) 670-1166 (800) 262-5070
FAX (310) 665-5110
www.carey.com

Celebrity Executive Car (310) 398-8779 (323) 850-8000
FAX (310) 398-6730

Classic Car Rental Connection (818) 728-0607
17514 Ventura Blvd. FAX (818) 728-0684
Encino, CA 91316 www.101classiccarrental.com

Classic Limos (800) 550-3125 (949) 495-3125
30251 Golden Lantern, E-510 FAX (949) 495-1652
Laguna Niguel, CA 92677 www.classiclimousines.com

CLS Transportation (800) 266-2577
FAX (310) 414-8126
www.clslimo.com

CPS Worldwide (888) 277-2776 (310) 463-9800
12400 Wilshire Blvd., Ste. 400 FAX (866) 636-6977
Los Angeles, CA 90025
www.californiaprotectiveservices.com

Crown Limousine L.A. (310) 737-0888 (800) 933-5466
FAX (310) 737-0890
www.crownlimola.com

Dav-El Limousines (310) 642-6666 (800) 922-0343
www.davel.com

Diva Limousine, Ltd. (800) 427-3482
www.divalimo.com

Dream One (800) 538-8799 (310) 670-5466
FAX (310) 670-0558
www.dreamonesedans.com

ELS Transportation (310) 410-8100
4720 171st St. FAX (310) 542-4108
Lawndale, CA 90260 www.elstransportation.com

Emerald Limousine Service (310) 591-6060
P.O. Box 83669 FAX (310) 750-9154
Los Angeles, CA 90083 www.limobyemerald.com

Encore Limousine Company (323) 753-4437
FAX (323) 753-4557
www.encorelimousine.com

Exclusive Sedan Service (818) 765-7311 (800) 400-7332
12580 Saticoy St. FAX (818) 765-0183
North Hollywood, CA 91605 www.exclusivesedan.com

Executive Limousine (310) 823-5466
4330 Lincoln Blvd. FAX (310) 822-5528
Marina del Rey, CA 90292 www.ezeclimo.com

Executive Productions (310) 456-8833
3951 Ridgemont Dr. FAX (310) 456-5692
Malibu, CA 90265

Executive Transit, Inc. (626) 568-4110 (800) 468-6529
FAX (626) 685-2626

Exquisite Limo and Sedan Service (310) 674-3326 (310) 420-0277
10834 S. Freeman Ave. FAX (310) 674-3138
Inglewood, CA 90304
www.exquisitelimoandsedanservice.com

Fleetwood Limousine (310) 645-6092 (800) 283-5893
FAX (310) 645-1245

Gemstar Limousine Service (310) 457-7307 (800) 922-5466
FAX (310) 457-6307
www.gemstarlimo.com

Greenwich Limousine (310) 657-5800
P.O. Box 321 FAX (818) 957-8078
Beverly Hills, CA 90213

Integrated Transportation Services (310) 845-1234 (800) 487-4255
3047 S. Robertson Blvd. FAX (310) 558-0748
Los Angeles, CA 90034 www.itslimo.com

Jack's Heaven (213) 819-5466 (213) 500-0077

Jackson Limousine Service (323) 734-9955 (800) 522-9955
FAX (323) 291-2669
www.jacksonlimo.com

Ⓐ **KLS Limousine Service Inc.** (310) 247-0804 (877) 936-5466
9663 Santa Monica Blvd., Ste. 773 FAX (310) 247-0805
Beverly Hills, CA 90210 www.klsla.com

Limos At Your Service (323) 646-1135
4858 W. Century Blvd. FAX (310) 645-9305
Los Angeles, CA 90045 www.limosatyourservice.net

Lokie Limousine Service (310) 815-9228
8720 Venice Blvd., Ste. 206 www.lokielimousine.com
Los Angeles, CA 90034

Music Express (818) 845-1502
(800) 255-4444
FAX (818) 845-1738
www.musiclimo.com

Red Carpet Limousine Service, Inc. (310) 398-9700
FAX (310) 398-9750
www.rcllimo.com

Regal Limousine Service (310) 446-0041
(800) 383-7028
P.O. Box 321
Beverly Hills, CA 90213
FAX (818) 957-8078
www.regallimousineservice.com

Secure Transportation (562) 941-0107
(800) 856-9994
13111 Meyer Rd.
Whittier, CA 90605
FAX (562) 906-2947
www.securetransportation.com

Silverado Coach Company, Inc. (818) 251-9700
(800) 544-7999
FAX (818) 884-4997
www.silveradocoach.com

Zimmac Sedan & Limo Service (310) 677-2220
(877) 677-2221
4858 W. Century Blvd., Ste. 104
Inglewood, CA 90304
FAX (310) 677-2221
www.zimmaclimo.com

24/7 Plan-It Locations (818) 376-6506 / (310) 770-8458
15500 Erwin St., Ste. 4009 FAX (818) 376-7606
Van Nuys, CA 91411 www.planitlocations.com

5 Star Film Locations Inc. (323) 654-3900 / (818) 970-0422
11244 Briarcliff Ln. FAX (323) 654-8838
Studio City, CA 91604 www.5starfilmlocations.com

A2Z Locations, Inc. (323) 667-3456
3171 Los Feliz Blvd., Ste. 308 FAX (323) 667-3434
Los Angeles, CA 90039 www.a2zlocations.com
(Architectural Properties, Bar and Restaurant, Castles, Churches, Coastal and Marine Locations, Colleges/Schools, Deserts, Estates, Historic Properties, Houses, International Locations, Museums, Office Buildings, Retail Spaces, Stages & Warehouses)

Access Locations, Inc. (310) 317-0781 / (310) 601-0644
24797 W. Saddle Peak FAX (310) 317-9508
Malibu, CA 90265 www.accesslocationsinc.com

All Pictures Media Locations (626) 243-0456 / (323) 377-3804
15 S. Raymond Ave., Ste. 200 FAX (626) 243-0455
Pasadena, CA 91105 www.allpicturesmedia.com
(Malibu to Los Angeles to Palm Springs Locations; Architectural Properties, Bar and Restaurant Locations, Estates, Houses, Office Buildings, Retail Spaces & Warehouses)

Amazing Film Locations/Stargazer (818) 993-7606 / (818) 704-6633
6501 Fallbrook Ave. FAX (818) 704-9821
West Hills, CA 91307 www.amazinglocations.com
(Architectural Properties, Bar and Restaurant Locations, Castles, Churches, Estates, Houses, Licensed Broker & Warehouses)

America Film Network, Inc. (818) 906-8945 / (818) 613-5962
4225 Woodman Ave. FAX (818) 267-5717
Sherman Oaks, CA 91423 www.americafilmnetwork.com
(Architectural Properties, Bar and Restaurant Locations, Castles, Churches, Marine Locations, Colleges/Schools, Deserts, Estates, Historic Properties, Houses, International Locations, Mountain Locations, Museums, Office Buildings, Retail Spaces, Stages & Warehouses)

Angela's Locations (818) 231-9626
4141 Falling Leaf Dr. FAX (818) 881-3049
Encino, CA 91316 www.angelaslocations.com

aProductionLocation.com (323) 874-0404 / (310) 561-2430
9663 Santa Monica Blvd., Ste. 490 FAX (323) 843-9808
Beverly Hills, CA 90210 www.aproductionlocation.com

Ascot Locations Service, Inc. (818) 843-3210
FAX (818) 843-3089
www.ascotlocations.com
(Coachella Valley and Palm Springs, Long Beach, Los Angeles and Ventura Counties & West Valley)

BEBWorld.com (323) 610-1587
www.bebworld.com
(Architectural Properties, Bar and Restaurant Locations, Castles, Estates, Houses, International Locations, Mountain Locations, Office Buildings, Retail Spaces, Stages & Warehouses)

California Film Commission Location Resource Center (323) 860-2960 / (800) 858-4749
7080 Hollywood Blvd., Ste. 900 FAX (323) 860-2972
Los Angeles, CA 90028 www.film.ca.gov

Cast Locations (323) 469-6616
536 N. Larchmont Blvd. FAX (323) 469-6599
Los Angeles, CA 90004 www.castlocations.com

CBAV, Inc./World Locations (310) 659-0599
8533 Sunset Blvd., Ste. 203 FAX (310) 659-3292
West Hollywood, CA 90069 www.worldlocations.com

Central Locations (323) 306-2020
P.O. Box 260231 FAX (800) 966-8539
Encino, CA 91426 www.filmlocations.la
(Architectural Properties, Bar and Restaurant Locations, Castles, Churches, Coastal and Marine Locations, Estates, Houses, Licensed Broker, Mountain Locations, Office Buildings, Stages & Warehouses)

Cinemafloat (949) 675-8888 / (714) 801-5553
1624 W. Oceanfront Walk FAX (949) 644-3073
Newport Beach, CA 92663
(Houses, Marine Locations & Piers)

Clean Strike Locations (562) 803-3701 / (562) 879-2207
12214 Lakewood Blvd., Bldg. 9 FAX (562) 803-3702
Downey, CA 90242 www.cleanstrikelocations.com

Cypress Sea Cove (310) 589-3344
33572 Pacific Coast Hwy FAX (310) 589-3343
Malibu, CA 90265 www.malibufilmlocations.com

Dennis Morgan Locations Inc. (818) 760-3876
FAX (866) 715-5545
www.dennismorganlocations.com
(Architectural Properties, Bar and Restaurant Locations, Castles, Churches, Coastal and Marine Locations, Colleges/Schools, Deserts, Estates, Houses, International Locations, Mountain Locations, Museums, Office Buildings, Retail Spaces, Stages & Warehouses)

EastWest Locations, Inc. (323) 769-3550 / (213) 509-1699
8491 Sunset Blvd., Ste. 206 FAX (323) 656-6324
West Hollywood, CA 90069 www.eastwestlocations.com

Elite Film Locations (818) 501-4553 / (818) 207-6410
4335 Van Nuys Blvd., Ste. 263 FAX (818) 530-7795
Sherman Oaks, CA 91403 www.elitefilmlocations.net
(Greater Los Angeles: Architectural Properties, Bar and Restaurant Locations, Beach Locations, Castles, Churches, Coastal and Marine Locations, Colleges/Schools, Deserts, Estates, Historic Properties, Hotels, Houses, Lofts, Map Services, Office Buildings, Ranches, Retail Spaces, Stages, Theaters & Warehouses)

The Event Division (310) 424-5112
9903 Santa Monica Blvd., Ste. 960 FAX (310) 277-0830
Beverly Hills, CA 90212 www.theeventdivision.net
(Bar and Restaurant Locations, Estates, Houses, Museums & Warehouses)

Far West Locations (310) 287-8310
3835-R E. Thousand Oaks Blvd. FAX (805) 446-6597
Thousand Oaks, CA 91362 www.farwestlocations.com

Fergusons' Film LA Property Management Co. (310) 858-7727 / (760) 399-9682
78710 Via Sonata FAX (760) 399-9685
La Quinta, CA 92253 www.locations2film.com
(Licensed Broker, L.A. Zone)

A Film Friendly Locations/ Joseph Darrell (323) 461-6386 / (310) 212-3243
FAX (310) 212-3242
www.jdls.com
(Architectural Properties, Bar and Restaurant Locations, Castles, Churches, Coastal and Marine Locations, Colleges/Schools, Deserts, Estates, Historic Properties, Houses, International Locations, Mountain Locations, Museums, Office Buildings, Retail Spaces, Stages & Warehouses)

Film Westside Locations (310) 710-2833
www.filmwestside.com

FilmWerx Locations, Inc. (323) 525-0008
4525 Wilshire Blvd., Ste. 204 FAX (323) 525-0009
Los Angeles, CA 90010 www.filmwerx.com

Fresno Film & Entertainment Commission (559) 621-8358
(559) 908-0539
2600 Fresno St., Ste. 2156-02 FAX (559) 457-1505
Fresno, CA 93721 www.fresnofilm.com
(Architectural Properties, Bar and Restaurant Locations, Churches, Colleges/Schools, Historic Properties, Houses, Museums, Office Buildings, Retail Spaces, Stages & Warehouses)

Golden Locations (310) 820-3312
(323) 260-4036
P.O. Box 16251 www.goldenlocations.com
Beverly Hills, CA 90209
(Churches)

Hollywood Locations (213) 534-3456
1201 W. Fifth St., Ste. F-170 FAX (213) 534-3459
Los Angeles, CA 90017 www.hollywoodlocations.com
(Licensed Broker)

A **HomeShootHome** (626) 794-1616
FAX (626) 737-6047
www.homeshoothome.com

Idaho Film Location Services (800) 783-1758
FAX (800) 783-1758
www.idaholocations.com

Image Locations, Inc. (310) 871-8004
(888) 411-2344
9663 Santa Monica Blvd., Ste. 842 FAX (213) 380-4307
Beverly Hills, CA 90210 www.imagelocations.com

Independent Locations (818) 222-5744
22655 DeKalb Dr. FAX (818) 222-5752
Calabasas, CA 91302 www.independentlocations.com
(Architectural Properties, Bar and Restaurant Locations, Castles, Churches, Coastal and Marine Locations, Colleges/ Schools, Deserts, Estates, Historic Properties, Houses, Map Service, Mountain Locations, Office Buildings, Retail Spaces, Stages & Warehouses)

iwantfilming.com (310) 373-3835
(877) 345-6464
4001 Pacific Coast Hwy, Ste. 104 FAX (310) 697-3283
Torrance, CA 90505 www.iwantfilming.com

Kodevco Locations/ Richard Korngute (323) 852-1817
(213) 300-1817
FAX (310) 454-0701
www.kodevco.com
(Architectural Properties, Houses, Office Buildings, Retail Spaces & Warehouses)

Landmark Locations, Inc. (310) 826-9660
(805) 908-1797
11726 San Vicente Blvd., Ste. 223 FAX (805) 496-1406
Los Angeles, CA 90049 www.landmark.locations.org
(Licensed Broker)

Legend Locations, LLC (323) 467-9265
6735 Yucca St., Ste. 311 FAX (323) 467-9266
Hollywood, CA 90028 www.legendlocations.com
(Architectural Properties, Bar and Restaurant Locations, Castles, Churches, Coastal and Marine Locations, Colleges/ Schools, Deserts, Estates, Houses, International Locations, Map Service, Mountain Locations, Office Buildings, Retail Spaces, Stages & Warehouses)

A **The Location Connection, Inc.** (310) 376-9797
(818) 422-8127
Raleigh Studios Manhattan Beach FAX (310) 376-9796
1600 Rosecrans Ave. www.locationconnection.com
Bldg. Five, Second Fl.
Manhattan Beach, CA 90266
(Coachella Valley, Los Angeles, Malibu, Orange County, San Fernando Valley, South Bay & Ventura County)

Location Network/Geoff White (323) 660-9100
(818) 426-2600
2395 Silver Lake Blvd., Ste. 11 FAX (323) 660-9003
Los Angeles, CA 90039 www.locationnetwork.com

Locations Plus (805) 969-0887
(805) 689-9434
755 Romero Canyon Rd. FAX (805) 695-0861
Santa Barbara, CA 93108 www.locationsplus.net
(Coastal and Marine Locations, Estates, Houses, Mountain Locations, Santa Barbara and Ventura Counties & Santa Ynez Valley)

Malibu Locations (310) 457-3926
29575 Pacific Coast Hwy, Ste. E FAX (310) 457-9308
Malibu, CA 90265 www.malibu-locations.com

Maverick Locations (310) 600-5020
www.mavericklocations.com
(Bar and Restaurant Locations, Churches, Coastal and Marine Locations, Deserts, Houses & Warehouses)

Media Locations, Inc. (323) 939-1912
(323) 202-8884
139 N. Highland Ave. FAX (323) 965-1088
Los Angeles, CA 90036 www.medialocationsinc.com
(Los Angeles County)

Meyler & Co. (310) 276-5717
8899 Beverly Blvd., Ste. 618 FAX (310) 276-5718
Los Angeles, CA 90048 www.meylerandco.com

Miles of Files/Bianca Gonzalez (805) 895-1325
817 Kentia Ave.
Santa Barbara, CA 93101

MNM Locations (310) 600-3011
FAX (310) 821-5506
www.mnmlocations.com
(Architectural Properties, Bar and Restaurant Locations, Churches, Coastal and Marine Locations, Colleges/Schools, Estates, Golf Courses, Historic Properties, International Locations, Licensed Broker, Mountain Locations, Office Buildings, Retail Spaces, Stages, Tennis Courts, Vineyards & Warehouses)

National Film Locations/ National Special Event Locations (310) 231-7045 (310) 231-7828
11740 Wilshire Blvd., Ste. A2306 FAX (310) 231-7047
Los Angeles, CA 90025

Pacific Design Center (310) 657-0800 (310) 360-6423
8687 Melrose Ave., Ste. M60 FAX (310) 652-8576
West Hollywood, CA 90069 www.pacificdesigncenter.com

Rancho Simi Recreation & Park District (805) 584-4400 (805) 584-4453
1692 Sycamore Dr. FAX (805) 527-2495
Simi Valley, CA 93065 www.rsrpd.org
(Churches, Lakes, Mountain Locations, Parks & Sports Fields/Facilities)

Real to Reel Locations (818) 785-7075
7021 Hayvenhurst Ave., Ste. 206 FAX (818) 785-9817
Van Nuys, CA 91406 www.rtrlocations.com
(Licensed Broker)

Reel World Locations (661) 296-3147 (310) 498-8775
19354 Opal Ln. www.reelworldlocations.com
Santa Clarita, CA 91350
(Architectural Properties, Bar and Restaurant Locations, Deserts, Estates, Houses, Office Buildings, Retail Spaces, Stages & Warehouses)

Ridgecrest Film Commission Location Library (760) 375-8202 (800) 847-4830
139 Balsam St., Ste. 1700 FAX (760) 375-9850
Ridgecrest, CA 93555 www.filmdeserts.com
(Mojave High Desert)

San Luis Obispo County Location & Casting (805) 547-9000
128 La Colina FAX (805) 969-9595
Pismo Beach, CA 93449

Santa Barbara Location Services/ aka Location Production Coordination (805) 969-5555 (805) 565-1562
1805 E. Cabrillo Blvd., Ste. B FAX (805) 969-9595
Santa Barbara, CA 93108
www.santabarbara-locations.com
(Ojai, San Luis Obispo, Santa Barbara, Santa Ynez Valley & Ventura)
Contact: Ronnie Haran Mellen

Skyline Locations (213) 689-0655
350 S. Grand Ave., Ste. 2240 FAX (213) 629-0733
Los Angeles, CA 90071 www.skylinelocations.com

Sources Location Library, Inc. (323) 464-5360 (323) 493-8844
FAX (323) 395-5575
www.locationlibrary.com

Stuart Raven Barter & Associates (323) 931-2177
5576 W. First St. FAX (323) 931-6374
Los Angeles, CA 90036 www.srba.com

Sunset Locations, Inc. (310) 360-1306
8730 Sunset Blvd., Ste. 485 FAX (310) 360-1362
West Hollywood, CA 90069 www.sunsetlocations.com
(Architectural Properties, Estates, Historic Properties, Houses, Licensed Broker, Office Buildings & Warehouses)

Toni Maier-On Location, Inc. (323) 469-9941
6253 Hollywood Blvd., Ste. 309 FAX (323) 469-9943
Hollywood, CA 90028 www.onlocation.com
(Architectural Properties, Malibu Locations, Office Buildings, Stages & Warehouses)

Universal Locations, Inc. (818) 845-4120
3314 W. Burbank Blvd. FAX (818) 845-4105
Burbank, CA 91505 www.universallocations.com
(Licensed Broker)

Unreel Locations (323) 953-6189
2950 Los Feliz Blvd., Ste. 206 FAX (323) 953-1637
Los Angeles, CA 90039 www.unreellocations.com
(Architectural Properties, Churches, Coastal and Marine Locations, Colleges/Schools, Historic Properties, Houses, Licensed Broker, Museums & Retail Spaces)

Ventura County Location & Casting Services (805) 641-3456
1239 Kingston Ln. FAX (805) 969-9595
Ventura, CA 93001

West Adams Locations (323) 766-0449 (323) 776-7649
FAX (323) 766-7634
www.westadamslocations.com

James Abke (323) 937-1010
www.zenobia.com

Ronald Abrams (310) 394-6066
(310) 880-5007
FAX (310) 458-0858
www.ronabrams.org

Ron Adams/Hero Locations - Scouting & Management (323) 461-1231
1245 N. Vine St., Ste. 300 FAX (323) 461-1299
Hollywood, CA 90038

All Major Productions Location (818) 344-5454
21221 Pacific Coast Hwy FAX (310) 456-5692
Malibu, CA 90265
(Bar and Restaurant Locations & Retail Spaces)

Dennis C. Alpert (818) 985-2739
(818) 378-6574
4945 Coldwater Canyon Ave.
Sherman Oaks, CA 91423

American Barricade, Inc. (714) 634-2663
(818) 955-8500
2141 S. Dupont Dr. FAX (714) 634-2666
Anaheim, CA 92806 www.americanbarricade.net
(Street Closures & Traffic Control and Plans)

Thom Anable (818) 590-0009
FAX (503) 206-6099
www.tanable.com

Angela's Locations (818) 231-9626
4141 Falling Leaf Dr. FAX (818) 881-3049
Encino, CA 91316 www.angelaslocations.com

Antelope Valley Film Office (661) 723-6090
(661) 510-4231
44933 Fern Ave. FAX (661) 723-5914
Lancaster, CA 93534 www.avfilm.com
(City of Lancaster, City of Palmdale & North Los Angeles County)

Jonathan Arroyo (323) 828-7664
FAX (213) 381-1980
www.creativescouts.com

Roger Barth (310) 877-3063

Ted Beauregard (323) 828-9481
(French and Spanish Speaking)

Steve Beimler/locationcompass (310) 877-3032
(Japanese & Spanish) www.locationcompass.com

Brad Bemis (310) 991-0959
www.bradbemis.com

Rob Benson (818) 760-0222
11522 Killion St.
North Hollywood, CA 91601

Alex Berechet (818) 554-8940
(818) 783-4423
5460 White Oak Ave., Ste. J108 FAX (818) 990-0387
Encino, CA 91316

Mike Bergemann (310) 849-2296
FAX (310) 919-3612
www.bergie.locations.org

Mike Besoli (626) 836-2225
(626) 932-8110
FAX (626) 836-2215
www.mikebesoli.com

Dorsey Bethune (310) 904-3115

Big Bear Locations (909) 584-8127
(818) 321-0091
FAX (909) 584-8527
www.bigbearlocations.com

Blockbuster Locations (818) 219-8101
(818) 501-8649
17451 Oak Creek Ct. FAX (310) 501-8659
Encino, CA 91316 www.blockbusterlocations.com

Bruce Boehner (213) 925-5379
FAX (213) 250-5379

Robert Bonk (213) 361-0746
FAX (626) 303-1277

Alasdair Boyd (213) 618-2643
boyd.locations.org

Kenny Brant (310) 871-8675
(Central, Northern and Southern California)

Laura Brown (310) 322-4499
(310) 592-1774

Michael J. Burmeister (818) 902-9646 (818) 400-4406
6540 Hayvenhurst Ave., Ste. 30 www.burmco.com
Lake Balboa, CA 91406

Jordan Burwick (310) 403-9332 (323) 668-1959
3908 Glenfeliz Blvd. www.jordanburwick.com
Los Angeles, CA 90039

California Location Scouting/ Ken Campbell (818) 503-0035
www.calocationscouting.com

Bruce Chudacoff (213) 300-4321 (310) 827-2660
FAX (310) 827-2660
(East Germany, PRC, United States & Zurich)

Cinemafloat (949) 675-8888 (714) 801-5553
1624 W. Oceanfront Walk FAX (949) 644-3073
Newport Beach, CA 92663
(Houses, Marine Locations & Piers)

Zack Clark (818) 642-7341
www.zclocations.com

Clean Wrap (310) 514-7579 (213) 530-8908
FAX (818) 507-5626
www.cleanwrap.biz

A **Club Ed** (661) 946-1515
42848 150th St. East FAX (661) 946-0454
Lancaster, CA 93535 www.avlocations.com
(Desert Landscapes)

Peter Cohn/ Solar Studios & Location Services (818) 240-1893 (310) 489-7801
1601 S. Central Ave. www.solarstudios.com
Glendale, CA 91204

Jack Constantine (818) 848-0826 (818) 445-2799
FAX (818) 235-0109
www.jackconstantine.com

Joni Coyote (626) 791-0087

Carey Crews (818) 986-9869 (818) 800-0913
3940 Laurel Canyon Blvd., Ste. 154
Studio City, CA 91604
www.locationcrews.smugmug.com

Steven Currie/Scout! (435) 645-5314 (310) 505-9342
FAX (435) 645-8036
www.scoututah.com

Rad Daly (818) 991-9466 (818) 203-9709
www.radscouting.com

Dennis Morgan Locations Inc. (818) 760-3876
FAX (866) 715-5545
www.dennismorganlocations.com
(Architectural Properties, Bar and Restaurant Locations, Castles, Churches, Coastal and Marine Locations, Colleges/Schools, Deserts, Estates, Houses, International Locations, Mountain Locations, Office Buildings, Retail Spaces, Stages & Warehouses)

Dennis Thomann Locations/ Digital Dennis (818) 780-8662
14942 Wyandotte St. FAX (818) 780-9617
Van Nuys, CA 91405 www.digitaldennis.com

Mark DeRobertis (626) 296-8655 (323) 697-7464
www.locationinvestigation.com

Scott Dewees (323) 666-6740 (310) 995-6740
www.scottdewees.com

Direct2 Locations (323) 766-1733
1105 S. Barrington Ave., Ste. 5 FAX (323) 372-3948
Los Angeles, CA 90049 www.direct2pro.com

Paul Dirks (818) 406-3433 (626) 394-3759

Clay Dodder (310) 315-1800 (310) 729-0665
FAX (310) 315-1831
www.clayscout.com

Wendy Donovan (323) 240-1188
www.wendydonovan.com

Tim Down (626) 437-7078 (626) 797-7124
2011 Glen Ave.
Pasadena, CA 91103

Robert Doyle (310) 394-0935

Dale Dreher (310) 600-5020
www.mavericklocations.com

Randall Duryea (310) 489-0547
www.nationscout.com

Jack R. English (323) 650-9850 (323) 219-4387
P.O. Box 2081
Beverly Hills, CA 90213

Albert Maximilian Epps (213) 479-7975
www.epps.locations.org

Liz Ervin (949) 362-0727 (949) 280-7695
www.encoredirectory.com

Thomas A. Farmer (310) 458-6025

David S. Ferdig (818) 398-3271
www.lunchwithdave.com

James J. Fitzpatrick (818) 506-8051
FAX (818) 506-1710

Chris Foels (818) 209-9787
FAX (310) 748-2232
www.creativescouts.com

Andrew Gardiner (323) 972-9624 (310) 371-7209
4450 W. 165th St. FAX (213) 341-0123
Lawndale, CA 90260 www.scout4locations.com

Jon Gentry (323) 908-3563 (917) 512-1751
www.imageevent.com/jongentry
(Architectural Properties, Bar and Restaurant Locations, Churches, Coastal and Marine Locations, Colleges/Schools, Deserts, Estates, Historic Properties, Houses, International Locations, Las Vegas Locations, Mountain Locations, Museums, Office Buildings & Retail Spaces)

Theo Gerike (484) 682-9010

Peter Gluck (323) 466-7722
www.petergluck.com

Marie-Paule Goislard (323) 661-0610 (213) 286-9192
(French) FAX (323) 644-1897
www.mpglocations.com

David T. Golden (310) 801-9899 (310) 837-9073
FAX (310) 837-4038
www.pixx.org

Bianca Gonzalez (805) 895-1325 (310) 474-3736

George Goodman (310) 213-5172

Jimmy Griffin (818) 681-1250
FAX (818) 891-9878

Bryan Grossmann (323) 228-5486
382 Havana Ave.
Long Beach, CA 90814

Cale Hanks (213) 500-7515
(323) 222-5144
FAX (323) 225-7726

Jof Hanwright/scout911 (310) 452-7660
www.scout911.com

Ronnie Haran Mellen (805) 969-2555
(805) 680-9595
2435 Sycamore Canyon Rd. FAX (805) 969-9595
Santa Barbara, CA 93108

Paul Hargrave (310) 397-2800
(310) 415-8870
FAX (310) 397-2867
www.paulhargrave.com

Howard Harnett (818) 841-4844
(818) 355-1891
FAX (818) 841-4817

Hart Brothers Livestock (951) 312-9009
(951) 677-6810
P.O. Box 514 FAX (951) 600-3805
Temecula, CA 92593
(Ranches)

Gahan Haskins (646) 567-9060
(917) 770-3223
www.riverboys.com

David Henriksen (818) 599-9823

George Herthel (310) 880-8208

Tom Holaday (213) 705-8500
(626) 798-9700

Ron Hugo (323) 876-6522
(323) 839-6047
www.ronhugo.com

Idaho Film Location Services (800) 783-1758
FAX (800) 783-1758
www.idaholocations.com

Inland Empire Film Commission (951) 779-6700
1201 Research Park Dr., Ste. 100 FAX (951) 779-0294
Riverside, CA 92507 www.filminlandempire.com
(Agriculture Properties, Airports, Bar and Restaurant Locations, Bridges, Casinos, Castles, Churches, Colleges/Schools, Deserts, Estates, Historic Properties, Houses, International Locations, Lakes, Mountain Locations, Museums, Office Buildings, Retail Spaces, Rivers, Riverside and San Bernardino Counties, Stages, Warehouses & Western Settings)

ITC Barricades, Inc. (714) 892-5858
(661) 816-6270
P.O. Box 858 FAX (714) 892-5887
Westminster, CA 92684 mysite.verizon.net/itcbarricades/
(Street Closures & Traffic Plans)

Jerry Jaffe (310) 403-4925
1603 Linden Ave. FAX (310) 270-4014
Venice, CA 90291 www.jerryjaffe.net

JCL Barricade Company (213) 622-9775
2334 E. Eighth St. FAX (213) 622-9790
Los Angeles, CA 90021 www.jclbarricade.com
(Street Closures & Traffic Plans)

John Richard Massengill Photography (831) 588-2572
(800) 330-3064
186 El Solyo Heights Dr. FAX (831) 335-8428
Felton, CA 95018 www.filminthesierras.com
(Architectural Properties, Bar and Restaurant Locations, Coastal and Marine Locations, Colleges/Schools, Deserts, Inyo and Mono Counties & Mountain Locations)

John A. Johnston (323) 461-9517
(323) 646-7226
2054 N. Argyle, Ste. 204
Los Angeles, CA 90068

Fred Jové/Locations Etcetera (661) 433-1138
(661) 269-2640
34505 Brock Ln.
Acton, CA 93510

Geoff Juckes/Location America (626) 791-3484
(626) 298-1900
www.locationamerica.com
(Aerials, Deserts, Mountain Locations, Remote Areas, Roads & Tropical Islands)

Stephen Kardell (310) 857-7844
FAX (562) 683-0409
www.stephenkardell.com

Larry Kelly (818) 620-4155
(818) 783-8050
FAX (818) 783-8051
www.larrykelly.tv

Halli Kristjansson (818) 281-9230
(818) 509-0526
12355½ Riverside Dr.
North Hollywood, CA 91607

La Classe Locations, Inc. (323) 660-9100
(323) 660-9003
2395 Silver Lake Blvd., Ste. 11 www.locationnetwork.com
Los Angeles, CA 90039

Simon Lampard (310) 455-2203
(310) 963-2203
FAX (310) 455-1393
www.lampardlocations.com

Nancy Lazarus (213) 500-7000
www.lazaruslocations.com

Greg Lazzaro (310) 850-2249
www.greglazzaro.com

Location Association/Bob Heberly (213) 507-4640
3206 Wyoming Ave. www.locationassociation.com
Burbank, CA 91505

The Location Connection, Inc. (310) 376-9797
(818) 422-8127
Raleigh Studios Manhattan Beach FAX (310) 376-9796
1600 Rosecrans Ave. www.locationconnection.com
Bldg. Five, Second Fl.
Manhattan Beach, CA 90266
(Coachella Valley, Los Angeles, Malibu, Orange County, San Fernando Valley & South Bay)

Location Network/Geoff White (323) 660-9100
(818) 426-2600
2395 Silver Lake Blvd., Ste. 11 FAX (323) 660-9003
Los Angeles, CA 90039 www.locationnetwork.com

Scott Allen Logan (310) 571-1555
(310) 433-0337
c/o Loganfilm, Inc., P.O. Box 825 FAX (310) 571-1556
Santa Monica, CA 90406 www.loganfilm.com

Long Beach Locations (562) 951-0306
(562) 900-1928
245 W. Broadway, Ste.190 FAX (562) 951-0347
Long Beach, CA 90802 www.lblocations.com

Lorin Miller Locations (916) 600-8442
(530) 888-6625
2525 Vineyard Dr.
Auburn, CA 95603

Bill Lose (310) 386-9919

Charlie Love (323) 646-7826

John C. Lowe (818) 355-5602
FAX (615) 410-7599
www.creativescouts.com

Melissa MacCracken (310) 344-3080
86 Dapplegray Ln.
Palos Verdes, CA 90274

Jim Maceo (626) 398-3000
(818) 424-4577
FAX (626) 398-6557

Flint Maloney (323) 254-3715
www.flintman.com

Nik Mansoor (818) 822-9292

Marbles (323) 472-5659
7510 W. Sunset Blvd., Ste. 230
Hollywood, CA 90046

Edward Mazurek (310) 980-4142
(310) 936-4606
1320 Pico Blvd., Ste. D
Santa Monica, CA 90406
www.3dlocations.com

Jim McCabe (310) 514-8776
(818) 414-5185

David McKinney (310) 990-9404
(310) 534-3463
www.prophotoscout.com

Beth Melnick (310) 779-5683
(503) 281-4741
northlight.locations.org

Robert Mendel/Location Scouting (213) 591-0510
www.mendel.locations.org

Michael N. Marks, Inc. (310) 306-1355
(310) 600-3011
7352 Trask Ave.
Playa del Rey, CA 90293
FAX (310) 821-5506

Miles of Files/Bianca Gonzalez (805) 895-1325
817 Kentia Ave.
Santa Barbara, CA 93101
(Santa Barbara; Spanish Speaking)

Aaron Millar (310) 278-8957
(310) 780-3547
FAX (310) 278-8957
www.aaronmillar.com

Barbara Miller (213) 393-5555
(626) 356-9913
www.millerlocations.com
(Domestic and International Locations)

David Moate/Reconnoitre (626) 794-8552

Mojave Production Services/ Jim Wheelan (760) 559-6983
FAX (818) 884-6858
(Mojave, Western Arizona and Western Nevada Deserts)

Judy Montgomery (323) 377-2336

Dennis Morley (310) 963-9400
FAX (323) 660-8997
www.dennismorley.com

Nick Morley (323) 848-7762
(213) 716-4298
FAX (323) 210-7153

Jeff Morris/LA Scout Planet (213) 798-7676
(661) 254-8650
24307 Magic Mtn. Pkwy, Box 46
Santa Clarita, CA 91355
FAX (661) 254-2853
www.lascoutplanet.com
(Architectural Properties, Bar and Restaurant Locations, Castles, Churches, Coastal and Marine Locations, Colleges/ Schools, Deserts, Estates, Historic Properties, Houses, Mountain Locations, Museums, Office Buildings, Roads and Highways, Street Closures & Warehouses)

David Nakata (818) 355-5517
www.creativescouts.com

Keith Nakata (323) 653-0455
811 N. Croft Ave.
Los Angeles, CA 90069
FAX (323) 653-6077

Galidan Nauber (213) 705-3212

Michael Neale (818) 994-1870
(818) 371-2300
FAX (818) 989-4561

Jeff Nelson (323) 461-5755
web.me.com/jeffdn/jeff_nelson_scout
(Architectural Properties, Bar and Restaurant Locations, Coastal and Marine Locations, Deserts, Houses, International Locations & Mountain Locations)

Elizabeth Nicole (323) 937-1010
www.zenobia.com

Kevin Noonan (310) 251-6880

Pacific Production Services, Inc. (323) 465-9179
(213) 360-7844
6513 Hollywood Blvd., Ste 214
Los Angeles, CA 90028
FAX (323) 465-9869
www.lafilmpermits.com
(Street Closures & Traffic Plans)

Michael Paolillo (310) 493-1671

Parlay Productions (310) 733-4430
(310) 270-7526
8500 Steller Dr., Bldg. 8
Culver City, CA 90232
FAX (310) 733-4439
www.parlayproductions.com

Pat Parrish (310) 652-5585
(310) 291-6618
8642 Gregory Way
Los Angeles, CA 90035
www.scout4ads.com

Marino Pascal (323) 254-9272
www.locationscout.com

Premier Events & Locations, LLC (805) 886-3495
P.O. Box 30917
Santa Barbara, CA 93105
FAX (805) 692-2685
www.pe-sb.com
(Architectural Properties, Bar and Restaurant Locations, Churches, Coastal and Marine Locations, Estates, Houses, International Locations, Mountain Locations, Office Buildings, Stages & Warehouses)

Reel World Locations (310) 498-8775
FAX (661) 296-3147
www.reelworldlocations.com

Osceola Refetoff/ Red Eye Productions (323) 465-5558
859 N. Las Palmas Ave.
Los Angeles, CA 90038
(International and Domestic Locations)

Will Regan (626) 441-8066
(626) 827-9800
FAX (626) 263-7630
www.willscout.com

Errol Reichow (805) 404-7871
FAX (818) 707-1940

Patrick Reinoso (818) 606-3081
(818) 883-3081
(Architectural Properties, Castles, Coastal and Marine Locations, Deserts, Historic Properties, International Locations, Mountain Locations, Office Buildings & Stages in Arizona, California, Nevada and Utah)

Renaissance Locations/ Paul Kruhm & Richard Latarewicz (310) 779-6221
(310) 466-0485
P.O. Box 66663 FAX (212) 859-7344
Los Angeles, CA 90066 www.renaissancelocations.com

Richard Muessel Company (310) 245-1990
7336 Santa Monica Blvd., Ste. 762 FAX (323) 512-5374
Los Angeles, CA 90046

Greg Robinson (562) 420-2276
(213) 895-8105
FAX (562) 420-2276

Santiago Romeo (818) 254-7110
(310) 666-5012
FAX (626) 380-1617

Gregg Ross (626) 398-8777
(818) 418-2993
FAX (626) 398-8779
www.greggross.com

Albie Salsich (310) 930-3620
(310) 446-6268

William Sandidge (323) 864-5530
(323) 662-2454
sandidge.locations.org

Santa Barbara Location Services/ aka Location Production Coordination (805) 969-5555
(805) 565-1562
1805 E. Cabrillo Blvd., Ste. B FAX (805) 969-9595
Santa Barbara, CA 93108 www.santabarbara-locations.com
(Ojai, San Luis Obispo, Santa Barbara, Santa Ynez Valley & Ventura)

The Scoutmaster/Jerry Tomson (310) 545-0290
1716 The Strand
Manhattan Beach, CA 90266

John Shaughnessy (818) 512-1658
www.creativescouts.com

Adam Silver (213) 709-8273
www.globallocationscouting.com

Skyline Locations (213) 689-0655
350 S. Grand Ave., Ste. 2240 FAX (213) 629-0733
Los Angeles, CA 90071 www.skylinelocations.com

Carol Smith (626) 437-3060
(626) 395-9574

Jeff Smith (310) 617-9147
(323) 876-5240
www.witsendlocations.com

Maria Smith (323) 937-1010
www.zenobia.com

Sharon Smith-Herring (310) 926-3700
(310) 372-1901
www.lagirlscout.com

Susan Snyder/Amazing Locations (310) 470-2208
(310) 570-0047
2023 Manning Ave. FAX (310) 559-5587
West Los Angeles, CA 90025

Gregory M. Strait (805) 955-9437
(323) 630-7824

Stuart Raven Barter & Associates (323) 931-2177
5576 W. First St. www.srba.com
Los Angeles, CA 90036

Sunset Locations, Inc. (310) 360-1306
8730 Sunset Blvd., Ste. 485 FAX (310) 360-1362
West Hollywood, CA 90069 www.sunsetlocations.com

Beth Tate/Location Access (310) 396-0305
www.btatelocations.com

Team Halprin, Inc. (310) 842-7000
9190 W. Olympic Blvd., Ste. 304 FAX (310) 842-7014
Beverly Hills, CA 90212 www.teamhalprin.com

Russ Thomas (818) 437-2560
(818) 753-8117
www.russfoundit.com

Danny Thomsen (626) 419-7766
www.dtlocations.com

Tom Lackey, Scott Bigbee & Associates (310) 395-8817
(310) 613-7322
FAX (310) 395-8817

Traffic Management, Inc. (562) 595-4278
2435 Lemon Ave. FAX (562) 424-0266
Signal Hill, CA 90755 www.trafficmanagement.com
(Street Closures & Traffic/Pedestrian Control)

Scott Trimble (310) 528-1241
(323) 372-4419
FAX (310) 362-8920
www.ststp.com

Vertical Adventures (949) 854-6250
(800) 514-8785
P.O. Box 7548 FAX (949) 854-5249
Newport Beach, CA 92658
(Deserts & Mountains)

Vincent Vanni (310) 713-8084
FAX (866) 227-7589
www.creativescouts.com

Capt. Troy Waters (310) 713-9193
(Coastal, Harbor and Marine Locations) FAX (310) 943-3328

West Coast Film Locations (310) 871-8675
P.O. Box 5720 FAX (661) 724-8808
Lancaster, CA 93539
(Antelope Valley)

Willie's On & Off Road Center (760) 257-3734
(760) 953-3303
48301 National Trails Hwy FAX (760) 257-3335
Newberry Springs, CA 92365 www.williesoffroad.com

Mel Wilson (213) 591-0719
(323) 936-3666
FAX (323) 936-3264
wilson.locations.org

Frank Yoshikane (714) 273-3103
FAX (866) 295-4599

Mark Zekanis (805) 512-4161
(805) 237-2356
FAX (805) 237-2356

Zenobia Agency, Inc. (323) 937-1010
(888) 639-6917
130 S. Highland Ave. FAX (323) 937-1133
Los Angeles, CA 90036 www.zenobia.com
(Reps for Location Managers and Scouts)

30th Street Garage (619) 234-4325
3335 30th St. FAX (619) 234-2055
San Diego, CA 92104 www.30thstreetgarage.com

9900 Club (310) 550-8444
9900 S. Santa Monica Blvd. FAX (310) 550-5969
Beverly Hills, CA 90212 www.thefriarsbh.com

Agua Dulce Movie Ranch (661) 251-2365
(661) 510-6958
34855 Petersen Rd. FAX (661) 268-7680
Agua Dulce, CA 91390 www.sosfilmworks.com

Andresen's Rancho Rosita (805) 491-3242
www.ranchorosita.com

Auto Club Speedway (909) 429-5000
Contact: Phil Tucker FAX (909) 429-5500
www.autoclubspeedway.com

Bella Vista Stable (818) 353-2161
10616 McBroom St.
Sunland, CA 91040

Bony Pony Ranch (310) 275-1075
12555 Yerba Buena Rd. FAX (310) 246-5725
Malibu, CA 90265 www.bonyponyranch.com

Bothwell Ranch (818) 347-9000
5300 Oakdale Ave. FAX (818) 587-9215
Woodland Hills, CA 91364

BPR Investment (818) 347-4434
7050 Valjean Ave. FAX (818) 347-7565
Van Nuys, CA 91406

Bridges Auditorium (909) 607-8580
450 N. College Way www.cuc.claremont.edu/bridges
Claremont, CA 91711

Canyon Ranch (805) 371-0097
(661) 803-2948
368 E. Carlisle Rd. FAX (805) 371-0091
West Lake Village, CA 91361
www.canyonranchfilmlocation.com

Caravan West Productions (661) 268-8300
35660 Jayhawker Rd. FAX (661) 268-8301
Agua Dulce, CA 91390 www.caravanwest.com

Chic Little Devil Style House (310) 403-6929
1206 Maple Ave., 11th Fl.
Los Angeles, CA 90015
www.chiclittledevilstylehouse.com

Cinespace (323) 817-3456
FAX (323) 860-9794
www.cinespace.info

City Loft (818) 613-5962
1275 E. Sixth St. davidberechet9822.sitewelder.com
Los Angeles, CA 90021

Cojo - Jalama Ranch (805) 736-7300
P.O. Box 1177 FAX (805) 736-8084
Lompoc, CA 93438 www.cojoranch.com

Cypress Sea Cove (310) 589-3344
33572 Pacific Coast Hwy FAX (310) 589-3343
Malibu, CA 90265 www.malibufilmlocations.com

Dance Studio No. 1 (310) 235-2193
2037 Granville Ave. www.danceno1.com
Los Angeles, CA 90025

Disney Ice (714) 535-7465
300 W. Lincoln Ave. FAX (714) 518-3220
Anaheim, CA 92805 www.anaheimice.com

Dry Gulch Ranch - Malibu (310) 457-3807
(310) 589-8311
12420 Yellow Hill Rd. FAX (310) 457-3807
Malibu, CA 90265 www.drygulchranch.com

Dusty Oak Ranch (818) 991-0714
(805) 495-3162
670 E. Carlisle Canyon Rd.
Westlake Village, CA 91361

Ebony Repertory Theatre @ The Nate Holden (323) 964-9768
4718 W. Washington Blvd. www.ebonyrep.org
Los Angeles, CA 90016

El Campeon Farms/ Windy Hill Ranch (805) 497-2766
(805) 732-9163
999 Potrero Rd. FAX (805) 497-0377
Thousand Oaks, CA 91361 www.elcampeonfarms.com

El Capitan Theatre & Entertainment Centre (323) 467-7674
(818) 516-3092
6838 Hollywood Blvd. FAX (323) 467-0922
Los Angeles, CA 90028 www.elcapitantickets.com

Epicenter Stadium - City of Rancho Cucamonga (909) 477-2760
10500 Civic Center Dr. FAX (909) 477-2761
Rancho Cucamonga, CA 91730 www.rcepicenter.com

Esprit (310) 305-3700
13900 Marquesas Way FAX **(310) 305-1743**
Marina del Rey, CA 90292 **www.espritmdr.com**

Fairplex (909) 865-4042
(909) 865-4041
1101 W. Mckinley Ave. FAX **(909) 623-9599**
Pomona, CA 91768 **www.fairplex.com**

The Forum (310) 330-7300
3900 W. Manchester Blvd. **www.thelaforum.com**
Inglewood, CA 90305
Contact: Devon Mackey

Gallery 1018 (310) 923-0660
(310) 295-1620
1018 S. Santa Fe Ave. **www.gallery1018.com**
Los Angeles, CA 90021

Gallery de Soto (323) 253-2255
108 W. Second St., Ste. 104 **www.gallerydesoto.com**
Los Angeles, CA 90012

Goathouse and TTS Studios (818) 982-9872
7303 Ethel Ave. FAX **(818) 982-9199**
North Hollywood, CA 91605 **www.ttsloft.com**
(Loft & Stage)

Gold Creek Ranch (818) 542-9355
8807 Gold Creek Rd. **www.goldcreekranch.com**
Lake View Terrace, CA 91342

Goldspirit Farm (818) 834-1272
12682 Kagel Canyon Rd. FAX **(818) 834-1902**
San Fernando, CA 91342 **www.goldspiritfarm.com**

Greek Theatre (323) 665-5857
2700 N. Vermont Ave. FAX **(323) 666-8202**
Los Angeles, CA 90027 **www.nederlander.com**

Hart Brothers Livestock (951) 312-9009
(951) 677-6810
P.O. Box 514 FAX **(951) 600-3805**
Temecula, CA 92593

Hollywood Park (310) 330-7248
Box 369 FAX **(310) 673-6278**
Inglewood, CA 90306 **www.hollywoodpark.com**
Contact: Deann Fruhling

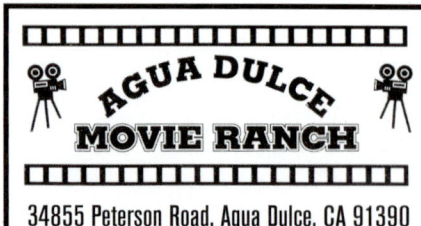

Hollywood Production Center (818) 480-3100
121 W. Lexington Dr. FAX **(818) 480-3199**
Glendale, CA 91203 **www.hollywoodpc.com**

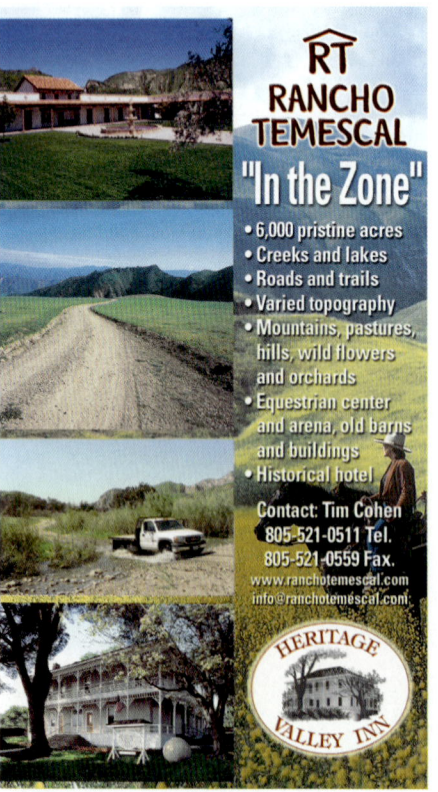

Honda Center (714) 704-2422
2695 E. Katella Ave. FAX (714) 704-2610
Anaheim, CA 92806 www.arrowheadpond.com
Contact: Jo-Ann Armstrong

House of Blues (323) 848-5193
(323) 848-5100
8430 Sunset Blvd. www.hob.com
West Hollywood, CA 90069
Contact: Maureen McGrath

Hummingbird Nest Ranch (805) 579-8000
2940 Kuehner Dr. FAX (805) 583-1527
Simi Valley, CA 93063 www.hummingbirdnestranch.com

The Huntington Library, Art Collections and Botanical Gardens (626) 405-2215
www.filmhuntington.org

Huron SubStation (323) 225-8909
(323) 251-4155
2640 Huron St. FAX (323) 225-8909
Los Angeles, CA 90065 www.huronsubstation.com

Ice Chalet (310) 541-6630
550 Deep Valley Dr. FAX (310) 541-8674
Avenue of the Peninsula Mall www.pvicechalet.com
Rolling Hills Estates, CA 90274

Inner-City Arts Campus (213) 627-9621
720 Kohler St. FAX (213) 627-6469
Los Angeles, CA 90021
www.inner-cityarts.org/images.html

A **JMJ Ranch** (805) 497-3018
930 W. Potrero Rd. FAX (805) 497-2122
Thousand Oaks, CA 91361 www.jmjranch.com

Jody Domingue Studios (323) 467-0098
(818) 577-9737
5770 Melrose Ave., Ste. 204
Los Angeles, CA 90038
www.jodydominguestudios.com

La Mirada Theatre for the Performing Arts (714) 994-6310
(562) 944-9801
14900 La Mirada Blvd. FAX (714) 994-5796
La Mirada, CA 90638 www.lamiradatheatre.com
Contact: Laura Moore

LA Music Center (213) 972-7211
(213) 972-3335
Contact: John Vassiliou www.musiccenter.org

Lane Ranch & Company (661) 942-0435
42220 10th St. West, Ste. 101 FAX (661) 942-7485
Lancaster, CA 93534 www.laneranch.net
(Desert Landscape)

Limoneira Orchards (866) 242-1828
1141 Cummings Rd. FAX (805) 525-8211
Santa Paula, CA 93060 www.limoneiraorchards.com

Los Angeles County Metropolitan Transportation Authority (Metro) (213) 922-5616
One Gateway Plaza FAX (213) 922-5654
Los Angeles, CA 90012 www.metro.net

M.J. Higgins (213) 247-0142
www.mjhiggins.com

Mid-Century Modern House (310) 274-7440
FAX (310) 274-9809
www.simonhousela.com

A **National Aerospace Training and Research Center/NASTAR** (866) 482-0933
Contact: Brienna Henwood www.nastarcenter.com

The Newhall Mansion at Piru (805) 625-3309
(805) 521-0866
829 N. Park St., P.O. Box 26 www.pirumansion.com
Piru, CA 93040

Oasis Locations (213) 553-9144
(213) 891-9030
940 S. Hill St., Ste. E FAX (213) 553-9145
Los Angeles, CA 90015 www.oasislocations.com

The Old Globe (619) 231-1941
(619) 234-5623
1363 Old Globe Way FAX (619) 231-9518
San Diego, CA 92101 www.theoldglobe.org
Contact: Debbie Ballard

Orpheum Theatre (877) 677-4386
(213) 626-5321
842 S. Broadway www.laorpheum.com
Los Angeles, CA 90014
Contact: Steve Needleman

Pacific Earth Resources/ Rogers Ranch (805) 987-8456
(800) 942-5296
305 W. Hueneme Rd. FAX (805) 986-5210
Camarillo, CA 93012 www.pacificearth.com

Paddison Farm (562) 863-4567 / (562) 972-4126
11951 E. Imperial Hwy
Norwalk, CA 90650
www.paddisonfarm.com

Paramount Ranch Locations (805) 530-1967
8800 Grimes Canyon Rd.
Moorpark, CA 93021
Contact: Lisa Francey
FAX (805) 523-1903
www.movielocationsca.com

The Studios at Paramount (323) 956-8811
The Studios at Paramount
New York Streets
5555 Melrose Ave.
Hollywood, CA 90038
www.thestudiosatparamount.com

Pier 59 Studios West (310) 829-5959
2415 Michigan Ave.
Santa Monica, CA 90404
FAX (310) 829-9550
www.pier59studioswest.com

The Polsa Rosa Ranch (661) 257-3456
www.polsarosa.com

Ⓐ **Rancho Temescal** (805) 521-0511 / (805) 889-1114
P.O. Box 378
Piru, CA 93040
FAX (805) 521-0559
www.ranchotemescal.com

RecCenter Studio (213) 413-9300 / (323) 868-4226
1161 Logan St.
Los Angeles, CA 90026
FAX (213) 413-9301
www.reccenterstudio.com

REDCAT (213) 237-2810
631 W. Second St.
Los Angeles, CA 90012
FAX (213) 237-2811
www.redcat.org

Renberg Theatre (323) 860-7336
The Village at Ed Gould Plaza
1125 N. McCadden Pl.
Los Angeles, CA 90038
FAX (323) 308-4103
www.lagaycenter.org

Riley's Farm & Apple Orchard (909) 797-7534 / (909) 790-8463
12261 Oak Glen Rd.
Oak Glen, CA 92399
FAX (909) 797-4524
www.rileysfarm.com

The Rockin' Horse Ranch (661) 268-0096 / (310) 961-1666
11837 Cardeene Rd.
Agua Dulce, CA 91390
www.therockinhorseranch.net

Rose Bowl (626) 577-3130 / (626) 577-3206
1001 Rose Bowl Dr.
Pasadena, CA 91103
Contacts: Julie Granillo & Erika Samarzich
FAX (626) 405-0992
www.rosebowlstadium.com

Santa Anita Park (626) 574-6373
285 W. Huntington Dr.
Arcadia, CA 91007
Contact: Pete Siberell
FAX (626) 821-1530
www.santaanita.com

Santa Monica Fitness & Office Space (310) 453-9604
3201 Santa Monica Blvd.
Santa Monica, CA 90404
www.loopnet.com/xnet/mainsite/listing/profile/profile.aspx?lid=15647821

SC Village (949) 489-9000 / (562) 867-9600
8900 McCarty Rd.
Chino, CA 91710
(Paintball Park)
FAX (562) 804-1514
www.scvillage.com

The Shrine Auditorium (213) 748-5116
649 W. Jefferson Blvd.
Los Angeles, CA 90007
FAX (213) 742-9922
www.shrineauditorium.com

Sky Drops Inc. (818) 633-2639
999 N. Mission Rd.
Los Angeles, CA 90033
www.skydrops.com

Solar Studios (818) 240-1893 / (310) 489-7801
1601 S. Central Ave.
Glendale, CA 91204
FAX (818) 242-1691
www.solarstudios.com

The Solomon Loft (626) 388-8342
www.filmdowntown.com

Staples Center (213) 742-7100
1111 S. Figueroa St.
Los Angeles, CA 90015
www.staplescenter.com

Studio 528, LLC (310) 428-6464
453 S. Spring St., Ste. 528
Los Angeles, CA 90013
www.studio528.com

Summit (818) 909-7933 / (818) 458-4495

Teatro Theater (310) 312-9772 / (310) 346-1649
626 Oxnard Blvd.
Oxnard, CA 93030
www.futurelighting.net

Tejon Ranch (661) 248-6890 / (661) 203-6261
4436 Lebec Rd., P.O. Box 1000
Lebec, CA 93243
FAX (661) 248-6773
www.tejonfilm.com

Tierra Rejada Ranch (805) 529-1766
15191 Read Rd.
Moorpark, CA 93021
FAX (805) 529-1470

Universal Studios Hollywood Theme Park (818) 622-6836
FAX (818) 622-0407
www.universalstudios.com/laps

Vasa Park (818) 889-3336 / (818) 889-2224
2854 Triunfo Canyon Rd.
Agoura Hills, CA 91301
FAX (818) 889-2416
www.vasa-park.com

Veluzat Motion Picture Ranch (661) 259-9669
P.O. Box 220597
Newhall, CA 91322
FAX (661) 259-3788
www.melodyranchstudio.com

Ventura Farms (805) 496-0767
235 W. Potrero Rd.
Thousand Oaks, CA 91361
www.venturafarms.com

Villa Malibu Luxury Rentals (310) 457-8484 / (310) 266-8126
6487 Cavalleri Rd., Ste. 224
Malibu, CA 90265
www.villamalibuliving.com

Ⓐ **Westfield, LLC** (818) 227-5507 / (310) 892-0043
6600 Topanga Canyon Blvd., Ste. 1M
Canoga Park, CA 91304
(Multiple Locations)
FAX (818) 999-0878
www.westfield.com

Westside Loft & Art Studio/ Spanish Style Home (310) 822-4504
3918 Alla Rd.
Los Angeles, CA 90066
FAX (310) 822-4504
www.amadeabailey.com

Willow Studios (213) 625-5771 / (310) 849-5452
1333-1335 Willow St.
Los Angeles, CA 90013
FAX (213) 625-0101
www.willowstudios.net

Winnetka Ranch (619) 468-9127
P.O. Box 915
Jamul, CA 91935
FAX (619) 468-9128
www.winnetkaranch.com

Writers Guild Theater (323) 782-4525
135 S. Doheny Dr.
Beverly Hills, CA 90211
Contact: Emal Nessary
www.wga.org

5 Star Motorhomes (800) 575-1710
FAX (626) 307-9100
www.5starmotorhomes.com

5th & Sunset Los Angeles (310) 979-0212
12322 Exposition Blvd. FAX (310) 979-0214
Los Angeles, CA 90064 www.5thandsunsetla.com

A-1 Portables (760) 949-4111
(800) 554-7723
17491 Lilac St. FAX (760) 949-4224
Hesperia, CA 92345
(Motorhomes & VIP Restrooms)

Action USA Production Vehicle Rental (805) 428-3744
(877) 428-7070
65 W. Easy St., Ste. 107 FAX (805) 522-0390
Simi Valley, CA 93065
www.usarv.us/production_vehicles.html

Action! Motorhome Rentals, Inc. (323) 712-7709
(562) 556-5008
FAX (562) 695-9060
www.actionmotorhomerentals.com

Action/Restroom Rentals (562) 595-7200
FAX (562) 595-7210
www.actionsiteservices.net
(Honeywagons, Portable Restrooms, Portable Toilets & V.I.P. Restrooms)

Adriana's Star Services, Inc. (310) 925-0967
(888) 527-7381
2542 Norte Vista Dr. FAX (909) 628-7708
Chino Hills, CA 91709 www.adrianastar.com

Al's Production Trailers (760) 373-5771
(805) 490-4399
P.O. Box 2442 FAX (760) 373-5771
California City, CA 93504 www.pridept.com
(Production Trailers)

All Day And Knight (818) 262-6568
(818) 262-3467
9536 Rudnick Ave. FAX (818) 341-6660
Chatsworth, CA 91311

Aloha Studio Rentals (661) 993-5393
30402 Clover Court FAX (661) 554-5497
Castaic, CA 91384 www.alohastudiorentals.com

America Traveler Studio Rentals (661) 273-7479
412 W. Sierra Hwy FAX (661) 273-1579
Acton, CA 93510 www.americatravelerinc.com

Andy Gump, Inc. (661) 251-7721
(800) 992-7755
26954 Ruether Ave. FAX (661) 251-7729
Santa Clarita, CA 91351 www.andygump.com
(Portable Toilets, Restrooms & Shower Trailers)

Apache Rental Group (818) 842-9944
(818) 842-9875
3910 W. Magnolia Blvd. FAX (818) 842-9269
Burbank, CA 91505 www.apacherentalgroup.com
(Motorhomes)

Base Camp Mobile Offices (818) 352-5750
1317 N. San Fernando Blvd., Ste. 503 FAX (818) 352-5750
Burbank, CA 91504

BBL Mobile, Inc. (800) 848-4140
(Honeywagons & Makeup Trailers) FAX (805) 241-8793
www.bblmobile.com

Bertrand Enterprises (760) 446-6600
1210 Graaf Ave. FAX (760) 446-2669
Ridgecrest, CA 93555
(Motorhomes)

Best Studio Rentals, Inc. (818) 441-4770
FAX (636) 327-3302

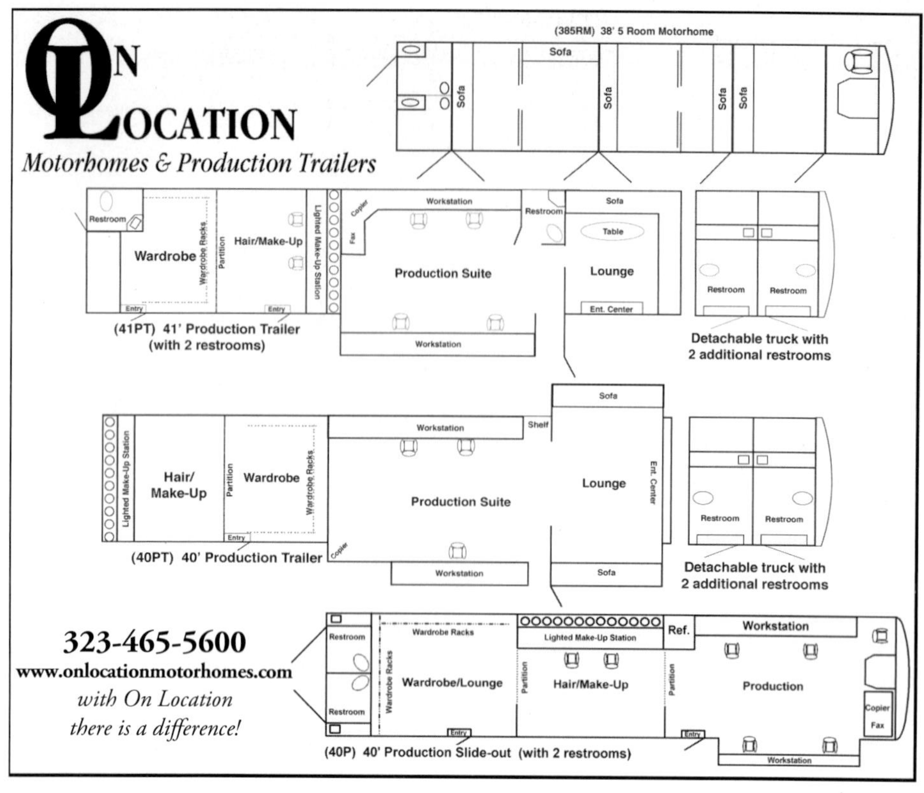

ON LOCATION
Motorhomes & Production Trailers
(385RM) 38' 5 Room Motorhome
(41PT) 41' Production Trailer
(with 2 restrooms)
Detachable truck with
2 additional restrooms
(40PT) 40' Production Trailer
Detachable truck with
2 additional restrooms
323-465-5600
www.onlocationmotorhomes.com
with On Location
there is a difference!
(40P) 40' Production Slide-out (with 2 restrooms)

Bill's Motorhome Rentals (818) 767-1481 (818) 219-6162
9555 Via Ricardo FAX **(818) 767-2814**
Burbank, CA 91504 **www.billsmotorhomes.com**

Blue Sky Production Equipment (818) 591-1761 (818) 253-6152
25734 Punto De Vista Dr.
Calabasas, CA 91302
www.blueskyproductionequipment.com

Bob's Production Trailers (661) 256-2991 (661) 406-2325
2200 Monje St. **www.bobspt.com**
Rosamond, CA 93560
(Motorhomes & Production Trailers)

Buboosky Production Vehicles (661) 993-9022 (661) 510-7650
FAX **(661) 513-9776**
www.buboosky.com

Century Studio Corporation (310) 287-3600 (888) 878-2437
8660 Hayden Pl., Ste. 100 FAX **(310) 287-3608**
Culver City, CA 90232 **www.centurystudio.com**
(Trailers)

Characters on Wheels (909) 393-6575 (310) 650-7046
15506 Dupont Ave. FAX **(909) 393-6275**
Chino, CA 91710 **www.stardeckrvs.com**

Chloe Enterprises, Inc. (818) 765-6500
3111 N. Kenwood St. FAX **(818) 765-2891**
Burbank, CA 91505
(Honeywagons)

Cinewagon, LLC (818) 822-0786 (818) 534-6402
P.O. Box 573511 FAX **(818) 881-4410**
Tarzana, CA 91357 **www.cinewagon.com**

Diamond Environmental Services, LLC (888) 744-7191
630 S. Hathaway FAX **(760) 290-3338**
Santa Ana, CA 92705 **www.diamondprovides.com**
(Honeywagons, Makeup Trailers, Mobile Offices, Motorhomes, Portable Restrooms, Portable Toilets, Shower Trailers, Star Trailers & V.I.P. Restrooms)

dk Coaches (661) 296-2232
29119 Mission Trail Ln.
Valencia, CA 91354

Eagle Portables Inc. (310) 955-7697
P.O. Box 1684 FAX **(866) 650-8205**
Lynwood, CA 90262 **www.eagleportables.com**
(Portable Restrooms & Portable Toilets)

Easy Rider Productions, Inc. (818) 822-8782 (877) 982-3279
P.O. Box 222034 FAX **(661) 288-1958**
Newhall, CA 91322 **www.easyriderprod.com**

El Monte RV (800) 337-2150 (562) 483-4983
12061 E. Valley Blvd. FAX **(626) 448-5836**
El Monte, CA 91732 **www.elmonterv.com/studio**
(Honeywagons, Makeup Trailers, Motorhomes, Star Trailers & Wardrobe Trailers)

Elliott Location Equipment (310) 915-1744 (505) 328-0909
www.elliottlocationequipment.com
(Honeywagons, Makeup Trailers, Mobile Offices, Production Trailers, Star Trailers, V.I.P. Restrooms & Wardrobe Trailers)

Euro-One Productions (323) 273-8638 (323) 255-2855
P.O. Box 1993 FAX **(323) 255-2855**
Los Angeles, CA 90078 **www.euro-one.net**
(Mobile Office/Dressing Room)

Frank's 5 Rooms (661) 298-7851 (818) 822-9474
16715 Gazeley St.
Santa Clarita, CA 91351
(Honeywagons, Motorhomes & Trailers)

Genie Production Vehicles (323) 447-0622 / (909) 917-9859
12188 Central Ave., Ste. 195 FAX (909) 591-2045
Chino, CA 91710 www.geniepv.com
(Makeup Trailers, Mobile Offices, Motorhomes, Portable Toilets, Production Trailers, Star Trailers & Wardrobe Trailers)

Holiday Studio Rentals (818) 252-7770 / (888) 466-8436
11473 Penrose St. FAX (818) 252-7723
Sun Valley, CA 91352 www.holidaysr.com

Hollywood Honeywagon & Production Vehicles (818) 763-1966 / (818) 535-9648
11160 Victory Blvd. FAX (818) 760-0551
North Hollywood, CA 91606
www.hollywoodhoneywagon.com
(Honeywagons, Makeup and Wardrobe Trailers, Motorhomes, Portable Restroom Units & Production Trailers)

Independent Honeywagon Rentals (520) 906-5761 / (818) 262-4432

King Kong Production Vehicles (323) 462-6646 / (949) 673-1999
FAX (949) 673-3993
www.kingkongtrailers.com
(Honeywagons, Makeup Trailers, Mobile Offices, Motorhomes, Portable Restrooms, Portable Toilets, Production Trailers, Shower Trailers, Star Trailers, V.I.P. Restrooms & Wardrobe Trailers)

Kohler Rental (310) 518-5118 / (866) 577-4797
1581 W. Wardlow Rd. FAX (310) 518-5028
Long Beach, CA 90810 www.kohlerrental.com
(Portable Restrooms)

LBS Rentals (818) 768-6170 / (818) 652-5784
11323 Sheldon St. FAX (818) 768-6079
Sun Valley, CA 91352 www.lbsrentals.com

Line 204 (323) 960-0113
1034 N. Seward St. FAX (323) 960-0163
Hollywood, CA 90038 www.line204.com

Mike Green RV's (818) 317-7099 / (541) 619-3934
24401 Valle del Oro, Ste. 201 FAX (323) 927-1546
Newhall, CA 91321 www.mikegreenrv.com
(Motorhomes, Portable Restrooms, Portable Toilets & V.I.P. Restrooms)

Mobile Base Camps/ Walter Moseneder (951) 694-0538
27499 Sierra Madre Dr. FAX (951) 346-4103
Murrieta, CA 92563 www.naturebase.com

Moe's Motorhome (805) 526-9252 / (805) 794-2500
2465 Pinewood Pl. www.moesmotorhome.com
Simi Valley, CA 93065

Moho to Go/MTG Trailers/ Beth Schroeder (424) 289-8174 / (562) 572-1565
10966 Westwood Blvd. FAX (424) 289-8174
Culver City, CA 90230 www.mtgtrailers.com

Motionpv (714) 454-6249
www.motionpv.com

Movie Movers Transportation Equipment (818) 252-7722 / (276) 650-3378
11473 Penrose St. FAX (818) 252-7723
Sun Valley, CA 91352 www.moviemovers.com

N.W. Production Services & RV Rental (800) 260-6646 / (949) 212-9735
190 Avenida La Cuesta FAX (949) 361-2836
San Clemente, CA 92672 www.nwproduction.com

A New Adventure, Inc. (818) 768-5899 / (805) 584-0232
3162 Anderson Dr. FAX (805) 584-0863
Simi Valley, CA 93065 www.anewadventure.com
(Makeup Trailers, Mobile Offices, Motorhomes, Shower Trailers, Star Trailers & Wardrobe Trailers)

No Boundary Productions (305) 491-2433 / (619) 981-0508
www.nbpro.biz

A **On Location Motorhomes** (323) 465-5600
P.O. Box 3087 FAX (909) 394-7423
San Dimas, CA 91773 www.onlocationmotorhomes.com
(Honeywagons, Makeup Trailers, Mobile Offices, Motorhomes, Portable Restrooms, Production Trailers, Star Trailers & Wardrobe Trailers)

Optimum Industries Inc. (909) 917-3913 / (909) 899-5756

Premiere Transportation (888) 771-0588
FAX (615) 261-2108
www.myluxurybus.com
(Makeup Trailers, Mobile Offices, Mobile Screening Rooms, Motorhomes & Star Trailers)

Prestige Star Trailers (310) 276-5922 / (818) 785-2981
6933 Whitaker Ave. FAX (818) 785-2681
Lake Balboa, CA 91406 www.prestigestartrailers.com
(Honeywagons, Production Trailers & Talent/Production Motorhomes)

Quixote Studios (323) 857-5050
1011 N. Fuller Ave. FAX (323) 851-5029
West Hollywood, CA 90046 www.quixote.com
(Motorhomes & Production Trailers)

Ray's Production Services (805) 649-9064 / (805) 687-1267
1187 Coast Village Rd., Ste. 362
Santa Barbara, CA 93108 www.raysmotorhomes.com

Redline RV Productions, LLC (714) 742-7901
7251 E. Lewis Dr. www.redlinervp.com
Orange, CA 92869
(Honeywagons & Star Trailers)

Risvold Ranch Property Rentals (805) 377-9675
FAX (805) 376-0772
www.risvoldranchproperties.com

Royal Restrooms (877) 922-9980
FAX (877) 922-9980
www.royalrestrooms.com
(Honeywagons, Portable Restrooms, Portable Toilets, Shower Trailers & V.I.P. Restrooms)

Silverstar Rentals (909) 322-4392

SirReel - LA & San Diego (888) 477-7335 / (760) 672-5522
(Production Trailers) FAX (888) 477-7313
www.sirreel.us

Sony Pictures Studios (310) 244-7016
10202 W. Washington Blvd. FAX (310) 244-7995
Culver City, CA 90232 www.sonypicturesstudios.com

Spartan Mobile Suites, Inc. (310) 587-3377
3727 W. Magnolia Blvd., Ste. 156 FAX (661) 702-0550
Burbank, CA 91505
(Mobile Screening Rooms & Star Trailers)

Star Waggons Production Trailers (818) 367-5946 / (888) 367-5946
13334 Ralston Ave. FAX (818) 362-1448
Sylmar, CA 91342 www.starwaggons.com
(Trailers)

StaR.V. Rentals (323) 864-8332
28109 Avenue Stanford FAX (661) 964-0550
Valencia, CA 91355 www.starvrentals.com

Steelgrave Production Services (818) 652-7377
(661) 298-8912
www.pmfarms.biz
(Honeywagons, Makeup Trailers, Production Trailers, Star Trailers & Wardrobe Trailers)

Studio Inn Corporation (818) 597-0606
5735 Parkmor Rd. FAX (818) 377-3213
Calabasas, CA 91302 www.studioinn.com

Suite Water Studio Enterprises, LLC (661) 510-7319
(661) 510-9260
11531 Davenport Rd.
Agua Dulce, CA 91390

Ⓐ **Susie's Production Vehicles** (661) 260-3500
(800) 299-6949
21226 Placerita Canyon Rd. FAX (866) 472-1450
Newhall, CA 91321 www.productionvehicles.com
(Motorhomes)

T&D Studio Support Services (818) 285-6667
8001 Langdon Ave., Ste. 1 FAX (818) 787-6480
Van Nuys, CA 91406
(Shower Trailers)

Tony's Production Trailers (818) 968-5259
2061 Krystal Ave. FAX (818) 833-0731
Lancaster, CA 93536

United Site Services (626) 698-3166
(626) 831-4517
4511 Rowland Ave. FAX (626) 254-0241
El Monte, CA 91734 www.unitedsiteservices.com
(Portable Restrooms, Portable Toilets, Shower Trailers & V.I.P. Restrooms)

VJ's Studio Equipment Rentals (818) 621-0701
12854 El Dorado Ave. FAX (818) 367-3048
Sylmar, CA 91342 www.vjstudiorentals.com

Advanced Records Management (323) 727-7277
1540 Church Rd. FAX **(323) 727-7070**
Montebello, CA 90640 **www.advancedrecords.com**
(Information Management, Retrieval and Storage)

Agua Dulce Water Trucks (818) 216-3680
14854 Lassen St. FAX **(818) 892-7710**
Mission Hills, CA 91345
(Transportation of Equipment and Picture Vehicles)

All Points Vanlines, Inc. (818) 771-9933
(800) 449-2347
FAX **(866) 771-9922**
www.allpointsvanlines.com

All-Safe Destruction, Inc. (310) 518-5022
2537-D Pacific Coast Hwy FAX **(951) 676-0506**
Torrance, CA 90505
(Transportation of Equipment and Props)

Baker Tanks (805) 525-1710
(Portable Storage Tanks) FAX **(805) 525-7861**
www.bakertanks.com

Bekins Moving & Storage (800) 994-6684
6300 Valley View St. **www.bekins.com**
Buean Park, CA 90620

Contain-it Storage (818) 982-6200
7361 Laurel Canyon Blvd. FAX **(818) 890-6110**
North Hollywood, CA 91605 **www.containitonline.com**
(Storage)

Cor-O-Van Moving & Storage (888) 544-3929
www.corovan.com

Dynamic L.A., Inc. (818) 771-1111
11755 Sheldon St. FAX **(818) 771-1159**
Sun Valley, CA 91352 **www.dynamicla.com**

File Keepers (323) 728-3133
(800) 332-3453
6277 E. Slauson Ave. FAX **(323) 728-1349**
Commerce, CA 90040 **www.filekeepers.com**
(File Management & Temperature-Controlled Storage)

Fine Art Shipping (310) 677-0011
(800) 421-7464
404 N. Oak St. FAX **(310) 677-8586**
Inglewood, CA 90302 **www.fineartship.com**

Flat Rate Moving (213) 404-1080
2445 E. 12th St., Bldg. C FAX **(213) 404-1086**
Los Angeles, CA 90021 **www.flatrate.com/la**

Gilbert Production Service, Inc. (323) 871-0006
4578 Worth St. FAX **(323) 264-2501**
Los Angeles, CA 90063 **www.gilbertproductionservice.com**
(Storage/Transportation of Equipment and Props)

Holiday Transfer Co./
Holiday Moving & Storage (310) 515-0900
1829 W. El Segundo Blvd., Ste. A FAX **(310) 515-5566**
Compton, CA 90222 **www.holidaytransferco.com**

Hollywood Parts (818) 255-0617
12580 Saticoy St., Bldg. C FAX **(818) 255-0613**
North Hollywood, CA 91605 **www.hollywoodparts.com**
(Asset Management Storage and Sales, File Management, Storage of Equipment, Storage of Props, Storage of Scenery, Storage of Vehicles, Temperature-Controlled Storage, Transportation of Equipment, Transportation of Props, Transportation of Scenery, Transportation of Vehicles & Wood Vaults)

Homer Mann Trucking (818) 834-0481
12000 Paxton St. FAX **(818) 834-0380**
Lakeview, CA 91342 **www.homermann.com**
(Transportation of Oversized Equipment and Props)

KLS Transportation (310) 327-3309
(Transportation of Equipment and Props) FAX **(310) 327-3305**

Lambert's Van & Storage, Inc. (310) 652-1555 / (800) 652-1555
P.O. Box 38250 FAX (818) 547-0956
Los Angeles, CA 90038 www.lambertsvanandstorage.com

Load Lock-N-Roll Moving-N-Storage (323) 962-6683 / (800) 660-5623
www.mrmove.us

Los Angeles Fine Arts & Wine Storage Company (310) 447-7700
2290 Centinela Ave. www.lafinearts&wine.com
West Los Angeles, CA 90064
(Humidity and Temperature-Controlled Security Rooms)

The Mobile Storage Group (800) 662-8810 / (310) 515-4804
15100 San Pedro St. FAX (310) 515-6685
Gardena, CA 90248 www.mobilestorage.com

Musicians Transfer (818) 558-1052
(Transportation of Musical Equipment) FAX (818) 558-1053

A **NorthStar Moving Corporation** (800) 275-7767 / (818) 727-0128
9120 Mason Ave. FAX (818) 727-7527
Chatsworth, CA 91311 www.northstarmoving.com

Noteworthy Moving Systems & Delivery (626) 441-6004 / (818) 241-4745
534 Lakeview Rd. FAX (626) 441-5679
Pasadena, CA 91105 www.noteworthymoving.com
(Rush Jobs & Transportation of Props)

Public Storage (800) 447-8673

Rene's Moving & Storage (323) 653-2141 / (310) 652-2200
(Wood Vaults) FAX (818) 547-0956

A **Scenic Expressions** (818) 409-3354
4000 Chevy Chase Dr. FAX (818) 244-4835
Los Angeles, CA 90039 www.scenicexpressions.com
(Storage/Transportation of Props and Scenery)

Schafer Bros. Piano Movers (310) 835-7231 / (800) 222-2888
1981 E. 213th St. FAX (310) 830-6615
Carson, CA 90810 www.pianomove.com

Sidelifter.com (877) 274-3354 / (916) 761-2442
Satelite Yard, 1941 W. Ninth St. FAX (916) 236-5793
Long Beach, CA 90810 www.sidelifter.com

Starving Students (800) 441-6683
1850 W. Sawtelle FAX (800) 825-1145
West Los Angeles, CA 90025 www.ssmovers.com

Studio Express Prop Transportation (818) 352-9402 / (818) 445-8175
10333 McVine Ave. FAX (818) 951-9883
Sunland, CA 91040 www.studioexpress.biz
(Storage/Transportation of Equipment and Props)

Studio Instrument Rentals/SIR (323) 957-5460
6465 Sunset Blvd. FAX (323) 957-5472
Hollywood, CA 90028 www.sirla.com
(Storage/Transportation of Musical Equipment)

Third Encore (818) 753-0148 / (800) 339-8850
10917 Vanowen St. FAX (818) 753-0151
North Hollywood, CA 91605 www.3rdencore.com
(Transportation of Musical Equipment)

Time Capsule Storage (661) 296-1111
25655 Springbrook Ave., Bldg. 2A www.tcsvalencia.com
Santa Clarita, CA 91350

United Valet Parking, Inc. (310) 642-7740
5839 Green Valley Circle, Ste. 202 FAX (310) 642-7753
Culver City, CA 90230

Western Studio Services (818) 842-9272
805 S. San Fernando Blvd. FAX (818) 842-0250
Burbank, CA 91502 www.westernstudioservice.com
(Storage/Transportation of Props)

Xpeditious Unlimited (310) 644-1286 / (310) 227-5106
12911 Simms Ave., Ste. E FAX (310) 644-4636
Hawthorne, CA 90250 www.xpeditiousunlimited.com

5th & Sunset Los Angeles (310) 979-0212
12322 Exposition Blvd. FAX (310) 979-0214
Los Angeles, CA 90064 www.5thandsunsetla.com

Beautiful Day Permits (626) 934-1280
2017 Scott Rd. FAX (626) 934-1281
West Covina, CA 91792
(Notification Services, Posting Services & Signature Services)

Children In Film (818) 901-0082
6539 Colbath Ave. FAX (818) 780-8262
Valley Glen, CA 91401 www.childreninfilm.com
(Children's Entertainment Work Permits)

Film Permits Unlimited, Inc./ Denise Wheeler (818) 347-9929
22025 Ventura Blvd., Ste. 101 FAX (818) 347-9784
Woodland Hills, CA 91364 www.filmpermits.com

Film This Production Services, Inc. (213) 763-9000 (213) 268-3297
155 W. Washington Blvd., Ste. 406 FAX (213) 763-9004
Los Angeles, CA 90015 www.filmthis.net

iManagement Group (310) 979-5729 (888) 549-2600
c/o Elkins Jones Insurance Agency FAX (310) 207-5441
12100 Wilshire Blvd., Ste. 300
Los Angeles, CA 90025 www.imanagementgroup.com
(Location Permit Insurance Requirements)

Inland Empire Film Commission (951) 779-6700
1201 Research Park Dr., Ste. 100 FAX (951) 779-0294
Riverside, CA 92507 www.filminlandempire.com
(Riverside and San Bernardino Counties)

Mammoth Location Services (760) 934-0628 (760) 914-0405
P.O. Box 24 FAX (760) 934-0700
Mammoth Lakes, CA 93546
www.mammothfilmlocations.com

Don Mann (310) 456-3399 (818) 640-8822
(Notification, Posting & Signature Services)

Ⓐ **Pacific Production Services, Inc.** (323) 465-9179 (213) 360-7844
6513 Hollywood Blvd., Ste. 214 FAX (323) 465-9869
Los Angeles, CA 90028 www.lafilmpermits.com
(Notification, Permit, Posting and Signature Services)

S.N.A.P.S./Signature, Notification And Posting Services (310) 883-5913 (888) 762-7701
FAX (888) 762-7781
www.filmpermitsignatures.com
(Posting, Notification and Signature Services)

Stanley Locations (818) 706-8022
591 E. Los Angeles FAX (888) 846-6011
Simi Valley, CA 93065

Tri-County Permit Services (805) 969-5555 (805) 565-1562
1805 E. Cabrillo Blvd., Ste. B
Santa Barbara, CA 93108
(San Luis Obispo, Santa Barbara & Ventura Counties)

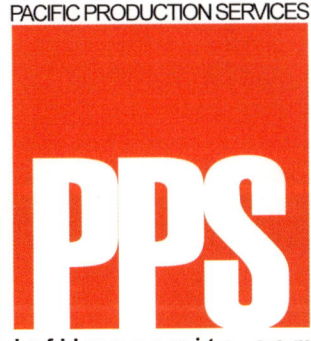

A-1 Portables (760) 949-4111
(800) 554-7723
17491 Lilac St. FAX (760) 949-4224
Hesperia, CA 92345

Action/Restroom Rentals (562) 595-7200
2121 Cover St. FAX (562) 595-7210
Long Beach, CA 90807 www.actionsiteservices.net

Andy Gump, Inc. (661) 251-7721
(800) 992-7755
26954 Ruether Ave. FAX (661) 251-7729
Santa Clarita, CA 91351 www.andygump.com

Clean Strike Rental & Cleaning (562) 803-3701
(562) 879-2207
12214 Lakewood Blvd., Bldg. 9 FAX (562) 803-3702
Downey, CA 90242 www.cleanstrikerentals.com

Diamond Environmental Services, LLC (888) 744-7191
630 S. Hathaway FAX (760) 290-3338
Santa Ana, CA 92705 www.diamondprovides.com

Elliott Location Equipment (310) 915-1744
(505) 328-0909
www.elliottlocationequipment.com

Hollywood Honeywagon & Production Vehicles (818) 763-1966
(818) 535-9648
11160 Victory Blvd. FAX (818) 760-0551
North Hollywood, CA 91606
www.hollywoodhoneywagon.com

King Kong Production Vehicles (323) 462-6646
(949) 673-1999
4000 Cohasset St. FAX (949) 673-3993
Burbank, CA 91505 www.kingkongtrailers.com

Kohler Co. (310) 518-5118
(866) 577-4797
1581 W. Wardlow Rd. FAX (310) 518-5028
Long Beach, CA 90810 www.kohlerrental.com

Royal Flush (818) 355-0301
www.aroyal-flush.com

Royal Restrooms (877) 922-9980
4470 W. Sunset Blvd., Ste. 121 FAX (877) 922-9980
Los Angeles, CA 90027 www.royalrestrooms.com

United Site Services (626) 698-3166
(626) 831-4517
4511 Rowland Ave. FAX (626) 254-0241
El Monte, CA 91734 www.unitedsiteservices.com

Africa Film Services (310) 273-9693
507 N. Almont Dr. FAX (310) 273-9698
Los Angeles, CA 90048 www.afsproductions.com
Contact: Dale Kushner

APU Productions (818) 681-3688
6701 E. Bacarro St. www.apuprod.com
Long Beach, CA 90815
(Peru & South American Region)

Association of Film Commissioners International (406) 495-8040
314 N. Main, Ste. 307 FAX (406) 495-8039
Helena, MT 59601 www.afci.org

Bajala Production Services (310) 990-9503
(310) 862-4201
FAX 011 52 624 142 6031
www.bajalaprod.com

Box Films - Chile (714) 849-6491
FAX (714) 849-6491
www.boxfilms.cl

CDI Virtual Brazil Films (818) 841-9446
2219 W. Olive Ave., Ste. 263 FAX (818) 506-1654
Burbank, CA 91506 www.brazilfilms.com

Cine South de Mexico (310) 573-9988
(800) 245-6639
Pedro Sainz de Baranda FAX (956) 584-9488
Ste. 139, Col. Avante www.filmmexico.com
Mexico City, DF 04460 Mexico
Contact: Mark Pittman

DMI Productions 00 44 1784 421 212
FAX 00 44 1784 421 213
www.dmiproductions.com

European Touch Productions (310) 686-6611
011 420 602 364 345
(Czech Republic & Prague) www.etpprague.com

Global Production Network (424) 245-4514
(310) 570-0065
FAX (323) 417-1599
www.globalproductionnetwork.com

The Good Film Company Ltd. (310) 228-6206
256 S. Robertson Blvd., Ste. 219
Beverly Hills, CA 90211
www.goodfilms.co.uk/eng/home.htm

Italian Film Commission (323) 879-0950
1801 Avenue of the Stars, Ste. 700 FAX (310) 203-8335
Los Angeles, CA 90067 www.filminginitaly.com

Mexico Tourism Board (310) 282-9112
1880 Century Park East, Ste. 511 FAX (310) 282-9116
Los Angeles, CA 90067 www.visitmexico.com
Contact: Jorge Gamboa-Patron

Milk & Honey Films (323) 993-9600
4401 Wilshire Blvd., Ste. 250 FAX (323) 993-9333
Los Angeles, CA 90010 www.milkandhoneyfilms.com
Contact: Howard Woffinden

Prana Studios, Inc. (323) 645-6500
1145 N. McCadden Pl. www.pranastudios.com
Los Angeles, CA 90038

Stillking Films (310) 466-9161
3530 Greenwood Ave. www.stillking.com
Los Angeles, CA 90066
(Bulgaria, Chile, Czech Republic, London, South Africa & Spain)
Contact: Doug Lewis

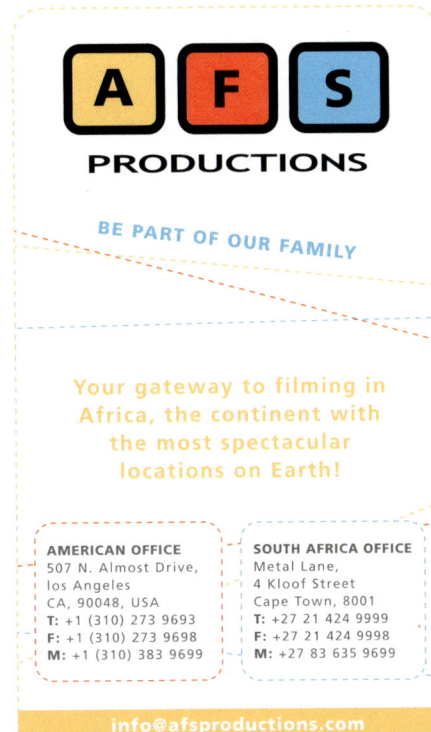

Vietnamese American Media, Inc. (714) 775-7772
5002 W. McFadden Ave., Ste. 14 FAX (714) 775-7772
Santa Ana, CA 92704
Contact: April Tran

1171 Production Group (323) 466-1171
1680 N. Vine St., Ste. 300 FAX (323) 466-1136
Hollywood, CA 90028 www.1171.com
Contacts: Grant Cihlar & Nancy Cihlar

Acme Design Group (818) 767-8888
11001 Fleetwood St. www.acme-designgroup.com
Sun Valley, CA 91352

AFS Productions (310) 273-9693
507 N. Almont Dr. FAX (310) 273-9698
Los Angeles, CA 90048 www.afsproductions.com
Contact: Dale Kushner

Albrecht Productions (858) 759-6522
(858) 581-3700
4686 Torrey Circle, Ste. B206
San Diego, CA 92130
Contact: Jacques Albrecht

All In One Productions (323) 780-8880
1111 Corporate Dr. FAX (323) 780-8887
Monterey Park, CA 91754 www.allinone-usa.com

Backlot Productions (323) 785-1078
1149 N. Gower St. FAX (323) 622-8726
Hollywood, CA 90038 www.backlotproductions.com

Bi-Coastal Concepts, Inc. (310) 208-6776
(305) 385-2204
11636 Montana Ave., Ste. 110 FAX (310) 208-6776
Los Angeles, CA 90049
Contact: Audrey Cohen

Black Dragon Entertainment, Inc. (323) 874-8888
FAX (323) 874-1058
www.blackdragon.com

Blueyed Pictures, Inc. (310) 444-7055
10960 Wilshire Blvd., Ste. 1750 FAX (310) 444-7050
Los Angeles, CA 90024 www.blueyedpictures.com

Bully Pictures (310) 745-1635
(310) 871-0385
858 Burrell St. FAX (310) 745-1645
Marina Del Rey, CA 90292 www.bullypictures.com

CDI Virtual Brazil Films (818) 841-9446
2219 W. Olive Ave., Ste. 263 FAX (818) 506-1654
Burbank, CA 91506 www.brazilfilms.com

Chiari Cook Company, Inc. (213) 304-0053
5822 W. Washington Blvd.
Culver City, CA 90232
Contacts: Jared Cook & Chiari Endo

CJE Productions, Inc. (310) 314-1950

Coastal Media Group (818) 880-9800
26660 Agoura Rd. FAX (818) 579-9026
Calabasas, CA 91302 www.coastalmediagroup.com

Cobalt Blue, LLC (818) 988-9093
15115 Lemay St. FAX (818) 988-9096
Van Nuys, CA 91405 www.cobaltbluefilms.com
Contact: Carl Beyer

The Company Pictures (310) 919-0950
(310) 806-1289
1901 S. Bundy Dr. www.thecompany.tv
Los Angeles, CA 90025

Concrete Images (310) 452-9644
(310) 480-8738
1301 Main St., Ste. 3 FAX (310) 452-9655
Venice, CA 90291 www.concreteimages.com

Crash Productions (310) 489-6848
713 N. Mansfield Ave. FAX (323) 939-9622
Los Angeles, CA 90038 www.crashproductions.com

DCM Productions (310) 545-2119
(310) 503-1631
1611 19th St. FAX (310) 545-5350
Manhattan Beach, CA 90266
Contact: Douglas Merrifield

Dorf Production Services (310) 476-8380
2554 Lincoln Blvd., Ste. 421 FAX (818) 789-6435
Venice, CA 90291
Contacts: Gary Dorf & Ilene Roberts

Dorf Production Services (310) 476-8380
15445 Ventura Blvd., Ste. 3312 FAX (818) 789-6435
Sherman Oaks, CA 91403
Contacts: Gary Dorf & Ilene Roberts

Encore Media LLC (310) 823-9233
5301 Beethoven St., Ste. 290 FAX (310) 823-9211
Los Angeles, CA 90066 www.encoremediallc.com

Engine Room (310) 860-9100
1040 N. Las Palmas, Bldg. 24 FAX (310) 860-9111
Los Angeles, CA 90038 www.engineroomvfx.com
Contacts: Michael Caplan & Dan Schmit

Epiphany Media (323) 960-4092
(323) 819-1001
5300 Melrose Ave. FAX (323) 960-4073
Hollywood, CA 90038 www.epiphanymedia.com

Espace Productions, Inc. (818) 543-3300
3905 San Fernando Rd., Studio A FAX (818) 543-7095
Glendale, CA 91204 www.espaceproductions.com

The Focus Studio (310) 399-9400
Four Rose Ave. FAX (310) 399-1180
Venice, CA 90291 www.thefocusstudio.com

FXF Productions, Inc. (310) 577-5009
1024 Harding Ave., Ste. 201 FAX (310) 577-1960
Venice, CA 90291 www.fxfproductions.com
Contacts: Eric Alan Donaldson & Lonnie Peralta

Gateway Productions, Inc. (323) 466-6236
Contact: Earl Mann FAX (818) 906-3539

Glory Productions (818) 730-4900
www.gloryproductions.com

HD Republic (310) 550-6885
FAX (310) 550-6253
www.hdrepublic.com

hi. Inc. (323) 605-3951
1752 N. Serrano Ave., Ste. 104 FAX (323) 395-0431
Los Angeles, CA 90027 www.hi-medias.com

Jack Provost/Associates (818) 988-8150
Contact: Jack Provost FAX (818) 988-8152

John Purdy, Inc. (323) 874-9802
7230 Franklin Ave., Ste. 326 FAX (323) 874-3119
Los Angeles, CA 90046
Contact: Jack Black

KGB Films (323) 610-0501
(818) 519-9575
6230 Wilshire Blvd., Ste. 71 FAX (323) 658-6568
Los Angeles, CA 90048 www.kgbfilms.com

L.A. Photosafari (310) 490-9574
(310) 201-5679
P.O. Box 34813 FAX (310) 558-3745
Los Angeles, CA 90034

Lena Production Services (310) 990-8223
(310) 399-2007
3121 Fifth St. FAX (310) 399-2425
Santa Monica, CA 90405
Contact: Bonnie Lena

LeTo Entertainment, LLC (310) 358-3282
(310) 621-1122
8840 Wilshire Blvd., Third Fl. FAX (310) 388-1403
Beverly Hills, CA 90211 www.letoentertainment.com

Lookout Entertainment (310) 798-3000
54 Hermosa Ave. FAX (310) 798-3001
Hermosa Beach, CA 90254
www.lookoutentertainment.com
Contact: Yvonne Bernard

Lyon Studios (949) 675-4790
222 21st St. FAX (949) 675-2139
Newport Beach, CA 92663 www.lyonstudios.com
Contacts: Naomi Killian & Curt Lyon

The M Company, Inc. (310) 577-3377
961 Marco Pl. FAX (310) 577-8877
Venice, CA 90291 www.mcompanyinc.com
Contact: Yen King

New Circuit Films, LLC (323) 871-8122
(818) 378-0033
6546 Hollywood Blvd., Ste. 213 FAX (818) 871-8122
Los Angeles, CA 90028 www.newcircuit.com

P.I.G./Protean Image Group (310) 399-9898
212 Main St. FAX (310) 399-9876
Venice, CA 90291 www.pigusa.com

Patrick Stewart Productions, LLC (818) 882-3700
Contact: Jennifer Nejman FAX (818) 882-3793
www.psptv.com

Proper Films (323) 472-5659
7510 W. Sunset Blvd., Ste. 230 FAX (323) 968-0098
Hollywood, CA 90046 www.properfilms.com

Revolver Films (310) 827-2441
4040 Del Rey Ave., Ste. 5 FAX (310) 827-2661
Marina del Rey, CA 90292 www.revolverfilmsla.com

Roaring Tiger Films (415) 241-7125
400 Treat Ave., Ste. E FAX (415) 861-4326
San Francisco, CA 94110 www.roaringtigerfilms.com

SCG Kino (310) 717-9264
Contact: Michael Schenk FAX (626) 791-6177
www.scgkino.com

Sim Video Los Angeles (323) 978-9000
738 Cahuenga Blvd. FAX (323) 978-9018
Hollywood, CA 90038 www.simvideola.com

Sincbox (310) 566-6700
11601 Wilshire Blvd., Ste. 2150 FAX (310) 566-6719
Los Angeles, CA 90025 www.sincbox.com

Slash Productions (323) 871-0201
(213) 810-5059
2086 Mound St. FAX (323) 871-0315
Los Angeles, CA 90068
Contacts: Antonia Holt & Scott Luhrsen

Spot On Media (800) 507-0159
(818) 209-6305
www.spotonmedia.tv
Contacts: Lisa Brandi, Shaun Greenspan, Igori Kamoevi & Andrew Webb

Stargate Stage (626) 403-8403
6827 Valjean Ave. FAX (626) 403-8444
Van Nuys, CA 91406 www.stargatefilms.com

Team Halprin, Inc. (310) 842-7000
FAX (310) 842-7014
www.teamhalprin.com

U.S. Production Services (310) 857-7780
578 Washington Blvd., Ste. 594 FAX (310) 496-0192
Marina del Rey, CA 90292
www.usproductionservices.com

Video Production Specialists (VPS) (866) 447-3877
FAX (310) 577-0850
www.videoproductionspecialists.com

Video Tech Services (310) 574-9385
(310) 505-4015
10866 Washington Blvd., Ste. 513 FAX (310) 577-0850
Culver City, CA 90232 www.videotechservices.com
Contact: Richard Larsen

Warped Pictures (310) 777-8828
(310) 999-1219
2447 Benedict Canyon FAX (310) 777-8805
Beverly Hills, CA 90210 www.warpedpictures.com
Contact: Volker Fleck

Western Branch Productions, Inc. (818) 762-3810
(818) 642-3810
4231 Beck Ave. FAX (818) 769-2847
Studio City, CA 91604 www.western-branch.com
Contact: Pete Vanlaw

Zystar Films, Inc. (310) 301-3313
Contact: Meryl Wallis Chase FAX (310) 301-9433
www.zystar.com

A-List Security, Inc. (213) 252-8927 (760) 497-9325
1625 W Olympic Blvd., Ste. M103 FAX (213) 252-8928
Los Angeles, CA 90015 www.a-listsecurity.com
(Location Bodyguards, Studio Security & Trained Law Enforcement Officers)

A.S.A. Security Services Division (323) 662-9787
P.O. Box 125 FAX (323) 662-1569
La Cañada, CA 91012 www.asatalent.com/crew
(Bodyguards, Off-Duty Police Officers, Security Guards & Set Security)

Absolute Protection Service, Inc. (310) 280-7277
419 N. Larchmont Blvd., Ste. 89 FAX (310) 280-7777
Los Angeles, CA 90004
www.absoluteprotectionservice.com
(Bodyguards, K-9 Units, Location and Studio Security, Off-Duty Officers & Unarmed Guards)

Absolute Protective Services, Inc. (213) 480-0128 (213) 272-2768
2330 W. Third St., Ste. 4 FAX (213) 480-0160
Los Angeles, CA 90057 www.apsprivatesecurity.com
(Armed Guards, Bodyguards, K-9 Units, Location Bodyguards, Location Security, Off-Duty Officers, Studio Security, Trained Law Enforcement Officers & Unarmed Guards)

Allways Chauffeurs & Bodyguards (310) 385-9088
FAX (310) 385-9038
www.allwaysdrivers.com

Angel Guarding Security (818) 482-6634
P.O. Box 11464 FAX (323) 739-0340
Glendale, CA 91225
(Armed Guards, Location Security, Security Only, Studio Security & Unarmed Guards)

Augie's Security (323) 343-8810 (213) 864-3848
533 Clifton St. FAX (323) 343-8800
Los Angeles, CA 90031 www.augiessecurity.com
(Location Security, Studio Security & Unarmed Guards)

Beach Cities Protective Services (877) 776-8282 (310) 930-2851
FAX (310) 831-0261
www.beachcitiesprotection.com
(Armed Guards, Bodyguards, Location Bodyguards, Location Security, Off-Duty Officers, Retired Officers, Studio Security, Trained Law Enforcement Officers & Unarmed Guards)

Bonanza Solutions, Inc. (818) 890-5951
P.O. Box 55729 FAX (661) 287-4485
Santa Clarita, CA 91385
(Location Bodyguards & Security)

C.A.S.T. Security, Inc. (562) 695-4558
6608 Gretna Ave. FAX (562) 908-9911
Whittier, CA 90606
(Security Only)

Celebrity Security (818) 469-9047 (866) 671-5637
FAX (661) 729-9323
www.joesstudioservices.com
(Armed Guards, Bodyguards, Location Bodyguards and Security, Off-Duty Officers, Retired Officers, Studio Security & Unarmed Guards)

Coleman Security & Investigations (CSI) (800) 965-4274
FAX (800) 845-1274
www.colemansecurityandinvestigations.com

CPS Worldwide (888) 277-2776 (310) 463-9800
12400 Wilshire Blvd., Ste. 400 FAX (866) 636-6977
Los Angeles, CA 90025
www.californiaprotectiveservices.com

EPS Security/ Empire Protective Services (562) 673-8164 (562) 219-0095
P.O. Box 1273
Norwalk, CA 90650
(Armed and Unarmed Security)

F.E.D. Security Armed Service (323) 578-7330
5029 Alhambra Ave. FAX (323) 222-5290
Los Angeles, CA 90032

FLI2 (214) 930-4311 (888) 411-3542
www.fli2.com
(Bodyguards, Location Bodyguards, Location Security, Studio Security & Trained Law Enforcement Officers)

Galahad Protective Services, Inc. (818) 780-1818
14320 Ventura Blvd., Ste. 612 FAX (818) 780-4848
Sherman Oaks, CA 91423 www.galahadinc.com

General Security Service, Inc. (323) 772-7377 / (800) 350-1944
14009 Crenshaw Blvd. FAX (310) 973-7627
Hawthorne, CA 90250
(Security Only)

Hollywood Production Security, Inc. (323) 461-3377 / (818) 961-7474
6520 Platt Ave., Ste. 681 FAX (818) 340-1940
West Hills, CA 91307
www.hollywoodproductionsecurity.com

Hollywood Security, Inc. (323) 851-4800
(Unarmed Security Guards) FAX (323) 417-4800
www.hollywoodsecurity.com

Johnson & Associates, Inc. (800) 496-0182 / (866) 211-7516
8581 Santa Monica Blvd., Ste. 305 FAX (858) 793-0471
West Hollywood, CA 90069 www.jnasecurity.com
(Armed Guards, Bodyguards, Location Bodyguards, Location Security, Off-Duty Officers, Security Only & Unarmed Guards)

Movie Guard (818) 262-5353
3727 W. Magnolia Blvd., Ste. 230
Burbank, CA 91510
(Bodyguards, Location Security & Off-Duty/Retired Officers)

North American Security, Inc. (323) 634-1911 / (310) 427-9196
4201 Wilshire Blvd., Ste. 440 FAX (323) 634-9111
Los Angeles, CA 90010

Picore Worldwide (818) 888-9659
FAX (818) 475-1882
www.picore.com
(Armed Guards, Bodyguards, Location Bodyguards, Location Security, Off-Duty Officers, Retired Officers, Studio Security, Trained Law Enforcement Officers & Unarmed Guards)

Praetorian Security Specialists (877) 210-8600 / (310) 493-4620
1339 Sycamore Dr. www.praesec.com
Simi Valley, CA 93065

Reel Security Corp. (818) 508-4750 / (310) 497-5782
4640 Lankershim Blvd., Ste. 212 FAX (818) 508-4751
North Hollywood, CA 91602 www.reelsecurity.com
(Armed Guards, Bodyguards, Location Bodyguards, Location Security, Off-Duty Officers, Retired Officers, Studio Security, Trained Law Enforcement Officers & Unarmed Guards)

Security Detection Metal Detectors (800) 261-8211 / (918) 629-3399
860 Carlton Privado FAX (866) 702-9303
Ontario, CA 91762 www.securitydetection.com
(Location & Studio Security)

SET Security, Inc. (818) 360-7686
P.O. Box 33356 FAX (818) 876-0544
Granada Hills, CA 91394
(Armed/Unarmed Security & Bodyguards)

SPI Entertainment Services (951) 544-4520
(Armed Guards, Bodyguards, Location Bodyguards, Location Security & Trained Law Enforcement Officers)

Starside Security & Investigation, Inc. (310) 417-9999 / (800) 782-7906
6080 Center Dr., Ste. 677 FAX (310) 362-0305
Los Angeles, CA 90045 www.starside.com
(Armed Guards, Bodyguards, Location Bodyguards, Location Security, Off-Duty Officers, Retired Officers, Studio Security, Trained Law Enforcement Officers & Unarmed Guards)

Strike Force Security Services (800) 672-6057 / (818) 787-6295
P.O. Box 26551 FAX (818) 276-1891
San Jose, CA 95159 www.strikeforcesecurity.com
Contact: Carole Moultout

Sully's Crew, Inc. Security Services/ Crew Protection (661) 250-2111
FAX (661) 250-3111
www.crewprotection.com
(Armed Guards, Bodyguards, Location Bodyguards, Studio Security & Unarmed Guards)

Westside Detectives, Inc. (323) 583-8660 / (323) 833-2383
6230 Wilshire Blvd., Ste. 59
Los Angeles, CA 90048
www.westsidedetectives.com
(Bodyguards, Investigations & Security)

World Executive Protection Group (818) 901-9300 / (818) 519-7622
FAX (818) 901-2800
www.eworldgroup.com

Adventures at Sea Charters (866) 872-7314
3101 West Coast Hwy www.boatcharter.com
Newport Beach, CA 92663
(Gondolas, Sailboats & Yachts)

Air One Charter (310) 743-0103
(877) 247-1359
6101 W. Centinela Ave., Ste. 375 FAX (310) 743-0140
Culver City, CA 90230 www.aironecharter.com
(Jets)

Aircraft Charter Holdings, LLC (866) 359-2487
(415) 464-0400
1657 S. Spaulding Ave. FAX (310) 492-5177
Los Angeles, CA 90019 www.aircharter.com
(Jets)

AirFlite Aviation Services (562) 490-6200
(800) 241-3548
3250 Airflite Way FAX (562) 490-6270
Long Beach, CA 90807 www.airflight.com
(Jets)

American Yacht Charters, Inc. (949) 673-4453
2901 West Coast Hwy, Ste.190 FAX (949) 673-0807
Newport Beach, CA 92663 www.aycharters.com
(Yachts)

Avjet Corporation (800) 342-8538
(818) 841-6190
4301 Empire Ave. FAX (818) 841-6209
Burbank, CA 91505 www.avjet.com
(Jets)

Blue Water Sailing (310) 823-5545
(Sailboats & Yachts) FAX (310) 823-5728
www.bluewatersailing.com

California Dreamin' (800) 373-3359
33133 Vista del Monte Rd. FAX (951) 699-0601
Temecula, CA 92591 www.californiadreamin.com
(Hot Air Balloons)

Chrysler Aviation, Inc. (818) 989-7900
(800) 995-0825
7120 Hayvenhurst Ave., Ste. 309
Van Nuys, CA 91406 www.chrysleraviation.com
(Jets)

Clay Lacy Aviation, Inc. (818) 989-2900
(800) 423-2904
7435 Valjean Ave. FAX (818) 909-9537
Van Nuys, CA 91406 www.claylacy.com
(Jets)

Elite Aviation, Inc. (818) 988-5387
7501 Hayvenhurst Pl. FAX (818) 988-2111
Van Nuys, CA 91406 www.eliteaviation.com
(Jets)

Elite Yacht Charters (310) 552-7968
468 N. Camden Dr., Ste. 200 FAX (310) 553-2551
Beverly Hills, CA 90210 www.eliteyacht.com
(Sailboats & Yachts)

Environmental Motors (818) 244-6938
109 Franklin Court FAX (818) 244-8463
Glendale, CA 91024 www.environmentalmotors.com
(Eco-Friendly Automobiles)

FantaSea Yachts & Yacht Club (310) 827-2220
4215 Admiralty Way FAX (310) 827-7453
Marina del Rey, CA 90292 www.fantaseayachts.com
(Yachts)

Golf Cars - LA, Inc. (661) 251-2201
16439 Sierra Hwy www.golfcars-la.com
Canyon Country, CA 91351

Gondola Company Of Newport Beach (949) 675-1212
3400 Via Oporto, Ste. 103 FAX (949) 675-8812
Newport Beach, CA 92663 www.gondolas.com
(Gondolas)

Heli-USA (818) 994-1445
(877) 863-5952
16303 Waterman Dr. FAX (818) 994-1447
Van Nuys, CA 91406 www.toflyla.com
(Helicopters)

Island Express Helicopter (310) 510-2525
(800) 228-2566
1175 Queens Hwy South FAX (310) 510-9671
Long Beach, CA 90802 www.islandexpress.com
(Helicopters)

Jet Productions (818) 781-4742
(877) 895-1790
7240 Hayvenhurst Ave., Ste. 148 FAX (818) 781-4743
Van Nuys, CA 91406 www.jetproductions.net
(Jets)

Maguire Aviation (818) 989-2300
(800) 451-7270
7155 Valjean Ave. FAX (818) 902-9386
Van Nuys, CA 91406
(Jets)

Meridian Teterboro (800) 882-2333
(Jets) www.meridianteb.com

Odyssey Yacht Charter, Inc. (310) 308-4643
(310) 823-9917
(Yachts) FAX (310) 823-9917
www.odysseyyacht.com

Paradise Bound Yacht Charters (800) 655-0850
4375 Admiralty Way
Marina del Rey, CA 90292
www.the-calculating-lady.com/captalex
(Sailboats & Yachts)

Pierpoint Landing (562) 983-9300
(Jets) FAX (562) 495-6252
www.pierpoint.net

Skytrails Aviation (877) 759-8724
16233 Vanowen St. FAX (818) 901-0272
Van Nuys, CA 91406 www.skytrails.com
(Jets)

Studio Jet (818) 769-3535
P.O. Box 4215 FAX (818) 301-2536
Valley Village, CA 91617 www.studiojet.com
(Jets)

Summit Helicopters (818) 890-0903
(818) 890-9592
12653 Osborne St., Ste. 35 www.summithelicopter.com
Pacoima, CA 91331
(Helicopters)

Sun Quest (818) 778-6520
(800) 529-7595
7415 Hayvenhurst Pl. FAX (818) 778-6526
Van Nuys, CA 91406 www.sunquestexec.com
(Jets)

Trans-Exec Air Service (310) 399-9435
(Jets) www.transexec.com

Auto Club Speedway (909) 429-5000
Contact: Phil Tucker
FAX **(909) 429-5500**
www.autoclubspeedway.com

Cinespace (323) 817-3456
6356 Hollywood Blvd., Second Fl.
Hollywood, CA 90028
FAX **(323) 860-9794**
www.cinespace.info

Disney Ice (714) 535-7465
300 W. Lincoln Ave.
Anaheim, CA 92805
Contact: Jill Legault
FAX **(714) 518-3220**
www.anaheimice.com

Ebony Repertory Theatre @ The Nate Holden (323) 964-9768
4718 W. Washington Blvd.
Los Angeles, CA 90016
www.ebonyrep.org

El Capitan Theatre & Entertainment Centre (323) 467-7674 (818) 516-3092
6838 Hollywood Blvd.
Los Angeles, CA 90028
FAX **(323) 467-0922**
www.elcapitantickets.com

Epicenter Stadium - City of Rancho Cucamonga (909) 477-2760
10500 Civic Center Dr.
Rancho Cucamonga, CA 91730
FAX **(909) 477-2761**
www.rcepicenter.com

Fairplex (909) 865-4042 (909) 865-4041
1101 W. Mckinley Ave.
Pomona, CA 91768
FAX **(909) 623-9599**
www.fairplex.com

The Forum (310) 330-7300
3900 W. Manchester Blvd.
Inglewood, CA 90305
Contact: Devon Mackey
www.thelaforum.com

Greek Theatre (323) 665-5857
2700 N. Vermont Ave.
Los Angeles, CA 90027
FAX **(323) 666-8202**
www.nederlander.com

Hollywood Park (310) 330-7248
Box 369
Inglewood, CA 90306
Contact: Deann Fruhling
FAX **(310) 673-6278**
www.hollywoodpark.com

Honda Center (714) 704-2422
2695 E. Katella Ave.
Anaheim, CA 92806
Contact: Jo-Ann Armstrong
FAX **(714) 704-2610**
www.arrowheadpond.com

House of Blues Concerts (323) 769-4600
Contact: Ingrid Gunn
FAX **(323) 769-4792**
www.hob.com

Ice Chalet (310) 541-6630
550 Deep Valley Dr.
Avenue of the Peninsula Mall
Rolling Hills Estates, CA 90274
FAX **(310) 541-8674**
www.pvicechalet.com

La Mirada Theatre for the Performing Arts (714) 994-6310 (562) 944-9801
14900 La Mirada Blvd.
La Mirada, CA 90638
Contact: Laura Moore
FAX **(714) 994-5796**
www.lamiradatheatre.com

LA Music Center (213) 972-7211 (213) 972-3335
135 N. Grand Ave.
Los Angeles, CA 90012
Contact: John Vassiliou
www.musiccenter.org

The Old Globe (619) 231-1941 (619) 234-5623
1363 Old Globe Way
San Diego, CA 92101
Contact: Debbie Ballard
FAX **(619) 231-9518**
www.theoldglobe.org

Orpheum Theatre (877) 677-4386 (213) 626-5321
842 S. Broadway
Los Angeles, CA 90014
Contact: Steve Needleman
www.laorpheum.com

REDCAT (213) 237-2810
631 W. Second St.
Los Angeles, CA 90012
FAX **(213) 237-2811**
www.redcat.org

Renberg Theatre (323) 860-7336
The Village at Ed Gould Plaza
1125 N. McCadden Pl.
Los Angeles, CA 90038
FAX **(323) 308-4103**
www.lagaycenter.org

Rose Bowl (626) 577-3130 (626) 577-3206
1001 Rose Bowl Dr.
Pasadena, CA 91103
Contacts: Julie Granillo & Erika Samarzich
FAX **(626) 405-0992**
www.rosebowlstadium.com

Santa Anita Park (626) 574-6373
285 W. Huntington Dr.
Arcadia, CA 91007
Contact: Pete Siberell
FAX **(626) 821-1530**
www.santaanita.com

The Shrine Auditorium (213) 748-5116
649 W. Jefferson Blvd.
Los Angeles, CA 90007
FAX **(213) 742-9922**
www.shrineauditorium.com

Staples Center (213) 742-7100
1111 S. Figueroa St.
Los Angeles, CA 90015
www.staplescenter.com

Universal Studios Hollywood Theme Park (818) 622-6836
(Theme Park Show Stages)
FAX **(818) 622-0407**
www.universalstudios.com/laps

Writers Guild Theater (323) 782-4525
135 S. Doheny Dr.
Beverly Hills, CA 90211
Contact: Emal Nessary
www.wga.org

American Barricade, Inc. (714) 634-2663 / (818) 955-8500
2141 S. Dupont Dr. FAX (714) 634-2666
Anaheim, CA 92806 www.americanbarricade.net
(Equipment & Services)

American Barrier Systems, Inc. (805) 648-2128 / (877) 774-4664
3989 Market St. FAX (805) 648-1543
Ventura, CA 93003 www.americanbarriers.com
(Equipment)

Castex Rentals (323) 462-1468
1044 Cole Ave. FAX (323) 462-3719
Hollywood, CA 90038 www.castexrentals.com
(Equipment)

Heavy Artillery Production Rentals (310) 295-1202
3200 S. La Cienega Blvd. FAX (310) 295-1202
Los Angeles, CA 90016 www.heavyartilleryrentals.com
(Equipment)

ITC Barricades, Inc. (714) 892-5858 / (661) 816-6270
P.O. Box 858 FAX (714) 892-5887
Westminster, CA 92684 mysite.verizon.net/itcbarricades/
(Equipment & Services)

JCL Barricade Company (213) 622-9775
2334 E. Eighth St. FAX (213) 622-9790
Los Angeles, CA 90021 www.jclbarricade.com
(Equipment & Services)

Pacific Production Services, Inc. (323) 465-9179 / (213) 360-7844
6513 Hollywood Blvd., Ste. 214 FAX (323) 465-9869
Los Angeles, CA 90028 www.lafilmpermits.com
(Equipment & Services)

RC Production Rentals (310) 621-7113
13105 Saticoy St. FAX (310) 943-0480
North Hollywood, CA 91605 www.rcproductionrentals.com
(Equipment)

Traffic Management, Inc. (562) 595-4278
2435 Lemon Ave. FAX (562) 424-0266
Signal Hill, CA 90755 www.trafficmanagement.com
(Equipment & Services)

Xpendable Rentals (323) 656-0905
5925 Santa Monica Blvd. FAX (323) 375-1711
Hollywood, CA 90038 www.xpendablerentals.com
(Equipment)

Altour (310) 571-6000
(800) 878-5847
12100 W. Olympic Blvd., Ste. 300 FAX **(310) 571-3157**
Los Angeles, CA 90064 **www.altour.com**

Beach Rentals US/ Carlson Wagonlit Travel (951) 239-1211
40168 Village Rd., Ste. 1334 **www.beachrentalsus.com**
Temecula, CA 92591

Intercontinental Visa Service (213) 625-7175
350 S. Figueroa St., Ste. 185 FAX **(213) 625-7170**
Los Angeles, CA 90071 **www.ivisaservice.com**
(Visa Service)

Judy Garland & Associates (310) 376-1337
(310) 849-1604
1181 Cypress Ave., Ste. A
Hermosa Beach, CA 90254

Larchmont Travel Service (323) 936-2830
6210 Wilshire Blvd., Ste. 205 FAX **(323) 417-4931**
Los Angeles, CA 90048 **www.concordworldtravel.com**
Mon–Fri 8:30am–5:30pm, Sat 11am–3pm

Montrose Travel (818) 553-3330
2355 Honolulu Ave. FAX **(818) 248-7358**
Montrose, CA 91020 **www.montrosetravel.com**
Mon–Fri 9am–5pm

Plaza Travel (818) 990-4053
(800) 347-4447
16530 Ventura Blvd., Ste. 106 FAX **(818) 789-5405**
Encino, CA 91436 **www.plazatravel.com**

PNR Travel (310) 574-6800
1726 Westwood Blvd. FAX **(310) 574-6801**
Los Angeles, CA 90024 **www.pnrtravel.com**
Mon–Fri 8:30am–5:30pm

Pothos, Inc. (619) 546-0621
(619) 757-4295
2260 El Cajon Blvd., Ste. 474 FAX **(413) 723-7838**
San Diego, CA 92104 **www.pothos.us**

Production Travel & Tours (818) 760-0327
Mon–Fri 9am–6pm FAX **(818) 760-8406**
www.adventureplanners.org

Rand-Fields Division of Pro-Travel Intl. (310) 274-7666
9171 Wilshire Blvd., Ste. 428 FAX **(310) 271-9597**
Beverly Hills, CA 90210 **www.protravelinc.com**
Mon–Fri 9am–5:30pm

Sabrina Brazil Travel (888) 456-2224
14320 Ventura Blvd., Ste. 246 FAX **(818) 789-4523**
Sherman Oaks, CA 91423 **www.sabrinabraziltravel.com**

The Travel Exchange (323) 848-8022
Mon–Fri 10am–5pm FAX **(323) 848-8023**

Travel Express LA (310) 728-1831
9200 Sunset Blvd., Ste. 320 FAX **(310) 728-1881**
West Hollywood, CA 90069 **www.travelexpressla.com**

Travel Management Group/TMG (512) 940-6118
6176 Outlook Ave. **www.tmg.la**
Los Angeles, CA 90042

Travel of America (626) 814-6350
(800) 228-8843
668 Arrow Grand Circle FAX **(626) 331-7051**
Covina, CA 91722
Mon–Fri 7am–6pm, Sat 10am–3pm

TravelStore (310) 689-5400
11601 Wilshire Blvd., Ste. 325 FAX **(310) 689-5401**
Los Angeles, CA 90025 **www.travelstoreusa.com**
Mon–Fri 8am–5pm

V.I.P. Travel Values (818) 501-0808
(800) 949-0908
16633 Ventura Blvd., Ste. 725 FAX **(818) 501-0988**
Encino, CA 91436 **www.bullrush.com**

Visas International (818) 859-7101
(800) 638-1517
3005 W. Victory Blvd. FAX **(818) 859-7103**
Burbank, CA 91505 **www.visasintl.com**
(Visa Service)
Mon–Fri 9am–5pm

Westside International Travel at Altour (310) 571-6090
FAX **(310) 689-5995**

A **Willett Travel** (818) 762-0676
(800) 994-5538
FAX **(818) 763-7806**
www.willetttravel.com
(Corporate, Production & Vacation Travel)
Mon–Fri 9am–5pm

California Weather & Earth Sciences, LLC (800) 843-7246
(760) 684-5761
(Worldwide Forecasts) FAX (760) 868-0906
www.califweather.com

CompuWeather (800) 825-4445
(323) 666-4411
FAX (800) 825-4441
www.filmweather.com
(24-Hour Live Meteorologists, Hurricane Surveillance, Live Forecasts, Nationwide Weather & Worldwide Weather)

Los Angeles Weather & Vicinity (805) 988-6610
(Recorded Forecasts)

Metro Weather Service (800) 488-7866
FAX (800) 768-7998
www.metroweather.com
(24-Hour Live Meteorologists for Nationwide and Worldwide Weather)

Pacific Coast Forecasting (818) 787-1287
(877) 359-4723
7530 Hayvenhurst Ave. FAX (818) 787-3187
Van Nuys, CA 91406 www.pcforecasting.com
(Worldwide Weather)

Weather Watch Service (863) 709-1221
(Worldwide Weather) FAX (863) 709-1221
www.weatherwatchservice.com

NOTES:

LA 411

L.A. COUNTY MUSEUM OF ART

L.A. STORY

INT. L.A. COUNTY MUSEUM OF ART - SUNDAY

Harris (Steve Martin) and Ariel look at paintings. Ariel holds a small home video camera. They both are looking around sneakily. They separate. Harris watches the guard from the corner of his eye. The guard disappears, momentarily, around a corner. Harris reaches down and pulls levers on his shoes. Roller-skate wheels pop out and he skates through the gallery while Ariel videotapes him.

INT. L.A. COUNTY MUSEUM OF ART - GALLERY - DAY

Harris, Sara (Victoria Tennent), Roland (Richard E. Grant) and Ariel are taking in a painting.

HARRIS

(Admiring)

I like the relationships. I mean, each character has his own story. The puppy is a bit too much, but you have to overlook things like that in these kinds of paintings. The way he's holding her... it's almost... filthy. I mean, he's about to kiss her and she's pulling away. The way the legs are sort of smashed up against her... Phew... Look how he's painted the blouse... sort of translucent. You can just make out her breasts underneath and it's sort of touching him about here. It's really... pretty torrid, don't you think? Then of course you have the onlookers peeking at them from behind the doorway like they're all shocked. They wish. Yeah, I must admit, when I see a painting like this, I get emotionally... erect.

The painting is revealed to be of a red rectangle.

SCREENPLAY BY:
Steve Martin

ALSO FILMED AT LACMA:
I Am Sam

LA 411

www.LA411.com

■ PICTURED:
LACMA

■ LOCATION:
Miracle Mile

■ PHOTOGRAPHER:
Michael Rueter
Michael Rueter Photography/L.A.-N.Y.
www.michaelrueter.com

Supporting production in Southern California for 31 years

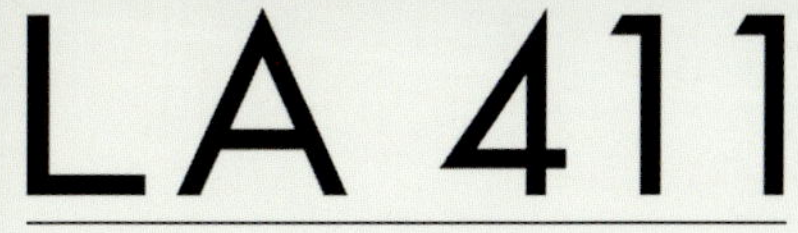

Production Support

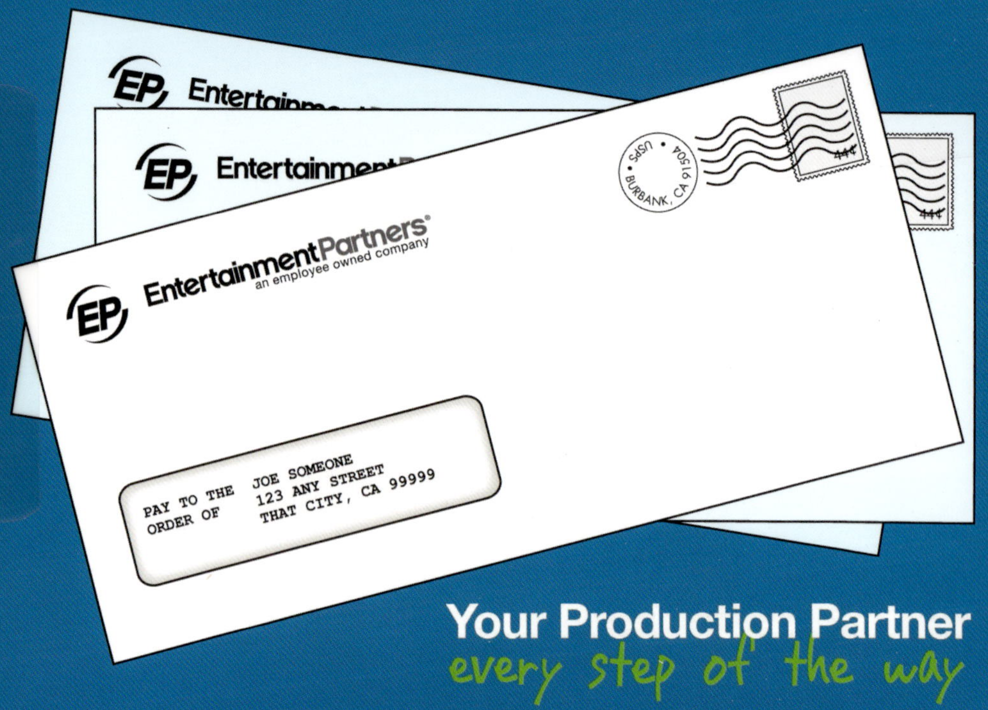

Your Production Partner
every step of the way

California

2835 N. Naomi St.
Burbank, CA 91504-2024
Phone: 818.955.6000
Support: 800.624.3472

Florida

2000 Universal Studios Plaza
Suite 620
Orlando, FL 32819-7606
Phone: 407.354.5900

Louisiana

3445 Causeway Blvd.
Suites 328 - 329
Metairie, LA 70002
Phone: 504.296.2502

New Mexico

5650 University Blvd., SE
Production Bldg. A, Room 231
Albuquerque, NM 87106
Phone: 505.227.2240

New York

875 6th Ave., 15th Floor
New York, NY 10001-3507
Phone: 646.473.9000

www.entertainmentpartners.com

Ⓐ ADVERTISER SYMBOL

Refer to the General Index for cross-referencing items in this section.

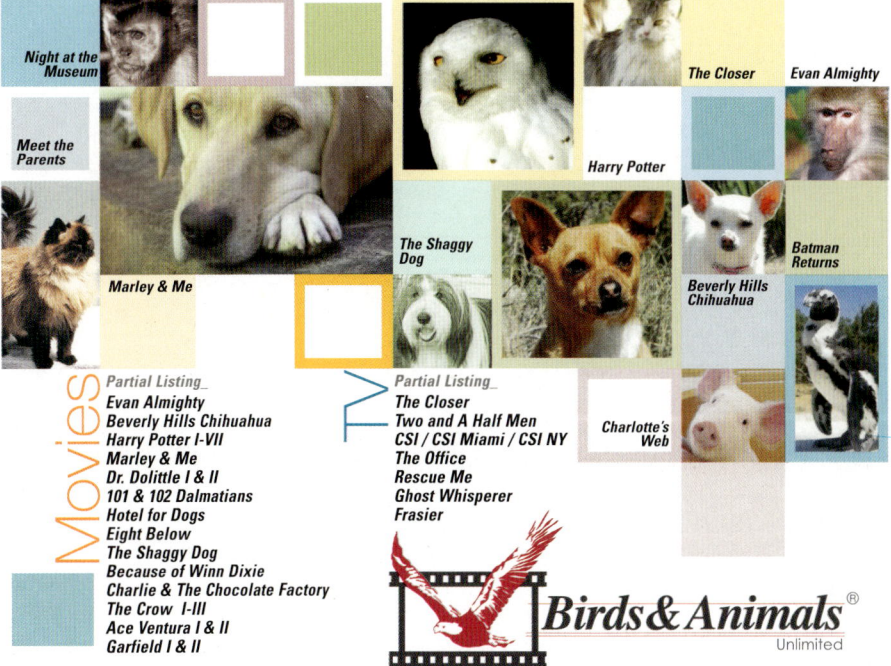

Accurate English (310) 892-3556
13101 Washington Blvd., Ste. 231
Los Angeles, CA 90066
(Accent Reduction & Dialect Coaching)

Robert Easton (818) 985-2222
www.roberteaston.org

Joel Goldes/The Dialect Coach (818) 879-1896
www.thedialectcoach.com

Peter Kelley (212) 431-4000
601 W. 26th St., Ste. 1762
New York, NY 10001
(Acting Coaching)
www.actingonfilm.com

Larry Moss Speech & Dialect Services (310) 395-4284

Kevin McDermott (310) 800-5691
(Acting Coaching)
www.theactorscircle.com

Wayne Dvorak Acting Studio (323) 462-5328
www.waynedvorak.com

1st Phil's Animal Rentals (805) 521-1100
P.O. Box 309 FAX (805) 521-0956
Piru, CA 93040 www.philsanimalrentals.com
(Baby Animals, Buffalo, Bulls, Chickens, Cows, Dogs, Donkeys, Ducks, Goats, Horses, Livestock, Pigs, Rabbits & Sheep)

A2Z Animals (661) 269-1999
FAX (661) 269-0989
www.a2zanimals.com

AAA Performing Animal Troupe (661) 722-1497
4154 W. Avenue North FAX (661) 722-1498
Palmdale, CA 93551 www.performinganimaltroupe.com
(Domestics, Exotics, Horses & Livestock)

Aaron's Animal Ark (818) 888-5548
18375 Ventura Blvd., Ste. 539 FAX (818) 888-5548
Tarzana, CA 91356
(Birds, Cats, Dogs, Elephants, Farm Animals, Raccoons, Reptiles & Squirrels)

Acting Dogs by Steven Ritt (661) 269-3647
(661) 268-8223
33040 Big Springs Rd. www.actingdogs.com
Acton, CA 93510

Action Bulls (805) 878-6948
P.O. Box 5175 FAX (805) 931-0961
Santa Maria, CA 93456
(Rodeo Animals)

Action Animal Rental (661) 268-0534
(323) 353-2281
11426 Sierra Hwy FAX (323) 295-3085
Agua Dulce, CA 91390 www.actionanimals.com

Action Reptiles (951) 897-8317
(Alligators, Amphibians, Insects, Lizards, Snakes, Tarantulas & Turtles)

All Stars Studio Animals (818) 421-4327
(Dogs) www.allstarsanimals.com

Alvin's Animal Rental (909) 823-9437
P.O. Box CB FAX (909) 822-2748
Bloomington, CA 92316 www.alvinanimalrentals.com
(Domestic and Wild Animals)

American Humane Association (818) 501-0123
(800) 677-3420
15366 Dickens St. FAX (818) 501-8725
Sherman Oaks, CA 91403 www.americanhumane.org/film

Animal Actors of Hollywood, Inc. (805) 495-2122
860 W. Carlisle Rd. FAX (805) 496-3053
Thousand Oaks, CA 91361 www.animalactors.net
(Barnyard, Birds, Cats, Deer, Dogs, Elephants, Ferrets, Foxes, Monkeys, Porcupines, Raccoons, Rats, Reptiles, Sloth, Squirrels & Wolves)

Animal Actors Sweet Sunshine (951) 609-1687
(877) 609-1687
FAX (951) 609-1687
www.animal-actors.com
(Birds, Cats, Dogs, Exotics, Elephants, Farm Animals, Horses, Insects, Livestock, Monkeys, Reptiles, Small Wildlife, Trick Horses & Wolves)

Animal Fantasy Shows (661) 944-1651
(661) 944-4888
P.O. Box 1260 FAX (661) 944-6773
Littlerock, CA 93543
(Dogs, Macaw Parrots & White and Bay Andalusian Horses)

Animal Savvy (661) 492-0776
16654 Soledad Canyon Rd., Box 151 FAX (661) 298-2532
Canyon Country, CA 91387 www.animalsavvy.net
(Birds, Cats, Dogs, Insects, Livestock, Rabbits, Rodents & Small Exotics)

Animal SuperModels (805) 320-3952
P.O. Box 7004 www.animalsupermodels.com
Thousand Oaks, CA 91360
(Birds, Cats, Dogs, Farm Animals & Horses)

Animals For You/Diana Smith (805) 521-1000
(Barnyard Animals & Livestock) FAX (805) 521-1010
www.animalsforyou.com

Animals of a Different Color (661) 252-3300
(805) 358-4818
16900 Forrest St. FAX (661) 252-9870
Canyon Country, CA 91351 www.animalcolorist.com
(Animal Colorist)

Aquatic Design (310) 822-7484
(310) 420-8379
4943 McConnell Ave., Ste. K FAX (310) 822-8644
Los Angeles, CA 90066 www.aquatic2000.com
(Fish)

STEVE MARTIN'S
WORKING WILDLIFE
DOGS
LARGE CATS
BEARS
PRIMATES
WOLVES / COYOTES
HOOF STOCK
FOREST ANIMALS
BIRDS
REPTILES
EXOTICS

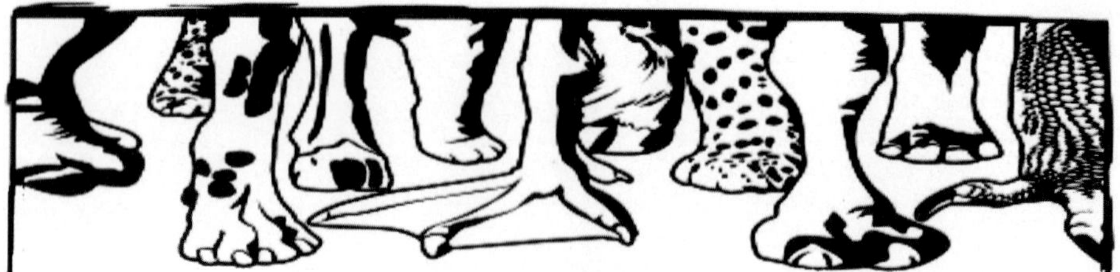

Ⓐ Bear...With Us (661) 724-0409 / (661) 886-1794
P.O. Box 469
Acton, CA 93510
www.bearwithme.org
(Bears)

Bee & Insect People Unlimited (800) 924-3097
FAX (909) 869-7391
(Bees, Insects, Spiders & Wasps)

Benay's Bird & Animal Source, Inc. (818) 881-0053
4776 Nomad Dr.
Woodland Hills, CA 91364
FAX (818) 888-5548
www.benaysanimals.com
(Birds, Cats, Coati, Dogs, Exotics, Farm Animals, Horses, Monkeys, Raccoons, Reptiles, Rodents, Sea Lions, Skunks, Squirrels & Wildlife)

Bill Rivers' Movieland Animals (210) 478-8808
FAX (951) 926-1854
www.movielandanimals.com
(American Buffaloes, Camels & Exotics)

Birdman (702) 896-4274
FAX (702) 896-4275
www.birdman.tv
(Condors, Crows, Eagles & Free Flying Birds)

Ⓐ Birds & Animals Unlimited (949) 830-7845
FAX (949) 830-5116
www.birdsandanimals.com
(Birds, Cats, Dogs, Exotics, Farm Animals, Horses, Insects, Livestock, Primates, Reptiles, Small Animals & Snakes)

Bob Dunn's Animal Services (818) 896-0394
16001 Yarnell St.
Sylmar, CA 91342
FAX (818) 364-0222
www.animalservices.com
(Birds, Chimps, Fish, Insects, Orangutans & Reptiles)

Boone's Animals for Hollywood, Inc. (661) 257-0630
FAX (661) 257-4274
www.boonesanimals.com
(Birds, Cats, Dogs & Rodents)

Bow Wow Productions (408) 621-0620 / (800) 926-9969
www.bowwowproductions.com
(Birds, Cats, Dogs, Exotics & Farm Animals)

Brian McMillan's Hollywood Animals (323) 665-9500 / (323) 481-4806
4103 Holly Knoll Dr.
Los Angeles, CA 90027
FAX (323) 665-9200
www.hollywoodanimals.com
(Domestics & Exotics)

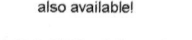

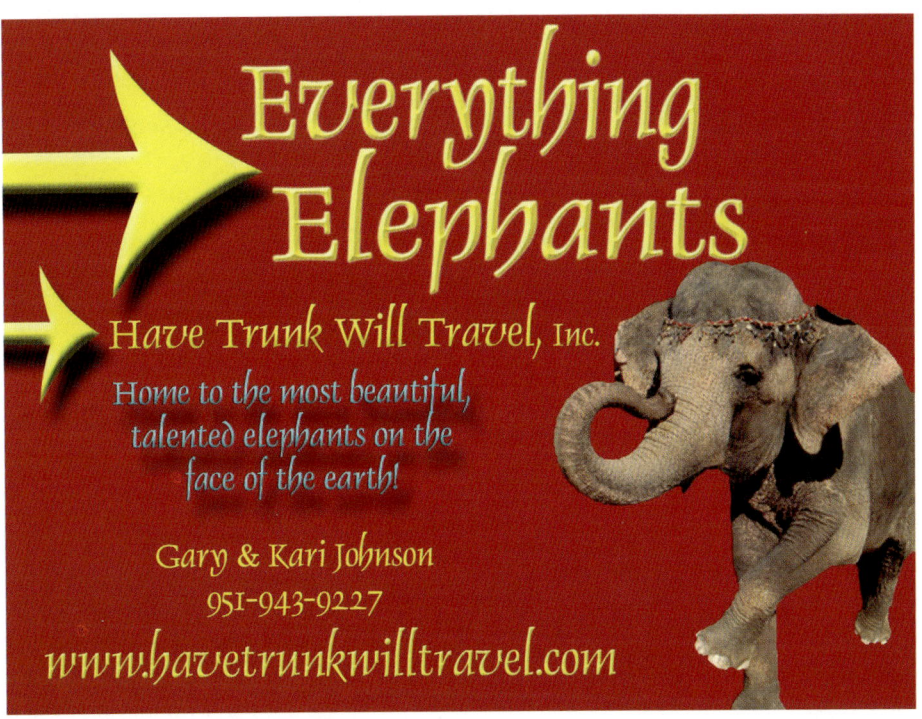

Brockett's Film Fauna, Inc. (805) 379-3141
437 W. Carlisle Rd. FAX (805) 379-4585
Thousand Oaks, CA 91361 www.brockettsfilmfauna.com
(Alligators, Amphibians, Birds, Cats, Crocodiles, Dogs, Insects, Reptiles, Small Animals, Snakes & Spiders)

Bugs Are My Business/ Steve Kutcher (626) 836-0322
1801 Oakview Ln. home.earthlink.net/~skutcher
Arcadia, CA 91006
(Butterflies, Insects, Small Animals & Spiders)

Caravan West Productions (661) 268-8300
35660 Jayhawker Rd. FAX (661) 268-8301
Agua Dulce, CA 91390 www.caravanwest.com
(Horses & Livestock)

Cats & Cockatoos of Hollywood (866) 264-6257
(623) 205-0245
www.cats-cockatoos.com
(Amphibians, Birds, Cats, Dogs, Exotics, Fishes, Horses & Reptiles)

Jennifer Conrad, DVM (310) 394-5877
(310) 948-6789
P.O. Box 445 FAX (310) 394-5877
Santa Monica, CA 90406
(On Set Veterinarian)

Cougar Hill Ranch (661) 533-3549
P.O. Box 132 FAX (661) 533-1590
Littlerock, CA 93543 www.cougarhillranch.com
(Birds, Domestics, Exotics, Farm Animals & Reptiles)

Creature Features Travelin' Zoo (310) 980-7305
www.creaturefeaturestravellingzoo.com
(Insects, Reptiles, Scorpions & Spiders)

Critters of the Cinema (661) 724-1929
(800) 233-3647
P.O. Box 378 FAX (661) 724-1868
Lake Hughes, CA 93532 www.crittersofthecinema.com
(Barnyard Animals, Birds, Cats, Dogs, Exotics & Reptiles)

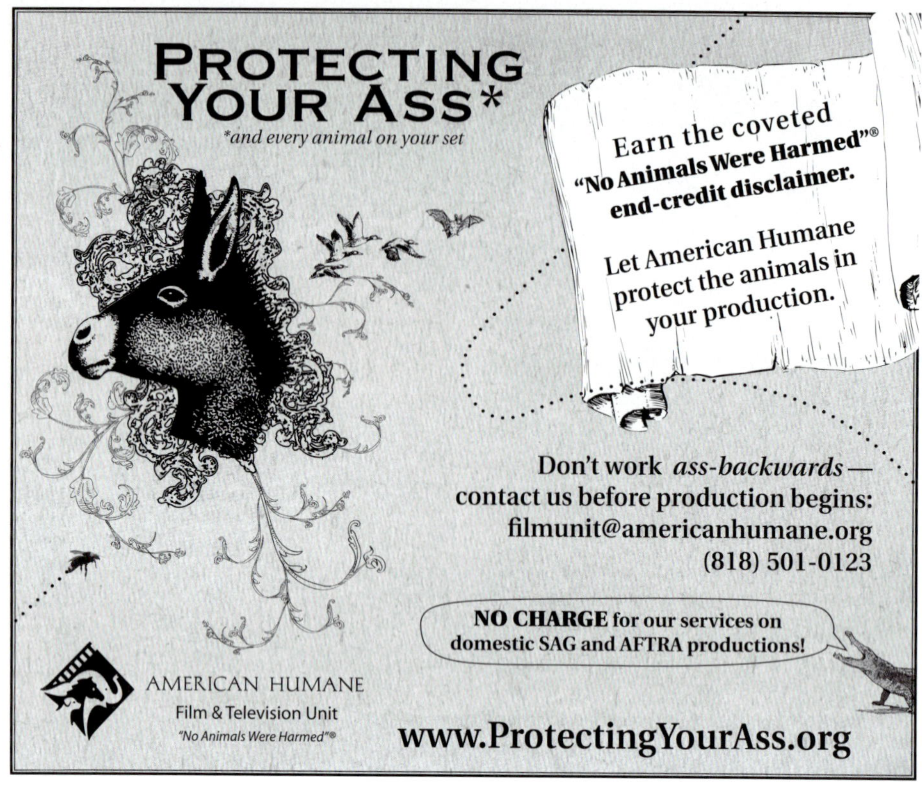

Doves Trained for TV (818) 340-4040
(Trained Doves and Pigeons) FAX (818) 340-2432
www.traineddoves.com

Dusty Promotions, LLC (866) 552-2262
(Horses) www.dustypromotions.com

The Elephant Store/Cheryl Shawver (805) 497-1238
850 W. Carlisle Rd. FAX (805) 496-3053
Thousand Oaks, CA 91361
(Birds, Dogs & Elephants)

Feature Creatures (805) 484-8999
(877) 364-4852
348 Mission Dr. FAX (805) 445-7599
Camarillo, CA 93010 www.tlc4dogs.net
(Domestics, Exotics & Farm Animals)

Gentle Jungle (661) 248-6195
P.O. Box 832 FAX (661) 248-6992
Lebec, CA 93243 www.gentlejungle.com
(Domestics, Exotics, Farm Animals & Horses)

Goin' Ape (661) 252-7816
(530) 823-2300
P.O. Box 9147 FAX (530) 823-1874
Auburn, CA 95604
(Primates)

Grisco's Animals (951) 685-4081
(951) 215-0980
P.O. Box 54 FAX (951) 685-2142
Mira Loma, CA 91752 www.griscosanimals.com
(Alligators, Barnyard Animals, Birds of Prey, Cats & Dogs)

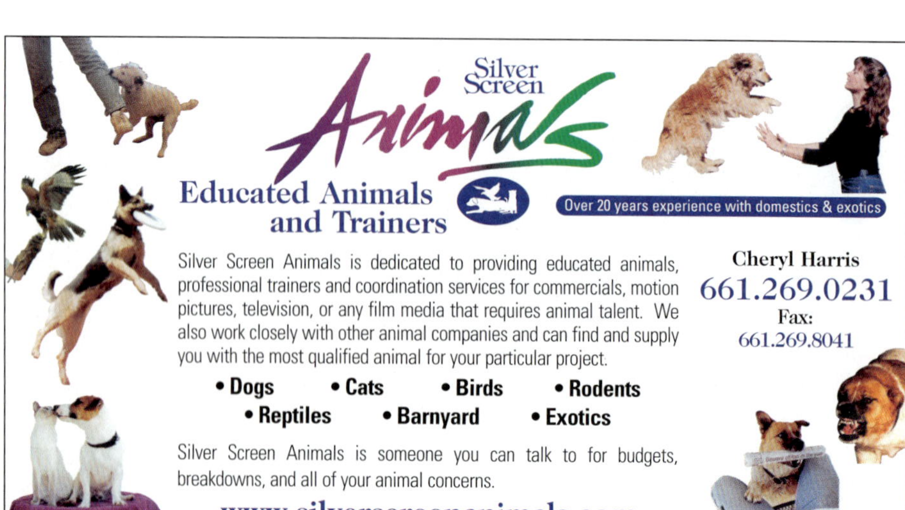

Hart Brothers Livestock (951) 312-9009
(951) 677-6810
FAX (951) 600-3805
(Barnyard Animals, Buffalo, Bulls, Cattle, Driving Horses, Farm Animals, Livestock & Riding and Trick Horses)

Ⓐ **Have Trunk Will Travel, Inc.** (951) 943-9227
(Elephants) FAX (951) 943-9563
www.havetrunkwilltravel.com

Horses for Productions (310) 457-7027
(310) 961-1584
2277 Decker Canyon Rd. www.horsesforproductions.com
Malibu, CA 90265
(Horses, Hunting Hounds, Ponies & Riders)

Jules Sylvester's Reptile Rentals Inc. (818) 706-0815
(818) 621-4101
FAX (818) 707-3537
www.reptilerentals.com
(Frogs, Insects, Reptiles, Rodents, Scorpions, Spiders & Tortoises)

Jungle Exotics (909) 887-3500
16215 Cajon Blvd. FAX (909) 887-0953
San Bernardino, CA 92407 www.junglexotics.com
(Cats, Dogs, Insects, Reptiles & Wild Animals)

Kathryn Segura PHD Animals (818) 744-4254
FAX (818) 980-1846
www.take1products.com
(Aquatics, Birds, Domestics, Exotics, Horses, Insects & Reptiles)

Kim's Exotic Critters (818) 353-2717
(818) 402-6880
FAX (818) 352-5513
www.movieanimals.com
(Barnyard Animals, Birds, Bugs, Cats, Dogs, Domestics, Exotics, Miniature Mules & Reptiles)

Ⓐ Lane Ranch & Company (661) 942-0435
42220 10th St. West, Ste. 101 FAX (661) 942-7485
Lancaster, CA 93534 www.laneranch.net
(Draft Animals, Liberty and Trick Horses & Livestock)

Le PAWS (310) 782-6573
438 Amapola Ave., Ste. 115 FAX (310) 381-3699
Torrance, CA 90501 www.lepawsagency.com
(Dogs)

Lundin Farm (661) 252-6140
(818) 618-9959
(Farm Animals & Horses) www.rrstar.net

Bernie Mailberg/Ro-Ed (562) 943-7978
14439 Broadway Court FAX (562) 943-1621
Whittier, CA 90604 www.roed.com
(Pigeon Wrangler)

Mark Jackson Animals (714) 649-3194
(714) 306-9986
P.O. Box 749 FAX (714) 649-2103
Trabuco Canyon, CA 92678 www.mjanimals.com

Merrill Carson Show & Ranch (818) 780-1735
(818) 782-5758
7905 Lloyd Ave. FAX (818) 780-7738
North Hollywood, CA 91605 www.merrillcarson.com
(Palominos)

Mike Boyle Ranches (805) 526-0321
(805) 230-9315
(Livestock & Trick Horses) FAX (805) 520-8037
www.mikeboyleranches.com

Moe DiSesso Trained Animals (661) 255-7969
24233 Old Rd. FAX (661) 255-8179
Santa Clarita, CA 91321 www.animalactors4hire.com
(Domestics & Small Exotics)

Movin' On Livestock Rental Co. (661) 252-8654
(661) 269-5952
20527 Soledad St. FAX (661) 250-8843
Canyon Country, CA 91351 www.movinonlivestock.com

Oliver Livestock (951) 741-1922
(951) 767-9493
38565 San Ignacio Rd. www.oliverlivestock.com
Hemet, CA 92544
(Farm Animals)

Omar's Exotic Birds, Inc. (310) 659-6552
(714) 315-6159
8729 Santa Monica Blvd. FAX (310) 659-6553
West Hollywood, CA 90069 www.omarsexoticbirds.com

Paws For Effect (661) 724-2201
(877) 729-7439
(Birds, Cats, Dogs, Exotics & Livestock) FAX (661) 724-2252
www.pawsforeffect.net

Randy Miller's Predators in Action (909) 585-9286
P.O. Box 1691 FAX (909) 585-9356
Big Bear City, CA 92314 www.predatorsinaction.com
(Black and Grizzly Bears, Cougars, Leopards, Lions, Tigers & White Tigers)

Roger Schumacher Animal Rental (909) 483-4733
P.O. Box 4919 FAX (909) 483-4734
Rancho Cucamonga, CA 91729
www.rogersanimalrentals.com

Ⓐ Rolling Thunder Ranch (661) 252-0461
(661) 478-1616
16163 Sierra Hwy FAX (661) 250-3907
Canyon Country, CA 91351 www.rollingthunderranch.com
(Barnyard Animals, Cows, Llamas, Raccoons, Sheep & Trick Horses)

Ⓐ Silver Screen Animals (661) 269-0231
34540 Brock Ln. FAX (661) 269-8041
Acton, CA 93510 www.silverscreenanimals.com
(Birds, Cats, Dogs, Exotics, Farm Animals, Raccoons, Reptiles, Rodents & Squirrels)

Steve Berens
Animals of Distinction, Inc. (661) 268-1057
P.O. Box 773
Acton, CA 93510
(Birds, Cats & Dogs)

Ⓐ Steve Martin's Working Wildlife (661) 245-2406
FAX (661) 245-3617
www.workingwildlife.com
(Bears, Black Leopards, Chimps, Dogs, Ferrets, Foxes, Lions, Orangutans, Raccoons, Reindeer, Reptiles, Skunks, Tigers & Wolves)

Studio Animal Services (661) 257-4798
28230 San Martinez Grande Canyon Rd. FAX (661) 257-4892
Castaic, CA 91384 www.studioanimals.com
(Barnyard Livestock, Birds, Cats, Dogs, Exotics & Squirrels)

Summersalt Equi-Service, Ltd./
800 Creatures (661) 803-1531
34162 Agua Dulce Canyon Rd.
Saugus, CA 91390
(Domestics, Horses & Insects)

A Tad Western
Production Company, Inc. (661) 268-0658
(661) 609-2033
(Horses & Livestock) FAX (661) 268-0438
www.atadwest.com

Talented Animals (310) 858-8722
1033 N. Carol Dr., Ste. 401 FAX (413) 215-9370
West Hollywood, CA 90069 www.talentedanimals.com
(Birds, Cats, Dogs, Exotics, Horses, Livestock, Primates, Reptiles, Rodents, Wild Animals & Wolves)

Geoffrey Vernon (310) 433-2003
(On-Set Veterinarian) FAX (310) 271-0986

War Horse & Militaria
Heritage Foundation (818) 694-9277
(Horses) FAX (818) 896-8310
www.warhorsefoundation.com

The Wild Bunch Ranch/
Jean Simpson (208) 456-3041
(877) 456-3041
FAX (208) 456-3041
www.thewildbunchranch.com

Wild Things Animal Rentals, Inc. (831) 455-1901
(800) 228-7382
(Domestics & Exotics) FAX (831) 455-1902
www.wildthingsinc.com

Wolves and Company (760) 244-3317
19150 Willow St.
Hesperia, CA 92345
(Domestics & Exotics)

Worldwide Movie Animals, LLC (661) 252-2000
(805) 630-5848
29264 Bouquet Canyon Rd. FAX (661) 252-2001
Santa Clarita, CA 91390
www.worldwidemovieanimals.com
(Beavers, Birds, Camels, Cats, Dogs, Emus, Foxes, Insects, Kangaroos, Monkeys, Ostriches, Porcupines & Snakes)

Ⓐ Entertainment Partners
(818) 955-6299
(646) 473-9000
FAX (818) 845-6507
www.entertainmentpartners.com

Film Budget Pro
(323) 574-9696
FAX (888) 699-9778
www.filmbudgetpro.com

KGB Films
6230 Wilshire Blvd., Ste. 71
Los Angeles, CA 90048
(323) 610-0501
(818) 519-9575
FAX (323) 658-6568
www.kgbfilms.com

Media Services
(310) 440-9696
(800) 333-7518
FAX (310) 472-9979
www.media-services.com

ScheduALL
(818) 754-3735
(818) 259-1508
FAX (818) 754-3739
www.scheduall.com

II Jam Casting & Productions (818) 890-2593
12531 Chanute St. FAX (818) 834-4515
Pacoima, CA 91331 www.twojamcasting.com
(Commercials, Real People & Webisodes)
Contacts: Lee Miguel & Nigel P. Miguel

AAA Urban Casting (310) 967-9954
(661) 255-5097
P.O. Box 800126 FAX (661) 255-5097
Valencia, CA 91380 www.aaaurbancasting.com
(Babies, Celebrities, Children, Circus/Variety Acts, Commercials, Film, Foreign Language Casting, Podcasting, Real People, Reality, TV, Voice Casting & Webisodes)

ABA - Antoinette Motion Picture Production/ Casting Services (310) 323-9028
8306 Wilshire Blvd., PMB 900 www.abaaa.com
Beverly Hills, CA 90211
(Commercials)
Contact: Antoinette Meier

Abesera Casting (323) 931-5622
400 N. Orange Dr. www.abeseracasting.tv
Los Angeles, CA 90036
(Children, Commercials, Film, Music Videos, Real People, Reality & TV)

Aisha Coley Casting (323) 882-4144
7336 Santa Monica Blvd., Ste. 611
Los Angeles, CA 90046
(Film & TV)

Akimas Casting (805) 649-8041
(805) 705-4110
P.O. Box 650 www.akimascastingandtalent.com
Santa Barbara, CA 93116
(Commercials)

Alice Ellis Casting (310) 314-1488
(Commercials) FAX (310) 314-2649
www.elliscasting.com

Alyson Horn Casting/ Studios@Orange (323) 874-8764
1020 N. Sycamore Ave. FAX (323) 874-6330
Los Angeles, CA 90038 www.alysonhorncasting.com
(Commercials)

Annelise Collins Casting (310) 586-1936
(310) 503-1967
3435 Ocean Park Blvd., Ste. 107 www.annelisecast.com
Santa Monica, CA 90405
(Commercials, Film & TV)

Annie Egian Casting (213) 308-5535
FAX (323) 660-2294
www.annieegiancasting.com
(Babies, Celebrities, Children, Circus/Variety Acts, Commercials, Film, Real People, TV & Voice Casting)

April Webster Casting (818) 526-4242
800 Main St., Ste. 310
Burbank, CA 91506
(Film & TV)

ASG Casting, Inc. (818) 762-0200
4144 Lankershim Blvd., Ste. 202 FAX (818) 753-9322
North Hollywood, CA 91602 www.asgcasting.com
(Commercials, Film & TV)
Contacts: Justin Radley & Arlene Schuster-Goss

AthleteSource Casting (310) 871-7956
13425 Ventura Blvd., Second Fl.
Sherman Oaks, CA 91423
www.athletesourcecasting.com
(Real People & Sports Casting)

Patrick Baca (323) 683-9020
606 N. Larchmont Blvd., Ste. 4B
Los Angeles, CA 90004
www.imdb.com/name/nm0045192/
(Film, Industrials, TV & Webisodes)

Bad Girls Casting (323) 468-6888
6660 Santa Monica Blvd., First Fl. FAX (323) 468-8811
Los Angeles, CA 90038 www.badgirlscasting.com
(Commercials, Film & Music Videos)

Barbara Bersell Casting (310) 470-1670
(Commercials, Film & TV)

Rise Barish (310) 456-9018
(310) 458-1100
1216 Fifth St. FAX (310) 457-3117
Santa Monica, CA 90401
(Commercials, Film & TV)

Bass Casting (323) 848-3737
8284 Santa Monica Blvd.
Los Angeles, CA 90046
(Film & TV)

Bebe Flynn Casting (323) 252-6026
(213) 382-8474
(Commercials, Film & Real People) FAX (213) 382-8564
www.bebeflynncasting.com

Beth Holmes Casting, Inc. (818) 980-9803
11340 Moorpark St. FAX (818) 980-2838
Studio City, CA 91602 www.bethholmescasting.com
(Commercials)
Contacts: Beth Holmes & Monica Lee-Eisenbeis

Betty Mae, Inc. (310) 396-6100
1009 Abbott Kinney, Second Fl. FAX (310) 396-1313
Venice, CA 90291
(Film & TV)

Beverly Long Casting (818) 754-6222
11425 Moorpark St. FAX (818) 754-6226
Studio City, CA 91602
(Commercials, Film & TV)

Billy DaMota Casting (818) 243-1263
(818) 903-6048
13425 Ventura Blvd., Ste. 200 FAX (818) 243-1720
Sherman Oaks, CA 91423 www.castboy.com
(Commercials, Film & TV)

Blanca Valdez Casting En Español (323) 876-5700
1001 N. Poinsettia Pl. FAX (323) 876-5297
West Hollywood, CA 90046 www.blancavaldez.com
(Spanish Language Casting)

Bluewater Ranch/ Casting Artists, Inc. (310) 395-1882
1433 Sixth St. www.bluewaterranch.com
Santa Monica, CA 90401
(Film & TV)

Charles Bogdan (323) 606-2636
(Commercials, Film & TV) www.charlesbogdan.com

De De Brinkman (310) 892-0003
(970) 920-4705
(Real People) FAX (970) 925-8378

broad-cast/Lien-Cowan Casting (323) 937-0411
7461 Beverly Blvd., Ste. 203 FAX (323) 937-2070
Los Angeles, CA 90036 www.broad-cast.tv
(Commercials)
Contact: Dan Cowan

Brown/West Casting (323) 938-2575
7319 Beverly Blvd., Ste. 10
Los Angeles, CA 90036
(Film & TV)

Bump It Casting/Balyndah Bumpus (213) 700-5139
5482 Wilshire Blvd., Ste. 363 FAX (323) 737-1430
Los Angeles, CA 90036
(Babies, Celebrities, Children, Commercials, Film, Real People, Reality, Spanish Language, TV, Voice Casting & Webisodes)

Burbank Casting/ Susan Turner' McMains (818) 559-2446
2829 N. Glenoaks, Stes. 106-148
Burbank, CA 91504 **www.susanturnercasting.com**
(Celebrities, Children, Commercials, Film, Industrials, Podcasting, Real People, Reality, TV, Voice Casting & Webisodes)

Burrows/Boland Casting (310) 503-4719
333 W. Washington Blvd., Ste. 309
Marina del Rey, CA 90292
(Film & TV) **www.burrowsboland.com**

Cami Patton Casting (818) 509-5779
4640 Lankershim Blvd., Ste. 511
North Hollywood, CA 91602
(Film & TV)

Carnes & Company (818) 445-0996
(Commercials)
Contact: Thomas Carnes

Carol Lefko Casting (310) 888-0007
P.O. Box 84509
Los Angeles, CA 90073
(Film & TV)

Carol Rosenthal Casting (213) 483-4200
www.rosenthalcasting.com
(Commercials, Film, Music Videos & PSAs)

Carrafiello Casting (818) 512-7710, (818) 817-4374
13425 Ventura Blvd., Second Fl. **www.ccasting.net**
Sherman Oaks, CA 91423
(Commercials, Film & TV)
Contacts: Meghan Carrafiello

Carroll Voiceover Casting Co. (323) 851-9966
6767 Forest Lawn Dr., Ste. 203 FAX **(323) 851-3973**
Los Angeles, CA 90068
(Commercials)
Contact: Carroll Kimble

Casting Brothers (818) 763-1361
Fifth Street Studios, 1216 Fifth St.
Santa Monica, CA 90401 **www.castingbrothers.com**
(Commercials, Industrials, Real People & Voice Casting)
Contacts: Alan Kaminsky & Joshua Rappaport

Casting by Lila Selik (310) 556-2444
P.O. Box 66369 **www.castingbylilaselik.com**
Los Angeles, CA 90066
(Commercials, Film & TV)

The Casting Connection (310) 924-9803, (310) 508-3033
5536 Carpenter Ave.
Valley Village, CA 91607
(Commercials, Film & TV)
Contacts: Mary Ann Phelps & Peter Szeliga

The Casting Couch, Inc./ Sande Alessi (818) 201-0466
13731 Ventura Blvd. **www.sandealessicasting.com**
Sherman Oaks, CA 91423
(Commercials, Film & TV)

Cathi Carlton Casting, Inc. (310) 581-3010
2701 Ocean Park Blvd., Ste. 250
Santa Monica, CA 90405 **www.cathicarltoncasting.com**
(Commercials)

Cervantes Nomad Casting (323) 330-1020
c/o 200 South Studios FAX **(323) 931-4992**
200 S. La Brea Ave., Ste. C **www.nomadcasting.com**
Los Angeles, CA 90036
(Commercials, Film, Real People & TV)
Contact: Toni Cervantes

CFB Casting (323) 993-5682, (323) 822-3688
(Film & TV)

Charisse Glenn Casting (818) 735-7372, (310) 656-4600
(Commercials) FAX **(818) 735-7964**
www.cgcasting.com

Christal Blue Casting (323) 960-5057
(Commercials, Film & TV) **www.christalblue.com**

Clair Sinnett Casting (310) 606-0813, (310) 606-5626
(Commercials, Film & TV) FAX **(310) 606-0823**
www.clairsinnettcasting.com
Contacts: Jamie Boalbey & Heather Shay

Combat Casting (310) 686-2718
6850 Vineland Ave., Ste. N FAX **(818) 509-9581**
North Hollywood, CA 91605 **www.combatcasting.com**

Craig Colvin & Co. (323) 785-7850
(Commercials, Film & TV)

crashcasting & Associates (323) 385-6537, (818) 817-4348
(Commercials & Real People) FAX **(818) 728-6785**
Contact: Rosanna

Creative Casting Services (818) 846-3200
(Children, Commercials & Real People) FAX **(818) 846-3099**

Currently Casting, Inc. (818) 613-7703
Michelle Metzner, CSA FAX **(818) 760-0355**
13636 Ventura Blvd., Ste. 411 **www.currentlycasting.net**
Sherman Oaks, CA 91423
(Commercials, Film, Music Videos, Podcasting, Reality, TV & Webisodes)
Contact: Michelle Metzner

Danielle Eskinazi Casting (323) 969-8200
7700 W. Sunset Blvd. FAX **(323) 969-0101**
West Hollywood, CA 90046 **www.daniellecasting.com**
(Commercials, Film & TV)

Danny Stoltz Casting (310) 728-9522
www.dannystoltzcasting.com
(Commercials & Real People)

David Glanzer Casting (213) 369-4345
7985 Santa Monica Blvd., Ste. 570 **www.dgcasting.com**
Los Angeles, CA 90046
(Film & TV)

David Kang Casting (323) 969-8200
7700 Sunset Blvd., Second Fl. FAX **(323) 969-0101**
Los Angeles, CA 90046 **www.davidkangcasting.net**
(Babies, Celebrities, Children, Circus/Variety Acts, Commercials, Film, Podcasting, Real People, TV & Webisodes)

Debe Waisman Casting (818) 752-7052, (310) 535-1325
11684 Ventura Blvd., PMB 415
Studio City, CA 91604
(Commercials)

Deborah Kurtz Casting, Inc. (310) 550-5300
8899 Beverly Blvd. FAX **(310) 248-5297**
Los Angeles, CA 90048
(Commercials, Film & TV)

Deedra Ricketts Casting (323) 807-5825
686 S. Arroyo Pkwy, Ste. 6 FAX **(323) 550-1173**
Pasadena, CA 91105 **www.ddcasting.com**
(Commercials)

DeHorter Majomi Casting (323) 957-1657
c/o CSA, 606 N. Larchmont Blvd., Ste. 4B **zdcasting.net**
Los Angeles, CA 90004
(Commercials, Film, TV & Webisodes)

Dickson/Arbusto Casting (323) 871-8501
P.O.Box 27668
Los Angeles, CA 90027
(Film & TV)

Digital Dogs Casting (323) 651-0123 / (323) 651-0888
P.O. Box 48229 FAX (323) 969-0101
Los Angeles, CA 90048 **www.digitaldogscasting.com**
(Commercials, Film and TV)
Contact: Robert B. Martin, Jr.

Dino Ladki Casting/Dino Ladki (310) 289-4962
8556 Rugby Dr. **www.dinoladkicasting.com**
West Hollywood, CA 90069
(Commercials, Film, Industrials, TV, Voice Casting & Webisodes)

Doron Ofir Casting (323) 203-1331 / (310) 779-6112
7250 Franklin Ave., Ste. 1006 FAX (310) 943-1598
Los Angeles, CA 90046 **www.popularproductions.net**

Dowd-Roman Casting (323) 665-1776 / (323) 330-1020
200 S. La Brea Ave., Second Fl. FAX (323) 954-0933
Los Angeles, CA 90036
(Babies, Celebrities, Children, Commercials, Foreign Language Casting, Industrials, Podcasting, Real People, Voice Casting & Webisodes)

Eastside Studios (323) 660-7874
4216 Fountain Ave. FAX (323) 660-7875
Los Angeles, CA 90029 **www.eastsidestudiosla.com**
(Commercials)
Contact: Doug Mangskau

Elaine Craig Voice Casting, Inc. (323) 469-8773
6464 Sunset Blvd., Ste. 1150 FAX (323) 469-6990
Hollywood, CA 90028 **www.elainecraig.com**
(Commerials, Foreign Language Casting & Voice Casting)

Face in the Crowd Casting/ Maryclaire Sweeters (310) 720-3117 / (310) 458-1100
www.faceinthecrowdcasting.com
(Commercials, Film, Foreign Language Casting, Real People, TV & Webisodes)

Far More Casting & Production (213) 281-9802
Contacts: Rosalinda Morales & Lidia Pires

Paula Ferguson (661) 297-3282
(Commercials) FAX (661) 297-5580

Flyy Casting (323) 969-8200 / (310) 210-6795
7700 W. Sunset Blvd., Ste. 200
Los Angeles, CA 90046

Francine Maisler Casting (310) 244-6945
10202 W. Washington Blvd., Jimmy Stewart Bldg., Ste. 207
Culver City, CA 90232
(Film & TV)

Gabrielle Schary Casting (310) 450-0835
2601 Ocean Park Blvd., Ste. 120 FAX (310) 450-7794
Santa Monica, CA 90405
www.gabriellescharycasting.com
(Commercials, TV, Voice Over Casting & Web)

Gerrie Wormser Casting (310) 277-3281
468 S. Roxbury Dr., Ste. 104
Beverly Hills, CA 90212
(Film & TV)

Headquarters Casting (310) 556-9001
3108 W. Magnolia Blvd. FAX (310) 861-5988
Burbank, CA 91505 **www.headquarterscasting.com**

Heidi Levitt Casting (323) 525-0800
7201 Melrose Ave., Ste. 203 **www.heidilevittcasting.com**
Los Angeles, CA 90046
(Film & TV)

Helgoth & Associates Casting (323) 462-5021
1312 N. Wilton Pl. FAX (323) 462-5021
Hollywood, CA 90028
www.helgothandassociatescasting.com
(Commercials, Film & TV)

Hispanic Talent Casting of Hollywood (323) 934-6465
2536 Hauser Blvd., Ste. 3
Los Angeles, CA 90016
(Commercials, Film & TV)

The Hollywood-Madison Group (818) 762-8008
11684 Ventura Blvd., Ste. 258 FAX (818) 762-8089
Studio City, CA 91604 **www.hollywood-madison.com**
(Celebrities)
Contact: Jonathan Holiff

House Casting (323) 769-0200
855 N. Cahuenga Blvd. FAX (323) 469-8901
Los Angeles, CA 90038 **www.housecasting.com**
(Babies, Celebrities, Children, Commercials, Film, Foreign Language Casting, Real People, TV, Voice Casting & Webisodes)

Ian Royston Casting (310) 720-7242
(Commercials, Film, Real People & Webisodes)

Idell James Casting (310) 230-9986
(Commercials) FAX (310) 230-8233

In The Twink of An Eye Casting (818) 623-2336 / (800) 821-2974
(Commercials) FAX (818) 623-2637

iProbe Multilingual Solutions, Inc. (888) 489-6035
www.iprobesolutions.com
(Foreign Language Voice Overs and Voice Casting)

J. S. Snyder & Assoc. (323) 465-4241
1801 N. Kingsley Dr., Ste. 202
Los Angeles, CA 90027
(Commercials, Film, Music Videos, New Media & TV)
Contacts: Bernard Abellada, Stephen Snyder & James Whipple

Jane Doe Casting (323) 692-1800
c/o The Casting Lounge **www.janedoecasting.com**
1035 S. La Brea Ave.
Los Angeles, CA 90019
(Commercials, Film & TV)

Jed and Company (310) 699-3715
321 Santa Monica Blvd., Third Fl. FAX (323) 464-0646
Santa Monica, CA 90401 **www.jedandco.com**
(Commercials)

Jeff Gerrard Casting (818) 782-9900
13425 Ventura Blvd., Second Fl. FAX (818) 782-0030
Sherman Oaks, CA 91423
(Commercials, Film & TV)
Contacts: Jeff & Justin

Jeff Hardwick Casting (818) 752-9898
3940 Laurel Canyon Blvd., Ste. 1158
Studio City, CA 91604
www.jeffhardwickcasting.com
(Commercials, Film & TV)

Jeff Rosenman Casting (323) 330-1020
200 S. La Brea Ave., Second Fl.
Los Angeles, CA 90036 **www.rosenmancasting.com**

Jessica J Casting (310) 498-6668 / (323) 330-1020
200 South Studios **www.jessicajcasting.com**
200 S. La Brea, Second Fl.
Los Angeles, CA 90036
(Babies, Celebrities, Children, Circus/Variety Acts, Commercials, Podcasting, Reality, TV & Webisodes)

Jessica Overwise Casting (310) 459-2686
17250 Sunset Blvd., Ste. 304 FAX (310) 459-0961
Pacific Palisades, CA 90272
(Commercials, Film & TV)

Joe Blake Casting (310) 581-3009
@ Ocean Park Casting FAX (310) 450-3758
2701 Ocean Park Blvd., Ste. 250
Santa Monica, CA 90405
(Commercials, Film & TV)

Julie Ashton Casting (323) 856-9000
6715 Hollywood Blvd., Ste. 203 FAX (323) 856-9010
Los Angeles, CA 90028
(Film & TV)

Junie Lowry-Johnson Casting (818) 733-4384
(323) 850-3171
100 Universal City Plaza, Bungalow 5165
Universal City, CA 91608
(Film & TV)

Kalmenson & Kalmenson Voice Casting (818) 377-3600
P.O. Box 260207 FAX (818) 377-3636
Encino, CA 91426 www.kalmenson.com
(Voice Overs)
Contacts: Catherine & Harvey Kalmenson

Kari Peyton Casting (323) 468-6888
6660 Santa Monica Blvd.
Los Angeles, CA 90038
(Film & TV)

Kathy Knowles Casting (310) 458-1100
(Commercials) FAX (310) 458-7878

Katie Carlson Kasting (310) 625-6244
(Non-Union, Real People & Union)

Katy Wallin Casting (818) 563-4121
1918 Magnolia Blvd., Ste. 206 FAX (818) 563-4318
Burbank, CA 91506 www.katywallin.com
(Commercials, Film & TV)

Lee Sonja Kissik (805) 688-3702
1660 Cougar Ridge Rd.
Buellton, CA 93427
(Commercials, Film & TV)

Landau McRae Casting (310) 458-1100
1216 Fifth St. FAX (310) 458-7878
Santa Monica, CA 90401 www.fifthstreetstudios.com
(Commercials, Film & TV)

Katherine Landau/Kat Kasting (310) 458-1100
(Commercials) FAX (310) 458-7878
www.fifthstreetstudios.com

Matthew Lessall (323) 965-2104
5225 Wilshire Blvd., Ste. 1203 www.lessallcasting.com
Los Angeles, CA 90036
(Commercials, Film, TV & Webisodes)

Linda Lowy Casting (323) 671-5438
4151 Prospect Ave., Cottages, Ste. 105
Los Angeles, CA 90027
(Film & TV)

Lisa Fields Casting (310) 274-9909
(Commercials, Film & TV) FAX (310) 274-9919
www.lisafieldscasting.com

Lisa Freiberger Casting (818) 990-9956
(Film & TV)

Lisa Pantone, Casting (818) 552-2772
(Commercial, Film &TV) www.lisapantone.com
Contact: Lisa Pantone

Loop Troop (818) 216-3678
827 Hollywood Way, Ste. 411 www.looptroop.com
Burbank, CA 91505
(ADR Group Voice Casting, Animation, Film & TV)
Contact: Terri Douglas

Louis Goldstein & Associates Casting (818) 817-4371
(805) 746-4650
(Commercials)
Contacts: Diane Silvester & Louis Goldstein

Lynne Quirion Casting (310) 492-6520
(818) 606-4533
13425 Ventura Blvd. www.lynnequirioncasting.com
Sherman Oaks, CA 91423
(Commercials, Film, Print, Real People, TV, Union & Voice Casting)
Contact: Lynne Quirion

M Casting (310) 248-5296
(213) 393-2758
8899 Beverly Blvd. FAX (310) 248-5297
Los Angeles, CA 90048
(Commercials)
Contacts: Marisa Munoz & Ray Munoz

Suzie Magrey (310) 497-7115
c/o On Your Mark Studio, 13425 Ventura Blvd., Ste. 200
Sherman Oaks, CA 91423
(Commercials)

Mambo Casting (323) 655-7200
489 S. Robertson Blvd., Ste. 104 FAX (323) 655-7221
Beverly Hills, CA 90211 www.mambocasting.com
(Commercials, Film, Hispanic Casting & TV)
Contact: Orlette Ruiz

Marci Liroff Casting (818) 784-5434
P.O. Box 57948 www.marciliroff.com
Sherman Oaks, CA 91413
(Film & TV)

Margarette & Kennedy Casting (818) 434-1339
(Commercials, Film & TV) FAX (818) 238-0333
Contact: Susan Margarette-Havins

Mariko Ballentine Casting (323) 401-1188
(818) 783-6693
www.marikoballentine.com

Mark Randall Casting (323) 465-7553
(323) 533-0572
1811 N. Whitley Ave., Ste. 401
Hollywood, CA 90028
(Celebrities, Children, Circus/Variety Acts, Commercials, Film, Print, Real People, Reality, TV & Webisodes)
Contact: Mark Randall

Mark Sikes Casting (818) 759-7648
c/o Pioneer Valley Productions www.marksikes.com
8909 24th St.
Los Angeles, CA 90034
(Film & TV)

Mark Teschner Casting (323) 671-5542
c/o The Prospect Studios, 4151 Prospect Ave.
General Hospital Bldg.
Los Angeles, CA 90027
(Film & TV)

Martin Casting & Associates (310) 775-6605
2329 Purdue Ave. www.martincasting.com
Los Angeles, CA 90064
(Union Commercials & TV)

McBride Casting (310) 581-3000
(310) 433-3177
2701 Ocean Park Blvd., Ste. 250 FAX (310) 450-3149
Santa Monica, CA 90405 www.mcbridecasting.com
(Babies, Children, Circus/Variety Acts, Commercials, Film, Real People, TV & Webisodes)

Valerie McCaffrey (818) 785-1886
4924 Balboa Blvd., Ste. 172
Encino, CA 91316
(Film & TV)

John McCarthy (323) 732-8118
1234 S. Gramercy Pl. FAX (323) 732-8818
Los Angeles, CA 90035
(Commercials, Film & TV)

Megan Foley Casting & Co. (818) 216-9350
(818) 817-4319
c/o On Your Mark Studios www.meganfoleycasting.com
13425 Ventura Blvd., Ste. 200
Sherman Oaks, CA 91423
(Commercials)
Contacts: Megan Foley-Marra, Chuck Marra & Kira Shea Smithson

Melissa Skoff Casting (818) 760-2058
(Film & TV) www.melissaskoff.com

Michael Donovan Casting (323) 876-9020
7805 Sunset Blvd., Ste. 200 FAX (323) 876-9021
Los Angeles, CA 90046
(Commercials, Film & TV)

Mimi Webb Miller Casting (310) 452-0863 / (310) 991-0863
321 Santa Monica Blvd., Third Fl. FAX (310) 581-5277
Santa Monica, CA 90401
(Real People & Union)

Mindy Marin Casting (310) 395-1882
1433 Sixth St.
Santa Monica, CA 90401
(Film & TV)

Molly Lopata Casting (818) 788-0673
13731 Ventura Blvd., Ste. A
Sherman Oaks, CA 91423
(Film & TV)

Monroe Casting (818) 640-4470
3100 Damon Way www.pixiemonroecasting.com
Burbank, CA 91505
(Commercials)

MTierney Casting (213) 422-2181
FAX (323) 262-2759
www.mtierneycasting.com
(Commercials, Films, Real People, Reality & TV)

Nancy Nayor Casting (323) 857-0151
6320 Commodore Sloat, Seventh Fl.
Los Angeles, CA 90048
(Film & TV)

O'Haver + Co./Jenny O'Haver (323) 650-9010 / (413) 528-6728
www.ohaver.net
(Commercials, Film, Foreign Language Casting, Real People & TV)

Gregory Orson (323) 469-6464
6464 Sunset Blvd., Ste. 970
Los Angeles, CA 90028
(Film & TV)

Pam Dixon Casting (310) 432-4852
10351 Santa Monica Blvd., Ste. 200 FAX (310) 432-4844
Los Angeles, CA 90025
(Film & TV)

Pam Gilles Casting (818) 779-7744 / (310) 463-2406
15450 Cabrito Rd. www.gillescasting.com
Van Nuys, CA 91406
(Commercials, Film, TV & Babies, Celebrities, Children, Circus/Variety, Commercials, Foreign Language Casting, Podcasting, Real People, Reality, TV, Voice Casting & Webisodes)
Contacts: Pam Gilles

Pamela Campus Casting (818) 897-1588
(Commercials, Film & TV)

Pamela Kaplan Casting (415) 902 6484
237 Keller St.
Petaluma, CA 94952
(Real People)

Parlay Productions (310) 733-4430 / (310) 270-7526
8500 Steller Dr., Bldg. 8 FAX (310) 733-4439
Culver City, CA 90232 www.parlayproductions.com

Patrick Cunningham Casting (323) 956-5435
Paramount Pictures, 5555 Melrose Ave.
Hollywood, CA 90038
(Babies, Celebrities, Children, Commercials, Film, Foreign Language Casting, Podcasting, Real People, Reality, TV, Voice Casting & Webisodes)

Paula Rosenberg Casting (310) 260-0129
818 12th St., Ste. 9
Santa Monica, CA 90403
(Film & TV)

Pemrick/Fronk Casting (818) 325-1289
14724 Ventura Blvd., PH
Sherman Oaks, CA 91403
(Film & TV)

Phyllis Ricci Casting (818) 761-8257
(Commercials)

Pitch Casting (323) 969-8200
7700 W. Sunset Blvd. FAX (323) 969-0101
West Hollywood, CA 90046 www.pitchcasting.com
(Commercials & Film)

popcasting (310) 990-4418
7273 Santa Monica Blvd. FAX (323) 785-7855
West Hollywood, CA 90046 www.popcastingla.com
(Babies, Children, Commercials, Film, Foreign Language Casting, Podcasting, Real People, Reality, TV & Webisodes)

Prime Casting & Payroll (323) 962-0377 / (323) 394-3399
6430 Sunset Blvd., Ste. 425 FAX (323) 466-4166
Hollywood, CA 90028 www.primecasting.com
(Babies, Children, Circus/Variety Acts, Commercials, Film, Industrials, Real People, TV & Webisodes)
Contact: Peter Alwazzan

Real People Casting (310) 827-9498
4732-D Villa Marina
Marina del Rey, CA 90292
(Commercials, Film & TV)
Contact: Sharon Lindsey

Reel Talent/Kids (805) 969-2222
1805 E. Cabrillo Blvd., Ste. B FAX (805) 969-9595
Santa Barbara, CA 93108
(Commercials)
Contact: Rachel Larreta

René Haynes Casting (818) 842-0187
P.O. Box 3399
Burbank, CA 91508
(Film & TV)

Renita Casting (323) 939-5992 / (310) 775-6611
c/o 310 Casting Studios www.renitacasting.com
2329 Purdue Ave.
Los Angeles, CA 90064
(Babies, Celebrities, Children, Circus/Variety Acts, Commercials, Film, Foreign Language Casting, Podcasting, Real People, Reality, TV, Voice Casting & Webisodes)

Richard Delancy Casting (818) 760-3110
11030 Aqua Vista St., Ste. 52 FAX (818) 760-1382
Studio City, CA 91602
(Babies, Children, Commercials, Film, Industrials, Real People, Reality, TV, Voice Casting & Webisodes)
Contacts: Michael Krieger & Ricky Montez

Ricki Maslar Casting (818) 729-9344
c/o Unconditional Entertainment
3607 Magnolia Blvd., Ste. 3
Burbank, CA 91607
(Film & TV)

Robi Reed & Associates (323) 463-6350
8200 Wilshire Blvd., Ste. 400
Beverly Hills, CA 90211
(Film & TV)

Rodeo Casting (323) 969-9125
7013 Willoughby Ave. FAX (323) 874-7729
Hollywood, CA 90038
(Commercials)
Contact: Britt Enggren

Ross Lacy Casting (323) 330-1020
FAX (323) 954-9391
www.rosslacycasting.com
(Babies, Celebrities, Children, Commercials, Film, TV & Webisodes)

Ruth Conforte Casting (818) 771-7287
P.O. Box 4474
Valley Village, CA 91617
(Commercials, Film, Industrials, TV & Voice Casting)
Contact: Ruth Conforte

Samuel Warren & Associates International Casting Services (323) 462-1510 (619) 264-4135
5205 Kearny Villa Way www.samuelwarren.com
San Diego, CA 92123
(Commercials, Film & TV)

Sanford Casting (323) 465-9999 (818) 908-1800
The Casting Underground FAX (818) 908-4325
1641 N. Ivar Ave. www.sanfordcasting.com
Los Angeles, CA 90028
(Commercials)

Sara Finn Casting (323) 460-7040
588 N. Larchmont Blvd.
Los Angeles, CA 90004
(Film & TV)

Brien Scott (818) 343-3669
18034 Ventura Blvd., Ste. 275 FAX (818) 343-3669
Encino, CA 91316
(Commercials, Film & TV)

Shane. A Casting Company (323) 468-6888 (323) 708-1574
c/o Silver Layne Studios FAX (323) 468-8811
6660 Santa Monica Blvd., First Fl. www.shanecasting.com
Los Angeles, CA 90038
(Commercials)

Shaner/Testa Casting (818) 954-7497
4000 Warner Blvd., Bldg. 261
Burbank, CA 91522
(Film & TV)

Sheila Manning Casting (310) 557-9990
332 S. Beverly Dr. FAX (310) 557-9998
Beverly Hills, CA 90212
(Commercials, Film & TV)

Ava Shevitt (310) 656-4600
Village Studio FAX (310) 656-4610
321 Santa Monica Blvd., Ste. 300 www.villagestudio.net
Santa Monica, CA 90401
(Commercials, Film & TV)

Shooting From The Hip Casting (818) 506-0613
Zydeco Studios, 11317 Ventura Blvd. FAX (818) 506-8858
Studio City, CA 91604
www.shootingfromthehipcasting.com
(Commercials, Film & TV)
Contact: Francene Selkirk-Ackerman

[skirts] (323) 692-1800
1035 S. La Brea Ave. FAX (323) 692-1810
Los Angeles, CA 90019 www.skirtscasting.com

Sobo Casting (323) 394-2154 (323) 854-1888
8899 Beverly Blvd., Ste. 206 www.sobocasting.com
Los Angeles, CA 90048
(Commercials, Film, Podcasting, TV & Webisodes)
Contacts: Amy Sobo & Jane Sobo

Spot Casting (323) 330-1020
200 S. La Brea Ave., Second Fl. www.spotcasting.net
Los Angeles, CA 90036
(Babies, Celebrities, Children, Commercials & TV)

Pamela Starks (323) 253-0205 (323) 330-1020
(Commercials & Film)

Steven Erdek Casting (310) 770-7226 (213) 924-8497
Castaway Studios, 8899 Beverly Blvd.
Los Angeles, CA 90048
(Commercials, Film & TV)

StormMaker Productions, Inc. (818) 760-4111
10551 Burbank Blvd. FAX (818) 760-4111
North Hollywood, CA 91601
www.stormmakerproductions.com
(Babies, Celebrities, Children, Circus/Variety Acts, Commercials, Film, Podcasting, Real People, Reality, TV, Voice Casting & Webisodes)

Streetwise Casting (310) 396-3184
578 Washington Blvd., Ste. 457 FAX (310) 827-4756
Marina Del Rey, CA 90292 www.streetwisecasting.com

Stuart Stone Casting/ Under The Rock Casting (323) 866-1811
8899 Beverly Blvd. www.stonecasting.tv
Los Angeles, CA 90048
(Children, Commercials, Film, Real People, Reality & Webisodes)
Contact: Stuart Stone

Susan Bluestein Casting (323) 468-4562
c/o Sunset Gower Studios
1438 N. Gower St., Bldg. 20, Box 25
Los Angeles, CA 90028
(Film & TV)

Susan Tyler Casting (818) 506-0400
c/o On Your Mark Studio, 13425 Ventura Blvd.
Sherman Oaks, CA 91423
(Celebrities, Commercials, Film, Foreign Language Casting, Podcasting, Reality, TV & Voice Casting)

Tammara Billik Casting (818) 623-1631
4000 Warner Blvd., Bldg. 190, Ste. 104
Burbank, CA 91522
(Film & TV)

Taylor Casting (310) 313-2090 (310) 600-6339
(Commercials & Real People)

Terry Berland Casting (310) 275-0601
2329 Purdue Ave. www.berlandcasting.com
Los Angeles, CA 90064
(Commercials)
Contacts: Terry Berland & Karmen Leech

TLC Booth, Inc. (323) 464-2788
6521 Homewood Ave.
Hollywood, CA 90028
(Commercials)
Contacts: Loree Booth & Leland Williams

Tolley Casparis Casting, Inc. (323) 931-3263
8899 Beverly Blvd. www.tolleycasting.com
Los Angeles, CA 90048
(Babies, Children, Circus/Variety Acts, Commercials, Film, Foreign Language Casting, Podcasting, Real People, TV, Voice Casting & Webisodes)

TypeCasting, Inc./James Levine (310) 775-6616 (818) 554-8019
310 Casting Studios FAX (310) 478-2100
2329 Purdue Ave. www.typecastinginc.com
Los Angeles, CA 90064
(Commercial, Film, Real People & TV)

Ulrich/Dawson/Kritzer Casting (818) 623-1818
4705 Laurel Canyon Blvd., Ste. 301
North Hollywood, CA 91607
(Commercials, Film & TV)

Valko/Miller Casting (818) 953-7743
3500 W. Olive Ave., Ste. 780
Burbank, CA 91505
(Film & TV)

Vicki Goggin & Associates Casting (818) 817-4330
13425 Ventura Blvd., Second Fl. www.vickigoggin.com
Sherman Oaks, CA 91423
(Commercials, TV & Webisodes)

Vicki Rosenberg & Associates (310) 369-3448
10201 W. Pico Blvd., Bldg. 80, Ste. 19
Los Angeles, CA 90035
(Film & TV)

The Voicecaster (818) 841-5300
1832 W. Burbank Blvd. FAX **(818) 841-2085**
Burbank, CA 91506 **www.voicecaster.com**
(Commercials)
Contacts: Gary Giambo, Huck Liggett & Martha Mayakis

Voices Voicecasting (818) 716-8865
11340 Moorpark St. **www.voicesvoicecasting.com**
North Hollywood, CA 91602
(Commercials)
Contact: Mary Lynn Wissner

The Walkie Talkies (818) 652-3049
(818) 652-3048
P.O. Box 3233 **www.trustthebeeps.com**
Granada Hills, CA 91394
(ADR Group Voice Casting)
Contacts: Joey Naber & Paula Price

Weber & Associates Casting (310) 449-3685
10250 Constellation Blvd., Ste. 2060
Los Angeles, CA 90067
(Film & TV)

Anissa Williams (323) 550-1205
c/o Castaway Studios, 8899 Beverly Blvd.
Beverly Hills, CA 90048
(Commercials)

Yumi Takada Casting (310) 372-7287
2105 Huntington Ln., Ste. A
Redondo Beach, CA 90278
(Commercials, Film & TV)

Debra Zane (310) 558-0400
5225 Wilshire Blvd., Ste. 536 FAX **(310) 558-0475**
Los Angeles, CA 90036
(Film & TV)

Zane/Pillsbury Casting (323) 769-9191
585 N. Larchmont Blvd.
Los Angeles, CA 90004
(Film & TV)

1 Space (323) 962-1455
6430 Sunset Blvd., Ste. 425 FAX (323) 466-4166
Hollywood, CA 90028 www.primecasting.com

1020 Studios (323) 883-0262
1020 N. Sycamore Ave. FAX (323) 874-6330
Los Angeles, CA 90038 www.1020studios.com

200 South, Inc. (323) 330-1020
200 S. La Brea Ave., Second Fl. FAX (323) 954-0933
Los Angeles, CA 90036 www.200south.com

310 Casting Studios (310) 775-6600
(310) 775-6601
2329 Purdue Ave. FAX (310) 478-2100
Los Angeles, CA 90064 www.310castingstudios.com

5th Street Studios (310) 458-1100
1216 Fifth St. FAX (310) 458-7878
Santa Monica, CA 90401

Alley Kat Studio (323) 462-1755
(323) 462-4546
1455 N. Gordon St. FAX (323) 962-3693
Hollywood, CA 90028 www.alleykatstudios.com

AuditionTape, Inc. (310) 289-4962
8556 Rugby Dr. FAX (501) 621-4152
West Hollywood, CA 90069 www.audition-tape.com

BB Casting (310) 963-8538
(818) 377-9538
520 Washington Blvd., Ste. 468 www.bbcasting.com
Marina del Rey, CA 90292

Big House Studios (818) 782-9900
FAX (818) 782-0030

Castaway Studios (310) 248-5296
8899 Beverly Blvd., Lobby FAX (310) 248-5297
Los Angeles, CA 90048 www.castawaystudios.com

Casting Cafe (310) 274-9909
9000 Santa Monica Blvd. FAX (310) 274-9919
West Hollywood, CA 90069 www.castingcafe.us

The Casting Group (818) 761-3242
4640 Lankershim Blvd., Ste. 305 FAX (818) 761-3494
North Hollywood, CA 91602 www.postsession.com

The Casting Lounge (323) 692-1800
1035 S. La Brea Ave. FAX (323) 692-1810
Los Angeles, CA 90019 www.thecastinglounge.com

The Casting Underground (323) 465-9999
1641 N. Ivar Ave. FAX (323) 465-6290
Hollywood, CA 90028

Chelsea Studios, Inc. (818) 817-4350
13425 Ventura Blvd., Second Fl. FAX (818) 728-6785
Sherman Oaks, CA 91423 www.chelseastudios.com

Cole Avenue Studios (323) 463-1600
1006 N. Cole Ave. FAX (323) 463-9566
Hollywood, CA 90038 www.coleavenuestudios.com

Eastside Studios (323) 660-7874
4216 Fountain Ave. FAX (323) 660-7875
Los Angeles, CA 90029 www.eastsidestudiosla.com

Exclusive Casting Studios (323) 969-8200
7700 W. Sunset Blvd., Second Fl. FAX (323) 696-0101
Los Angeles, CA 90046 www.exclusivecastingstudios.com

Hollywood Production Center (818) 480-3100
121 W. Lexington Dr. FAX (818) 480-3199
Glendale, CA 91203 www.hollywoodpc.com

Kalmenson & Kalmenson Voice Casting (818) 377-3600
P.O. Box 260207 FAX (818) 377-3636
Encino, CA 91426 www.kalmenson.com

LoudMouth Studios (818) 980-9803
11340 Moorpark St. FAX (818) 980-2838
Studio City, CA 91602 www.loudmouthstudios.com
Contacts: Beth Holmes, Jim Holmes & Monica Lee-Eisenbeis

MetaTheatre on Melrose (323) 852-6963
7801 Melrose Ave., Ste. 3 FAX (323) 852-6963
Los Angeles, CA 90046 www.anthonymeindl.com

MysticArt Pictures (818) 563-4121
1918 Magnolia Blvd., Ste. 206 FAX (818) 563-4318
Burbank, CA 91506 www.mysticartpictures.com
Contacts: Tim Safford & Katy Wallin

Ocean Park Casting (310) 581-3000
2701 Ocean Park Blvd., Ste. 250 FAX (310) 450-3149
Santa Monica, CA 90405 www.oceanparkcasting.com

On Your Mark Studios (818) 817-4300
13425 Ventura Blvd., Ste. 200 FAX (818) 728-6785
Sherman Oaks, CA 91423 www.onyourmarkstudios.com

Rodeo Studios (323) 969-9125
7013 Willoughby Ave. FAX (323) 874-7729
Hollywood, CA 90038

Samuel Warren & Associates International Casting Services (323) 462-1510
(619) 264-4135
5205 Kearny Villa Way www.samuelwarren.com
San Diego, CA 92123

San Luis Obispo County Location & Casting (805) 547-9000
128 La Colina FAX (805) 969-9595
Pismo Beach, CA 93449

Screenland Studios (818) 508-2288
10501 Burbank Blvd. www.screenlandstudios.com
North Hollywood, CA 91601
Contacts: Karen Apostolina & Steve Apostolina

Sessions West Studios, Inc. (310) 450-9228
2601 Ocean Park Blvd., Ste. 120 FAX (310) 450-7794
Santa Monica, CA 90405 www.sessionsweststudios.com

Silver Layne Studios (323) 468-6888
6660 Santa Monica Blvd., First Fl. FAX (323) 468-8811
Los Angeles, CA 90038

Solar Studios (818) 240-1893
(310) 489-7801
1601 S. Central Ave. FAX (818) 242-1691
Glendale, CA 91204 www.solarstudios.com

StormMaker Productions, Inc. (818) 760-4111
10551 Burbank Blvd. FAX (818) 760-4111
North Hollywood, CA 91601
www.stormmakerproductions.com

studio/stage (323) 463-3900
520 N. Western Ave. FAX (323) 463-3933
Los Angeles, CA 90004 www.studio-stage.com

Talent Network (310) 230-5773
(310) 570-6275
800 Hampton Dr., Ste. I FAX (310) 861-0318
Venice, CA 90291
www.talentnetworkusa.biz/studio.html

Village Studio (310) 656-4600
321 Santa Monica Blvd., Third Fl. FAX (310) 656-4610
Santa Monica, CA 90401 www.villagestudio.net

Eddie Baytos (818) 985-4533
(818) 304-4123
FAX (818) 985-4533
www.eddiebaytos.com

Kim Blank (323) 935-3341
(323) 547-2970
FAX (323) 937-4975

bloc, Inc. (323) 954-7730
5651 Wilshire Blvd., Ste. C
Los Angeles, CA 90036
(Choreography/Dance Agency)
FAX (323) 954-7731
www.blocagency.com

Bobby Ball Talent Agency (818) 506-8188
FAX (818) 506-8588

Donna Boise (562) 861-9227
FAX (562) 861-9227

Jordi Caballero (310) 562-9340
www.latinchoreography.com

Carol Cetrone (213) 483-3915
(323) 669-8619

Clear Talent Group/CTG (818) 509-0121
(818) 509-0207
10950 Ventura Blvd.
Studio City, CA 91604
(Dance)
FAX (818) 509-7729
www.cleartalentgroup.com

DDO Artists Agency (323) 462-8000
6725 Sunset Blvd., Ste. 230
Los Angeles, CA 90028
(Reps for Choreographers)
FAX (323) 462-0100
www.ddoagency.com

Joanne DiVito (818) 760-3160
FAX (818) 760-3160

Entertainment Plus Productions, Inc./Doug Johnson (323) 969-1756
(310) 770-4582
FAX (310) 287-0595
www.eplusproductions.com

Myrna Gawryn (310) 837-9388

Deborah Greenfield (818) 633-3577
(33) 645507742
www.rosanegraflamenco.org

JoAnn F. Jansen (323) 851-8012
FAX (323) 851-6317
www.joannjansen.com

Kazarian/Spencer & Associates, Inc. (818) 755-7571
11969 Ventura Blvd., Third Fl.
Studio City, CA 91604
(Reps for Choreographers)
FAX (818) 755-7574
www.ksawest.com

La Premiere Productions/Neisha Folkes (213) 999-1223
123 S. Figueroa St., Ste. 535
Los Angeles, CA 90012
www.neishafolkes.com

Jennifer Li (323) 481-4475
FAX (323) 665-7904

Ted Lin (310) 440-1471
(310) 869-7361

McDonald/Selznick Associates (323) 957-6680
953 N. Cole Ave.
Hollywood, CA 90038
(Reps for Choreographers)
FAX (323) 957-6688
www.msaagency.com

Mime and Movement by Lorin Eric Salm (818) 300-7473
(866) 444-6463
(Mime and Movement Coach)
www.movement-coach.com

More Zap Productions (310) 477-2118
(323) 850-8665
www.morezap.com

Pack The House Productions (310) 862-4855
www.pthproductions.com

Travis Payne (323) 665-6680
(323) 957-6680
FAX (323) 665-6681
www.travispayne.net

Fatima Robinson (323) 664-7900
(310) 859-8513
www.foresight-studios.com

Karen Russell-Budge (310) 281-1956

Mic Thompson (323) 240-2828
(800) 485-4147
www.micsmatch.com

1 On 1 Computing Technologies (818) 992-0584 (818) 254-5448
5824 Kentland Ave. FAX (818) 887-7247
Woodland Hills, CA 91367 www.1on1comp.com
(Consulting, Hardware, Networking and Troubleshooting for Mac and PC, Networks & Software, Systems Design & Troubleshooting)

318, Inc. (310) 581-9500
830 Colorado Ave. FAX (310) 581-9515
Santa Monica, CA 90401 www.318.com

Acacia Systems (562) 437-7690 (310) 546-6336
265 Park Ave. FAX (562) 439-7636
Long Beach, CA 90803 www.acaciasystems.com
(Consulting, Multimedia Training & Networking)

Action Computer Service (310) 552-2722 (213) 703-6218
FAX (310) 286-7850
(Consulting, Networking and Troubleshooting for Macintosh and PCs)

ActiveQuest, Inc. (661) 295-3890
25655 Springbrook Ave., Bldg. 2A www.activequest.com
Santa Clarita, CA 91350

Agenda Media Services, Inc. (818) 990-5343
5445 Balboa Blvd., Ste. 112 FAX (818) 990-5344
Encino, CA 91316 www.agenda.net
(Consulting, Networking & Software)

Alchemy Productions Inc./ MacAlchemist (310) 439-2028
4047 Van Buren Pl., Ste. 2 www.macalchemist.com
Culver City, CA 90232

Alpha Lex Systems Integration (818) 407-9200
FAX (818) 407-9204
www.alphalex.com
(Consulting, Multimedia Software & Systems Design)

Chaparral Software & Consulting Services (818) 225-1247
5737 Kanan, Ste. 589 FAX (818) 225-1248
Agoura Hills, CA 91301 www.chapsoft.com
(Database and Network Consultants for Macintosh)

Christian Boyce and Associates (310) 452-3720
3435 Ocean Park Blvd., Ste. 107 FAX (310) 392-4989
Santa Monica, CA 90405 www.christianboyce.com
(Macintosh Consultants)

Computech Support Services (310) 237-6065
3272 Motor Ave., Ste. F FAX (310) 845-9536
Los Angeles, CA 90035 www.computechsos.com

Computer Business Solutions/ Jerry Zeldes (818) 907-6773 (818) 587-1462
15233 Ventura Blvd., Ste. 1010 FAX (818) 501-0245
Sherman Oaks, CA 91403
(Accounting and AICP Bidding Systems for PCs)

CrownPeak (310) 841-5920
5880 W. Jefferson Blvd., Ste. G www.crownpeak.com
Los Angeles, CA 90016

DriveSavers Data Recovery (800) 440-1904
(Data Recovery) www.drivesavers.com

egad, inc. (818) 558-6968
434 N. Niagara FAX (818) 954-6317
Burbank, CA 91502 www.egad.com
(Media Vault Management Systems)
Contact: Peter Zaharkiv

EP's Global & Movie Magic Applications (818) 955-6299
2835 N. Naomi St. FAX (818) 845-6507
Burbank, CA 91504
(Accounting, Budgeting and Scheduling Software)

Erik Adams Computer Consulting (818) 802-7719
(Hardware, Network Support & Software) FAX (213) 596-5181
www.cinesat.net

filmmakersoftware (310) 452-1183
www.filmmakersoftware.com
(Databases & Production Software for Independent Filmmakers)

Final Draft, Inc. (818) 995-8995
(800) 231-4055
26707 W. Agoura Rd., Ste. 205 FAX (818) 995-4422
Calabasas, CA 91302 www.finaldraft.com
(Screenwriting Software)

FMS Techniques, Inc. (323) 965-7300
13538 Cantara St. FAX (818) 997-6541
Van Nuys, CA 91402 www.techniques.com
(Macintosh Consultants)

Stephen Goepel (818) 781-7025
(818) 404-7570
(Multimedia Consultant)

iCare4Macs (818) 414-4051
(310) 476-5243
17216 Saticoy St., Ste. 310 FAX (818) 301-1961
Van Nuys, CA 91406 www.icare4macs.com
(Macintosh Consulting)

ICS, Inc. (818) 609-7648
(800) 684-5009
6038 Tampa Ave. FAX (818) 705-4933
Tarzana, CA 91356 www.click2tech.com
(Network Support, Networking & PC)

Illuvatar, LLC (310) 753-1774
(714) 965-5918
P.O. Box 8506 FAX (714) 969-5918
Fountain Valley, CA 92728 www.illuvatar.com
(Consulting, Mac, Network Support, PC, Systems Design & Troubleshooting)

imagistic (818) 706-9100
4333 Park Terrace Dr., Ste. 120 FAX (818) 706-9103
Westlake Village, CA 91361 www.imagistic.com

InEntertainment, Inc. (323) 456-1580
6404 Wilshire Blvd., Ste. 960 FAX (323) 782-4900
Los Angeles, CA 90048 www.inentertainment.com
(Software)

IT4LA, Inc. (323) 936-4900
8033 Sunset Blvd., Ste. 228 FAX (323) 937-2445
Los Angeles, CA 90046 www.it4la.com
(Hardware, Networks & Software)

JDK Consulting (818) 705-8050
16752 Addison St. FAX (818) 474-7012
Encino, CA 91436
(AICP/AICE Software)

Jungle Software (818) 508-7090
12711 Ventura Blvd., Ste. 345 FAX (818) 487-7865
Studio City, CA 91604 www.junglesoftware.com
(Databases & Production Software for Independent Filmmakers)

LAComputerBuddy (818) 530-1655
11144 Balboa Blvd., Ste. 217 www.lacomputerbuddy.com
Granada Hills, CA 91344

The Mac Network (866) 622-7247
(626) 583-9122
573 S. Lake Ave., Ste. 7 FAX (866) 309-5721
Pasadena, CA 91101 www.themacnetwork.com

Mac Talk (818) 225-9327
22510 Ventura Blvd. www.mactalk.com
Woodland Hills, CA 91364

Mac Talk (805) 804-3009
228 E. Thompson Blvd. www.mactalk.com
Ventura, CA 93003
(Consulting, Hardware, Networks and Software for Macintosh)

Mac Universe (818) 876-2589
19100 Ventura Blvd., Ste. A www.macuniverse.com
Tarzana, CA 91356
(Macintosh Consultants)

MacEnthusiasts (800) 948-6902
10600 W. Pico Blvd. FAX (310) 559-3428
Los Angeles, CA 90064 www.macenthusiasts.com

MacFAQulty (310) 435-9972
137 N. Larchmont, Ste. 137 FAX (419) 715-1159
Los Angeles, CA 90004 www.macfaqulty.com
(Macintosh Consultants)

MacMan (323) 215-5668
www.macmannow.com

Mann Consulting (818) 907-6266
(888) 746-8227
FAX (818) 340-3355
www.mann.com
(Consulting, Hardware, Networks and Software for Macintosh and PCs)

Media Services (310) 440-9696
(800) 333-7518
500 S. Sepulveda Blvd., Fourth Fl. FAX (310) 472-9979
Los Angeles, CA 90049 www.media-services.com
(Accounting and AICP/AICE Actualizing/Bidding Software)

MESoft (323) 882-6658
3575 Cahuenga Blvd. West, Ste. 222 FAX (323) 446-7353
Los Angeles, CA 90068 www.mesoft.com
(Commercial Production, Mac, Media Vault Management Systems, PC, Shot Logging Software, Storyboarding Software & Television Commercial Information Database)

Mocha Media, Inc. (323) 462-5765
(818) 535-1988
1523 Gordon St., Ste. 5 FAX (323) 462-5766
Los Angeles, CA 90028 www.mochamedia.com

Moviola Digital Education Center (323) 467-1116
(323) 467-3107
1135 N. Mansfield Ave. FAX (323) 466-2522
Los Angeles, CA 90038 www.moviola.com/edu
(Education & Training)

New Agenda Inc. (818) 355-3677
P.O. Box 251313 www.newagendainc.com
Los Angeles, CA 90025

The Personal Computer Specialists (213) 700-4861
(949) 429-5131
www.personalcomputerspecialists.com

The Production Resource (818) 637-4896
(888) 345-1920
www.powerbid.com
(AICP/AICE Software & Powerbid: Bidding and Actualizing Software for Macintosh and PCs)

Production Suppliers (818) 340-0545
(818) 439-8066
FAX (818) 340-3355
www.prosuppliers.com
(Commercial Production, Consulting, Hardware, Mac, PC, Systems Design & Troubleshooting)

Productivity Consulting (626) 794-3637
4051 Canyon Dell Dr. FAX (626) 794-3886
Altadena, CA 91001 www.proconsult.com
(Consulting, Database Design, Mac, Multimedia Training, Network Support, Networking, PC, Scheduling Software, Systems Design, Training & Troubleshooting)

ScheduALL (818) 754-3735
(818) 259-1508
(Consulting & Scheduling Software) FAX (818) 754-3739
www.scheduall.com

A **Showbiz Software** (310) 440-9600
(800) 333-7518
500 S. Sepulveda Blvd., Fourth Fl. FAX (310) 472-9979
Los Angeles, CA 90049 www.showbizsoftware.com
(Accounting and AICP/AICE Actualizing/Bidding Software)

Strategic Data Solutions (310) 452-8786
1350 Abbot Kinney Blvd. FAX **(310) 909-8678**
Venice, CA 90291 **www.strategicdata.com**
(Network Consultants for Macintosh and PCs)

Transistor 8 (310) 314-3345
10228 Deerfield Ln. FAX **(310) 314-3385**
Northridge, CA 91324 **www.transistor8.com**
(Consulting, Hardware and Networks for Macintosh and PCs)

UnderlineMedia (303) 719-2623
www.underlinemedia.com

V.2 Consulting, Inc. (818) 528-5394
(415) 989-9889
15125 Ventura Blvd., Ste. 203 FAX **(415) 358-4085**
Sherman Oaks, CA 91403 **www.v2consulting.com**
(Consulting, Database Design, Mac, Media Vault Management Systems, Network Support, Networking, Systems Design, Training & Troubleshooting)

Wide Screen Software LLC (818) 764-3639
(Sun Tracking Software for Mac and PC) FAX **(818) 764-3639**
www.wide-screen.com

Wiredrive (310) 823-8238
4212 Glencoe Ave. **www.wiredrive.com**
Marina del Rey, CA 90292
(Online Reel Creation and Production Tools)

Wizard Consulting Group (818) 706-8877
(818) 483-4686
4039 Liberty Canyon Rd. FAX **(888) 524-5024**
Agoura Hills, CA 90301 **www.wizardconsultinggroup.com**
(Consulting for IBM and Mac & Database Design)

The Writers' Store (310) 441-5151
(866) 229-7483
2040 Westwood Bl. **www.writersstore.com**
Los Angeles, CA 90025
(Budgeting and Scriptwriting Software)

Xytech Systems Corporation (818) 303-7800
2835 N. Naomi St., Ste. 310 FAX **(818) 303-7801**
Burbank, CA 91504 **www.xytechsystems.com**
(Facility Management Software)

Zylan (800) 995-2652
11301 W. Olympic Blvd., Ste. 492 **www.zylan.net**
Los Angeles, CA 90064
(Consulting, Hardware and Software for MacIntosh and PCs)

All States Office Machines, Inc. (818) 755-9568 (800) 464-1941
10712 Valley Spring Ln. FAX **(818) 755-9569**
Universal City, CA 91602 **www.allstatesofficesupply.com**

Alliant Event Services, Inc. (909) 622-3306 (800) 851-5415
196 University Pkwy FAX **(909) 622-3917**
Pomona, CA 91768 **www.alliantevents.com**
(Copiers, Desktop Computers, Laptops, Monitors, Printers & Projectors)

American Surplus (818) 993-5355
18643 Parthenia St.
Northridge, CA 91324
(Office Furniture)

Batchelor Business Machine (818) 222-2152
5169 Douglas Fir Rd., Ste. 6 FAX **(310) 278-2117**
Calabasas, CA 91302 **www.ibmtypewriters.com**
(Typewriters)

C.P. Four (323) 466-8201
706 N. Cahuenga Blvd. FAX **(323) 467-2749**
Hollywood, CA 90038 **www.omegacinemaprops.com**
(Macintosh)

Cal Business Systems & Supply (310) 470-3435 (818) 980-0373
1920 Pandora Ave., Ste. 7 FAX **(310) 470-3557**
Los Angeles, CA 90025 **www.calbusiness.us**
(Copiers & Fax Machines)

Computech Support Services (310) 237-6065
3272 Motor Ave., Ste. F FAX **(310) 845-9536**
Los Angeles, CA 90035 **www.computechsos.com**

Copier Rental, Inc. (714) 898-7772 (800) 655-8802
7341 Garden Grove Blvd., Ste. C FAX **(714) 898-7705**
Garden Grove, CA 92841 **www.rentcopiers.com**
(Copiers & Fax Machines)

Copyrite Solutions Inc. (818) 503-0015
7532 Atoll Ave. FAX **(818) 503-0543**
North Hollywood, CA 91605 **www.copyritesolutions.net**

Ⓐ **CRE - Computer & A/V Solutions** (877) 266-7725 (888) 444-1059
5732 Buckingham Pkwy FAX **(877) 440-5252**
Culver City, CA 90230
www.computerrentals.com/products/mac/mac_rentals_specialist.php
(Desktop Computers, Fax Machines, Laptops, Macintosh, Monitors, PC, Plasmas, Printers & Projectors)

Dean Security Safe Co. (818) 997-1234 (800) 827-7534
8616 Woodman Ave. FAX **(818) 894-0280**
Arleta, CA 91331 **www.deansafe.com**

Ⓐ **Docusource** (562) 447-2600 (949) 337-7117
10450 Pioneer, Ste. 1 FAX **(562) 447-2614**
Santa Fe Springs, CA 90670 **www.docusource.com**

EcoToner (818) 895-2006 (877) 326-8663
19360 Rinaldi Ave., Ste. 355 FAX **(877) 329-4326**
Porter Ranch, CA 91326 **www.ecotoner.com**
(Fax Machines & Printers)

GreenBear Technologies Computer Rentals (888) 292-0978 (818) 239-1740
7524 Clybourn Ave. FAX **(818) 504-1748**
Los Angeles, CA 91352 **www.greenbear.us**
(Computers, Copiers, Desktops, Fax Machines, Laptops, Mac, Monitors, Networking, PC, Plasmas, Printers & Projectors)

Ⓐ **Hi-Tech Computer Rental** (818) 841-0677 (213) 387-6861
172 W. Verdugo Ave. FAX **(818) 841-0575**
Burbank, CA 91502 **www.htcr.net**

Hopper's Office & Drafting Furniture (323) 254-7362 (800) 762-7717
2901 Fletcher Dr. FAX **(323) 254-8226**
Los Angeles, CA 90065 **www.draftingfurniture.com**
(Office Furniture)

House of Business Machines (818) 501-3013 (818) 501-2255
4351 Woodman Ave. FAX **(818) 501-3838**
Sherman Oaks, CA 91423 **www.hbmla.com**
(Copiers, Fax Machines, Printers & Typewriters)

Lasercare (310) 202-4200 (800) 527-3720
3375 Robertson Pl. FAX **(310) 202-4202**
Los Angeles, CA 90034 **www.lasercare.com**
(Printers)

LCS (310) 476-8380
15445 Ventura Blvd., Ste. 3312 FAX **(818) 789-6435**
Sherman Oaks, CA 91403

LCS (310) 476-8380
2554 Lincoln Blvd., Ste. 421 FAX **(818) 789-6435**
Venice, CA 90291
(Compact Refrigerators, Copiers, Fax Machines, Microwave Ovens, Phone Systems, Printers & Shredders)

Line 204 (323) 960-0113
1034 N. Seward St. FAX **(323) 960-0163**
Hollywood, CA 90038 **www.line204.com**

Mac City Computers (818) 505-8992
11026 Ventura Blvd., Ste. 1 FAX **(818) 505-8992**
Studio City, CA 91604

Mac Talk (805) 804-3009
228 E. Thompson Blvd. **www.mactalk.com**
Ventura, CA 93003
(Macintosh)

Mac Talk (818) 225-9327
22510 Ventura Blvd. **www.mactalk.com**
Woodland Hills, CA 91364

MacEnthusiasts (800) 615-0492
10600 W. Pico Blvd. FAX **(310) 945-3329**
Los Angeles, CA 90064 **www.macenthusiasts.com**
(Desktop Computers, Fax Machines, Laptops, Macintosh, Monitors, Printers, Projectors & Televisions)

A **Marathon Services, Inc.** (818) 280-0510 (800) 325-3130
9259 Eton Ave. FAX **(818) 280-0191**
Chatsworth, CA 91311 **www.marathonservice.com**
(Copiers, Fax Machines & Printers)

A **NTS Office Machines** (818) 905-9446
4854 Van Nuys Blvd. FAX **(818) 905-8725**
Sherman Oaks, CA 91403 **www.ntsofficemachines.com**
(Copiers, Fax Machines & Printers)

Office Furniture LA (323) 750-6206
7625 Crenshaw Blvd. FAX (323) 750-6208
Los Angeles, CA 90043 www.laofficefurniture.com
(Office Furniture)

Perfect Copy Products (818) 997-9120
5914 Kester Ave. FAX (818) 901-9320
Van Nuys, CA 91411 www.perfectcopyproducts.com
(Copiers & Fax Machines)

Power Flow Computer Rental Center (818) 762-3801
(800) 797-3321
FAX (818) 762-3811
www.computerrentalcenter.com

A **Quality Business Machines** (310) 330-4733
(800) 927-1601
233 E. Hillcrest Blvd. FAX (310) 674-6145
Inglewood, CA 90301 www.qbminc.com
(Copiers & Fax Machines)

R.C. Gear (323) 465-3900
(800) 714-8099
6100 Melrose Ave. FAX (323) 465-3600
Los Angeles, CA 90038 www.rc-gear.com
(PC Laptops and Monitors)

Rack Innovations, Inc. (818) 847-0200
(800) 557-8861
2801 W. Empire Ave. FAX (888) 262-1726
Burbank, CA 91504 www.marketec.com
(A/V Furniture)

RenderCore (866) 627-3149
FAX (213) 623-3149
www.rendercore.com

Rush Computer Rentals (800) 343-7368
(818) 374-7308
6060 Sepulveda Blvd. FAX (818) 374-7350
Van Nuys, CA 91411 www.rushcomputer.com
(Copiers, Desktop Computers, Fax Machines, Laptops, Macintosh, Monitors, PC, Printers & Projectors)

Santa Monica Lock & Safe Co., Inc. (310) 450-5101
(800) 696-9499
2208 Pico Blvd. FAX (310) 450-9563
Santa Monica, CA 90405
(Safes & Vaults)

So Cal Office Technologies (800) 736-7979
707 Wilshire Blvd., Ste. 3650 www.socal-office.com
Los Angeles, CA 90017
(Copiers, Fax Machines, Printers & Scanners)

Studio Office Services (310) 392-4767
(323) 816-7938
2222 Fifth St., Ste. 302 FAX (310) 392-4768
Santa Monica, CA 90405 www.studioofficeservices.com
(Office Supply Sales)

TMG Copier Rental (310) 326-5100
(800) 267-9261
FAX (310) 326-4976
www.copierrental.com
(Copiers, Desktop Computers, Fax Machines, PC, Printers & Projectors)

Transistor 8 (310) 314-3345
10228 Deerfield Ln. FAX (310) 314-3385
Northridge, CA 91324 www.transistor8.com
(Computers)

Wexler Video (818) 846-9381
(800) 939-5371
1111 S. Victory Blvd. FAX (818) 846-9399
Burbank, CA 91502 www.wexlervideo.com

1020 Studios (323) 883-0262
1020 N. Sycamore Ave. FAX (323) 874-6330
Los Angeles, CA 90038 www.1020studios.com

310 Casting Studios (310) 775-6600
(310) 775-6601
2329 Purdue Ave. FAX (310) 478-2100
Los Angeles, CA 90064 www.310castingstudios.com

The Andrita Media Center (323) 344-4500
3030 Andrita St. FAX (323) 344-4800
Los Angeles, CA 90065 www.andritastudios.com

Beth Melsky Satellite Casting (310) 451-1515
(212) 505-5000
1528 Sixth St., Ste. 100 FAX (310) 393-2697
Santa Monica, CA 90401 www.bethmelsky.com
(Video Conferencing)

The Casting Frontier (323) 300-6129
P.O. Box 291640 www.castingfrontier.com
Los Angeles, CA 90029
(Digital Casting)

Coastal Media Group (818) 880-9800
26660 Agoura Rd. FAX (818) 579-9026
Calabasas, CA 91302 www.coastalmediagroup.com
(Video Conferencing)

Dashstream.com (310) 403-2689
1206 Pico Blvd., Ste. 23 FAX (310) 664-1124
Santa Monica, CA 90405 www.dashstream.com
(Digital Casting)

Eastside Studios (323) 660-7874
4216 Fountain Ave. FAX (323) 660-7875
Los Angeles, CA 90029 www.eastsidestudiosla.com

Envision Studios (310) 451-1515
1528 Sixth St., Ste. 100 FAX (310) 293-2697
Santa Monica, CA 90401 www.envisionstudios.tv

Exclusive Studios (323) 969-8200
7700 W. Sunset Blvd. FAX (323) 969-0101
Los Angeles, CA 90046 www.exclusivecastingstudios.com

**Hollywood Telephone/
Will Communications** (310) 536-9777
2627 Manhattan Beach Blvd., Ste. 211 FAX (310) 536-9276
Redondo Beach, CA 90278 www.willcommunications.com
(Video Conferencing)

IMA/Interactive Multimedia Artists (760) 602-9165
6580 Corte Cisco www.imavideo.com
Carlsbad, CA 92009

Let There Be Light (310) 770-0463
1423 Second St., Ste. 203 www.castingondemand.com
Santa Monica, CA 90401
(Digital Casting)

Nydrle, Inc. (310) 659-8844
670 N. La Peer Dr. FAX (310) 659-7733
West Hollywood, CA 90069 www.nydrle.com

Pacific Television Center (310) 287-3800
3440 Motor Ave., Circular Bldg. FAX (310) 287-3808
Los Angeles, CA 90034 www.pactv.com
(Video Conferencing)

Sample Digital, Inc. (310) 459-3045
844 Seward St. FAX (310) 861-0263
Los Angeles, CA 90038 www.sampledigital.com

Ava Shevitt (310) 656-4600
Village Studio FAX (310) 656-4610
321 Santa Monica Blvd., Ste. 300 www.villagestudio.net
Santa Monica, CA 90401

Voicebank.net (877) 294-9910
(661) 294-9912
25000 Avenue Stanford FAX (661) 294-9764
Valencia, CA 91355 www.voicebank.net

The Acme Resource Network for the Designing Arts (310) 358-0321
www.theacme.com
(Design & Film, Television and Video Production)

Advertising Age (310) 860-6420
6500 Wilshire Blvd., Ste. 2300 www.adage.com
Los Angeles, CA 90048

Adweek Directories (646) 654-5220
770 Broadway, Seventh Fl. www.adweek.com/directories
New York, NY 10003
(Advertising, Marketing & Media)

Adweek/West (323) 525-2270
5055 Wilshire Blvd., Seventh Fl. FAX (323) 525-2391
Los Angeles, CA 90036 www.adweek.com

The Alternative Pick (212) 675-4176
1123 Broadway, Ste. 7A FAX (212) 675-4403
New York, NY 10010 www.altpick.com
(Design, Illustration & Photography for Film, Print and Television)

Animation Magazine (818) 991-2884
30941 W. Agoura Rd., Ste. 102 FAX (818) 991-3773
Westlake Village, CA 91361 www.animationmagazine.net

Backstage/West (323) 525-2225
(323) 525-2356
5055 Wilshire Blvd., Fifth Fl. FAX (323) 525-2354
Los Angeles, CA 90036 www.backstage.com

Billboard (323) 525-2299
5055 Wilshire Blvd., Ste. 700 FAX (323) 525-2395
Los Angeles, CA 90036 www.billboard.com

The Black Book (800) 841-1246
740 Broadway, Second Fl. www.blackbook.com
New York, NY 10003
(Illustration & Photography)

Blu-Book Production Directory (323) 525-2369
5055 Wilshire Blvd., Sixth Fl. FAX (323) 525-2393
Los Angeles, CA 90036 www.hcdonline.com
(Commerical, Film and Television Production)

Breakdown Services, Ltd./ Commercial Express (310) 276-9166
2140 Cotner Ave., Third Fl. FAX (310) 276-8829
Los Angeles, CA 90025 www.breakdownservices.com
(Information Service for Talent Agents)

Cinefex (805) 383-0800
(909) 781-1917
79 Daily Dr., Ste. 309 FAX (805) 383-0803
Camarillo, CA 93010 www.cinefex.com

Debbies Book (626) 798-7968
www.debbiesbook.com
(Advertising, Film Production & Television Production)

DGA Directory of Members (310) 289-2082
FAX (310) 289-5384
www.dga.org

DGA Quarterly (310) 289-5333
7920 Sunset Blvd. www.dga.org
Los Angeles, CA 90046

Digital Content Producer (866) 505-7173
www.digitalcontentproducer.com

Emmy (ATAS Magazine) (818) 754-2800
5220 Lankershim Blvd. FAX (818) 761-2827
North Hollywood, CA 91601 www.emmys.tv

Encore (949) 362-0727
(949) 280-7695
25171 La Jolla Way, Ste. A www.encoredirectory.com
Laguna Niguel, CA 92677
(Directory for Orange County and San Diego)

Ⓐ **Entertainment Partners** (818) 955-6299
(818) 955-6000
2835 N. Naomi St. FAX (818) 845-6507
Burbank, CA 91504
(Payroll Production Guide)

Entertainment Publishers (310) 440-5800
(800) 820-7601
11693 San Vicente Blvd., Ste. 206 FAX (310) 440-5812
Los Angeles, CA 90049
www.entertainmentpublisher.com
(Guild and Union Contracts)

"Extra" Work For Brain Surgeons (310) 277-3001
(310) 277-1007
c/o Hollywood OS FAX (818) 333-2280
3108 West Magnolia Blvd. www.hollywoodos.com
Burbank, CA 91505
(Extras Casting and Talent Directory)

Hollywood Creative Directory (323) 525-2334
(800) 815-0503
5055 Wilshire Blvd. FAX (323) 525-2393
Los Angeles, CA 90036 www.hcdonline.com
(Film and Television Production & Talent)

The Industry Labor Guide (310) 440-5800
(800) 820-7601
11693 San Vicente Blvd., Ste. 206 FAX (310) 440-5812
Los Angeles, CA 90049 www.entertainmentpublisher.com
(Contract Breakdowns)

International Cinematographers Guild (IA Local 600) (323) 876-0160
7755 Sunset Blvd. FAX (323) 876-6383
Los Angeles, CA 90046 www.cameraguild.com

Kemps Film, TV & Video Handbook (949) 888-5013
www.kftv.com
(International Film, Television and Video Production)

Kids' Acting for Brain Surgeons (310) 277-3001
(310) 277-1007
3108 W. Magnolia Blvd. FAX (818) 333-2280
Burbank, CA 91505 www.hollywoodos.com

The Knowledge (011) 44 173 237 7047
CMP Information Ltd. FAX (011) 44 173 237 7440
Sovereign House Sovereign Way, Tonbridge
Kent TN9 1RW United Kingdom
www.theknowledgeonline.com

LA 411 (800) 545-2411
5900 Wilshire Blvd., 30th Fl. www.la411.com
Los Angeles, CA 90036
(Commercial, Film, Music Video, Television and Video Production for Southern California)

The Mercury Production Report (866) 263-7287
P.O. Box 864 www.mercuryprods.com
Kilauea, HI 96754

The Musicians Atlas (973) 509-9898
www.musiciansatlas.com

New York 411 (800) 545-2411
(646) 746-6891
360 Park Ave. South, 14th Fl. FAX (646) 746-6894
New York, NY 10010 www.newyork411.com
(Commercial, Film, Music Video, Television and Video Production for NY, NJ and CT)

P3-Production Update Magazine (323) 315-9477
c/o Sunset Gower Studios FAX (323) 297-6661
1438 N. Gower St. www.p3update.com
Hollywood, CA 90026

Players Directory (310) 247-3058
2210 W. Olive Ave. FAX (310) 601-4445
Burbank, CA 91506 www.playersdirectory.com
(Casting)

Pollstar (559) 271-7900
4697 W. Jacquelyn Ave. FAX (559) 271-7979
Fresno, CA 93722 www.pollstaronline.com
(Music Industry)

Producers Masterguide (212) 777-4002
(212) 995-5555
60 E. Eighth St., 34th Fl. FAX (212) 777-4101
New York, NY 10003 www.producers.masterguide.com
(Commercial, Film, Television and Video Production)

Production Reference Services (310) 275-8002
2140 Cotner Ave., Third Fl. www.prodrefservice.com
Los Angeles, CA 90025
(Advertising, Film Production, Marketing, Media, Multimedia Production & Television Production)

Production Weekly (800) 284-2230
FAX (310) 868-2594
www.productionweekly.com

The Reel Directory (415) 531-9760
P.O. Box 1910 www.reeldirectory.com
Boyes Hot Springs, CA 95416
(Advertising, Casting, Commercial Production, Design, Film Production, Guild and Union Contracts, Illustration, Media, Multimedia Production, Music Industry, Music Video Production, Payroll Production Guide, Photography, Talent, Television Production & Video Production)

Reel West Productions, Inc. (604) 451-7335
(888) 291-7335
4012 Myrtle St. FAX (604) 451-7305
Burnaby, BC V5C 4G2 Canada www.reelwest.com
(Film, Multimedia Production and Video)

Shoot Commercial Production Directory (323) 960-8035
(818) 884-2440
650 N. Bronson Ave., Ste. B253 FAX (323) 960-8036
Los Angeles, CA 90004

Shoot Magazine (323) 960-8035
650 N. Bronson Ave., Ste. B253 FAX (323) 960-8036
Los Angeles, CA 90004 www.shootonline.com

Variety, Inc. (323) 617-9100
5900 Wilshire Blvd., 30th Fl. www.variety.com
Los Angeles, CA 90036

Videomaker Magazine (530) 891-8410
(800) 284-3226
P.O. Box 4591 FAX (530) 891-8443
Chico, CA 95927 www.videomaker.com

Wisconsin Production Guide (414) 852-8855
www.badgerguide.com

Workbook (323) 856-0008
(800) 547-2688
6762 Lexington Ave. FAX (323) 856-0443
Los Angeles, CA 90038 www.workbook.com
(Advertising, Design, Illustration & Photography)

Written By, The Magazine of the Writers Guild of America, West (323) 782-4522
7000 W. Third St. FAX (323) 782-4802
Los Angeles, CA 90048 www.wga.org

Archer Norris (213) 437-4000
333 S. Grand Ave., Ste. 3680 FAX **(213) 437-4011**
Los Angeles, CA 90071 **www.archernorris.com**

Blake & Wang P.A. (310) 295-1198
1801 Century Park East, 24th Fl. FAX **(310) 943-2363**
Los Angeles, CA 90067 **www.blakewang.com**

Leon Gladstone/
Berger Kahn Entertainment Division (310) 821-9000
4551 Glencoe Ave., Ste. 300 **www.bergerkahn.com**
Marina del Rey, CA 90292

Law Offices of Greg S. Bernstein (310) 247-2790
(310) 247-2799
9601 Wilshire Blvd., Ste. 240 FAX **(310) 247-2791**
Beverly Hills, CA 90210 **www.thefilmlaw.com**

Law Offices of Mark Litwak (310) 859-9595
433 N. Camden Dr., Ste. 1010 FAX **(310) 859-0806**
Beverly Hills, CA 90210 **www.marklitwak.com**

Macfarlane Law (310) 280-9445
3780 Selby Ave. FAX **(310) 280-0176**
Los Angeles, CA 90034 **www.macfarlane-law.com**

Marc Moses Law (310) 940-4557
445 S. Figueroa St., Ste. 2700 FAX **(310) 843-9960**
Los Angeles, CA 90071

Nathalie Hoffman & Assocs. (310) 448-8885
(International Business Transactions) FAX **(310) 448-8886**

Owen Sloane/
Berger Kahn Entertainment Division (310) 821-9000
4551 Glencoe Ave., Ste. 300 **www.bergerkahn.com**
Marina del Rey, CA 90292

Zuber & Taillieu, LLP (310) 807-9700
10866 Wilshire Blvd., Ste. 300 FAX **(310) 807-9701**
Los Angeles, CA 90024 **www.ztllp.com**

AAA Urban Casting (661) 255-5097
(310) 967-9954
P.O. Box 800126 www.aaaurbancasting.com
Valencia, CA 91380
(Large Crowds, TV Audiences, Union & Non-Union)
Contacts: Alan Armani, Ursula Presley & Angel Princess

Advanced Casting & Talent (323) 645-2327
11054 Ventura Blvd. FAX (323) 395-5510
Studio City, CA 91604

Akimas Casting (805) 649-8041
(805) 705-4110
P.O. Box 650 www.akimascastingandtalent.com
Santa Barbara, CA 93116

Alice Ellis Casting (310) 314-1488
FAX (310) 314-2649
www.elliscasting.com

Atmosphere Casting (888) 858-7090
2528 12th Ave. FAX (323) 316-9611
Los Angeles, CA 90018

Background Artists (888) 442-2867
12021 Wilshire Blvd., Ste. 632 FAX (888) 442-2867
Los Angeles, CA 90025 www.backgroundartists.tv

Background Talent Services (818) 760-7090
FAX (818) 762-7225
www.backgroundtalent.net

Bill Dance Casting (818) 754-6634
4605 Lankershim Blvd., Ste. 110 FAX (818) 754-6643
North Hollywood, CA 91602

Bump It Casting/Balyndah Bumpus (213) 700-5139
5482 Wilshire Blvd., Ste. 363 FAX (323) 737-1430
Los Angeles, CA 90036
(Large Crowds & TV Audiences)

Burbank Casting/Michelle Gabriel (818) 559-2446
2829 N. Glenoaks Blvd. FAX (818) 480-4314
Bldg. 106, Ste. 148 www.burbankcasting.com
Burbank, CA 91504

Caravan West Productions (661) 268-8300
35660 Jayhawker Rd.
Agua Dulce, CA 91390
FAX (661) 268-8301
www.caravanwest.com

Carol Grant Casting (818) 237-0282
FAX (413) 778-7115
www.carolgrantcasting.com

The Casting Couch, Inc./
Sande Alessi (818) 201-0466
13731 Ventura Blvd.
Sherman Oaks, CA 91423
www.sandealessicasting.com

Ⓐ **Central Casting** (818) 562-2700
220 S. Flower St.
Burbank, CA 91502
FAX (818) 562-2786
www.centralcasting.org

Christal Blue Casting (323) 960-5057
FAX (818) 893-9200
www.christalblue.com

Cline Entertainment (760) 242-5391
P.O. Box 3077
Apple Valley, CA 92307
FAX (760) 946-2822
www.clinecasting.com

Ⓐ **Combat Casting** (310) 686-2718
6850 Vineland Ave., Ste. N
North Hollywood, CA 91605
FAX (818) 509-9581
www.combatcasting.com

Creative Extras Casting (310) 391-9041
(310) 913-1310
2461 Santa Monica Blvd., Ste. 501
Santa Monica, CA 90404
FAX (310) 391-9043

Crowd In A Box (877) 927-6939
(416) 275-0422
(Inflatable Extras)
www.crowdinabox.com

Debbie Sheridan Casting (800) 820-5305
13547 Ventura Blvd., Ste. 311
Sherman Oaks, CA 91423
FAX (800) 820-5305
www.dsctalent.com

Ⓐ **Extra Extra Casting, Inc.** (310) 552-1888
FAX (310) 728-6574
www.extraextracastings.com

Gonzo Bros. (310) 828-4989
www.gonzobrothers.com
(Cardboard Crowds & Inflatable Figures)

Headquarters Casting (310) 556-9001
3108 W. Magnolia Blvd. FAX (310) 861-5988
Burbank, CA 91505 www.headquarterscasting.com

Hollywood OS (310) 277-3001
(310) 277-1007
3108 W. Magnolia Blvd. FAX (818) 333-2280
Burbank, CA 91505 www.hollywoodos.com

A **Idell James Casting** (310) 230-9986
FAX (310) 230-8233

Jeff Olan Casting, Inc. (818) 285-5462
(818) 377-4475
14044 Ventura Blvd., Ste. 209 FAX (818) 285-5470
Sherman Oaks, CA 91423 www.jeffolancasting.com

Magic Casting (805) 688-3702
1660 Cougar Ridge Rd. magiccasting.mysite.com
Buellton, CA 93427
Contact: Chrystine Urban

Nandinee Productions (310) 876-0404
(310) 408-8404
FAX (310) 876-0436
www.nandineeproductions.com

Prime Casting & Payroll (323) 962-0377
(323) 394-3399
6430 Sunset Blvd., Ste. 425 FAX (323) 466-4166
Hollywood, CA 90028 www.primecasting.com
(Large Crowds, Stand-Ins & TV Audiences)

Producer's Casting Agency - Palisades (310) 459-0229
FAX (310) 459-4954

Star Casting/Cheryl Faye (661) 510-3466
FAX (661) 254-2853

Sunset Casting (310) 398-7141
P.O. Box 1996
Venice, CA 90291
(Non-Union Only)

Ugly Models & Unique Characters (818) 201-0466
13731 Ventura Blvd.
Sherman Oaks, CA 91423
(Commercials)

AFEX - Associated Foreign Exchange, Inc. (818) 386-2702 (888) 307-2339
16133 Ventura Blvd., Ste. 900 FAX (818) 386-2709
Encino, CA 91436 www.afex.com
(Currency Exchange)

Citibank (818) 845-9956
FAX (818) 845-0879

The Jacobson Group (310) 444-5255
11835 W. Olympic Blvd., Ste. 1285 FAX (310) 444-5256
Los Angeles, CA 90064 www.jacobsongrp.com

The Library (213) 985-4225
453 S. Spring St., Ste. 601 FAX (213) 975-9553
Los Angeles, CA 90013

Markay Financial Corporation (818) 998-6125
20407 Strathern St. FAX (818) 998-6127
Canoga Park, CA 91306 www.markay.com
(Consultants & Equipment Financing and Leasing)

Rose Greene Financial Services (310) 399-1200
2665 30th St., Ste. 111 FAX (310) 399-0911
Santa Monica, CA 90405 www.rosegreene.com

The Shindler Perspective, Inc. (818) 223-8345
16060 Ventura Blvd., Ste. 105 - 246 FAX (480) 247-4190
Encino, CA 91436 www.ishindler.com
(Consultants, Currency Exchange, Equipment Financing, Equipment Leasing & Film Finance)

Union Bank of California (213) 236-7700 (213) 236-6176
445 S. Figueroa St., Plaza Level FAX (213) 236-7734
Los Angeles, CA 90071 www.uboc.com
(Film Finance)

Wells Fargo (310) 210-4571
333 S. Grand Ave., Ste. 2000
Los Angeles, CA 90071

Steve Altes (818) 434-8469
(Male Hand Model) (661) 799-7829
FAX (661) 799-7829
www.stevealtes.com

LáShan Anderson (310) 729-1978
(323) 882-0025
FAX (310) 314-3365
www.bylashan.com
(African-American Foot, Hand and Leg Model & Child-Sized Hands)

Linda Ashton (310) 475-2111
(Female Hand Model) www.cesdtalent.com

Elizabeth Atkins (310) 475-2111
(Female Foot Model) www.cesdtalent.com

Nick Ballard (310) 475-2111
(Male Hand Model) www.cesdtalent.com

Te-See Bender (818) 988-5772
(Female Hand Model) (818) 642-5187
FAX (818) 988-5777

Laura-Shay Bentley (310) 878-2897
www.laura-shay.com
(Female Foot Model, Hand Model and Leg Model & On-Camera Writing)

Ⓐ Body Parts Models (310) 275-8263
2023 Coldwater Canyon Dr. (702) 496-8469
Beverly Hills, CA 90210 FAX (310) 273-5878
www.bodypartsmodels.com
(Reps for Body Parts Models)

Paul McCarthy Boyington (310) 475-2111
(Male Foot Model) www.cesdtalent.com

Ms. Marlon Braccia (310) 251-7252
www.askyogimarlon.com/gallery/Parts/
(Female Foot, Hand and Leg Model & On-Camera Writing)

Gerald Brodin (818) 636-9842
(Male Hand Model) (818) 260-9960
FAX (818) 526-0070
www.geraldbrodin.com

Marc Buccola (310) 475-2111
(Male Hand Model) www.cesdtalent.com

C.E.S.D. Talent Agency (310) 475-2111
10635 Santa Monica Blvd., Ste. 130 FAX (310) 475-1929
Los Angeles, CA 90025 www.cesdtalent.com
(Reps for Body Parts Models)

JC Caballero (310) 231-7010
(Male Hand Model) FAX (310) 231-7013
www.jordicaballero.com/handsbody

Brian Chase (310) 475-2111
(Male Hand Model) www.cesdtalent.com

Elisha Choice (213) 804-2511
(African-American Female Hand Model) FAX (323) 257-0636

Jenna Chong (626) 755-5653
(Hand Model) www.jennachong.com

Mia Crowe (323) 428-8434
www.handsupermodel.com
(Female Foot, Hand and Leg Model & On-Camera Writing)

Mary Culmone (310) 475-2111
(Female Hand Model) www.cesdtalent.com

Charles Davis (310) 475-2111
(Male Hand Model) www.cesdtalent.com

Cheryl Dent (310) 251-2149
(Hand Model) www.cheryldent.com

Juliet Diamond (310) 994-7935
(Child-Sized Hands)

Traci Dority (310) 418-2433
(Female Hand Model) (310) 418-2433

Denise Feir (818) 710-8055
(Child-Sized Hands)

Chris Gardner (310) 475-2111
(Male Hand Model) www.cesdtalent.com

Mike Garibaldi (707) 224-7370
(Hand Model)

Susan Gayle (818) 990-8650
(Child-Sized Hands)

Paulette Gilbert (805) 374-6090
(Hand Model) (805) 660-7868

Kimberly Girard (310) 475-2111
(Female Foot Model) www.cesdtalent.com

Laura Grayson (323) 899-9090 / (323) 512-5332
(Hand Model) FAX (323) 512-5332

Garon Grisby (310) 475-2111
(Male Hand Model) www.cesdtalent.com

Steve Harris (310) 475-2111
(Male Hand Model) www.cesdtalent.com

Anicka Haywood (310) 475-2111
(Female Foot Model) www.cesdtalent.com

Kelly Hornbaker (310) 306-6000 / (310) 345-2331
(Male Foot and Hand Model)

Tom Howard (661) 775-9566 / (661) 755-3839
(Hand Model)

Janine Jordae (818) 415-2929 / (818) 845-7434
www.janinejordae.com
(Female Foot and Hand Model & On-Camera Writing)

Alison Nicole Karp (310) 968-7370

Bill Karp (213) 999-9890 / (323) 876-7721
(Hand Model)

Tracy Kay (310) 475-2111
(Female Foot Model) www.cesdtalent.com

Horace Knight (310) 475-2111
(Male Hand Model) www.cesdtalent.com

Linda Kruse (818) 370-4649 / (818) 414-3606
(Female Hand Model) www.tvhandmodel.com

Breney Kurylo (714) 686-1313 / (562) 325-2030
(Child-Sized Hands)

Joel Lambert (310) 475-2111
(Male Hand Model) www.cesdtalent.com

Henry LeBlanc (323) 993-8615 / (323) 365-3333
(Hand Model) FAX (323) 938-2156
www.henryshands.com

Rebecca Levinson-Gaither (818) 404-1069
(Child-Sized Hands)

Joycelyne Lew (323) 466-3100 / (213) 999-5514
(Foot, Hand and Leg Model) FAX (323) 469-7138
www.joycelyne.com

Roger Lim (310) 475-2111
(Male Hand and Foot Model) www.cesdtalent.com

Louisa Maccan (310) 990-2704 / (310) 990-2704
FAX (310) 496-3008
www.ladyhands.com
(Female Hand Model & On-Camera Writing)

Susan McWilliams (310) 475-2111
(Female Hand Model) www.cesdtalent.com

Jodi Novak (310) 995-4410
(Child-Sized Hands)

Laila Odom (310) 475-2111
(Female Hand Model) www.cesdtalent.com

Linda O'Neil (310) 475-2111
(Female Hand Model) www.cesdtalent.com

Sondra Prosper (310) 475-2111
(Female Hand Model) www.cesdtalent.com

Chelsea Rangsikitpho (310) 475-2111
(Female Hand Model) www.cesdtalent.com

Tamia Richmond (310) 475-2111
(Female Hand and Foot Model) www.cesdtalent.com

Jennifer Robinson (310) 475-2111
(Female Hand Model) www.cesdtalent.com

Simeon Russell (310) 475-2111
(Male Hand Model) www.cesdtalent.com

Alan Safier (818) 766-2433
(Hand Model)

Laurel Schaefer (818) 846-3200
(Hand Model) FAX (818) 846-3099

Noah Schuffman (310) 475-2111
(Male Hand and Foot Model) www.cesdtalent.com

April Scott (310) 475-2111
(Female Hand and Foot Model) www.cesdtalent.com

Douglas Stockley (310) 475-2111
(Male Hand Model) www.cesdtalent.com

Lisa Tobin (818) 571-4499 / (818) 501-2002
(Child-Sized Hands)

Adele Uddo (310) 980-2992

Rick Wagner (310) 433-3900
(Hand Model) FAX (323) 464-9300
www.rickwagnerhands.com

Eric Weldon (310) 475-2111
(Male Hand Model) www.cesdtalent.com

Amy Weller (310) 475-2111
(Female Hand and Foot Model) www.cesdtalent.com

Sheri Weller (323) 253-0519
(Hand Model) www.sheristoweweller.com

David Lloyd Wilson (310) 475-2111
(Male Hand Model) www.cesdtalent.com

Gerold Markus Wunstel (310) 699-4335
(Foot and Hand Model) www.geroldactor.com

Tanya York (818) 788-4050
(Child-Sized Hands) FAX (818) 788-4011
www.yorkentertainment.com

Melissa Yvonne Lewis (310) 475-2111
(Female Hand and Foot Model) www.cesdtalent.com

Abacus Insurance Brokers, Inc. (310) 207-5432
12300 Wilshire Blvd., Ste. 100 FAX (310) 207-8526
Los Angeles, CA 90025 www.abacusins.com

AON/Albert G. Ruben Insurance Services, Inc. (310) 234-6800 (800) 752-9157
10880 Wilshire Blvd., Ste. 700 FAX (847) 953-2480
Los Angeles, CA 90024 www.albertgruben.com

Brilliant Insurance Services (818) 264-0300
20720 Ventura Blvd., Ste. 270 FAX (818) 264-0699
Woodland Hills, CA 91364 www.movieinsure.com

Cal-Surance Associates, Inc. (800) 762-7800
681 S. Parker, Ste. 200 www.calsurance.com
Orange, CA 92868

Claim Specialists International, Ltd. (213) 347-0250
550 South Hope St., Ste. 1625 FAX (213) 347-0266
Los Angeles, CA 90071

CMM Entertainment (818) 224-6142
21045 Califa St., Ste. 100 www.cmmentertainment.com
Woodland Hills, CA 91367

Dewitt Stern Of California Insurance Services (818) 623-5400
10969 Ventura Blvd. FAX (818) 623-5500
Studio City, CA 91604 www.dewittstern.com

Film Emporium Insurance Services (323) 464-5144
Sunset Gower Studios FAX (323) 464-7348
1438 N. Gower St., Bldg. 35, Box 71
Los Angeles, CA 90028 www.filmemporium.com

Film Finances (310) 275-7323
9000 Sunset Blvd., Ste. 1400 FAX (310) 275-1706
West Hollywood, CA 90069 www.filmfinances.com
(Completion Bond Guarantors)

First Tower Insurance Agency (866) 441-0321 (562) 821-0321
10002 Pioneer Blvd., Ste. 104 FAX (562) 949-7146
Santa Fe Springs, CA 90670 www.firsttower.com

Frankel & Associates Insurance (800) 696-3023 (310) 271-5582
9233 W. Pico Blvd., Ste. 226 FAX (310) 887-1758
Los Angeles, CA 90035 www.frankelins.com

Gallagher Entertainment (818) 539-1220
505 N. Burbank Blvd., Ste. 600 FAX (818) 539-1520
Glendale, CA 91203 www.ajgrms.com/entertainment

A **Heffernan Insurance Brokers/ InsureMyEquipment.com** (213) 236-0511 (626) 379-6280
811 Wilshire Blvd., Ste. 1801 FAX (213) 243-1233
Los Angeles, CA 90017 www.insuremyequipment.com

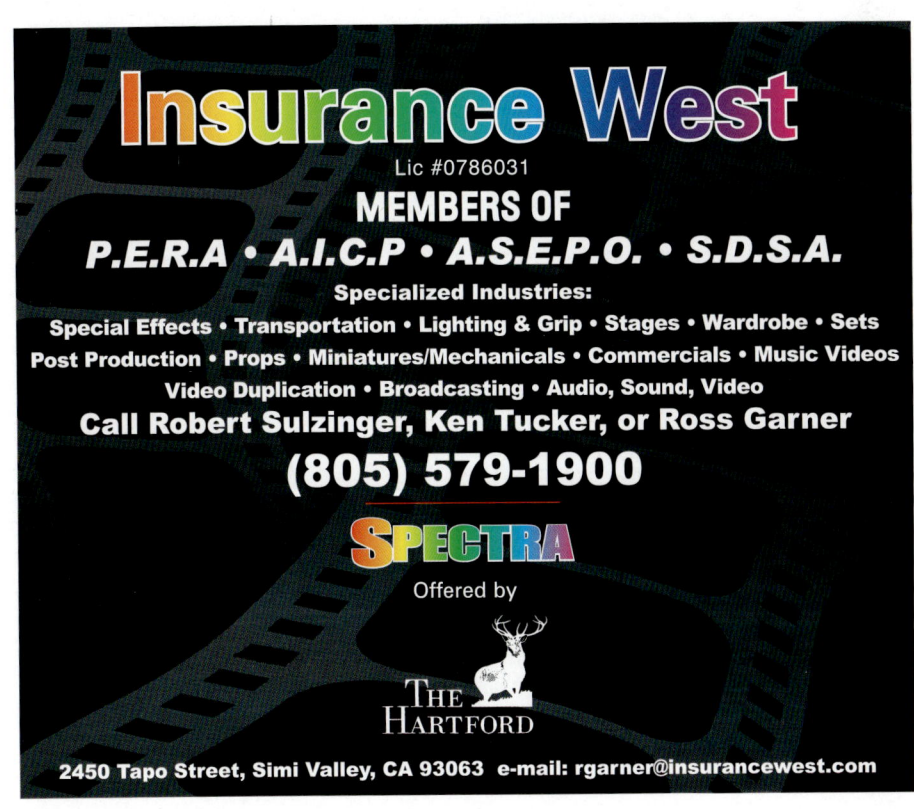

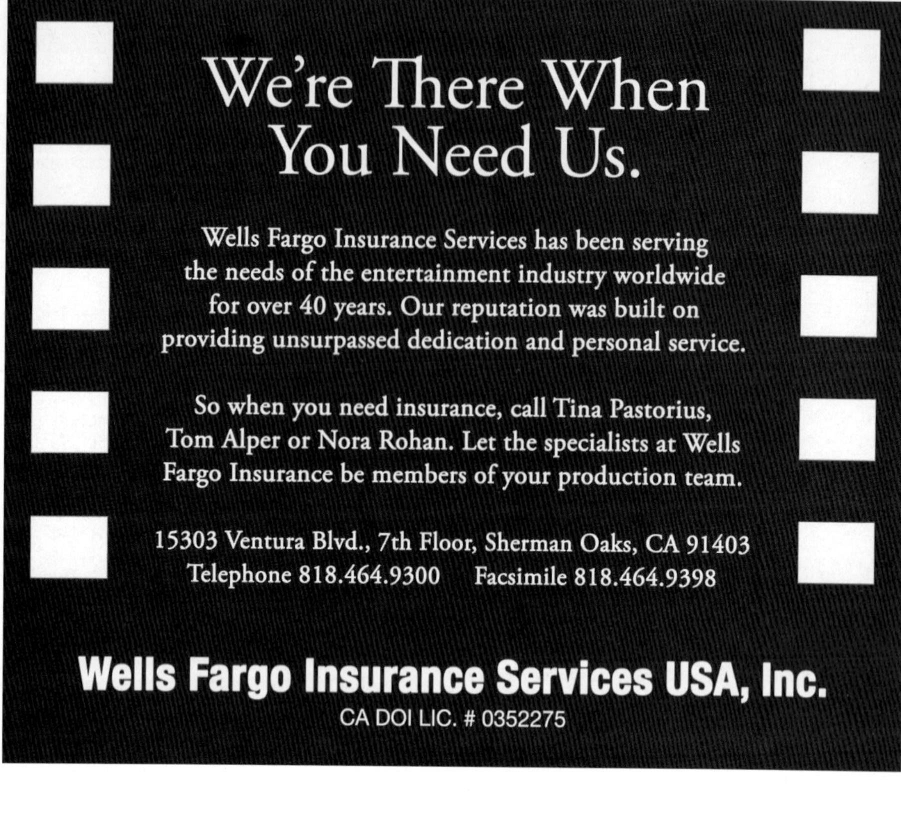

iManagement Group (310) 979-5729
(888) 549-2600
c/o Elkins Jones Insurance Agency FAX (310) 207-5441
12100 Wilshire Blvd., Ste. 300
Los Angeles, CA 90025 **www.imanagementgroup.com**

Infiniti Pacific Insurance Services (800) 957-6542
FAX (571) 323-0715
www.infinitipacific.com

International Film Guarantors (310) 309-5660
2828 Donald Douglas Loop North FAX (310) 309-5696
Second Fl. **www.ifgbonds.com**
Santa Monica, CA 90405
(Completion Bond Guarantors)

Jim Miller Financial Services (818) 880-4164
(213) 503-5448
4505 Las Virgenes Rd., Ste. 202 FAX (818) 880-0733
Calabasas, CA 91302 **www.jamesrmiller.com**

John Wm. Hart III Insurance Agency, Inc. (310) 789-5865
1800 Century Park East, Ste. 600 FAX (800) 858-6693
Los Angeles, CA 90067 **www.johnhartinsurance.com**

Kaercher Campbell & Associates Insurance Brokerage (310) 556-4766
FAX (310) 551-6874
www.kaerchercampbell.com

Marsh Risk & Insurance Services (213) 346-5200
(213) 346-5003
777 S. Figueroa St., 27th Fl. FAX (213) 346-5922
Los Angeles, CA 90017

MIB Insurance Services (310) 775-9020
111 N. Sepulveda Blvd., Ste. 245 FAX (310) 374-2305
Manhattan Beach, CA 90266 **www.mediainsurance.com**

Peacock Insurance Agency (949) 252-8777
2082 SE Bristol St., Ste. 2
Newport Beach, CA 92660

Premier Class Insurance Services, Inc. (562) 821-0321 / (866) 441-0321
10002 Pioneer Blvd., Ste. 104 FAX **(562) 949-7146**
Santa Fe Springs, CA 90670 **www.premierclass.net**

Sterling Grant and Associates, LLC (877) 954-7200
FAX **(602) 954-9624**
www.sterling-grant.com

Steven Randall Peterson Commercial Insurance Services (805) 643-2477 / (800) 441-7077
21 S. California St., Ste. 407 FAX **(805) 643-3874**
Ventura, CA 93001

Ⓐ **Robert Sulzinger/Insurance West** (805) 579-1900
2450 Tapo St. FAX **(805) 579-1916**
Simi Valley, CA 93063 **www.insurancewest.com**

Supple-Merrill & Driscoll, Inc. (626) 795-9921
550 El Dorado St. FAX **(626) 577-6656**
Pasadena, CA 91101 **www.productioninsurance.com**

Taylor & Taylor, Ltd. (818) 981-9700 / (212) 490-8511
15060 Ventura Blvd., Ste. 210 FAX **(818) 981-9703**
Sherman Oaks, CA 91403 **www.taylorinsurance.com**

Tom C. Pickard & Co., Inc. (800) 726-3701
820 Pacific Coast Hwy FAX **(800) 318-9840**
Hermosa Beach, CA 90254 **www.tcpinsurance.com**

Truman Van Dyke Co. (323) 883-0012
6767 Forest Lawn Dr., Ste. 301 FAX **(323) 883-0024**
Los Angeles, CA 90068
(Completion Bond Guarantors)

United Agencies, Inc. (800) 800-5880
100 N. First St., Ste. 301 FAX **(877) 901-5522**
Burbank, CA 91502 **www.unitedagencies.com**

USI Entertainment Insurance Services (818) 251-3000
21600 Oxnard St., Eighth Fl. FAX **(818) 251-1800**
Woodland Hills, CA 91367 **www.usi.biz.com**

Ⓐ **Wells Fargo Insurance Services** (818) 464-9300
15303 Ventura Blvd., Seventh Fl. FAX **(818) 464-9398**
Sherman Oaks, CA 91403 **www.wellsfargo.com**

Zeboray Insurance Services (949) 498-7017 / (800) 829-8445
P.O. Box 1044 **www.zeboray.com**
San Clemente, CA 92674

A-1 King Cleaning (323) 469-0781 (323) 702-0587
1607 N. El Centro, Ste. 6 FAX (818) 547-1553
Hollywood, CA 90028 **www.a1king.com**
(Carpet Cleaning, Dirt Removal, Floor Service, Hauling, Hot Pressure Washing, Janitorial Only, Layout Board, Pressure Cleaning, Steam Cleaning, Trash Collection & Window Cleaning)

A. Mullins Janitorial & Floor Maintenance (323) 933-8288 (310) 275-4950
5030 W. Washington Blvd. FAX (323) 933-8107
Los Angeles, CA 90016

AK Exterior Steam Cleaning (661) 373-7727
19425 Soledad Canyon, Ste. 137
Canyon Country, CA 91351
(Steam Cleaning)

All-Ways Steam Cleaning (818) 834-6555 (800) 347-8633
10515 Foothill Blvd.
Sylmar, CA 91342
(Pressure Cleaning)

Bailey Bobcat Service/Studio Cats (818) 982-4356
(Dirt Removal, Hauling, Location Site Prep & Pressure Cleaning)

Best Janitorial Services/LMS (818) 988-6644
14740 Keswick St. FAX (818) 988-7922
Van Nuys, CA 91405

Bin Rental (818) 786-5805 (877) 246-7368
9871 San Fernando Rd.
Pacoima, CA 91331

Board Sily (818) 590-5878

Clean Strike Rental & Cleaning (562) 803-3701 (562) 879-2207
12214 Lakewood Blvd., Bldg. 9 FAX (562) 803-3702
Downey, CA 90242 **www.cleanstrikerentals.com**
(Carpet Cleaning, Dirt Removal, Dumpsters, Floor Service, Hauling, Hot Pressure Washing, Layout Board, Location Site Prep, Pressure Cleaning, Steam Cleaning, Trash Collection & Window Cleaning)

Clean Up Your Act (323) 962-7280 (323) 316-8447
336 N. Bronson Ave.
Los Angeles, CA 90004
(Janitorial Only)

Clean Wrap (310) 514-7579 (213) 530-8908
FAX (818) 507-5626
www.cleanwrap.biz

Cleaner Image Janitorial (310) 346-5439 (310) 544-1028
FAX (310) 832-2097
www.cleanerimage.net
(Carpet Cleaning, Floor Service, Janitorial Service, Pressure Wash & Window Cleaning)

Diamond's Cleaning Service & Family, Inc. (818) 471-9099
833 N. Vista St. **www.diamondscleaningservices.com**
North Hollywood, CA 90046
(Carpet Cleaning)

Executive Building Services (626) 584-5757
260 S. Los Robles Ave., Ste. 101 FAX (626) 584-0178
Pasadena, CA 91101

Express Layout Boards, Inc. (661) 255-0602
(661) 857-1715
24504 Apple St. FAX (661) 255-0602
Santa Clarita, CA 91321

The Ground Floor (818) 887-6413
15812 Arminta St. FAX (818) 780-8554
Van Nuys, CA 91406 www.groundfloor.org
(Floor Service, Marble Polishing & Stone Restoration)

Holt Enterprises, Inc. (213) 924-9371
FAX (323) 661-0157

It's A Blast, Inc. (805) 955-9809
(877) 252-7848
2235 First St., Ste. 119 FAX (805) 955-0144
Simi Valley, CA 93065 www.itsablast.net
(Hot Pressure Washing)

A **Lavaughn's High Pressure System** (626) 794-2666
(818) 427-8820
44 W. Loma Alta Dr. FAX (626) 794-2666
Altadena, CA 91001
(Steam Cleaning)

Metropolis Disposal (818) 901-2020
(800) 650-6165
7740 Burnet Ave. FAX (818) 778-1895
Van Nuys, CA 91405 www.metropolis-disposal.com

On Location Disposal (626) 890-2652
(866) 423-1282
P.O. Box 3441 www.on-locationdisposal.com
El Monte, CA 91733
(Trash Bin Rental)

Pacific Powerwash (310) 200-8228
(866) 987-9274
www.pacificpowerwash.net
(Hot Pressure Washing, Pressure Cleaning & Steam Cleaning)

Safe Sets Recycling Corp. (310) 359-0754
2118 Wilshire Blvd., Ste. 314 FAX (310) 828-6477
Santa Monica, CA 90403 www.safesetsrecycling.org
(Recycling Service for Sets)

Thoreau Janitorial (310) 822-8017
5301 Beethovan St., Ste. 101 FAX (310) 822-5867
Los Angeles, CA 90066
(Janitorial Services)

Trailer Trash (818) 706-3423
(818) 590-2455
5737 Kanan Rd., Ste. 531 FAX (818) 706-1660
Agoura Hills, CA 91362 www.trailertrashla.com
(Hauling, Trash Bin Rental & Trash Collection)

Tudor Company (626) 458-6000
115 W. California Blvd., Ste. 243 FAX (626) 458-6086
Pasadena, CA 91105 www.tudorcompany.com

Water Dogs Pressure Washing (818) 392-8449
2517 Honolulu Ave. FAX (818) 248-3138
Montrose, CA 91020
(Pressure Cleaning)

Wrap Patrol (310) 836-6321
(Grip and Lighting Strikes) FAX (310) 636-1020

15/40 Productions (310) 848-1150
3133 Jack Northrop Ave. FAX (310) 848-1121
Hawthorne, CA 90250 www.1540productions.com

360 Designworks/ 360 Propworks Inc. (310) 323-3326
1441 W. 132nd St. FAX (310) 323-3352
Los Angeles, CA 90249 www.360designworks.com
(Corporate Event Planning, Event Show Production & Event Staffing)

Abbey Events (310) 900-0099 (323) 201-4200
1520 S. Maple Ave. FAX (323) 201-4299
Montebello, CA 90640 www.abbeyeventservices.com

Acme Design Group (818) 767-8888
11001 Fleetwood St. www.acme-designgroup.com
Sun Valley, CA 91352

Along Came Mary (323) 931-9082
5265 W. Pico Blvd. FAX (323) 936-8249
Los Angeles, CA 90019 www.alongcamemary.com

Bill Ferrell Co. (818) 994-1952 (866) 994-1952
14744 Oxnard St. FAX (818) 994-9670
Van Nuys, CA 91411 www.billferrell.com

Black Tie Catering and Events/ BT Daily (310) 337-9900
5741 Buckingham Pkwy, Ste. D FAX (310) 337-9916
Culver City, CA 90230 www.blacktieevent.com
(Caterers, Corporate Event Planning & Event Staffing)

Brent Bolthouse Productions (323) 848-9300
7966 Beverly Blvd., First Fl. FAX (323) 525-2425
Los Angeles, CA 90048

Celebrity Events (323) 848-2300
1800 Century Park East, Ste. 600
Los Angeles, CA 90067 www.celebrityinternational.com

Event Management Productions (760) 340-6003
73-647 Sun Ln. FAX (760) 437-3292
Palm Desert, CA 92260 www.eventproducer.com
(Event Show Production)

Events in Motion (323) 962-7660
6525 Sunset Blvd., Ste. G2 FAX (323) 962-7647
Hollywood, CA 90028 www.eventsinmotion.com

Fortune Entertainment (818) 760-0560
11253 Peachgrove St., Ste. 104 FAX (818) 760-0558
North Hollywood, CA 91601 www.efortune.com

L.A. Circus (323) 751-3486
7531 La Salle Ave. FAX (323) 778-2025
Los Angeles, CA 90047

Marilyn Jenett Locations (310) 475-0211
1933 Manning Ave. www.marilynjenettlocations.com
Los Angeles, CA 90025
(Location Coordinator)

Ocean Park Productions (310) 452-9585
2712 Second St. FAX (310) 452-9587
Santa Monica, CA 90405
www.oceanparkproductions.com

The Studios at Paramount (323) 956-8398
The Studios at Paramount Special Events
5555 Melrose Ave.
Los Angeles, CA 90038
www.paramountspecialevents.com

ProAdvance (310) 645-1910
8726 S. Sepulveda Blvd., Ste. 1441 FAX (323) 417-5133
Los Angeles, CA 90045 www.proadvance.com

Randy Fuhrman Events (818) 461-9111
12950 Blairwood Dr. FAX (818) 461-9222
Studio City, CA 91604 www.randyfuhrmanevents.com

Charlie Scola (310) 214-9158
www.charliescola.com

Scott Topper Productions (818) 640-6100 (310) 575-0200
11684 Ventura Blvd., Ste. 870
Studio City, CA 91604
www.scotttopperproductions.com

Silver Birches (626) 796-1431
650 S. Raymond Ave. FAX (626) 568-3274
Pasadena, CA 91105 www.silverbirches.net

Stoelt Productions (323) 463-3700
1962 S. La Cienega FAX (323) 463-3303
Los Angeles, CA 90034 www.stoeltproductions.com

Taste Catering, Inc. (949) 215-7373
FAX (949) 215-7494
www.tastecateringcafe.com
(Caterers, Corporate Event Planning, Entertainment, Event Show Production, Event Staffing, Party Supplies & Rentals)

Academy of Motion Picture Arts & Sciences - Margaret Herrick Library (310) 247-3020
333 S. La Cienega Blvd.
Beverly Hills, CA 90211
www.oscars.org/library/index.html

Act One Script Clearance, Inc. (818) 240-2416
(818) 240-2417
230 N. Maryland Ave., Ste. 208 FAX **(818) 240-2418**
Glendale, CA 91206 **www.actonescript.com**
(Research & Script Clearance)

Action Sports/Scott Dittrich Films (310) 459-2526
(212) 681-6565
P.O. Box 301 FAX **(310) 456-1743**
Malibu, CA 90265 **www.sdfilms.com**

Aero Associates (310) 337-1938
(310) 332-4383
Aviation Research Library, 8033 Emerson Ave.
Los Angeles, CA 90045
(Aviation History)

American Society of Composers, Authors & Publishers (ASCAP) (323) 883-1000
7920 Sunset Blvd., Ste. 300 FAX **(323) 883-1049**
Los Angeles, CA 90046 **www.ascap.com**
(Music Research)

Munish Asnani/ Visual Research & Treatment Design (323) 383-5663
www.munishasani.com
(Footage Research for Treatment Design)

Back In Time (760) 715-7721
P.O. Box 184 **www.backintime.com**
Del Mar, CA 92014
(Historical Consulting)

BBC Motion Gallery, Los Angeles (818) 299-9720
4144 Lankershim Blvd., Ste. 200 FAX **(818) 299-9763**
North Hollywood, CA 91602 **www.bbcmotiongallery.com**
(Clips, Footage and Text Resource Library, Sound/Radio Archive & Stock Footage Clearances)

Broadcast Music, Inc. (BMI) (310) 659-9109
8730 Sunset Blvd., Third Fl. West FAX **(310) 657-6947**
Los Angeles, CA 90069 **www.bmi.com**
(Music Research & Performance Rights)

California Film Commission Location Resource Center (323) 860-2960
(800) 858-4749
7080 Hollywood Blvd., Ste. 900 FAX **(323) 860-2972**
Los Angeles, CA 90028 **www.film.ca.gov**

Carolyn Chriss Research (310) 909-8760
4017 Weslin Ave.
Sherman Oaks, CA 91423
home.earthlink.net/~caroza3/carolynchrissresearch
(Footage, Historical, Literary and Photo Research)

Center for the Study of Political Graphics (323) 653-4662
8124 W. Third St., Ste. 211 FAX **(323) 653-6991**
Los Angeles, CA 90048 **www.politicalgraphics.org**
(Political Poster Archive)

Clearance Domain, LLC (310) 898-1233
(661) 252-1231
(Clips, Research & Script Clearance) FAX **(661) 252-4087**
www.clearancedomain.com

Clearance Unlimited (818) 988-5599
6848 Firmament Ave. FAX **(818) 988-5577**
Van Nuys, CA 91406 **www.clearances.net**
(Artist, Copyright, Footage, Music and Script Clearance & Title Search)

Clearly Right Entertainment, Inc. (310) 709-7909
950 N. Kings Rd., Ste. 346
West Hollywood, CA 90069
www.clearlyrightentertainment.com
(Art Clearances, Clearances, Clips, Film Copyright Research, Footage Clearance, Footage Research, Intellectual Property, Internet, Music Clearances, Music Research, Photography Clearances, Photography Research, Research, Stock Footage Clearances & Talent)

Costume Rentals Corporation (818) 753-3700
11149 Vanowen St. FAX **(818) 753-3737**
North Hollywood, CA 91605 **www.costumerentalscorp.com**

Creative Clearance (818) 728-4622
FAX **(818) 332-7070**
www.creativeclearance.com
(Clearances, Clips, Copyrights, Errors and Omissions, Film Copyright Research, Footage Clearance, Music Clearances, Music Research, Photography Clearances, Script Clearances, Stock Footage Clearances, Talent & Title Search)

Creative Musical Services (818) 426-7727
13547 Ventura Blvd., Ste. 358
Sherman Oaks, CA 91423
www.creativemusicalsvcs.com
(Music Clearance Library and Supervision)

Elizabeth Bardsley & Associates, Inc. (818) 563-4008
3727 W. Magnolia Blvd., Ste. 450 FAX **(818) 823-1938**
Burbank, CA 91510 **www.elizabethbardsley.com**
(Research Services & Script Annotations)

Evan M. Greenspan, Inc./EMG (818) 762-9656
4181 Sunswept Dr., Second Fl. FAX **(818) 762-2624**
Studio City, CA 91604 **www.clearance.com**
(Music Clearance)

Film Art LA (323) 461-4900
5241 Melrose Ave. FAX **(323) 461-4959**
Hollywood, CA 90038 **www.filmartla.com**
(Art and Photography Copyright Clearance and Research)

Film Bank, Inc./Corbis Motion (866) 473-5264
(323) 602-5750
3455 S. La Cienega Blvd. FAX **(323) 602-5837**
Los Angeles, CA 90016 **www.corbismotion.com**
(Stock Footage Clearance)

Film Superlist - Motion Pictures in The Public Domain (323) 655-4968
8391 Beverly Blvd., Ste. 321
Los Angeles, CA 90048
(Film Copyright Research)

Fox Studios (310) 369-2782
Research Library, 10201 W. Pico Blvd. FAX **(310) 369-3645**
Los Angeles, CA 90035 **www.foxstudios.com**

Global Brainstorm Research/ Carey Ann Strelecki (310) 993-3700
FAX **(818) 508-6635**
www.globalbrainstorm.com
(Art Clearances, Art Research, Clearances, Copyrights, Footage Clearance, Footage Research, Internet, Photography Clearances, Photography Research, Research, Script Clearances, Script Research, Stock Footage Clearances & Talent)

Global ImageWorks, LLC (201) 384-7715
65 Beacon St. FAX **(201) 501-8971**
Haworth, NJ 07641 **www.globalimageworks.com**

The History Source (310) 493-2636
14403 Addison St., Ste. 17 **www.thehistorysource.net**
Sherman Oaks, CA 91423

Hollywood Script Research (818) 553-3633
448 W. Maple FAX (818) 553-3624
Glendale, CA 91204 **www.hollywoodscriptresearch.com**
(Errors and Omissions & Legal Research)

IndieClear Script Clearance (323) 828-8280
(323) 871-9223
6532 1/2 La Mirada Ave. FAX (323) 871-9220
Los Angeles, CA 90038 **www.indieclear.com**
(Script Clearance and Research)

Joan Pearce Research Associates (323) 655-5464
8111 Beverly Blvd., Ste. 308 FAX (323) 655-4770
Los Angeles, CA 90048 **home.earthlink.net/~jpra/**
(Errors and Omissions & Research)

Just Imagine Research Library, Inc. (818) 764-5644
6910 Farmdale Ave. FAX (818) 764-6655
North Hollywood, CA 91605
(Architecture, Art & Photography)

Debra Lemonds (818) 563-2928
468 E. Providencia Ave., Ste. A FAX (818) 563-1680
Burbank, CA 91501
(Art Research & Photography Clearances and Research)

License It (310) 289-7232
9903 Santa Monica Blvd., Ste. 1103 FAX (310) 772-0985
Beverly Hills, CA 90212
(Artist, Footage, Internet and Music Clearance)

Lillian Michelson Research Library (818) 695-6445
Dreamworks SKG, 1000 Flower St. FAX (818) 695-7081
Glendale, CA 91201
(History; By Appointment Only)

Liquid Courage Music (310) 838-5656
3002 Midvale Ave., Ste. 210 FAX (310) 441-7558
Los Angeles, CA 90034
(Music Supervision)

Louis B. Mayer Library/
American Film Institute (323) 856-7654
(323) 856-7600
2021 N. Western Ave. **www.afi.com**
Los Angeles, CA 90027

Marshall/Plumb
Research Associates, Inc. (818) 848-7071
4150 Riverside Dr., Ste. 209 FAX (818) 848-7702
Burbank, CA 91505 **www.marshall-plumb.com**
(Script Research)

Miss Information (323) 270-9298
(213) 200-4063
P.O. Box 27814 FAX (323) 667-1717
Los Angeles, CA 90027 **www.miss-info.net**

Mophonics (310) 452-0331
200 Westminister Ave. FAX (310) 452-0356
Venice, CA 90291 **www.mophonics.com**
(Clearances, Copyrights, Intellectual Property, Internet, Music Clearances, Music Research, Music Supervision, Research & Talent)

Museum of Television & Radio (310) 786-1000
465 N. Beverly Dr. FAX (310) 786-1086
Beverly Hills, CA 90210 **www.mtr.org**
(Archives & Research Library)

Nickerson Research (323) 965-9990
FAX (323) 965-9991
www.nickersonresearch.com
(Footage, Photo, Talent and Text Clearance and Research)

PAC (323) 931-9962
(Historic Footage and Music Performance Research)

Pacifica Radio Archives (818) 506-1077
(800) 735-0230
3729 Cahuenga Blvd. FAX (818) 506-1084
North Hollywood, CA 91604
www.pacificaradioarchives.org
(Public Radio Programming & Sound Actualities)

PicturesNow.com (415) 435-1076
(Historic Photo Library) FAX (415) 435-5027
www.picturesnow.com

Richard J. Riordan - Central Library (213) 228-7000
630 W. Fifth St. **www.lapl.org**
Los Angeles, CA 90071
(Public Library)

Searchworks (323) 469-3783
2558 Verbena Dr. FAX (323) 464-0824
Los Angeles, CA 90068 **www.searchworks.com**
(Footage, Photo, Script and Talent Clearance and Licensing)

Seeling-Lafferty Research, LLC (310) 391-1801
12829 Rose Ave. FAX (310) 391-3561
Los Angeles, CA 90066
(Permission, Script Clearance and Title Research)

Southern California
Genealogical Society &
Family Research Library (818) 843-7247
417 Irving Dr. FAX (818) 843-7262
Burbank, CA 91504 **www.scgsgenealogy.com**

Sue Terry Associates (818) 506-0500
P.O. Box 56719
Sherman Oaks, CA 91403
(Art Clearances, Art Research, Copyrights, Costume Research, Footage Clearance, Footage Research, Historical Consulting, Literary Research, Music Research, Photography Clearances, Photography Research, Public Library, Research & Stock Footage Clearances)

TellAVision (310) 230-5303
1060 20th St., Ste. 8 FAX (310) 388-5550
Santa Monica, CA 90403 **www.tellavisionagency.com**
(Reps for Footage & Visual Research/Treatment Design Companies)

Ten Music (310) 305-3800
312 Venice Way FAX (310) 305-3811
Venice, CA 90291 **www.tenmusic.tv**
(Music Supervision)

Western Costume Co. (818) 760-0902
11041 Vanowen St. FAX (818) 508-2190
North Hollywood, CA 91605 **www.lawardrobesupplies.com**
(Costume Research Library)

Westside Detectives, Inc. (323) 583-8660
(323) 833-2383
6230 Wilshire Blvd., Ste. 59 **www.westsidedetectives.com**
Los Angeles, CA 90048
(Intellectual Property & Trademark Infringement)

Alexsasha Lauren's Excellent Massage (310) 927-0297

Allen Edwards Salon & Serenity Spa (310) 394-2878
FAX (310) 394-3477
www.allenedwards.com

Lama Amin (818) 762-9223
(818) 321-3539
www.magicfingersla.com

An Ancient Touch (818) 980-3060
(818) 437-8041
10458½ Moorpark St. FAX (818) 980-3060
Toluca Lake, CA 91602 www.anancienttouch.com

Aroma Spa & Sports (213) 387-2111
3680 Wilshire Blvd. www.aromaresort.com/spa.html
Los Angeles, CA 90010

Jennifer Astman-Posen (310) 480-8855
www.jenmassagela.com

Tanja Barnes (310) 439-8754
www.tanjabarnes.com

Karen Becker-Burns Massage Therapy (818) 543-1739
(310) 282-0997
9845 S. Santa Monica Blvd. www.lamedicinewoman.com
Beverly Hills, CA 90212

Carrie Becks/A-1 Massage & Massage Therapists (310) 678-7601
345 Richmond St. FAX (310) 227-8205
El Segundo, CA 90245

Belle Visage Day Spa (818) 907-0502
13207 Ventura Blvd. www.bellevisage.com
Studio City, CA 91604

Beverly Hot Springs (323) 734-7000
308 N. Oxford Ave. www.beverlyhotsprings.com
Los Angeles, CA 90004

Bodies in Motion (310) 836-8000
12100 Olympic Blvd. FAX (310) 775-8650
Los Angeles, CA 90064 www.bodiesinmotion.com

Body Energizers on Location/Diane Hubner (310) 394-4334
www.bodyenergizers.net

Jennifer Bratton/A Positive Change (310) 428-0568
www.servemehere.com/jenniferlbratton

Brooks Massage Therapy (323) 937-8839
(323) 937-8781
7619-21 Beverly Blvd. www.brooksmassage.com
Los Angeles, CA 90036

Burke Williams Spa (310) 587-3366
1358 Fourth St. www.burkewilliamsspa.com
Santa Monica, CA 90405
(See Web Site for Additional Locations)

Center for Wellbeing (626) 355-2443
20 N. Baldwin Ave. FAX (626) 355-2445
Sierra Madre, CA 91024 www.centerwellbeing.com

Jason Chase/JC Massage (310) 210-3033
1807 Marine St. www.healingacademy.net
Santa Monica, CA 90405

Rachel Cohen (310) 838-0849
FAX (310) 838-1922

Creative Chakra/Sandie West (310) 823-9378
3401 Pacific Ave., Ste. 2A, 2B & 1C FAX (310) 424-2905
Marina del Rey, CA 90292 www.creativechakra.com

Anna Dekker/The Dutch Touch (310) 630-7577
(310) 581-5302
www.dedutchtouch.com

DuBunné Day Spa and Massage Center (310) 326-9062
23725 Arlington Ave. FAX (310) 326-7056
Torrance, CA 90501 www.dubunnedayspa.com

Dr. Caren M. Elin, D.C. (805) 344-1414
(805) 448-1424
FAX (805) 344-4255

Equinox Fitness Club & Spa (310) 552-0420
www.equinoxfitness.com

Exhale Spa (310) 899-6222
1422 Second St. FAX (310) 899-6022
Santa Monica, CA 90401 www.exhalespa.com

Final Touch Massage Therapy (310) 704-0806
www.finaltouchmt.com

Deb Fingerman (213) 400-4475

Four Seasons Hotel Spa (310) 273-2222
FAX (310) 859-3824
www.fourseasons.com

Go Massage (888) 506-2772
(818) 783-1700
www.gomassage.com

A Great Massage Company/Merle Deborah Levine (818) 755-4699
(818) 315-6282
FAX (818) 752-2484

Amy Hall/Hands on Healing Bodywork (800) 840-2639

Healing Choices (805) 449-2646
901 Greenwich Dr. FAX (805) 449-2647
Thousand Oaks, CA 91360 www.chiro.net

Healing Choices (818) 266-7599
13202 Washington Blvd. FAX (805) 449-2647
Los Angeles, CA 90066 www.chiro.net
(Chiropractic)

Heidi's Fabulous Fatigue Fighters Worldwide (310) 488-5297
(917) 301-2022
FAX (212) 996-1958
www.fabulousfatiguefighters.com

Helen Hodgson/U Knead Massage (323) 573-6344
www.ukneadmassage.com

Mari Hotaki/Magic Hands (310) 582-8293

Infinite Circle/Debra Tourigny (310) 567-4445
P.O. Box 12442
Marina del Rey, CA 90295

Kinara Spa (310) 657-9188
656 N. Robertson Blvd. FAX (310) 657-9184
Los Angeles, CA 90069 www.kinaraspa.com

The Kneaded Experience (877) 242-4752
FAX (818) 205-9517
www.kneadedexperience-la.com

Carole Koenig (323) 935-7464
(323) 610-1997
www.ckmassagetherapy.com

Kimberly Korljan/Deep Work (310) 542-5773
FAX (310) 542-5773
www.deepwork.com

LA Body Points (310) 941-8464
www.labodypoints.com/chair_massage

Le Petite Retreat day spa (323) 466-1028
331 N. Larchmont Blvd. FAX (323) 462-4008
Los Angeles, CA 90004 www.lprdayspa.com

Elaine Lew (310) 874-4768
P.O. Box 64226 elainemassage.moonfruit.com
Los Angeles, CA 90064

Lulur Day Spa (310) 659-4100
645½ N. Robertson Blvd. FAX (310) 659-4117
Beverly Hills, CA 90069 www.lulurspa.com

Massage By Angie (818) 231-9441
(818) 231-4094
www.massagebyangie.com

The Massage Company (310) 358-1999
1106 N. La Cienega Blvd., Ste. 206
West Hollywood, CA 90069 www.messagecoweho.com

The Massage Express Co. (310) 806-0831
FAX (310) 401-7748
www.themassageexpress.com

Massage Therapy Center, Inc. (310) 444-8989
2130 S. Sawtelle Blvd., Ste. 207 www.massagenow.com
Los Angeles, CA 90025

Meta Touch
Custom Therapeutic Massage (310) 397-3422
4441 Sepulveda Blvd. FAX (310) 915-9532
Culver City, CA 90230 www.metatouch.com

Kim Moise, N.P. (323) 360-8366
FAX (310) 441-5032
www.kimlanmoise.com

Larry Nesti/Massage for Health (818) 266-3833
4149 Murietta Ave.
Sherman Oaks, CA 91423

Ole Henriksen Face/Body (310) 854-7700
(800) 327-0331
8622-A W. Sunset Blvd. FAX (310) 854-1869
Los Angeles, CA 90069 www.olehenriksen.com

Ona Spa (323) 931-4442
7373 Beverly Blvd. FAX (323) 931-9992
Los Angeles, CA 90036 www.onaspa.com

Production Massage (818) 434-8874
FAX (818) 688-0101
www.productionmassage.com

Pure Bodywork (310) 396-6800
FAX (310) 396-6855
www.purebodywork.com/set.html

Gloria Ramos/On Set Massage (818) 445-1727
(323) 202-6899
P.O. Box 361223 www.onsetmassage.com
Los Angeles, CA 90036

Nianna Rose (310) 980-2555

Sea Mountain Inn Resort Spa (877) 928-2827
Astral Ocean www.seamountaininn.com
Desert Hot Springs, CA 92240

A Shaman in the City/Dr. Mark (310) 394-6986
(877) 674-2626
1431 Ocean Ave., Ste. 1118 www.shaman.cc
Santa Monica, CA 90401

Smiling Lion Sun (619) 920-0863

Spa by Diane Loring, Inc. (805) 641-0022
www.spaventura.com

Spa Connections (888) 660-3636
www.spa-connections.com

Spa On Location, Inc. (310) 453-0210
(310) 497-1607
2461 Santa Monica Blvd., Ste. 404 FAX (310) 396-3066
Santa Monica, CA 90404 www.spaonlocation.com
(Mobile Spa)

The SpaMobile (310) 774-6390
8950 W. Olympic Blvd., Ste. 93 FAX (310) 861-9067
Beverly Hills, CA 90211 www.thespamobile.com
(Mobile Spa)

Trilogy Spa (310) 318-3511
1301 Manhattan Ave. FAX (310) 374-6452
Hermosa Beach, CA 90254 www.trilogyspa.com

Seppo J. Viljanen (323) 851-6000
(818) 599-6056
www.sportscentertltc.com

Deirdre Wagner (310) 570-0056
www.shentherapy.info

Yada Yada Yoga (310) 274-2665
www.yadayoga.com

Zykoff Bodywork (310) 275-7673
9009 Beverly Blvd. www.zykoffbodywork.com
West Hollywood, CA 90048

A-1 Courier (213) 622-4000
655 S. Flower St., Ste. 280
Los Angeles , CA 90017
www.a-1courier.com

Academy Messenger Service (323) 655-8224
FAX (323) 655-8386
www.academymessenger.com

Accurate Express (323) 906-1000
FAX (323) 906-9633
www.accurateexpress.net

Action Messenger Service (323) 654-2333
(800) 474-2587
1311 N. Highland Ave.
Los Angeles, CA 90028
FAX (323) 654-8889
www.actionmessenger.com

Ad Delivery (323) 852-1301
FAX (323) 852-9181

Beverly Hills Express Courier (213) 346-1000
(800) 481-9009
350 S. Figueroa, Ste. 196
Los Angeles, CA 90071
FAX (310) 657-3198

CitySprint (310) 258-0800
(800) 734-7328
FAX (310) 410-9331

Classic Couriers (323) 461-3741
(323) 769-3412
1601 N. El Centro Ave.
Hollywood, CA 90028
FAX (323) 957-3110
www.classic-couriers.com

Deliver LA (310) 478-8000
(800) 653-3548
10537 Santa Monica Blvd., Ste. 200
Los Angeles, CA 90025
FAX (310) 470-4564
www.deliverla.com

Efficient Delivery Service (818) 817-2700
7065 Hayvenhurst Ave., Ste. 7
Van Nuys, CA 91406
FAX (818) 205-9883
www2.efficientdeliveryservice.com/entrack/index.asp

Entertainment Delivery Group (888) 838-2929
FAX (818) 838-2939
www.entertainmentdelivery.net

Fox Messenger (800) 474-2536
FAX (213) 250-8714

KBS Dailies/Film Messenger Service (310) 842-6880
3336 S. Robertson Blvd.
Los Angeles, CA 90034
FAX (310) 842-6888
www.kbsmessenger.com

Messenger Express (818) 754-1234
5503 Cahuenga Blvd., Ste. 100
North Hollywood, CA 91601
FAX (818) 754-1031

Now Messenger Service (818) 842-5444
2906 W. Magnolia Blvd.
Burbank, CA 91505
FAX (818) 842-7153
www.nowmessengerservice.net

PDL Concepts, Inc. (800) 995-8819
21213-B Hawthorne Blvd., Ste. 5637
Torrance, CA 90503
FAX (562) 948-4554
www.pdlonline.com

Reels On Wheels Unlimited (914) 576-6300
(213) 620-9787
FAX (914) 633-6932
www.reelsonwheels.com

Rocket Messenger Service (323) 469-7155
(818) 341-9786
P.O. Box 3506
Chatsworth, CA 91311
FAX (818) 993-3407
www.rocketmessenger.com

Santa Monica Express Messenger Service (310) 458-6000
(800) 245-4502
12424 Wilshire Blvd., Ste. 740
Santa Monica, CA 90025
FAX (310) 395-9004
www.smexpress.com

Security Couriers, Inc. (818) 789-3999
(888) 863-7736
FAX (818) 789-3888
www.securitycouriers.com

Sequoia Messenger Service (323) 465-0709
(818) 906-2009
20061 Saticoy St., Ste. 202
Winnetka, CA 91306
FAX (818) 906-2616
www.sequoiamessenger.com

Sterling Messenger Services (310) 839-7000
(323) 299-7500
P.O. Box 34758
Los Angeles, CA 90034
FAX (310) 839-9999
www.sterlingdelivery.com

Sunrise Delivery Service, Inc. (818) 789-5121
FAX (818) 789-5333
www.sunrisedelivery.com

Team Delivery Systems (310) 590-1500
5839 Green Valley Circle, Ste. 105
Culver City, CA 90230
FAX (310) 410-9331
www.teamdelivery.com

Time Machine (213) 975-9850
(800) 734-8463
1533 Wilshire Blvd.
Los Angeles, CA 90017
FAX (800) 977-2077
www.timemachinenetwork.com

United Express (310) 556-1883
(818) 787-1883
1888 Century Park East, Ste. 105
Los Angeles, CA 90067
FAX (310) 556-7700

Universal Courier (310) 410-4500
(323) 463-3975
5839 Green Valley Circle, Ste. 105
Culver City, CA 90230
FAX (310) 410-9331
www.universalcourier.com

Westside Express, Inc./ Nationwide Express (310) 470-4470
(800) 207-2222
FAX (310) 470-2557

A and C Harbour Lites, Ltd. (310) 926-9552
P.O. Box 9279 FAX (310) 356-3579
Marina Del Rey, CA 90295
(Marine Coordination)

All Water Productions (808) 216-4553
(310) 567-4308
(Marine Coordination) www.allwaterproductions.com

Aquatic Cinema (310) 864-2000
www.aquaticcinema.com

A **Aquavision** (562) 433-2863
(562) 688-3038
3708 E. Fourth St. FAX (562) 433-2863
Long Beach, CA 90814 www.aquavision.net
(Marine Coordination)

Camera Craft (714) 330-9900
(714) 964-6920
www.cameracraftonline.com

Cat Production Services/ Extreme Sports Filming (562) 596-7105
(Marine Coordination) www.extremesportsfilming.com

Cinema Aquatics (818) 365-7999
(805) 207-5797
www.cinemaaquatics.com

Cinema Safety & Marine Services, Inc. (310) 614-0206
(805) 207-5797
1534 N. Moorpark Rd., Ste. 108 FAX (805) 241-3954
Thousand Oaks, CA 91360 www.cinemasafety.com
(Marine Coordination)

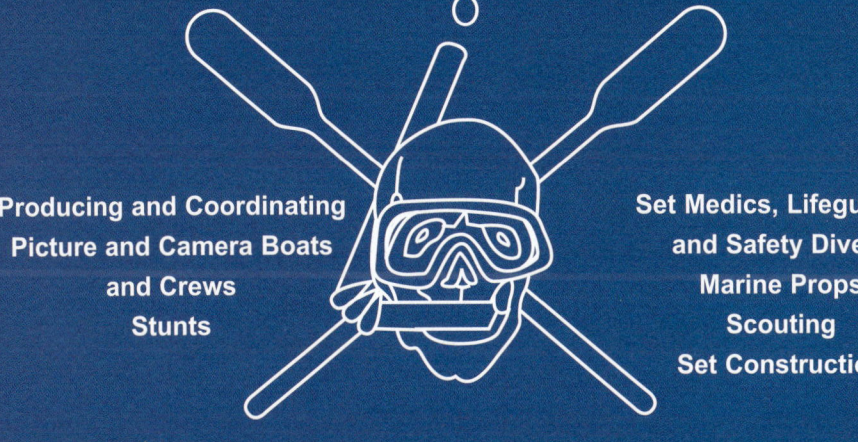

CineMarine Team - Cinema Rentals, Inc. (661) 222-7342 (877) 877-9605
25876 The Old Road, Ste. 174 FAX **(661) 253-3643**
Stevenson Ranch, CA 91381 **www.cinemarineteam.com**
(Marine Coordination)

Executive Yacht Management, Inc. (310) 306-2555
644 Venice Blvd. FAX **(310) 306-1147**
Marina del Rey, CA 90291 **www.yacht-management.com**
(Marine Coordination)

Marine Crew, Inc. (305) 586-6664 (760) 889-3107
(Marine Coordination) **www.marinecrew.net**

Motion Picture Marine (310) 822-1100
616 Venice Blvd. FAX **(310) 822-2679**
Marina del Rey, CA 90291 **www.motionpicturemarine.com**
(Marine Coordination)

A **Nautical Film Services** (562) 594-9276 (310) 729-6920
P.O. Box 50066 FAX **(562) 594-9242**
Long Beach, CA 90815 **www.nauticalfilmservices.com**
(Marine Coordination)

Jimmy O'Connell (310) 968-0549 (310) 452-5774
306 Market St., Ste. A FAX **(310) 452-5774**
Venice, CA 90291

Offshore Grip Marine, Inc. (310) 547-3515
23852 Pacific Coast Hwy, Ste. 764 FAX **(310) 943-3328**
Malibu, CA 90265 **www.offshoregripmarine.com**
(Marine Coordination)

Premiere Yacht Charters (619) 410-5222 (619) 808-2822
1380 Harbor Island Dr. **www.premiereyachtcharters.com**
San Diego, CA 92101

Privateer Lynx (866) 446-5969 (949) 274-5785
(Marine Coordination) FAX **(949) 723-1958**
www.privateerlynx.org

US Camera Boats LLC (949) 230-9327
FAX **(949) 492-7783**
www.uscameraboats.com

Capt. Troy Waters (310) 713-9193
(Marine Coordinator) FAX **(310) 943-3328**

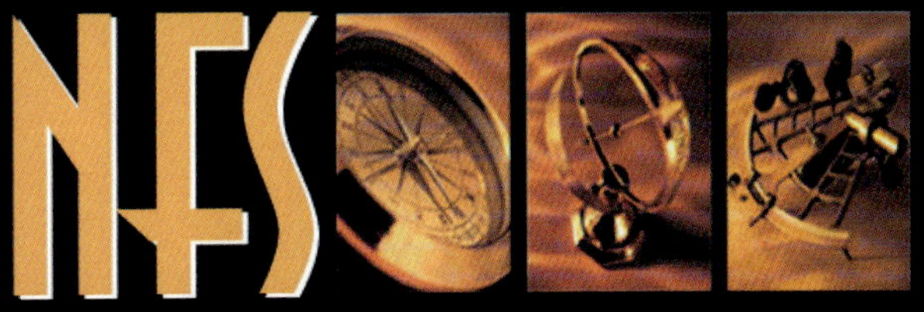

Nautical Film Services

Safety, Service and Success Since 1984

Full Service Marine Management For The Entertainment Industry

TELEVISION
FILM
PRINT
EVENTS
COMMERCIALS

- Modern & Historical Picture Vessels
- Camera, Support & Safety Vessels
- Worldwide Nautical Locations & Logistics

For information about NFS, please contact:

Michael Neipris
PRESIDENT

OFFICE: **562.594.9276**
MOBILE: **310.729.6920**
E-MAIL: **info@nauticalfilmservices.com**
WEB: **www.nauticalfilmservices.com**

Nautical Film Services

Mei-Ling Andreen (818) 259-0821
(818) 622-3793
(Traveling Notary) FAX **(818) 622-0728**

ASAP Traveling Notary Public (818) 780-8121
(800) 266-8279
(24-Hour Service & Traveling Notary) **1800anotary.com**

Film Auditors, Inc. (213) 413-0033
849 N. Occidental Blvd. FAX **(213) 413-0088**
Los Angeles, CA 90026 **www.filmauditors.com**

Mobile Notary (310) 475-1764
(323) 650-3164
(24-Hour Service)

Paragon Language Services, Inc. (323) 966-4655
(800) 499-0299
5657 Wilshire Blvd., Ste. 310 FAX **(323) 651-1867**
Los Angeles, CA 90036 **www.paragonls.com**

Sandra Robles (818) 471-6994

Traveling Notary Public/ Michele Lamorie (310) 274-4832
(310) 417-3437
P.O. Box 66738 FAX **(310) 337-1231**
Los Angeles, CA 90066

Zoom Mobile Notary Services (213) 487-0414
(323) 719-7313
137 N. Larchmont Blvd., Ste. 575 FAX **(213) 487-1610**
Los Angeles, CA 90004 **www.zoommobilenotary.com**

Payroll & Production Accountants

ABS Payroll & Production Accounting Services (818) 848-9200 (877) 284-5600
3500 W. Olive Ave.
Burbank, CA 91505
www.abspayroll.net

The Accounting Group (818) 333-4555
FAX (818) 333-4556

American Residuals & Talent, Inc. (805) 526-9119
1409 Kuehner Dr., Ste. 206 FAX (805) 306-9419
Simi Valley, CA 93063 www.artpayoll.com
(Celebrity Contracts, Payroll & SAG/AFTRA Commercial Signatory Services)

American Residuals & Talent, Inc. (209) 296-4087
14755 Diamond View Dr. FAX (209) 296-0627
Pioneer, CA 95666 www.artpayoll.com
(Celebrity Contracts, Payroll, SAG/AFTRA Commercial Signatory & Union Compliance Signatory)

The Audit Trail, Inc. (818) 786-0825
5907 Noble Ave. FAX (818) 786-0829
Van Nuys, CA 91411 www.audittrail.org

CAPS Universal (310) 280-0755
5880 W. Jefferson Blvd., Ste. H FAX (310) 280-0889
Los Angeles, CA 90016 www.capsuniversalpayroll.com
(Celebrity Contracts, Payroll, Production Software, SAG/AFTRA Commercial Signatory Services & Union Compliance Signatory)

Cast & Crew Entertainment Services (818) 848-6022
100 E. Tujunga Ave. FAX (818) 848-9556
Burbank, CA 91502 www.castandcrew.com

Audrey S. Cohen (310) 208-6776 (305) 385-2204
(Production Accountant) FAX (310) 208-6776

Daugherty Accounting Services, Inc. (818) 901-8208
FAX (818) 901-8208

Dolphingirl Productions, Inc. (562) 688-8999 (562) 531-8999
5421 Whitewood Ave. FAX (562) 634-3898
Lakewood, CA 90712
(SAG/AFTRA Commercial Signator Services)

EMS, Inc. (818) 386-0905
16027 Ventura Blvd., Ste. 102 FAX (818) 386-9341
Encino, CA 91436 www.emspayroll.com

Entertainment Partners (818) 955-6299 (646) 473-9000
2835 N. Naomi St. FAX (818) 845-6507
Burbank, CA 91504 www.entertainmentpartners.com
(Production Software)

Film Auditors, Inc. (213) 413-0033
849 N. Occidental Blvd. FAX (213) 413-0088
Los Angeles, CA 90026 www.filmauditors.com

Film Budget Pro (323) 574-9696
FAX (888) 699-9778
www.filmbudgetpro.com
(Budgeting, Production Software & Scheduling)

The Jacobson Group (310) 444-5255
11835 W. Olympic Blvd., Ste. 1285 FAX (310) 444-5256
Los Angeles, CA 90064 www.jacobsongrp.com

Douglas W. McHenry (805) 208-3281

Ⓐ **Media Services** (310) 440-9696 / (800) 333-7518
500 S. Sepulveda Blvd., Fourth Fl. FAX **(310) 472-9979**
Los Angeles, CA 90049 **www.media-services.com**

Lisa Mitchell (310) 801-8860
(Auditor & Production Accountant)

Ⓐ **NPI Production Services, Inc.** (818) 566-7878 / (866) 296-2267
2550 Hollywood Way, Ste. 430 FAX **(818) 566-7879**
Burbank, CA 91505 **www.npiproductionservices.com**
(Payroll & SAG/AFTRA Commercial Signatory Services)

Oberman, Tivoli, Miller & Pickert, Inc. (310) 471-9300 / (310) 471-9356
500 S. Sepulveda Blvd., Fourth Fl. FAX **(310) 471-4702**
Los Angeles, CA 90049 **www.media-services.com**

PayReel (800) 352-7397 / (303) 526-4900
FAX **(303) 526-4901**
www.payreel.com

Marilyn Penn-Lindley (310) 827-2094 / (310) 780-8683
FAX **(951) 361-1446**
(Post Production Accounting & Production Accountant)

PES Payroll (818) 729-0080
(800) 301-1992
4100 W. Burbank Blvd. FAX (818) 295-3886
Burbank, CA 91505 **www.pespayroll.com**

Prime Casting & Payroll (323) 962-0377
(323) 394-3399
6430 Sunset Blvd., Ste. 425 FAX (323) 466-4166
Hollywood, CA 90028 **www.primecasting.com**

Randemonium, Inc. (818) 505-0400
4555 Radford Ave. FAX (818) 505-0599
Studio City, CA 91607
(SAG/AFTRA Commercial Signatory Services & Union Compliance Signatory)

Rice Gorton Pictures, Ltd. (323) 665-6200
2870 Los Feliz Pl., Ste. 301 FAX (323) 665-4222
Los Angeles, CA 90039
(Post Production Accounting)

Sessions Payroll Management, Inc. (818) 841-5202
303 N. Glenoaks Blvd., Ste. 810 FAX (818) 841-9112
Burbank, CA 91502 **www.sessionspayroll.com**

Talent Partners (818) 556-4700
FAX (818) 955-7789
www.talentpartners.com

TEAM (818) 558-3261
901 W. Alameda Ave., Ste. 100 FAX (818) 558-3263
Burbank, CA 91506 **www.teamservices.net**
(Celebrity Contracts, Payroll, SAG/AFTRA Commercial Signatory Services & Union Compliance Signatory)

Michele Varon, C.P.A. (818) 386-1900
4064 Weslin Ave. FAX (818) 386-1901
Sherman Oaks, CA 91423
(Production Accountant)

AAA Custom Engravers (818) 989-8010
15948 Leadwell St. FAX (818) 989-8020
Van Nuys, CA 91406
(Engraving)

Action Ad Specialties, Inc. (818) 762-7680
FAX (818) 762-9750
www.actionadpromos.com
(Apparel, Embroidery, Hats, Silkscreening & T-Shirts)

Active Ad Specialties (310) 558-3533
(800) 866-8684
10746 Francis Pl., Ste. 305 FAX (310) 558-0503
Los Angeles, CA 90034 www.activeadspecialties.com
(Merchandising)

Adapt Consulting, Inc. (818) 782-6974
13618 Lemay St. FAX (818) 782-6975
Van Nuys, CA 91401 www.adaptadspecialty.com
(Apparel, Bags, Hats, Merchandising & T-Shirts)

B & H Company (310) 719-7004
(800) 996-6003
120 W. 157th St. FAX (310) 719-9894
Gardena, CA 90248 www.bhcompany.com
(Embroidery & Silkscreening)

The Bag Ladies (310) 822-1706
(800) 359-2247
4214 Glencoe Ave. FAX (310) 574-9960
Marina del Rey, CA 90292 www.bag-ladies.com
(Bags)

Banners and Flags Unlimited (805) 528-5018
P.O. Box 7004 FAX (805) 528-3529
Los Osos, CA 93412 www.bannermarketinggroup.com
(Apparel, Bags, Embossing, Embroidery, Hats, Laser Printing, Merchandising, Packaging, Silkscreening & T-Shirts)

Bare Reflections (818) 765-5304
12547 Sherman Way, Ste. J FAX (818) 765-1830
North Hollywood, CA 91605

Big 10 Industries, Inc. (310) 280-1610
6006 Washington Blvd. FAX (310) 280-1611
Culver City, CA 90232 www.big10.com
(Embroidery, Engraving, Silkscreening & Tie-Dye)

Bovary and Butterfly (323) 933-7448
(310) 430-4321
5225 Wilshire Blvd., Ste. 100 FAX (323) 933-1315
Los Angeles, CA 90036 www.bovaryandbutterfly.com

Brand Central Promotions (800) 828-1943
(800) 828-1943
FAX (888) 934-7942
www.bcpromo.com
(Apparel, Bags, Embossing, Embroidery, Hats, Laser Printing, Merchandising, Packaging, Silkscreening & T-Shirts)

Brand-It Promotions (310) 318-8585
FAX (310) 318-5854
www.branditpromotions.com

Brownstone Screen Printers (818) 985-7283
5709 Cahuenga Blvd. FAX (818) 753-9155
North Hollywood, CA 91601 www.bspplus.com
(Embroidery & Silkscreening)

CC&C Embroidery House Corporation (661) 250-3460
(888) 882-5621
26841 Ruether Ave., Ste. C FAX (661) 250-3921
Canyon Country, CA 91351 www.embroideryhouse.com
(Embroidery & Screenprinting)

Classy Tees (323) 654-4103
7810 Romaine St., Ste. 3
Los Angeles, CA 90046
(Silkscreening)

Coastal Printworks, Inc. (818) 503-0781
7344 Hinds Ave. FAX (818) 503-0977
North Hollywood, CA 91605 www.coastalprintworks.com
(Crew and Promotional Apparel, Embroidery & Screenprinting)

Corporate Images, Inc. (805) 498-9018
(800) 439-8939
3563 Old Conejo Rd. FAX (805) 498-9017
Newbury Park, CA 91320 www.corporateimages.com
(Apparel, Bags, Embossing, Embroidery, Hats, Laser Printing, Merchandising, Packaging, Silkscreening & T-Shirts)

D art Company (310) 890-6251
www.d-artcompany.com

David K's T-Shirt Printing (310) 204-3812
8926 Venice Blvd. www.davidkla.com
Culver City, CA 90232
(Embroidery & Silkscreening)

EKF Promotions (818) 786-2996
19528 Ventura Blvd., Ste. 232 FAX (818) 578-6439
Tarzana, CA 91356 www.ekfpromo.com
(Apparel, Bags, Embossing, Hats, Merchandising, Packaging, Silkscreening & T-Shirts)

Ellen's Silkscreening & Promotional Products (626) 441-4415
(888) 545-9711
1506 Mission St. FAX (626) 441-2788
South Pasadena, CA 91030 www.ellenssilkscreening.com
(Embroidery & Silkscreening)

Event Apparel (818) 252-7622
(818) 419-2450
11355 Penrose St. FAX (818) 252-1112
Sun Valley, CA 91352 www.eventapparel.com

Gamble Gear, LLC (310) 435-3307
(Promotional Apparel Manufacturing) www.gamblegear.com

Get Smart Promotions (818) 808-0812
4570 Van Nuys Blvd., Ste. 313
Sherman Oaks, CA 91403
www.getsmartpromotions.com
(Crew and Promotional Apparel & Merchandising)

Golden Fleece Designs, Inc. (818) 848-7724
(800) 468-7245
441 S. Victory Blvd. FAX (818) 566-7100
Burbank, CA 91502
(Canvas Products Manufacturing)

Hartt Trophy & Engraving Co. (323) 462-7309
(323) 462-3516
620 N. Larchmont Blvd. FAX (323) 462-2127
Los Angeles, CA 90004

I.D. Me Promotions (818) 774-9500
18401 Burbank Blvd., Ste. 116 FAX (818) 774-9510
Tarzana, CA 91356 www.idmepromotions.com
(Advertising Space, Embroidery, Merchandising, Promotional Products & Silkscreening)

Imprint Revolution (310) 474-4472
10681 W. Pico Blvd. FAX (310) 474-1340
West Los Angeles, CA 90064 www.imprintrevolution.com
(Embroidery, Heat Pressing, Promotional Products & Silkscreening)

Inner Circle Graphics (310) 392-9784
(800) 404-9784
706 Lincoln Blvd. FAX (310) 399-0359
Venice, CA 90291 www.innercirclegraphics.com
(Embroidery & Silkscreening)

The Logo Shop (818) 501-8000
4533 Van Nuys Blvd., Ste. 202 FAX (818) 501-8099
Sherman Oaks, CA 91403 www.thelogoshop.com
(Crew and Promotional Apparel)

Merch Graphics (866) 356-3724
3520 Cadillac Ave., Ste. G FAX (714) 556-2301
Costa Mesa, CA 92626 www.merchgraphics.com
(Apparel, Bags, Embossing, Embroidery, Hats, Laser Printing, Merchandising, Packaging, Silkscreening & T-Shirts)

Outdoor Services (818) 501-8299
FAX (818) 501-6756
(Advertising Space: Billboards & Bus Shelters)

Perlman Creative Group (310) 709-2091
P.O. Box 4016 www.perlmancreative.com
Newport Beach, CA 92661
(Graphic Design & Packaging)

platine cookies (310) 559-9933
10850 Washington Blvd. FAX (310) 559-9934
Culver City, CA 90232 www.platinecookies.com
(Custom Cookies and Brownies)

Promoting You, Inc. (818) 610-0045
20501 Ventura Blvd., Ste. 180 FAX (818) 708-3023
Woodland Hills, CA 91364 www.promotingyouinc.com

Quick Draw (310) 477-6770
2244 Federal Ave. www.quickdraw1.com
Los Angeles, CA 90064
(Embroidery, Promotional Products & Screenprinting)

Roots (310) 858-8343
(310) 577-8026
371 N. Beverly Dr. FAX (310) 858-8229
Beverly Hills, CA 90210 www.roots.com
(Embroidery)

Sichel Embroidered Crew Apparel (818) 255-0862
(800) 729-0361
10847 Sherman Way FAX (818) 255-3913
Sun Valley, CA 91352
(Embroidery)

Star Treatment Gift Services (818) 781-9016
(800) 444-9059
15210 Stagg St. FAX (818) 781-9230
Van Nuys, CA 91405 www.startreatment.com

Sweatsedo (310) 398-6845
5504 Sepulveda Blvd. FAX (310) 313-1714
Culver City, CA 90230 www.sweatsedo.com
(Apparel & Embroidery)

A Unique Presentation (310) 202-8787
(888) 358-8787
3675 Dunn Dr. FAX (310) 202-8383
Los Angeles, CA 90034 www.auniquepresentation.com
(Embroidery & Silkscreening)

we-designstudio (323) 284-5130
P.O. Box 411223 FAX (561) 455-9644
Los Angeles, CA 90041 www.wedesignstudio.com

World Emblem Intl. (800) 766-0448
3465 E. Cedar Ave. FAX (800) 880-2073
Ontario, CA 91761 www.worldemblem.com
(Apparel, Bags, Embroidery, Hats, Laser Printing, Silkscreening & T-Shirts)

LA 411 **Stunt Coordinators & Performance Drivers** LA 411

Absolute Action/Tom McComas (310) 251-6254
(Coordinator)

Accelerated Action/Stanton Barrett (818) 599-4521
(704) 905-0171
(Coordinator) FAX (704) 721-9082
www.acceleratedaction.com

Robert Alonzo (310) 656-5151
www.innovativeartists.com

Dennis C. Alpert/Wheels on Film (818) 985-2739
(818) 378-6574
FAX (818) 985-2739

Jim Arnett (323) 856-3000
www.thegelleragency.com

Dean Bailey (818) 886-8687
(800) 360-3562
3763 Barry Ave.
Mar Vista, CA 90066

Bill Young's Precision Driving Team (310) 202-9872
(310) 476-6229
453 S. Barrington Ave. FAX (310) 476-6229
Los Angeles, CA 90049

Bobby Ore Motorsports LLC (818) 880 5678
(Coordinator) FAX (863) 655-6262
www.bobbyoremotorsports.com

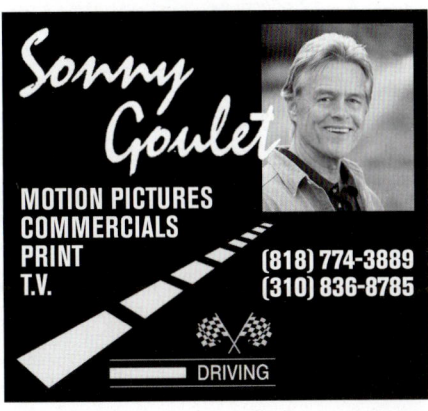

Bondelli Driving Team (818) 654-1055
(818) 795-1999
FAX (818) 957-6390
www.mbdrivingteam.com

Eddie Braun (818) 980-2123
(310) 339-7367
FAX (310) 545-4906
www.driversinc.com

Charlie Brewer (323) 462-2301
(310) 991-7150
FAX (323) 931-1744
www.stuntsunlimited.com

Eddie Brown (818) 994-4199
FAX (310) 459-7374
www.driversinc.com

Ⓐ **Rocky Capella** (800) 400-3124
(323) 462-2301
(Coordinator)
www.rockycapella.com

R.J. Chambers (661) 295-6789
29034 Sheridan Rd.
Val Verde, CA 91384
FAX (661) 295-0123

Cinema Drivers/
Tom Anthony's Driving Team (661) 250-9617
(877) 654-9550
3418 N. Knoll Dr.
Hollywood, CA 90068
www.cinemadrivers.com

Marcel Cozza (714) 981-3029

Shawn Crowder (310) 913-2935
(818) 347-0671

Tamra Crowder (818) 970-0959
(818) 982-9447

Wally Crowder (818) 774-3889
(805) 443-1550
FAX (805) 491-0708
www.stuntplayers.com

Jeff Danoff/Ramp Rentals (323) 462-2301
(661) 803-2210
P.O. Box 1063
Canyon Country, CA 91386
FAX (661) 285-7748
www.jeffdanoff.com

Mark & Chandra DeAlessandro/
VisionFit Unlimited (818) 980-2123
FAX (661) 253-3264
www.dynamikduo.com

Peter DeMarzo/
Performance Driving Specialists (949) 733-8755
(949) 478-9152
10 Starflower
Irvine, CA 92604

Chad Di Marco (714) 847-1501
(714) 596-6952
17161 Palmdale St.
Huntington Beach, CA 92647
FAX (714) 848-0561

DKO Industries, Inc. (818) 435-2159
(818) 652-8854
8801 Whitaker Ave.
Northridge, CA 91343
(Coordinator)
FAX (818) 936-0194

Dream Wave Productions, LLC/
Gregory Brazzel (805) 479-7446
5360 East Ave., Ste. T-10
Palmdale, CA 93552
(Coordinator)
FAX (661) 533-4829

Drivers East (800) 803-3992
www.driverseast.com

Ⓐ **Drivers Inc.** (818) 994-4199
620 Resolano Dr.
Pacific Palisades, CA 90272
(Rigging)
FAX (310) 459-7374

Dumenigo, Inc. (818) 766-4334
(818) 515-2114
FAX (661) 252-3505
www.jaysondumenigo.com

Georgia Durante (818) 508-0122
(818) 508-7618
FAX (818) 508-0322
www.performancetwo.com

Corey Eubanks (805) 368-0800
P.O. Box 427
Santa Ynez, CA 93460
FAX (805) 686-4639

Executive Productions (310) 456-8833
3951 Ridgemont Dr.
Malibu, CA 90265
(Coordinator)
FAX (310) 456-5692

ExpertDrivers.com (949) 922-3013
12 Genoa
Laguna Niguel, CA 92677
(Referral Service)
FAX (949) 495-8050
www.expertdrivers.com

femmefatale motorsports/
Kathy Jarvis (310) 666-4758
FAX (323) 843-9486
www.ffmotorsports.com

Brent Fletcher (818) 944-4199
FAX (310) 459-7374
www.driversinc.com

Mike Garibaldi (707) 224-7370

The Geller Agency (323) 856-3000
1547 Cassil Pl.
Hollywood, CA 90028
(Reps for Stunt Coordinators)
FAX (323) 856-3009
www.thegelleragency.com

Al Goto/AK Goto Productions, Inc. (818) 980-2123
P.O. Box 8493
Calabasas, CA 91372
(Coordinator)
www.algoto.com

Ⓐ **Sonny Goulet** (714) 899-3939
(818) 774-3889
FAX (714) 899-3939
www.sonnygouletdriving.com

Allan Graf (310) 288-8000
www.paradigmagency.com

J. Bud Graves (818) 335-2130
(415) 336-6257
FAX (818) 761-8383

John & Candace Hateley (661) 268-1942
(323) 462-2301
10810 Zorro Way
Santa Clarita, CA 91390
FAX (661) 268-1992

Art Hickman (206) 947-7126
(818) 825-5502

Michael Hilow (818) 554-2803
(Coordinator & Rigging)

Kelly Hine (818) 994-4199
FAX (310) 459-7374
www.driversinc.com

Hit The Mark (949) 697-4042
(Coordinator)
FAX (949) 497-0157
www.thedrivingconnection.com

Steve Holladay (805) 740-6018
(323) 462-2301
FAX (805) 735-7205
www.camerabikes.com

Hollywood Picture Cars/Scott Bosés (323) 466-2277
1028 N. La Brea Ave.
Hollywood, CA 90038
FAX (323) 466-6541
www.hollywoodpicturecars.com

Tom Howard (661) 775-9566
(661) 755-3839

International Stunt Association (ISA) (818) 501-5225
4454 Van Nuys Blvd., Ste. 214 FAX (818) 501-5656
Sherman Oaks, CA 91403 www.isastunts.com

Marc Isaac (310) 393-0793
(310) 352-5856
FAX (310) 393-0793

Jackknife King (661) 251-4200
FAX (661) 251-5165
www.hollywoodfires.com

Penny Johnson (818) 710-1186
(818) 384-2429

JTGrey Performance Driving LLC (310) 310-0572
(Coordinator) www.jtgrey.com

Bill Karp (213) 999-9890
(323) 876-7721

Kazarian/Spencer & Associates, Inc. (818) 755-7565
11969 Ventura Blvd., Third Fl. FAX (818) 755-7525
Studio City, CA 91604 www.ksawest.com
(Referral Service)

Steve Kelso/K4 Motorsports, Inc. (818) 713-0552
(323) 462-2301
www.k4motorsports.com

Hubie Kerns Jr. (310) 459-7819
(818) 980-2123
(Coordinator) FAX (310) 459-7374

Jim Kirby (562) 595-8886
(Coordinator) FAX (562) 595-6566
www.laprepinc.com

Kim Robert Koscki (818) 681-8317
(661) 288-1118

L.A. Motorsports (818) 222-6954
(877) 526-6867
FAX (866) 294-3266
www.lamsports.com

Mark Lonsdale (310) 829-1738
(Coordinator) FAX (310) 829-0868
www.frogmen.com

Freddy Lopez (818) 985-2739
(818) 292-1562

Peter MacDonald (310) 288-8000
www.paradigmagency.com

Eddie Marazzito (661) 904-2292
(818) 982-9447
www.rainbowindustries.ws/eddie

McCabe Performance Driving (818) 360-4662
(818) 519-0474
(Coordinator) FAX (818) 360-4662
www.mccabedriving.com

Shawn McConnell (818) 985-2739
(818) 980-2123

Mike McCoy (818) 994-4199
FAX (310) 459-7374
www.driversinc.com

Rhys Millen (714) 847-2158
17471 Apex Circle FAX (714) 848-6821
Huntington Beach, CA 92647 www.rmrproducts.com

Steve Millen (714) 540-7909
(949) 645-1224
2251 Santiago Dr. FAX (714) 540-4150
Newport Beach, CA 92660

Rick Miller (818) 970-1099
(661) 799-7570
FAX (661) 799-2522

Motion Picture Stunts International (310) 880-9282
26910 The Old Road www.motionpicturestunts.com
Ste. 148
Valencia, CA 91381

Eddie Mulder (818) 994-4199
FAX (310) 459-7374
www.driversinc.com

National Alliance of Stunt Performers (818) 508-0122

Chris Nielsen/Stunt Driver Inc. (310) 709-5561
(818) 980-2123
www.thestuntdriver.com

Eric Norris (310) 656-5151
www.innovativeartists.com

Guy Norris (310) 273-6700
www.utaproduction.com

David Ottenberg (805) 995-2965
P.O. Box 521 FAX (805) 995-2821
Cayucos, CA 93430 www.cayucoscreekbarn.com

Greg Pene/GP Performance Driving (909) 240-8401
1943 N. Campus Ave., Ste. B234
Upland, CA 91784

Performance Two, Inc. (818) 508-0122
(818) 508-7618
5235 Goodland Ave. FAX (818) 508-0322
North Hollywood, CA 91607 www.performancetwo.com

Allan Poppleton (310) 656-5151
www.innovativeartists.com

Nick Powell (310) 288-8000
www.paradigmagency.com

R.S.O. Productions (661) 803-7349
(Coordinator & Driver)

Branko Racki (310) 273-6700
www.utaproduction.com

Doriana Richman (818) 222-6954
(310) 480-5302
FAX (866) 294-3266
www.lamsports.com

Roger Richman (818) 222-6954
(310) 890-0505
FAX (866) 294-3266
www.lamsports.com

John Ross (323) 839-7840
(310) 710-1632
FAX (818) 985-0000
www.insidestunts.com

Markos Rounthwaite (310) 656-5151
www.innovativeartists.com

George Marshall Ruge (310) 288-8000
(Coordinator) www.paradigmagency.com

Rich Rutherford (949) 300-6029
360 One, Inc., 5401 Camino Mojado FAX (949) 361-2739
San Clemente, CA 92673 www.richrutherford.com

Errol Sack (661) 252-7629
(805) 432-9149
12059 Davenport Rd. FAX (661) 251-5165
Agua Dulce, CA 91390 www.errolsack.com

Eric Schwab (310) 288-8000
www.paradigmagency.com

Ben Scott (661) 269-2134
(805) 279-0229
(Coordinator) FAX (661) 269-4013

Jeff Scott (213) 709-9190
(323) 469-9980
(Coordinator)

Peter Stader (805) 520-1777
(818) 886-8687
(Coordinator)

Gregg Stern (310) 292-0915
FAX (505) 982-0163

Tom Struthers (310) 273-6700
www.unitedtalent.com

Stunt Coordinators, Inc. (818) 886-5417
(818) 254-7270
2016 Rayshire St. www.stuntcoordinatorsinc.com
Thousand Oaks, CA 91362
(Coordinator)

Stuntmen's Association of Motion Pictures (818) 766-4334
10660 Riverside Dr., Second Fl., Ste. E FAX (818) 766-5943
Toluca Lake, CA 91602 www.stuntmen.com
(Referral Service)

Stunts for Commercials (661) 295-6789
29034 Sheridan Rd. FAX (661) 295-0123
Val Verde, CA 91384

Stunts In Trucks (818) 766-2200
(818) 980-2123
25111 Rye Canyon Loop FAX (818) 766-2011
Santa Clarita, CA 91321 www.fastrucks.com
(Coordinator)

Stuntwomen's Association of Motion Pictures (818) 762-0907
12457 Ventura Blvd., Ste. 208 FAX (818) 762-9534
Studio City, CA 91604 www.stuntwomen.com
(Referral Service)

Stuntworld, Inc./Gianni Biasetti (310) 666-3004
(909) 797-7621
www.stuntworldinc.com

Olivia Summers (818) 970-4108
www.oliviasummers.com

Team Hutchinson (323) 650-2072
(323) 377-2499
(Coordinator) FAX (949) 951-7153
www.teamhutchinson.com

Team Right (310) 908-9198
FAX (310) 376-7872
www.teamright.com

Tony Hunt Motorsports (310) 782-4892
www.tonyhunt.com

Greg Tracy (562) 714-7191
FAX (562) 856-8187
www.driversinc.com

United Stuntwomen's Association, Inc. (USA) (818) 508-4651
FAX (818) 508-7074
www.usastunts.com

Jim Vickers (310) 288-8000
www.paradigmagency.com

Shelly Ward (818) 255-5850
FAX (818) 255-5450
www.shellywardent.com

Jack Weimer (818) 504-4131
(818) 448-2000

Dr. T.J. White (323) 469-9980
(877) 377-8868
P.O. Box 2832 www.drstunt.com
Toluca Lake, CA 91610

Audrey Williams (818) 985-2739
(818) 219-1568

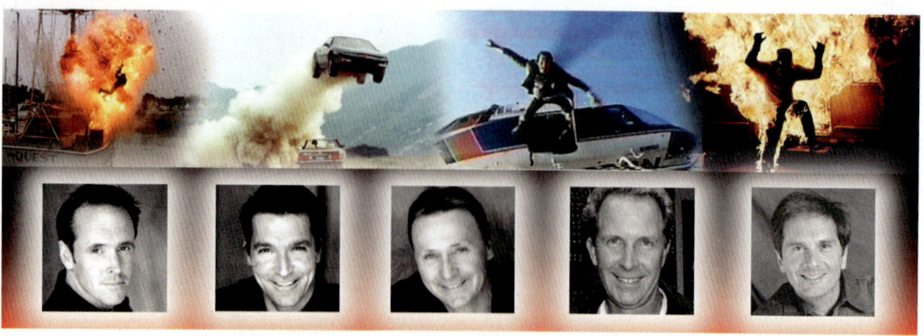

Stunt Coordinators—Aerial & Specialty

Absolute Action/Tom McComas (310) 251-6254
(General Stunts & Skydiving)

Accelerated Action/Stanton Barrett (818) 599-4521
(704) 905-0171
7337 Pacific View Dr. FAX (704) 721-9082
Los Angeles, CA 90068 **www.acceleratedaction.com**
(Handgliding, Paragliding, Scuba Diving & Skiing)

Action Productions, LLC (818) 203-5900
www.jasongray.tv
(Aerial Coordination, Bungee Jumping, Extreme Rigging, Fencing, Fight Choreography, General Stunts, Marine Coordination, Martial Arts, Rigging, Rope Rescue, Scuba Diving, Stunt Coordination, Sword Fighting, Trampolines, Trick Horseback Riding & Wirework)

Active Media Circle/Nick Brett (818) 980-2123
FAX (818) 980-1329
www.activemediacircle.com

Adrenaline Nation/Scott Smith (310) 686-0778
FAX (818) 509-1751
www.adrenalinenation.com
(Aerial, Aerial Coordination, BASE Jumping, Coordination, Rigging, Skydiving, Skysurfing, Stunt Coordination, Wingsuit Skydiving & Wingwalking)

Ⓐ **Aerial Stunt Service/Joe Jennings** (310) 543-2222
3128 Via La Selva **www.aerialstuntservice.com**
Palos Verdes Estates, CA 90274
(Aerial Coordination, BASE Jumping, Paragliding, Skydiving, Skysurfing & Wingsuit Skydiving)

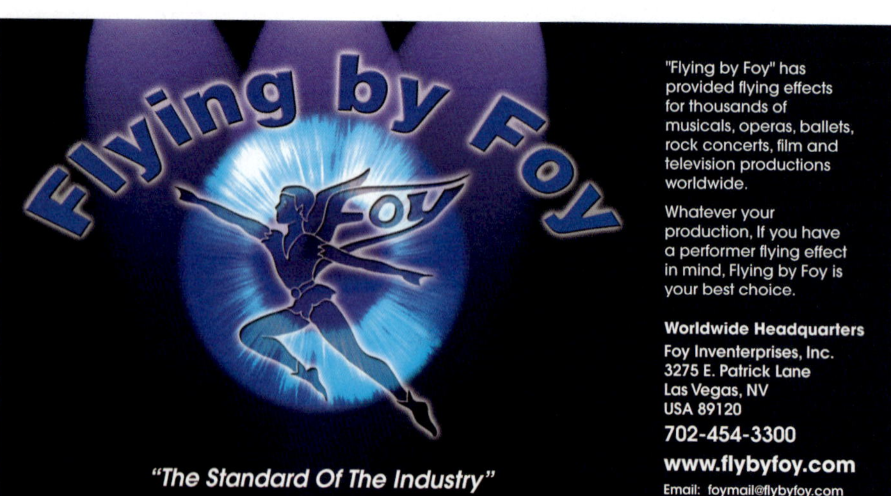

Aerobatic Hang Gliding, Inc. (760) 822-5667
585 N. Twin Oaks Valley Rd., Ste. D www.johnheiney.com
San Marcos, CA 92069
(Hang Gliding)

Alpine Training Services (626) 434-3636
417-B W. Foothill Blvd., Ste. 528 FAX (626) 857-0252
Glendora, CA 91741 www.atsfilmworks.com
(Canyoneering, Extreme Rigging, Kayaking, Rock Climbing, Rope Rescue & Wirework)

Aquavision/Bob Anderson (562) 433-2863
(562) 688-3038
3708 E. Fourth St. FAX (562) 433-2863
Long Beach, CA 90814 www.aquavision.net
(Aquatic, General Stunts & Rigging)

Jim Arnett (323) 856-3000
www.thegelleragency.com

Dave Barlia (818) 207-9696
www.davebarlia.com
(BASE and Bungee Jumping & Wingsuit Skydiving)

Beckman Rigging/BRS Rigging (310) 532-3933
(661) 510-2518
13516 S. Mariposa Ave. FAX (310) 532-3993
Gardena, CA 90247 www.brsrigging.com

Branam Enterprises (310) 637-4727
(877) 295-3390
310 S. Long Beach Blvd. FAX (310) 637-4735
Compton, CA 90221 www.branament.com
(Flying & General Stunts)

Brand X Action Specialists (818) 701-9239
(661) 268-0658
32901 Agua Dulce FAX (818) 886-8754
Agua Dulce, CA 91350 www.brandxstunts.org

Eddie Braun (818) 980-2123
(310) 339-7367
FAX (310) 545-4906

Charlie Brewer (323) 462-2301
(310) 991-7150
(General Stunts) FAX (323) 931-1744
www.stuntsunlimited.com

Bungee America, Inc./Ron Jones (310) 322-8892
P.O. Box 8925 www.bungeeamerica.com
Calabasas, CA 91302
(Bungee Jumping & Rope Rescue)

California Dreamin' (800) 373-3359
33133 Vista del Monte Rd. FAX (951) 699-0601
Temecula, CA 92591 www.californiadreamin.com

Rocky Capella/RCP-SF Stunt Group (800) 400-3124
(323) 462-2301
www.rockycapella.com
(Coordination, Fight Choreography, General Stunts, Stunt Coordination & Wirework)

R.J. Chambers (661) 295-6789
29034 Sheridan Rd. FAX (661) 295-0123
Val Verde, CA 91384

Eric Chen (323) 932-9888
(714) 900-9974
(Martial Arts) www.usawushu.com

Wally Crowder (818) 774-3889
(805) 443-1550
FAX (805) 491-0708
www.stuntplayers.com
(Fight Choreography, General Stunts, Marine Coordination, Rigging & Scuba Diving)

Dumenigo, Inc. (818) 766-4334
(818) 515-2114
FAX (661) 252-3505
www.jaysondumenigo.com

Ian Eyre (323) 363-6225
(818) 774-3889
(General Stunts) www.imdb.com/name/nm0264226/

Flyboyz Productions (909) 234-3943
27580 Fallingstar Ln. www.flyboyz.com
Saugus, CA 91350
(Skydiving)

Hartley Folstad (909) 597-8511
(Aerial & Wingwalking) FAX (909) 597-8511
www.silverwingswingwalking.com

Frogmen Unlimited/Mark Lonsdale (661) 821-1210
(310) 405-2655
(Aquatic) www.frogmen.com

The Geller Agency (323) 856-3000
1547 Cassil Pl. FAX (323) 856-3009
Hollywood, CA 90028 www.thegelleragency.com
(Reps for Stunt Coordinators)

Dale Gibson (818) 980-2123
9655 Wentworth St. FAX (818) 951-4335
Sunland, CA 91040 www.2stunts.com
(Coordination, Sword Fighting Choreography, General Stunts, Stunt Coordination, Sword Fighting & Trick Horseback Riding)

Got Rigging?/ Michael Li & Norbert Phillips (818) 391-4883
20040 Curassow Court FAX (661) 250-8133
Canyon Country, CA 91351
(Extreme Rigging)

Got Stunts? (310) 766-5867
www.gotstunts.com
(BASE Jumping, General Stunts, Skydiving & Skysurfing)

Piergiorgio Gusso/TwinAir (818) 988-7573
7552 Hayvenhurst Pl. FAX (818) 988-7578
Van Nuys, CA 91406 www.twinair.net

Hollywood Stuntworks (661) 294-3816
(818) 980-2123
28261 W. Parker Rd. FAX (661) 295-8956
Castaic, CA 91384 www.hollywoodstuntworks.com
(General Stunts)

Craig Hosking (661) 251-5151
(Aerial) FAX (661) 251-5140

Impact Stunts (323) 932-8869
1150 S. La Brea Ave. FAX (323) 932-8895
Los Angeles, CA 90019 www.impactstunts.com
(Fight Choreography, Martial Arts, Weapons & Wirework)

International Stunt Association (ISA) (818) 501-5225
4454 Van Nuys Blvd., Ste. 214 FAX (818) 501-5656
Sherman Oaks, CA 91403 www.isastunts.com

Capt. Lance Julian (808) 224-0801
(323) 856-3000
(Marine Coordinator) FAX (323) 856-3009
www.thegelleragency.com

Kim K. Kahana Jr. (818) 888-2935
(323) 462-2301
P.O. Box 6214 FAX (818) 888-2951
Woodland Hills, CA 91365 www.dttrampolines.com
(Aerial Coordination, General Stunts, Rigging, Stunt Coordination & Trampolines)

KCW Studios (626) 698-0029
318 S. Date Ave. FAX (626) 943-0190
Alhambra, CA 91803 www.kcwstudios.com
(BASE Jumping, Bungee Jumping, Coordination, Extreme Rigging, Fencing, General Stunts, Referral Service, Rigging, Rope Rescue, Skydiving, Skysurfing, Stunt Coordination, Sword Fighting, Trampolines & Trick Horseback Riding)

Hubie Kerns Jr. (310) 459-7819
(818) 980-2123
(General Stunts) FAX (310) 459-7374

L.A. Motorsports (818) 222-6954
(877) 526-6867
FAX (866) 294-3266
www.lamsports.com

Lane Leavitt/Leavittation, Inc. (661) 252-7551
25982 Sand Canyon Rd. FAX (661) 250-8526
Santa Clarita, CA 91387 www.stuntrev.com
(Flying & General Stunts)

Ray Lykins (310) 922-3852
(818) 774-3889
(General Stunts) FAX (310) 458-4162
www.raylykins.com

Eric Mansker (818) 363-8202
(818) 980-2123
(General Stunts)

Peter J. McKernan Jr. (310) 458-9176
(310) 993-4486
(Aerial) FAX (310) 393-4227

Mike Ryan Stunt Services (818) 766-2200
(818) 404-8230
25111 Rye Canyon Loop FAX (818) 766-2011
Santa Clarita, CA 91321 www.fastrucks.com

Motion Picture Stunts International (310) 880-9282
26910 The Old Road, Ste. 148
Valencia, CA 91381 www.motionpicturestunts.com

Victor Paul (626) 284-3432
(323) 469-9980
(Sword Master)

Jimmy Romano (323) 469-9980
(818) 430-6411
(General Stunts)

John Ross (323) 839-7840
(310) 710-1632
FAX (818) 985-0000
www.insidestunts.com
(Coordination, General Stunts, Rigging, Scuba Diving, Skiing & Trampolines)

John D. Sarviss (661) 270-0565
(818) 980-2123
39120 Bouquet Canyon Rd. www.radicalcameracars.com
Leona Valley, CA 93551
(Aerial)

Peter Stader (805) 520-1777
(818) 886-8687
(General Stunts) FAX (805) 520-0310

Steve Stafford/Studio Wings (805) 320-9500
855 Aviation Dr. FAX (805) 987-4720
Camarillo, CA 93010 www.studiowings.com

A **Stunt Coordinators, Inc.** (818) 254-7270
2016 Rayshire St. FAX (805) 494-1493
Thousand Oaks, CA 91362
www.stuntcoordinatorsinc.com

Stunt Grunts, Inc. (818) 257-0605
22222 Horizon Pl. FAX (818) 993-4841
Chatsworth, CA 91311 www.stuntgrunts.com
(Extreme Rigging, Fight Choreography, General Stunts, Scuba Diving, Stunt Coordination, Trick Horseback Riding & Wirework)

Stunt Wings/Adventure Sports (818) 367-2430
(818) 266-0874
12623 Gridley St. FAX (818) 367-5363
San Fernando, CA 91342 www.stuntwings.com
(Aerial Coordination, Hang Gliding, Paragliding, Stunt Coordination & Ultralight Aviation)

Stuntmen's Association of Motion Pictures (818) 766-4334
10660 Riverside Dr. FAX (818) 766-5943
Second Fl., Ste. E www.stuntmen.com
Toluca Lake, CA 91602
(Referral Service)

Stunts for Commercials (661) 295-6789
29034 Sheridan Rd. FAX (661) 295-0123
Val Verde, CA 91384
(Stunt Coordination)

Stuntwomen's Association of Motion Pictures (818) 762-0907
12457 Ventura Blvd., Ste. 208 FAX (818) 762-9534
Studio City, CA 91604 www.stuntwomen.com
(Referral Service)

Stuntworld, Inc./Gianni Biasetti (310) 666-3004
(909) 797-7621
www.stuntworldinc.com

SwordPlay/Tim Weske (818) 421-2926
(818) 980-2123
64 E. Magnolia Blvd. FAX (818) 566-4357
Burbank, CA 91502 www.timweske.com

John Tamburro (818) 896-2700
(661) 713-6671
(Aerial Coordination) FAX (818) 896-2771
www.blackstarhelicopters.com

Team Hutchinson (323) 650-2072
(323) 377-2499
(General Stunts) FAX (949) 951-7153
www.teamhutchinson.com

Thornton Aircraft Company (626) 795-8604
7520 Hayvenhurst Ave. FAX (626) 795-8606
Van Nuys, CA 91406 www.thorntonaircraft.com
(Aerial)

United Stuntwomen's Association, Inc. (USA) (818) 508-4651
FAX (818) 508-7074
www.usastunts.com

Vertical Adventures/Bob Gaines (949) 854-6250
(800) 514-8785
P.O. Box 7548 FAX (949) 854-5249
Newport Beach, CA 92658 www.verticaladventures.com
(Mountain Climbing)

Dick Ziker (323) 462-2301

Action Specialists (661) 775-8530 / (818) 915-4691
28313 Industry Dr. FAX (661) 775-8531
Valencia, CA 90355 www.actionspecialists.com
(Flying and Stunt Rigging Equipment)

Adventure Sport Aviation, Inc. (909) 215-0960
2095 Goetz Rd. www.adventuresportsaviation.com
Perris, CA 92570
(Parachutes & Stunt Rigging Equipment)

Ⓐ **Beckman Rigging/BRS Rigging** (310) 532-3933 / (661) 510-2518
13516 S. Mariposa Ave. FAX (310) 532-3993
Gardena, CA 90247 www.brsrigging.com
(Flying and Stunt Rigging Equipment)

Bikes..Camera..Action! (310) 995-2084
1105 Bonilla
Topanga, CA 90290
(Adjustable Jump Ramps for Bikes, Skateboards and Skates)

Branam/West Coast Theatrical (310) 637-4727 / (877) 295-3390
310 S. Long Beach Blvd. FAX (310) 637-4735
Compton, CA 90221 www.branament.com
(Flying and Stunt Rigging Equipment)

Caso Brothers (310) 703-4470 / (310) 670-6434
6430 W. 85th St.
Los Angeles, CA 90045
(Mats, Pads & Trampolines)

Ⓐ **DT Trampolines Inc.** (818) 888-2935 / (800) 649-4945
P.O. Box 6214 FAX (818) 888-2951
Woodland Hills, CA 91365 www.dttrampolines.com
(Mats, Pads, Stunt Rigging Equipment & Trampolines)

Fisher Technical Services Rentals (702) 251-0700 / (866) 942-4098
FAX (702) 251-0400
www.fishertechnical.com

Ⓐ **Got Rigging?/ Michael Li & Norbert Phillips** (818) 391-4883
20040 Curassow Court FAX (661) 250-8133
Canyon Country, CA 91351
(Flying and Stunt Rigging Equipment)

Hollywood Stuntworks (661) 294-3816 / (818) 980-2123
28261 W. Parker Rd. FAX (661) 295-8956
Castaic, CA 91384 www.hollywoodstuntworks.com
(Flying and Stunt Rigging Equipment)

Icarus Rigging (323) 660-4112
3531 Casitas Ave. FAX (323) 660-6135
Los Angeles, CA 90039 www.icarusrigging.com

International Stunt Association (ISA) (818) 501-5225
4454 Van Nuys Blvd., Ste. 214 FAX (818) 501-5656
Sherman Oaks, CA 91403 www.isastunts.com
(Mats, Pads & Stunt Rigging Equipment)

Jack Rubin & Sons, Inc. (818) 562-5100
520 S. Varney St. FAX **(818) 562-5101**
Burbank, CA 91502 **www.wirerope.net**
(Cord, Hardware Fasteners, Harnesses, Flying Equipment, Safety Gear, Stunt Rigging Equipment and Supplies, Velcro & Webbing)

Leavittation, Inc. (661) 252-7551
25982 Sand Canyon Rd. FAX **(661) 250-8526**
Santa Clarita, CA 91387 **www.stuntrev.com**
(Articulated Crash Dummies, Mats, Pads & Stunt Rigging Equipment)

Lowy Enterprises, Inc. (310) 763-1111
1970 E. Gladwick St. FAX **(310) 763-1111**
Rancho Dominguez, CA 90220 **www.lowyusa.com**
(Cord, Elastic, Hardware Fasteners, Harnesses, Safety and Stunt Rigging, Thread, Velcro & Webbing)

Rick's Stunt Car Service/ Motion Picture Driving Clinic (818) 341-9526 (818) 796-1497
8560 Variel Ave.
Canoga Park, CA 91304
(Articulated Stunt Mannequins)

S & S Stunt Equipment Rental, Inc. (818) 980-2123
13136 Saticoy Ave., Ste. N. FAX **(805) 494-9424**
North Hollywood, CA 91605 **www.stuntequipment.com**
(Mats, Pads & Stunt Rigging Equipment)

Spohn Ranch, Inc. (877) 489-3539
15131 Clark Ave., Ste. B FAX **(626) 330-5503**
City of Industry, CA 91745 **www.spohnranch.com**
(BMX, MX, Skateboard and Stunt Ramps)

Stuntworld, Inc./Gianni Biasetti (310) 666-3004 (909) 797-7621
www.stuntworldinc.com

VER Sales, Inc. (818) 567-3000 (800) 229-0518
2509 N. Naomi St. FAX **(818) 567-3018**
Burbank, CA 91504 **www.versales.com**
(Safety and Stunt Rigging Equipment & Supplies)

Yerkes Productions (818) 344-4231 (323) 462-2301
(Mats, Pads & Stunt Rigging Equipment)

A.S.A. Talent & Modeling Division (323) 662-9787
P.O. Box 125 FAX (323) 662-1569
La Cañada, CA 91011 www.asatalent.com/crew

Abrams Artists Agency (310) 859-0625
(310) 859-1417
9200 Sunset Blvd., Ste. 1130 FAX (310) 276-6193
West Hollywood, CA 90069
(Talent Only)

Artist Management Agency (714) 558-7373
(619) 233-6655
261 N. Bush St. www.artistmanagementagency.com
Santa Ana, CA 92701
(Talent & Voice-Overs)

AthleteSource Casting (310) 871-7956
13425 Ventura Blvd., Second Fl.
Sherman Oaks, CA 91423
(Athletes) www.athletesourcecasting.com

Baldwin Talent, Inc. (310) 827-2422
8055 W. Manchester Ave., Ste. 550
Playa del Rey, CA 90293
(Commercial Talent)

Beauty Models/BC4 (323) 466-0600
5900 Wilshire Blvd. FAX (323) 466-1605
Hollywood, CA 90036 www.beautymodelsla.com

bloc, Inc. (323) 954-7730
5651 Wilshire Blvd., Ste. C FAX (323) 954-7731
Los Angeles, CA 90036 www.blocagency.com

Bobby Ball Talent Agency (818) 506-8188
4116 W. Magnolia Blvd., Ste. 205 FAX (818) 506-8588
Burbank, CA 91505 www.bobbyballagency.com
(Athletes, Body Parts Models, Children, Commercial Talent, Models, Talent & Voice-Over Artists)

Body Parts Models (310) 275-8263
(702) 496-8469
2023 Coldwater Canyon Dr. FAX (310) 273-5878
Beverly Hills, CA 90210 www.bodypartsmodels.com
(Body Parts Models)

Brady, Brannon, Rich (323) 852-9559
5670 Wilshire Blvd., Ste. 820 FAX (323) 852-9579
Los Angeles, CA 90036
(Talent & Voice-Overs)

Brand Model & Talent Agency, Inc. (714) 850-1158
601 N. Baker FAX (714) 850-0806
Santa Ana, CA 92703 www.brandmodelandtalent.com

C.E.S.D. Talent Agency (310) 475-2111
10635 Santa Monica Blvd., Ste. 130 FAX (310) 475-1929
Los Angeles, CA 90025 www.cesdtalent.com

Cassell-Levy, Inc./CL, Inc. (323) 461-3971
843 N. Sycamore Ave. FAX (323) 461-1134
Hollywood, CA 90038 www.clinc.com
(Talent & Voice-Overs)

The Cindy Romano Talent Agency (760) 323-3333
P.O. Box 1951
Palm Springs, CA 92263
www.cindyromanomodelingandtalentagency.com

Clear Talent Group/CTG (818) 509-0121
(818) 509-0207
10950 Ventura Blvd. FAX (818) 509-7729
Studio City, CA 91604 www.cleartalentgroup.com
(Choreographers)

Click Models Management (310) 246-0800
9057 Nemo St. FAX (310) 858-1701
West Hollywood, CA 90069 www.clickmodel.com
(Models Only)

Colleen Cler Agency (818) 841-7943
178 S. Victory Blvd., Ste. 108 FAX (818) 841-4541
Burbank, CA 91502 www.colleencler.com
(Children Through Young Adults)

Creative Artists Agency (CAA) (424) 288-2000
FAX (424) 288-2900
www.caa.com

D2 Models (310) 820-1020
(888) 820-1001
11693 San Vicente Blvd., Ste. 823 FAX (323) 372-3948
Los Angeles, CA 90049 models.direct2pro.com
(Children, Commercial Talent, Models & Talent)

DDO Artists Agency (323) 462-8000
6725 Sunset Blvd., Ste. 230 FAX (323) 462-0100
Los Angeles, CA 90028 www.ddoagency.com
(Reps for Choreographers)

Dominique Model and Talent (714) 969-7250
(Talent) www.dominiquemodelandtalent.com

Elite Model Management (310) 274-9395
345 N. Maple Dr., Ste. 397 FAX (310) 278-7520
Beverly Hills, CA 90210 www.elitemodel.com
(Models Only)

The Endeavor Agency (310) 248-2000
9601 Wilshire Blvd., Third Fl. FAX (310) 248-2020
Beverly Hills, CA 90210

Film Artists Associates (818) 883-5008
21044 Ventura Blvd., Ste. 215
Woodland Hills, CA 91364
(Talent Only)

The Ford Agency (310) 276-8100
9200 W. Sunset Blvd. FAX (310) 276-9299
Hollywood, CA 90029 www.fordmodels.com

Hollywood Voices (323) 466-3595
P.O. Box 85042 www.hollywoodvoices.net
Los Angeles, CA 90072
(Voice-Overs Only)

Horses for Productions (310) 457-7027
(310) 961-1584
2277 Decker Canyon Rd. www.horsesforproductions.com
Malibu, CA 90265
(Champions, Jockeys & Riders)

The House of Representatives (310) 772-0772
211 S. Beverly Dr., Ste. 208 FAX (310) 772-0998
Beverly Hills, CA 90212

International Creative Management - ICM (310) 550-4000
10250 Constellation Blvd. www.icmtalent.com
Los Angeles, CA 90067
(Talent & Voice-Overs)

Kazarian/Spencer & Associates, Inc. (818) 769-9111
11969 Ventura Blvd., Third Fl. FAX (818) 769-1824
Studio City, CA 91604 www.ksawest.com
(Talent & Voice-Overs)

LA Models & LA Talent (323) 436-7700
7700 W. Sunset Blvd. FAX (323) 436-7755
Los Angeles, CA 90046 www.lamodels.com
(Models Only)

LA Talent (323) 436-7777
7700 W. Sunset Blvd. FAX (323) 436-7788
Los Angeles, CA 90046 www.latalent.com

Light/Wilhelmina (323) 653-5700
7257 Beverly Blvd., Ste. 200 FAX (323) 653-4262
Los Angeles, CA 90036 www.wilhelmina.com

McDonald/Selznick Associates (323) 957-6680
953 N. Cole Ave. FAX **(323) 957-6688**
Hollywood, CA 90038 **www.msaagency.com**
(Choreographers, Dancers, Models, Production Designers, Singers & Talent)

MGA/Mary Grady Agency (818) 763-8400
269 S. Beverly Dr., Ste. 1088 **www.mgatalent.com**
Los Angeles, CA 90212

Nous Model Management, Inc./ Nu Talent Agency (310) 385-6900 (310) 385-6907
117 N. Robertson Blvd. FAX **(310) 385-6910**
Los Angeles, CA 90048 **www.nousmodels.com**

Otto Models & Talent (323) 650-2200
1460 N. Sweetzer Ave. FAX **(323) 650-1134**
West Hollywood, CA 90069 **www.ottomodels.com**
(Athletes, Body Parts Models, Commercial Talent, Models & Talent)

Periwinkle Entertainment Productions (714) 776-5820
P.O. Box 2486 FAX **(714) 635-1711**
Anaheim, CA 92814
(Circus and Variety Acts)

Premier West Entertainment/ Divas in Training (818) 231-1491 (888) 340-7444
3760 Cahuenga Blvd. West, Ste. 103
Studio City, CA 91604 **www.divasintraining.com**

Privilege Talent Agency (818) 386-2377
P.O. Box 260860 FAX **(818) 986-7513**
Encino, CA 91426

S.I.M. Agency (310) 694-3563
10940 Wilshire Blvd., Ste. 1600 FAX **(866) 849-3106**
Los Angeles, CA 90024 **www.sim-agency.com**
(Children, Commercial Talent, Models & Talent)

San Diego Model Management (619) 296-1018 (619) 296-2373
438 Camino del Rio South, Ste. 116 FAX **(619) 296-3422**
San Diego, CA 92108 **www.sdmodel.com**
(Athletes, Body Parts Models, Children, Commercial Talent, Models & Talent)

Stage 9 Talent (323) 460-6006
1249 N. Lodi Pl. FAX **(323) 462-3535**
Hollywood, CA 90038

Susan Nathe & Associates (323) 653-7573
8281 Melrose Ave., Ste. 200 FAX **(323) 653-1179**
Los Angeles, CA 90046
(Commercial Talent & Theatrical Talent)

Sutton, Barth & Vennari (323) 938-6000
145 S. Fairfax Ave., Ste. 310 FAX **(323) 935-8671**
Los Angeles, CA 90036
(Talent & Voice-Overs)

Trio Talent Agency (323) 851-6886
1502 Gardner St. FAX **(323) 851-6882**
Los Angeles, CA 90046 **www.triotalentagency.com**
(Choreographers & Talent)

VOX, Inc. (323) 655-8699
5670 Wilshire Blvd., Ste. 820 FAX **(323) 852-1472**
Los Angeles, CA 90036 **www.voxusa.net**
(Talent & Voice-Overs)

William Morris Agency (LA) (310) 859-4000
One William Morris Pl. FAX **(310) 285-9010**
Beverly Hills, CA 90212 **www.wmeentertainment.com**
(Talent & Voice-Overs)

Ⓐ Entertainment Partners (818) 955-6299
(646) 473-9000
2835 N. Naomi St. FAX (818) 845-6507
Burbank, CA 91504 www.entertainmentpartners.com

Hadity & Associates, Inc. (646) 792-2217
One West St., Ste. 100 www.hadity.com
New York, NY 10004

The Incentives Office (310) 982-1340
1507 Seventh St., Ste. 157 www.theincentivesoffice.com
Santa Monica, CA 90401

Tax Credits, LLC (866) 652-3170
45 Knightsbridge Rd. www.taxcreditsllc.com
Piscataway, NJ 08854

A & D Music Incorporated (949) 768-7110 (949) 500-6307
22322 Colonna Dr. FAX (949) 716-7667
Laguna Hills, CA 92653 www.admusic.net
(Music)

A and C Harbour Lites, Ltd. (310) 926-9552
P.O. Box 9279 FAX (310) 356-3579
Marina Del Rey, CA 90295
(Boat Handling, Marine, Scuba Diving & Water Safety)
Contact: Capt. Seth Chase

Abacus Consulting & Chinese Translation Services (626) 487-8909 (626) 282-9186
401 N. Garfield Ave., Ste. 1 FAX (626) 282-9252
Alhambra, CA 91801
(Chinese Culture) www.certifiedchinesetranslation.com

Adam Williams, Magic & Illusion (310) 289-9852
(Illusion & Magic) FAX (310) 271-4822
www.magicsnow.com

Aerial Action Productions/ Reel Orange (949) 548-4524
316 La Jolla Dr. FAX (949) 548-0749
Newport Beach, CA 92663 www.reelorange.com
(Aerial & White Water)
Contact: Art Vitarelli

Airboyd/Boyd Kelly (818) 535-2693
www.airboyd.com
(Aviation, Police Procedures & SAG Airplane Pilot)
Contact: Boyd Kelly

Andersen Physical Therapy (626) 354-4421 (626) 568-4997
(Physical Therapy) www.callthept.com

Aquavision (562) 433-2863 (562) 688-3038
3708 E. Fourth St. FAX (562) 433-2863
Long Beach, CA 90814 www.aquavision.net
(Marine Coordination & Scuba Diving)
Contact: Bob Anderson

AthleteSource Casting (310) 871-7956
13425 Ventura Blvd., Second Fl.
Sherman Oaks, CA 91423
www.athletesourcecasting.com
(Action and Olympic Sports)

David Avadon (310) 397-5539
3414 Centinela Ave. www.davidavadon.com
Los Angeles, CA 90066
(Con Games, Pickpocketing & Sleight of Hand)

Bear Creek Pottery (951) 769-3400 (951) 306-9379
4988 W. Ramsey St. FAX (951) 769-3400
Banning, CA 92220 www.bearcreekpottery.com
(Ceramics & Pottery)
Contact: Paul L. Bradford

Carrie Becks/A-1 Medical Advisor (310) 227-8200 (310) 678-7601
345 Richmond St. FAX (310) 227-8205
El Segundo, CA 90245 www.redm33.com

Bikes..Camera..Action! (310) 995-2084
1105 Bonilla
Topanga, CA 90290
(Bicycle Racing & Rollerblading)
Contact: Rick Denman

Bob Marriott's Flyfishing Store (714) 525-1827
2700 W. Orangethorpe Ave. FAX (714) 525-5783
Fullerton, CA 92833 www.bobmarriotts.com
(Fly-Fishing)

Paul K. Bronston, M.D. (310) 301-9426
One Jib St., Ste. 202 FAX (310) 823-2433
Marina del Rey, CA 90292
(Medical)

Call the Cops (888) 548-0911
(Homicide, Narcotics, Patrol and Vice Procedure, Police Dialogue & SWAT Tactics)
Contact: Randy Walker

Cannon's Great Escapes (818) 385-7092
P.O. Box 703 FAX (818) 581-4130
Yucaipa, CA 92399 www.cannonsgreatescapes.com
(Escapes, Illusion & Magic)

Caravan West Productions (661) 268-8300
35660 Jayhawker Rd. FAX (661) 268-8301
Agua Dulce, CA 91390 www.caravanwest.com
(Firearms Instructor, Westerns - 1860–1910)
Contact: Peter Sherayko

Cinema Aquatics (818) 365-7999 (805) 207-5797
(Marine) www.cinemaaquatics.com

Cinema Rentals, Inc. (661) 222-7342 (877) 877-9605
25876 The Old Rd., Ste. 174 FAX (661) 253-3643
Stevenson Ranch, CA 91381 www.cinemarentals.com
(Marine and Underwater Safety)
Contact: Jim Pearson

Cinema Safety & Marine Services, Inc. (310) 614-0206 (805) 207-5797
1534 N. Moorpark Rd., Ste. 108 FAX (805) 241-3954
Thousand Oaks, CA 91360 www.cinemasafety.com
(Medical, Scuba Diving, Underwater & Water Safety)

Cinemafloat (949) 675-8888 (714) 801-5553
1624 W. Oceanfront Walk FAX (949) 644-3073
Newport Beach, CA 92663
(Marine)
Contact: Joseph Cleary

Combat Casting (310) 686-2718
6850 Vineland Ave., Ste. N FAX (818) 509-9581
North Hollywood, CA 91605 www.combatcasting.com
(Military, Police & SWAT)

Customs by Eddie Paul, A Division of EP Industries, Inc. (310) 643-8515 (310) 259-0542
2305 Utah Ave. FAX (310) 643-8520
El Segundo, CA 90245 www.deadlinetv.net
(Automotive, Motorcycle & Underwater)

Debbie Merrill's Skate Great USA (310) 821-5489 (310) 625-0059
P.O. Box 3452 www.skategreat.com
Santa Monica, CA 90408
(Ice, In-Line and Roller Skating)
Contact: Debbie Merrill

Dennis Conner Sports, Inc. (619) 523-5131
2907 Shelter Island Dr., Ste. 105 FAX (619) 523-5279
San Diego, CA 92106 www.stars-stripes.com
(Marine & Sailing)

John Dietsch/Flyfishing Consultant (310) 979-7170
12233 W. Olympic Blvd., Ste. 314 FAX (310) 979-7173
Los Angeles, CA 90064 www.flyfishfilms.com
(Fly-Fishing)

Don Wayne Magic, Inc. (818) 763-3192
(Illusion & Magic) www.donwaynemagic.com

Doves Trained for TV (818) 340-4040
(Magic Cosultant) FAX (818) 340-2432
www.amosmagic.com

DT Trampolines Inc. (818) 888-2935 / (800) 649-4945
P.O. Box 6214 FAX **(818) 888-2951**
Woodland Hills, CA 90365 **www.dttrampolines.com**
Contact: Birgit Schier

Donna Duffy, R.N. (310) 545-2895 / (310) 704-9131
(Medical)

The Etiquette Company (949) 493-6700
29 St. Kitts FAX **(949) 493-6700**
Dana Point, CA 92629 **www.theetiquettecompany.com**
(Etiquette)

Executive Yacht Management, Inc. (310) 306-2555
644 Venice Blvd. FAX **(310) 306-1147**
Marina del Rey, CA 90291 **www.yacht-management.com**
(Marine)
Contact: L. Ring

Art Fransen (951) 736-9440
FAX **(951) 453-3580**
www.supertrap.com
(Homicide, Narcotics, Police Procedure & SWAT Tactics)

Frogmen Unlimited/Mark Lonsdale (661) 821-1210 / (310) 405-2655
(Aquatic Action & Diving) **www.frogmen.com**

Steven Guerrero (310) 864-2000
(Marine) **www.aquaticcinema.com**

Gunmetal Group, LLC (818) 414-5381
11271 Ventura Blvd., Ste. 369 FAX **(661) 251-6041**
Studio City, CA 91604 **www.gunmetalgroup.com**
(Military & Tactical)

Bob Hamer, FBI (310) 801-0083
(FBI & Law Enforcement)

Franz Harary/ Odyssey in Illusion, Inc. (323) 871-1796 / (323) 855-9886
8300 Maple Dr. **www.harary.com**
Los Angeles, CA 90046
(Illusion & Magic)

Harlan's Heroes (818) 566-1660 / (818) 439-9664
FAX **(818) 566-1887**
www.harlans-heroes.com
(Military: Korea, Vietnam, World War I & World War II)

The History Source (310) 493-2636
14403 Addison St., Ste. 17 **www.thehistorysource.net**
Sherman Oaks, CA 91423
(History)

Hollywoodivers.com (323) 969-9875 / (877) 657-2822
(Diving & Marine) FAX **(323) 969-9734**
www.hollywoodivers.com

Interorbital Systems (661) 965-0771 / (323) 463-6529
1394 Barnes St., Bldg. 7, Mojave Spaceport
Mojave, CA 93501 **www.interorbital.com**
(Aerospace, Rocket and Space Systems)
Contact: Randa Milliron

Steve Kutcher (626) 836-0322
1801 Oakview Ln. **home.earthlink.net/~skutcher**
Arcadia, CA 91006
(Biology, Entomology & Science)

Edward Lear, Esq. (310) 642-6900 / (866) 522-2642
5200 W. Century Blvd., Ste. 345 FAX **(310) 642-6910**
Los Angeles, CA 90045
(Civil and Criminal Law & Trial Scenes)

Gary Leffew/Anything Rodeo (805) 878-6948
P.O. Box 517
Santa Maria, CA 93456
(Rodeo)

Marie London, RN BSN (323) 465-2050 / (323) 687-6304
(Medical) FAX **(818) 234-4521**

Los Angeles Police Department (213) 485-4302
1358 N. Wilcox Ave. **www.lapd.org**
Hollywood, CA 90028

The Magic Castle (323) 851-3313
7001 Franklin Ave. **www.magiccastle.com**
Hollywood, CA 90028
(Magic)
Contact: James G. Williams

Nina Marino, ESQ (310) 557-0007
9454 Wilshire Blvd., Ste. 500 FAX **(310) 557-0008**
Beverly Hills, CA 90212 **www.kaplanmarino.com**
(Criminal Law)

Robin McCarthy (818) 883-6223
(Ice Skating)
Contacts: Robin McCarthy & Bonnie Harris

Bobbi McRae (310) 922-2777 / (818) 767-2121
(Figure and Hockey Skating)

Doug Merrifield (310) 545-2119 / (310) 503-1631
1611 19th St. FAX **(310) 545-5350**
Manhattan Beach, CA 90266
(Diving & Marine)

Mime and Movement by Lorin Eric Salm (818) 300-7473 / (866) 444-6463
(Mime and Movement) **www.movement-coach.com**

Brandon Molale (310) 493-5158 / (323) 469-9980
(Football) **www.brandonmolale.com**

Monad Railway Equipment Co. (562) 404-8641 / (562) 522-7894
15220 Valley View Ave. FAX **(562) 404-8541**
La Mirada, CA 90638 **www.monadrailway.com**
(Railroads & Trains)
Contact: Lon Orlenko

Motion Picture Marine (310) 822-1100
616 Venice Blvd. FAX **(310) 822-2679**
Marina del Rey, CA 90291 **www.motionpicturemarine.com**
(Marine Coordination)

Jimmy O'Connell (310) 968-0549 / (310) 452-5774
306 Market St., Ste. A FAX **(310) 452-5774**
Venice, CA 90291

David O'Leary (805) 493-4844 / (805) 558-6754
3211 Winterbrook Court
Thousand Oaks, CA 91360
(Firefighting & Medical)

One-on-One Sports Consultants (408) 261-8480 / (408) 892-1030
4250 Albany Dr., Ste. F109
San Jose, CA 95129

Stephen Patt, M.D. (310) 582-1114
2001 Santa Monica Blvd., Ste. 888-W
Santa Monica, CA 90404
(Medical)

Perris Valley Skydiving (951) 657-3904
2091 Goetz Rd. FAX **(951) 657-6178**
Perris, CA 92570 **www.skydiveperris.com**
Contact: Patrick Conaster

Reel Deal Technical Advisors (310) 780-0618
P.O. Box 1444
Manhattan Beach, CA 90266
(Homicide, Military, Narcotics, Police-Patrol, Special Ops, SWAT & Vice)
Contact: Chic Daniel

Howard Richman (818) 344-3306
soundfeelings.com/products/music_instruction/piano_lessons.htm
(Piano)

John Sakas (310) 908-9198 / (888) 240-7100
2408 Carnegie Ln., Ste. 3 FAX (310) 376-7872
Redondo Beach, CA 90278
(Martial Arts)

Schwartz Oil Company, Inc. (661) 259-4000 / (818) 365-9214
27241 Henry Mayo Dr. FAX (661) 257-0137
Valencia, CA 91355 www.socifuel.com
(HAZWOPER)

State Fire Marshal - Motion Picture/ Entertainment Unit (626) 305-1908
602 E. Huntington Dr., Ste. A FAX (626) 305-5175
Monrovia, CA 91016 www.fire.ca.gov
Contact: Deputy Adams

Studio Sea Management, Inc. (310) 276-8158 / (818) 519-4399
P.O. Box 15368 FAX (888) 297-5945
Beverly Hills, CA 90209
(Marine)
Contact: Ransom Walrod

Stunt Wings/Joe Greblo (818) 367-2430 / (818) 266-0874
12623 Gridley St. FAX (818) 367-5363
Sylmar, CA 91342 www.stuntwings.com
(Hang Gliding, Paragliding & Ultralight Aircraft)

SwordPlay/Tim Weske (818) 421-2926 / (818) 980-2123
64 E. Magnolia Blvd. FAX (818) 566-4357
Burbank, CA 91502 www.timweske.com
(Fencing and Sword Fight Choreography)

Richard Theiss/RTSea Prods. (949) 733-8572
P.O. Box 51417 FAX (949) 733-8572
Irvine, CA 92619 www.rtsea.com
(Marine Action & Scuba Diving)

US Air Force Motion Picture Office (310) 235-7522 / (310) 235-7511
10880 Wilshire Blvd., Ste. 1240 FAX (310) 235-7500
Los Angeles, CA 90024
Contact: Charles Davis

US Army Office of Public Affairs (310) 235-7621 / (310) 235-7622
10880 Wilshire Blvd., Ste. 1250 FAX (310) 235-6075
Los Angeles, CA 90024
www.defenselink.mil/faq/pis/PC12FILM.html

US Coast Guard Motion Picture & Television Office (310) 235-7817
10880 Wilshire Blvd., Ste. 1210 FAX (310) 235-7851
Los Angeles, CA 90024
www.defenselink.mil/faq/pis/PC12FILM.html

US Marine Corps Motion Picture & Television Liason Office (310) 235-7272
10880 Wilshire Blvd., Ste. 1230 FAX (310) 235-7274
Los Angeles, CA 90024

US Navy Office Entertainment Industry Liason (310) 235-7481 / (310) 235-6266
10880 Wilshire Blvd., Ste. 1220 FAX (310) 235-7856
Los Angeles, CA 90024
Contacts: Rosalie Clark & Robert Anderson

Vertical Adventures (949) 854-6250 / (800) 514-8785
P.O. Box 7548 FAX (949) 854-5249
Newport Beach, CA 92658
(Mountain Climbing)
Contact: Bob Gaines

Vietnamese American Media, Inc. (714) 775-7772
5002 W. McFadden Ave., Ste. 14 FAX (714) 775-7772
Santa Ana, CA 92704
(Vietnam War)
Contact: April Tran

War Horse & Militaria Heritage Foundation (818) 694-9277
(Military Cavalry) FAX (818) 896-8310
www.warhorsefoundation.com

Warriors, Inc. (818) 349-6640
16129 Tupper St. FAX (818) 688-3939
North Hills, CA 91343 www.warriorsinc.com
(Firearms Instruction, History, Intelligence, Korean War, Marines, Martial Arts, Military, Special Operations, Vietnam War, World War I & World War II)

Westside Detectives, Inc. (323) 583-8660 / (323) 833-2383
6230 Wilshire Blvd., Ste. 59
Los Angeles, CA 90048
www.westsidedetectives.com
(Missing Persons and Private Detective Procedures)

WW2 Military Vehicle Rentals, Ltd. (949) 632-4345
www.ww2militaryvehiclerentals.com

A+ The Employment Co., Inc. (818) 840-0998
4111 W. Alameda Ave., Ste. 303 FAX **(818) 840-8563**
Burbank, CA 91505 **www.theemploymentco.com**

AD Personnel (310) 284-3939
1180 S. Beverly Dr., Ste. 715 FAX **(310) 284-3940**
Los Angeles, CA 90035 **www.adpersonnel.com**
(Foreign Language Transcription, Permanent Personnel, Temporary Personnel, Transcription & Word Processing)

Alpha Dog Transcriptions (818) 785-6818
6314 Ethel Ave. FAX **(818) 782-3756**
Van Nuys, CA 91401 **www.alphadogtranscriptions.com**
(Scripts & Transcription)

Angel City Transcription (818) 939-0396
(818) 605-6925
13652 Leadwell St. FAX **(323) 936-1219**
Van Nuys, CA 91405 **www.angelcityscripts.com**
(Scripts & Transcription)

BAM Transcription (818) 505-0990
(310) 600-6595
10061 Riverside Dr., Ste. 917 FAX **(818) 506-1462**
Toluca Lake, CA 91602 **www.bamtranscription.com**
(Scripts & Transcription)

Brocato Transcription Services (818) 846-1128
3607 W. Magnolia Blvd., Ste. 8 FAX **(818) 846-0262**
Burbank, CA 91505
www.brocatotranscriptionservices.com
(Scripts & Transcription)

Comar Agency (310) 248-2700
9615 Brighton Way, Ste. 313 FAX **(310) 288-0205**
Beverly Hills, CA 90210
(Permanent and Temporary Personnel)

The Continuity Company (310) 968-4302
8726D S. Sepulveda Blvd., Ste. B22
Los Angeles, CA 90045
(Scripts & Transcription)

Daily Transcripts (310) 734-8853
(310) 417-4838
6701 Center Dr. West, Ste. 1111 FAX **(424) 203-3072**
Los Angeles, CA 90045 **www.dailytranscription.com**
(Transcription)

Flying Fingers Transcripts (818) 557-0580
927 W. Olive Ave., Ste. B FAX **(818) 557-0590**
Burbank, CA 91506 **www.flyingfingerstranscripts.com**
(Foreign Language Transcription, Transcription & Word Processing)

Force One Entertainment (310) 271-5217
702 N. Bedford FAX **(310) 271-2439**
Beverly Hills, CA 90210
www.forceoneentertainment.com
(Permanent and Temporary Personnel)

Hollywood Transcribing (818) 437-9970
15061 Moorpark St. **www.hollywoodtranscribing.com**
Sherman Oaks, CA 91403

Huntington Court Reporters & Transcription, Inc. (626) 792-7250
(800) 586-2988
1450 W. Colorado Blvd., Ste. 100 FAX **(626) 792-8760**
Pasadena, CA 91105 **www.huntingtoncr.com**
(Transcription & Foreign Language Transcription)

iProbe Multilingual Solutions, Inc. (888) 489-6035
www.iprobesolutions.com
(Foreign Language Transcription)

JR Media Services, Inc. (818) 557-0200
(818) 398-9306
2501 W. Burbank Blvd., Ste. 200 FAX **(818) 557-0201**
Burbank, CA 91505 **www.jrmediaservices.com**

Brenda Marshall (818) 766-8735
(Resumes, Scripts & Word Processing) FAX **(818) 762-6225**
www.brendamarshall.net

MSG, Inc. Transcription Service (310) 826-4563
(310) 288-6598
2118 Wilshire Blvd., Ste. 1003
Santa Monica, CA 90403

Production Transcripts (818) 265-1541
(888) 349-3022
3736 San Fernando Rd. FAX **(213) 947-1585**
Glendale, CA 91204 **www.productiontranscripts.com**
(Transcription)

RNK Productions, LLC (818) 742-5189
356 E. Olive Ave., Ste. 108 **www.rnkproductions.com**
Burbank, CA 91502
(Scripts & Transcription)

Script Changes (310) 995-3098
www.scriptchanges.com
(Script Coordinators, Scripts, Transcription & Word Processing)

The Script Specialists (818) 380-3090
15303 Ventura Blvd., Ste. 900 FAX **(818) 901-1605**
Sherman Oaks, CA 91403 **www.thescriptspecialists.com**
(Scripts & Transcription)

Sound Transcription Service (818) 908-2404
7336 Santa Monica Blvd., Ste. 603
West Hollywood, CA 90046

Studio Transcription Services, a division of STS Media Services, Inc. (818) 563-3004
P.O. Box 10213 **www.studiotranscription.com**
Burbank, CA 91510
(Foreign Language Transcription, Scripts, Transcription & Word Processing)

Talk 2 TYPE Transcriptions (818) 986-6982
FAX **(818) 986-1343**
www.talk2type.net

transcript exchange (818) 237-5671
12400 Ventura Blvd., Ste. 626
Studio City, CA 91604 **www.transcriptexchange.com**
(Transcription)

The Transcription Company (818) 848-6500
4100 W. Burbank Blvd., Third Fl. FAX **(818) 556-4150**
Burbank, CA 91505 **www.transcripts.net**
(Scripts & Transcription)

Transcriptions Overnight (310) 995-3098
www.transcriptionsovernight.com
(Scripts, Transcription & Word Processing)

Word of Mouth Transcription Services (818) 904-9044
(818) 780-7346
6710 Calhoun Ave. FAX **(818) 780-7346**
Van Nuys, CA 91405 **www.wordofmouthtranscripts.com**
(Scripts & Transcription)

Words Plus (323) 655-7492
(323) 243-3150
6621 W. Fifth St. FAX **(323) 655-2048**
Los Angeles, CA 90048 **www.wordsplus1.com**

WP Plus (323) 255-5515
2858 El Roble Dr.
Los Angeles, CA 90041
(Scripts & Transcription)

1-Stop Translation (213) 480-0011
3700 Wilshire Blvd., Ste. 630 FAX (213) 232-3223
Los Angeles, CA 90010 www.1stoptr.com

Abacus Consulting & Chinese Translation Services (626) 487-8909 (626) 282-9186
401 N. Garfield Ave., Ste. 1 FAX (626) 282-9252
Alhambra, CA 91801
www.certifiedchinesetranslation.com
(Cantonese, Mandarin & Spanish)

ABC WordExpress Worldwide Language Services (800) 570-0700 (310) 260-7700
8306 Wilshire Blvd., Ste. 200 FAX (800) 570-5950
Beverly Hills, CA 90211 www.wordexpress.net
(Localization & Transcription)

Agnew Tech-II (805) 494-3999
741 Lakefield Rd., Ste. C FAX (805) 494-1749
Westlake Village, CA 91361 www.agnew.com

Lisa Azuma (310) 430-3143
(Japanese, Localization & Transcription)

Philippe Bergeron (818) 932-9491
(French & French-Canadian)

Blague Communications (818) 769-5661
11417 Moorpark St. FAX (818) 769-5996
North Hollywood, CA 91602
www.blaguecommunications.com

Blue 105 (818) 563-4335
2600 W. Olive Ave., Fifth Fl. FAX (818) 563-4223
Burbank, CA 91505 www.blue105.com
(Arabic, Brazilian Portuguese, Chinese, Danish, Dutch, French, German, Greek, Hebrew, Italian, Japanese, Korean, Norwegian, Spanish & Swedish)

Marina Brodskaya (650) 387-3168
(Russian) FAX (650) 857-9094

Claudette Roland Translation Services (310) 475-4347
P.O. Box 24035
Los Angeles, CA 90024
(Localization & Transcription)

Bernadette Colomine (213) 484-4984 (213) 247-9414
(French) FAX (213) 484-4984

Communicate Japan (818) 842-6506
P.O. Box 4253 FAX (818) 842-5106
Burbank, CA 91503 www.communicatejapan.com
(Japanese)

Cosmos Lingua Translation Services (323) 935-4100 (323) 459-9531
269 S. Beverly Dr., Ste. 542 FAX (323) 935-4446
Beverly Hills, CA 90212 www.cosmoslingua.com

CTS LanguageLink (800) 208-2620
9920 Jordan Circle, Ste. A FAX (360) 693-9292
Santa Fe Springs, CA 90670 www.ctslanguagelink.com

Laura D'Auri, Esq. (310) 270-5779
(Italian)

European Captioning Institute (ECI) (818) 238-4231
303 N. Glenoaks Blvd., Ste. 200 FAX (818) 238-4266
Burbank, CA 91502 www.ecisubtitling.com
(Localization and Transcription; 100+ Languages Including Armenian, Brazilian Portuguese, Bulgarian, Canadian French, Cantonese, Danish, Finish, French, German, Greek, Hindi, Italian, Japanese, Korean, Latin Spanish, Mandarin, Norwegian, Polish, Portuguese, Russian, Spanish, Swedish, Turkish & Vietnamese)

Executive Linguist Agency, Inc. (310) 376-1409 (800) 522-2320
500 S. Sepulveda Blvd., Ste. 300 FAX (310) 376-9285
Manhattan Beach, CA 90266 www.executivelinguist.com

Exotic Languages Agency (800) 303-7200 (714) 704-1874
333 City Blvd. West, Ste. 630 FAX (714) 704-1870
Orange, CA 92868 www.ela1.com

French a la Carte/Katherine Vallin (323) 493-5533 (323) 822-9401
1632 N. Laurel Ave., Ste. 116 www.french-a-la-carte.com
West Hollywood, CA 90046
(French & Spanish)

French Language Services (310) 215-1092
www.frenchlanguageservices.com
(French & French-Canadian)

A Frenchman in LA (310) 237-6438
www.afrenchman.com
(African, Asian, European, Indian and Middle-Eastern Languages Localization, Transcription and Translation)

Gilmour Translations (626) 355-5257
(French & Italian) home.earthlink.net/~ngilmour

Nanette Gobel (310) 801-2164
(French, German & Localization)

Esther M. Hermida (310) 890-3129 (949) 234-0043
(Spanish) www.certifiedspanishinterpreter.com

In Other Words (323) 697-8130
818 N. Doheny Dr., Ste. 407 FAX (310) 446-3022
Los Angeles, CA 90069 www.iowtrans.com

iProbe Multilingual Solutions, Inc. (888) 489-6035
www.iprobesolutions.com
(6912 Languages & Transcription Including Arabic, Dutch, Finnish, French, French Canadian, Cantonese, Chinese, Danish, German, Greek, Hebrew, Hindi, Italian, Japanese, Korean, Mandarin, Norwegian, Polish, Portuguese, Russian, Spanish, Swedish, Turkish, Urdu & Vietnamese)

Japanese Media Translation (323) 229-9161
(Japanese)

JBI Studios (818) 592-0056
21432 Wyandotte FAX (818) 592-6994
Canoga Park, CA 91303 www.jbistudios.com
(Asian and European Languages)

JR Media Services, Inc. (818) 557-0200 (818) 398-9306
2501 W. Burbank Blvd., Ste. 200 FAX (818) 557-0201
Burbank, CA 91505 www.jrmediaservices.com

The Kitchen, a TM Systems Company (818) 306-5300 (310) 270-8214
12711 Ventura Blvd., Ste. 217 www.thekitchen.tv
Studio City, CA 91604
(Transcription)

Addie Akemi Kohzu (818) 207-2555 (818) 501-5435
(Japanese Localization)

Language.net (310) 399-1790
804 Main St. FAX (310) 399-1901
Venice, CA 90291 www.language.net
(All Languages, Localization & Transcription)

Linguatheque (818) 549-9591 (800) 440-5344
FAX (818) 549-9593
www.linguatheque.com

Melissa MacCracken (310) 344-3080

Marcland International Communications (818) 557-6677
www.marcland.com

My Own Private Japan (310) 749-9091
(888) 909-9185
(Japanese) FAX (888) 909-9185
www.myownprivatejapan.com

OneWorld Language Solutions (323) 848-7993
(Asian and European Languages) FAX (323) 848-7995
www.oneworldlanguage.com

Paragon Language Services, Inc. (323) 966-4655
(800) 499-0299
5657 Wilshire Blvd., Ste. 310 FAX (323) 651-1867
Los Angeles, CA 90036 www.paragonls.com

Post Modern Edit, LLC (949) 608-8700
2941 Alton Pkwy FAX (949) 608-8729
Irvine, CA 92606 www.postmodernedit.com
(Arabic, Chinese, Danish, Dutch, French, German, Greek, Hebrew, Hindi, Italian, Japanese, Korean, Norwegian, Portuguese, Spanish, Swedish & Tamil)

The Sign Language Company (818) 763-1215
12050 Guerin St., Ste. 204 FAX (818) 763-3708
Studio City, CA 91604 www.signlanguageco.com

Jacqueline Stine (661) 298-9243
(818) 209-0070
18637 Nathan Hill Rd.
Santa Clarita, CA 91351
(Spanish)

STS Foreign Language Services/ a division of STS Media Services, Inc. (818) 563-3004
P.O. Box 10213 www.stsforeignlanguage.com
Burbank, CA 91510
(Arabic, Armenian, Bengali, Chinese, Dutch, Finnish, French, German, Greek, Haitian French Creole, Hebrew, Hindi, Italian, Japanese, Khmer, Korean, Latin, Portuguese, Russian, Spanish, Swedish, Tamil, Thai & Ukrainian)

Technicolor Creative Services - Burbank (818) 480-5100
(310) 801-7300
www.technicolor.com

Toro Bravo (323) 363-7746
(Spanish) www.torobravo.us

V & J Translations (310) 721-4716
1225 12th St., Ste. 9 FAX (310) 313-3220
Santa Monica, CA 90401 www.vjtrans.com
(Chinese, French, German, Italian, Japanese, Korean, Portuguese, Romanian, Russian & Spanish)

V & L International, LLC (310) 822-1781
(212) 292-4228
751 17th St. FAX (310) 822-1761
Santa Monica, CA 90402 www.vnli.com

Voicegroup, Inc. (818) 973-2770
3500 W. Olive Ave., Third Fl. FAX (818) 998-2770
Burbank, CA 91505 www.voicegroup.com

Marie Zelenka-Hootsmans (310) 237-6438
www.baesjou.net
(African, Asian, European, Indian and Middle-Eastern Languages Localization, Transcription and Translation)

9900 Club (310) 550-8444
9900 S. Santa Monica Blvd. FAX (310) 550-5969
Beverly Hills, CA 90212 www.thefriarsbh.com

Air Hollywood (818) 890-6801
(877) 466-2587
13240 Weidner St. FAX (818) 890-7041
Pacoima, CA 91331 www.airhollywood.com

Autry National Center (323) 667-2000
4700 Western Heritage Way FAX (323) 660-5721
Los Angeles, CA 90027 www.autrynationalcenter.org
Contact: Special Events Coordinator

Avalon (323) 462-6031
(323) 462-8900
1735 Vine St. FAX (323) 462-0579
Hollywood, CA 90028 www.avalonhollywood.com
Contact: Barney Holm

Boardner's (323) 462-9621
1652 N. Cherokee Ave. FAX (323) 462-8858
Hollywood, CA 90028 www.boardners.com
Contact: Tricia La Belle

The Bungalow Club (323) 964-9494
(323) 936-5270
7174 Melrose Ave. FAX (323) 964-9452
Los Angeles, CA 90046 www.thebungalowclub.com

Cafe-Club Fais Do-Do (323) 954-8080
5257 W. Adams Blvd. www.faisdodo.com
Los Angeles, CA 90016

Calamigos (818) 972-5940
LA Equestrian Center FAX (818) 972-5946
480 Riverside Dr. www.calamigosequestrian.com
Burbank, CA 91506
Contact: Alison Court

Cinespace (323) 817-3456
6356 Hollywood Blvd., Second Fl. FAX (323) 860-9794
Hollywood, CA 90028 www.cinespace.info

Cozy's Blues Club (818) 986-6000
(818) 882-6042
14058 Ventura Blvd. FAX (818) 501-0606
Sherman Oaks, CA 91423 www.cozysblues.com
Contact: Steve Rakoczy

The Derby (323) 663-8979
4500 Los Feliz Blvd. FAX (323) 663-5641
Los Angeles, CA 90027 www.the-derby.com
Contact: Tammie Gower

El Cid (323) 668-0318
4212 W. Sunset Blvd. www.elcidla.com
Los Angeles, CA 90029
Contact: Tobin Shea

El Rey Theatre (323) 936-6400
Contact: Tessa Swallow FAX (323) 936-5657
www.theelrey.com

Equestrian Center (818) 972-5940
480 Riverside Dr. FAX (818) 973-1048
Burbank, CA 91506 www.la-equestriancenter.com
Contact: Mina Behboudei

Fox Studios (310) 369-3663 / (310) 369-4636
10201 W. Pico Blvd. FAX (310) 369-3978
Los Angeles, CA 90035 www.foxstudios.com

Gallery 1018 (310) 923-0660 / (310) 295-1620
1018 S. Santa Fe Ave. www.gallery1018.com
Los Angeles, CA 90021

The Hideout (310) 429-1851
112 W. Channel Rd. www.santamonicahideout.com
Santa Monica, CA 90402

The Highlands (323) 461-9820
6801 Hollywood Blvd., Ste. 433 FAX (323) 461-9802
Hollywood, CA 90028 www.thehighlandshollywood.com

House of Blues (323) 848-5193 / (323) 848-5100
8430 Sunset Blvd. www.hob.com
West Hollywood, CA 90069
Contact: Maureen McGrath

Jillian's Universal (818) 985-9213 / (818) 985-8234
1000 Universal Studios Blvd. FAX (818) 985-9513
Ste. G103 www.jilliansbilliards.com
Universal City, CA 91608

The Jim Henson Company (323) 802-1500
1416 N. La Brea Ave. FAX (323) 802-1825
Hollywood, CA 90028 leasing.henson.com/events.html

Joseph's Cafe (323) 462-8697
1775 N. Ivar Ave. FAX (323) 462-0614
Los Angeles, CA 90028 www.josephscafe.com

The Kress (323) 785-5000 / (323) 785-5005
6608 Hollywood Blvd. FAX (323) 785-5019
Hollywood, CA 90028

LACMA (The Los Angeles County Museum Of Art) (323) 857-6039 / (323) 857-4768
5905 Wilshire Blvd. FAX (323) 857-6021
Los Angeles, CA 90036 www.lacma.org

The Larchmont (323) 467-4068
5657 Melrose Ave. FAX (323) 467-8343
Hollywood, CA 90038
Contacts: Ben Freed & Tatiana Lonny

Laugh Factory (323) 656-1336
8001 Sunset Blvd. FAX (323) 656-2563
Los Angeles, CA 90046 www.laughfactory.com

Lucky Strike Lanes (323) 467-7776
6801 Hollywood Blvd., Ste. 143 FAX (323) 467-9997
Hollywood, CA 90028 www.bowlluckystrike.com

Lucky Strike Lanes (714) 937-5263
20 City Blvd. West, Bldg. G, Ste. 2
Orange, CA 92868 www.bowlluckystrike.com

Maggiano's Little Italy Banquets (323) 965-2777
189 The Grove Dr. FAX (323) 965-8662
Los Angeles, CA 90036 www.maggianos.com/banquet

The Magic Castle (323) 851-3313
7001 Franklin Ave. www.magiccastle.com
Hollywood, CA 90028
Contact: James G. Williams

Museum of Television & Radio (310) 786-1000
465 N. Beverly Dr. FAX (310) 786-1086
Beverly Hills, CA 90210 www.mtr.org

My House (323) 960-3300
7080 Hollywood Blvd. www.myhousehollywood.com
Hollywood, CA 90028
Contact: Billie Jo Neidlinger

NBC Universal Studio Special Events (818) 777-9466 / (800) 892-1979
100 Universal City Plaza FAX (818) 866-0293
Bldg. 1280-10 www.filmmakersdestination.com
Universal City, CA 91608

Ⓐ **Pacific Design Center** (310) 657-0800 / (310) 360-6423
8687 Melrose Ave., Ste. M60 FAX (310) 652-8576
West Hollywood, CA 90069
Contact: Diana Arone www.pacificdesigncenter.com

Pacific Park (310) 260-8744
380 Santa Monica Pier FAX (310) 899-1826
Santa Monica, CA 90401 www.pacpark.com
Contact: Kristin Wasiluk

The Studios at Paramount (323) 956-8398
The Studios at Paramount Special Events
5555 Melrose Ave.
Los Angeles, CA 90038
www.paramountspecialevents.com

Park Plaza (213) 384-5281
607 S. Park View St. FAX (213) 383-8392
Los Angeles, CA 90057 www.parkplazaevents.com

Pearl (310) 358-9191
665 N. Robertson Blvd. www.pearl90069.com
West Hollywood, CA 90069

Pickwick Bowl/Pickwick Ice Center (818) 845-5300
1001 Riverside Dr. FAX (818) 846-6424
Burbank, CA 91506 www.pickwickgardens.com
Contact: Sherrie Dickinson

Pinz Bowling Center (818) 769-7600
12655 Ventura Blvd. FAX (818) 509-1284
Studio City, CA 91604 www.pinzbowlingcenter.com
Contact: Eleda Cohen

Raleigh Studio Cafe (323) 871-5660
Raleigh Studios, 5300 Melrose Ave. FAX (323) 871-4433
Hollywood, CA 90038
Contact: Taylor Peeples

RecCenter Studio (213) 413-9300 / (323) 868-4226
1161 Logan St. FAX (213) 413-9301
Los Angeles, CA 90026 www.reccenterstudio.com

Red Buddha Lounge (323) 962-2913 / (323) 309-2166
6423 Yucca St. www.theredbuddha.com
Los Angeles, CA 90028

Smoke House Restaurant (818) 845-3731
4420 Lakeside Dr. FAX (818) 845-3181
Burbank, CA 91505 www.smokehouse1946.com
Contact: Israel Aviles

Three Clubs (323) 462-6441
1123 N. Vine St. www.threeclubs.com
Los Angeles, CA 90038

Union Station (213) 617-0111
800 N. Alameda St., Ste. 100 FAX (213) 617-0171
Los Angeles, CA 90012

Villa Malibu Luxury Rentals (310) 457-8484 / (310) 266-8126
6487 Cavalleri Rd., Ste. 224 www.villamalibuliving.com
Malibu, CA 90265

World Cafe (310) 395-3648 / (310) 392-1661
2820 Main St. FAX (310) 392-8440
Santa Monica, CA 90405 www.worldcafela.com
Contact: Leslie Paonessa

NOTES:

NOTES:

THE FORMOSA CAFE

L.A. CONFIDENTIAL

INT. FORMOSA - ENTRANCE - DAY

Exley (Guy Pearce) and Jack (Kevin Spacey) enter.

EXLEY
Check the bar. I got the restaurant.

RESTAURANT

Exley scans. There's Stompanato with a girl who looks amazingly like "LANA TURNER."

Engrossed, Stomapanato doesn't look up till Exley's nearly on top of him.

STOMPANATO
Hey, you want an autograph, write to M-G-M.

EXLEY
Since when do two-bit hoods and hookers give out autographs?

STOMPANATO
What?

As Stompanato stands, Exley flashes his badge.

EXLEY
L.A.P.D. Sit down.

"LANA"
Who in the hell do you think you are?

EXLEY
Take a walk, honey, before I haul your ass downtown.

STOMPANATO
You are making a large mistake.

As Jack arrives, Lana tosses a drink in Exley's face.

"LANA"
Get away from our table!

EXLEY
(grabs her wrist)
Shut up. Being cut to look like Lana Turner doesn't mean you are Lana Turner.

Jack pulls him aside.

JACK
She is Lana Turner.

EXLEY
What?

JACK
She IS Lana Turner.

SCREENPLAY BY:
Brian Helgeland & Curtis Hanson, based on the novel by James Ellroy

ALSO FILMED AT THE FORMOSA CAFE:
Swingers

Camera & Sound Equipment

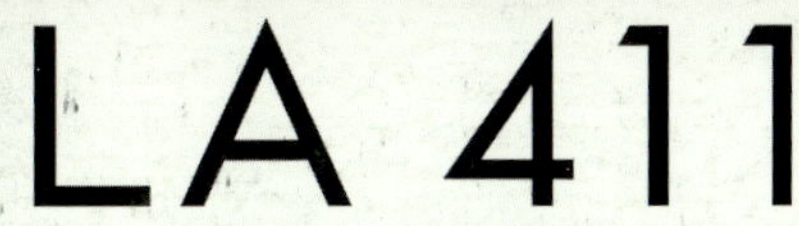

www.LA411.com

PICTURED:
Formosa Café

LOCATION:
West Hollywood

PHOTOGRAPHER:
Michael Rueter
Michael Rueter Photography/L.A.-N.Y.
www.michaelrueter.com

Supporting production in Southern California for 31 years

A ADVERTISER SYMBOL

Refer to the General Index for cross-referencing items in this section.

Aerial Equipment

Aerial Action Productions/ Reel Orange (949) 548-4524
316 La Jolla Dr. FAX (949) 548-0749
Newport Beach, CA 92663 www.reelorange.com
Aircraft: Fixed Wing Aircraft & Ultralights
Camera Mounts: Fixed Wing Aerial Camera Platforms
Cameras: 16mm, 35mm, Digital & POV Helmet Cameras
Services: Aerial Coordination, Aerial Production & Pilots

Aerial Cinema Systems/ Helicopters West, Inc. (661) 270-0565 (818) 980-2123
39120 Bouquet Canyon Rd.
Leona Valley, CA 93551
Aircraft: Fixed Wing Aircraft, Helicopters & Warbirds
Camera Mounts: Gyro-Stabilized, Nose, Outside, POV & Side Mounts
Equipment: Police Searchlight & Safety and Cargo Equipment
Services: Aerial Coordination, Aerial Production & Pilots

Aerial Film Unit by Corporate Helicopters (800) 345-6737 (858) 505-5650
3753 John J. Montgomery Dr., Ste. 2 FAX (858) 505-5658
San Diego, CA 92123 www.corporatehelicopters.com
Aircraft: Helicopters
Camera Mounts: Camera Platforms, Gyro-Stabilized Mounts, Helicopter Mounts, Nose Mounts, Side Mounts & Wescam Mounts
Camera Mounts/Systems: Wescam
Cameras: Betacam, Digital Video, Gyro-Stabilized Camera Systems & High Def
Equipment: Air to Ground Radios, Fuel Truck & Night Sun Searchlights
Services: Aerial Coordination, Aerial Production, Helicopter Refueling & Pilots

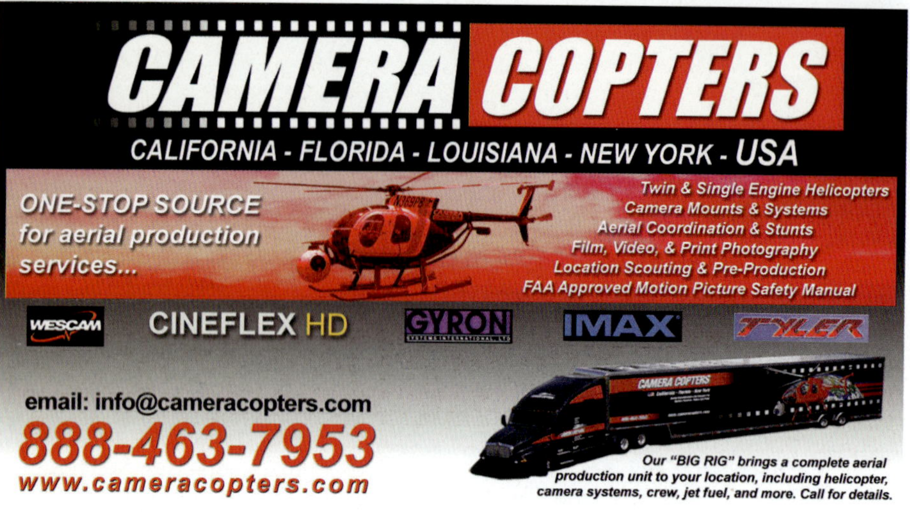

Aerial Filmworks (310) 998-7009
(808) 281-1921
www.aerialfilmworks.com
Aerial Equipment: Gyro-Stabilized 5-Axis Camera Systems & HDTV Helicopter and Lear Jet Camera Systems
Camera Mounts: Fixed Wing Camera Mount, Gyro-Stabilized Mounts, Helicopter Mounts & Nose Mounts
Cameras: Gyro-Stabilized Camera Systems & High Def
Services: Aerial Production

Aerial Shot Productions (661) 799-0154
(661) 607-7266
24077 WhiteWater Dr. www.aerialshotproductions.com
Valencia, CA 91354
Aircraft: Fixed-Wing UAV RC Helicopters
Equipment: Aerial Camera Mounts and Systems

Ⓐ **Aerial Stunt Service/Joe Jennings** (310) 543-2222
3128 Via La Selva www.aerialstuntservice.com
Palos Verdes Estates, CA 90274
Camera Mounts: Aircraft POV and Gyro-Stabilized Mounts
Cameras: 16mm, 35mm, Gyro-Stabilized and POV Helmet Cameras & Skydiving
Equipment: BASE Jumping Equipment, Heavy Drop Cargo Chutes, Parachutes & Skydiving Equipment
Services: Aerial Coordination & Pilots

Aerial Video Systems/AVS (818) 954-8842
712 S. Main St. FAX (818) 954-9122
Burbank, CA 91506 www.aerialvideo.com
Aerial Equipment: Gyro-Stabilized 5-Axis Camera Systems & HDTV Helicopter and Lear Jet Camera Systems
Cameras: Aerial Cameras, Gyro-Stabilized Camera Systems, HDTV, Helmet & High Def
Services: Aerial Production

- Bell JetRanger turbine helicopter
- Cineflex HD/SD stabilized aerial camera system
- 4:2:2 HDCAM Record Deck, multiple format and frame rates with videotape included
- Seasoned production pilot
- Experienced Cineflex aerial HD cinematographer
- Open front seat with director monitor

For more information call:
1.866. HELINET (435-4638)
www.helinet.com

HELINET AVIATION

McKERNAN

MOTION PICTURE AVIATION

AVIATION SPECIALISTS FOR THE MOTION PICTURE INDUSTRY

EXPERIENCE AND KNOWLEDGE:

- MOTION PICTURE PILOTS ASSOCIATION MEMBER
- COMMERCIAL HELICOPTER PILOTS
- COMMERCIAL FIXED WING PILOTS
- AERIAL COORDINATORS

LEADING SUPPLIER OF:

- HELICOPTER CAMERASHIPS
- TYLER CAMERA MOUNTS
- GYRO STABILIZED MOUNTS

PARTIAL LIST OF CREDITS:

RED DAWN-THE GREEN HORNET
VALENTINE'S DAY-PUBLIC ENEMIES
STATE OF PLAY-FLIGHT OF THE DRAGON
YOUNG AMERICANS-LAND OF THE LOST
TRAUMA-FLASH FORWARD-CSI
TOUR OF DUTY-AIRWOLF

DEMO REEL AVAILABLE UPON REQUEST

AVAILABLE SERVICES:

- DEPT. OF DEFENSE SUPPORT CONSULTANT
- STUNT COORDINATOR
- FAA MOTION PICTURE MANUAL
- STORYBOARD & SCRIPT CONSULTING
- FIXED WING / HELICOPTER
- PEEL PAINTING / MOCK UPS
- PICTURE AIRCRAFT
- PERMITS & INSURANCE

CONTACT INFORMATION:

OFFICE: 310.458.9176 · CELL: 310.993.4486 · SERVICE: 323.469.9980
WWW.HELICOPTERGUY.COM · EMAIL: PETER@HELICOPTERGUY.COM

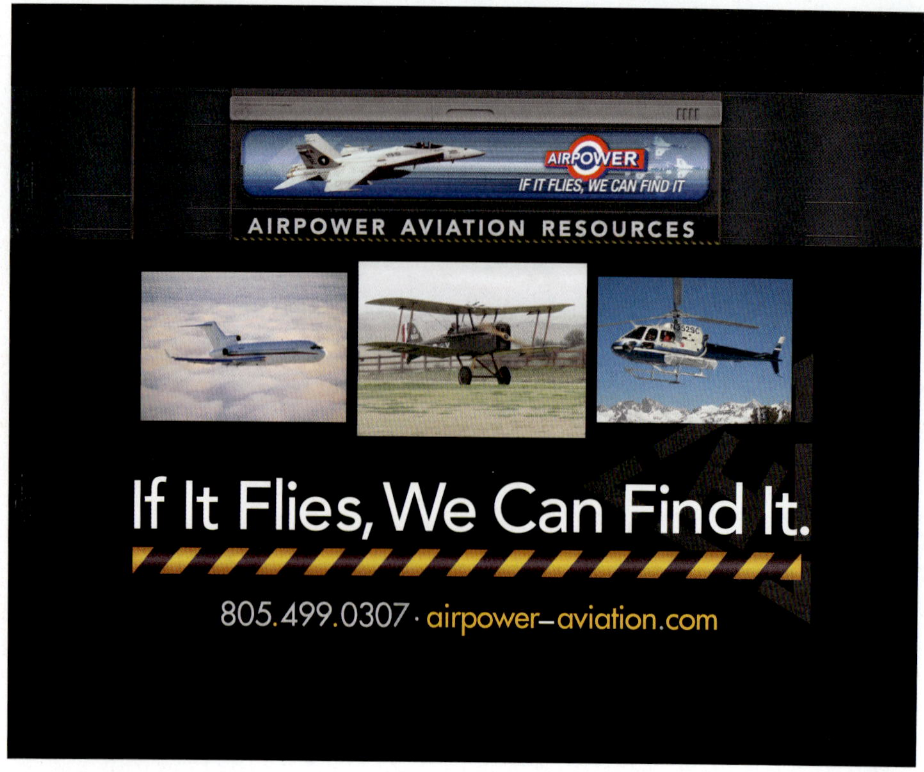

Aerobatic Hang Gliding, Inc. (760) 822-5667
585 N. Twin Oaks Valley Rd., Ste. D **www.johnheiney.com**
San Marcos, CA 92069
Aircraft: Hang Gliders
Camera Mounts: Hang Glider Mounts & Ultralight
Services: Aerial Coordination

Ⓐ **Airpower Aviation Resources** (805) 402-0052
702 Paseo Vista FAX **(805) 498-0357**
Thousand Oaks, CA 91320 **www.airpower-aviation.com**
Aircraft: Civilian and Military Fixed Wing Aircraft & Helicopters
Services: Aerial Coordination, Aerial Production & Pilots

Altitude Aviation (310) 379-4448 (310) 489-8938
2309 Pacific Coast Hwy, Ste. 204 FAX **(310) 937-7112**
Hermosa Beach, CA 90254 **www.altitudeaviation.com**
Aircraft: Fixed Wing Aircraft & Helicopters
Services: Aerial Coordination & Pilots

Beckman Rigging/BRS Rigging (310) 532-3933 (661) 510-2518
13516 S. Mariposa Ave. FAX **(310) 532-3993**
Gardena, CA 90247 **www.brsrigging.com**

Blackstar Helicopters Inc. (818) 896-2700
10500 Airpark Way, Hangar M4 FAX **(818) 896-2771**
Pacoima, CA 91331 **www.blackstarhelicopters.com**

Branam/West Coast Theatrical (310) 637-4727 (877) 295-3390
310 S. Long Beach Blvd. FAX **(310) 637-4735**
Compton, CA 90221 **www.branament.com**
Equipment: Aerial Camera Cable Systems

Briles Wing & Helicopter, Inc. (818) 994-1445
16303 Waterman Dr. FAX **(818) 994-1447**
Van Nuys, CA 91406 **www.toflyla.com**
Aircraft: Helicopters

California Dreamin' (800) 373-3359
33133 Vista del Monte Rd. FAX **(951) 699-0601**
Temecula, CA 92591 **www.californiadreamin.com**
Aircraft: Bi-Planes & Hot Air Balloons

Ⓐ **Camera Copters, Inc.** (888) 463-7953 (305) 793-7033
23421 Balmoral Ln. **www.cameracopters.com**
West Hills, CA 91307
Aircraft: Helicopters
Camera Mounts: Gyro-Stabilized Camera Systems
Services: Aerial Coordination & Pilots

Celebrity Helicopters (877) 999-2099
961 W. Alondra Blvd. FAX **(877) 999-2099**
Compton, CA 90220 **www.celebheli.com**
Aircraft: Fixed Wing Aircraft & Helicopters
Services: Aerial Coordination, Aerial Production, Consultation & Pilots

Cinema Rentals, Inc. (661) 222-7342 (877) 877-9605
25876 The Old Rd., Ste. 174 FAX **(661) 253-3643**
Stevenson Ranch, CA 91381 **www.cinemarentals.com**
Camera Mounts: Remote-Controlled Helicopter Mounts

Ⓐ **Clay Lacy Aviation, Inc.** (818) 989-2900 (800) 423-2904
7435 Valjean Ave. FAX **(818) 909-9537**
Van Nuys, CA 91406 **www.claylacy.com**
Aircraft: Fixed Wing Aircraft
Camera Mounts: Fixed Wing Aerial Camera Platforms
Services: Aerial Coordination, Aerial Production & Pilots

Flyboyz Productions (909) 234-3943
27580 Fallingstar Ln. **www.flyboyz.com**
Saugus, CA 91350
Aircraft: Fixed Wing Aircraft, Helicopters, Hot Air Balloons & Ultralights
Cameras: Helmet & Wingbelly
Equipment: Heavy Cargo Chutes & Parachutes
Services: Aerial Coordination & Aerial Production

Ⓐ **Flying-Cam, Inc.** (310) 581-9276
3100 Donald Douglas Loop North FAX **(310) 581-9278**
Ste. 203 **www.flying-cam.com**
Santa Monica, CA 90405
Cameras: Remote-Controlled Helicopter Cameras

Gear-Up Elsinore, Inc. (619) 659-0698
P.O. Box 1536 FAX **(619) 659-0698**
Alpine, CA 91903
Equipment: Parachutes

Guardian Helicopters, Inc. (818) 442-9904
16425 Hart St. FAX **(818) 442-9901**
Van Nuys, CA 91406 **www.guardianhelicoptersusa.com**
Aircraft: Helicopters & Fixed Wing Aircraft
Camera Mounts: Nose, Spacecam, Tyler & Wescam
Equipment: Air to Ground Radios, Fuel Trucks, Mock-Ups, Props & Search Lights
Services: Aerial Coordination, Ground Safety & Pilots

Gyron Aerial Systems (626) 584-8722
39 E. Walnut St. FAX **(626) 584-4069**
Pasadena, CA 91103 **www.gyron.com**
Camera Mounts: Gyron Gyro-Stabilized

Hangar 1 Productions (213) 483-6898
1910 W. Sunset Blvd., Ste. 900 FAX **(213) 483-4185**
Los Angeles, CA 90026 **www.hangar1project.com**
Aircraft: Fixed-Wing Aircraft & Helicopter
Camera Mounts/Systems: Gyron, Spacecam, Tyler & Wescam
Equipment: Air to Ground Radios, Fuel Trucks & Night Sun Searchlights
Services: Aerial Coordination, Ground Safety, Pilots & Second Unit Directors

Heli-Flite (800) 340-1969
6873 Flight Rd. FAX **(951) 359-5019**
Riverside, CA 92504
Aircraft: Gyrocopters, Gyroplanes & Helicopters
Camera Mounts: Aerial Platforms
Equipment: Safety Equipment
Services: Aerial Coordination, Aerial Production & Pilots

Heli-USA (818) 994-1445 (877) 863-5952
16303 Waterman Dr. FAX **(818) 994-1447**
Van Nuys, CA 91406 **www.toflyla.com**
Aircraft: Helicopters

Ⓐ **Helinet Aviation Services** (818) 902-0229 (800) 221-8389
16644 Roscoe Blvd. FAX **(818) 902-9278**
Van Nuys, CA 91406 **www.helinet.com**
Aircraft: Helicopters
Camera Mounts: Aerial Camera Mounts
Cameras: Cineflex HD Gyro-Stabilized Camera Systems

Horizon Helicopters, Inc. (818) 879-3636
11271 Ventura Blvd., Ste. 430 FAX **(818) 701-4040**
Studio City, CA 91604
Aircraft: Helicopters

Hosking Aviation (661) 251-5151
FAX **(435) 649-9904**
Aircraft: Bi-Wing, Fixed Wing Aircraft & Helicopters
Equipment: Fuel Trucks & Safety Equipment
Services: Aerial Coordination & Pilots

Largo Industries (310) 486-0415 (310) 822-7940
649 Palms Blvd. FAX **(310) 305-9188**
Venice, CA 90291 **www.fred-north.com**
Equipment: Air to Ground Radios, Arri 435, Gyro-Stabilized System & Nose and Side Mounts
Services: Aerial Coordination, Ground Safety & Pilots

Los Angeles Helicopters (562) 377-0396 (800) 976-4354
4235 Donald Douglas Dr. **www.lahelicopters.com**
Long Beach, CA 90808

Mauiscape Helicopters (808) 877-7272 (888) 440-7272
FAX **(808) 893-0775**
www.mauiscape.com
Aircraft: Helicopters
Camera Mounts: Camera Platforms, Gyro-Stabilized Mounts, Helicopter Mounts, Nose Mounts, Side Mounts, Tyler Camera Mounts, Vibration Isolation Mounts & Wescam Mounts
Camera Mounts/Systems: Spacecam, Tyler & Wescam
Equipment: Air to Ground Radios, Aircraft Intercom Systems, Overwater Safety Equipment & Safety Equipment
Services: Aerial Coordination, Consultation, Ground Safety Consultation, Pilots & Ground Safety Personnel and Pilots

Ⓐ **McKernan Motion Picture Aviation** (310) 458-9176 (310) 993-4486
FAX **(310) 393-4227**
www.helicopterguy.com
Aerial Equipment: Gyro-Stabilized 5-Axis Camera Systems & Stab-C/Gyron
Aircraft: Fixed Wing Aircraft, Hang Gliders, Helicopters, Military Fixed-Wing Aircraft, Ultralights & Warbirds
Camera Mounts/Systems: Gyron, Spacecam, Tyler & Wescam
Camera Mounts: Belly Mounts & Camera Platforms
Services: Aerial Coordination

MicroFlight, Inc. (949) 583-9571 (714) 883-2334
FAX **(949) 855-9186**
www.microflight.net
Aircraft: Remote-Controlled Airplanes, Blimps and Helicopters

Motion Picture Marine (310) 822-1100
616 Venice Blvd. FAX **(310) 822-2679**
Marina del Rey, CA 90291 **www.motionpicturemarine.com**
Camera Mounts: Perfect Horizon Camera Stabilized Head

Nettmann Systems International (818) 623-1661
6910 Tujunga Ave. FAX **(818) 623-1671**
North Hollywood, CA 91605
www.camerasystems.com/agents.htm
Aerial Equipment: Film Video-HDTV Helicopter and Lear Jet Camera Systems, Gyro-Stabilized 5-Axis Camera Systems, Stab-C/Gyron FS, Super-G & Vectorvision

Orbic Helicopters, Inc. (818) 988-6532 (818) 989-9986
16700 Roscoe Blvd. FAX **(818) 988-2014**
Van Nuys, CA 91406 **www.orbichelicopters.com**
Aircraft: Helicopters

Philip Pastuhov (805) 320-3304
Camera Mounts: Aerial Fixed Wing Camera and POV Mounts
Equipment: Aircraft Intercom System

Perris Valley Skydiving (951) 657-3904
2091 Goetz Rd. FAX **(951) 657-6178**
Perris, CA 92570 **www.skydiveperris.com**
Aircraft: Fixed Wing Aircraft
Camera Mounts: Wing Mounts
Cameras: POV Helmet Cameras
Equipment: Parachutes & Skydiving Equipment
Services: Aerial Coordination

Pictorvision Inc (818) 785-9282 (800) 876-5583
7701 Haskell Ave., Ste. B FAX **(818) 785-9787**
Van Nuys, CA 91406 **www.pictorvision.com**
Camera Mounts: 5-Axis Gyro-Stabilized Camera Systems, Helicopter Mounts, Nose Mounts & Side Mounts
Cameras: 35mm, High Def, SD, Wescam & XR

Producers Air Force (818) 845-5970 (818) 795-7463
One Orange Grove Terrace FAX **(818) 845-4033**
Burbank, CA 91501 **www.producersairforce.com**
Equipment: Air to Ground Radios
Services: Aerial Production, Aerial Coordination & Consultation

RF Film, Inc. (866) 985-3456
FAX **(866) 986-3456**
www.rffilm.com

Skydive Elsinore, LLC (951) 245-9939 (877) 843-5867
20701 Cereal St. FAX **(951) 245-3661**
Lake Elsinore, CA 92530 **www.skydiveelsinore.com**
Aircraft: Fixed Wing Aircraft
Camera Mounts: Fixed Wing Aerial Camera Platforms
Equipment: Parachutes & Skydiving Equipment
Services: Aerial Coordination & Pilots

South Coast Helicopters, Inc. (714) 751-3515 (714) 997-0469
2950 Airway Ste. C-1 FAX **(714) 751-4705**
Costa Mesa, CA 92626
Aircraft: Helicopters
Equipment: Air to Ground Radios, Fuel Trucks & Night Sun
Services: Aerial Coordination, Ground Safety Personnel & Pilots

SpaceCam Systems, Inc (818) 889-6060
31111 Via Colinas, Ste. 201 FAX **(818) 889-6062**
Westlake Village, CA 91362 **www.spacecam.com**
Camera Mounts: Gyro-Stabilized Camera Mounts & Spacecam
Cameras: 35mm, 35mm VistaVision, 65mm, HDTV & Spacecam
Services: Stabilized Shooting Coordination

Stearman Flight Center (909) 597-8511
7000 Merrill Ave., Ste. 53 FAX **(909) 597-8511**
Chino, CA 91710 **www.silverwingswingwalking.com**
Aircraft: Vintage Airplanes

Studio Wings (805) 320-9500
855 Aviation Dr. FAX **(805) 987-4720**
Camarillo, CA 93010 **www.studiowings.com**
Aircraft: Fixed Wing Aircraft & Helicopters
Equipment: Police Helicopter Search Lights
Services: Aerial Coordination, Aerial Production & Pilots

Stunt Wings/Adventure Sports (818) 367-2430 (818) 266-0874
12623 Gridley St. FAX **(818) 367-5363**
San Fernando, CA 91342 **www.stuntwings.com**
Aircraft: Hang Gliders, Hot Air Balloons, Parachutes, Paragliders & Ultralight Aircraft
Camera Mounts: Hang Gliding & Ultralight Camera Mounts
Cameras: Lightweight Gyro-Stabilized
Services: Aerial Coordination

Ⓐ **Thornton Aircraft Company** (626) 795-8604
7520 Hayvenhurst Ave. FAX **(626) 795-8606**
Van Nuys, CA 91406 **www.thorntonaircraft.com**
Aircraft: Fixed-Wing Aircraft, Jets, Military Fixed-Wing Aircraft & Warbirds
Services: Aerial Coordination & Pilots

Ⓐ **Tyler Camera Systems** (818) 989-4420 (800) 390-6070
14218 Aetna St. FAX **(818) 989-0423**
Van Nuys, CA 91401 **www.tylermount.com**
Camera Mounts: Gyro-Stabilized Helicopter Camera Mounts

VertiView Helicopter (310) 822-6790 (800) 447-3585
13428 Maxella Ave., Ste. 261 FAX **(310) 821-4010**
Marina del Rey, CA 90292 **www.call4ideas.com**
Aircraft: Helicopter

Wolfe Air Aviation Ltd. (626) 584-4060
39 E. Walnut St. FAX **(626) 584-4069**
Pasadena, CA 91103 **www.wolfeair.com**
Camera Mounts: Vectorvision

Wolfe Air Aviation, Ltd. (626) 584-4060
39 E. Walnut St. FAX **(626) 584-4069**
Pasadena, CA 91103 **www.wolfeair.com**
Aircraft: Fixed Wing Aircraft & Helicopters

Paul Barth (888) 463-7953
(305) 793-7033
www.cameracopters.com

Chuck Bordon (805) 732-9694

Bravo Aviation, Inc. (310) 263-7669
(562) 755-5083
Ports O'Call Village, Berth 75 FAX (310) 263-7679
San Pedro, CA 90732 www.bravoair.com

Vance Colvig (818) 762-6336

Craig Dyer (310) 383-0777
10500 Airpark Way, Hangar M4 FAX (818) 896-2771
Pacoima, CA 91331
www.blackstarhelicopters.com/craigdyer.html
(Helicopter Pilot)

Cliff Fleming (714) 751-3515
(714) 997-0469
FAX (714) 751-4705
www.moviepilots.com

Hartley Folstad (909) 597-8511
(Fixed Wing Pilot) FAX (909) 597-8511
www.silverwingswingwalking.com

Ⓐ **David Gene Gibbs** (661) 254-6451
(818) 321-2689
FAX (661) 254-3940

Guardian Helicopters, Inc. (818) 442-9904
16425 Hart St. FAX (818) 442-9901
Van Nuys, CA 91406 www.guardianhelicoptersusa.com
(Helicopter Pilot)

Piergiorgio Gusso/TwinAir (818) 988-7573
7552 Hayvenhurst Pl. FAX (818) 988-7578
Van Nuys, CA 91406 www.twinair.net

Desiree Horton (818) 879-3636
(Helicopter Pilot) FAX (818) 701-4040

Craig Hosking (661) 251-5151
FAX (661) 251-5140

Evan Jensen/Hangar 1 Productions (213) 483-6898
1910 W. Sunset Blvd., Ste. 900 FAX (213) 483-4185
Los Angeles, CA 90026 www.hangar1project.com
(Helicopter Pilot)

Esteban Jimenez (323) 500-8336
(818) 988-7573
7552 Hayvenhurst Pl. www.copterpilot.com
Van Nuys, CA 91406
(Gyroplane Pilot & Helicopter Pilot)

Peter J. McKernan Jr. (310) 458-9176
(310) 993-4486
FAX (310) 393-4227

Peter J. McKernan Sr. (310) 993-4486
(310) 458-9176
FAX (310) 939-4227
www.helicopterguy.com

John Ward Nielsen (323) 939-9540
(323) 939-7719
(Helicopter Pilot) FAX (323) 939-7775

Fred North (310) 486-0415
(310) 822-7940
649 Palms Blvd. FAX (310) 305-9188
Venice, CA 90291 www.fred-north.com

Robin Petgrave (310) 938-2727
(877) 999-2099
(Helicopter Pilot) FAX (310) 898-1220
www.celebheli.com

Alan D. Purwin (818) 902-0229
(800) 221-8389
FAX (818) 902-9278
www.helinet.com

Dan Rudert (310) 993-2380
(661) 250-8150
(Helicopter Pilot) FAX (661) 250-8587
www.moviepilots.com

John D. Sarviss (661) 270-0565
(818) 980-2123
39120 Bouquet Canyon Rd. www.radicalcameracars.com
Leona Valley, CA 93551

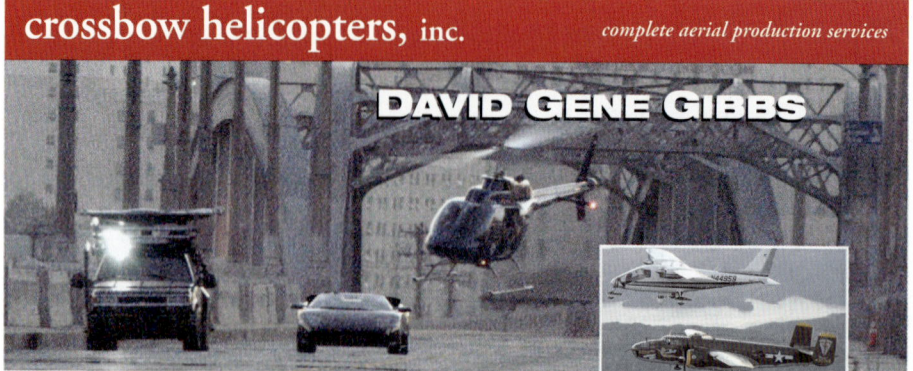

Ivor Shier/Corporate Helicopters (858) 505-5650
(800) 345-6737
(Helicopter Pilot) FAX (858) 505-5658
www.corporatehelicopters.com

Rick Shuster (805) 231-1006
(805) 493-5044
(Aerial Coordinator & Helicopter Pilot) FAX (805) 493-0530
www.moviepilots.com

Glenn J. Smith (800) 210-7800
(562) 997-0224
(Helicopter Pilot) FAX (562) 997-0324
www.airliftconstruction.com

Steve Stafford/Studio Wings (805) 320-9500
855 Aviation Dr. FAX (805) 987-4720
Camarillo, CA 93010 www.studiowings.com

Lance Strumpf (818) 402-1775
(818) 994-1445
16303 Waterman Dr. FAX (818) 994-1447
Van Nuys, CA 91406 www.toflyla.com

Chuck Tamburro (818) 881-6408
(818) 489-0256
(Helicopter Pilot) FAX (818) 881-6462

John Tamburro (818) 896-2700
(661) 713-6671
(Helicopter Pilot) FAX (818) 896-2771
www.blackstarhelicopters.com

Greg Vernon/Hangar 1 Productions (213) 483-6898
1910 W. Sunset Blvd., Ste. 900 FAX (213) 483-4185
Los Angeles, CA 90026 www.hangar1project.com

Action Trax/Dan Wynands (818) 980-2123 (818) 903-3314
2879 Irongate Pl. FAX **(805) 241-1137**
Thousand Oaks, CA 91362 **www.camerabikes.tv**
(ATVs, High Speed Camera Motorcycles, Off-Road Camera Vehicles, Side Platform Camera Bikes & Solo Camera Bikes)

Adventure Equipment/Ultimate Arm (818) 618-9988
5506 Colodny Dr. FAX **(805) 375-2211**
Agoura Hills, CA 91301 **www.ultimatearm.com**

Allan Padelford Camera Cars (661) 268-1330
www.apcamcars.com
(360° Roof Mounted Motorized Crane Arm, Hi-Speed Camera Cars with 3 Axis Remote Heads, Maverick Insert Bike, Process Trailers & Technocranes)

Burbank Kawasaki (818) 848-6627 (818) 749-5676
1329 N. Hollywood Way FAX **(818) 848-6630**
Burbank, CA 91505 **www.burbankkawasaki.com**
(ATVs, Jet Skis & Motorcycles)

Camera Cars Unlimited, Inc. (818) 889-9903
5331 Derry Ave., Ste. A FAX **(818) 889-4970**
Agoura Hills, CA 91301 **www.cameracarsunlimited.com**
(Crane Ready Camera Car, Off-Road and Standard Camera Cars, Process Trailers & Tow Dollies)

Camera Craft (714) 330-9900 (714) 964-6920
(Camera Boats) **www.cameracraftonline.com**

Carpenter Camera Cars **(818) 362-3261**
13681 Fenton Ave. FAX **(818) 367-3241**
Sylmar, CA 91342 **www.cameracars.com**
(2-Axle Insert Cars, 3-Axle Insert Cars, Air-Ride Process Trailers, ATVs, Chase Cars, High Speed Camera Cars, Mini High Speed Camera Cars, Process Trailers/Trucks & Tow Dollies)

Chapman/
Leonard Studio Equipment, Inc. **(818) 764-6726** **(888) 883-6559**
12950 Raymer St. FAX **(888) 502-7263**
North Hollywood, CA 91605 **www.chapman-leonard.com**
(Apollo Trailers, Camera Car Cranes & Tow Dollies)

Exotic Pursuits, Inc. **(818) 980-2123** **(818) 903-3314**
P.O. Box 46609 **www.exoticpursuits.com**
Los Angeles, CA 90046
(Chase Cars & High Speed Camera Cars)

Filmotechnic International Corp. **(310) 215-3004**
7743 Densmore Ave. FAX **(323) 622-8740**
Van Nuys , CA 91406 **www.russianarm.com**
(High Speed Camera Cars & Off-Road Gyro-Stabilized Equipment)

Dean Goldsmith/
Camera Car Industries **(818) 998-4798**
12473 San Fernando Rd. FAX **(818) 833-5962**
Sylmar, CA 91342 **www.cameracarindustries.com**
(3 Axis Remote Camera Car Cranes)

Griptrix, Inc. (818) 982-2510
12767 Saticoy St. FAX (818) 982-8830
North Hollywood, CA 91605 www.griptrix.com
(Electric Camera Dolly)

Holladay Camera Bikes (805) 740-6018
(323) 462-2301
FAX (805) 735-7205
www.camerabikes.com
(Bikes, High Speed Camera Motorcycles, Platforms & Sidecars)

L.A. Motorsports (818) 222-6954
(877) 526-6867
(Hi-Speed) FAX (866) 294-3266
www.lamsports.com

A **Performance Filmworks, Inc.** (310) 721-4812
(800) 360-3562
3763 Barry Ave. FAX (310) 313-4875
Mar Vista, CA 90066 www.performancefilmworks.com
(5 Axis High Speed and Off-Road Gyro-Stabilized Equipment & Camera ATVs, Bikes and Solo)

Pursuit Systems Inc. (818) 579-7250
7255 Radford Ave. www.pursuitsystems.com
North Hollywood, CA 91605

Radical Camera Cars (661) 270-0565
(818) 980-2123
39120 Bouquet Canyon Rd. www.radicalcameracars.com
Leona Valley, CA 93551
(Camera Racing Go Carts, High Speed Camera Cars, Hovercrafts, Off-Road Camera Cars & Process Trucks)

Safari Technologies (866) 449-7447
(818) 585-6653
FAX (805) 830-1158
www.safaritechnologies.net

Shelly Ward Enterprises (818) 255-5850
7255 Radford Ave. FAX (818) 255-5450
North Hollywood, CA 91605 www.shellywardent.com

Shotmaker Camera Cars & Cranes (818) 623-1700
(877) 708-7708
10909 Vanowen St. FAX (818) 623-1710
North Hollywood, CA 91605 www.shotmaker.com
(Air-Ride Process Trailers, Camera Car Cranes, Crane Ready Camera Cars, Process Trailers/Trucks, Remote Cranes & Tow Dollies)

Snowblind Snowmobiles (213) 247-4777
11429 Hayvenhurst Ave. www.mtnx.com
Granada Hills, CA 91344
(Camera Sleds & Snowmobiles)

Specialty Camera Cars (818) 364-2600
17116 Goya St. FAX (818) 364-2622
Granada Hills, CA 91344 www.specialtycameracars.com
(2 and 3 Axle Insert Cars, High Speed Camera Cars, Process Trailers, Remote Crane & Tow Dollies)

Vehicle Effects (818) 355-2676
(818) 846-7506
FAX (818) 846-7576
www.vehicleeffects.com
(High Performance and High Speed Off-Road Camera Cars & Process Trailers)

A

Abel Cine Tech, Inc. (818) 972-9078 / (888) 700-4416
801 S. Main St., Ste. A FAX (818) 972-2673
Burbank, CA 91506 www.abelcine.com
16mm: Aaton, Super 16mm & Xterà
16mm Arri: Aaton
Heads: Cartoni, O'Connor & Sachtler
High Def: 1080i, 24P, 65mm, 720P, Mini DVs, Multi-Camera Systems, Panasonic, Phantom High-Speed and PS Technik Adaptors, Sony & Ultraprimes
Lenses: Angenieux, Animorphic, Canon, Century, Cooke, Elite, Fujinon, Telephoto, Variable, Zeiss & Zooms
Video: Digital, JVC, Panasonic & Sony
Other: Multi-Camera Systems, Splash Housing & Splashbags
Accessories: CamTram System, Digital Micro Force Zoom Control, Filters, Heads, Jibs, MovieTube Lens Adapter, Remote Heads, Underwater Housings & Visual FX Camera Systems

Aerocrane Rentals LLC (818) 252-7700
9824 Glen Oaks Blvd. FAX (818) 252-7709
Sun Valley, CA 91352 www.aerocranerentals.com
Accessories: High-Speed Vistavision, Motion Control Rigs & Visual FX Camera Systems

Alan Gordon Enterprises, Inc. (323) 466-3561
5625 Melrose Ave. FAX (323) 871-2193
Los Angeles, CA 90038 www.alangordon.com
16mm: Bell/Howell, Bolex, Canon Scoopic, Eclair & G.S.A.P.
16mm Arri: 16-M, 16-S, 16BL, SR2, SR2HS, SR3 & Super16
35mm Arri: 2C, 35-3 & BL4S
Heads: Bogen, Cartoni, O'Connor & Sachtler Fluid Head
Lenses: Primes & Zooms
Video: Canon & Sony Digital Video Cameras and DV Steadicam
Other: Stop Motion & Video Assist Cameras

Atlantic Cine Equipment (818) 794-9410 / (410) 340-9674
1026 Griswold Ave. www.aceeast.com
San Fernando, CA 91340

Birns & Sawyer, Inc. (323) 466-8211 / (818) 766-2525
Camera & Sales Division FAX (323) 466-7049
6381 De Longpre Ave. www.birnsandsawyer.com
Hollywood, CA 90028
16mm: Aaton XTR-Prod & A-Minima
16mm Arri: SR2, SR2HS, SR3 & SR3HS
35mm: Aaton 35-3
35mm Arri: 35-3, 435, 535B, Arri 2C, BL-Evolution, BL4S & Moviecam Compact
Heads: Arri, Cartoni, Lambda Head, O'Connor, Ronford, Sachtler & Weaver-Steadman
High Def: Cooke S4s, Multi-Camera Systems, Panasonic and Sony Mini DVs, PS Technik Adaptors, SDX 900 & Ultra Primes

Camera Support (818) 557-1400 / (800) 995-5427
2827 N. San Fernando Blvd. FAX (818) 557-1323
Burbank, CA 91504 www.camerasupport.com
16mm: Aaton XTR Prod and Accessories
Accessories: Camera Pedestals, Jibs & Steadicam Systems
Heads: 2 and 3 Axis Remote Heads
High Def: 720P and 1080I Cameras & Accessories
Video: Digital Video Cameras & Accessories
Other: Multi-Camera Systems

Camtec Motion Picture Cameras (818) 841-8700
4221 W. Magnolia Blvd. FAX (818) 841-8777
Burbank, CA 91505 www.camtec.tv
16mm: Aaton A-Minima & Arri SR2, SR2HS, SR3 and SR3HS
35mm: Arri 235, 35-III, 435 and 535b, Arricam & Reflex Eyemo
High Def: Panasonic Varicam
Lenses: Arri Ultra, Cooke S4, Hawk 150-450, Hawk V Anamorphics, Innovision Probe 2 Plus, Optimo Zoom, Revolution & Variable Primes
Accessories: Arri Wireless Lens Control, Cartoni Lambda, Digital Hard Drive Combo Units, Preston FIZ & Video Directors Finder

Cinema Rentals, Inc. (661) 222-7342 / (877) 877-9605
25876 The Old Road, Ste. 174 FAX (661) 253-3643
Stevenson Ranch, CA 91381 www.cinemarentals.com
35mm: Stunt, Crash and Underwater Cameras
Video: Digital Underwater Video & Lipstick Cameras

Clairmont Camera (818) 761-4440
4343 Lankershim Blvd. FAX (818) 761-0861
North Hollywood, CA 91602 www.clairmont.com
16mm: Aaton A-Minima
16mm Arri: SR335mm: Aaton 35-3, Moviecam Compact and SuperLight, SuperAmerica & Wilcam VistaVision
35mm Arri: 35-3, 435, 535, BL3, BL4S, GT & ST
High Def: Panasonic 24F & Sony F900
Other: Power Pods & Strobes

CrashCam Industries (310) 990-3418
www.edgutentag.com
35mm: Reflexed Eyemo Crash Systems
35mm Arri: 2C and 35-3 Crash Systems
Accessories: Arri 235/Preston FIZ Units

Dalsa (818) 884-7000
6160 Variel Ave. FAX (818) 884-7022
Woodland Hills, CA 91367 www.dalsa.com/dc
Heads: Arri, O'Connor & Weaver-Steadman
High Def: 24P, Panasonic, PS Technik Adaptors & Sony
Lenses: Angenieux, Animorphic, Arri Master Series and Ultra, Cooke & Optimo Zoom
Accessories: C-Motion & Sliders

Digital Wings (323) 851-3825 / (202) 438-9199
3480 Barham Blvd., Ste. 322 FAX (323) 851-0470
Los Angeles, CA 90068 www.digitalwings.com
16mm: Arri SR3 & Nizo 801 Macro
Heads: Mini-Worrell & Sachtler
Lenses: Zeiss
Video: Panasonic AJ-200, AJ-215 & DVX-100

DIMENSION 3 (818) 592-0999
5240 Medina Rd.
Woodland Hills, CA 91364
Accessories: 3D Stereoscopic Camera/Lens Systems for Arriflex, Panavision and Video Cameras

Doggicam, Inc. (818) 845-8470
1500 W. Verdugo Ave. FAX (818) 845-8477
Burbank, CA 91506 www.doggicam.com
16mm: Doggicam
35mm: Doggicam
Other: Body-Mount, Bulldog Wireless Remote Head, Doggimount, Lightweight Remote Sparrow Head, Power Slide, Remote Follow Focus, Rhino Clamps & Super Slide

Geo Film Group, Inc. (818) 376-6680 / (877) 436-3456
7625 Hayvenhurst Ave., Ste. 46 FAX (818) 376-6686
Van Nuys, CA 91406 www.geofilm.com
35mm: Body Mount, Helmet, ManCam, Mini Vistavision & Pogo
35mm Arri: 235, 2C, 35-3 & 435-ESO
Other: Arri 2C Crash Housing, Eyemo Crash Systems & POV Camera

Geronimo Creek Film Company (323) 997-0202
P.O. Box 6006 FAX (323) 417-4915
Burbank, CA 91510 www.geronimocreek.com
16mm: Arri SR2.9 Super 16mm
Heads: Ronford Support
Lenses: Zeiss MK2 Super Speed Primes & Canon 8-64
T2.4Video: CEI 5 Flicker Free Color Video Assist & Sony 8"
Portable Monitor w/ Playback System
Accessories: ARRI AKS

Gyron Aerial Systems (626) 584-8722
39 E. Walnut St. FAX (626) 584-4069
Pasadena, CA 91103 www.gyron.com
Arri: Gyron Camera System
High Def: Gyron Camera System

Hill Digital (818) 445-9211
9714 La Canada Way www.hilldigital.com
Sunland, CA 91040
35mm: Moviecam Compact
Other: Ultra Hi-Speed Cameras (6-2500 FPS)
Video: 24 Frame & Video Assist

Hollywood Camera, Inc. (818) 972-5000
(818) 720-8404
3100 N. Damon Way FAX (818) 972-5010
Burbank, CA 91505 www.hollywoodcamera.com
16mm: Aaton XTR-Prod & A-Minima
16mm Arri: SR2, SR2HS, SR3 & SR3HS
35mm: Fries High Speed Reflex Visual Effects
Camera Packages
35mm Arri: 2C, 35-3, BL-4, BL4S, 435 Advanced, 535B &
Moviecam Compact
Heads: Arri, Cartoni, Lambda Head, O'Connor, Ronford,
Sachtler and Weaver-Steadman Remote Heads
High Def: Panasonic 720p VariCam, PS Technik Adaptors, SDX
900, Sony F900 & Mini DVs
Lenses: Cooke S4s, Zeiss Standard and Superspeeds & Zeiss
Ultra Primes

HydroFlex Underwater Camera & Lighting Systems (310) 301-8187
301 E. El Segundo Blvd. FAX (310) 821-9886
El Segundo, CA 90245 www.hydroflex.com
16mm: Aaton and Arri SR Underwater Housings
35mm Arri: 35-3, 435 Pan-Arri Surf & Shallow and Deep Water
Housings and Accessories
65mm: IMAX, Iwerks 3D & Panavision Underwater Housings
High Def: HD Housings & Splashbags
Heads: HydroHead 2 and 3 Axis Waterproof Remote Heads
Video: Sony FX1 and Z1 & Mini DV Housings
Other: Light Meter Housing, Splashbags & Waterproof
Video Monitors

Ⓐ **Indie Rentals** (323) 465-7700
(323) 571-9476
7022 W. Sunset Blvd. FAX (323) 297-2773
Hollywood, CA 90028 www.indierentals.com

Infinite Siege (323) 578-4440

Innovision Optics (310) 453-4866
1719 21st St. FAX (310) 453-4677
Santa Monica, CA 90404 www.innovisionoptics.com
Lenses: Boroscope Lenses & Probe Lens System
Video: RadCam Miniature Camera Car
Other: 3-Axis Remote Head Cams, Portable Table Top Motion
Control Systems & Rollvision Wireless

Keslow Camera (310) 636-4600
11260 Playa Court FAX (310) 915-5335
Culver City, CA 90230 www.keslowcamera.com
16mm Arri: SR3 & SR3HS
35mm Arri: 435ES, 535B, Arricam Studio and Lite & Moviecam
Compact and SL
High Def: RED Cameras
Lenses: Angenieux, Canon, Cooke, Leica Telephoto,
Revolution & Zeiss

Libertypak (323) 258-5336
(888) 303-6539
5387 Vincent Ave. www.libertypak.com
Los Angeles, CA 90041
Other: Lithium Ion Battery Belts

Millisecond Cinematography (323) 395-0507
(212) 937-3468
Other: Millisecond FAX (323) 395-0507
www.mscine.com

Motion Picture Marine (310) 822-1100
616 Venice Blvd. FAX (310) 822-2679
Marina del Rey, CA 90291 www.motionpicturemarine.com
Heads: Perfect Horizon Camera Stabilization Head

Moviola/Moviola Cameras (323) 467-3107
(800) 327-3724
1135 N. Mansfield Ave. FAX (323) 464-1518
Los Angeles, CA 90038 www.moviola.com

Nebtek (818) 782-5466
11152 Fleetwood St., Ste. 3 FAX (801) 467-0307
Van Nuys, CA 91406 www.nebtek.com
Heads: Power Pod

Nettmann Systems International (818) 623-1661
6910 Tujunga Ave. FAX (818) 623-1671
North Hollywood, CA 91605 www.camerasystems.com
Heads: Gyro-Stabilized, Gyron FS, Mini-Mote & Stab-C

New Deal Studios, Inc. (310) 578-9929
4105 Redwood Ave. FAX (310) 578-7370
Los Angeles, CA 90066 www.newdealstudios.com
35mm: Fries/Mitchell
65mm: Fries/Mitchell
Other: Motion Control Systems & Video Assist

Old School Cameras (310) 710-6525
(323) 462-0914
920 N. Citrus Ave. FAX (323) 462-5935
Hollywood, CA 90038 www.oldschoolcameras.com
16mm: Arri SR3 HS, Bolex, Éclair & Super16
35mm: Arri 35-2C, Arri 435, Eyemo Reflex Crash
Cameras & Moviecam
Heads: O'Connor & Sachtler
High Def: 4K & RED Cameras
Lenses: Slant-Focus, Zeiss & Zooms
Super 8mm: Beaulieu, Canon & Crystal SyncVideo: Panasonic
Accessories: Sliders, Steadicam Systems &
Underwater Housings

Ⓐ **Oppenheimer Cine Rental** (310) 286-2104
(877) 467-8666
16mm: Aaton XTR-Prod & XTR+ FAX (206) 467-9165
16mm Arri: SR2, SR2HS & SR3 www.oppcam.com
35mm: Aaton 35-3 & Moviecam Compact and SuperLight
35mm Arri: 2C, 35-3, 435, BL3 & BL4
Heads: 3 Axis Remote Heads, Mako, Power Pod Remote Head,
Weaver-Steadman & Wireless
High Def: 1080i, 4K & 720P
Lenses: Cooke S4, Oppenheimer Camera,
Optimo Zoom & Zeiss
Accessories: Boat Mounts, Helicopter Mounts, Jibs, Splash
Housing, Steadicam Systems & Underwater Housings
Other: Tyler Helicopter Mounts

Otto Nemenz International, Inc. (323) 469-2774
870 Vine St. FAX (323) 469-1217
Hollywood, CA 90038 www.ottonemenz.com
16mm Arri: SR3 & SR3HS
35mm: Arricam 235, LT and ST, Eyemo, Moviecam Compact
Mark2 & Moviecam Compact SL
35mm Arri: 2C, 35-3, 3C, 435, 535, 535B, BL3, BL4 & BL4S
Heads: 3 Axis Nodal Head, Arri Gearhead II & Power Pod
Remote Head
Lenses: 17-80 T2.3 Angeneiux, 24-290mm T2.8, Angenieux
Optimo, Cooke S4 Primes & Zeiss Ultra and Variable Primes
Other: Color Video

Pace Technologies (818) 565-0005
2117 Empire Ave. FAX (818) 565-0006
Burbank, CA 91504 www.pacehd.com
Accessories: Underwater and Wet Environment Camera Systems

Pacific Motion Control, Inc. (818) 768-1573
(661) 644-1516
9812 Glenoaks Blvd. FAX (818) 768-1575
Sun Valley, CA 91352 www.pacificmotion.net
Heads: Motion Control Frame Accurate Sorensen Heads (2 or
3 Axis), Remote/Repeatable Aerohead (2 or 3 Axis), Remote/
Repeatable Talon & Sorensen Mini Head (2 or 3 Axis)
Accessories: Camera Sync Systems, Lynx C-50 Motion Control
Camera Motor, Motion Control Systems, Preston System
(Optional Kuper Interface) Remote Heads &
Time-Lapse Controller

Panavision (818) 316-1000
Corporate Headquarters FAX **(818) 316-1111**
6219 DeSoto Ave. **www.panavision.com**
Woodland Hills, CA 91367
35mm: Millennium XL, Panaflex, Panaflex G, Panaflex G2 & Panaflex Platinum
35mm Arri: 435ES and III, Arri 435 & Arri 235
High Def: Genesis Camera System, Sony F-23, Panavision/ Sony F-900 & F-900R
Lenses: Anamorphic and Spherical, Angenieux Zooms, Close-Focus, Cooke Zooms, Frazier, High Def Primo Digital Zooms and Primes, Hylen Lens System, Optimo Zooms, Primo Series and Zooms, Slant-Focus & Zeiss
Other: 65mm Studio Handheld Lightweight Camera & Panavision Remote Cranes and Heads

Panavision Hollywood (323) 464-3800
6735 Selma Ave. FAX **(323) 469-5175**
Hollywood, CA 90028 **www.panavision.com**
16mm: Aaton XTR-Prod & Panaflex 16
16mm Arri: SR2 Hi-Speed, SR3 & SR3 Hi-Speed
35mm: Aaton 35 III, Gold and Gold II, Millennium, Millennium XL, Mitchell Mark II, Pan-Arri IIC, Pan-Arri III, Pan-Arri IIIC, Pan-Arri 435ES, Panastar I, Panastar II, Panavision Lightweight II & Platinum
High Def: Panavision
Lenses: Anamorphic and Spherical, Angenieux, Baltar, Close-Focus, Frazier, Innovision Probe II, Kowa, Periscope, Portrait, Primo Series, Slant-Focus, Swing and Tilts & Zeiss

Photo-Plus (818) 766-6868
(800) 759-5722
4141 Elmer Ave. **www.ronvidor.com**
Studio City, CA 91602
Other: GPI Steadicam Pro System

Photo-Sonics, Inc. (818) 531-3240
820 S. Mariposa St. FAX **(818) 531-3258**
Burbank, CA 91506 **www.photosonics.com**

Pictorvision Inc (818) 785-9282
(800) 876-5583
FAX **(818) 785-9787**
16mm: Super 16 **www.pictorvision.com**
Cameras: High Def & SD
Accessories: 5 Axis Gyro-Stabilized Camera Systems, Cineflex, Pictorvision Eclipse, Wescam & XR

Preston Cinema Systems (310) 453-1852
1659 11th St., Ste. 100 FAX **(310) 453-5672**
Santa Monica, CA 90404 **www.prestoncinema.com**
Accessories: Digital Lens Control, Digital Micro Force Zoom Control & FI+Z and Light Ranger Auto Focus Systems

Pro8mm (818) 848-5522
2805 W. Magnolia Blvd. FAX **(818) 848-5956**
Burbank, CA 91505 **www.pro8mm.com**
Super 8mm: Beaulieu, Canon, Crystal Sync & Nizo

Rocky Mountain Motion Pictures (323) 461-9900
(435) 649-1030
937 N. Citrus Ave. FAX **(323) 461-0100**
Los Angeles, CA 90038 **www.rmmp.com**
16mm Arri: SR2 & SR3
35mm: Moviecam Compact and SL
35mm Arri: 35-3, 435, 435ES & Eyemo Crash Cameras
Heads: Arri Gearhead 2, O'Connor, Ronford, Sachtler & Weaver Steadman
Lenses: Angenieux, Cooke, Cooke S-4 Primes, Lo-Angle Prism, Periscope, Revolution Lens & Zeiss

The Slider (805) 496-5289
(818) 344-5284
FAX **(805) 496-4802**
www.theslider.com
Accessories: 32" Video and Mitchell Mount Minisliders & 3', 4', 6', 8' Manual and Motorized Sliders

Slow Motion, Inc. (818) 982-4400
7211 Clybourn Ave.
Sun Valley, CA 91352

SpaceCam Systems, Inc (818) 889-6060
31111 Via Colinas, Ste. 201 FAX **(818) 889-6062**
Westlake Village, CA 91362 **www.spacecam.com**
Accessories: Boat and Car Crane and Helicopter Gyro-Stabilized Camera Mounts

Speed Vision Technologies, Inc. (858) 356-0855
(858) 967-0401
4485 Sunset Bluffs Way FAX **(858) 356-0901**
San Diego, CA 92130 **www.speedvisiontech.com**
High Def: 720P
Lenses: Angenieux, Boroscope and Probe, Kowa, Telephoto, Variable Primes & Zooms
Video: Digital & High Def

Super 8 Film Cameras & 2nd Unit (310) 276-8196
(800) 470-4602
8630 Wilshire Blvd. **www.super8guy.com**
Beverly Hills, CA 90211
16mm: Bolex REX-4 & Canon Scoopic 16M
Heads: Bogen Camera Support & SteadyTracker
Lenses: Angenieux Zooms, Bolex Gel Filters, Kern Zooms & Switar 6, 10, 16, 25, 26 Macro, 50 and 75mm
Super16: Bolex SBM
Super 8mm: Beaulieu 4008 Pro, Canon 1014XL-S Crystal Sync & Nizo 801 Macro
Video: Panasonic Lumix GH1 HD 1080 24P Camera, 7-14, 14-140 & 45-200 LensAccessories: Super 8 Video Tap/Assist Packages

Swiss Crane (310) 235-1953
(800) 316-0067
11771 1/2 Pico Blvd. FAX **(310) 235-1131**
Los Angeles, CA 90064 **www.activeremote.com**
Heads: 3 Axis Remote, Power Pod 2000 & Power Pod Plus with Wireless Preston Follow Focus

TCH/The Camera House (818) 997-3802
7351 Fulton Ave. FAX **(818) 997-3885**
North Hollywood, CA 91605 **www.thecamerahouse.com**
16mm: Arri SR3
35mm: Arri 35-2C, 35-3, 435 ES, 535 B, SR3, Arricam Studio and Light & Moviecam SL and Compact
Heads: Arri, Cartoni, O'Connor, Ronford & Sachtler
Lenses: Cooke, Prime, Telephoto, Variable, Zeiss & Zoom

Tyler Camera Systems (818) 989-4420
(800) 390-6070
14218 Aetna St. FAX **(818) 989-0423**
Van Nuys, CA 91401 **www.tylermount.com**
Accessories: Gyro-Stabilized Helicopter Camera Mounts

Ultravision, Inc. (310) 829-9130
1815 24th St., Unit B FAX **(310) 829-9131**
Santa Monica, CA 90404 **www.ultravisioninc.com**
16mm Arri: SR2 & SR3
35mm: Compact and SuperAmerica, Eyemo Reflex Crash Cameras & Moviecam SL
35mm Arri: 35-3, BL3 & BL4

Video Assist Systems, Inc. (818) 606-8901
FAX **(818) 222-5862**
www.videoassistsystems.com
Accessories: Color Video Doors and Taps for Arriflex & Video Transmitters

Weekend Video & Company (323) 376-9191
High Def: Sony and Panasonic HD/1080i/23.98P

Wolfe Air Aviation Ltd. (626) 584-4060
39 E. Walnut St. FAX **(626) 584-4069**
Pasadena, CA 91103 **www.wolfeair.com**
Camera Systems: Vectorvision

Wolfe Air Aviation, Ltd. (626) 584-4060
39 E. Walnut St. FAX **(626) 584-4069**
Pasadena, CA 91103 **www.wolfeair.com**
Camera Systems: Vectorvision

Wooden Nickel Lighting Inc. (818) 761-9662
6920 Tujunga Ave. FAX **(818) 985-0717**
North Hollywood, CA 91605
www.woodennickellighting.com
16mm Arri: SR2
35mm: Mitchell Fries High Speed
35mm Arri: 3 & BL3
Lenses: Angenieux, Cooke & Zeiss

5th & Sunset Los Angeles (310) 979-0212
12322 Exposition Blvd. FAX (310) 979-0214
Los Angeles, CA 90064 www.5thandsunsetla.com

A B Sea Photo (310) 645-8992
9136 S. Sepulveda Blvd. FAX (310) 645-3645
Los Angeles, CA 90045 www.absea.net/rentals
(Underwater Cameras and Equipment)

Ambient Digital, LLC (805) 415-4100
(323) 460-5199
6444 Santa Monica Blvd. www.ambientdsr.com
Los Angeles, CA 90038
(Computer Controlled Multiple Still Camera Systems, Imaging Supplies & Panoramic Photography)

Bel Air Camera Superstore (310) 208-5150
(800) 200-4999
10925 Kinross Ave. FAX (310) 208-7472
Los Angeles, CA 90024 www.belaircamera.com

Calumet Photographic, Inc. (323) 466-1238
1135 N. Highland Ave. FAX (323) 466-1906
Hollywood, CA 90038 www.calumetphoto.com

Capture Digital (323) 512-2046
1011 N. Fuller Ave., Ste. M FAX (323) 512-2035
Los Angeles, CA 90046 www.capturedigital.com

Elephant Eye Media, Inc./EEM (310) 399-5560
212 Marine St., Ste. 209 FAX (310) 399-5553
Santa Monica, CA 90405 www.elephanteyemedia.com

Pasadena Camera Rental, Inc. (626) 796-3300
41 E. Walnut St. FAX (626) 432-6731
Pasadena, CA 91103 www.samyscamera.com

Pix (323) 936-8488
211 S. La Brea Ave. FAX (323) 936-5209
Los Angeles, CA 90036 www.pixcamera.com

Reel EFX, Inc. (818) 762-1710
(213) 308-7289
5539 Riverton Ave. FAX (818) 762-1734
North Hollywood, CA 91601 www.reelefx.com
(Computer Controlled Multiple Still Camera System)

Samy's Camera (323) 938-2420
(800) 321-4726
431 S. Fairfax Ave. FAX (323) 937-2919
Los Angeles, CA 90036 www.samys.com

Samy's Camera (310) 450-4551
585 Venice Blvd. FAX (310) 450-8590
Venice, CA 90291 www.samys.com

Motion Control

Aerocrane Rentals LLC (818) 252-7700
9824 Glen Oaks Blvd. FAX (818) 252-7709
Sun Valley, CA 91352 www.aerocranerentals.com

Bazzar Effects (310) 600-1539
13810 Calfa St. FAX (818) 997-1929
Van Nuys, CA 91401 www.bazzareffects.com

Ⓐ **Camera Control, Inc.** (310) 581-8343
3317 Ocean Park Blvd. FAX (310) 581-8340
Santa Monica, CA 90405 www.cameracontrol.com

Fisher Technical Services Rentals (702) 251-0700
(866) 942-4098
FAX (702) 251-0400
www.fishertechnical.com

General Lift, LLC (310) 414-0717
209 E. El Segundo Blvd. FAX (310) 414-0705
El Segundo, CA 90245 www.general-lift.com

Image G/Ikonographics (818) 761-6644
10900 Ventura Blvd. www.imageg.com
Studio City, CA 91604

Innovision Optics (310) 453-4866
1719 21st St. FAX (310) 453-4677
Santa Monica, CA 90404 www.innovisionoptics.com

New Deal Studios, Inc. (310) 578-9929
4105 Redwood Ave. FAX (310) 578-7370
Los Angeles, CA 90066 www.newdealstudios.com

Ⓐ **Pacific Motion Control, Inc.** (818) 768-1573
9812 Glenoaks Blvd. FAX (818) 768-1575
Sun Valley, CA 91352 www.pacificmotion.net
Cranes: Motion Control/Repeatable Cranes: Gazelle (Portable 6' Arm), Graphlite (Portable 10' or 13' Arm), Telescoping Cranes: Super Scorpio Technocrane (30' or 37' Arm)
Dollies: Motion Control/Repeatable Zebra (Portable 2' or 6' Arm) & The Bogie
Accessories: CGI Rig Interface Models, Frame Accurate Motion Control Heads, Kuper Motion Control Systems, Model Movers, Motion Control Lighting Cues, Motion Control Track (Straight or 360° Curved), Motor Driver Systems, Preston System with Kuper Interface, Remote/Repeatable Heads (Aerohead & Talon) & Turn Tables

Absolute Sound (818) 244-4799
(818) 399-3419
FAX (818) 244-0884

Jack Bornoff (818) 905-0356

Cunningham Sound (818) 424-6611

Ⓐ **Cutting Edge Productions, Inc.** (310) 326-4500
(818) 503-0400
22904 Lockness Ave. FAX (310) 326-4715
Torrance, CA 90501 www.cuttingedgeproductions.tv

Delicate Productions, Inc. (805) 388-1800
874 Verdulera St. FAX (805) 388-1037
Camarillo, CA 93010 www.delicate.com

Director's Choice Sound (818) 766-9050
(323) 854-3236
6062 Shadyglade Ave. FAX (818) 766-9250
North Hollywood, CA 91606
www.directorschoicesound.com

Forté Sound/Margaret Nathans (213) 304-1605
(323) 478-0245
FAX (323) 478-0255

Gary Raymond Sound Systems (805) 492-5858
P.O. Box 1722
Thousand Oaks, CA 91358

Impact Audio (800) 323-0490
(213) 494-9492
FAX (800) 323-0490

Christopher Lennon (323) 459-6997
FAX (818) 766-9250

Napalm Sound (213) 923-0200
www.napalmsound.com

Planet 00:00:03 Sound Co./Tim Hays (818) 789-8799
(877) 737-6863
12400 Ventura Blvd., Ste. 500 FAX (818) 789-8329
Studio City, CA 91604 www.planet3soundco.com

Pro-Tools Playback (310) 863-5092
(805) 732-7946
2006 Graham Ave., Ste. A www.protoolsplayback.com
Redondo Beach, CA 90278

Production Sound Services/ Jim Machowski (310) 266-7086
(303) 949-9090

Roll Sound, Inc./ Robert Dreebin & Alex Lamm (310) 629-2476
(818) 540-5979
19712 Mayall St. FAX (818) 772-2614
Chatsworth, CA 91311 www.rollsound.biz

Skyland Sound, Inc. (310) 390-3520

Wilcox Sound and Communications (818) 557-3377
4545 Chermak St. FAX (818) 557-3367
Burbank, CA 91505

Ametron Audio Video
(323) 466-4321
(323) 464-1144
1546 N. Argyle Ave.
FAX (323) 871-0127
Hollywood, CA 90028
www.ametron.com

Big Time Picture Company, Inc. (310) 207-0921
12210 1/2 Nebraska Ave. FAX (310) 826-0071
Los Angeles, CA 90025 www.bigtimepic.com

Comtel Pro Media (818) 450-1100
2201 N. Hollywood Way FAX (818) 450-1144
Burbank, CA 91505 www.comtelpromedia.com

Eastman Kodak
(323) 962-9053
(800) 621-3456
1017 N. Las Palmas Ave., Ste. 100 FAX (800) 648-9805
Hollywood, CA 90038 www.kodak.com/go/motion
(Film Only)

Edgewise Media Services, Inc.
(323) 769-0900
(800) 824-3130
1215 N. Highland Ave. FAX (323) 466-6815
Hollywood, CA 90038 www.edgewise-media.com

Edgewise Media Services, Inc.
(714) 919-2020
(800) 444-9330
917 E. Katella Ave. FAX (714) 919-2010
Anaheim, CA 92805 www.edgewise-media.com

EVS/Express Video Supply, Inc.
(818) 552-4590
(800) 238-8480
1620 Flower St. FAX (818) 552-4591
Glendale, CA 91201 www.evsonline.com
(New and Recycled Video Stock)

Film Emporium (323) 464-5144
Sunset Gower Studios FAX (323) 464-7348
1438 N. Gower St., Bldg. 35, Box 72
Hollywood, CA 90028 www.filmemporium.com

Film Source LA
(818) 484-3236
(866) 537-1114
FAX (818) 688-0101
www.filmsourcela.com

Fujifilm USA, Inc.
Motion Picture Divison (888) 424-3854
2220 W. Magnolia Blvd. FAX (323) 465-8279
Burbank, CA 91506 www.fujifilmusa.com
(Film Only)

Media Distributors
(818) 980-9916
(888) 889-3130
10960 Ventura Blvd. FAX (818) 980-9265
Studio City, CA 91604 www.mediadistributors.com

Moviola/Moviola Cameras
(323) 467-3107
(800) 468-3107
1135 N. Mansfield Ave. FAX (323) 464-1518
Hollywood, CA 90038 www.moviola.com
(Video Only)

MSE Media Solutions
(323) 721-1656
(800) 626-1955
6013 Scott Way FAX (323) 721-1506
Los Angeles, CA 90040 www.msemedia.com

Pro8mm (818) 848-5522
2805 W. Magnolia Blvd. FAX (818) 848-5956
Burbank, CA 91505 www.pro8mm.com
(Super 8 & Super 16)

ProMediaSupplies.com (336) 664-1004
(High Def Tape & New Video Stock) FAX (336) 605-3212
www.promediasupplies.com

Reel Good
(323) 876-5427
(213) 303-6886
7758 Sunset Blvd. FAX (323) 876-5428
Los Angeles, CA 90046
(Film Only)

Revolt Pro Media (818) 904-0001
7625 Hayvenhurst Ave., Ste. 32 FAX (818) 904-0005
Van Nuys, CA 91406 www.revoltpromedia.com
(High Def Tape & New Video Stock & Recycled Video Stock)

Spectra Film & Video (818) 762-4545
5626 Vineland Ave. FAX (818) 762-5454
North Hollywood, CA 91601
www.spectrafilmandvideo.com

SplitReel, Inc. (323) 528-1832

The Tape Company
(818) 566-9898
(800) 851-3113
2721 W. Magnolia Blvd. FAX (818) 566-8989
Burbank, CA 91505 www.thetapecompany.com

TapeStockOnline.com
(888) 322-8273
(310) 352-4230
2034 E. Lincoln Ave., Box 426 FAX (310) 352-4233
Anaheim, CA 92806 www.tapestockonline.com
(Video Only)

Videotape Products, Inc.
(818) 566-9898
(800) 422-2444
2721 W. Magnolia Blvd. FAX (818) 566-8989
Burbank, CA 91505 www.myvtp.com
(Video Only)

A West Coast Film Company, LLC (818) 980-6131
4804 Laurel Canyon Blvd., Ste. 547 FAX (818) 980-6181
North Hollywood, CA 91607

Westside Media Group
(310) 979-3500
(818) 779-8600
12233 W. Olympic Blvd., Ste. 152 FAX (310) 979-3503
West Los Angeles, CA 90064 www.wmgmedia.com
(High Def Tape & New Video Stock)

Absolute Rentals (818) 842-2828
2633 N. San Fernando Blvd. FAX **(818) 842-8815**
Burbank, CA 91504 **www.absoluterentals.com**

Action Audio & Visual (323) 461-4290 (888) 406-8164
10834 Burbank Blvd., Ste. A-100 FAX **(323) 461-4292**
North Hollywood, CA 91601
www.actionaudioandvisual.com
(Analog, Audio Props, DAT Recording Tape, Digital Multi-Track Portable Recorders, Expendables, Microphones, Mixing Boards, Playback Systems, Schoeps, Specialty Mics, Theatrical Sound Systems, Underwater Communications & Wireless Systems)

Advanced Audio Rental Inc. (818) 955-7100
733 N. Victory Blvd. FAX **(818) 955-7176**
Burbank, CA 91502 **www.advancedaudiorentals.com**

Alan Gordon Enterprises, Inc. (323) 466-3561
5625 Melrose Ave. FAX **(323) 871-2193**
Los Angeles, CA 90038 **www.alangordon.com**
(Analog & DAT Recording Tape)

All Electronics Corporation (818) 904-0524 (800) 826-5432
14928 Oxnard St. FAX **(818) 781-2653**
Van Nuys, CA 91411 **www.allelectronics.com**

Alliant Event Services, Inc. (909) 622-3306 (800) 851-5415
196 University Pkwy FAX **(909) 622-3917**
Pomona, CA 91768 **www.alliantevents.com**

Alternative Rentals (310) 204-3388
5805 W. Jefferson Blvd. FAX **(310) 204-3384**
Los Angeles, CA 90016 **www.alternativerentals.com**
(Schoeps, Specialty Mics, Wireless Systems & Zaxcom Digital Multi-Track Portable Recorders)

Ametron Audio Video (323) 466-4321 (323) 464-1144
1546 N. Argyle Ave. FAX **(323) 871-0127**
Hollywood, CA 90028 **www.ametron.com**

Angelcom Audio (562) 948-3154
FAX **(562) 948-5324**
www.angelcomaudio.com
(P.A. Systems, Playback Systems & Speakers)

Astro Audio Video Lighting, Inc. (818) 549-9915 (800) 427-8768
6615 San Fernando Rd. FAX **(818) 549-9921**
Glendale, CA 91201 **www.astroavl.com**

ATK Audiotek (661) 705-3700
28238 Avenue Crocker FAX **(661) 705-3707**
Valencia, CA 91355 **www.atkaudiotek.com**

Audio Applications (714) 508-1858
14791 Myford Rd. FAX **(714) 508-2362**
Tustin, CA 92780 **www.videoapps.com**
(Digital Audio Workstations, Microphones, Playback Systems, Speakers & Wireless Systems)

Audio Rents, Inc. (323) 874-1000
1541 N. Wilcox Ave. FAX **(323) 460-2676**
Los Angeles, CA 90028 **www.audiorents.com**
(Analog, Audio Props, Digital Audio, Digital Multi-Track, Microphones, Playback Systems, Players, Preamps, Speakers, Specialty Microphones, Theatrical Sound Systems, Vintage Gear & Wireless Systems)

Broadcast Store (818) 998-9100
9420 Lurline Ave., Ste. C FAX **(818) 998-9106**
Chatsworth, CA 91311 **www.broadcaststore.com**

CBS Studio Center (818) 655-6311
4024 Radford Ave. FAX **(818) 655-5819**
Studio City, CA 91604 **www.cbssc.com**

Ⓐ CineLUX Sound Services Inc. (818) 566-3000 / (888) 246-3589
3210 W. Burbank, Ste. A
Burbank, CA 91505
www.cinelux.tv

Coffey Sound & Communications, Inc. (323) 876-7525 / (888) 293-3030
3325 Cahuenga Blvd. West FAX (323) 876-4775
Hollywood, CA 90068 www.coffeysound.com

Ⓐ Cutting Edge Productions, Inc. (310) 326-4500 / (818) 503-0400
22904 Lockness Ave. FAX (310) 326-4715
Torrance, CA 90501 www.cuttingedgeproductions.tv
(Analog, Audio Props, DAT Recording Tape, DV, Expendables, Microphones, Playback Systems, Players, Preamps, Speakers, Specialty Microphones, Theatrical Sound Systems, Vintage Gear & Wireless Systems)

Darryl Linkow Film & Video Sound (818) 597-8855
5924 Chesebro Rd.
Agoura Hills, CA 91301
(Audio Props, DAT Recording Tape, Digital Multi-Track Portable Recorders, Microphones, Speakers & Wireless Systems)

Delicate Productions, Inc. (805) 388-1800
874 Verdulera St. FAX (805) 388-1037
Camarillo, CA 93010 www.delicate.com

DVCarney (310) 595-4562
www.dvcarney.com
(Analog, Digital Audio Workstations, Digital Multi-Track Portable Recorders, Microphones, Playback Systems, Preamps, Speakers & Specialty Microphones)

ELM, Ltd. (818) 508-5995
13659 Victory Blvd., Ste. 583 www.elmlimited.com
Van Nuys, CA 91401

Farr Out Productions, LLC (310) 902-5944
FAX (818) 830-3608
www.farroutpro.com
(Digital Multi-Track Portable Recorders, Microphones, Playback Systems, Speakers, Specialty Microphones & Wireless Systems)

Gary Raymond Sound Systems (805) 492-5858
P.O. Box 1722
Thousand Oaks, CA 91358

HydroFlex Underwater Camera & Lighting Systems (310) 301-8187
301 E. El Segundo Blvd. FAX (310) 821-9886
El Segundo, CA 90245 www.hydroflex.com
(Underwater Communications and Speakers)

I.M. Sound (928) 282-2043 / (323) 314-0948
351 N. Laurel Ave. www.ikemagal.com
Los Angeles, CA 90048

J.L. Fisher, Inc. (818) 846-8366
1000 W. Isabel St. FAX (818) 846-8699
Burbank, CA 91506 www.jlfisher.com

Lex Products Corp. (818) 768-4474
11847 Sheldon St. FAX (818) 768-4040
Sun Valley, CA 91352 www.lexproducts.com
(Power Distribution Systems and Cables for Sound Equipment)

Location Sound Corporation (818) 980-9891 / (800) 228-4429
10639 Riverside Dr. FAX (818) 980-9911
North Hollywood, CA 91602 www.locationsound.com
(DAT Recording Tape, Digital Multi-Track Portable Recorders, Expendables, Microphones, Playback Systems, Players, Preamps, Speakers, Specialty Microphones, Walkies & Wireless Systems)

McNulty Nielsen, Inc. (310) 704-1713
6930 1/2 Tujunga Ave. FAX (323) 372-3768
North Hollywood, CA 91605 www.mcnultynielsen.com
(Analog, Audio Props, Digital Multi-Track Portable Recorders, DV, Expendables, Microphones, Playback Systems, Players, Preamps, Speakers, Theatrical Sound Systems & Wireless Systems)

Nelson Sound, Inc. (818) 545-8451 / (800) 487-0787
345 Mira Loma Ave. FAX (818) 545-8467
Glendale, CA 91204 www.nelsonsound.com

Pace Technologies (818) 565-0005
2117 Empire Ave. FAX (818) 565-0006
Burbank, CA 91504 www.pacehd.com
(Underwater Communications)

Planet 00:00:03 Sound Co./ Tim Hays (818) 789-8799 / (877) 737-6863
12400 Ventura Blvd., Ste. 500 FAX (818) 789-8329
Studio City, CA 91604 www.planet3soundco.com

Productionsound (818) 842-8662 / (818) 295-8662
FAX (818) 842-8662

Silver Pixel Productions (818) 415-9572
FAX (805) 531-0079
www.silverpixelproductions.com

SSR Sound System Rentals (323) 839-7705
www.ssrrentals.com
(Audio Props, Microphones, Speakers & Wireless Systems)

Studio On Wheels (818) 419-0323
(Mobile Recording Facilities) FAX (562) 698-3513
www.recordingtruck.com

Towards 2000, Inc. (818) 557-0903
215 W. Palm Ave., Ste. 204 FAX (818) 557-0596
Burbank, CA 91502 www.t2k.com

Warner Bros. Studio Facilities - Production Sound & Video (818) 954-2511
4000 Warner Blvd., Bldg. 28 FAX (818) 954-2491
Burbank, CA 91522 www.wbsf.com

Wexler Video (818) 846-9381 / (800) 939-5371
1111 S. Victory Blvd. FAX (818) 846-9399
Burbank, CA 91502 www.wexlervideo.com

Wilcox Sound and Communications (818) 557-3377
4545 Chermak St. FAX (818) 557-3367
Burbank, CA 91505

World of Video & Audio (310) 659-5959 / (866) 900-3827
8717 Wilshire Blvd. FAX (310) 659-8247
Beverly Hills, CA 90211 www.wova.com
(DAT Recording Tape, DV, Microphones, Players, Playback Systems, Preamps, Speakers, Specialty Mics & Wireless Systems)

Greenberg Teleprompting
L.A.'s #1 Choice for Prompting
25 Years In Show Business
Studio / Broadcast
Nationwide Prompting Services
Corporate / Live Events
PowerPoint Notes Pages
Bi-Lingual Operators
L.A. Office
818.838.4437 • Fax 818.838.0447
Orange County
714.288.8553 • Fax 714.288.8901
www.greenprompt.com • email: scripts@greenprompt.com

Teleprompting & Cue Card Services

Ⓐ AcuPrompt Teleprompting Services (818) 576-1291
(866) 576-1291
19145 Parthenia St., Ste. A FAX (818) 576-9981
Northridge, CA 91324 www.acuprompt.com

Christopher Augustine (323) 572-0800
(323) 806-8070

Ⓐ Bev Feldman's StarPrompt (818) 790-7418
FAX (818) 790-6521
www.starprompt.tv

State-of-the-art equipment.
State-of-the-industry service.

CUE TECH
TELEPROMPTING
www.cue-tech.com

Contact Pamela Kutsunai at
818-487-2700

Fax: 818-487-2750 · Email: info@cue-tech.com
5527 Satsuma Avenue
North Hollywood, California 91601

Award Shows Commercials Film & Video
Live Speeches Award Shows Commercials
Film & Video Live Speeches Award Shows
Commercials Film & Video Live Speeches
Award Shows Commercials Film & Video
Live Speeches Award Shows Commercials
Film & Video Live Speeches Award Shows
Commercials Film & Video Live Speeches
Award Shows Commercials Film & Video
Live Speeches Award Shows Commercials
Film & Video Live Speeches Award Shows
Commercials Film & Video Live Speeches
Award Shows Commercials Film & Video
Live Speeches Award Shows Commercials
Film & Video Live Speeches Award Shows
Commercials Film & Video Live Speeches
Award Shows Commercials Film & Video
Live Speeches Award Shows Commercials
Film & Video Live Speeches Award Shows
Commercials Film & Video Live Speeches
Award Shows Commercials Film & Video
Live Speeches Award Shows Commercials
Film & Video Live Speeches Award Shows
Commercials Film & Video Live Speeches
Award Shows Commercials Film & Video
Live Speeches Award Shows Commercials
Film & Video Live Speeches Award Shows
Commercials Film & Video Live Speeches
Award Shows Commercials Film & Video
Live Speeches Award Shows Commercials
Film & Video Live Speeches Award Shows
Commercials Film & Video Live Speeches
Award Shows Commercials Film & Video
Live Speeches Award Shows Commercials
Film & Video Live Speeches Award Shows
Commercials Film & Video Live Speeches
Award Shows Commercials Film & Video
Live Speeches Award Shows Commercials

California Teleprompter (858) 945-2076
P.O. Box 13024 FAX (858) 945-2076
La Jolla, CA 92039 www.calteleprompter.com

Crystal Pyramid Productions (619) 644-3000
(800) 365-8433
7323 Rondel Court FAX (619) 644-3001
San Diego, CA 92119 www.crystalpyramid.com

Ⓐ **Cue Tech Teleprompting** (818) 487-2700
5527 Satsuma Ave. FAX (818) 487-2750
North Hollywood, CA 91601 www.cue-tech.com

Ⓐ **Greenberg Teleprompting** (818) 838-4437
(714) 288-8553
FAX (818) 838-0447
www.greenprompt.com

Ⓐ **iPromptLA** (310) 837-0389
1220 24th St., Ste. 6 FAX (310) 837-0806
Santa Monica, CA 90404 www.ipromptla.com

Mary Stec's Channel Cue Cards (818) 991-8224
(818) 606-7895
(Cue Cards) FAX (818) 991-8839

McNulty Nielsen, Inc. (310) 704-1713
(310) 704-1997
6930 1/2 Tujunga Ave. FAX (323) 372-3768
North Hollywood, CA 91601 www.mcnultynielsen.com

On Air Prompting (818) 406-2582
140 E. Tujunga Ave. www.onairprompting.com
Burbank, CA 91502

A PC Prompting Systems (818) 831-6554
18320 Ankara Court FAX (818) 831-6574
Northridge, CA 91326 www.pcprompting.com

Prompt Response (888) 776-6787
13700 S. Broadway FAX (949) 218-8105
Los Angeles, CA 90061 www.promptresponse.tv

Prompt Response (949) 218-8103
(888) 776-6787
34812 Doheny Pl. FAX (949) 218-8105
Capistrano Beach, CA 92624 www.promptresponse.tv

A ProPrompt, Inc./Compu=Prompt (323) 465-9441
5723 Melrose Ave., Ste. 204 FAX (323) 465-3587
Los Angeles, CA 90038 www.proprompt.com

Q Systems Teleprompting (858) 538-9300
(800) 538-9301
FAX (561) 828-2747
www.qsystemswest.com

Tele-Cue (858) 272-7022
(858) 735-7913
4458 Caminito Cuarzo FAX (858) 272-7023
San Diego, CA 92117 www.telecueteleprompting.com

Vivi-Q Teleprompting Services, Inc. (818) 236-2177
2355 Honolulu Ave., Ste. 201 FAX (818) 236-2846
Montrose, CA 91020 www.vivi-q.com

Video Assist Services

Rob Abbey (310) 991-0884
(310) 589-5838

Peter Albert/On-Set Digital, Inc. (562) 633-2333
(800) 495-7328
8741 Rose St.
Bellflower, CA 90706
(Digital)

Leonardo Arterberry III (323) 466-7232
(Digital) www.videorama.com

AVS (818) 954-8842
712 S. Main St. FAX (818) 954-9122
Burbank, CA 91506 www.aerialvideo.com

Awesome Playback/Bob Lund (310) 391-0550
(310) 365-2305
(Digital & Tape-Based)

Christopher Blakely (323) 466-6660
(213) 509-7798
(Digital & Tape-Based) FAX (310) 399-9227

BlueScreen, LLC/Bob Kertesz (323) 467-7572
(Digital) www.bluescreen.com

Kevin Boyd/K.P.B Digital For Film (323) 350-3446
(Digital) www.kpbdigitalforfilm.com

Jeff Burrage/Digital Split (310) 791-7278
(310) 614-3920
FAX (310) 378-7299

Bob Chambers (805) 777-1779
(818) 486-7707
(Digital) FAX (805) 777-1799

Mark Chapman (323) 466-7232
(213) 610-7746
www.videorama.com

ChillowVision, LLC (323) 810-3456
11021 Wagner St. FAX (310) 395-1920
Culver City, CA 90230 www.chillowvision.com
(Digital)

Cinelogic, Inc. (818) 772-4777
(818) 359-3589
(Digital) www.videoassist.com

Ⓐ **Cogswell Video Services, Inc.** (661) 257-9087
27636 Avenue Scott, Ste. B FAX (661) 257-9478
Valencia, CA 91355 www.cogswellvideo.com
(Digital)

Keith Collea (310) 823-0508
(520) 907-2211
(Digital) FAX (815) 642-4444
www.red-rail.com

Crystal Pyramid Productions (619) 644-3000
(800) 365-8433
7323 Rondel Court FAX (619) 644-3001
San Diego, CA 92119 www.crystalpyramid.com
(Digital & Tape Based)

Director's Choice Video/ Robert Morales (818) 766-9050
(323) 854-3236
(Digital) FAX (818) 766-9250
www.directorschoicevideo.com

DVassist/Anthony DeSanto (805) 279-1016
(805) 499-6602
(Digital & Tape-Based)

Scott M. Goldman/Video Systems (310) 441-9836
(310) 292-9284
(Digital) FAX (310) 474-5282

Scott Hammar/Happy Jaq Video (310) 770-0377
5158 Canoga Ave. FAX (818) 346-5396
Woodland Hills, CA 91364

Kevin Hawks/ Circle Take Video Assist (805) 241-0457
(805) 490-3621
FAX (805) 241-6050

Hill Digital (818) 445-9211
9714 La Canada Way www.hilldigital.com
Sunland, CA 91040

Hoodman Corp. (800) 818-3946
(310) 222-8608
20445 Gramercy Pl., Ste. 201 FAX (310) 222-8623
Torrance, CA 90501 www.hoodmanusa.com

Impact AV (213) 494-9492
(800) 323-0490
635 Dimmick Dr. FAX (323) 225-1389
Los Angeles, CA 90065
(Digital)

Inter Video (818) 843-3624
2211 N. Hollywood Way FAX (818) 843-6884
Burbank, CA 91505 www.intervideo24.com
(Digital)

Rich Jackson/Lucky Jackson DV (818) 262-7505
(818) 753-0533

Brett Junod (310) 592-0997
(Digital)

Brett Kelly/Kelly Video (818) 883-7932
(818) 389-1583

L.A. Video Assist (818) 368-8144
(Digital)

Man In The Box Video Assist/
Dempsey Tillman (818) 517-8865
FAX (818) 887-0682
www.maninthebo xvideo.com

Andy Minzes/Ready To Roll Video (818) 842-2977
(818) 321-2117
405 N. Sparks St. FAX (818) 842-5273
Burbank, CA 91506
(Digital)

Michael Moretti/Lost Dog Video (310) 722-8351
845 Second St. FAX (310) 483-7872
Hermosa Beach, CA 90254 www.lostdogvideo.com
(Digital)

Nebtek (818) 782-5466
11152 Fleetwood St., Ste. 3 FAX (818) 768-8348
Sun Valley, CA 91352 www.nebtek.com
(Digital)

Ocean Video/Jeb Johenning (310) 859-7573
(213) 300-2000
(Digital) FAX (310) 275-8676
www.oceanvideo.com

On Tap Video Playback Systems (310) 222-8614
(310) 488-8410
(Digital) FAX (310) 222-8624
www.hoodmanusa.com

Anthony Perkins (310) 651-1099
www.chillowvision.com

Play It Again Sam/Sam Harrison (661) 263-6070
(661) 803-9372
(Digital)

Play It Again Video (310) 450-1846
(213) 509-7798
185 Pier Ave., Ste. 104 FAX (310) 399-9227
Santa Monica, CA 90405 www.mainstreetmediainc.com

RF Film, Inc. (866) 985-3456
FAX (866) 986-3456
www.rffilm.com

Erick H. Schultz/EZ Video (310) 542-3202
(310) 430-2468
(Digital) FAX (310) 542-3202

TV Productions, Inc. (818) 763-4098
3704 Mound View Ave.
Studio City, CA 91604
(Digital)

Mike Uguccioni/PreFX (310) 403-1556
(Digital)

Videorama! Industries, LLC/
Howard Van Emden (323) 466-7232
1119 N. Hudson Ave. FAX (323) 466-7228
Hollywood, CA 90038 www.videorama.com
(Digital)

Video Assist Systems, Inc. (818) 606-8901
(Digital) FAX (818) 222-5862
www.videoassistsystems.com

Video Hawks (818) 889-9655
P.O. Box 7525 FAX (818) 889-9755
Westlake Village, CA 91359 www.videohawks.com
(Digital)

Video Playback and Back and Back (310) 418-2963
(310) 750-6477
5508 Manitowac Dr.
Palos Verdes, CA 90275

Video Tech Services (310) 574-9385
(310) 505-4015
10866 Washington Blvd., Ste. 513 FAX (310) 577-0850
Culver City, CA 90232 www.videotechservices.com

VideoAxis, Inc. (818) 223-8884
(818) 642-5471
23958 Craftsman Rd. FAX (818) 223-9559
Calabasas, CA 91302

Videodrone (818) 508-6214
(323) 855-4278
(Digital) FAX (818) 508-6214

Warner Bros. Studio Facilities -
Production Sound Rentals (818) 954-2511
4000 Warner Blvd., Bldg. 28 FAX (818) 954-2901
Burbank, CA 91522 www.wbsf.com

Charlie Westfall/
Chas. Westfall Video (818) 509-7800
(818) 970-8962
(Digital) FAX (818) 769-1773

Wolf Seeberg Video (310) 822-4973
(Digital) FAX (310) 305-8918
www.wolfvid.com

A B Sea Photo (310) 645-8992
9136 S. Sepulveda Blvd. FAX **(310) 645-3645**
Los Angeles, CA 90045 **www.absea.net**
(24P, Broadcast Systems, Digital, HDV, High Def, Underwater Housings & Underwater Systems)

Aaron & Le Duc (310) 452-2034
2210 Third St., Ste. 316 **www.leducdesign.com**
Santa Monica, CA 90405

Abel Cine Tech, Inc. (818) 972-9078
(888) 700-4416
801 S. Main St., Ste. A FAX **(818) 972-2673**
Burbank, CA 91506 **www.abelcine.com**
(24P, Broadcast Systems, Digital, HDV, High Def, Mini DV, Monitors, Phantom HD High Speed Camera, Projectors, Recorders, Specialty Cameras & Underwater Housings)

Absolute Rentals (818) 842-2828
2633 N. San Fernando Blvd. FAX **(818) 842-8815**
Burbank, CA 91504 **www.absoluterentals.com**
(3/4" SP Video Systems, Analog and Digital Video Systems, Betacam and Betacam SP Systems, Broadcast and Digital Betacam Systems, Broadcast Video Camera Systems, DV Camera Systems, DVC Pro, DVCAM, Facilities, Flatscreens, HD Camera Systems, HD-CAM HDV, Hi-8, High Def, Mini DV, Mini DV 24P, Mini DV Video Camera Systems, Monitors, PAL, Panasonic/Sony HD Cameras and VTR Systems, Portable Avid Systems, Projectors, Recorders, Remote Heads, Sony DV, Sony PD 150 VX2000 DCCam, Sony UVX 1800 BETACAM SP VTR, Sound, Specialty Cameras, Video Camera Systems, Video Equipment Repair & Video Recorders)

Action Audio & Visual (323) 461-4290
(888) 406-8164
10834 Burbank Blvd., Ste. A-100 FAX **(323) 461-4292**
North Hollywood, CA 91601
www.actionaudioandvisual.com
(24P, Analog Systems, Betacam, Broadcast Systems, Digiprimes, Digital, HDV, Hi-8, High Def, Magliner, Mini DV, Monitors, Multi-Camera Systems, Playback Systems, Recorders, Remote Heads, Sound Equipment, Specialty Cameras, Steadicam Systems, Ultimatte, Video Assist Systems & Wireless Monitoring)

Advanced Video, Inc. (323) 469-0707
723 N. Cahuenga Blvd.
Hollywood, CA 90038

Aerial Video Systems/AVS (818) 954-8842
712 S. Main St. FAX **(818) 954-9122**
Burbank, CA 91506 **www.aerialvideo.com**
(High Def, Lipstick Cameras, RF/Microwave Wireless Video, Specialty Cameras, Video Assist Systems & Wireless Monitoring)

Alan Gordon Enterprises, Inc. (323) 466-3561
5625 Melrose Ave. FAX **(323) 871-2193**
Los Angeles, CA 90038 **www.alangordon.com**
(Digital Beta and Video Cameras and Systems & Mini DV 24P)

Alternative Rentals (310) 204-3388
5805 W. Jefferson Blvd. FAX **(310) 204-3384**
Los Angeles, CA 90016 **www.alternativerentals.com**
(24P, DVC Pro, HD-CAM, HDV, Projectors, Wireless Monitoring & Zeiss)

A **American Hi Definition, Inc.** (818) 222-0022
7635 Airport Business Pkwy FAX (818) 222-0818
Van Nuys, CA 91406 www.hi-def.com
(Video Camera Projectors, Screens and Systems)

American Video Group (310) 477-1535
2542 Aiken Ave. www.americanvideogroup.com
Los Angeles, CA 90064
(Digital Betacam Camera Systems)

Ametron Audio Video (323) 466-4321
(323) 464-1144
1546 N. Argyle Ave. FAX (323) 871-0127
Hollywood, CA 90028 www.ametron.com
(Video Camera Systems)

Artistic Resources Corporation (323) 965-5200
535 N. Brand Blvd., Ste. 235 FAX (323) 965-5209
Glendale, CA 91203 www.artisticresources.com

Backstage Equipment, Inc. (818) 504-6026
(800) 692-2787
8052 Lankershim Blvd. FAX (818) 504-6180
North Hollywood, CA 91605 www.backstageweb.com
(Cameras, Magliners, Remote Heads, Sound & Video Carts)

Band Pro Film & Digital, Inc. (818) 841-9655
3403 W. Pacific Ave. FAX (818) 841-7649
Burbank, CA 91505 www.bandpro.com
(Video Camera Systems)

Barber Tech (818) 982-7775
(877) 887-6388
40125 20th St. West FAX (661) 339-3235
Palmdale, CA 93551 www.barbertvp.com
(Film Simulation Process Cameras & Projectors)

Barcon Video Productions (818) 248-9161
3653 Mesa Lila Ln. FAX (818) 249-8884
Glendale, CA 91208 www.barcon.com

Bexel (818) 847-1298
(800) 225-6185
2701 N. Ontario St. FAX (818) 847-1238
Burbank, CA 91504 www.bexel.com
(Broadcast and Digital Betacam Systems)

Big Door (310) 546-6100
P.O. Box 3577 FAX (310) 546-4069
Manhattan Beach, CA 90266 www.bigdoor.tv
(Betacam Systems)

Birns & Sawyer, Inc. (323) 466-8211
(818) 766-2525
Camera & Sales Division FAX (323) 466-1868
6381 De Longpre Ave. www.birnsandsawyer.com
Hollywood, CA 90028

BlueScreen, LLC/Bob Kertesz (323) 467-7572
www.bluescreen.com
(Blue and Green Screen Facilities & Portable Ultimatte)

Briggs Video, Inc./Peter Ney (661) 250-8258
4111 W. Vanowen Pl. FAX (661) 250-8259
Burbank, CA 91505 www.briggsvideo.com
(Betacam SP Systems)

Broadcast Store (818) 998-9100
9420 Lurline Ave., Ste. C FAX (818) 998-9106
Chatsworth, CA 91311 www.broadcaststore.com
(Video Camera Systems)

Mobile Production Facilities

Designed for broadcast entertainment video production, the Background Images mobile production facilities and highly experienced Union Operators take the show on the road! Equipped with the latest in broadcast production technology and multiple expandos. These mobile production facilities are high-tech as well as spacious and comfortable environments to work in.

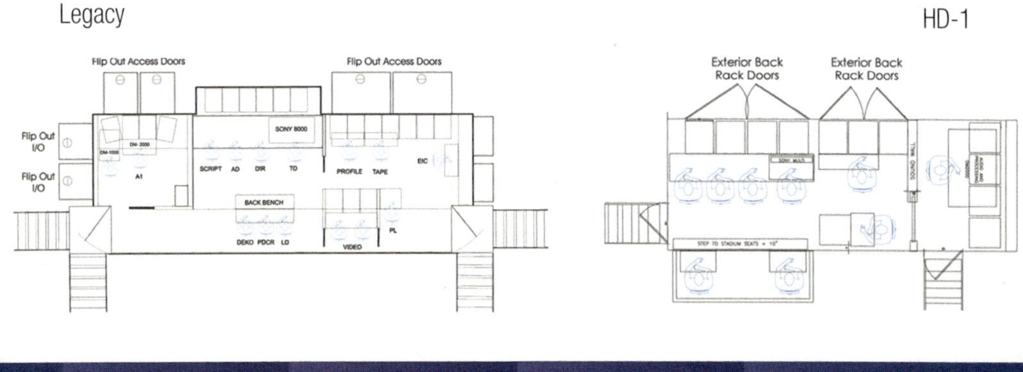

Los Angeles
28908 N. Ave
Paine Unit B
Valencia, CA 91355
661.257.5710

Atlanta
1320 Ellsworth Industrial Blvd.
Unit A17
Atlanta, GA 30318
404.352.8848

Visit **www.bgimages.com/trucks/mobileunits.html** to download specifications, monitor wall layout or take an interactive tour.

Broadcast ENG Package Available.

See our ad for Displays in Video Display & Projection.

Ⓐ C-Mount Industries, Inc. (310) 464-6888
FAX (310) 464-6888
www.cmountindustries.com
(24P, Camera Crews, HDV, Lipstick Cameras, Mini DV, Monitors, Production Trucks, Specialty Cameras, Underwater Housings, Wireless Monitoring & Wireless Video)

Cinema Rentals, Inc. (661) 222-7342
(877) 877-9605
25876 The Old Road, Ste. 174 FAX (661) 253-3643
Stevenson Ranch, CA 91381 www.cinemarentals.com
(Digital and Hi-8 Underwater Video & Lipstick Cameras)

Claude Booth Company Equipment Repairs (310) 980-3229
(310) 993-4901
12534 Valley View, Ste. 128 FAX (714) 894-4095
Los Angeles, CA 92845 www.claudebooth.net
(Video Camera and Equipment Repair)

Crash Productions (310) 489-6848
713 N. Mansfield Ave. FAX (323) 939-9622
Los Angeles, CA 90038 www.crashproductions.com
(Betacam SP & Digital)

Creative Technology Los Angeles (818) 779-2400
14000 Arminta St. FAX (818) 779-2401
Panorama City, CA 91402 www.ctinternational.com
(Video Camera Systems)

Crystal Pyramid Productions (619) 644-3000
(800) 365-8433
7323 Rondel Court FAX (619) 644-3001
San Diego, CA 92119 www.crystalpyramid.com
(Betacam SP and DV Camera Systems, Blue and Green Screen, HDV, High Def, Portable AVID Systems & Underwater Camera Systems and Housings)

Ⓐ Cutting Edge Productions, Inc. (310) 326-4500
(818) 503-0400
22904 Lockness Ave. FAX (310) 326-4715
Torrance, CA 90501 www.cuttingedgeproductions.tv
(¾", 24P, Analog Systems, Betacam, Blue Screen Facilities, Broadcast Systems, Digital, Flatscreens, Flypacks, Green Screen Facilities, HDV, Hi-8, High Def, Mini DV, Monitors, Multi-Camera Systems, Playback Systems, Production Trucks, Projectors, Recorders & Sound Equipment)

Dalsa (818) 884-7000
6160 Variel Ave. FAX (818) 884-7022
Woodland Hills, CA 91367 www.dalsa.com/dc
(24P, Analog and Digital Video Systems, Digiprimes, Green Screen Facilities, HDV, High Def, Lipstick Cameras, Monitors, Sound Equipment, Specialty Cameras & Wireless Monitoring)

Deck Hand, Inc. (818) 557-8403
1905 Victory Blvd., Ste. 8 FAX (818) 557-8406
Glendale, CA 91201 www.deckhand.com
(D-5, Digi Beta, DVCAM, DVCPro, DVCPro HD, HD and SD Deck Rentals, HDCAM, HDCAM SR, HDV, High Def, Monitors & Recorders)

Digital Antics (818) 621-5134
3619 W. Magnolia Blvd. FAX (818) 567-2949
Burbank, CA 91505 www.darental.com
(Digital Betacams, DV Cameras & HD Camera Systems)

Epiphany Media (323) 819-1001
5300 Melrose Ave. www.epiphanymedia.com
Hollywood, CA 90038
(Betacam, Betacam SP, Blue Screen Facilities, Broadcast Systems, Digital Betacam Systems, DVCAMs, Flatscreens, Flypacks, Green Screen Facilities, High Def, Multi-Camera Systems & Ultimatte)

EVS/Express Video Supply, Inc. (818) 552-4590
(800) 238-8480
1620 Flower St. FAX (818) 552-4591
Glendale, CA 91201 www.evsonline.com

Filmtools (818) 845-8066
(888) 807-1900
1400 W. Burbank Blvd. FAX (818) 845-8138
Burbank, CA 91506 www.filmtools.com
(Camera Carts)

G. John Slagle Productions (310) 514-3233
(310) 871-6269
22 Golden Spur Ln. FAX (310) 514-1545
Rancho Palos Verdes, CA 90275 www.slaglevideo.com
(Video Camera Systems)

Gear Monkey (714) 705-6088
(877) 411-4445
630 The City Dr., Ste. 175 FAX (714) 705-6080
Orange, CA 92868 www.gearmonkeyrentals.com
(Digital Betacam Systems, Monitors & Video Recorders)

Hermosa Pictures (310) 909-8525
1850 Industrial St., Ste. 307 FAX (310) 349-3441
Los Angeles, CA 90021 www.hermosapictures.com
(24P, Analog Systems, Betacam, Broadcast Systems, Camera Carts, Digiprimes, Digital, High Def, Mini DV, Monitors, Multi-Camera Systems & Sound Equipment)

Hy-Tone Productions (310) 456-3052
75-550 Calle Del Sur
Indian Wells, CA 92210
(Betacam SP and Mini DV Video Camera Systems)

Illuminate – Arts, Media & Entertainment (323) 969-8822
3575 Cahuenga Blvd. West, Fourth Fl. FAX **(323) 969-8840**
Los Angeles, CA 90068 **www.illuminatehollywood.com**
(24P, Analog Systems, Betacam, Blue/Green Screen Facilities, Broadcast Systems, Digiprimes, Digital Downconversions/ Dailies, Endoscopic Lenses, Flatscreens, HDV, Hi-8, High Def Camera and Record Packages, Mini DV, Monitors, Multi-Camera Systems, Playback Systems, Portable AVID Systems, Production Trucks, Projectors, Recorders, Remote Heads, Sound Equipment, Specialty Cameras, Steadicam Systems, Ultimatte, Video Assist Systems & Wireless Monitoring)

Imagecraft (818) 954-0187
99 E. Providencia Ave. FAX **(818) 954-0189**
Burbank, CA 91502 **www.imagecraft.tv**

A **Indie Rentals** (323) 465-7700 (323) 571-9476
7022 W. Sunset Blvd. FAX **(323) 297-2773**
Hollywood, CA 90028 **www.indierentals.com**
(24P, Digital, Flatscreens, High Def, Mini DV, Monitors, Multi-Camera Systems, Playback Systems, Projectors, Sound Equipment, Specialty Cameras, Steadicam Systems, Video Assist Systems & Wireless Monitoring)

Indigo Systems (805) 964-9797
50 Castilian Dr. FAX **(805) 685-2711**
Goleta, CA 93117 **www.indigosystems.com**
(Infrared Cameras)

Innovision Optics (310) 453-4866
1719 21st St. FAX **(310) 453-4677**
Santa Monica, CA 90404 **www.innovisionoptics.com**
(Endoscopic Lenses, HD Probe Lens System, Miniature Cameras & Miniature Remote Camera Cars)

Inter Video (818) 843-3624
2211 N. Hollywood Way FAX **(818) 843-6884**
Burbank, CA 91505 **www.intervideo24.com**
(24 fps Playback Systems, Betacam SP & PAL)

KCET Studios (323) 953-5258 (818) 692-5766
4401 Sunset Blvd. FAX **(323) 953-5496**
Los Angeles, CA 90027 **www.kcetstudios.com**
(Broadcast Systems, Camera Carts, Digi Beta, Digital, Endoscopic Lenses, Flatscreens, Flypacks, Green Screen Facilities, HDV, High Def, Infrared Cameras, Lipstick Cameras, Magliner, Mini DV, Monitors, Multi-Camera Systems, Playback Systems, Portable AVID Systems, Production Trucks, Projectors, Recorders, Remote Heads, Repair, Sound Equipment, Specialty Cameras, Video Assist Systems & Wireless Monitoring)

Mad Dog Video, Inc. (818) 985-7766
5510 Satsuma Ave. FAX **(818) 508-6794**
North Hollywood, CA 91601 **www.maddogvideo.com**
(Beta SP, Digital Betacam, DV Cam, HD & Mini DV)

Mark Mardoyan (818) 996-5566
(24P, Flypacks & Production Trucks) FAX **(818) 996-4082**
markmardo.synthasite.com

Moviola/Moviola Cameras (323) 467-3107 (800) 468-3107
1135 N. Mansfield Ave. FAX **(323) 464-1518**
Hollywood, CA 90038 **www.moviola.com**
(DVCAMs)

National Mobile Television (310) 782-9945
2740 California St. **www.nmtv.com**
Torrance, CA 90503
(Production Trucks)

Old School Cameras (310) 710-6525 (323) 462-0914
920 N. Citrus Ave. FAX **(323) 462-5935**
Hollywood, CA 90038 **www.oldschoolcameras.com**
(HDV, High Def, Mini DV, Monitors, Sound Equipment & Wireless Monitoring)

Photo-Plus (818) 766-6868 (800) 759-5722
4141 Elmer Ave. **www.ronvidor.com**
Studio City, CA 91602
(GPI Steadicam Pro System & Video Recorders)

Pictorvision Inc (818) 785-9282 (800) 876-5583
7701 Haskell Ave., Ste. B FAX **(818) 785-9787**
Van Nuys, CA 91406 **www.pictorvision.com**
(High Def, Remote Heads & SD)

POV-HD (310) 866-9300
(POV Cameras & Specailized Mounts)

Pro-Cam Video Systems, Inc. (818) 954-9300 (800) 818-8433
140 E. Tujunga Ave. FAX **(818) 954-9450**
Burbank, CA 91502 **www.pro-cam.tv**
(Digital Video Camera Systems)

A **Schulman Mobile Video** (323) 785-2528
1320 N. Wilton Pl. FAX **(323) 785-2529**
Hollywood, CA 90028 **www.schulmanmv.com**
(Digital Satellite Production Trucks)

Silver Pixel Productions (818) 415-9572
FAX **(808) 531-0079**
www.silverpixelproductions.com
(Betacam, Digital, HDV, High Def & Mini DV)

Sim Video Los Angeles (323) 978-9000
738 Cahuenga Blvd. FAX **(323) 978-9018**
Hollywood, CA 90038 **www.simvideola.com**
(Betacam SP Systems)

SJC Mobile Video (661) 257-5881 (818) 652-0359
28625 Braxton Ave. FAX **(661) 257-5883**
Valencia, CA 91355 **www.sjcvideo.com**
(Broadcast Systems, Digital, Multi-Camera Systems & Production Trucks)

Sonnanstine Engineering (310) 962-1429
5510 Satsuma Ave. **www.soneng.com**
North Hollywood, CA 91601
(Video Camera and Equipment Repair)

Sony Electronics Inc. (323) 352-5001
2706 Media Center Dr., Ste. 130 FAX **(323) 352-5039**
Los Angeles, CA 90065
(24P, Betacam, Broadcast Systems, HDV, High Def, Mini DV, Monitors, Playback Systems, Projectors, Recorders & Repair)

Sterling Productions (626) 675-0994
600 N. Louise St., Ste. 8 **www.sterlingproductionstv.com**
Glendale, CA 91206
(Beta, DV and High Def Camera Systems)

Stone Electronics (323) 931-2838
7928 Beverly Blvd. FAX **(323) 931-7116**
Los Angeles, CA 90048 **www.stoneelectronics.com**
(Repair)

Studio Exchange, Inc. (818) 840-1351
816 N. Victory Blvd. **www.studio-exchange.com**
Burbank, CA 91502
(Video Camera Systems)

Sweetwater Digital Productions/ SVP, Inc. (818) 902-9500
7635 Airport Business Park Way FAX **(818) 902-0140**
Van Nuys, CA 91406 **www.svptv.com**
(24P, BetaSP, Digibeta and HD Video Camera Systems, Flypacks, High Def, Multi-Camera Systems, Production Trucks & Projectors)

Gary Taillon (805) 443-3806
2168 Meadow Brook Court
Thousand Oaks, CA 91362

Technical Audio Video Corp./ George Meyer (310) 820-1113 (310) 820-3480
12418 Santa Monica Blvd. FAX **(310) 826-9769**
West Los Angeles, CA 90025
(Video Equipment Repair) **www.technicalaudiovideo.com**

Touring Video, Inc. (818) 953-8700 (800) 773-8687
827 Hollywood Way, Ste. 424 FAX **(818) 953-8707**
Burbank, CA 91505 **www.touringvideo.com**
(Production Trucks)

Twelve Tone Productions (323) 633-1000 (323) 633-3853
P.O. Box 36356 FAX **(323) 934-3491**
Los Angeles, CA 90036
www.twelvetoneproductions.com
(24P, Green Screen Facilities, HDV & Multi-Camera Systems)

Upstage, LLC (818) 787-5294
5920 Lemona Ave. FAX **(818) 778-0140**
Van Nuys, CA 91411
(Facilities)

Video Applications, Inc. (714) 508-1858 (800) 835-5432
14791 Myford Rd. FAX **(714) 508-2362**
Tustin, CA 92780 **www.videoapps.com**
(Betacam, Digital, Flatscreens, HDV, High Def, Lipstick Cameras, Mini DV, Monitors, Multi-Camera Systems, Playback Systems, Projectors, Recorders, Sound Equipment, Specialty Cameras & Video Projection Systems)

Video Assist Systems, Inc. (818) 606-8901
(Monitors & Video Assist Systems) FAX **(818) 222-5862**
www.videoassistsystems.com

Video Equipment Rentals (818) 956-1444 (800) 794-1407
912 Ruberta Ave. FAX **(818) 241-4519**
Glendale, CA 91201 **www.verrents.com**
(Video Camera Systems)

Video Gear (858) 356-0200
11760 Sorento Valley Rd., Ste. M FAX **(858) 356-0204**
San Diego, CA 92121 **www.video-gear.com**
(Dolly Systems, HDV, Mini DV, Steadicam Systems & Sound Equipment)

Video Production Specialists (VPS) (866) 447-3877
FAX **(310) 577-0850**
www.videoproductionspecialists.com
(Beta SP & Digibeta Video Camera Systems)

Videowerks (310) 393-8754 (310) 780-4156
3435 Ocean Park Blvd., Ste. 107 FAX **(310) 399-1829**
Santa Monica, CA 90405 **www.videowerks.com**
(Betacam SP, DV Camera Systems, DVC Pro 50 24P, HDV & High Def)

Visionary Forces Broadcast Rentals (818) 562-1960
148 S. Victory Blvd. FAX **(818) 562-1270**
Burbank, CA 91502 **www.visionaryforces.com**
(¾", 24P, Betacam, HDV, High Def, Mini DV, Monitors & Recorders)

VTR Interchange, Inc. (818) 985-1467
1407 Foothill Blvd., Ste. 221 FAX **(909) 593-4327**
La Verne, CA 91750 **www.vtrinterchange.com**
(24P, Analog Systems, Betacam, Broadcast Systems, Digital, Flatscreens, Flypacks, Green Screen Facilities, HDV, High Def, Mini DV, Monitors, Multi-Camera Systems, Playback Systems, Production Trucks, Projectors, Recorders, Repair, Video Assist Systems & Wireless Monitoring)

Ⓐ **Westcoast Video Productions, Inc.** (818) 785-8033 (800) 477-8417
14141 Covello St., Ste. 9A FAX **(818) 785-8035**
Van Nuys, CA 91405 **www.wvpinc.com**
(Betacams & Broadcast Video Camera Systems)

Wexler Video (818) 846-9381 (800) 939-5371
1111 S. Victory Blvd. FAX **(818) 846-9399**
Burbank, CA 91502 **www.wexlervideo.com**

Wintech Video (818) 501-6565
4455 Van Nuys Blvd. FAX **(818) 501-6566**
Sherman Oaks, CA 91403 **www.wintechvideo.com**
(Betacam Video Camera Systems)

World Wide Digital Services, Inc. (818) 841-1669
171 W. Magnolia Blvd. FAX **(818) 841-0239**
Burbank, CA 91502 **www.worldwidela.com**
(Analog and Digital Video Camera Systems & Recorders)

Yada/Levine Video Productions (323) 461-1616
1253 Vine St., Ste. 21A FAX **(323) 461-2288**
Hollywood, CA 90038 **www.yadalevine.com**
(24P, Betacam, Betacam SP, Digital Betacam, HDV, High Def & Mini DV)

Action Audio & Visual (323) 461-4290 (888) 406-8164
10834 Burbank Blvd., Ste. A-100 FAX (323) 461-4292
North Hollywood, CA 91601
www.actionaudioandvisual.com

American Hi Definition, Inc. (818) 222-0022
7635 Airport Business Pkwy FAX (818) 222-0818
Van Nuys, CA 91406 www.hi-def.com
(Video Projection)

Audio Visual Brokers (626) 625-3020
207 N. Aspan Ave., Ste. 2 FAX (626) 256-8319
Azusa, CA 91702 www.projectorbrokers.com

AYMA Entertainment (323) 788-8445 (323) 851-9671
P.O. Box 254 FAX (323) 851-9671
Hollywood, CA 90078 www.aymaent.com

Ⓐ **Background Images, Inc.** (661) 257-5710
28908 N. Paine Ave., Ste. B www.bgimages.com
Valencia, CA 91335

Big Red Productions, Inc. (714) 842-4338 (714) 402-2291
FAX (718) 842-4798
www.bigredprod.com

Blu Laser Digital, LLC (877) 258-7291 (480) 522-0196
FAX (480) 452-0139
www.blulaserdigital.com
(24 fps Computer Playback, 24 fps Video Playback, 24P HD Process Projection, 30 fps Computer Playback, 30 fps Video Playback, Film/Video Synchronizing Control, Flatscreens, Front Screen Projections, High-Output Large Screen Video Projection, LCD Screens, LED Screens, Mobile LED Screens, Plasma Screens, Rear Screen Projections, Video Playback, Video Projection & Video Walls)

Cinematography Electronics, Inc. (818) 706-3334
5321 Derry Ave., Ste. G FAX (818) 706-3335
Agoura Hills, CA 91301
www.cinematographyelectronics.com
(Film/Video Synchronizing Control)

Ⓐ **Cutting Edge Productions, Inc.** (310) 326-4500 (818) 503-0400
22904 Lockness Ave. FAX (310) 326-4715
Torrance, CA 90501 www.cuttingedgeproductions.tv
(24 fps Computer Playback, 24 fps Video Playback, 24P HD Process Projection, 30 fps Computer Playback, 30 fps Video Playback, Cabling, Film/Video Synchronizing Control, Flatscreens, Front Screen Projections, High-Output Large Screen Video Projection, LCD Screens, Photography Consultants, Plasma Screens, Rear Screen Projections, Video Playback & Video Projection)

Cygnet Video (661) 296-0374
27355 Chesterfield Dr. FAX (661) 297-8526
Valencia, CA 91354 www.cygnetvideo.com
(24/30 fps Computer and Video Playback & 24P HD Process Projection)

ELM, Ltd. (818) 508-5995
13659 Victory Blvd., Ste. 583 www.elmlimited.com
Van Nuys, CA 91401

Future Lighting (310) 312-9772 (310) 346-1649
(Front/Rear Projection) www.futurelighting.net

Make Your Project Shine

Headquartered in Los Angeles, with a location in Atlanta, Background Images Inc. is your premier one stop service provider for all your Video Display, Audio and Lighting needs.

Our team consists of industry veterans from both sides of the globe, bringing world-class skills and ideas to your table. With our passion for new technology and our innovative thinking, we can ensure that all aspects of your event, no matter what the scale, will be of the highest quality.

Professional Presentation & Event Production Equipment | 24 / 7 Support

- Pre-Production & Budgeting
- Experienced Union Operators & Technicians
- Mobile Production Facilities
- Broadcast ENG Packages
- Multi Display Show Control
- HD/SD Camera Packages
- Large & Multi-Screen Video Projection
- Lighting
- Plasma
- LCD Screens
- LED Screens
- Audio Systems

See our ad for Mobile Production Units under Video Cameras & Equipment.

Los Angeles
661.257.5710
Atlanta
404.352.8848

www.bgimages.com

Courtney M. Goodin (323) 937-4978
(323) 465-9441
FAX (323) 935-6698
(24 fps Computer Playback, 24 fps Video Playback, 24P HD Process Projection, 30 fps Computer Playback, 30 fps Video Playback, Film/Video Synchronizing Control, LCD Screens & Video Playback)

Hill Digital (818) 445-9211
9714 La Canada Way www.hilldigital.com
Sunland, CA 91040
(24/30 fps Video Playback)

I-MAG Video A/V, Inc. (818) 956-1444
(818) 291-4080
1563 Irving Ave. www.i-magvideo.com
Glendale, CA 91201
(Front and Rear Screen Projections, LED Systems & Video Playback)

Impact Video (818) 972-1774
3088 Clybourn Ave. FAX (818) 972-1329
Burbank, CA 91505 www.impactav.com
(LED Screens & Video Walls)

Independent Studio Services, Inc./ISS (818) 951-5600
9545 Wentworth St. FAX (818) 951-2850
Sunland, CA 91040 www.issprops.com
(24/30 fps Video Playback)

Innovative Design Technologies (800) 558-3080
(818) 376-1920
7635 Airport Business Park Way FAX (818) 376-1915
Van Nuys, CA 91406
(Projection & Video Walls)

Inter Video (818) 843-3624
2211 N. Hollywood Way FAX (818) 843-6884
Burbank, CA 91505 www.intervideo24.com
(24/30 fps Computer and Video Playback)

JumboScreen (818) 540-4282
(866) 665-8626
3262 Futura Point FAX (805) 492-3879
Thousand Oaks, CA 91362 www.jumboscreen.com
(Mobile LED Video Screen)

Mann Consulting (818) 907-6266
(888) 746-8227
FAX (818) 340-3355
www.mann.com
(24/30 fps Computer Graphics & Video Playback)

Todd A. Marks/Production Suppliers (818) 340-0545
(818) 439-8066
FAX (818) 340-3355
www.prosuppliers.com
(24 fps Computer Playback, 24 fps Video Playback, 24P HD Process Projection, 30 fps Computer Playback, 30 fps Video Playback, Cabling, Computer Graphics, Film/Video Synchronizing Control, Flatscreens, Front Screen Projections, High-Output Large Screen Video Projection, LCD Screens, LED Screens, Mobile LED Screens, Photography Consultants, Plasma Screens, Rear Screen Projections, Video Playback, Video Projection & Video Walls)

John Monsour (323) 650-5706
2062 Stanley Hills Dr.
Los Angeles, CA 90046
(24 fps Computer Screen Graphics, Photography Consultant & Video Playback)

New Deal Studios, Inc. (310) 578-9929
4105 Redwood Ave. FAX (310) 578-7370
Los Angeles, CA 90066 www.newdealstudios.com
(Blue and Green Screen)

Ⓐ **Playback Technologies** (818) 556-5030
135 N. Victory Blvd. FAX (818) 556-5034
Burbank, CA 91502 www.playbacktech.com
(24/30 fps Computer and Video Playback)

Liz Radley (818) 262-8363

Reaction Audio Visual (949) 600-8235
(877) 273-6887
9951 Muirlands FAX (949) 600-8238
Irvine, CA 92618 www.reactionav.com
(Flatscreens, Front and Rear Screen Projections, LCD Screens, Plasma Screens & Video Projection)

Screenworks NEP (805) 497-7160
(800) 868-2898
370 N. Westlake Blvd., Ste. 210 FAX (805) 497-8301
Westlake Village, CA 91362 www.screenworksnep.com
(LED Screens, Mobile LED Screens & Video Projection)

Mike Shaheen (805) 520-4989
(818) 202-1177
(24 fps Video Playback)

Sweetwater Digital Productions/SVP, Inc. (818) 902-9500
7635 Airport Business Park Way FAX (818) 902-0140
Van Nuys, CA 91406 www.svptv.com
(24 fps Computer Playback, 24 fps Video Playback, 24P HD Process Projection, 30 fps Computer Playback, 30 fps Video Playback, Flatscreens, Front Screen Projections, High-Output Large Screen Video Projection, LCD Screens, LED Screens, Mobile LED Screens, Photography Consultants, Plasma Screens, Rear Screen, Projections, Video Playback, Video Projection & Video Walls)

Gary Taillon (805) 443-3806
2168 Meadow Brook Court
Thousand Oaks, CA 91362

Ira D. Toles (310) 457-2830
(310) 560-5555
(24/30 fps Video Playback)

Towards 2000, Inc. (818) 557-0903
215 W. Palm Ave., Ste. 204 FAX (818) 557-0596
Burbank, CA 91502 www.t2k.com
(Projection & Video Walls)

Vidcom/Mark I. Scott (661) 297-6697
(818) 335-1354
21201 Georgetown Dr. FAX (661) 297-6697
Saugus, CA 91350 www.markiscott.com
(24/30 fps Computer and Video Playback, CRT, LCD, LED, Plasma, Projection & Video Walls)

Video Applications, Inc. (714) 508-1858
(800) 835-5432
14791 Myford Rd. FAX (714) 508-2362
Tustin, CA 92780 www.videoapps.com
(Flatscreens, Front Screen Projections, High-Output Large Screen Video Projection, Plasma Screens, Rear Screen Projections, Video Playback & Video Projection)

Video Production Specialists (VPS) (866) 447-3877
FAX (310) 577-0850
www.videoproductionspecialists.com
(24/30 fps Video Playback, Projection & Video Walls)

Warner Bros. Studio Facilities - Production Sound & Video (818) 954-2511
4000 Warner Blvd., Bldg. 28 FAX (818) 954-2491
Burbank, CA 91522 www.wbsf.com

NOTES:

LA 411

POINT FERMIN

SAN PEDRO

THE BIG LEBOWSKI

WIND-SWEPT BLUFF - DAY

Walter (John Goodman), holding a bright red coffee can with a blue plastic lid, and the Dude (Jeff Bridges) stand at the edge of the bluff.

WALTER

Donny was a good bowler, and a good man He was...He was a man who loved the outdoors, and bowling, and as a surfer explored the beaches of southern California. He died as so many of his generation, before his time. In your wisdom you took him, Lord. As you took so many bright flowering young men, at Khe San and Lan Doc and Hill 364 ... and so, Theodore Donald Karabotos, in accordance with what your dying wishes might well have been, we commit your mortal remains to the bosom of the Pacific Ocean which you loved so well.

AS HE SHAKES OUT THE ASHES:

WALTER

Goodnight, sweet prince.

The wind has blown all of the ashes into the Dude..

WALTER (Cont.)
(brushing off the Dude)

Sh*t, I'm sorry Dude.

DUDE

Goddamnit Walter! You f**king a***ole!

WALTER

Dude! Dude, I'm sorry!

DUDE

You make everything a f**king travesty!

WALTER

Dude, I'm--it was an accident!

DUDE

What about that sh*t about Vietnam!

WALTER

Dude, I'm sorry--

DUDE

What the f**k does Vietnam have to do with anything! What the f**k were you talking about?!

WALTER

Sh*t Dude, I'm sorry--

DUDE

You're a f**k, Walter!

He gives Walter a weak shove. Walter seems dazed, then wraps his arms around the Dude.

WALTER

Awww, f**k it Dude. Let's go bowling.

SCREENPLAY BY:
Ethan & Joel Coen

ALSO FILMED AT POINT FERMIN:
Chinatown

High Def, Digital Cinema & 3D

LA 411

www.LA411.com

PICTURED:
Pt. Fermin

LOCATION:
San Pedro

PHOTOGRAPHER:
Michael Rueter
Michael Rueter Photography/L.A.-N.Y.
www.michaelrueter.com

Supporting production in Southern California for 31 years

Ⓐ ADVERTISER SYMBOL

Refer to the General Index for cross-referencing items in this section.

Christie (714) 236-8610
10550 Camden Dr. FAX **(714) 503-3375**
Cypress, CA 90630 **www.christiedigital.com**

Cinedigm Digital Cinema Corp. (323) 463-2144
6255 Sunset Blvd., Ste. 1025 FAX **(323) 463-1319**
Hollywood, CA 90028 **www.cinedigm.com**

Deluxe Digital Cinema (818) 525-3445
300 S. Flower St. FAX **(818) 525-3443**
Burbank, CA 91502
www.bydeluxe.com/services_digital_initiatives.php

Dolby Laboratories, Inc. (818) 823-2800
3601 W. Alameda Ave. FAX **(818) 557-0890**
Burbank, CA 91505
www.dolby.com/consumer/technology/dolby-digital-cinema.html
(3-D Glasses & Projectors)

Doremi Labs, Inc. (818) 562-1101
1020 Chestnut St. FAX **(818) 562-1109**
Burbank, CA 91506 **www.doremilabs.com**

Dvidea 33 1 55 43 79 00
Paris Innovation Masséna, Hall B FAX **33 1 55 43 75 01**
Seventh Fl., 15 rue Jean-Baptiste Berlier **www.dvidea.com**
Paris 75013 France

Kodak (323) 464-6131
6700 Santa Monica Blvd. FAX **(323) 468-1568**
Los Angeles, CA 90038
motion.kodak.com/us/en/motion/products/distribution_and_exhibition/_kodak_digital_cinema/tms.htm
(TMS: Theatre Management System)

Real D (310) 385-4000
100 N. Crescent Dr., Ste. 120 FAX **(310) 385-4001**
Beverly Hills, CA 90210 **www.reald.com**
(Projectors)

Sony Corporation (201) 930-1000
One Sony Dr. **pro.sony.com**
Park Ridge, NJ 07656

Technicolor Digital Cinema (818) 260-4907
2233 N. Ontario St. **www.technicolordigitalcinema.com**
Burbank, CA 91504

Texas Instruments (972) 995-2011
P.O. Box 660199 **www.dlp.com**
Dallas, TX 75266
(Projectors)

XDC Inc. (973) 575-7811
Nine Law Dr., Ste. 200 FAX **(973) 575-7812**
Fairfield, NJ 07004 **www.xdcinema.com**

Digital Cinema Content Management & Storage Manufacturers

Archion Technologies
(888) 655-8555
(818) 840-0777
824 N. Victory Blvd.
Burbank, CA 91502
FAX **(818) 840-0877**
www.archion.com

BlueArc
44 (0) 1344 408 200
Queensgate House, Cookham Rd.
Bracknell RG12 1RB United Kingdom
FAX **44 (0) 1344 408 202**
www.bluearc.com

EditShare
(617) 782-0479
119 Braintree St., Ste. 705
Boston, MA 02134
FAX **(617) 782-1071**
www.editshare.com

Facilis Technology Inc.
(800) 620-7022
577 Main St.
Hudson, MA 01749
FAX **(978) 562-9022**
www.facilis2.com

G-Technology
(310) 449-4670
3528 Hayden Ave., Second Fl. South
Culver City, CA 90232
FAX **(310) 449-4599**
www.g-technology.com

Infortrend Corporation
(408) 988-5088
2200 Zanker Rd., Ste. 130
San Jose, CA 95131
FAX **(408) 988-6288**
www.infortrend.com

Isilon Systems, Inc.
(206) 315-7500
3101 Western Ave.
Seattle, WA 98121
FAX **(206) 315-7501**
www.isilon.com

JMR Electronics, Inc.
(818) 993-4801
8968 Fullbright Ave.
Chatsworth, CA 91311
www.jmr.com

Rorke Data, Inc. Information
(800) 328-8147
(952) 829-0300
7626 Golden Triangle Dr.
Eden Prairie, MN 55344
FAX **(952) 829-0988**
www.rorke.com

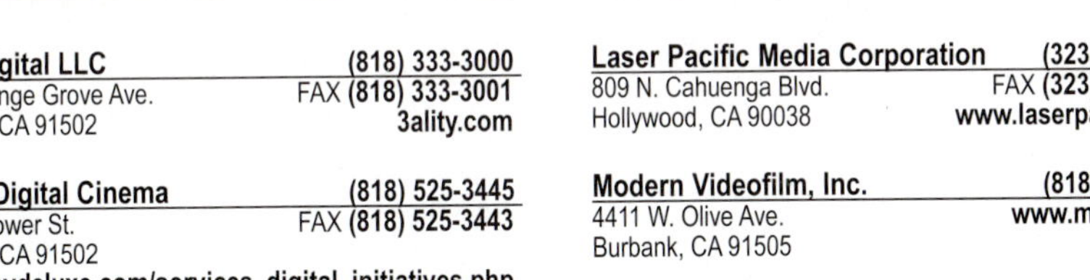

Digital Cinema Packages/Post

3ality Digital LLC
(818) 333-3000
55 E. Orange Grove Ave.
Burbank, CA 91502
FAX **(818) 333-3001**
3ality.com

Deluxe Digital Cinema
(818) 525-3445
300 S. Flower St.
Burbank, CA 91502
FAX **(818) 525-3443**
www.bydeluxe.com/services_digital_initiatives.php

Digital Jungle Post Production
(323) 962-0867
6363 Santa Monica Blvd.
Hollywood, CA 90038
FAX **(323) 962-9960**
www.digijungle.com

Dolby Laboratories, Inc.
(818) 823-2800
3601 W. Alameda Ave.
Burbank, CA 91505
FAX **(818) 557-0890**
www.dolby.com/consumer/technology/dolby-digital-cinema.html

Efilm
(323) 463-7041
1146 N. Las Palmas Ave.
Hollywood, CA 90038
FAX **(323) 465-7342**
www.efilm.com

Laser Pacific Media Corporation
(323) 462-6266
809 N. Cahuenga Blvd.
Hollywood, CA 90038
FAX **(323) 464-3233**
www.laserpacific.com

Modern Videofilm, Inc.
(818) 840-1700
4411 W. Olive Ave.
Burbank, CA 91505
www.mvfinc.com

Qube Cinema, Inc.
(818) 392-8155
4640 Lankershim Blvd., Ste. 601
North Hollywood, CA 91602
FAX **(818) 301-0401**
www.qubecinema.com

Stereomedia
(818) 442-7538
12185 Laurel Terrace Dr.
Studio City, CA 91604
FAX **(818) 761-3510**
www.3dstereomedia.com

Stereoscope Studios
(818) 729-0372
727 N. Victory Blvd.
Burbank, CA 91502
FAX **(818) 729-0374**
www.stereo3d.tv

Technicolor Digital Cinema
(818) 260-4907
2233 N. Ontario St.
Burbank, CA 91504
www.technicolordigitalcinema.com

3ality Digital LLC (818) 333-3000
55 E. Orange Grove Ave. FAX (818) 333-3001
Burbank, CA 91502 3ality.com
(3-D Cameras)

A B Sea Photo (310) 645-8992
9136 S. Sepulveda Blvd. FAX (310) 645-3645
Los Angeles, CA 90045 www.absea.net
(Underwater Housings)

Aaron & Le Duc (310) 452-2034
2210 Third St., Ste. 316 www.leducdesign.com
Santa Monica, CA 90405
(1080i, 24P, 4K Cameras, Canon, HD-CAM, HDSR & HDV, Panasonic & Sony)

Abel Cine Tech, Inc. (818) 972-9078
(888) 700-4416
801 S. Main St., Ste. A FAX (818) 972-2673
Burbank, CA 91506 www.abelcine.com
(1080i, 24P, 720P, Accessories, D-5, Decks, HD-CAM, HDSR, HDV, Monitors, Panasonic, Phantom HD High-Speed Camera, Projectors, PS Technik Adaptors, SDX 900, Sony & VTR Systems)

Absolute Rentals (818) 842-2828
2633 N. San Fernando Blvd. FAX (818) 842-8815
Burbank, CA 91504 www.absoluterentals.com
(1080i, 24P, 720P and 1080i HD Camera Systems, HD Facilities, HD Online Final Cut Pro Editorial Facility, HD-CAM, HDSR, HDV, Panasonic/Sony HD Cameras and TVR Systems, Projectors, Screens and Video Camera Systems, SDX 900, Sony and Panasonic Mini DVx & Video Projection Systems)

Action Audio & Visual (323) 461-4290
(888) 406-8164
10834 Burbank Blvd., Ste. A-100 FAX (323) 461-4292
North Hollywood, CA 91601
www.actionaudioandvisual.com
(1080i, 24P, 720P, Accessories, Converters, Cooke S4s, Decks, HD-CAM, HDSR, HDV, Monitors, Multi-Camera Systems, Panasonic, Portable Ultimatte, PS Technik Adaptors, SDX 900, Sony, Sync Generators, Ultra Primes, Wireless Monitoring & Zeiss Digiprimes)

Alan Gordon Enterprises, Inc. (323) 466-3561
5625 Melrose Ave. FAX (323) 871-2193
Los Angeles, CA 90038 www.alangordon.com

All In One Productions (323) 780-8880
1111 Corporate Dr. FAX (323) 780-8887
Monterey Park, CA 91754 www.allinone-usa.com

Alliant Event Services, Inc. (909) 622-3306
(800) 851-5415
196 University Pkwy FAX (909) 622-3917
Pomona, CA 91768 www.alliantevents.com
(Multi-Camera Packages)

Alternative Rentals (310) 204-3388
5805 W. Jefferson Blvd. FAX (310) 204-3384
Los Angeles, CA 90016 www.alternativerentals.com
(24P, DVC Pro HD, HD-CAM, HDV, Projectors, Wireless Monitoring & Zeiss)

A **American Hi Definition, Inc.** (818) 222-0022
7635 Airport Business Pkwy FAX (818) 222-0818
Van Nuys, CA 91406 www.hi-def.com
(Screens, Projectors & Video Camera Systems)

American Video Group (310) 477-1535
2542 Aiken Ave. www.americanvideogroup.com
Los Angeles, CA 90064

Ametron Audio Video (323) 466-4321
(323) 464-1144
1546 N. Argyle Ave. FAX (323) 871-0127
Hollywood, CA 90028 www.ametron.com

Artistic Resources Corporation (323) 965-5200
535 N. Brand Blvd., Ste. 235 FAX (323) 965-5209
Glendale, CA 91203 www.artisticresources.com

Atlantic Cine Equipment (818) 794-9410
(410) 340-9674
1026 Griswold Ave. www.aceeast.com
San Fernando, CA 91340

B2 Services, Inc. (818) 566-8769
3818 Burbank Blvd. FAX (818) 566-1378
Burbank, CA 91505 www.b2servicesinc.com
(1080i, 24P, 720P, D-5, Decks, DVC-Pro, HD-CAM, HDSR, HDV & Monitors)

Band Pro Film & Digital, Inc. (818) 841-9655
3403 W. Pacific Ave. FAX (818) 841-7649
Burbank, CA 91505 www.bandpro.com

Bexel (818) 841-5051
(800) 225-6185
2701 N. Ontario St. FAX (818) 841-1572
Burbank, CA 91504 www.bexel.com

Big Door (310) 546-6100
P.O. Box 3577 FAX (310) 546-4069
Manhattan Beach, CA 90266 www.bigdoor.tv

Birns & Sawyer, Inc. (323) 466-8211
(818) 766-2525
6381 De Longpre Ave. FAX (323) 466-1868
Hollywood, CA 90028 www.birnsandsawyer.com
(Cooke S4s, Mini DVs, Multi-Camera Systems, Panasonic, PS Technik Adaptors, SDX 900, Sony & Ultra Primes)

BlueScreen, LLC/Bob Kertesz (323) 467-7572
137 N. Larchmont Blvd., Ste. 508 www.bluescreen.com
Los Angeles, CA 90004
(Blue and Green Screen Facilities & Portable Ultimatte)

Briggs Video, Inc./Peter Ney (661) 250-8258
4111 W. Vanowen Pl. FAX (661) 250-8259
Burbank, CA 91505 www.briggsvideo.com

Broadcast Store (818) 998-9100
9420 Lurline Ave., Ste. C FAX (818) 998-9106
Chatsworth, CA 91311 www.broadcaststore.com

Brown Bag Films and Hi Def (310) 455-0633
608 Fernwood Pacific Dr. FAX (310) 455-0633
Topanga, CA 90290 www.films-and-hi-def.com

Cablecam Inc. (818) 349-4955
21303 Itasca St. FAX (818) 349-3879
Chatsworth, CA 91311 www.cablecam.com

Camera Support (818) 557-1400
(800) 995-5427
2827 N. San Fernando Blvd. FAX (818) 557-1323
Burbank, CA 91504 www.camerasupport.com
(720P and 1080i HD Camera Systems, Accessories, Multi-Camera Concert Packages & HD Online Final Cut Pro Editorial Facility)

Cimavision, Inc. (310) 614-3644
www.cimavisioninc.com

Cinema Rentals, Inc. (661) 222-7342
(877) 877-9605
25876 The Old Road., Ste. 174 FAX (661) 253-3643
Stevenson Ranch, CA 91381 www.cinemarentals.com

Clairmont Camera (818) 761-4440
4343 Lankershim Blvd. FAX (818) 761-0861
North Hollywood, CA 91602 www.clairmont.com

Coastal Media Group (818) 880-9800
26660 Agoura Rd. FAX (818) 579-9026
Calabasas, CA 91302 www.coastalmediagroup.com

Crescent Hollywood, LLC (310) 745-0491
(213) 280-9690
6031 Acacia St. FAX (310) 745-0691
Los Angeles, CA 90056 www.crescenthollywood.com
(1080i, 24P, 720P, Accessories, Converters, Decks, DVC-Pro, Editing Facilities, Monitors, Multi-Camera Concert Packages, Multi-Camera Systems & Panasonic)

Ⓐ **Cutting Edge Productions, Inc.** (310) 326-4500
(310) 367-0416
22904 Lockness Ave. FAX (310) 326-4715
Torrance, CA 90501 www.cuttingedgeproductions.tv
(1080i, 24P, 720P, Blue Screen Facilities, Decks, Green Screen Facilities, HDV, Monitors, Multi-Camera Concert Packages, Multi-Camera Systems, Production Trucks, Projectors, Sony & VTR Systems)

Dalsa (818) 884-7000
6160 Variel Ave. FAX (818) 884-7022
Woodland Hills, CA 91367 www.dalsa.com/dc
(1080i, 24P, 4K Cameras, 720P, Accessories, Converters, Cooke S4s, Decks, DVC-Pro, Green Screen Facilities, HD-CAM, HDSR, HDV, Monitors, Panasonic, PS Technik Adaptors, SDX 900, Sony, Ultra Primes, VTR Systems, Wireless Monitoring & Zeiss Digiprimes)

Ⓐ **Deck Hand, Inc.** (818) 557-8403
1905 Victory Blvd., Ste. 8 FAX (818) 557-8406
Glendale, CA 91201 www.deckhand.com
(D-5, DVCPro HD, HDCAM, HDCAM SR & HDV)

Doggicam, Inc. (818) 845-8470
1500 W. Verdugo Ave. FAX (818) 845-8477
Burbank, CA 91506 www.doggicam.com

editSource (310) 572-7230
(310) 466-3624
12044 Washington Blvd. FAX (310) 572-7238
Los Angeles, CA 90066 www.theeditsource.com

EVS/Express Video Supply, Inc. (818) 552-4590
(800) 238-8480
1620 Flower St. FAX (818) 552-4591
Glendale, CA 91201 www.evsonline.com

Farr Out Productions, LLC (310) 902-5944
FAX (818) 830-3608
www.farroutpro.com
(1080i, 24P, 720P, HDV, HDX900, Panasonic, Sony & Wireless Video Monitoring)

Fellpro (310) 490-5185
(310) 318-3962
FAX (310) 318-1128
www.fellpro.com

Gemini 3D (310) 395-4739
www.gemini3dcamera.com

Gyron Systems International, A Division of Wolfe Air Aviation, Ltd. (626) 584-8722
39 E. Walnut St. FAX (626) 584-4069
Pasadena, CA 91103 www.gyron.com

HD Camera Rentals (323) 737-1314
4117 W. Jefferson Blvd. FAX (310) 861-0163
Los Angeles, CA 90016 www.hdcamerarentals.com
(4K Cameras, Accessories, Cooke S4s, Decks, DVC-Pro, HD-CAM, HDSR, Multi-Camera Concert Packages, Multi-Camera Systems, PS Technik Adaptors, SDX 900, Sony XDCAM, Ultra Primes, VTR Systems & Wireless Monitoring)

HD Cinema (310) 434-9500
12233 Olympic Blvd., Ste. 134 FAX (310) 434-9600
Los Angeles, CA 90064 www.hd-cinema.com

HD Prod Video LA, LLC (818) 400-2900
(661) 287-0092
25626 Christie Court www.hdprola.com
Stevenson Ranch, CA 91381

HD Wave Productions (818) 415-1869
(612) 281-1869
3650 Barham Blvd., Ste. T223 FAX (866) 510-0159
Toluca Lake, CA 90068 www.hdwave.com

Ⓐ **Helinet Aviation Services** (818) 902-0229
(866) 435-4638
16644 Roscoe Blvd. FAX (818) 902-9278
Van Nuys, CA 91406 www.helinet.com

Hermosa Pictures (310) 909-8525
1850 Industrial St., Ste. 307 FAX (310) 349-3441
Los Angeles, CA 90021 www.hermosapictures.com
(1080i, 24P, 720P, Accessories, Canon, Monitors, Multi-Camera Systems, Panasonic & Sony)

Hollywood Camera, Inc. (818) 972-5000
(818) 720-8404
3100 N. Damon Way FAX (818) 972-5010
Burbank, CA 91505 www.hollywoodcamera.com

Home Planet Productions (805) 965-9848
(818) 422-4144
FAX (805) 965-2329
www.homeplanetproductions.com

HVS Productions (858) 573-0987
(619) 992-9714
7270 Engineer Rd., Ste. A FAX (858) 569-0094
San Diego, CA 92111 www.hvsprod.com

Indie Rentals (323) 465-7700
(323) 571-9476
7022 W. Sunset Blvd. FAX (323) 297-2773
Hollywood, CA 90028 www.indierentals.com
(1080i, 24P, 720P, Accessories, Converters, Editing Facilities, HDV, Monitors, Multi-Camera Systems, Panasonic, Projectors, PS Technik Adaptors, Sony & Wireless Monitoring)

Innovision Optics (310) 453-4866
1719 21st St. FAX (310) 453-4677
Santa Monica, CA 90404 www.innovisionoptics.com

John Sharaf Photography (310) 451-4048
(310) 650-6996
16132 Alcima Ave. FAX (310) 454-6768
Pacific Palisades, CA 90272 www.sharaf.net

Kasdin Productions (310) 914-4847
2117 Colby Ave. www.kasdin.com
Los Angeles, CA 90025

kosmos innertainment group (310) 490-5369
(310) 433-2154
FAX (310) 641-8439
www.redone4rent.com
(1080i, 24P, 4K Cameras, 720P, Converters, HDV, Monitors, Multi-Camera Concert Packages, Multi-Camera Systems, Projectors, RED Cameras & Sony)

Les Sechler Specialty Products (310) 420-5146
32545-B Golden Lantern St., Ste. 114 FAX (615) 599-8020
Dana Point, CA 92629

Monte Vista Pictures (951) 764 2343
31915 Rancho California Rd., Ste. 200-135
Oceanside, CA 92591
www.montevistapictures.com

Moviola/Moviola Cameras (323) 467-3107
(800) 468-3107
1135 N. Mansfield Ave. FAX (323) 464-1518
Los Angeles, CA 90038 www.moviola.com

National Mobile Television (310) 782-9945
2740 California St. www.nmtv.com
Torrance, CA 90503
(1080i, 24P, 720P & Production Trucks)

Nettmann Systems International (818) 623-1661
FAX (818) 623-1671
www.camerasystems.com

Old School Cameras (310) 710-6525
(323) 462-0914
920 N. Citrus Ave. FAX (323) 462-5935
Hollywood, CA 90038 www.oldschoolcameras.com
(1080i, 24P, 4K Cameras, 720P, Converters, Editing Facilities, HD-CAM, HDV, Monitors, Panasonic, RED Cameras, Sony, Wireless Monitoring & Zeiss Super Speed Primes)

Pace Technologies (818) 565-0005
2117 Empire Ave. FAX (818) 565-0006
Burbank, CA 91504 www.pacehd.com

Panavision (818) 316-1000
Corporate Headquarters FAX (818) 316-1111
6219 DeSoto Ave. www.panavision.com
Woodland Hills, CA 91367

Pictor Productions, Inc./Sam Painter (323) 876-7302
(213) 999-1985
FAX (323) 876-7303

Pictorvision Inc (818) 785-9282
(800) 876-5583
7701 Haskell Ave., Ste. B FAX (818) 785-9787
Van Nuys, CA 91406 www.pictorvision.com

Pivotal Post (818) 760-6000
4142 Lankershim Blvd. FAX (818) 760-6011
North Hollywood, CA 91602 www.pivotalpost.com
(1080i, 24P, HD Online Final Cut Pro Editorial Facility, HD-CAM, HDSR, HDV, Projectors & Video Projection Systems)

POV-HD (310) 866-9300
(POV Cameras & Specailized Mounts)

Pro HD Rentals, Inc. (310) 453-3301
1448 19th St. FAX (310) 453-3310
Santa Monica, CA 90404 www.prohdrentals.com

Pro-Cam Video Systems, Inc. (818) 954-9300
(800) 818-8433
140 E. Tujunga Ave. FAX (818) 954-9450
Burbank, CA 91502 www.pro-cam.tv

RED Digital Cinema (949) 206-7900
20291 Valencia Circle FAX (949) 206-7990
Lake Forest, CA 92630 www.red.com

RentHD.com/Lightpost Productions (818) 955-7678
1701 W. Burbank Blvd., Ste. 201 FAX (818) 955-5181
Burbank, CA 91506 www.renthd.com
(24p, 720P and 1080i HD Camera Systems, HD Facilities, HD Online Final Cut Pro Editorial Facility, HD-CAM, HDV, Panasonic HD Cameras, Sony HDSR & VTR Systems)

Revolver Films (310) 827-2441
4040 Del Rey Ave., Ste. 5 FAX (310) 827-2661
Marina del Rey, CA 90292 www.revolverfilmsla.com

Schulman Mobile Video (323) 785-2528
1320 N. Wilton Pl. FAX (323) 785-2529
Hollywood, CA 90028 www.schulmanmv.com
(HD Production Trucks)

Sim Video Los Angeles (323) 978-9000
738 Cahuenga Blvd. FAX (323) 978-9018
Hollywood, CA 90038 www.simvideola.com

Sony Corporation (201) 930-1000
One Sony Dr. pro.sony.com
Park Ridge, NJ 07656

Spectrum HD (310) 979-7170
12233 W. Olympic Blvd., Ste. 314 FAX (310) 979-7173
Los Angeles, CA 90064 www.spectrumhd.com

Speed Vision Technologies, Inc. (858) 356-0855
(858) 967-0401
4485 Sunset Bluffs Way FAX (858) 356-0901
San Diego, CA 92130 www.speedvisiontech.com
(720P & Accessories)

Stereomedia (818) 442-7538
12185 Laurel Terrace Dr. FAX (818) 761-3510
Studio City, CA 91604 www.3dstereomedia.com

T-stop, inc. (323) 708-4555
(888) 411-7331
5627 Melrose Ave. FAX (610) 808-4555
Los Angeles, CA 90038 www.t-stopinc.com
(1080i, 24P, 4K Cameras, 720P, Accessories, DVC-Pro, Monitors, Panasonic & Red Cameras)

Gary Taillon (805) 443-3806
2168 Meadow Brook Court
Thousand Oaks, CA 91362

TCH/The Camera House (818) 997-3802
(818) 427-6219
7351 Fulton Ave. FAX (818) 997-3885
North Hollywood, CA 91605 www.thecamerahouse.com

Touring Video, Inc. (818) 953-8700
(800) 773-8687
FAX (818) 953-8707
www.touringvideo.com

Twelve Tone Productions (323) 633-1000
P.O. Box 36356 FAX (323) 934-3491
Los Angeles, CA 90036
www.twelvetoneproductions.com
(1080i, 24P, 720P, Accessories, Green Screen Facilities, HD-CAM, HDV & Multi-Camera Systems)

Tyler Camera Systems (818) 989-4420
(800) 390-6070
14218 Aetna St. FAX (818) 989-0423
Van Nuys, CA 91401 www.tylermount.com

Uptown 6 (323) 274-2552
6460 Odin St. FAX (310) 497-7954
Los Angeles, CA 90068 www.uptown6.com
(1080i, 24P, 720P, Accessories, Monitors & Panasonic)

Video Applications, Inc. (714) 508-1858
(800) 835-5432
14791 Myford Rd. FAX (714) 508-2362
Tustin, CA 92780 www.videoapps.com
(1080i, 720P, Converters, D-5, Decks, DVC-Pro, HD-CAM, Monitors, Multi-Camera Systems, Panasonic, Projectors, Sony & Video Projection Systems)

Video Equipment Rentals (818) 956-1444
(800) 794-1407
912 Ruberta Ave. FAX (818) 241-4519
Glendale, CA 91201 www.verrents.com
(1080i, 24P, 720P, Accessories, D-5, Decks, DVC-Pro, HD-CAM, HDSR, HDV, Monitors, Multi-Camera Systems, Panasonic & Projectors)

Video Gear Source (818) 557-8225
3619 W. Magnolia Blvd. FAX (818) 559-5684
Burbank, CA 91505 www.videogearsource.com

Video Production Specialists (VPS) (866) 447-3877
FAX (310) 577-0850
www.videoproductionspecialists.com
(24P, HDV, Screens and Video Camera Systems & Video Projection Systems)

Videowerks (310) 393-8754
(310) 780-4156
3435 Ocean Park Blvd., Ste. 107 FAX (310) 399-1829
Santa Monica, CA 90405 www.videowerks.com
(1080i, 24P, 720P, DVC-Pro, HDV & Panasonic)

Visionary Forces Broadcast Rentals **(818) 562-1960**
148 S. Victory Blvd. FAX **(818) 562-1270**
Burbank, CA 91502 **www.visionaryforces.com**
(1080i, 24P, 720P, Converters, D-5, Decks, DVC-Pro, HD-CAM, HDSR, HDV, Monitors, Panasonic, Sony, Sync Generators & VTR Systems)

Westcoast Video Productions, Inc. **(818) 785-8033** **(800) 477-8417**
14141 Covello St., Ste. 9A FAX **(818) 785-8035**
Van Nuys, CA 91405 **www.wvpinc.com**

Westside Media Group **(310) 979-3500** **(818) 779-8600**
12233 W. Olympic Blvd., Ste. 152 FAX **(310) 979-3503**
West Los Angeles, CA 90064 **www.wmgmedia.com**
(1080i, 24P, 4K Cameras, 720P, D-5, DVC-Pro, Editing Facilities, HD-CAM, HDSR, HDV, Monitors & Sync Generators)

Wexler Video **(818) 846-9381** **(800) 939-5371**
1111 S. Victory Blvd. FAX **(818) 846-9399**
Burbank, CA 91502 **www.wexlervideo.com**

Wintech Video **(818) 501-6565**
4455 Van Nuys Blvd. FAX **(818) 501-6566**
Sherman Oaks, CA 91603 **www.wintechvideo.com**

World Wide Digital Services, Inc. **(818) 841-1669**
171 W. Magnolia Blvd. FAX **(818) 841-0239**
Burbank, CA 91502 **www.worldwidela.com**

Zona Productions, Inc. **(323) 876-0132**
(HD Facilities)

Affusion Media/ Visual Data Media Services Inc. (818) 558-3363
145 W. Magnolia Blvd. FAX (818) 845-2550
Burbank, CA 91502 www.visualdatainc.com

All In One Productions (323) 780-8880
1111 Corporate Dr. FAX (323) 780-8887
Monterey Park, CA 91754 www.allinone-usa.com

Brown Bag Films and Hi Def (310) 455-0633
608 Fernwood Pacific Dr. FAX (310) 455-0633
Topanga, CA 90290 www.films-and-hi-def.com

CCI Digital, Inc. (818) 562-6300
2921 W. Alameda Ave. FAX (818) 562-8222
Burbank, CA 91505 www.ccidigital.com

Copy Right Video (310) 315-4151
1554 18th St. FAX (310) 582-1554
Santa Monica, CA 90404 www.copyrightvideo.com

Custom Video (310) 543-4901
707 Torrance Blvd., Ste. 105 www.customvideo.tv
Redondo Beach, CA 90277

A **Deck Hand, Inc.** (818) 557-8403
1905 Victory Blvd., Ste. 8 FAX (818) 557-8406
Glendale, CA 91201 www.deckhand.com

DG FastChannel (323) 603-5220
(800) 324-5672
3330 Cahuenga Blvd. West, Fourth Fl. FAX (323) 603-5300
Los Angeles, CA 90068 www.dgfastchannel.com

Digital Jungle Post Production (323) 962-0867
6363 Santa Monica Blvd. FAX (323) 962-9960
Hollywood, CA 90038 www.digijungle.com

Dub-It.com (323) 993-9570
(888) 993-8248
1110 N. Tamarind Ave. FAX (323) 962-3446
Hollywood, CA 90038 www.dub-it.com

Duplitech Corporation (310) 781-1101
2637 Manhattan Beach Blvd. FAX (310) 781-1109
Redondo Beach, CA 90278 www.duplitech.com

The Edit Bay (714) 978-7878
571 N. Poplar St., Ste. I FAX (714) 978-7858
Orange, CA 92868 www.theeditbay.com

Five Star Video/1555 TV (818) 558-1679
3400 W. Alameda Ave., Ste. A FAX (818) 558-4367
Burbank, CA 91505 www.1555.tv

HD Creative Services (323) 461-3715
723 N. Cahuenga Blvd. www.hdcreativeservices.com
Hollywood, CA 90038

Level 3 Post (818) 840-7200
(818) 840-7889
2901 W. Alameda, Third Fl. www.level3post.com
Burbank, CA 91505

Lightning Media (818) 556-2777
3723 W. Olive Ave. FAX (818) 556-2770
Burbank, CA 91505 www.lightningmedia.com

Lightning Media (323) 957-9255
1415 N. Cahuenga Blvd. FAX (323) 330-6217
Hollywood, CA 90028 www.lightningmedia.com

New & Unique Videos (619) 644-3000
(800) 365-8433
7323 Rondel Court FAX (619) 644-3001
San Diego, CA 92119 www.newuniquevideos.com

The Studios at Paramount (323) 956-3041
The Studios at Paramount FAX (323) 862-2242
Post Production Services www.thestudiosatparamount.com
5555 Melrose Ave.
Los Angeles, CA 90038

Point360 (818) 556-5700
(866) 968-4336
1133 N. Hollywood Way FAX (818) 556-5753
Burbank, CA 91505 www.point360.com

Point360 (310) 481-7000
(866) 968-4336
12421 W. Olympic Blvd. FAX (323) 466-7406
Los Angeles, CA 90064 www.point360.com

Post Digital Services (323) 845-0812
1258 N. Highland Ave., Ste. 210 FAX (323) 845-0812
Hollywood, CA 90038 www.postdigitalservices.com

Post Media Group, Inc. (310) 289-5959
337 S. Robertson Blvd. www.postmediagroup.tv
Beverly Hills, CA 90211

Santa Monica Video, Inc. (310) 451-0333
(800) 843-3827
1505 11th St. FAX (310) 458-3350
Santa Monica, CA 90401 www.santamonicavideo.com

Tylie Jones & Associates, Inc. (818) 955-7600
3620 W. Valhalla Dr. FAX (818) 955-8551
Burbank, CA 91505 www.tylie.com

Victory Studios LA (818) 769-1776
10911 Riverside Dr., Ste. 100 FAX (818) 760-1280
North Hollywood, CA 91602 www.victorystudiosla.com

Westside Media Group (310) 979-3500
(818) 779-8600
12233 W. Olympic Blvd., Ste. 152 www.wmgmedia.com
West Los Angeles, CA 90064

World of Video & Audio (310) 659-5959
(866) 900-3827
8717 Wilshire Blvd. FAX (310) 659-8247
Beverly Hills, CA 90211 www.wova.com

Aaron & Le Duc (310) 452-2034
2210 Third St., Ste. 316 www.leducdesign.com
Santa Monica, CA 90405

Absolute Rentals (818) 842-2828
2633 N. San Fernando Blvd. FAX (818) 842-8815
Burbank, CA 91504 www.absoluterentals.com

Address One (310) 838-7783
(323) 465-4415
c/o Raleigh Studios FAX (323) 960-4961
662 N. Van Ness Ave., Ste. 301 www.addressone.tv
Los Angeles, CA 90004

AlphaDogs, Inc. (818) 729-9262
1612 W. Olive Ave., Ste. 200 FAX (818) 729-8537
Burbank, CA 91506 www.alphadogs.tv

Alternative Rentals (310) 204-3388
5805 W. Jefferson Blvd. FAX (310) 204-3384
Los Angeles, CA 90016 www.alternativerentals.com

Artistic Resources Corporation (323) 965-5200
535 N. Brand Blvd., Ste. 235 FAX (323) 965-5209
Glendale, CA 91203 www.artisticresources.com

Audio Video Systems International (818) 888-7625
5101 Tendilla Ave. FAX (818) 730-5047
Woodland Hills, CA 91364 www.usedvideo.net

Avid (818) 557-2520
(800) 949-2843
101 S. First St., Ste. 200 FAX (818) 557-2558
Burbank, CA 91502 www.avid.com

B2 Services, Inc. (818) 566-8769
3818 Burbank Blvd. FAX (818) 566-1378
Burbank, CA 91505 www.b2servicesinc.com

Big Time Picture Company, Inc. (310) 207-0921
12210½ Nebraska Ave. FAX (310) 826-0071
Los Angeles, CA 90025 www.bigtimepic.com

Broadcast Store (818) 998-9100
9420 Lurline Ave., Ste. C FAX (818) 998-9106
Chatsworth, CA 91311 www.broadcaststore.com

Brown Bag Films and Hi Def (310) 455-0633
608 Fernwood Pacific Dr. FAX (310) 455-0633
Topanga, CA 90290 www.films-and-hi-def.com

Catalyst Post Services (818) 841-4952
3029 W. Burbank Blvd. FAX (818) 566-4175
Burbank, CA 91505 www.catalystpost.com

Christy's Editorial (818) 845-1755
(800) 556-5706
3625 W. Pacific Ave. FAX (818) 845-1756
Burbank, CA 91505 www.christys.net

Crescent Hollywood, LLC (310) 745-0491
(213) 280-9690
6031 Acacia St. FAX (310) 694-8555
Los Angeles, CA 90056 www.crescenthollywood.com

D-Tech/Digital Storage Rentals (323) 876-8700
(323) 850-8854
3575 Cahuenga Blvd., Ste. 125-1 FAX (323) 850-8865
Los Angeles, CA 90068 www.digirent.com

A **Deck Hand, Inc.** (818) 557-8403
1905 Victory Blvd., Ste. 8 FAX (818) 557-8406
Glendale, CA 91201 www.deckhand.com

The Digital Difference (310) 581-8800
1201 Olympic Blvd. FAX (310) 581-8808
Santa Monica, CA 90404 www.digdif.com

Digital Systems Media (949) 215-7151
(877) 629-7810
17702 Mitchell North, Ste. 110 FAX (949) 215-6399
Irvine, CA 92614 www.digitalsystemsmedia.com

Drive This! (310) 345-4304
(800) 910-7646
FAX (626) 963-5706
www.drivethis.tv

editSource (310) 572-7230
12044 Washington Blvd. FAX (310) 572-7238
Los Angeles, CA 90066 www.theeditsource.com

Electric Picture Solutions (818) 766-5000
3753 Cahuenga Blvd. West FAX (818) 623-7547
Studio City, CA 91604 www.electricpicturesolutions.com

Firestarter Rentals (310) 420-5146
880 W. First St., Ste. 513 FAX (866) 450-6716
Los Angeles, CA 90012

Fotokem Nonlinear Services (818) 729-0007
900 W. Alameda Ave. FAX (818) 441-5199
Burbank, CA 91506 www.fotokem.com

Global Entertainment Partners/GEP (818) 380-8133
3747 Cahuenga Blvd. West FAX (818) 954-0211
Studio City, CA 91604 www.gepartners.com

Go Edit, Inc. (818) 284-6260
5614 Cahuenga Blvd. FAX (818) 985-6260
North Hollywood, CA 91601 www.goedit.tv

HD Creative Services (323) 461-3715
723 N. Cahuenga Blvd. www.hdcreativeservices.com
Hollywood, CA 90038

Hollywood-DI (323) 850-3550
1041 N. Formosa Ave., Bldg. 10 FAX (323) 850-3551
Los Angeles, CA 90046 www.hollywooddi.com

Hula Post Production (818) 954-0200
3747 Cahuenga Blvd. West FAX (818) 954-0211
Studio City, CA 91604 www.hulapost.com

Jurifilm Entertainment (310) 915-9559
(877) 587-4345
4404 Westlawn Ave. FAX (310) 391-4217
Los Angeles, CA 90066 www.jurifilm.com

Kasdin Productions (310) 914-4847
www.kasdin.com

Key Code Media, Inc. (818) 303-3900
11530 Ventura Blvd. FAX (818) 303-3901
Studio City, CA 91604 www.keycodemedia.com

LA Digital Post, Inc. (310) 954-8650
(818) 487-5000
2260 Centinela Ave. FAX (310) 954-8686
West Los Angeles, CA 90064 www.ladigital.com

LA Digital Post, Inc. (818) 487-5000
(310) 954-8650
11311 Camarillo St. FAX (818) 487-5015
Toluca Lake, CA 91602 www.ladigital.com

M.G. Digital, Inc. (310) 558-3907
(310) 558-3424
8500 Steller Dr., Ste. 1 FAX (310) 559-7800
Culver City, CA 90232 www.mgdigital.us

Matchframe Video (818) 840-6800
610 N. Hollywood Way FAX (818) 840-2726
Burbank, CA 91505 www.matchframevideo.com

Moviola/J & R Film Company
1135 N. Mansfield Ave.
Hollywood, CA 90038
(323) 467-3107
(800) 468-3107
FAX (323) 464-1518
www.moviola.com

Orbit Digital
12233 W. Olympic Blvd., Ste. 134
Los Angeles, CA 90064
(324) 298-2250
FAX (323) 850-3801
www.orbitdigital.com

Pivotal Post
4142 Lankershim Blvd.
North Hollywood, CA 91602
(818) 760-6000
(818) 760-6007
FAX (818) 760-6012
www.pivotalpost.com

Pixel Plantation
4111 W. Alameda Ave., Ste. 301
Burbank, CA 91505
(818) 566-7777
www.pixelplantation.com

Planet Post
(858) 573-9303
(619) 435-0888
www.planetpost.net

Post Media Group, Inc.
337 S. Robertson Blvd.
Beverly Hills, CA 90211
(310) 289-5959
www.postmediagroup.tv

Precision Productions + Post
10718 McCune Ave.
Los Angeles, CA 90034
(310) 839-4600
FAX (310) 839-4601
www.precisionpost.com

Promax Systems, Inc.
16 Technology Dr., Ste. 106
Irvine, CA 92618
(949) 727-3977
(800) 977-6629
FAX (949) 727-3546
www.promax.com

QSR Systems
(323) 200-2155
FAX (661) 257-6380
www.qsrsystems.com

Runway, Inc.
10575 Virginia Ave.
Culver City, CA 90232
(310) 636-2000
(888) 297-2843
FAX (310) 636-2034
www.runway.com

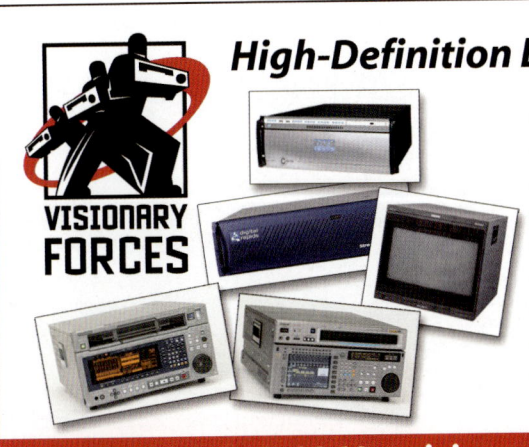

Sim Video Los Angeles
738 Cahuenga Blvd.
Hollywood, CA 90038
(323) 978-9000
FAX (323) 978-9018
www.simvideola.com

Thumbwar
5700 Melrose Ave., Ste. 302
Los Angeles, CA 90038
(310) 910-9030
FAX (310) 910-9031
thumbwar.tv

Touring Video, Inc.
827 Hollywood Way, Ste. 424
Burbank, CA 91505
(818) 953-8700
(800) 773-8687
FAX (818) 953-8707
www.touringvideo.com

TV Magic, Inc.
107 W. Valencia Ave.
Burbank, CA 91502
(818) 841-6886
www.tvmagic.tv

TV Pro Gear
1630 Flower St.
Glendale, CA 91201
(818) 246-7100
FAX (818) 246-1945
www.tvprogear.com

Video Equipment Rentals
912 Ruberta Ave.
Glendale, CA 91201
(818) 956-1444
(800) 794-1407
FAX (818) 241-4519
www.verrents.com

A **Visionary Forces Broadcast Rentals**
148 S. Victory Blvd.
Burbank, CA 91502
(818) 562-1960
FAX (818) 562-1270
www.visionaryforces.com

Westside Media Group
12233 W. Olympic Blvd., Ste. 152
West Los Angeles, CA 90064
(310) 979-3500
(818) 779-8600
FAX (310) 979-3503
www.wmgmedia.com

Wexler Video
1111 S. Victory Blvd.
Burbank, CA 91502
(818) 846-9381
(800) 939-5371
FAX (818) 846-9399
www.wexlervideo.com

Accom (650) 328-3818
1490 O'Brien Dr. FAX (650) 327-2511
Menlo Park, CA 94025 www.accom.com
(Video Editing Systems, Processing Tools and Storage)

AccuScene Corporation 44 (0) 1383 828 880
Unit Four FAX 44 (0) 1383 828 882
Dunfermline Business Centre www.accuscene.com
12 Att Ave.
Dunfermline, Fife KY11 3BZ United Kingdom
(Compact Display Products/Viewfinders)

Acrodyne Industries (Ai) (888) 881-4447
10706 Beaver Dam Rd. www.acrodyne.com
Cockeysville, MD 21030
(Transmitters)

AJA Video (530) 274-2048
(800) 251-4224
443 Crown Point Circle, Ste. C FAX (530) 274-9442
Grass Valley, CA 95945 www.aja.com
(Interface Tools & Video Converters)

Amphibico (514) 333-8666
459 Deslauriers FAX (514) 333-1339
Montreal, QC H4N 1W2 Canada www.amphibico.com
(Underwater Camera Housings and Accessories)

Angenieux 33 477 90 78 00
(Lenses) FAX 33 477 90 78 03
www.angenieux.com

Apple, Inc. (408) 996-1010
One Infinite Loop www.apple.com
Cupertino, CA 95014
(Video Editing Systems and Monitors)

Astro Systems, Inc. (626) 336-7001
(877) 882-7876
418 Cloverleaf Dr., Ste. C FAX (626) 336-7005
Baldwin Park, CA 91706 www.astro-systems.com
(Video Monitors and Processing Tools)

Auto Desk (415) 507-5000
111 McInnis Pkwy FAX (415) 507-5100
San Rafael, CA 94903 www.autodesk.com/ME
(Video Editing and FX Systems)

Avica Technology Corporation (310) 450-9090
1201 Olympic Blvd. FAX (310) 450-5353
Santa Monica, CA 90404 www.avicatech.com
(Exhibition Software Systems & Post Production)

Avid (818) 557-2520
(800) 949-2843
101 S. First St., Ste. 200 FAX (818) 557-2558
Burbank, CA 91502 www.avid.com
(Video Editing and FX Systems)

Band Pro Film & Digital, Inc. (818) 841-9655
3403 W. Pacific Ave. FAX (818) 841-7649
Burbank, CA 91505 www.bandpro.com
(Prime Lenses)

Blackmagic Design (408) 954-0500
1551 McCarthy Blvd., Ste. 106 FAX (408) 954-0508
Milpitas, CA 95035 www.blackmagic-design.com
(Video Cards)

BOXX Technologies, Inc. (512) 835-0400
(877) 877-2699
10435 Burnet Rd., Ste. 120 FAX (512) 835-0434
Austin, TX 78758 www.boxxtech.com
(Video Editing and FX Systems)

Canon (800) 321-4388
One Canon Plaza www.cannonbroadcast.com
Lake Success, NY 11042
(Lenses)

CELCO (909) 481-4648
8660 Red Oak Ave. FAX (909) 481-6899
Rancho Cucamonga, CA 91730 www.celco.com
(Film Recorders)

Chyron Corporation (631) 845-2000
Five Hub Dr. FAX (631) 845-3895
Melville, NY 11747 www.chyron.com
(Video Graphics Systems)

Cobalt Digital, Inc. (217) 344-1243
(800) 669-1691
2406 E. University Ave. FAX (217) 344-1245
Urbana, IL 61802 www.cobaltdigital.com
(Video Conversion Tools)

Compix Media (310) 320-8937
2730 Monterey St., Ste. 103 FAX (310) 320-8938
Torrance, CA 90503 www.compixmedia.com
(Character Generators)

da Vinci Systems, Inc. (954) 688-5600
4397 NW 124 Ave. FAX (954) 575-5936
Coral Springs, FL 33065 www.davsys.com
(Color Image Enhancement and Restoration Tools)

Digital Projection, Inc. (770) 420-1350
55 Chastain Rd., Ste. 115 FAX (770) 420-1360
Kennesaw, GA 30144 www.digitalprojection.com
(DLP-Based Projection Systems)

Digital Vision, Inc. (818) 769-8111
4605 Lankershim Blvd., Ste. 700 FAX (818) 769-1888
North Hollywood, CA 91602 www.digitalvision.se
(Video Processing Tools)

Doggicam, Inc. (818) 845-8470
1500 W. Verdugo Ave. FAX (818) 845-8477
Burbank, CA 91506 www.doggicam.com
(Remote Heads)

Dolby Laboratories, Inc. (818) 823-2800
3601 W. Alameda Ave. FAX (818) 557-0890
Burbank, CA 91505 www.dolby.com
(Audio Processing Systems)

Doremi Labs, Inc. (818) 562-1101
1020 Chestnut St. FAX (818) 562-1109
Burbank, CA 91506 www.doremilabs.com
(Disk Recorders & Video Servers)

Draper, Inc. (800) 238-7999
411 S. Pearl St. FAX (765) 987-7142
Spiceland, IN 47385 www.draperinc.com
(Front and Rear Projection Screens)

DSC Laboratories (905) 673-3211
3565 Nashua Dr. FAX (905) 673-0929
Mississauga, ON L4V 1R1 Canada www.dsclabs.com
(Camera Test Systems)

DVS Digital Video, Inc. (818) 846-3600
300 E. Magnolia Blvd., Ste. 102 FAX (818) 846-3648
Burbank, CA 91502 www.dvsus.com
(Video Processing Tools)

Electrosonic (818) 333-3631
3420 N. San Fernando Blvd. FAX (818) 566-4923
Burbank, CA 91504 www.electrosonic.com
(Display and Projection Systems)

Evertz (905) 335-3700
212 N. Evergreen St. FAX (905) 335-3573
Burbank, CA 91505 www.evertz.com
(Video Processing Tools)

eyeon Software, Inc. (416) 686-8411
(Video Compositing and FX Systems) FAX (416) 698-9315
www.eyeonline.com

Faraday Technology, Ltd. 44 (0) 1782 661501
(Delay Lines & Filters) FAX **44 (0) 1782 630101**
www.faradaytech.co.uk

Folsom Research, Inc. (916) 859-2500
(888) 414-7226
11101-A Trade Center Dr. FAX **(916) 859-2515**
Rancho Cordova, CA 95670 **www.folsom.com**
(Video Processing Tools)

FOR-A Corporation of America (714) 894-3311
11125 Knott Ave., Ste. A FAX **(714) 894-5399**
Cypress, CA 90630 **www.for-a.com**
(Video Processing Tools)

Fujinon, Inc. (973) 633-5600
10 High Point Dr. FAX **(973) 633-5216**
Wayne, NJ 07470 **www.fujinon.com**
(Lenses)

Gyron Systems International,
A Division of Wolfe Air Aviation, Ltd. (626) 584-8722
39 E. Walnut St. FAX **(626) 584-4069**
Pasadena, CA 91103 **www.gyron.com**
(Aerial Equipment)

Harris Corp. (818) 717-6800
(800) 231-9673
(Video Graphics Systems) FAX **(818) 525-2587**
broadcast.harris.com

Iconix (800) 783-1080
418 Chapala St. **www.iconixvideo.com**
Santa Barbara, CA 93101
(HD Video Camera Systems)

Ikegami Electronics (USA), Inc. (201) 368-9171
37 Brook Ave. FAX **(201) 569-1626**
Maywood, NJ 07607 **www.ikegami.com**

IMAGICA Corp. of America (310) 277-1790
1840 Century Park East, Ste. 750 FAX **(310) 277-1791**
Los Angeles, CA 90067 **www.imagica-la.com**
(Projection Systems)

JVC Professional Products (973) 317-5000
1700 Valley Rd. FAX **(973) 317-5030**
Wayne, NJ 07470 **www.jvc.com/pro**
(HD Pro-Camcorders and Systems)

Key Digital Systems (914) 667-9700
521 E. Third St. FAX **(914) 668-8666**
Mount Vernon, NY 10553 **www.keydigital.com**
(Video Processing Tools)

Keywest Technology (913) 492-4666
(800) 331-2019
14563 W. 96th Terrace FAX **(913) 322-1864**
Lenexa, KS 66215 **www.keywesttechnology.com**
(Video Processing Tools)

KTech Telecommunications, Inc. (818) 773-0333
21540 Prairie St., Ste. B FAX **(818) 773-8330**
Chatsworth, CA 91311 **www.ktechtelecom.com**
(Video Processing Tools)

Leader Instruments Corporation (714) 527-9300
(800) 645-5104
6484 Commerce Dr. **www.leaderusa.com**
Cypress, CA 90630
(Video Monitors and Accessories)

LSI Logic (800) 372-2447
1621 Barber Ln. **www.lsi.com**
Milpitas, CA 95035
(Communications Semiconductors)

Maxell Corporation of America (201) 794-5900
22-08 Route 208 FAX **(201) 796-8790**
Fair Lawn, NJ 07410 **www.maxell.com**
(Tape Stock)

Maximum Throughput, Inc. (514) 925-3350
(888) 684-1011
1751 Richardson St., Ste. 5-204 FAX **(514) 925-3378**
Montreal, QC H3K 1G6 Canada **www.max-t.com**
(Network-Attached Storage Devices)

Miller Camera Support, LLC (973) 857-8300
216 Little Falls Rd. FAX **(973) 857-8188**
Cedar Grove, NJ 07009 **www.miller.com.au**

Miranda (514) 333-1772
(Video Processing Tools) FAX **(514) 333-9828**
www.miranda.com

Multidyne (516) 671-7278
(800) 488-8378
191 Forest Ave. FAX **(516) 671-3362**
Locust Valley, NY 11560 **www.multidyne.com**
(Fiber Optic Transport Products)

NEC (800) 338-9549
395 N. Service Rd., Ste. 407 **www.necus.com**
Melville, NY 11747
(Display Systems/Monitors)

Nettmann Systems International (818) 623-1661
FAX **(818) 623-1671**
www.camerasystems.com
(Aerial Camera Systems & Remote Heads)

Norpak Corporation (613) 592-4164
(TV Data Broadcasting Tools) FAX **(613) 592-6560**
www.norpak.ca

OpTex 44 (0) 20 8236 1212
(Lenses) FAX **44 (0) 20 8236 1414**
www.optexint.com

P & S Technik 49 89 45 09 82 30
FAX **49 89 45 09 82 40**
www.pstechnik.de
(Digital Image Converters, Lenses & Optics)

Panasonic Broadcast &
Television Systems Co. (323) 436-3500
(323) 436-3615
3330 Cahuenga Blvd. West
Los Angeles, CA 90068 **www.panasonic.com/broadcast**

Panavision (818) 316-1000
Corporate Headquarters FAX **(818) 316-1111**
6219 DeSoto Ave. **www.panavision.com**
Woodland Hills, CA 91367
(Camera Lenses and Systems)

Pinnacle Systems, Inc. (650) 526-1600
280 N. Bernardo Ave. FAX **(650) 526-1601**
Mountain View, CA 94043 **www.pinnaclesys.com**
(Video Editing and FX Systems)

Pixel Power, Inc. (818) 276-4515
(954) 943-2026
400 S. Victory Blvd., Ste. 309 FAX **(818) 450-0763**
Burbank, CA 91502 **www.pixelpower.com**
(Video Graphics Systems)

PixelTools Corporation (408) 374-5327
10721 Wunderlich Dr. FAX **(408) 374-8074**
Cupertino, CA 95014 **www.pixeltools.com**
(Software Encoding and Repair Utilities)

Quantel, Inc. 44 (0) 1635 48222
(Video Editing and FX Systems) FAX **44 (0) 1635 815815**
www.quantel.com

QuStream (256) 726-9200
(800) 328-1008
103 Quality Circle, Ste. 210 FAX **(256) 726-9271**
Huntsville, AL 35805 **www.pesa.com**
(Routing Switcher Systems)

QuVIS (785) 272-3656
(800) 554-8116
2921 Wanamaker Dr., Ste. 107 FAX **(785) 272-3657**
Topeka, KS 66614 **www.quvis.com**
(Video Processing Tools and Storage)

R.C. Gear (323) 465-3900
(800) 714-8099
6100 Melrose Ave. FAX (323) 465-3600
Los Angeles, CA 90038 **www.rc-gear.com**
(Character Generators & Video Graphics Systems)

RED Digital Cinema (949) 206-7900
20291 Valencia Circle FAX (949) 206-7990
Lake Forest, CA 92630 **www.red.com**

Sachtler Corporation of America (516) 867-4900
709 Executive Blvd. FAX (845) 268-9324
Valley Cottage, NY 10989 **www.sachtler.com**
(Camera Support Equipment)

Sencore (605) 339-0100
(800) 736-2673
3200 Sencore Dr. **www.sencore.com**
Sioux Falls, SD 57107
(Broadcast Facility Systems & Video Servers)

Sharp Electronics Corporation (201) 529-8200
(866) 484-7825
Professional Display Division FAX (201) 529-9636
Sharp Plaza, Mail Stop One **www.sharpusa.com**
Mahwah, NJ 07495
(Display and Projection Tools, Projection Systems & Video Monitors)

Sierra Video Systems (530) 478-1000
P.O. Box 2462 FAX (530) 478-1105
Grass Valley, CA 95945 **www.sierravideo.com**
(Modular Terminal Equipment & Routing Switchers)

Snell & Wilcox, Inc. (818) 556-2616
3519 Pacific Ave. FAX (818) 556-2626
Burbank, CA 91505 **www.snellwilcox.com**
(Video Processing Tools)

Sonnet Technologies, Inc. (949) 587-3500
(949) 587-3526
Eight Autry FAX (949) 457-6350
Irvine, CA 92618 **www.sonnettech.com**

Sony Electronics Inc. Broadcast & Production Solutions Division (201) 930-1000
www.sony.com/hdcamsr

Stradis (404) 320-0110
1800 Century Blvd. NE, Ste. 1225 FAX (404) 320-3132
Atlanta, GA 30345 **www.stradis.com**
(MPEG-2 Video Decoders)

Sun Microsystems (650) 960-1300
(800) 555-9786
4150 Network Circle **www.sun.com**
Santa Clara, CA 95054
(Video Servers and Systems)

Teleview 82 70 7018 8900
(Receivers) FAX 82 31 703 9223
www.teleview.co.kr

Teranex (407) 858-6000
7800 Southland Blvd., Ste. 250 FAX (407) 858-6048
Orlando, FL 32809 **www.teranex.com**
(Converters, Noise Reducers & Post Processors)

Thomson Grass Valley (818) 729-7700
(800) 547-8949
2255 N. Ontario St., Ste. 150 FAX (818) 729-7777
Burbank, CA 91504 **www.thomsongrassvalley.com**
(Cameras & Video Processing Tools)

Tyler Camera Systems (818) 989-4420
(800) 390-6070
14218 Aetna St. FAX (818) 989-0423
Van Nuys, CA 91401 **www.tylermount.com**
(Gyro-Stabilized Helicopter Camera Mounts)

Utah Scientific (801) 575-8801
4750 Wiley Post Way, Ste. 150 FAX (801) 537-3099
Salt Lake City, UT 84116 **www.utsci.com**
(Switchers)

Visual Matrix Corporation (818) 843-4831
P.O. Box 11028 FAX (818) 843-6544
Burbank, CA 91504 **www.visual-matrix.com**
(Converters)

5th Wall Entertainment (323) 461-0600
6311 Romaine St., Ste. 7135 www.5thwall.tv
Hollywood, CA 90038
(Color Correction, Compositing & Online)

60Hz, Inc. (310) 264-8498
1660 Stanford St. FAX (310) 264-8497
Santa Monica, CA 90404 www.60-hz.com

Aaron & Le Duc (310) 452-2034
2210 Third St., Ste. 316 www.leducdesign.com
Santa Monica, CA 90405
(Color Correction, Compositing, Computer Graphics, Down/Upconversions, File Transfers, Non-Linear Online & Titling/Character Generation)

Absolute Films (626) 442-6454
(323) 692-1010
1441 Huntington Dr., Bldg. 301 FAX (626) 448-1930
South Pasadena, CA 91030 www.absolutefilms.net
(Color Correction, Computer Graphics, File Transfers, Film To HD/Datacine, Linear and Non-Linear Online, Titling/Character Generation & Upconversions)

Absolute Post (818) 842-7966
2633 N. San Fernando Blvd. FAX (818) 842-8815
Burbank, CA 91504 www.absolutepost.tv
(Color Correction, Compositing, Computer Graphics, Downconversions, File Transfers, Film to HD/Telecine, HD to Film Transfers, Linear and Non-Linear Online & Titling/Character Generation)

Aftershock Digital (323) 658-5700
8222 Melrose Ave., Ste. 304 FAX (323) 658-5200
Los Angeles, CA 90046 www.editkings.com
(Color Correction, Compositing, Computer Graphics, Down/Upconversions, File Transfers & Non-Linear Online)

All In One Productions (323) 780-8880
1111 Corporate Dr. FAX (323) 780-8887
Monterey Park, CA 91754 www.allinone-usa.com
(Color Correction, Compositing, Computer Graphics, Down/Upconversions, File Transfers, Non-Linear Online & Titling/Character Generation)

AlphaDogs, Inc. (818) 729-9262
1612 W. Olive Ave., Ste. 200 FAX (818) 729-8537
Burbank, CA 91506 www.alphadogs.tv
(Color Correction, Compositing, File Transfers, Non-Linear Offline & Non-Linear Online)

Arsenal FX (310) 453-5400
1522A Cloverfield www.arsenalfx.tv
Santa Monica, CA 90404
(Color Correction, Compositing, Computer Graphics, Non-Linear Offline, Non-Linear Online & Tape to Tape Correction)

Ascent Media - Creative Services (310) 434-7000
520 Broadway, Fifth Fl. www.ascentmedia.com
Santa Monica, CA 90401
(Color Correction, Compositing, Down/Upconversions, File Transfers, Film to HD/Datacine and Telecine, HD to Film Transfers, Linear and Non-Linear Online & Titling/Character Generation)

Autonomy, Inc. (323) 662-7048
www.autonomy.tv
(Color Correction, Compositing, Computer Graphics, File Transfers, Non-Linear Online, Titling/Character Generation & Upconversions)

Black Dragon Entertainment, Inc. (323) 874-8888
FAX (323) 874-1058
www.blackdragon.com
(Computer Graphics, Non-Linear Offline and Online & Tape to Tape Color Correction)

Bobine Telecine Post (310) 582-1240
1447 Cloverfield Blvd., Ste. 101 FAX (310) 582-1245
Santa Monica, CA 90404 bobinetelecine.com
(Color Correction, Compositing, Down/Upconversions, File Transfers, Film to HD/Telecine and Datacine & HD to Film Transfers)

CCI Digital, Inc. (818) 562-6300
2921 W. Alameda Ave. FAX (818) 562-8222
Burbank, CA 91505 www.ccidigital.com
(Color Correction, Compositing, Computer Graphics, Down/Upconversions, File Transfers, Film to HD/Telecine and Datacine, Linear and Non-Linear Online & Titling/Character Generation)

Cerulean FX (310) 576-1344
1558 10th St., Ste. D www.ceruleanfx.com
Santa Monica, CA 90401
(Color Correction)

Company 3 LA (310) 255-6600
1661 Lincoln Blvd., Ste. 400 FAX (310) 255-6602
Santa Monica, CA 90404
(Color Correction, Compositing, Down/Upconversions, File Transfers, Film to HD/Telecine and Datacine & Linear and Non-Linear Online)

Different by Design (310) 689-2470
(310) 569-8038
12233 W. Olympic Blvd., Ste. 120 FAX (310) 689-2471
Los Angeles, CA 90064 www.dxdproductions.com
(Color Correction, Downconversions, File Transfers, Non-Linear Online & Titling/Character Generation)

Digital Cinema Post (310) 264-4184
3000 Olympic Blvd. FAX (310) 388-5885
Santa Monica, CA 90404
www.bravermanproductions.com
(Color Correction, Non-Linear Online & Titling/Character Generation)

DVS Intelestream (310) 447-1111
(818) 841-6750
2133 S. Bundy Dr. FAX (310) 447-1050
Los Angeles, CA 90064 www.dvs.tv
(Color Correction, Down/Upconversions & HD to Film Transfers)

Encore Hollywood (323) 466-7663
6344 Fountain Ave. FAX (323) 467-5539
Hollywood, CA 90028 www.encorehollywood.com
(Color Correction, Compositing, Computer Graphics, Down/Upconversions, File Transfers, Film to HD/Telecine, Linear and Non-Linear Online & Titling/Character Generation)

Fancy Film (323) 661-0391
4212 Santa Monica Blvd. www.fancyfilm.com
Los Angeles, CA 90029
(Color Correction, Compositing, Down/Upconversions, File Transfers, Non-Linear Offline, Non-Linear Online & Titling/Character Generation)

FILMLOOK Media and Post/ FILMLOOK Inc. (818) 845-9200
2917 W. Olive Ave. FAX (818) 845-9238
Burbank, CA 91505 www.filmlook.com
(Captions, Color Correction, Computer Graphics, Downconversions, Duplication, File Transfers, Non-Linear Offline, Non-Linear Online, Subtitles, Tape to Tape Correction, Titling/Character Generation & Upconversions)
Contacts: Anna Cordova & Robert Faber

FotoKem (818) 846-3101
(818) 846-3102
2801 W. Alameda Ave. FAX (818) 841-2130
Burbank, CA 91505 www.fotokem.com
(Color Correction, Compositing, Down/Upconversions, File Transfers, Film to HD/Telecine and Datacine, HD to Film Transfers, Linear and Non-Linear Online & Titling/Character Generation)

FXF Productions, Inc. (310) 577-5009
1024 Harding Ave., Ste. 201 FAX (310) 577-1960
Venice, CA 90291 www.fxfproductions.com

A Gosch Production (818) 729-0000
2227 W. Olive Ave. www.goschproductions.com
Burbank, CA 91506
(Color Correction, Compositing, Computer Graphics, File Transfers, Down/Upconversions, Linear and Non-Linear Online & Titling/Character Generation)

Happy Pixel Post (310) 392-8047
1826 14th St. www.happypixelstudios.com
Santa Monica, CA 91404
(Color Correction, Compositing, Computer Graphics & Online)

HD Cinema (310) 434-9500
12233 Olympic Blvd., Ste. 134 FAX (310) 434-9600
Los Angeles, CA 90064 www.hd-cinema.com
(Color Correction, Compositing, Computer Graphics, Downconversions, File Transfers, Non-Linear Online & Titling/Character Generation)

HD Pictures & Post, Inc. (310) 264-2575
12233 West Olympic Blvd., Ste.120 FAX (310) 689-2471
Los Angeles, CA 90064 www.hdpicturesandpost.com

HD Wave Productions (818) 415-1869
(612) 281-1869
3650 Barham Blvd., Ste. T223 FAX (866) 510-0159
Toluca Lake, CA 90068 www.hdwave.com
(Color Correction, Compositing, Computer Graphics, Down/Upconversions, File Transfers, Non-Linear Online & Titling/Character Generation)

HTV - High Technology Video (323) 969-8822
(818) 760-7600
3575 Cahuenga Blvd. West, Ste. 490 FAX (323) 969-8860
Los Angeles, CA 90068 www.htvinc.net
(Color Correction, Compositing, Computer Graphics, Downconversions, File Transfers, Film to HD/Telecine and Datacine, HD to Film Transfers, Non-Linear Online & Titling/Character Generation)

The Institution Post (818) 566-7801
423 N. Fairview St. www.the-institution.com
Burbank, CA 91505

Inter Video (818) 843-3624
2211 N. Hollywood Way FAX (818) 843-6884
Burbank, CA 91505 www.intervideo24.com

iO Film (323) 822-4444
1415 Cahuenga Blvd. FAX (323) 467-7300
Hollywood, CA 90028 www.iofilm.net
(Film to HD/Telecine and Scanning, HD to Film Transfers & Non-Linear Online)

LA Digital Post, Inc. (310) 954-8650
(818) 487-5000
2260 Centinela Ave. FAX (310) 954-8686
West Los Angeles, CA 90064 www.ladigital.com
(Avid Systems, Color Correction, Compositing, Duplication, Final Cut Pro Systems, Graphics, HD Editing, HD Online, HD/SD Finishing, Offline, Standards Conversions & Visual FX)

LA Digital Post, Inc. (818) 487-5000
(310) 954-8650
11311 Camarillo St. FAX (818) 487-5015
Toluca Lake, CA 91602 www.ladigital.com
(Avid Systems, Color Correction, Compositing, Duplication, Final Cut Pro Systems, Graphics, HD Editing, HD Online, HD/SD Finishing, Offline, Standards Conversions & Visual FX)

Laser Pacific Media Corporation (323) 462-6266
809 N. Cahuenga Blvd. FAX (323) 464-3233
Hollywood, CA 90038 www.laserpacific.com
(Color Correction, Compositing, Down/Upconversions, File Transfers, Film to HD/Telecine and Datacine, HD to Film Transfers, Linear Online & Titling/Character Generation)

Level 3 Post (818) 840-7200
(818) 840-7889
2901 W. Alameda, Third Fl. www.level3post.com
Burbank, CA 91505
(Color Correction, Compositing, Computer Graphics, Down/Upconversions, File Transfers, Film to HD/Telecine, Non-Linear Online & Titling/Character Generation)

Lightning Media (818) 556-2777
3723 W. Olive Ave. FAX (818) 556-2770
Burbank, CA 91505 www.lightningmedia.com
(Downconversions & File Transfers)

Lightning Media (323) 957-9255
1415 N. Cahuenga Blvd. FAX (323) 330-6217
Hollywood, CA 90028 www.lightningmedia.com
(Downconversions & File Transfers)

Lightning Media (310) 453-3777
1831 Centinela Ave. FAX (310) 453-7818
Santa Monica, CA 90404 www.lightningmedia.com
(Downconversions & File Transfers)

Los Feliz Post (323) 512-7678
6767 Forest Lawn Dr., Ste. 115 FAX (323) 845-9998
Los Angeles, CA 90068 www.lfpost.com
(Color Correction, Down/Upconversions, Non-Linear Online & Titling/Character Generation)

Matchframe Video (818) 840-6800
610 N. Hollywood Way FAX (818) 840-2726
Burbank, CA 91505 www.matchframevideo.com
(Color Correction, Compositing, Downconversions, Duplication, File Transfers, Film to HD/Telecine, Linear and Non-Linear Online, Standards Conversions, Tape to Tape Correction, Titling/Character Generation & Upconversions)

Pixel Blues, Inc. (818) 766-4600
411 W. Alameda Blvd. Ste. 401 FAX (818) 766-4601
North Hollywood, CA 91602 www.pixelblues.com
(Color Correction, Compositing, Computer Graphics, Down/Upconversions, File Transfers, Non-Linear Online & Titling/Character Generation)

Pixel Plantation (818) 566-7777
4111 W. Alameda Ave., Ste. 301 www.pixelplantation.com
Burbank, CA 91505
(Color Correction, Compositing, Computer Graphics, Downconversions, Duplication, Non-Linear Offline, Non-Linear Online & Upconversions)

Point360 (323) 957-5500
(866) 968-4336
1147 Vine St. FAX (323) 466-7406
Hollywood, CA 90038 www.point360.com
(Color Correction, Computer Graphics, Down/Upconversions, File Transfers, Film to HD/Telecine and Datacine, Linear and Non-Linear Online & Titling/Character Generation)

Point360 (310) 481-7000
12421 W. Olympic Blvd. FAX (310) 207-8404
Los Angeles, CA 90064 www.point360.com
(Compositing, File Transfers, Non-Linear Online & Titling/Character Generation)

Point360 (818) 556-5700
(866) 968-4336
1133 N. Hollywood Way FAX (818) 556-5753
Burbank, CA 91505 www.point360.com
(Captions, Color Correction, Compositing, Computer Graphics, Downconversions, Duplication, File Transfers, Film to HD/Datacine, Film to HD/Telecine, HD to Film Transfers, Linear Online, Non-Linear Online, Standards Conversions, Subtitles, Tape to Tape Correction, Titling/Character Generation & Upconversions)

Post and Beam (310) 828-1128
3025 Olympic Blvd., Ste. 112 FAX (310) 828-8211
Santa Monica, CA 90404 www.postandbeam.tv

Post Digital Services (323) 845-0812
1258 N. Highland Ave., Ste. 210 FAX (323) 845-0812
Hollywood, CA 90038 www.postdigitalservices.com
(Captions, Color Correction, Compositing, Computer Graphics, Downconversions, Duplication, File Transfers, HD to Film Transfers, Linear Offline, Non-Linear Offline, Non-Linear Online, Standards Conversions, Subtitles, Tape to Tape Correction, Titling/Character Generation & Upconversions)

The Post Group (323) 462-2300
6335 Homewood Ave. FAX (323) 462-0836
Hollywood, CA 90028 www.postgroup.com
(Color Correction, Compositing, Computer Graphics, Down/Upconversions, File Transfers, Film to HD/Telecine and Datacine, HD to Film Transfers, Linear and Non-Linear Online & Titling/Character Generation)

Post Logic Studios (323) 461-7887
1800 N. Vine St., Ste. 100 FAX (323) 461-7790
Los Angeles, CA 90028 www.postlogic.com
(Color Correction, Compositing, Computer Graphics, Down/Upconversions, File Transfers, Film to HD/Telecine and Datacine, HD to Film Transfers, Linear and Non-Linear Online & Titling/Character Generation)

Post Media Group, Inc. (310) 289-5959
337 S. Robertson Blvd. www.postmediagroup.tv
Beverly Hills, CA 90211

Precision Productions + Post (310) 839-4600
10718 McCune Ave. FAX (310) 839-4601
Los Angeles, CA 90034 www.precisionpost.com
(Color Correction, Compositing, Computer Graphics, Downconversions, File Transfers, HD to Film Transfers, Non-Linear Online & Titling/Character Generation)

Prime Digital Media Services (661) 964-0220
28111 Avenue Stanford FAX (661) 964-0550
Valencia, CA 91355 www.primedigital.com
(Color Correction, Compositing, Computer Graphics, Down/Upconversions, File Transfers, HD to Film Transfers, Linear and Non-Linear Online & Titling/Character Generation)

Qube Cinema, Inc. (818) 392-8155
4640 Lankershim Blvd., Ste. 601 FAX (818) 301-0401
North Hollywood, CA 91602 www.qubecinema.com
(Digital Cinema Servers and Software & Digital Film Mastering)

Raycom Post (818) 846-0101
4450 Lakeside Dr., Ste. 300 FAX (818) 846-0277
Burbank, CA 91505 www.raycompost.com
(Captions, Color Correction, Computer Graphics, Down/Upconversions, Duplication, File Transfers & Non-Linear Online)

Red Dog Post & Design (310) 237-6438
www.reddogpost.com
(Captions, Color Correction, Compositing, Linear and Non-Linear Online, Standards Conversions & Subtitles)

Ring of Fire (310) 966-5055
1538 20th St. FAX (310) 966-5056
Santa Monica, CA 90404 www.ringoffire.com
(Compositing, Computer Graphics, Down/Upconversions, File Transfers, Linear and Non-Linear Online & Titling/Character Generation)

RIOT LA (310) 434-6000
702 Arizona Ave. FAX (310) 434-6510
Santa Monica, CA 90401 www.rioting.com
(Color Correction, Compositing, Computer Graphics, Down/Upconversions, File Transfers, Film to HD/Telecine and Datacine, HD to Film Transfers, Linear and Non-Linear Online & Titling/Character Generation)

Rocket Dailies (310) 701-5999
19360 Rinaldi St., Ste. 428
Northridge, CA 91326
(Color Correction, Down/Upconversions, Film to HD/Telecine and Datacine, HD to Film Transfers & Titling/Character Generation)

Shapeshifter (323) 876-3444
3405 Cahuenga Blvd. West FAX (323) 876-3444
Los Angeles, CA 90068 www.shapeshifter.biz
(Color Correction, Compositing, Computer Graphics, Downconversions, File Transfers, Non-Linear Online, Titling/Character Generation & Upconversions)

Solventdreams (323) 906-9700
4222 Santa Monica Blvd. FAX (323) 906-9711
Los Angeles, CA 90029 www.solventdreams.com
(Color Correction, Compositing, Computer Graphics, Down/Upconversions, Linear and Non-Linear Online & Titling/Character Generation)

Spectrum HD (310) 979-7170
12233 W. Olympic Blvd., Ste. 314 FAX **(310) 979-7173**
Los Angeles, CA 90064 **www.spectrumhd.com**

SSI/Advanced Post Services (323) 969-9333
7165 Sunset Blvd. FAX **(323) 969-8333**
Los Angeles, CA 90046 **www.ssipost.com**
(Color Correction, Compositing, Computer Graphics, Down/Upconversions, File Transfers, Film to HD/Telecine and Datacine, HD to Film Transfers, Linear and Non-Linear Online & Titling/Character Generation)

SSI/Advanced Post Services (323) 874-9344
7155 Santa Monica Blvd. FAX **(323) 850-7189**
Los Angeles, CA 90046 **www.ssipost.com**
(Color Correction, Compositing, Computer Graphics, Down/Upconversions, File Transfers, Film to HD/Telecine and Datacine, HD to Film Transfers, Linear and Non-Linear Online & Titling/Character Generation)

Stargate Digital (626) 403-8403
1001 El Centro St. FAX **(626) 403-8444**
South Pasadena, CA 91030 **www.stargatefilms.com**
(Compositing, Computer Graphics, Down/Upconversions, File Transfers, HD to Film Transfers, Linear and Non-Linear Online & Titling/Character Generation)

STEELE Studios (310) 656-7770
5737 Mesmer Ave. FAX **(310) 656-7771**
Culver City, CA 90230 **www.steelevfx.com**
(Color Correction, Compositing, Computer Graphics, Downconversions, Duplication, File Transfers, Linear Offline, Linear Online, Titling/Character Generation, Tape to Tape Correction & Upconversions)

Stewart Sound Factory (714) 973-3030
204 N. Broadway, Ste. N FAX **(714) 973-2530**
Santa Ana, CA 92701 **www.stewartsound.com**

Switch Studios (310) 301-1800
316 S. Venice Blvd. FAX **(310) 496-1964**
Venice, CA 90291 **www.switch-studios.com**
(Color Correction, Compositing, Computer Graphics, File Transfers, Non-Linear Online & Titling/Character Generation)

The Syndicate (310) 260-2320
1207 Fourth St., Ste. 200 FAX **(310) 260-2420**
Santa Monica, CA 90401 **www.syndicate.tv**
(Color Correction, Compositing, Computer Graphics, Down/Upconversions, File Transfers, Film to HD/Telecine and Datacine, Linear and Non-Linear Online & Titling/Character Generation)

Technicolor Creative Services - Hollywood (323) 817-6937
6040 Sunset Blvd. **www.technicolor.com**
Hollywood, CA 90028
(Color Correction, Compositing, Computer Graphics, Down/Upconversions, File Transfers, Film to HD/Telecine and Datacine, HD to Film Transfers, Linear and Non-Linear Online & Titling/Character Generation)

Universal Studios Digital Services (818) 777-1111
100 Universal City Plaza, Bldg. 3153 FAX **(818) 866-5258**
Universal City, CA 91608
www.filmmakersdestination.com
(Color Correction, Duplication, Editing, Encoding & Telecine)

Vendetta Post (310) 587-9100
225 Santa Monica Blvd., Ninth Fl. FAX **(310) 587-9299**
Santa Monica, CA 90401 **www.vendettapost.com**
(Computer Graphics & Non-Linear Online)

Victory Studios LA (818) 769-1776
10911 Riverside Dr., Ste. 100 FAX **(818) 760-1280**
North Hollywood, CA 91602 **www.victorystudiosla.com**
(Color Correction, Downconversions, Duplication, File Transfers, Non-Linear Offline, Non-Linear Online, Title/Character Generation & Upconversions)

View Studio, Inc. (805) 745-8814
385 Toro Canyon Rd. **www.viewstudio.com**
Carpinteria, CA 93013
(Color Correction & Compositing)

West Post Digital (310) 857-5000
1703 Stewart St. FAX **(310) 857-5060**
Santa Monica, CA 90404 **www.westpostdigital.com**
(Color Correction, Compositing, Computer Graphics, Down/Upconversions, Non-Linear Online & Titling/Character Generation)

Westside Media Group (310) 979-3500
(818) 779-8600
12233 W. Olympic Blvd., Ste. 152 FAX **(310) 979-3503**
West Los Angeles, CA 90064 **www.wmgmedia.com**
(Color Correction, Duplication, Film Transfers, Standards Conversions & Subtitles)
Contacts: Scott Ellison, Lewis Lipstone & Shirley Lipstone

World of Video & Audio (310) 659-5959
(866) 900-3827
8717 Wilshire Blvd. FAX **(310) 659-8247**
Beverly Hills, CA 90211 **www.wova.com**
(DVCPro, HDCam and HDV Downconversions & Upconversions)

Alternative Rentals (310) 204-3388
FAX **(310) 204-3384**
www.alternativerentals.com

American Film Institute (AFI) (323) 856-7600
2021 N. Western Ave. FAX **(323) 467-4578**
Los Angeles, CA 90027 **www.afi.com**

Ⓐ **American Hi Definition, Inc.** (818) 222-0022
7635 Airport Business Pkwy FAX **(818) 222-0818**
Van Nuys, CA 91406 **www.hi-def.com**

Arenas (323) 785-5535
3375 Barham Blvd. FAX **(323) 785-5560**
Los Angeles, CA 90068
www.arenasgroup.com/info-screen.html

Big Time Picture Company, Inc. (310) 207-0921
12210 1/2 Nebraska Ave. FAX **(310) 826-0071**
Los Angeles, CA 90025 **www.bigtimepic.com**

The Charles Aidikoff Screening Room (310) 274-0866
150 S. Rodeo Dr., Ste. 140 FAX **(310) 550-1794**
Beverly Hills, CA 90212 **www.aidikoff.tv**

Cinespace (323) 817-3456
6356 Hollywood Blvd., Second Fl. FAX **(323) 860-9794**
Hollywood, CA 90028 **www.cinespace.info**

The Culver Studios (310) 202-1234
9336 W. Washington Blvd. FAX **(310) 202-3536**
Culver City, CA 90232 **www.theculverstudios.com**

Dalsa (818) 884-7000
6160 Variel Ave. FAX **(818) 884-7022**
Woodland Hills, CA 91367 **www.dalsa.com/dc**

Delicate Productions, Inc. (805) 388-1800
874 Verdulera St. FAX **(805) 388-1037**
Camarillo, CA 93010 **www.delicate.com**

Dick Clark Screening Room (310) 255-4699
2900 Olympic Blvd., First Fl.
Santa Monica, CA 90404
www.dickclarkproductionstheatre.com

Fine Arts Theatre (310) 701-8925
(310) 659-3875
8556 Wilshire Blvd. FAX **(310) 861-9005**
Beverly Hills, CA 90211 **www.studioscreenings.com**

Fox Studios (310) 369-2406
(310) 369-4636
10201 W. Pico Blvd. FAX **(310) 369-0503**
Los Angeles, CA 90035 **www.foxpost.com**

Goethe-Institut (323) 525-3388
5750 Wilshire Blvd., Ste. 100 FAX **(323) 934-3597**
Los Angeles, CA 90036 **www.goethe.de/losangeles**

Hollywood-DI (323) 850-3550
1041 N. Formosa Ave. FAX **(323) 850-3551**
Fairbanks Theater **www.hollywooddi.com**
West Hollywood, CA 90046

LACMA (The Los Angeles County Museum Of Art) (323) 857-6039
(323) 857-4768
5905 Wilshire Blvd. FAX **(323) 857-6021**
Los Angeles, CA 90036 **www.lacma.org**

Los Angeles Center Studios (213) 534-3000
1201 W. Fifth St., Ste. T-110 FAX **(213) 534-3001**
Los Angeles, CA 90017 **www.lacenterstudios.com**

Los Angeles Film School Theater (323) 860-0789
6363 Sunset Blvd., Ste. 500 **www.lafilm.edu**
Los Angeles, CA 90028

Pacific Design Center/ SilverScreen Theater (310) 657-0800
8687 Melrose Ave. FAX **(310) 652-8576**
West Hollywood, CA 90069
www.pacificdesigncenter.com

The Studios at Paramount (323) 956-5520
The Studios at Paramount
Post Production Services
5555 Melrose Ave.
Los Angeles, CA 90038
www.thestudiosatparamount.com

PlasterCITY Digital Post Facility (323) 469-9800
6500 Sunset Blvd. FAX **(323) 462-4620**
Los Angeles, CA 90028 **www.plastercitypost.com**

Raleigh Studios (323) 960-3456
5300 Melrose Ave. FAX **(323) 871-5600**
Hollywood, CA 90038 **www.raleighstudios.com**

Sony Pictures Studios (310) 244-5721
10202 W. Washington Blvd.
Culver City, CA 90232 **www.sonypicturesstudios.com**

Spartan Mobile Suites, Inc. (310) 587-3377
3727 W. Magnolia Blvd., Ste. 156 FAX **(661) 702-0550**
Burbank, CA 91505

Switch Studios (310) 301-1800
316 S. Venice Blvd. FAX **(310) 496-1964**
Venice, CA 90291 **www.switch-studios.com**

Theatrical Concepts, Inc. (818) 597-1100
3030 Triunfo Canyon Rd. FAX **(818) 597-0202**
Agoura Hills, CA 91301 **www.theatrical.com**

Warner Bros. Studio Facilities - Projection (818) 954-2144
4000 Warner Blvd. FAX **(818) 954-7915**
Burbank, CA 91522 **www.wbpostproduction.com**

Wilshire Screening Room (310) 701-8925
(310) 659-3875
8670 Wilshire Blvd., Ste. 112 FAX **(310) 861-9005**
Beverly Hills, CA 90211 **www.studioscreenings.com**

Action Footage/ Warren Miller Entertainment (800) 729-3456
(Extreme/Adventure Sports) www.warrenmiller.com

Action Sports/Scott Dittrich Films (310) 459-2526 (212) 681-6565
P.O. Box 301 FAX (310) 456-1743
Malibu, CA 90265 www.sdfilms.com
(Animals, Nature, People & Sports)

AeronauticPictures.com (805) 985-2320
P.O. Box 1748 www.aeronauticpictures.com/royalty-free-stock-footage/
Ojai, CA 93024
(Aerial & Location)

All-Stock (310) 317-9996 (800) 323-0079
P.O. Box 1705 www.all-stock.com
Pacific Palisades, CA 90272
(Animals, Nature, People & Sports)

America by Air Stock Footage Library (800) 488-6359
154 Euclid Blvd. FAX (413) 235-1462
Lantana, FL 33462 www.hdfootage.com
(Aerials, Contemporary & International)

Animation Trip (858) 793-1900
3830 Valley Center Dr., Ste. 705-833 FAX (858) 793-1942
San Diego, CA 92130 www.animationtrip.com/licensing
(Computer Animation)

Apex Stock (323) 443-2580 (888) 250-2739
6725 W. Sunset Blvd., Ste. 490 FAX (323) 443-2579
Hollywood, CA 90028 www.apexstock.com

Artbeats (541) 863-4429 (800) 444-9392
1405 N. Myrtle Rd. FAX (541) 863-4547
Myrtle Creek, OR 97457 www.artbeats.com
(Aerials, Backgrounds, Effects, Establishments, Lifestyles, Nature & Reference)

BBC Motion Gallery, Los Angeles (818) 299-9720 (800) 966-5424
4144 Lankershim Blvd., Ste. 200 FAX (818) 299-9763
North Hollywood, CA 91602 www.bbcmotiongallery.com
(Arts, Bloopers, Communications, Current Events, Destinations, Entertainment, Historical, Leisure, Lifestyles, Medicine, Music, Natural History, News, Politics, Reality, Science, Stock, Technology, Travel and Locations, Universal Newsreels & Wildlife)

BBC Motion Gallery, New York (212) 705-9399
747 Third Ave. FAX (212) 705-9342
New York, NY 10017 www.bbcmotiongallery.com
(Arts, Bloopers, Communications, Current Events, Destinations, Entertainment, Historical, Leisure, Lifestyles, Medicine, Music, Natural History, News, Politics, Reality, Science, Stock, Technology, Travel and Locations, Universal Newsreels & Wildlife)

BBC Motion Gallery, Toronto (416) 362-3223
130 Spadina Ave., Ste. 401 FAX (416) 362-3553
Toronto, ON M5V 2L4 Canada www.bbcmotiongallery.com
(Arts, Bloopers, Communications, Current Events, Destinations, Entertainment, Historical, Leisure, Lifestyles, Medicine, Music, Natural History, News, Politics, Reality, Science, Stock, Technology, Travel and Locations, Universal Newsreels & Wildlife)

BlackLight Films (323) 436-7070 (323) 436-2229
3371 Cahuenga Blvd. West FAX (323) 436-2230
Hollywood, CA 90068 www.blacklightfilms.com

Blue Sky Stock Footage/Bill Mitchell (310) 305-8384 (877) 992-5477
P.O. Box 24439 FAX (310) 305-8985
Santa Fe, NM 87502 www.blueskyfootage.com
(All Subjects)

Budget Films, Inc. (323) 660-0187 (323) 660-0800
4427 Santa Monica Blvd. FAX (323) 660-5571
Los Angeles, CA 90029 www.budgetfilms.com
(Beauty, Clouds, Deserts, Fireworks, Moon, National Parks, Nature & Sunsets)

Camera One (206) 523-3456
8523 15th Ave. NE FAX (206) 523-3668
Seattle, WA 98115 www.cameraone.us
(Aerials, Archeology, Caribbean, Cities, Clouds, Eclipse, Europe, Landscapes, Lightning, Moons, National Parks, Natural and Traffic/Urban Time-Lapse, Nature, Northwest, Outdoor Sports, Scenics, Southwest, Storms, Sunrises and Sunsets, Underwater, Whitewater & Wildlife)

CelebrityFootage (310) 360-9600
320 South Almont Dr. FAX (310) 360-9696
Beverly Hills, CA 90211 www.celebrityfootage.com
(Award Ceremonies, Celebrities, Entertainment, Events, Hollywood, Movie Premieres, People, Red Carpet Arrivals & Stars)

Cinegraph (312) 939-1300
47 W. Polk St., Ste. 100-113 FAX (312) 341-1709
Chicago, IL 60605 www.cinegraph.com
(Destinations, Nature & Scenics)

Classic Images (310) 277-0400 (800) 949-2547
469 S. Bedford Dr. FAX (310) 277-0412
Beverly Hills, CA 90212 www.classicimg.com
(1890s–Present, Aerials, Americana, Archival, Cartoons, Cityscapes, Commercials, Educational, Historical, Hollywood, Industry, Music, Nature, Newsreel, Sports, Technology, Time-Lapse, Travel, Underwater, Vintage TV and Film & Wildlife)

Collegiate Images (954) 343-8000 (818) 625-1606
13450 Sunrise Blvd., Ste. 70 FAX (954) 343-8001
Sunrise, FL 33323
(College Sports)

The Communications Group, Inc. (919) 828-4086 (888) 479-3456
P.O. Box 50157 FAX (919) 832-7797
Raleigh, NC 27650 www.cgfilm.com
(Aerials, Boston, North Carolina Cities, Farms and Landscapes & The Big Dig)

DV/HDcuts (310) 497-5636
P.O. Box 24439 FAX (505) 438-0924
Santa Fe, NM 87502 www.dvcuts.com
(Airplanes, Americana, Cityscapes, Clouds, Deserts, Driving Shots, Experimental, Highways, Historical Landmarks, International People and Scenery, Landscapes, Lightning, Mountains, Nature, Oceans, Rivers, Seasons, Stars/Comets/Planets, Storms, Suns and Moon, Time-Lapse, Traffic, Trains, Transportation & Underwater)

Fish Films Footage World (818) 905-1071
4548 Van Noord Ave. FAX (818) 905-0301
Studio City, CA 91604 www.footageworld.com
(Aerials, Alaska, Animals, Cities, Extreme Sports, Implosions, Nature, Time-Lapse, Travel, Underwater, Weather & Wildlife)

The Footage Store (818) 556-6080
2121 Scott Rd., Ste. 201 FAX (818) 556-6080
Burbank, CA 91504 www.footagestore.com
(Beauty, Nature, Scenics, Time Lapse & Wildlife)

FootageBank HD/ footagehead Royalty Free (310) 822-1400 (888) 653-1400
1733 Abbot Kinney Blvd., Ste. C FAX (310) 822-4100
Venice, CA 90291 www.footagebank.com
(Aerials, Animals, Cities, Landscapes, News, Space, Technology, Time-Lapse, Travel, Underwater & Worldwide Locations)

Framepool Inc. (386) 428-0586
(800) 331-1314
3033 Silver Palm Dr. FAX **(866) 928-6637**
Edgewater, FL 32141 **www.framepool.com**
(Aerials, Agriculture, Animals, Architecture, Cityscapes, Clouds, Contemporary, Cultures, Deserts, Flowers, Forests, International People and Scenery, Landscapes, Lightning, Lifestyles, Mountains, Nature, Rivers, Skies, Space, Sports, Suns and Moons, Technology, Time-Lapse & Wildlife)

Framepool Inc. (310) 402-4626
(800) 331-1314
10905 Ohio Ave., Ste. 116 FAX **(866) 928-6637**
Los Angeles, CA 90024 **www.framepool.com**
(Aerials, Aerospace, Agriculture, Animals, Cityscapes, Clouds, Commercials, Contemporary, Cultures, Deserts, Flowers, International People and Scenery, Landscapes, Lightning, Lifestyles, Mountains, Nature, Scenic, Seasons, Space, Stars/Comets/Planets, Storms, Time-Lapse, Traffic, Transportation, Underwater & Wildlife)

Global ImageWorks, LLC (201) 384-7715
65 Beacon St. FAX **(201) 501-8971**
Haworth, NJ 07641 **www.globalimageworks.com**
(All Subjects)

Greg Hensley Productions (970) 984-3158
www.greghensley.com

The Hollywood Film Registry (310) 456-8184
5473 Santa Monica Blvd., Ste. 408 FAX **(323) 957-2159**
Los Angeles, CA 90029
(All Subjects)

Home Planet Productions (805) 965-9848
(818) 422-4144
FAX **(805) 965-2329**
www.homeplanetproductions.com

Howard Hall Productions (858) 259-8989
2171 La Amatista Rd. FAX **(858) 792-1467**
Del Mar, CA 92014 **www.howardhall.com**
(Aerials, Animals, Clouds, Landscapes, Mountains, Nature, Oceans, Skies, Suns and Moons, Time-Lapse, Underwater & Wildlife)

Image Bank Films and Archive Films by Getty Images (800) 462-4379
6300 Wilshire Blvd., 16th Floor FAX **(323) 202-4207**
Los Angeles, CA 90048 **www.gettyimages.com**
(Archival & Contemporary)

Inter Video (818) 843-3624
FAX **(818) 843-6884**
www.intervideo24.com
(Aviation, Computer Graphics, Medical, News, Space, Sports, Travel & Weather)

LA News Service (310) 345-1437
713 Hamden Pl. FAX **(310) 230-0817**
Pacific Palisades, CA 90342 **www.highdefinition.net**

National Geographic Digital Motion (310) 734-5302
(877) 730-2022
9100 Wilshire Blvd., Ste. 401E FAX **(310) 858-5801**
Beverly Hills, CA 90212 **www.ngdigitalmotion.com**
(Archeology, Architecture, Ceremonies, Cities, Landmarks, Natural Disasters, Natural History, People, Wildlife & World Scenes)

New & Unique Videos (619) 644-3000
(800) 365-8433
7323 Rondel Court FAX **(619) 644-3001**
San Diego, CA 92119 **www.newuniquevideos.com**
(Aerials, Animals, Archival Film, Beaches and Sunsets, Bloopers, Cities, Islands, Contemporary, Corporate, Agricultural, Current Events, Industrial, International, Lifestyles, Medical, Military, People, San Diego, Scenics, Southern California, Sports, Travel and Locations, Technological, Underwater & Wildlife)

NHL Hockey Archive (201) 750-5860
(201) 750-5800
240 Pegasus Ave. FAX **(201) 750-5850**
Northvale, NJ 07647 **www.nhlhockeyarchive.com**
(NHL Hockey)

Oddball Film + Video (415) 558-8112
(415) 558-8122
275 Capp St. FAX **(415) 558-8116**
San Francisco, CA 94110 **www.oddballfilm.com**
(Americana, International, Nature, Timelapse & Wildlife)

Producers Library (818) 752-9097
(800) 944-2135
10832 Chandler Blvd. FAX **(818) 752-9196**
North Hollywood, CA 91601 **www.producerslibrary.com**
(Cities, Nature, News, Red Carpet & Scenics)

Reel Orange (949) 548-4524
316 La Jolla Dr. FAX **(949) 548-0749**
Newport Beach, CA 92663 **www.reelorange.com**
(Aerials, Environmental & Grand Canyon)

Silverman Stock Footage (917) 470-9104
210 Douglass St. **www.silvermanstockfootage.com**
Brooklyn, NY 11217
(Aerials, Airplanes, Americana, Animals, Architecture, Archival, Cityscapes, Clouds, Contemporary, Cultures, Deserts, Extreme Sports, Flowers, International People, Landscapes, Lifestyles, Nature, Oceans, Scenics, Space, Storms, Suns and Moons, Time-Lapse, Traffic & Underwater)

Sports Cinematography Group (310) 785-9100
(212) 744-5333
73 Market St. FAX **(310) 564-7500**
Venice, CA 90291 **www.sportscinematographygroup.com**
(Sports)

StormStock (817) 276-9500
P.O. Box 122020 FAX **(817) 795-1132**
Arlington, TX 76012 **www.stormstock.com**
(Blizzards, Beaches, Caribbean, Clouds, Disasters, Environmental, Fires, Flash Floods, Hail, Hurricane Katrina, Hurricanes, Landscapes, Lightning, Microbursts, Natural Disasters, Natural History, Nature, Oceans, Radar, Science, Seasons, Skies, Storm Clouds, Storms, Sunrises, Sunsets, Time-Lapse, Tornadoes, Traffic & Waves)

Thought Equity Motion (866) 815-6599
4130 Cahuenga Blvd., Ste. 315 **www.thoughtequity.com**
Universal City, CA 91602
(All Subjects)

Universal Studios Stock Footage Library (818) 777-1695
100 Universal Plaza FAX **(818) 866-0763**
Bldg. 2313A, Lower Level **www.filmmakersdestination.com**
Universal City, CA 91608
(Selected Subjects)

US Air Force Motion Picture Office (310) 235-7522
(310) 235-7511
10880 Wilshire Blvd., Ste. 1240 FAX **(310) 235-7500**
Los Angeles, CA 90024
(Air Force)

US Army Office of Public Affairs (310) 235-7621
(310) 235-7622
10880 Wilshire Blvd., Ste. 1250 FAX **(310) 235-6075**
Los Angeles, CA 90024
(US Army) **www.defenselink.mil/faq/pis/PC12FILM.html**

Video Tape Library, Inc./VTL (323) 656-4330
1525 N. Crescent Heights Blvd., Ste. 2 FAX **(323) 656-8746**
Los Angeles, CA 90046 **www.videotapelibrary.com**
(Aerials, Americana, Animals, Archival, Bloopers, Cities, Cultures, Extreme and Recreational Sports, Historical, Landmarks, Landscapes, Lifestyles, News, People, Professionals, Time-Lapse, Travel Locations & Underwater)

Wings Wildlife Production, Inc. (949) 830-7845
Two McLaren, Ste. A FAX **(949) 830-5116**
Irvine, CA 92618 **www.wildlifelibrary.com**
(African and North American Wildlife)

Wish You Were Here Film & Video, Inc. (866) 347-8625
(818) 371-9649
www.wywhstock.com
(Aerials, Destinations, Landmarks, Scenics, Time-Lapse & Wildlife)

WTTW Digital Archives (773) 509-5412
5400 N. St. Louis Ave. FAX **(773) 509-5307**
Chicago, IL 60625 **www.wttwdigitalarchives.com**
(Cityscapes, Flowers, Music Performance/Concerts, National Parks, Rural, Scenics, Trains, Tsunami Disaster and Relief, U.S. Landmarks & U.S. Troops/Iraq)

Ametron Audio Video
(323) 466-4321
(323) 464-1144
FAX (323) 871-0127
www.ametron.com

Broadcast Store
(818) 998-9100
9420 Lurline Ave., Ste. C
Chatsworth, CA 91311
FAX (818) 998-9106
www.broadcaststore.com

Edgewise Media Services, Inc.
(323) 769-0900
(800) 824-3130
1215 N. Highland Ave.
Hollywood, CA 90038
FAX (323) 466-6815
www.edgewise-media.com

Edgewise Media Services, Inc.
(714) 919-2020
(800) 444-9330
917 E. Katella Ave.
Anaheim, CA 92805
FAX (714) 919-2010
www.edgewise-media.com

EVS/Express Video Supply, Inc.
(818) 552-4590
(800) 238-8480
1620 Flower St.
Glendale, CA 91201
FAX (818) 552-4591
www.evsonline.com

Film Source LA
(818) 484-3236
(866) 537-1114
FAX (818) 688-0101
www.filmsourcela.com

Media Distributors
(818) 980-9916
(888) 889-3130
10960 Ventura Blvd.
Studio City, CA 91604
FAX (818) 980-9265
www.mediadistributors.com

Moviola/Moviola Cameras
(323) 467-3107
(800) 468-3107
1135 N. Mansfield Ave.
Los Angeles, CA 90038
FAX (323) 464-1518
www.moviola.com

MSE Media Solutions
(323) 721-1656
(800) 626-1955
6013 Scott Way
Los Angeles, CA 90040
FAX (323) 721-1506
www.msemedia.com

ProMediaSupplies.com
(336) 664-1004
FAX (336) 605-3212
www.promediasupplies.com

Revolt Pro Media
(818) 904-0001
7625 Hayvenhurst Ave., Ste. 32
Van Nuys, CA 91406
FAX (818) 904-0005
www.revoltpromedia.com

The Tape Company
(818) 566-9898
(800) 851-3113
2721 W. Magnolia Blvd.
Burbank, CA 91505
FAX (818) 566-8989
www.thetapecompany.com

TapeStockOnline.com
(888) 322-8273
(310) 352-4230
2034 E. Lincoln Ave., Box 426
Anaheim, CA 92806
FAX (310) 352-4233
www.tapestockonline.com

Videotape Products, Inc.
(818) 566-9898
(800) 422-2444
2721 W. Magnolia Blvd.
Burbank, CA 91505
FAX (818) 566-8989
www.myvtp.com

Westside Media Group
(310) 979-3500
(818) 779-8600
12233 W. Olympic Blvd., Ste. 152
West Los Angeles, CA 90064
FAX (310) 979-3503
www.wmgmedia.com

NOTES:

LA 411

CLASSIC LOS ANGELES FILM LOCATIONS

THE HOLLYWOOD ROOSEVELT HOTEL

ALMOST FAMOUS

INT. ARIZONA RAMADA INN LOBBY - NIGHT

All enter the lobby like warriors, in a pack. The hotel chairs are spotted with curious hangers-on, decked out and lounging. Dick is already stationed, as always, at the front desk.

DICK

Jeff, Tony... Keys... keys... keys... room list...

He gives key and a stack of messages to Russell (Billy Crudup), and turns to William (Patrick Fugit) who he makes feel more important. Penny (Kate Hudson) is nearby with her suitcase tackle box purse.

DICK (Cont.)

The Enemy! Here you go, here's the key to your palatial suite, room list, plus let me give you a luggage tag. You're Number 42.

CLERK

Is this Mr. Miller? You have a message from Elaine (Frances McDormand).

WILLIAM

Thanks.

CLERK

She's a handful.

WILLIAM

I know.

William cooly takes the folded message, doesn't look at it, and tries to pretend this embarrassing moment didn't happen. Jeff (Jason Lee) exchanges a look with Russell.

ON RUSSELL who approaches William.

RUSSELL

Come by in a few minutes. We'll do the interview.

William exits and goes to join Penny. Jeff approaches, regarding William standing with Penny and the girls. Intrigue is swirling in the lobby.

JEFF

I'm worried, man.

RUSSELL

Naw, we can trust him. He's a fan.

JEFF

But it's Rolling Stone. He looks harmless, but he does represent the magazine that trashed Eric Clapton, broke up Cream, ripped Led Zeppelin, and wrote that lame story about the Allman Brothers Band that bummed Duane out before he died. Don't forget the Rules. This little sh*t is the Enemy. He writes what he sees.

(beat)

But it would be cool to be on the cover.

SCREENPLAY BY:

Cameron Crowe

ALSO FILMED AT THE HOLLYWOOD ROOSEVELT HOTEL:

Catch Me If You Can, The Fabulous Baker Boys

LA 411

www.LA411.com

■ PICTURED:
Roosevelt Hotel

■ LOCATION:
Hollywood

■ PHOTOGRAPHER:
Michael Rueter
Michael Rueter Photography/L.A.-N.Y.
www.michaelrueter.com

Supporting production in Southern California for 31 years

when it's time to
GET OFF THE GROUND
NOW OFFERING FACILITY RENTAL
GRIP
And Rigging Equipment
Labor and Rentals
NOW FEATURING
VARIABLE HIGH SPEED CHAIN MASTER HOISTS!
24 Hour Service
Grip Friendly
Trucking Available
Ask About Long Haul
Manlifts & Crank Ups
Complete Rigging Accessories
Metal Fabrication
Welding MIG & TIG
Rigging Labor
Huge
Inventory of:
Trussing & Accessories
Speed Grids 12" and 20"
Decking
Motor Controllers (up to 48-way)
Speed Rail / Lightboxes
Curtain Systems
Motorized Light Travelers
Motorized I-Beam Trolleys
I-Beam Tracks
Curved
Super Truss Mother Grids
Ground Support
Self Climbing Towers
Radius Truss
Staging
Turntables
Custom Platforms & Catwalks
Truss decks & stages, handrails
Fall Protection
Winches
www.branament.com
Call (310) 637-4727
Fax (310) 637-4735
SINCE 1977
BRANAM
Need a demo or rehearsal facility?
BOOK NOW!
you're ready for
BRANAM
310 S. Long Beach Blvd. Compton, CA 90221
Grip & Lighting Equipment

Ⓐ ADVERTISER SYMBOL

Refer to the General Index for cross-referencing items in this section.

8 Ball Manufacturing LLC (661) 252-3344 / (661) 212-7901
16016 Baker Canyon Rd. www.8ballcamerasupport.com
Saugus, CA 91390
Accessories: Sliders 24" to 72"

Active Remote Systems, LLC (310) 235-1953 / (800) 316-0067
11771 1/2 Pico Blvd. FAX (310) 235-1131
Los Angeles, CA 90064 www.activeremote.com
Arms: Modular Swiss Jib w/41' Reach
Cranes: 15', 21', 30' and 50' Technocranes and Aerocrane & Super TechnoCranes
Dollies: Barby & Hot Dog
Accessories: 2 and 3 Axis Remote Heads, Hot Gears, Libra Heads, Mo-Sys System, Power Pod 2000, Power Pod Plus, Scorpio & Z-Axis Heads

ADP Camera Cranes, Inc./ David Rhea (818) 972-2728 / (714) 315-9495
124 N. Naomi St. FAX (818) 972-2728
Burbank, CA 91505
Arms: CamMate 5'-40'
Cranes: Jib Arms

Adventure Equipment/Ultimate Arm (818) 618-9988
5506 Colodny Dr. FAX (805) 375-2211
Agoura Hills, CA 91301 www.ultimatearm.com

Aerocrane Rentals LLC (818) 252-7700
9824 Glen Oaks Blvd. FAX (818) 252-7709
Sun Valley, CA 91352 www.aerocranerentals.com
Cranes: Enlouva IIIA and IVA, Phoenix 40', Super Aerocrane 30', Super35 Aerocrane 35' & Super Scorpio Technocrane 30' and 37'
Arms: Aero Jib
Accessories: 2 and 3 Axis Aerohead, Aerohead Light & VFX Digital Repeat Aerohead

Aerotech Remote (818) 359-9252 / (818) 703-7345
9314 Huston Rd. FAX (818) 703-7345
Chatsworth, CA 91311

Ahern Entertainment (818) 834-7669
12215 Montague St. FAX (818) 686-1982
Pacoima, CA 91331 www.ahernentertainment.com

Alan Gordon Enterprises, Inc. (323) 466-3561
5625 Melrose Ave. FAX (323) 871-2193
Los Angeles, CA 90038 www.alangordon.com
Arms: Focus Microjib, Intel-A-Jib, Porta-Jib, Trovato & Trovato Jr. Jib Arms
Dollies: Cameleon, Cricket, Doorway, Egripment Dinky Dolly, Elemack & Spyder
Accessories: Glidecam Stabilization System & Matthews Steel Track

Any Point of View, Inc. (818) 219-1667 / (818) 504-6500
FAX (818) 394-6300
www.anypov.com
Accessories: 2 and 3 Axis Remote Heads, Digital Hot Gears & Remote Follow Focus Systems, Steadicam Systems & Vinten Quatro Studio Air Pedestals
Arms: 4'-40' Jimmy Jib Triangles

Atlantic Cine Equipment (818) 794-9410 / (410) 340-9674
1026 Griswold Ave. www.aceeast.com
San Fernando, CA 91340

Barber Tech (818) 982-7775 / (877) 887-6388
40125 20th St. West FAX (661) 339-3235
Palmdale, CA 93551 www.barbertvp.com
Booms: 20' Barber Boom & Barber Baby Boom
Accessories: Camera Car Shock Mount & Remote Focus & Zoom

Bazzar Effects (310) 600-1539
13810 Calfa St. FAX (818) 997-1929
Van Nuys, CA 91401 www.bazzareffects.com
Accessories: 2 & 3 Axis Motion Control Heads, Kuper Motion Control, Lynx, Model Movers, Motion Control, Pan/Tilt Heads, Preston, Stepper-Driver Packages & Turn Tables
Cranes: Black Widow & Mantis
Dollies: Stealth & Doorway

Big Shot Camera Cranes/ Brian Gaetke (818) 729-9339
FAX (818) 729-9331
www.bigshot.tv
Arms: 80' Akela Crane, 55' Akela Crane Jr. & 30' Jimmy Jib
Accessories: Remote Hot Head

Bikes..Camera..Action! (310) 995-2084
1105 Bonilla
Topanga, CA 90290
Accessories: Super Light Camera Mounts for Bicycles, Hang Gliders, Motorcycles and Ultralight Planes

Birns & Sawyer, Inc. (818) 766-2525 (323) 466-8211
5275 Craner Ave. FAX (818) 766-3833
North Hollywood, CA 91601 www.birnsandsawyer.com
Arms: Porta-Jib & Porta-Jib Dual and Traveller
Dollies: Cameleon, Losmandy, Porta-Glide, Sierra & Studio

Ⓐ **Branam/West Coast Theatrical** (310) 637-4727 (877) 295-3390
310 S. Long Beach Blvd. FAX (310) 637-4735
Compton, CA 90221 www.branament.com
Accessories: Aerial Camera Winch Systems

Ⓐ **Cablecam Inc.** (818) 349-4955
21303 Itasca St. FAX (818) 349-3879
Chatsworth, CA 91311 www.cablecam.com
Accessories: Cable-Suspended Camera Tracking Systems & Mounts

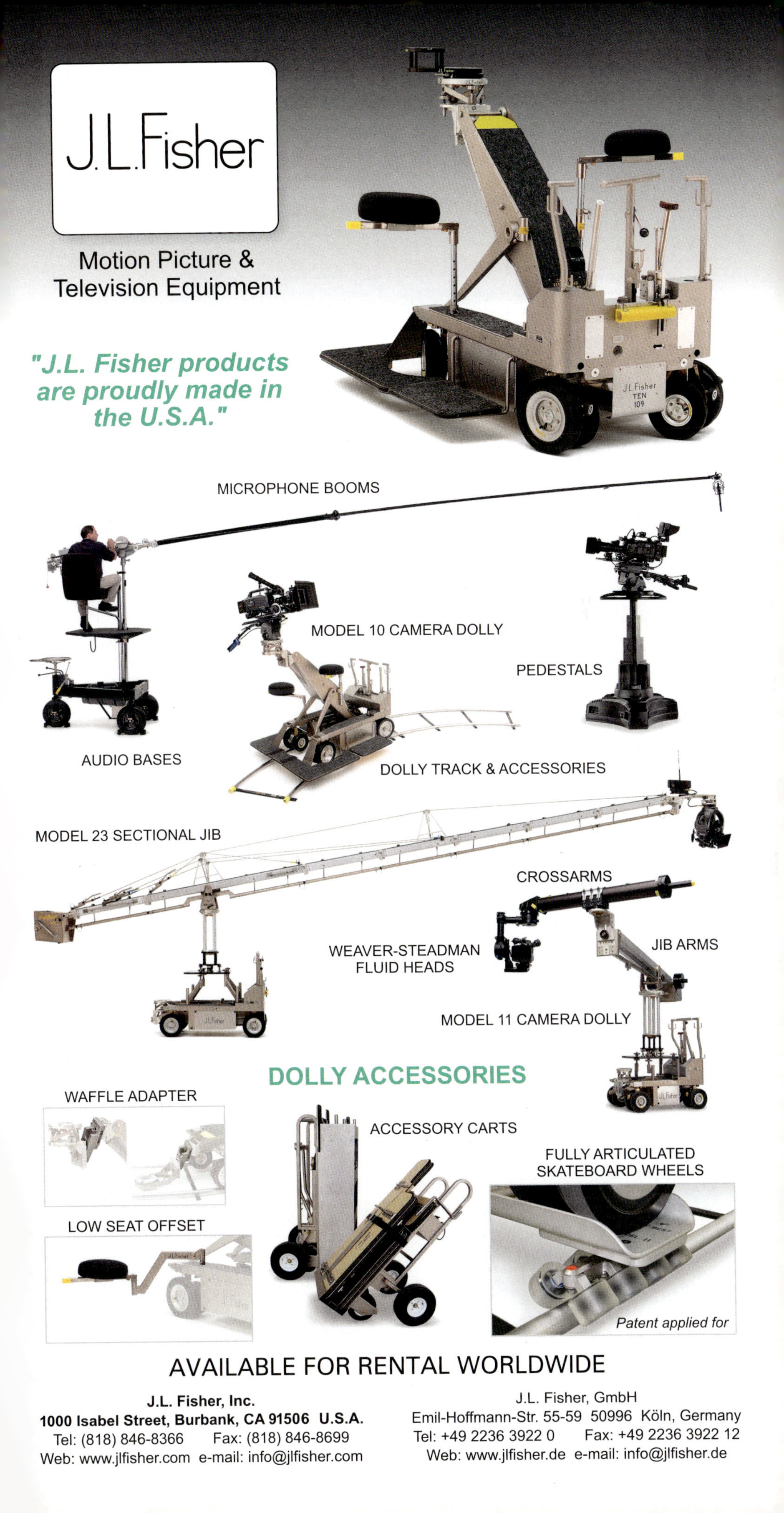

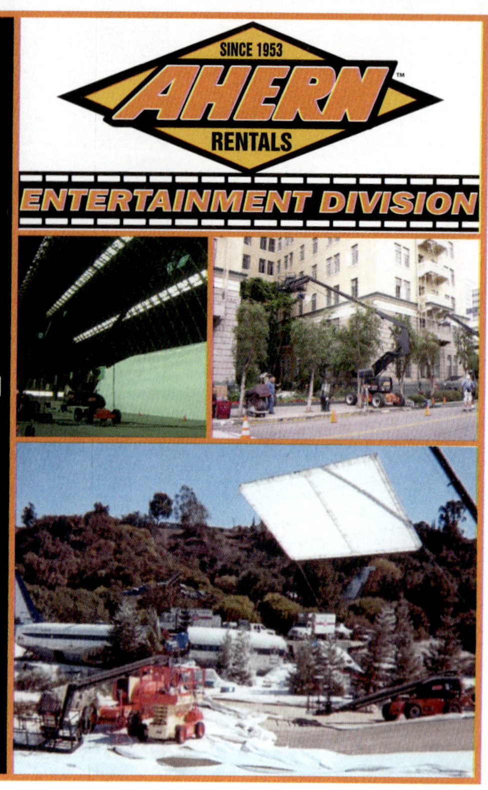

Camera Control, Inc. (310) 581-8343
3317 Ocean Park Blvd. FAX (310) 581-8340
Santa Monica, CA 90405 www.cameracontrol.com
Cranes: Live Action & Miniature Motion Control Cranes: Milo and Milo Long Arm Motion Control Systems & Talos Motion Control Rig
Dollies: Modular Motion Control Rig
Accessories: Motion Control Heads, Sleds and Turntables, Ultihead Motion Control Systems, CGI Rig Models, Flair Motion Control Systems, Motion Control Sliders, Model Movers & Remote/Repeatable Heads

Camera Support (818) 557-1400
(800) 995-5427
2827 N. San Fernando Blvd. FAX (818) 557-1323
Burbank, CA 91504 www.camerasupport.com
Arms: 6'–40' Jib SystemsAccessories: 2 and 3 Axis Remote Heads, CamRail Systems, Lencin and Vinten Fulmar Pedestals, Pan/Tilt Heads & Steadicam Systems

Champion Crane Rental, Inc. (818) 781-3497
(323) 875-1248
12521 Branford St. FAX (818) 896-6202
Pacoima, CA 91331 www.championcrane.us
Cranes: 40'–265' Reach
Accessories: Camera Baskets, Light Bars & Rain Bars

Ⓐ **Chapman/Leonard Studio Equipment, Inc.** (818) 764-6726
(888) 883-6559
12950 Raymer St. FAX (888) 502-7263
North Hollywood, CA 91605 www.chapman-leonard.com
Arms: Lenny Plus, Lenny II Plus, Lenny Mini, Plus III & Stinger Jib Arm w/ Glider
Cranes: Nike, Super Apollo, Super Nova, Titan II & Zeus
Dollies: Hustler IV, Hybrid III, Olympian, Peewee, Sidewinder, Super Peewee II, Super Peewee III & Super Peewee IV
Accessories: Bases: ATB, CS, Hy Hy Maverik, Olympian III & Raptor

Chris Rhodes Productions (310) 850-0710 (888) 200-2383
P.O. Box 691901 FAX (323) 874-5076
Los Angeles, CA 90069 www.technocrane.net
Arms: 6'–40' CamMate Jib System 2000 & 17', 24', 30' and 50' Telescopic Cranes
Dollies: Dolly w/ TrackAccessories: Remote Pan/Tilt Heads & Z-Axis/Dutch Head

Cinemoves, Inc./Technocrane, Ltd. (818) 782-9051
FAX (818) 475-5406
www.cinemoves.com
Cranes: Super TechnoCranes & TechnoCranes
Dollies: Filou Rig Runner Trackable Remote Camera System

A **Cranium, Inc.** (818) 903-4343 (888) 272-6486
13770 Purple Ridge Ave. FAX (818) 890-6093
Kagel Canyon, CA 91342 www.cranium.tv
Cranes: 17', 24', 30' and 45' Telescoping Camera Cranes (Moviebird Technocranes), Aerojib 8', Felix 18', Foxy 23', Galaxy 60', Giraffe 30' & Phoenix 40'
Dollies: Felix Wide and Narrow Base & Galaxy, Giraffe and Phoenix Wide Base
Heads: 2-Axis Mo-Sys Lambda and Nettman Cam-Remote, 3-Axis Scorpio & Stabilized Scorpio 4
Accessories: 2 and 3 Axis Remote Heads, Mo-Sys Lambda & Scorpio III

Digital Wings (323) 851-3825 (202) 438-9199
3480 Barham Blvd., Ste. 322 FAX (323) 851-0470
Los Angeles, CA 90068 www.digitalwings.com
Cranes: Triangle Jimmy Jib
Dollies: Phantom
Accessories: Dolly Track, Steadicam Systems & Track Wheel Sets

Doggicam, Inc. (818) 845-8470
1500 W. Verdugo Ave. FAX (818) 845-8477
Burbank, CA 91506 www.doggicam.com
Accessories: Body-Mount, Bulldog Wireless Remote Head, Doggimount, Lightweight Remote Sparrow Head, Power Slide, Remote Follow Focus, Rhino Clamps & Super Slide

Phillip Ebeid/Summit Cranes (818) 909-7933
www.summitcranes.com
Cranes: Portable Jimmy Jib & Remote Head 6'–31' Reach

El Monte Film Works (818) 209-5056
Arms: CamMate & Jib Arms
Dollies: Cruiser Dolly
Accessories: Dolly Tracks, Preston, Remote Follow Focus, Remote Heads & Remote Zooms

Filmotechnic International Corp. (310) 215-3004
7743 Densmore Ave. FAX (323) 622-8740
Van Nuys , CA 91406 www.russianarm.com
Cranes: Russian Arm
Accessories: Flight Head & Shock Absorber CAR Mount System

Filmotechnic USA (310) 884-9700 (562) 480-0012
20432 S. Santa Fe Ave., Ste C FAX (562) 685-0810
Carson, CA 90810 www.filmotechnic-usa.com
Arms: Russian Arm, Pursuit Arm & Ultimate Arm
Cranes: Cablecam, Cross Country, Libra Heads, Russian Crane, Pursuit Crane, Super TechnoCranes & TechnoCranes
Accessories: 2 Axis Remote Heads, 3 Axis Aerohead, 3 Axis Remote Heads, 4 Axis Remote Heads, Aerial Camera Winch Systems, ATV Mounts, Cable-Suspended Systems, Camera Car Mounts, Dutch Heads, Flight Head, High Speed Camera Tracking Systems, Libra Heads, Megamount, Motorcycle Camera Mounts, Pan/Tilt Heads, Perfect Horizon, Power Pods, Preston, Remote Camera Systems, Remote Follow Focus, Remote Heads, Remote Zoom, Scorpio & Shock Mounts

Fisher Technical Services Rentals (702) 251-0700 (866) 942-4098
FAX (702) 251-0400
www.fishertechnical.com

Fluid Pictures, Inc./ Eastwood Productions (818) 704-7873 (818) 355-5936
www.fluidpicturesinc.com
Arms: 7'-40' Jimmy Jib w/ 3rd Axis Head, Dolly and Track
Accessories: 5'-15' and 10'-33' Telescoping Column Towercams, Remote Heads & Steadicams

Focal Motion Inc. (818) 653-6287
www.focalmotion.com
Accessories: Pan/Tilt Heads
Arms: Jimmy Jib

Focus on Cars (310) 762-1370
20434 S. Santa Fe Ave. FAX (310) 763-7110
Long Beach, CA 90810 www.southbaystudios.com
Accessories: ATV and Car Camera Mounts

GCS/General Crane Services, Inc. (805) 578-2292 (818) 571-0944
1606 River Wood Court www.craneservices.com
Simi Valley, CA 93063

General Lift, LLC (310) 414-0717
209 E. El Segundo Blvd. FAX (310) 414-0705
El Segundo, CA 90245 www.general-lift.com
Arms: Jib Systems
Cranes: Genuflex Mk III
Dollies: Genuflex Mk III, Motion Control Systems & Zebra Motion Control
Accessories: 2 and 3 Axis Remote Heads, Arriflex Motorized Gearhead & Kuper Motion Control Computers

Geo Film Group, Inc. (818) 376-6680 (877) 436-3456
7625 Hayvenhurst Ave., Ste. 46 FAX (818) 376-6686
Van Nuys, CA 91406 www.geofilm.com
Arms: Jan Jib & Maxi JibCranes: Extreme, Javelin & Technocrane

Gold Coast Crane Service (805) 230-1114 (818) 414-1980
FAX (805) 494-8533
Accessories: Box Spreader Bars, Camera Baskets, Light Bars, Man Baskets & Rain Bars

Dean Goldsmith/ Camera Car Industries (818) 998-4798
12473 San Fernando Rd. FAX (818) 833-5962
Sylmar, CA 91342 www.cameracarindustries.com
Accessories: 3 Axis Remote Camera Systems

Grip Jet (818) 424-4747 (800) 474-7538
Box 47, 12653 Osborne St. FAX (818) 897-4747
Pacoima, CA 91331 www.gripjet.com
Accessories: Bazookas, Condor Mounts & Ladder Pods

Griptrix, Inc. (818) 982-2510
12767 Saticoy St. FAX (818) 982-8830
North Hollywood, CA 91605 www.griptrix.com
Dollies: Electric Camera Dolly

Holladay Camera Bikes (805) 740-6018 (323) 462-2301
Accessories: Motorcycle Camera Mounts FAX (805) 735-7205
www.camerabikes.com

Hot Gears (818) 780-2708
16644 Roscoe Blvd., Ste. 34 FAX (818) 989-5408
Van Nuys, CA 91406
Accessories: 2 and 3 Axis Remote Heads

Image G/Ikonographics (818) 761-6644
10900 Ventura Blvd. www.imageg.com
Studio City, CA 91604
Cranes: Bulldog I 16' and 22' Motion Control Cranes, Bulldog II 22' and 32' Motion Control Cranes, Gazelle Motion Control Portable System (6' Arm), Graphlite & Hyena Motion Control Portable System
Dollies: Greyhound Motion Control Portable System & Rocket Sled Motion Control Portable System
Accessories: 3', 4', 6' Sliders and Silent Sliders, 360° Axis, Dolly Track, Gazelle, Graphite, Kuper, Model Movers, Motion Control, Motion Control Accessories, Pan/Tilt Heads Frame Accurate Motion Control Heads, Sorensen Design Track and Turn Table & Zebra

Innovision Optics (310) 453-4866
1719 21st St. FAX (310) 453-4677
Santa Monica, CA 90404 www.innovisionoptics.com
Arms: Z-Jib Zero Gravity Arm
Accessories: 3-Axis Remote Head, High Speed Camera Tracking Systems, Pan/Tilt Heads & Rotation/Linear Motion Control Tables

A **J.L. Fisher, Inc.** (818) 846-8366
1000 W. Isabel St. FAX (818) 846-8699
Burbank, CA 91506 www.jlfisher.com
Arms: Fisher Jib 20, 21, 22 and 23
Booms: Fisher Microphone w/6'–29' Reach
Dollies: Fisher 9, 10 and 11Heads: Vector 700
Accessories: Quattro Pedestal

JB Slider (818) 345-3127
(818) 388-2898
19159 Rosita St. FAX (818) 705-0753
Tarzana, CA 91356 www.jbslider.com
Accessories: 2' and 3' Sliders

Jib Solutions, Inc. (818) 367-6337
(818) 321-2224
15021 Briarhill Dr. FAX (818) 367-3081
Sylmar, CA 91342 www.video8film.com
Arms: 15' and 24' Technojib Telescoping Jib Arms, Jimmy Jibs & Triangle Jimmy
Cranes: Jib Arms
Accessories: 2 Axis Remote Heads, Dutch Heads & Remote Heads

Jibmasters, Inc. (310) 993-5456
(805) 496-6999
1248 Willsbrook Court FAX (805) 494-9999
Westlake Village, CA 91361 www.jibmasters.com
Arms: 30' Reach
Accessories: Dutch Head & Wide Angle Lenses

Jibology (310) 721-9816
FAX (323) 939-9754
www.jibology.com
Accessories: Remote ZoomArms: Jimmy Jib
Cranes: Jib Arms & Triangle Jimmy Jib

JibWorks/Mark Koonce (213) 680-1448
www.jibworks.com
Accessories: Dutch Heads, Hot Heads, Pan/Tilt Heads, Remote Camera Systems, Remote Follow Focus & Remote Zoom
Arms: Jimmy Jib, Porta-Jibs & Triangle Jimmy
Dollies: GatorCam

KCW Studios (626) 698-0029
318 S. Date Ave. FAX (626) 943-0190
Alhambra, CA 91803 www.kcwstudios.com

Tracy Kilbourne (818) 888-9825
(818) 439-5949
FAX (818) 888-9826
Arms: Triangle Jib Arms w/ 30' Reach
Accessories: Dutch Control & Remote Heads

Line 204 (323) 960-0113
1034 N. Seward St. FAX (323) 960-0163
Hollywood, CA 90038 www.line204.com

Logan Cinema Equipment Rental (323) 702-8502
Arms: Jimmy Jib www.watchreels.com/mhofstein

Motion Picture Marine (310) 822-1100
616 Venice Blvd. FAX (310) 822-2679
Marina del Rey, CA 90291 www.motionpicturemarine.com
Accessories: Perfect Horizon Camera Stabilization Head

Motor Reflex (818) 761-7749
P.O. Box 7153 www.motorreflex.com
Burbank, CA 91510
Accessories: Kuper Motion Control and Stepper-Driver Packages, Motion Control Drive Units and Accessories, Preston FIZ-to-Moco Blackboxes & TruePos Track Encoder/Display

Willy Nemeth/Good Medicine Hat (541) 840-3366
(541) 476-0598
Accessories: ATV and Car Camera Mounts

Nettmann Systems International (818) 623-1661
6910 Tujunga Ave. FAX (818) 623-1671
North Hollywood, CA 91605 www.camerasystems.com
Accessories: Cam-Remote/Mini-Mote, Gyro-Stabilized 5-Axis Remote Heads: Gyron FS/Stab-C and Stab-C Compact & Kenworthy/Nettman Snorkel

Wayne Norman (818) 558-3705
www.jimmyjibs.com

Oppenheimer Cine Rental (310) 286-2104
(877) 467-8666
FAX (206) 467-9165
www.oppcam.com
Cranes: 42' Braced Super Swiss Jib Crane
Accessories: Power Pod Remote Head

Pacific Motion Control, Inc. (818) 768-1573
(661) 644-1516
9812 Glenoaks Blvd. FAX (818) 768-1575
Sun Valley, CA 91352 www.pacificmotion.net
Cranes: Motion Control/Repeatable Cranes: Gazelle (Portable 6' Arm), Graphlite (Portable 12' Arm) and The Milo, Telescoping Cranes: Super Scorpio Technocrane (30' or 37' Arm)
Dollies: Bogey & Motion Control/Repeatable Zebra (Portable 2' or 6' Arm)
Accessories: 2 Axis Remote Heads, 3 Axis Aerohead, Aeroheads, CGI Rig Interface Models, Flair Motion Control, Frame Accurate Motion Control Heads, Kuper Motion Control, Lynx, Model Movers, Motion Control Lighting Cues, Motion Control Track (Straight or 360° Curved), Motor Driver Systems, Preston, Remote Camera Systems, Remote/Repeatable Heads, Stepper-Driver Packages, Turn Tables & Zebra

Panavision Remote Systems (818) 316-1000
Corporate Headquarters FAX (818) 316-1111
6219 DeSoto Ave. www.panavision.com
Woodland Hills, CA 91367
Cranes: 100' Strada, 15', 20', 30' and 50' Technocranes, Felix, Foxy, Libra Heads, Panacart-Techno Combo, Phoenix, Strada/ Steadicam Hook and Release, Pictorvision XR & TechnoDolly
Accessories: CruiseCam, GoMobile-Techno Combo, HotHeads, Manual and Motorized Sliders, Panacart-Techno Combo, PowerPods, Towercam & TowerCam FX and XS

Pictorvision Inc (818) 785-9282
(800) 876-5583
7701 Haskell Ave., Ste. B FAX (818) 785-9787
Van Nuys, CA 91406 www.pictorvision.com
Accessories: 5 Axis Gyro-Stabilized Camera Systems, Cineflex, Pictorvision Eclipse, Wescam & XR

Pursuit Systems Inc. (818) 579-7250
7255 Radford Ave. www.pursuitsystems.com
North Hollywood, CA 91605

R.A. Jones Enterprises (818) 999-1411
5676 Penfield Ave. FAX (818) 999-0077
Woodland Hills, CA 91367
Cranes: Aquapod Underwater Remote Head and Crane

Safari Technologies (866) 449-7447
(818) 585-6653
P.O. Box 5417 FAX (805) 830-1158
Palm Springs, CA 92263 www.safaritechnologies.net
Arms: SR4 Car Mount
Accessories: Remote Pan/Tilt Heads

Service Vision USA (818) 623-1970
12035 Sherman Way FAX **(818) 759-6911**
North Hollywood, CA 91605 **www.servicevisionusa.com**
Cranes: 30' SuperScorpio Crane with 8' Extention & 9'–50' Carbon Fibre
Accessories: 2 and 3 Axis Remote Heads, 3 Axis Remote Camera Systems, 360° Axis, Gyro Stabilized Remote Heads, Remote Follow Focus, Remote Heads, Remote Pan/Tilt Heads, Scorpio III, Scorpio Mini Head & Scorpio Stabilized Head

(A) **The Slider** (805) 496-5289
(818) 344-5284
FAX **(805) 496-4802**
www.theslider.com
Accessories: 32" Video and Mitchell Mount Minisliders & 3', 4', 6', 8' Manual and Motorized Sliders

Spydercam (877) 933-7226
(303) 941-1900
28130 Avenue Crocker, Ste. 322 **www.spydercam.com**
Santa Clarita, CA 91355
Accessories: 2-D and 3-D Suspended Camera Systems & Rigging Systems

Straight Shoot'r Cranes, Inc. (818) 609-8310
18434 Oxnard St., Ste H FAX **(818) 609-8311**
Tarzana, CA 91356 **www.straightshootr.com**
Accessories: Pan/Tilt Heads
Cranes: Jib Arms

Techno-Jib Rentals (818) 917-5677
(888) 520-2090
www.technojibrentals.com

Telescopic Camera Cranes, Inc. (310) 947-5126
(818) 355-5721
www.telescopiccameracranes.com

Terra-Flite (323) 223-2709
3811 San Rafael Ave.
Los Angeles, CA 90065
Arms: 16' Gyro-Stabilized Arm w/ 8' Reach & 9' Vertical Range and 14" Min. Height

Climate Control Systems

Action Portable Air Conditioning (888) 508-3394
FAX (888) 508-3394
(Portable Air Conditioning and Heating Units & Spot Coolers)

Ⓐ Aggreko Event Services (818) 767-7288
(888) 918-4874
FAX (818) 762-7782
11180 Penrose St.
Sun Valley, CA 91352
www.aggreko.com/equipserv/event-services.asp
(Air Conditioning Units & Heaters)

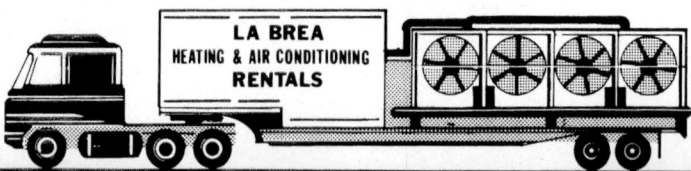

Ⓐ Air on Location, Inc. (818) 307-4558
(Portable Air Conditioning Units) FAX (818) 712-6933

Atlas Sales & Rentals, Inc. (800) 972-6600
(310) 320-9800
20410 Gramercy Pl. FAX (310) 320-9870
Torrance, CA 90501 www.atlassales.com
(Portable Air Conditioning Units, Fans and Heaters & Spot Coolers)

Ⓐ Cinema Air, Inc. (805) 732-6517
FAX (805) 526-6905
www.cinemaair.com
(Portable Air Conditioning Units and Heating Units & Spot Coolers)

DJ Safety, Inc. (323) 221-0000
(818) 445-2381
2623 N. San Fernando Rd. FAX (323) 221-0001
Los Angeles, CA 90065 www.djsafety.com
(Pool Heating)

Elegant Mist, LLC (310) 428-5180
FAX (310) 564-0439
www.elegantmist.com

GE/Showpower Energy Rentals (310) 604-9676
(877) 797-4768
18420 S. Santa Fe Ave. www.gepower.com
Rancho Domiguez, CA 90220
(Portable Air Conditioning Units)

Kohler Rental (310) 518-5118
(866) 577-4797
1581 W. Wardlow Rd. FAX (310) 518-5028
Long Beach, CA 90810 www.kohlereventservices.com

Kreiger Sales (323) 721-5894
(800) 573-4437
6930 Telegraph Rd. FAX (323) 721-1276
Los Angeles, CA 90040 www.rapidcool.net
(Misting System)

La Brea Air, Inc. (800) 452-2732 (310) 258-9100
5601 W. Slauson Ave., Ste. 262 FAX **(310) 258-9110**
Culver City, CA 90230 **www.labrearentals.com**
(Air Conditioning and Heating Equipment and Systems)

Line 204 (323) 960-0113
1034 N. Seward St. FAX **(323) 960-0163**
Hollywood, CA 90038 **www.line204.com**

Malibu Mobile Air (818) 706-3423 (818) 590-2455
5737 Kanan Rd., Ste. 531 FAX **(818) 706-1660**
Agoura Hills, CA 91301
(Air Conditioning Units, Heating Units & Portable Units)

Mike's Heating and Cooling Service, Inc. (626) 286-4133 (626) 372-2811
4504 Halkett Ave. FAX **(626) 286-7709**
Rosemead, CA 91770
www.mikesheatingandcoolingservice.com

Sony Pictures Studios (310) 244-6926
10202 W. Washington Blvd. FAX **(310) 244-8090**
Culver City, CA 90232 **www.sonypicturesstudios.com**
(Blowers, Pool Heaters, Portable Air Conditioning Units & Ventilation Fans)

Studio Air Conditioning, Inc. (818) 222-4143
5171 N. Douglas Fir Rd., Ste. 6 FAX **(818) 222-2092**
Calabasas, CA 91302 **www.studioair.com**
(Air Conditioning Units & Heaters)

Sunbelt Rentals (818) 996-7100
18251 Napa St. **www.sunbeltrentals.com**
Northridge, CA 91325

Sunbelt Rentals (714) 923-1890
1600 W. Katella Ave. FAX **(714) 923-1891**
Orange, CA 92867 **www.sunbeltrentals.com**

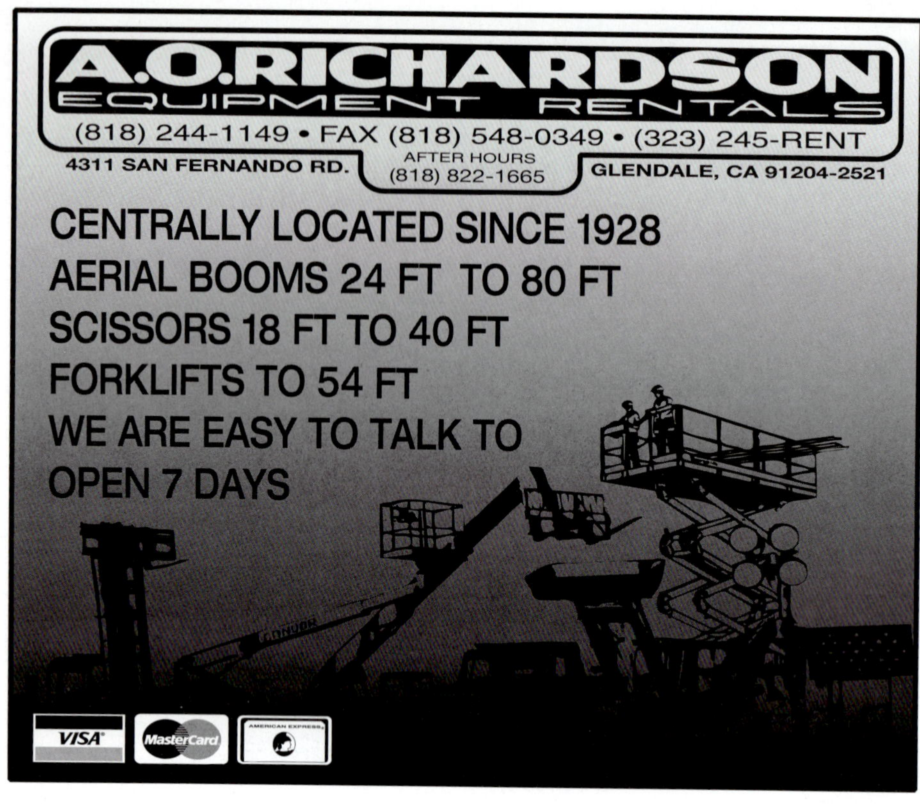

24/7 Studio Equipment (818) 840-8247 / (818) 391-4104
3111 N. Kenwood St. FAX (818) 847-0941
Burbank, CA 91505 www.247studioequipment.com

A-1 Coast Rental (310) 326-1910 / (800) 932-6278
24000 Crenshaw Blvd. FAX (310) 326-1547
Torrance, CA 90505 www.a1coastrentals.com

A-Line Crane Rental Services, Inc. (714) 261-3536 / (800) 524-7972
18032-C Lemon Dr., Ste. 212 FAX (714) 744-5802
Yorba Linda, CA 92886 www.alinecranes.com

A **A.O. Richardson** (818) 242-3129 / (818) 242-0888
4311 San Fernando Rd. FAX (818) 548-0349
Glendale, CA 91204 www.aorichardson.com

B & G Industrial Rentals (310) 327-0804 / (800) 536-3019
1627 W. 130th St. FAX (310) 327-9174
Gardena, CA 90249 www.bgrentalsinc.com
(24-Hour Service)

Bailey Bobcat Service/Studio Cats (818) 982-4356

Contractors Equipment Rentals (562) 432-2954
2020 W. Pacific Coast Hwy FAX (562) 437-4949
Long Beach, CA 90810

First Call Studio Equipment (818) 771-9351 / (818) 254-5232
12458 Gladstone Ave. FAX (818) 901-6333
Sylmar, CA 91342 www.1stcallequip.com
(Gator Tractor Trailers)

Kohler Rental (310) 518-5118 / (866) 577-4797
1581 W. Wardlow Rd. FAX (310) 518-5028
Long Beach, CA 90810 www.kohlereventservices.com

Power Trip Rentals (310) 667-4433 / (310) 292-0974
2950 E. Harcourt St. FAX (310) 604-3233
Rancho Dominguez, CA 90221 www.powertriprentals.net

Sunbelt Rentals (818) 349-1210 / (866) 677-5438
18251 Napa St. FAX (818) 701-9113
Northridge, CA 91325 www.sunbeltrentals.com

Sunstate Equipment Company (888) 456-4560 / (800) 870-9110
17310 S. Main St. FAX (949) 699-1054
Carson, CA 90248 www.sunstateequip.com

Sunstate Equipment Company (888) 456-4560 / (800) 870-9110
4460 E. La Palma Ave. FAX (949) 699-1054
Anaheim, CA 92807 www.sunstateequip.com

Sunstate Equipment Company (888) 456-4560 / (800) 870-9110
32311 Dunlap Blvd. FAX (949) 699-1054
Yucaipa, CA 92399 www.sunstateequip.com

Sunstate Equipment Company (888) 456-4560 / (800) 870-9110
5590 Eastgate Mall FAX (949) 699-1054
San Diego, CA 92121 www.sunstateequip.com

Sunstate Equipment Company (888) 456-4560 / (800) 870-9110
205 W. Magnolia Blvd. FAX (714) 779-9767
Burbank, CA 91502 www.sunstateequip.com

United Rentals (818) 842-5288
203 W. Olive Ave. FAX (818) 842-9970
Burbank, CA 91502 www.unitedrentals.com

Acey Decy Lighting (818) 408-4444
200 Parkside Dr. FAX (818) 408-2777
San Fernando, CA 91340 www.aceydecy.com

Angstrom Lighting (323) 462-4246
(866) 275-9211
837 N. Cahuenga Blvd. FAX (323) 462-8190
Hollywood, CA 90038 www.angstromlighting.com

Anytime - Hollywood (323) 461-8483
755 N. Lillian Way FAX (323) 461-2338
Hollywood, CA 90038 www.anytime-rentals.com

Apache Rental Group (818) 842-9944
(818) 842-9875
3910 W. Magnolia Blvd. FAX (818) 842-9269
Burbank, CA 91505 www.apacherentalgroup.com

Birns & Sawyer, Inc. (323) 466-8211
(818) 766-2525
6381 De Longpre Ave. FAX (323) 466-7049
Hollywood, CA 90028 www.birnsandsawyer.com

Board Brothers (323) 600-3964
12939 Hamlin St.
North Hollywood, CA 91606
(Layout Boards)

Board Patrol (818) 508-4633
(323) 965-1478
(Layout Boards) FAX (818) 508-4638
www.theboardpatrol.com

Board Sily (818) 590-5878
(Layout Boards)

Board Stiff, Inc. (310) 516-7881
(323) 855-4640
1847 W. 144th St. FAX (310) 516-7882
Gardena, CA 90249 www.boardstiff.com
(Layout Board)

Ⓐ **Bulbtronics** (323) 461-6262
(800) 654-8542
1054 N. Cahuenga Blvd. FAX (323) 461-7307
Hollywood, CA 90038 www.bulbtronics.com

Castex Rentals (323) 462-1468
1044 Cole Ave. FAX (323) 462-3719
Hollywood, CA 90038 www.castexrentals.com

Concept Lighting, Inc. (818) 767-1122
11274 Goss St. FAX (818) 768-9900
Sun Valley, CA 91352 www.conceptlight.com

The Culver Studios (310) 202-3338
9336 W. Washington Blvd. FAX (310) 202-3516
Culver City, CA 90232 www.theculverstudios.com

Entertainment Lighting Services (ELS) (818) 769-9800
(800) 622-6628
11440 Sheldon St. FAX (818) 769-2100
Sun Valley, CA 91352 www.elslights.com
(Lighting Expendables & Production Expendables)

Expendable Supply Store (818) 407-7800
(800) 233-7830
12800 Foothill Blvd. FAX (818) 407-7875
Sylmar, CA 91342 www.hollywoodrentals.com

Expendables Plus (818) 841-8282
2040 N. Lincoln St. FAX (818) 841-3345
Burbank, CA 91504 www.cinelease.com

The Expendables Recycler (818) 901-9796
5812 Columbus Ave. FAX (818) 901-6010
Van Nuys, CA 91411 www.expendablesrecycler.com
(Camera and Lighting Expendables)

Express Layout Boards, Inc. (661) 255-0602
(661) 857-1715
24504 Apple St. FAX (661) 255-0602
Santa Clarita, CA 91321

Filmtools (818) 845-8066
(888) 807-1900
1400 W. Burbank Blvd. FAX **(818) 845-8138**
Burbank, CA 91506 **www.filmtools.com**
(Camera Expendables)

Fox Studios (310) 369-2528
(310) 369-4636
Studio Supply, 10201 W. Pico Blvd. FAX **(310) 369-4078**
Los Angeles, CA 90035 **www.foxstudios.com**
(Camera Expendables, Construction and Paint Supplies & Production Office Expendables)

GAM Products, Inc. (323) 935-4975
(888) 426-2656
4975 W. Pico Blvd. FAX **(323) 935-2002**
Los Angeles, CA 90019 **www.gamonline.com**

Hollywood Center Studios (323) 860-0000
1040 N. Las Palmas Ave. FAX **(323) 860-8105**
Hollywood, CA 90038 **www.hollywoodcenter.com**

Hollywood Rentals/ESS/Olesen (818) 407-7800
12800 Foothill Blvd. FAX **(818) 407-7875**
Sylmar, CA 91342 **www.hollywoodrentals.com**

Jack Rubin & Sons, Inc. (818) 562-5100
520 S. Varney St. FAX **(818) 562-5101**
Burbank, CA 91502 **www.wirerope.net**

Kinetic Lighting (310) 837-3204
(800) 908-3842
7672 N. Clybourne Ave. FAX **(310) 837-8695**
Los Angeles, CA 91352 **www.kineticlighting.com**

Lay'd Out (310) 455-4384
(310) 963-2203
P.O. Box 252 FAX **(310) 455-1393**
Topanga, CA 90290 **www.laydout.org**
(Layout Boards)

Lexus Lighting, Inc. (818) 768-4508
11225 Dora St. FAX **(805) 641-3273**
Sun Valley, CA 91352 **www.lexuslighting.com**

Line 204 (323) 960-0113
1034 N. Seward St. FAX **(323) 960-0163**
Hollywood, CA 90038 **www.line204.com**

Location Junkies (310) 215-3111
(310) 741-6162
3452 Moore St. FAX **(310) 743-6855**
Los Angeles, CA 90066 **www.locationjunkies.com**
(Layout Boards)

Location Sound Corporation (818) 980-9891
(800) 228-4429
10639 Riverside Dr. FAX **(818) 980-9911**
North Hollywood, CA 91602 **www.locationsound.com**
(Production Expendables)

LocoMats (818) 376-8386
7064 Gerald Ave. FAX **(818) 376-8648**
Van Nuys, CA 91406 **www.locomats.com**

The Lot (323) 850-3180
(323) 850-2832
1041 N. Formosa Ave. **www.skyepartners.com**
West Hollywood, CA 90046

Maggie's Layout Board (818) 344-6601
18653 Ventura Blvd., Ste. 450 FAX **(818) 344-3566**
Tarzana, CA 91356 **www.maggieslayoutboard.net**

Mat Men (323) 632-4368
(310) 704-5939
2160 E. Woodlyn Rd. FAX **(310) 943-1852**
Pasadena, CA 91104
(Layout Boards)

Miller Production Services (310) 287-0466
3520 Helms Ave. FAX **(310) 287-0467**
Culver City, CA 90232

MPR Photographic Rentals (310) 762-1360
South Bay Studios FAX **(310) 639-2055**
20434 S. Santa Fe Ave. **www.southbaystudios.com**
Long Beach, CA 90810

Out of Frame Production Rentals (323) 462-1898
1126 N. Citrus Ave. FAX **(323) 462-1897**
Hollywood, CA 90038 **www.outofframela.com**
(Camera Expendables, Layout Boards, Lighting Expendables & Production Expendables)

Paladin Group, Inc. (323) 874-7758
(323) 851-8222
7351 Santa Monica Blvd. FAX **(323) 851-7328**
Los Angeles, CA 90046

Panavision Panastore (818) 316-1000
Corporate Headquarters FAX **(818) 316-1111**
6219 DeSoto Ave. **www.panastore.com**
Woodland Hills, CA 91367
(Camera Expendables)

The Studios at Paramount (323) 956-5114
The Studios at Paramount
Grip & Lighting Expendables
5555 Melrose Ave.
Hollywood, CA 90038
www.thestudiosatparamount.com

Pasadena Camera Rental, Inc. (626) 796-3300
41 E. Walnut St. FAX **(626) 432-6731**
Pasadena, CA 91103 **www.samyscamera.com**

Paskal Lighting (818) 896-5233
12685 Van Nuys Blvd. FAX **(818) 485-0157**
Pacoima, CA 91331 **www.paskal.com**

Premier Lighting & Production Co. (818) 762-0884
(800) 770-0884
12023 Victory Blvd. FAX **(818) 762-0896**
North Hollywood, CA 91606 **www.premier-lighting.com**

Quixote Studios (323) 957-9933
(818) 553-2960
4585 Electronics Pl. FAX **(323) 957-9944**
Griffith Park, CA 90039 **www.quixote.com**

Ragtime Rentals, Inc. (323) 769-0650
6011 Waring Ave. FAX **(323) 461-8065**
Hollywood, CA 90038 **www.ragtimerentals.com**

Raleigh Studios Lighting & Grip (323) 960-3456
5300 Melrose Ave. FAX **(323) 871-5644**
Hollywood, CA 90038 **www.raleighstudios.com**

Rose Brand (818) 505-6290
(800) 360-5056
10616 Lanark St. FAX **(818) 505-6293**
Sun Valley, CA 91352 **www.rosebrand.com**

Sequoia Illumination (818) 563-1000
(888) 647-2777
2428 N. Ontario St. FAX **(818) 563-1001**
Burbank, CA 91504 **www.sequoiaillumination.com**

Set Stuff, Inc. (323) 993-9500
1105 N. Sycamore Ave. FAX **(323) 993-9506**
Hollywood, CA 90038 **www.setstuffrentals.com**

ShowBiz Enterprises, Inc. (818) 989-7007
15541 Lanark St. FAX **(818) 989-8272**
Van Nuys, CA 91406 **www.showbizenterprises.com**

Siren Studios (323) 467-3559
(323) 960-9045
6063 W. Sunset Blvd. FAX **(323) 461-6744**
Hollywood, CA 90028 **www.sirenstudios.com**

SirReel - LA & San Diego (760) 672-5522
(888) 477-7335
(Production Expendables) FAX **(888) 477-7313**
www.sirreel.us

Skye Rentals (323) 462-5934
920 N. Citrus Ave. FAX **(323) 462-5935**
Hollywood, CA 90038 **www.skyerentals.com**
(Camera Expendables, Layout Boards, Lighting Expendables & Production Expendables)

Studio Depot/Mole-Richardson Co. (323) 851-0111
900 N. La Brea Ave. FAX **(323) 851-7854**
Hollywood, CA 90038 **www.studiodepot.com**

Studio Inn Expendables (818) 880-4770
5735 Parkmor Rd. FAX **(818) 377-3213**
Calabasas, CA 91302 **www.studioinn.com**

Studio Stockroom, LLC (866) 575-7666
FAX **(866) 571-7666**
www.studiostockroom.com

Superior Studio Specialties (323) 278-0100
(800) 354-3049
2239 S. Yates Ave. FAX **(323) 278-0111**
Commerce, CA 90040 **www.superiorstudio.com**

TCH/The Camera House (818) 997-3802
7351 Fulton Ave. FAX **(818) 997-3885**
North Hollywood, CA 91605 **www.thecamerahouse.com**

TM Motion Picture Equipment Rentals, Inc. (818) 846-3100
101 E. Linden Ave. FAX **(818) 846-3217**
Burbank, CA 91502 **www.tmequipmentrentals.com**

Visions In Color, Inc. (818) 566-1114
2101 W. Burbank Blvd. FAX **(818) 566-6817**
Burbank, CA 91506
(Bulbs & Lighting Expendables)

Warner Bros. Studio Facilities - Mill Store (818) 954-4444
4000 Warner Blvd., Bldg. 44 FAX **(818) 954-5753**
Burbank, CA 91522 **www.wbsf.com**

Westside Production Services (310) 244-2700
5933 W. Slauson Ave. FAX **(310) 244-2702**
Culver City, CA 90230 **www.westsidelighting.com**

Acey Decy Lighting (818) 408-4444
200 Parkside Dr. FAX (818) 408-2777
San Fernando, CA 91340 www.aceydecy.com

Action Grip, LLC (818) 389-7618
33483 Domino Hill Rd. FAX (661) 268-0429
Agua Dulce, CA 91390 www.actiongripllc.com

Albuquerque Studios (505) 227-2000
5650 University Blvd. SE FAX (505) 227-2001
Albuquerque, NM 87106 www.abqstudios.com

Alliance Grip Trucks (213) 819-1777
2617 Corralitas Dr. FAX (323) 666-0828
Los Angeles, CA 90039 www.alliancegrip.com

American Grip (818) 768-8922
8468 Kewen Ave. FAX (818) 768-0564
Sun Valley, CA 91352 www.americangrip.com

Angstrom Lighting (323) 462-4246 (866) 275-9211
837 N. Cahuenga Blvd. FAX (323) 462-8190
Hollywood, CA 90038 www.angstromlighting.com

Anytime Production Rentals (323) 461-8483
755 N. Lillian Way FAX (323) 461-2338
Hollywood, CA 90038 www.anytime-rentals.com

Backstage Equipment, Inc. (818) 504-6026 (800) 692-2787
8052 Lankershim Blvd. FAX (818) 504-6180
North Hollywood, CA 91605 www.backstageweb.com

Beckman Rigging/BRS Rigging (310) 532-3933 (661) 510-2518
13516 S. Mariposa Ave. FAX (310) 532-3993
Gardena, CA 90247 www.brsrigging.com

Berkeley Avenue Productions (310) 579-2277 (512) 296-7804
155 W. Washington Blvd., Ste. 650
Los Angeles, CA 90015 www.berkeleyavenue.com

Bill Ferrell Co. (818) 994-1952 (866) 994-1952
14744 Oxnard St. FAX (818) 994-9670
Van Nuys, CA 91411 www.billferrell.com

Birns & Sawyer, Inc. (818) 766-2525 (323) 466-8211
Lighting Division, 5275 Craner Ave. FAX (818) 766-3833
North Hollywood, CA 91601 www.birnsandsawyer.com

Borrmann Metal Center (818) 846-7171 (800) 801-2677
110 W. Olive Ave. FAX (818) 846-9347
Burbank, CA 91502 www.borrmannmetalcenter.com

Ⓐ **Branam/West Coast Theatrical** (310) 637-4727 (877) 295-3390
310 S. Long Beach Blvd. FAX (310) 637-4735
Compton, CA 90221 www.west-coast-theatrical.com

Bullet Grip, Inc. (818) 832-8707
18926 San Jose St. FAX (818) 832-8807
Northridge, CA 91326 www.bulletgrip.com

Bundle-Up Rentals (818) 787-3700
13556 Hart St. FAX (818) 787-3791
Van Nuys, CA 91405

Cam Film Services (818) 957-6180
5201 Castle Rd.
La Cañada Flintridge, CA 91011

Castex Rentals (323) 462-1468
1044 Cole Ave. FAX (323) 462-3719
Hollywood, CA 90038 www.castexrentals.com

CBS Studio Center (818) 655-5711
4024 Radford Ave. FAX (818) 655-5443
Studio City, CA 91604 www.cbssc.com

Century Studio Corporation (310) 287-3600 (888) 878-2437
8660 Hayden Pl., Ste. 100 FAX (310) 287-3608
Culver City, CA 90232 www.centurystudio.com

Chapman/Leonard Studio Equipment, Inc. (818) 764-6726 (888) 883-6559
12950 Raymer St. FAX (888) 502-7263
North Hollywood, CA 91605 www.chapman-leonard.com

Cine Power & Light, Inc. (818) 846-0123
805 S. San Fernando Rd., Bldg. 2 FAX (818) 846-0111
Burbank, CA 91502 www.cinepowerlight.com

Cinelease, Inc. (818) 841-8282
2040 N. Lincoln St. FAX (818) 954-9641
Burbank, CA 91504 www.cinelease.com

Cinessential Films (323) 422-6480
FAX (323) 467-8754

Cineworks, Inc. (818) 252-0001
8125 Lankershim Blvd. FAX (818) 252-0003
North Hollywood, CA 91605 www.cineworksinc.com

The Company Pictures (310) 919-0950 (310) 806-1289
1901 S. Bundy Dr. www.thecompany.tv
Los Angeles, CA 90025

Concept Lighting, Inc. (818) 767-1122
11274 Goss St. FAX (818) 768-9900
Sun Valley, CA 91352 www.conceptlight.com

Crosslight Grip & Lighting (323) 965-7676 (310) 721-0356
5429 Washington Blvd. FAX (323) 965-7675
Los Angeles, CA 90016 www.crosslight.tv

The Culver Studios (310) 202-1234
9336 W. Washington Blvd. FAX (310) 202-3516
Culver City, CA 90232 www.theculverstudios.com

Dan Reilly Grip Rentals (661) 702-8971 (661) 803-3132
30956 N. Stone Creek Rd. FAX (661) 702-8972
Castaic, CA 91384

Digital Film Studios (818) 771-0019
11800 Sheldon St., Ste. C FAX (818) 771-0575
Sun Valley, CA 91352 www.digitalfilmstudios.com

Digital Wings (323) 851-3825 (202) 438-9199
3480 Barham Blvd., Ste. 322 FAX (323) 851-0470
Los Angeles, CA 90068 www.digitalwings.com

ElectraLynn Lighting & Grip, Ltd. (818) 506-4692
www.electralynn.com

Entertainment Lighting Services (ELS) (818) 769-9800 (800) 622-6628
11440 Sheldon St. FAX (818) 769-2100
Sun Valley, CA 91352 www.elslights.com

EZ Grip Equipment Rentals (818) 366-2043

First Call Grip Equipment (818) 848-5801 (818) 381-3137
1317 N. San Fernando Blvd., Ste. 503 FAX (818) 848-5801
Burbank, CA 91504

FM Grip & Lighting, Inc. (818) 383-6376 (818) 897-9111
10312 Norris Ave., Ste. D FAX (818) 897-9113
Pacoima, CA 91331 www.fmgrip.com

Fox Studios (310) 369-4747 / (310) 369-4636
Grip Department, 10201 W. Pico Blvd. FAX (310) 969-1456
Los Angeles, CA 90035 www.foxstudios.com

Geronimo Creek Film Company (323) 997-0202
FAX (323) 417-4915
www.geronimocreek.com

Greg Mustin Rentals (805) 374-6060 / (805) 559-7612
FAX (805) 374-6060

Grip Brothers, Inc. (661) 259-5602
25538 Via Ventana FAX (661) 259-5053
Valencia, CA 91381

The Grip Company (818) 421-6695 / (818) 474-7261
595 Fresh Meadows Rd. FAX (818) 886-5039
Simi Valley, CA 93065 www.thegripco.com

Grip Jet (818) 424-4747 / (800) 474-7538
Box 47, 12653 Osborne St. FAX (818) 897-4747
Pacoima, CA 91331 www.gripjet.com

HALA Lighting & Grip (818) 883-4771 / (818) 288-6004
15844 Strathern St. FAX (818) 883-4871
Van Nuys, CA 91406 www.halastudios.com

Hollywood Rentals/ESS/Olesen (818) 407-7800
12800 Foothill Blvd. FAX (818) 407-7875
Sylmar, CA 91342 www.hollywoodrentals.com

Icarus Rigging (323) 660-4112
3531 Casitas Ave. FAX (323) 660-6135
Los Angeles, CA 90039 www.icarusrigging.com

Indie Rentals (323) 465-7700 / (323) 571-9476
7022 W. Sunset Blvd. FAX (323) 297-2773
Hollywood, CA 90028 www.indierentals.com

Industrial Metal Supply Co. (818) 729-3333 / (800) 339-6033
8300 San Fernando Rd. FAX (818) 729-3334
Sun Valley, CA 91352 www.industrialmetalsupply.com

J.L. Fisher, Inc. (818) 846-8366
1000 W. Isabel St. FAX (818) 846-8699
Burbank, CA 91506 www.jlfisher.com

Jack Rubin & Sons, Inc. (818) 562-5100
520 S. Varney St. FAX (818) 562-5101
Burbank, CA 91502 www.wirerope.net

JG Productions (310) 836-4323
FAX (310) 836-4307

Kevin Coon Grip Truck Rental (661) 298-0248 / (661) 645-7168
16969 Forrest St.
Canyon Country, CA 91351

L.A. Grip & Lighting (818) 703-5956
23469 Justice St. FAX (818) 703-5956
West Hills, CA 91304

LAgrip (910) 616-3801
11000 Morrison St., Ste. 307 www.lagrip.com
North Hollywood, CA 91601

lapinegrip Co. (818) 765-6335 / (310) 365-9534
13105 Saticoy St. FAX (310) 919-3155
North Hollywood, CA 91605 www.lapinegrip.com

Leonetti Company (818) 890-6000
10601 Glenoaks Blvd. FAX (818) 890-6116
Pacoima, CA 91331 www.leonetticompany.com

Lexus Lighting, Inc. (818) 768-4508
11225 Dora St. FAX (805) 641-3273
Sun Valley, CA 91352 www.lexuslighting.com

Lightshapes (818) 753-4883 / (818) 516-4606
4547 Biloxi Ave. FAX (818) 753-0181
Toluca Lake, CA 91602 www.light-shapes.com

Los Angeles Rag House (818) 276-1130
100 E. Santa Anita Ave. FAX (818) 842-2150
Burbank, CA 91502 www.laraghouse.com

The Lot (323) 850-2832 / (310) 901-7352
1041 N. Formosa Ave. FAX (323) 850-2909
West Hollywood, CA 90046 www.skyepartners.com

Matthews Studio Equipment (818) 843-6715 / (800) 237-8263
2405 Empire Ave. FAX (323) 849-1525
Burbank, CA 91504 www.msegrip.com

McNulty Nielsen, Inc. (310) 704-1713
6930 1/2 Tujunga Ave. FAX (323) 372-3768
North Hollywood, CA 91605 www.mcnultynielsen.com

Miller Production Services (310) 287-0466
3520 Helms Ave. FAX (310) 287-0467
Culver City, CA 90232

Mobile Movie Studio (818) 429-4085 / (806) 773-4243
FAX (818) 845-3485
www.mobilemoviestudio.com

Modern Studio Equipment, Inc. (818) 764-8574
7428 Bellaire Ave. FAX (818) 764-2958
North Hollywood, CA 91605 www.modernstudio.com

Monster Lighting (818) 261-5108 / (310) 614-5385
5117 Strohm Ave. FAX (818) 301-2008
North Hollywood, CA 91601 www.monsterlighting.com

MPR Photographic Rentals (310) 762-1360
South Bay Studios FAX (310) 639-2055
20434 S. Santa Fe Ave. www.southbaystudios.com
Long Beach, CA 90810

NBC Universal Grip Department (818) 777-2291 / (800) 892-1979
100 Universal City Plaza, Bldg. 4250-1 FAX (818) 866-0105
Universal City, CA 91608
www.filmmakersdestination.com

Occidental Studios, Inc. (213) 384-3331
201 N. Occidental Blvd. FAX (213) 384-2684
Los Angeles, CA 90026 www.occidentalstudios.com

Out of Frame Production Rentals (323) 462-1898
1126 N. Citrus Ave. FAX (323) 462-1897
Hollywood, CA 90038 www.outofframela.com

Pacific LightSmith, LLC (310) 677-8458 / (310) 261-4751
P.O. Box 9119 FAX (310) 677-8458
Marina del Rey, CA 90295

Paladin Group, Inc. (323) 874-7758 / (323) 851-8222
7351 Santa Monica Blvd. FAX (323) 851-7328
Los Angeles, CA 90046

The Studios at Paramount (323) 956-5114
The Studios at Paramount
Grip Services **www.thestudiosatparamount.com**
5555 Melrose Ave.
Los Angeles, CA 90038

Pasadena Camera Rental, Inc. (626) 796-3300
41 E. Walnut St. FAX **(626) 432-6731**
Pasadena, CA 91103 **www.samyscamera.com**

Paskal Lighting (818) 896-5233
12685 Van Nuys Blvd. FAX **(818) 485-0157**
Pacoima, CA 91331 **www.paskal.com**

Premier Lighting & Production Co. (818) 762-0884 (800) 770-0884
12023 Victory Blvd. FAX **(818) 762-0896**
North Hollywood, CA 91606 **www.premier-lighting.com**

PRG (818) 252-2600
9111 Sunland Blvd. FAX **(818) 252-2620**
Sun Valley, CA 91352 **www.prg.com**

R.A. Jones Enterprises (818) 999-1411
5676 Penfield Ave. FAX **(818) 999-0077**
Woodland Hills, CA 91367

The Rag Place, Inc. (818) 765-3338
13160 Raymer St. FAX **(818) 765-3860**
North Hollywood, CA 91605 **www.theragplace.com**

Ragtime Rentals, Inc. (323) 769-0650
6011 Waring Ave. FAX **(323) 461-8065**
Hollywood, CA 90038 **www.ragtimerentals.com**

Raleigh Studios (323) 960-3456
5300 Melrose Ave. FAX **(323) 960-4712**
Hollywood, CA 90038 **www.raleighstudios.com**

The Rosenthal Group (818) 252-1010
10625 Cohasset St. FAX **(818) 252-1070**
Sun Valley, CA 91352 **www.therosenthalgroup.com**

Samy's Camera (323) 938-2420 (800) 321-4726
431 S. Fairfax Ave. FAX **(323) 937-2919**
Los Angeles, CA 90036 **www.samys.com**

Samy's Camera (310) 450-4551
585 Venice Blvd. FAX **(310) 450-8590**
Venice, CA 90291 **www.samys.com**

Sequoia Illumination (818) 563-1000 (888) 647-2777
2428 N. Ontario St. FAX **(818) 563-1001**
Burbank, CA 91504 **www.sequoiaillumination.com**

Silver Sage/Sage Lighting & Grip (818) 384-5529
11024 Balboa Blvd., Ste. 106 FAX **(818) 831-7788**
Granada Hills, CA 91344 **www.sagelightingusa.com**

Skye Lighting (323) 462-5934
920 N. Citrus Ave. FAX **(323) 462-5935**
Hollywood, CA 90038 **www.skyerentals.com**

Sony Pictures Studios (310) 244-5827
10202 W. Washington Blvd.
Culver City, CA 90232 **www.sonypicturesstudios.com**

Studio Depot/Mole-Richardson Co. (323) 851-0111
900 N. La Brea Ave. FAX **(323) 851-7854**
Hollywood, CA 90038 **www.studiodepot.com**

Sun Valley Cabinets (818) 767-2228
7554 Clybourn Ave. FAX **(818) 767-4427**
Sun Valley, CA 91352 **www.sunvalleycabinets.com**

TDS Grip & Canvas, LLC (818) 402-2009 (818) 876-0060
4838 Heaven Ave.
Woodland Hills, CA 91364

TM Motion Picture Equipment Rentals, Inc. (818) 846-3100
101 E. Linden Ave. FAX **(818) 846-3459**
Burbank, CA 91502 **www.tmequipmentrentals.com**

Tomzilla, Inc. (818) 841-6400 (800) 424-7477
157 W. Providencia Ave. FAX **(818) 841-9948**
Burbank, CA 91502 **www.filmzilla.biz**

United Rentals (562) 695-0748
3455 San Gabriel River Pkwy FAX **(562) 615-2191**
Pico Rivera, CA 90660 **www.unitedrentals.com**

A **VER Sales, Inc.** (818) 567-3000 (800) 229-0518
2509 N. Naomi St. FAX **(818) 567-3018**
Burbank, CA 91504 **www.versales.com**

Warner Bros. Studio Facilities - Grip Department (818) 954-1590
4000 Warner Blvd. FAX **(818) 954-4806**
Burbank, CA 91522 **www.wbsf.com**

Westside Production Services (310) 244-2700
5933 W. Slauson Ave. FAX **(310) 244-2702**
Culver City, CA 90230 **www.westsidelighting.com**

White Stewdio Service (818) 904-9114 (818) 400-3456
P.O. Box 524
North Hollywood, CA 91603

Wooden Nickel Lighting Inc. (818) 761-9662
6920 Tujunga Ave. FAX **(818) 985-0717**
North Hollywood, CA 91605
www.woodennickellighting.com

Workhorse Productions, Inc. (323) 791-7757
6368 Santa Monica Blvd. FAX **(323) 395-5647**
Los Angeles, CA 90038 **www.workhorseproductions.us**

Hoisting & Lift Equipment/Cherry Pickers

24/7 Studio Equipment (818) 840-8247 (818) 391-4104
3111 N. Kenwood St. FAX (818) 847-0941
Burbank, CA 91505 www.247studioequipment.com
(Booms, Camera Baskets, Forklifts, Man Baskets, Non-Reflective Booms, Offset Jibs, Rigging & Scissorlifts)

A-Line Crane Rental Services, Inc. (714) 261-3536 (800) 524-7972
18032-C Lemon Dr., Ste. 212 FAX (714) 744-5802
Yorba Linda, CA 92886 www.alinecranes.com

B & G Industrial Rentals (310) 327-0804 (800) 536-3019
1627 W. 130th St. FAX (310) 327-9174
Gardena, CA 90249 www.bgrentalsinc.com
(Air Winches, Chain Hoists, Forklifts & Scaffolding)

Ⓐ **Beckman Rigging/BRS Rigging** (310) 532-3933 (661) 510-2518
13516 S. Mariposa Ave. FAX (310) 532-3993
Gardena, CA 90247 www.brsrigging.com
(Chain Hoists & Truss Systems)

Ⓐ **Branam/West Coast Theatrical** (310) 637-4727 (877) 295-3390
310 S. Long Beach Blvd. FAX (310) 637-4735
Compton, CA 90221 www.west-coast-theatrical.com
(Chain Hoists & Truss Systems)

California Crane Rental (562) 907-4492 (800) 772-7263
8509 Chetle Ave. FAX (562) 907-4495
Santa Fe Springs, CA 90670
www.californiacraneandrigging.com
(Cranes, Man Baskets, Non-Reflective Flat Black Booms & Offset Jibs)

Champion Crane Rental, Inc. (818) 781-3497 (323) 875-1248
12521 Branford St. FAX (818) 896-6202
Pacoima, CA 91331 www.championcrane.us
(Truck Cranes)

Contractors Crane Service (818) 785-5758 (818) 898-1019
7009 Valjean Ave. FAX (818) 785-6952
Van Nuys, CA 91406 www.contractorscrane.com

Entertainment Lighting Services (ELS) (818) 769-9800 (800) 622-6628
11440 Sheldon St. FAX (818) 769-2100
Sun Valley, CA 91352 www.elslights.com
(Chain Hoists, Light Bars, Rigging & Truss Systems)

First Call Studio Equipment (818) 771-9351 (818) 254-5232
12458 Gladstone Ave. FAX (818) 901-6333
Sylmar, CA 91342 www.1stcallequip.com
(Booms, Forklifts, Man Baskets, Manlifts, Personnel Lifts & Scissorlifts)

Gold Coast Crane Service (805) 230-1114 (818) 414-1980
FAX (805) 494-8533
(Box Spreader Bars, Camera Baskets, Light Bars, Man Baskets & Rain Bars)

Kish Rigging, Inc. (805) 532-1300
5400 Commerce Ave. FAX (805) 532-1332
Moorpark, CA 93021 www.kishrigging.com
(Chain Hoists & Truss Systems)

L.A. Propoint, Inc. (818) 767-6800
10870 La Tuna Canyon FAX (818) 767-3900
Sun Valley, CA 91352 www.lapropoint.com
(Box Spreader Bars, Chain Hoists, Light Bars, Rigging & Truss Systems)

Mike Brown Grandstands, Inc. (909) 593-1444
(800) 266-2659
(Scaffolding)
FAX (909) 593-1745
www.mbgs.com

ShowRig (310) 538-4175
15823 S. Main St.
Los Angeles, CA 90248
(Chain Hoists & Truss Systems)
FAX (310) 538-4180
www.sgps.net

Skjonberg Controls, Inc. (805) 650-0877
1363 Donlon St., Ste. 6
Ventura, CA 93003
FAX (805) 650-0360
www.skjonberg.com

Studio City Rentals (818) 543-0300
900 Grand Central Ave.
Glendale, CA 91201
FAX (818) 543-0310
www.studiocityrental.com

United Rentals (805) 644-7319
3665 Market St.
Ventura, CA 93003
FAX (805) 644-2409
www.unitedrentals.com

United Rentals (858) 565-7122
5580 Kearny Villa
San Diego, CA 92123
FAX (858) 565-6279
www.unitedrentals.com

United Rentals (661) 948-2654
43631 Sierra Hwy
Lancaster, CA 93543
FAX (661) 951-0685
www.unitedrentals.com

United Rentals (818) 340-5881
7755 Canoga Ave.
Canoga Park, CA 91304
FAX (818) 340-0035
www.unitedrentals.com

United Rentals (562) 695-0748
3455 San Gabriel River Pkwy
Pico Rivera, CA 90660
(Booms, Forklifts, Scaffolding & Scissorlifts)
FAX (562) 615-2191
www.unitedrentals.com

United Rentals (818) 842-5288
203 W. Olive Ave.
Burbank, CA 91502
(Booms, Forklifts, Scaffolding & Scissorlifts)
FAX (818) 842-9970
www.unitedrentals.com

Van Nuys Scaffold (818) 988-9750
(800) 773-7328
17960 Tulson St.
Granada Hills, CA 91344
FAX (661) 252-7873

A & M Production Services (818) 562-9678
(818) 404-3777
624 N. Victory Blvd. FAX (818) 562-9674
Burbank, CA 91502 www.amlighting.com
(Lighting)

Ace Rentals Inc (818) 255-5995
11950 Sherman Rd. FAX (818) 255-5355
North Hollywood, CA 91605 www.acegenerators.com
(24-Hour Service, Fueling Service, Generators & Small Generators)

Acey Decy Lighting (818) 408-4444
200 Parkside Dr. FAX (818) 408-2777
San Fernando, CA 91340 www.aceydecy.com

Adept Lighting (805) 701-2344
3505 N. Quarzo Circle FAX (805) 523-8660
Thousand Oaks, CA 91362 www.adeptlighting.com
(24-Hour Service, Fluorescent Lighting & Generators)

Aero Balloons/Lights Up Industries (213) 741-0124
1500 S. Griffith Ave. FAX (213) 867-0009
Los Angeles, CA 90021 www.lightsup.net
(Giant Tungsten/HMI Lighting Balloons & Tube and Weather Balloons)

Aerolight, Inc. Balloon Lighting (818) 606-4240
(866) 785-2376
11328 Goss St. FAX (818) 698-0371
Sun Valley, CA 91352 www.aerolightballoons.com
(24-Hour Service, HMIs, Lighting Balloons & Tube Balloons)

Aggreko Event Services (818) 767-7288
(888) 918-4874
11180 Penrose St. FAX (818) 767-7782
Sun Valley, CA 91352
www.aggreko.com/equipserv/event-services.asp
(Generators)

Airstar Space Lighting (818) 753-0066
(800) 217-9001
10950 Burbank Blvd. FAX (818) 753-0067
North Hollywood, CA 91601 www.airstar-light.us
(Tungsten/HMI Lighting Balloons)

Albuquerque Studios (505) 227-2000
5650 University Blvd. SE FAX (505) 227-2001
Albuquerque, NM 87106 www.abqstudios.com

Alliant Event Services, Inc. (909) 622-3306
(800) 851-5415
196 University Pkwy FAX (909) 622-3917
Pomona, CA 91768 www.alliantevents.com

American Mobile Power Co. (818) 845-5474
3300 W. Burbank Blvd.
Burbank, CA 91505
(Generators)

Ample Power (877) 224-9030
3840 Brittany Ln. FAX (818) 276-8421
La Crescenta, CA 91214 www.amplepowergenerators.com

Angstrom Lighting (323) 462-4246
(866) 275-9211
837 N. Cahuenga Blvd. FAX (323) 462-8190
Hollywood, CA 90038 www.angstromlighting.com
(Theatrical Lighting)

ArcLight Efx, Inc. (818) 394-6330
9338 San Fernando Rd. FAX (818) 252-3486
Sun Valley, CA 91352 www.arclightefx.com
(Lighting)

ASAP Generators (818) 487-0500
(Generators)

Astro Audio Video Lighting, Inc. (818) 549-9915
(800) 427-8768
6615 San Fernando Rd. FAX (818) 549-9921
Glendale, CA 91201 www.astroavl.com

Ⓐ **At Power, LLC** (877) 576-1099
(818) 424-1396
5722 Telephone Rd., Ste. C12-104 FAX (877) 576-1099
Ventura, CA 93003 www.atpower.biz
(24-Hour Service, Fueling Service, Generators, Light Towers, Small Generators & Transformers)

Available Light/JT Services (760) 505-1605 / (800) 439-1605
5251 Dixon Rd.
Oceanside, CA 92056
FAX (760) 643-1608
www.jtservices.com

BEBEE Generators (310) 605-5001
2301 E. Gladwick St.
Rancho Dominguez, CA 90220
FAX (310) 605-5002

Bender ET, Inc. (800) 382-2953
2117 Floyd St.
Burbank, CA 91504
FAX (818) 565-3552
www.bender.org
(Electrical Safety Equipment/GFCI)

Berkeley Avenue Productions (310) 579-2277 / (512) 296-7804
155 W. Washington Blvd., Ste. 650
Los Angeles, CA 90015
www.berkeleyavenue.com

Birns & Sawyer, Inc. (818) 766-2525 / (323) 466-8211
5275 Craner Ave.
North Hollywood, CA 91601
FAX (818) 766-3833
www.birnsandsawyer.com

Booster Lighting (818) 771-9959 / (818) 974-0434
(Lighting Equipment)
FAX (818) 771-9959
www.boosterlighting.com

Bundle-Up Rentals (818) 787-3700
13556 Hart St.
Van Nuys, CA 91405
FAX (818) 787-3791

Burbank Kawasaki (818) 848-6627
1329 N. Hollywood Way
Burbank, CA 91505
FAX (818) 848-6630
www.burbankkawasaki.com
(Small Generators)

Cam Film Services (818) 957-6180
5201 Castle Rd.
La Cañada Flintridge, CA 91011
(Lighting)

Castex Rentals (323) 462-1468
1044 Cole Ave.
Hollywood, CA 90038
FAX (323) 462-3719
www.castexrentals.com
(Generators, HMIs & Kino Flos)

CBS Studio Center (818) 655-5465
4024 Radford Ave.
Studio City, CA 91604
FAX (818) 655-5904
www.cbssc.com

Century Studio Corporation (310) 287-3600 / (888) 878-2437
8660 Hayden Pl., Ste. 100
Culver City, CA 90232
FAX (310) 287-3608
www.centurystudio.com
(Lighting)

Cine Power & Light, Inc. (818) 846-0123
805 S. San Fernando Rd., Bldg. 2
Burbank, CA 91502
FAX (818) 846-0111
www.cinepowerlight.com

Cinelease, Inc. (818) 841-8282
2040 N. Lincoln St.
Burbank, CA 91504
FAX (818) 954-9641
www.cinelease.com

Cinematography Electronics, Inc. (818) 706-3334
5321 Derry Ave., Ste. G
Agoura Hills, CA 91301
FAX (818) 706-3335
www.cinematographyelectronics.com
(Line Frequency Meters)

Cinemills Corporation (818) 843-4560 / (800) 325-7674
2021 Lincoln St.
Burbank, CA 91504
FAX (818) 843-7834
www.cinemills.com
(Lighting)

Cinerep/Amps (818) 882-2677
20420 Corisco St.
Chatsworth, CA 91311
FAX (818) 882-2447
www.cinerepamps.com
(24-Hour Service, Fueling Service, Generators & Small Generators)

Cineworks, Inc. (818) 252-0001
8125 Lankershim Blvd.
North Hollywood, CA 91605
FAX (818) 252-0003
www.cineworksinc.com
(Lighting)

City Lights Motion Picture Lighting (213) 952-8243

The Company Pictures (310) 919-0950 / (310) 806-1289
1901 S. Bundy Dr.
Los Angeles, CA 90025
(Lighting)
www.thecompany.tv

Concept Lighting, Inc. (818) 767-1122
11274 Goss St.
Sun Valley, CA 91352
FAX (818) 768-9900
www.conceptlight.com

Contrast Lighting Services, Inc. (818) 225-1099
FAX (818) 225-0499

Copy That Lighting (818) 522-1620
25852 McBean Pkwy, Ste. 535
Santa Clarita, CA 91355
(Blue and Green Screen & Fluorescent Lighting)
FAX (818) 812-9183

The Culver Studios (310) 202-1234
9336 W. Washington Blvd.
Culver City, CA 90232
(Lighting)
FAX (310) 202-3516
www.theculverstudios.com

D-Zyn Elements (818) 332-0819
7324 Reseda Blvd., Ste. 254
Reseda, CA 91335
(Lighting Design)
FAX (818) 332-1479
www.d-zyns.com

DADCO (818) 768-8886 / (818) 982-9764
11273 Goss St.
Sun Valley, CA 91352
(24-Hour Service, Generators & Small Generators)
FAX (818) 765-0914
www.dadcopowerandlights.com

Davis Fluorescent Lighting (310) 836-4860 / (800) 300-2852
8530 Venice Blvd.
Los Angeles, CA 90034
(Lighting)
FAX (310) 836-0289

Delicate Productions, Inc. **(805) 388-1800**
874 Verdulera St. FAX **(805) 388-1037**
Camarillo, CA 93010 **www.delicate.com**

Digital Film Studios **(818) 771-0019**
11800 Sheldon St., Ste. C FAX **(818) 771-0575**
Sun Valley, CA 91352 **www.digitalfilmstudios.com**

Digital Wings **(323) 851-3825**
(202) 438-9199
3480 Barham Blvd., Ste. 322 FAX **(323) 851-0470**
Los Angeles, CA 90068 **www.digitalwings.com**

Direct Lighting, Inc. **(661) 254-6836**
(661) 645-2609
24307 Magic Mountain Pkwy, Ste. 293 FAX **(661) 294-9587**
Valencia, CA 91355 **www.directlighting.net**
(Lighting)

ElectraLynn Lighting & Grip, Ltd. **(818) 506-4692**
www.electralynn.com

Elevation Zero, Inc. **(818) 502-1763**
(310) 251-2684
747 Milford St. FAX **(818) 502-1707**
Glendale, CA 91203
(Lighting)

Entertainment Lighting Services (ELS) **(818) 769-9800**
(800) 622-6628
11440 Sheldon St. FAX **(818) 769-2100**
Sun Valley, CA 91352 **www.elslights.com**
(Blacklight, Bulbs, Electrical Safety Equipment, Fiber Optics, Fluorescent Lighting, HMIs, LED Lighting, Light Towers, Soft Box Lighting, Strobe Lighting, Theatrical Lighting & Xenon Lighting)

Feldman Production Services **(818) 790-7069**
4648 El Camino Corto FAX **(818) 790-6521**
La Cañada Flintridge, CA 91011 **www.combotruck.com**
(Chimeras, Fluorescent Lighting, Green Screen, HMIs & Lighting)

Finnlight **(310) 456-9464**
(310) 968-1986
www.finnlight.com
(Lighting, Lighting Equipment & Softbox Lighting)

First Call Studio Equipment **(818) 771-9351**
(818) 254-5232
12458 Gladstone Ave. FAX **(818) 901-6333**
Sylmar, CA 91342 **www.1stcallequip.com**
(24-Hour Service & Light Towers)

Fisher Light **(818) 752-2626**
(800) 888-0187
5521 Cleon Ave. FAX **(818) 752-6316**
North Hollywood, CA 91601 **www.fisherlight.com**
(Balloon Lights)

FM Grip & Lighting **(818) 383-6376**
267 W. Alameda Ave. FAX **(818) 260-9150**
Burbank, CA 91502 **www.fmgrip.com**
(Lighting)

Fox Studios **(310) 369-1133**
(310) 369-4636
Set Lighting Department FAX **(310) 969-8850**
10201 W. Pico Blvd. **www.foxstudios.com**
Los Angeles, CA 90035

GE/Showpower Energy Rentals **(310) 604-9676**
(877) 797-4768
18420 S. Santa Fe Ave. **www.gepower.com**
Rancho Domiguez, CA 90220
(Fueling Service & Generators)

Geronimo Creek Film Company **(323) 997-0202**
P.O. Box 6006 FAX **(323) 417-4915**
Burbank, CA 91510 **www.geronimocreek.com**
(Lighting)

Goodwin Production and Design Services **(805) 499-7040**
(818) 414-6699
(Lighting) FAX **(805) 499-7078**

Henderson Lighting & Grip, Inc. **(858) 279-3743**
3743 Cameo Ln.
San Diego, CA 92111

Hero Productions, Inc. **(323) 257-0454**
FAX **(323) 256-8969**
www.heroproductions.net
(24-Hour Service, Chimeras, Dedo Lighting, Green Screen, HMIs, Small Generators, Soft Box Lighting & Theatrical Lighting)

Hollywood Center Studios (323) 860-0000
1040 N. Las Palmas Ave. FAX (323) 860-8105
Hollywood, CA 90038 www.hollywoodcenter.com
(Lighting)

Ⓐ **Hollywood Rentals/ESS/Olesen** (818) 407-7800
12800 Foothill Blvd. FAX (818) 407-7875
Sylmar, CA 91342 www.hollywoodrentals.com
(Lighting)

HydroFlex Underwater Camera & Lighting Systems (310) 301-8187
301 E. El Segundo Blvd. FAX (310) 821-9886
El Segundo, CA 90245 www.hydroflex.com
(Fluorescent, HMI & Incandescent Underwater Lighting Systems)

Illumination Dynamics (818) 686-6400
(866) 544-4843
10232 Glenoaks Blvd. FAX (818) 686-6776
Pacoima, CA 91331 www.illuminationdynamics.com

Indie Rentals (323) 465-7700
(323) 571-9476
7022 W. Sunset Blvd. FAX (323) 297-2773
Hollywood, CA 90028 www.indierentals.com
(Fluorescent Lighting, Lighting, Small Generators & Soft Box Lighting)

Innovision Optics (310) 453-4866
1719 21st St. FAX (310) 453-4677
Santa Monica, CA 90404 www.innovisionoptics.com
(Dedo Lighting & Fiber Optics)

Irish Fuel (310) 909-3508
FAX (310) 659-1266
(24-Hour Service, Fueling Service & Small Generators)

JCR Lighting (310) 376-4223
(310) 993-5768
125 34th St.
Hermosa Beach, CA 90254
(Lighting)

Kennedy Lighting Company, Inc. (310) 378-0039
(310) 486-0882
FAX (310) 378-1269

Kinetic Lighting (310) 837-3204
(800) 908-3842
7672 N. Clybourne Ave. FAX (310) 837-8695
Los Angeles, CA 91352 www.kineticlighting.com
(Blacklight, Bulbs & Theatrical Lighting)

Kino Flo, Inc. (818) 767-6528
2840 N. Hollywood Way FAX (818) 767-7517
Burbank, CA 91505 www.kinoflo.com
(Lighting)

Kohler Rental (310) 518-5118
(866) 577-4797
1581 W. Wardlow Rd. FAX (310) 518-5028
Long Beach, CA 90810 www.kohlerrental.com
(Generators)

Leonetti Company (818) 890-6000
10601 Glenoaks Blvd. FAX (818) 890-6116
Pacoima, CA 91331 www.leonetticompany.com
(24-Hour Service, Blue Screen, Bulbs, Chimeras, Fluorescent Lighting, Green Screen, HMIs & Lighting Balloons)

Lex Products Corp. (818) 768-4474
11847 Sheldon St. FAX (818) 768-4040
Sun Valley, CA 91352 www.lexproducts.com
(Cables, Dimming and Control Systems, Electrical Safety Equipment, Electrical Switches and Panels & Power Distribution Systems)

Lexus Lighting, Inc./ Xenons by Lexus (818) 768-4508
11225 Dora St. FAX (805) 641-3273
Sun Valley, CA 91352 www.lexuslighting.com

Libertypak (323) 258-5336
(888) 303-6539
5387 Vincent Ave. www.libertypak.com
Los Angeles, CA 90041
(Lithium Ion Battery Belts)

Light It! LLC (866) 871-2102
FAX (866) 871-2152
(Bulbs, Chimeras, Dedo Lighting, Electrical Safety Equipment, Fluorescent Lighting, HMIs, Lithium Ion Battery Belts, Small Generators & Soft Box Lighting)

The Lightning Co., LLC (818) 207-8400
20434 S. Santa Fe Ave. FAX (818) 279-0558
Long Beach, CA 90802 www.tlcfx.com

Lights/Camera/Action, Inc. (323) 525-1976
217 S. Lorraine Blvd. FAX (323) 525-1905
Los Angeles, CA 90004
(Lighting)

Litepanels, Inc. (818) 752-7009
10932 Burbank Blvd. FAX (818) 752-2437
North Hollywood, CA 91601 www.litepanels.com
(Lighting)

The Lot (323) 850-3180
(323) 850-2832
1041 N. Formosa Ave. www.skyepartners.com
West Hollywood, CA 90046
(Lighting)

LumaPanel/T8 Technology Co. (310) 358-6685
FAX (310) 496-2789
www.lumapanel.com

M7 Studio Lighting (310) 822-1263
131 Galleon St., Ste. 2
Marina del Rey, CA 90292
(Lighting)

McNulty Nielsen, Inc. (310) 704-1713
6930 1/2 Tujunga Ave. FAX (323) 372-3768
North Hollywood, CA 91601 www.mcnultynielsen.com
(24-Hour Service, Blue Screen, Bulbs, Chimeras, Fluorescent Lighting, Green Screen, HMIs, Line Frequency Meters, Small Generators, Soft Box Lighting & Theatrical Lighting)

Miller Production Services (310) 287-0466
3520 Helms Ave. FAX (310) 287-0467
Culver City, CA 90232
(Generators)

Mobile Lighting, Inc. (760) 431-7198
(619) 417-4943
6912 Goldfinch Pl.
Carlsbad, CA 92011

Monster Lighting (818) 261-5108
(310) 614-5385
5117 Strohm Ave. FAX (818) 301-2008
North Hollywood, CA 91601 www.monsterlighting.com
(HMIs, Fluorescents Lighting, Generators & Soft Box Lighting)

Ⓐ **Musco Lighting** (641) 673-0411
(800) 825-6020
15320 Valencia Ave. FAX (888) 397-8736
Fontana, CA 92335 www.musco.com

NBC Universal Set Lighting Department (818) 777-2291
(800) 892-1979
100 Universal City Plaza, Bldg. 4250-1 FAX (818) 866-0105
Universal City, CA 91608 www.filmmakersdestination.com
(Bulbs, Electrical Safety Equipment, Fluorescent Lighting, Generators, HMIs, Lighting Balloons, Strobe Lighting & Theatrical Lighting)

Ⓐ **New Mexico Lighting & Grip Co.** (505) 227-2500
2301 E. Gladwick St. FAX (505) 227-2510
Rancho Dominguez, CA 90220 www.nmlgc.com
(Lighting)

Ⓐ **Night Lights by Bebee, Ltd.** (310) 605-5001
2301 E. Gladwick St. FAX (310) 605-5002
Rancho Dominguez, CA 90220
(Lighting)

Occidental Studios, Inc. (213) 384-3331
201 N. Occidental Blvd. FAX (213) 384-2684
Los Angeles, CA 90026 www.occidentalstudios.com
(Lighting)

Ⓐ **On the Spot Lighting Rentals, Inc.** (818) 368-8143
(818) 414-2367
FAX (818) 368-8143
www.onthespotlightingandpower.com

Out of Frame Production Rentals (323) 462-1898
1126 N. Citrus Ave. FAX (323) 462-1897
Hollywood, CA 90038 www.outofframela.com
(Blue Screen, Generators, Green Screen & Small Generators)

Pace Technologies (818) 565-0005
2117 Empire Ave. FAX (818) 565-0006
Burbank, CA 91504 www.pacehd.com
(HMI and Incandescent Underwater Lighting Systems)

Pacific LightSmith, LLC (310) 677-8458
(310) 261-4751
P.O. Box 9119 FAX (310) 677-8458
Marina del Rey, CA 90295

Paladin Group, Inc. (323) 874-7758
(323) 851-8222
7351 Santa Monica Blvd. FAX (323) 851-7328
Los Angeles, CA 90046

Ⓐ **The Studios at Paramount** (323) 956-5391
The Studios at Paramount
Set Lighting www.thestudiosatparamount.com
5555 Melrose Ave.
Hollywood, CA 90038
(Lighting)

Parenti Productions – Lighting Design (323) 988-0738
P.O. Box 41926 FAX (323) 988-0738
Los Angeles, CA 90041 www.parentiproductions.com
(Lighting Design)

Pasadena Camera Rental, Inc. (626) 796-3300
41 E. Walnut St. FAX (626) 432-6731
Pasadena, CA 91103 www.samyscamera.com

Paskal Lighting (818) 896-5233
12685 Van Nuys Blvd. FAX (818) 485-0157
Pacoima, CA 91331 www.paskal.com

Peterson Systems International (626) 357-7051
2350 E. Central Ave. FAX (626) 303-3066
Duarte, CA 91010 www.yjams.com

Photo-Sonics, Inc. (818) 531-3240
820 S. Mariposa St. FAX (818) 531-3258
Burbank, CA 91506 www.photosonics.com
(High Intensity Soft Box Lighting)

Portable Power, Inc. (818) 365-3366
628 Celis St. FAX (818) 365-3399
San Fernando, CA 91340 www.portablepowerinc.com
(Generators)

Power Source Generators (818) 262-2618
(323) 463-5555
1111 N. Beachwood Dr. FAX (323) 463-5556
Los Angeles, CA 90038
(Generators)

Power Trip Rentals (310) 667-4433
(310) 292-0974
2950 E. Harcourt St. FAX (310) 604-3233
Rancho Dominguez, CA 90221 www.powertriprentals.net
(24-Hour Service, Fueling Service, Generators, Light Towers & Small Generators)

Premier Lighting & Production Co. (818) 762-0884
(800) 770-0884
12023 Victory Blvd. FAX (818) 762-0896
North Hollywood, CA 91606 www.premier-lighting.com

PRG (818) 252-2600
9111 Sunland Blvd. FAX (818) 252-2620
Sun Valley, CA 91352 www.prg.com
(HMIs, Lighting Balloons & Theatrical Lighting)

Prima Equipment Co. (818) 984-2024
5275 Craner Ave.
North Hollywood, CA 91615
(Fluorescent Lighting, Repairs & Soft Box Lighting)

Production Equipment Services, Inc. (818) 779-2114
15021 Keswick St. FAX (818) 779-2119
Van Nuys, CA 91405 www.pe-services.net
(Generator Repairs)

Quinn Power Systems (562) 463-6040
(562) 463-6000
3500 Shepherd St. www.quinnpower.com
City of Industry, CA 90601
(Generators)

Rain For Rent (805) 525-3306
(805) 331-0175
333 S. 12th St. FAX (805) 525-7663
Santa Paula, CA 93061 www.rainforrent.com
(Generators)

Raleigh Studios (323) 960-3456
5300 Melrose Ave. FAX (323) 871-5600
Hollywood, CA 90038 www.raleighstudios.com
(Lighting)

Ⓐ **The Rosenthal Group** (818) 252-1010
10625 Cohasset St. FAX (818) 252-1070
Sun Valley, CA 91352 www.therosenthalgroup.com

Samy's Camera (323) 938-2420
(800) 321-4726
431 S. Fairfax Ave. FAX (323) 937-2919
Los Angeles, CA 90036 www.samys.com

Samy's Camera (310) 450-4551
585 Venice Blvd. FAX (310) 450-8590
Venice, CA 90291 www.samys.com

Sequoia Illumination (818) 563-1000
(888) 647-2777
2428 N. Ontario St. FAX (818) 563-1001
Burbank, CA 91504 www.sequoiaillumination.com

SGPS, Inc. (310) 538-4175
15823 S. Main St. FAX (310) 538-4180
Los Angeles, CA 90248 www.sgps.net
(Lighting)

Side Efx Company (818) 968-8711
7011 Willoughby Ave., Bldg. 2 FAX (267) 989-5354
Hollywood, CA 90038 www.sideefxco.com
(Lighting)

Silver Sage/Sage Lighting & Grip (818) 384-5529
11024 Balboa Blvd., Ste. 106 FAX (818) 831-7788
Granada Hills, CA 91344 www.sagelightingusa.com

Sky Productions (818) 442-1527
www.skyproduction.net
(24-Hour Service, Blacklight, Dedo Lighting, Electrical Safety Equipment, Fluorescent Lighting, Generators, Light Towers, Lighting Balloons & Theatrical Lighting)

Skylight Balloon Lighting (866) 765-4448
www.skylightballoon.com

SMS Generators, Inc. (818) 361-2151
11619 Pendleton St. FAX (818) 768-5303
Sun Valley, CA 91352 www.smsgenerators.com
(24-Hour Service, Fueling Service, Generators & Lighting Crane Trucks)

Sony Pictures Studios (310) 244-5810
10202 W. Washington Blvd. FAX **(310) 244-2365**
Culver City, CA 90232 **www.sonypicturesstudios.com**
(Lighting)

Source Lighting & Grip Rentals, Inc. (323) 463-5555
1111 N. Beachwood Dr. **www.sourcefilmstudio.com**
Los Angeles, CA 90038
(Blue Screen, Chimeras, Dedo Lighting, Generators, Green Screen, HMIs, Incandescent Underwater Lighting Systems & Small Generators)

Sourcemaker Balloon Lighting (800) 930-3944
(Lighting Balloons) **www.lightingballoons.com**

Stage Tech (562) 407-1133
14523 Marquardt Ave. FAX **(562) 407-1306**
Santa Fe Springs, CA 90630 **www.stage-tech.com**
(Lighting)

Star Power Generators (818) 982-2200
7416 Varna Ave., Ste. F FAX **(818) 982-2229**
North Hollywood, CA 91605
www.starpowergenerators.com
(24-Hour Service & Generators)

Studio Depot/Mole-Richardson Co. (323) 851-0111
900 N. La Brea Ave. FAX **(323) 851-7854**
Hollywood, CA 90038 **www.studiodepot.com**

Sun Lighting Services, Inc. (818) 898-1550
26652 Oak Terrace Pl. FAX **(818) 898-1552**
Valencia, CA 91381

Sunbelt Rentals (818) 996-7100
18251 Napa St. **www.sunbeltrentals.com**
Northridge, CA 91325

Sunbelt Rentals (714) 923-1890
1600 W. Katella Ave. FAX **(714) 923-1891**
Orange, CA 92867 **www.sunbeltrentals.com**

Team Imagination, Inc. (310) 541-7790
916 Silver Spur Rd., Ste. 110 FAX **(310) 541-8797**
Rolling Hills Estates, CA 90274
(Lighting) **www.teamimagination.com**

TM Motion Picture Equipment Rentals, Inc. (818) 846-3100
101 E. Linden Ave. FAX **(818) 846-3439**
Burbank, CA 91502 **www.tmequipmentrentals.com**

Towards 2000, Inc. (818) 557-0903
215 W. Palm Ave., Ste. 204 FAX **(818) 557-0596**
Burbank, CA 91502 **www.t2k.com**
(Lighting)

Unilux/Blue Feather Lighting (818) 701-5404
(800) 635-2743
19630 Lanark St. FAX **(818) 701-5404**
Reseda, CA 91335 **www.unilux.com**
(Strobe Lighting)

United Rentals (818) 842-5288
203 W. Olive Ave. FAX **(818) 842-9970**
Burbank, CA 91502 **www.unitedrentals.com**
(Generators with Light Towers)

Visual Terrain, Inc. (818) 786-3500
14141 Covello St., Ste. 4B FAX **(818) 786-3501**
Van Nuys, CA 91405 **www.visualterrain.net**
(Lighting)

Warner Bros. Studio Facilities - Set Lighting (818) 954-2575
4000 Warner Blvd. FAX **(818) 954-4806**
Burbank, CA 91522 **www.wbsf.com**
(Lighting)

Waywest Lighting & Camera, Inc. (949) 588-7822
(714) 381-0100
22432 Lombardi FAX **(949) 588-7922**
Laguna Hills, CA 92653 **www.waywest.tv**
(Lighting)

Westside Production Services (310) 244-2700
5933 W. Slauson Ave. FAX **(310) 244-2702**
Culver City, CA 90230 **www.westsidelighting.com**

Wooden Nickel Lighting Inc. (818) 761-9662
6920 Tujunga Ave. FAX **(818) 985-0717**
North Hollywood, CA 91605
(Lighting) **www.woodennickellighting.com**

Workhorse Productions, Inc. (323) 791-7757
6368 Santa Monica Blvd. FAX **(323) 395-5647**
Los Angeles, CA 90038 **www.workhorseproductions.us**
(Chimeras, Generators, HMIs, Small Generators, Soft Box Lighting & Strobe Lighting)

XenoPro (818) 752-4040
5521 Cleon Ave. FAX **(818) 752-6316**
North Hollywood, CA 91601 **www.xenopro.com**
(Xenon Lighting)

Zilla Lighting For Film (Tomzilla) (818) 841-6400
(800) 424-7477
157 W. Providencia Ave. FAX **(818) 841-9948**
Burbank, CA 91502 **www.zillalighting.com**

A & S Case Company
(818) 509-5920
(800) 394-6181
5260 Vineland Ave.
FAX (818) 509-1397
North Hollywood, CA 91601
www.ascase.com
(Camera and Equipment Cases)

Abbey Events
(310) 900-0099
(323) 201-4200
1520 S. Maple Ave.
FAX (323) 201-4299
Montebello, CA 90640
www.abbeyeventservices.com
(Canopies, Heaters, Helium Tanks & Tents)

Absolute Rentals
(818) 842-2828
2633 N. San Fernando Blvd.
FAX (818) 842-8815
Burbank, CA 91504
www.absoluterentals.com
(Camera and Equipment Cases & Camera Expendables)

Accelerated Rentals and Location Services Corp.
(661) 251-3135
FAX (661) 299-5991
www.acceleratedrentals.com

ACME Production Rentals
(818) 730-4899

Alliant Event Services, Inc.
(909) 622-3306
(800) 851-5415
196 University Pkwy
FAX (909) 622-3917
Pomona, CA 91768
www.alliantevents.com

American Barricade, Inc.
(714) 634-2663
(818) 955-8500
2141 S. Dupont Dr.
FAX (714) 634-2666
Anaheim, CA 92806
www.americanbarricade.net
(Traffic Safety Equipment)

American Barrier Systems, Inc.
(805) 648-2128
(877) 774-4664
3989 Market St.
FAX (805) 648-1543
Ventura, CA 93003
www.americanbarriers.com
(Barricades)

Antelope Valley Locations and Production Services
(661) 946-1515
42848 150th St. East
FAX (661) 946-0454
Lancaster, CA 93535
www.avlocations.com

Anvil Cases/Calzone Case Co.
(626) 968-4100
(800) 359-2684
15730 Salt Lake Ave.
FAX (626) 968-1703
City of Industry, CA 91745
www.anvilcases.com

Anytime - Hollywood
(323) 461-8483
755 N. Lillian Way
FAX (323) 461-2338
Hollywood, CA 90038
www.anytime-rentals.com
(Canopies, Chairs, Coolers, Heaters, Misters & Tables)

Apache Rental Group
(818) 842-9944
(818) 842-9875
3910 W. Magnolia Blvd.
FAX (818) 842-9269
Burbank, CA 91505
www.apacherentalgroup.com
(Canopies, Chairs, Coolers, Heaters & Tables)

Atomic Production Supplies
(818) 566-8811
2621 N. Ontario St.
FAX (818) 566-8311
Burbank, CA 91504
www.atomicproductionsupplies.com
(Canopies, Chairs, Coolers & Tables)

Backstage Equipment, Inc.
(818) 504-6026
(800) 692-2787
8052 Lankershim Blvd.
FAX (818) 504-6180
North Hollywood, CA 91605
www.backstageweb.com
(Camera, Magliner, Remote Head, Sound & Video Carts)

California Ice & Propane
(818) 224-4423
21215 Devonshire St.
FAX (818) 224-2650
Chatsworth, CA 91311
(Heaters & Propane)

Camera Essentials
(323) 666-8936
(323) 666-8875
2620 1/2 Hyperion Ave.
FAX (323) 666-0214
Los Angeles, CA 90027
www.cameraessentials.com
(Camera and Equipment Raincovers, Ditty Bags & Film Changing Tents)

Cases by Masco
(951) 326-3000
43178 Business Park Dr., Ste. 100
FAX (951) 326-3040
Temecula, CA 92590
www.casesbymasco.com
(Camera and Equipment Cases)

Castex Rentals
(323) 462-1468
1044 Cole Ave.
FAX (323) 462-3719
Hollywood, CA 90038
www.castexrentals.com
(Canopies, Directors Chairs, Tables, Traffic Safety Equipment & Wardrobe Racks)

CineBags
(818) 662-0605
(Bags & Pouches)
FAX (818) 662-0613
www.cinebags.com

Cineworks, Inc. (818) 252-0001
8125 Lankershim Blvd. FAX (818) 252-0003
North Hollywood, CA 91605 www.cineworksinc.com

Clean Strike Rental & Cleaning (562) 803-3701
(562) 879-2207
12214 Lakewood Blvd., Bldg. 9 FAX (562) 803-3702
Downey, CA 90242 www.cleanstrikerentals.com
(Dumpsters & Portable Restrooms)

DeWayne Events (661) 251-4342
16520 Diver St. FAX (661) 251-2488
Canyon Country, CA 91387
(Canopies & Tents)

Dortons, Inc. (323) 751-3486
(951) 685-6014
6319 Eucalyptus FAX (323) 778-2025
Riverside, CA 92509
(Tents)

Earl Hays Press (818) 765-0700
10707 Sherman Way FAX (818) 765-5245
Sun Valley, CA 91352

Enterprise Printers and Production Supplies (323) 876-3530
1021 Lillian Way FAX (323) 876-4398
Los Angeles, CA 90038 www.enterpriseprinters.com
(Production Boards & Strips)

Ⓐ **Environmental Noise Control/ Behrens & Associates** (800) 679-8633
(310) 679-8623
13806 Inglewood Ave. FAX (310) 679-8676
Hawthorne, CA 90250
www.environmental-noise-control.com
(Acoustical Blankets & Panels)

Golf Cars - LA, Inc. (661) 251-2201
16439 Sierra Hwy www.golfcars-la.com
Canyon Country, CA 91351

Ⓐ **Golf Cars and Industrial Vehicles, Inc.** (818) 765-4102
7440 Greenbush Ave. FAX (818) 765-4112
North Hollywood, CA 91605 www.gcivyamaha.com

Heavy Artillery Production Rentals (310) 295-1202
3200 S. La Cienega Blvd. FAX (310) 295-1202
Los Angeles, CA 90016 www.heavyartilleryrentals.com
(Bullhorns, Chairs, Cones, Coolers, Director Chairs, Heaters, Misters, Mobile Services, Tables, Tents, Traffic Safety Equipment, Walkies & Wardrobe Racks)

Hollywood Chairs (760) 471-6600
1801 Diamond St. www.hollywoodchairs.com
San Marcos, CA 92078
(Directors Chairs)

Hollywood Tentworks (877) 883-3131
(818) 890-0214
10244 Norris Ave. FAX (877) 883-3132
Pacoima, CA 91331 www.tentworks.com
(A/C, Canopies, Chairs, Heaters, Portable Stages, Tables & Tents)

Innerspace Cases (818) 767-3030
(800) 806-7689
11555 Cantara St., Ste. I FAX (818) 767-6118
North Hollywood, CA 91605 www.innerspacecases.com

International E-Z UP, Inc. (951) 781-0843
1601 Iowa Ave. FAX (951) 781-0586
Riverside, CA 92507 www.ezup.com
(Tents)

ITC Barricades, Inc. (714) 892-5858
(661) 816-6270
P.O. Box 858 FAX (714) 892-5887
Westminster, CA 92684 mysite.verizon.net/itcbarricades/
(Traffic Safety Equipment)

JCL Barricade Company (213) 622-9775
2334 E. Eighth St. FAX (213) 622-9790
Los Angeles, CA 90021 www.jclbarricade.com
(Barricades & Posting Signs)

Kayam Theatre and Concert Tent Company (213) 484-5010
831 Gretna Green Way, Ste. 104 www.kayam.co.uk
Los Angeles, CA 90049
(Tents)

Lex Products Corp. (818) 768-4474
11847 Sheldon St. FAX (818) 768-4040
Sun Valley, CA 91352 www.lexproducts.com
(Audio, Data and Power Cables, Dimming and Control Systems, Electrical Switches and Panels & Power Distribution Systems)

Line 204 (323) 960-0113
1034 N. Seward St. FAX (323) 960-0163
Hollywood, CA 90038 www.line204.com
(Canopies, Chairs, Coolers & Tables)

Melmat, Inc. (714) 379-4555
(800) 635-6289
5333 Industrial Dr. FAX (714) 379-4554
Huntington Beach, CA 92649 www.melmat.com

Mike Brown Grandstands, Inc. (909) 593-1444
(800) 266-2659
FAX (909) 593-1745
www.mbgs.com
(Bleachers, Crowd Control Barricades, Disabled Persons Lifts and Ramps, Grandstands, Portable Stages, Stanchions & Turnstiles)

Miller Production Services (310) 287-0466
3520 Helms Ave. FAX (310) 287-0467
Culver City, CA 90232
(Canopies, Chairs, Heaters, Misters, Tables & Traffic and Crowd Control Equipment)

Out of Frame Production Rentals (323) 462-1898
1126 N. Citrus Ave. FAX (323) 462-1897
Hollywood, CA 90038 **www.outofframela.com**
(Barricades, Bullhorns, Camera Expendables, Canopies, Chairs, Cones, Coolers, Directors Chairs, Heaters/AC, Misters, Tables, Traffic Control, Walkies & Wardrobe Racks)

Pacific Production Services, Inc. (323) 465-9179
(213) 360-7844
6513 Hollywood Blvd., Ste. 214 FAX (323) 465-9869
Los Angeles, CA 90028 **www.lafilmpermits.com**
(Safety and Traffic Equipment)

Panavision Panastore (818) 316-1000
Corporate Headquarters FAX (818) 316-1111
6219 DeSoto Ave. **www.panavision.com**
Woodland Hills, CA 91367
(Accessories & Camera Expendables)

Print Technology (310) 273-9450
(877) 613-9450
8899 Beverly Blvd., Ste. 803 FAX (310) 273-8450
Los Angeles, CA 90048 **www.print-technology.com**
(Business Forms & Stationery Systems)

The Production Truck, Inc. (818) 459-0425
711 Ruberta Ave. FAX (818) 459-0427
Glendale, CA 91201 **www.theproductiontruck.com**
(Chairs, Coolers, Directors Chairs, Heaters, Tents & Wardrobe Racks)

Quixote Studios (323) 960-9191
1000 N. Cahuenga Blvd. FAX (323) 960-3366
Los Angeles, CA 90038 **www.quixote.com**
(Canopies, Chairs, Coolers, Misters & Tables)

RC Production Rentals (310) 621-7113
13105 Saticoy St. FAX (310) 943-0480
North Hollywood, CA 91605 **www.rcproductionrentals.com**
(Bags, Barricades, Bullhorns, Camera Carts, Camera Expendables, Canopies, Chairs, Cones, Coolers, Directors Chairs, Heaters, Street Closures, Tables, Tents, Traffic Control, Traffic Safety Equipment, Walkies & Wardrobe Racks)

Rock Bottom Rentals (646) 660-4221
(800) 794-5444
1310 Westwood Blvd. FAX (877) 809-4502
Los Angeles, CA 90024 **www.rockbottomrentals.com**
(Canopies, Chairs, Coolers, Cones & Tables)

Set Stuff, Inc. (323) 993-9500
1105 N. Sycamore Ave. FAX (323) 993-9506
Hollywood, CA 90038 **www.setstuffrentals.com**
(Air Conditioners, Canopies, Coolers, Directors Chairs, Heaters, Tables, Tents & Traffic Safety Equipment)

SirReel - LA & San Diego (760) 672-5522
(888) 477-7335
FAX (888) 477-7313
www.sirreel.us

Skye Rentals (323) 462-5934
920 N. Citrus Ave. FAX (323) 462-5935
Hollywood, CA 90038 **www.skyerentals.com**
(Barricades, Bullhorns, Camera Carts, Camera Cases, Camera Expendables, Canopies, Chairs, Cones, Coolers, Directors Chairs, Equipment Cases, Heaters, Misters, Tables, Tents, Traffic Control, Traffic Safety Equipment, Walkies & Wardrobe Racks)

Sun Aired Bag Company (310) 372-7225
524 Cypress Ave. FAX (310) 372-5825
Hermosa Beach, CA 90254 **www.sunaired.com**
(Mesh Clothing Bags)

Sunset Gators (310) 704-5939
(323) 632-4368
(Gators) FAX (626) 798-9747
www.sunsetgators.com

T.Z. Case (909) 392-8806
(888) 892-2737
1786 Curtiss Court FAX (909) 392-8406
La Verne, CA 91750 **www.tzcase.com**
(Camera and Equipment Cases)

Tent Kings of Los Angeles (818) 720-5126
(310) 880-5128
3238 N. San Fernando Blvd. FAX (818) 557-8320
Burbank, CA 91504 **www.tentkings.com**

Traffic Management, Inc. (562) 595-4278
2435 Lemon Ave. FAX (562) 424-0266
Signal Hill, CA 90755 **www.trafficmanagement.com**
(Barricades, Cones, Crowd Control Equipment, Street Closures, Traffic Control, Traffic Plans & Traffic Safety Equipment)

Workhorse Productions, Inc. (323) 791-7757
6368 Santa Monica Blvd. FAX (323) 395-5647
Los Angeles, CA 90038 **www.workhorseproductions.us**
(Camera Expendables, Canopies, Chairs, Cones, Coolers, Crowd Control Equipment, Directors Chairs, Film Changing Tents, Heaters, Tables, Tents, Traffic Control, Traffic Safety Equipment, Walkies & Wardrobe Racks)

World Supply (323) 851-1350
(800) 399-6753
3425 W. Cahuenga Blvd. FAX (323) 851-1922
Hollywood, CA 90068 **www.worldsupply.org**
(Production Boards)

A Wynning Event (310) 279-5114
(310) 729-2590
433 N. Camden Dr., Ste. 400 FAX (310) 274-5105
Beverly Hills, CA 90210 **www.awynningevent.com**
(Chairs, Heaters, Tables & Tents)

Xpendable Rentals (323) 656-0905
5925 Santa Monica Blvd. FAX (323) 375-1711
Hollywood, CA 90038 **www.xpendablerentals.com**
(Barricades, Bullhorns, Camera Carts, Canopies, Chairs, Cones, Coolers, Directors Chairs, Heaters, Helium Tanks, Misters, Road Signs, Tables, Tents, Traffic Safety Equipment, Walkies & Wardrobe Racks)

Trucks & Vans

Accelerated Rentals and Location Services Corp. (661) 251-3135
(Utility Vehicles) FAX (661) 299-5991
www.acceleratedrentals.com

Affordable West, Inc. (323) 467-7182
1040 N. La Brea Ave. FAX (323) 467-6520
Hollywood, CA 90038

Ⓐ **Avon Studio Transportation** (323) 850-0826
(800) 432-2866
7080 Santa Monica Blvd. FAX (323) 467-4239
Los Angeles, CA 90038 www.avonrents.com

Beverly Hills Rent-A-Car (323) 464-5900
(310) 901-0135
800 N. La Brea FAX (323) 464-2506
Los Angeles, CA 90038 www.bhrentacar.com

Budget Truck Rental (213) 749-9104
www.budgettruck.com

California Rent-A-Car (310) 477-2727
11725 Santa Monica Blvd. FAX (310) 477-9176
Los Angeles, CA 90025 www.productioncarrental.com
(Pickups)

California Truck Rental (562) 699-3434
2555 Pellissier Pl. FAX (562) 699-3493
Whittier, CA 90601

cameratruck.com (818) 540-6189
(818) 865-0007
FAX (818) 865-6099
www.cameratruck.com

Cine Power & Light, Inc. (818) 846-0123
805 S. San Fernando Rd., Bldg. 2 FAX (818) 846-0111
Burbank, CA 91502 www.cinepowerlight.com

Ⓐ **Galpin Studio Rentals** (323) 957-3333
(800) 256-6219
1763 N. Ivar Ave. FAX (323) 856-6790
Hollywood, CA 90028 www.galpinstudiorentals.com
(Camera Vans, Cargo Vans, Crew Cabs, High Cubes, Liftgate Trucks, Pickups, Production Cubes, Stake Beds & Wardrobe Cubes)

Galpin Studio Rentals (818) 891-1751
(800) 256-6219
8353 Sepulveda Blvd. FAX (818) 778-3027
North Hills, CA 91343 www.galpinstudiorentals.com

Heavy Artillery Production Rentals (310) 295-1202
3200 S. La Cienega Blvd. FAX (310) 295-1202
Los Angeles, CA 90016 www.heavyartilleryrentals.com
(Production Cubes)

Hertz Equipment Rental Corporation (818) 762-9282
(888) 777-2700
5556 Vineland Ave. FAX (818) 762-9440
North Hollywood, CA 91601 www.hertzequip.com

Hollywood Rentals/ESS/Olesen (818) 407-7800
12800 Foothill Blvd. FAX (818) 407-7875
Sylmar, CA 91342 www.hollywoodrentals.com
(Production Vans with Twin Generators)

Lexus Lighting, Inc. (818) 768-4508
11225 Dora St. FAX (805) 641-3273
Sun Valley, CA 91352 www.lexuslighting.com
(Camera and Lighting Trucks)

N Motion Studio Rentals (888) 878-2531 (818) 837-4595
13101 Foothill Blvd. FAX (818) 837-4590
Sylmar, CA 91342 **www.unitedtruckcenters.com**

NBC Universal Transportation (818) 777-2966
100 Universal City Plaza FAX (818) 866-1521
Bldg. 8166, First Fl. **www.filmmakersdestination.com**
Universal City, CA 91608
(Cargo Vans, Crew Cabs, Flatbeds, High Cubes, Liftgate Trucks, Pickups, Production Cubes, Stake Beds, Tractors, Trailers, Twin Generator Vans & Utility Vehicles)

The Studios at Paramount (323) 956-5151
The Studios at Paramount
Transportation **www.thestudiosatparamount.com**
5555 Melrose Ave.
Los Angeles, CA 90038

Penske Truck Leasing Co. (213) 628-1255 (800) 222-0277
2300 E. Olympic Blvd. FAX (213) 488-1590
Los Angeles, CA 90021 **www.gopenske.com**

Sequoia Illumination (818) 563-1000 (888) 647-2777
2428 N. Ontario St. FAX (818) 563-1001
Burbank, CA 91504 **www.sequoiaillumination.com**

Skye Rentals (323) 462-5934
920 N. Citrus Ave. FAX (323) 462-5935
Hollywood, CA 90038 **www.skyerentals.com**
(Production Cubes & Stake Beds)

Sony Pictures Studios (310) 244-7016
10202 W. Washington Blvd. FAX (310) 244-7995
Culver City, CA 90232 **www.sonypicturesstudios.com**

Specialty Car Locators (818) 554-5062 (661) 310-2715
P.O Box 55334 FAX (661) 554-7063
Valencia, CA 91385
www.specialtycarlocators.com/equipmentforrent.htm
(Crew Cab Stakebeds)

Studio Equipment Rentals, Inc. (661) 714-0858
45259 23rd St. FAX (661) 942-7125
Lancaster, CA 93536
(Utility Vehicles)

Super 8 Film Cameras & 2nd Unit (310) 276-8196 (800) 470-4602
8630 Wilshire Blvd. FAX (310) 276-8196
Beverly Hills, CA 90211 **www.justneeds2.com**
(Camera and Lighting Van)

Suppose U Drive Truck Rental Service (818) 243-3151 (800) 404-8800
3809 San Fernando Rd. FAX (818) 243-7968
Glendale, CA 91204 **www.supposeudrive.com**

TCH/The Camera House (818) 997-3802
7351 Fulton Ave. FAX (818) 997-3885
North Hollywood, CA 91605 **www.thecamerahouse.com**

U-Haul (800) 528-4285 (800) 468-4285
www.uhaul.com

The Walt Disney Studios - Transportation Department (818) 560-1285
500 S. Buena Vista St.
Burbank, CA 91521

Warner Bros. Studio Facilities - Transportation Department (818) 954-4106
4000 Warner Blvd. FAX **(818) 954-4471**
Burbank, CA 91522 **www.wbsf.com**

Westside Production Services (310) 244-2700
5933 W. Slauson Ave. FAX **(310) 244-2702**
Culver City, CA 90230 **www.westsidelighting.com**

Willie's On & Off Road Center (760) 257-3734
(760) 953-3303
48301 National Trails Hwy FAX **(760) 257-3335**
Newberry Springs, CA 92365 **www.williesoffroad.com**
(Off-Road Vehicles)

Workhorse Productions, Inc. (323) 791-7757
6368 Santa Monica Blvd. FAX **(323) 395-5647**
Los Angeles, CA 90038 **www.workhorseproductions.us**
(Cargo Vans, High Cubes & Production Cubes)

NOTES:

CLASSIC LOS ANGELES FILM LOCATIONS

WALT DISNEY CONCERT HALL

IRON MAN

INT. STARK ENTERPRISES - DAY

Tony Stark (Robert Downey Jr.) addresses the media among whom is sexpot reporter Christine Everheart. Stark is flanked by his military advisor, Jim "Rhodey" Rhodes (Terrence Howard).

STARK
There's been speculation that I was involved in the events that occurred on the freeway and the rooftop...

CHRISTINE EVERHEART
I'm sorry, Mr. Stark, but do you honestly expect us to believe that that was a bodyguard in a suit that conveniently appeared, despite the fact that...

STARK
I know that it's confusing. It is one thing to question the official story, and another thing entirely to make wild accusations, or insinuate that I'm a superhero.

CHRISTINE EVERHEART
I never said you were a superhero.

STARK
Didn't? Mmm-mmm. Well, good, because that would be outlandish and, uh, fantastic. I'm just not the hero type. Clearly. With this laundry list of character defects, all the mistakes I've made, largely public.

RHODEY
(whispers to Tony)
Just stick to the cards, sir.

STARK
Yeah, okay.

Stark holds up his notes and pauses, then puts them down.

STARK (Cont.)
The truth is... I am Iron Man.

SCREENPLAY BY:
Mark Fergus & Hawk Ostby and Art Marcum & Matt Holloway, based on characters created by Stan Lee, Don Heck, Larry Lieber & Jack Kirby

ALSO FILMED AT THE BRADBURY BUILDING:
The Soloist

Props & Wardrobe

Ⓐ ADVERTISER SYMBOL

Refer to the General Index for cross-referencing items in this section.

Atmospheric Effects

Reelistic F/X, Inc. **(818) 346-2484**
21318 Hart Street
Canoga Park, CA 91303
(Pyrotechnics & Special Mechanical FX)
FAX (818) 346-2710
www.r-fx.com

Snow Business Hollywood **(818) 884-3009**
21318 Hart Street
Canoga Park, CA 91303
FAX (818) 884-3110
www.snowbusinesshollywood.com

With more types of snow than the Eskimo and Inuit languages have words for, Snow Business Hollywood can supply exactly the effect you require, from a single snow flake to a terrifyingly "safe" avalanche.

Aerial Film Unit by Corporate Helicopters (800) 345-6737 / (858) 505-5650
3753 John J. Montgomery Dr., Ste. 2 FAX (858) 505-5658
San Diego, CA 92123 **www.corporatehelicopters.com**
(Helicopters)

Airpower Aviation Resources (805) 402-0052
FAX (805) 498-0357
www.airpower-aviation.com

Altitude Aviation (310) 379-4448 / (310) 489-8938
2309 Pacific Coast Hwy, Ste. 204 FAX (310) 937-7112
Hermosa Beach, CA 90254 **www.altitudeaviation.com**

Blackstar Helicopters Inc. (818) 896-2700
10500 Airpark Way, Hangar M4 FAX (818) 896-2771
Pacoima, CA 91331 **www.blackstarhelicopters.com**

Camera Copters, Inc. (888) 463-7953 / (305) 793-7033
23421 Balmoral Ln. **www.cameracopters.com**
West Hills, CA 91307

Hangar 1 Productions (213) 483-6898
1910 W. Sunset Blvd., Ste. 900 FAX (213) 483-4185
Los Angeles, CA 90026 **www.hangar1project.com**

Helinet Aviation Services (818) 902-0229 / (800) 221-8389
FAX (818) 902-9278
www.helinet.com

Jet Productions (818) 781-4742 / (877) 895-1790
FAX (818) 781-4743
www.jetproductions.net

McKernan Motion Picture Aviation (310) 458-9176 / (310) 993-4486
FAX (310) 393-4227
www.helicopterguy.com

Stearman Flight Center (909) 597-8511
7000 Merrill Ave., Ste. 53 FAX (909) 597-8511
Chino, CA 91710 **www.silverwingswingwalking.com**
(Bi-Planes, Fixed-Wing Aircraft & Vintage)

Studio Wings (805) 320-9500
855 Aviation Dr. FAX (805) 987-4720
Camarillo, CA 93010 **www.studiowings.com**

Stunt Wings/Adventure Sports (818) 367-2430 / (818) 266-0874
12623 Gridley St. FAX (818) 367-5363
San Fernando, CA 91342 **www.stuntwings.com**

Thornton Aircraft Company (626) 795-8604
7520 Hayvenhurst Ave. FAX (626) 795-8606
Van Nuys, CA 91406 **www.thorntonaircraft.com**
(Fixed-Wing Aircraft, Jets & Military)

LA 411 **Animatronics, Puppets & Makeup FX** LA 411

1313FX (818) 441-3797
www.1313fx.com

Aardzark (818) 556-3500
707 S. Main St. FAX (818) 450-0777
Burbank, CA 91506
(Animatronics, Characters and Creatures, Makeup FX & Puppets)

All Effects Company, Inc. (818) 298-3730
20902 Enrique St. www.allfx.com
Woodland Hills, CA 91364

Almost Human Special Make Up EFX (310) 838-6993
3650 Eagle Rock Blvd. FAX (310) 838-6999
Los Angeles, CA 90065 www.almosthuman.net
(Makeup FX & Prosthetics)

Altered Anatomy, Inc. (818) 765-1992
(909) 653-3658
(Animatronics & Puppets) FAX (909) 653-9468
www.bnt4cncrp.com

Amalgamated Dynamics, Inc. (818) 882-8638
20100 Plummer St. FAX (818) 882-7327
Chatsworth, CA 91311 www.studioadi.com
(Animatronics, Creatures, Makeup FX & Puppets)

American Makeup and FX (336) 264-2302
(818) 780-5002
13536 Saticoy St. FAX (818) 780-5002
Van Nuys, CA 91402 www.amefx.com
(Articulated Urethane Dummies, Body Suits, Body Parts, Cadavers, Castings, Character/Creature Body Suits, Characters, Creatures, Custom Animal FX, Full Body Suits, Hand Puppets, Life-Like Replicas, Makeup FX and Prosthetics, Masks, Sculpting, Sculpture, Slip Rubber Masks, Special FX Props & Statues)

Ⓐ **Anatomorphex/The Sculpture Studio** (818) 768-2880
8210 Lankershim Blvd., Ste. 14 www.anatomorphex.com
North Hollywood, CA 91605
(Animatronics, Creatures, Makeup FX & Puppets)

Animal Makers, Inc. (805) 523-1900
11911 Discovery Court, Ste. 411 FAX (805) 523-1903
Moorpark, CA 93021 www.animalmakers.com/store
(Animatronics, Articulated Dummies, Characters, Computer Enhanced Puppetry, Creatures, Foam Sculpting, Life-Like Replicas, Masks, Mechanical Puppets, Models, Prosthetics, Puppets, Radio-Controlled Puppets, Remote-Controlled FX, Robotics, Sculpting & Special FX Props)

Animated FX, Inc./ Dave Nelson & Norman Tempia (818) 879-9440
FAX (818) 879-9441
www.animatedfx.net
(Animatronics, Characters, Marionettes, Mechanical Puppets, Puppets & Radio-Controlled Puppets)

Arteffex/Dann O'Quinn (818) 506-5358
911 Mayo St. FAX (323) 255-4599
Los Angeles, CA 90042 www.acfxo.com
(Animatronics, Casting, Characters, Creatures, Foam Sculpting, Hand Puppets, Makeup FX, Masks, Mechanical Puppets, Miniatures, Models, Oversized Props, Prosthetics, Puppets, Radio-Controlled Puppets, Remote-Controlled FX, Robotics, Sculpting, Special FX Props & Statues)

Artistic Innovation Studios, Inc. (661) 296-7007
(Makeup FX & Prosthetics) FAX (661) 513-0229
www.aistudiosinc.com

Autonomous F/X, Inc. (818) 901-6005
14300 Calvert St. FAX (818) 901-6089
Van Nuys, CA 91401 www.autonomousfx.com

Bellfx, LLC (818) 590-4992
1908 First St. www.bellfx.com
San Fernando, CA 91340
(Animatronics, Puppetry & Robotics)

Bischoff's Taxidermy & Animal EFX (818) 843-7561
54 E. Magnolia Blvd. FAX (818) 567-2443
Burbank, CA 91502 www.bischoffs.net
(Custom Animal EFX)

Bob Baker Marionettes (213) 250-9995
1345 W. First St. FAX (213) 250-1120
Los Angeles, CA 90026 www.bobbakermarionettes.com
(Puppet Makers)

Ⓐ **The Character Shop** (805) 306-9441
4735 Industrial St., Ste. 4-B FAX (805) 306-9444
Simi Valley, CA 93063 www.character-shop.com
(Aliens, Animatronics, Animals, Characters and Creatures, Makeup FX, Marionettes, Prosthetics, Puppets, Remote-Controlled Articulation & Robotics)

Chiodo Bros. Productions, Inc. (818) 842-5656
110 W. Providencia Ave. FAX (818) 848-0891
Burbank, CA 91502 www.chiodobros.com
(Prosthetics & Puppets)

Cosmic Ant (323) 913-0030
(323) 717-8777
FAX (323) 913-0030
www.cosmicant.com
(Creatures, Makeup FX, Prosthetics & Puppets)

Creative Character Engineering (818) 901-0507
16110 Hart St. FAX (818) 901-8417
Van Nuys, CA 91406 www.creativecharacter.com
(Animatronics, Creatures, Makeup FX, Prosthetics & Ultra-Realistic Rental Babies)

The Creature Company (323) 319-6501
(661) 433-5283
17334 Queensglen Ave. FAX (866) 762-9974
Palmdale, CA 93591 www.creaturecompany.com
(Animatronics, Articulated Dummies, Body Suits, Cadavers, Castings, Characters, Creatures, Foam Sculpting, Hand Puppets, Life-Like Replicas, Makeup FX, Marionettes, Masks, Mechanical Puppets, Miniatures, Models, Molds, Oversized Props, Prosthetics, Puppets, Radio-Controlled Puppets, Remote-Controlled FX, Robotics, Sculpting, Special FX Props, Statues & Vacuum-Forming)

Creature Effects, Inc. (323) 850-3228
3325 Cahuenga Blvd. FAX (323) 850-3280
Los Angeles, CA 90068 www.creaturefxinc.com
(Animatronics, Body Suits, Creatures, Makeup FX, Prosthetics Puppets & Special FX Props)

Ⓐ **Crisis FX** (818) 504-4151
(818) 504-2159
8210 Lankershim Blvd., Ste. 5 FAX (818) 504-1704
North Hollywood, CA 91605 www.crisisfx.com
(Animatronics, Castings, Makeup FX, Molds & Statues)

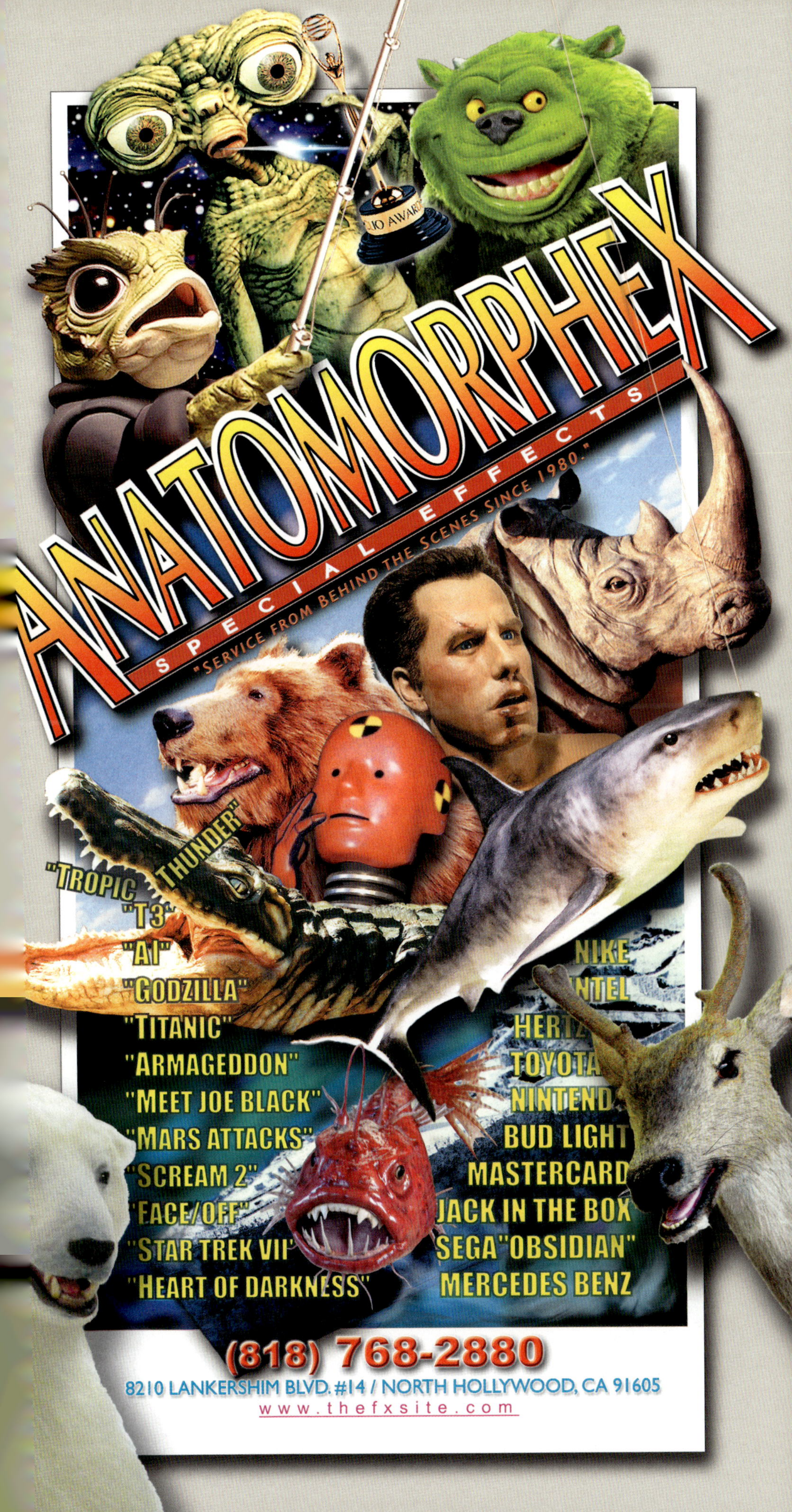
ANATOMORPHEX
SPECIAL EFFECTS
"SERVICE FROM BEHIND THE SCENES SINCE 1980."
CLIO AWARD
"TROPIC THUNDER"
"T3"
"AI"
"GODZILLA"
"TITANIC"
"ARMAGEDDON"
"MEET JOE BLACK"
"MARS ATTACKS"
"SCREAM 2"
"FACE/OFF"
"STAR TREK VII"
"HEART OF DARKNESS"
NIKE
TOYOTA
BUD LIGHT
MASTERCARD
JACK IN THE BOX
SEGA "OBSIDIAN"
MERCEDES BENZ
(818) 768-2880
8210 LANKERSHIM BLVD. #14 / NORTH HOLLYWOOD, CA 91605
www.thefxsite.com

CWSFX (818) 568-5361
FAX (818) 563-6724
www.cwsfx.com
(Animatronics, Articulated Dummies, Body Suits, Cadavers, Castings, Characters, Creatures, Hand Puppets, Life-Like Replicas, Makeup FX, Masks, Mechanical Puppets, Molds, Prosthetics, Puppets, Radio-Controlled Puppets, Robotics, Sculpting, Special FX Props & Statues)

Douglas White Effects (818) 785-4148
6859 Valjean Ave., Ste. 7 FAX (818) 785-2567
Van Nuys, CA 91406 www.dweffects.com

Dynamic Design International, LLC/ Darren Perks (818) 923-8798 (818) 439-8447
(Prosthetics) FAX (623) 386-6826
www.dynamicdesignintl.com

An Eye 4 Detail (626) 791-7962
1044 N. Hudson Ave.
Pasadena, CA 91104
(Animatronics, Articulated Dummies, Body Suits, Castings, Characters, Creatures, Foam Sculpting, Marionettes, Miniatures, Models, Oversized Props, Puppets & Sculpting)

Festival Artists, Inc. (626) 334-9388 (626) 303-6042
120 N. Aspan Ave. FAX (626) 969-8595
Azusa, CA 91702 www.festivalartists.org
(Oversized Props & Welding)

Film Illusions, Inc. (626) 974-5896
1735 S. Grand Ave. FAX (626) 974-5806
Glendora, CA 91740 www.filmillusions.com
(Animatronics & Puppets)

Flix FX, Inc. (818) 765-3549 (877) 326-8433
7327 Lankershim Blvd., Ste. 4 FAX (818) 765-0135
North Hollywood, CA 91605 www.flixfx.com
(Animatronics & Puppets)

Gary J. Tunnicliffe's Two Hours in the Dark, Inc. (818) 837-1045
12473 Gladstone Ave., Ste. Q FAX (818) 837-1842
Sylmar, CA 91342 www.2hoursinthedark.com

Global Effects, Inc. (818) 503-9273
7115 Laurel Canyon Blvd. FAX (818) 503-9459
North Hollywood, CA 91605 www.globaleffects.com
(Creature Suits, Makeup FX & Vacuum-Forming)

Ric Heitzman (323) 308-8013
(Puppetry) www.richeitzman.com

Image Creators, Inc. (310) 710-7128 (310) 202-8286
www.imagecreators.net
(Animal Puppets, Animatronics, Body Suits, Creatures, Prosthetics, Remote-Controlled FX & Robotics)

Imagivations (818) 767-6767
11585 Sheldon St. FAX (818) 767-3637
Sun Valley, CA 91352 www.imagivations.com
(Foam Sculpting, Miniatures, Models & Remote-Controlled Props)

Independent Studio Services, Inc./ISS (818) 951-5600
9545 Wentworth St. www.issprops.com
Sunland, CA 91040

Industrial Monsters & Props/IMP FX (818) 772-6540
FAX (818) 772-8749
www.impfx.com
(Animatronics, Articulated Dummies, Body Suits, Cadavers, Castings, Characters, Computer Enhanced Puppetry, Creatures, Foam Sculpting, Hand Puppets, Life-Like Replicas, Makeup FX, Marionettes, Masks, Mechanical Puppets, Models, Molds, Oversized Props, Prosthetics, Puppets, Radio-Controlled Puppets, Remote-Controlled FX, Robotics, Sculpting, Special FX Props & Statues)

Jim Henson's Creature Shop (323) 802-1525 (818) 953-3030
1416 N. La Brea Ave. FAX (323) 802-1891
Los Angeles, CA 90028 www.creatureshop.com
(Animatronics & Puppets)

Kent Allen Jones (310) 429-9422
(Sculpture) www.portfolios.com/kentjones

Kevin Marks Effects (818) 613-2746
(Prosthetics & Special FX Makeup)

Scott Land (626) 599-9992 (818) 429-3275
P.O. Box 1125 FAX (626) 599-9993
Monrovia, CA 91017 www.thepuppetman.com
(Marionettes & Puppets)

Legacy Effects (818) 782-0870
340 Parkside Dr. FAX (818) 792-4322
San Fernando, CA 91340 www.stanwinstonstudio.com
(Animatronics, Casting, Characters and Creatures, Creature Suits, Makeup FX, Mechanical Puppets, Molds, Remote-Controlled FX and Robotics, Prosthetics & Puppets)

Makeup & Effects Laboratories, Inc./MEL (818) 982-1483
7110 Laurel Canyon Blvd., Bldg. E FAX (818) 982-5712
North Hollywood, CA 91605 www.melefx.com
(Animatronics, Miniatures, Oversized and Soft Props, Radio-Controlled Puppets & Vacuum-Forming)

The Mannequin Gallery (818) 834-5555
12350 Montague St., Ste. E FAX (818) 834-5558
Pacoima, CA 91331 www.mannequingallery.com
(Mannequins & Sculpting)

Marc's Creature Company (800) 787-1778 (661) 645-6023
21125 Centre Pointe Pkwy FAX (661) 254-7371
Santa Clarita, CA 91350
www.marcscreaturecompany.com
(Animatronics, Articulated Dummies, Castings, Characters, Creatures, Hand Puppets, Life-Like Replicas, Makeup FX, Marionettes, Masks, Mechanical Puppets, Molds, Prosthetics, Puppets, Radio-Controlled Puppets, Remote-Controlled FX, Robotics, Sculpting, Special FX Props, Statues, Vacuum-Forming & Welding)

Ⓐ **Masters FX, Inc./Todd Masters** (818) 834-3000 (604) 683-5311
FAX (818) 834-9755
www.mastersfx.com
(Animatronic Puppets, Articulated Urethane Dummies & Masks)

Michael Burnett Productions, Inc. (818) 768-6103
P.O. Box 16627 FAX (815) 550-1247
North Hollywood, CA 91615 www.mbpfx.com
(Animatronics, Creatures, Full Body Suits, Makeup FX, Mechanical Puppets & Slip Rubber Masks)

Mike Tristano & Co. (818) 888-6970 (818) 522-0969
14431 Ventura Blvd., Ste. 185 FAX (818) 888-6447
Sherman Oaks, CA 91423
(Body Parts, Cadavers, Makeup FX & Prosthetics)

Multivision FX (818) 843-3266 (818) 288-6839
1112 N. Glenoaks Blvd. FAX (818) 843-3266
Burbank, CA 91504 www.multivisionfx.com
(Animatronics, Characters and Creatures, Creature Suits, Makeup FX & Prosthetics)

NAC Co. (805) 376-0206 (805) 405-7337
1772-J E. Avenida de Los Arboles FAX (805) 376-8407
Thousand Oaks, CA 91362 www.naceffects.com
(Animatronics, Remote-Controlled FX, Robotics & Special FX Props)

NBC New York Prosthetics Shop (212) 664-4093
30 Rockefeller Plaza www.filmmakersdestination.com
New York, NY 10112

Optic Nerve Studios, Inc. (818) 771-1007
9818 Glenoaks Blvd. FAX **(818) 771-1009**
Sun Valley, CA 91352 **www.opticnervefx.com**
(Animatronics, Characters and Creatures, Creature Suits, Full Body Suits, Miniatures, Prosthetics & Special FX Makeup)

Pacific Vision Productions, Inc. (626) 441-4869
210 Pasadena Ave. **www.pacificvision.com**
South Pasadena, CA 91030
(Animatronics, Electronics & Rigging)

Christine Papalexis (323) 665-8062
FAX **(323) 665-1214**
(Hand and Remote-Controlled Puppets, Marionettes & Puppet Fabrication)

Pat Brymer Creations (323) 259-0400
136 N. Avenue 61, Ste. 102 FAX **(323) 259-0358**
Los Angeles, CA 90042 **www.pbcreations.com**
(Puppets & Rigging)

Patrick Tatopoulos Designs, Inc. (818) 859-0368
1951 Ontario St. FAX **(818) 841-8883**
Burbank, CA 91505 **www.tatopoulosstudios.net**
(Animatronics, Characters and Creatures, Creature Suits, Makeup FX, Miniatures, Prosthetics & Remote Controlled Puppets)

PerformFX (818) 847-0030
(661) 609-4499
2301 Empire Ave. **www.performfx.com**
Burbank, CA 91504
(Animatronics, Characters and Creatures, Makeup FX, Marionettes, Molds, Prosthetics, Puppeteered and Remote-Controlled FX & Puppets)

Puppet Studio (818) 506-7374
10903 Chandler Blvd. FAX **(818) 506-7374**
North Hollywood, CA 91601 **www.puppetstudio.com**
(Computer Enhanced Puppetry, Hand Puppets, Marionettes & Puppet FX)

Ralis Special Makeup Effects (818) 209-8046
(213) 622-3936
3727 W. Magnolia Blvd., Ste. 407 FAX **(213) 622-3987**
Burbank, CA 91505 **www.ralisfx.com**
(Makeup FX & Prosthetics)

René and His Artists Productions (818) 848-6809
707-A Main St. FAX **(818) 848-3112**
Burbank, CA 91506
(Body Suits, Marionettes, Radio-Controlled Puppets & Ventriloquist Figures)

RSP, Inc./Robert Short (310) 457-4499
7117 Dume Dr. FAX **(310) 457-4499**
Malibu, CA 90265 **www.robertshort.com**
(Special FX Makeup & Visual FX Design and Supervision)

Rubens Display World (909) 923-5671
(909) 923-5672
1482 E. Francis St. FAX **(909) 923-5670**
Ontario, CA 91761 **www.rubensdisplay.com**
(Mannequins)

Smith FX, Inc. (818) 601-8800
www.shaunsmithfx.com

Spectral Motion, Inc. (818) 956-6080
1849 Dana St. FAX **(818) 956-6083**
Glendale, CA 91201 **www.spectralmotion.com**
(Animatronics, Body Suits, Characters and Creatures, Makeup FX, Miniatures, Models, Prosthetics, Puppets & Vacuum-Forming)

Stevie FX (818) 915-3615
(818) 206-0144
(Creatures, Makeup FX & Prosthetics) FAX **(818) 206-0169**
www.steviefx.com

Sticks & Stones (818) 352-9538
FAX **(818) 352-9538**
www.sticksandstonesfx.com
(Animatronics, Makeup FX, Prosthetics & Puppets)

Sunset Optometric Center Inc. (323) 668-2702
4445 Sunset Blvd. FAX **(323) 668-1210**
Los Angeles, CA 90027 **www.sunsetoptometriccenter.com**

Techworks Studios, Inc. (818) 559-5536
FAX **(661) 298-0929**
www.techworksstudios.com
(Animatronics, Creatures, Makeup FX, Prosthetics, Puppets, Robots & Sculpting)

Tony Urbano & Tim Blaney Puppetry (310) 572-1917
11664 National Blvd., Ste. 148 FAX **(310) 572-1917**
Los Angeles, CA 90064
(Marionettes, Puppeteered FX & Puppets)

Acrylic Airlines Inc. (310) 664-7036
46 Thornton Ave. **www.dispensaryart.com**
Venice, CA 90291
(Art Rentals, Cleared Artwork Rentals, Cleared Artwork Sales, Custom Artwork, Digital Fabrication, Fabrication, Fine Art Rentals, Fine Art Reproduction, Poster Art & Sculptures)

Art O'Rama (310) 314-9884
(Cleared Artwork Rentals and Sales) **www.artorama.tv**

Art Pic (818) 503-5999
6826 Troost Ave. FAX **(818) 503-5995**
North Hollywood, CA 91605 **www.artpic2000.com**
(Art Rentals)

Artagogo (310) 398-2224
(310) 753-9991
(Fine Art Rentals) **www.artagogo.net**

Artisan's Editions (818) 370-3613
2121 N. Buena Vista St. FAX **(818) 845-6692**
Burbank, CA 91504 **www.artisanseditions.com**
(Fine Art Reproduction)

Munish Asnani (323) 383-5663
www.munishasani.com

The Canvas Peddler (818) 985-8830
5543 Satsuma Ave. FAX **(818) 985-5554**
North Hollywood, CA 91601
(Custom Framing)

Chris' Art Resource/C.A.R. (323) 669-1604
(323) 665-7566
1035 N. Myra Ave. **www.chrisrentsart.com**
Los Angeles, CA 90029
(Art Rentals)

D.R.G. Enterprises, Inc. (818) 908-0100
14810 Oxnard St. FAX **(818) 908-0505**
Van Nuys, CA 91411
(Custom Framing)

Dina Art Ltd. (323) 469-4073
(310) 508-5563
6433 W. Sunset Blvd. FAX **(323) 469-4072**
Los Angeles, CA 90028 **www.dinaart.com**
(Cleared Artwork Rentals and Sales, Custom Framing, Fabrication & Poster Art)

Bridget Duffy (310) 675-2715
(310) 422-2910
5016 W. 118th St. FAX **(310) 675-2400**
Hawthorne, CA 90250 **www.duffyart.com**

Film Art LA (323) 461-4900
5241 Melrose Ave. FAX **(323) 461-4959**
Hollywood, CA 90038 **www.filmartla.com**
(Cleared Art Rentals & Digital Fine Art Reproductions)

Galerie Lakaye (323) 460-7333
(Art Rentals) FAX **(323) 460-7330**
www.galerielakaye.com

Gallery of Functional Art (310) 829-6990
Bergamot Station FAX **(310) 829-5707**
2525 Michigan Ave., Ste. E3 **www.galleryoffuctionalart.com**
Santa Monica, CA 90404
(Contemporary & Eclectic)

Ghettogloss Gallery (323) 871-8100
6109 Melrose Ave. FAX **(323) 871-8330**
Los Angeles, CA 90038 **www.ghettogloss.com**

H. Studio (818) 767-8448
(800) 242-8992
8640 Tamarack Ave. FAX **(818) 767-5334**
Sun Valley, CA 91352 **www.hstudio.com**
(Acrylic Sculptures)

Hollywood Studio Gallery (323) 462-1116
1035 N. Cahuenga Blvd. FAX **(323) 462-5113**
Hollywood, CA 90038
(Fabrication)

Jules & Jim (818) 985-2434
6651 Irvine Ave.
North Hollywood, CA 91606
(Custom Artwork Props)

Kevin Barry Fine Art Associates (323) 951-1860
8210 Melrose Ave. FAX **(323) 951-1866**
Los Angeles, CA 90046
(Art Rentals & Framing)

Lacy Primitive & Fine Art (310) 271-0807
1240 Sierra Alta Way FAX **(310) 271-0806**
Los Angeles, CA 90069 **www.lacyprimitiveandfineart.com**
(Abstract, Contemporary and Minimalist Painting Art Rentals)

M.J. Higgins Fine Art & Furnishings (213) 617-1700
400 S. Main St., Ste. 103 FAX **(213) 617-1777**
Los Angeles, CA 90013 **www.mjhiggins.com**
(Art Rentals, Cleared Artwork Rentals and Sales, Custom Artwork, Fabrication, Fine Art Rentals and Reproduction, Los Angeles-Based Contemporary Art & Sculptures)

Mardine Davis Art Consulting (323) 468-8800
652 N. Larchmont Blvd. FAX **(323) 468-8387**
Los Angeles, CA 90004 **www.mardinedavisart.com**
(Cleared Artwork Rentals, Cleared Artwork Sales, Custom Framing, Digital Fabrication, Fine Art Rentals, Fine Art Reproduction, Poster Art & Sculptures)

Modern Props (323) 934-3000
5500 W. Jefferson Blvd. FAX **(323) 934-3155**
Los Angeles, CA 90016 **www.modernprops.com**
(Cleared Contemporary Art Rentals)

Nicole Elias Art (323) 578-5083
(323) 461-6717
(Fine Art Rentals)

Pacific Imaging (818) 764-8500
12712 Saticoy St. FAX **(818) 764-8505**
North Hollywood , CA 91605
(Fine Art Reproduction & Poster Art)

The Studios at Paramount (323) 956-3729
The Studios at Paramount
Sign Shop & Graphic Services
5555 Melrose Ave.
Hollywood, CA 90038
www.thestudiosatparamount.com

Perrell Fine Art (323) 933-8630
145 N. La Brea, Ste. E FAX **(323) 933-8629**
Los Angeles, CA 90036 **www.perrellfineart.com**
(Art Framing and Rentals)

Pinacoteca Picture Props (323) 965-2722
5735 W. Adams Blvd. FAX **(323) 965-2730**
Los Angeles, CA 90016 **www.pinaprops.com**
(Art Rentals)

Santa Monica Fine Art Studios (310) 453-3632
1834 Franklin St. FAX **(310) 453-3632**
Santa Monica, CA 90404 **www.tanjarector.com**
(Art Rentals)

Sculpture and Paintings by Bruce Gray (323) 223-4059
688 S. Avenue 21 **www.brucegray.com**
Los Angeles, CA 90031
(Art Rentals, Cleared Artwork Rentals, Cleared Artwork Sales, Custom Artwork, Fabrication, Fine Art Rentals & Sculptures)

Sports and the Arts
(Art Rentals)
(818) 762-7133
(818) 400-9390
FAX (818) 762-7122
www.sportart.net

Stone Art
419 Wilshire Blvd.
Santa Monica, CA 90401
(Framing)
(310) 395-6303
FAX (310) 395-8871

Studio P
1248 Palmetto St.
Los Angeles, CA 90013
(Digital Fine Art Fabrication)
(213) 613-1759
FAX (213) 613-1760
www.studiopinc.com

Sunny Meyer Fine Art
(Art Restoration)
(818) 985-6630
www.oldart.com

U-Frame It
13630 Sherman Way
Van Nuys, CA 91405
(Cleared Artwork Sales, Custom Framing, Poster Art & Restoration)
(818) 781-4500
(818) 402-8579
FAX (818) 781-7479
www.uframeitgallery.com

Doug Wright/Prop Art
(323) 461-5842
(323) 868-5831

Arts & Crafts Supplies

Aaron Bros.
(888) 372-6464
(818) 243-7661
www.aaronbrothers.com

Baller Hardware
(Art Supplies)
(323) 665-4149
www.ballerhardware.com

Bead Box
(Appliqués, Beads, Jewels & Trims)
(818) 342-2481

Blick Art Materials
7301 W. Beverly Blvd.
Los Angeles, CA 90036
(323) 933-9284
FAX (323) 933-9794
www.dickblick.com

Blick Art Materials
11531 Santa Monica Blvd.
West Los Angeles, CA 90025
(310) 479-1416
www.dickblick.com

Blick Art Materials
44 S. Raymond Ave.
Pasadena, CA 91105
(626) 795-4985
www.dickblick.com

The Button Store
8344 W. Third St.
Los Angeles, CA 90048
(323) 658-5473
FAX (323) 782-0940

Buy-Lines Co., Inc.
5444 Melrose Ave.
Hollywood, CA 90038
(Czech Glass Beads)
(323) 463-4855

Cameraflauge
6840 Vineland Ave.
North Hollywood, CA 91605
(Paints)
(818) 762-1059
(213) 304-9323
FAX (818) 762-0207
www.cameraflauge.com

Cane & Basket Supply Co.
1283 S. Cochran Ave.
Los Angeles, CA 90019
(Bamboo, Raffia & Sea Grass)
(323) 939-9644
FAX (323) 939-7237
www.caneandbasket.com

Carter Sexton Artists' Materials
(818) 763-5050
www.cartersexton.com

Continental Art Supplies
(818) 345-1044
www.continentalart.com

Graphaids, Inc.
3030 S. La Cienega Blvd.
Culver City, CA 90232
(310) 204-1212
(800) 866-6601
FAX (310) 204-5730
www.graphaids.com

Graphaids, Inc.
12400 Santa Monica Blvd.
West Los Angeles, CA 90025
(310) 820-0445
FAX (310) 820-5506
www.graphaids.com

Kit Kraft, Inc.
12109 Ventura Pl.
Studio City, CA 91604
(Beads, Jewels, Paints & Trims)
(818) 509-9739
www.kitkraft.biz

McManus & Morgan, Inc.
2506 W. Seventh St.
Los Angeles, CA 90057
(Fine Art Papers & Stationery)
(213) 387-4433
FAX (213) 387-3454
www.mcmanusmorgan.com

Michael's Arts & Crafts
1427 Fourth St.
Santa Monica, CA 90401
(310) 393-9634
(800) 642-4235
FAX (310) 395-2096
www.michaels.com

Michael's Arts & Crafts
18131 Ventura Blvd.
Tarzana, CA 91356
(818) 881-7555
(800) 642-4235
FAX (818) 996-3639
www.michaels.com

Mittel's Art Center
2016 Lincoln Blvd.
Santa Monica, CA 90405
(Framing, Paints & Papers)
(310) 399-9500
www.mittels.net

Mittel's Art Center
22100 Ventura Blvd.
Woodland Hills, CA 91364
(Framing, Paints & Papers)
(818) 710-0517
www.mittels.net

Moskatels
(Craft Supplies)
(213) 689-4830
FAX (213) 622-3803

Pearl Art & Craft Supplies, Inc.
1250 S. La Cienega Blvd.
Los Angeles, CA 90035
(310) 854-4900
FAX (310) 854-4908
www.pearlpaint.com

Swain's
537 N. Glendale Ave.
Glendale, CA 91206
(818) 243-3129
www.swainsart.com

Universal Rugs and Oil Paintings
741 W. Broadway
Glendale, CA 91204
(818) 548-0110
FAX (818) 548-0114
www.universalhomedecor.com

Utrecht Art Supply Center
11677 Santa Monica Blvd.
West Los Angeles, CA 90025
(310) 478-5775
(800) 223-9132
FAX (310) 478-5675
www.utrechtart.com

World Supply
3425 W. Cahuenga Blvd.
Hollywood, CA 90068
(323) 851-1350
(800) 399-6753
FAX (323) 851-1922

LA 411 Atmospheric/Lighting Special FX & Pyrotechnics LA 411

Alpha Wolf Special Effects (213) 700-2054
(818) 429-9382
www.alphawolfprods.com
(Atmospheric FX, Confetti Special FX and Cannon Systems, Fog FX/Machines, Mechanical FX, Powderman, Projections, Pyrotechnics, Rain FX/Machines, Smoke FX/Machines, Snow FX/Machines, Special FX Coordinator, Weather FX/Machines & Wind FX/Machines)

ANA Special Effects, Inc. (818) 909-6999
7021 Hayvenhurst Ave. FAX (818) 782-0635
Van Nuys, CA 91406 www.anaspecialeffects.com

Angstrom Lighting (323) 462-4246
(866) 275-9211
837 N. Cahuenga Blvd. FAX (323) 462-8190
Hollywood, CA 90038 www.angstromlighting.com
(Fog Machines)

Artistry In Motion Confetti, Inc. (818) 994-7388
15101 Keswick St. FAX (818) 994-7688
Van Nuys, CA 91405 www.artistryinmotion.com
(Confetti Special FX and Cannon Systems)

Automatrix Effects/David Waine (323) 469-0088
2623 N. San Fernando Rd. FAX (323) 395-0570
Los Angeles, CA 90065 www.automatrixfx.com

Bill Ferrell Co. (818) 994-1952
(866) 994-1952
14744 Oxnard St. FAX (818) 994-9670
Van Nuys, CA 91411 www.billferrell.com
(Confetti Special FX and Cannon Systems)

Boom Boom Effects (818) 772-6699
11100-8 Sepulveda Blvd., Ste. 339 FAX (818) 772-6689
Mission Hills, CA 91345

Calbor Enterprises Two, Inc. (818) 760-3222
(818) 262-5329
10646 Chiquita St. FAX (818) 760-2238
Toluca Lake, CA 91602 www.pyro-fx.net
(Confetti Special FX and Cannon Systems, Fog FX/Machines, Powderman, Public Display Fireworks, Pyrotechnics, Rain FX/Machines, Smoke FX/Machines, Snow FX/Machines, Special FX Coordinator, Weather FX/Machines & Wind FX/Machines)

Jerry Chavez (818) 985-0494
(818) 400-4615
(Pyrotechnics) FAX (818) 985-0415

Cinefx/Josh Hakian (818) 889-7217
3737 Patrick Henry Pl. FAX (818) 889-7217
Agoura Hills, CA 91301
(Mechanical FX & Pyrotechnics)

Controlled Airstreams (818) 597-1977
32180 Mulholland Hwy FAX (818) 597-0536
Malibu, CA 90265
(Atmospheric FX)

Dan Murphy Special Effects (661) 269-9353
www.murphy-special-effects.com
(Atmospheric FX, Mechanical FX, Pyrotechnics & Special FX Coordinator)

Dan Donley (805) 493-5990
(213) 200-2810
(Public Display Fireworks)

Eddie Surkin Special FX/ Etan Enterprises (818) 342-1952
(818) 203-5466
6127 Melvin Ave. FAX (818) 342-1952
Tarzana, CA 91356
(Pyrotechnic Special FX)

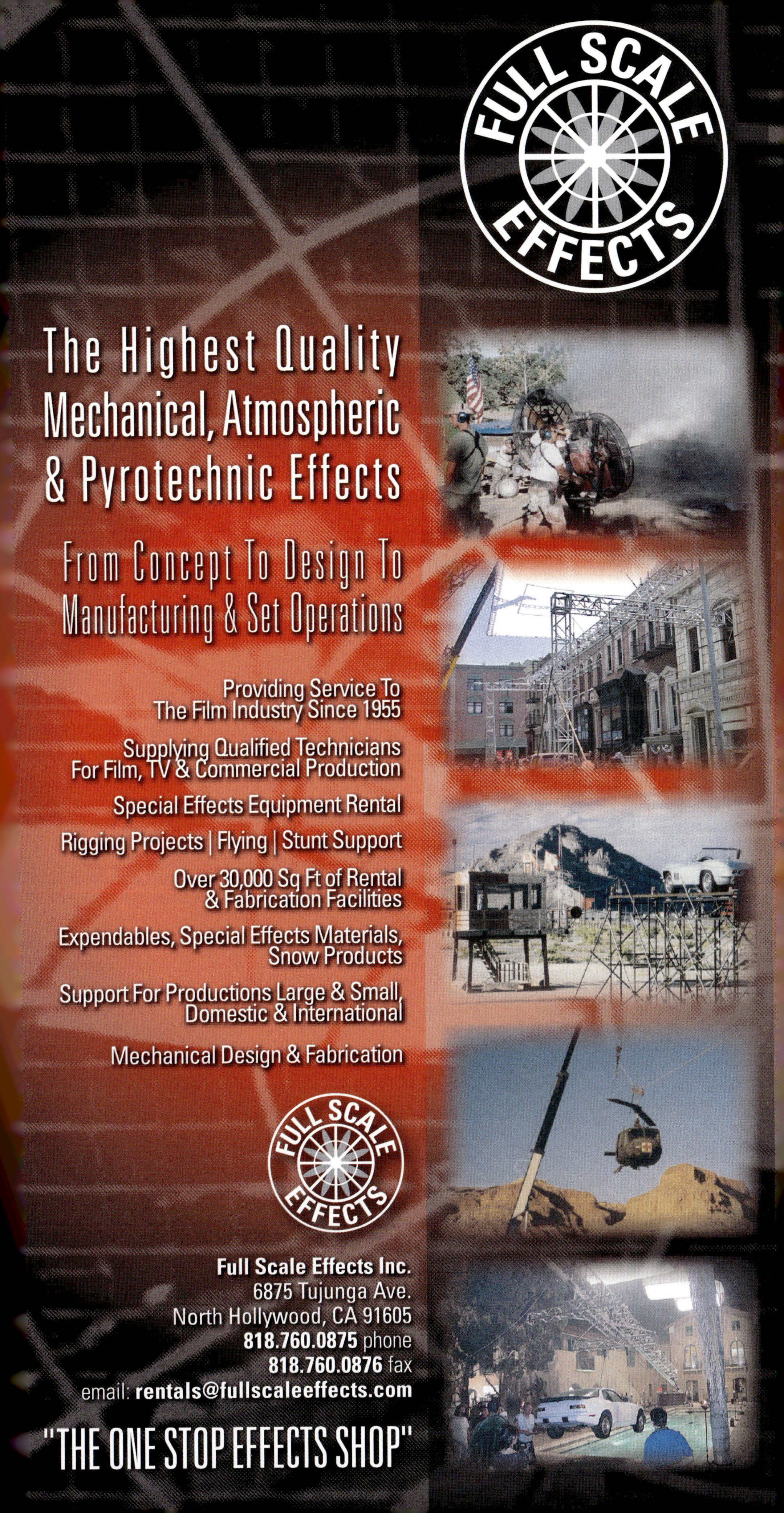

The Effects Group (323) 876-0992
(Atmospheric FX & Pyrotechnics) FAX (323) 876-0288
www.theeffectsgroup.net

F/X Concepts, Inc./Lou Carlucci (818) 508-1094
P.O. Box 1008 FAX (818) 508-1094
Santa Clarita, CA 91386
(Fog, Smoke and Wind Machines)

Filmtrix, Inc. (818) 808-9321
P.O. Box 809 www.filmtrix.com
North Hollywood, CA 91603
(Special FX Coordinator)

Flix FX, Inc. (818) 765-3549 (877) 326-8433
7327 Lankershim Blvd., Ste. 4 FAX (818) 765-0135
North Hollywood, CA 91605 www.flixfx.com
(Fog, Rain, Snow and Wind Effects)

Flutter Fetti (877) 321-1999 (504) 522-0300
FAX (504) 522-0304
www.flutterfetti.com

Ⓐ **Full Scale Effects** (818) 760-0875 (818) 760-0042
6875 Tujunga Ave. FAX (818) 760-0876
North Hollywood, CA 91605 www.fullscaleeffects.com

Future Lighting (310) 312-9772 (310) 346-1649
(Cloud and Fire Wall Projections) www.futurelighting.net

Gary F. Bentley Special Effects Systems (323) 664-1509 (323) 365-2914
(Atmospheric and Mechanical FX) FAX (323) 661-7320

Jet Effects (818) 764-5644
6910 Farmdale Ave. FAX (818) 764-6655
North Hollywood, CA 91605 www.jeteffects.net

Knott Limited Special Effects (323) 876-2356
6919 Treasure Trail FAX (323) 876-2356
Los Angeles, CA 90068
(Atmospheric FX & Miniature Pyrotechnics)

Laser Magic Productions (818) 981-7983
13455 Ventura Blvd., Ste. 237 www.laser-magic.com
Sherman Oaks, CA 91423
(Laser FX)

Lazarus Lighting Design (818) 956-3211 (800) 553-5554
14701C Arminta St. FAX (818) 956-3233
Van Nuys, CA 91402 www.lldco.com
(Fiber Optic Special FX Lighting)

The Lightning Co., LLC (818) 207-8400
20434 S. Santa Fe Ave. FAX (818) 279-0558
Long Beach, CA 90802 www.tlcfx.com

Long Beach Ice (888) 438-1956 (562) 438-8129
1600 Cherry Ave. FAX (562) 856-1356
Long Beach, CA 90813 www.longbeachice.com
(Atmospheric FX & Snow FX/Machines)

Luminys Systems Corp. (323) 461-6361 (800) 321-3644
6601 Santa Monica Blvd. FAX (323) 461-3067
Hollywood, CA 90038 www.lightningstrikes.com
(Lightning FX)

MagicSnow Systems (310) 289-9852
8581 Santa Monica Blvd., Ste. 219 www.magicsnow.com
Los Angeles, CA 90069
(Snow Machines)

Neil Marquis (818) 780-0118 (213) 280-4552

Mini-Fog/Prop Services Unlimited (323) 462-2272 (213) 968-1068
(Compact Fog Generators) FAX (323) 469-9204

NBC Universal Property (818) 777-2784
100 Universal City Plaza FAX (818) 866-1543
Universal City, CA 91608
www.filmmakersdestination.com

Newhall Ice Co. (661) 259-0893 (818) 362-9742
22502 Fifth St. FAX (661) 259-0691
Newhall, CA 91321
(Snow Machines)

North Hollywood Ice Co. (818) 762-2237 (323) 465-5538
5257 Craner Ave. FAX (818) 762-6750
North Hollywood, CA 91601
(Snow Machines) www.northhollywoodice.com

The Studios at Paramount (323) 956-5140
The Studios at Paramount FAX (323) 862-2325
Manufacturing and Special Effects
5555 Melrose Ave.
Hollywood, CA 90038
www.thestudiosatparamount.com
(Environmental Effects & Steam Effects)

Rain For Rent (805) 525-3306 (805) 331-0175
333 S. 12th St. FAX (805) 525-7663
Santa Paula, CA 93061 www.rainforrent.com
(Rain Machines, Pumps & Tanks)

Reel EFX, Inc. (818) 762-1710 (213) 308-7289
5539 Riverton Ave. FAX (818) 762-1734
North Hollywood, CA 91601 www.reelefx.com
(Atmospheric FX)

Reelistic FX, Inc./John Gray (818) 346-2484 (818) 621-2484
21318 Hart St. FAX (818) 346-2710
Canoga Park, CA 91303 www.r-fx.com

Reliable Snow Service (661) 269-2093 (661) 305-8274
(Snow Machines) FAX (661) 269-2237

Renegade Effects Group (818) 980-8848
11312 Hartland St. FAX (818) 980-8849
North Hollywood, CA 91605 www.renegadeeffects.com

Ⓐ **Roger George Rentals** (818) 994-3049
14525 Bessemer St. FAX (818) 994-9432
Van Nuys, CA 91411 www.rogergeorge.com
(Weather FX Machines)

RPI Entertainment & Media Group (323) 960-9014 (323) 656-9014
1031 N. Laurel Ave., Ste. 3 FAX (775) 252-6627
Hollywood, CA 90046 www.rpientertainment.com
(Atmospheric FX, Blacklights, Confetti Special FX and Cannon Systems, Fiber Optics, Fog FX/Machines, Laser FX, Lightning FX, Projections, Public Display Fireworks, Pyrotechnics, Smoke FX/Machines, Snow FX/Machines & Special FX Lighting)

Schwartz Oil Company, Inc. (661) 259-4000 (818) 365-9214
27241 Henry Mayo Dr. FAX (661) 257-0137
Valencia, CA 91355 www.socifuel.com
(Pyrotechnics)

Jeff Scott (213) 709-9190 (323) 469-9980
(Atmospheric FX & Pyrotechnics)

Set Stuff, Inc. (323) 993-9500
1105 N. Sycamore Ave. FAX (323) 993-9506
Hollywood, CA 90038 www.setstuffrentals.com
(Diffusion Smokers & Fog, Pyrotechnic, Snow and Wind FX)

Shannon Luminous Materials, Inc. (714) 550-9931 (800) 543-4485
304 N. Townsend St., Ste. A FAX (714) 550-9938
Santa Ana, CA 92703 www.blacklite.com
(Blacklight Paint, Blacklights & Coatings)

Sky-Tracker Moving Xenon/ Searchlights (949) 350-7101 (800) 472-2353
(Special FX Lighting) FAX (949) 305-0918
www.skytrackerusa.com

Sno-FX (323) 876-0992
(Snow) FAX (323) 876-0288
www.theeffectsgroup.net

Ⓐ **Snow Business Hollywood, Inc.** (818) 884-3009
21318 Hart St. FAX (818) 884-3110
Canoga Park, CA 91303
www.snowbusinesshollywood.com

Ⓐ **Special Effects Unlimited, Inc.** (323) 466-3361
1005 Lillian Way FAX (323) 466-5712
Hollywood, CA 90038 www.specialeffectsunlimited.com
(Atmospheric and Mechanical FX & Pyrotechnics)

Spectrum Effects Enterprises, Inc. (323) 871-4445 (661) 510-5633
Raleigh Studios FAX (661) 244-4469
5300 Melrose Ave., Ste. 101D www.spectrumeffects.com
Hollywood, CA 90038
(Pyrotechnics)

State Fire Marshal - Motion Picture/Entertainment Unit (626) 305-1908
602 E. Huntington Dr., Ste. A FAX (626) 305-5175
Monrovia, CA 91016 www.fire.ca.gov
(Pyrotechnics Only)

Stutsman Effects, Inc. (310) 457-6661 (310) 922-4705
29859 Harvester Rd. FAX (310) 457-4061
Malibu, CA 90265
(Atmospheric and Mechanical FX, Pyrotechnics & Special FX Coordinator)

Surefire Special Effects, Inc. (310) 345-7288
P.O. Box 488 FAX (714) 693-0382
Atwood, CA 92811 www.surefirefx.com

Tesla Technology Research (626) 359-1373 (626) 589-6141
2527 Treelane Ave. www.ttr.com
Monrovia, CA 91016
(Atmospheric and Lightning FX & Electric Arcs)

TLC-Creative Special Effects (310) 822-6790 (800) 447-3585
13428 Maxella Ave., Ste. 261 FAX (310) 821-4010
Los Angeles, CA 90292 www.tlc-call4ideas.com
(Laser Special FX)

Ultimate Effects (661) 298-3033 (818) 253-5947
16805 Sierra Hwy FAX (661) 298-3029
Canyon Country, CA 91351 www.ultimateeffects.com

Unilux/Blue Feather Lighting (818) 701-5404 (800) 635-2743
19630 Lanark St. FAX (818) 701-5404
Reseda, CA 91335 www.unilux.com
(Strobe Lighting FX)

Joseph Viskocil (310) 823-9600 (310) 625-3107
(Pyrotechnics)

Warner Bros. Studio Facilities - Special Effects (818) 954-1365
4000 Warner Blvd. FAX (818) 954-1424
Burbank, CA 91522 www.wbsf.com

West EFX, Inc. (818) 762-1059 (213) 304-9323
6840 Vineland Ave. FAX (818) 762-0207
North Hollywood, CA 91605 www.westefx.com

YLS Entertainment (714) 995-4588
10853 Portal Dr. FAX (562) 598-4123
Los Alamitos, CA 90720 www.ylsentertainment.com
(Laser Display FX and Systems)

A and C Harbour Lites, Ltd. (310) 926-9552
P.O. Box 9279 FAX (310) 356-3579
Marina Del Rey, CA 90295
(Barges, Camera/Picture Boats, Canoes, Charters, Charts, Inflatables, Jet Skis, Kayaks, KiteBoards, Maps, Marine Props, Nautical Equipment/Supplies, Nautical Props, Powerboats, Sailboats, Submarines, Support Boats, Surfboards, Tugboats & Yachts)

Action Watersports (310) 827-2233 (310) 827-2567
4144 Lincoln Blvd. FAX (310) 305-8046
Marina del Rey, CA 90292 www.actionwatersports.com
(Kayaks, Kite Boards, Skate Boards, Snow Boards & Surf Boards)

Aerial Action Productions/ Reel Orange (949) 548-4524
316 La Jolla Dr. FAX (949) 548-0749
Newport Beach, CA 92663 www.reelorange.com
(Canoes, Kayaks & White Water Camera and Picture Rafts)

Antiques of the Sea (562) 592-1752
P.O. Box 23, 16811 Pacific Coast Hwy FAX (562) 592-3026
Sunset Beach, CA 90742 www.antiquesofthesea.com
(Nautical Props)

Aqua Rescue (323) 707-3411 (323) 707-3415
(Inflatables, Jet Skis & Nautical Props) FAX (818) 293-0049
www.aquarescue.com

Aquavision (562) 433-2863 (562) 688-3038
3708 E. Fourth St. FAX (562) 433-2863
Long Beach, CA 90814 www.aquavision.net
(Camera and Picture Boats & Marine Props)

Argo Charters/Kimberly Lynn (760) 345-7529 (760) 567-7291
(Rare Boats)

Burbank Kawasaki (818) 848-6627
1329 N. Hollywood Way FAX (818) 848-6630
Burbank, CA 91505 www.burbankkawasaki.com
(Jet Skis)

Cal-Western Boat Company (562) 983-3600 (562) 984-2000
(Yachts) FAX (562) 983-3603
www.marinefilmyachtservices.com

California Sailing Academy (310) 821-3433 (310) 821-3434
14025 Panay Way FAX (310) 821-4141
Marina del Rey, CA 90292
www.californiasailingacademy.com
(Camera and Picture Boats & Nautical Antiques)

Captain Dave's Marine Services, Inc. (562) 437-4772 (877) 345-9009
1951 Golden West St., PMB 223 FAX (562) 354-7103
Huntington Beach, CA 92648
(Barges, Camera/Picture Boats, Canoes, Inflatables, Kayaks, Marine Coordination, Marine Props, Nautical Equipment/ Supplies, Nautical Props, Powerboats, Sailboats, Submarines, Support Boats, Tugboats & Yachts)

CAT Marine Production Services (562) 596-7105 (714) 235-7578
FAX (714)-771-3356
www.extremesportsfilming.com
(Barges, Camera/Picture Boats, Canoes, Charters, Charts, Hovercrafts, Inflatables, Jet Skis, Kayaks, KiteBoards, Maps, Marine Props, Nautical Equipment/Supplies, Nautical Props, Powerboats, Sailboats, Submarines, Support Boats, Surfboards, Tugboats, White Water Rafts & Yachts)

Catalina Island Channel Express (310) 519-1212 (800) 995-4386
Berth 95 FAX (310) 548-7389
San Pedro, CA 90731 www.catalinaexpress.com

The Catamaran Store (818) 764-3015 (818) 764-8334
11629 Vanowen St.
North Hollywood, CA 91605

Cinema Aquatics (818) 365-7999 (805) 207-5797
www.cinemaaquatics.com

Cinema Safety & Marine Services, Inc. (310) 614-0206 (805) 207-5797
1534 N. Moorpark Rd., Ste. 108 FAX (805) 241-3954
Thousand Oaks, CA 91360 www.cinemasafety.com
(Barges, Camera/Picture Boats, Canoes, Inflatables, Jet Skis, Kayaks, Support Boats, Surfboards & White Water Rafts)

Cinemafloat (949) 675-8888 (714) 801-5553
1624 W. Oceanfront Walk FAX (949) 644-3073
Newport Beach, CA 92663
(Barges, Camera and Picture Boats, Marine Props & Tugboats)

CineMarine Team - Cinema Rentals, Inc. (661) 222-7342 (877) 877-9605
25876 The Old Road, Ste. 174 FAX (661) 253-3643
Stevenson Ranch, CA 91381 www.cinemarineteam.com
(Camera and Picture Boats)

Dennis Conner Sports, Inc. (619) 523-5131
2907 Shelter Island Dr., Ste. 105 FAX (619) 523-5279
San Diego, CA 92106 www.stars-stripes.com
(America's Cup Sailboats & Camera Boats)

Elite Yacht Charters (310) 552-7968
468 N. Camden Dr., Ste. 200 FAX (310) 553-2551
Beverly Hills, CA 90210 www.eliteyacht.com

Executive Yacht Management, Inc. (310) 306-2555
644 Venice Blvd. FAX (310) 306-1147
Marina del Rey, CA 90291 www.yacht-management.com
(Camera, Picture and Support Boats)

Hornblower Cruises & Events (310) 301-6000
Fisherman's Village, 13755 Fiji Way www.hornblower.com
Marina del Rey, CA 90292

Instinct Charters (949) 470-3800
24182 Okeechobee Ln. FAX (949) 470-3800
Lake Forest, CA 92630

M. G. Marine (310) 645-0196 (310) 650-8913
8324 Altavan Ave.
Los Angeles, CA 90045

Motion Picture Marine (310) 822-1100
616 Venice Blvd. FAX (310) 822-2679
Marina del Rey, CA 90291
www.motionpicturemarine.com
(Camera and Picture Boats & Nautical Props)

Nautical Decor Newport Trading Co. (949) 723-9696 (949) 673-7353
2810 Newport Blvd.
Newport Beach, CA 92663
(Nautical Props)

Nautical Film Services (562) 594-9276 (310) 729-6920
P.O. Box 50066 FAX (562) 594-9242
Long Beach, CA 90815 www.nauticalfilmservices.com

Naval Historical Education Foundation (949) 300-5616 (949) 500-9966
1727 Superior Ave. FAX (949) 548-3921
Costa Mesa, CA 92627 www.jollyboats.org
(Jolly Boats, Long Boats & Naval Equipment/Supplies)

Jimmy O'Connell (310) 968-0549
(310) 452-5774
306 Market St., Ste. A FAX **(310) 452-5774**
Venice, CA 90291

Offshore Grip Marine, Inc. (310) 547-3515
23852 Pacific Coast Hwy, Ste. 764 FAX **(310) 943-3328**
Malibu, CA 90265 **www.offshoregripmarine.com**
(Barges, Camera and Picture Boats, Inflatables, Jet Skis, Kayaks, Marine Props, Nautical Equipment/Supplies, Nautical Props, Powerboats, Sailboats, Submarines, Support Boats, Tugboats & Yachts)

Picture Vehicles Unlimited (818) 766-2200
25111 Rye Canyon Loop FAX **(818) 766-2011**
Santa Clarita, CA 91321 **www.picturevehicles.com**

Pine Knot Concessions (909) 866-2628
(909) 866-9512
41725 Big Bear Blvd. FAX **(909) 866-4485**
Ste. C, P.O. Box 1916 **www.pineknotlanding.com**
Big Bear Lake, CA 92315
(Picture Boats)

Premiere Yacht Charters (619) 410-5222
(619) 808-2822
1380 Harbor Island Dr. **www.premiereyachtcharters.com**
San Diego, CA 92101
(Barges, Camera/Picture Boats, Canoes, Charters, Charts, Inflatables, Jet Skis, Kayaks, KiteBoards, Maps, Marine Props, Nautical Equipment/Supplies, Nautical Props, Powerboats, Sailboats, Submarines, Support Boats, Surfboards, Tugboats, White Water Rafts & Yachts)

Privateer Lynx (866) 446-5969
(949) 274-5785
(Early 19th Century Tallship) FAX **(949) 723-1958**
www.privateerlynx.org

The Ronin Company (310) 770-3090
4712 Admiralty Way, Ste. 390 FAX **(818) 788-9023**
Marina del Rey, CA 90292 **www.roninyachtcharters.com**
(Sailboats, Sport Cruisers & Yachts)

SeaMist Skippers of Marina del Rey (310) 398-8830
(800) 398-8830
FAX **(310) 821-6786**
www.seamist-skippers.com

Ship's Trader (818) 884-9088
21235 San Miguel St. **www.antiquesofadventure.com**
Woodland Hills, CA 91364
(Charters & Nautical Props)

Studio Sea Management, Inc. (310) 276-8158
(818) 519-4399
P.O. Box 15368 FAX **(888) 297-5947**
Beverly Hills, CA 90209
(Camera and Picture Boats)

Capt. Troy Waters (310) 713-9193
FAX **(310) 943-3328**
(Barges, Camera/Picture Boats, Inflatables, Jet Skis, Marine Props, Nautical Props, Powerboats, Sailboats, Submarines, Support Boats, Tugboats & Yachts)

West Coast Water Tenders (661) 250-2585
(661) 510-8128
FAX **(661) 250-2584**
www.westcoasth20.com

All Powder Coating/Waag (818) 989-5008
16000 Strathern FAX (818) 989-5226
Van Nuys, CA 91406 www.waag.com

Alpine Carpet One (310) 773-3422
3961 S. Sepulveda Blvd. www.alpinecarpetone.com
Culver City, CA 90230

ALSA Corporation (323) 581-5200
2640 E. 37th St. FAX (323) 589-4400
Vernon, CA 90058 www.alsacorp.com
(Chrome Finishing)

Anawalt Lumber Co. (323) 464-1600
1001 N. Highland Ave. FAX (323) 464-3997
Hollywood, CA 90038 www.anawaltlumber.com

Anawalt Lumber Co. (818) 769-4421
11000 Burbank Blvd. FAX (818) 769-1279
North Hollywood, CA US 91601 www.anawaltlumber.com

Anawalt Lumber Co. (310) 652-6202
641 N. Robertson Blvd. FAX (310) 652-3010
West Hollywood, CA 90069 www.anawaltlumber.com

Anawalt Lumber Co. (310) 478-0324
11060 W. Pico Blvd. FAX (310) 478-1916
Los Angeles, CA 90064 www.anawaltlumber.com

Andrews Powder Coating, Inc. (818) 700-1030
9801 Independence Ave. FAX (818) 700-0904
Chatsworth, CA 91311 www.powdercoater.com
(Metal Finishing)

Angel's Onyx (818) 998-4549
(805) 522-3346
P.O. Box 941585 www.angelsonyx.com
Simi Valley, CA 93094
(Cultured Marble & Onyx)

Astek Wallcovering, Inc. (818) 901-9876
(800) 432-7930
15924 Arminta St. FAX (818) 901-9891
Van Nuys, CA 91406 www.astekwallcovering.com
(Custom and Period Wall Coverings, Window Films & Wood Veneers)

ATC Distributing Corporation (818) 982-0514
(800) 445-6759
12110 Sherman Way FAX (818) 982-8932
North Hollywood, CA 91605
(Formica, Laminating, Metals & Wood Veneers)

Aul Pipe Tubing and Steel (323) 267-1200
2701 Bonnie Beach Pl. FAX (323) 267-1258
Los Angeles, CA 90023

B & B Hardware (310) 390-9413
12450 W. Washington Blvd. FAX (310) 390-1625
Los Angeles, CA 90066

B & T Industrial Supply, Inc. (818) 982-3475
13008 Sherman Way FAX (818) 982-3624
North Hollywood, CA 91605 www.btindustrial.com

Baller Hardware (323) 665-4149
www.ballerhardware.com

Bobco Metals Company (213) 748-5171
(800) 262-2605
2000 S. Alameda St. FAX (213) 748-5824
Los Angeles, CA 90058 www.bobcometal.com

Borrmann Metal Center (818) 846-7171
(800) 801-2677
110 W. Olive Ave. FAX (818) 846-9347
Burbank, CA 91502 www.borrmannmetalcenter.com

Bourget Flagstone Co. (310) 829-4010
1810 Colorado Ave. FAX (310) 829-6261
Santa Monica, CA 90404 www.bourgetbros.com
(Stone)

California Do It Center (818) 845-8301
(818) 407-3888
3221 W. Magnolia Blvd. FAX (818) 846-9214
Burbank, CA 91505 www.doitcenter.com

California Do It Center (805) 497-2753
3775 Thousand Oaks Blvd. FAX (805) 497-9289
Thousand Oaks, CA 91360 www.doitcenter.com

California Panel & Veneer (562) 926-5834
14055 Artesia Blvd. FAX (562) 926-3139
Cerritos, CA 90703 www.calpanel.com
(Formica & Plywood)

California Quarry Products (661) 942-3992
(Bulk Landscape Materials)

Catalina Paint (818) 347-7775
6941 Topanga Canyon Blvd. FAX (818) 347-7632
Canoga Park, CA 91303 www.catalinapaint.com

Catalina Paint (818) 772-8888
8814 Reseda Blvd. www.catalinapaint.com
Northridge, CA 91324

Catalina Paint (818) 765-2629
7107 Radford Ave. FAX (818) 764-7065
North Hollywood, CA 91605 www.catalinapaint.com

Culver City Industrial Hardware (310) 398-1251
5429 S. Sepulveda Blvd. www.culverhardware.com
Culver City, CA 90230

Decorator's Laminating Service (323) 933-5877
(Coating & Laminating) FAX (323) 934-8476

Design Hardware (323) 930-1330
6053 W. Third St. FAX (323) 930-0459
Los Angeles, CA 90036 www.designhardware.com
(Bathroom Fixtures & Door Hardware)

Dunn-Edwards (323) 464-4157
(800) 735-4632
FAX (323) 464-1607
www.dunnedwards.com

Emser Tile (323) 650-2000
(323) 650-2010
8431 Santa Monica Blvd. FAX (323) 650-1589
Los Angeles, CA 90069 www.emsertile.com
(Granite, Marble, Slate & Tile)

Expo Design Center (310) 824-8400
10861 Weyburn Ave. www.expo.com
Los Angeles, CA 90024

Expo Design Center (858) 974-0600
7803 Othello Ave. www.expo.com
San Diego, CA 92111

Expo Design Center (310) 921-1400
1519 Hawthorne Blvd. www.expo.com
Redondo Beach, CA 90278

Fox Studios (310) 369-2528
(310) 369-4636
Studio Supply, 10201 W. Pico Blvd. FAX (310) 369-4078
Los Angeles, CA 90035 www.foxstudios.com
(Custom Doors and Windows & Wood Moulding)

Frazee Paint Co. (323) 467-2468
(800) 477-9991
(Color Matching) FAX (323) 467-7834
www.frazeepaint.com

Harters Distributors (818) 899-9917
(Formica)

The Home Depot (818) 246-9600
(800) 553-3199
5040 San Fernando Rd.
Glendale, CA 91204
www.homedepot.com

The Home Depot (310) 822-3330
12975 W. Jefferson Blvd.
Los Angeles, CA 90066
www.homedepot.com

The Home Depot (323) 461-3303
5600 Sunset Blvd.
Los Angeles, CA 90028
FAX (213) 860-3147
www.homedepot.com

The Home Depot (818) 764-9600
11600 Sherman Way
North Hollywood, CA 91605
www.homedepot.com

The Home Depot (805) 983-3823
(805) 983-0653
401 W. Esplanade Dr.
Oxnard, CA 93030
www.homedepot.com

The Home Depot (818) 716-9141
6345 Variel Ave.
Woodland Hills, CA 91367
www.homedepot.com

The Home Depot (858) 277-8910
4255 Genesee
San Diego, CA 92117
www.homedepot.com

The Home Depot (619) 280-0230
5920 Fairmount Ave.
San Diego, CA 92120
www.homedepot.com

Industrial Metal Supply Co. (818) 729-3333
(800) 339-6033
8300 San Fernando Rd.
Sun Valley, CA 91352
FAX (818) 729-3334
www.industrialmetalsupply.com

Jeffrey Stevens (310) 652-3050
Pacific Design Center
8687 Melrose Ave., Ste. B404
West Hollywood, CA 90069
(Wallcoverings)
FAX (310) 652-8230
www.jeffreystevens.com

Koontz Hardware (310) 652-0123
8914 Santa Monica Blvd.
West Hollywood, CA 90069
FAX (310) 652-7123
www.koontz.com

Linoleum City (323) 469-0063
(800) 559-2489
4849 Santa Monica Blvd.
Hollywood, CA 90029
(Carpeting, Linoleum & Tile)
FAX (323) 465-5866
www.linoleumcity.com

Mann Brothers Paint (323) 936-5168
758 N. La Brea Ave.
Hollywood, CA 90038
FAX (323) 936-1980
www.mannbrothers.com

Mark's Paints (818) 766-3949
4830 Vineland Ave.
North Hollywood, CA 91601
FAX (818) 766-0068
www.markspaint.com

NAC Co. (805) 376-0206
(805) 405-7337
1772-J E. Avenida de Los Arboles
Thousand Oaks, CA 91362
FAX (805) 376-8407
www.naceffects.com

NBC Universal Property (818) 777-2784
100 Universal City Plaza
Universal City, CA 91608
FAX (818) 866-1543
www.filmmakersdestination.com

Newhall Paint Store (661) 259-3454
FAX (661) 259-5864
www.newhallpaintstore.com

Nova Color Artists Acrylic Paint (310) 204-6900
5894 Blackwelder St.
Culver City, CA 90232
FAX (310) 838-2094
www.novacolorpaint.com

Orchard Supply Hardware/OSH (818) 557-2755
641 N. Victory Blvd.
Burbank, CA 91502
FAX (818) 557-2753
www.osh.com

Orchard Supply Hardware/OSH (323) 871-1707
5525 Sunset Blvd.
Hollywood, CA 90028
FAX (323) 871-5985
www.osh.com

Orchard Supply Hardware/OSH (310) 571-3838
(310) 571-3839
2020 S. Bundy Dr.
West Los Angeles, CA 90025
FAX (310) 571-3841
www.osh.com

Reliable Hardware Company (818) 753-8558
11319 Vanowen St.
North Hollywood, CA 91605
FAX (818) 753-4778
www.reliablehardware.com

Rompage Hardware (323) 467-2129
FAX (323) 467-1639

Rose Brand (818) 505-6290
(800) 360-5056
10616 Lanark St.
Sun Valley, CA 91352
FAX (818) 505-6293
www.rosebrand.com

Scenery West (818) 765-8661
11461 Hart St.
North Hollywood, CA 91605
FAX (818) 765-5495
www.scenerywest.com

Sepulveda Building Materials (310) 217-0134
359 E. Gardena Blvd.
Gardena, CA 90248
(Landscape Materials & Masonry)
FAX (310) 217-0193
www.sepulveda.com

SOS Metals (310) 217-8848
FAX (310) 217-8088
www.sosmetals.com

Southland Lumber & Supply Co., Inc. (323) 776-3530
(310) 641-8150
FAX (310) 641-5243

Spectra Paint Center (626) 793-5155
456 S. Rosemead Blvd.
Pasadena, CA 91107
FAX (626) 793-6503
www.spectrapaint.com

Spectra Paint Center (818) 786-5610
7615 Balboa Blvd.
Van Nuys, CA 91406
FAX (818) 786-5433
www.spectrapaint.com

Sprayco Service Center (323) 934-5669
1198 S. La Brea Ave.
Los Angeles, CA 90019
(Paint & Painting Equipment)
FAX (323) 934-3025
www.spraycoservicecenter.com

Spraylat Corporation (310) 559-2335
FAX (310) 836-6094
www.spraylat.com

Stock Building Supply (818) 842-2177
640 N. Victory Blvd.
Burbank, CA 91502
FAX (818) 842-2679
www.stocksupply.com

Stock Building Supply (323) 469-1951
6641 Santa Monica Blvd.
Hollywood, CA 90038
FAX (323) 469-5027
www.stocksupplly.com

Stock Building Supply (323) 478-2200
3250 San Fernando Rd.
Los Angeles, CA 90065
FAX (323) 478-2201
www.stocksupply.com

Stock Building Supply (310) 390-3621
3860 Grandview Blvd.
Los Angeles, CA 90066
FAX (310) 881-2000
www.stocksupply.com

Stock Building Supply (818) 982-6046
(800) 478-3779
7151 Lankershim Blvd.
North Hollywood, CA 91605
FAX (818) 982-9564
www.stocksupply.com

Tashman Screens & Hardware (323) 656-7028
FAX (323) 656-0213
www.tashmans.com

Tell Steel
(562) 435-0821
(800) 734-8355
FAX (562) 437-6894
www.tellsteel.com

TTS Products (323) 268-1347
2822 E. Olympic Blvd. FAX (323) 268-8093
Los Angeles, CA 90023

The Wallpaper Bin (818) 407-1831
9250 Reseda Blvd. FAX (818) 407-1832
Northridge, CA 91324 www.wallpaperbinla.com

Warner Bros. Studio Facilities - Mill Store (818) 954-4444
4000 Warner Blvd., Bldg. 44 FAX (818) 954-5753
Burbank, CA 91522 www.wbsf.com

West Coast Sign Supply (213) 487-6666
1700 W. Pico Blvd. FAX (213) 487-6660
Los Angeles, CA 90015 www.westcoastsignsupply.com

West Coast Sign Supply (818) 785-8777
14332 Calvert St. FAX (818) 785-8778
Van Nuys, CA 91411 www.westcoastsignsupply.com

Wildfire, Inc. - Lighting & Visual Effects
(310) 755-6780
(800) 937-8065
2908 Oregon Court, Ste. G1 FAX (310) 755-6781
Torrance, CA 90503 www.wildfirefx.com
(Fixtures & Paints/Painting Equipment)

Zal Industrial
(323) 262-0259
(800) 327-8289
4905 Telegraph Rd. FAX (323) 262-6050
Los Angeles, CA 90022 www.zalindustrial.com

Abbey Events
(310) 900-0099
(323) 201-4200
1520 S. Maple Ave.
FAX (323) 201-4299
Montebello, CA 90640
www.abbeyeventservices.com

Action Portable Air Conditioning (888) 508-3394
(Tents)
FAX (888) 508-3394

Anytime - Hollywood (323) 461-8483
755 N. Lillian Way
FAX (323) 461-2338
Hollywood, CA 90038
www.anytime-rentals.com
(Canopies)

Anza Tents
(310) 320-6200
(888) 637-8086
375 Maple Ave.
FAX (310) 781-8227
Torrance, CA 90503
www.anzatents.com
(Tents)

Apache Rental Group
(818) 842-9944
(818) 842-9875
3910 W. Magnolia Blvd.
FAX (818) 842-9269
Burbank, CA 91505
www.apacherentalgroup.com
(Canopies)

Atomic Production Supplies (818) 566-8811
2621 N. Ontario St.
FAX (818) 566-8311
Burbank, CA 91504
www.atomicproductionsupplies.com
(Canopies)

Berlyn Enterprises/Pro Canopy
(818) 701-7100
(888) 404-7750
9612 Owensmouth Ave.
FAX (818) 349-0500
Chatsworth, CA 91311
www.procanopy.com

Camera Essentials
(323) 666-8936
(323) 666-8875
2620 1/2 Hyperion Ave.
FAX (323) 666-0214
Los Angeles, CA 90027
www.cameraessentials.com
(Tents)

Castex Rentals (323) 462-1468
1044 Cole Ave.
FAX (323) 462-3719
Hollywood, CA 90038
www.castexrentals.com
(Canopies)

Chester's Circus & Carnival Equipment
(323) 751-3486
(951) 233-6014
(Canvas Tenting)
FAX (323) 778-2025

Classic Tents (310) 328-5060
540 Hawaii Ave.
www.classictentrentals.com
Torrance, CA 90503
(Tents)

Creative Inflatables
(626) 579-4454
(800) 446 3528
9872 Rush St.
FAX (626) 579-5561
South El Monte, CA 91733
www.creativeinflatables.com
(Tents)

DeWayne Events (661) 251-4342
16520 Diver St.
FAX (661) 251-2488
Canyon Country, CA 91387

Dortons, Inc.
(323) 751-3486
(951) 685-6014
6319 Eucalyptus
FAX (323) 778-2025
Riverside, CA 92509
(Tents)

Eide Industries, Inc.
(562) 402-8335
(800) 422-6827
16215 Piuma Ave.
FAX (562) 924-2233
Cerritos, CA 90703
www.eideindustries.com
(Canopies)

Exclusive Tent Rentals
(626) 966-3817
(323) 377-0650
(Tents)
FAX (626) 966-0137
www.exclusivetentrentals.com

Hollywood Tentworks (877) 883-3131
10244 Norris Ave.
FAX (877) 883-3132
Pacoima, CA 91331
www.tentworks.com

International E-Z UP, Inc. (951) 781-0843
1601 Iowa Ave.
FAX (951) 781-0586
Riverside, CA 92507
www.ezup.com
(Tents)

Kayam Theatre and Concert Tent Company (213) 484-5010
831 Gretna Green Way, Ste. 104
www.kayam.co.uk
Los Angeles, CA 90049
(Tents)

L.A. Circus
(323) 751-3486
(951) 685-6014
7531 La Salle Ave.
FAX (323) 778-2025
Los Angeles, CA 90047
(Tents)

Line 204 (323) 960-0113
1034 N. Seward St.
FAX (323) 960-0163
Hollywood, CA 90038
www.line204.com
(Canopies)

Miller Production Services (310) 287-0466
3520 Helms Ave.
FAX (310) 287-0467
Culver City, CA 90232
(Canopies)

Out of Frame Production Rentals (323) 462-1898
1126 N. Citrus Ave.
FAX (323) 462-1897
Hollywood, CA 90038
www.outofframela.com
(Canopies)

The Production Truck, Inc. (818) 459-0425
711 Ruberta Ave.
FAX (818) 459-0427
Glendale, CA 91201
www.theproductiontruck.com
(Tents)

Quixote Studios (323) 960-9191
1000 N. Cahuenga Blvd.
FAX (323) 960-3366
Los Angeles, CA 90038
www.quixote.com
(Canopies)

Rock Bottom Rentals
(310) 315-2600
(800) 794-5444
1310 Westwood Blvd.
FAX (310) 582-1178
Los Angeles, CA 90024
www.rockbottomrentals.com
(Canopies)

Set Stuff, Inc. (323) 993-9500
1105 N. Sycamore Ave.
FAX (323) 993-9506
Hollywood, CA 90038
www.setstuffrentals.com
(Tents)

Skye Rentals (323) 462-5934
920 N. Citrus Ave.
FAX (323) 462-5935
Hollywood, CA 90038
www.skyerentals.com

Studio Air Conditioning, Inc. (818) 222-4143
5171 N. Douglas Fir Rd., Ste. 6
FAX (818) 222-2092
Calabasas, CA 91302
www.studioair.com
(Tents)

Tent Kings of Los Angeles
(818) 720-5126
(310) 880-5128
3238 N. San Fernando Blvd.
FAX (818) 557-8320
Burbank, CA 91504
www.tentkings.com
(Tents)

A Wynning Event
(310) 279-5114
(310) 729-2590
433 N. Camden Dr., Ste. 400
FAX (310) 274-5105
Beverly Hills, CA 90210
www.awynningevent.com

Xpendable Rentals (323) 656-0905
5925 Santa Monica Blvd.
FAX (323) 375-1711
Hollywood, CA 90038
www.xpendablerentals.com
(Canopies)

All Powder Coating/Waag (818) 989-5008
16000 Strathern FAX (818) 989-5226
Van Nuys, CA 91406 www.waag.com

Automatrix Effects/David Waine (323) 469-0088
2623 N. San Fernando Rd. FAX (323) 395-0570
Los Angeles, CA 90065 www.automatrixfx.com

B and R Scenery, Inc. (805) 388-8555
486 Constitution Ave. FAX (805) 388-9996
Camarillo, CA 93012 www.bandrscenery.com
(Car Manipulation, Lifts & Turntables)

Tony Berardinelli (818) 506-5598
FAX (818) 506-5598

The Big American Dream Co. (818) 504-2404
11174 Fleetwood St. FAX (818) 504-2458
Sun Valley, CA 91352 www.bestbadco.com

Camera Ready Cars (714) 444-1700
11161 Slater Ave. FAX (714) 444-0700
Fountain Valley, CA 92708 www.metalcrafters.com
(Automotive Display Stands)

Cantos Collection (310) 780-6002 (213) 303-2228
P.O. Box 34813 FAX (213) 558-3745
Los Angeles, CA 90034 www.cantoscollection.com

Coach Engineering/Dave Weiner (818) 563-2399 (818) 406-5130
805 S. San Fernando Rd. FAX (818) 563-1399
Burbank, CA 91502 www.coachengineering.com
(Buses)

Customs by Eddie Paul, A Division of EP Industries, Inc. (310) 643-8515 (310) 259-0542
2305 Utah Ave. FAX (310) 643-8520
El Segundo, CA 90245 www.deadlinetv.net
(Automotive Display Stands, Car Manipulation & Car Mounts)

DH Automotive (323) 842-8393
www.dhautoworks.com

DKO Industries, Inc. (818) 435-2159 (818) 652-8854
8801 Whitaker Ave. FAX (818) 936-0194
Northridge, CA 91343

Evanspeed (909) 985-6308
(Dynamometer Equipment) FAX (909) 985-6308

Executive Productions (310) 456-8833
3951 Ridgemont Dr. FAX (310) 456-5692
Malibu, CA 90265

Focus on Cars (310) 762-1370
20434 S. Santa Fe Ave. FAX (310) 763-7110
Long Beach, CA 90810 www.southbaystudios.com

Ghostlight Industries Inc. (818) 898-1938
956 Griswold Ave. FAX (818) 898-1948
San Fernando, CA 91340 www.ghostlightla.com
(Buses, Car Manipulation, Car Mounts & Lifts)

Hollywood Picture Cars/Scott Bosés (323) 466-2277
1028 N. La Brea Ave. FAX (323) 466-6541
Hollywood, CA 90038 www.hollywoodpicturecars.com

Hot Air Airbrushing (661) 255-2959 (661) 313-5437
FAX (661) 255-2959

Industrial Artists (626) 355-1913
803 Woodland Dr.
Sierra Madre, CA 91024

Jeffries Automotive Styling (323) 851-5678 (818) 980-5367
3077 Cahuenga Blvd.
Los Angeles, CA 90068

Kit Car/Kit Riedel (818) 888-0900 (818) 404-7936

L.A. Motorsports (818) 222-6954 (877) 526-6867
FAX (866) 294-3266
www.lamsports.com

L.A. Prep, Inc. (562) 595-8886
2700 Signal Pkwy www.laprepinc.com
Signal Hill, CA 90806
(Automotive Display Stands, Car Manipulation, Car Mounts, Lifts & Turntables)

Mr. Vintage Machine (213) 369-0281
www.mistervintagemachine.com

NAC Co. (805) 376-0206 (805) 405-7337
1772-J E. Avenida de Los Arboles FAX (805) 376-8407
Thousand Oaks, CA 91362 www.naceffects.com

Willy Nemeth/Good Medicine Hat (541) 840-3366 (541) 476-0598
(Car Mounts)

The Studios at Paramount (323) 956-5140
The Studios at Paramount FAX (323) 862-2325
Manufacturing and Special Effects
5555 Melrose Ave.
Hollywood, CA 90038
www.thestudiosatparamount.com

Performance Filmworks, Inc. (310) 721-4812 (800) 360-3562
FAX (310) 313-4875
www.performancefilmworks.com

Picture Car Warehouse (213) 534-3775
LA Center Studios FAX (213) 534-3779
1201 W. Fifth St., Box 34 www.picturecarwarehouse.net
Los Angeles, CA 90017

Picture Vehicles Unlimited (818) 766-2200
25111 Rye Canyon Loop FAX (818) 766-2011
Santa Clarita, CA 91321 www.picturevehicles.com

Precision Prep (818) 504-6590
9828 Glenoaks Blvd. FAX (818) 504-6623
Sun Valley, CA 91352

Promotional Products (619) 258-9010 (800) 258-9010
10062 Vista Parque FAX (888) 258-9010
Lakeside, CA 92040 www.vehicledisplays.com
(Automotive Display Stands)

Pursuit Systems Inc. (818) 579-7250
7255 Radford Ave. www.pursuitsystems.com
North Hollywood, CA 91605

Rainbow Industries (818) 982-9447 (818) 982-9457
7355 Fulton Ave. www.rainbowindustries.ws
North Hollywood, CA 91605

Rick's Stunt Car Service/ Motion Picture Driving Clinic (818) 341-9526 (818) 796-1497
8560 Variel Ave.
Canoga Park, CA 91304

Schwartz Oil Company, Inc. (661) 259-4000 (818) 365-9214
27241 Henry Mayo Dr. FAX (661) 257-0137
Valencia, CA 91355 www.socifuel.com
(Mobile Refueling Systems & Studio Fueling Trucks)

Shelly Ward Enterprises (818) 255-5850
FAX (818) 255-5450
www.shellywardent.com

Sierra Mobile Window Tinting (818) 376-0661 (661) 251-9536
7837 Sepulveda Blvd., Ste. 14 FAX (818) 376-0655
Van Nuys, CA 91405 www.sierratint.com

Sunset Glass Tinting (310) 391-3400 (323) 735-7713
4859 Slauson Ave., Ste. 288 www.sunsettinting.com
Los Angeles, CA 90056

Swift Car Mounts/Bruce Swift (818) 341-4537 (818) 808-9500
8800 Winnetka Ave. www.home.earthlink.net/~bswift52
Northridge, CA 91324
(Car Mounts)

Unique Movie Cars, Inc. (888) 345-6227
FAX (702) 566-6194

Vehicle Effects (818) 355-2676 (818) 846-7506
909 N. Victory Blvd. FAX (818) 846-7576
Burbank, CA 91502 www.vehicleeffects.com

Jack Weimer (818) 504-4131 (818) 448-2000
10949 Tuxford St.
Sun Valley, CA 91352

Color-Correct Props

Color Correct, USA (310) 904-0500
3644 Eastham Dr.
Culver City, CA 90232

Comp 24 (818) 562-6676
(818) 621-4632
1919 Empire Ave. FAX (818) 842-4623
Burbank, CA 91504 **www.comp24.com**

Dennis Curtin Studio, Inc. (310) 827-8850
1919 Empire Ave. FAX (818) 842-4623
Burbank, CA 91504 **www.denniscurtin.com**

So Cal Production Source (310) 699-2787
FAX (310) 618-0129
www.scpsunlimited.com

ABC Studios - Costume Department (818) 553-4800
545 Circle Seven Dr. FAX **(818) 545-0468**
Glendale, CA 91201

Action Sets and Props/ WonderWorks (818) 992-8811
7231 Remmet Ave. FAX **(818) 347-4330**
Canoga Park, CA 91303 **www.wonderworksweb.com**
(Spacesuits)

Alek Adorian (323) 937-4416
7222 Melrose Ave. **www.alekadorian.com**
Los Angeles, CA 90046
(Dance and Evening Gowns, Rental & Theater Costume Construction and Design)

Alva's Dance and Theatrical Supply (310) 519-1314
1417 W. Eighth St. FAX **(310) 831-6110**
San Pedro, CA 90732 **www.alvas.com**
(Dance Costume Rentals)

Anatomorphex/The Sculpture Studio (818) 768-2880
8210 Lankershim Blvd., Ste. 14 **www.anatomorphex.com**
North Hollywood, CA 91605
(Full Costume Construction)

Arteffex/Dann O'Quinn (818) 506-5358
911 Mayo St. FAX **(323) 255-4599**
Los Angeles, CA 90042 **www.acfxo.com**
(Animal/Character Costumes, Custom Costume Construction, Mascots, Masks & Special FX Costumes)

Baron California Hats (818) 563-3025
1619 W. Burbank Blvd. FAX **(818) 563-4025**
Burbank, CA 91506 **www.baronhats.com**
(Rentals)

Bittersweet Butterfly Fancy Lingerie and Flowers (323) 660-4303
1406 Micheltorena FAX **(323) 665-9114**
Los Angeles, CA 90026 **www.bittersweetbutterfly.com**
(Contemporary, Evening Gowns, Rentals, Undergarments, Vintage & Wedding Gowns)

Bon Choix Couture, Inc. (818) 729-9994
1223 S. Flower St. FAX **(818) 729-9995**
Burbank, CA 91502 **www.bonchoixcouture.com**
(Beading, Construction, Contemporary, Custom, Dancewear, Embroidery, Full Costume Construction, Full Costume Design, Furs, Futuristic Costuming, Gloves, Horseback Riding Apparel, Knitwear, Leather, Military, Period–Present, Police, Special FX Costumes, Undergarments, Uniforms & Western Wear)

Broken Horn (626) 337-4266
1022 Leorita St. FAX **(626) 337-4283**
Baldwin Park, CA 91706 **www.brokenhornsaddlery.com**
(English and Western Riding Apparel and Tack)

Lynda Burdick (323) 662-7612
(Hats) FAX **(323) 662-7612**
www.lyndahats.com

Poppy Cannon-Reese (310) 477-5116
(707) 292-6957
www.poppycannonreese.com

Caravan West Productions (661) 268-8300
35660 Jayhawker Rd. FAX **(661) 268-8301**
Agua Dulce, CA 91390 **www.caravanwest.com**
(1860–1910 Vintage Western Wear)

Chic Little Devil Style House (310) 403-6929
1206 Maple Ave., 11th Fl.
Los Angeles, CA 90015
www.chiclittledevilstylehouse.com

Cinnabar (818) 842-8190
4571 Electronics Pl. FAX **(818) 842-0563**
Los Angeles, CA 90039 **www.cinnabar.com**
(Full Costume Construction and Design)

Nina Correa (310) 390-6761
(Full Costume Construction) FAX **(310) 398-3889**

Costume Rentals Corporation (818) 753-3700
11149 Vanowen St. FAX **(818) 753-3737**
North Hollywood, CA 91605 **www.costumerentalscorp.com**

Design World (323) 661-0393
(323) 896-1942
1620 N. Kingsley Dr. FAX **(323) 662-6976**
Los Angeles, CA 90027
(Full Costume Construction and Design)

Douglas White Effects (818) 785-4148
6859 Valjean Ave., Ste. 7 FAX **(818) 785-2567**
Van Nuys, CA 91406 **www.dweffects.com**

Eastern Costume Company (818) 982-3611
7243 Coldwater Canyon Ave. FAX **(818) 982-1905**
North Hollywood, CA 91605 **www.easterncostume.com**
(Beading, Construction, Contemporary, Custom, Dancewear, Design, Embroidery, Ethnic Apparel, Evening Gowns, Flight Gear, Full Costume Construction, Full Costume Design, Furs, Futuristic Costuming, Gloves, Hats, Horseback Riding Apparel, Knitwear, Leathers, Mascots, Military, Period–Present, Police, Religious Garments, Rentals, Screenprinting, Shoes/Boots, Spacesuits, Undergarments, Uniforms, Wedding Gowns & Western Wear)

An Eye 4 Detail (626) 791-7962
1044 N. Hudson Ave.
Pasadena, CA 91104
(Animal, Character and Special FX Costume Construction)

Gamila M. Fakhry-Smith (818) 506-1683
FAX (818) 506-5756
(Period–Present Sci Fi and Special FX Costume Construction and Design)

Filmmaker Production Services Company (877) 730-3772
(505) 341-1824
FAX (505) 341-1833
www.filmmakerproductionservices.com

Ⓐ **Fox Studios** (310) 369-1897
(310) 369-4636
Wardrobe Department FAX (310) 369-2487
10201 W. Pico Blvd. www.foxstudios.com
Los Angeles, CA 90035
(Contemporary, Custom & Rentals)

Francine Lecoultre Design Studio (323) 664-1636
FAX (323) 664-1676
(Period, Sculptural and Special FX Costume Construction)

Gaspar Gloves (323) 441-1986
(323) 702-7620
1224 S. San Julian St., Ste. 4 FAX (323) 227-6993
Los Angeles, CA 90015 www.gasparglov es.com

Dana Gillette (323) 874-6630
(323) 533-5078
(Construction and Design & Elvis Jumpsuits) FAX (323) 874-6630

Global Effects, Inc. (818) 503-9273
7115 Laurel Canyon Blvd. FAX (818) 503-9459
North Hollywood, CA 91605 www.globaleffects.com
(Actor Climate Systems & Futuristic, Medieval Armor, Period and Special FX Costume Construction)

Golyester Antiques (323) 931-1339
136 S. La Brea Ave.
Los Angeles, CA 90036
(Vintage Costumes and Textile Rentals)

Gregory's Tux Shop (818) 980-5480
12051 Magnolia Blvd. FAX (818) 980-5084
North Hollywood, CA 91607 www.tuxedosonline.com

James Hayes (323) 660-9892
(213) 503-0710
1832 Maltman Ave. FAX (323) 661-4287
Los Angeles, CA 90026
(Period–Present Construction and Design)

Ⓐ **The Hollywood Studio Collection** (818) 812-6068
(818) 812-6092
8841 Wilbur Ave. FAX (818) 885-7004
Northridge, CA 91324 www.backlotprops.com
(Animal/Character Costumes, Armor, Beading, Contemporary, Dancewear, Ethnic Apparel, Evening Gowns, Flight Gear, Full Costume Construction, Full Costume Design, Furs, Futuristic Costuming, Gloves, Hats, Horseback Riding Apparel, Knitwear, Leathers, Mascots, Masks, Military, Period, Period–Present, Police, Religious Garments, Rentals, Shoes/Boots, Spacesuits, Special FX Costumes, Undergarments, Uniforms, Vintage & Wedding Gowns)

Hollywood Toys & Costumes (323) 464-4444
(800) 554-3444
6600 Hollywood Blvd. FAX (323) 464-4644
Hollywood, CA 90028
www.yourhollywoodcostumes.com
(Animal Walkaround Costume Rentals)

Image Creators, Inc. (310) 710-7128
(310) 202-8286
www.imagecreators.net
(Animal, Character, Creature and Special FX Costume Construction)

J & M Costumers, Inc. (818) 760-1991
5708 Gentry Ave. FAX (818) 980-4449
North Hollywood, CA 91607 www.jmcostumers.com

Kaptain Bubble Leather (818) 353-9400
(818) 203-3835
(Leather Designer) www.bubbleleather.com

KCL Productions (310) 990-1478
(310) 739-2534
21337 Rambla Vista www.kclproductions.com
Malibu, CA 90265
(Animal/Character Costumes, Construction, Custom, Design, Full Costume Construction, Full Costume Design, Mascots, Masks, Special FX Costumes & Walk Arounds)

Kowboyz (818) 625-1926
(505) 984-1256
FAX (505) 98-7620
(Cowboy Boots, Clothing, Hats, Leathers & Vintage)

L.A. Circus (323) 751-3486
(951) 685-6014
7531 La Salle Ave. FAX (323) 778-2025
Los Angeles, CA 90047

Leahpatra Knitwear (310) 951-9095
(Knitwear) www.leahpatra.com

Louise Green Millinery Co. (310) 479-1881
1616 Cotner Ave. FAX (310) 479-2838
Los Angeles, CA 90025 www.louisegreen.com
(Custom & Period Hats)

Makeup & Effects Laboratories, Inc./MEL (818) 982-1483
7110 Laurel Canyon Blvd., Bldg. E FAX (818) 982-5712
North Hollywood, CA 91605 www.melefx.com
(Hard and Soft Walkarounds)

Margaretrose Custom Clothing Design (323) 852-4787
306 S. Edinburgh Ave. FAX (323) 852-4789
Los Angeles, CA 90048 www.margaretrosedesign.net
(Contemporary, Custom, Dancewear, Design, Evening Gowns, Full Costume Construction, Full Costume Design, Uniforms & Wedding Gowns)

Mia Gyzander Costumes, Inc. (310) 559-0570
10510 Rose Ave. FAX (310) 559-0580
Los Angeles, CA 90034 www.miagyzander.com
(Construction & Design)

Motion Picture Costumes & Supplies, Inc. (818) 557-1247
3811 Valhalla Dr. FAX (818) 557-1695
Burbank, CA 91505
(1776–Present Costumes and Uniforms)

Musotica Wear, Inc. (818) 252-7800
(213) 618-3636
3727 W. Magnolia Blvd., Ste. 452 FAX (818) 527-7803
Burbank, CA 91505 www.musotica.com
(Animal/Character Costumes, Contemporary, Custom, Dancewear, Evening Gowns, Full Costume Design, Faux Furs, Gloves, Hats, Knitwear, Leathers, Military, Police, Shoes/Boots, Special FX Costumes & Undergarments)

Muto-Little (323) 469-1618
519 N. Larchmont Blvd. FAX (323) 469-0298
Los Angeles, CA 90004
(Costume Construction)

NBC Universal Costume Department (818) 777-2722
100 Universal City Plaza FAX (818) 866-1544
Bldg. 4250/3054 www.filmmakersdestination.com
Universal City, CA 91608
(Vintage and Contemporary Clothing and Accessories)

Norcostco California Costume (818) 567-0753
(800) 220-6915
3606 W. Magnolia Blvd. FAX (818) 567-1961
Burbank, CA 91505 www.norcostco.com
(Theatrical Costume Rentals)

One Night Affair (310) 474-7808
1726 S. Sepulveda Blvd. www.onenightaffair.com
West Los Angeles, CA 90025
(Designer Evening and Wedding Gown Rentals)

Susan Ottevanger (805) 223-5870
709 W. Channel Islands Blvd., Ste. 34 www.seewater.com
Port Hueneme, CA 93041
(Custom Costume Construction)

Palace Costume and Prop Co. (323) 651-5458
835 N. Fairfax Ave. FAX (323) 658-7133
Los Angeles, CA 90046 www.palacecostume.com
(1850s–Present Costume Rentals)

Pat Brymer Creations (323) 259-0400
136 N. Avenue 61, Ste. 102 FAX (323) 259-0358
Los Angeles, CA 90042 www.pbcreations.com
(Animal/Character Costumes & Custom)

Producers Air Force (818) 845-5970
(818) 795-7463
One Orange Grove Terrace FAX (818) 845-4033
Burbank, CA 91501 www.producersairforce.com
(Flight Gear)

Prop Masters, Inc. (818) 846-3915
2721 W. Empire Ave. FAX (818) 846-1278
Burbank, CA 91504 www.propmastersinc.com
(Armor, Character Walkarounds, Space Suits & Special FX Costumes)

Repeat Performance (323) 938-0609
318 N. La Brea Ave. FAX (323) 938-2235
Los Angeles, CA 90036 www.rpcostumerentals.com
(1800s–1960s Authentic Period Costume Rentals)

reVamp (213) 488-3387
834 S. Broadway, Ste. 1200 FAX (775) 366-0036
Los Angeles, CA 90014 www.revampvintage.com

Silvia's Costumes (323) 666-0680
(323) 666-0702
4964 Hollywood Blvd. FAX (323) 666-6397
Los Angeles, CA 90027 www.silviascostumes.com
(Hand Embroidery & Period–Present Costume Construction and Design)

Somper Furs (310) 273-5262
2270 W. Washington Blvd. FAX (310) 273-7270
Los Angeles, CA 90018 www.somperfurs.com
(Cashmere Capes, Furs & Leathers)

Sony Pictures Studios (310) 244-7260
(310) 244-5995
5300 Alla Rd. www.sonypicturesstudios.com
Los Angeles, CA 90066

Denyse Specktor/The Big Yarn (805) 267-0909
1237 S. Victoria Ave.
Oxnard, CA 93035

Sticks & Stones (818) 352-9538
FAX (818) 352-9538
www.sticksandstonesfx.com
(Full Costume Construction and Design; No Rentals)

Super Suit Factory (213) 700-1827
472 S. El Molino Ave., Ste. 9 www.supersuitfactory.com
Pasadena, CA 91101
(Animal/Character and Special FX Constumes)

Susan Nininger Studio (323) 222-6217
(213) 819-0640
(Contemporary, Period and Sculptural Costume Construction)

Suss Design (323) 954-9637
7352 Beverly Blvd. FAX (323) 954-9674
Los Angeles, CA 90036 www.sussdesign.com
(Knitwear)

Sword & The Stone (818) 562-6548
723 N. Victory Blvd. FAX (818) 562-6549
Burbank, CA 91502 www.swordandstone.com
(Armor, Chain Mail and Leather Costumes)

Total Fabrication, Inc. (818) 375-1022
(877) 362-6322
FAX (818) 375-1023
www.totalfab.com
(Armor, Animal and Character Costume Construction and Design, Full Costume Construction, Full Costume Design, Futuristic Costuming, Mascots, Masks & Special FX Costumes)

United American Costume/ American Costume (818) 764-2239
12980 Raymer St. FAX (818) 765-7614
North Hollywood, CA 91605
(1700s–Present Costumes and Uniforms)

United Pacific Studios (213) 489-2001
729 E. Temple St. FAX (213) 489-2098
Los Angeles, CA 90012 www.unitedpacificstudios.com

Ursula's Costumes, Inc. (310) 582-8230
(310) 582-8231
2516 Wilshire Blvd. FAX (310) 582-8233
Santa Monica, CA 90403 www.ursulascostumes.com
(Costumes, Makeup, Masks & Wigs)

Candace Walters (877) 232-3455
(928) 300-6636
FAX (928) 282-0786
www.victoriancowgirl.com
(Period–Present Costume Construction and Design)

Warner Bros. Studio Facilities - Costume Department (818) 954-1297
(800) 375-3085
4000 Warner Blvd., Bldg. 153 FAX (818) 954-3685
Burbank, CA 91522 www.wbsf.com

Ellene Warren (310) 559-5363
(Beading, Custom Knit and Crochet, Full Costume Design, Knitwear; No Rentals)

Western Costume Co. (818) 760-0902
11041 Vanowen St. FAX (818) 508-2190
North Hollywood, CA 91605
www.lawardrobesupplies.com
(Character, Contemporary, Military & Period)

Aero Shade (323) 655-2411
FAX (323) 655-3180
www.aeroshadeco.com

American Screen & Window Coverings, Inc. (626) 453-0888
1903 Central Ave. FAX (626) 453-0768
South El Monte, CA 91733

Black Sheep Enterprises (818) 909-2299
15745 Stagg St. FAX (818) 909-2288
Van Nuys, CA 91406 www.blacksheepent.net
(Theatrical Drapery Fabrication and Rigging)

Blindsgalore.com (877) 702-5463
6555 Nancy Ridge Dr., Ste. 100 FAX (858) 643-9282
San Diego, CA 92121 www.blindsgalore.com

Dazian Rentals (818) 287-3811
(877) 232-9426
7120 Case Ave. FAX (818) 287-3812
North Hollywood, CA 91605 www.dazian.com

Eide Industries, Inc. (562) 402-8335
(800) 422-6827
16215 Piuma Ave. FAX (562) 924-2233
Cerritos, CA 90703 www.eideindustries.com
(Awnings)

A Fox Studios (310) 369-2616
Drapery Department FAX (310) 369-4785
10201 W. Pico Blvd. www.foxstudios.com
Los Angeles, CA 90035
(Custom Drapery Fabrication, Rentals & Upholstery)

G & G Design Associates (310) 538-6400
16131 S. Maple Ave. www.ggda.net
Gardena, CA 90248

Grosh Scenic Rentals (323) 662-1134
(877) 363-7998
4114 Sunset Blvd. FAX (323) 664-7526
Los Angeles, CA 90029 www.grosh.com

Melrose Drapery (323) 464-8404
6053 1/2 Melrose Ave. www.melrosedrapery.com
Los Angeles, CA 90038

NBC Universal Property (818) 777-2784
100 Universal City Plaza FAX (818) 866-1543
Universal City, CA 91608 www.filmmakersdestination.com

Omega/Cinema Props (323) 466-8201
5857 Santa Monica Blvd. FAX (323) 467-7473
Hollywood, CA 90038 www.omegacinemaprops.com

Patmar Company (323) 666-2502
(800) 341-5757
4715 Melrose Ave. FAX (323) 666-5445
Los Angeles, CA 90029 www.patmarcompany.com
(Window Treatments Only)

Rose Brand (818) 505-6290
(800) 360-5056
10616 Lanark St. FAX (818) 505-6293
Sun Valley, CA 91352 www.rosebrand.com
(Theatrical Draperies)

S & K Theatrical Draperies, Inc. (818) 503-0596
(800) 341-3165
7313 Varna Ave. FAX (818) 503-0599
North Hollywood, CA 91605
www.sktheatricaldraperies.com

Sew What? Inc. (310) 639-6000
1978 E. Gladwick St. FAX (310) 639-6036
Rancho Dominguez, CA 90220 www.sewwhatinc.com
(Curtains, Custom, Rentals & Theatrical Drapery)

ShowBiz Enterprises, Inc. (818) 989-7007
15541 Lanark St. FAX (818) 989-8272
Van Nuys, CA 91406 www.showbizenterprises.com
(Theatrical Draperies)

Stern's Draperies, Inc. (818) 789-3838
FAX (818) 789-0222

Triangle Scenery (323) 662-8129
1215 Bates Ave. FAX (323) 662-8120
Los Angeles, CA 90029 www.tridrape.com

Valley Drapery/Linen Trees (818) 892-7744
16616 Schoenborn St. FAX (818) 892-7884
North Hills, CA 91343 www.valleydrapery.com

Warner Bros. Studio Facilities - Drapery Department (818) 954-1831
4000 Warner Blvd. FAX (818) 954-3428
Burbank, CA 91522 www.wbsf.com

Aaron Cleaners (310) 392-1843
(Same Day Service Before 9am)

Apple Cleaners (310) 208-1985
(Same Day Service Before 9:30am)

Brown's Cleaners (310) 451-8531

Door to Door Valet Cleaners (310) 318-8047
(310) 871-1141
901 Manhattan Ave. FAX (310) 318-3183
Manhattan Beach, CA 90266
www.doortodoorcleaners.com

Effrey's (310) 858-7400

Four Seasons Cleaners (323) 848-9158
8042 Santa Monica Blvd.
Los Angeles, CA 90046
(Same Day Service Before Noon)

George's Cleaning (310) 826-6380
12120 Santa Monica Blvd.
Los Angeles, CA 90025

Highland Express (323) 938-2884
(One Hour Service Available)

Hill Top Cleaners (818) 761-6668
(Same Day Service Before 10am) FAX (818) 761-7780
www.hilltopcleaners.com

Holly Hills (323) 469-1466
(Same Day Service Before 11am)

Hollyway Cleaners (323) 654-1271
(Same Day Service Before Noon)

La Cienega One Hour (310) 659-7474
(Same Day Service Before 11am) FAX (310) 659-2612

Leonard's (310) 274-9073
(Same Day Service Before 10:30am)

Merry Go Round Cleaners (310) 275-1782
8550 W. Third St. FAX (310) 275-3014
Los Angeles, CA 90048 www.merrygoroundcleaners.com
(Same Day Service Before 10am)

Milt & Edie's Dry Cleaners (818) 846-4734
4021 W. Alameda Ave. FAX (818) 972-2739
Burbank, CA 91506 www.miltandediesdrycleaners.com
(Four-Hour Service Available)

Peter's Magnolia Cleaners (323) 654-1383
(323) 653-0060
(Same Day Service Before 10am)

Premier Suede/
Leather & Specialty Cleaners (949) 244-0943
(800) 245-2378
3419 Via Lido, Ste. 167
Newport Beach, CA 92663
(Same Day Service Before 9:30am)

Antique Mall-Sherman Oaks (818) 906-0338
14034 Ventura Blvd. www.soantiquemall.com
Sherman Oaks, CA 91423
(Antique–Present, Costume Jewelry Design, Estate Jewelry, Fine Jewelry, Period, Rentals, Vintage, Watches & Wedding Rings)

Avi Traditional Silversmithing (818) 506-4478
(818) 506-4113
11131 Vanowen St., Ste. C FAX (818) 506-4478
North Hollywood, CA 91605 www.avisilversmith.com

Dr. Elise Brisco/
Hollywood Vision Center (323) 954-5800
955 S. Carrillo Dr., Ste. 105 FAX (323) 954-5807
Los Angeles, CA 90048 www.hollywoodvision.com
(Special FX Contact Lenses)

Buckin' Ham Palace (760) 568-5111
(760) 408-2055
(Antique, Costume Jewelry Design, Period, Rentals, Reproductions, Vintage & Watches)

ByLaShan Jewelry (310) 729-1978
(323) 882-0025
FAX (310) 314-3365
www.bylashan.com

Chic Little Devil Style House (310) 403-6929
1206 Maple Ave., 11th Fl.
Los Angeles, CA 90015
www.chiclittledevilstylehouse.com

Crystalarium (310) 652-8006
8500 Melrose Ave., Ste. 105 FAX (310) 652-8007
West Hollywood, CA 90069 www.crystalarium.com
(Custom Gold and Silver Jewelry & Gemstones)

Face Value (818) 348-1320
5305 Tendilla Ave. www.facevalueprops.com
Woodland Hills, CA 91364
(Vintage and Contemporary Eyeglasses and Watches)

Femme Metale Inc. (951) 279-9737
2556 Avenida Del Vista, Ste. 201 FAX (951) 279-9747
Corona, CA 92882 www.femmemetale.com

Gail Freeman
Antique & Estate Jewelry (818) 632-0044
6433 Topanga Canyon Blvd., Ste. 211
Woodland Hills, CA 91303
(Antique and Estate Jewelry)

Dr. Jonathan Gording, Optometry (310) 470-4289
2035 Westwood Blvd. FAX (310) 474-3423
West Los Angeles, CA 90025 www.drgording.com
(Special FX Contact Lenses)

The Hand Prop Room, L.P. (323) 931-1534
5700 Venice Blvd. FAX (323) 931-2145
Los Angeles, CA 90019 www.hpr.com

Harry Winston Jewelers (310) 271-8554
310 N. Rodeo Dr. FAX (310) 271-8526
Beverly Hills, CA 90210 www.harrywinston.com

History for Hire (818) 765-7767
7149 Fair Ave. FAX (818) 765-7871
North Hollywood, CA 91605 www.historyforhire.com
(Antique–Contemporary Watches)

Image Optics (818) 981-3343
16745 Saticoy St., Ste. 102 FAX (818) 780-5498
Sherman Oaks, CA 91403
(Antique–Present Eyeglasses, Rentals, Purchase & Product Placement)

Junk for Joy Vintage, Etc. (818) 569-4903
3314 W. Magnolia Blvd. www.junkforjoy.com
Burbank, CA 91505
(Period and Vintage Jewelry and Eyewear)

L. Wilmington & Co. (213) 624-8314
611 Wilshire Blvd., Ste. 1103 FAX (213) 624-7438
Los Angeles, CA 90017 www.lwilmington.com
(Custom Jewelry)

l.a. Eyeworks (714) 957-8255
South Coast Plaza FAX (714) 957-0790
3333 Bristol St., Ste. 1010 www.laeyeworks.com
Costa Mesa, CA 92626
(Eyeglasses & Sunglasses)

l.a. Eyeworks (323) 653-8255
7407 Melrose Ave. FAX (323) 653-8176
Los Angeles, CA 90046 www.laeyeworks.com

Liza Shtromberg Jewelry (323) 913-1444
2120 N. Hillhurst Ave. FAX (323) 913-1427
Los Angeles, CA 90027 www.lizashtromberg.com
(Handmade Silver and Gold Designer Jewelry)

Montana Eyes (310) 917-4474
709 Montana Ave. FAX (310) 917-4473
Santa Monica, CA 90403

Claude Morady (310) 275-3104
9615 Brighton Way, Ste. 338 FAX (310) 275-3754
Beverly Hills, CA 90210
(Antique–Contemporary Estate Jewelry)

Oliver Peoples (310) 657-2553
8642 Sunset Blvd. FAX (310) 657-7308
West Hollywood, CA 90069 www.oliverpeoples.com
(Eyeglasses & Sunglasses)

Optical Outlook (310) 447-8630
11677 San Vicente Blvd.
Los Angeles, CA 90049
www.dandeutschopticaloutlook.com
(Eyeglasses & Sunglasses)

Optical Outlook (818) 752-8606
12050 Ventura Blvd. FAX (818) 752-3043
Studio City, CA 91604
www.dandeutschopticaloutlook.com

Optical Outlook (310) 652-9144
8555 Sunset Blvd. FAX (310) 652-9108
West Hollywood, CA 90069
www.dandeutschopticaloutlook.com

Palace Costume and Prop Co. (323) 651-5458
835 N. Fairfax Ave. FAX (323) 658-7133
Los Angeles, CA 90046 www.palacecostume.com
(Ethnic and Period Jewelry)

The Pasadena Antique
Center & Annex (626) 449-7706
(626) 449-9445
444 & 480 S. Fair Oaks Ave. FAX (626) 449-3386
Pasadena, CA 91105 www.pasadenaantiquecenter.com
(Antique–Present, Costume Jewelry Design & Vintage)

Prop Specs (323) 935-7776
FAX (323) 935-7778
www.propspecs.com
(Antique–Present Eyeglasses and Sunglasses)

Skinny Dog Design Group, Inc. (562) 436-7237
1750 E. Florida St. www.jewelrypropshop.com
Long Beach, CA 90802
(Costume Jewelry Design, Fine Jewelry, Gemstones, Period, Rentals, Reproductions & Wedding Rings)

Specs Appeal (323) 650-0988
7976 Santa Monica Blvd. FAX (323) 650-1579
Los Angeles, CA 90046 www.specsappealonline.com
(Contact Lenses, Eyeglasses & Sunglasses)

Spirited Bead & Klews Gallery, Inc. (661) 823-1930
(661) 823-1395
FAX (661) 823-1930
www.klewexpressions.com
(Ethnic and Modern Polymer Clay Jewelry)

Thanks for the Memories/TFTM (323) 852-9407
8319 Melrose Ave. FAX (323) 852-9407
Los Angeles, CA 90069
(Antique–Present, Costume Jewelry Design, Estate Jewelry, Period, Rentals, Vintage & Watches)

Van Cleef & Arpels of California, Inc. (310) 276-1161
300 N. Rodeo Dr. FAX (310) 276-8835
Beverly Hills, CA 90210

Wanna Buy a Watch?, Inc. (323) 653-0467
8465 Melrose Ave. FAX (323) 653-9101
West Hollywood, CA 90069 www.wannabuyawatch.com
(Antique–Contemporary Watches and Wedding Rings)

Zirconite Direct (213) 236-0809
110 E. Ninth St., Ste. A1090 www.zirconite.com
Los Angeles, CA 90079

Adam Basma Bazaar, Inc. (323) 931-7766 / (323) 934-9493
5998 W. Pico Blvd. FAX (323) 931-7765
Los Angeles, CA 90035 www.adambasma.com
(Antique, Theatrical Fabrics, Treating, Trims, Upholstery & Vintage Textiles)

Archive Edition Textiles/ Textile Artifacts (310) 676-2424
12575 Crenshaw Blvd. FAX (310) 676-2242
Hawthorne, CA 90250 www.archiveedition.com
(Antique and Vintage Fabrics and Trim, Linens, Reproduction Antique Fabrics, Upholstery & Vintage Textiles)

B. Black & Sons/King's Road (213) 624-9451
548 S. Los Angeles St. FAX (213) 624-9457
Los Angeles, CA 90013 www.bblackandsons.com

Caldelle Leather (310) 314-8800
1649 12th St. FAX (310) 314-8877
Santa Monica, CA 90404 www.caldelle.com

Calico Corners (818) 766-1120
FAX (818) 766-8725
www.calicocorners.com

California Flameproofing & Processing Co., Inc. (626) 792-6981
170 N. Halstead St. FAX (626) 792-1071
Pasadena, CA 91107 www.californiaflameproof.com

Cameraflauge (818) 762-1059 / (213) 304-9323
6840 Vineland Ave. FAX (818) 762-0207
North Hollywood, CA 91605 www.cameraflauge.com
(Blue/Green Screen Suits)

Dazian Fabrics (818) 287-3800 / (877) 432-9426
7120 Case Ave. FAX (818) 287-3810
North Hollywood, CA 91605 www.dazian.com

Diamond Foam Company (323) 931-8148
611 S. La Brea Ave. FAX (323) 931-2086
Los Angeles, CA 90036
www.diamondandfoamfabrics.com

A Dyeing Art (818) 246-5440
325 Mira Loma Ave. FAX (818) 246-5448
Glendale, CA 91204 www.adyeingart.com
(Fabric Dyeing)

F & S Fabrics (310) 475-1637
10629 W. Pico Blvd. FAX (310) 470-0228
Los Angeles, CA 90064

F & S Fabrics (310) 475-1637
10654 W. Pico Blvd. FAX (310) 470-0228
Los Angeles, CA 90064
(Upholstery)

Firetect (661) 298-8801 / (800) 380-8801
26951 Ruether Ave., Ste. D FAX (661) 298-8851
Canyon Country, CA 91351 www.firetect.com
(Flameproofing)

Foam Mart (818) 848-3626 / (800) 943-8362
628 N. Victory Blvd. FAX (323) 849-4245
Burbank, CA 91502 www.foammart.com
(Upholstery Fabrics & Vinyls)

Francine Lecoultre Design Studio (323) 664-1636
(Fabrics & Dyeing) FAX (323) 664-1676

Golyester Antiques (323) 931-1339
136 S. La Brea Ave.
Los Angeles, CA 90036
(Vintage Textiles)

J. Robert Scott, Inc. (310) 680-4226
8737 Melrose Ave. FAX (310) 659-4994
West Hollywood, CA 90069 www.jrobertscott.com

Jeffrey Stevens (310) 652-3050
FAX (310) 652-8230
www.jeffreystevens.com

Lee's Decorative Showcase (818) 988-5337 / (800) 347-5337
16531 Saticoy St. FAX (818) 988-5955
Van Nuys, CA 91406
(Decorative Trimming, Fabrics & Tassels)

Maison et Café (323) 939-9860
148 S. La Brea Ave. FAX (323) 939-8036
Los Angeles, CA 90036 www.cafemidi.com

Michael Levine, Inc. (213) 622-6259
920 S. Maple Ave. FAX (213) 683-0504
Los Angeles, CA 90015

Norm's (310) 559-4323
FAX (310) 836-0387

Oriental Silk Import & Export (323) 651-2323
8377 Beverly Blvd. FAX (323) 651-2323
Los Angeles, CA 90048 www.orientalsilk.com

Robbins Fabrics, Inc. (323) 724-6180
2524 W. Beverly Blvd. FAX (323) 724-6985
Montebello, CA 90640 www.robbinsfabrics.com

Rose Brand (818) 505-6290 / (800) 360-5056
10616 Lanark St. FAX (818) 505-6293
Sun Valley, CA 91352 www.rosebrand.com
(Theatrical Fabrics and Fabric Treating)

Sew What? Inc. (310) 639-6000
1978 Gladwick St. FAX (310) 639-6036
Rancho Dominguez, CA 90220 www.sewwhatinc.com

Denyse Specktor/The Big Yarn (805) 267-0909
1237 S. Victoria Ave.
Oxnard, CA 93035
(Knitting Supplies)

The Way We Wore (323) 937-0878
334 S. La Brea Ave. FAX (323) 936-6578
Los Angeles, CA 90036 www.thewaywewore.com
(Vintage Textiles)

Caravan West Productions (661) 268-8300
35660 Jayhawker Rd. FAX (661) 268-8301
Agua Dulce, CA 91390 www.caravanwest.com

FX House Associates (650) 855-9461
P.O. Box 1536 FAX (650) 855-9268
Palo Alto, CA 94302 www.fxha.com

Global Effects, Inc. (818) 503-9273
7115 Laurel Canyon Blvd. FAX (818) 503-9459
North Hollywood, CA 91605 www.globaleffects.com

The Hand Prop Room, L.P. (323) 931-1534
5700 Venice Blvd. FAX (323) 931-2145
Los Angeles, CA 90019 www.hpr.com

Independent Studio Services, Inc./ISS (818) 951-5600
9545 Wentworth St. www.issprops.com
Sunland, CA 91040

LCW Props (818) 243-0707
6439 San Fernando Rd. FAX (818) 243-1830
Glendale, CA 91201 www.lcwprops.com

Mike Tristano & Co. (818) 522-0969
(Armor, Edged Weapons, Guns & Period) FAX (818) 888-6447
www.moviegunguy.com

Omega/Cinema Props (323) 466-8201
5857 Santa Monica Blvd. FAX (323) 461-3643
Hollywood, CA 90038 www.omegacinemaprops.com

Sacred Sword, Inc. (818) 509-9581
6850 Vineland Ave., Ste. L www.militaryprops.com
North Hollywood, CA 91605

Sword & The Stone (818) 562-6548
723 N. Victory Blvd. FAX (818) 562-6549
Burbank, CA 91502 www.swordandstone.com

Tactical Edge Group (818) 361-5569
www.propguys.com/weapons/

AAA Custom Engravers (818) 989-8010
15948 Leadwell St. FAX (818) 989-8020
Van Nuys, CA 91406
(Engraving)

AAA Flag & Banner Mfg. Co. (323) 932-8500
712 N. La Brea Ave. FAX (323) 936-3532
Los Angeles, CA 90038 www.aaaflag.com

AAA Flag & Banner Mfg. Co. (310) 276-1178
8954 W. Pico Blvd. www.aaaflag.com
Los Angeles, CA 90035

Aalco Signs & Graphics (323) 728-2957
2856 S. Vail Ave. FAX (323) 728-9409
City of Commerce, CA 90040
(Signage)

Alex Pitt Photography (323) 665-4492
www.alexpittphotography.com

Alley Kat Graphic (818) 480-8610
3209 W. Valley Heart Dr. FAX (818) 566-1145
Burbank, CA 91505 www.alleykatgraphic.com

Alpha Sign Company (818) 788-9401
13831 Ventura Blvd. FAX (818) 788-0478
Sherman Oaks, CA 91423 www.alphasign.com
(Sign Fabrication)

American Signs & Graphics (310) 203-9252
(323) 938-7446
311 N. Robertson Blvd., Ste. 161 FAX (323) 938-7447
Beverly Hills, CA 90211 www.americansignsinc.com
(Banners, Custom Signs, Graphics, Repair & Waterjet Lettering)

Art & Scenic Design Studios (323) 706-3904
(Billboards, Graphics, Hand Lettering, Hand Painting, Logos & Sign Painting)

Art, Signs & Graphics (818) 503-7997
6939 Farmdale Ave. FAX (818) 503-7999
North Hollywood, CA 91605
www.artsignsandgraphics.com

B and R Scenery, Inc. (805) 388-8555
486 Constitution Ave. FAX (805) 388-9996
Camarillo, CA 93012 www.bandrscenery.com
(Custom, Electric Sign Fabrication, Full-Service Sign Shop, Letters, Logos, Sign Fabrication & Signs)

Banners and Flags Unlimited (805) 528-5018
P.O. Box 7004 FAX (805) 528-3529
Los Osos, CA 93412 www.bannermarketinggroup.com
(Banners, Flags, Graphics, Labels, Point of Purchase Displays, Posters & Signage)

Ⓐ **Beyond Image Graphics, Inc.** (818) 547-0899
1853 Dana St. FAX (818) 547-1470
Glendale, CA 91201 www.beyondimagegraphics.com

Burbank Sign Co. (818) 846-1298
454 N. Moss St. FAX (818) 846-0005
Burbank, CA 91502 www.burbanksign.com
(Hand Lettering and Painting & Vintage Aircraft Nose Art)

Carwraps, Inc. (818) 718-0774
(866) 972-7227
8821 Shirley Ave. FAX (866) 211-2424
Northridge, CA 91324 www.carwraps.net
(Banners, Billboards, Custom Lettering, Digital Prints, Displays, Graphics, Hand Lettering, Letters, Logos, Posters, Point of Purchase Displays, Signage, Vehicle Graphics & Vehicle Wraps)

Charisma Design Studio, Inc. (818) 252-6611
(800) 891-8617
8414 San Fernando Rd. FAX (818) 252-6610
Sun Valley, CA 91352 www.charismadesign.com
(Waterjet Cutting)

Cinnabar (818) 842-8190
4571 Electronics Pl. FAX (818) 842-0563
Los Angeles, CA 90039 www.cinnabar.com
(Billboards)

Classic Letters, Inc. (310) 787-4343
(800) 398-6777
22129½ Vermont Ave. FAX (310) 787-4340
Torrance, CA 90502 www.classicletters.com

Coast Kites, Inc./Beagle Easel (213) 749-1262
(562) 276-5483
2201 Compton Ave.
Los Angeles, CA 90011

Colby Poster Printing Company (213) 747-5108
(800) 956-7707
1332 W. 12th Pl. FAX (213) 747-3209
Los Angeles, CA 90015 www.colbyposter.com
(Billboards, Posters & Signage)

Collins Signs (818) 686-6581
(818) 929-7809
10518 Johanna Ave. FAX (818) 806-3229
Shadow Hills, CA 91040 www.collins-signs.com
(Banners, Billboards, Custom Lettering, Digital Prints, Displays, Flags, Full-Service Shop, Graphics, Hand Lettering, Labels, Letters, Logos, Point of Purchase Displays, Posters, Printed Inserts, Sign Painting & Signage)

we do excellence
dimensional signs
large format Digital Outputs
Backlit Prints
Canvas Printing Stretching
5'x10' CNC Routing
Dimensional Signage
Custom Wall Murals
Vehicle Wrap Graphics
custom decals/labels
Design and Layout
Vinyl Graphics
Vinyl Lettering
Mounting, Laminating and Finishing
Custom Die-Cut Standees
large format graphics/signs
Trade Show/ Exhibit Graphics
Printed Banners
Custom Decals/Labels
vehicle graphics
Beyond Image Graphics Inc.
853 Dana St. Glendale, CA 91201 • 818 547-0899 beyondimagegraphics.com

Concept Design Productions (626) 932-0082
(800) 846-0717
718 Primrose Ave. FAX (626) 932-0072
Monrovia, CA 91016 www.conceptdesigninc.com

Continental Scenery, Inc. (818) 768-8075
7802 Clybourn Ave. FAX (818) 768-6939
Sun Valley, CA 91352 www.continentalscenery.com

Ⓐ **D'ziner Sign Co.** (323) 467-4467
(877) 397-6736
1536 N. Highland Ave. FAX (323) 467-4494
Hollywood, CA 90028 www.showbizsigns.com

Dangling Carrot Creative (661) 295-6610
28308 Constellation Rd. FAX (661) 295-6699
Valencia, CA 91355 www.danglingcarrotcreative.com

Dazian Fabrics (818) 287-3800
(877) 432-9426
7120 Case Ave. FAX (818) 287-3810
North Hollywood, CA 91605 www.dazian.com
(Custom Banners and Displays)

Dennis Curtin Studio, Inc. (310) 827-8850
1919 Empire Ave. FAX (818) 842-4623
Burbank, CA 91504 www.denniscurtin.com

Designer Diner (818) 621-4751
(Signs & Graphics)

Designing Letters (310) 702-4042
4032 Marcasel Ave. FAX (310) 398-6002
Los Angeles, CA 90066 www.designingletters.com
(Custom Lettering, Graphics, Hand Lettering, Hand Painting, Letters & Logos)

DesignTown, USA (310) 840-2940
(888) 386-9717
3644 Eastham Dr. FAX (310) 840-2935
Culver City, CA 90232 www.designtownusa.com
(Banners, Billboards, Custom Lettering, Digital Prints, Displays, Electric Sign Fabrication, Flags, Full-Service Shop, Graphics, Hand Lettering, Hand Painting, Labels, Letters, License Plates, Logos, Newspapers, Point of Purchase Displays, Posters, Printed Inserts, Repair, Sign Painting, Signage, Vacuum-Formed Signs, Vehicle Wraps, Waterjet Cutting & Waterjet Lettering)

Earl Hays Press (818) 765-0700
10707 Sherman Way FAX (818) 765-5245
Sun Valley, CA 91352
(Generic Labels, License Plates, Newspapers & Printed Inserts)

Flix FX, Inc. (818) 765-3549
(877) 326-8433
7327 Lankershim Blvd., Ste. 4 FAX (818) 765-0135
North Hollywood, CA 91605 www.flixfx.com
(Vinyl Graphics & Vacuum-Formed Signs)

Ⓐ **Fox Studios** (310) 369-2762
(310) 369-4636
Sign Shop, 10201 W. Pico Blvd. FAX (310) 286-9462
Los Angeles, CA 90035 www.foxstudios.com
(Full-Service Sign Shop)

The Hand Prop Room, L.P. (323) 931-1534
5700 Venice Blvd. FAX (323) 931-2145
Los Angeles, CA 90019 www.hpr.com

Heaven or Las Vegas Neon (310) 636-0081
11814 W. Jefferson Blvd. FAX (310) 636-1959
Culver City, CA 90230 www.rentneon.com
(Signage)

Ⓐ **Hollywood Sign Company** (323) 463-1171
(800) 894-2744
1036 N. Cole Ave. FAX (323) 463-3934
Hollywood, CA 90038 www.hollywoodsigncompany.com

i Communications, Inc. (818) 252-1300
7648 San Fernando Rd. FAX (818) 252-1385
Sun Valley, CA 91352 www.icommnetwork.net
(Signage)

JCL Graphics (213) 622-9775
2334 E. Eighth St. FAX (213) 622-9790
Los Angeles, CA 90021 www.bannersuperstore.com

Laser Edge, Inc. (310) 450-5200
2401 Lincoln Blvd. FAX (310) 450-5288
Santa Monica, CA 90405 www.laseredge.net
(Digital Prints)

Liquid Language, The Art of Lettering (949) 458-3770
FAX (949) 458-3770
www.liquidlanguage.com

Living Color Graphics (323) 468-9931
(323) 468-9037
FAX (323) 468-9037
www.livingcolorgraphics.com

Mandex Led Motion Displays (805) 497-8006
(818) 825-9664
2350 Young Ave. FAX (818) 889-4569
Thousand Oaks, CA 91360 www.ledsignage.com

Mark Anthony Printing Service (213) 610-8845
3019 Vail Ave. FAX (323) 890-1007
City of Commerce, CA 90040

Michael Salerno & Associates (323) 223-6089
600 Moulton Ave., Ste. 404
Los Angeles, CA 90031

Movieart, Inc. (818) 765-1780
(800) 429-0476
13136 Saticoy St., Stes. D & E FAX (818) 765-0258
North Hollywood, CA 91605 www.movieart.com

NBC Universal Graphic Design & Sign Shops (818) 777-2350
100 Universal City Plaza FAX (818) 866-0209
Bldg. 4250/3054 www.filmmakersdestination.com
Universal City, CA 91608

New Image Graphics & Printing (323) 876-1102
7109 Sunset Blvd. FAX (323) 874-8838
Los Angeles, CA 90046 www.newimagegraphic.com

Olympus Enterprises, Inc. (818) 252-1110
(888) 843-7285
9063 San Fernando Rd. FAX (818) 252-5777
Sun Valley, CA 91352 www.olympusent.com

Omega/Cinema Props (323) 466-8201
5857 Santa Monica Blvd. FAX (323) 461-3643
Hollywood, CA 90038 www.omegacinemaprops.com

A **The Studios at Paramount** (323) 956-3729
The Studios at Paramount
Sign Shop & Graphic Services
5555 Melrose Ave.
Hollywood, CA 90038
www.thestudiosatparamount.com

Perlman Creative Group (310) 709-2091
P.O. Box 4016 www.perlmancreative.com
Newport Beach, CA 92661
(Banners, Billboards, Digital Prints, Displays, Full-Service Shop, Graphics, Labels, Logos, Newspapers, Point of Purchase Displays, Posters, Printed Inserts & Signage)

Production Graphics (818) 638-8102
341 Mira Loma FAX (818) 638-8104
Glendale, CA 91204 www.production-graphics.com

Prolab Digital Imaging (310) 625-4411
5441 W. 104th St. FAX (310) 204-6939
Los Angeles, CA 90045 www.prolabdigital.com

Really Fake Digital (323) 221-6995
696 Moulton Ave., Ste. B FAX (323) 227-9033
Los Angeles, CA 90031 www.reallyfake.com
(Custom, Digital Imaging, Graphics & Signage)

Rembrandt Graphics, Inc. (818) 552-6584
1225 Los Angeles St. FAX (818) 552-6601
Glendale, CA 91204 www.rembrandtgraphics.com
(Graphic Props & Signage)

Scenic Express, Inc. (323) 254-4351
3019 Andrita St. FAX (323) 254-4411
Los Angeles, CA 90065 www.scenicexpress.net

Sew What? Inc. (310) 639-6000
1978 Gladwick St. FAX (310) 639-6036
Rancho Dominguez, CA 90220 www.sewwhatinc.com

Sign Comm (213) 383-2111
3224 Beverly Blvd. FAX (213) 383-2128
Los Angeles, CA 90057 www.signcomm91.com

Sign Makers (323) 932-9231
5772 W. Venice Blvd. FAX (323) 932-8605
Los Angeles, CA 90019 www.signmakers.com
(Banners & Signs)

Sign Zone (323) 465-8200
(866) 744-6966
4873 Melrose Ave. FAX (323) 465-8202
Los Angeles, CA 90029 www.signzonela.com

Signtist, LLC (323) 658-5222
353 S. Fairfax Ave. FAX (323) 658-5226
West Hollywood, CA 90291 www.signtist.com

Signtist, LLC (310) 581-5637
2010 Lincoln Blvd. FAX (310) 581-5639
Venice, CA 90291 www.signtist.com

Solbrook Display Corporation (818) 761-3297
10620 Magnolia Blvd. FAX (818) 761-7697
North Hollywood, CA 91601 www.solbrook.com

Studio Graphics (818) 951-5600
9545 Wentworth St. FAX (818) 951-2886
Sunland, CA 91040 www.issprops.com
(Generic Labels, License Plates, Newspapers & Signage)

Superior Sign Studios (323) 933-2445
1408 S. Redondo Blvd. FAX (323) 933-2446
Los Angeles, CA 90019

Total Look Studios Hollywood (323) 962-0009
(323) 854-6775
1617 N. El Centro, Ste. 9
Hollywood, CA 90028
www.christopherxavierlozano.com
(Banners, Billboards, Custom Lettering, Digital Prints, Displays, Graphics, Logos, Posters, Printed Inserts & Signage)

The Unknown Artist (714) 662-0662
1565 Scenic Ave., Ste. C FAX (714) 662-0428
Costa Mesa, CA 92626 www.unknownartist.com

The Walt Disney Studios - Sign Graphics Department (818) 560-5488
500 S. Buena Vista St. FAX (818) 563-3987
Burbank, CA 91521

Warner Bros. Studio Facilities - Sign Shop (818) 954-1815
4000 Warner Blvd. FAX (818) 954-2806
Burbank, CA 91522 www.wbsf.com

WE Design Studio (213) 706-1265
(323) 284-5130
P.O. Box 411223 FAX (561) 455-9644
Los Angeles, CA 90041 www.designstudio.com

WestOn Letters (818) 503-9472
7259 N. Atoll Ave. FAX (818) 503-9475
North Hollywood, CA 91605 www.westonletters.com
(Letters, Logos & Sign Systems)

Zing Graphics (562) 946-0304
12309 Telegraph Rd. FAX (562) 946-0303
Santa Fe Springs, CA 90670 www.zinggraphics.com
(Banners, Billboards, Custom Lettering, Digital Prints, Displays, Flags, Full-Service Shop, Graphics, Logos, Point of Purchase Displays, Posters, Repair & Signage)

Almost Christmas Prop Shoppe/ Cathy Christmas (310) 286-0921
(310) 748-4521
5057 Lankershim Blvd. FAX (818) 285-9630
North Hollywood, CA 91601 www.cathychristmas.com

Bittersweet Butterfly Lingerie and Flowers (323) 660-4303
1406 Micheltorena FAX (323) 665-9114
Los Angeles, CA 90026 www.bittersweetbutterfly.com
(Cacti & Floral Design)

California Nursery Specialties/ Cactus Ranch (818) 894-5694
(Cactus & Succulent Plants) FAX (818) 894-7794
www.california-cactus-succulents.com

Great Greens, Inc./Randy Martens (805) 643-3486
2960 N. Ventura Ave. FAX (805) 643-1954
Ventura, CA 93001

Green Scapes (661) 255-3205
(818) 599-6908
26191 Bouquet Canyon Rd. FAX (661) 255-8858
Santa Clarita, CA 91350 www.greenscapesgreen.com

Green Set, Inc. (818) 764-1231
11617 Dehougne St. FAX (818) 764-1423
North Hollywood, CA 91605 www.greenset.com

Instant Jungle International (714) 850-9227
(800) 447-4007
2560 S. Birch St. FAX (714) 850-9228
Santa Ana, CA 92707 www.instantjungle.com

Jackson Shrub Supply, Inc. (818) 982-0100
11505 Vanowen St. FAX (818) 982-1310
North Hollywood, CA 91605 www.jacksonshrub.com

Kimura Bonsai & Landscape (818) 343-4090
17230 Roscoe Blvd. FAX (818) 343-6101
Northridge, CA 91325

Make Be-Leaves (818) 597-7790
(800) 634-1402
5311 Derry Ave., Ste. C FAX (818) 597-7799
Agoura Hills, CA 91301 www.makebe-leaves.com
(Silk Flowers, Plants and Trees)

Omega/Cinema Props (323) 466-8201
5857 Santa Monica Blvd. FAX (323) 461-3643
Hollywood, CA 90038 www.omegacinemaprops.com

Pacific Sod (805) 986-8277
(800) 942-5296
305 W. Hueneme Rd. FAX (805) 986-5210
Camarillo, CA 93012 www.pacificsod.com
(Grass, Sod & Wildflower Sod)

The Plant Connection (818) 787-9171
(323) 874-9102
FAX (818) 787-8619

Sandy Rose Floral, Inc. (818) 980-4371
6850 Vineland Ave., Ste. C FAX (818) 980-4598
North Hollywood, CA 91605 www.sandyrose.com

Superior Studio Specialties (323) 278-0100
(800) 354-3049
2239 S. Yates Ave. FAX (323) 278-0111
Commerce, CA 90040 www.superiorstudio.com
(Artificial Plants and Flowers)

Tic-Tock (800) 893-6688
(323) 874-3034
1603 N. La Brea Ave. FAX (323) 874-6134
Hollywood, CA 90028 www.tictock.com
(Floral Set Design)

Advanced Foam (310) 515-0466
1745 W. 134th St. FAX (310) 515-3548
Gardena, CA 90249 www.advancedfoam.com

Ⓐ **Atlas Foam Products** (818) 837-3626
12836 Arroyo St. FAX (818) 837-1114
Sylmar, CA 91342 www.atlasfoam.com

Burman Industries (818) 782-9833
13536 Saticoy St. FAX (818) 782-2863
Van Nuys, CA 91402 www.burmanfoam.com

Daniels Engraving Co., Inc. (818) 837-3222
571 Fifth St. FAX (818) 837-1002
San Fernando, CA 91340 www.danielsdse.com

DeRouchey Urethane Creations Inc. (949) 240-1960
(949) 289-0211
24771 Anchor Lantern St. FAX (949) 361-4810
Dana Point, CA 92629
www.deroucheyurethanefoam.com
(24-Hour Service, Mobile Units & Spray Urethane Foam)

Diamond Foam Company (323) 931-8148
801 S. La Brea Ave. FAX (323) 931-2086
Los Angeles, CA 90036 www.diamondandfoamfabrics.com

Festival Artists, Inc. (626) 334-9388
(626) 303-6042
120 N. Aspan Ave. FAX (626) 969-8595
Azusa, CA 91702 www.festivalartists.org
(Mobile Units & Spray Urethane Foam)

Foam Mart (818) 848-3626
(800) 943-8362
628 N. Victory Blvd. FAX (323) 849-4245
Burbank, CA 91502 www.foammart.com

Foam Sales and Marketing (818) 558-5717
1005 W. Isabel St. FAX (818) 558-5724
Burbank, CA 91506 www.foamsalesmarketing.com

Foamway.com (323) 908-3493
(514) 998-6935
FAX (450) 687-2326
www.foamway.com

Lee's Decorative Showcase (818) 988-5337
(800) 347-5337
16531 Saticoy St. FAX (818) 988-5955
Van Nuys, CA 91406

Storyland Studios/Foam Works (951) 674-0998
(800) 218-1932
590 Crane St. FAX (951) 674-0245
Lake Elsinore, CA 92530 www.foamworks.com

West Coast Sign Supply (213) 487-6666
1700 W. Pico Blvd. FAX (213) 487-6660
Los Angeles, CA 90015 www.westcoastsignsupply.com

West Coast Sign Supply (818) 785-8777
14332 Calvert St. FAX (818) 785-8778
Van Nuys, CA 91411 www.westcoastsignsupply.com

Winters Foam Systems, Inc. (760) 499-1999
(877) 456-4969
1308 N. Inyo St., Ste. B FAX (760) 499-1998
Ridgecrest, CA 93555 www.glowsource.com
(Spray Urethane Foam)

A.B.E. Office Furniture (626) 443-4223
(800) 564-4223
3400 N. Peck Rd. FAX (626) 443-6245
El Monte, CA 91731 www.abefurniture.com
(Office)

Accessory Preview, Inc. (323) 931-2050
353 N. La Brea Ave. FAX (323) 931-2090
Los Angeles, CA 90036 www.accessorypreview.com
(Accessories, Antique–Contemporary & Eclectic)

Acme Design Group (818) 767-8888
11001 Fleetwood St. www.acme-designgroup.com
Sun Valley, CA 91352

Antique Mall-Sherman Oaks (818) 906-0338
14034 Ventura Blvd. www.soantiquemall.com
Sherman Oaks, CA 91423
(Accessories, Antique–Contemporary, Deco, Eclectic, Glassware, Hand Props, Lighting, Period & Vintage)

Aquatic Design (310) 822-7484
(310) 420-8379
4943 McConnell Ave., Ste. K FAX (310) 822-8644
Los Angeles, CA 90066 www.aquatic2000.com
(Aquariums)

Arte de Mexico (818) 753-4510
(818) 769-5090
5356 Riverton Ave. FAX (818) 769-9425
North Hollywood, CA 91601 www.artedemexico.com
(Antique, Eclectic & Mexican)

Bits, Pieces & Leaves (818) 505-6550
(818) 505-8562
12608 Ventura Blvd. FAX (818) 505-1036
Studio City, CA 91604
(Garden & Patio)

Bleu Moon (310) 855-0788
344 N. La Cienega Blvd. www.bleumoon.us
Los Angeles, CA 90048
(Accessories, Antique, Custom, Eclectic, Garden and Patio, Lighting, Office, Reproductions, Rugs, Tapestries, Upholstery & Vintage)

Brook Furniture Rental (818) 386-2158
15125 Ventura Blvd. FAX (818) 386-0351
Sherman Oaks, CA 91403 www.bfr.com

Chestnuts & Papaya (323) 937-8450
459½ S. La Brea Ave. FAX (323) 937-7940
Los Angeles, CA 90036 www.chestnutsandpapaya.com

Chestnuts & Papaya (323) 937-8450
5000 W. Adams Blvd. FAX (323) 937-7940
Los Angeles, CA 90016 www.chestnutsandpapaya.com

Connoisseur Antiques (323) 658-8432
8468 Melrose Pl. FAX (323) 658-7285
Los Angeles, CA 90069 www.connoisseurantiques.com
(European Antique Furniture and Accessories)

Contents Ltd. (323) 655-2700
8268 Melrose Ave. FAX (323) 655-2706
Los Angeles, CA 90046 www.contentsltd.com
(Accessories, Acrylic, Antique–Contemporary, Custom, Deco, Eclectic, Garden and Patio, Glassware, Modern, Office, Period, Reproductions, Rugs, Tapestries, Upholstery & Vintage)

Cort Furniture Rental (310) 652-2678
(800) 576-2266
8484 Wilshire Blvd. FAX (310) 657-5615
Beverly Hills, CA 90211 www.cort1.com
(Home & Office)

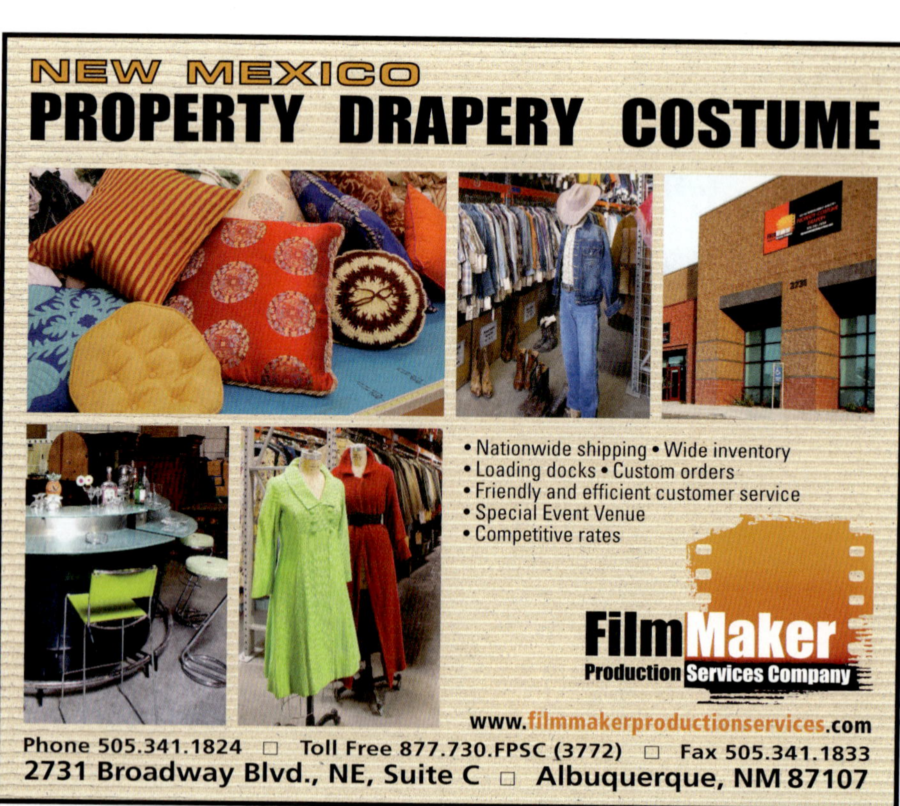

Cort Furniture Rental (818) 907-5496
(800) 576-2266
14140 Ventura Blvd. FAX (818) 907-6415
Sherman Oaks, CA 91423 www.cort1.com
(Home & Office)

Crest Office Furniture (800) 833-4848
2840 N. Lima St., Ste. 110 www.crestoffice.com
Burbank, CA 91504

Decadence Home Decor (310) 360-7221
8922 Beverly Blvd. FAX (310) 360-0874
West Hollywood, CA 90048
www.decadencehomedecor.com
(Contemporary Furniture)

Denmark 50 (323) 650-5222
(323) 852-1939
7974 Melrose Ave.
Los Angeles, CA 90046
(Mid-Century & Modern)

Design Direct (818) 761-4066
Pacific Design Center, P.O. Box 1295
Studio City, CA 91614
(Contemporary and Period Fabric and Furniture)

A **Designer 8* Studio Rental** (323) 962-2062
(800) 709-7007
6525 Sunset Blvd., Ste. G-2 FAX (310) 764-0394
Hollywood, CA 90028 www.designer8studiorental.com
(Custom & Modern Chic)

Designer's Furniture Resource (818) 244-3061
300 S. Brand Blvd. FAX (818) 244-1740
Glendale, CA 91204 www.dfglendale.com
(Classic)

Detelich Gallery (310) 260-9667
(800) 595-8192
1654 Ocean Ave. FAX (310) 260-9787
Santa Monica, CA 90401 www.detelichgallery.com
(Antique Mission Furniture and Lighting)

Dialogica (310) 888-0008
8820 Beverly Blvd. FAX (310) 888-8750
Los Angeles, CA 90048 www.dialogica.com
(Contemporary Furniture and Rugs & Lighting)

Diva (310) 278-3191
8801 Beverly Blvd. www.divafurniture.com
Los Angeles, CA 90048
(Contemporary)

Dozar Office Furnishings (310) 559-9292
9937 Jefferson Blvd., Ste. 100 FAX (310) 559-9009
Culver City, CA 90232 www.dozarrents.com
(Accessories, Contemporary, Custom, Eclectic & Office)

Emmerson Troop (323) 653-9763
8111 Beverly Blvd. FAX (323) 653-5445
Los Angeles, CA 90046 www.emmersontroop.com
(Antique–Modern & Asian)

A **Filmmaker Production Services Company** (877) 730-3772
(505) 341-1824
FAX (505) 341-1833
www.filmmakerproductionservices.com

Fine Custom Upholstery (310) 837-5541
8929 National Blvd. FAX (310) 837-3842
Los Angeles, CA 90034 www.finecustomupholstery.com
(Custom, Deco & Upholstery)

Galerie Lakaye (323) 460-7333
FAX (323) 460-7330
www.galerielakaye.com

H. Studio (818) 767-8448
(800) 242-8992
8640 Tamarack Ave. FAX (818) 767-5334
Sun Valley, CA 91352 www.hstudio.com
(Acrylic & Modern)

Harry Art Furniture, Art Deco & Antiques (310) 559-7863
8834 National Blvd. FAX (310) 559-3387
Culver City, CA 90232 www.coolharryfurniture.com
(1950s and 1960s Custom Art Furniture, Antiques & Art Deco)

Hollywood Parts (818) 255-0617
12580 Saticoy St., Bldg. C FAX (818) 255-0613
North Hollywood, CA 91605 www.hollywoodparts.com
(Asset Management, Storage and Sales, Antique–Contemporary, Bondage Themed Equipment and Furniture, Custom, Deco, Garden and Patio, Glassware, Hand Props, Lighting, Modern, Office, Period, Prop House, Reproductions, Rugs, Tapestries & Vintage)

Hopper's Office & Drafting Furniture (323) 254-7362
(800) 762-7717
2901 Fletcher Dr. FAX (323) 254-8226
Los Angeles, CA 90065 www.draftingfurniture.com
(Drafting & Office)

House of Brienza, Inc. (310) 839-9254
2358 S. Robertson Blvd. FAX (310) 839-3254
Los Angeles, CA 90034 www.houseofbrienza.com
(Antique, Custom & Pine)

House of Props, Inc. (323) 463-3166
1117 N. Gower St. FAX (323) 463-8302
Hollywood, CA 90038
(Antiques, China, Desktop Accessories, Fine Art, Hand Props & Lamps)

J. Green, Inc. (310) 428-0635
917 Lake St. www.jgreenfurniture.com
Venice, CA 90291
(Custom, Fine Wood & Upholstery)

Jan's & Co., Inc. (323) 735-6455
(323) 735-6392
1934 W. Adams Blvd. FAX (323) 735-6240
Los Angeles, CA 90018 www.jansantiques.com
(French Antiques)

Jefferson West, Inc. (310) 558-3031
9310 Jefferson Blvd. FAX (310) 558-4296
Culver City, CA 90232 www.jeffersonwest.com
(Antiques)

Jonathan Adler (323) 658-8390
8125 Melrose Ave. FAX (323) 658-8930
Los Angeles, CA 90046 www.jonathanadler.com
(Modern)

La Brea Antique Collection (323) 938-9444
334 N. La Brea Ave. FAX (323) 930-1323
Los Angeles, CA 90036 www.labreamodern.com

Lawrence of La Brea (323) 935-1100
671 S. La Brea Ave. FAX (323) 935-1199
Los Angeles, CA 90036 www.lawrenceoflabrea.com
(Antique–Present Rugs)

Lennie Marvin Enterprises, Inc. (818) 841-5882
3110 Winona Ave. FAX (818) 841-2896
Burbank, CA 91504 www.propheaven.com
(Antique–Present Prop House)

Living Room (323) 665-5070
(213) 448-0511
3531 Sunset Blvd. FAX (323) 665-7056
Los Angeles, CA 90026 www.livingroomhome.com

Loja Designs (310) 450-6940
1409 Abbot Kinney Blvd. FAX (310) 450-6944
Venice, CA 90291 www.lojadesigns.com
(Modern)

Los Feliz Rattan & Wicker Showroom (818) 848-8462

M.J. Higgins Fine Art & Furnishings (213) 617-1700
400 S. Main St., Ste. 103 FAX (213) 617-1777
Los Angeles, CA 90013 www.mjhiggins.com
(1950s–1960s, Accessories, Antique–Contemporary, Custom, Eclectic, Lighting, Period, Reproductions & Vintage)

Pat McGann (310) 657-8708
746 N. La Cienega Blvd. FAX (310) 358-0977
West Hollywood, CA 90069 www.patmcganngallery.com
(20th Century Design, Antiques & Art)

Modern Chair Rental (562) 943-2500
1301 South Beach Blvd., Ste. C FAX (562) 943-2511
La Habra, CA 90631 www.modernchairrental.com
(Accessories, Acrylic, Antique, Antique–Contemporary, Contemporary, Custom, Deco, Modern, Office, Prop House, Reproductions & Vintage)

Modern One (323) 651-5082
(323) 651-0946
7956 Beverly Blvd. FAX (323) 651-1130
Los Angeles, CA 90048
(Contemporary)

Ⓐ **Modern Props** (323) 934-3000
5500 W. Jefferson Blvd. FAX (323) 934-3155
Los Angeles, CA 90016 www.modernprops.com
(Art Deco, Contemporary and Modern Home and Office Accessories and Furniture)

Modernica (213) 683-1963
2118 E. Seventh Pl. FAX (213) 623-7565
Los Angeles, CA 90021 www.modernicaprops.net
(Accessories, Acrylic, Antique, Antique–Contemporary, Contemporary, Custom, Deco, Eclectic, Garden and Patio, Glassware, Hand Props, Lighting, Modern, Office, Period, Prop House, Reproductions, Rugs, Tapestries, Upholstery & Vintage)

Monte Allen Slipcovers & Upholstering (310) 207-7676
2326 Centinela Ave. FAX (310) 207-7677
West Los Angeles, CA 90064 www.monteallen.com
(Antique–Contemporary)

Mosaik (323) 525-0337
7378 Beverly Blvd. FAX (323) 525-0341
Los Angeles, CA 90036 www.e-mosaik.com
(Antique, Eclectic, Garden and Patio, Lighting, Moroccan & Rugs)

NBC Universal Property (818) 777-2784
100 Universal City Plaza FAX (818) 866-1543
Universal City, CA 91608 www.filmmakersdestination.com
(Custom)

Niedermaier Furniture (323) 782-1888
(310) 497-6000
P.O.Box 691013 www.niedermaier.com
West Hollywood, CA 90069

Noble Forge (818) 765-5004
7416 Varna Ave., Ste. D FAX (661) 286-1166
North Hollywood, CA 91355 www.nobleforge.com
(Blacksmiths, Custom Metalwork & Fireplace Screens)

Nouveau Craft (818) 506-4113
11131 Vanowen St., Ste. C FAX (818) 506-8766
North Hollywood, CA 91605

Off the Wall (323) 930-1185
7325 Melrose Ave. FAX (323) 930-1595
Los Angeles, CA 90046 www.offthewallantiques.com
(1920s–50s Art Deco)

Office Connection (949) 756-8882
1392 McGaw Ave. FAX (949) 756-8883
Irvine, CA 92614 www.office-connection.net
(Office Furniture)

Office Furniture LA (323) 750-6206
7625 Crenshaw Blvd. FAX (323) 750-6208
Los Angeles, CA 90043 www.laofficefurniture.com

Old Pine Furnishings (818) 507-7077
1830 Dana St. FAX (818) 507-8799
Glendale, CA 91201 www.oldpinefurnishings.com
(Antique, Country, Garden & Patio)

Old World Rugs (310) 659-6354
260 S. Robertson Blvd.
Beverly Hills, CA 90211
(Native American and Oriental Rugs & European Tapestries)

Ⓐ **Omega/Cinema Props** (323) 466-8201
5857 Santa Monica Blvd. FAX (323) 461-3643
Hollywood, CA 90038 www.omegacinemaprops.com
(Antique–Present Prop House)

Omega/Cinema Props (323) 466-8201
CP Two, 5755 Santa Monica Blvd. FAX (323) 962-0345
Hollywood, CA 90038 www.omegacinemaprops.com
(Antique–Present Prop House)

Omega/Cinema Props (323) 466-8201
CP Three, 1107 N. Bronson Ave. FAX (323) 467-7473
Hollywood, CA 90038 www.omegacinemaprops.com
(Antique–Present Prop House)

Omega/Cinema Props (323) 466-8201
CP Four, 706 N. Cahuenga Blvd. FAX (323) 467-2749
Hollywood, CA 90038 www.omegacinemaprops.com
(Antique–Present Prop House)

Pacific Orient Traders (310) 306-1520
(310) 889-4109
5320 McConnell Ave. FAX (310) 306-1530
Los Angeles, CA 90066 www.pacificorienttraders.com

The Pasadena Antique Center & Annex (626) 449-7706
(626) 449-9445
444 & 480 S. Fair Oaks Ave. FAX (626) 449-3386
Pasadena, CA 91105 www.pasadenaantiquecenter.com
(Accessories, Antique–Contemporary, Deco, Eclectic, Garden and Patio, Glassware, Hand Props, Lighting, Modern, Mission, Rugs & Vintage)

The Patio Collection (310) 453-0026
2512 Santa Monica Blvd. FAX (310) 453-0029
Santa Monica, CA 90404 www.patiocollections.com

Period Props (818) 848-7767
(818) 807-6677
1536 N. Evergreen St.
Burbank, CA 91505
(Prop House)

Pinacoteca (323) 965-2722
5735 W. Adams Bl. FAX (323) 965-2730
Los Angeles, CA 90016 www.pinacotecaprops.com

Prop Services West - Hollywood (323) 461-3371
7017 Santa Monica Blvd. FAX (323) 461-4571
Hollywood, CA 90038 www.pswprophouse.com
(Accessories, Antique–Contemporary, Eclectic, Mission, Prop House & Rugs)

Prop Services West - LA (323) 290-2600
4625 Crenshaw Blvd. FAX (323) 290-2607
Los Angeles, CA 90043 www.pswprophouse.com
(Accessories, Antique–Contemporary, Eclectic, Mission, Prop House & Rugs)

RC Vintage (818) 765-7107
(323) 462-4510
7100 Tujunga Ave. FAX (818) 765-7197
North Hollywood, CA 91605 www.rcvintage.com
(Vintage–Contemporary Prop House)

Retro Gallery (323) 936-5261
1100 S. La Brea Ave. FAX (323) 936-5262
Los Angeles, CA 90019 www.retroglass.com
(20th Century Glassware)

Riad Decor (323) 782-1064
(310) 877-7194
6136 W. Pico Blvd. FAX (323) 782-1082
Los Angeles, CA 90035 www.riadecor.com
(Indian, Indonesian & Moroccan)

The Rug Warehouse (310) 838-0450
3260 Helms Ave. FAX (310) 838-3868
Los Angeles, CA 90034 www.therugwarehouse.com
(Antique–Modern Rugs)

Sculpture and Paintings by Bruce Gray (323) 223-4059
688 S. Avenue 21 www.brucegray.com
Los Angeles, CA 90031
(Aluminum and Steel Sculpture, Art Furniture, Contemporary, Custom, Eclectic, Garden and Patio, Mobiles & Modern)

Shelter Furniture (323) 937-3222
7920 Beverly Blvd. FAX (323) 937-0639
Los Angeles, CA 90048
(Modern)

Silk Roads Design Gallery (323) 857-5588
145 N. La Brea Ave. FAX (323) 933-9364
Los Angeles, CA 90036 www.silkroadsgallery.com
(Antiques, Asian Art & Furnishings)

Sleep Exquisite (310) 478-3800
11727 Gateway Blvd. www.sleepexquisite.com
West Los Angeles, CA 90064
(Futons, Japanese Bedding & Tatami Platforms)

Sonny Black Dungeon Furniture (323) 939-2376
5128 Venice Blvd. FAX (323) 939-2376
Los Angeles, CA 90019 www.dungeonfurniture.com
(Bondage Themed Equipment and Furniture)

Sony Pictures Studios (310) 244-5999
5300 Alla Rd. FAX (310) 244-0999
Los Angeles, CA 90066 www.sonypicturesstudios.com

Sunny Meyer Fine Art (818) 985-6630
(Art Rentals) www.oldart.com

Sweet Smiling Home, Inc. (213) 687-9630
1317 Palmetto St. FAX (213) 687-9638
Los Angeles, CA 90013 www.sweetsmilinghome.com
(Antique and Contemporary Chinese and Indonesian Furniture)

Thanks for the Memories/TFTM (323) 852-9407
8319 Melrose Ave. FAX (323) 852-9407
Los Angeles, CA 90069
(Accessories, Antique–Contemporary, Deco, Garden and Patio, Glassware, Hand Props, Lighting, Modern, Office, Period, Rugs, Tapestries, Upholstery & Vintage)

Universal Patio Furniture (818) 762-9088
11055 Ventura Blvd. FAX (818) 762-8249
Studio City, CA 91604 www.unifurn.com
(Patio Furniture)

Warisan (323) 938-3960
7470 Beverly Blvd. FAX (323) 938-3959
Los Angeles, CA 90036 www.warisan.com
(Asian Antiques)

Warner Bros. Studio Facilities - Property (818) 954-2181
4000 Warner Blvd. FAX (818) 954-4965
Burbank, CA 91522 www.wbsf.com

Wertz Bros. Antique Mart (310) 452-1800
(310) 477-4251
1607 Lincoln Blvd. FAX (310) 452-1821
Santa Monica, CA 90404

Wertz Brothers Furniture, Inc. (310) 477-4251
11879 Santa Monica Blvd. FAX (310) 477-5136
West Los Angeles, CA 90025
(Used Home Furnishings)

Woven Accents (310) 652-6520
(800) 222-7847
525 N. La Cienega Blvd. FAX (310) 652-6594
Los Angeles, CA 90048 www.wovenonline.com
(Antique and Modern Rugs & Tapestries)

Zipper: Art Form & Function (323) 951-0620
8316 W. Third St. FAX (323) 951-0621
Los Angeles, CA 90048
(Contemporary Designer)

California Attractions, Ltd. (818) 999-6255
7023 Canoga Ave., Ste. B
Canoga Park, CA 91303
(Carnival Equipment)

Candyland Amusements (818) 266-4056
18653 Ventura Blvd., Ste. 235 FAX (818) 345-7988
Tarzana, CA 91356 **www.candylandamusements.com**

Chester's Circus & Carnival Equipment (323) 751-3486
(951) 233-6014
(Carnival and Circus Equipment) FAX (323) 778-2025

Ⓐ **Christiansen Amusements, Inc.** (800) 300-6114
(760) 735-8542
P.O. Box 997 FAX (760) 735-8543
Escondido, CA 92033 **www.amusements.com**
(Carnival Rides, Food Concessions & Games)

Creative Inflatables (626) 579-4454
(800) 446 3528
9872 Rush St. FAX (626) 579-5561
South El Monte, CA 91733 **www.creativeinflatables.com**
(Custom Inflatable Props, Jumpers, Misting Stations, Slides & Tents)

DeWayne Events (661) 251-4342
16520 Diver St. FAX (661) 251-2488
Canyon Country, CA 91387
(Carnival and Circus Equipment)

Dortons, Inc. (323) 751-3486
(951) 685-6014
6319 Eucalyptus FAX (323) 778-2025
Riverside, CA 92509
(Carnival and Circus Props)

Ⓐ **Family Amusement Corporation** (323) 660-8180
(800) 262-6467
876 N. Vermont Ave. FAX (323) 660-8976
Los Angeles, CA 90029 **www.familyamusement.com**
(Antique Slot Machines, Arcade and Video Games, Billiard Tables, Jukeboxes, Pinball Machines & Simulators)

Family Entertainment (310) 821-4490
(800) 379-4626
333 Washington Blvd., Ste. 360 FAX (310) 821-0522
Marina del Rey, CA 90292 **www.familyentertainment.biz**
(Carnival Rides & Gaming Equipment)

Grissom BIT Services (760) 801-8283
(Carnival Rides & Games) FAX (760) 737-8144

Franz Harary/ Odyssey in Illusion, Inc. (323) 871-1796 / (323) 855-9886
8300 Maple Dr.
Los Angeles, CA 90046
www.harary.com
(Magical Illusions)

Hollywood Magic, Inc. (323) 464-5610
6614 Hollywood Blvd.
Hollywood, CA 90028
FAX **(323) 464-0162**
(Magic Tricks & Novelties)

Hollywood Picture Cars/Scott Bosés (323) 466-2277
1028 N. La Brea Ave.
Hollywood, CA 90038
FAX **(323) 466-6541**
www.hollywoodpicturecars.com
(Jukeboxes, Penny Arcade Games & Pinball Machines)

L.A. Circus (323) 751-3486 / (951) 685-6014
7531 La Salle Ave.
Los Angeles, CA 90047
FAX **(323) 778-2025**
(Vintage–Modern Carnival and Circus Props & Canvas Tents)

Lucky Entertainment (310) 277-9666
10271 Almayo Ave., Ste. 101
West Los Angeles, CA 90064
FAX **(310) 284-8151**
www.luckyentertainment.com
(Artificial Cake, Carnival and Gambling Equipment, Jukeboxes, Refreshment Carts & Video Games)

North American Amusements, Inc. (909) 357-7130
11101 Calabash Ave.
Fontana, CA 92337
FAX **(909) 357-7136**
www.shamrockshows.com
(Carnival Rides, Food Concessions & Gaming Equipment)

Ⓐ **Play-Well** (626) 793-0603
686 S. Fair Oaks Ave.
Pasadena, CA 91105
FAX **(626) 793-2552**
www.playwell.com
(Outdoor Residential Play Equipment)

RC Vintage (818) 765-7107 / (323) 462-4510
7100 Tujunga Ave.
North Hollywood, CA 90028
FAX **(818) 765-7197**
www.rcvintage.com

Soap Plant/Wacko/La Luz de Jesus (323) 663-0122 / (323) 666-7667
4633 Hollywood Blvd.
Los Angeles, CA 90027
FAX **(323) 663-0243**
www.soapplant.com

Team Play Events (818) 889-3336 / (818) 889-2224
2854 Triunfo Canyon Rd.
Agoura Hills, CA 91301
FAX **(818) 889-2416**
www.teamplayevents.com
(Billiard Tables, Carnival Equipment, Carnival Rides, Casino Equipment, Circus Equipment, Classic Video Arcade Games, Food Concessions, Games, Gaming Equipment, Inflatables, Jumpers, Misting Stations, Novelties, Pinball Machines, Refreshment Carts, Simulators, Slides, Tents & Video Games)

The Train Shack (818) 842-3330 / (800) 572-9929
1030 N. Hollywood Way
Burbank, CA 91505
FAX **(818) 842-4562**
www.trainshack.com
(Toy Trains & Accessories)

A to Z Glass (323) 723-3449
(800) 734-4933
FAX (323) 728-5506

Adamm's Stained Glass (310) 451-9390
1426 Fourth St. FAX (310) 451-9386
Santa Monica, CA 90401 www.adammsgallery.com
(Beveled, Carved, Custom, Etched, Fabrication, Leaded, Restoration, Sculpted, Stained & Translucent)

A **Alfonso's Breakaway Glass, Inc.** (818) 768-7402
(866) 768-7402
8070 San Fernando Rd. FAX (818) 767-6969
Sun Valley, CA 91352 www.alfonsosbreakawayglass.com

All New Glass & Mirror Co. (323) 936-5245
FAX (323) 936-0280

Alva's Dance and Theatrical Supply (310) 519-1314
1417 W. Eighth St. FAX (310) 831-6110
San Pedro, CA 90732 www.alvas.com

ANA Special Effects, Inc. (818) 909-6999
7021 Hayvenhurst Ave. FAX (818) 782-0635
Van Nuys, CA 91406 www.anaspecialeffects.com
(Breakaway)

Charisma Design Studio, Inc. (818) 252-6611
(800) 891-8617
8414 San Fernando Rd. FAX (818) 252-6610
Sun Valley, CA 91352 www.charismadesign.com
(Etched, Sculpted & Waterjet Cutting)

Classic Glass Co. (818) 519-0344
FAX (805) 375-3017
(Carved, Etched, Leaded, Mirror, Stained & Tempered)

Continental Glazing (661) 295-8100
25050 Avenue Kearny, Ste. 115
Valencia, CA 91355

Giroux Glass, Inc. (213) 747-7406
850 W. Washington Blvd. FAX (213) 747-8778
Los Angeles, CA 90015 www.girouxglass.com
(Breakaway, Etched, Glazed & Mirror)

Hollywood Glass Company (323) 661-7774
(323) 665-8829
5119 Hollywood Blvd. FAX (323) 661-7261
Los Angeles, CA 90027

I.M.G. Glass & Mirror (818) 968-0987
FAX (805) 579-0743
(Beveled, Breakaway, Carved, Custom, Decorative, Etched, Fabrication, Glazed, Leaded, Mirror, Motion Effects, Restoration, Tempered, Translucent & Waterjet Cutting)

International Glass Block (323) 585-6368
(323) 585-6392
1316 E. Slauson Ave. FAX (323) 587-4421
Los Angeles, CA 90011 www.vetromosaico.com
(Glass Blocks)

James Thomas Stained & Leaded Glass (818) 763-5693
4375 Tujunga Ave. FAX (818) 763-5692
Studio City, CA 91604
(Beveled, Etched, Leaded & Stained)

Motion Picture Glass (818) 885-8700
9607 Canoga Ave. FAX (818) 885-8701
Chatsworth, CA 91311

Pacific GlassWorks, Inc. (310) 444-9191
FAX (310) 444-9161
www.pacificglassworks.com

Rohan Glass Co., Inc. (818) 984-1000
(323) 877-6000
12442 Oxnard St. FAX (323) 877-7447
North Hollywood, CA 91606 www.rohanglass.com

Ruben's Glass & Mirrors (323) 937-4774
616 S. La Brea Ave. FAX (323) 937-0215
Los Angeles, CA 90036 www.rubens-glass.com

Shower Door Doctor (818) 781-4957
(800) 540-0555
(Mirror & Tempered) FAX (818) 762-2524

Special Effects Technologies, Inc. (310) 490-6406
3644 Eastham Dr. FAX (213) 947-1327
Culver City, CA 90232 www.effectstech.com
(Custom Glass, Etched & Motion Effects)

Superior Glass Service (323) 663-1165
(800) 237-3366
FAX (323) 663-1168
www.framelessdepot.com

UltraGlas, Inc. (818) 772-7744
(800) 777-2332
9200 Gazette Ave. FAX (818) 772-8231
Chatsworth, CA 91311 www.ultraglas.com
(Decorative, Embossed & Translucent)

A & S Case Company (818) 509-5920 (800) 394-6181
5260 Vineland Ave. FAX (818) 509-1397
North Hollywood, CA 91601 www.ascase.com
(Wardrobe Cases)

Apache Rental Group (818) 842-9944 (818) 842-9875
3910 W. Magnolia Blvd. FAX (818) 842-9269
Burbank, CA 91505 www.apacherentalgroup.com
(Wardrobe Supplies)

Atomic Production Supplies (818) 566-8811
2621 N. Ontario St. FAX (818) 566-8311
Burbank, CA 91504 www.atomicproductionsupplies.com
(Wardrobe Supplies)

Ball Beauty Supplies (323) 655-2330 (800) 588-0244
416 N. Fairfax Ave. www.ballbeauty.com
Los Angeles, CA 90036

Beauty Company (310) 475-3531
10863 W. Pico Blvd.
West Los Angeles, CA 90064

Cal-East Imports (310) 278-2520
232 S. Beverly Dr., Ste. 211 FAX (310) 278-4761
Beverly Hills, CA 90212
(Hairpieces & Wigs)

Cases for Visual Arts, Inc. (818) 981-4238 (818) 693-6304
(Portable Makeup Stations) FAX (818) 501-4215
www.casesforvisualarts.com

Castex Rentals (323) 462-1468
1044 Cole Ave. FAX (323) 462-3719
Hollywood, CA 90038 www.castexrentals.com
(Hangers, Makeup Cases, Makeup Supplies, Makeup Tables, Portable Makeup Stations, Wardrobe Mirrors & Wardrobe Racks)

Charlie Wright, Ltd. (818) 347-4566
19720 Ventura Blvd., Ste. 106 FAX (818) 346-1043
Woodland Hills, CA 91364 www.wrighthair.com
(Wigs)

Chic Little Devil Style House (310) 403-6929
1206 Maple Ave., 11th Fl.
Los Angeles, CA 90015
www.chiclittledevilstylehouse.com

Cinema Secrets (818) 846-0579
4400 Riverside Dr. FAX (818) 846-0431
Burbank, CA 91505 www.cinemasecrets.com
(Hair and Makeup Supplies)

Dinair (818) 780-4777
5315 Laurel Canyon Blvd., Ste. 201 FAX (818) 780-4748
North Hollywood, CA 91607 www.dinair.com
(Hair and Makeup Supplies)

Extensions Plus (818) 881-5611
17738 Sherman Way FAX (818) 881-5220
Reseda, CA 91335 www.extensions-plus.com
(Hair and Wig Extensions)

Favian Wigs by Natascha (818) 346-1104
23547 Hatteras St. FAX (818) 346-1338
Woodland Hills, CA 91367
(Wigs)

Fred Segal Apothia (323) 651-1935
8118 Melrose Ave. FAX (323) 653-2178
Los Angeles, CA 90046 www.apothia.com

Frend's Beauty Supply (818) 769-3834 (323) 877-4828
5270 Laurel Canyon Blvd. FAX (818) 769-8124
North Hollywood, CA 91607
www.frendsbeautysupply.com

Galaxy Manufacturing Co. (323) 728-3980 (800) 876-4599
5411 Sheila St. FAX (323) 728-5971
Los Angeles, CA 90040 www.galaxymfg.com
(Barber and Beauty Salon Equipment)

Hair and Compounds (818) 997-8810
(Custom European Hair and Extensions) FAX (818) 997-8860
www.haircompounds.com

Hair Extensions By Sara Sierra (626) 826-7313
1124 S. Cajon Ave.
West Covina, CA 91791

Industry Hair (818) 562-1858
(By Appointment Only)

Innerspace Cases (818) 767-3030 (800) 806-7689
11555 Cantara St., Ste. I FAX (818) 767-6118
North Hollywood, CA 91605 www.innerspacecases.com
(Makeup and Wardrobe Cases)

The Joe Blasco Makeup Center (323) 467-4949 (800) 553-1580
1670 Hillhurst Ave., Ste. 202 FAX (323) 664-7142
Los Angeles, CA 90027 www.joeblasco.com

Larchmont Beauty Center (323) 461-0162
208 N. Larchmont Blvd. FAX (323) 461-0164
Los Angeles, CA 90004 www.larchmontbeauty.com

Line 204 (323) 960-0113
1034 N. Seward St. FAX (323) 960-0163
Hollywood, CA 90038 www.line204.com
(Wardrobe Supplies)

Lorac Cosmetics, Inc. (818) 678-3939 (800) 845-0705
FAX (818) 678-3930
www.loraccosmetics.com

M.A.C. (310) 659-6201 (800) 588-0070
(Makeup) www.maccosmetics.com

Make Believe, Inc. (310) 396-6785
3240 Pico Blvd. FAX (310) 396-1936
Santa Monica, CA 90405 www.makebelieve.to
(Hair and Makeup Supplies)

Miller Production Services (310) 287-0466
3520 Helms Ave. FAX (310) 287-0467
Culver City, CA 90232
(Wardrobe Supplies)

Naimie's Beauty Supply (818) 655-9922
12640 Riverside Dr. FAX (818) 655-9999
Valley Village, CA 91607 www.naimies.com

Norcostco California Costume (818) 567-0753 (800) 220-6915
3606 W. Magnolia Blvd. FAX (818) 567-1961
Burbank, CA 91505 www.norcostco.com
(Theatrical Makeup)

Ole Henriksen Face/Body (310) 854-7700
8622-A W. Sunset Blvd. FAX (310) 854-1869
Los Angeles, CA 90069 www.olehenriksen.com
(Skin Care Products)

Origins (626) 564-1790
(Makeup) www.origins.com

Out of Frame Production Rentals (323) 462-1898
1126 N. Citrus Ave. FAX (323) 462-1897
Hollywood, CA 90038 www.outofframela.com
(Makeup Tables, Portable Makeup Stations, Wardrobe Mirrors, Wardrobe Racks & Wardrobe Supplies)

The Outfitter (323) 469-9421 (323) 461-7822
6626 Hollywood Blvd. FAX (323) 462-4730
Hollywood, CA 90028
(Wigs)

Quixote Studios (323) 960-9191
1000 N. Cahuenga Blvd. FAX (323) 960-3366
Los Angeles, CA 90038 www.quixote.com
(Wardrobe Supplies)

Riquette International (310) 551-5253
269 S. Beverly Dr., Ste. 200 FAX (310) 551-5254
Beverly Hills, CA 90212 www.riquette.com
(Hair and Makeup Supplies)

Rock Bottom Rentals (310) 315-2600 (800) 794-5444
1310 Westwood Blvd. FAX (310) 582-0023
Los Angeles, CA 90024 www.rockbottomrentals.com
(Wardrobe Supplies)

Salon Equipment International (562) 461-2972 (877) 461-2972
16640 Bellflower Blvd. FAX (562) 925-2461
Bellflower, CA 90706 www.salonequipment.com
(Barber and Beauty Equipment)

Set Stuff, Inc. (323) 993-9500
1105 N. Sycamore Ave. FAX (323) 993-9506
Hollywood, CA 90038 www.setstuffrentals.com
(Makeup Tables, Racks & Wardrobe Mirrors)

Studio Makeup Academy (323) 465-4002
1438 N. Gower St., Studio 308
Hollywood, CA 90028
www.studiomakeupacademy.com

Sun Aired Bag Company (310) 372-7225
524 Cypress Ave. FAX (310) 372-5825
Hermosa Beach, CA 90254 www.sunaired.com
(Wardrobe Bags)

T.Z. Case (909) 392-8806 (888) 892-2737
1786 Curtiss Court www.tzcase.com
La Verne, CA 91750
(Makeup Cases)

Temptu (213) 739-1800
201 N. Westmoreland Ave., Ste. 133 www.temptu.com
Los Angeles, CA 90004
(Airbrush Equipment and Accessories, Portable Makeup Stations, Skin Care Products & Theatrical Makeup)

A **Travel Auto Bag Co. Inc.** (800) 940-0095
FAX (212) 302-8267
www.travelautobag.com
(Hangers, Makeup Cases, Steamers, Wardrobe Bags, Wardrobe Cases, Wardrobe Racks & Wardrobe Supplies)

UVASUN (323) 651-4540 (323) 646-2004
8242 W. Third St., Ste. 100 FAX (323) 651-4150
Los Angeles, CA 90048 www.uvasun.com
(Air Brush Tanning & Tanning Beds)

West Hollywood Beauty Supply & Salon (323) 656-2237
www.westhollywoodbeauty.com

Wigged Out/Carol F. Doran (818) 352-4701
FAX (818) 352-4701
web.mac.com/wiggedout
(Facial Hair, Hair and Wig Extensions, Hairpieces & Wigs)

Wilshire Beauty (323) 937-2001
5401 Wilshire Blvd. www.wilshirebeauty.com
Los Angeles, CA 90036

Wilshire Wigs & Accessories (818) 761-9447
5241 Craner Ave. FAX (818) 761-9779
North Hollywood, CA 91601 www.wilshirewigs.com

Cal Ice Company (310) 590-1260
229 Glasgow Ave.
Engelwood, CA 90301
(Block, Crushed, Cubed, Dry & Snow)

California Ice & Propane (818) 224-4423
21215 Devonshire St. FAX (818) 224-2650
Chatsworth, CA 91311
(Block, Carved, Crushed, Cubed & Dry)

Ice FX (818) 785-1143
(888) 830-8383
14243 Bessemer St. www.unionice.com/icefx.htm
Van Nuys, CA 91401
(Custom Cut, Dry, Photo & Snow)

LA Ice Art (310) 670-1444
(323) 578-4244
229 S. Glasgow Ave. www.laiceart.com
Inglewood, CA 90301
(Block & Sculpted)

Long Beach Ice (888) 438-1956
(562) 438-8129
1600 Cherry Ave. FAX (562) 856-1356
Long Beach, CA 90813 www.longbeachice.com
(Beverage, Block, Crushed, Cubed, Custom Cut, Dry, Fabrication, Photo, Sculpted, Shards & Snow)

Robin McCarthy (818) 883-6223
4918 Escobedo Dr.
Woodland Hills, CA 91364
(Portable Plastic Ice Skating Surfaces)

Michael Plesh and Company (818) 768-4444
(Fabrication & Fake Ice Cubes) www.propmakers.com

Newhall Ice Co. (661) 259-0893
(818) 362-9742
22502 Fifth St. FAX (661) 259-0691
Newhall, CA 91321
(24-Hour Service; Block, Crushed, Cubed & Dry)

North Hollywood Ice Co. (818) 762-2237
(323) 465-5538
5257 Craner Blvd. FAX (818) 762-6750
North Hollywood, CA 91601
(Dry & Photo) www.northhollywoodice.com

Reliable Snow Service (661) 269-2093
(661) 305-8274
(Beverage, Clear Block & Dry) FAX (661) 269-2237

Special Effects Technologies, Inc. (310) 490-6406
3644 Eastham Dr. FAX (213) 947-1327
Culver City, CA 90232 www.effectstech.com
(Fake Ice Cubes and Shards & Fabrication)

Willy Bietak Productions, Inc. (310) 576-2400
1404 Third St. Promenade, Ste. 200 FAX (310) 576-2405
Santa Monica, CA 90401 www.bietakproductions.com
(Portable Ice Skating Surfaces)

Alpha Medical Resources, Inc. (818) 504-9090
7990 San Fernando Rd. **www.alphamedprops.com**
Sun Valley, CA 91352

Angelus Medical & Optical Co., Inc. (310) 769-6060
13007 S. Western Ave. FAX **(310) 769-1999**
Gardena, CA 90249 **www.angelusmedical.com**
(Dental, Medical & Optical Props)

Carrie Becks/A-1 Medical Advisor (310) 227-8200
(310) 678-7601
345 Richmond St. FAX **(310) 227-8205**
El Segundo, CA 90245 **www.redm33.com**
(Ultrasound Equipment)

C.P. Two (323) 466-8201
5755 Santa Monica Blvd. FAX **(323) 962-0345**
Hollywood, CA 90038 **www.omegacinemaprops.com**

Dapper Cadaver (818) 771-0818
www.bjwinslow.com

E.C. Prop Rentals, Inc. (818) 764-2008
11846 Sherman Way FAX **(818) 764-2374**
North Hollywood, CA 91605 **www.ecprops.com**

Galaxy Manufacturing Co. (323) 728-3980
(800) 876-4599
5411 Sheila St. FAX **(323) 728-5971**
Los Angeles, CA 90040 **www.galaxymfg.com**
(Chiropractic and Massage Tables & Dental and Medical Equipment)

The High Wheelers (626) 288-0820
(626) 576-8648
9344 E. Valley Blvd. **www.highwheelers.com**
Rosemead, CA 91770
(Medical Equipment)

History for Hire (818) 765-7767
7149 Fair Ave. FAX **(818) 765-7871**
North Hollywood, CA 91605 **www.historyforhire.com**

Independent Studio Services, Inc./ISS (818) 951-5600
9545 Wentworth St. FAX **(818) 951-2850**
Sunland, CA 91040 **www.issprops.com**

LCW Props (818) 243-0707
6439 San Fernando Rd. FAX **(818) 243-1830**
Glendale, CA 91201 **www.lcwprops.com**

Lennie Marvin Enterprises, Inc. (818) 841-5882
3110 Winona Ave. FAX **(818) 841-2896**
Burbank, CA 91504 **www.propheaven.com**

Lynn Harding Antique Instruments of the Professions and Sciences (805) 646-0204
103 W. Aliso St. FAX **(805) 646-0204**
Ojai, CA 93023
(Antique Scientific Instruments)

Med + Rent, Inc. (818) 834-5800
FAX **(818) 834-5900**
www.medrent.com
(Dental, Hospital, Lab and Medical Props)

Modern Props (323) 934-3000
5500 W. Jefferson Blvd. FAX **(323) 934-3155**
Los Angeles, CA 90016 **www.modernprops.com**

Morgue Prop Rentals (323) 226-9018
www.morgueproprentals.com

MyMedSource (888) 755-9370
3305 E. Miraloma Ave., Ste. 176 FAX **(888) 755-9371**
Anaheim, CA 92806 **www.mymedsource.com**

Pacific Coast Nuclear Associates (714) 961-0237
16881 Chestnut St. FAX **(714) 961-1738**
Yorba Linda, CA 92886
(Medical Equipment)

Pico Medical Rents & Sells (323) 936-4104
(800) 676-0400
6035 W. Pico Blvd. FAX **(323) 936-3454**
Los Angeles, CA 90035 **www.shoppicomedical.com**

Premiere Props (818) 768-3800
11500 Sheldon St. FAX **(818) 768-3808**
Sun Valley, CA 91352
(Contemporary and Period Props)

The Rational Past (310) 903-3663
FAX **(310) 476-6278**
www.therationalpast.com

Technical Props, Inc. (818) 761-4993
FAX **(818) 761-5059**

A & D Music Incorporated (949) 768-7110
22322 Colonna Dr. FAX **(949) 716-7667**
Laguna Hills, CA 92653 **www.admusic.net**
(Amplifiers, Antique, D.J. Gear, Drums, Guitars, Harps, Horns, Keyboard Instruments, Microphones, Percussion, Rare Instruments, Speakers & Strings)

Adam's Music (310) 839-3575
10612 W. Pico Blvd. FAX **(310) 839-0167**
Los Angeles, CA 90064 **www.adamsmusic.com**
(Amplifiers, Antique, Drums, Guitars, Horns, Keyboard Instruments, Microphones, Percussion, Pianos, Rare Instruments, Speakers & Strings)

Drum Doctors (818) 244-8123
520 Commercial St. FAX **(818) 244-8120**
Glendale, CA 91203 **www.drumdoctors.com**

Drum Fetish (213) 359-0328
(323) 397-4320
(Drums)

Enchanted Melodies/CNS (818) 894-5694
8925 Densmore Ave. FAX **(818) 894-7794**
North Hills, CA 91343
(Antique Circus Organ with Operator)

Harps Unlimited (818) 986-3262
14122 Dickens St.
Sherman Oaks, CA 91423
(Harps & Rare Instruments)

Harpworld Music Company (818) 891-1023
(818) 903-6830
P.O. Box 28-0189 **www.harpworld.com**
Northridge, CA 91328
(Antique–Present Harps, Harp Cases & Music Stands)

Hollywood Piano Company (818) 954-8500
(888) 697-4266
1033 Hollywood Way **www.hollywoodpiano.com**
Burbank, CA 91505

Kasimoff-Blüthner Piano Co. (323) 466-7707
337 N. Larchmont Blvd. FAX **(323) 466-7708**
Los Angeles, CA 90004 **www.bluthnerlosangeles.com**
(Antique, Celesta, Harpsichords, Keyboard Instruments, Pianos & Rare Instruments)

L.A. Percussion Rentals (310) 666-8152
FAX **(310) 868-0646**
www.lapercussionrentals.com
(Amplifiers, Drums, Keyboard Instruments, Microphones, Orchestral, Percussion, Rare Instruments & Speakers)

Music Prop Services (818) 982-4100
7309 Clybourn Ave., Ste. 6 **www.musicprops.com**
Sun Valley, CA 91352
(Amplifiers, D.J. Gear, Drums, Guitars, Horns, Large Speakers, Microphones, Pianos, Strings, Set Dressing & Prop House)

Norman's Rare Guitars (818) 344-8300
18969 Ventura Blvd. FAX **(818) 344-1260**
Tarzana, CA 91356 **www.normansrareguitars.com**
(Amps, Fretted String Instruments & Guitars)

Studio Instrument Rentals/SIR (323) 957-5460
6465 Sunset Blvd. FAX **(323) 957-5472**
Hollywood, CA 90028 **www.sirla.com**

Third Encore (818) 753-0148
(800) 339-8850
10917 Vanowen St. FAX **(818) 753-0151**
North Hollywood, CA 91605 **www.3rdencore.com**
(Musical Instruments)

American Signs & Graphics (310) 203-9252
(323) 938-7446
311 N. Robertson Blvd., Ste. 161 FAX (323) 938-7447
Beverly Hills, CA 90211 www.americansignsinc.com

Concept Design (626) 932-0082
(800) 846-0717
718 Primrose Ave. FAX (626) 932-0072
Monrovia, CA 91016 www.conceptdesigninc.com
(Fabrication)

The Hand Prop Room, L.P. (323) 931-1534
5700 Venice Blvd. FAX (323) 931-2145
Los Angeles, CA 90019 www.hpr.com
(Hand Props Only)

Ⓐ **Heaven or Las Vegas Neon** (310) 636-0081
11814 W. Jefferson Blvd. FAX (310) 636-1959
Culver City, CA 90230 www.rentneon.com

Hollywood Neon, Inc. (323) 852-9611
7456 Melrose Ave. FAX (323) 852-0031
Los Angeles, CA 90046 www.hollywoodneon.com

Neon by Ohashi (323) 258-8701
6267 Saylin Ln. FAX (323) 258-4917
Los Angeles, CA 90042 www.ohashineon.com
(Fabrication)

Nights of Neon, Inc. (818) 756-4791
13815 Saticoy St. FAX (818) 756-4744
Van Nuys, CA 91402 www.nightsofneon.com
(Fabrication & Props)

RC Vintage (818) 765-7107
(323) 462-4510
7100 Tujunga Ave. FAX (818) 765-7197
North Hollywood, CA 90028 www.rcvintage.com
(Period–Present Signage)

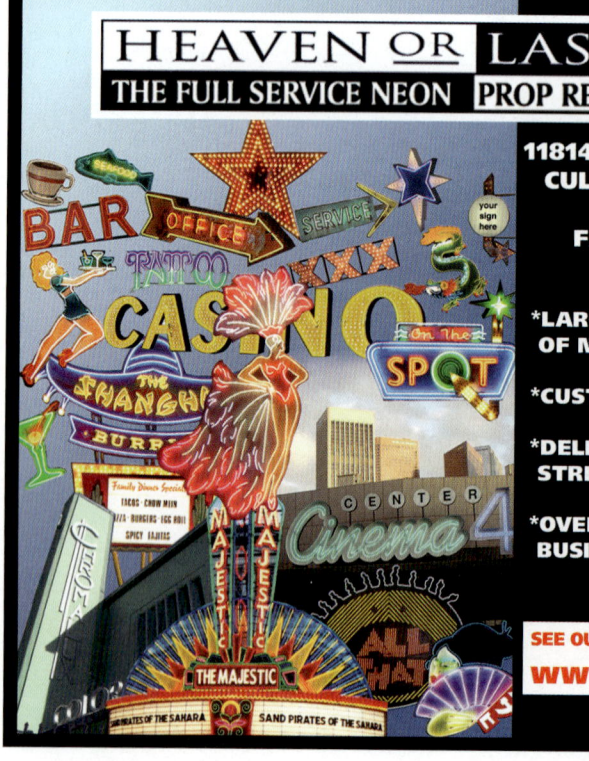

Ahead Stereo (323) 931-8873
7428 Beverly Blvd. FAX (323) 937-7285
Los Angeles, CA 90036 www.aheadstereo.com
(Sound Equipment Rentals)

Alan Gordon Enterprises, Inc. (323) 466-3561
5625 Melrose Ave. FAX (323) 871-2193
Los Angeles, CA 90038 www.alangordon.com
(Antique and Classic Motion Picture Cameras and Projectors & Prop Cameras)

Apex Electronics (818) 767-7202
(323) 875-1308
8909 San Fernando Rd. FAX (818) 767-1341
Sun Valley, CA 91352 www.apexelectronic.com
(Aircraft and Military Electronics)

Apex Jr. (818) 248-0416
3045 Orange Ave. FAX (818) 248-0490
La Crescenta, CA 91214 www.apexjr.com

Coast Recording Props (323) 462-6070
(323) 462-6058
6223 Santa Monica Blvd. FAX (323) 462-6064
Hollywood, CA 90038
(Prop Cameras & Radio Station and Recording Studio Props)

CRE - Computer & A/V Solutions (800) 427-2382
(888) 444-1059
5732 Buckingham Pkwy FAX (877) 440-5252
Culver City, CA 90230
www.computerrentals.com/products/mac/mac_rentals_specialist.php
(Computer and Video Props, Graphic Displays, LED Electronic Displays, Projectors & Rentals)

Face Value (818) 348-1320
5305 Tendilla Ave. www.facevalueprops.com
Woodland Hills, CA 91364
(Prop Cameras & Vintage Cameras, Microphones and Radios)

The Hand Prop Room, L.P. (323) 931-1534
5700 Venice Blvd. FAX (323) 931-2145
Los Angeles, CA 90019 www.hpr.com
(Prop Cameras)

Inter Video (818) 843-3624
2211 N. Hollywood Way FAX (818) 843-6884
Burbank, CA 91505 www.intervideo24.com
(Computer and Video Props & Prop Cameras)

Jordan's House of Betas (310) 428-7786
1549 1/2 S. Wooster St. www.jordanshouseofbetas.com
Los Angeles, CA 90035
(News Beta Cameras & Prop Cameras)

MacEnthusiasts (800) 948-6901
10600 W. Pico Blvd. FAX (310) 287-1088
Los Angeles, CA 90064 www.macenthusiasts.com
(Mac Computers, Projectors & Rentals)

Mandex Led Motion Displays (805) 497-8006
(818) 825-9664
2350 Young Ave. FAX (818) 889-4569
Thousand Oaks, CA 91360 www.ledsignage.com
(LED Electronic Displays)

Practical Props (818) 982-3198
11754 Vose St. FAX (818) 980-7894
North Hollywood, CA 91605 www.practicalprops.com

Prolab Digital Imaging (310) 625-4411
5441 W. 104th St FAX (310) 204-6939
Los Angeles, CA 90045 www.prolabdigital.com

Satellite America, Inc. (818) 710-9348
22030 Ventura Blvd., Ste. E FAX (818) 710-1423
Woodland Hills, CA 91364
(Satellite Dishes)

SJC Mobile Video (661) 257-5881
28625 Braxton Ave. FAX (661) 257-5883
Valencia, CA 91355 www.sjcvideo.com
(Prop Cameras)

So Cal Production Source (310) 699-2787
FAX (310) 618-0129
www.scpsunlimited.com
(Aircraft, Antique, Cameras, Computer, Dummy Equipment, Electronic, Electronic Surveillance Equipment, Graphic Displays, LED Electronic Displays, Microphones, Military, News Beta Cameras, Projectors, Prop Cameras, Radio Station and Recording Studio, Radios, RED Cameras, Rentals, Satellite Dishes, Sound Equipment, Still Cameras, Supplies, Televisions, Video & Vintage)

Studio Prop Rentals, Inc. (661) 775-1655
(818) 679-4000
28306 Constellation Rd. FAX (661) 255-9726
Valencia, CA 91355 www.studioproprentals.com
(Cameras, Computers, Contemporary News Beta Cameras and Accessories, Electronics, Props, Radios, Rentals, Sound Equipment & Telephones)

This Town Productions (213) 926-7000
1155 N. La Cienega Blvd., PH 7 FAX (702) 926-7009
West Hollywood, CA 90069 www.thistown.tv
(Prop Cameras & Vintage Audio and Video Props)

1 A Allstar Picture Cars (818) 609-0777 (310) 463-4489
17757 Victory Blvd. FAX (818) 609-0666
Reseda, CA 91335 www.allstarpicturecars.com
(Antique–Present, Classics, Exotics, Motorcycles, Sports Cars, Taxis & Trucks)

1 A Constant Change Picture Vehicles (818) 355-8824 (818) 908-1948
15500 Erwin St., Ste. 328 FAX (818) 787-7755
Van Nuys, CA 91411 www.seemyrentals.com
(Ambulances, ATVs, Buses, Cabin Cruisers, Camera Cars, Classic–Contemporary, Convertibles, Domestics, European, Exotics, Farm Vehicles, Fire Trucks, Helicopters, Jeeps, Limousines, Military Vehicles, Motorcycles, Muscle Cars, Police Cars, RVs, Salvage, Scooters, Sports Cars, Storage, Taxis, Trailers, Trucks & Vehicle Coordination and Transportation)

2 Wheel Devil (323) 225-2224 (213) 793-1937
(Antique Motorcycles)

310 Picture Cars (310) 678-8007
6709 La Tijera Blvd., Ste. 247 www.picturecardiv.com
Los Angeles, CA 90045
(Ambulances, Buses, Cigarette Boats, Classics, Damaged, Emergency, Exotics, Fire Trucks, Limousines, Lowriders, Military Vehicles, Motorcycles, Muscle Cars, Taxis, Vehicle Coordination & Vehicle Transportation)

A-Z Bus Sales, Inc. (951) 781-7188 (800) 437-5522
1900 S. Riverside Ave. FAX (951) 778-2950
Colton, CA 92324 www.a-zbus.com

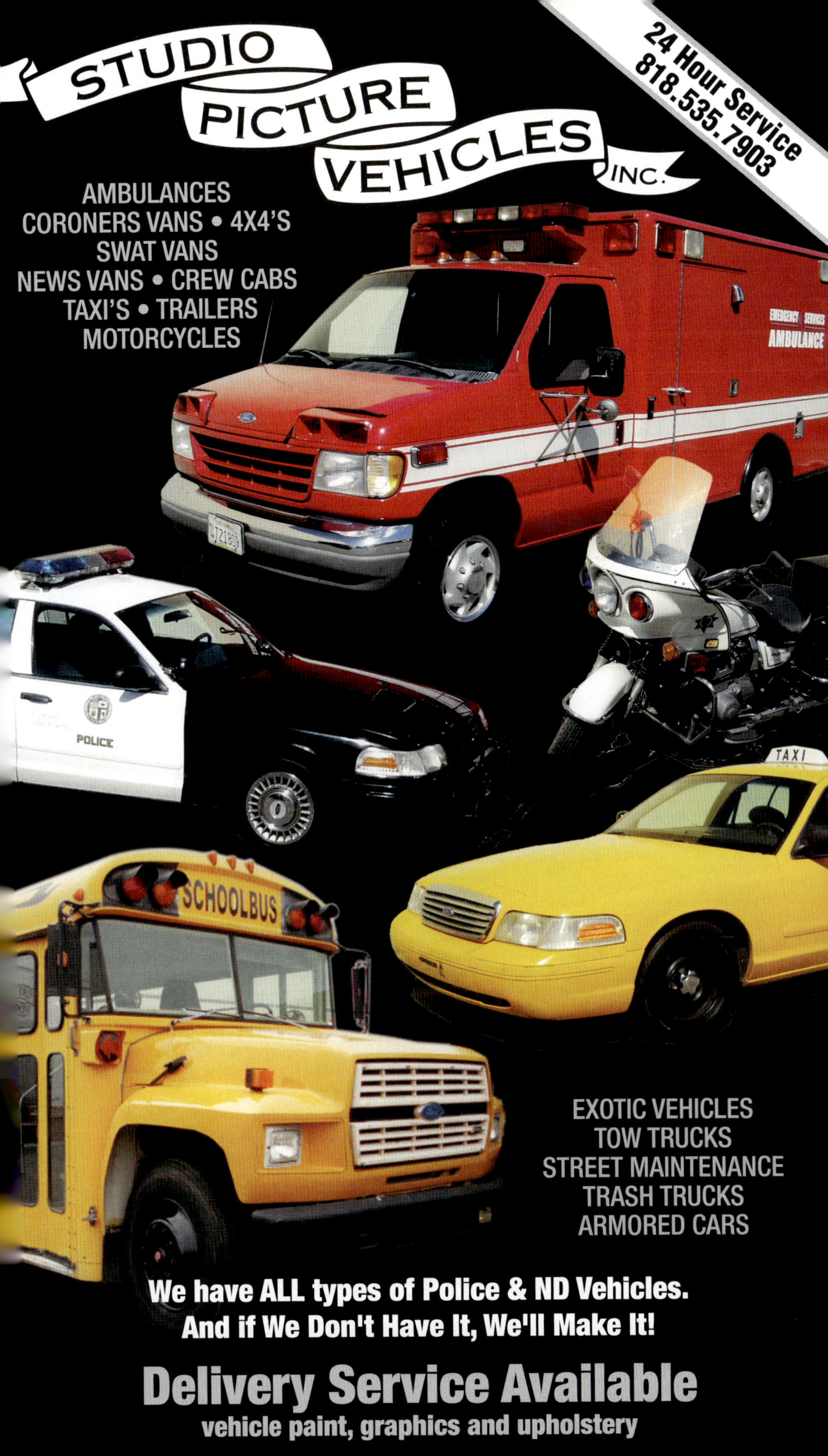

STUDIO PICTURE VEHICLES INC.
24 Hour Service
818.535.7903
AMBULANCES
CORONERS VANS • 4X4'S
SWAT VANS
NEWS VANS • CREW CABS
TAXI'S • TRAILERS
MOTORCYCLES
EMERGENCY SERVICES
AMBULANCE
POLICE
TAXI
SCHOOLBUS
EXOTIC VEHICLES
TOW TRUCKS
STREET MAINTENANCE
TRASH TRUCKS
ARMORED CARS

ABA Antique Autos, Inc./ ABA Picture Vehicles (310) 323-9028
8306 Wilshire Blvd., PMB 900 www.abaaa.com
Beverly Hills, CA 90211
(Contemporary and Vintage Buses, Cars, Horse and Buggy & Trucks)

Action Antique Period Picture Cars (562) 693-5641
2684 Turnbull Canyon Rd.
City of Industry, CA 91745
(Antiques, Antique Mechanic's Tools & Classic Cars and Trucks)

Advanced Fire & Rescue Services (818) 837-7336
(661) 299-4801
16205 Lost Canyon Rd. FAX (661) 298-3069
Canyon Country, CA 91387 www.advancedfire.com
(Fire Engines & Rescue Vehicles)

All Major Productions (818) 344-5454
21221 Pacific Coast Hwy FAX (310) 456-5692
Malibu, CA 90265
(Classic–Contemporary Cars, Motorcycles & Vehicle Transportation)

All Vehicle Services (818) 609-0777
(Antique–Contemporary Buses, Cars, Convertibles, Emergency Vehicles, Limousines, Motorcycles, Trucks and Vehicle Transportation)

Arista Picture Vehicles (562) 928-8581
(562) 462-8118
8132 Firestone Blvd., Ste. 41 FAX (562) 928-8444
Downey, CA 90241
(Antique–Present, Buses, Classics, Convertibles, Exotics, Fire Trucks, Motorcycles, Police and Sports Cars & Taxis)

Armytrucks, Inc. (661) 252-8511
(818) 523-6013
(Military Vehicles) FAX (661) 252-8561
www.armytrucks.com

Avon Studio Transportation (323) 850-0826
(800) 432-2866
7080 Santa Monica Blvd. FAX (323) 467-4239
Los Angeles, CA 90038 www.avonrents.com
(Contemporary)

Avon Studio Transportation (310) 277-4455
(800) 432-2866
9224 Olympic Dr. FAX (310) 277-0675
Beverly Hills, CA 90212 www.avonrents.com

Avon Studio Transportation (310) 392-8618
(800) 432-2866
2411 Lincoln Blvd. FAX (310) 399-0901
Santa Monica, CA 90405 www.avonrents.com

B & R Police Motorcycle Studio Rentals (818) 994-6673
(310) 399-7370
P.O. Box 5669 FAX (310) 452-7274
Santa Monica, CA 90409 www.pmsrentals.com
(Classic–Contemporary)

Barry's Reel Vehicles (661) 254-8114
FAX (661) 254-8115

Ⓐ **Beverly Hills Rent-A-Car** (818) 623-6700
(310) 901-0135
11647 Ventura Blvd. FAX (818) 623-0400
Studio City, CA 91604 www.bhrentacar.com
(Camera Cars, Classics, Exotics, Sports Cars, Trucks & Vehicle Transportation)

Bircheff's Army Trucks (909) 214-8413
(909) 985-6862
(Jeeps, Military Vehicles & Vintage) FAX (909) 989-2030
www.armytruckrental.com

Bongorama (310) 569-0354
www.blackhorsemedia.com
(Classic, High Performance, Hot Rods, Lowriders, Muscle Cars, Salvage, Sports Cars, Stunt Cars, Vehicle Coordination & Vehicle Transportation)

Bothwell Ranch (818) 347-9000
5300 Oakdale Ave. FAX (818) 587-9215
Woodland Hills, CA 91364
(Antiques & Classics)

Burbank Kawasaki (818) 848-6627
(818) 749-5676
1329 N. Hollywood Way FAX (818) 848-6630
Burbank, CA 91505 www.burbankkawasaki.com
(ATVs, Jet Skis & Motorcycles)

★Exotics ★Vintage ★Classics ★Trucks
★Rolls Royce ★Bentley ★Ferrari ★Aston Martin
Specializing in the Rare and Unusual

(888) 64-ROLLS

(818) 905-6267 • Fax (818) 906-1249 • rollsroyce1@earthlink.net
Visit us at www.classicautorental.com

Callaway Picture Cars (310) 447-2677
P.O. Box 17 FAX (510) 583-5011
Sunol, CA 94586
(Antique and Vintage Cars)

Cantos Collection (310) 780-6002
(213) 303-2228
P.O. Box 34813 FAX (213) 558-3745
Los Angeles, CA 90034 www.cantoscollection.com
(Antique—Present Buses, Cars, Convertibles, Limousines, Motorcycles, Performance Cars & Trucks)

Cat Production Services/ Extreme Sports Filming (562) 596-7105
www.extremesportsfilming.com
(Ambulances, Antique, ATVs, Buses, Cabin Cruisers, Camera Cars, Carriages, Cigarette Boats, Classic, Contemporary, Convertibles, Cutaways, Damaged, Domestics, Emergency Vehicles, European, Exotics, Farm Vehicles, Fire Trucks, Fishing Boats, Futuristic, Hearses, Helicopter, High Performance, Horse and Buggy, Hot Rods, HumVees, Jeeps, Limousines, Lowriders, Luxury, Military Vehicles, Motorboats, Motorcycles, Muscle Cars, Police Vehicles, Rescue Vehicles, RVs, Salvage, Scooters, Semi Trucks, Sleighs, Sports Cars, Storage, Stunt Cars, Tanks, Taxis, Tractor Trailers, Trailers, Trains, Troop Carriers, Trucks, Vehicle Coordination, Vehicle Transportation, Vintage, Wagons, Water Trucks, Woodies & Yachts)

Cinema Vehicle Services (818) 780-6272
12580 Saticoy St. FAX (818) 780-1340
North Hollywood, CA 91605 www.cinemavehicles.com
(Classic–Contemporary)

Classic Auto Rental Services (818) 905-6267
(888) 647-6557
15445 Ventura Blvd., Ste. 60 FAX (818) 906-1249
Sherman Oaks, CA 91413 www.classicautorental.com
(Bentleys, Classics, Exotics, Rolls-Royces & Vintage)

Classic Car Rental Connection (818) 728-0607
(818) 804-9203
17514 Ventura Blvd. FAX (818) 728-0684
Encino, CA 91316 www.101classiccarrental.com
(Antiques & Classics)

Classic Car Suppliers (310) 659-1711
1484 Sunset Plaza Dr. www.classiccarsuppliers.com
West Hollywood, CA 90069
(Antiques, Classics, Convertibles, Exotics & High Performance Cars)

Classic Limos (800) 550-3125
(949) 495-3125
30251 Golden Lantern, E-510 FAX (949) 495-1652
Laguna Niguel, CA 92677 www.classiclimousines.com
(Classics, Limousines & Vintage)

X BEVERLY HILLS MARINA DEL REY NEWPORT BEACH LAS VEGAS HOLLYWOOD

Classy Chassis Rentals (818) 321-9022
18375 Ventura Blvd., Ste. 260 FAX **(818) 881-0130**
Tarzana, CA 91356 **www.classychassisrentals.com**
(1950 Oldsmobile & 1957 Bentley)

Coach Engineering/Dave Weiner (818) 563-2399
(818) 406-5130
805 S. San Fernando Rd. FAX **(818) 563-1399**
Burbank, CA 91502 **www.coachengineering.com**
(Bus Cutaways & Buses)

Cornwell & Sheridan Motors, Classic Auto Rentals (310) 217-9060
(310) 995-8973
15700 S. Broadway FAX **(310) 516-9427**
Gardena, CA 90248 **www.old-cars.net**
(Antiques, Army Jeeps, Classics, Convertibles, Exotics, High Performance, Limousines, Motorcycles & Vintage Cars)

Corvette Mike (714) 630-0700
(714) 342-2570
1133 N. Tustin Ave. FAX **(714) 630-1810**
Anaheim, CA 92807 **www.corvettemike.com**
(Classic Corvettes)

Customs by Eddie Paul, A Division of EP Industries, Inc. (310) 643-8515
(310) 259-0542
2305 Utah Ave. FAX **(310) 643-8520**
El Segundo, CA 90245 **www.deadlinetv.net**
(Futuristic, High Performance, Hot Rods, Motorcycles & Stunt Cars)

DH Automotive (323) 842-8393
www.dhautoworks.com

Dougs Vintage Trailers (760) 949-3115
12567 Empire Pl. **www.dougsvintagetrailers.com**
Victorville, CA 92392
(Camera Cars & Trailers)

Dream Machines of America (323) 936-6141
105 S. Fairfax Ave. FAX **(323) 936-2305**
Los Angeles, CA 90036 **www.fordmustangs.org**
(Antiques & Classics)

Dream One (800) 538-8799
(310) 670-5466
(Limousines) FAX **(323) 933-1677**
www.dreamonesedans.com

EagleRider Motorcycle Rentals (310) 536-6777
11860 S. La Cienega Blvd. FAX **(310) 536-6776**
Los Angeles, CA 90250 **www.eaglerider.com**

Executive Productions (310) 456-8833
3951 Ridgemont Dr. FAX **(310) 456-5692**
Malibu, CA 90265
(Antique, Contemporary, Exotics & Rare Cars)

EZ 1 Movie Cars (310) 717-3099
1450 W. 228th St., Ste. 27
Torrance, CA 90501

Five-Star Military Vehicles (714) 847-8687
(310) 740-6931
FAX **(714) 841-0317**
www.militaryvehicles.com
(HumVees, Jeeps, Land Rovers, Tanks & Troop Carriers)

Ⓐ **Galpin Studio Rentals** (323) 957-3333
(800) 256-6219
1763 N. Ivar Ave. FAX **(323) 856-6790**
Hollywood, CA 90028 **www.galpinstudiorentals.com**
(Classic–Contemporary Cars, Motorcycles and Tractor Trailers)

Ⓐ **Galpin Studio Rentals** (818) 891-1751
(800) 256-6219
8353 Sepulveda Blvd. FAX **(818) 778-3027**
North Hills, CA 91343 **www.galpinstudiorentals.com**

Ghostlight Industries Inc. (818) 898-1938
956 Griswold Ave. FAX **(818) 898-1948**
San Fernando, CA 91340 **www.ghostlightla.com**
(Classic, Contemporary, Domestics, Emergency Vehicles, Exotics, Farm Vehicles, Hearses, Hot Rods, Limousines, Military Vehicles, Police Vehicles, Rescue Vehicles, Sports Cars, Tanks, Taxis, Trucks, Vehicle Coordination and Transportation & Vintage)

Hardline Products Marine Group (805) 581-4700
(805) 732-5341
677 Cochran St. FAX **(805) 581-0022**
Simi Valley, CA 93065
www.hardlineproducts.com/marinegroup
(Cabin Cruisers, Cigarette Boats, Fishing Boats, Jet Boats, PWC & Yachts)

Michael Harper-Smith (818) 705-8655
5375 Tampa Ave. FAX **(818) 996-3741**
Tarzana, CA 91356 **www.eurofilmcars.com**
(European Vehicles Only: Cars, Double-Decker Buses, Limousines, London Taxis, Motorcycles, Scooters, Trucks & Vans)

The High Wheelers (626) 288-0820
(626) 576-8648
9344 E. Valley Blvd. **www.highwheelers.com**
Rosemead, CA 91770
(Antique and Double-Decker Buses & Classic Cars)

Hollywood Fire Authority (909) 593-3964
(909) 227-1794
www.hollywoodfire.biz
(Ambulances, Emergency Vehicles, Fire Trucks & Rescue Vehicles)

Hollywood Fires (661) 252-7629
FAX **(661) 251-5165**
www.hollywoodfires.com

Hollywood Picture Cars/Scott Bosés (323) 466-2277
1028 N. La Brea Ave. FAX **(323) 466-6541**
Hollywood, CA 90038 **www.hollywoodpicturecars.com**
(Antique–Contemporary)

Ⓐ **Hot Shot Picture Cars** (818) 365-5656
1621 First St. FAX **(818) 365-4595**
San Fernando, CA 91340 **www.hotshotpicturecars.com**
(Ambulances, Antique, ATVs, Buses, Cabin Cruisers, Camera Cars, Carriages, Cigarette Boats, Classic, Contemporary, Convertibles, Cutaways, Damaged, Domestics, Emergency Vehicles, European, Exotics, Farm Vehicles, Fire Trucks, Fishing Boats, Futuristic, Hearses, Helicopters, High Performance, Horse and Buggy, Hot Rods, HumVees, Jeeps, Limousines, Luxury, Military Vehicles, Motorboats, Motorcycles, Muscle Cars, Police, Rescue Vehicles, RVs, Salvage, Scooters, Semi Trucks, Sleighs, Sports Cars, Storage, Stunt Cars, Tanks, Taxis, Tractor Trailers, Trailers, Trains, Troop Carriers, Trucks, Vehicle Coordination, Vehicle Transportation, Vintage, Wagons, Water Trucks, Woodies & Yachts)

Howard Brown & Sons Auto Sales, Inc. (818) 767-2121
(310) 922-2777
11040 Olinda St. FAX **(818) 767-2320**
Sun Valley, CA 91352 **www.hbsas.com**
(Antique, ATVs, Buses, Classic, Contemporary, Convertibles, Cutaways, Damaged, Domestics, European, Exotics, Farm Vehicles, Hearses, High Performance, Hot Rods, Jeeps, Limousines, Lowriders, Luxury, Motorboats, Motorcycles, Muscle Cars, Police Vehicles, RVs, Salvage, Scooters, Sports Cars, Stunt Cars, Taxis, Trucks & Vintage)

Hypercycle (818) 988-8860
(818) 261-7104
15941 Arminta St. FAX **(818) 988-8834**
Van Nuys, CA 91406 **www.hypercycle.com**

Jeffries Automotive Styling (323) 851-5678
(818) 980-5367
3077 Cahuenga Blvd.
Los Angeles, CA 90068
(Antiques, Classics, Exotics, Futuristic and Stunt Cars & Hot Rods)

Jimmy's 411 Classics (310) 739-5795
2220 S. Beverly Glen, Ste. 305 FAX (310) 556-3115
Los Angeles, CA 90064 www.411classics.com

Ⓐ **Joe Ortiz Fire Trucks** (818) 768-1678
(818) 974-2218
11340 Allegheny St. FAX (818) 768-1907
Sun Valley, CA 91352
(Ambulances & Fire Trucks)

John Sarviss Stunt Equipment (661) 270-0565
(818) 980-2123
39120 Bouquet Canyon Rd. www.radicalcameracars.com
Leona Valley, CA 93551
(Stunt Camera Cars)

K4 Motorsports, Inc. (818) 713-0552
(323) 462-2301
24907 Anza Dr. FAX (818) 422-3763
Valencia, CA 91355 www.k4motorsports.com
(Race Cars & Stunt Cars)

Ⓐ **Kick Ass Cars and Bikes** (310) 278-9309
FAX (310) 278-9322
www.kickasscarsandbikes.com

L.A. Motorsports (818) 222-6954
(877) 526-6867
FAX (866) 294-3266
www.lamsports.com
(Classic–Contemporary Racing Vehicles & Vehicle Transportation)

Lane Ranch & Company (661) 942-0435
42220 10th St. West, Ste. 101 FAX (661) 942-7485
Lancaster, CA 93534 www.laneranch.net
(Antique Cars, Farm Vehicles and Trucks)

Mel Underwood Water Trucks, Inc. (818) 361-9176
(800) 675-4855
13201 Foothill Blvd. FAX (818) 361-9617
Sylmar, CA 91342
(Water Trucks)

Motion Picture Vehicle Service (818) 997-8630
14547 Titus St. FAX (818) 997-8636
Panorama City, CA 91402
www.motionpicturevehicleservices.com
(Exotics, Limousines, Military, Motorcycles, Police, Rescue Vehicles, Taxis & Trucks)

Mr. Vintage Machine (213) 369-0281
www.mistervintagemachine.com
(Antique, Buses, Classic, Convertibles, Customs, European, Exotics, Fire Trucks, Hearses, High Performance, Hot Rods, Imports, Jeeps, Lowriders, Luxury, Micro Cars, Mopeds, Motorboats, Motorcycles, Muscle Cars, Off Road Vehicles, RVs, Scooters, Semi Trucks, Sidecars, Specialty Vehicles, Sports Cars, Stock Cars, Trailers, Trucks, Vans, Vehicle Coordination, Vintage, Wagons & Woodies)

NationwidePictureCars.Com (310) 659-1711
www.nationwidepicturecars.com
(Classic–Contemporary Cars, Motorcycles and Trucks)

OC Film Cars (714) 515-4095
1801 E. Katella Ave., Ste. 3001 www.ocfilmcars.com
Anaheim, CA 92805

Olympic Rent A Car (310) 751-6501
9230 W. Olympic Blvd., Ste. 204
Beverly Hills, CA 90212 www.olympicrentacar.com

Ⓐ **Picture Car Warehouse** (213) 534-3775
LA Center Studios FAX (213) 534-3779
1201 W. Fifth St., Box 34 www.picturecarwarehouse.net
Los Angeles, CA 90017
(Antiques–Present, Classics, Convertibles, Exotics, High Performance, Military, Motorcycles, Police, Sports Cars & Trucks)

Picture Cars (818) 769-0999
5518 Vineland Ave. FAX (818) 769-6250
North Hollywood, CA 91601
(Antique–Present, Classics, Convertibles, Exotics, Motorcycles, Police and Sports Cars & Taxis)

Picture Vehicles Unlimited (818) 766-2200
2511 Rye Canyon Loop FAX (818) 766-2011
Santa Clarita, CA 91321 www.picturevehicles.com
(Classics, Exotics, Race Cars & Semi Trucks)

Regional Transit Service (951) 684-5926
(951) 233-7732
2805 Cadet St. FAX (951) 352-4596
Riverside, CA 92504 www.rts-regionaltransitservice.com
(Buses, City Transit Buses & Vintage)

Rent-A-Wreck (310) 826-7555
12333 W. Pico Blvd. FAX (310) 207-0681
Los Angeles, CA 90064

San Bernardino Railroad Historical Society (562) 438-9613
(1927 Steam Locomotive) www.sbrhs.org

Scooters Bellissimo/Go, Scoot Go! (626) 523-7224
1730 La Senda Pl. www.scootersbellissimo.com
South Pasadena, CA 91030
(Scooters)

Secure Transportation (562) 941-0107
(800) 856-9994
13111 Meyer Rd. FAX (562) 906-2947
Whittier, CA 90605 www.securetransportation.com
(Hearses & Limousines)

Showmobiles, Inc. (818) 762-0700
(888) 974-0300
FAX (818) 762-0710
www.showmobilesinc.com
(Antique–Contemporary Buses, Cars, Convertibles, Emergency Vehicles, Limousines, Motorcycles and Trucks)

Silverado Coach Company, Inc. (818) 251-9700
(800) 544-7999
(Antiques, Classics & Rare Cars) FAX (818) 884-4997
www.silveradocoach.com

Specialty Car Locators (818) 554-5062
(661) 310-2715
P.O Box 55334 FAX (661) 554-7063
Valencia, CA 91385
www.specialtycarlocators.com/equipmentforrent.htm
(Classic–Contemporary Military Vehicles, Police Cars and Taxis)

Specialty Vehicle Association (818) 882-2927
(818) 523-3532
4121 Paredo Way, Ste. E FAX (818) 882-2927
Simi Valley, CA 93063
(Classic–Contemporary Cars, Motorcycles and Trucks)

Ⓐ **Studio Picture Vehicles** (818) 765-1201
(818) 781-4223
7502 Wheatland Ave. FAX (818) 506-4789
Sun Valley, CA 91352
(Ambulances, Detective Cars, Police Cars & Street Vehicles)

Terence of London (818) 364-7474
13175 San Fernando Rd.
Sylmar, CA 91342
(British Taxis & Double-Decker Buses)

Transformedia (310) 210-9272
2107 Curtis Ave., Ste. B
Redondo Beach, CA 90278
(Picture Vehicle Coordination)

Ann G. Troy (805) 729-1923
1187 Coast Village Rd., Ste. 1-461 FAX (805) 969-2631
Montecito, CA 93108
(Picture Vehicle Coordination)

Unique Movie Cars, Inc. (888) 345-6227
FAX (702) 566-6194
(Antiques, Contemporary and Futuristic Cars & Stunt Vehicles)

Vehicle Center (626) 288-1541
(Four-Door Jeeps) FAX (626) 288-9559

Vehicle Effects
(818) 355-2676
(818) 846-7506
FAX (818) 846-7576
www.vehicleeffects.com
(Classic–Contemporary Muscle Cars and Trucks & Picture Vehicle Coordination)

Veluzat Motion Picture Rentals
(661) 259-7788
(661) 259-9669
P.O. Box 220597
FAX (661) 259-3788
Newhall, CA 91322
www.melodyranchstudio.com
(US/Foreign Military Vehicles)

VintageTrailerCrazy.com
(949) 689-3964
33175 Hwy 79 South, Ste. A-424
Temecula, CA 92592
www.vintagetrailercrazy.com
(Custom Vintage Trailers, Hot Rods, RVs & Woodies)

Warner Bros. Studio Facilities - Fire Department
(818) 954-3269
4000 Warner Blvd.
FAX (818) 954-6957
Burbank, CA 91522
www.wbsf.com
(Fire Engines & Rescue Vehicles)

The Wood N' Carr
(562) 498-8730
2345 Walnut Ave.
FAX (562) 985-3360
Signal Hill, CA 90755
www.woodncarr.net
(Camera Cars, Exotics & Woodies)

WW2 Military Vehicle Rentals, Ltd.
(949) 632-4345
www.ww2militaryvehiclerentals.com
(Jeeps, Military Vehicles, Tanks, Troop Carriers, Trucks, Vehicle Coordination & Vehicle Transportation)

Plastics, Plexiglas & Fiberglass

LA 411

Aquatic Design
(310) 822-7484
(310) 320-8379
4943 McConnell Ave., Ste. K
Los Angeles, CA 90066
FAX **(310) 822-8655**
www.aquatic2000.com
(Customized Aquariums)

California Quality Plastics
(909) 930-5535
2226 Castle Harbor Pl. South
Ontario, CA 91761
FAX **(909) 930-5540**
www.calplastics.com

Calsak Plastics
(310) 928-4100
(877) 777-0405
19801 S. Rancho Way, Ste. B
Rancho Dominguez, CA 90220
FAX **(310) 928-4111**
www.calsakplastics.com

Circle K Products
(951) 695-1955
P.O. Box 909
Temecula, CA 92593
FAX **(951) 695-0605**
(Liquid Plastics, Mold-Making & Silicones)

Flix FX, Inc.
(818) 765-3549
(877) 326-8433
7327 Lankershim Blvd., Ste. 4
North Hollywood, CA 91605
FAX **(818) 765-0135**
www.flixfx.com
(Vacuum-Forming)

Ⓐ **Fox Studios**
(310) 369-2712
(310) 369-4636
Staff Shop, 10201 W. Pico Blvd.
Los Angeles, CA 90035
FAX **(310) 969-1006**
www.foxstudios.com
(Acrylics, Fiberglass, Resin & Vacuum-Forming)

Ⓐ **Graphic Spider/Custom Acrylic**
(310) 844-7640
13004 S. Figueroa
Los Angeles, CA 90061
FAX **(310) 844-7641**
www.graphicspider.com
(3-D Cnc Milling, Acrylics, Aquariums, Custom, Fabrication, Cut Letters, Fiberglass, Liquid Plastics, Plastics, Plexiglas, Resins, Signage & Wood Cutting)

Makeup & Effects Laboratories, Inc./MEL
(818) 982-1483
7110 Laurel Canyon Blvd., Bldg. E
North Hollywood, CA 91605
FAX **(818) 982-5712**
www.melefx.com
(Mold-Making & Vacuum-Forming)

NBC Universal Staff Shop
(818) 777-2337
100 Universal City Plaza, Bldg. 4250-1
Universal City, CA 91608
FAX **(818) 723-5952**
www.filmmakersdestination.com
(Acrylics, Custom, Fabrication, Fiberglass, Mold-Making, Plexiglas, Resins, Thermo Forming & Vacuum-Forming)

The Studios at Paramount
(323) 956-5140
The Studios at Paramount
Manufacturing and Special Effects
5555 Melrose Ave.
Los Angeles, CA 90038
FAX **(323) 862-2325**
www.thestudiosatparamount.com

Planet Plastics
(909) 393-8222
14954 La Palma Dr.
Chino, CA 91710
FAX **(909) 393-2552**
www.planetplastics.com
(Acrylics & Plastics)

Plastic Depot
(818) 843-3030
2907 San Fernando Blvd.
Burbank, CA 91504
FAX **(818) 843-5451**
www.plasticdepotofburbank.com
(Acrylics, Fiberglass & Plastics)

Plastic Mart
(310) 268-1404
11665 Santa Monica Blvd.
Los Angeles, CA 90025
FAX **(310) 268-1411**
www.plasticmart.net
(Plastics & Plexiglas)

Projex International
(661) 268-0999
(877) 251-9095
9555 Hierba Rd.
Agua Dulce, CA 91390
FAX **(661) 268-1885**
www.projexinternational.com
(Fiberglass Fabrication and Props & Mold-Making)

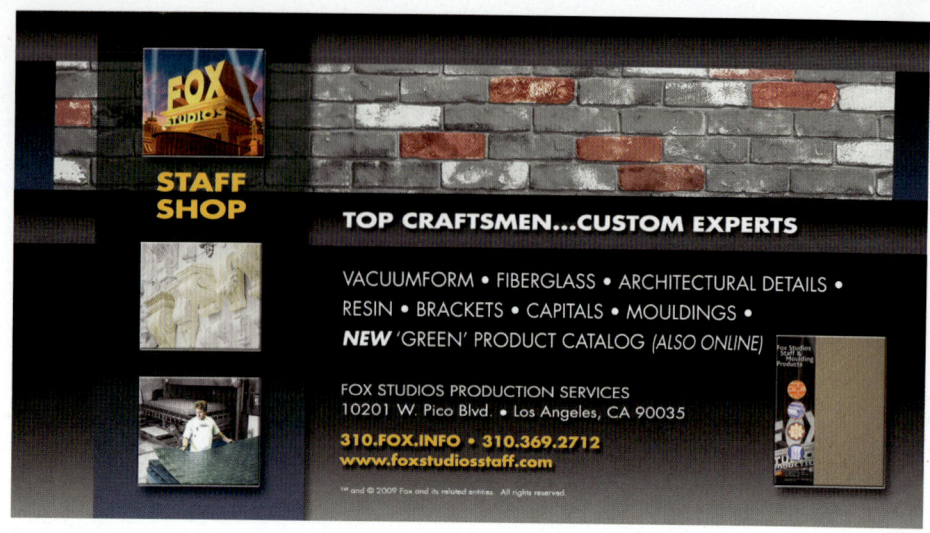

Prop Masters, Inc. (818) 846-3915
2721 W. Empire Ave. FAX (818) 846-1278
Burbank, CA 91504 www.propmastersinc.com
(Fabrication, Mold-Making & Vacuum-Forming)

Regal Piedmont Plastics (562) 404-4014
(800) 400-7342
17000 Valley View FAX (562) 404-2855
La Mirada, CA 90638 www.regalpiedmontplastics.com
(Plastics & Plexiglas)

Rose Brand (818) 505-6290
(800) 360-5056
10616 Lanark St. FAX (818) 505-6293
Sun Valley, CA 91352 www.rosebrand.com

Sabic Polymershapes (562) 942-9381
(866) 437-7427
9905 Pioneer Blvd. FAX (562) 801-6267
Santa Fe Springs, CA 90670
www.sabicpolymershapes.com
(Acrylics, Adhesives, Custom, Epoxies, Fabrication, Mold-Making Materials, Mylars, Plastics, Plexiglas, Silicones, Thermo Forming, Urethanes, Vacuum-Forming & Vinyls)

Scenery West (818) 765-8661
11461 Hart St. FAX (818) 765-5495
North Hollywood, CA 91605 www.scenerywest.com

Specialty Resources Company (818) 759-1190
11651 Hart St. FAX (818) 759-0081
North Hollywood, CA 91605 www.aliendecor.com
(Acrylics, Fiberglass, Hoses & Plastics)

Vinyl Technology, Inc. (626) 443-5257
200 Railroad Ave. FAX (626) 443-0531
Monrovia, CA 91016
(Fabrication)

Walco Materials Group (760) 520-1020
(800) 297-4541
2121 Chablis Court, Ste. 100 FAX (760) 520-1025
Escondido, CA 92029 www.walcomaterials.com
(Adhesives, Epoxies, Mold-Making, Silicones & Urethanes)

Warner Bros. Studio Facilities - Staff Shop (818) 954-2269
4000 Warner Blvd., Bldg. 44 FAX (818) 954-2016
Burbank, CA 91522 www.wbsf.com

West Coast Sign Supply (213) 487-6666
1700 W. Pico Blvd. FAX (213) 487-6660
Los Angeles, CA 90015 www.westcoastsignsupply.com

West Coast Sign Supply (818) 785-8777
14332 Calvert St. FAX (818) 785-8778
Van Nuys, CA 91411 www.westcoastsignsupply.com

Clearance Domain LLC (800) 562-1231
(310) 898-1233
FAX (888) 562-5120
www.clearancedomain.com

Creative Entertainment Services (818) 748-4800
2550 N. Hollywood Way, Ste. 100 FAX (818) 847-8625
Burbank, CA 91505 www.acreativegroup.com

Davie-Brown Entertainment (310) 979-1980
2225 S. Carmelina Ave. FAX (310) 820-7277
Los Angeles, CA 90064 www.davie-brown.com

Hadler Public Relations, Inc. (310) 557-0415
(818) 552-7300
801 N. Brand Blvd., Ste. 620 FAX (310) 557-8418
Glendale, CA 91203

HERO Entertainment Marketing, Inc. (818) 764-7414
10777 Sherman Way FAX (818) 764-7415
Sun Valley, CA 91352 www.heropp.com

I.S.M. Entertainment, Inc. (831) 475-1472
343 Soquel Ave., Ste. 523 FAX (831) 475-1473
Santa Cruz, CA 95062 www.ismentertainment.com

Keppler Entertainment, Inc. (310) 658-8000
225 24th St. www.brandmatch.com
Manhattan Beach, CA 90266

Larry Dorn Associates/ World Backgrounds (323) 935-6266
5919 W. Third St., Ste. 1D FAX (323) 935-9523
Los Angeles, CA 90036 www.worldbackgrounds.com

Motion Picture Magic (818) 953-7494
3605 W. Pacific Ave. FAX (818) 953-7113
Burbank, CA 91505 www.motionpicturemagic.com

Norm Marshall & Associates (818) 982-3505
11059 Sherman Way FAX (818) 503-1936
Sun Valley, CA 91352 www.normmarshall.com

Pier 3 Entertainment (310) 376-5115
811 N. Catalina Ave., Ste. 1308 FAX (310) 318-5858
Redondo Beach, CA 90277
www.pier3entertainment.com

Prop Fabrication & Mechanical FX

1 On 1 Computing Technologies (818) 992-0584 (818) 254-5448
5824 Kentland Ave. FAX (818) 887-7247
Woodland Hills, CA 91367 **www.1on1comp.com**
(Motion Control Rigs, Robotics, Robotic Props & Turntables)

360 Designworks/ 360 Propworks Inc. (310) 323-3326
1441 W. 132nd St. FAX (310) 323-3352
Los Angeles, CA 90249 **www.360designworks.com**
(Action Props, Custom, Foam Sculpting, FX Props, Mechanical FX, Miniatures, Models, Oversized Props, Product Pours, Prop Fabrication, Prototyping, Rigging, Sculpted Props & Welding)

Animatronics Metal Fabrication Mechanical FX Action Props Custom Vehicles Robotics
Prop Fabrication Models CNC Machining CNC Routing Acrylic Tanks CNC Tube Bending
Automotive FX Hydraulics Turntables Moldmaking The Vacu-form Factory "The FLIX Stage"
FLIX FX
WHERE FORM FITS FUNCTION
The Mechanical Effects and Prop Fabrication Experts
818 765 3549
Introducing: THE FLIX INSERT STAGE
• Television Commercials
• Motion Pictures and Television
• Stage Shows and Theatrical Events
• Themed Entertainment Venues
• Museum Displays and Interactives
• Retail Fixtures and Displays
• Tradeshows and Special Events
Whether it pops, slides, twirls, rolls by at 30 miles per hour, or is just "sitting pretty", our reputation for being the "Go To" guys for Mechanical EFX is only rivaled by our ability to create Spectacular Props. We can help you achieve the same high quality of design and fabrication for your project. Call or e-mail Marc at: marc@flixfx.com
CHEEZ-IT
Our approach is simple... Innovate!
Over 2500 Commercials
Since 1991
View Extraordinary Examples of our Work @
www.flixfx.com
Toll free: 877-326-8433
7327 Lankershim Blvd. #4, North Hollywood, CA 91605
CA Contractor

Ⓐ Action Sets and Props/ WonderWorks (818) 992-8811
7231 Remmet Ave. FAX (818) 347-4330
Canoga Park, CA 91303 www.wonderworksweb.com
(Foreground Miniatures, FX Props & Space Suits)

Alfonso's Breakaway Glass, Inc. (818) 768-7402 (866) 768-7402
8070 San Fernando Rd. FAX (818) 767-6969
Sun Valley, CA 91352
www.alfonsosbreakawayglass.com

All Access Staging & Productions (310) 784-2464
1320 Storm Pkwy FAX (310) 517-0899
Torrance, CA 90501 www.allaccessinc.com
(Turntables)

All Effects Company, Inc. (818) 298-3730
20902 Enrique St. www.allfx.com
Woodland Hills, CA 91364

All Sets (310) 430-0971 (310) 430-0970
2529 N. San Fernando Rd. FAX (323) 221-9600
Los Angeles, CA 90065 www.allsets.com
(Action Props, Artificial Foods, Breakaways, Computer-Controlled, Custom, Electronics, Foam Sculpting, FX Props, Gadgetry, Hydraulics, Mechanical FX, Miniatures, Models, Oversized Props, Prop Fabrication, Prototyping, Radio-Controlled, Remote-Controlled, Rigging, Robotics, Rubber Props, Sculpted Props, Skeleton Replication, Toy Fabrication, Weapon Fabrication & Welding)

Altered Anatomy, Inc. (818) 765-1992 (909) 653-3658
20841 Bakal Dr. FAX (909) 653-9468
Riverside, CA 92508 www.bnt4cncrp.com
(Prop and Toy Fabrication, Rapid Prototyping & Vacuum-Forming)

ANA Special Effects, Inc. (818) 909-6999
7021 Hayvenhurst Ave. FAX (818) 782-0635
Van Nuys, CA 91406 www.anaspecialeffects.com
(Action Props & Breakaways)

Anatomorphex/The Sculpture Studio (818) 768-2880
8210 Lankershim Blvd., Ste. 14 www.anatomorphex.com
North Hollywood, CA 91605
(Mechanical FX, Miniatures, Models & Statues)

Animal Makers, Inc. (805) 523-1900
11991 Discovery Court, Ste. 411 FAX (805) 523-1903
Moorpark, CA 93021 www.animalmakers.com/store
(Computer-Controlled, Mechanical FX, Models, Prop Fabrication, Radio-Controlled, Robotics, Sculpted Props & Skeleton Replication)

Arteffex/Dann O'Quinn (818) 506-5358
911 Mayo St. FAX (323) 255-4599
Los Angeles, CA 90042 www.acfxo.com
(Action Props, Custom, Foam Sculpting, FX Props, Gadgetry, Mechanical FX, Miniatures, Models, Motion Control Systems, Oversized Props, Prop Fabrication, Radio-Controlled, Remote-Controlled, Robotics, Rubber Props & Sculpted Props)

Artistic Entertainment Services (626) 334-9388
120 N. Aspan FAX (626) 969-8595
Azusa, CA 91702

Automatrix Effects/David Waine (323) 469-0088
2623 N. San Fernando Rd. www.automatrixfx.com
Los Angeles, CA 90065

B and R Scenery, Inc. (805) 388-8555
486 Constitution Ave. FAX (805) 388-9996
Camarillo, CA 93012 www.bandrscenery.com
(Prop Fabrication, Turntables & Welding)

Bear Creek Pottery (951) 769-3400 (951) 306-9379
4988 W. Ramsey St. FAX (951) 769-3400
Banning, CA 92220 www.bearcreekpottery.com
(Ceramics & Pottery)

Ⓐ Beckman Rigging/BRS Rigging (310) 532-3933 (661) 510-2518
13516 S. Mariposa Ave. FAX (310) 532-3993
Gardena, CA 90247 www.brsrigging.com
(Flying & Rigging)

Bellfx, LLC (818) 590-4992
1908 First St. www.bellfx.com
San Fernando, CA 91340
(Action Props, Mechanical FX, Prototypes & Robotics)

Benchmark Scenery, Inc. (818) 507-1351
1757 Standard Ave. FAX (818) 507-1354
Glendale, CA 91201
(Turntables)

Bill Ferrell Co. (818) 994-1952
(866) 994-1952
14744 Oxnard St. FAX (818) 994-9670
Van Nuys, CA 91411 www.billferrell.com
(Motion Control Systems, Revolving Stages & Turntables)

Bone Clones, Inc. (818) 709-7991
21416 Chase St., Ste. 1 FAX (818) 709-7993
Canoga Park, CA 91304 www.boneclones.com
(Human and Animal Bone, Skeleton and Skull Replications)

Greg Bonura (661) 269-2978
(805) 341-3124
(Gadgetry & Hand and Specialty Props) FAX (661) 269-0546

Boom Boom Effects (818) 772-6699
11100-8 Sepulveda Blvd., Ste. 339 FAX (818) 772-6689
Mission Hills, CA 91345
(Action Props)

Branam/West Coast Theatrical (310) 637-4727
(877) 295-3390
310 S. Long Beach Blvd. FAX (310) 637-4735
Compton, CA 90221 www.branament.com
(Flying & Rigging)

Bravo! Productions (562) 435-0065
110 W. Ocean Blvd., Ste. 537 FAX (562) 435-4421
Long Beach, CA 90802 www.bravoevents-online.com
(Fabricated, Miniature, Oversized and Sculpted Props)

Charisma Design Studio, Inc. (818) 252-6611
(800) 891-8617
8414 San Fernando Rd. FAX (818) 252-6610
Sun Valley, CA 91352 www.charismadesign.com
(Waterjet Cutting)

Cinefx/Josh Hakian (818) 889-7217
3737 Patrick Henry Pl. FAX (818) 889-7217
Agoura Hills, CA 91301
(Mechanical FX)

Cinema Production Services, Inc. (818) 989-2164
7631 Haskell Ave. FAX (818) 989-2174
Van Nuys, CA 91406 www.cpsfx.com

Cinnabar (818) 842-8190
4571 Electronics Pl. FAX (818) 842-0563
Los Angeles, CA 90039 www.cinnabar.com
(Foam Sculpting, Miniatures, Models, Props, Prop Fabrication, Prototyping & Welding)

Circle K Products (951) 695-1955
P.O. Box 909 FAX (951) 695-0605
Temecula, CA 92593
(Action Props, Miniatures, Models, Prop Fabrication, Rubber Props & Skeleton Replication)

Scott Cosgrove (818) 224-2142
(209) 765-0696
(Rigging)

Custom Movie Props (310) 466-2910
www.custommovieprops.com
(Action Props, Electronics, Fiberglass, Metal Fabrication, Miniatures & Models)

Customs by Eddie Paul, A Division of EP Industries, Inc. (310) 643-8515
(310) 259-0542
2305 Utah Ave. FAX (310) 643-8520
El Segundo, CA 90245 www.deadlinetv.net
(Action Props, Custom, Foam Sculpting, FX Props, Gadgetry, Hydraulics, Marine Equipment, Mechanical FX, Miniatures, Models, Oversized Props, Prop Fabrication, Prototyping, Radio-Controlled, Remote-Controlled, Rigging, Robotics, Sculpted Props, Skeleton Replication, Toy Fabrication, Turntables, Vacuum-Forming, Weapon Fabrication & Welding)

Dennis Curtin Studio, Inc. (310) 827-8850
1919 Empire Ave. FAX (818) 842-4623
Burbank, CA 91504 www.denniscurtin.com

Design Setters Corporation (818) 846-6256
2909 Thornton Ave. FAX (818) 846-1095
Burbank, CA 91504 www.designsetters.com

DesignTown, USA (310) 840-2940
3644 Eastham Dr. FAX (310) 840-2935
Culver City, CA 90232 www.designtownusa.com
(Action Props, Breakaways, Custom, Electronics, Foam Sculpting, FX Props, Gadgetry, Mechanical FX, Miniatures, Models, Oversized Props, Pottery, Prop Fabrication, Prototyping, Rubber Props, Sculpted Props, Vacuum-Forming, Waterjet Cutting & Welding)

Don Wayne Magic, Inc. (818) 763-3192
10907 Magnolia Blvd., Ste. 467 FAX (818) 985-4953
North Hollywood, CA 91601 www.donwaynemagic.com
(FX and Magic Props)

Douglas White Effects (818) 785-4148
6859 Valjean Ave., Ste. 7 FAX (818) 785-2567
Van Nuys, CA 91406 www.dweffects.com
(Molds & Remote-Controlled Props)

DowDesign (949) 650-3000
(Miniatures) FAX (949) 722-6353
www.dowdesign.com

The Effects Group (323) 876-0992
(Mechanical FX) FAX (323) 876-0288
www.theeffectsgroup.net

Effects in Motion (818) 346-2484
21318 Hart St. FAX (818) 346-2710
Canoga Park, CA 91303 www.effectsinmotion.com
(Motion Control Rigs)

Elden Design/Elden Sets, Props and Backdrops (323) 550-8922
2767 W. Broadway www.eldenworks.com/rickelden
Eagle Rock, CA 90041
(Custom, Flying, Gadgetry, Oversized Props, Prop Fabrication, Prototyping, Rigging & Sculpted Props)

Electronic Design & Development (818) 298-0827
27735 Rainier Rd. www.electronicdad.com
Castaic, CA 91384

F/X Concepts, Inc./Lou Carlucci (818) 508-1094
P.O. Box 1008 FAX (818) 508-1094
Santa Clarita, CA 91386
(Mechanical Special FX Props)

Festival Artists, Inc. (626) 334-9388
(626) 303-6042
120 N. Aspan Ave. FAX (626) 969-8595
Azusa, CA 91702 www.festivalartists.org
(Foam Sculpting, Oversized Props & Welding)

Filmtrix, Inc. (818) 808-9321
P.O. Box 809 www.filmtrix.com
North Hollywood, CA 91603
(Rigging)

Flanders Control Cables (626) 792-7384
340 S. Fair Oaks Ave. FAX (626) 792-5341
Pasadena, CA 91105 www.flandersco.com
(Mechanical FX and Rigging)

A Flix FX, Inc. (818) 765-3549 (877) 326-8433
7327 Lankershim Blvd., Ste. 4 FAX **(818) 765-0135**
North Hollywood, CA 91605 **www.flixfx.com**
(Action Props, Artificial Foods, Custom, Electronics, Foam Sculpting, FX Props, Gadgetry, Hydraulics, Mechanical FX, Miniatures, Models, Oversized Props, Prop Fabrication, Prototyping, Radio-Controlled, Remote-Controlled, Robotics, Rubber Props, Turntables, Vacuum-Forming & Welding)

Fox Studios (310) 369-2712 (310) 369-4636
Staff Shop, 10201 W. Pico Blvd. FAX **(310) 969-1006**
Los Angeles, CA 90035 **www.foxstudios.com**
(Acrylic, Custom Fabrication, Fiberglass, Plaster, Resin & Vaccuum-Forming)

Full Scale Effects (818) 760-0875 (818) 760-0042
6875 Tujunga Ave. FAX **(818) 760-0876**
North Hollywood, CA 91605 **www.fullscaleeffects.com**

GF Productions, Inc. (661) 702-1483 (661) 816-5597
781 Melrose Ave. FAX **(661) 702-1485**
Pasadena, CA 91106 **www.gfproductionsinc.com**

Gilderfluke & Co., Inc. (818) 840-9484 (800) 776-5972
205 S. Flower St. FAX **(818) 840-9485**
Burbank, CA 91502 **www.gilderfluke.com**
(Motion Control Systems)

Global Effects, Inc. (818) 503-9273
7115 Laurel Canyon Blvd. FAX **(818) 503-9459**
North Hollywood, CA 91605 **www.globaleffects.com**
(Action, Rubber and Special Mechanical FX Props, Miniatures & Robotics)

Grant McCune Design, Inc. (818) 779-1920
6836 Valjean Ave. FAX **(818) 781-9108**
Van Nuys, CA 91406 **www.gmdfx.com**
(Mechanical FX, Miniatures, Models & Prototypes)

The Hand Prop Room, L.P. (323) 931-1534
5700 Venice Blvd. FAX **(323) 931-2145**
Los Angeles, CA 90019 **www.hpr.com**
(Fabrication)

Rufus Herrick (805) 496-0249 (206) 232-7100

HM Design (818) 985-8636
6353 Teesdale Ave. FAX **(818) 985-8636**
North Hollywood, CA 91606

HMS Creative Productions (818) 764-6151
1317 N. San Fernando Blvd., Ste. 144 FAX **(818) 764-0620**
Burbank, CA 91504 **www.hms-studios.com**
(Custom, Foam Sculpting, Metal Fabrication, Miniatures, Models, Product Pours, Prop Fabrication, Prototyping, Rubber Props, Sculpted Props, Toy Fabrication, Welding & Vacuum-Forming)

Hollywood Welding (323) 465-3137 (323) 816-0440
1045 N. Hudson Ave. FAX **(323) 465-5941**
Hollywood, CA 90038
(Fabrication & Welding)

I.D.F. Studio Scenery (818) 982-7433
6844 Lankershim Blvd. FAX **(818) 982-7435**
North Hollywood, CA 91605 **www.idfstudioscenery.com**

Icarus Rigging (323) 660-4112
3531 Casitas Ave. FAX **(323) 660-6135**
Los Angeles, CA 90039 **www.icarusrigging.com**
(Mechanical FX and Rigging)

Imagivations (818) 767-6767
11585 Sheldon St. FAX **(818) 767-3637**
Sun Valley, CA 91352 **www.imagivations.com**

Independent Studio Services, Inc./ISS (818) 951-5600
9545 Wentworth St. **www.issprops.com**
Sunland, CA 91040

Industrial Artists (626) 355-1913
803 Woodland Dr.
Sierra Madre, CA 91024
(Action Props & Custom Turntables)

Innovision Optics (310) 453-4866
1719 21st St. FAX **(310) 453-4677**
Santa Monica, CA 90404 **www.innovisionoptics.com**
(Portable Tabletop Motion Control Systems)

Ironwood (818) 265-2055
1514 Flower St. FAX **(818) 265-1680**
Glendale, CA 91201 **www.ironwoodscenic.com**
(Rigging)

Jet Effects (818) 764-5644
6910 Farmdale Ave. FAX **(818) 764-6655**
North Hollywood, CA 91605 **www.jeteffects.net**
(Fabrication, Miniatures & Prop FX)

Kinderspiel (323) 876-6549 (323) 216-0403
3103 Lincoln Park Ave. **www.kinder-spiel.net**
Los Angeles, CA 90031
(Fountains, Oversized Props, Sculptures & Statues)

Knott Limited Special Effects (323) 876-2356
(Mechanical FX) FAX **(323) 876-2356**

L.A. Propoint, Inc. (818) 767-6800
9051 Sunland Blvd. FAX **(818) 767-3900**
Sun Valley, CA 91352 **www.lapropoint.com**
(Action Props, FX Props, Gadgetry, Hydraulics, Mechanical FX, Motion Control Systems, Prototyping, Rigging, Turntables & Welding)

L.A. Rigging (818) 848-6264
FAX **(818) 848-9012**
(Computer-Controlled and Mechanical Rigging)

Peter McKinney (310) 863-5984
FAX **(310) 356-3815**
www.360designworks.com
(Action Props, Custom, FX Props, Mechanical FX, Miniatures, Models, Oversized Props, Product Pours, Prop Fabrication, Prototyping, Rigging & Welding)

Merritt Productions, Inc. (818) 760-0612
10845 Vanowen St. **www.merrittproductions.com**
North Hollywood, CA 91605
(Action Props, Mechanical FX & Miniatures)

Michael Plesh and Company (818) 768-4444
www.propmakers.com
(Ceramics, Custom, Oversized Props & Prototypes)

Modelwerkes/Gene Rizzardi (818) 314-8211 (661) 298-0627
www.modelwerkes.com
(Action Props, Breakaways, Custom, Foam Sculpting, FX Props, Gadgetry, Mechanical FX, Miniatures, Models, Prop Fabrication, Prototyping. Remote-Controlled, Rubber Props, Sculpted Props & Vacuum-Forming)

Modern Props (323) 934-3000
5500 W. Jefferson Blvd. FAX **(323) 934-3155**
Los Angeles, CA 90016 **www.modernprops.com**
(Contemporary, Electronic and Futuristic Props)

Murphy Metalworks, Inc. (661) 269-9353
(Prop Fabrication & Welding) **www.murphymetalworks.com**

NAC Co. (805) 376-0206 (805) 405-7337
1772-J E. Avenida de Los Arboles FAX **(805) 376-8407**
Thousand Oaks, CA 91362 **www.naceffects.com**
(Action Props, Flying and Rigging, Mechanical FX, Motion Control Systems, Prototypes & Robotics)

New Deal Studios, Inc. (310) 578-9929
4105 Redwood Ave. FAX (310) 578-7370
Los Angeles, CA 90066 www.newdealstudios.com
(Mechanical FX, Miniatures & Models)

Optic Nerve Studios, Inc. (818) 771-1007
9818 Glenoaks Blvd. FAX (818) 771-1009
Sun Valley, CA 91352 www.opticnervefx.com
(Action Props, Breakaways, Futuristic, Mechanical FX, Miniatures, Models, Prop-Fabrication, Robotics & Vacuum-Forming)

Susan Ottevanger (805) 223-5870
709 W. Channel Islands Blvd., Ste. 34 www.seewater.com
Port Hueneme, CA 93041
(Soft Goods)

Pacific Vision Productions, Inc. (626) 441-4869
210 Pasadena Ave. www.pacificvision.com
South Pasadena, CA 91030

A **The Studios at Paramount** (323) 956-5140
The Studios at Paramount FAX (323) 862-2325
Manufacturing and Special Effects
5555 Melrose Ave.
Los Angeles, CA 90038
www.thestudiosatparamount.com

Patrick Tatopoulos Designs, Inc. (818) 859-0368
1951 Ontario St. FAX (818) 841-8883
Burbank, CA 91505 www.tatopoulosstudios.net
(Action Props, Fabrication, Mechanical FX, Metal Fabrication, Minatures, Molds and Remote, Prototyping, Robotics, Sculpted Props & Space Suits)

Peter Geyer Action Props, Inc. (818) 768-0070
8235 Lankershim Blvd., Ste. G www.actionprops.com
North Hollywood, CA 91605

Pottery Manufacturing & Distributing, Inc. (310) 323-7772
18881 S. Hoover St. FAX (310) 323-6613
Gardena, CA 90248 www.potterymfg.com
(Concrete, Glazed & Terra Cotta Pottery)

Precision Turntable Services (661) 252-8444
28155 La Veda Ave. www.precisionturntables.com
Santa Clarita, CA 91387
(Turntables)

Prop Masters, Inc. (818) 846-3915
2721 W. Empire Ave. FAX (818) 846-1278
Burbank, CA 91504 www.propmastersinc.com
(Action and Oversized Props, Miniatures, Molds, Sculpting & Vacuum-Forming)

Prop Services Unlimited/Jim Fox (323) 462-2272
(213) 968-1068
(Mechanical FX & Prop Rigging) FAX (323) 469-9204

Pure Imagination Co. (818) 609-9629
FAX (866) 238-7703
www.pureimaginationco.com
(Action Props, Foam Sculpting, Gadgetry, Miniatures, Models, Prop Fabrication, Radio-Controlled, Remote-Controlled, Rubber Props Sculpted Props & Toy Fabrication)

Rando Productions, Inc. (818) 982-4300
11939 Sherman Rd. FAX (818) 982-4320
North Hollywood, CA 91605 www.randoproductions.com
(Hydraulics & Mechanical and Motion Control Rigging and Turntables)

Reel EFX, Inc. (818) 762-1710
(213) 308-7289
5539 Riverton Ave. FAX (818) 762-1734
North Hollywood, CA 91601 www.reelefx.com
(Mechanical FX)

Reelistic FX, Inc./John Gray (818) 346-2484
(818) 621-2484
(Action Props & Mechanical FX) FAX (818) 346-2710
www.r-fx.com

Renegade Effects Group (818) 980-8848
11312 Hartland St. FAX (818) 980-8849
North Hollywood, CA 91605 www.renegadeeffects.com
(Miniatures, Models & Vacuum-Forming)

Scenery West (818) 765-8661
11461 Hart St. FAX (818) 765-5495
North Hollywood, CA 91605 www.scenerywest.com
(Oversized Props)

Sculptors Pride Design Studios (626) 256-4779
902 S. Primrose Ave.
Monrovia, CA 91016
(Architectual, Miniatures & Oversized and Sculpted Props)

The Shape Shop (310) 532-4391
16709 Gramercy Pl., Ste. B www.theshapeshop.net
Torrance, CA 90247
(Custom, Miniatures, Models, Molds, Oversized Props, Prototyping & Vacuum-Forming)

Shelly Ward Enterprises (818) 255-5850
(Turntables) FAX (818) 255-5450
www.shellywardent.com

A **Snow Business Hollywood, Inc.** (818) 884-3009
21318 Hart St. FAX (818) 884-3110
Canoga Park, CA 91303
www.snowbusinesshollywood.com
(Ice Cubes, Icicles, Igloos & Snowmen)

So Cal Production Source (310) 699-2787
FAX (310) 618-0129
www.scpsunlimited.com
(Action Props, Artificial Foods, Breakaways, Ceramics, Computer-Controlled, Custom, Electronics, Extreme Sports, Flying, Foam Sculpting, FX Props, Gadgetry, Hydraulics, Lasercutting, Marine Equipment, Mechanical FX, Miniatures, Models, Motion Control Systems, Oversized Props, Pottery, Product Pours, Prop Fabrication, Prototyping, Radio-Controlled, Remote-Controlled, Rigging, Robotics, Rubber Props, Sculpted Props, Skeleton Replication, Toy Fabrication, Turntables, Vacuum-Forming, Waterjet Cutting, Weapon Fabrication & Welding)

Special Effects Technologies, Inc. (310) 490-6406
3644 Eastham Dr. FAX (213) 947-1327
Culver City, CA 90232 www.effectstech.com
(Motion Rigging, Prop Making, Tabletop Rigs & Turntables)

A **Special Effects Unlimited, Inc.** (323) 466-3361
1005 Lillian Way FAX (323) 466-5712
Hollywood, CA 90038 www.specialeffectsunlimited.com
(Mechanical FX)

Specialty International (818) 349-0810
20730 Dearborn St. FAX (818) 349-0910
Chatsworth, CA 91311 www.specialtyinternational.com
(Laser Cutting, Metal Fabrication & Welding)

Spectral Motion, Inc. (818) 956-6080
1849 Dana St. FAX (818) 956-6083
Glendale, CA 91201 www.spectralmotion.com
(Action Props, Mechanical FX, Miniatures, Models, Molds, Robotics & Space Suits)

Spectrum Effects Enterprises, Inc. (323) 871-4445
(661) 510-5633
Raleigh Studios FAX (661) 244-4469
5300 Melrose Ave., Ste. 101D www.spectrumeffects.com
Hollywood, CA 90038
(Mechanical FX)

Standard Engineering Co. (323) 277-3270
(800) 248-8500
5920 Alameda St. FAX (323) 277-3273
Huntington Park, CA 90255
(Belt and Roller Conveyors)

F. Lee Stone/Stonefx (818) 999-0339
(818) 642-2850
9201 Grundy Ln. FAX (818) 999-1042
Chatsworth, CA 91311
(Mechanical FX)

Studio Art & Technology (818) 951-5620
9545 Wentworth St. FAX (818) 951-2882
Sunland, CA 91040
www.issprops.com/manufacturing.aspx
(Electronics, Hydraulics, Miniatures, Rigging & Welding)

Stunt Wings/Adventure Sports (818) 367-2430 (818) 266-0874
12623 Gridley St. FAX (818) 367-5363
San Fernando, CA 91342 **www.stuntwings.com**
(Action Props, Extreme Sports, Flying & Specialized Rigging)

Stutsman Effects, Inc. (310) 457-6661 (310) 922-4705
FAX (310) 457-4061
(Action Props, Hydraulics, Mechanical FX, Miniatures, Rigging & Welding)

Sword & The Stone (818) 562-6548
723 N. Victory Blvd. FAX (818) 562-6549
Burbank, CA 91502 **www.swordandstone.com**
(Edged Weapons Fabrication, Jewelry, Metal Armor & Silver and Bronze Casting)

Techworks Studios, Inc. (818) 559-5536
FAX (661) 298-0929
www.techworksstudios.com
(Action Props, Bone Replications, FX Props, Gadgetry, Prop Fabrication, Robotic Props, Robotics, Sculpted Props, Silicone Rubber Props & Space Suits)

Trans FX, Inc. - TFX (805) 485-6110 (888) 876-7339
2361 Eastman Ave. FAX (805) 532-1645
Oxnard, CA 93030 **www.transfx.com**
(Mock-Ups & Model Makers)

Tribal Scenery (818) 558-4045
3216 Vanowen St. FAX (818) 558-4356
Burbank, CA 91505 **www.tribalscenery.com**

Ultra Effects (805) 499-1506 (818) 292-1906
501-I S. Reino Rd., Ste. 378 FAX (805) 499-1506
Newbury Park, CA 91320 **www.ultraeffects.net**
(Models, RC Vehicles & Robotics)

The Village Art Project (818) 985-9357 (310) 210-9300
11602 Ventura Blvd. FAX (818) 985-8211
Studio City, CA 91604 **www.thevillageartproject.com**
(Ceramics & Pottery)

Vision Scenery Corporation (818) 567-2818
26 E. Providencia Ave. FAX (818) 567-2839
Burbank, CA 91502
(Action Props, Artificial Foods, Breakaways, Custom, Electronics, Foam Sculpting, FX Props, Gadgetry, Hydraulics, Mechanical FX, Miniatures, Models, Oversized Props, Product Pours, Prop Fabrication, Prototyping, Radio-Controlled, Remote-Controlled, Rigging, Robotics, Rubber Props, Sculpted Props, Skeleton Replication, Toy Fabrication, Turntables, Vacuum-Forming, Waterjet Cutting, Weapon Fabrication & Welding)

The Walt Disney Studios (818) 560-5510
Property Department FAX (818) 559-7433
500 S. Buena Vista St.
Burbank, CA 91521

Warner Bros. Studio Facilities - Special FX Department (818) 954-1365
4000 Warner Blvd. FAX (818) 954-1424
Burbank, CA 91522 **www.wbsf.com**
(Prop Manufacturing & Special FX Rentals)

West EFX, Inc. (818) 762-1059 (213) 304-9323
6840 Vineland Ave. FAX (818) 762-0207
North Hollywood, CA 91605 **www.westefx.com**

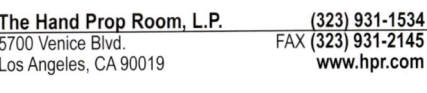

The Hand Prop Room, L.P. (323) 931-1534
5700 Venice Blvd. FAX (323) 931-2145
Los Angeles, CA 90019 www.hpr.com

LCW Props (818) 243-0707
6439 San Fernando Rd. FAX (818) 243-1830
Glendale, CA 91201 www.lcwprops.com

Modern Props (323) 934-3000
5500 W. Jefferson Blvd. FAX (323) 934-3155
Los Angeles, CA 90016 www.modernprops.com

NBC Universal Property (818) 777-2784
100 Universal City Plaza FAX (818) 866-1543
Universal City, CA 91608
www.filmmakersdestination.com

Omega/Cinema Props (323) 466-8201
5857 Santa Monica Blvd. FAX (323) 461-3643
Hollywood, CA 90038 www.omegacinemaprops.com

Prop Services West - Hollywood (323) 461-3371
7017 Santa Monica Blvd. FAX (323) 461-4571
Hollywood, CA 90038 www.pswprophouse.com

Prop Services West - LA (323) 290-2600
4625 Crenshaw Blvd. FAX (323) 290-2607
Los Angeles, CA 90043 www.pswprophouse.com

RC Vintage (818) 765-7107
(323) 462-4510
7100 Tujunga Ave. FAX (818) 765-7197
North Hollywood, CA 90028 www.rcvintage.com

Sony Pictures Studios (310) 244-5999
5300 Alla Rd. FAX (310) 244-0999
Los Angeles, CA 90066 www.sonypicturesstudios.com

Warner Bros. Studio Facilities - Property (818) 954-2181
4000 Warner Blvd. FAX (818) 954-4965
Burbank, CA 91522 www.wbsf.com

Alpine Fixtures & Sheet Metal, Inc.
(323) 734-7200
(323) 766-6040
FAX (323) 734-0058

Angel Appliances
8545 Sepulveda Blvd.
Sepulveda, CA 91343
(818) 892-7227
(877) 835-6030
FAX (818) 892-3524
www.angelappliances.com

Antique Stove Heaven
5414 S. Western Ave.
Los Angeles, CA 90062
(1800s–1950s)
(323) 298-5581
FAX (323) 298-0029
www.antiquestoveheaven.com

Bleau-Bush Co., Inc.
(323) 735-1561
FAX (323) 735-0874

C.P. Two
5755 Santa Monica Blvd.
Hollywood, CA 90038
(323) 466-8201
www.omegacinemaprops.com

The Dish Factory
(213) 687-9500
(213) 687-9501
FAX (213) 617-0074
www.dishfactory.com

Gourmet Depot
(Kitchen Appliance Replacement Parts)
(800) 543-7549
(415) 777-5144
FAX (415) 495-5141
www.thegourmetdepotco.com

History for Hire
7149 Fair Ave.
North Hollywood, CA 91605
(Period Equipment)
(818) 765-7767
FAX (818) 765-7871
www.historyforhire.com

LA Party Rents
13520 Saticoy St.
Van Nuys, CA 91402
(818) 989-4300
(310) 785-0000
FAX (818) 989-3593
www.lapartyrents.com

Lennie Marvin Enterprises, Inc.
3110 Winona Ave.
Burbank, CA 91504
(818) 841-5882
FAX (818) 841-2896
www.propheaven.com

Objects
3650 Holdrege Ave.
Los Angeles, CA 90016
(Contemporary Kitchen Dressing)
(310) 839-6363
FAX (310) 839-6262
www.ob-jects.com

Ⓐ **Rick Enterprises**
4320 W. Vanowen St.
Burbank, CA 91505
(818) 847-1144
FAX (818) 847-1119

Star Restaurant Equipment & Supply Co.
6178 Sepulveda Blvd.
Van Nuys, CA 91411
(818) 782-4460
FAX (818) 782-8179
www.starkitchen.com

Surfas
(310) 559-4770
FAX (310) 559-4983

Tavern Soda Service
(818) 349-1414
FAX (818) 349-9819
(Antique–Present Bar Setups, Beer Taps and Soda Equipment)

Williams-Sonoma
339 N. Beverly Dr.
Beverly Hills, CA 90210
(310) 274-9127
www.williams-sonoma.com

Williams-Sonoma
142 S. Lake Ave.
Pasadena, CA 91101
(626) 795-5045
www.williams-sonoma.com

Williams-Sonoma
Fashion Square
Sherman Oaks, CA 91423
(818) 906-2787
www.williams-sonoma.com

Specialty Props

1st Phil's Animal Rentals (805) 521-1100
P.O. Box 309 FAX (805) 521-0956
Piru, CA 93040 www.philsanimalrentals.com
(Carriages & Wagons)

AAT Fabrication (818) 780-9310
(800) 200-4228
16760 Stagg St., Ste. 217 FAX (800) 805-0039
Van Nuys, CA 91406 www.aatfabrication.com/props
(Aquariums)

ABC Caskets Factory (323) 268-1783
(866) 369-5457
1705 N. Indiana St. FAX (323) 268-5215
Los Angeles, CA 90063 www.abettercasket.com
(Casket Fabrication and Rental & Cemetery Lowering Device)

Acquabella Fountain Restorations (310) 582-1149
(661) 822-6552
www.acquabellawaterfeatures.com
(Fountains & Ponds)

Action Sets and Props/ WonderWorks (818) 992-8811
7231 Remmet Ave. FAX (818) 347-4330
Canoga Park, CA 91303 www.wonderworksweb.com
(Outer Space Props)

Adam Basma Bazaar, Inc. (323) 934-9493
(310) 854-3500
1551 S. La Cienega Blvd. www.adambasma.com
Los Angeles, CA 90035
(Middle Eastern)

Ⓐ Aero Mock-Ups, Inc. (818) 982-7327 / (888) 662-5877
13126 Saticoy St. FAX (818) 982-0122
North Hollywood, CA 91605 www.aeromockups.com
(Aircraft, Aircaft Interiors & Airline Props)

Air Designs (818) 768-6639
11900 Wicks St. FAX (818) 768-6675
Sun Valey, CA 91352 www.airdesigns.net
(Automotive Props & Diner and Restaurant Equipment)

Ⓐ Air Hollywood (818) 890-6801 / (877) 466-2587
13240 Weidner St. FAX (818) 890-7041
Pacoima, CA 91331 www.airhollywood.com
(Airline Props)

Airpower Aviation Resources (805) 402-0052
702 Paseo Vista FAX (805) 498-0357
Thousand Oaks, CA 91320 www.airpower-aviation.com

Almost Christmas Prop Shoppe/ Cathy Christmas (310) 286-0921 / (310) 748-4521
5057 Lankershim Blvd. FAX (818) 285-9630
North Hollywood, CA 91601 www.cathychristmas.com
(Christmas Decorations and Lights)

Alva's Ballet Barres (310) 519-1314 / (800) 403-3447
1417 W. Eighth St. FAX (310) 831-6110
San Pedro, CA 90732 www.alvas.com
(Ballet Bars & Dancers Props)

American Hot Tub Co. (818) 957-8827 / (818) 439-3730
2520 Foothill Blvd. FAX (818) 957-8830
La Crescenta, CA 91214 www.americansoftub.com
(Portable Hot Tubs & Spas)

Apex Electronics (818) 767-7202 / (323) 875-1308
8909 San Fernando Rd. FAX (818) 767-1341
Sun Valley, CA 91352 www.apexelectronic.com
(Aircraft, Electronics & Military Props)

Armstrong's Antique Plumbing & Lighting (714) 761-1320 / (714) 488-7300
2820 W. Orange Ave. FAX (714) 761-1320
Anaheim, CA 92804
(1890s–1940s)

Ⓐ Big Events, Inc. (760) 477-2655
1613 Ord Way FAX (760) 477-2656
Oceanside, CA 92056 www.bigeventsonline.com

Bindery (323) 962-2109 / (323) 428-7222
5720 Melrose Ave. www.charlenematthews.com
Los Angeles, CA 90038
(Bookbinding & Book Props)

Bischoff's Taxidermy & Animal EFX (818) 843-7561
54 E. Magnolia Blvd. FAX (818) 567-2443
Burbank, CA 91502 www.bischoffs.net
(Furs, Hides & Lifesized Mounted Animals)

Bob Gail Special Events (310) 202-5200
3321 La Cienega Pl. FAX (310) 839-4558
Los Angeles, CA 90016 www.bobgail.com
(Prop House)

Bugs Are My Business/ Steve Kutcher (626) 836-0322
1801 Oakview Ln. home.earthlink.net/~skutcher
Arcadia, CA 91006
(Preserved Butterflies and Insects & Rubber Bugs)

Ⓐ C & C Fence Co., Inc. (818) 983-1959 / (800) 660-3382
12822 Sherman Way FAX (818) 765-2729
North Hollywood, CA 91605 www.candcfence.com
(Chain Link, Iron and Metal Fences)

C.P. Four (323) 466-8201
706 N. Cahuenga Blvd. FAX (323) 467-2749
Hollywood, CA 90038 www.omegacinemaprops.com

California Casket Company (310) 390-9969 / (800) 787-1400
12553 W. Venice Blvd. FAX (310) 390-2272
Los Angeles, CA 90066 www.calcasket.com
(Caskets, Gravemarkers & Urns)

California Casket Company (310) 390-9969
(800) 787-1400
3153 Glendale Blvd. FAX (310) 390-2272
Glendale, CA 90039 www.calcasket.com
(Caskets, Gravemarkers & Urns)

Cannon's Great Escapes (818) 385-7092
P.O. Box 703 FAX (818) 581-4130
Yucaipa, CA 92399 www.cannonsgreatescapes.com
(Handcuffs, Manacles & Restraints)

Ⓐ **Caravan West Productions** (661) 268-8300
35660 Jayhawker Rd. FAX (661) 268-8301
Agua Dulce, CA 91390 www.caravanwest.com
(1860–1910 Firearms, Cannons and Western Props)

Cinema Crates/
Hallenbeck's General Store & Cafe (818) 985-5916
5510 Cahuenga Blvd. FAX (818) 985-0113
North Hollywood, CA 91601 www.hallenbecks.net
(Barrels, Crates, Gym Lights & Period General Store Props)

Complete Props (818) 445-1480
(Silent Paper and Plastic Bags) www.silentbags.com

Concept Design (626) 932-0082
(800) 846-0717
718 Primrose Ave. FAX (626) 932-0072
Monrovia, CA 91016 www.conceptdesigninc.com
(Exhibit and Theatrical Props & Podiums)

Creative Inflatables (626) 579-4454
(800) 446 3528
9872 Rush St. FAX (626) 579-5561
South El Monte, CA 91733 www.creativeinflatables.com
(Custom Inflatable Props)

Crowd In A Box (877) 927-6939
(416) 275-0422
(Inflatable Extras) FAX (888) 601-2910
www.crowdinabox.com

Crystalarium (310) 652-8006
8500 Melrose Ave., Ste. 105 FAX (310) 652-8007
West Hollywood, CA 90069 www.crystalarium.com
(Crystals, Mineral Specimens & Sculpture)

Damian Canvas Works (310) 822-2343
4230 Del Rey Ave., Ste. 405
Marina del Rey, CA 90292
www.damiancanvasworks.com

Dekra-Lite (714) 436-0705
(800) 436-3627
3102 W. Alton Ave. FAX (714) 436-0612
Santa Ana, CA 92704 www.dekra-lite.com
(Christmas Decorations and Lighting)

Design Models, Inc. (310) 726-0933
1215-B E. El Segundo Blvd. FAX (310) 726-0934
El Segundo, CA 90245

DIMENSION 3 (818) 592-0999
5240 Medina Rd.
Woodland Hills, CA 91364
(3D Viewing Glasses)

E.C. Prop Rentals, Inc. (818) 764-2008
11846 Sherman Way FAX (818) 764-2374
North Hollywood, CA 91605 www.ecprops.com
(Commercial & Industrial)

Engineered Storage Systems, Inc. (626) 961-0961
15034 E. Proctor Ave. FAX (626) 330-2235
City of Industry, CA 91746 www.engineeredstorage.com
(Industrial Equipment, Lockers, Pallet Racks & Shelving)

Film Flies (818) 845-9039
(818) 398-6409
145 S. Glenoaks Blvd., PMB 435 www.filmflies.com
Burbank, CA 91502
(Lifelike and Lifesize Replicas of Bees, Bugs, Houseflies, Insects and Wasps)

Flix FX, Inc. (818) 765-3549
(877) 326-8433
FAX (818) 765-0135
7327 Lankershim Blvd., Ste. 4
North Hollywood, CA 91605
www.flixfx.com
(Large Aquariums & Shimmer Tanks)

The Folk Tree (626) 795-8733
(626) 793-4828
FAX (626) 793-4841
217 S. Fair Oaks Ave.
Pasadena, CA 91105
www.folktree.com
(Latin American and World Crafts)

G & F Carriages (909) 820-4600
(866) 590-0054
FAX (909) 820-4903
2175 S. Willow Ave.
Bloomington, CA 92316
www.gandfcarriages.com
(Horse Drawn Carriages & Wagons)

Galerie Lakaye (323) 460-7333
FAX (323) 460-7330
www.galerielakaye.com

Gonzo Bros. (310) 828-4989
www.gonzobrothers.com
(Cardboard Crowds & Inflatable Figures)

Goodies Props, Inc. (818) 252-1892
FAX (818) 504-2927
9990 Glenoaks Blvd.
Sun Valley, CA 91352
(Prop House)

Gustintaero (818) 890-5983
FAX (818) 897-4988
www.gustintaero.com
(Aircraft Mock-Ups)

A **The Hand Prop Room, L.P.** (323) 931-1534
FAX (323) 931-2145
5700 Venice Blvd.
Los Angeles, CA 90019
www.hpr.com

Hart Brothers Livestock (951) 312-9009
(951) 677-6810
FAX (951) 600-3805
P.O. Box 514
Temecula, CA 92593
(Chuck Wagon, Cowboy Gear, Stagecoach & Wagons)

HEF Studio Pool Service, LLC (818) 439-6234
FAX (818) 758-8440
www.hefpool.com
(Pool and Water Tank Maintenance)

History for Hire (818) 765-7767
FAX (818) 765-7871
7149 Fair Ave.
North Hollywood, CA 91605
www.historyforhire.com
(Prop House)

Hollywood Cinema Production Resources (310) 258-0123
(310) 869-8909
FAX (310) 258-0124
P.O. Box 88459
Los Angeles, CA 90009
www.hollywoodcpr.org
(Prop House)

Hollywood Parts (818) 255-0617
(818) 445-6676
FAX (818) 255-0613
12580 Saticoy St., Bldg. C
North Hollywood, CA 91605
www.hollywoodparts.com
(Asset Management, Props/Wardrobe from Productions & Storage and Sales)

The Home Beer, Wine & Cheesemaking Shop (818) 884-8586
(800) 559-9922
FAX (818) 224-3812
22836-2 Ventura Blvd.
Woodland Hills, CA 91364
www.homebeerwinecheese.com
(Barrels, Bottles, Caps & Corks)

Independent Studio Services, Inc./ISS (818) 951-5600
www.issprops.com
9545 Wentworth St.
Sunland, CA 91040
(Period–Present Prop House)

The Inflatable Crowd Company, Inc. (310) 399-8101
FAX (310) 399-8202
1011 Pico Blvd., Ste. 4
Santa Monica, CA 90405
www.inflatablecrowd.com
(Inflatable Mannequins)

Ingalls Conveyors, Inc. (323) 837-9900
(800) 826-4554
FAX (323) 837-9990
140 E. Whittier Blvd.
Montebello, CA 90640
www.ingallsconveyors.com
(Adjustable and Roller Speed Belt Conveyors)

Jets & Props (818) 505-0199
(818) 324-0884
FAX (818) 505-0199
www.jetsandprops.com
(Aviation Props)

Lane Ranch & Company (661) 942-0435
FAX (661) 942-7485
42220 10th St. West, Ste. 101
Lancaster, CA 93534
www.laneranch.net
(Farm Props, Mechanical Bulls, Wagons & Windmills)

Lennie Marvin Enterprises, Inc. (818) 841-5882
FAX (818) 841-2896
3110 Winona Ave.
Burbank, CA 91504
www.propheaven.com
(Prop House)

A **Lifestyle Pool & Spa** (818) 997-3255
FAX (818) 997-3026
5830 Sepulveda Blvd.
Van Nuys, CA 91411
www.lifestylepoolspa.com
(Pools & Spas)

Living Art Aquatic Design (310) 822-7484
FAX (310) 822-8644
4943 McConnell Ave., Ste. K
Los Angeles, CA 90066
www.aquatic2000.com
(Aquarium Rentals & Water Tanks)

Liz's Antique Hardware (323) 939-4403
FAX (323) 939-4387
453 S. La Brea Ave.
Los Angeles, CA 90036
www.lahardware.com
(Antique and Contemporary Hardware and Lighting & Reproductions)

Lundin Farm (661) 252-6140 / (818) 618-9959
(Farm Props) www.rrstar.net

Lynn Harding Antique Instruments of the Professions and Sciences (805) 646-0204
103 W. Aliso St. FAX (805) 646-0204
Ojai, CA 93023
(Antique Scientific Instruments)

Medical Purchasing Corp. (323) 753-5575
5419 S. Vermont
Los Angeles, CA 90037

Mike Tristano & Co. (818) 522-0969
FAX (818) 888-6447
www.moviegunguy.com
(Guns and Accessories, Military Props and Equipment, Modern and Period Firearms & Weapons)

Model Trains by René (818) 848-6809
707-A Main St. FAX (818) 848-3112
Burbank, CA 91506

Modern Props (323) 934-3000
5500 W. Jefferson Blvd. FAX (323) 934-3155
Los Angeles, CA 90016 www.modernprops.com
(Contemporary, Electronic and Futuristic Props)

Mosaik (323) 525-0337
7378 Beverly Blvd. FAX (323) 525-0341
Los Angeles, CA 90036 www.e-mosaik.com
(Moroccan Props)

A **Mr. Pool/P.M. Sales** (818) 345-1528
18441 Vanowen St. FAX (818) 345-0292
Reseda, CA 91335 www.mr-pool.com
(Galvanized Steel, Glass Tanks, Vinyl Lined & Wood Pools)

N.S. Aerospace Props (818) 765-1087 / (323) 877-0107
7429 Laurel Canyon Blvd. FAX (818) 765-8969
North Hollywood, CA 91605 www.nortonsalesinc.com
(Rocket Components, Engines, Fittings, Gauges & Valves)

NAC Co. (805) 376-0206 / (805) 405-7337
1772-J E. Avenida de Los Arboles FAX (805) 376-8407
Thousand Oaks, CA 91362 www.naceffects.com

NatureMaker (760) 438-4244 / (800) 872-1889
6225 El Camino Real FAX (760) 438-4344
Carlsbad, CA 92009 www.naturemaker.com
(Foam, Metal, Preserved, Silk and Wood Faux Trees)

NBC Universal Graphic Design & Sign Shops (818) 777-2350
100 Universal City Blaza FAX (818) 866-0209
Bldg. 4250/3054 www.filmmakersdestination.com
Universal City, CA 91608
(Generic Product Props, Grave Markers, Signs and Banners & Vehicle Graphics)

NBC Universal Property (818) 777-2784
100 Universal City Plaza FAX (818) 866-1543
Universal City, CA 91608 www.filmmakersdestination.com

Oceanic Arts (562) 698-6960
12414 E. Whittier Blvd. FAX (562) 945-0868
Whittier, CA 90602 www.oceanicarts.net
(Tropical Polynesian Building and Decorating Materials)

Omega/Cinema Props (323) 466-8201
5857 Santa Monica Blvd. FAX (323) 461-3643
Hollywood, CA 90038 www.omegacinemaprops.com
(Prop House)

Pacific Miniatures (714) 447-4478
2021 Raymer Ave. FAX (714) 447-4465
Fullerton, CA 92833 www.pacmin.com
(Aircraft Miniatures)

The Studios at Paramount (323) 956-5140
The Studios at Paramount FAX (323) 862-2325
Manufacturing and Special Effects
5555 Melrose Ave.
Hollywood, CA 90038
www.thestudiosatparamount.com

The Pasadena Antique Center & Annex (626) 449-7706 / (626) 449-9445
444 & 480 S. Fair Oaks Ave. FAX (626) 449-3386
Pasadena, CA 91105 www.pasadenaantiquecenter.com
(Vintage African-American, Asian and Latin Books, Electronics, Ephemera, Fountains, Medical Props, Memorabilia, Records, Statues, Toys and Tribal Art)

Period Props (818) 848-7767 / (818) 807-6677
1536 N. Evergreen St.
Burbank, CA 91505
(Prop House)

Plastica (323) 655-1051
8405 W. Third St. www.plasticashop.com
Los Angeles, CA 90048
(Collectible and Vintage Plastic Items)

Political Campaign Buttons (323) 655-4968
8391 Beverly Blvd., PMB 321
Los Angeles, CA 90048

Practical Props (818) 982-3198
11754 Vose St. FAX (818) 980-7894
North Hollywood, CA 91605 www.practicalprops.com
(Lamps, Lighting Fixtures & Radios)

Prop Services West - Hollywood (323) 461-3371
7017 Santa Monica Blvd. FAX (323) 461-4571
Hollywood, CA 90038 www.pswprophouse.com
(Home Furnishings & Prop House)

Prop Services West - LA (323) 290-2600
4625 Crenshaw Blvd. FAX (323) 290-2607
Los Angeles, CA 90043 www.pswprophouse.com
(Home Furnishings & Prop House)

RC Vintage (818) 765-7107 / (323) 462-4510
7100 Tujunga Ave. FAX (818) 765-7197
North Hollywood, CA 91605 www.rcvintage.com
(1940s–60s Diner Equipment, Casino Equipment, Gas Station Props, Jukeboxes, Lighting Fixtures and Street Dressing)

Reign Trading Co. (626) 307-7755
(Mexican) FAX (626) 307-7744
www.reigntrading.com

Rent a Center (818) 505-1903
6300 Laurel Canyon Blvd. FAX (818) 505-8413
North Hollywood, CA 91606 www.rentacenter.com

Reseda Discount Pottery & Fountains (818) 345-1832
7313 Reseda Blvd. FAX (818) 705-4582
Reseda, CA 91335 www.resedadiscountpottery.com
(Fountains, Pottery & Statues)

Sacred Sword, Inc. (818) 509-9581
6850 Vineland Ave., Ste. L www.militaryprops.com
North Hollywood, CA 91605
(Military)

Safari Ethiopian Store (323) 935-5749
1049 S. Fairfax Ave. www.ethiopiandesign.com
Los Angeles, CA 90019
(African Artifacts, Cloth and Jewelry)

San Bernardino Railroad Historical Society (562) 438-9613
(1927 Steam Locomotive) www.sbrhs.org

Skinny Dog Design Group, Inc. (562) 436-7237
1750 E. Florida St. www.jewelrypropshop.com
Long Beach, CA 90802
(Jewelry)

So Cal Production Source (310) 699-2787
FAX (310) 618-0129
www.scpsunlimited.com
(Motion Capture Props & Rapid Prototyping)

Soap Plant/Wacko/La Luz de Jesus (323) 663-0122
(323) 666-7667
4633 Hollywood Blvd. FAX (323) 663-0243
Los Angeles, CA 90027 www.laluzdejesus.com
(Rare Artwork, Books, Props & Toys)

Standard Engineering Co. (323) 277-3270
(800) 248-8500
5920 Alameda St. FAX (323) 277-3273
Huntington Park, CA 90255
(Belt and Roller Conveyors)

Studio Prop Rentals, Inc. (661) 775-1655
(818) 679-4000
28306 Constellation Rd. FAX (661) 255-9726
Valencia, CA 91355 www.studioproprentals.com
(Prop House & Rentals)

Studio Prop Services (818) 482-1115
23679 Calabasas Rd., Ste. 353 FAX (818) 224-2911
Calabasas, CA 91302 www.studiopropservices.com
(Custom Props)

Stuntworld, Inc./Gianni Biasetti (310) 666-3004
(909) 797-7621
www.stuntworldinc.com
(Basejumping Gear, Parachutes, Rigging & Skydiving Gear)

Sweet Smiling Home, Inc. (213) 687-9630
1317 Palmetto St. FAX (213) 687-9638
Los Angeles, CA 90013 www.sweetsmilinghome.com
(Architectural Elements, Objets D'Art, Religious Icons, Stone Statues & Tribal and Vintage Textiles)

Tail Man Mermaids & More (310) 530-0616
(Aquatic Props & Mermaid/Merman Tails) FAX (310) 530-0616
www.mermaidrentals.com

Towards 2000, Inc. (818) 557-0903
215 W. Palm Ave., Ste. 204 FAX (818) 557-0596
Burbank, CA 91502 www.t2k.com
(Discotheque, Laser & Robotic Lighting Equipment)

Valley Martial Arts Supply (818) 769-0436
(800) 508-0825
5638 Lankershim Blvd. FAX (818) 769-3257
North Hollywood, CA 91601 www.valleymartialarts.com
(Swords)

Vedanta Bookshop (323) 465-7114
(800) 816-2242
1946 Vedanta Pl. FAX (323) 465-9568
Hollywood, CA 90068 www.vedanta.com

Vinyl Technology, Inc. (626) 443-5257
200 Railroad Ave. FAX (626) 443-0531
Monrovia, CA 91016 www.vinyltechnology.com
(Fabrication)

Vision Scenery Corporation (818) 567-2818
26 E. Providencia Ave. FAX (818) 567-2839
Burbank, CA 91502 www.visionscenery.com

Action Watersports (310) 827-2233 / (310) 827-2567
4144 Lincoln Blvd. FAX (310) 305-8046
Marina del Rey, CA 90292 www.actionwatersports.com
(Jet Skis & Sailboards)

Burbank Kawasaki (818) 848-6627
1329 N. Hollywood Way FAX (818) 848-6630
Burbank, CA 91505 www.burbankkawasaki.com
(Jet Skis, Motorcycles, Off-Road Sport Vehicles & Scooters)

Cat Production Services/ Extreme Sports Filming (562) 596-7105
www.extremesportsfilming.com
(Cabin Cruisers, Cigarette Boats, Classic, Dune Buggies, Fishing Boats, Jet Skis, Motorcycles, Off-Road, Sailboards, Scooters, Sea-Doos, Watercraft & Yachts)

EagleRider Motorcycle Rentals (310) 536-6777
11860 S. La Cienega Blvd. FAX (310) 536-6776
Los Angeles, CA 90250 www.eaglerider.com
(Harley-Davidsons)

Golf Cars - LA, Inc. (661) 251-2201
16439 Sierra Hwy www.golfcars-la.com
Canyon Country, CA 91351

Hardline Products Marine Group (805) 581-4700 / (805) 732-5341
677 Cochran St. FAX (805) 581-0022
Simi Valley, CA 93065
www.hardlineproducts.com/marinegroup
(Cabin Cruisers, Cigarette Boats, Fishing Boats, Jet Boats, PWC & Yachts)

Honda of Hollywood (323) 466-7191 / (800) 371-3718
6525 Santa Monica Blvd. FAX (323) 372-3200
Hollywood, CA 90038 www.honda4u.com
(BMW, Honda, Kawasaki and Suzuki Motorcycles, Jet Skis & Sea-Doos)

Honda of North Hollywood (818) 766-6134 / (800) 800-6134
5626 Tujunga Ave.
North Hollywood, CA 91601
(Motorcycles & Sea-Doos)

Hypercycle (818) 988-8860 / (818) 261-7104
15941 Arminta St. FAX (818) 988-8834
Van Nuys, CA 91406 www.hypercycle.com

LA's Jet-Skier Fun Team (310) 569-1099
(Jet Skis & Watercraft) FAX (727) 528-8665
www.jetskifun.com

Scooters Bellissimo/Go, Scoot Go! (626) 523-7224
1730 La Senda Pl. www.scootersbellissimo.com
South Pasadena, CA 91030
(Scooters)

Snowblind Snowmobiles (213) 247-4777
11429 Hayvenhurst Ave. www.mtnx.com
Granada Hills, CA 91344

Vehicle Effects (818) 355-2676 / (818) 846-7506
909 N. Victory Blvd. FAX (818) 846-7576
Burbank, CA 91502 www.vehicleeffects.com

Willie's On & Off Road Center (760) 257-3734 / (760) 953-3303
48301 National Trails Hwy FAX (760) 257-3335
Newberry Springs, CA 92365 www.williesoffroad.com
(Dune Buggies & Off-Road Sport Vehicles)

Adventure 16 Wilderness Outfitters (310) 473-4574
11161 W. Pico
Los Angeles, CA 90064
www.adventure16.com

Archery House (858) 254-4058
P.O. Box 87788 FAX (760) 231-1146
San Diego, CA 92138 www.usarcheryhouse.com
(Archery)

Beverly Hills Bike Shop (310) 275-2453
854 S. Robertson Blvd. FAX (310) 657-9611
Los Angeles, CA 90035 www.bhbikeshop.com

Big Five Sporting Goods (818) 842-5479
510 N. Victory Blvd. www.big5sportinggoods.com
Burbank, CA 91502

Big Five Sporting Goods (818) 246-1100
144 N. Central Ave. www.big5sportinggoods.com
Glendale, CA 91203

Big Five Sporting Goods (323) 651-2909
6601 Wilshire Blvd. www.big5sportinggoods.com
Los Angeles, CA 90048

Big Five Sporting Goods (818) 769-5526
12033 Ventura Pl. www.big5sportinggoods.com
Studio City, CA 91604

Bikes..Camera..Action! (310) 995-2084
1105 Bonilla
Topanga, CA 90290
(Bicycles & Racing Equipment)

Bob Marriott's Flyfishing Store (714) 525-1827
2700 W. Orangethorpe Ave. FAX (714) 525-5783
Fullerton, CA 92833 www.bobmarriotts.com

Captain Nemo U/W Operations (310) 626-7083
904 Silver Spur Rd., Ste. 386 FAX (310)534 4185
Rolling Hills Estates, CA 90274
(Scuba Equipment)

Champs (310) 652-4041
www.champssports.com

Curtis Gym Equipment (818) 897-2804
10275 Glenoaks Blvd., Ste. 7 FAX (818) 838-1149
Pacoima, CA 91331
(Exercise Equipment Rental)

Dive N' Surf (310) 372-8423
504 N. Broadway FAX (310) 372-0937
Redondo Beach, CA 90277 www.divensurf.com

Divers' Discount.com (800) 347-2822
1752 Langley Ave. FAX (949) 221-9323
Irvine, CA 92614 www.diversdiscount.com

Doc's Ski Haus (310) 828-3492
(888) 832-6122
2929 Santa Monica Blvd. FAX (310) 828-1472
Santa Monica, CA 90404 www.docsskihaus.com
(Skiing & Snowboarding)

DT Trampolines Inc. (818) 888-2935
(800) 649-4945
P.O. Box 6214 FAX (818) 888-2951
Woodland Hills, CA 91365 www.dttrampolines.com

Fitwest, Inc. (760) 734-1832
(800) 783-3125
FAX (760) 734-1835
www.fitwestinc.com

Fold-A-Goal (323) 734-2507
(800) 542-4625
4856 W. Jefferson Blvd. FAX (323) 734-0731
Los Angeles, CA 90016 www.fold-a-goal.com
(Soccer Equipment)

Hollywood Fitness Trainers (818) 955-2645
(877) 702-2348
22647 Ventura Blvd., Ste. 262 www.wizardofyouth.com
Woodland Hills, CA 91364
(Exercise and Gymnasium Equipment)

Hollywoodivers.com (323) 969-9875
(877) 657-2822
(Scuba Gear) FAX (323) 969-9734
www.hollywoodivers.com

I. Martin Imports/Bicycles (323) 653-6900
8330 Beverly Blvd. FAX (323) 653-5670
Los Angeles, CA 90048 www.imartin.com

Masterbuilt Boxing & Wrestling Rings (323) 225-9628
FAX (323) 225-0327

Merchant of Tennis (310) 855-1946
1118 S. La Cienega Blvd. FAX (310) 652-9905
Los Angeles, CA 90035 www.merchantoftennis.com

On Track (800) 697-2999
108 E. Prospect Ave. FAX (818) 563-9705
Burbank, CA 91502 www.ontrackandfield.com
(Track and Field Equipment)

Out-Fit (800) 376-3339
(805) 584-1500
725 Cochran St., Ste. B FAX (805) 584-1518
Simi Valley, CA 93065 www.out-fit.net

Play It Again Sports (818) 879-5083
30317 Canwood St. FAX (818) 879-9297
Agoura Hills, CA 91301 www.playitagainsports.com
(New & Used)

Quantum Rock Extreme Sports (310) 378-2171
P.O. Box 4032 FAX (310) 378-9383
Rolling Hills Estates, CA 90274 www.quantumrock.com
(Rock Climbing Walls)

R.E.I. Co-Op (310) 727-0728
1800 Rosecrans Ave., Ste. E FAX (310) 727-0735
Manhattan Beach, CA 90266 www.rei.com

R.E.I. Co-Op (818) 831-5555
18605 Devonshire St. FAX (818) 831-3235
Northridge, CA 91324 www.rei.com

R.E.I. Co-Op (714) 543-4142
1411 Village Way FAX (714) 543-7850
Santa Ana, CA 92705 www.rei.com

The Racket Doctor (323) 663-6601
3214 Glendale Blvd. FAX (323) 663-4329
Los Angeles, CA 90039 www.racketdoctor.com

Reel Bikes (714) 287-8989
8464 Indianapolis Ave. FAX (714) 969-1173
Huntington Beach, CA 92646
www.members.aol.com/teambike/reelbikes.html
(Bicycles, Exercise Equipment & Period)

Rent Fitness Equipment.com (877) 736-8348
14201 S. Main St. FAX (310) 943-2761
Los Angeles, CA 90061 www.rentfitnessequipment.com
(Exercise Equipment)

Roger Dunn Golf Shop (818) 763-3622
4744 Lankershim Blvd. FAX (818) 763-4101
North Hollywood, CA 91602
www.worldwidegolfshops.com

Safety Cycle Shop (323) 464-5765
1014 N. Western Ave. www.safetycycle.com
Los Angeles, CA 90029

Santa Monica Surf Shop (310) 315-7244
2934 Wilshire Blvd. FAX **(310) 453-8405**
Santa Monica, CA 90403
www.santamonicasurfshop.com

Score, American Soccer Co., Inc. (310) 830-6161
(800) 626-7774
726 E. Anaheim St. FAX **(800) 426-1222**
Wilmington, CA 90744 **www.scoresports.com**
(Soccer Equipment)

Scuba Haus (310) 828-2916
2501 Wilshire Blvd. FAX **(310) 829-5083**
Santa Monica, CA 90403 **www.scubahaus.com**

Sport Chalet (818) 558-3500
201 E. Magnolia Blvd., Ste. 145 FAX **(818) 567-2020**
Burbank, CA 91501 **www.sportchalet.com**

Sport Chalet (310) 657-3210
Beverly Connection FAX **(310) 657-2201**
100 N. La Cienega Blvd. **www.sportchalet.com**
Los Angeles, CA 90048

Sport Chalet (818) 790-9800
920 Foothill Blvd. FAX **(818) 790-1051**
La Cañada Flintridge, CA 91011 **www.sportchalet.com**

Sport Chalet (310) 821-9400
13455 Maxella Ave. FAX **(310) 823-0485**
Marina del Rey, CA 90292 **www.sportchalet.com**

Sports Authority (818) 727-2200
8700 Tampa Ave. FAX **(818) 727-9836**
Northridge, CA 91324 **www.sportsauthority.com**

Sportsrobe/ Sports Studio Ventures, LLC (310) 559-3999
(800) 666-2787
8654 Hayden Pl. FAX **(310) 559-4767**
Culver City, CA 90232 **www.sportsstudio.net**
(Period–Present Athletic Costume & Equipment)

Val Surf & Sports (818) 769-6977
4810 Whitsett Ave. FAX **(818) 769-4318**
Valley Village, CA 91617 **www.valsurf.com**

Valley Martial Arts Supply (818) 769-0436
(800) 508-0825
5638 Lankershim Blvd. FAX **(818) 769-3257**
North Hollywood, CA 91601 **www.valleymartialarts.com**
(Boxing, Martial Arts & Wrestling)

VS Athletics (310) 534-0305
(800) 676-7463
4035 S. Higuera St. FAX **(888) 415-5212**
San Luis Obispo, CA 93401 **www.vsathletics.com**
(Display Clocks & Track and Field Equipment)

Studio Prop Rentals

NBC Universal Property (818) 777-2784
100 Universal City Plaza FAX **(818) 866-1543**
Universal City, CA 91608
www.filmmakersdestination.com

NBC Universal Stock Units (818) 777-1126
100 Universal City Plaza, Bldg. 3156 FAX **(818) 866-1363**
Universal City, CA 91608
www.filmmakersdestination.com

Sony Pictures Studios (310) 244-5999
5300 Alla Rd. FAX **(310) 244-0999**
Los Angeles, CA 90066 **www.sonypicturesstudios.com**

United Pacific Studios (213) 489-2001
729 E. Temple St. FAX **(213) 489-2098**
Los Angeles, CA 90012 **www.unitedpacificstudios.com**

Warner Bros. Studio Facilities - Property (818) 954-2181
4000 Warner Blvd. FAX **(818) 954-4965**
Burbank, CA 91522 **www.wbsf.com**

Studio Services

Barneys New York (310) 276-4400
FAX (310) 777-5842
www.barneys.com

Bloomingdale's (310) 360-2714
8500 Beverly Blvd., Beverly Center FAX (310) 360-2752
Los Angeles, CA 90048 www.bloomingdales.com
Contact: Jennifer Stoelt

Bloomingdale's (818) 325-2301
14060 Riverside Dr., Fashion Square FAX (818) 325-2240
Sherman Oaks, CA 91423 www.bloomingdales.com
Contact: Bobbe Aiona

Fred Segal (323) 651-4129
8100 Melrose Ave. FAX (323) 651-5238
Los Angeles, CA 90046
Contact: Sandy Melvin

Giorgio Armani (310) 271-5555
436 N. Rodeo Dr. www.giorgioarmani.com
Beverly Hills, CA 90210

Guess?, Inc. (213) 765-3100
(212) 730-7200
1444 S. Alameda St. FAX (213) 765-5915
Los Angeles, CA 90021 www.guess.com
Contacts: Leilani Augustine & Nina Flood

Macy's (310) 659-9660
Beverly Center, 8500 Beverly Blvd. FAX (310) 657-2798
Los Angeles, CA 90048
Contact: Stacy Davis

Macy's (818) 379-7855
Fashion Square, 14000 Riverside Dr., Third Fl.
Sherman Oaks, CA 91423
Contact: Karen Furno

Monopoly (323) 655-0704
8421 W. Third St. FAX (213) 625-8169
Los Angeles, CA 90048
Contact: Mikhail Vortman

Nordstrom (818) 592-4622
Topanga Plaza, 6602 Topanga Canyon Blvd.
Canoga Park, CA 91303
Contact: Wendy Laurence-Williams

Nordstrom (818) 502-1683
(818) 502-9922
Glendale Galleria, 200 W. Broadway FAX (818) 502-2142
Glendale, CA 91210 www.nordstrom.com
Contact: Gretchen Hengel

Nordstrom (310) 254-1670
Westside Pavillion FAX (310) 254-2778
10830 W. Pico Blvd. www.nordstrom.com
Los Angeles, CA 90064
Contact: Debra Hastain

Saks Fifth Ave. (310) 271-6726
(310) 887-5546
Contacts: Pui Ko & Fernando Meneses

Sy Devore (818) 783-2700
12930 Ventura Blvd., Store 124 FAX (818) 501-4302
Studio City, CA 91604 www.sydevore.com
Contact: Danny Marsh

Tailoring & Alterations

Antoine's Tailoring (310) 275-8045

Nina Correa (310) 390-6761
FAX (310) 398-3889

Costume Rentals Corporation (818) 753-3700
11149 Vanowen St. FAX (818) 753-3737
North Hollywood, CA 91605
www.costumerentalscorp.com

Design World (323) 661-0393
(323) 896-1942
1620 N. Kingsley Dr.
Los Angeles, CA 90027

Fox Studios (310) 369-1897
(310) 369-4636
Wardrobe Department FAX (310) 369-2487
10201 W. Pico Blvd. www.foxstudios.com
Los Angeles, CA 90035

Hans the Tailor (323) 653-2957

J & M Costumers, Inc. (818) 760-1991
5708 Gentry Ave. FAX (818) 980-4449
North Hollywood, CA 91607 www.jmcostumers.com

NBC Universal Costume Department (818) 777-2722
100 Universal City Plaza FAX (818) 866-1544
Bldg. 4250/3054 www.filmmakersdestination.com
Universal City, CA 91608

Silvia's Costumes (323) 666-0680
(323) 666-0702
4964 Hollywood Blvd. FAX (323) 666-6397
Los Angeles, CA 90027 www.silviascostumes.com

Warner Bros. Studio Facilities - Costume Department (818) 954-1297
(800) 375-3085
4000 Warner Blvd., Bldg. 153 FAX (818) 954-3685
Burbank, CA 91522 www.wbsf.com

Wild Lotus (310) 659-0210
(323) 356-6284
8539 W. Sunset Blvd., Ste. 18 www.wildlotususa.com
West Hollywood, CA 90069

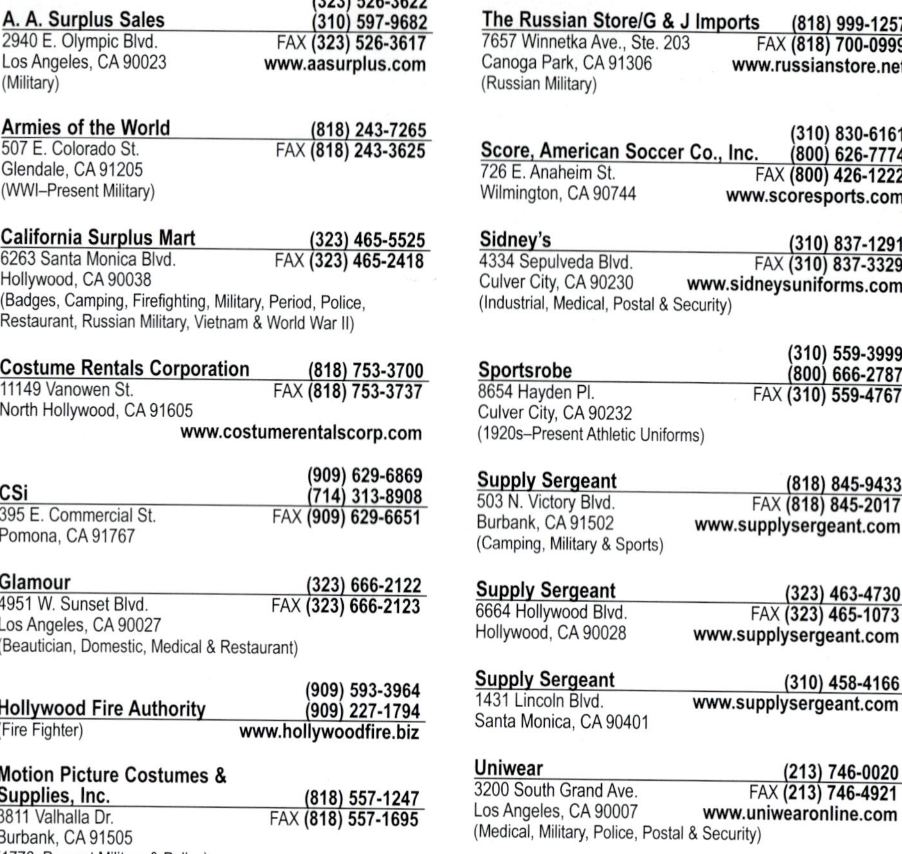

A. A. Surplus Sales (323) 526-3622 (310) 597-9682
2940 E. Olympic Blvd. FAX (323) 526-3617
Los Angeles, CA 90023 www.aasurplus.com
(Military)

Armies of the World (818) 243-7265
507 E. Colorado St. FAX (818) 243-3625
Glendale, CA 91205
(WWI–Present Military)

California Surplus Mart (323) 465-5525
6263 Santa Monica Blvd. FAX (323) 465-2418
Hollywood, CA 90038
(Badges, Camping, Firefighting, Military, Period, Police, Restaurant, Russian Military, Vietnam & World War II)

Costume Rentals Corporation (818) 753-3700
11149 Vanowen St. FAX (818) 753-3737
North Hollywood, CA 91605
www.costumerentalscorp.com

CSi (909) 629-6869 (714) 313-8908
395 E. Commercial St. FAX (909) 629-6651
Pomona, CA 91767

Glamour (323) 666-2122
4951 W. Sunset Blvd. FAX (323) 666-2123
Los Angeles, CA 90027
(Beautician, Domestic, Medical & Restaurant)

Hollywood Fire Authority (909) 593-3964 (909) 227-1794
(Fire Fighter) www.hollywoodfire.biz

Motion Picture Costumes & Supplies, Inc. (818) 557-1247
3811 Valhalla Dr. FAX (818) 557-1695
Burbank, CA 91505
(1776–Present Military & Police)

R.D.D. USA (213) 742-0666
3200 South Grand Ave. FAX (213) 742-9366
Los Angeles, CA 90007 www.rddusa.com
(Camping, Military & Security)

The Russian Store/G & J Imports (818) 999-1257
7657 Winnetka Ave., Ste. 203 FAX (818) 700-0999
Canoga Park, CA 91306 www.russianstore.net
(Russian Military)

Score, American Soccer Co., Inc. (310) 830-6161 (800) 626-7774
726 E. Anaheim St. FAX (800) 426-1222
Wilmington, CA 90744 www.scoresports.com

Sidney's (310) 837-1291
4334 Sepulveda Blvd. FAX (310) 837-3329
Culver City, CA 90230 www.sidneysuniforms.com
(Industrial, Medical, Postal & Security)

Sportsrobe (310) 559-3999 (800) 666-2787
8654 Hayden Pl. FAX (310) 559-4767
Culver City, CA 90232
(1920s–Present Athletic Uniforms)

Supply Sergeant (818) 845-9433
503 N. Victory Blvd. FAX (818) 845-2017
Burbank, CA 91502 www.supplysergeant.com
(Camping, Military & Sports)

Supply Sergeant (323) 463-4730
6664 Hollywood Blvd. FAX (323) 465-1073
Hollywood, CA 90028 www.supplysergeant.com

Supply Sergeant (310) 458-4166
1431 Lincoln Blvd. www.supplysergeant.com
Santa Monica, CA 90401

Uniwear (213) 746-0020
3200 South Grand Ave. FAX (213) 746-4921
Los Angeles, CA 90007 www.uniwearonline.com
(Medical, Military, Police, Postal & Security)

Aardvark's (310) 392-2996
85 Market St.
Venice, CA 90291

Archive Edition Textiles/ Textile Artifacts (310) 676-2424
12575 Crenshaw Blvd. FAX (310) 676-2242
Hawthorne, CA 90250 www.archiveedition.com
(Antique and Vintage Lace and Trim & Reproduction Antique Fabrics)

Buffalo Exchange (323) 938-8604
(323) 938-9204
131 N. La Brea Ave. FAX (520) 622-7015
Los Angeles, CA 90036 www.buffaloexchange.com
(Contemporary–Vintage)

The Button Store (323) 658-5473
8344 W. Third St. FAX (323) 782-0940
Los Angeles, CA 90048
(Antique & Vintage)

Catwalk (323) 951-9255
459 N. Fairfax Ave. FAX (323) 951-9258
Los Angeles, CA 90036
www.catwalkdesignervintage.com
(Antique, Contemporary, Designer, Hats, Purses, Rentals, Undergarments, Victorian & Vintage)

Chuck's Vintage (323) 653-5386
7515 Melrose Ave. www.chucksvintage.com
Los Angeles, CA 90046

Daddyo's (818) 760-6750
10361 Margate St.
North Hollywood, CA 91601
(Vintage 1900s–80s)

Decades, Inc. (323) 655-0223
8214½ Melrose Ave. www.decadesinc.com
Los Angeles, CA 90046
(1960s–70s Vintage Couture)

Mister Freedom (323) 653-2014
7161 Beverly Blvd. FAX (323) 932-9590
Los Angeles, CA 90036 www.misterfreedom.com
(Antique, Original, Rentals, Used, Victorian, Vintage & Western)

Gotta Have It! (310) 392-5949
1516 Pacific Ave.
Venice, CA 90291

Hubba Hubba (818) 845-0636
3220 W. Magnolia Blvd.
Burbank, CA 91505

Iguana Vintage Clothing (818) 907-6716
14422 Ventura Blvd. www.iguanaclothing.com
Sherman Oaks, CA 91403

It's a Wrap! Production Wardrobe Sales (818) 567-7366
3315 W. Magnolia Blvd. www.itsawraphollywood.com
Burbank, CA 91505
(Period–Present)

Jet Rag (323) 939-0528

Junk for Joy Vintage, Etc. (818) 569-4903
3314 W. Magnolia Blvd. www.junkforjoy.com
Burbank, CA 91505
(Original 1950s–80s)

Lily (310) 724-5757
9044 Burton Way
Beverly Hills, CA 90211

Meow (562) 438-8990
2210 E. Fourth St. www.meowvintage.com
Long Beach, CA 90814
(1940s–80s)

Out of the Closet (323) 934-1956
360 N. Fairfax Ave. FAX (323) 934-1750
Los Angeles, CA 90028 www.outofthecloset.org
(Antique, Contemporary, Designer, Jewelry, Original, Shoes, Used & Vintage)

Out of the Closet (323) 664-4394
6210 Sunset Blvd. FAX (323) 467-6258
Los Angeles, CA 90028 www.outofthecloset.org

Out of the Closet (323) 664-4394
3160 Glendale Blvd. FAX (323) 662-0988
Los Angeles, CA 90039 www.outofthecloset.org

Ozzie Dots - Costume & Vintage Clothing (323) 663-2867
4637 Hollywood Blvd. FAX (323) 663-0501
Los Angeles, CA 90027 www.ozziedots.com
(Hats, Purses, Undergarments, Victorian, Vintage & Western)

The Paper Bag Princess (310) 385-9036
(416) 925-2603
8818 W. Olympic Blvd. FAX (310) 385-9052
Beverly Hills, CA 90211 www.thepaperbagprincess.com
(1920s–Present Designer Apparel)

The Pasadena Antique Center & Annex (626) 449-7706
(626) 449-9445
444 & 480 S. Fair Oaks Ave. FAX (626) 449-3386
Pasadena, CA 91105 www.pasadenaantiquecenter.com
(Victorian–1970s Clothing, Hats and Purses & Western)

Playclothes (818) 755-9559 / (818) 755-9558
11422 Moorpark St. FAX (818) 755-9515
North Hollywood, CA 91602
www.vintageplayclothes.com
(1920s–80s Vintage Costumes)

Polkadots and Moonbeams (323) 651-1746 / (800) 210-8051
8367 W. Third St. **www.polkadotsandmoonbeams.com**
Los Angeles, CA 90048

Ragg Mopp (323) 666-0550
3816 W. Sunset Blvd.
Los Angeles, CA 90026
www.myspace.com/raggmoppvintage

Ravishing Resale (323) 655-8480
8127 W. Third St.
Los Angeles, CA 90048
(Vintage–Contemporary)

Re-Mix Vintage Shoes (323) 936-6210
7605½ Beverly Blvd. FAX (323) 202-4014
Los Angeles, CA 90036 **www.remixvintageshoes.com**
(Never Worn)

Resurrection Vintage Clothing (323) 651-5516
8006 Melrose Ave. **www.ressurectionvintage.com**
Los Angeles, CA 90046

A **reVamp** (213) 488-3387
834 S. Broadway, Ste. 1200 FAX (775) 366-0036
Los Angeles, CA 90014 **www.revampvintage.com**

Rock and Rodeo (323) 937-8450
459½ S. La Brea Ave. FAX (323) 937-7940
Los Angeles, CA 90036 **www.rockandrodeo.com**

Slow Clothing (323) 655-3725
7474 Melrose Ave. **www.slow7474.com**
Los Angeles, CA 90046

Squaresville (323) 669-8464
1800 N. Vermont Ave.
Los Angeles, CA 90027

The Studio Wardrobe Department (323) 467-9455 / (818) 503-1490
1357 N. Highland Ave. **www.studiowardrobe.com**
Hollywood, CA 90028
(1940s–Contemporary)

Unique Vintage (818) 953-2877
2013 W. Magnolia Blvd. **www.unique-vintage.com**
Burbank, CA 91506
(Contemporary, Original & Vintage)

Vintage American Clothing (310) 490-4173
12818 S. Normandie Ave. FAX (310) 538-5459
Gardena, CA 90249 **www.vintageamericanclothing.com**

Wasteland, Inc. (323) 653-3028
7428 Melrose Ave.
Los Angeles, CA 90046

The Way We Wore (323) 937-0878
334 S. La Brea Ave. FAX (323) 936-6578
Los Angeles, CA 90036 **www.thewaywewore.com**
(20th Century, Antique, Designer, Hats, Lace, Original, Purses, Trim, Undergarments, Used, Victorian, Vintage & Western)

A-1 Water Trucks (805) 680-0372 (805) 685-5000
P.O. Box 1552 FAX (805) 683-2361
Santa Barbara, CA 93116 www.a1water.net
(Water Trucks: 2000–4000 Gallons)

A **Agua Dulce Water Trucks** (818) 216-3680
14854 Lassen St. FAX (818) 892-7710
Mission Hills, CA 91345
(Water Trucks: 2500 & 4000 Gallons)

Alotta H20 Water Truck Services (714) 692-0692
23300 Azela Circle FAX (714) 692-1162
Yorba Linda, CA 92887 www.alottah2o.com
(Water Trucks: 2000–2800 Gallons)

Antelope Valley Locations and Production Services (661) 946-1515
42848 150th St. East FAX (661) 946-0454
Lancaster, CA 93535 www.avlocations.com

Bertrand Enterprises (760) 446-6600
1210 Graaf Ave. FAX (760) 446-2669
Ridgecrest, CA 93555
(Water Trucks: 4000 Gallons)

Blast Off Enterprises (760) 751-7007 (760) 519-9012
P.O. Box 2550 FAX (760) 751-8421
Valley Center, CA 92082
(Water Trucks: 2500–4000 Gallons)

Carters Effects & Wetshots (310) 623-7817 (760) 963-4306
P.O. Box 2831 www.budpharm.com
Wrightwood, CA 92397
(Bulk Hot Water, Fire Trucks & Water Trucks: 2000–4000 Gallons)

Earthworks Trucks & Equipment (760) 559-7111
9481 Mariposa Rd. FAX (760) 243-7554
Hesperia, CA 92344

Four C's Equipment (661) 619-3542
7751 Citation Ln. FAX (661) 845-0719
Bakersfield, CA 93307
(Water Trucks: 4000 Gallons)

Hollywood Fires (661) 252-7629
12059 Davenport Rd. FAX (661) 251-5165
Agua Dulce, CA 91390 www.hollywoodfires.com

Jensen Water Trucks (310) 455-2463
1137 Fernwood Pacific Dr. FAX (310) 455-0168
Topanga, CA 90290
(Fire Trucks: 1000 Gallons & Water Trucks: 2500 & 4000 Gallons)

Ⓐ **Mel Underwood Water Trucks, Inc.** (818) 361-9176
(800) 675-4855
13201 Foothill Blvd. FAX (818) 361-9617
Sylmar, CA 91342
(Water Trucks: 2000–4500 Gallons)

Michelle's AAA Equipment Rentals, Inc. (800) 367-9287
(Water Trucks: 2000 & 4000 Gallons)

Ⓐ **RMR Equipment Rentals** (661) 510-8516
(661) 257-3303
(Water Trucks: 2500 & 4000 Gallons) FAX (661) 294-8522
www.rmrwatertrucks.com

Sid's Watertrucks (818) 606-6008
(805) 579-3773
P.O. Box 1282 FAX (805) 579-3714
Reseda, CA 91337
(Water Trucks: 2500–4000 Gallons)

Silver Bullet Water Trucks (951) 681-3537
P.O. Box 324 FAX (951) 681-3598
Norco, CA 92860
(Water Trucks: 2500 Gallons)

Water in Motion Co. (818) 266-4907
(818) 266-4919
4000 Cohasset FAX (909) 624-9031
Burbank, CA 91504

Weber Water Truck Rentals (760) 325-4894
(760) 272-9134
28404 Taos Court FAX (760) 327-3549
Palm Springs, CA 92234
(Water Trucks: 4000 Gallons)

West Coast Water Tenders (661) 250-2585
(661) 510-8128
FAX (661) 250-2584
www.westcoasth20.com

CLASSIC LOS ANGELES FILM LOCATIONS

THE BRADBURY BUILDING

(500) DAYS OF SUMMER

INT. OFFICE WAITING AREA – DAY

Tom (Joseph Gordon-Levitt), in a suit, with architecture sketches, waits in the foyer. A VERY CUTE GIRL is sitting in another chair, also waiting. She smiles. He smiles back.

GIRL
Have I seen you before?

TOM
I, uh, don't know. I don't think so.

GIRL
Do you go to St. Patrick's? Not to pray or anything but to stand outside?

TOM
I do! I love that church. It's like my favorite structure in the city.

GIRL
If only it wasn't near that horrible mirrored thing.

TOM
Yes! Exactly. I totally agree!

GIRL
Yeah. I think I've seen you there.

TOM
You have? Really? Hmm. I didn't see you.

GIRL
It happens. You probably weren't looking.

A MAN comes out and calls Tom's name.
Halfway through the doorway, Tom pauses and looks back at the girl.

NARRATOR
If Tom had learned anything, it was that you can't ascribe great cosmic significance to a simple earthly event. Coincidence, that's all anything ever is. There are no miracles. There's no such thing as fate. Nothing is meant to be. He was sure of it now. Tom was...pretty sure.

TOM
When this is over...uh...would you like to grab a cup of coffee or something?

GIRL
I'm sorta supposed to meet someone.

TOM
Oh. Got it...no problem.

He turns back around and shakes it off.

GIRL
OK. Why not?

TOM
Great! So I'll wait for you here. My name's Tom.

GIRL
Nice to meet you. I'm Autumn.

SCREENPLAY BY:
Scott Neustadter & Michael H. Weber

ALSO FILMED AT THE BRADBURY BUILDING:
Blade Runner

LA 411

www.LA411.com

PICTURED:
Bradbury Building

LOCATION:
Downtown Los Angeles

PHOTOGRAPHER:
Michael Rueter
Michael Rueter Photography/L.A.-N.Y.
www.michaelrueter.com

Supporting production in Southern California for 31 years

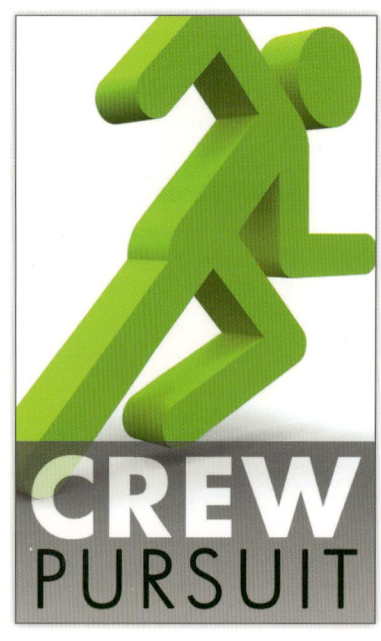

Ⓐ ADVERTISER SYMBOL

Refer to the General Index for cross-referencing items in this section.

411 Creatives (310) 568-2733
10736 Jefferson Blvd., Ste. 820 **www.411creatives.com**
Culver City, CA 90230
(Reps for Storyboard Artists)

A.S.A. Medical Services Division (323) 662-9787
P.O. Box 125 FAX **(323) 662-1569**
La Cañada, CA 91012 **www.asatalent.com/crew**
(EMTs, Lifeguards, Nurses, Paramedics, Rescue Technicians, Safety Consultants, Set Medics & Studio Teachers/ Welfare Workers)

Action Artists Agency (323) 337-4666
1444 1/4 Glendale Blvd. FAX **(323) 395-5663**
Los Angeles, CA 90026 **www.action-artists.com**
(Reps for Set Sketchers and Storyboard Artists)

Agency Celebrity Artists (310) 775-5723
(214) 930-9875
www.agencycelebrityartists.com
(Reps for Hair and Makeup Artists)

All Crew Agency (818) 206-0144
2920 W. Olive Ave., Ste. 201 FAX **(818) 206-0169**
Burbank, CA 91505 **www.allcrewagency.com**
(Reps for Costume Designers, Directors of Photography, First Assistant Directors, Hair and Makeup Artists, Producers, Production Designers, Production Managers, Prosthetics Artists, Script Supervisors and Sound Mixers)

Ambitious Entertainment (818) 990-8993
www.ambitiousent.com
(Reps for Art Directors/Production Designers, Commercial Directors and Directors of Photography)

Artist Untied (323) 933-0200
(415) 957-0500
FAX **(415) 957-0555**
www.artistuntied.com
(Reps For Hair and Makeup Artists, Prop Stylists and Wardrobe Stylists)

Artists by Timothy Priano (310) 274-0032
345 N. Maple Dr., Ste. 397 FAX **(310) 278-7520**
Beverly Hills, CA 90210
www.artistsbytimothypriano.com
(Reps for Hair and Makeup Artists and Wardrobe Stylists)

artists' services (323) 445-4910
(415) 824-4423
www.artists-services.com
(Reps for Hair and Makeup Artists, Prop Masters & Wardrobe Stylists)

ArtMix Beauty (310) 943-8102
2332 S. Centinela Ave., Ste. C FAX **(310) 943-8101**
Los Angeles, CA 90064 **www.artmixbeauty.com**
(Reps for Hair and Makeup Artists and Wardrobe Stylists)

ArtMix Photography (310) 943-8100
(718) 596-2400
2332 S. Centinela Ave., Ste. C FAX **(310) 943-8101**
Los Angeles, CA 90064 **www.artmixphotography.com**
(Reps for Stills Photographers)

@baby! baby!/Lynn Raines (818) 905-0790
(818) 216-8666
2830 S. Robertson Blvd. FAX **(818) 501-0768**
Los Angeles, CA 90034 **www.atbabybaby.com**
(Referral for Baby Wranglers, Nurses and Studio Teachers/ Welfare Workers)

Beauty & Photo (323) 549-3100
3737 Greenwood Ave. FAX **(323) 549-9881**
Los Angeles, CA 90066 **www.beautyandphoto.com**
(Reps for Hair and Makeup Artists)

Casala, Ltd. (818) 780-7180
6539 Colbath Ave. FAX **(818) 780-8262**
Valley Glen, CA 91401 **www.childreninfilm.com**
(Referral for Medics, Nurses and Studio Teachers/Welfare Workers)

Célestine Agency (310) 998-1977
1548 16th St. FAX **(310) 998-1978**
Santa Monica, CA 90404 **www.celestineagency.com**
(Reps for Hair and Makeup Artists, Set Decorators and Wardrobe Stylists)

Cherie Represents (323) 937-9095
845 S. Mansfield Ave., Ste. 1 FAX **(323) 937-3300**
Los Angeles, CA 90036 **www.cheriereps.com**
(Reps for Hair and Makeup Artists and Wardrobe Stylists)

Cloutier (310) 394-8813
1026 Montana Ave. FAX **(310) 394-8863**
Santa Monica, CA 90403 **www.cloutieragency.com**
(Reps for Hair and Makeup Artists and Wardrobe Stylists)

Crew Connection (800) 352-7397
(303) 526-4900
FAX **(303) 526-4901**
www.crewconnection.com
(Nationwide and International Crew Booking)

Crystal Agency (323) 906-9600
(323) 788-1336
4237 Los Nietos Dr. FAX **(323) 443-3752**
Los Angeles, CA 90027 **www.crystalagency.com**
(Reps for Hair and Makeup Artists and Wardrobe Stylists)

Dattner Dispoto & Associates (310) 474-4585
10635 Santa Monica Blvd., Ste. 165 FAX **(310) 474-6411**
Los Angeles, CA 90025 **www.ddatalent.com**
(Reps for Directors of Photography & Production Designers)

Dawn to Dusk Agency (323) 850-6783
(212) 431-8631
8306 Wilshire Blvd., Ste. 412
Beverly Hills, CA 90211 **www.dawn2duskagency.com**
(Reps for Hair and Makeup Artists and Wardrobe Stylists)

Digital Artists Agency/DAA (310) 788-3918
13323 Washington Blvd., Ste. 304 FAX **(310) 788-3415**
Los Angeles, CA 90066 **www.d-a-a.com**
(Reps for Visual FX Artists)

Dion Peronneau Agency (323) 299-4043
5482 Wilshire Blvd., Ste. 1512 FAX **(323) 299-4269**
Los Angeles, CA 90036 **www.dionperonneau.com**
(Reps for Hair and Makeup Artists and Wardrobe Stylists)

A **The Directors Network** (818) 906-0006
3685 Motor Ave., Ste. 220 FAX **(818) 301-2224**
Los Angeles, CA 90034 **www.thedirectorsnetwork.com**
(Reps for Commercial Directors)

The Endeavor Agency (310) 248-2000
9601 Wilshire Blvd., Third Fl. FAX **(310) 248-2020**
Beverly Hills, CA 90210

Ennis, Inc. (310) 587-3512
www.ennisinc.com
(Reps for Hair and Makeup Artists and Wardrobe Stylists/ Costume Designers)

Epiphany Artist Group, Inc. (323) 660-6353
FAX **(323) 660-0094**
(Reps for Hair and Makeup Artists and Wardrobe Stylists)

Exclusive Artists Management (323) 436-7766
7700 Sunset Blvd., Ste. 205 FAX **(323) 436-7799**
Los Angeles, CA 90046 **www.eamgmt.com**
(Reps for Hair and Makeup Artists and Wardrobe Stylists)

Famous Frames, Inc. (310) 642-2721
(800) 530-3375
5839 Green Valley Circle, Ste. 104 FAX **(310) 642-2728**
Culver City, CA 90230 **www.famousframes.com**
(Reps for Storyboard Artists)

FIRE House Management (888) 839-0101
FAX **(888) 839-2943**
www.firehousemanagement.com
(Reps for Hair and Makeup Artists and Wardrobe Stylists)

Frameworks Storyboards (323) 665-7736
983 Manzanita St. FAX **(323) 662-4381**
Los Angeles, CA 90029 **www.frameworks-la.com**
(Reps for Storyboard Artists)

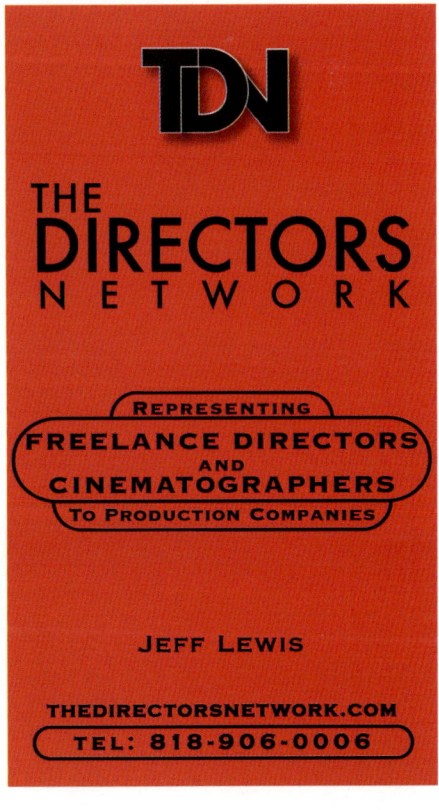

Fred Segal Beauty (310) 550-1800
9250 Wilshire Blvd., Ste. 210 FAX **(310) 550-1501**
Beverly Hills, CA 90212 **www.fredsegalbeauty.com**
(Reps for Hair and Makeup Artists and Wardrobe Stylists)

The Geller Agency (323) 856-3000
1547 Cassil Pl. FAX **(323) 856-3009**
Hollywood, CA 90028 **www.thegelleragency.com**
(Reps for Costume Designers, Directors of Photography, Editors, First Assistant Directors, Production Designers and Stunt Coordinators)

The Gersh Agency (310) 274-6611
(212) 997-1818
P.O. Box 5617 **www.gershagency.com**
Beverly Hills, CA 90210
(Reps for Costume Designers, Directors of Photography, Editors, Producers and Production Designers)

A **Innovative Artists** (310) 656-5151
1617 Broadway, Third Fl. FAX **(310) 656-5156**
Santa Monica, CA 90404 **www.innovativeartists.com**
(Reps for Art Directors/Production Designers, Directors of Photography, Producers and Wardrobe Stylists/ Costume Designers)

International Creative Management - ICM (310) 550-4000
10250 Constellation Blvd. **www.icmtalent.com**
Los Angeles, CA 90067
(Reps for Costume Designers, Directors of Photography, Editors, Producers and Production Designers)

iTalent Company (818) 284-6423
FAX **(866) 755-0708**
www.italentco.com
(Reps for Directors of Photography, Editors, Hair and Makeup Artists and Wardrobe Stylists/Costume Designers)

The Jacob & Kole Agency (323) 460-4767
6715 Hollywood Blvd., Ste. 216 FAX **(323) 460-4804**
Los Angeles, CA 90028 **www.jacobandkoleagency.com**
(Reps for Directors of Photography and Production Designers)

Jeannine Angelique and Associates (310) 401-3211
www.jeannineangelique.com
(Reps for Director/Cameramen, Directors of Photography & Production Designers)

Karlee Artist Management (323) 512-8002
(323) 913-0700
2658 Griffith Park Blvd., Ste. 171 FAX **(323) 878-0068**
Los Angeles, CA 90039 **www.karleeartist.com**
(Reps for Hair and Makeup Artists and Wardrobe Stylists)

LA Rep (213) 446-1720
FAX **(323) 656-1756**
(Reps for Hair and Makeup Artists, Stills Photographers and Wardrobe Stylists)

Leslie Alyson (310) 601-2355
1801 Century Park East, Ste. 700 **www.lesliealyson.com**
Los Angeles, CA 90067
(Reps for Hair and Makeup Artists)

MacGowan Spencer Agency (323) 525-0235
(Reps for Hair and Makeup Artists) FAX **(310) 887-4843**
www.macgowanspencer.com

The Mack Agency (818) 753-6300
5726 Woodman Ave., Ste. 4 FAX **(818) 753-6311**
Van Nuys, CA 91401 **www.themackagency.net**
(Reps for Directors of Photography and Production Designers)

Magnet LA (323) 297-0250
6363 Wilshire Blvd., Ste. 650 FAX **(323) 297-0249**
Los Angeles, CA 90048 **www.magnetla.com**
(Reps for Art Directors, Hair and Makeup Artists and Wardrobe Stylists)

Marsh, Best & Associates (310) 285-0303
9150 Wilshire Blvd., Ste. 220 FAX **(310) 285-0218**
Beverly Hills, CA 90212 **www.marshbest.com**
(Reps for Costume Designers, Directors of Photography, Editors, Production Designers and Sound Production Mixers)

The Mirisch Agency (310) 282-9940
1925 Century Park East, Ste. 1070 FAX **(310) 282-0702**
Los Angeles, CA 90067 **www.mirisch.com**
(Reps for Camera Operators, Costume Designers, Directors of Photography, Editors, Producers, Production Designers & Visual Effects Supervisors)

Montana Artists Agency (323) 845-4144
7715 W. Sunset Blvd., Third Fl. FAX **(323) 845-4155**
Los Angeles, CA 90046 **www.montanartists.com**
(Reps for Directors of Photography, Hair & Makeup Artists, Producers, Production Designers and Wardrobe Stylists/ Costume Designers)

MS Management (323) 935-8455
FAX **(323) 935-3143**
www.ms-management.com
(Reps for Hair Stylists, Make-up Artists and Wardrobe Stylists)

The Murtha Agency (310) 822-9113
4240 Promenade Way, Ste. 232 FAX **(310) 822-6662**
Marina Del Rey, CA 90292 **www.murthaagency.com**
(Reps for Costume Designers, Directors of Photography, Editors & Producers)

New York Office (323) 468-2240
(212) 545-7895
6605 Hollywood Blvd., Ste. 200 FAX **(323) 468-2244**
Los Angeles, CA 90028 **www.nyoffice.net**
(Reps for Costume Designers, Directors of Photography, Editors, Hair and Makeup Artists and Production Designers)

On Location Education (818) 541-9077
(800) 800-3378
400 Columbus Ave., Ste. 7S FAX **(914) 747-2750**
Los Angeles, CA 90046 **www.onlocationeducation.com**
(Referral for Studio Teachers/Welfare Workers)

Opus Beauty (323) 856-8540
6442 Santa Monica Blvd., Ste. 200B FAX **(323) 871-8311**
Los Angeles, CA 90038 **www.opusbeauty.com**
(Reps for Hair and Makeup Artists and Wardrobe Stylists)

Orlando Management (818) 781-9233
15134 Martha St. **www.orlandomanagement.com**
Sherman Oaks, CA 91411
(Reps for Directors of Photography and Production Designers)

Paradigm, A Talent & Literary Agency (310) 288-8000
360 N. Crescent Dr. FAX **(310) 288-2000**
Beverly Hills, CA 90210 **www.paradigmagency.com**
(Reps for Costume Designers, Directors of Photography, Editors, Makeup Artists, Producers & Production Designers)

Partos Company (310) 458-7800
227 Broadway, Ste. 204 FAX **(310) 587-2250**
Santa Monica, CA 90401 **www.partos.com**
(Reps for Directors of Photography, Production Designers and Wardrobe Stylists)

Photogenics (310) 733-2550
8549 Higuera St. FAX **(310) 815-8632**
Culver City, CA 90232 **www.photogenicsmedia.com**
(Reps for Hair and Makeup Artists and Wardrobe Stylists)

Radiant Artists (323) 463-0022
6715 Hollywood Blvd., Ste. 220 FAX **(323) 375-0231**
Los Angeles, CA 90028 **www.radiantartists.com**
(Reps for Directors of Photography and Production Designers)

The Rappaport Agency (323) 464-4481
6311 Romaine St., Ste. 7204 FAX **(323) 464-5030**
Hollywood, CA 90038 **www.rappagency.com**
(Reps for Stills Photographers)

Rescues Unlimited, Inc. (800) 966-0883
P.O. Box 3086 FAX **(800) 966-1329**
Covina, CA 91722
(Reps for Rescue Technicians)

The Rex Agency (323) 664-6494
4446 Ambrose Ave. FAX **(323) 664-6112**
Los Angeles, CA 90027 **www.therexagency.com**
(Reps for Art Directors, Hair and Makeup Artists and Wardrobe Stylists)

Ria Images (323) 876-2761 / (213) 448-8545
7440 Palo Vista Dr. FAX (323) 876-4666
Los Angeles, CA 90046 www.btlartists.com
(Reps for Directors of Photography and Production Designers)

Rouge Artists, Inc. (310) 822-2898 / (310) 570-1150
2433 Boone Ave. FAX (310) 827-7367
Venice, CA 90291 www.rougeartists.com
(Reps for Hair and Makeup Artists and Wardrobe Stylists)

Russell Todd Agency (818) 985-1130
5238 Goodland Ave. FAX (818) 985-1134
Valley Village, CA 91607 www.russelltoddagency.com
(Reps for Steadicam Operators)

The Schneider Entertainment Agency (818) 222-5200
22287 Mulholland Hwy, Ste. 210 FAX (818) 222-5284
Calabasas, CA 91302
www.schneiderentertainment.com
(Reps for Directors of Photography, Hair and Makeup Artists and Steadicam Operators)

Sesler & Company (310) 966-4005 / (416) 504-1223
11840 Jefferson Blvd. FAX (323) 988-0930
Culver City, CA 90230 www.seslercompany.com
(Reps for Directors of Photography)

Sheldon Prosnit Agency (310) 652-8778
800 S. Robertson Blvd., Ste. 6 FAX (310) 652-8772
Los Angeles, CA 90035 www.lspagency.net
(Reps for Directors of Photography and Production Designers)

The Skouras Agency (310) 395-9550
1149 Third St., Third Fl. FAX (310) 395-4295
Santa Monica, CA 90403 www.skouras.com
(Reps for Directors of Photography and Production Designers)

Stacy Cheriff Agency (310) 314-2606
10923 Ayres Ave. www.stacycheriffagency.com
Los Angeles, CA 90064
(Reps for Directors of Photography)

Sternworld Creative Management (310) 439-1903
923 Marco Pl. FAX (310) 439-1904
Venice, CA 90291 www.sternworld.net
(Reps for Design, Marketing, Music and Promotion Companies)

Streetlights Production Assistant Program (323) 960-4540
(Production Assistant Training and Crews) FAX (323) 960-4546
www.streetlights.org

The Studio Teachers (IA Local 884) (818) 559-9600 / (818) 559-9797
www.thestudioteachers.com
(Referral for Studio Teachers)

Suzanna Camejo & Associates/ Artists For The Environment (310) 479-4470
(Reps for Directors of Photography, Editors and Production Designers)

TAMU Artist Agency (310) 721-0735
137 S. Robertson Blvd., Ste. 111 FAX (323) 571-3498
Beverly Hills, CA 90211 www.tamuartistagency.com
(Reps for Hair and Makeup Artists and Wardrobe Stylists)

Ⓐ **TDN Artists** (818) 906-0006
3685 Motor Ave., Ste. 220 FAX (818) 301-2224
Los Angeles, CA 90034 www.tdnartists.com
(Reps for Directors of Photography, Editors & Production Designers)

@Teacher! Teacher! (310) 559-1918 / (310) 880-2310
FAX (818) 501-0768
(Referral for Baby Wranglers, Nurses and Studio Teachers/ Welfare Workers)

TellAVision (310) 230-5303
1060 20th St., Ste. 8 FAX (310) 388-5550
Santa Monica, CA 90403 www.tellavisionagency.com
(Reps for 3-D FX Artists, Storyboard Artists & Visual Research/ Treatment Design)

Tracey Mattingly, LLC (323) 462-5000
FAX (323) 462-5001
www.traceymattingly.com
(Reps for Hair and Makeup Artists and Wardrobe Stylists)

United Talent Agency (310) 273-6700
9560 Wilshire Blvd., Ste. 500 FAX (310) 247-1111
Beverly Hills, CA 90212 www.utaproduction.com
(Reps for Costume Designers, Directors of Photography and Production Designers)

Video Tech Services (310) 574-9385 / (310) 505-4015
10866 Washington Blvd., Ste. 513 FAX (310) 577-0850
Culver City, CA 90232 www.videotechservices.com
(Reps for Camera Operators, Gaffers and Lighting Directors, Sound Production Mixers and Video Assist and VTR Operators)

The Wall Group LA (310) 276-0777
329 N. Wetherly Dr., Ste. 207 FAX (310) 276-0107
Beverly Hills, CA 90211 www.thewallgroup.com
(Reps for Hair and Makeup Artists)

WatchReels.com (818) 953-4930
84 E. Santa Anita FAX (818) 688-3991
Burbank, CA 91502 www.watchreels.com

Workgroup, Ltd. (310) 246-0446 / (212) 675-6334
(Reps for Hair and Makeup Artists) FAX (415) 674-1950
www.workgroup-ltd.com

Zenobia Agency, Inc. (323) 937-1010 / (888) 639-6917
130 S. Highland Ave. FAX (323) 937-1133
Los Angeles, CA 90036 www.zenobia.com
(Reps for Food Stylists, Hair and Makeup Artists, Location Scouts, Prop Stylists & Wardrobe Stylists)

A A A Amphibious Medics (818) 219-5522
(877) 878-9185
FAX (818) 301-2665
www.amphibiousmedics.com
(Ambulances, Lifeguards, Medics, Nurses, Safety Consultants & Safety Divers)

A.S.A. Medical Services Division (323) 662-9787
P.O. Box 125 FAX (323) 662-1569
La Cañada, CA 91012 www.asatalent.com/crew
(Ambulances, EMTs, Lifeguards, Nurses, Paramedics, Safety Consultants and Divers & Set Medics)

Martin L. Alpert, M.D. (310) 393-0739
(On Set, Travel and Tropical Physician) FAX (310) 395-2063

Alpha Ambulance, Inc. (323) 937-0308
(323) 370-3073
425 S. Fairfax Ave., Ste. 205 FAX (323) 937-4893
Los Angeles, CA 90036 www.aambulance.com
(Ambulances, EMTs, Lifeguards, Medics & Rescue Technicians)

American Rescue Services, Inc. (323) 664-5816
(323) 377-4062
1582 Altivo Way
Los Angeles, CA 90026
(EMTs, Lifeguards, Medics, Nurses, Safety Divers & Paramedics)

Aqua Rescue (323) 707-3411
(323) 707-3415
FAX (818) 293-0049
www.aquarescue.com
(Lifeguards, Medics, Safety Divers & Underwater Safety)

Aquavision (562) 433-2863
(562) 688-3038
3708 E. Fourth St. FAX (562) 433-2863
Long Beach, CA 90814 www.aquavision.net
(Referral for Lifeguards, Medics, Safety Consultants, Safety Divers, Swiftwater Rescue Technicians & Technical Advisors)

@baby! baby!/Lynn Raines (818) 905-0790
(818) 216-8666
2830 S. Robertson Blvd. FAX (818) 501-0768
Los Angeles, CA 90034 www.atbabybaby.com
(Referral for Nurses)

Steve Baruch (661) 373-8270
FAX (661) 554-1785
www.moviemedx.com
(EMTs, Lifegaurds, Medics, Production Safety Coordination, Safety Divers & Technical Advisors)

Cory L. Berg (323) 644-1289
(323) 497-9774
(Paramedic) FAX (323) 644-1289

Sandra Leigh Bolish (661) 645-7347

Kasi Brown (310) 962-8682
(EMT)

Casala, Ltd. (818) 780-7180
6539 Colbath Ave. FAX (818) 780-8262
Valley Glen, CA 91401
(Referral for Lifeguards, Nurses and Paramedics)

Tom Case (661) 273-8649
(661) 755-6073

Cinema Safety & Marine Services, Inc. (310) 614-0206
(805) 207-5797
1534 N. Moorpark Rd., Ste. 108 FAX (805) 241-3954
Thousand Oaks, CA 91360 www.cinemasafety.com
(Lifeguards, Medics, Nurses, Rescue Technicians, Safety Consultants, Safety Divers, Technical Advisors & Underwater)

Code Blue Medics (661) 644-3422
(800) 272-0785
24307 Magic Mountain Pkwy, Ste. 361 FAX (661) 253-0135
Santa Clarita, CA 91355 www.codebluemedics.com
(Ambulances, EMTs, Lifeguards, MDs, Medics, Nurses, Paramedics, Rescue Technicians, Safety Consultants, Technical Advisors & Travel Medicine)

Sean Cussen (562) 618-4357

Robert Cymbal (818) 219-0520
(818) 360-0120
FAX (818) 360-2408
(Lifeguards, Marine Coordination, Medics, Rescue Technicians, Safety Divers & Technical Advisors)

Entertainment Industry Physicians (323) 464-2151
7080 Hollywood Blvd., Ste. 1101 FAX (323) 464-2903
Hollywood, CA 90028

First Aid Services of San Diego, Inc. (619) 708-5555
(888) 457-5273
5907 Erlanger St. FAX (858) 457-1641
San Diego, CA 92122 www.firstaidservices.com
(Ambulances, EMTs, Lifegaurds, Medics, Nurses & Technical Advisors)

Tammy Yazgulian Frost (818) 655-5341
(661) 904-1520
FAX (818) 655-8570

Gerber Ambulance Service (310) 466-8476
(310) 466-8476
FAX (310) 542-1152
www.gerberambulance.com
(Ambulances, EMT's, Nurses & Paramedics)

Timothy Hall (661) 755-7855 / (661) 259-1389
(EMT & Medic)

Healthy Traveler Clinic (626) 584-1200
1250 E. Green St., Ste. 100 FAX (626) 584-2900
Pasadena, CA 91106 www.healthytraveler.com
(Travel Medicine)

Joshua Humphrey (310) 270-7032
(Medic & Safety Diver) www.aquamonsters.com

Jon P. Ko (818) 355-2506
(EMT, Medic, Safety Consultant & Travel Medicine)

Liberty Ambulance (310) 846-4011 / (310) 846-4012
14109 Pontlavoy Ave. FAX (310) 846-4022
Santa Fe Springs, CA 90670 www.libertyambulance.com

Joel Markman (310) 488-3724
FAX (310) 399-2592
(EMT, Lifeguard, Medic & Technical Advisor)

Michael Matus (818) 505-8072 / (818) 632-8072
FAX (707) 516-3573

McCormick Ambulance (310) 349-8901 / (888) 349-8944
13933 Crenshaw Blvd. www.mccormickambulance.com
Hawthorne, CA 90250
(Ambulances, EMTs, Medics, Paramedics & Technical Advisors)

Paul Nolan (661) 252-6134 / (661) 433-8255

David O'Leary (805) 493-4844 / (805) 558-6754
(Paramedic)

A **Passport Health** (323) 297-0700 / (888) 499-7277
333 South Hope St., Ste. C145 FAX (323) 549-9423
Los Angeles, CA 90071 www.passporthealthusa.com
(Travel Medicine)

Stephen Patt, M.D. (310) 582-1114
(Cast Exams, Safety Consultant, Technical Advisor & Travel Medicine)

Rescue Services International (661) 942-0264 / (800) 989-5027
FAX (800) 989-5031

Rescues Unlimited, Inc. (800) 966-0883
P.O. Box 3086 FAX (800) 966-1329
Covina, CA 91722
(Rescue Technicians)

Terri L. Rock, M.D. (310) 319-1566
FAX (310) 319-2468
(On Set Family Physician & Travel Medicine)

Stat Housecalls (888) 556-3669
1601 N. Sepulveda Blvd., Ste. 639 FAX (888) 556-3669
Manhattan Beach, CA 90266 www.stathousecalls.com
(Cast Exams, EMTs, Medics, Nurses, Rescue Technicians, Safety Consultants, Technical Advisors & Travel Medicine)

Symons Event Safety (909) 880-2979 / (866) 728-3754
P.O. Box 10333 FAX (909) 880-9279
San Bernardino, CA 92423 www.symonseventsafety.com
(Ambulances, EMTs, Medics, Nurses, Paramedics, Rescue Technicians, Safety Consultants, Technical Advisors & Travel Medicine)

@Teacher! Teacher! (310) 559-1918 / (310) 880-2310
(Referral for Nurses) FAX (818) 501-0768

Kim Thio (805) 732-3488 / (805) 492-2772
(Paramedic) FAX (805) 492-2772
www.studiomedical.com

Tower I.D. Medical Associates, Inc. (310) 358-2300
8635 W. Third St., Ste. 1180W FAX (310) 358-2308
Los Angeles, CA 90048
(Travel Medicine)

Lynn Wyett (818) 929-3203 / (818) 348-4441

Fanae Aaron (323) 463-0022
www.radiantartists.com

Gabriel Abraham (323) 578-2112
www.gabrielabraham.com

Ken Adam (310) 282-9940
www.mirisch.com

Heidi Adams (213) 880-1229
www.showreelsonline.com/the_mack_agency/heidi_adams

Jeb Adams (818) 338-9296
(818) 681-4179
(Art Director & Production Designer)

Carter Addy (310) 871-9627
(Art Director & Set Decorator) FAX (310) 871-9627
www.carteraddy.com

Maher Ahmad (310) 288-8000
www.paradigmagency.com

Floyd Albee (310) 395-9550
www.skouras.com

All Crew Agency (818) 206-0144
2920 W. Olive Ave., Ste. 201 FAX (818) 206-0169
Burbank, CA 91505 www.allcrewagency.com
(Reps for Production Designers)

James Allen (818) 762-2747
FAX (818) 762-2747

Justin Allen (323) 856-8540
www.opusbeauty.com

Jade Altman (323) 855-5515
(323) 664-5234
www.depict33.com

Patricia Altman (323) 855-6710
(323) 664-5234
www.depict33.com

Miranda Amador (310) 557-8458
FAX (310) 557-8458

Ambitious Entertainment (818) 990-8993
www.ambitiousent.com
(Reps for Art Directors/Production Designers)

Ruth Ammon (323) 845-4144
www.montanartists.com

Nathan Amondson (818) 753-6300
www.themackagency.net

Amy Ancona (310) 274-6611
www.gershagency.com

Susan Anderson (323) 664-6494
www.therexagency.com

Fred Andrews (310) 656-5151
www.innovativeartists.com

Conrad E. Angone (323) 664-9756

Atli Arason (818) 753-6300
www.themackagency.net

Steve Arnold (310) 395-9550
(818) 326-1440
(Production Designer) www.steve-arnold.com

William Arnold (323) 845-4144
www.montanartists.com

Michelle Ashley (323) 449-1538
(Set Decorator) FAX (323) 851-2249

Jody Asnes (310) 246-3190
(917) 575-2026

Alan Au (310) 392-8422
(310) 428-1951

Paul Austerberry (310) 458-7800
www.partos.com

Ken E. Averill (323) 697-6057
(818) 368-4755
www.kenaverill.com

Paul Avery (323) 468-2240
www.nyoffice.net

Ramsey Avery (323) 845-4144
www.montanartists.com

Phillip Barker (310) 474-4585
www.dattnerdispoto.com

Guy Barnes (310) 822-9113
www.murthaagency.com

Walter Barnett (323) 856-8540
www.opusbeauty.com

Benoit Barouh (323) 460-4767
www.jacobandkoleagency.com

K.K. Barrett (310) 273-6700
www.utaproduction.com

Francesca Bartoccini (310) 282-9940
(323) 712-0650
(Art Director & Production Designer) www.bartoccini.com

Edward Bash (818) 249-6979
(323) 376-4047
FAX (818) 249-8179

Larry Basso/Basso Design (323) 401-8801
www.bassodesign.com

Amelia Battaglio (310) 703-7251
(917) 405-8758
www.detaglia.com

Stephen Beatrice (310) 274-6611
www.gershagency.com

Eric Beauchamp (310) 659-5151
(310) 251-5113
FAX (310) 659-5156
www.ericbeauchamp.com

Sophie Becher (310) 285-0303
www.marshbest.com

Judy Becker (310) 273-6700
www.utaproduction.com

Jeffrey Beecroft (626) 398-3337
(626) 786-2310
(Production Designer) www.jeffreybeecroft.com

Stefan Beese/Beesign - Production Design (323) 620-3348
FAX (928) 222-7040
www.beesign-la.com

Chase Harlan (310) 401-3211
www.jeannineangelique.com

Sandy Harris (310) 274-0032
www.artistsbytimothypriano.com

Stan Harris (646) 246-3722
(818) 599-8911
www.devedog.com

Brentan Harron (310) 288-8000
www.paradigmagency.com

Clayton Hartley (310) 288-8000
www.paradigmagency.com

Tom Hartman (310) 458-7800
www.partos.com

Helen Harwell (310) 428-3940
(Art Director & Production Designer)

Sean Haworth (310) 282-9940
(Production Designer) www.mirisch.com

Rick Heinrichs (310) 285-0303
www.marshbest.com

Ric Heitzman (323) 308-8013
www.richeitzman.com

Mark Helf (323) 664-6494
www.therexagency.com

Ron Hellman (323) 297-0250
www.magnetla.com

Stephen Hendrickson (310) 282-9940
www.mirisch.com

Dan Hennah (310) 285-0303
www.marshbest.com

Dunn Henry (310) 288-8000
www.paradigmagency.com

Jennifer Herwitt (310) 652-3681
(213) 220-8698
(Set Decorator) FAX (310) 360-1029
www.herwitt.com

Jeremy Hindle (310) 273-6700
www.utaproduction.com

Roberta Hoeft (310) 274-0032
www.artistsbytimothypriano.com

Richard Holland (310) 273-6700
www.utaproduction.com

Paul Holt (323) 845-4144
www.montanartists.com

Aaron Hom (323) 937-1010
www.zenobia.com

Brock Houghton (323) 449-6924

Jan Houllevigue (323) 468-2240
www.nyoffice.net

Angela Howard (323) 468-2240
www.nyoffice.net

David K. Huang (818) 399-9049

Richard Hudolin (310) 282-9940
www.mirisch.com

Denise Hudson (310) 288-8000
www.paradigmagency.com

Clark Hunter (310) 288-8000
www.paradigmagency.com

Jon Hutman (310) 274-6611
www.gershagency.com

Mark Hutman (310) 274-6611
www.gershagency.com

Suzuki Ingerslev (310) 288-8000
www.paradigmagency.com

Innovative Artists (310) 656-5151
1617 Broadway, Third Fl. FAX (310) 656-5156
Santa Monica, CA 90404 www.innovativeartists.com
(Reps for Art Directors/Production Designers)

International
Creative Management - ICM (310) 550-4000
10250 Constellation Blvd. www.icmtalent.com
Los Angeles, CA 90067
(Reps for Production Designers)

Colin D. Irwin (323) 856-3000
www.thegelleragency.com

Kalina Ivanov (310) 285-0303
www.marshbest.com

Andrew Jackness (310) 822-9113
www.andrewjackness.com

Gemma Jackson (310) 395-9550
www.skouras.com

Regan Jackson (310) 652-8778
www.lspagency.net

The Jacob & Kole Agency (323) 460-4767
6715 Hollywood Blvd., Ste. 216 FAX (323) 460-4804
Los Angeles, CA 90028 www.jacobandkoleagency.com
(Reps for Production Designers)

Bruton Jones (310) 288-8000
www.paradigmagency.com

Chris Jones (323) 468-2240
www.nyoffice.net

Elizabeth Jones (323) 468-2240
www.nyoffice.net

Steven Jones-Evans (310) 274-6611
www.gershagency.com

Francois Jordaan (310) 458-7800
www.partos.com

Johnny Josselyn (213) 810-4003
FAX (323) 446-8484
www.johnnyjos.com

Chester Kaczenski (310) 652-8778
www.lspagency.net

Corey Kaplan (310) 656-5151
www.innovativeartists.com

Kevin Kavanaugh (310) 395-9550
www.skouras.com

Jaeson Kay (818) 206-0144
www.allcrewagency.com

Michael Keeling (310) 458-7800
www.partos.com

Victor Kempster (310) 395-9550
www.skouras.com

Morgan Kennedy (310) 474-4585
www.dattnerdispoto.com

K.J.B. Kiely (323) 935-1127
(213) 706-8162
FAX (323) 930-5611

Lilly Kilvert (310) 273-6700
www.utaproduction.com

Steve Kimmel (310) 652-8778
(Production Designer) FAX (323) 669-0343
www.lspagency.net

David King (323) 845-4144
www.montanartists.com

Holli Kingsbury (310) 274-0032
www.artistsbytimothypriano.com

Paul Kirby (310) 395-9550
www.skouras.com

Sonja Klaus (310) 288-8000
www.paradigmagency.com

Miljen Kljakovic (310) 285-0303
www.marshbest.com

Ray Kluga (310) 656-5151
www.innovativeartists.com

Christian Svanes Kolding (310) 848-7310
www.christiansvaneskolding.com

David Korins (323) 468-2240
www.nyoffice.net

Doug Kraner (310) 656-5151
www.innovativeartists.com

Michael Krantz (323) 460-4767
www.jacobandkoleagency.com

Francois-Renaud Labarthe (310) 652-8778
www.lspagency.net

Charlie Lagola (310) 288-8000
www.paradigmagency.com

Bill Lakoff (818) 261-9448
FAX (818) 994-1526
www.wtldesignsinc.com

Neil Lamont (310) 652-8778
www.lspagency.net

Peter Lamont (310) 652-8778
www.lspagency.net

Suttirat Larlarb (323) 845-4144
www.montanartists.com

Richard Lassalle (310) 274-6611
www.gershagency.com

Julian LaVerdiere (310) 395-9550
www.skouras.com

Steve Lawrence (310) 395-9550
www.skouras.com

David Lazan (310) 656-5151
www.innovativeartists.com

Lauryn LeClere (818) 760-7746
(818) 681-2114
FAX (818) 760-7748
www.lecleredesign.com

Charles Lee (310) 652-8778
www.lspagency.net

Jonathan Lee (310) 285-0303
www.marshbest.com

Steven Legler (310) 314-4077
(310) 962-4952
(Art Director & Production Designer) FAX (310) 314-4067
www.leglerart.com

Dan Leigh (310) 285-0303
www.marshbest.com

Douglas C. Lewis (562) 424-5476
(213) 700-7424
(Set Decorator) FAX (562) 424-5603

Richard B. Lewis (310) 282-9940
www.richardblewisdesign.com

George Liddle (310) 822-9113
www.murthaagency.com

Stephen Lineweaver (310) 656-5151
www.innovativeartists.com

Barbara Ling (310) 395-9550
www.skouras.com

Tom Lisowski (323) 856-3000
www.thegelleragency.com

Sharon Lomofsky (310) 274-6611
www.gershagency.com

Santo Loquasto (310) 288-8000
www.paradigmagency.com

Cory Lorenzen (310) 274-6611
www.gershagency.com

Johanna Lowe (310) 274-0032
www.artistsbytimothypriano.com

Richard C. Lowe (310) 664-1001
FAX (310) 664-1001
www.lowejinx.com

Joseph Lucky (310) 288-8000
www.paradigmagency.com

Hugo Luczyc-Wyhowski (310) 395-9550
www.skouras.com

Patrick Lumb (310) 273-6700
(Production Designer) www.patricklumb.com

Nicholas Lundy (310) 656-5151
www.innovativeartists.com

Jeffrey Luther (661) 722-9251
(661) 400-5829
(Art Director & Production Designer)

Marcos Lutyens (310) 282-9940
www.mirisch.com

The Mack Agency (818) 753-6300
5726 Woodman Ave., Ste. 4 FAX (818) 753-6311
Van Nuys, CA 91401 www.themackagency.net
(Reps for Production Designers)

Magnet LA (323) 297-0250
6363 Wilshire Blvd., Ste. 650 FAX (323) 297-0249
Los Angeles, CA 90048 www.magnetla.com
(Reps for Art Directors)

Grant Major (310) 273-6700
www.utaproduction.com

Aran Mann (310) 274-6611
www.gershagency.com

Jeff Mann (310) 474-4585
www.ddatalent.com

Michael Manson (213) 300-6010
(Art Director & Production Designer) FAX (323) 843-5361

Marsh, Best & Associates (310) 285-0303
9150 Wilshire Blvd., Ste. 220 FAX (310) 285-0218
Beverly Hills, CA 90212 www.marshbest.com
(Reps for Production Designers)

Paul Martin (310) 652-8778
(323) 578-1946
www.lspagency.net

Anastasia Masaro (310) 822-9113
www.murthaagency.com

Happy Massee (310) 288-8000
www.paradigmagency.com

Jacqui Masson (213) 483-4400
(213) 220-3530
(Set Decorator) FAX (213) 483-4400

Gary Matteson (323) 340-1447
(323) 573-7753
www.garymattesondesign.com

Arthur Max (310) 822-9113
www.murthaagency.com

Caty Maxey (310) 656-5151
www.innovativeartists.com

Vincent Mazeau (323) 463-0100
www.magnetla.com

Andrew McAlpine (310) 285-0303
www.marshbest.com

Alex McDowell (818) 753-6300
www.themackagency.net

Stephen J. McHale (805) 405-4123
FAX (818) 475-1453

Peter McKinney (310) 863-5984
FAX (310) 356-3815
www.mckinneyprodesign.com
(Art Director, Production Designer & Set Decorator)

Jason McKnight (323) 856-8540
www.opusbeauty.com

Deborah McLean (323) 937-1010
www.zenobia.com

Cabot McMullen (310) 600-3693
(818) 284-6423
FAX (866) 755-0708
www.cmi-nyc.com

Anthony Medina (310) 656-5151
www.innovativeartists.com

Irwin Mehlman (310) 399-6942
(310) 350-9683
FAX (310) 399-6442

Bekka Melino (323) 468-2240
www.nyoffice.net

Greg Melton (310) 288-8000
www.paradigmagency.com

Carlos Menendez (310) 474-4585
www.dattnerdispoto.com

Andrew Menzies (310) 656-5151
www.innovativeartists.com

Philip Messina (310) 395-9550
www.skouras.com

Tom Meyer (310) 273-6700
www.utaproduction.com

Elizabeth Mickle (310) 288-8000
www.paradigmagency.com

Louise Middleton (818) 284-6423
www.italentco.com

Bruce Miller (310) 652-8778
www.lspagency.net

Chris Anthony Miller (818) 781-9233
www.orlandomanagement.com

Michelle Milosh (323) 660-1102
(323) 377-3721

Michelle Minch (626) 441-8975
(626) 695-1227
FAX (626) 441-8118
www.michelleminch.com

The Mirisch Agency (310) 282-9940
1925 Century Park East, Ste. 1070 FAX (310) 282-0702
Los Angeles, CA 90067 www.mirisch.com
(Reps for Production Designers)

Nigel Mitchell (818) 781-9233
www.nigelrmitchell.com

Tim Moen (310) 822-2898
www.rougeartists.com

Montana Artists Agency (323) 845-4144
7715 W. Sunset Blvd., Third Fl. FAX (323) 845-4155
Los Angeles, CA 90046 www.montanartists.com
(Reps for Production Designers)

Jose Montano (310) 395-9550
www.skouras.com

Cecilia Montiel (323) 460-4767
www.jacobandkoleagency.com

Elizabeth Moore (818) 990-8993
(323) 459-8160
www.eamoore.com

Dan Morski (818) 881-4358
(323) 497-7502
FAX (818) 881-3208
www.danmorski.com

John Mott (323) 856-3000
www.thegelleragency.com

Scott P. Murphy (323) 845-4144
www.montanartists.com

The Murtha Agency (310) 822-9113
4240 Promenade Way, Ste. 232 FAX (310) 822-6662
Marina Del Rey, CA 90292 www.murthaagency.com
(Reps for Production Designers)

Jane Musky (310) 395-9550
www.skouras.com

John Myhre (310) 285-0303
www.marshbest.com

Rika Nakanishi (818) 753-6300
www.themackagency.net

Ariana Nakata (310) 458-7800
www.partos.com

Janet Nelson (310) 395-9550
(323) 851-1512
www.skouras.com

Joseph Nemec (310) 288-8000
www.paradigmagency.com

New York Office (323) 468-2240
(212) 545-7895
6605 Hollywood Blvd., Ste. 200 FAX (323) 468-2244
Los Angeles, CA 90028 www.nyoffice.net
(Reps for Production Designers)

Jill Nicholls (323) 297-0250
www.magnetla.com

Patricia Norris (310) 822-9113
www.murthaagency.com

Michael Novotny (310) 652-8778
www.lspagency.net

John Nyomarkay (310) 652-8778
www.lspagency.net

Brian O'Hara/O'Hara Design Group (310) 828-3830
FAX (310) 828-3840
www.oharadesigngroup.com

Paul Oberman (310) 652-8778
www.lspagency.net

Luca Ognibene (310) 458-7800
www.partos.com

Michael Okowita (310) 288-8000
www.paradigmagency.com

Brian Ollman (818) 206-0144
www.allcrewagency.com

Gary A. Olson (818) 761-8426
(818) 749-6577
(Prop Master)

Orlando Management (818) 781-9233
15134 Martha St. www.orlandomanagement.com
Sherman Oaks, CA 91411
(Reps for Production Designers)

Stefano Maria Ortolani (310) 822-9113
www.murthaagency.com

Laurent Ott (310) 652-8778
www.lspagency.net

Chuck Parker (310) 656-5151
www.innovativeartists.com

Salvador Parra (310) 652-8778
www.lspagency.net

Partos Company (310) 458-7800
227 Broadway, Ste. 204 FAX (310) 587-2250
Santa Monica, CA 90401 www.partos.com
(Reps for Production Designers)

Owen Paterson (310) 273-6700
www.utaproduction.com

Janet Patterson (310) 285-0303
www.marshbest.com

Tiffany Payne (818) 753-6300
www.themackagency.net

Randall Peacock (323) 297-0250
www.magnetla.com

Tule Peak (310) 652-8778
www.lspagency.net

Paul Peters (310) 288-8000
www.paradigmagency.com

Kirk Petruccelli (323) 845-4144
www.montanartists.com

Nigel Phelps (310) 273-6700
www.utaproduction.com

Kevin Phipps (310) 285-0303
www.marshbest.com

Kevin Pierce (818) 206-0144
www.allcrewagency.com

Herbert Pinter (310) 822-9113
www.murthaagency.com

Dave Pirinelli (213) 434-7523
web.mac.com/dpart2/
dave_pirinelli_production_design/home.html

Agustin Plotquin (310) 430-0971
(310) 430-0970
FAX (323) 221-9600
www.allsets.com

Nick Plotquin (310) 430-0971
(310) 430-0970
FAX (323) 221-9600
www.allsets.com

Patti Podesta (310) 288-8000
www.paradigmagency.com

Peter Politanoff (310) 288-8000
www.paradigmagency.com

Gideon Ponte (310) 273-6700
www.unitedtalent.com

Katterina Powers (310) 288-8000
www.paradigmagency.com

Anthony Pratt (310) 285-0303
www.marshbest.com

Kim Healy Pretti (818) 325-5086
www.kimpretti.com

Clement Price-Thomas (310) 395-9550
www.skouras.com

Laird Pulver (818) 206-0144
www.allcrewagency.com

Dan Quellette (323) 460-4767
www.jacobandkoleagency.com

Robert J. Quinn (818) 888-0991
(818) 517-6155

Jean Rabasse (323) 460-4767
www.jacobandkoleagency.com

Radiant Artists (323) 463-0022
6715 Hollywood Blvd., Ste. 220 FAX (323) 375-0231
Los Angeles, CA 90028 www.radiantartists.com
(Reps for Production Designers)

Steve Ralph (213) 400-9340
(262) 567-9813
www.steveralphdesign.com

Gary Randall (818) 504-9211
(323) 376-3046
FAX (818) 504-9949
www.garyrandalldesigns.com

Ida Random (310) 395-9550
www.skouras.com

Bjorn Reddington (213) 280-6460
FAX (805) 684-8717

Duncan Reed (213) 300-4280
FAX (323) 962-1730
www.duncanreed.com

Jeremy Reed (310) 273-6700
www.utaproduction.com

Seth Reed (310) 288-8000
www.paradigmagency.com

Kim Rees (951) 377-6570
(323) 463-0022
www.radiantartists.com

Peter Remmers (818) 522-9904
www.rfdinc.tv

Chuck Renaud (917) 204-6034
(323) 254-4420
(Production Designer)
www.chuckrenaud.com

The Rex Agency (323) 664-6494
4446 Ambrose Ave.
Los Angeles, CA 90027
(Reps for Art Directors)
FAX (323) 664-6112
www.therexagency.com

Vincent Reynaud (310) 652-8778
www.lspagency.net

Norman Reynolds (310) 395-9550
www.skouras.com

Judy Rhee (212) 634-8157
(Production Designer)

Andy Rhodes (310) 395-9550
www.skouras.com

Ria Images (323) 876-2761
(213) 448-8545
7440 Palo Vista Dr.
Los Angeles, CA 90046
(Reps for Production Designers)
FAX (323) 876-4666
www.btlartists.com

Steve Rick (323) 788-8468
(Prop Master)

Mark Ricker (310) 395-9550
www.skouras.com

Jon Riggs (949) 489-1898
(949) 232-6346
(Prop Master & Set Decorator)

Deborah Riley (310) 285-0303
www.marshbest.com

Marc Rizzo/Rizzo Design (818) 437-6520
(Art Director & Production Designer)
www.rizzodesign.com

Nanci B. Roberts (818) 951-3226
(818) 395-5419
FAX (818) 951-3316

Mary Margaret Robinson (323) 656-6131
(Production Designer, Set Buyer & Set Decorator)

Barry Robison (310) 273-6700
www.utaproduction.com

Bruce Rod (323) 227-4958
www.brucerodtv.com

Alan Roderick-Jones (310) 457-3029
(310) 985-4265
www.alanrjstudios.com

Jan Roelfs (310) 395-9550
www.skouras.com

Evan Rohde (310) 652-8778
www.lspagency.net

Philip Rosenberg (310) 274-6611
(772) 708-1700

Anne Ross (310) 968-0007
www.anneross.com

David Ross (310) 943-8102
www.artmixbeauty.com

Bruno Rubeo (310) 285-0303
www.marshbest.com

Edward L. Rubin (310) 656-5151
www.innovativeartists.com

Beth Rubino (310) 822-9113
www.murthaagency.com

Nina Ruscio (310) 285-0303
www.marshbest.com

Chris Ryan (818) 761-7118
(818) 416-7912
(Prop Master)

Jefferson Sage (310) 395-9550
www.skouras.com

Wendy Samuels (310) 503-9255
(310) 202-6466
(Art Director & Production Designer)
FAX (310) 876-2742
www.wendysamuels.com

William Sandell (310) 274-6611
www.gershagency.com

Tom Sanders (310) 273-6700
www.utaproduction.com

Gerard Santos (323) 297-0250
www.magnetla.com

Darcy Scanlin (323) 468-2240
www.nyoffice.net

Tino M. Schaedler (818) 753-6300
www.themackagency.net

Curtis Schnell (310) 652-8778
www.lspagency.net

Jeff Schoen (818) 781-9233
www.orlandomanagement.com

Oliver Scholl (310) 274-6611
www.gershagency.com

Pam Scholtens (310) 274-0032
www.artistsbytimothypriano.com

Jason Schuster (310) 577-2216
(310) 918-4266
FAX (310) 306-9025

Stephen Scott (310) 652-8778
www.lspagency.net

Miriam Seger (213) 705-8003

Francois Seguin (310) 285-0303
www.marshbest.com

Bella Serrell (323) 463-0022
www.radiantartists.com

Sharon Seymour (310) 395-9550
www.skouras.com

Bob Shaw (310) 822-9113
www.murthaagency.com

Michael Shaw (917) 691-6756
www.mshawdesign.com

Phil Shearer (818) 990-8993
www.ambitiousent.com

Sheldon Prosnit Agency (310) 652-8778
800 S. Robertson Blvd., Ste. 6
Los Angeles, CA 90035
(Reps for Production Designers)
FAX (310) 652-8772
www.lspagency.net

Richard Sherman (310) 274-6611
www.gershagency.com

Bruce Shibley (310) 663-9163
FAX (866) 312-9846
www.bruceshibley.com

Naomi Shohan (310) 822-9113
www.murthaagency.com

Maya Sigel (323) 460-4767
www.jacobandkoleagency.com

Ross Silverman (323) 683-5263

Beatrice Sisul (323) 460-4767
www.jacobandkoleagency.com

David Skinner (323) 460-4767
www.jacobandkoleagency.com

The Skouras Agency (310) 395-9550
1149 Third St., Third Fl.
Santa Monica, CA 90403
(Reps for Production Designers)
FAX (310) 395-4295
www.skouras.com

Naomi Slodki (323) 663-8616
(323) 972-6480
FAX (323) 667-1452

Penn Smith (661) 254-5547
(818) 259-0967
FAX (661) 254-4905
www.pennsmithdesign.com

Rusty Smith (310) 274-6611
www.gershagency.com

Wayne T. Smith (310) 405-6937
(011) 642 7 472 3787
(Art Director & Production Designer) FAX (011) 649 410 6550

Mark Snelgrove (310) 652-8778
www.lspagency.net

David L. Snyder (310) 656-5151
www.innovativeartists.com

Tom Southwell (323) 460-4767
www.jacobandkoleagency.com

Johannes Spalt (323) 463-0022
www.radiantartists.com

Jim Spencer (310) 288-8000
www.paradigmagency.com

Carol Spier (310) 285-0303
www.marshbest.com

Jon Spirson (818) 590-1183

Neil Spisak (310) 395-9550
www.skouras.com

Annie Spitz (310) 652-8778
www.lspagency.net

Carl Sprague (310) 288-8000
www.paradigmagency.com

Anthony Rivero Stabley (323) 440-1455

Allan Starski (310) 282-9940
www.mirisch.com

Craig Stearns (310) 656-5151
www.innovativeartists.com

Gary Steele (310) 273-6700
www.utaproduction.com

James Steuart (310) 288-8000
www.paradigmagency.com

Eve Stewart (310) 474-4585
www.dattnerdispoto.com

Jane Stewart (310) 288-8000
www.paradigmagency.com

Missy Stewart (310) 273-6700
www.unitedtalent.com

Arnd Stockhausen (213) 595-4755
FAX (818) 246-2080
www.filmdesign.biz

John Stoddart (310) 395-9550
www.skouras.com

David Stone (310) 471-5568
(310) 880-1539
FAX (310) 471-1638
www.davidstonedesign.net
(Art Director, Production Designer & Prop Master)

Garreth Stover (310) 285-0303
www.marshbest.com

Carol Strober (323) 661-4881
(Production Designer)
FAX (310) 661-5223
www.carolstrober.com

Patrick Sullivan (310) 288-8000
www.paradigmagency.com

Suzanna Camejo & Associates/ Artists For The Environment (310) 479-4470
(Reps for Production Designers)

Christopher Tandon (310) 288-8000
www.paradigmagency.com

Yohei Taneda (310) 285-0303
www.marshbest.com

Mark Tanner (310) 474-4585
www.dattnerdispoto.com

TDN Artists (818) 906-0006
3685 Motor Ave., Ste. 220
Los Angeles, CA 90034
(Reps for Art Directors/Production Designers)
FAX (818) 301-2224
www.tdnartists.com

Sue Tebbutt (310) 652-8778
www.lspagency.net

Dale Thaw (310) 869-3516
FAX (866) 807-6895
www.dalethaw.com

Wynn Thomas (310) 285-0303
www.marshbest.com

Kevin Thompson (310) 273-6700
www.utaproduction.com

Bradley Thordarson (213) 200-8308
(Production Designer)
www.bradleythordarson.com

Jodie Tillen (310) 656-5151
www.innovativeartists.com

Hughes Tissandier (310) 652-8778
www.lspagency.net

Ethan Tobman (310) 943-8102
www.artmixbeauty.com

Matt Tognacci (818) 990-8993
www.ambitiousent.net

Nick Tortorici (310) 822-2898
www.rougeartists.com

Ginger Tougas (323) 460-4767
www.jacobandkoleagency.com

Richard Toyon (310) 288-8000
www.paradigmagency.com

Luca Tranchino (310) 395-9550
www.skouras.com

Bernardo Trujillo (310) 652-8778
www.lspagency.net

United Talent Agency (310) 273-6700
9560 Wilshire Blvd., Ste. 500 FAX (310) 247-1111
Beverly Hills, CA 90212 www.utaproduction.com
(Reps for Production Designers)

Katherine Vallin (323) 493-5533
(323) 822-9401
(Production Designer)

Kristen Vallow (310) 458-7800
www.partos.com

Sandy Veneziano (310) 822-9113
www.murthaagency.com

Edward Verreaux (310) 273-6700
www.utaproduction.com

Jay Vetter (310) 282-9940
www.mirisch.com

Jamie Vickers (310) 505-2445
www.partos.com

Ron Volz (310) 720-2002
FAX (323) 937-3939
www.ronvolz.com

Patrizia Von Brandenstein (310) 282-9940
www.mirisch.com

Graham (Grace) Walker (310) 656-5151
www.innovativeartists.com

Michael Walker (310) 458-7800
www.partos.com

Tom Walsh (310) 656-5151
www.innovativeartists.com

Thom Ward (818) 206-0144
www.allcrewagency.com

David Wasco (310) 273-6700
www.utaproduction.com

Dennis Washington (310) 822-9113
www.murthaagency.com

Dan Webster (310) 652-8778
www.lspagency.net

Loren Weeks (323) 845-4144
www.montanartists.com

Dan Weil (310) 273-6700
www.utaproduction.com

Inbal Weinberg (310) 652-8778
www.lspagency.net

Marla Weinhoff (310) 474-4585
www.marlaweinhoffstudio.com

Bo Welch (310) 273-6700
www.unitedtalent.com

David Weller/David Weller Design (310) 398-1982
(Production Designer) www.wellerdesign.com

Ford Wheeler (310) 652-8778
www.lspagency.net

Mike Whetstone (310) 652-8778
www.lspagency.net

Martin Whist (626) 524-6900
(310) 273-6700
www.whistdesign.com

Ise White (310) 274-0032
www.artistsbytimothypriano.com

Mark White (310) 652-8778
www.lspagency.net

Francis Whitebloom (310) 458-7800
www.partos.com

Ben Whittaker (310) 401-3211
www.jeannineangelique.com

Teri Whittaker (310) 401-3211
www.jeannineangelique.com

Jennifer Williams (310) 652-8778
www.lspagency.net

Adele Wilson (818) 340-7576
(818) 219-9650
(Set Decorator)

Dave Wilson (310) 458-7800
www.partos.com

Charles Wood (310) 285-0303
www.marshbest.com

Mark Worthington (323) 460-4767
www.jacobandkoleagency.com

Jack Wright III (323) 868-7490
(415) 868-9023
(Art Director & Production Designer)

Richard Wright (310) 652-8778
www.lspagency.net

Stuart Wurtzel (310) 282-9940
www.mirisch.com

Michael Wylie (323) 314-5468
(Production Designer)

Eugenio Zanetti (310) 285-0303
www.marshbest.com

Baby Wranglers

A.S.A. Studio Teachers Association (323) 662-9787
FAX (323) 662-1569
www.asatalent.com/crew

Maxine Abarbara (818) 518-7115
FAX (818) 347-9347

@baby! baby!/Lynn Raines (818) 905-0790
(818) 216-8666
FAX (818) 501-0768
www.atbabybaby.com

A. Kathleen Chambers-Schelhorse (310) 606-0115

Carol Hart (323) 663-3512
(323) 841-9192
FAX (323) 661-2124

Alicia Kalvin (310) 980-0290
(310) 459-6875
www.studioteacher.org

Jill McKay (310) 836-8877
(310) 617-8245

Stacey Parzik (818) 385-0000
(818) 648-1667
www.partiesbystacey.com

Cyndi Raymond (323) 428-2906
FAX (323) 938-7714
www.cyndiraymond.com

Linda Stone Shure (310) 837-7542
(310) 488-1826
FAX (310) 204-5683

Linda Stanley (310) 372-1449
(602) 740-5598

Jack Stern (818) 970-7540

The Studio Teachers (IA Local 884) (818) 559-9600
(818) 559-9797
www.thestudioteachers.com

Janie Teller (310) 820-4522
(646) 331-9456

Jimmy Wagner (818) 755-0076
FAX (818) 762-5156
www.jimmywagner.us

Saena Yi (310) 801-7921

John Abbene (310) 457-3290

Ramon Almanza (310) 387-9601
(First AC & High Def)

Jack Arnet (818) 782-8635
(818) 203-2026
(Aerial & Tyler Equipment) FAX (818) 780-1279

Chuck Bemis (323) 656-2246
(323) 397-8454

Paul Brady (818) 540-6189
(Second AC) FAX (818) 865-6099
www.cameratruck.com

Bob Brown (661) 254-6900
(805) 341-6673
FAX (661) 254-6900
us.imdb.com/name/nm0113141/

Donald Burghardt (661) 803-4577
(First AC)

Michael Caparelli (323) 447-3637
FAX (323) 666-7479

Richard Carlson (818) 888-9117
(818) 298-8624
FAX (818) 888-7723

April Castaneda (702) 835-3581
(818) 330-9505
www.aprilcastaneda.com

Stephen Craker (323) 270-5259
(503) 588-2071
(Second AC)

Ronnie Dennis (818) 519-8167

Vito DePalma (818) 706-1095
(818) 606-3011

Del DePierro (213) 300-7771
(Motion Control) www.deldepierro.com

Maurizio Nino Dotto (818) 359-5122
(First AC, High Def, Motion Control, Remote Heads & Steadicam)

Robert Eber (310) 913-1707
FAX (310) 450-8264

David Eubank (818) 766-7500
www.davideubank.com
(First AC, High Def, Remote Heads & Steadicam)

Stephen Franklin (310) 739-6614

Nicholas Fry (323) 709-7366
www.nicholasfryphotography.com

Jeff Gershman (818) 469-8404

Alan M. Gitlin (818) 906-8684
(818) 266-6321
(High Def)

A. Barry Gordon (818) 368-5069
(818) 416-2999
FAX (818) 368-8515

Bob Hall (818) 887-0823
(818) 618-0823
(Steadicam) FAX (801) 365-9617

George Hesse (310) 306-8497
(310) 801-8967
(First AC & High Def)

Jay Anthony (Tony) Jones (310) 546-7908
(310) 918-7407
(Steadicam & Underwater) www.jayanthonyjones.com

Kit Kalionzes (310) 390-9234
(310) 614-6487

Robert Lowell (818) 489-5969
(First AC)

John Malvino (323) 965-1062
(415) 924-6631

Vincent Mata (818) 422-7174
(818) 703-8339
(First AC) FAX (818) 762-1178

Lee Morris (323) 251-3839

Javier Muñoz (818) 846-6416
FAX (818) 846-6416
(High Def, Remote Heads, Second AC & Second Unit)

Ryne A. Niner (805) 405-7197
(805) 241-9565
FAX (805) 241-9584
www.nineraks.com

David Ortiz (714) 536-5149
(714) 745-5149

Leslie Otis (310) 395-5539

Clint Palmer (626) 794-8361
(818) 261-6463
(Aerial & Special FX)

Ronald Henry Raschke (805) 798-1545
(805) 649-3477

Michael Riba (805) 920-9006
(818) 430-8612
(Remote Heads, Second Unit & Steadicam)

David Riley (323) 664-1630

Rob Rubin (818) 706-3203
(818) 216-2162
(Aerial, Remote Heads, Second AC & Underwater)

Jon Sharpe (818) 346-4604
(818) 419-2064

Cory Shiozaki (310) 523-4100
(310) 729-6541

Andy Sydney (818) 783-2341
(818) 231-3359
(High Def, Steadicam & Underwater) FAX (818) 830-0444

Adan Torres (818) 974-2672
(818) 974-2672
(First AC, High Def & Second AC)

Greg Ulrich (661) 904-2219
(First AC, Motion Control, Remote Heads, Second Unit & Special FX)

Jon Zarkos (310) 798-5265
(310) 365-7856

Eric Zimmerman (818) 753-6300
(310) 849-1948
(Aerial, Steadicam & Underwater)

Dan Adams (310) 828-2628
(310) 828-7745

Steven A. Adelson (604) 506-6552
(818) 985-1130
(Steadicam)

William S. Arnot (917) 417-4701
(818) 985-1130
(Steadicam) www.russelltoddagency.com

Dan Ayers (818) 425-7252
(Steadicam) www.steadidan.com

Wayne Baker (818) 991-9676
(818) 472-1780
(Aerial & Underwater) FAX (818) 991-9677

Eddie Barber (818) 982-7775
(Barber Booms) FAX (818) 982-7773
www.barbertvp.com

Tim Bellen (818) 985-1130
(Steadicam) www.russelltoddagency.com

Brian Bernstein (818) 999-2055

George Bianchini (310) 399-6300
(Steadicam) www.steadygeorge.com

Maceo Bishop (818) 985-1130
www.russelltoddagency.com

Tom Boyd (818) 623-8255
(818) 974-1937
(Underwater) www.taboyd.com

Kurt Braun (818) 752-0100
(High Def, Second Unit & Steadicam)

Joe Broderick (818) 848-5182
(818) 968-2805
(Steadicam)

Art Brown (310) 576-4992
(High Def & Underwater)

Scott Browner (805) 370-1014
(818) 298-5440

Bill Brummond (310) 780-7911
(Steadicam) FAX (310) 364-0014

Greg Bubb (310) 663-9665
(Steadicam)

Joseph W. Calloway (626) 798-8222
(626) 827-7331
FAX (626) 798-4577
www.callowayfilms.com
(Action Sports, Aerial, High Def, Remote Heads, Second Unit & Underwater)

Dave Chameides (323) 377-3324
(Steadicam)

Ted Chu (310) 254-5396
(Aerial, High Def, Remote Heads & Second Unit)

Stephen Clancy (818) 203-5008
(Steadicam)

Jeff L. Clark (661) 312-6131
(Steadicam) www.jeffclarksteadicam.com

Jeffrey R. Clark (661) 295-1325
(805) 506-1959
(Aerial, Skiing & Steadicam) www.jefclark.com

Marcis Cole (310) 578-0036
(Steadicam)

Barry Conrad (818) 248-9161
FAX (818) 249-8884
www.barcon.com

Lyndel Crosley (818) 424-6186

Richard Crow (310) 944-4367
(Steadicam) www.gotsteadicam.com

Britt Cyrus (818) 667-9654
(818) 757-1430

Rick Davidson (323) 913-3402
(323) 327-2705
(Steadicam) www.russelltoddagency.com

Collin Davis (626) 737-0457
(310) 729-9803

Richard W. Davis (661) 424-9288
(818) 681-8742
(Steadicam)

Dan R. Dayton (661) 547-8604
(760) 249-6889
(Aerial)

John Pierre Dechene (818) 889-6749
(Aerial, High Def, Remote Heads, Second Unit, Special FX & Underwater)

Rick Denman (310) 455-2084
(310) 995-2084

Joel Deutsch (310) 628-5400
www.evidenceproductions.com

Glenn Di Vincenzo (818) 366-7525
(818) 437-5551
(Steadicam)

David Dougherty (818) 782-3503
(213) 718-5132
(Barber Boom)

Rick Drapkin (818) 261-6977
(Aerial, Remote Heads, Steadicam & Underwater)

Phillip Ebeid (818) 909-7933
(818) 458-4495
(Aerial & Remote Heads) www.summitcranes.com

Jason Ellson (323) 363-4074
(Steadicam) www.schneiderentertainment.com

David Emmerichs (323) 962-7800
(Remote Heads & Steadicam) FAX (323) 962-7878
www.schneiderentertainment.com

Farr Out Productions, LLC (310) 902-5944
(Reps for Camera Operators) FAX (818) 830-3608
www.farroutpro.com

Jerome Fauci (843) 795-5402
(310) 809-4345
(Steadicam) FAX (818) 808-0042
www.gocamerasupport.com

Kenn Ferro (818) 985-1130
(Steadicam) www.russelltoddagency.com

Lance Fisher (323) 935-4803
(323) 868-5108
web.mac.com/lancefisher

Eric Fletcher (818) 566-9875
(Steadicam) www.russelltoddagency.com

Candide Franklyn (818) 222-5200
www.schneiderentertainment.com

Tom (Frisby) Fraser (818) 216-5306
(High Def, Remote Heads, Second Unit & Special FX)

David J. Frederick (310) 261-3541
(310) 474-6299
(Steadicam) www.soc.org

Illya Friedman (818) 634-4311

Buddy Fries (310) 670-9663

Brian Gaetke (818) 219-2043
FAX (818) 729-9331

Kirk Gardner (818) 222-5200
www.schneiderentertainment.com

Harry K. Garvin (323) 816-6336
(Steadicam) www.russelltoddagency.com

Rusty Geller (818) 808-0042
(011) 6189 295 4481
(Steadicam) www.rustygeller.com

Christopher George (818) 974-0434
(Steadicam)

Robert Gersicoff (818) 763-1036
(Aerial & Remote Control)

Kristin Glover (310) 398-1541
(310) 365-6305
FAX (310) 398-9896

Bob Gorelick (310) 915-0627
(310) 869-9959
(Steadicam) FAX (310) 915-0157
www.schneiderentertainment.com

Christopher Gosch (310) 857-6664
(310) 999-1877
(Steadicam) FAX (310) 857-6664
www.thecompany.tv

Dylan Goss (310) 989-3131
(Aerial)

Bruce Alan Greene (818) 985-1130
(High Def & Steadicam) www.brucealangreene.com

Charles E. Hammerschmitt (909) 337-0006
(Steadicam)

Mark Hardin (818) 761-7749
(Motion Control & Special FX) www.markhardin.com

Joshua Harrison (818) 985-1130
www.russelltoddagency.com

Kent Harvey (310) 699-3674
(Aerial, High Def & Second Unit) FAX (310) 202-0305
www.khfilms.com

Chris Hayes (917) 626-9050
(323) 876-0160
(Action Sports, High Def, Motion Control, Remote Heads, Second Unit & Special FX)

Sandy Hays (818) 985-1130
(Steadicam) www.russelltoddagency.com

M. Todd Henry (310) 545-5545
(310) 224-0148
FAX (310) 545-7305

Jerry Hill (818) 772-9256
(Steadicam) FAX (818) 772-9251
www.steadimoves.com

Jeffrey M. Hoffman (805) 927-0453
(310) 779-1887

Keith Holland (323) 856-4728
www.keithholland.com
(Action Sports, Aerial, High Def, Motion Control, Second Unit, Special FX & Underwater)

Timothy K. Hubbard (310) 325-7083
(310) 251-1507
FAX (310) 326-5340

Colin Hudson (818) 222-5200
www.schneiderentertainment.com

Jeffrey Hunt (818) 317-2140
(Steadicam)

Gene Jackson (323) 935-5342

Alec Jarnagin (917) 804-6606
(818) 985-1130
www.floatingcamera.com

Simon Jayes (818) 402-2389
(818) 980-4834
(Remote Heads & Steadicam) FAX (818) 753-8190

Joe Jennings (310) 543-2222
www.aerialstuntservice.com
(Aerial, Helicopter & Skydiving)

Peter Jensen (310) 791-7010
(Steadicam) FAX (310) 791-0780

Horace Jordan (818) 846-4441
(818) 587-8766

Peter Jordan (310) 866-9300
(POV)

Jacques Jouffret (310) 459-0700
(818) 985-1130
(Steadicam) FAX (310) 459-7885
www.russelltoddagency.com

John Joyce (818) 985-1130
(Steadicam) www.russelltoddagency.com

Ross Judd (818) 362-7202
(818) 469-2028
(Steadicam) FAX (818) 362-8233
members.dslextreme.com/users/rossteadijudd

Mark Karavite (818) 985-1130
www.russelltoddagency.com

Lawrence Karman (310) 450-4728
(310) 351-7016
(Steadicam)

Michael Kelem (310) 486-2008
(310) 230-3433
(Aerial, High Def & Second Unit)

Dan Kneece (310) 822-5751
(818) 985-1130
(Steadicam) www.imdb.com/name/nm0460638/

Bud Kremp (818) 985-1130
www.russelltoddagency.com

Dean Krueger (951) 764 2343

Mark LaBonge (818) 222-5200
(Steadicam) www.schneiderentertainment.com

Aaron Land (310) 305-1400
(High Def) www.happypixelstudios.com

Erwin Landau (818) 448-2639
(Steadicam) FAX (818) 769-0293
www.landaucamera.com

Michael Levine (310) 489-6848
FAX (323) 939-9622
www.crashproductions.com

Tommy Lohmann (818) 222-5200
(Steadicam) www.schneiderentertainment.com

John Longenecker (310) 276-8196
(800) 470-4602
(Second Unit) FAX (310) 246-1841
www.johnlongenecker.com

David Luckenbach (213) 369-7077
(805) 646-9745
www.davidluckenbach.com
(Remote Heads, Steadicam & Underwater)

Jesse MacDonald (310) 710-6525
www.jessemacdonald.com
(Action Sports, High Def, Motion Control, Remote Heads, Second Unit, Special FX, Steadicam & Underwater)

Jeff Mart (818) 324-3741
(818) 985-1130
(Steadicam) www.russelltoddagency.com

Cedric Martin (310) 998-7154
(Steadicam) FAX (818) 245-9338
www.cedricmartin.com

Michael May (661) 254-2629
(661) 917-0259
(Steadicam)

Mike McGowan (818) 985-1130
(Steadicam) www.russelltoddagency.com

Scott Meyer (818) 730-4900
www.scottfilms.com

Jody Miller (310) 251-0057
(818) 985-1130
(Steadicam) FAX (310) 399-3419
www.russelltoddagency.com

Mark E. Moore (818) 222-5200
(Steadicam) www.schneiderentertainment.com

Nathan Nebeker (323) 395-0507
FAX (323) 395-0507
www.mscine.com

Mark Nelson (619) 291-2403
(Action Sports & High Def) FAX (619) 291-2475
www.visualconcepts.tv

Randy Nolen (818) 876-0041
(818) 807-2398
(Steadicam) FAX (818) 876-0041

Neal Norton (818) 985-1130
(Steadicam) www.russelltoddagency.com

Mark O'Kane (818) 883-0075
(Steadicam)

Brad Olander (760) 944-4475
(Steadicam) www.olandercamera.com

Lucio Olivieri (818) 913-1688

Gerry O'Malley (626) 441-4842
(626) 484-0150
(Steadicam)

Charles Papert (323) 350-8822
(Steadicam) FAX (323) 843-9357
www.charlespapert.com

Andrew Parke (310) 367-1140
(310) 473-2664
www.andrewparke.com
(Action Sports, Aerial, High Def, Second Unit & Underwater)

David Parrish (818) 765-6037
FAX (818) 764-3639
www.wide-screen.com/david.html

Bruce Pasternack (818) 999-9796
(818) 943-9796
(Remote Heads) FAX (818) 999-9796

Chris Patterson (310) 962-3498
FAX (310) 962-3498
www.chrispattersonfilms.com

Christopher Paul (323) 468-2240
www.nyoffice.net

Ascanio Pignatelli (310) 913-2313
FAX (206) 202-3750

Serge T. Poupis (818) 972-5000
FAX (818) 972-5010
www.hollywoodcamera.com

Cynthia Pusheck (323) 497-8489
(Underwater)

Brooks Robinson (661) 287-1555
(661) 904-4788
(Steadicam) FAX (661) 287-3353
www.russelltoddagency.com

Peter Rosenfeld (818) 222-5200
www.schneiderentertainment.com

Andrew Rowlands (818) 222-5200
(Steadicam) www.schneiderentertainment.com

Russell Todd Agency (818) 985-1130
5238 Goodland Ave. FAX (818) 985-1134
Valley Village, CA 91607 www.russelltoddagency.com
(Reps for Steadicam Operators)

Michael Santy (415) 309-2365

The Schneider Entertainment Agency (818) 222-5200
22287 Mulholland Hwy, Ste. 210 FAX (818) 222-5284
Calabasas, CA 91302
www.schneiderentertainment.com
(Reps for Steadicam Operators)

Andy Shuttleworth (323) 850-1248
(323) 573-2032
(Steadicam) FAX (323) 850-1276

John Skotchdopole (310) 994-7114

Paul Sommers (818) 542-3016
(213) 400-8693
(Steadicam) FAX (818) 236-3628
www.paulsommers.com

Michael Stumpf (323) 697-6090
(Steadicam) www.russelltoddagency.com

Paul Taylor (818) 985-1130
(Steadicam) www.russelltoddagency.com

Taj Teffaha (714) 612-7691
(Steadicam)

Rick Tiedemann (818) 985-1130
(954) 583-3326
(Steadicam)

Henry Tirl (818) 222-5200
(Steadicam) **www.schneiderentertainmentagency.com**

Eric Tramp (909) 214-7202
(Steadicam)

Bela Trutz (310) 901-5411
(310) 455-7000
(Steadicam)

Joseph Valentine (310) 399-8000
(310) 245-0345
FAX (775) 782-6403

Ron G. Veto (818) 344-5284
(818) 372-5585
(Steadicam)

Video Tech Services (310) 574-9385
(310) 505-4015
10866 Washington Blvd., Ste. 513 FAX (310) 577-0850
Culver City, CA 90232 **www.videotechservices.com**
(Reps for Camera Operators)

Ronald Vidor (818) 766-6868
(800) 759-5722
(Steadicam & Underwater) **www.ronvidor.com**

Stefan von Bjorn (323) 478-1500
(323) 363-7711
(Steadicam) FAX (323) 478-1554
www.stefanvonbjorn.com

Richard S. Walden (818) 244-3159
(Aerial, Action Sports, High Def, Motion Control, Remote Heads, Second Unit & Special FX)

David Waldman (323) 841-9253
www.david-waldman.com

Michael Walker (818) 621-4492
FAX (818) 888-1923

Ralph Watson (310) 822-9113
(Steadicam) **www.murthaagency.com**

Dana D. Winseman (626) 372-6090
www.linkedin.com/pub/8/b51/ab5

Andreas Wood (323) 369-9461
(818) 703-9372
(Steadicam) FAX (818) 703-9372
www.andreaswood.com

Ian Woolston-Smith (203) 470-3885
(310) 402-5130
(Steadicam) **www.iancam.com**

Elizabeth Ziegler (818) 989-4420
(818) 469-6732
(Steadicam) FAX (818) 989-0423

Steven A. Adelson (604) 506-6552
(818) 985-1130

William S. Arnot (917) 417-4701
(818) 985-1130
www.russelltoddagency.com

Dan Ayers (818) 425-7252
www.steadidan.com

Tim Bellen (818) 985-1130
www.russelltoddagency.com

George Bianchini (310) 399-6300
www.steadygeorge.com

Maceo Bishop (818) 985-1130
www.russelltoddagency.com

Kurt Braun (818) 752-0100

Joe Broderick (818) 848-5182
(818) 968-2805

Bill Brummond (310) 780-7911
FAX (310) 364-0014

Greg Bubb (310) 663-9665

Dave Chameides (323) 377-3324

Stephen Clancy (818) 203-5008

Jeff L. Clark (661) 312-6131
www.jeffclarksteadicam.com

Jeffrey R. Clark (661) 295-1325
(805) 506-1959
www.jefclark.com

Marcis Cole (310) 578-0036

Richard Crow (310) 944-4367
www.gotsteadicam.com

Rick Davidson (323) 913-3402
(323) 327-2705
www.russelltoddagency.com

Richard W. Davis (661) 424-9288
(818) 681-8742

Glenn Di Vincenzo (818) 366-7525
(818) 437-5551

Rick Drapkin (818) 261-6977

Jason Ellson (323) 363-4074
www.schneiderentertainment.com

David Emmerichs (323) 962-7800
FAX (323) 962-7878
www.schneiderentertainment.com

Jerome Fauci (843) 795-5402
(310) 809-4345
FAX (818) 808-0042
www.gocamerasupport.com

Kenn Ferro (818) 985-1130
www.russelltoddagency.com

Eric Fletcher (818) 566-9875
www.russelltoddagency.com

David J. Frederick (310) 261-3541
(310) 474-6299
www.soc.org

Harry K. Garvin (323) 816-6336
www.russelltoddagency.com

Rusty Geller (818) 808-0042
(011) 6189 295 4481
www.rustygeller.com

Christopher George (818) 974-0434

Mark Goellnicht (818) 985-1130
www.russelltoddagency.com

Bob Gorelick (310) 915-0627
(310) 869-9959
FAX (310) 915-0157
www.schneiderentertainment.com

Christopher Gosch (310) 857-6664
(310) 999-1877
FAX (310) 857-6664
www.thecompany.tv

Bruce Alan Greene (818) 985-1130
www.brucealangreene.com

David Allen Grove (818) 284-6423
www.italentco.com

Charles E. Hammerschmitt (909) 337-0006

Joshua Harrison (818) 985-1130
www.russelltoddagency.com

Sandy Hays (818) 985-1130
www.russelltoddagency.com

Jerry Hill (818) 772-9256
FAX (818) 772-9251
www.steadimoves.com

Jeffrey Hunt (818) 317-2140
www.russelltoddagency.com

Simon Jayes (818) 402-2389
(818) 980-4834
FAX (818) 753-8190

Peter Jensen (310) 791-7010
FAX (310) 791-0780

Jacques Jouffret (310) 459-0700
(818) 985-1130
FAX (310) 459-7885
www.russelltoddagency.com

John Joyce (818) 985-1130
www.russelltoddagency.com

Ross Judd (818) 362-7202
(818) 469-2028
FAX (818) 362-8233
members.dslextreme.com/users/rossteadijudd

Mark Karavite (818) 985-1130
www.russelltoddagency.com

Lawrence Karman (310) 450-4728
(310) 351-7016

Dan Kneece (310) 822-5751
(818) 985-1130
www.imdb.com/name/nm0460638/

Bud Kremp (818) 985-1130
www.russelltoddagency.com

Mark LaBonge (818) 222-5200
www.schneiderentertainment.com

Erwin Landau (818) 448-2639
FAX (818) 769-0293
www.landaucamera.com

Tommy Lohmann (818) 222-5200
www.schneiderentertainment.com

David Luckenbach (213) 369-7077
(805) 646-9745
www.davidluckenbach.com

Jeff Mart (818) 324-3741
(818) 985-1130
www.russelltoddagency.com

Cedric Martin (310) 998-7154
FAX (818) 245-9338
www.cedricmartin.com

Michael May (661) 254-2629
(661) 917-0259

BJ McDonnell (818) 985-1130
www.russelltoddagency.com

Mike McGowan (818) 985-1130
www.russelltoddagency.com

Christopher TJ McGuire (661) 839-7432
(310) 652-8778
www.ar-mcguire.com

Mark Meyers (818) 985-1130
www.russelltoddagency.com

Jody Miller (310) 251-0057
(818) 985-1130
FAX (310) 399-3419
www.russelltoddagency.com

Mark E. Moore (818) 222-5200
www.schneiderentertainment.com

Randy Nolen (818) 876-0041
(818) 807-2398
FAX (818) 876-0041

Brian Nordheim (818) 985-1130
www.russelltoddagency.com

Neal Norton (818) 985-1130
www.russelltoddagency.com

Mark O'Kane (818) 883-0075
(800) 906-3082
FAX (818) 883-0014

Brad Olander (760) 944-4475
www.olandercamera.com

Gerry O'Malley (626) 441-4842
(626) 484-0150

Charles Papert (323) 350-8822
FAX (323) 843-9357
www.charlespapert.com

Brooks Robinson (661) 287-1555
(661) 904-4788
FAX (661) 287-3353
www.russelltoddagency.com

Andrew Rowlands (818) 222-5200
www.schneiderentertainment.com

Russell Todd Agency (818) 985-1130
5238 Goodland Ave. FAX (818) 985-1134
Valley Village, CA 91607 www.russelltoddagency.com
(Reps for Steadicam Operators)

The Schneider Entertainment Agency (818) 222-5200
22287 Mulholland Hwy, Ste. 210 FAX (818) 222-5284
Calabasas, CA 91302
www.schneiderentertainment.com
(Reps for Steadicam Operators)

Andy Shuttleworth (323) 850-1248
(323) 573-2032
FAX (323) 850-1276

Paul Sommers (818) 542-3016
(213) 400-8693
FAX (818) 236-3628
www.paulsommers.com

Daniel Stilling (818) 284-6423
www.italentco.com

Michael Stumpf (323) 697-6090
www.russelltoddagency.com

Paul Taylor (818) 985-1130
www.russelltoddagency.com

Taj Teffaha (714) 612-7691

Rick Tiedemann (818) 985-1130
(954) 583-3326

Henry Tirl (818) 222-5200
www.schneiderentertainmentagency.com

Eric Tramp (909) 214-7202

Bela Trutz (310) 901-5411
(310) 455-7000

Ron G. Veto (818) 344-5284
(818) 372-5585

Ron Vidor (818) 206-0144
www.allcrewagency.com

Ronald Vidor (818) 766-6868
(800) 759-5722
www.ronvidor.com

Stefan von Bjorn (323) 478-1500
(323) 363-7711
FAX (323) 478-1554
www.stefanvonbjorn.com

Ralph Watson (310) 822-9113
www.murthaagency.com

Ian Woolston-Smith (203) 470-3885
(310) 402-5130
www.iancam.com

Andreas Wood (323) 369-9461
(818) 703-9372
FAX (818) 703-9372
www.andreaswood.com

Elizabeth Ziegler (818) 989-4420
(818) 469-6732
FAX (818) 989-0423

Action! Craft Service (323) 793-5263
(Breakfasts, Juices & Smoothies) FAX (323) 466-0010

All Set Certified Craft Services (323) 350-3269
(818) 972-2970
FAX (818) 972-2970
www.popcornpopp.com

Aloha Craft Service/ Janice Fernandez (714) 396-2168

Ambrosia Craft Service (310) 649-0564
FAX (310) 649-0264

Andrea's Craft Service Co. (323) 822-0377
FAX (323) 654-8289

Andy's WitchCraft (323) 666-3259
(213) 926-4681
P.O. Box 461572
Los Angeles, CA 90046

Ate 1 Ate (818) 915-2850
47 Seaview Terrace, Ste. A
Santa Monica, CA 90401

Big Bites Craft Service (818) 769-6188
FAX (818) 769-6188

Bite Me Crafts Service (909) 239-4969
(888) 424-8363
2703 Recinto Ave. FAX (888) 424-8363
Rowland Heights, CA 91748

Breakfast Brothers (310) 880-0406

Silvie Camber/Good and Plenty (310) 821-0657
(626) 688-6054
FAX (310) 821-0657

Craft Du Monde/Kelli Michna (310) 500-0742
FAX (310) 791-1300
www.craftdumonde.com

Craftabilities/Peppermint Patti (323) 874-4550
(323) 243-1803
(Catering For Non-Union/Crowd Extras) FAX (323) 874-3831

The Crafty Canuck (310) 717-1219
7800 Midfield Ave. www.craftycanuck.net
Los Angeles, CA 90045
(24-Hour Service, Breakfast, Coffee Services, Juices & Smoothies)

The Crafty Greek (323) 557-0363
(323) 876-8373
P.O. Box 46131 FAX (323) 876-8373
Los Angeles, CA 90046 www.craftygreek.com

The Crafty Otter/Gail Otter (213) 483-6792
P.O. Box 853 www.craftyotter.com
Venice, CA 90294

Custom Breakfast Catering (661) 254-8119
(661) 904-5188
(Breakfast)

A Cut Above Craft Service (213) 590-7487

Fatty's Craft Service (818) 298-3073

First Choice (310) 741-0014

First Resort Craft Service/ Drew Marks (818) 503-7176
(310) 490-8508

Getting Fresh Craft Service (818) 416-9813
www.gettingfreshcrafty.com

Girls Gone Crafty (626) 675-3694
(626) 200-5755

A Good Craft (323) 559-1144
www.agoodcraft.com
(24-Hour Service, Coffee Service, Juices & Smoothies)

Help Me Rhonda Crafts Service (760) 559-6984
P.O. Box 5418 FAX (818) 884-6858
West Hills, CA 91308

Heydorff & Associates (818) 243-4686
(818) 819-6444

Hollands-White (213) 447-4799
(213) 250-2313
FAX (213) 250-2313
www.hollands-white.com

The Hungry Eye (213) 994-0347
FAX (818) 841-3665

Jimmy Campbell Craft Services/ Breakfast (310) 621-4352
www.jimmycampbellcrafty.com

Karl Kashiwagi (323) 651-5097
(323) 447-3542

Kit & Kaboodle (310) 270-7836
(310) 770-2294
2633 Lincoln Blvd., Ste. 430 www.knkcraftservices.com
Santa Monica, CA 90405

Krafty Man (310) 691-0451
(24-Hour Service, Breakfasts, Coffee Service, Juices & Smoothies)

Krafty World/Daniel Poole (818) 845-7388
(818) 298-3073

Laura Bagano, Inc. (818) 701-0857
(818) 472-2864
FAX (818) 701-0888

Tammy Levine/Tammy's Treats (213) 368-4732

The LillyPad Crafts Service (818) 282-5914
www.thelillypad.org

Main Street Munchies (323) 650-5947
www.mainstreetmunchies.com
(Breakfasts, Cappuccinos & Smoothies)

Beverly McIntyre/Heart & Soul (818) 505-9240
(818) 624-7856

Mojave Film Services (760) 799-4414
P.O. Box 2205 FAX (877) 327-6265
Joshua Tree, CA 92252 www.mojavefilmservices.com
(24-Hour Service, Breakfasts, Catering For Non-Union/Crowd Extras, Coffee Service, Juices, Lunch, Mobile Kitchen Facilities, Second Meals & Smoothies)

Nelly's Craft Service (818) 288-0755
8442 Forsythe St. FAX (818) 352-4808
Sunland, CA 91040

Off The Shelf Craft Division LLC (310) 990-4973
9854 National Blvd., Ste. 234 FAX (310) 440-0794
Los Angeles, CA 90034

Patrick's Location Catering (805) 388-5544
FAX (805) 388-5544
(24-Hour Service & Mobile Kitchen Facilities)

Perkside Coffee (818) 231-5281
7300 Oak Park Ave. www.perkside.com
Van Nuys, CA 91406
(24-Hour Service, Coffee Service & Smoothies)

Pit Stop Coffee (310) 882-8181
www.pitstopcoffee.net
(24-Hour Service, Breakfasts, Catering For Non-Union/Crowd Extras, Coffee Service, Lunch & Second Meals)

She's Crafty (818) 974-9566
(818) 376-0836
FAX (818) 376-0836

Smoothies Craft Service (818) 535-2654
(818) 535-0866

Taste Catering, Inc. (949) 215-7373
FAX (949) 215-7494
www.tastecateringcafe.com
(24-Hour Service, Breakfasts, Catering For Non-Union/Crowd Extras, Coffee Service, Juices, Lunch, Mobile Kitchen Facilities, Second Meals & Smoothies)

Team Banzai Craft Service (626) 664-4760

A Touch of Craft Company: (310) 994-6759
Frank & Judy Lau (310) 393-0381

Patrick Blewett (805) 415-4100
(323) 460-5199
www.ambientdsr.com

Paul Brady (818) 540-6189
FAX (818) 865-6099
www.digitalimagingtechnician.com

Susan A. Campbell (818) 879-1900
(818) 203-9190

Jeffrey R. Clark (661) 295-1325
(805) 506-1959
www.jefclark.com

Keith Collea (310) 577-3757
(520) 907-2211
FAX (815) 642-4444
www.redcamstudios.com

Dan Coplan (323) 627-0773
(818) 762-3373
www.dancoplan.com

Britt Cyrus (818) 667-9654

Doug DeGrazzio (626) 797-1528
(818) 404-4265
FAX (626) 398-6413

David DeMore (818) 764-8918

Michael Ellis (310) 399-5560
FAX (310) 399-5553
www.elephanteyemedia.com

Elise Gannett (310) 399-5560
FAX (310) 399-5553
www.elephanteyemedia.com

Cliff Hsui (818) 389-1786
FAX (323) 978-9018

Dale Hunter (818) 706-1911
(818) 516-0303
FAX (818) 706-1911

Jay Anthony (Tony) Jones (310) 546-7908
(310) 918-7407
www.jayanthonyjones.com

Gerard J. R. Keenan (310) 494-4044
(818) 434-6474
www.hd-24p.com

Chris Keller (310) 399-5560
FAX (310) 399-5553
www.elephanteyemedia.com

Scott Meyer (818) 730-4900
www.scottfilms.com

Evan Nesbitt (323) 463-0476
(323) 314-5928
FAX (323) 463-0477
www.evannesbitt.com

Ryne A. Niner (805) 405-7197
(805) 241-9565
FAX (805) 241-9584
www.nineraks.com

Ethan Phillips (213) 819-2449

Philip D. Schwartz (310) 260-6424
(310) 699-2980
www.watchreels.com/philipschwartz

Ryan M. Sheridan (818) 635-8071
FAX (818) 345-7663
www.sheridandesign.com

Bill Sturcke (805) 501-3289

Steve Tacon (310) 283-0953
(310) 306-7893

Gary Taillon (805) 443-3806

Tom Tcimpidis (818) 366-4837

Derek Wan (323) 788-3883
FAX (323) 780-8887
www.allinone-usa.com

Robert D. Zeigler (818) 893-7545
(818) 816-0363
FAX (818) 894-8807

Hisham Abed (310) 288-8000
www.paradigmagency.com

Ivan Abel (323) 468-2240
www.nyoffice.net

Nasar Abich Jr. (310) 652-8778
www.lspagency.net

Phil Abraham (310) 395-9550
(Film & High Def) www.skouras.com

Damian Acevedo (323) 468-2240
(Film & High Def) www.nyoffice.net

Steve Ackerman (818) 832-7919
(Film & High Def) FAX (818) 832-9458

Tom Ackerman (310) 274-6611
www.gershagency.com

Lance Acord (310) 474-4585
www.dattnerdispoto.com

Henry Adebonojo (818) 206-0144
(Film & High Def) www.allcrewagency.com

Eric Adkins (213) 482-9227
(213) 276-0287
(Film & High Def)

Andrew Adolphus (323) 468-2240
www.nyoffice.net

Yannick Agliardi (323) 788-8445
(High Def) www.aymaent.com

Brian Agnew (310) 652-8778
www.lspagency.net

Magni Agustsson (310) 652-8778
www.lspagency.net

Lloyd Ahern (818) 222-5200
www.schneiderentertainment.com

Maxime Alexandre (310) 273-6700
www.unitedtalent.com

All Crew Agency (818) 206-0144
2920 W. Olive Ave., Ste. 201 FAX (818) 206-0169
Burbank, CA 91505 www.allcrewagency.com
(Reps for Directors of Photography)

Russ T. Alsobrook (626) 441-4472
(626) 755-4191

Gonzalo Amat (310) 288-8000
www.paradigmagency.com

Ambitious Entertainment (818) 990-8993
www.ambitiousent.com
(Reps for Directors of Photography)

Giacomo Ambrosini (323) 468-2240
(Film & High Def) www.nyoffice.net

Mitch Amundsen (310) 274-6611
www.gershagency.com

Eric Roy Anderson (661) 245-5929
(310) 740-7678
(Film, High Def & Second Unit) www.ericroyanderson.com

Tarin Anderson (310) 652-8778
www.lspagency.net

Daniel Andreas (310) 986-3370
(Film & High Def) www.24pcine.com

Tim Angulo (818) 206-0144
(805) 680-8108
www.allcrewagency.com

Daniel Aranyo (310) 652-8778
www.lspagency.net

Daniel Ardilley (310) 652-8778
(Film & High Def) www.lspagency.net

David A. Armstrong (310) 656-5151
www.innovativeartists.com

John Aronson (310) 822-9113
FAX (310) 822-6662
www.murthaagency.com

Howard Atherton (310) 822-9113
www.murthaagency.com

Bernard Auroux (310) 717-1428
(Film & High Def) www.bernardauroux.com

Chris Austin (213) 999-7060
(Film & High Def)

Tsuneo Azuma (310) 399-2270
(310) 717-6442
(Film & High Def) www.zumamoon.us

Joaquin Baca-Asay (310) 314-2606
www.stacycheriffagency.com

Kirk Bachman (310) 457-9366
(310) 579-5357
FAX (310) 457-1829
www.kirkbachman.com
(Film, High Def, Remote Heads & Second Unit)

Magdalena Gorka Bachman (323) 460-4767
www.jacobandkoleagency.com

Fredrik Backar (310) 458-7800
www.partos.com

Rebecca Baehler (323) 460-4767
(Film & High Def) www.jacobandkoleagency.com

Christopher Baffa (310) 288-8000
www.paradigmagency.com

John Bailey (310) 273-6700
(Film & High Def) www.utaproduction.com

Ian Baker (310) 395-9550
www.skouras.com

Ted L. Baker (310) 373-0274
(310) 266-7274
(High Def) FAX (310) 373-0274
www.tedbakerdp.com

Tony Balderrama (310) 314-2606
www.stacycheriffagency.com

Alex Barber (310) 474-4585
www.dattnerdispoto.com

Mia Barker (310) 395-9550
www.skouras.com

Jeff Barklage (818) 906-0006
(Film & High Def) www.tdnartists.com

Michael Walker Barnard (818) 222-5200 / (310) 828-8239
(Second Unit) FAX (310) 828-1923

Michael Barrett (310) 569-6594 / (310) 273-6700
www.utaproduction.com

John S. Bartley (310) 822-9113
(Film & High Def) www.murthaagency.com

Miroslaw Baszak (323) 460-4767
www.jacobandkoleagency.com

Bojan Bazelli (310) 474-4585
www.dattnerdispoto.com

Rhet Bear (310) 656-5151 / (626) 893-2375
(Film & High Def) FAX (310) 656-5156
www.rhetbear.com

Affonso Beato (310) 285-0303
www.marshbest.com

Christophe Beaucarne (323) 460-4767
www.jacobandkoleagency.com

Adam Beckman (310) 474-4585
(Film & High Def) www.ddatalent.com

John Behring (661) 298-8868 / (818) 416-4868
(Film & High Def)

Bruce Benedict (949) 837-5311 / (949) 929-1178
FAX (949) 837-9668
www.brucebenedictphoto.com
(Action Sports, Film, High Def & Second Unit)

Peter Benison (818) 206-0144
www.allcrewagency.com

Bill Bennett (310) 458-7800 / (323) 223-2709
FAX (310) 587-2250
www.wfb4.com
(Action Sports, Aerial, Film , High Def, Remote Heads & Second Unit)

Jeremy Benning (310) 966-4005
www.seslercompany.com

Andreas Berger (310) 458-7800
www.partos.com

Gabriel Beristain (310) 822-9113
www.murthaagency.com

Michael D. Bernard (310) 474-4585 / (213) 353-9900
(Film & High Def) www.dattnerdispoto.com

Lana Bernberg (323) 845-4144
(Film & High Def) www.montanartists.com

Steven Bernstein (323) 845-4144
(Film & High Def) www.montanartists.com

Leslie Bernstien (626) 354-6200
(High Def, Second Unit & Special FX) FAX (323) 666-0214
www.xlntpictures.com

Barry Berona (323) 791-3676 / (212) 564-7892
www.barryberona.com
(Film, High Def, Second Unit & Special FX)

Alain Betrancourt (310) 395-9550
(Film & High Def) www.skouras.com

John Beymer (310) 288-8000
www.paradigmagency.com

Adam Biddle (818) 753-6300
(Film & High Def) www.themackagency.net

Scott Billups (818) 990-8993
(Film & High Def) www.ambitiousent.com

Ivan Bird (310) 474-4585
www.dattnerdispoto.com

Hans Bjerno (909) 393-1704

Stephen Blackman (323) 463-0022
www.radiantartists.com

Larry Blanford (310) 285-0303
www.marshbest.com

Roberto Blasini (818) 284-6423
www.italentco.com

Robert Blatman (949) 246-7480 / (949) 218-2022
(Action Sports, Aerial, Film, High Def & Second Unit)

Philipp Blaubach (310) 274-6611
www.gershagency.com

Sebastian Blendov (310) 314-2606
www.stacycheriffagency.com

Nigel Bluck (310) 395-9550
www.skouras.com

Kip Bogdahn (310) 314-2606
(Film & High Def) www.stacycheriffagency.com

Oliver Bokelberg (310) 274-6611
www.gershagency.com

Peter Bonilla (323) 819-2348 / (323) 656-3363
(Film & High Def) www.peterbonilla.com

Michael Bonvillain (323) 845-4144
www.montanartists.com

Eli Born (310) 288-8000
www.paradigmagency.com

Harlan Bosmajian (310) 656-5151
(Film & High Def) www.innovativeartists.com

Richard Bowen (310) 880-4715 / (510) 525-3377

Stephen Bower (818) 781-9233 / (917) 861-8344
(Film, High Def & Underwater) www.stephenbower.com

David Boyd (323) 845-4144
www.montanartists.com

John Boyd (818) 990-8993
www.ambitiousent.com

Russell Boyd (310) 822-9113
www.murthaagency.com

Geoff Boyle (310) 288-8000
www.paradigmagency.com

Kurt Brabbee (818) 284-6423
www.italentco.com

John Brawley (310) 288-8000
www.paradigmagency.com

Collin Brink (323) 468-2240
www.nyoffice.net

Robert Brinkmann (310) 822-9113
www.murthaagency.com

Mark Brinster (818) 990-8993
(Film & High Def) www.ambitiousent.com

Alice Brooks (323) 468-2240
(Film & High Def) www.italentco.com

Gordon Brown (818) 781-9233
www.orlandomanagement.com

Eigil Bryld (310) 395-9550

Bobby Bukowski (310) 474-4585
(Film & High Def) www.dattnerdispoto.com

Don Burgess (310) 274-6611
www.gershagency.com

Jo Burn (310) 285-0303
www.marshbest.com

Tony Burns (818) 206-0144
www.allcrewagency.com

David Burr (310) 822-9113
www.murthaagency.com

Stephen H. Burum (310) 822-9113
www.murthaagency.com

Bill Butler (310) 656-5151
(Film & High Def) www.innovativeartists.com

Scott Buttfield (310) 395-9550
www.skouras.com

Patrick Cady (310) 274-6611
www.gershagency.com

Brian Callahan (323) 876-7302
(Film & High Def) FAX (323) 876-7303

Jerry G. Callaway (818) 222-5200
(Second Unit) www.schneiderentertainment.com

Thomas Callaway (323) 856-3000
www.thegelleragency.com

Joseph W. Calloway (626) 798-8222
(626) 827-7331
FAX (626) 798-4577
www.callowayfilms.com
(Action Sports, Aerial, Film, High Def, Remote Heads, Second Unit, Special FX & Underwater)

Antonio Calvache (323) 845-4144
(High Def) www.montanartists.com

Tom Camarda (323) 573-4166
(323) 666-3352
(Film & High Def) FAX (323) 221-5086
www.tomcamarda.net

Paul Cameron (310) 474-4585
(Film & High Def) www.dattnerdispoto.com

Tom Campbell (805) 965-4951
(Film & High Def) FAX (805) 965-7449
www.tomcampbell.com

Matt Cantrell (661) 245-3581
(661) 619-2601
FAX (661) 245-3581

Yves Cape (310) 652-8778
www.lspagency.net

Marco Cappetta (818) 896-0977
(818) 648-3609
(Aerial, Film, High Def & Second Unit) www.cinemarco.com

Bob Carmichael (323) 856-3000
(Second Unit) www.thegelleragency.com

Russell Carpenter (310) 288-8000
www.paradigmagency.com

James Carter (310) 656-5151
(Film & High Def) www.innovativeartists.com

Ron Carter (213) 610-9954
(Film & High Def)

Lula Carvalho (310) 274-6611
www.gershagency.com

Paolo Cascio (818) 974-3800
www.pchollywood.com
(Film, High Def, Remote Heads & Second Unit)

Pedro Castro (310) 652-8778
(Film & High Def) www.pedrocastro.net

Sarah Cawley (310) 288-8000
www.paradigmagency.com

Doug Chamberlain (310) 656-5151
www.innovativeartists.com

Robert Chappell (323) 460-4767
www.jacobandkoleagency.com

Chuy Chavez (310) 274-6611
www.gershagency.com

Claudio Chea (310) 656-5151
www.innovativeartists.com

Enrique Chediak (310) 273-6700
(Film & High Def) www.unitedtalent.com

Christopher Chomyn (213) 300-2126
(Film & High Def) www.chrischomyn.com

James Chressanthis (310) 652-8778
(323) 493-8505
(Film & High Def) FAX (310) 455-1947
www.chressanthis.com

Dana Christiaansen (310) 457-5958

Chunghoon Chung (310) 474-4585
www.dattnerdispoto.com

C.P. Cima (310) 614-3644
(Film & High Def) www.cimavisioninc.com

David Claessen (310) 288-8000
(Film & High Def) www.paradigmagency.com

Bob Clark (818) 822-1254
(404) 557-5274
(Film & High Def) www.whatfilm.biz

Curtis Clark (323) 460-4767
(Film & High Def) www.jacobandkoleagency.com

Manuel Alberto Claro (310) 652-8778
www.lspagency.net

Jonathon Cliff (310) 458-7800
www.partos.com

Patrice Lucien Cochet (310) 274-6611
www.gershagency.com

Chuck Cohen (323) 856-3000
www.thegelleragency.com

Joseph Colangelo (818) 753-6300
www.themackagency.net

Peter L. Collister (310) 274-6611
www.gershagency.com

Ed Colman (310) 306-5306
(800) 224-1130
(Film & Miniatures) FAX (310) 306-0248
www.superdailies.com

Marino Colmano (818) 362-5170
(Film & High Def) www.marinocolmano.com

Stephen C. Confer (310) 398-5615
(310) 849-1934
(Film, High Def & Remote Heads)

Barry Conrad (818) 248-9161
FAX (818) 249-8884
www.barcon.com

Benjamin Cooke (310) 656-5151
www.innovativeartists.com

Jack Cooperman (909) 336-1535
(Aerial, Miniatures & Special FX)

Robert Copeland (310) 399-0440
FAX (310) 399-2550

Ericson Core (310) 274-6611
www.gershagency.com

Simon Coull (310) 860-3741
(Film & High Def) www.simoncoull.com

Mick Coulter (310) 395-9550
www.skouras.com

Brandon Cox (310) 656-5151
www.innovativeartists.com

Tom Cox (661) 803-0091
(Aerial, Film & High Def)

Nelson Cragg (323) 856-3000
(310) 288-8000
www.thegelleragency.com

Lol Crawley (310) 652-8778
www.lspagency.net

Crew Connection (800) 352-7397
(303) 526-4900
FAX (303) 526-4901
www.crewconnection.com
(Referral for for Directors of Photography)

Tony Croll (310) 288-4545

Jeff Cronenweth (310) 474-4585
(Film & High Def) www.dattnerdispoto.com

Tony Cutrono (818) 206-0144
www.allcrewagency.com

Stefan Czapsky (310) 474-4585
(Film & High Def) www.dattnerdispoto.com

Edward G. Dadulak (818) 400-2900
(661) 287-0092
(Film, High Def & Second Unit) www.hdprola.com

Paul Daley (310) 314-2606
www.stacycheriffagency.com

Shane Daly (310) 474-4585
www.dattnerdispoto.com

Lee Daniel (310) 274-6611
www.gershagency.com

Greg Daniels (310) 937-1905
(310) 386-4112

David Darby (909) 626-7785
(212) 564-7892
(Film & High Def) FAX (909) 625-6925
www.daviddarby.com

Dattner Dispoto & Associates (310) 474-4585
10635 Santa Monica Blvd., Ste. 165 FAX (310) 474-6411
Los Angeles, CA 90025 www.ddatalent.com
(Reps for Directors of Photography)

Allen Daviau (310) 395-9550
(Film & High Def) www.skouras.com

Andrew Davis (310) 401-3211
www.jeannineangelique.com

Collin Davis (310) 729-9803
(Film & High Def)

Don Davis (310) 474-4585
(Film & High Def) www.dattnerdispoto.com

Doug Davis (714) 536-6868
(714) 376-5738
(Film & High Def) FAX (714) 536-6868
web.mac.com/d2films

Elliot Davis (310) 395-9550
www.skouras.com

Brent Deal (818) 781-9233
(Film & High Def) www.orlandomanagement.com

Benoit Debie (310) 652-8778
www.lspagency.net

John de Borman (310) 274-6611
www.gershagency.com

Anghel Decca (310) 273-6700
(Film & High Def) www.unitedtalent.com

Bruno Delbonnel (310) 273-6700
(Film & High Def) www.utaproduction.com

Ricardo Della Rosa (310) 652-8778
www.lspagency.net

Frankie DeMarco (310) 652-8778
www.lspagency.net

Peter Deming (310) 285-0303
www.marshbest.com

Jim Denault (917) 224-1810
(310) 274-6611
(Film & High Def)

Maurice DePas (818) 292-6531
(Film)

Caleb Deschanel (310) 274-6611
www.gershagency.com

Joel Deutsch (310) 628-5400
(Film & High Def) www.evidenceproductions.com

Craig DiBona (323) 856-3000
(Film & High Def) www.thegelleragency.com

Billy Dickson (310) 288-8000
www.paradigmagency.com

Ketil Dietrichson (310) 652-8778
(Film & High Def) www.lspagency.net

Joe di Gennaro (818) 749-4957
(Film & High Def) FAX (818) 761-2377
homepage.mac.com/joe.digennaro/

Phil Dillon (818) 906-0006
(Film & High Def) www.tdnartists.com

Andrew Dintenfass (818) 753-6300
(Film & High Def) www.themackagency.net

Scott Dittrich (310) 459-2526
(Action Sports) www.sdfilms.com

Mark Doering-Powell (818) 259-0112
(818) 932-9329
FAX (818) 932-9090
(Film, High Def, Second Unit, Special FX & Underwater)

Patrick Michael Dolan (310) 480-0507
(Film)

Lawrence Dolkart (323) 463-0022
(Film & High Def) www.radiantartists.com

Peter Donahue (310) 474-4585
(Film & High Def) www.dattnerdispoto.com

Dicran (Deke) Donelian (310) 395-9550
(212) 387-7955
(Film & High Def) www.dekedonelian.com

Jack Donnelly (323) 460-4767
(914) 764-0917
(Film & High Def) www.jacobandkoleagency.com

Rob Doumitt (213) 952-8243

Dave Drez (310) 314-2606
www.stacycheriffagency.com

David DuBois (310) 652-8778
www.lspagency.net

Predrag Dubravcic (323) 460-4767
www.jacobandkoleagency.com

Shawn Dufraine (323) 845-4144
(Film & High Def) www.montanartists.com

Simon Duggan (310) 288-8000
www.paradigmagency.com

Ray Dumas (310) 966-4005
(Film & High Def) www.seslercompany.com

Keith Dunkerley (310) 656-5151
www.innovativeartists.com

David M. Dunlap (845) 677-8644
(310) 288-8000
(Film & High Def)

Andrew Dunn (310) 395-9550
www.skouras.com

Giles Dunning (310) 652-8778
(Film & High Def) www.lspagency.net

Lex DuPont (310) 288-8000
www.paradigmagency.com

Marcos Durian (818) 753-6300
www.themackagency.net

Patrick Duroux (323) 460-4767
www.jacobandkoleagency.com

Marcelo Durst (310) 458-7800
www.partos.com

Chris Duskin (310) 288-8000
www.paradigmagency.com

John Ealer (323) 468-2240
(Film) www.nyoffice.net

Timothy Eaton (866) 535-1972
(Film & High Def) www.veritestudios.com

Mark Eberle (818) 906-0006
www.tdnartists.com

Robert Eberlein (310) 277-0070
(Film, High Def & Special FX)

Eric Edwards (310) 656-5151
(Film) www.innovativeartists.com

David Eggby (310) 822-9113
(Film & High Def) www.murthaagency.com

Ron Egozi (917) 690-0573
(310) 656-5151
www.ronegozi.com

Jody Eldred (310) 821-3047
(310) 989-5639
FAX (310) 821-5447
www.miraclesofthepassion.com/jodybio.htm
(Action Sports, Aerial, Film, High Def & Underwater)

Mark Ellensohn (310) 503-0133
(Film & High Def) FAX (818) 502-1707

Paul Elliott (310) 285-0303
www.marshbest.com

Frederick Elmes (310) 822-9113
www.murthaagency.com

Robert Elswit (310) 273-6700
(Film & High Def) www.utaproduction.com

Ross Emery (310) 474-4585
www.dattnerdispoto.com

Kevin Emmons (818) 906-0006
(719) 330-0201
(Film & High Def) FAX (719) 488-9111
www.emmonsdp.com

Eric Engler (818) 753-6300
(323) 937-7877
(Film & High Def) www.themackagency.net

Lukas Ettlin (310) 282-9940
(Film & High Def) www.mirisch.com

Will Eubank (310) 288-8000
www.paradigmagency.com

Jallo Faber (310) 273-6700
www.utaproduction.com

B. Sean Fairburn (818) 621-3912
(Film & High Def) www.seanfairburn.com

Marco Fargnoli (818) 284-6423
www.italentco.com

Farr Out Productions, LLC (310) 902-5944
(Reps for Directors of Photography) FAX (818) 830-3608
www.farroutpro.com

Jim Fealy (310) 474-4585
(Film) www.dattnerdispoto.com

Gary Feblowitz (818) 415-1869
(612) 281-1869
(Film & High Def) FAX (952) 912-0519
www.hdwave.com

Ruurd M. Fenenga (323) 782-1854
(High Def) www.highdef.nl

Michael Ferris (310) 456-1530
(310) 749-5850
(High Def & Underwater) FAX (310) 456-1433

Michael Fimognari (310) 288-8000
www.paradigmagency.com

Russell Fine (310) 474-4585
(Film & High Def) (917) 940-0765
www.dattnerdispoto.com

Steven Finestone (310) 838-5698
(Film & High Def) (310) 713-9994
FAX (310) 558-4711

Bruce L. Finn (310) 317-1557
(Film & High Def) (323) 845-4144
FAX (310) 317-1558
www.montanartists.com

Michael Fitzmaurice (310) 458-7800
(Film) www.partos.com

John Fleckenstein (323) 874-2975

Tim Fleming (310) 274-6611
www.gershagency.com

John C. Flinn III (310) 656-5151
www.innovativeartists.com

Eduardo Flores Torres (310) 282-9940
www.mirisch.com

Larry Fong (323) 460-4767
(Film & High Def) www.jacobandkoleagency.com

Stephane Fontaine (323) 460-4767
www.jacobandkoleagency.com

Crille Forsberg (310) 273-6700
(Film & High Def) www.utaproduction.com

Ian Forsyth (323) 460-4767
(Film & High Def) www.jacobandkoleagency.com

Eric Foster (310) 401-3211
(Film & High Def) www.jeannineangelique.com

Robert Fraisse (310) 288-8000
www.paradigmagency.com

Greig Fraser (310) 273-6700
www.utaproduction.com

Patrick Fraser (323) 363-6125
(Film & High Def) (818) 753-6300
www.themackagency.net

Walt Fraser (310) 656-5151
www.innovativeartists.com

Jonathan Freeman (310) 274-6611
www.gershagency.com

Adam Frisch (310) 652-8778
www.lspagency.net

Jim Frohna (310) 395-9550
www.skouras.com

Tak Fujimoto (310) 395-9550
www.skouras.com

Guy Furner (310) 475-8767
(Film & High Def) (212) 924-8505
FAX (212) 924-8544

Scott Galinsky (310) 288-8000
www.paradigmagency.com

Joe Gallagher (323) 856-3000
www.thegelleragency.com

Christopher Gallo (818) 753-6300
(Film & High Def) www.themackagency.net

Omer Ganai (310) 273-6700
(Film & High Def) www.utaproduction.com

Robert Gantz (310) 656-5151
www.innovativeartists.com

William Garcia (818) 206-0144
(Film & High Def) www.allcrewagency.com

Greg Gardiner (310) 288-8000
www.paradigmagency.com

James Gardner (310) 966-4005
(Film & High Def) www.seslercompany.com

Kirk Gardner (818) 222-5200
(Second Unit) www.schneiderentertainment.com

Mark Garrett (310) 288-8000
www.paradigmagency.com

Eric Gautier (310) 652-8778
www.lspagency.net

Ryan Gaw (323) 845-4144
(Film & High Def) www.montanartists.com

David Geddes (310) 656-5151
www.innovativeartists.com

The Geller Agency (323) 856-3000
1547 Cassil Pl. FAX (323) 856-3009
Hollywood, CA 90028 www.thegelleragency.com
(Reps for Directors of Photography)

Darren Genet (310) 656-5151
www.innovativeartists.com

Dejan Georgevich (310) 656-5151
www.innovativeartists.com

The Gersh Agency (310) 274-6611
(212) 997-1818
P.O. Box 5617 www.gershagency.com
Beverly Hills, CA 90210
(Reps for Directors of Photography)

Helge Gerull (310) 395-9550
(Film & High Def) www.skouras.com

Mike Gerzevitz (310) 439-0101
(Film & High Def) (310) 967-4878
www.mikegerz.com

Jack Gill (310) 288-8000
www.paradigmagency.com

Pierre Gill (310) 288-8000
www.paradigmagency.com

Dan Gillham (323) 468-2240
(Film & High Def) www.nyoffice.net

Xavi Gimenez (310) 652-8778
www.lspagency.net

Michael Goi (310) 288-8000
www.paradigmagency.com

Stephen Goldblatt (310) 395-9550
www.skouras.com

Adriano Goldman (310) 395-9550
www.skouras.com

Paul Goldsmith (310) 474-4585
www.dattnerdispoto.com

Dana Gonzales (310) 652-8778
(Film & High Def) www.lspagency.net

Frederic Goodich (310) 430-6793
www.fredericgoodich.com

Ronald C. Goodman (818) 889-6060
(Aerial) FAX (818) 889-6062
www.spacecam.com

Christopher Gosch (310) 857-6664
(310) 999-1877
FAX (310) 857-6664
www.thecompany.tv

Stuart Graham (323) 460-4767
www.jacobandkoleagency.com

Kevin Graves (323) 856-3000
(Film & High Def) www.thegelleragency.com

Jack Green (310) 274-6611
www.gershagency.com

Jesse Green (310) 395-9550
(Film & High Def) www.skouras.com

Adam Greenberg (310) 274-6611
www.gershagency.com

Bryan Greenberg (323) 656-7818
(Film & High Def) FAX (323) 656-3202

Robbie Greenberg (310) 458-7800
(Film) www.partos.com

David Gribble (310) 652-8778
www.lspagency.net

Xavier Perez Grobet (310) 474-4585
www.dattnerdispoto.com

Derek Grover (310) 291-1372
(Film & High Def)

Tom Grubbs (310) 457-5539
(Film & High Def)

Keith Gruchala (818) 633-3577
www.keithgruchala.com
(Action Sports, Aerial, Film, High Def, Special FX & Steadicam)

Alexander Gruszynski (310) 288-8000
www.paradigmagency.com

Jim Gucciardo (917) 518-6266
www.jimgucciardo.com

Ottar Gudnason (310) 474-4585
www.dattnerdispoto.com

Eric Guichard (323) 460-4767
www.jacobandkoleagency.com

Sanji F. Gupta (818) 906-0006
www.tdnartists.com

Eric J. Haase (310) 656-5151
(Film & High Def) www.innovativeartists.com

Karl Hahn (323) 460-4767
www.jacobandkoleagency.com

Conrad W. Hall (310) 395-9550
www.skouras.com

Dennis S. Hall (310) 656-5151
www.innovativeartists.com

Geoffrey Hall (310) 288-8000
www.paradigmagency.com

Warren Hansen (323) 460-4767
(323) 365-4427
(Film & High Def) www.warrenhansen.com

Anthony Hardwick (310) 463-9894
(310) 288-8000
(Film & High Def) www.paradigmagency.com

Russell Harper (310) 401-3211
www.russellharper.net

Randy Hart (818) 768-4508
(Film & High Def) FAX (818) 768-4270

Peter Hartmann (310) 966-4005
(Film & High Def) www.seslercompany.com

Jason Harvey (818) 753-6300
www.themackagency.net

Kent Harvey (310) 699-3674
(Film, High Def & Second Unit) FAX (310) 202-0305
www.khfilms.com

Kim Haun (818) 501-4898
(Film & High Def) FAX (818) 788-5633
www.kimhaun.com

Simon Hawken (323) 463-0022
www.radiantartists.com

Peter Hawkins (213) 604-5999
(323) 468-2240
FAX (323) 468-2244
www.nyoffice.net

Bob Hayes (310) 390-9190
(310) 717-6625
www.floatinglantern.net
(Film, High Def, Remote Heads, Second Unit & Special FX)

Bill Heath (818) 781-9233
www.orlandomanagement.com

Matthew Heckerling (310) 282-9940
www.mirisch.com

Bernd Heinl (818) 284-6423
www.italentco.com

Wolfgang Held (323) 468-2240
(Film & High Def) www.nyoffice.net

David Hellman (310) 395-9550
www.skouras.com

Richard Henkels (310) 652-8778
www.lspagency.net

David Hennings (310) 656-5151
www.innovativeartists.com

Scott Henriksen (323) 460-4767
(Film & High Def) www.jacobandkoleagency.com

David Herrington (323) 845-4144
www.montanartists.com

Karl Herrmann (310) 282-9940
www.mirisch.com

Ron Hersey (323) 856-3000
www.thegelleragency.com

Gregg Heschong (818) 547-9697
(Film & High Def) FAX (818) 547-9698

Joshua Hess (310) 395-9550
www.skouras.com

Henner Hofmann (310) 282-9940
(Film & High Def) www.mirisch.com

Michael Hofstein (323) 702-8502
(Aerial & Special FX) www.watchreels.com/mhofstein

Julian Hohndorf (310) 314-2606
www.stacycheriffagency.com

Philip Holahan (818) 222-5200
www.schneiderentertainment.com

Adam Holender (310) 288-8000
www.paradigmagency.com

Doug Holgate (949) 631-4311
(949) 375-4997
(Aerial) FAX (949) 631-4835

Peter Holland (310) 288-8000
www.paradigmagency.com

Nathan Hope (310) 822-9113
(Film & High Def) www.murthaagency.com

Doug Hostetter (818) 753-6300
www.themackagency.net

Tom Houghton (323) 821-3351
(212) 690-1007
(Film & High Def) FAX (212) 690-1026
www.tomhoughton.com

John Houtman (310) 966-4005
www.seslercompany.com

Robert Howard (310) 413-6683
(310) 256-3469

Steve Howell (661) 799-0154
(661) 607-7266
(Aerial) www.stevehowelldp.com

Gil Hubbs (310) 454-1181
(Film & High Def)

Angus Hudson (310) 288-8000
www.paradigmagency.com

Tim Hudson (310) 401-3211
www.jeannineangelique.com

David Huey (818) 679-2994
(Film & High Def) FAX (818) 848-4478

Kent Hughes (818) 468-6068
(Aerial, Film, High Def & Remote Heads)

Paula Huidobro (310) 656-5151
www.innovativeartists.com

Rob Humphreys (310) 458-7800
www.partos.com

Jim Hunter (323) 252-0909
(Film & High Def) www.jim-hunter.com

Mott Hupfel (310) 474-4585
(Film & High Def) www.dattnerdispoto.com

Shane Hurlbut (310) 274-6611
www.gershagency.com

Philip Hurn (818) 206-0144
(Film & High Def) www.allcrewagency.com

Tom Hurwitz (323) 460-4767
(212) 928-4466
(Film & High Def) www.tomhurwitz.com

Slavomir Idziak (310) 395-9550
www.skouras.com

Jacob Ihre (310) 395-9550
www.skouras.com

Tony Imi (818) 206-0144
www.allcrewagency.com

Innovative Artists (310) 656-5151
1617 Broadway, Third Fl. FAX (310) 656-5156
Santa Monica, CA 90404 www.innovativeartists.com
(Reps for Directors of Photography)

International Creative Management - ICM (310) 550-4000
10250 Constellation Blvd. www.icmtalent.com
Los Angeles, CA 90067
(Reps for Directors of Photography)

John Inwood (310) 248-4022
(917) 690-4313
(Film & High Def) FAX (310) 276-3207
www.watchreels.com/johninwood

Judy Irola (323) 856-3000
(Film & High Def) www.thegelleragency.com

Matthew Irving (310) 656-5151
www.innovativeartists.com

Mark Irwin (310) 288-8000
www.paradigmagency.com

Toby Irwin (310) 273-6700
www.utaproduction.com

Levie Isaacks (310) 656-5151
www.innovativeartists.com

Mai Iskander (646) 515-5995
(310) 458-7800
(Film & High Def) www.partos.com

iTalent Company (818) 284-6423
9701 Wilshire Blvd., 10th Fl. FAX (866) 755-0708
Beverly Hills, CA 90212 www.italentco.com
(Reps for Directors of Photography)

Dale Iwamasa (310) 768-2920
(Film & High Def)

The Jacob & Kole Agency (323) 460-4767
6715 Hollywood Blvd., Ste. 216 FAX (323) 460-4804
Los Angeles, CA 90028 www.jacobandkoleagency.com
(Reps for Directors of Photography)

Frederik Jacobi (323) 468-2240
www.nyoffice.net

Alan Jacoby (310) 801-9297
(818) 206-0144
www.vortexfilms.com

Igor Jadue-Lillo (323) 460-4767
(Film & High Def) www.jacobandkoleagency.com

Peter James (310) 395-9550
www.skouras.com

Alec Jarnagin (917) 804-6606
(818) 985-1130
(Film & High Def) www.floatingcamera.com

Johnny E. Jensen (310) 656-5151
www.innovativeartists.com

Jon Joffin (310) 474-4585
www.dattnerdispoto.com

Christopher W. Johnson (424) 456-0090
(Action Sports, Aerial, Film, High Def, Second Unit, Special FX, Steadicam & Underwater)

David Johnson (310) 274-6611
www.gershagency.com

Hugh Johnson (310) 822-9113
www.murthaagency.com

Shelly Johnson (310) 274-6611
www.gershagency.com

J. Wesley Jones (310) 282-9940
www.mirisch.com

Kevin Jones (323) 460-4767
(Film & High Def) www.jacobandkoleagency.com

Bengt Jan Jonsson (310) 656-5151
www.innovativeartists.com

Imre Juhasz (323) 788-4132
+36 30 372 4894
(Film & High Def) www.imrejuhasz.net

Pergrin Jung (310) 454-9036
(310) 849-1771
FAX (310) 454-9084
www.pergrinjung.com

Kristian Kachikis (310) 474-4585
(Film & High Def) www.dattnerdispoto.com

Emmanuel Kadosh (310) 288-8000
www.paradigmagency.com

Nicholas Karakatsanis (310) 652-8778
www.lspagency.net

Daniel Karp (818) 990-8993
(Film & High Def) www.ambitiousent.com

Michael Karp (818) 515-8917
(Miniatures & Special FX) members.aol.com/mckarp

Stephen Kazmierski (323) 845-4144
www.montanartists.com

Glen Keenan (310) 966-4005
www.seslercompany.com

Steve Keith-Roach (310) 273-6700
www.utaproduction.com

Gavin Kelly (323) 856-3000
www.thegelleragency.com

Kira Kelly (323) 463-0022
www.radiantartists.com

Ken Kelsch (818) 781-9233
(Film & High Def) www.orlandomanagement.com

Victor J. Kemper (310) 282-9940
www.mirisch.com

Wayne Kennan (818) 889-1023
(Film & High Def)

Francis Kenny (310) 274-6611
www.gershagency.com

Joe Kessler (310) 433-1901

Scott Kevan (310) 274-6611
www.gershagency.com

Kyle Kibbe (310) 474-4585
(Film) www.dattnerdispoto.com

Jan Kiesser (310) 656-5151
(Film & High Def) www.innovativeartists.com

Shawn Kim (310) 652-8778
www.lspagency.net

Adam Kimmel (213) 840-9791
(212) 228-7523
(Film & High Def)

Jim Kimura (323) 559-1110
FAX (626) 398-1387
www.tdnartists.com
(Aerial, Film, High Def, Remote Heads, Second Unit, Special FX & Underwater)

Sean Kirby (310) 652-8778
www.lspagency.net

Alar Kivilo (310) 273-6700
(Film & High Def) www.utaproduction.com

Rainer Klausmann (310) 285-0303
www.marshbest.com

David Klein (310) 288-8000
www.paradigmagency.com

Thomas Kloss (310) 652-8778
(Film & High Def) www.lspagency.net

James Kniest (310) 966-4005
www.seslercompany.com

Douglas Koch (310) 966-4005
www.seslercompany.com

Matthias Koenigswieser (310) 652-8778
www.lspagency.net

Lajos Koltai (310) 395-9550
www.skouras.com

Pete Konczal (310) 652-8778
www.lspagency.net

Tanja Koop (310) 285-0303
www.marshbest.com

Petra Korner (310) 656-5151
www.innovativeartists.com

Jon Kranhouse (310) 459-8844
(Aerial & Special FX) www.hydrooptix.com

Tom Krueger (323) 460-4767
(Film & High Def) www.jacobandkoleagency.com

Alwin Kuchler (310) 274-6611
www.gershagency.com

Ben Kufrin (818) 284-6423
www.italentco.com

Ellen Kuras (310) 273-6700
(Film & High Def) www.utaproduction.com

Toyomichi Kurita (310) 285-0303
www.marshbest.com

Roy Kurtluyan (818) 378-0033
FAX (323) 871-8122
www.newcircuit.com
(Action Sports, Film, High Def, Second Unit, Special FX & Underwater)

Flavio Labiano (310) 474-4585
www.dattnerdispoto.com

Joseph Labisi (310) 962-6394
(Film & High Def) www.josephlabisi.com

Ed Lachman (310) 273-6700
(Film) www.utaproduction.com

Kjell Lagerroos (310) 474-4585
www.dattnerdispoto.com

Alex Lamarque (310) 652-8778
www.laspagency.net

Rod Lamborn (323) 468-2240
(Film & High Def) www.nyoffice.net

Ken Lamkin (818) 206-0144
www.allcrewagency.com

Stöps Langensteiner (310) 652-8778
(Film & High Def) www.lspagency.net

Christophe Lanzenberg (310) 273-6700
(Film & High Def) www.utaproduction.com

David Lanzenberg (310) 395-9550
www.skouras.com

Andre Lascaris (310) 656-5151
www.innovativeartists.com

Dan Laustsen (310) 285-0303
www.marshbest.com

Michael Paul Lawler (323) 663-8716
(Miniatures & Visual FX)

John Lawrence (310) 962-7133
(Film & High Def) www.jlcamera.com

Jim LeBlanc (619) 778-4433
(Film & High Def)

John Le Blanc (323) 257-8881
FAX (323) 258-9549

Patti Lee (310) 288-8000
www.paradigmagency.com

Philip Lee (323) 574-5617
(818) 284-6423
(Film & High Def) FAX (818) 753-0571
www.italentco.com

Jason Lehel (310) 656-5151
www.innovativeartists.com

David Lena (310) 480-7007
FAX (310) 399-2425
www.davidlena.com
(Action Sports, Aerial, Film, High Def & Second Unit)

Denis Lenoir (310) 652-8778
(Film & High Def)

John R. Leonetti (310) 274-6611
(Film & High Def) www.gershagency.com

Yorick LeSaux (310) 652-8778
www.lspagency.net

Andrew Lesnie (310) 273-6700
(Film & High Def) www.utaproduction.com

Philippe Le Sourd (310) 395-9550
www.skouras.com

Michael Levine (310) 489-6848
FAX (323) 939-9622
www.crashproductions.com

Jordan Levy (310) 314-2606
(Film & High Def) www.stacycheriffagency.com

Peter Levy (310) 822-9113
www.murthaagency.com

Sam Levy (310) 474-4585
www.dattnerdispoto.com

Rain Li (310) 656-5151
www.innovativeartists.com

Matthew Libatique (310) 273-6700
(Film & High Def) www.utaproduction.com

Charles Libin (323) 460-4767
(Film & High Def) www.luminaria.net/reels/reelindex.html

John Lichtwardt (818) 781-9233
www.orlandomanagement.com

Andy Lilien (323) 460-4767
(Film & High Def) www.jacobandkoleagency.com

Jong Lin (310) 652-8778
www.lspagency.net

Karl Walter Lindenlaub (310) 395-9550
www.skouras.com

Ralph Linhardt (818) 781-9233
www.orlandomanagement.com

Martin Linss (310) 288-8000
www.paradigmagency.com

Philip Linzey (310) 288-8000
(Film & High Def) www.paradigmagency.com

Jay P. Lipa (818) 781-9233
www.orlandomanagement.com

Jeanne Lipsey (310) 395-9550
(Film & High Def) www.skouras.com

Walt Lloyd (818) 753-6300
(Film & High Def) www.themackagency.net

Mateo Londono (310) 474-4585
(Film) www.dattnerdispoto.com

Gordon Lonsdale (310) 656-5151
(Film & High Def) www.innovativeartists.com

Rick Lopez (323) 468-2240
www.nyoffice.net

Patrick Loungway (818) 519-1190

Emmanuel Lubezki (323) 460-4767
(Film & High Def) www.jacobandkoleagency.com

Franz Lustig (323) 460-4767
www.jacobandkoleagency.com

John Lynch (310) 395-9550
www.skouras.com

Chris Mably (310) 458-7800
www.partos.com

Julio Macat (310) 652-8778
www.lspagency.net

William MacCollum (323) 363-4140
(Film & High Def) FAX (323) 843-9634
www.watchreels.com/williammaccollum

Jesse MacDonald (310) 710-6525
www.jessemacdonald.com
(Action Sports, Film, High Def, Remote Heads, Second Unit & Special FX)

Rob Macey (818) 281-3925
(High Def) FAX (818) 240-8715
www.nothingfilms.com

The Mack Agency (818) 753-6300
5726 Woodman Ave., Ste. 4 FAX (818) 753-6311
Van Nuys, CA 91401 www.themackagency.net
(Reps for Directors of Photography)

Peter Mackay (818) 341-5101
(212) 564-7892
FAX (818) 341-5141
www.petermackay.net

Dylan Macleod (310) 966-4005
www.seslercompany.com

Glen MacPherson (310) 822-9113
www.murthaagency.com

Eric Maddison (310) 474-4585
www.dattnerdispoto.com

Chris Magee (310) 928-3453
(Aerial, Film & High Def) www.chrismagee.com

Paul Maibaum (310) 288-8000
www.paradigmagency.com

Maz Makhani (310) 248-2000
(Film & High Def) www.mazmakhani.com

Denis Maloney (310) 656-5151
www.innovativeartists.com

Matt Mania (818) 781-9233
(Film & High Def) www.orlandomanagement.com

Teodoro Maniaci (310) 274-6611
www.gershagency.com

Chris Manley (310) 652-8778
www.lspagency.net

Gary C. Manske (619) 523-5000
(Special FX) FAX (619) 225-2244
ckmanske.googlepages.com/home

Billy D. Marchese (310) 422-7971
(Film & High Def) www.dezartcinematic.com

Mark Nelson (619) 291-2403
(Action Sports & High Def) FAX (619) 291-2475
www.visualconcepts.tv

Barry Markowitz (323) 460-4767
(Film & High Def) www.jacobandkoleagency.com

Adam Marsden (310) 966-4005
www.seslercompany.com

Marsh, Best & Associates (310) 285-0303
9150 Wilshire Blvd., Ste. 220 FAX (310) 285-0218
Beverly Hills, CA 90212 www.marshbest.com
(Reps for Directors of Photography)

Nicola Marsh (310) 656-5151
www.innovativeartists.com

Pascal Marti (323) 468-2240
(Film) www.nyoffice.net

Alejandro Martinez (310) 652-8778
www.lspagency.net

Thomas Marvel (310) 474-4585
(Film & High Def) www.dattnerdispoto.com

Steve Mason (310) 822-9113
www.murthaagency.com

Brandon Mastrippolito (323) 845-4144
(Film & High Def) www.montanartists.com

Harry Mathias (805) 379-9003
(High Def)

James Matlosz (310) 474-4585
(Film & High Def) www.ddatalent.com

Shawn Maurer (310) 656-5151
(Film & High Def) www.innovativeartists.com

Tim Maurice-Jones (310) 273-6700
(Film & High Def) www.utaproduction.com

Jamie Maxtone-Graham (323) 856-3000
www.thegelleragency.com

Joe Maxwell (310) 652-8778
(Film & High Def) www.lspagency.net

Marco Mazzei (310) 652-8778
(Film & High Def) www.marcomazzei.net

Don McAlpine (310) 274-6611
www.gershagency.com

Craig McCourry (310) 928-3470
www.mccourry.com

Sam McCurdy (310) 288-8000
www.paradigmagency.com

Michael McDonough (310) 652-8778
www.lspagency.net

Russ McElhatton (323) 856-3000
www.thegelleragency.com

Stephen McGehee (310) 652-8778
www.lspagency.net

Patrick McGowan (310) 458-7800
www.partos.com

Martin McGrath (323) 460-4767
www.jacobandkoleagency.com

Tom McGrath (310) 474-4585
(Film & High Def) www.dattnerdispoto.com

Bruce McGregor (818) 980-6116
(415) 383-1007
www.highdefvisions.com

Kieran McGuigan (310) 273-6700
www.unitedtalent.com

Christopher TJ McGuire (661) 839-7432
www.ar-mcguire.com

Derek McKane (310) 395-9550
(Film & High Def) www.skouras.com

Robert McLachlan (310) 273-6700
(Film & High Def) www.utaproduction.com

Geary McLeod (310) 288-8000
www.paradigmagency.com

Stephen McMahon (310) 393-5065
(Film & High Def)

Todd McMullen (818) 222-5200
www.schneiderentertainment.com

Stephen McNutt (310) 656-5151
(Film & High Def) www.innovativeartists.com

Joe Meade (310) 395-9550
(Film & High Def) www.skouras.com

Igor Meglic (310) 413-7908
(Film & High Def)

Phil Meheux (310) 395-9550
www.skouras.com

Sharone Meir (310) 274-6611
www.gershagency.com

Alex Melman (310) 274-6611
www.gershagency.com

Adam Meltzer (323) 864-9130
(Film & High Def) www.meltzerdp.com

Nick Mendoza Jr. (818) 848-1269
(818) 288-8921
(Film & High Def) www.nickdp.com

Chris Menges (310) 285-0303
www.marshbest.com

Peter Menzies Jr. (310) 395-9550
www.skouras.com

Hilda Mercado (323) 460-4767
www.jacobandkoleagency.com

Simon Mestel (310) 966-4005
www.seslercompany.com

Rexford Metz (562) 692-2286
(310) 480-9172
(Aerial, Underwater & Visual FX) FAX (562) 692-2286
www.rexfordmetz.com

William Meurer (818) 640-4789
(Film & High Def) FAX (323) 466-8211

Scott Meyer (818) 730-4900
(Film & High Def) www.scottfilms.com

Sion Michel (323) 428-7751
(Film & High Def) www.sionmichel.com

Jose Luis Mignone (818) 995-7579
(818) 645-6823

Robin Miller (818) 781-9233
www.orlandomanagement.com

Charles E. Mills (818) 222-5200
www.schneiderentertainment.com

Dan Mindel (310) 395-9550

Charles Minsky (805) 969-9946
(310) 656-5151
FAX (805) 969-7575

Claudio Miranda (310) 474-4585
(Film & High Def) www.dattnerdispoto.com

The Mirisch Agency (310) 282-9940
1925 Century Park East, Ste. 1070 FAX (310) 282-0702
Los Angeles, CA 90067 www.mirisch.com
(Reps for Directors of Photography)

Danny Moder (310) 474-4585
www.ddatalent.com

Amir Mokri (818) 753-6300
(Film & High Def) www.themackagency.net

Tony Molina (310) 474-4585
(Film & High Def) www.dattnerdispoto.com

William H. Molina (210) 379-0961
(Film & High Def) homepage.mac.com/molinadp/WHM

Jo Molitoris (310) 474-4585
www.dattnerdispoto.com

Mike Molloy (310) 285-0303
www.marshbest.com

Montana Artists Agency (323) 845-4144
7715 W. Sunset Blvd., Third Fl. FAX (323) 845-4155
Los Angeles, CA 90046 www.montanartists.com
(Reps for Directors of Photography)

Joseph Montgomery (805) 773-6550
(213) 500-3304
(Film & High Def) FAX (805) 773-6136

Luc Montpellier (310) 288-8000
www.paradigmagency.com

George Mooradian (818) 505-0050
(818) 753-6300
(Film & High Def) FAX (818) 505-0050
www.themackagency.net

Donald M. Morgan (818) 830-0513
(Film & High Def)

Damien Morisot (323) 468-2240
(Film) www.nyoffice.net

Michael R. Morris (818) 951-5359
(323) 496-0191
(Film & Second Unit) www.michaelrmorris.net

Robert Morris (323) 845-4144
(Film & High Def) www.montanartists.com

David Morrison (323) 463-0022
(Film & High Def) www.radiantartists.com

Steven Moses (323) 460-4767
(310) 545-1235
www.jacobandkoleagency.com

Peter Moss (818) 906-0006
(Film & High Def) www.tdnartists.com

George Motz (323) 460-4767
(212) 627-0092
(Film & High Def) www.jacobandkoleagency.com

David Moxness (310) 474-4585
www.dattnerdispoto.com

Eric Moynier (818) 206-0144
(Film & High Def) www.allcrewagency.com

M. David Mullen (323) 468-2240
(Film & High Def) www.nyoffice.net

Robby Muller (310) 822-9113
www.murthaagency.com

Patrick Murguia (310) 285-0303
www.marshbest.com

J. Michael Muro (323) 845-4144
www.montanartists.com

Fred Murphy (310) 274-6611
www.gershagency.com

Fletcher Murray (818) 841-9660
(Film & High Def) FAX (818) 841-8370
www.theassociation.tv

The Murtha Agency (310) 822-9113
4240 Promenade Way, Ste. 232 FAX (310) 822-6662
Marina Del Rey, CA 90292 www.murthaagency.com
(Reps for Directors of Photography)

Jeffrey Mygatt (310) 288-8000
www.paradigmagency.com

Hiro Narita (310) 282-9940
(Film, High Def & Second Unit) www.mirisch.com

Guillermo Navarro (310) 458-7800
(Film) www.partos.com

Michael Negrin (310) 656-5151
(Film & High Def) www.innovativeartists.com

David Negron Jr. (323) 856-3000
www.thegelleragency.com

Arlene Donnelly Nelson (310) 474-4585
www.ddatalent.com

Otto Nemenz (323) 469-2774
(310) 459-3320
FAX (323) 469-1217

Alex Nepomniaschy (310) 656-5151
www.innovativeartists.com

Evan Nesbitt (323) 463-0476
(323) 314-5928
(Film, High Def & Second Unit) FAX (323) 463-0477
www.evannesbitt.com

Mathias Neumann (310) 474-4585
www.dattnerdispoto.com

New York Office (323) 468-2240
(212) 545-7895
6605 Hollywood Blvd., Ste. 200 FAX (323) 468-2244
Los Angeles, CA 90028 www.nyoffice.net
(Reps for Directors of Photography)

Robert New (323) 856-3000
www.thegelleragency.com

Spencer Newman (310) 358-7619
www.sourcetv.com
(Action Sports, Aerial, Film, High Def, Remote Heads, Second Unit, Special FX & Underwater)

Yuri Neyman (818) 486-4916
(323) 436-7593
(Film & High Def)

Christopher Nibley (818) 509-0613
(Film, High Def, Second Unit & Special FX) www.nibley.com

Bridger Nielson (323) 460-4767
(Film & High Def) www.jacobandkoleagency.com

Carl Nilsson (310) 474-4585
(Film & High Def) www.dattnerdispoto.com

Chris Norr (323) 845-4144
(Film & High Def) www.montanartists.com

David Norton (310) 395-9550
(Film & High Def) www.skouras.com

Barry Norwood (310) 401-3211
(Film & High Def) www.jeannineangelique.com

Crescenzo G.P. Notarile (323) 464-3901
(213) 300-3901
(Film & High Def) FAX (323) 464-3909
www.watchreels.com/crescenzo

David B. Nowell (661) 251-3456
(Aerial & Second Unit) FAX (661) 251-3864

Vasco Nunes (323) 468-2240
(Film) www.nyoffice.net

Giles Nuttgens (310) 474-4585
www.dattnerdispoto.com

Brian O'Connell (310) 384-6185
(Film & High Def) www.brianoconnell.com

Sean O'Dea (310) 474-4585
(310) 880-0537
(Film & High Def) www.dattnerdispoto.com

Rene Ohashi (310) 966-4005
(Film & High Def) www.seslercompany.com

Daryn Okada (310) 822-9113
www.murthaagency.com

Thomas Olgeirsson (310) 545-8592
(703) 577-6195
(Film & High Def) www.olgeirsson.com

Patrick D. O'Mara (310) 540-8411
(310) 901-5514
(Film & High Def) FAX (310) 545-0136

Trent Opaloch (310) 966-4005
www.seslercompany.com

Yaron Orbach (310) 652-8778
www.lspagency.net

Orlando Management (818) 781-9233
15134 Martha St. www.orlandomanagement.com
Sherman Oaks, CA 91411
(Reps for Directors of Photography)

Melissa Orndorff (323) 664-6494
(Film & High Def) www.therexagency.com

Tim Orr (310) 273-6700
www.unitedtalent.com

Jeff Orsa (323) 460-4767
(High Def) www.jacobandkoleagency.com

Oktay Ortabasi (818) 845-3230
(Film, High Def & Second Unit) FAX (818) 688-8180
www.dreamingtreeproductions.com

Michael D. O'Shea (310) 822-9113
www.murthaagency.com

Richard Oshen (626) 794-5777
(626) 922-5777
FAX (626) 794-4477
www.eye-light.org

Hernan Michael Otaño (917) 796-3997
(310) 288-8000

Toshiaki Ozawa (310) 474-4585
(Film & High Def) www.dattnerdispoto.com

Chuck Ozeas (310) 458-7800
(Film & High Def) www.partos.com

Michael Ozier (310) 285-9000
(Film & High Def) www.michaelozier.com

Vince Pace (818) 759-7322
(Film & High Def) FAX (818) 759-7323
www.pacehd.com

Angelo Pacifici (310) 313-3762
(818) 990-8993
(Film & High Def) FAX (310) 745-1949
www.ambitiousent.com

Sam Painter (323) 876-7302
(213) 999-1985
(High Def) FAX (323) 876-7303

Gary Palmer (310) 440-4001
www.thesuninmotion.com

Anthony Palmieri (310) 282-9940
www.mirisch.com

Robert Papais (310) 458-7800
www.partos.com

Phedon Papamichael (310) 656-5151
(Film & High Def) www.innovativeartists.com

Charles Papert (323) 350-8822
FAX (323) 843-9357
www.charlespapert.com

Paradigm,
A Talent & Literary Agency (310) 288-8000
360 N. Crescent Dr. FAX (310) 288-2000
Beverly Hills, CA 90210 www.paradigmagency.com
(Reps for Directors of Photography)

Gyola Pardos (310) 395-9550
www.skouras.com

Andrij Parekh (310) 395-9550
(Film & High Def) www.andrijparekh.com

Lee Ford Parker (310) 928-3165
(Second Unit & Special FX) FAX (209) 668-4010
www.mocoman.com

Dino Parks (310) 285-0303
www.marshbest.com

Phil Parmet (310) 288-8000
www.paradigmagency.com

Barry Parrell (310) 966-4005
(Film & High Def) www.seslercompany.com

Partos Company (310) 458-7800
227 Broadway, Ste. 204 FAX (310) 587-2250
Santa Monica, CA 90401 www.partos.com
(Reps for Directors of Photography)

Vincent Passeri (818) 753-6300
www.themackagency.net

Philip Pastuhov (805) 320-3304
(415) 389-9019
(Aerial, Film & High Def) FAX (415) 381-4154

Chris Patterson (310) 962-3498
(Film & High Def) FAX (310) 962-3498
www.chrispattersonfilms.com

Peter Pau (310) 274-6611
www.gershagency.com

Daniel C. Pearl (323) 525-1976
FAX (323) 525-1905
www.danielpearldp.com
(Film, High Def, Remote Heads, Special FX & Underwater)

Brian Pearson (310) 822-9113
www.murthaagency.com

Christopher Pearson (310) 288-8000
www.paradigmagency.com

Nicola Pecorini (310) 395-9550
www.skouras.com

Bob Pendar-Hughes (323) 463-0022
www.radiantartists.com

Lonnie Peralta (310) 628-8158
(310) 577-5009
(Film, High Def & Second Unit) FAX (310) 577-1960
www.lonnieperalta.com

Luis Perez (310) 474-4585
(Film) www.dattnerdispoto.com

Dave Perkal (323) 845-4144
(310) 625-6541
(Film & High Def) www.montanartists.com

Michael Pescasio (310) 288-8000
www.paradigmagency.com

Ray Peschke (818) 206-0144
(Film & High Def) www.allcrewagency.com

Barry Peterson (310) 273-6700
www.utaproduction.com

Lowell Peterson (310) 288-8000
www.paradigmagency.com

Sebastian Pfaffenbichler (310) 395-9550
(Film & High Def) www.skouras.com

Aaron Phillips (310) 395-9550
(Film) www.skouras.com

David Phillips (212) 643-2859
(310) 474-4585
(Film & High Def) www.dattnerdispoto.com

Garry Phillips (310) 285-0303
www.marshbest.com

Jeffrey Phillips (818) 781-9233
www.orlandomanagement.com

Sean MacLeod Phillips (310) 395-4739

André Pienaar (310) 458-7800
(Film & High Def) www.partos.com

Tony Pierce-Roberts (310) 395-9550
(Film & High Def) www.skouras.com

Timothy Pike (310) 395-9550
(Film & High Def) www.skouras.com

Michael Pinkey (818) 781-9233
(Film & High Def) www.watchreels.com/pinkey

Tom Piozet (805) 965-9848
(818) 422-4144
(High Def) FAX (805) 965-2329
www.homeplanetproductions.com

Ekkehart Pollack (310) 656-5151
www.innovativeartists.com

Jake Polonsky (310) 474-4585
www.dattnerdispoto.com

Zoran Popovic (310) 656-5151
www.innovativeartists.com

Christopher Popp (323) 856-3000
(Film, High Def & Second Unit) www.thegelleragency.com

Steven Poster (213) 819-0000
(310) 205-5812

Thierry Pouget (323) 468-2240
www.nyoffice.net

Tico Poulakakis (310) 966-4005
www.seslercompany.com

Munn Powell (310) 273-6700
www.utaproduction.com

Jaron Presant (310) 401-3211
www.jaronpresant.com

Tom Priestley (310) 288-8000
(Film & High Def) www.paradigmagency.com

Robert Primes (310) 282-9940
(323) 851-8444
(Film & High Def) FAX (323) 851-4493
www.innovativeartists.com

Christopher Probst (310) 652-8778
www.lspagency.net

Wei K. Pun (310) 314-2606
www.stacycheriffagency.com

Lawrence Purcell (323) 666-5911
(Film & High Def) FAX (323) 662-9969

Cynthia Pusheck (323) 497-8489
homepage.mac.com/cpush/menu13.html
(Film, High Def, Second Unit & Underwater)

Roger Quillin (323) 512-7660
(310) 801-1731
(Aerial, Film & High Def) www.lostsquadron.com/q

Declan Quinn (323) 460-4767
(Film & High Def) www.jacobandkoleagency.com

Atanas Radev (323) 304-2995 / (818) 206-0144
(Film & High Def) www.allcrewagency.com

Radiant Artists (323) 463-0022
6715 Hollywood Blvd., Ste. 220 FAX (323) 375-0231
Los Angeles, CA 90028 www.radiantartists.com
(Reps for Directors of Photography)

Stephen Ramsey (310) 429-2541 / (323) 650-4974
(Film & High Def)

Joel Ransom (818) 781-9233
www.orlandomanagement.com

Krishna Rao (310) 288-8000
www.paradigmagency.com

Jeff Ravitz (818) 786-3500 / (818) 681-1495
(High Def) FAX (818) 786-3501
www.visualterrain.net

Ossi Rawi (310) 285-0303
www.marshbest.com

Richard Rawlings (310) 822-9113
www.murthaagency.com

Richard Reens (818) 906-0006
www.thedirectorsnetwork.com

Larry Reibman (310) 376-0673 / (310) 251-2956
(Film & High Def)

Neil Reichline (818) 342-3664 / (818) 400-1014
(Action Sports, Film & High Def) neilreichline.zenfolio.com

Manfred Reiff (310) 401-3211
(Film & High Def) www.manfredreiff.com

Tami Reiker (310) 474-4585
www.dattnerdispoto.com

Gosta Reiland (310) 395-9550
www.skouras.com

Marc Reshovsky (818) 753-6300
www.themackagency.net

William Rexer II (310) 395-9550
(Film & High Def) www.skouras.com

Ria Images (323) 876-2761 / (213) 448-8545
7440 Palo Vista Dr. FAX (323) 876-4666
Los Angeles, CA 90046 www.btlartists.com
(Reps for Directors of Photography)

Robert Richardson (310) 395-9550
www.skouras.com

Ross Richardson (310) 395-9550
(Film & High Def) www.skouras.com

Bob Richman (323) 460-4767
(Film & High Def) www.jacobandkoleagency.com

Anthony Richmond (310) 273-6700
(Film & High Def) www.utaproduction.com

Tom Richmond (310) 273-6700
(Film & High Def) www.utaproduction.com

Rene Richter (323) 845-4144
www.montanartists.com

Jan Richter-Friis (310) 474-4585
(Film) www.dattnerdispoto.com

Lisa Rinzler (310) 274-6611
www.gershagency.com

Heimo Ritzinger (818) 906-0006
www.tdnartists.com

Neil Roach (323) 460-4767
www.jacobandkoleagency.com

Timm Roarke (323) 460-4767
www.jacobandkoleagency.com

Eric Robbins (310) 401-3211
www.jeannineangelique.com

Jim Roberson (323) 856-3000
(Film & High Def) www.thegelleragency.com

Eliot Rockett (323) 856-3000
(Film & High Def) www.thegelleragency.com

Bill Roe (310) 822-9113
www.murthaagency.com

Glenn Roland (310) 475-0937
(Aerial, Film, High Def & Special FX) FAX (310) 475-0939
www.glennrolandfilms.com

Serge Roman (323) 876-2761 / (213) 448-8545
www.btlartists.com

Pete Romano (310) 301-8187 / (310) 282-9940
(Underwater) FAX (310) 301-3065

Charles Rose (310) 251-9931 / (310) 657-6840
(Film & High Def) FAX (310) 657-6840

Jamie Rosenberg (917) 566-7705 / (866) 625-7050
www.tdnartists.com
(Action Sports, Aerial, Film, High Def, Remote Heads & Special FX)

Jim Rosenthal (818) 252-1010
(Film & High Def) FAX (818) 252-1070

Chuck Rosher (310) 788-0684 / (818) 298-1999
(Film & High Def) www.oraclecreative.com

Pierre Rouger (310) 474-4585
www.dattnerdispoto.com

Philippe Rousselot (310) 274-6611
www.gershagency.com

Andrew Rowlands (818) 222-5200
www.schneiderentertainment.com

Mauricio Rubinstein (323) 460-4767
www.jacobandkoleagency.com

David Rudd (323) 845-4144 / (310) 573-9080
FAX (310) 573-1511
www.directorofphoto.com
(Film, High Def, Remote Heads & Second Unit)

Martin Ruhe (310) 474-4585
www.dattnerdispoto.com

Danny Ruhlmann (310) 474-4585
www.dattnerdispoto.com

Manel Ruiz (310) 474-4585
www.dattnerdispoto.com

Juan Ruiz-Anchia (310) 274-6611
www.gershagency.com

Ruben Fernandez Russ (323) 460-4767
www.jacobandkoleagency.com

Richard Rutkowski (323) 460-4767
(212) 732-9331
(Film & High Def) www.360d.com/rr

Nic Sadler (323) 460-4767
(Film & High Def) www.nicsadler.com

Mehran Salamati (818) 780-2708
(310) 455-7201
(Film & High Def) FAX (818) 989-5408
www.hotgears.com

Gilbert Salas (310) 314-2606
www.stacycheriffagency.com

Andres Sanchez (310) 683-0709
www.andresdp.com
(Aerial, Film, High Def, Remote Heads & Second Unit)

Tony Sanders (714) 444-3000
(Film & High Def) FAX (714) 444-3001
www.sandersstudio.tv

Linus Sandgren (310) 395-9550
www.skouras.com

Adam Santelli (310) 401-3211
(Film & High Def) www.jeannineangelique.com

Matthew J. Santo (310) 395-9550
www.skouras.com

Peter Santoro (818) 326-8548
(818) 769-7688
(Film & High Def) FAX (818) 985-8131

Germano Saracco (310) 463-8538
(Film & High Def) www.germanosaracco.com

Isi Sarfati (310) 282-9940
www.mirisch.com

Chris Sargent (310) 395-9550
www.skouras.com

Kevin Sarnoff (310) 413-9293
www.kevinsarnoff.com

Harris Savides (310) 395-9550
(Film & High Def) www.skouras.com

Malik H. Sayeed (310) 474-4585
www.dattnerdispoto.com

Giorgio Scali (310) 248-2000
(Film & High Def)

Richard Schaefer (714) 508-9700
www.lightingcameraman.com

Tobias Schliessler (310) 395-9550
www.skouras.com

Rohn Schmidt (310) 288-8000
www.paradigmagency.com

Dan Schmit (310) 860-9100
(Film & High Def) FAX (310) 860-9111

Greg Schmitt (323) 463-0022
www.radiantartists.com

The Schneider Entertainment Agency (818) 222-5200
22287 Mulholland Hwy, Ste. 210 FAX (818) 222-5284
Calabasas, CA 91302
www.schneiderentertainment.com
(Reps for Directors of Photography)

Aaron Schneider (310) 656-5151
www.innovativeartists.com

Megan Schoenbachler (323) 468-2240
(Film) www.nyoffice.net

Nancy Schreiber (323) 845-4144
(Film & High Def) www.montanartists.com

Frederick Schroeder (310) 288-8000
www.paradigmagency.com

Mark Schulze (619) 644-3000
(800) 365-8433
(Action Sports, High Def & Underwater) FAX (619) 644-3001
www.crystalpyramid.com

Samantha Schutz (323) 468-2240
www.nyoffice.net

Philip D. Schwartz (310) 260-6424
(310) 699-2980
www.watchreels.com/philipschwartz
(Film, High Def, Remote Heads & Second Unit)

John Schwartzman (310) 822-9113
www.murthaagency.com

Lawrence Schweich (213) 215-3191
(Film & High Def) www.lawrenceschweich.com

Carlo Scialla (909) 399-0200
(212) 564-7892
FAX (212) 564-7849
www.sradp.com
(Film, High Def, Special FX & Underwater)

Richard Scudder (323) 252-0966
(Second Unit) www.richardscudder.com

John Seale (310) 822-9113
www.murthaagency.com

Robert Seaman (818) 206-0144
www.allcrewagency.com

Christian Sebaldt (818) 265-4040
(Film) www.shortstackfilmworks.com

Andrzej Sekula (310) 274-6611
www.gershagency.com

Peter Selesnick (323) 460-4767
(Film & High Def) www.jacobandkoleagency.com

Randolph Sellars (818) 249-1247
(503) 231-0194
(Film & High Def)

Ken Seng (310) 274-6611
(718) 755-7100
(Film, High Def & Underwater) www.gershagency.com

Ben Seresin (310) 395-9550
www.skouras.com

Michael Seresin (310) 395-9550
www.skouras.com

Edwardo Serra (310) 273-6700
(Film & High Def) www.utaproduction.com

Sesler & Company (310) 966-4005
(416) 504-1223
11840 Jefferson Blvd. FAX (323) 988-0930
Culver City, CA 90230 www.seslercompany.com
(Reps for Directors of Photography)

Jamie Sewell (323) 460-4767
www.jacobandkoleagency.com

Byron Shah (310) 274-6611
www.gershagency.com

Afshin Shahidi (310) 401-3211
(Film & High Def) www.jeannineangelique.com

Neil Shapiro (310) 395-9550
www.skouras.com

John Sharaf (310) 451-4048
(310) 650-6996
(Film & High Def) FAX (310) 454-6768
www.sharaf.net

Bill Sheehy (310) 546-1085

Sheldon Prosnit Agency (310) 652-8778
800 S. Robertson Blvd., Ste. 6 FAX (310) 652-8772
Los Angeles, CA 90035 www.lspagency.net
(Reps for Directors of Photography)

Jas Shelton (310) 652-8778
www.lspagency.net

Lawrence Sher (818) 284-6423
www.italentco.com

Stephen Sheridan (310) 282-9940
(Film & High Def) www.mirisch.com

Therese Sherman (818) 729-9000
(818) 402-0706
www.explodedviewla.com

Andrew Shulkind (310) 282-9940
www.andrewshulkind.com
(Film, High Def, Remote Heads, Second Unit, Special FX, Steadicam & Underwater)

Sidney Sidell (310) 652-8778
(661) 799-8560
(Film & High Def) FAX (661) 799-8570
www.innovativeartists.com

Matthew J. Siegel (310) 722-8872
www.siegeldp.com
(Film, High Def, Second Unit & Special FX)

Newton Thomas Sigel (310) 474-4585
(Film & High Def) www.dattnerdispoto.com

Josh Silfen (323) 468-2240
www.nyoffice.net

Michael Simmonds (310) 652-8778
www.lspagency.net

John Simmons (818) 753-6300
(Film & High Def) www.themackagency.net

Geoffrey Simpson (310) 822-9113
www.murthaagency.com

Patrick Simpson (818) 753-6300
(Film & High Def) www.themackagency.net

Santosh Sivan (310) 288-8000
www.paradigmagency.com

Harold Skinner (818) 516-1766
(Film & High Def) www.hjskinner.com

The Skouras Agency (310) 395-9550
1149 Third St., Third Fl. FAX (310) 395-4295
Santa Monica, CA 90403 www.skouras.com
(Reps for Directors of Photography)

G. John Slagle (310) 514-3233
(310) 892-6447
(Film & High Def) FAX (310) 514-1545
www.slaglevideo.com

Deirdre Slevin (323) 845-4144
www.montanartists.com

Adam Sliwinski (818) 206-0144
www.allcrewagency.com

Michael Slovis (323) 856-3000
(Film & High Def) www.thegelleragency.com

Don Matthew Smith (510) 658-1604
(Film & High Def) www.jacobandkoleagency.com

Larry Smith (310) 395-9550
www.skouras.com

Noah David Smith (917) 882-9127
(818) 906-0006
www.noahdavidsmith.com

Steven Douglas Smith (888) 345-6464
(310) 401-3211
(Film & High Def) www.directorofphotography.org

Troy Smith (818) 222-5200
www.schneiderentertainment.com

Ben Smithard (310) 474-4585
www.dattnerdispoto.com

Peter Smokler (310) 230-4325
(310) 962-2506
(Film & High Def) FAX (310) 459-4625
www.chimponachain.com/Smokler12-271.mov

Reed Smoot (310) 314-2606
www.stacycheriffagency.com

Jim Sofranko (845) 657-2099
(323) 468-2240
(Film) FAX (845) 657-5876
www.nyoffice.net

Bing Sokolsky (818) 769-9154
(Film & High Def) FAX (818) 769-2950
www.bingsokolsky.com

Eduardo Martinez Solares (310) 652-8778
www.lspagency.net

Paul Sommers (818) 542-3016
(213) 400-8693
www.paulsommers.com

Todd Antonio Somodevilla (323) 463-0022
(Film & High Def) www.radiantartists.com

Christopher Soos (323) 463-0022
(Film & High Def) www.radiantartists.com

Peter Sova (310) 656-5151
(Film & High Def) www.innovativeartists.com

Glynn Speeckaert (310) 474-4585
www.dattnerdispoto.com

Dante Spinotti (310) 822-9113
www.murthaagency.com

Stephen St. John (310) 474-4585
www.dattnerdispoto.com

Terry Stacey (310) 273-6700
(Film & High Def) www.utaproduction.com

Stacy Cheriff Agency (310) 314-2606
10923 Ayres Ave. www.stacycheriffagency.com
Los Angeles, CA 90064
(Reps for Directors of Photography)

Florian Stadler (323) 377-2242
(310) 314-2606
(Film & High Def) www.florianstadler.com

John Stanier (310) 395-9550
(Film & High Def) www.skouras.com

Brendan Steacy (310) 966-4005
www.seslercompany.com

Robert Steadman (310) 459-0083
FAX (310) 459-5415

Ueli Steiger (310) 458-7800
(Film) www.partos.com

Henrik Stenberg (310) 474-4585
www.dattnerdispoto.com

David P. Stern (818) 788-7876
(818) 907-7012

Susan Stitt (310) 652-8778
www.lspagency.net

David Stockton (310) 474-4585
www.dattnerdispoto.com

Rogier Stoffers (323) 460-4767
(Film & High Def) www.jacobandkoleagency.com

John Stokes (310) 822-9113
www.murthaagency.com

Dan Stoloff (310) 288-8000
(Film & High Def) www.paradigmagency.com

Ivan Strasburg (310) 652-8778
www.lspagency.net

Daryl Studebaker (323) 363-5491
(Film & High Def)

David G. Stump (323) 650-5662
(Film, High Def & Visual FX) FAX (323) 650-5663

Vladimir Subotic (323) 468-2240
www.nyoffice.net

Tim Suhrstedt (310) 656-5151
www.innovativeartists.com

Bruce Surtees (310) 274-6611
www.gershagency.com

Peter Suschitzky (310) 395-9550
www.skouras.com

Darko Suvak (310) 273-6700
(Film & High Def) www.utaproduction.com

Suzanna Camejo & Associates/ Artists For The Environment (310) 479-4470
(Reps for Directors of Photography)

Brian Sweeney (661) 257-4371
(661) 713-4371
(Film & High Def) FAX (661) 257-8905

Rob Sweeney (310) 288-8000
www.paradigmagency.com

Eric Swenson (888) 965-4321
(Film & High Def) FAX (888) 965-4321
www.ericvfx.com

Jeremy Sykes (619) 435-0888
(Film & High Def) www.sykesfilm-tv.com

Hubert Taczanowski (310) 288-8000
www.paradigmagency.com

Yasu Tanida (310) 822-9113
www.murthaagency.com

Gabor Tarko (310) 314-2606
www.stacycheriffagency.com

Gale Tattersall (323) 845-4144
(Film & High Def) www.montanartists.com

Jonathan Taylor (310) 652-8778
www.lspagency.net

Nick Taylor (626) 201-9901
(323) 460-4767
www.jacobandkoleagency.com
(Aerial, Film, High Def, Remote Heads & Second Unit)

Rodney Taylor (310) 474-4585
(Film & High Def) www.dattnerdispoto.com

TDN Artists (818) 906-0006
3685 Motor Ave., Ste. 220 FAX (818) 301-2224
Los Angeles, CA 90034 www.tdnartists.com
(Reps for Directors of Photography)

Marten Tedin (310) 395-9550
(Film & High Def) www.skouras.com

Manuel Teran (310) 285-0303
www.marshbest.com

Gary Thieltges (323) 668-2331
(818) 845-8470
(Film & High Def) FAX (818) 845-8477
www.doggicam.com

Simon Thirlaway (310) 652-8778
www.lspagency.net

John Thomas (310) 656-5151
www.innovativeartists.com

Mike Thomas (714) 761-4163

Don Thorin (310) 288-8000
www.paradigmagency.com

Rich Thorne (323) 856-3000
www.thegelleragency.com

Romeo Tirone (310) 288-8000
(Film & High Def) www.paradigmagency.com

Peter Tischhauser (310) 314-2606
(323) 822-0793
FAX (323) 822-0793
www.stacycheriffagency.com

John Toll (310) 822-9113
www.murthaagency.com

Salvatore Totino (310) 395-9550
www.skouras.com

Luciano Tovoli (323) 460-4767
www.jacobandkoleagency.com

Eric Treml (310) 474-4585
(Film & High Def) www.dattnerdispoto.com

Massimiliano Trevis (310) 288-8000
www.paradigmagency.com

Sergey Trofimov (310) 288-8000
www.paradigmagency.com

Wyatt Troll (310) 474-4585
www.dattnerdispoto.com

Chris Tufty (323) 222-3302
(213) 713-4534
FAX (323) 222-3306
www.christufty.com
(Film, High Def, Remote Heads & Second Unit)

Andrew Turman (310) 395-9550
(310) 962-6287
(Film, High Def, Remote Heads & Special FX)

Kasper Tuxen (310) 652-8778
www.lspagency.net

Franck Tymezuk (310) 458-7800
www.partos.com

Matt Uhry (310) 401-3211
(Film & High Def) www.jeannineangelique.com

David Ungaro (310) 652-8778
www.lspagency.net

United Talent Agency (310) 273-6700
9560 Wilshire Blvd., Ste. 500 FAX (310) 247-1111
Beverly Hills, CA 90212 www.utaproduction.com
(Reps for Directors of Photography)

Jordan Valenti (310) 652-8778
(Film & High Def) www.lspagency.net

Sean Valentini (310) 966-4005
www.seslercompany.com

Stephane Vallee (310) 458-7800
www.partos.com

Theo Van de Sande (310) 288-8000
(Film & High Def) www.paradigmagency.com

Brett Van Dyke (310) 966-4005
www.seslercompany.com

Joost van Gelder (310) 273-6700
www.unitedtalent.com

Hoyte Van Hoytema (310) 273-6700
www.unitedtalent.com

Joost Van Starrenburg (323) 460-4767
(Film & High Def) www.jacobandkoleagency.com

Riego Van Wersch (323) 460-4767
www.jacobandkoleagency.com

Checco Varese (917) 559-4276
(310) 273-6700
(Film & High Def) www.checcovarese.com

Mark Vargo (310) 288-8000
www.paradigmagency.com

Sonnel Velazquez (310) 401-3211
www.jeannineangelique.com

Jan Velicky (310) 273-6700
www.utaproduction.com

Billy Velten (818) 906-0006
(Film & High Def) www.tdnartists.com

Jeffrey Venditti (310) 656-5151
(310) 663-7677
(Film & High Def) FAX (310) 656-5156
www.jeffvenditti.com

Steven Vernon (310) 617-6813
(818) 753-6300
(Film & High Def) FAX (310) 338-9725
www.themackagency.net

Carlos Veron (310) 395-9550
www.skouras.com

Rey Villalobos (310) 656-5151
www.innovativeartists.com

Amy Vincent (310) 288-8000
(Film & High Def) www.paradigmagency.com

Lyle Vincent (310) 822-9113
www.murthaagency.com

Tuomo Virtanen (310) 458-7800
www.partos.com

Stefan von Bjorn (323) 478-1500
(323) 363-7711
(Film & High Def) FAX (323) 478-1554
www.stefanvonbjorn.com

Wedigo Von Schultzendorff (310) 395-9550
www.skouras.com

Christos Voudouris (323) 468-2240
(Film) www.nyoffice.net

Steven Wacks (323) 633-1000
FAX (323) 934-3491
www.twelvetoneproductions.com

Thaddeus Wadleigh (310) 455-0633
(Film & High Def) www.films-and-hi-def.com

William Wages (310) 656-5151
www.innovativeartists.com

David Wagreich (310) 652-8778
(Film & High Def) www.lspagency.net

David Waldman (323) 841-9253
(Film & High Def) www.david-waldman.com

Rick Walker (818) 993-1099
(Film & High Def) FAX (818) 993-0062

Garry Waller (805) 217-7141
(Film & High Def) www.murthaagency.com

Chris Walling (323) 856-3000
(Film & High Def) www.thegelleragency.com

Derek Wan (323) 788-3883
(Film & High Def) FAX (323) 780-8887
www.allinone-usa.com

Kevin Ward (818) 701-7676
(Film & High Def) www.shoottothrill.net

Vincent Warin (310) 395-9550
www.skouras.com

Pete Warrilow (818) 888-6100
(Film & High Def) www.petewarrilow.com

David Waterston (310) 474-4585
(Film & High Def) www.dwaterston.com

Colin Watkinson (310) 401-3211
www.colinwatkinson.com

William Webb (818) 284-6423
www.italentco.com

Curtis Wehr (310) 656-5151
(Film & High Def) www.innovativeartists.com

Mark Weingartner (818) 222-5200
www.schneiderentertainment.com

Byron Werner (310) 401-3211
www.jeannineangelique.com

Clay Westervelt (818) 990-8993
(Film & High Def) www.ambitiousent.com

Tony Westman (310) 656-5151
www.innovativeartists.com

Haskell Wexler (310) 395-9550
(310) 395-0090
FAX (310) 458-6768

Howard Wexler (310) 396-3416 / (310) 880-2219
(Film & High Def) FAX (310) 452-1466
www.howardwexler.com

Julian Whatley (310) 474-4585
(Film & High Def) www.dattnerdispoto.com

James Whitaker (310) 395-9550
www.skouras.com

Nicole Hirsch Whitaker (323) 463-0022
(Film & High Def) www.radiantartists.com

Joseph White (323) 856-3000
www.thegelleragency.com

Tristan Whitman (818) 906-0006
www.tdnartists.com

Kenneth Wiatrak (818) 985-1582 / (818) 425-8310
(Film, High Def & Visual FX) FAX (818) 766-4584
www.wiatrak.us

Jo Willems (310) 474-4585
(Film & High Def) www.dattnerdispoto.com

Mark Williams (310) 474-4585
www.dattnerdispoto.com

Matthew Williams (818) 550-8227 / (818) 590-4528
(Film & High Def) FAX (818) 843-6850
www.williamsdp.com

David Wilson (323) 463-0022
www.radiantartists.com

Nathan Wilson (310) 401-3211
(Film & High Def) www.jeannineangelique.com

Scott Winig (310) 458-7800
www.partos.com

Nicholas Wise (323) 468-2240
www.nyoffice.net

Alexander Witt (310) 822-9113
www.murthaagency.com

Anthony Wolberg (310) 395-9550 / (718) 643-0017
(Film & High Def) www.skouras.com

Dariusz Wolski (310) 395-9550
www.skouras.com

Michael Wood (310) 395-9550
www.skouras.com

Oliver Wood (310) 822-9113
www.murthaagency.com

Mark Woods (818) 206-0144 / (626) 826-6314
(Film & High Def) www.markwoods.com

Ian Woolston-Smith (203) 470-3885 / (310) 402-5130
www.iancam.com
(Aerial, Film, High Def, Remote Heads, Second Unit & Steadicam)

Joseph Yacoe (818) 753-6300
(Film & High Def) www.themackagency.net

Yoshikatsu Yasaki (310) 458-7800
www.partos.com

Steve Yedlin (310) 656-5151
(Film & High Def) www.innovativeartists.com

Robert D. Yeoman (310) 822-9113
www.murthaagency.com

Gary Young (818) 206-0144
www.allcrewagency.com

Alexis Zabe (310) 652-8778
www.lspagency.net

Haris Zambarloukos (310) 273-6700
www.unitedtalent.com

Peter Zeitlinger (310) 652-8778
www.lspagency.net

Massimo Zeri (310) 827-4305 / (310) 869-0831
www.massimozeri.com

John Zilles (310) 474-4585
(Film & High Def) www.dattnerdispoto.com

Eric Zimmerman (818) 753-6300 / (310) 849-1948
c/o The Mack Agency www.themackagency.net

Joe Zizzo (310) 395-9550
(Film & High Def) www.skouras.com

Jake Zortman (310) 779-8655
(Film & High Def) www.jakezortman.com

Vilmos Zsigmond (818) 753-6300
(Film & High Def) www.themackagency.net

Pete Zuccarini (310) 274-6611
www.gershagency.com

Kenneth Zunder (310) 288-8000
www.paradigmagency.com

Anthony Adler (323) 856-3000
www.thegelleragency.com

All Crew Agency (818) 206-0144
2920 W. Olive Ave., Ste. 201 FAX (818) 206-0169
Burbank, CA 91505 www.allcrewagency.com
(Reps for First Assistant Directors)

Benita Allen (310) 652-8778
www.lspagency.net

Bryan Altham (818) 990-0070
(818) 391-3678
www.quitbotheringme.com

Todd Amateau (310) 652-8778
www.lspagency.net

Emie H. Amemiya (323) 463-3033

Roger Barth (310) 877-3063

Mike Bell (818) 929-0475
www.mikebell.tv

Brian Bender (323) 876-3030
(415) 699-6200
FAX (415) 504-6603

Anne Berger (310) 399-4435
(Spanish) (310) 430-4591
FAX (310) 399-4435

Christopher A. Berger (310) 394-8041
(310) 502-2446

Lee Blaine (626) 808-9760
(310) 428-4420
FAX (626) 798-8074
www.leeblaine.com

Jason Blumenfeld (310) 435-3547

Craig Borden (323) 856-3000
www.thegelleragency.com

Kevin Brady (310) 937-8955
(310) 502-9099
FAX (310) 937-7025

J. Stephen Buck (760) 402-5199
(760) 944-8596

Thomas McAuley Burke (310) 239-0761

Jim Burnett (505) 897-4126
(310) 418-3020
FAX (505) 897-4776

Patrick Burns (818) 908-3361

Todd Burrows (818) 437-0015

Nelson Cabrera (310) 699-3133

John Callas (310) 393-4519
(310) 344-5334
FAX (310) 395-4412

Cole Campbell (626) 893-6242

Lisa Campbell-Demaine (323) 650-4817
(818) 404-1914

Steve Carmendy (310) 829-9207
(310) 463-4874

Randy Carter (818) 242-4088
(818) 206-0144
www.allcrewagency.com/home/talent.php5?id=2

John Castor (323) 225-3392
(323) 646-7953

Jonathan Chambers (904) 982-7711
(310) 736-6597
FAX (904) 620-9272
www.jonathanchambers.net

Brent Clark (805) 512-6601
FAX (805) 652-1941

Audrey S. Cohen (310) 208-6776
(305) 385-2204
FAX (310) 208-6776

Tom Cooney (818) 705-2619
(818) 929-1234
FAX (818) 343-6746

Dave Darmour (310) 393-9004 / (323) 363-3930

Trent De Haan (310) 822-8989 / (310) 729-7979

Joel DeLoach (323) 436-7433

Theodore de Rose (310) 980-3854 / 66 (0) 81395 8046
www.imdb.com/name/nm1282830/

Steve Dietrich (818) 760-2915 / (818) 422-3470
FAX (818) 980-2028

Michael J. Dill-Cruz (310) 980-9221 / (310) 707-6659
FAX (310) 980-9221

Paul DiStefano (818) 753-9753

Bob Donaldson (323) 856-3000
www.thegelleragency.com

Brian Donnelly (310) 880-9400

A **Gary Dorf** (310) 476-8380
FAX (818) 789-6435

Dale Dreher (323) 777-3410 / (310) 600-5020
www.hazardtown.com

Larry Droguett (206) 979-7724
FAX (818) 755-4504

Alan Edmisten (310) 379-4015

Jodi Ehrlich (323) 462-3456
(French)

Brian J. Ellis (818) 206-0144
FAX (818) 206-0169
www.allcrewagency.com

Sergio Ercolessi (310) 652-8778
www.lspagency.net

Luc Etienne (310) 273-6700
www.unitedtalent.com

Leslie M. Evers (310) 600-7373

Tom Fauntleroy (805) 898-1035 / (805) 570-8320

Jim Feyereisen (310) 877-1112
FAX (310) 999-6535

James J. Fitzpatrick (818) 506-8051
FAX (818) 506-1710

Richard Fox (323) 856-3000
www.thegelleragency.com

Ruth Frazier (818) 848-9129 / (818) 288-0815
FAX (818) 558-5772

Bruce Fritzberg (323) 822-7881 / (818) 231-2260

Walter Gasparovic (310) 273-6700
www.utaproduction.com

Kent Gates (661) 294-8694 / (818) 667-5368
www.freewebtown.com/callsheet/

The Geller Agency (323) 856-3000
1547 Cassil Pl.
FAX (323) 856-3009
Hollywood, CA 90028
www.thegelleragency.com
(Reps for First Assistant Directors)

Ken Gilbert (805) 374-6090 / (805) 208-1753

Frank Glenn (310) 822-9496 / (310) 963-0645

Cellin Gluck (310) 454-5594 / (310) 382-0303
FAX (310) 496-3046

Stephen Goepel (818) 781-7025 / (818) 404-7570

Marty Gold (818) 892-3665

Travis A. Gold (818) 968-3653

Tim Goldberg (310) 877-1081 / (310) 450-1220
FAX (310) 319-1392
www.oceanparkpix.com

Rosser Goodman (818) 519-9575 / (818) 206-0144
www.kgbfilms.com

Tommy Gormley (310) 273-6700
www.utaproduction.com

Janice K. Goto (415) 990-4470 / (415) 383-1225

James Grasso (310) 455-7169

Michael Gray (805) 558-6671

Cherie R. Hankal (310) 720-6385

Mark Hansson (323) 665-7718 / (323) 646-0402
FAX (323) 665-3080

Sam Harris (818) 206-0144
www.allcrewagency.com

J. Michael Haynie (805) 443-7118

Jonathan Haze (818) 763-3041 / (818) 314-7997
FAX (818) 763-3042

Rafael C. Herrera (310) 221-3456
FAX (818) 785-2663

Carol Lang Herrick (805) 496-0249 / (206) 232-7100

Glen A. Hettinger (661) 255-0953 / (661) 400-4577
www.glenhettinger.com

Bill Hoyt (818) 389-8341 / (818) 488-1271

Wickham Irwin (818) 489-5212 / (818) 889-7733

C. Hardy James (503) 702-3544 / (310) 472-4734
FAX (503) 824-2751

Jeff January (323) 856-3000
www.thegelleragency.com

Scott Javine (818) 645-2808

Michael A. Kahler (310) 938-2938

Doron Kauper (818) 907-6028
FAX (818) 804-5121
www.wrappersystems.com

Thomas A. Keith (818) 754-1357
(213) 300-9451

Jack Kelly (310) 375-7423
(310) 683-8585
FAX (310) 347-4028

Jay Kelman (310) 390-4747
(310) 386-0098

Michael Klick (310) 204-2986
(310) 720-2986
FAX (310) 204-5155

Ned Kopp (323) 467-1817
(415) 467-1817

Erwin Kramer (310) 446-1866
(310) 266-8146
FAX (310) 446-1856
www.erwinkramer.com

Coni Lancaster (310) 823-3115
(310) 749-8962
FAX (310) 823-8366

Rock Lane (310) 393-1997
(310) 480-3245
FAX (310) 393-8527

Rick Lange (310) 489-0033
(323) 851-8012
FAX (323) 851-6317

Roger La Page (818) 368-3243
(818) 468-7191
FAX (818) 368-3243

Bill Latka (310) 990-1938

Richard Levin (818) 206-0144
www.allcrewagency.com

Jeff Lewis (310) 717-1752

Ed Licht (818) 206-0144
www.allcrewagency.com

Jules Lichtman (310) 652-8778
www.lspagency.net

Josef Lieck (310) 652-8778
www.lspagency.net

Timothy Lonsdale (818) 206-0144
www.allcrewagency.com

Tim Lovekin (310) 344-6918

Sonny Lowe (310) 994-8097
(French)

Scott Luhrsen (323) 871-0201
(323) 791-1909
FAX (323) 871-0315

Earl Mann (818) 906-3309
(818) 371-1135

Gary Marcus (310) 273-6700
www.unitedtalent.com

John Marias (310) 394-4214
(310) 245-4204
FAX (310) 395-2590

Sandy Martin (323) 851-3755
(213) 509-7722
FAX (323) 851-4359

Richard Marvin (818) 563-2073
(213) 760-9204

Steve Marvin (505) 820-3334
(818) 563-2073
FAX (505) 820-3334

Bonnie Matchinga (323) 851-7623
(323) 851-5151
FAX (323) 851-9598

Eugene Mazzola (206) 499-8984
(626) 296-6943
www.eugenemazzola.com

Austin McCann (310) 456-6005

Kevin P. McCarthy (323) 782-3969
(323) 253-5319

Gregory McCollum (818) 952-5374
(818) 535-7794
FAX (818) 952-5379

Josh McLaglen (310) 273-6700
www.utaproduction.com

Peter Merwin (818) 618-6101
(818) 953-8920

Scott Metcalfe (805) 405-1590
(310) 823-2781

Liz T. Miles (310) 993-0022
web.mac.com/liztmiles/

Milos Milicevic (310) 273-6700
www.unitedtalent.com

Bobby Miller (949) 494-3263
FAX (949) 494-7945

Roger Mills (818) 242-0532

Leslie Miretti (310) 399-2000
FAX (310) 459-8484

Linda Montanti (310) 274-8898

Richard Muessel (310) 245-1990
FAX (323) 512-5374

Kieran Mullaney (818) 508-5979
(818) 903-9305

Justin Muller (310) 273-6700
www.utaproduction.com

Jack Nayer (310) 301-3020
(718) 622-5046
FAX (718) 636-9446

Steve Nemiroff (310) 473-4100
FAX (310) 473-4100

M. Margaret O'Brien-Sparks (818) 388-9726
(818) 997-1993
FAX (818) 997-1993

Robin Randal Oliver (323) 856-3000
www.thegelleragency.com

Princess O'Mahoney (818) 908-0098

Pamela O'Mara (310) 540-8411
(310) 901-5515
FAX (310) 545-0136

Paul Papanek (323) 732-0776

Randy Pearl (310) 989-7656

Julian Petrillo (323) 856-3000
www.thegelleragency.com

Thomas D. Phillips (818) 469-5322
FAX (888) 504-4339
www.phillipsnewmedia.com

Steven Pomeroy (323) 533-8714

Cynthia Potthast (323) 653-9801
(818) 359-1100

Bruce Pratt (310) 990-4286
(818) 222-4052
FAX (818) 222-4062

Jack Provost (818) 988-8150
FAX (818) 988-8152

Kari Rantala (805) 984-3468
(805) 469-6536
FAX (805) 984-3468

Ron Rapiel (310) 390-5454
(310) 890-1100

Rhonda L. Raulston (626) 695-8921

Jolyon Reese (818) 206-0144
www.allcrewagency.com

Randy Rennolds (818) 846-2334
FAX (818) 567-1123

Craig Respol (818) 346-4641
(310) 776-1229

Lynn Reynolds (323) 851-4662
(541) 601-7913
FAX (541) 552-0852
www.lynnreynolds.com

Jody Rosenthal (310) 317-0489
(310) 804-2684
FAX (310) 317-0420

Ethan Ross (310) 990-1655

Lisa Satriano (310) 273-6700
www.unitedtalent.com

James Sbardellati (818) 631-8459
FAX (818) 248-8459

Larry Schreiner (310) 874-2164

Robert Schultz (213) 500-7787

Marty Eli Schwartz (310) 273-6700
www.unitedtalent.com

Jan Scott (310) 833-1770

Jeffrey J. Scruton (310) 454-8290
FAX (310) 459-4051

Larry Serraino (661) 607-6528
FAX (661) 254-6402

Jerry Shanks (818) 506-0502
FAX (818) 506-0502

Jim Shippee (310) 480-5988

TK Shom (310) 652-8778
www.lspagency.net

Thom Sidoti (310) 600-6669
www.agavefilms.com

Scott Siegal (626) 794-7760
(213) 713-0154

Tim Silver (310) 739-7356
(310) 399-5122
(French)

Eric Siss (310) 628-7226

Al Smith (310) 452-3751
(310) 864-8550

Matthew D. Smith (310) 293-8747

Chris Soldo (310) 968-6877
(805) 969-7920

Jonathan Southard (323) 856-3000
www.thegelleragency.com

Marlon Staggs (323) 790-0440

Tony Steinberg (323) 856-3000
www.thegelleragency.com

Dan Steinbrocker (310) 410-1000
FAX (310) 410-0008

Brad Stevenson (213) 716-7893
(818) 222-8251

Kennedy Taylor (323) 253-4649
(Japanese)

Debby Timmons (818) 906-2093

Jeff Tuttle (626) 824-1222

Marc Vance (310) 890-2414

Christian Van Fleet (562) 577-7526

Pete Vanlaw (818) 762-3810
(818) 506-6977
FAX (818) 769-2847
www.western-branch.com

Jey Wada (323) 855-9595

Martin Walters (310) 273-6700
www.unitedtalent.com

John Warran (818) 951-7052
(818) 621-6662
FAX (818) 951-6057
www.johnwarran.com

Bobby Weinstein (310) 306-1960
FAX (310) 306-1820

Ree Whitford (818) 424-9988
(818) 505-1060

Rick Whiting (310) 392-6000
(415) 332-6462
(Spanish) FAX (415) 332-6462

David A. Wilson (818) 340-7576

Katarina Wittich (323) 221-1023
FAX (323) 276-0216

Ian Woolf (818) 704-4237
(818) 970-4237
FAX (818) 704-6706

Cyrus Yavneh (310) 823-1515
FAX (310) 823-7975

Don Yorkshire (818) 760-7474
(818) 632-7475
FAX (818) 760-7016

Raymond Zarro (310) 460-2424
FAX (310) 399-7614

Jack Ziga (323) 664-9862
(323) 465-9862

Joel R. Zimmerman (310) 399-9906
(310) 993-5703
www.joelzimmerman.com

Leslie Zurla (818) 762-4346
(818) 207-1743
FAX (818) 506-8483

Nir Adar (323) 937-1010
www.zenobia.com

Valerie Aikman-Smith (323) 463-9990
(323) 365-1994
FAX (323) 463-9991
www.valerieaikman-smith.com

Alphonse Culinary Engineer (562) 733 8954
(Food Stylist)

Shellie Anderson (818) 427-6168
(Food Stylist) www.shellieanderson.com

Alise Arato (323) 937-1010
www.zenobia.com

Associates James & Julia/ Julia Weinberg (310) 274-2383
1015 Gayley Ave., Ste. 210
Los Angeles, CA 90024
(Home Economist)
FAX (310) 821-0232
www.foodstylists.com

Oona Austin (323) 656-4452
(253) 549-2475
(Food Stylist) FAX (323) 656-4452

Carolyn L. Avelino (714) 532-6852
(714) 323-0173
FAX (714) 532-6853

Lisa Barnet (626) 376-5932
www.lisabarnet.com

Camille's (626) 202-5214
(626) 791-4081
(Food Stylist) FAX (866) 222-7760
www.camilleskitchen.com

Jean E. Carey (949) 509-4774
(Home Economist)

Debbie Castaldi (310) 503-7107
(310) 398-2375
FAX (310) 398-2375

Sienna DeGovia (323) 376-3762
(Food Stylist) www.siennacake.com

Paris DeJesus (951) 536-3374
(951) 780-1341

Marti DeLucia-Brown (714) 425-7492

Cheryl Dent (310) 251-2149
(Food Stylist & Home Economist) www.cheryldent.biz

B.J. Doerfling (818) 991-0581
(Food Stylist & Home Economist) FAX (818) 991-0581

Suzy Eaton (323) 937-1010
www.zenobia.com

Edible Style/Wendy Loring Blasdel (818) 507-5914
(818) 903-4483
FAX (818) 548-2557

Eleanor (323) 240-8482
(323) 342-0064
FAX (323) 441-8425
www.ebgraphicdesign.com/foodstyles

Elizabeth James & Associates, Inc. (949) 632-5410
FAX (562) 592-9412
www.foodstylists.com

Food Savvy Incorporated/ Andy Sheen-Turner (323) 333-0070
(Food Stylist) www.foodsavvywebsite.com

Kris Foreman (310) 277-4550
(310) 871-2642

Beth Fortune (310) 948-0631
www.bethfortune.com

Tobi Frank-Martin (310) 552-7921
(818) 667-7565
(Home Economist) FAX (818) 222-4385

Saba Gaziyani (323) 937-1010
www.zenobia.com

Gourmet Proppers, Ltd./ Bonnie Belknap (818) 566-4140
(Food Stylist) FAX (818) 563-2218
www.gourmetproppers.com

Victoria Granof (323) 937-1010
www.zenobia.com

Ronnda Hamilton (323) 251-6991
FAX (323) 512-5144

Alice M. Hart/Food for Film Stylists (323) 877-2376
www.foodforfilm.com

Jean Hodges/Showgrits (818) 567-2405
(Food Stylist) FAX (818) 567-0038
www.showgrits.com

Mark Holcomb (949) 215-7373
(Food Stylist) FAX (949) 215-7494
www.tastecateringcafe.com

Kimberly Huson (310) 396-2403
(310) 739-6664
FAX (310) 396-0683
www.stylefood.com

Johanna Lowe (310) 274-0032
www.artistsbytimothypriano.com

Maelle (323) 697-9763
(Food Stylist) www.maelle.com

Sylvia Marmolejo (323) 936-9893
(Food Stylist) FAX (323) 936-1503
www.smstyling.com

Deborah McLean (323) 937-1010
www.zenobia.com

Janet Miller (310) 670-0854
(310) 614-7179
(Home Economist) FAX (310) 670-0854
www.zenobia.com

Nathan Fong & Associates Culinary Film Design (818) 342-4222
(604) 685-1825
FAX (604) 685-1825
www.fongonfood.com

Esther Nieuwenhuis (323) 654-9840
(213) 713-5832

Marjorie Ohrnstein (323) 658-6144
(323) 573-9622
www.funfoodcatering.com

David Pogul (619) 283-8030
(Food Stylist)

Judy Peck Prindle (323) 939-7009
FAX (323) 939-4219

Carrie Ann Purcell (323) 937-1010
www.zenobia.com

Marina Rodríguez (310) 478-4738
(310) 948-0951

Carolyn Sato (310) 502-1391

David Shalleck/VOLOCHEF (415) 775-8552
(415) 713-1967
(Food Stylist)
FAX (415) 775-1140
www.volochef.com

Lorraine Shapiro (323) 653-8899
(Home Economist)
FAX (323) 653-8899

Susan Southcott (310) 390-0383
(310) 621-2232
FAX (310) 390-2343

Norman Stewart (310) 285-8361
www.zenobia.com

Denise Stillman (949) 496-4841
www.stylistforfood.com

Debi Halpert Storosh (310) 397-3300
(310) 890-0527
(Home Economist)

Jen Tauritz Gotch (323) 937-1010
www.zenobia.com

Helene Tsukasa (310) 477-7997
(310) 251-3180
(Food Stylist)

Yona Tulk (323) 939-7770
FAX (323) 939-7770

Patricia J. Winters (310) 286-2242
FAX (310) 286-2244

Zenobia Agency, Inc. (323) 937-1010
(888) 639-6917
130 S. Highland Ave.
Los Angeles, CA 90036
(Reps For Food Stylists)
FAX (323) 937-1133
www.zenobia.com

Victor Abbene (818) 700-1398
(310) 505-4212
FAX (818) 700-1319

David Adams (626) 224-3672
(626) 852-7810
(Electrician)

Steve Adams (310) 962-0935
(310) 398-2293

Richard Alarian (805) 207-9100

Karl Alexander (818) 307-9404
(818) 889-7206
FAX (818) 889-7668
www.karlalexanderbooks.com

Michael Ambrose (213) 598-8179
www.imdb.com/name/nm0003307/

Daniel Anaya (213) 446-0833

Ronald Anderson (520) 419-1490
(800) 577-9635
FAX (520) 623-3144
www.mistyproductionservice.com

Dean Andolsek (818) 785-5254
FAX (818) 785-5354
www.sideefxco.com

Daniele R. Benoit (818) 701-5404
www.unilux.com

Norm Berens (310) 376-1853
(310) 936-3830
FAX (310) 376-2981

Bjorn Boisen (310) 261-4751

Randall Burak (818) 363-3305
(818) 599-5121
FAX (818) 363-3305

Russell Caldwell (310) 463-7431
FAX (818) 474-7016

Joseph W. Calloway (626) 798-8222
(626) 827-7331
(Lighting Designer & Lighting Director) FAX (626) 798-4577
www.callowayfilms.com

Dwight D. Campbell (818) 957-6180
(818) 419-6532

Brett Carleton (323) 997-0202
FAX (323) 417-4915
www.brettcarleton.com

Glenn Corbett (818) 424-1396
(Gaffer) FAX (877) 576-1099

Doug Dale (805) 584-1240
(805) 377-6042
FAX (805) 584-1240

JoAnn Day (661) 943-8020
(818) 281-5854
www.chinditinc.net

David Devlin (212) 439-1106
(213) 368-4660
FAX (310) 496-2789
www.daviddevlin.com

Rob Doumitt (213) 952-8243

Jack English (818) 645-6046
(Gaffer)

Christian Epps (323) 632-5632
(Lighting Designer & Lighting Director) www.in2light.tv

Joly Erickson (818) 701-1963

Jerry Feldman (818) 219-1806
www.jerryfeldmandp.com

Tom Feldman (818) 790-7069
(Lighting Director) FAX (818) 790-6521
www.tomfeldman.com

Richard Foley (818) 729-9000
(818) 402-0707
FAX (818) 729-9033
www.explodedviewla.com

John Gilmour (805) 485-7067
(805) 901-9817

Randy Glass (949) 498-4956
(949) 697-1484
FAX (949) 492-6256

William R. Glasscock (818) 340-7788
(818) 903-7788
(Gaffer) FAX (818) 655-8390

Norm Glasser (805) 492-6006
FAX (805) 492-1006

Mark Goodwin (805) 499-7040
(818) 414-6699
FAX (805) 499-7078

Barry Gross (323) 646-8914

Ted Hayash (818) 653-5786
www.tedhayash.com

Rick Heebner (818) 606-4322

Myron Hyman (661) 510-8457

Robert Jason (310) 612-3471
FAX (310) 542-4193

Joe Jorden (818) 789-1499
(818) 517-0990

Irv Katz (310) 399-5985

Michael Wm. Katz (310) 396-9387
www.imdb.com/name/nm0441797/

Kevin Kelley (818) 535-7169

Greg Kendrick (949) 588-7822
(714) 381-0100
FAX (949) 588-7922
www.waywest.tv

Larry Kennedy (310) 378-0039
(310) 486-0882
FAX (310) 378-1269

Len Levine (310) 663-1359

Chris Lewis (818) 897-4392
(818) 517-4162
FAX (818) 897-3554
(Gaffer, Lighting Designer & Lighting Director)

Brad Lipson (818) 355-7157

Geordie MacDonald (818) 784-2871
(818) 425-3551

Mel Maxwell (818) 762-3032

Tim McArdle (818) 368-8143
(818) 414-2367
(Lighting Director) FAX (818) 368-8143

Rob McCarthy (661) 254-7470
(661) 609-2034
(Gaffer & Lighting Director) FAX (661) 254-1454

Jim McEachen (805) 640-7200
(310) 709-4705

Jeff McGrath (310) 545-1532
(310) 567-1023
FAX (310) 374-1639

Alan McKay (818) 848-5470

Charles A. McNamara (323) 839-5949
(973) 204-7002
web.mac.com/charliemcnamara

Patrick Melly (310) 398-7082
(310) 488-1299
FAX (310) 398-7182

David Morton (661) 296-9070

Tim Morton (818) 941-5053
(817) 681-1309
(Gaffer, Lighting Designer & Lighting Director)

Kevin Mulvey (818) 753-4883
(818) 516-4606
FAX (818) 753-0181
www.light-shapes.com
(Gaffer, Lighting Designer & Lighting Director)

Patrick M. Murray (818) 632-6320
(Gaffer)

Michael Off (818) 679-9332
(800) 508-8020
FAX (818) 848-6934
(Gaffer, Lighting Designer & Lighting Director)

Bruce Olinder (310) 838-2111
FAX (310) 838-3033

Gustavo Oliva (310) 717-3790

Michael Palmer (310) 489-6453
FAX (562) 925-4872

Aldo Parenti (323) 988-0738
(Lighting Design) FAX (323) 988-0738
www.parentiproductions.com

Michael Parsons (310) 753-7040
FAX (310) 837-1211

Tim Phelps (619) 250-7829
(619) 691-0556
FAX (213) 625-0174
(Gaffer, Lighting Designer & Lighting Director)

Rudy Pohlert (818) 222-7462
(818) 458-1066
FAX (818) 225-0499

Raman N. Rao (310) 365-6955
(Gaffer & Lighting Director)

Jeff Ravitz (818) 786-3500
(818) 681-1495
(Lighting Designer) FAX (818) 786-3501
www.visualterrain.net

Gerald A. Rhodes (661) 252-6358
(661) 803-0869
www.jeryrig.com

John C. Rogers (310) 376-4223
(310) 993-5768

Karen Roseme (760) 935-4086
(323) 697-8382
FAX (760) 935-4086

Jim Rosenthal (818) 252-1010
FAX (818) 252-1070

Andrea Sachs (818) 497-5777

Brad Sargent (818) 398-0864
(Electrician, Gaffer & Lighting Director)

Roger Sassen (818) 348-5909
(818) 429-2413
FAX (818) 702-0689

A. Iggy Scarpitti (323) 653-0802
(323) 810-7878
FAX (323) 651-9383

Bill Silic (818) 898-1550
(805) 559-4525
FAX (818) 898-1552

Harold Skinner (818) 516-1766
www.hjskinner.com

Alex Skvorzov (661) 254-9043
(818) 359-0900
FAX (661) 254-8395

Scott A. Spencer (818) 674-2132
FAX (805) 578-6074

Stuart Spohn (626) 254-0570

Gary Tandrow (818) 762-8943
(818) 915-6818
FAX (818) 762-2190

JT Teiper (760) 505-1605
(760) 643-1600
FAX (760) 643-1608
www.jtservices.com

Jon Tower (310) 573-1777
(310) 650-8560
FAX (310) 230-1222

Joel Unangst (213) 481-2520

Video Tech Services (310) 574-9385
(310) 505-4015
10866 Washington Blvd., Ste. 513 FAX (310) 577-0850
Culver City, CA 90232
(Reps for Gaffers and Lighting Directors)

Tom Voelpel (661) 255-3342
FAX (661) 255-3394

Mark Vuille (310) 798-1062
(310) 629-0176
www.light-works.net

Larry Wallace (310) 822-1263
(Gaffer)

Joseph Warren (805) 581-9341
(805) 501-1439

Kenneth Wheeland (310) 455-1401
(310) 663-9411

Elan Yaari (310) 392-2446
(310) 210-2741
FAX (310) 392-4887

Daniel Anaya
(213) 446-0833

William S. Arnot
(917) 417-4701
(818) 985-1130
www.russelltoddagency.com

Michel Barrère
(323) 654-3445
(323) 821-4310

Jeff Beebe
(Key Grip)
(661) 252-9303
(661) 645-1305

Pat Campea Jr.
(Underwater)
(818) 885-5161
(818) 970-0248
FAX (818) 885-5161

Brett Carleton
(323) 997-0202
FAX (323) 417-4915
www.brettcarleton.com

Kevin Coon
(661) 298-0248
(661) 645-7168

Rick Davis
(818) 599-4749
www.grip411.com

Jerry Deats
(818) 366-2043

Robert Devine
(805) 492-4882

Marty Eichmann
(661) 251-7532

R. Shawn Ensign
(310) 546-4860

Jerry Giacalone
(805) 341-2692
(805) 496-0249
FAX (805) 496-4802

John Gilmour
(Key Grip)
(805) 485-7067
(805) 901-9817

Gregg Guellow
(818) 985-2038
(818) 482-4309
FAX (818) 763-7451

Jorge Guzman
(Key Grip & Underwater)
(310) 836-4323
FAX (310) 836-4307

Billy Haas
(818) 886-9027
(818) 207-4803

Joshua Humphrey
(Underwater)
(310) 270-7032
www.aquamonsters.com

Jack P. Johnson
(818) 606-3900
(818) 542-9355

Casey Jones
(818) 782-3723
FAX (818) 787-8907

Greg Karamov
(818) 508-5235
(818) 434-8661
FAX (818) 508-5235

Irv Katz
(310) 399-5985

Michael Kenner
(818) 424-4747
(800) 474-7538
FAX (818) 897-4747
www.gripjet.com

Kevin Kernohan
(818) 366-8099
(818) 943-9055
FAX (818) 366-0852

Thomas Levy
(Underwater)
(415) 515-5547
(415) 669-7777
FAX (415) 669-7777

Gregory Lorick
(310) 600-3522
(310) 440-3414
FAX (310) 440-3454

Bill Luna
(805) 527-7859
FAX (805) 583-4100

David MacDonald
(818) 244-3063

Bill Manning
(Best Boy, Dolly Grip & Key Grip)
(818) 703-5956
FAX (818) 703-5956

Michael E. Matteson
(818) 640-3117
(818) 893-9192
FAX (818) 895-2562

Tom D. May
(818) 879-9845
(818) 846-3100
FAX (818) 846-3459

Rob Meckler
(310) 600-7539

Michael Milella
(818) 891-0101
(818) 606-5030
FAX (818) 892-5054
(Best Boy, Dolly Grip, Jib Operator & Key Grip)

Bob Miyamoto
(310) 645-3885

Greg Mustin
(805) 374-6060
(805) 559-7612

Willy Nemeth
(541) 840-3366
(541) 476-0598

Glen Noorda
(805) 482-9773
(818) 607-6938

George Palmer
(310) 455-7062

George Peters
(805) 375-1414
(818) 618-9988
FAX (805) 375-1153
www.ultimatearm.com

Tim Pogoler
(818) 281-1616
www.timcoworks.com
(Best Boy, Jib Operator, Key Grip, Motion Control, Rigging Grip & Underwater)

Dan Reilly
(661) 702-8971
(661) 803-3132
FAX (661) 702-8972

Josh Rich
(Key Grip & Underwater)
(310) 450-1927
(310) 251-9317
FAX (310) 450-1927

Scott M. Robinson
(Underwater)
(310) 544-6682
FAX (310) 544-4034

Terry Ruffner
(661) 312-3645
(661) 259-8881

Jimmie Salazar
(310) 375-4008

Mark Sannes
(310) 316-4034
(310) 415-0056
FAX (310) 540-2763

T.D. Scaringi
(Underwater)
(818) 402-2009
(818) 876-0060

Pat Sheetz (818) 894-2060

James Shelton (818) 957-1577
(818) 370-7715
FAX (818) 957-1599

Michael Shore (310) 420-1443

Craig Shumard (818) 768-1573
(661) 644-1516
(Motion Control) FAX (818) 768-1575
www.pacificmotion.net

Chett Spinney (818) 341-2256
(805) 469-7176
FAX (818) 341-2274

John Stabile (818) 886-0869
(818) 421-6695
FAX (818) 886-5039

Mark Stanley (818) 489-4700
FAX (818) 831-3907

Bruce J. Swift (818) 341-4537
(818) 808-9500
www.home.earthlink.net/~bswift52/
(Best Boy, Dolly Grip, Key Grip, Rigging Grip & Underwater)

Michael G. Uva (310) 901-3287
(310) 366-5822
www.kastandkrew.com
(Best Boy, Dolly Grip, Jib Operator, Key Grip, Motion Control, Rigging Grip & Underwater)

Jean-Pierre Visier (310) 670-2265
(Underwater)

Donald Vos (818) 848-5801
(818) 381-3137
(Key Grip) FAX (818) 848-5801

Stewart White (818) 904-9114
(818) 400-3456

Adir Abergel (323) 297-0250
(Hair) www.magnetla.com

Amanda Abizaid (323) 937-1010
www.zenobia.com

Heidi Aburas (323) 767-3373
(Body Painting, Grooming, Makeup, Special FX Makeup & Wigs)

Brandy Adams (323) 937-9095
www.cheriereps.com

Cindy Adams (310) 274-0032
www.artistsbytimothypriano.com

Matt Adams (310) 733-2550
(Hair) www.photogenicsmedia.com

Sallie Adams (818) 206-0144
www.allcrewagency.com

A Agency Celebrity Artists (310) 775-5723
(214) 930-9875
www.agencycelebrityartists.com
(Reps for Hair and Makeup Artists)

Agostina (323) 436-7766
(Makeup) www.eamgmt.com

Misa Aikawa (310) 709-8596
www.misamakeup.com
(Body Painting, Hair, Makeup, Special FX Makeup & Wigs)

Taylor Alderson (310) 210-9510

Alejandra (310) 274-0032
(Grooming & Hair) www.artistsbytimothypriano.com

Jan Alexander (818) 222-5200
(Hair) www.schneiderentertainment.com

Alicia (562) 430-1827
(562) 787-2426
www.makeupandhairbyalicia.com

All Crew Agency (818) 206-0144
2920 W. Olive Ave., Ste. 201 FAX (818) 206-0169
Burbank, CA 91505 www.allcrewagency.com
(Reps for Hair and Makeup Artists)

Shirlena Allen (323) 850-6783
(Hair) www.dawn2duskagency.com

Gabriel Almodovar (310) 550-1800
(Makeup) www.fredsegalbeauty.com

Keith Alston (323) 937-1010
(Makeup) www.zenobia.com

Ana-Maria (310) 274-0032
(Manicurist) www.artistsbytimothypriano.com

David (Leroy) Anderson (310) 288-8000
(Makeup) www.paradigmagency.com

Kelly Andrus-Radinsky (818) 592-6331

Enzo Angileri (310) 394-8813
(Hair) www.cloutieragency.com

Alma Anguiano (310) 485-0404
www.mkartists.com

Jonathan Antin (310) 733-2550
(Hair) www.photogenicsmedia.com

Raina Antle (323) 385-3163
(Colorist, Grooming, Hair & Makeup) www.rainaantle.com

Teddy Antolin (323) 549-3100
(Hair) www.beautyandphoto.com

Terri Apanasewicz (310) 394-8813
(Makeup) www.cloutieragency.com

Alan Apone (310) 601-2355
www.lesliealyson.com

Kathy Aragon (310) 274-0032
www.artistsbytimothypriano.com

Gregory Arlt (323) 436-7766
(Makeup) www.eamgmt.com

Elena Arroy (818) 887-9535
(818) 825-0706
FAX (818) 887-9535
www.elenaarroy.com

Artemis (323) 906-9600
(Artemis) www.crystalagency.com

Artist Untied (323) 933-0200
(415) 957-0500
(Reps for Hair and Makeup Artists) FAX (415) 957-0555
www.artistuntied.com

Artists by Timothy Priano (310) 274-0032
345 N. Maple Dr., Ste. 397 FAX (310) 278-7520
Beverly Hills, CA 90210
www.artistsbytimothypriano.com
(Reps for Hair and Makeup Artists)

artists' services (323) 445-4910 (415) 824-4423
8581 Santa Monica Blvd., Ste. 437
West Hollywood, CA 90069 www.artists-services.com
(Reps for Hair & Makeup Artists)

ArtMix Beauty (310) 943-8102
2332 S. Centinela Ave., Ste. C FAX (310) 943-8101
Los Angeles, CA 90064 www.artmixbeauty.com
(Reps for Hair and Makeup Artists)

Gracie Atherton (323) 445-4910
www.artists-services.com

Barbara Augustus-Johnson (323) 856-8928
FAX (818) 988-9784

Tena Austin (323) 876-4692
(Grooming & Makeup) FAX (323) 876-0292

Riad Azar (323) 856-8540
(Hair) www.opusbeauty.com

Miriam Azoulay (646) 234-3227 (323) 465-5584
(Makeup) www.margaretmaldonado.com

Amanda B. (323) 938-5225

Billy B (323) 462-5000
(Makeup) www.traceymattingly.com

David Babaii (323) 462-5000
(Hair) www.traceymattingly.com

Nancy Baca (323) 874-1107 (213) 359-3235

Jake Bailey (323) 462-5000
(Makeup) www.traceymattingly.com

Vivian Baker (310) 601-2355
www.lesliealyson.com

Lucy Baldock (310) 998-1977
www.celestineagency.com

Lynn Barber (818) 222-5200
(Makeup) www.schneiderentertainment.com

Cori Bardo (310) 998-1977
(Hair) www.celestineagency.com

Scott Barnes (310) 300-2906 (917) 270-1521
(Makeup) FAX (310) 300-2901
www.scottbarnes.tv

Frederique Barrera (213) 359-5899
www.frederiqueb.com
(Grooming, Makeup & Special FX Makeup)

Joshua Barrett (310) 274-0032
(Grooming & Hair) www.artistsbytimothypriano.com

Pauline Barry (415) 290-9532
www.paulinebarry.com

Mary Jean Beach (909) 590-1688
(Makeup) www.makeupbymaryjean.com

Beauty & Photo (323) 549-3100
3737 Greenwood Ave. FAX (323) 549-9881
Los Angeles, CA 90066 www.beautyandphoto.com
(Reps for Hair and Makeup Artists)

Hether Beckrest (310) 246-0446
www.workgroup-ltd.com

Sabrina Bedrani (323) 462-5000
(Makeup) www.traceymattingly.com

Kiki Benet (323) 462-5000
(Makeup) www.traceymattingly.com

Marco Berardini (310) 394-8813
(Makeup) www.cloutieragency.com

Miles Berdache (323) 445-4910
www.artists-services.com

Bridget Bergman (310) 493-0113

Marsha Bialo (310) 447-8300
(Manicurist) www.bpolished.com

Lucia Bianca (818) 845-8899
(Makeup) FAX (818) 845-8899

Kate Biscoe (323) 839-0550 (212) 741-0202
(Makeup) FAX (323) 666-5277

John Blaine (310) 822-2898
(Hair) www.rougeartists.com

Andre Blaise (310) 822-2898
(Hair) www.rougeartists.com

Luca Blandi (310) 274-0032
(Hair) www.artistsbytimothypriano.com

Oscar Blandi (310) 274-0032
(Hair) www.artistsbytimothypriano.com

Norma Blaque (323) 906-9600
(Hair) www.crystalagency.com

Morgan Blaul (310) 274-0032
www.artistsbytimothypriano.com

Gaea Bogue (510) 717-2533
(Grooming, Hair & Makeup) www.gaeab.com

Elan Bongiorno (310) 998-1977
(Makeup) www.celestineagency.com

Ben Bornstein (818) 284-6423
(Makeup) www.italentco.com

Jenn Bouley-Gemmell (323) 854-2220
FAX (310) 372-1782

Marissa Bourbonnais (323) 850-6783
(Makeup) www.dawn2duskagency.com

Ashley Bourdon (310) 274-0032
www.artistsbytimothypriano.com

Kareen Boursier (323) 937-1010
www.zenobia.com

Alexis Brazel (323) 664-6494
(Makeup) www.therexagency.com

June Brickman (818) 917-2792

Dawn Broussard (323) 297-0250
(Makeup) www.magnetla.com

Jenni Brown (310) 291-5117

Tamara Brown (323) 933-0200
www.artistuntied.com

Natalia Bruschi (310) 550-1800
(Hair) www.fredsegalbeauty.com

Belinda Bryant (213) 620-8505 (213) 393-3600
(Body Painting, Grooming, Makeup & Special FX Makeup)

Kara Yoshimoto Bua (323) 462-5000
(Makeup) www.traceymattingly.com

Jennifer Budner (310) 266-2155
(Makeup) FAX (760) 544-9009

Michelle Buhler (818) 284-6423
(Makeup) www.italentco.com

Michele Burke (818) 574-7111
(Body Painting, Makeup & Special FX Makeup)

Barney Burman (818) 284-6423
(Makeup) www.italentco.com

Michael Burnett (818) 768-6103
(Makeup) FAX (818) 768-6136
www.mbpfx.com

Gina Burrus (714) 717-8736
FAX (714) 846-6130
www.ginaburrus.com
(Body Painting, Grooming, Makeup & Special FX Makeup)

Mary Burton (310) 278-8086
(Makeup) FAX (310) 278-7046

Martha Callender (323) 906-8230
(818) 489-3429
(Makeup; French & Spanish)

Jocelyn Callot (323) 664-6494
(Makeup) www.therexagency.com

Rudy Calvo (323) 299-4043
(Makeup) www.dionperonneau.com

Adam Campbell (323) 462-5000
(Hair) www.traceymattingly.com

Coleen Campbell-Olwell (323) 436-7766
(Makeup) www.eamgmt.com

Nicole Cap (310) 274-0032
www.artistsbytimothypriano.com

Laverne Caracuzzi (805) 494-6484
(Makeup)

Jodi Cardenas (310) 274-0032
(Manicurist) www.artistsbytimothypriano.com

Jamie Cardillo-Lee (212) 582-8052
(310) 739-0405
FAX (213) 477-2324
www.elevationtalent.com
(Body Painting, Grooming, Hair & Makeup)

Kim Carillo (310) 998-1977
(Makeup) www.celestineagency.com

Will Carillo (310) 246-0446
(Hair) www.workgroup-ltd.com

Siobhan Carmody (818) 206-0144
(Makeup) www.allcrewagency.com

Damien Carney (323) 664-6494
(Hair) www.therexagency.com

Diana Carreiro (310) 274-0032
www.artistsbytimothypriano.com

Will Carrillo (310) 998-1977
(Hair) www.celestineagency.com

Terri Carter (323) 299-4043
(Makeup) www.dionperonneau.com

Célestine Agency (310) 998-1977
1548 16th St. FAX (310) 998-1978
Santa Monica, CA 90404 www.celestineagency.com
(Reps for Hair and Makeup Artists)

Joanne Cervelli-Smith (310) 395-7770

Amy Chance (310) 998-1977
(Makeup) www.celestineagency.com

Cassie Chapman (323) 445-4910
www.artists-services.com

Betten Chaston (323) 937-1010
www.zenobia.com

Rose Chatterton (818) 284-6423
(Hair) www.italentco.com

Cherie Represents (323) 937-9095
845 S. Mansfield Ave., Ste. 1 FAX (323) 937-3300
Los Angeles, CA 90036 www.cheriereps.com
(Reps for Hair and Makeup Artists)

Racine Christensen (310) 246-0446
www.workgroup-ltd.com

Von Christmas (323) 512-8002
(Manicurist) www.karleeartist.com

Anna Chu (310) 274-0032
(Hair) www.artistsbytimothypriano.com

Veronica Chu (310) 274-0032
www.artistsbytimothypriano.com

Lori Cincotta (310) 463-3579

Jackie Cioffa (310) 274-0032
(Makeup) www.artistsbytimothypriano.com

Jenni Clark (818) 516-8929
www.jenniclark.com

Jeremy Clark (310) 274-0032
(Hair) www.artistsbytimothypriano.com

Cloutier (310) 394-8813
1026 Montana Ave. FAX (310) 394-8863
Santa Monica, CA 90403 www.cloutieragency.com
(Reps for Hair and Makeup Artists)

Dian Bethune Coble (323) 856-0551
(323) 646-1071
FAX (323) 461-3703
(Body Painting, Grooming, Hair, Makeup & Wigs)

COCO (626) 422-0351
(626) 862-3957
(Makeup)

Lauren Kaye Cohen (323) 462-5000
(Makeup) www.traceymattingly.com

Connie Cole (310) 395-1073
(310) 502-2434
(Grooming, Hair & Makeup) FAX (310) 395-1073

Claire Coleman (323) 937-1010
www.zenobia.com

Kim Collea (310) 823-0508
(520) 906-9076
FAX (815) 642-4444

Tyler Colton (310) 998-1977
www.celestineagency.com

Josh Comen (310) 288-8000
(Special FX Makeup) www.paradigmagency.com

Jerry Constantine (310) 288-8000
(Special FX Makeup) www.paradigmagency.com

Colleen Conway (323) 297-0250
(Hair) www.magnetla.com

Cooper (310) 998-1977
www.celestineagency.com

Fran Cooper (310) 943-8102
(Makeup) www.artmixbeauty.com

Michelle Coursey (310) 274-0032
(Makeup) www.artistsbytimothypriano.com

David Cox (310) 998-1977
(Hair) www.celestineagency.com

Anthony Cristiano (310) 274-0032
(Hair) www.artistsbytimothypriano.com

Crystal Agency (323) 906-9600
(323) 788-1336
4237 Los Nietos Dr. FAX (323) 443-3752
Los Angeles, CA 90027 www.crystalagency.com
(Reps for Hair and Makeup Artists)

Tracey Cunningham (310) 274-0032
(Hair) www.artistsbytimothypriano.com

Donna D. (310) 274-0032
(Manicurist) www.artistsbytimothypriano.com

Laura d. (310) 550-1800
(Hair) www.fredsegalbeauty.com

Elizabeth Dahl (323) 469-9035
(310) 562-6370
(Makeup) www.makeupbyelizabeth.com

Francelle Daly (323) 297-0250
(Makeup) www.magnetla.com

Burke Daniel (310) 274-0032
(Makeup) www.artistsbytimothypriano.com

Cyndi Daniels (310) 274-0032
(Manicurist) www.artistsbytimothypriano.com

Danilo (323) 297-0250
(Hair) www.magnetla.com

Davide (310) 274-0032
www.artistsbytimothypriano.com

Lawrence Davis (323) 512-8002
(Hair) www.karleeartist.com

Nettie Davis (323) 578-9039
(Grooming & Manicurist) www.nettiedavis.com

Dawn to Dusk Agency (323) 850-6783
(212) 431-8631
8306 Wilshire Blvd., Ste. 412
Beverly Hills, CA 90211 www.dawn2duskagency.com
(Reps for Hair and Makeup Artists)

Beatrice De Alba (310) 601-2355
www.lesliealyson.com

Paul DéArmas (310) 550-1800
(Hair) www.fredsegalbeauty.com

Deception Tattoos & FX/Tanner (310) 729-4405
(Tattoo FX Artist) www.deceptionbodyart.com

Danielle Decker (310) 943-8102
www.artmixbeauty.com

Athena Demetrios (310) 435-9029
(530) 334-5213
(Makeup)

Sterfon Demings (818) 206-0144
(Hair) www.allcrewagency.com

Olaf Derlig (323) 436-7766
(Grooming, Hair & Makeup) www.eamgmt.com

Angela DiCarlo (323) 468-2240
www.nyoffice.net

Dickey (323) 664-6494
(Hair) www.therexagency.com

Debra Dietrich (818) 206-0144
(Hair) www.allcrewagency.com

Betsy diFrancesca (323) 937-1010
www.zenobia.com

Denise M. Dillaway (310) 600-8654
(Grooming, Hair & Makeup) www.denisedillaway.com

Jay Diola (323) 935-8455
(Hair) www.ms-management.com

Dion Peronneau Agency (323) 299-4043
5482 Wilshire Blvd., Ste. 1512 FAX (323) 299-4269
Los Angeles, CA 90036 www.dionperonneau.com
(Reps for Hair and Makeup Artists)

Monica DiVenti (310) 450-4160

Tihomira Dobranova (323) 304-2996
(Makeup) www.tihomira.com

Kyra Dorman (310) 274-0032
www.artistsbytimothypriano.com

Lucie Doughty (310) 739-3375
(Colorist & Hair) FAX (310) 391-9149
www.luciedoughty.com

Jorjee Douglass (323) 664-6494
www.therexagency.com

Linda Dowds (818) 284-6423
(Makeup) www.italentco.com

Wendy Doyle (323) 937-1010
www.zenobia.com

Bari Dreiband-Burman (818) 980-6587
(Makeup) www.burmanstudio.com

Margo Ducharme (310) 274-0032
www.artistsbytimothypriano.com

Jacqueline Duffy (310) 550-1800
(Makeup) www.fredsegalbeauty.com

Rosie Duprat-Fort (818) 206-0144
(Makeup) www.allcrewagency.com

France DuShane (323) 933-0200
www.artistuntied.com

Lauren Ehrenfield (310) 998-1977
www.celestineagency.com

Georgie Eisdell (323) 436-7766
(Grooming, Hair & Makeup) www.eamgmt.com

Lisa Eldridge (323) 297-0250
www.magnetla.com

Gloria Elias-Foeillet (323) 549-3100
(Makeup) www.beautyandphoto.com

Elle (310) 274-0032
(Manicurist) www.artistsbytimothypriano.com

Alexis Ellen (888) 839-0101
(Makeup) www.firehousemanagement.com

Elsbeth (323) 935-8455
(Manicurist) www.ms-management.com

Ennis, Inc. (310) 587-3512
(Reps for Hair and Makeup Artists) www.ennisinc.com

Epiphany Artist Group, Inc. (323) 660-6353
(Reps for Hair and Makeup Artists) FAX (323) 660-0094

Daniel Erdman (323) 462-5000
(Hair) www.traceymattingly.com

Mary Erickson (877) 242-6878
www.lamakeup.com

Andrea Escorcia (310) 274-0032
(Manicurist) www.artistsbytimothypriano.com

Gunn Espegard (213) 999-5212
(323) 512-7180
www.gunnespegard.com

Exclusive Artists Management (323) 436-7766
7700 Sunset Blvd., Ste. 205 FAX (323) 436-7799
Los Angeles, CA 90046 www.eamgmt.com
(Reps for Hair and Makeup Artists)

Fabiola (310) 927-7080
(Makeup; Spanish)

Helena Faccenda (323) 462-5000
www.traceymattingly.com

Joe Farulla (818) 284-6423
(Makeup) www.italentco.com

Karen Faye (818) 985-5110
(213) 509-7208
www.karen-faye.com

Hillary Fenton (310) 274-0032
www.artistsbytimothypriano.com

Kathryn Miles Fenton (818) 988-7038
(Makeup)

Nancy Ferguson (818) 883-8808
(Makeup)

Eric Ferrell (323) 299-4043
(Makeup) www.dionperonneau.com

Debra Ferullo (323) 462-5000
(Makeup) www.traceymattingly.com

Jeffrey Fetzer (323) 937-1010
www.zenobia.com

Ray Filipowicz (888) 839-0101
(Makeup) www.firehousemanagement.com

Kiki Finley (323) 935-8455
(Makeup) www.ms-management.com

FIRE House Management (888) 839-0101
(Reps for Hair and Makeup Artists) FAX (888) 839-2943
www.firehousemanagement.com

Sean Flanigan (310) 601-2355
www.lesliealyson.com

Toby Fleischman (323) 436-7766
(Makeup) www.eamgmt.com

Rebeca Flores (323) 937-1010
www.zenobia.com

Lisa Forster (323) 937-1010
www.zenobia.com

Mary Jo Fortin (310) 457-6446

Karen Fraker (805) 649-9064
(805) 455-0563
www.karenfraker.com

Nicole Frank (818) 222-5200
(Hair) www.schneiderentertainment.com

Fred Segal Beauty (310) 550-1800
9250 Wilshire Blvd., Ste. 210 FAX (310) 550-1501
Beverly Hills, CA 90212 www.fredsegalbeauty.com
(Reps for Hair and Makeup Artists)

Robin Fredriksz (323) 297-0250
www.magnetla.com

Brett Freedman (310) 998-1977
www.celestineagency.com

Edward French (818) 340-4852
(818) 317-9997
(Makeup) FAX (818) 340-4837
www.edwardfrench.com

Beth Fricke (310) 274-0032
(323) 243-0583
www.artistsbytimothypriano.com/artists/bethfricke
(Manicurist)

Alan Friedman (818) 881-1473

Elisabeth Fry (310) 601-2355
(Makeup) www.lesliealyson.com

Kelcey Fry (323) 962-0295
(818) 469-0026
www.lipspink.com

Kiyomi Fukazawa (310) 497-3681
(Hair & Makeup) www.kiyomimakeup.com

Dennis G. (323) 297-0250
(Hair) www.magnetla.com

Toni G. (818) 284-6423
www.italentco.com

Eric Gabriel (323) 664-6494
(Hair) www.therexagency.com

Mary E. Gaffney (213) 407-5392
(Makeup)

Jane Galli (310) 601-2355
www.lesliealyson.com

Craig Gangi (323) 462-5000
(Hair) www.traceymattingly.com

Michelle Garbin (310) 283-5118
(Makeup)

Lisa Garner (310) 274-0032
(Grooming & Makeup) www.artistsbytimothypriano.com

Cheryl Gates (310) 775-5723
www.agencycelebrityartists.com

Asia Geiger (310) 998-1977
www.celestineagency.com

Giovanni Giuliano (310) 998-1977
(Hair) www.celestineagency.com

Madlyn Gnoffo (310) 274-0032
(Makeup) www.artistsbytimothypriano.com

Lorri Goddard-Clark (323) 664-6494
(Colorist) www.therexagency.com

Tamara Gold (310) 801-1342
www.theredlipstickreporter.com
(Body Painting, Grooming & Makeup)

Jan Golden (818) 458-2569
www.goldenjan.com

Carolina Gonzalez (310) 274-0032
(Makeup) www.artistsbytimothypriano.com

Rachel Goodwin (323) 297-0250
(Makeup) www.magnetla.com

Laura Gorman (310) 274-0032
www.artistsbytimothypriano.com

Casey Gouveia (310) 998-1977
www.celestineagency.com

April Greaves (310) 998-1977
(Makeup) www.celestineagency.com

Caprice Green (323) 549-3100
(Hair) www.beautyandphoto.com

Kimberly Greene (818) 291-1884
(Makeup)

Rodney Groves (323) 856-8540
(Hair) www.opusbeauty.com

Lori Guidroz (323) 664-6494
(Hair) www.therexagency.com

Nico Guilis (310) 482-9802
(Makeup)

Luis Guillermo (310) 274-0032
(Grooming & Hair) www.artistsbytimothypriano.com

Susan Haddon (310) 998-1977
www.celestineagency.com

Sharon Hagen (310) 480-8489

Gail Hagopian (818) 225-1080
(818) 645-6135
(Makeup) FAX (818) 225-1080

Monique Hahn (626) 676-1389
(323) 664-8685
(Grooming, Hair & Makeup) www.moniquemakeup.com

Nedra Hainey (818) 506-3652
(818) 919-6017
FAX (818) 509-7715

Mindy Hall (323) 466-4441
(310) 415-2294
FAX (323) 460-4442
www.miltonagency.com

Keiko Hamaguchi (310) 998-1977
(Hair) www.celestineagency.com

Nathan Hamilton (213) 280-2750
(Makeup)

Paula Jane Hamilton (213) 705-0202
(Body Painting & Makeup) www.paulajanehamilton.com

Jamal Hammadi (323) 297-0250
(Hair) www.magnetla.com

Su Han (323) 436-7766
(Makeup) www.eamgmt.com

Jonathan Hanousek (323) 436-7766
(Hair) www.eamgmt.com

Julie Harris (310) 274-0032
(Makeup) www.artistsbytimothypriano.com

Pat Harris (310) 594-6568
(Makeup & Special FX Makeup)

Clifford Hashimoto (323) 445-4910
www.artists-services.com

Noah Hatton (323) 512-8002
(Hair) www.karleeartist.com

Brian Haugen (310) 274-0032
www.artistsbytimothypriano.com

Heather Hawkins (323) 937-1010
www.zenobia.com

Dawn Haynes (323) 850-6783
(Men's Grooming) www.dawn2duskagency.com

Andrea Helgadottir (310) 733-2550
(Makeup) www.photogenicsmedia.com

Sharin Helgestad (818) 780-7766
(213) 792-6677

Bridget Henry (310) 274-0032
www.artistsbytimothypriano.com

Adrienne Herbert (310) 998-1977
(Grooming & Makeup) www.celestineagency.com

Valerie Hernandez (323) 856-8540
www.opusbeauty.com

Kerry Herta (310) 822-2898
www.rougeartists.com

Hikari (310) 998-1977
(Hair) www.celestineagency.com

Voni Hinkle (818) 284-6423
www.italentco.com

Jenna Hipp (310) 998-1977
(Manicurist) www.celestineagency.com

Steven Hoeppner (310) 274-0032
www.artistsbytimothypriano.com
(Grooming, Hair & Makeup)

Ursula Holder (310) 550-1800
(Hair) www.fredsegalbeauty.com

Byrd Holland (818) 558-1954
(Makeup) FAX (818) 558-1954

Bryan Hollingshead (323) 937-1010
(Grooming & Makeup) www.zenobia.com

Adrienne Houle (323) 937-1010
(Makeup) www.zenobia.com

Maryellen Howe (323) 937-1010
www.zenobia.com

Daniel Howell (323) 297-0250
(Hair) www.magnetla.com

Claudia Humburg (310) 733-2550
www.photogenicsmedia.com
(Body Painting, Hair & Makeup)

Paul Hyett (818) 206-0144
(Makeup & Special FX Makeup) www.allcrewagency.com

Annie Ing (310) 998-1977
(Makeup) www.celestineagency.com

Melanie Inglessis (323) 856-8540
(Makeup) www.opusbeauty.com

Paul Innis (323) 856-8540
(Makeup) www.opusbeauty.com

Filippo ioco (323) 512-8002
(Body Painting) www.karleeartist.com

Danielle Irene (310) 274-0032
(Hair) www.artistsbytimothypriano.com

Bradley Irion (310) 274-0032
(Hair) www.artistsbytimothypriano.com

Thea Istenes (310) 733-2550
(Makeup) www.photogenicsmedia.com

iTalent Company (818) 284-6423
9701 Wilshire Blvd., 10th Fl. FAX (866) 755-0708
Beverly Hills, CA 90212 www.italentco.com
(Reps for Hair and Makeup Artists)

Debbie Jacks (310) 274-0032
www.artistsbytimothypriano.com

Darico Jackson (323) 906-9600
(Hair) www.crystalagency.com

Amanda Jacobellis (310) 858-1970
www.makeupmandy.com

Ashley Javier (323) 297-0250
(Hair) www.magnetla.com

David John (310) 550-1800
(Hair) www.fredsegalbeauty.com

Dale Johnson (310) 274-0032
www.artistsbytimothypriano.com

Michael Johnson (310) 274-0032
(Grooming & Hair) www.artistsbytimothypriano.com

Rosie Johnston (323) 436-7766
(Makeup) www.eamgmt.com

Dean Jones (336) 264-2302
(818) 780-5002
FAX (818) 780-5002
www.amandfx.com

Valerie Joslin (310) 459-8917
(310) 801-7289

Allyson Joyner (213) 216-1328
FAX (818) 554-7212
www.ajoliegroup.com

Jeff Judd (323) 666-6333
(323) 719-9321
(Body Painting & Makeup) www.jeffjuddinc.com

Julieanna Justus (310) 550-1800
www.fredsegalbeauty.com

Kali (310) 998-1977
(Hair) www.celestineagency.com

Michael Kanyon (310) 998-1977
(Hair) www.celestineagency.com

Persefone Karakosta (818) 284-6423
(Makeup) www.italentco.com

Karlee Artist Management (323) 512-8002
(323) 913-0700
2658 Griffith Park Blvd., Ste. 171 FAX (323) 878-0068
Los Angeles, CA 90039 www.karleeartist.com
(Reps for Hair and Makeup Artists)

Bethany Karlyn (310) 822-2898
(Makeup) www.rougeartists.com

Katinka (310) 489-9908
(310) 306-8484
www.katinkamakeup.com

Janice Kavanagh (310) 288-0818
(310) 486-6266
FAX (310) 288-0812

Kelly Kavanagh (818) 284-6423
(Makeup) www.italentco.com

Kazumi (888) 839-0101
www.firehousemanagement.com

Trisha Kelley (818) 508-1533
(818) 809-9980

Cammy Kelly (310) 274-0032
www.artistsbytimothypriano.com

David Keough (310) 998-1977
(Hair) www.celestineagency.com

Noriko Kerns (323) 664-6494
www.therexagency.com

Estreya Kesler (310) 903-7013

Shannon Kim (310) 451-4477
(Hair) www.thomaschasehair.com

Anthea King (310) 274-0032
(Grooming & Makeup) www.artistsbytimothypriano.com

Connie King (310) 775-5723
www.agencycelebrityartists.com

Kiyoshi (323) 856-8540
(Makeup) www.opusbeauty.com

Tonga Knight (704) 807-7447
(704) 392-7358

Hannah Knowlton (310) 550-1800
(Hair) www.fredsegalbeauty.com

Martina Kohl (310) 392-7083
(310) 614-8353
www.martinakohl.com

Yuji Kojima (323) 664-6494
www.therexagency.com

Klexius Kolby (323) 512-8002
(Makeup) www.karleeartist.com

Nina Kraft (310) 486-6236
(Makeup)

Uzmee Krakovszki (323) 906-9600
(Hair, Makeup & Men's Grooming) www.crystalagency.com

Corina Kramer (323) 445-4910
www.artists-services.com

Emi Kudo (323) 512-8002
(Manicurist) www.karleeartist.com

Peter Kukla (310) 200-4164

Kimmi Kyees (310) 998-1977
(Manicurist) www.celestineagency.com

LA Rep (213) 446-1720
3219 Laurel Canyon Blvd. FAX (323) 656-1756
Studio City, CA 91604
(Reps for Hair and Makeup Artists)

Steven Lake (323) 436-7766
(Hair) www.eamgmt.com

Natasha Lakic (323) 664-6494
(Makeup) www.therexagency.com

Alex LaMarsh (323) 933-0200
www.artistuntied.com

Marci Landgraf (323) 937-1010
www.zenobia.com

Marie Larkin (323) 656-8340
(323) 842-3580
(Hair)

Didier Lavergne (310) 282-9940
(Makeup) www.mirisch.com

Rosemary Lawrence (626) 797-0104
FAX (323) 761-6418

Debbie Leavitt (310) 394-8813
(Manicurist) www.cloutieragency.com

Marie-Josee LeDuc (310) 733-2550
(Makeup) www.photogenicsmedia.com

Adruitha Lee (818) 284-6423
(Hair) www.italentco.com

Kate Lee (323) 297-0250
(Makeup) www.magnetla.com

Norma Lee (323) 654-5790
(818) 774-5441
(Hair)

Sonia Lee (323) 436-7766
www.eamgmt.com

Barbara Leister-Lamelza (323) 436-7766
(Grooming, Hair & Makeup) www.eamgmt.com

Lisa Leming (714) 914-6397
www.lisaleming.com

Mauricio Lemus (707) 712-0180
(Grooming, Hair, Makeup & Wigs) www.mauriciolemus.net

Sam Leonardi (323) 462-5000
(Hair) FAX (323) 462-5001
www.traceymattingly.com

Leslie Alyson (310) 601-2355
1801 Century Park East, Ste. 700 www.lesliealyson.com
Los Angeles, CA 90067
(Reps for Hair and Makeup Artists)

Mara Levarre (310) 274-0032
(Makeup) www.artistsbytimothypriano.com

Hilda Levierge (323) 664-6494
(Makeup) www.therexagency.com

Angela Levin (323) 462-5000
(Makeup) www.traceymattingly.com

Tracey Levy (818) 284-6423
(Makeup) www.italentco.com

Joycelyne Lew (323) 466-3100
(213) 999-5514
FAX (323) 469-7138

Stephen Lewis (323) 436-7766
(Grooming, Hair & Makeup) www.eamgmt.com

Aaron Light (310) 998-1977
(Hair) www.celestineagency.com

Oona Lind (323) 664-6494
www.therexagency.com

Jessica Liparoto (323) 436-7766
www.eamgmt.com

Livio (310) 943-8102
(Hair) www.artmixbeauty.com

Jeanine Lobell (323) 297-0250
(Makeup) www.magnetla.com

Lolita (323) 299-4043
www.dionperonneau.com

Sherrie Long (213) 302-0313
(415) 608-9220
www.sherrielong.com
(Grooming, Hair, Makeup, Manicurist, Special FX Makeup & Wigs)

Leslie Lopez (310) 276-0777
(Makeup) www.thewallgroup.com

Frances Lordan (323) 937-1010
www.zenobia.com

Barbara Lorenz (310) 657-0028
(818) 789-2717
(Hair) FAX (818) 905-8824

Lottie (323) 664-6494
(Makeup) www.therexagency.com

Naomi Lowde-Priestley (323) 850-8834
FAX (323) 882-8273

Billy Lowe (310) 430-4045
(Hair) www.billylowe.com

Christopher Xavier Lozano (323) 962-0009
(323) 854-6775
www.tlshollywood.com

Tammy Ly (323) 937-1010
(Manicurist) www.zenobia.com

Juanita Lyon (310) 998-1977
www.celestineagency.com

Sharon Roewe Lyons (310) 775-5723
www.agencycelebrityartists.com

Min Min Ma (310) 246-0446
www.workgroup-ltd.com

Helene Macaulay (310) 274-0032
(Makeup) www.artistsbytimothypriano.com

Sheryl Macauley (323) 937-1010
(Manicurist) www.zenobia.com

MacGowan Spencer Agency (323) 525-0235
(Reps for Hair and Makeup Artists) FAX (310) 887-4843
www.macgowanspencer.com

Magnet LA (323) 297-0250
6363 Wilshire Blvd., Ste. 650 FAX (323) 297-0249
Los Angeles, CA 90048 www.magnetla.com
(Reps for Hair and Makeup Artists)

Mai-Li (310) 395-8286
(Makeup)

Tré Major (323) 850-6783
(Hair) www.dawn2duskagency.com

Tre' Majors (323) 856-8540
www.opusbeauty.com

Donna Malatino (310) 804-7391
www.donnamalatino.com
(Colorist, Grooming, Hair, Makeup & Wigs)

Cervando Maldonado (323) 462-5000
www.traceymattingly.com

Annie Maniscalco (818) 763-3300
(818) 468-4527
FAX (818) 763-3300

Monet Mansano (323) 937-1010
(Makeup) www.zenobia.com

Melanie Manson (310) 880-2825
(818) 700-0311
FAX (818) 700-0311
www.melaniemanson.com
(Body Painting, Grooming, Makeup & Special FX Makeup)

Manuella (310) 274-0032
(Grooming & Hair) www.artistsbytimothypriano.com

Christian Marc (310) 998-1977
www.celestineagency.com

Cassi Mari (213) 712-5935
(310) 287-8082

Richard Marin (310) 394-8813
(Hair) www.cloutieragency.com

Michelle Marre (310) 306-1596
(Makeup) FAX (310) 821-1799

Anne Marso (310) 570-7027
(Grooming, Hair & Makeup) FAX (310) 393-8937
www.annemarso.com

Glenn Marziali (310) 274-0032
(Makeup) www.artistsbytimothypriano.com

Steven Mason (323) 436-7766
(Hair) www.eamgmt.com

Todd Masters (818) 834-3000
(604) 683-5311
(Special FX Makeup) FAX (818) 834-9755
www.mastersfx.com

Mary Mastro (310) 601-2355
www.lesliealyson.com

Robin Mathews (818) 284-6423
(Makeup & Special FX Makeup) www.italentco.com

Matin (310) 274-0032
(Makeup) www.artistsbytimothypriano.com

Hazuki Matsushita (310) 709-0400
www.hazukimakeup.com

Dawn Mattocks (323) 251-3305
(323) 251-0447
FAX (323) 663-8025
www.makeupwithmattocks.com
(Body Painting, Colorist, Grooming, Hair, Makeup, Manicurist, Special FX Makeup & Wigs)

Randi Måvestrand (310) 951-3966
(Makeup) www.randimavestrand.com

Francesca Maxwell (818) 509-9707
(818) 259-9223
FAX (818) 509-9707

Amber Maynard (323) 348-6334
(310) 451-4477
(Hair)

Meaganne McCandess (323) 933-0200
www.artistuntied.com

Meghan McClain (310) 943-8102
(Makeup) www.artmixbeauty.com

Tania McComas (818) 222-5200
(Makeup) www.schneiderentertainment.com

Lori McCoy Bell (818) 222-5200
(Hair) www.schneiderentertainment.com

Christian McCullock (323) 462-5000
(Makeup) www.traceymattingly.com

Jon David McHargue (310) 775-5723
www.agencycelebrityartists.com

Thomas McKiver (310) 274-0032
(Hair) www.artistsbytimothypriano.com

Emma McMahon (310) 550-1800
(Hair) www.fredsegalbeauty.com

Brittany McMaster (310) 550-1800
(Hair) www.fredsegalbeauty.com

Antoinette Meier (310) 323-2180
www.abaaa.com

Patrick Melville (310) 274-0032
(Hair) www.artistsbytimothypriano.com

Melvone (310) 733-2550
(Makeup) www.photogenicsmedia.com

Ivan Mendoza (310) 246-0446
www.workgroup-ltd.com

Myke Michaels (818) 219-7662
(818) 905-9059
www.wolfpackfilmworks.com
(Hair, Makeup & Special FX Makeup)

David Michaud (213) 675-0199
(Hair & Makeup) FAX (323) 936-7547
www.michaudbeauty.com

Miki (323) 462-5000
(Hair) www.traceymattingly.com

Emanuel Millar (310) 601-2355
www.lesliealyson.com

Jean Whitman Miller (949) 497-3263
(Hair) FAX (949) 494-7945

Meleesa Miller (323) 937-9095
(Hair) www.cheriereps.com

Patty Miller (818) 843-5208
(213) 217-0914
(Hair)

Karan Mitchell (323) 462-5000
(Makeup) www.traceymattingly.com

Laura Mohberg (323) 462-5000
(Makeup) www.traceymattingly.com

Julie A. Mollo (323) 665-1635
(323) 459-2789
FAX (323) 665-2339
www.juliemakeup.com

Montana Artists Agency (323) 845-4144
7715 W. Sunset Blvd., Third Fl. FAX (323) 845-4155
Los Angeles, CA 90046 www.montanartists.com
(Reps for Hair and Makeup Artists)

Damian Monzillo (323) 854-2887
(Hair) www.scissorandcomb.com

Mylah Morales (323) 856-8540
(Makeup) www.opusbeauty.com

Patricia Morales (323) 462-5000
(Hair) www.traceymattingly.com

Mordechai (310) 274-0032
(Hair) www.artistsbytimothypriano.com

Morgan (310) 943-8102
(Hair) www.artmixbeauty.com

Anne Morgan (310) 601-2355
www.lesliealyson.com

Sharon Morrisey (310) 550-1800
(Hair) www.fredsegalbeauty.com

Joanie Moscatello (818) 216-5067
(Manicurist) www.eamgmt.com

Gil Mosko (818) 908-1087
(Makeup & Special FX Makeup) FAX (818) 908-1262
www.gmfoam.com

Motoko (323) 436-7766
(Makeup) www.eamgmt.com

Autumn Moultrie (323) 436-7766
(Makeup) www.eamgmt.com

Sammy Mourabit (310) 998-1977
(Makeup) www.celestineagency.com

Donald Mowat (310) 467-4152
(323) 957-4602
(Makeup)

Tracy Moyer (310) 998-1977
www.celestineagency.com

MS Management (323) 935-8455
(Reps for Hair and Makeup Artists) FAX (323) 935-3143
www.ms-management.com

Nellie Muganda (323) 937-1010
www.zenobia.com

Quinn Murphy (310) 274-0032
(Makeup) www.artistsbytimothypriano.com

William Murphy (323) 856-8540
(Makeup) www.opusbeauty.com

Roz Music (323) 297-0250
www.magnetla.com

Barbara Mutnick (310) 274-0032
(Manicurist) www.artistsbytimothypriano.com

Neeko (323) 512-8002
(Hair) www.karleeartist.com

Thomas Nellen (818) 222-5200
(Makeup) www.schneiderentertainment.com

Beau Nelson (310) 274-0032
(Makeup) www.artistsbytimothypriano.com

Glenn Neufeld (310) 288-8000
(Special FX Makeup) www.paradigmagency.com

Nenci Nevarez (310) 398-7014
(702) 256-8910
www.myspace.com/nencistudio
(Colorist, Grooming, Hair, Makeup & Wigs)

New York Office (323) 468-2240
(212) 545-7895
6605 Hollywood Blvd., Ste. 200 FAX (323) 468-2244
Los Angeles, CA 90028 www.nyoffice.net
(Reps for Hair and Makeup Artists)

Davy Newkirk (323) 462-5000
(Hair) www.traceymattingly.com

Khoa Nguyen (310) 550-1800
(Hair) www.fredsegalbeauty.com

Alex Noble (818) 206-0144
(Makeup) www.allcrewagency.com

Douglas Noe (818) 206-0144
www.allcrewagency.com

Gloria Noto (323) 664-6494
(Makeup) www.therexagency.com

Jennifer Nudelman (323) 906-9600
(Makeup) www.crystalagency.com

Walton Nunez (310) 550-1800
(Hair) www.fredsegalbeauty.com

Glenn Nutley (310) 998-1977
(Grooming, Hair & Makeup) www.celestineagency.com

Elaine Offers (323) 436-7766
(Makeup) www.eamgmt.com

Olive (323) 664-6494
(Makeup) www.therexagency.com

Bridget O'Neill (323) 874-5796
(Grooming & Makeup) FAX (323) 874-5797

Opus Beauty (323) 856-8540
6442 Santa Monica Blvd., Ste. 200B FAX (323) 871-8311
Los Angeles, CA 90038 www.opusbeauty.com
(Reps for Hair and Makeup Artists)

Valli O'Reilly (323) 937-1010
www.zenobia.com

Carlos Ortiz (310) 394-8813
(Hair) www.cloutieragency.com

Kat O'Shea (310) 274-0032
www.artistsbytimothypriano.com

Ermahn Ospina (818) 284-6423
(Makeup) www.italentco.com

Charlotte Ostergren (310) 822-2898
(Makeup) www.rougeartists.com

Yvonne Ouellette (949) 218-3948
(714) 293-0223
FAX (949) 218-3958
www.yvonneouellette.com

Dina Ousley (818) 308-8500
FAX (818) 308-8501
www.dinair.com

Shane Paish (310) 998-1977
(Makeup) www.celestineagency.com

Julia Palmer (323) 512-8002
(Manicurist) www.karleeartist.com

Yiotis Panayiotou (310) 998-1977
(Hair) www.celestineagency.com

George Papanikolas (323) 436-7766
(Colorist) www.eamgmt.com

Hyun Park (323) 906-9600
(Hair) www.crystalagency.com

Tena Parker Baker (661) 714-4665
(Hair) FAX (310) 390-9154

Bunny Parker (818) 222-5200
(Hair) www.schneiderentertainment.com

Deborah Patino (818) 371-9719
www.deborahpatino.com
(Grooming, Makeup & Special FX Makeup)

Cole Patterson (678) 438-7500
(818) 481-2222
(Makeup) www.lastlooksinc.com

Jeffrey Paul (323) 436-7766
(Grooming, Hair & Makeup) www.eamgmt.com

Samuel Paul (323) 935-8455
(323) 512-8002
(Makeup) www.ms-management.com

Denise Pauly (818) 506-7762
(818) 416-8549
FAX (818) 553-6654
denisepauly.com

Frankie Payne (323) 856-8540
(Hair) www.opusbeauty.com

Kristen Paynter (917) 834-4444
(323) 468-2240
www.kpaynter.com

Joanna Pensinger (323) 436-7766
(Grooming) www.eamgmt.com

Rachael Perrin (310) 274-0032
www.artistsbytimothypriano.com

Vicki Peters (323) 937-1010
www.zenobia.com

Randi Petersen (310) 274-0032
(Hair) www.artistsbytimothypriano.com

Shannon Pezatta (323) 299-4043
(Makeup) www.dionperonneau.com

Daniel Phillips (818) 206-0144
www.allcrewagency.com

Marilyn Patricia Phillips (818) 482-0588
(Hair) FAX (818) 848-1915

Shawn Phillips (310) 775-5723
www.agencycelebrityartists.com

Phayvanh Phongsa (310) 550-1800
(Hair) www.fredsegalbeauty.com

Photogenics (310) 733-2550
8549 Higuera St. FAX (310) 815-8632
Culver City, CA 90232 www.photogenicsmedia.com
(Reps for Hair and Makeup Artists)

Carol Pierce (310) 629-9729

Jennifer Pitt (323) 462-5000
(Makeup) www.traceymattingly.com

Stephanie Pohl (310) 274-0032
(Hair) www.artistsbytimothypriano.com

Lisa Postma (310) 998-1977
(Manicurist) www.celestineagency.com

Marilyn Poucher (818) 257-8002
(Makeup)

Toany Preusse (310) 775-5723
www.agencycelebrityartists.com

Vanessa Price (323) 664-6494
(Hair) www.therexagency.com

Jojo Proud (818) 206-0144
www.allcrewagency.com

Q Hardy (323) 299-4043
(Hair) www.dionperonneau.com

Serena Radaelli (310) 394-8813
(Hair) www.cloutieragency.com

Renee Rael (323) 933-0200
www.artistuntied.com

Robert Ramos (310) 998-1977
(Hair) www.celestineagency.com

Stephen Ramsey (310) 274-0032
(Grooming & Hair) www.artistsbytimothypriano.com

Carol Raskin (818) 206-0144
www.allcrewagency.com

Julie Rea (323) 935-8455
(Hair) www.ms-management.com

Darrell Redleaf (818) 769-9021
FAX (818) 769-0323
www.darrellredleaf.com
(Colorist, Grooming, Hair, Makeup & Wigs)

Laini Reeves (323) 462-5000
(Hair) www.traceymattingly.com

Brigitte Reiss-Andersen (310) 274-0032
(Makeup) www.artistsbytimothypriano.com

Michael P. Reitz (323) 874-6008
(Hair) FAX (323) 874-6009

The Rex Agency (323) 664-6494
4446 Ambrose Ave. FAX (323) 664-6112
Los Angeles, CA 90027 www.therexagency.com
(Reps for Hair and Makeup Artists)

Deanne Reynolds (310) 733-2550
www.photogenicsmedia.com

Leah Rial (323) 882-6822
(323) 702-2356
(Makeup) FAX (323) 882-6767

Julia Richardson (916) 925-7434
(415) 515-9840
(Makeup) www.californiamakeup.com

Andrea Richter (323) 299-4043
(Makeup) www.dionperonneau.com

Krystal Riddle (310) 550-1800
(Hair) www.fredsegalbeauty.com

Riku (310) 998-1977
(Makeup) www.celestineagency.com

Carlos Rittner (323) 937-1010
(Makeup) www.zenobia.com

Helen Robertson (310) 998-1977
(Makeup) www.celestineagency.com

Lia Robin (818) 515-9840
(661) 255-5505
FAX (661) 255-8315
www.liarobin.com

Wendy Robin (808) 371-8242
(888) 986-9333
FAX (808) 356-0804
www.studiowofhonolulu.com
(Body Painting, Makeup & Special FX Makeup)

Jeannia Robinette (323) 462-5000
(Makeup) www.traceymattingly.com

Todd Robinson (310) 775-5723
www.agencycelebrityartists.com

Ruth Roche (310) 274-0032
(Hair) www.artistsbytimothypriano.com

Bob Romero (818) 981-3338
(818) 953-6625
(Makeup) FAX (818) 981-3339
www.bobromero.com

Roque (323) 462-5000
(Hair) www.traceymattingly.com

Roshar (888) 839-0101
(Makeup) www.firehousemanagement.com

Charles Gregory Ross (818) 206-0144
www.allcrewagency.com

Rouge Artists, Inc. (310) 822-2898
(310) 570-1150
2433 Boone Ave. FAX (310) 827-7367
Venice, CA 90291 www.rougeartists.com
(Reps for Hair and Makeup Artists)

Celena Rubin (310) 502-3223
www.artofmakeup.com

Lisa Ruckh (213) 716-1723
www.beautybylisa.com
(Body Painter, Hair, Makeup, Special FX Makeup & Wigs)

Tania D. Russell (415) 777-9099
www.fordartists.com

Patrice Ryan (213) 700-2765

Robert Ryan (310) 864-6936
(Makeup) FAX (424) 208-3813
www.bobryandesign.com

Maital Sabban (323) 935-8455
(Makeup) www.ms-management.com

Sara Saltanovitz (310) 274-0032
www.artistsbytimothypriano.com
(Grooming, Hair & Makeup)

Stephan Salyers (323) 848-6952
(Makeup) web.mac.com/stephensalyers

Martin Samel (310) 601-2355
www.lesliealyson.com

Samelia (310) 822-2898
www.rougeartists.com

Gina Sandler (213) 509-0785
www.ginasandler.com
(Body Painting, Grooming, Makeup & Special FX Makeup)

Kathleen Sandoval (323) 937-1010
(Makeup) www.zenobia.com

Maria Sandoval (818) 822-7453
(Hair) FAX (866) 350-7389

Vanessa Scali (323) 462-5000
(Makeup) www.traceymattingly.com

Julie Schiffer (323) 223-3400
(Makeup) FAX (323) 223-3400

The Schneider Entertainment Agency (818) 222-5200
22287 Mulholland Hwy, Ste. 210 FAX (818) 222-5284
Calabasas, CA 91302
www.schneiderentertainment.com
(Reps for Hair and Makeup Artists)

Ulli Schober (310) 998-1977
(Makeup) www.celestineagency.com

Janeen Schreyer (818) 222-5200
(Makeup) www.schneiderentertainment.com

Kristan Serafino (323) 856-8540
(Hair) www.opusbeauty.com

Peter Serraino (661) 755-6849

Tatiana Sery (310) 274-0032
(Manicurist) www.artistsbytimothypriano.com

Shatsy (323) 464-8081
(323) 646-4730
(Makeup) FAX (323) 464-5575

Yvette Shelton (323) 850-6783
(Hair) www.dawn2duskagency.com

Kate Shorter (323) 661-2605
(323) 646-9816

Shyena (323) 436-7766
(Makeup) www.eamgmt.com

Rea Ann Silva (310) 822-2898
(Makeup) www.rougeartists.com

Arlene Silver (323) 906-9574
(310) 210-7935
FAX (323) 906-9574

Joe J. Simon (310) 274-0032
(Makeup) www.artistsbytimothypriano.com

Mili Simon (323) 937-1010
www.zenobia.com

Sharon Simon (661) 296-5996
(818) 389-7303
FAX (661) 296-5996
(Body Painting, Makeup & Special FX Makeup)

Larry Sims (323) 436-7766
(Hair) www.eamgmt.com

Veronica Sjoen (323) 933-0200
www.artistuntied.com

Mikal Sky (310) 694-7933
(310) 663-1914
FAX (213) 748-3654
www.skyboxmakeup.com
(Body Painting, Colorist, Grooming, Hair, Makeup, Manicurist, Special FX Makeup & Wigs)

Robin Slater (310) 202-1494
(310) 345-7095
www.imakeup.com

Dina Sliwiak (323) 468-2240
www.nyoffice.net

Elizabeth Sloan (213) 706-3562
www.elizabethsloan.com/make-up
(Grooming, Hair & Makeup)

Mike Smithson (818) 206-0144
(Makeup) www.allcrewagency.com

Bryin Smoot (310) 274-0032
www.artistsbytimothypriano.com

Patti Song (310) 394-8813
(Colorist) FAX (310) 394-8863
www.cloutieragency.com/pattisong

Natalie MacGowan Spencer (323) 525-0235
(Grooming, Hair & Makeup) FAX (310) 887-4843
www.macgowanspencer.com

Paul Starr (323) 297-0250
(Makeup) www.magnetla.com

Molly Stern (323) 297-0250
(Makeup) www.magnetla.com

Tanya Stine (323) 299-4043
(Hair) www.dionperonneau.com

Charles Baker Strahan (310) 274-0032
(Hair) www.artistsbytimothypriano.com

Jo Strettell (310) 394-8813
(Makeup) www.cloutieragency.com

Collier Strong (310) 394-8813
(Makeup) www.cloutieragency.com

Anouck Sullivan (310) 246-0446
www.workgroup-ltd.com

Sarah Sullivan (323) 556-3455
(310) 408-0861
(Makeup) www.margaretmaldonado.com

Tracy Sutter (310) 394-8813
(Manicurist) FAX (310) 394-8863
www.cloutieragency.com

Tabitha (310) 274-0032
(Manicurist) www.artistsbytimothypriano.com

Michelle Tabor (323) 937-9095
www.cheriereps.com

Solina Tabrizi (818) 284-6423
(Hair) www.italentco.com

Joyce Taft (310) 274-0032
www.artistsbytimothypriano.com
(Grooming, Hair & Makeup)

Talent, Concept & Design (818) 571-4492
(818) 729-7924
FAX (818) 729-7924
www.welshdragonpictures.com
(Hair, Makeup, and Special FX Makeup Crew)

Rob Talty (323) 856-8540
www.opusbeauty.com

Tamami (323) 664-6494
(Makeup) www.therexagency.com

TAMU Artist Agency (310) 721-0735
137 S. Robertson Blvd., Ste. 111 FAX (323) 571-3498
Beverly Hills, CA 90211 www.tamuartistagency.com
(Reps for Hair and Makeup Artists)

Stacy Morgan Taylor (949) 240-7770
(949) 235-0203
(Body Painting, Grooming, Hair, Makeup & Wigs)

Peggy Teague (818) 704-1410
(818) 929-8814
(Makeup) FAX (818) 704-1410

Peg Thielen (818) 506-6161
(Grooming & Makeup) www.pegthielen.com

Vaniece Thomas (323) 512-8002
(Makeup) www.karleeartist.com

Dominie Till (818) 206-0144
www.allcrewagency.com

Kim Todd (323) 299-4043
www.dionperonneau.com

Tokyo (310) 246-0446
www.workgroup-ltd.com

D. Garen Tolkin (323) 436-7766
(Grooming, Hair & Makeup) www.eamgmt.com

Peter Tothpal (310) 601-2355
www.lesliealyson.com

Mark Townsend (323) 297-0250
(Hair) www.magnetla.com

Tracey Mattingly, LLC (323) 462-5000
(Reps for Hair and Makeup Artists) FAX (323) 462-5001
www.traceymattingly.com

Patrick Tumey (310) 998-1977
(Makeup) www.celestineagency.com

Tina Turnbow (310) 274-0032
(Makeup) www.artistsbytimothypriano.com

Kerrie Urban (310) 274-0032
www.artistsbytimothypriano.com

Matthew Vanleeuwen (323) 462-5000
(Makeup) www.traceymattingly.com

Terrie Velazquez-Owen (818) 284-6423
(Hair) www.italentco.com

Kim Verbeck (323) 436-7766
(Grooming) www.eamgmt.com

Melanie Verkins (818) 248-6044
(818) 388-2204
FAX (818) 248-6044

Robert Vetica (323) 297-0250
(Hair) www.magnetla.com

Lona Vigi (323) 297-0250
(Hair) www.magnetla.com

Johnny Villanueva (323) 462-5000
(Hair) www.traceymattingly.com

Anne Visconti (323) 934-9810
(Hair & Wigs)

Gina Viviano (310) 274-0032
(Manicurist) www.artistsbytimothypriano.com

Angela Vriese (310) 550-1800
(Makeup) www.fredsegalbeauty.com

Bertrand W. (323) 462-5000
(Hair) www.traceymattingly.com

Vickie Waite (805) 427-2310
(805) 492-3680
FAX (805) 492-3680
www.bridalbeauty.info

Ewan Walker (323) 299-4043
(Makeup) www.dionperonneau.com

The Wall Group LA (310) 276-0777
329 N. Wetherly Dr., Ste. 207 FAX (310) 276-0107
Beverly Hills, CA 90211 www.thewallgroup.com
(Reps for Hair and Makeup Artists)

Ken Wallace (310) 288-8000
(Special FX Makeup) www.paradigmagency.com

Melissa Walsh (323) 549-3100
www.beautyandphoto.com

Greta Weatherby (323) 445-4910
www.artists-services.com

Laura Weathersby (310) 274-0032
www.artistsbytimothypriano.com

Rhiannon Webb (310) 775-5723
www.agencycelebrityartists.com

Charlene Wee (818) 625-5985
(Makeup)

Rick Wellman (310) 274-0032
(Colorist) www.artistsbytimothypriano.com

Angie Wells (818) 415-7212
(310) 497-7212
(Makeup & Special FX Makeup) FAX (310) 656-5758
www.angiewells.com

Barry White (323) 512-8002
(Grooming) www.karleeartist.com

Michael White (818) 206-0144
(Hair) www.allcrewagency.com

Brad Wilder (310) 601-2355
www.lesliealyson.com

Prisca Wille (323) 868-5760
(323) 936-0090
FAX (323) 257-0696
www.prisca.com

Michelle Wilson (323) 578-2133
www.michelledoesmakeup.com
(Grooming, Hair & Makeup)

Ellen Wong (805) 984-7298
(310) 570-7242
celebrity-network.net/makeup/ellenwong/home.html
(Grooming & Makeup)

Natalie Wood (818) 206-0144
(Makeup) **www.allcrewagency.com**

Workgroup, Ltd. (310) 246-0446
(212) 675-6334
(Reps for Hair and Makeup Artists) FAX **(415) 674-1950**
www.workgroup-ltd.com

John Wright (323) 856-8540
(Makeup) **www.opusbeauty.com**

Vera Yurtchuk (818) 884-0517
(Grooming,Makeup & Special FX Makeup)

Zenobia Agency, Inc. (323) 937-1010
(888) 639-6917
130 S. Highland Ave. FAX **(323) 937-1133**
Los Angeles, CA 90036 **www.zenobia.com**
(Reps for Hair and Makeup Artists)

Zulica (323) 937-1010
www.zenobia.com

Donny Abrams (310) 600-7499
(Line Producer)

Mitch Ackerman (310) 656-5151
www.innovativeartists.com

Penny Adams (310) 288-8000
(Line Producer) www.paradigmagency.com

Paul M. Addis (818) 990-8993
www.ambitiousent.com

Brian Ades (310) 503-8080

Gilbert Adler (310) 273-6700
www.unitedtalent.com

Neal Ahern (310) 288-8000
(Line Producer) www.paradigmagency.com

Julie Alford-Sawyer (310) 529-1992
(Line Producer)

All Crew Agency (818) 206-0144
2920 W. Olive Ave., Ste. 201 FAX (818) 206-0169
Burbank, CA 91505 www.allcrewagency.com
(Reps for Producers)

Mark Allan (310) 288-8000
www.paradigmagency.com

Donald V. Allen (310) 390-5522
FAX (310) 390-6520

Kelly Amato (310) 374-2786
(310) 600-8224

Emie H. Amemiya (323) 463-3033

Karen Anderson (310) 815-8897
FAX (310) 815-1269
www.epiphanypictures.com

William Artope (213) 741-9301
(310) 466-1040
FAX (213) 741-2303
www.wildeyedent.com

Ken Ashe (310) 855-4238
FAX (512) 532-6194

Louise Barlow (310) 993-8172
www.louisebarlow.com

LuAnn Barry-Goldman (310) 474-2439
FAX (310) 474-5282

Jane Bartelme (310) 273-6700
www.unitedtalent.com

Bill Beasley (310) 273-6700
www.unitedtalent.com

Brian Bell (310) 288-8000
www.paradigm.com

Marc Benardout (323) 697-8154
FAX (413) 691-8154
www.birthmarc.com

Robert Bennett (310) 550-6885
FAX (310) 550-6253
www.hdrepublic.com

Linda Berenstein Mason (323) 650-4449
(Line Producer)

Lester Berman (310) 288-8000
www.paradigmagency.com

Yvonne M. Bernard (310) 382-4535
FAX (310) 798-3001

Tim Berry (818) 206-0144
www.allcrewagency.com

Stuart Besser (310) 288-8000
www.paradigmagency.com

Michael Beugg (310) 285-0303
www.marshbest.com

Dolly Tarazon Billinger (818) 506-5829
(818) 645-6115
(Line Producer)

Dennis Bishop (310) 288-8000
www.paradigmagency.com

Stuart Black (310) 821-2221
(310) 804-1479
FAX (310) 821-4106

Laurie Boccaccio (213) 706-3484
(Line Producer)

Hope Grossman Bolois (818) 905-7972
FAX (818) 784-3050

Ron Bozman (310) 273-6700
www.unitedtalent.com

Drew Bracken (818) 606-5478
FAX (818) 831-8047

Steven Brandman (310) 656-5151
www.innovativeartists.com

Barbara Brentano (562) 366-4234
(310) 266-9980
(Spanish) FAX (562) 439-8242

Adam Brightman (310) 288-8000
www.paradigmagency.com

Terri Lee Brook (818) 559-8656
(310) 720-3477
FAX (818) 559-1569

G. Mac Brown (914) 968-2330
(310) 273-6700
www.unitedtalent.com

Pola Brown (323) 528-2755

Rick Brown (310) 922-1946

Steven Brown (310) 656-5151
www.innovativeartists.com

Pieter Jan Brugge (310) 273-6700
www.utaproduction.com

Gary Bryman (310) 612-6767

Shirley Bukrey-Lloyd (310) 306-1502
(Spanish)

Alexander Buono (310) 288-8000
www.paradigmagency.com

Patrick Burns (818) 908-3361

Thomas Busch (310) 288-8000
(Line Producer) www.paradigmagency.com

Marol Butcher (323) 906-9088
(323) 497-0097

John Callas (310) 393-4519
(310) 344-5334
FAX (310) 395-4412

Joseph Caracciolo Jr. (310) 282-9940
(917) 796-7056
www.mirisch.com

Katie Carlson (310) 625-6244

Don Carmody (310) 282-9940
www.mirisch.com

Wayne Carmona (310) 288-8000
(Line Producer) www.paradigmagency.com

Mark Castro (626) 564-8195
(213) 309-7680
FAX (626) 628-3959

Bruce Catania (818) 990-8993
www.ambitiousent.com

Ed Cathell (310) 285-0303
www.marshbest.com

Ronnie Chong (310) 288-8000
www.paradigmagency.com

David Coatsworth (310) 273-6700
www.unitedtalent.com

Lisa Cochran (310) 288-8000
(Line Producer) www.paradigmagency.com

Audrey S. Cohen (310) 208-6776
(305) 385-2204
FAX (310) 208-6776

Robert P. Cohen (310) 656-5151
www.innovativeartists.com

Mark Cooper (310) 288-8000
www.paradigmagency.com

John Corser (213) 200-1477
(800) 245-3149
FAX (323) 843-9486
www.corser.com

Brian Cowan (310) 288-8000
(Line Producer) www.paradigmagency.com

Clint Cowen (323) 656-7415
(323) 497-8117

Kristen Cox (818) 749-6608
FAX (323) 851-1659
www.16x9productions.com

Scott Craig (323) 665-2069
(213) 364-4894

Chris Crawford (323) 912-9175
(323) 646-1375

Anthony Santa Croce (310) 282-9940
www.mirisch.com

Ruthie Crossley (323) 735-6811
(310) 918-5352

Terry Crotzer (818) 990-8993
www.ambitiousent.com

Bill Curran (310) 392-1035
(310) 729-4701

Michelle Currinder (213) 703-6424

Douglas Curtis (310) 282-9940
www.mirisch.com

Madelyn Curtis (310) 459-8976

Russell Curtis (818) 994-1802

Jim Czarnecki (310) 474-4585
www.dattnerdispoto.com

J. Miles Dale (310) 285-0303
www.marshbest.com

Betsy Danbury (818) 284-6423
(Line Producer) www.italentco.com

Dave Darmour (310) 393-9004
(323) 363-3930

Rick Days (323) 221-9003

Joe Dea (818) 990-8993
www.ambitiousent.com

Heather Dear (805) 696-6901
(Line Producer)

Andrew Denyer (310) 795-3084

Maurice DePas (818) 292-6531

Diana De Vries (323) 864-7975
(Line Producer) FAX (310) 358-3174

Kimberly Dickens (310) 288-8000
www.paradigmagency.com

Steve Dietrich (818) 760-2915
(818) 422-3470
FAX (818) 980-2028

Kat Dillon (310) 399-7839

Joe Dishner (818) 284-6423
(Line Producer) www.italentco.com

Karen Dixon (310) 386-8082
www.karendandcompany.com

Robert Doherty (310) 656-5151
www.innovativeartists.com

Anita Zommers Dollens (310) 874-3757
(808) 735-8447
FAX (310) 919-3075

Carr Donald (818) 419-7400
FAX (818) 508-1193

Brian Donnelly (310) 880-9400

Sarah J. Donohue (818) 206-0144
www.allcrewagency.com

Gary Dorf (310) 476-8380
FAX (818) 789-6435

Janice Doskey (914) 261-2267
(866) 545-8878
(French)

Ned Doyle (310) 480-4190
(973) 763-6679

(323) 896-5889

Henri Dragonas (323) 822-9884
(Line Producer) FAX (323) 822-9244

Valerie Druckman (323) 654-5402

Peggy Dunn (310) 398-4867
(310) 200-3979

James R. Dyer (310) 273-6700
www.unitedtalent.com

Bob Engelman (310) 288-8000
www.paradigmagency.com

Buddy Enright (310) 285-0303
www.marshbest.com

Edy H. Enriquez (310) 836-9011
(323) 252-0904
FAX (310) 836-9010
www.x1fx.com

Leslie M. Evers (310) 600-7373
(Line Producer)

Marty Ewing (310) 288-8000
(Line Producer) www.paradigmagency.com

Dawn Fanning (626) 695-1112
(626) 791-5811
FAX (626) 791-9611

Denise Daniels Fanning (213) 399-9831

Franny Faull (310) 614-0992

Tom Fauntleroy (805) 898-1035
(805) 570-8320

Thom Fennessey (323) 650-2500

Greg Ferguson (818) 519-8764

Barry Fink (310) 880-0311
(310) 822-2350
(Line Producer)

Debbie A. Fisher (310) 475-8767

Karin Fittante (323) 937-1010
www.zenobia.com

Michael Flynn (310) 273-6700
www.utaproduction.com

D.J. Ford (323) 731-4214
(818) 621-5184

Michael Fottrell (310) 288-8000
www.paradigmagency.com

JP Fox (310) 351-2549

Billy Frank (818) 981-2327
FAX (818) 981-2440
www.mihp.tv

Ruth Frazier (818) 848-9129
(818) 288-0815
FAX (818) 558-5772

Franny Freiberger (818) 415-5554

Jeff Freilich (310) 288-8000
(Line Producer) www.paradigmagency.com

Nona Sue Friedman (323) 468-9975
(310) 562-2161

Bruce Fritzberg (323) 822-7881
(818) 231-2260

Nancy Fulton-Rogers (310) 376-7757
(310) 880-3338

Oliver Fuselier (310) 600-5825

Ursula Gabel (310) 489-6352

Karen Gainer (818) 558-7006

Debbie Galloway (818) 424-2353
(Line Producer)

Pat Garvin (310) 453-2597
FAX (310) 453-2347

Kent Gates (818) 667-5368
www.freewebtown.com/callsheet/

Steve Gerbson (818) 990-8993
www.ambitiousent.com

The Gersh Agency (310) 274-6611
(212) 997-1818
P.O. Box 5617 www.gershagency.com
Beverly Hills, CA 90210
(Reps for Producers)

Jason Gilbert (310) 804-0436

Ken Gilbert (805) 374-6090
(805) 208-1753

Peter Giuliano (310) 273-6700
www.unitedtalent.com

Hilary Glaholt (310) 710-2717

Leora Glass (323) 938-9553
(213) 709-8000

Cellin Gluck (310) 454-5594
(310) 382-0303
FAX (310) 454-5523

Nanette Gobel (310) 801-2164

Marty Gold (818) 892-3665

Jon Goldberg (310) 401-1122
(310) 936-2077

Phillip M. Goldfarb (310) 656-5151
www.innovativeartists.com

Jared Goldman (310) 288-8000
(Line Producer) www.paradigmagency.com

Nigel Goldsack (310) 285-0303
www.marshbest.com

Andrew Golov (310) 474-4585
www.dattnerdispoto.com

John Gomez (805) 587-2982

Gregory E. Goodman (310) 273-6700
www.unitedtalent.com

Arthur Gorson (323) 876-3331
(Line Producer) FAX (323) 876-4666
www.wildindigo.tv

Janice K. Goto (415) 990-4470
(415) 383-1225

David Grace (310) 656-5151
www.innovativeartists.com

Robert Graf (310) 273-6700
www.unitedtalent.com

Callum Greene (310) 273-6700
www.unitedtalent.com

Katy Greene (310) 406-8800

Susan Gross (310) 829-6202

Jacqueline Hakim (310) 871-7181

Barbara A. Hall (310) 285-0303
www.marshbest.com

Naia Hall (323) 650-4893

Ken Halsband (310) 288-8000
(Line Producer) www.paradigmagency.com

Greg A. Hampson (310) 288-8000
(Line Producer) www.paradigmagency.com

Shari Hanson (562) 433-8502

John Hardy (818) 284-6423
(Line Producer) FAX (866) 755-0708
www.italentco.com

Cheddy Hart (818) 206-0144
www.allcrewagency.com

Jim Hart (310) 288-8000
www.paradigmagency.com

David Hartley (310) 288-8000
(Line Producer) www.paradigmagency.com

Joel Hatch (310) 288-8000
www.paradigmagency.com

Tracy Hauser (310) 293-2752

Jamie Haynes (310) 305-7139
FAX (310) 827-7367

Jonathan Haze (818) 763-3041
(818) 314-7997
FAX (818) 763-3042

Allison Heath (310) 729-3302

Bob Heath (310) 288-8000
(Line Producer) www.paradigmagency.com

Laura Brown Heflin (310) 322-0007
(310) 779-7955

Paul Hellerman (310) 288-8000
www.paradigmagency.com

Youree Henley (323) 497-9600

Kendall Henry (323) 462-5934
(626) 688-0409
(Line Producer)

Carol Lang Herrick (805) 496-0249
(206) 232-7100

Peter Heslop (310) 288-8000
(Line Producer) www.paradigmagency.com

Paul Hettler (415) 608-6758
(415) 381-1606
FAX (415) 381-1030

Cynthia Hill (310) 753-9991
www.artagogo.net

Victor Ho (310) 285-0303
www.marshbest.com

Ulla Hoeller (310) 589-0030
(323) 394-1248
(French & German) FAX (310) 526-7702

Sam Hoffman (310) 288-8000
(Line Producer) www.paradigmagency.com

Nick Holden (310) 858-8981
(Line Producer)

Lisa Hollingshead (310) 880-7556
(323) 828-5780

Antonia Holt (323) 871-0201
(213) 810-5059
(French) FAX (323) 871-0315

John Hopgood (818) 760-6923
(Line Producer)

Craig Houchin (818) 951-5959
www.craighouchin.com

Chantal Houle (310) 953-9166
(French) www.chantalhoule.com

Scott Howard (818) 789-5032

Michael Huens (323) 365-5797
www.wolvesatthedoor.com

Holly D. Hughes (818) 951-6889

Joseph Iberti (310) 282-9940
www.mirisch.com

International Creative Management - ICM (310) 550-4000
10250 Constellation Blvd. www.icmtalent.com
Los Angeles, CA 90067
(Reps for Producers)

Caroline Jaczko (310) 288-8000
www.paradigmagency.com

Polly Johnson (310) 721-1276

Bronston Jones (310) 849-4994
www.attackads.tv

Stephen Jones (310) 273-6700
www.unitedtalent.com

Anna Joseph (310) 628-9233
(310) 823-4852
FAX (310) 822-8859

John Joseph (818) 990-8993
www.ambitiousent.com

Georgia Kacandes (310) 273-6700
www.unitedtalent.com

Elena Kakoullis (213) 446-6262
FAX (213) 626-5330

Mark Kalbfeld (310) 497-1645
(818) 879-9955

Avram Butch Kaplan (310) 288-8000
www.paradigmagency.com

Jan Katz (310) 821-2221
(310) 804-0913
FAX (310) 821-4106

Doron Kauper (818) 907-6028
FAX (818) 804-5121
www.wrappersystems.com

Dessa Kaye (818) 766-7318

Richard Kaylor (310) 463-3845

Jay Kelman (310) 390-4747
(310) 386-0098
FAX (310) 915-6650

Kristy Kessler (310) 968-7713

Ric Kidney (310) 273-6700
www.unitedtalent.com

Todd King (310) 288-8000
www.paradigmagency.com

Nancy Kissock (310) 475-5615
FAX (310) 475-5615

Michael Klick (310) 204-2986
(310) 720-2986
FAX (310) 204-5155

Kim Knight (310) 274-0032
www.artistsbytimothypriano.com

Rob Knox (323) 876-6435
FAX (323) 446-8339

Buzz Koenig (310) 282-9940
www.mirisch.com

Teresa E. Kounin (310) 273-8677

Chris Kraft (323) 791-5135
FAX (323) 372-3614

Erwin Kramer (310) 446-1866
(Line Producer) (310) 266-8146
FAX (310) 446-1856
www.erwinkramer.com

Paul Kurta (818) 406-3020

Coni Lancaster (310) 823-3115
FAX (310) 823-8366

Patti Lancaster (310) 479-1424
FAX (310) 445-3301

Christopher Landry (818) 206-0144
www.allcrewagency.com

Kathy Landsberg (310) 288-8000
(Line Producer) www.paradigmagency.com

Henry Lange (310) 288-8000
(Line Producer) www.paradigmagency.com

Roger La Page (818) 368-3243
(818) 468-7191
FAX (818) 368-3243

Marc Lasko (310) 479-4100

Bill Latka (310) 990-1938

Mary Leonard (626) 791-9790
www.maryleonard.net

Darcy Leslie-Parsons (310) 963-6629
(310) 837-2817

Deven LeTendre (626) 577-6894
(818) 414-2020
FAX (626) 577-6814

Diane Leuci (631) 827-2784
(Line Producer)

Herb Linsey (323) 874-9487

Sonny Lowe (310) 994-8097
(French)

Lindy Lucas (310) 877-1066
FAX (818) 242-4429
www.lindylucas.com

Martha Lucas (213) 481-7109
(323) 376-9699

Scott Luhrsen (323) 871-0201
(323) 791-1909
FAX (323) 871-0315

Margot Lulick (310) 288-8000
(Line Producer) www.paradigmagency.com

Scott Lumpkin (310) 288-8000
www.paradigmagency.com

Daniel Lupi (310) 273-6700
www.unitedtalent.com

Tim Lynch (310) 704-5568
FAX 310-496-1438
www.woodshedfilms.com

Don MacBain (310) 910-1220

Peter MacGregor-Scott (310) 282-9940
www.mirisch.com

Neil Machlis (310) 282-9940
www.mirisch.com

Paul Manix (818) 414-2229

Earl Mann (818) 906-3309
(818) 371-1135

John Marias (310) 394-4214
(310) 245-4204
FAX (310) 395-2590

Gina Marsh (310) 285-0303
www.marshbest.com

Theresa Marth (818) 760-7174
(818) 404-9314

Byron A. Martin (818) 206-0144
www.allcrewagency.com

Keegan Martin (818) 990-8993
www.ambitiousent.com

Sandy Martin (323) 851-3755
(213) 509-7722
FAX (323) 851-4359

Fatima Martins (310) 899-0923
(Portuguese & Spanish)

Molly Mayeux (818) 284-6423
(Line Producer) www.italentco.com

Lisa McClelland (310) 457-3290
(310) 924-2022

Maura McCoy (310) 266-7511
(310) 301-3575

Michael McDonnell (310) 474-4585
www.dattnerdispoto.com

Steve McGlothen (310) 656-5151
www.innovativeartists.com

Kimberly McGregor (310) 474-4585
www.dattnerdispoto.com

Christopher McKinnon (310) 572-7929
(213) 494-7404
www.afewgoodideas.com

Mark McNair (310) 273-6700
www.utaproduction.com

Craig McNeil (310) 288-8000
www.paradigmagency.com

Samuel L. Mercer (310) 285-0303
www.marshbest.com

Adam Merims (310) 273-6700
www.unitedtalent.com

Richard Middleton (310) 656-5151
www.innovativeartists.com

Anita Miller (805) 909-2104

Bobby Miller (949) 494-3263
FAX (949) 494-7945

Jeff Miller (323) 851-2001
(310) 344-9404
FAX (323) 851-2061

Terry Miller (310) 288-8000
(Line Producer) www.paradigmagency.com

Roger Mills (818) 242-0532

Leslie Miretti (310) 399-2000
FAX (310) 459-8484

The Mirisch Agency (310) 282-9940
1925 Century Park East, Ste. 1070 FAX (310) 282-0702
Los Angeles, CA 90067 www.mirisch.com
(Reps for Producers)

Scott Mislan (310) 880-9043
www.imdb.com/name/nm0006502/

Tom E. Mitchell (818) 990-2355
FAX (818) 990-5215

Kim Monaco (310) 994-1529

Philip A. Mondello (213) 399-7624

Montana Artists Agency (323) 845-4144
7715 W. Sunset Blvd., Third Fl. FAX (323) 845-4155
Los Angeles, CA 90046 www.montanartists.com
(Reps for Producers)

Alexander J. Moon (323) 428-8641

Leanne Moore (310) 288-8000
(Line Producer) www.paradigmagency.com

Sharon Morov (310) 383-6572

Caylyn Eastin Morris (310) 963-1522

JJ Morris (323) 868-8806

Pamela Morrow (310) 306-8320
(310) 490-7771

Robyn L. Moskow (562) 434-6918
(213) 910-8855

Samson Mucke (310) 656-5151
www.innovativeartists.com

Jack Murray (310) 288-8000
www.paradigmagency.com

The Murtha Agency (310) 822-9113
4240 Promenade Way, Ste. 232 FAX (310) 822-6662
Marina Del Rey, CA 90292 www.murthaagency.com
(Reps for Producers)

Matt Myers (310) 288-8000
(Line Producer) www.paradigmagency.com

Tina Nakane (213) 500-4700

Rick Nathanson (310) 288-8000
www.paradigmagency.com

Jack Nayer (310) 301-3020
(718) 622-5046
FAX (718) 636-9446

Cindy Nelson (310) 274-0032
www.artistsbytimothypriano.com

Michael Nelson (310) 285-0303
www.marshbest.com

Todd Nelson (213) 384-0810
(213) 220-1028
www.braska.com

Merilee Newman (310) 384-6184
(310) 399-7463

David Nicksay (310) 273-6700
www.unitedtalent.com

Elizabeth Nicole (323) 937-1010
www.zenobia.com

Beryt Nisenson (713) 256-8044
(323) 638-5870
(Line Producer; Medical Projects) FAX (713) 400-9151
www.berytn.com

Kevin Noonan (310) 251-6880

Vanessa Norris-Nalle (818) 437-0470
(714) 849-6491

Nellie Nugiel (310) 288-8000
(Line Producer) www.paradigmagency.com

M. Margaret O'Brien-Sparks (818) 388-9726
(818) 997-1993
FAX (818) 997-1993

Gary Odom (818) 990-8993
www.ambitiousent.com

Colleen O'Donnell (818) 591-1953
(818) 437-1133

Jennifer Ogden (310) 282-9940
www.mirisch.com

Pamela O'Mara (310) 540-8411
(310) 901-5515
FAX (310) 545-0136

Karri O'Reilly (323) 691-5539
www.karrioco.com

Ken Ornstein (310) 288-8000
(Line Producer) www.paradigmagency.com

Wayne Nelson Page (818) 990-8993
www.ambitiousent.com

Paul Papanek (323) 732-0776

Brian Parker (310) 656-5151
www.innovativeartists.com

Beth Pearson (310) 567-5725
(310) 457-6195
FAX (818) 889-2193

Emily Perez (310) 804-7479
FAX (818) 352-2667
www.photographers.com/red9

David Persoff (323) 791-3840
(Line Producer)

Diana Phillips (310) 285-0303
www.marshbest.com

Piazzie (323) 937-1096

Danya Pink (310) 288-8000
www.paradigmagency.com

Denise Pouchet (818) 566-1381
FAX (818) 566-1381

Rick Powers (310) 710-9397

Greg Prange (310) 288-8000
www.paradigmagency.com

Erik Press (213) 324-2366

Patricia Priest (727) 612-6277
(323) 466-3288

Tom Prince (310) 822-9113
www.murthaagency.com

Jack Provost (818) 988-8150
FAX (818) 988-8152

Roger Pugliese (818) 206-0144
www.allcrewagency.com

Nakiya Ramsey (310) 500-0223
(310) 215-3234

Ron Rapiel (310) 390-5454
(310) 890-1100

Kevin Reidy (310) 656-5151
www.innovativeartists.com

Randy Rennolds (818) 846-2334
FAX (818) 567-1123

Craig Repass (310) 420-1955
(818) 591-8807

Craig Respol (818) 346-4641
(310) 776-1229

Lynn Reynolds (323) 851-4662
(541) 601-7913
FAX (541) 552-0852

Kathryn L. Rhodes (310) 475-0709

Guy Riedel (310) 288-8000
www.paradigmagency.com

Christina Ritzmann (310) 454-4805
(310) 613-4854
FAX (310) 454-4818

Selwyn Roberts (310) 288-8000
www.paradigmagency.com

Gary Robinson (310) 247-0818
FAX (310) 858-2254
www.sharpcut.com

Denise Rocchietti (818) 783-3214
(818) 519-4660

Vicki Dee Rock (310) 288-8000
www.paradigmagency.com

David Roessell (310) 288-8000
(Line Producer) www.paradigmagency.com

Karen Rohrbacher (310) 488-1959
(310) 459-4708
(Line Producer)

Jake Rose (310) 288-8000
(Line Producer) www.paradigmagency.com

Louise Rosner (310) 273-6700
www.unitedtalent.com

Richard Rothschild (310) 288-8000
(Line Producer) www.paradigmagency.com

Edward Royce (949) 752-7761
FAX (949) 752-2034
www.roycemultimedia.com

Kelly Andrea Rubin (310) 498-1805

Danny Rubio (310) 392-2302
(310) 435-9260
FAX (310) 392-2302

Steve Ruggieri (310) 503-6911
(818) 368-0666
FAX (818) 360-0237

Jeremiah Samuels (310) 273-6700
www.unitedtalent.com

Amy M. Samuelson (310) 463-1238

Rayna Saslove (323) 939-9309
(323) 440-5827

Cat Sautter (760) 439-6600
FAX (760) 439-6688

Robert Schmidt (818) 842-1929

Sascha Schneider (310) 288-8000
(Line Producer) www.paradigmagency.com

Sarah Schoessler (310) 577-0877
(310) 259-0600
FAX (310) 919-1877

John D. Schofield (310) 273-6700
www.unitedtalent.com

Larry Schreiner (310) 874-2164

Jan Scott (310) 833-1770

Don Scotti (818) 506-3060
(310) 990-0646
FAX (323) 460-6063

Jeffrey J. Scruton (310) 454-8290
FAX (310) 459-4051

Paige Seidel (213) 810-6526

Hani Selim (310) 452-9644
(310) 480-8738
FAX (310) 452-9655
www.concreteimages.com

Larry Serraino (661) 607-6528
FAX (661) 254-6402

Harvey Shapiro (310) 395-4546
(310) 702-9855
(Line Producer) FAX (310) 395-4546

Kim Shapiro (818) 389-6888

Robert Shapiro (310) 282-9940
www.mirisch.com

Roee Sharon (323) 447-4618

Kyra Shelgren (818) 207-4330
(Line Producer)

Dona Shine (818) 519-7972

Jim Shippee (310) 480-5988

Michael Shores (323) 791-9433
(Line Producer) www.heavenanimage.com

Jason Shubb (310) 288-8000
(Line Producer) www.paradigmagency.com

Thom Sidoti (310) 600-6669
www.agavefilms.com

Scott Siegal (626) 794-7760
(213) 713-0154

Marc Siegel (323) 653-3550
FAX (323) 653-3553

Jeffrey Silver (310) 273-6700
www.unitedtalent.com

Tim Silver (310) 739-7356
(310) 399-5122

Rudd Simmons (310) 285-0303
www.marshbest.com

Jimmy Simons (310) 288-8000
www.paradigmagency.com

Eric Siss (310) 628-7226

Jay Sisson (213) 820-3075
(Spanish)

Enzo Sisti (310) 822-9113
www.murthaagency.com

Lindsay Skutch (805) 687-9852
(805) 341-3554

Ginger Sledge (310) 285-0303
www.marshbest.com

Al Smith (310) 452-3751
(310) 864-8550

Iain Smith (310) 285-0303
www.marshbest.com

Daniel Sollinger (818) 206-0144
www.allcrewagency.com

Jeanne Stack (310) 457-5645
(310) 600-1599

Marlon Staggs (323) 790-0440

Suzanne Stanford (310) 989-5787

Michelle Stark (323) 851-7055
(323) 401-5656

Sharon Starr (818) 994-7017

Gregg Stern (310) 292-0915
FAX (505) 982-0163

Philip Steuer (310) 273-6700
www.unitedtalent.com

Brad Stevenson (213) 716-7893
(818) 222-8251

Nancy Rae Stone (818) 284-6423
(Line Producer) www.italentco.com

Steven Strachan (310) 459-1299

Cristen Car Strubbe (310) 273-6700
www.utaproduction.com

Joel Tabbush (818) 481-9396
(773) 325-9901
www.tabbush.com

Michele Tamme (818) 701-9908
(818) 804-8797

Maryann Tanedo (310) 288-7868

Sal Tassone (310) 455-7822
(310) 403-0007
(French, Italian & Spanish) FAX (310) 455-1245

Lisa Tauscher (310)422-7981

Eileen Terry (310) 663-9370
(808) 780-8707
(Line Producer)

Debbie Tietjen (310) 418-3632

Michael Tillman (323) 938-1756
(323) 788-3383

Debby Timmons (818) 906-2093

Lisa Timmons (818) 708-8589

Steven Tobenkin (310) 621-1122
FAX (310) 388-1403

Joanne Toll (310) 288-8000
www.paradigmagency.com

Clayton Townsend (310) 395-9550
www.skouras.com

Lee Trask (310) 396-5023

Judy Trotter (805) 695-0499
(805) 705-2150

Maureen Tunney (818) 907-9456
(818) 645-7149
(Line Producer)

Jeff Tuttle (626) 824-1222

Richard Vane (310) 273-6700
www.unitedtalent.com

Kelly Van Horn (310) 282-9940
www.mirisch.com

Pete Vanlaw (818) 762-3810
(818) 506-6977
FAX (818) 769-2847
www.western-branch.com

Jim Van Wyck (310) 282-9940
www.mirisch.com

Chrisann Verges (310) 273-6700
www.unitedtalent.com

Susan Vogelfang (310) 306-2648
(Line Producer)

Allan Wachs (310) 589-4841
(310) 467-5131

Mark Walejko (310) 344-8949

E. Bennett Walsh (310) 285-0303
www.marshbest.com

Peter Ware (310) 288-8000
www.paradigmagency.com

Francine Weiner (818) 419-4800
(Line Producer)

Bobby Weinstein (310) 306-1960
FAX (310) 306-1820

Danielle Weinstock (310) 288-8000
(Line Producer) www.paradigmagency.com

Dara Weintraub (310) 273-6700
www.unitedtalent.com

Phyllis Weisband-Fibus (818) 760-8111
FAX (818) 760-8112

Jaki West (310) 374-2082
(Line Producer)

Jon Douglas West (818) 761-4488
(310) 888-4592
FAX (818) 761-2112

Kathy Wheelock (818) 901-0987
FAX (818) 988-5314

Ree Whitford (818) 424-9988
(818) 505-1060

Rick Whiting (310) 392-6000
(415) 332-6462
FAX (415) 332-6462

Shannon Wickliffe (323) 422-8834
(619) 961-5669
(Line Producer) www.shannonwickliffe.com

Jan Wieringa (323) 871-9000
(323) 363-1110
FAX (323) 962-8028
www.zoofilm.net

William C. Wiles (949) 702-3313
(949) 640-6246
FAX (949) 640-6518

Michael Williams (818) 206-0144
www.allcrewagency.com

Tom Wilson (323) 662-7976
www.nobodyproductions.com

Ken Winber (310) 780-3636

Stan Wlodkowski (310) 273-6700
www.unitedtalent.com

David Wolfson (818) 371-5678
(512) 345-5197
FAX (512) 345-5668
www.spoonfilms.com

Jason Wolk (213) 804-4743
(Spanish) www.jasonwolk.net

Johanna Woollcott (310) 390-3778
(310) 592-6120

Steve Woroniecki (310) 344-1442

Craig Wyrick-Solari (310) 288-8000
(Line Producer) www.paradigmagency.com

Lila Yacoub (310) 285-0303
www.marshbest.com

Diana Young (310) 862-4201
(310) 990-9503
www.bajalaprod.com

Gabrielle Yuro (310) 500-8153

Raymond Zarro (310) 460-2424
FAX (310) 399-7614

Don Zepfel (310) 282-9940
www.mirisch.com

Jack Ziga (323) 664-9862
(323) 465-9862

Joel R. Zimmerman (310) 399-9906
(310) 993-5703
www.joelzimmerman.com

Joseph Zolfo (310) 288-8000
(Line Producer) www.paradigmagency.com

Leslie Zurla (818) 762-4346
(818) 207-1743
FAX (818) 506-8483

Beth Alonso (310) 228-8268
FAX (866) 291-0439

Lisa Azuma (310) 430-3143
(Japanese)

Lisa Bemel (310) 600-9625
(212) 452-2314

Pepper Carlson (310) 261-4099
FAX (310) 681-0238
www.peppercarlson.com

Julie Clark (818) 766-3974
(818) 692-5631

Danielle Flores (323) 953-6408

Kris Homsher (310) 600-2116
(310) 909-7070
FAX (310) 861-1868

Tambre Leighn (310) 994-4043
www.coachingbytambre.com

Jibralta Merrill (818) 980-2091

Katie Mustard (213) 618-8105
www.katiemustard.com

Michyl-Shannon Quilty (818) 415-7359
www.imdb.com/name/nm1025085/

Suzanne E. Sebastian (805) 452-0561
(805) 687-0354

Patricia M. Soto (310) 641-1300

Christy Taylor (310) 704-5939
FAX (626) 798-9747
www.sirenstudios.com

Shawn Tolleson (310) 880-0144

Ann G. Troy (805) 729-1923

Lois Walker (323) 467-1067

Philip Wright (626) 523-6173
FAX (323) 395-5540

Julie Zafiratos (323) 497-9796
www.imdb.com/name/nm1270657/

Brian Ades (310) 503-8080
(UPM)

Gonul Aldogan (310) 600-3957

Linda Aliber-Karson (323) 936-7938
(UPM)

All Crew Agency (818) 206-0144
2920 W. Olive Ave., Ste. 201 FAX (818) 206-0169
Burbank, CA 91505 www.allcrewagency.com
(Reps for Production Managers)

Bridget Allen (323) 243-4685
44 779 980 5735
www.sketchpictures.com

Laura Anderson (323) 936-4247
(323) 646-6569
(UPM)

Donnalee Austen (323) 333-1010
(UPM)

Greg Bartlett (310) 345-7815
(UPM) FAX (310) 861-5796

Yvette Bergeron (310) 398-0199
(UPM) FAX (310) 313-4875

Sarah Brunie (818) 243-1514

Shirley Bukrey-Lloyd (310) 306-1502
(Spanish; UPM)

Randy Carter (818) 242-4088
(818) 206-0144
www.allcrewagency.com/home/talent.php5?id=2
(UPM)

Carrie Lynn Certa (818) 206-0144
www.allcrewagency.com

Lori Berk Chapman (213) 700-7180
(818) 980-9040
(UPM) FAX (818) 980-9788

Devon Clark (310) 453-5250
(310) 795-0237
(UPM)

William Coleman (323) 791-7055
(UPM)

Chris Crawford (323) 912-9175
(323) 646-1375
(UPM)

Crew Connection (800) 352-7397
(303) 526-4900
(Referral for Production Managers) FAX (303) 526-4901
www.crewconnection.com

Michelle Currinder (213) 703-6424

Stacey Daarstad (951) 764-9225

Lisa Dabao (310) 283-3924

Gina D'Agostino (909) 744-2618

Pedro Aragão De Oliveira (310) 729-0327
(UPM)

Laurie Devine (818) 968-2806
(UPM)

Cathy Diaz (818) 774-8782

Kevan Dirinpour (310) 293-2371
(French) FAX (310) 388-3184

Karen Dixon (310) 386-8082
www.karendandcompany.com

Bob Dohrmann (310) 397-2628

Janice Doskey (914) 261-2267
(866) 545-8878
(French; UPM)

Dale Dreher (323) 777-3410
(310) 600-5020
www.hazardtown.com

Don Dunn (818) 259-1589
(UPM) www.dunnfilms.com

Dana Eudaily (310) 985-4532
(310) 985-4532
(UPM)

Stephanie E. Evans (818) 257-3220
(UPM)

Denise Daniels Fanning (213) 399-9831
(UPM)

Andrea Fein-Primack (818) 998-7598
(310) 386-3386

Lauri Fetch (805) 495-4021

Debbie A. Fisher (310) 475-8767
(UPM)

Angela Frisbie (818) 209-9342
(415) 740-6188
FAX (818) 508-9068

Maureen Gibson (818) 381-7810
(UPM) FAX (818) 352-2280
www.mospace.net

Nanette Gobel (310) 801-2164

Rosser Goodman (818) 519-9575
(818) 206-0144
(UPM) www.kgbfilms.com

Susan Gross (310) 829-6202

Ari Hakim (310) 489-7739

Allison Heath (310) 729-3302
(UPM)

Lori Hoffman (310) 391-0706
(UPM)

Nick Holden (310) 858-8981
(UPM)

Anna Holland (818) 585-7733

Denyse Hurley (805) 640-0218
(323) 791-5399

Candes Kehn (818) 203-0313
(UPM)

Mirjam Kositchek (310) 702-9520
(UPM)

Andre Kusmierz (310) 415-8025
(UPM)

Brooke Lawrence (310) 560-9787
(UPM)

Bonnie Lena (310) 990-8223
(310) 399-2007
FAX (310) 399-2425
(German; UPM)

Josie Leonard-Straub (310) 552-3414
(213) 503-6123
FAX (310) 286-7850
(UPM)

Valerie Lindblom (323) 669-7938
(323) 896-3321
(UPM)

Lindy Lucas (310) 877-1066
FAX (818) 242-4429
www.lindylucas.com
(UPM)

Fatima Martins (310) 899-0923
(Portuguese & Spanish)

Terry Maxfield (213) 399-0047

Stephen McDaniel (310) 699-1912
(UPM)

Susan McGonigle (310) 770-7715
(858) 467-1494

Jibralta Merrill (818) 980-2091
(French; UPM)

Moira Michiels (310) 963-1750
(UPM)

Doreen Murphy (818) 956-1279
(323) 573-3231
FAX (818) 956-1280

Steve Nemiroff (310) 473-4100
FAX (310) 473-4100
(UPM)

Nancy Noever (310) 480-8685
(UPM)

John O'Rourke (323) 856-3000
www.thegelleragency.com

Benjamin Oswald (323) 222-2212

Kathy Palmer (310) 339-0987

Hoon Park (310) 503-0974
FAX (310) 507-0194
(UPM)

Piazzie (323) 937-1096

Patrick Porter (310) 455-0294

Nakiya Ramsey (310) 500-0223
(310) 215-3234

Craig Repass (310) 420-1955
(818) 591-8807

Scott H. Rice (323) 656-5006
(213) 804-4080
FAX (323) 656-0736
(UPM)

Pablo Richards (323) 868-5039
(UPM)

Gilbert Riley (310) 804-7513
(UPM)

Ted Robbins (323) 816-3474

Steven Rood (310) 478-5202
(310) 980-1700

Adam Roodman (818) 997-3337
(310) 570-7775
(UPM)

Jessica Roulston (310) 754-9447
www.imdb.com/name/nm0745730/

Jeremy Rubin (818) 332-4005
www.jeremyrubin.com/resume.htm
(UPM)

Steve Ruggieri (310) 503-6911
(818) 368-0666
FAX (818) 360-0237
(UPM)

Michael Schlenker (310) 560-0274
(UPM)

Robert Schmidt (818) 842-1929
(UPM)

Yari Schutzer (323) 933-5781
www.yari.biz
(UPM)

Rob Sexton (310) 793-1097
(310) 903-6800

Kathleen E. Simons (818) 497-8889
(423) 239-4949
FAX (423) 239-2232
(UPM)

Susan Smith (310) 821-9428
(310) 383-7357
FAX (310) 821-9428

Suzanne Stanford (310) 989-5787
(UPM)

Dawn Stennes (323) 394-4331
(UPM)

Keith Stephenson (323) 819-1001
(323) 654-8413
www.epiphanymedia.com
(UPM)

Mike Sterner (619) 644-3000
FAX (619) 644-3001
www.crystalpyramid.com
(UPM)

Sherry Sternosky (310) 383-7720

Chris Stoerchle (818) 623-0779
(310) 880-0013
FAX (818) 450-0476
www.6degreesofe.com

Valerie Thomas (310) 390-4676
(310) 877-3058
(UPM)

Katherine Lee Thumann (310) 396-2976
(UPM)

Joel Todaro (310) 990-7386
(UPM)

James S. Unger (310) 994-2454
(323) 656-3667

Gary M. Van Fleet (818) 645-3841
(UPM)

Sandra Vaughan (818) 585-3571
(530) 235-1922
(UPM)

Leslie D. Waldman (818) 985-8976
(UPM)

Karen Waters (310) 821-5636
(310) 463-5922

Shannon Wickliffe (323) 422-8834
(619) 961-5669
(UPM)
www.shannonwickliffe.com

Sean Zaccheo (310) 844-4117
(UPM)
www.zaccheofilms.com

Julie Zafiratos (323) 497-9796
(UPM)
www.imdb.com/name/nm1270657/

Brandy Zazueta (562) 425-1989
(562) 716-9054
(UPM)

Advanced Images/Tony Haig (310) 399-0269
FAX (310) 399-0269

Charles Allen (626) 795-1053
www.charlesallen.com

Allan Amato (888) 839-0101
www.firehousemanagement.com

Anna Englert Photography (858) 459-9205
(858) 344-1771
P.O. Box 202
La Jolla, CA 92038
www.annaenglert.com

Elizabeth Annas (818) 509-8400
(818) 201-7671
FAX (818) 509-0098

ArtMix Photography (310) 943-8100
(718) 596-2400
2332 S. Centinela Ave., Ste. C
Los Angeles, CA 90064
(Reps for Stills Photographers)
FAX (310) 943-8101
www.artmixphotography.com

Sherry Rayn Barnett (818) 766-8787
FAX (818) 766-4587
www.sherrybarnettphotography.com

Carl Schneider Photography (310) 379-1833
(800) 540-6008
www.carlschneider.com

Lionel Cassini (818) 633-2697
www.lionelcassini.com

Saint Clic (818) 606-9002
www.saintclic.com

Byron J. Cohen (818) 782-1155
(818) 416-9989
FAX (818) 782-1166
www.byronjcohen.com

Richard Corman (310) 943-8100
www.artmixphotography.com

David Fairchild Photography (310) 316-5547
501 S. Catalina Ave.
Redondo Beach, CA 90277
www.davidfairchildstudio.com

Davis Photographic (213) 434-3344
(562) 343-5898
382 Molino Ave., Ste. 2
Long Beach, CA 90814
www.davisphotographic.com

Lionel DeLuy (323) 664-6494
www.therexagency.com

Roberto D'Este (310) 943-8100
(212) 989-4996
www.artmixphotography.com

Jerry De Wilde (323) 662-6491
www.dewildephotography.com

James Dimmock (310) 943-8100
www.jamesdimmock.com

Fernando Escovar (818) 726-7269
(888) 310-2020
www.fotographer.com

Kevin Estrada (818) 607-6057
FAX (267) 375-2475
www.moviestills.net

Don Flood (310) 943-8100
www.artmixphotography.com

Jesse Frohman (310) 943-8100
www.artmixphotography.com

David Guilburt (310) 457-8260
FAX (310) 457-8262
www.davidguilburt.com

Amy Guip (310) 943-8100
www.artmixphotography.com

Matt Gunther (310) 943-8100
www.artmixphotography.com

A Dean Hendler (818) 508-9155
(818) 601-1177
www.deanhendler.com

David Henriksen (818) 599-9823

Pierre J. Hörmann (310) 930-6335
(310) 568-9045
FAX (310) 568-9045

Michael Jacobs/MJP (323) 461-0240
(323) 839-4625
FAX (505) 345-7883
www.mjphoto.com

Jim Cox Photography (310) 657-3600
www.jimcox.net

John P. Johnson (818) 438-1035
www.johnjohnsonphoto.com

Kelvin Jones (310) 390-5161
www.kelvinjonesphotography.com

Ben Kaller (213) 446-1720

Naomi Kaltman (310) 943-8100
www.artmixphotography.com

Ⓐ Karl Larsen Photography (310) 663-1206
FAX (617) 812-0273
www.karllarsen.com

Kenneth Dolin Photography (310) 276-9937
www.kennethdolin.com

Christopher Kilkus (323) 664-6494
www.therexagency.com

Heinz Kohler (213) 620-0015
FAX (213) 620-0016
www.kohlerphotos.com

Kubeisy Photography (818) 885-1545
(888) 478-4557
FAX (805) 522-8731
www.digitography.tv

Kyla Photography (310) 262-1125
www.kylaphoto.com

LA Rep (213) 446-1720
3219 Laurel Canyon Blvd. FAX (323) 656-1756
Studio City, CA 91604
(Reps for Stills Photographers)

R. Dean Larson (323) 654-8352
(323) 654-8368

David Lena (310) 480-7007
FAX (310) 399-2425
www.davidlena.com

Lisa Dare Photography (818) 352-3747
(818) 370-2480
FAX (818) 352-3747
www.lisadare.com

Christine Loss (818) 366-2043

Christopher Xavier Lozano (323) 962-0009
(323) 854-6775
www.tlshollywood.com

Kevin Lynch (310) 943-8100
www.artmixphotography.com

Anthony Mandler (310) 943-8100
www.artmixphotography.com

Lynn McAfee (818) 761-1317

Ⓐ Michael Rueter Photography (818) 268-3630
www.michaelrueter.com

Michael Douglas Middleton (805) 583-8859
FAX (805) 583-8859

Keith Nakata (323) 653-0455
FAX (323) 653-6077

Robert Anthony Nese (323) 258-9629
(818) 247-2149

Stanley D. Newton (310) 202-8547
(310) 710-2541
www.stanleynewtonphoto.com

Guy Noffsinger (310) 386-0972
www.yourphotoguy.com

Yoshi Ohara (310) 327-0056
FAX (310) 327-0808
www.marznet.com

Abe Perlstein (805) 528-8585
(805) 234-1253
www.abes3dworld.blogspot.com

Alex Pitt (323) 665-4492
www.alexpittphotography.com

The Rappaport Agency (323) 464-4481
6311 Romaine St., Ste. 7204 FAX (323) 464-5030
Hollywood, CA 90038 www.rappagency.com
(Reps for Stills Photographers)

Kai Regan (310) 943-8100
(212) 989-4996
www.artmixphotography.com

Fredric Reshew (323) 664-6494
www.therexagency.com

robert/robert (323) 933-5487
3191 Casitas Ave., Ste. 110 www.robertrobert.com
Studio City, CA 90039

Mike Ruiz (323) 664-6494
www.therexagency.com

Sam Urdank Photography (310) 877-8319
www.samurdank.com

Richard Scudder (323) 252-0966
www.richardscudder.com

Sherburne Photography (310) 570-9094
www.sherburnephotography.com

SheShooter/Carey Hendricks (818) 563-2511
(323) 440-8823
www.sheshooter.com

Michele K. Short (213) 255-0451
www.michelekshort.com

Daniel Shudo (310) 729-8848
(310) 479-6711
www.danielshudo.com

Stacy Hammond Photography (310) 923-4232
(517) 281-5549
www.flickr.com/photos/stacyhammond

Erik Thureson (818) 404-3600
(818) 402-0320
www.lightbox57.com

Derek Van Oss/DVO Photo (323) 743-8078
(917) 922-0742
FAX (800) 316-5087
www.dvophoto.com

Joseph Viles (818) 565-8003
(818) 556-1557
FAX (818) 558-5101
www.josephviles.com

Ben Watts (310) 943-8100
www.benwatts.com

James White (310) 943-8100
www.artmixphotography.com

Gyslain Yarhi (323) 664-6494
www.therexagency.com

Jack L. Zelman (818) 284-6423
www.italentco.com

Gregg E. Amodei
(805) 493-1409
(805) 844-1409

Christopher Amy
(French & Spanish)
(310) 836-1650
(310) 678-8202

artists' services
8581 Santa Monica Blvd., Ste. 437
West Hollywood, CA 90069
(Reps for Prop Masters)
(323) 445-4910
(415) 824-4423
www.artists-services.com

David Baker
(310) 850-1911

Jeff Barber
(Prop Stylist)
(213) 507-0809
(310) 327-1777

Jeffrey Bellamy
(Set Decorator)
(626) 403-0394
(626) 824-0094

Greg Bonura
(661) 269-2978
(805) 341-3124
FAX (661) 269-0546

Edwin Brewer
(323) 422-0064

John Brunot
(818) 262-9305

R. Spencer Burt
(Set Decorator)
(310) 489-4743
(310) 478-4738

Jerry Chavez
(818) 400-4615
(818) 985-0494

Barry Conner
(818) 991-0904
(818) 314-0523
FAX (818) 991-1934

Kirk DeMusiak
(Set Decorator & Underwater)
(310) 827-1978
(310) 963-6994
FAX (310) 827-3298
www.kirkdemusiak.com

Jeff Dombro
(661) 253-3512
(818) 426-7888

Dan Donley
(Underwater)
(805) 493-5990
(213) 200-2810

Jonathan Drake
(818) 825-0705
(818) 887-9535
FAX (818) 887-9535

Steven P. Duchscherer
(818) 708-3647

Steven Eaton
(Set Decorator)
(661) 297-3504
(818) 422-5004

Robert Feffer
(Prop Stylist & Set Decorator)
(818) 886-1154
(818) 681-7239

Stephen Flynn
(213) 248-9530

Jim Fox
(Prop Rigs)
(323) 462-2272
(213) 968-1068
FAX (323) 469-9204

Marc Gannes
(818) 348-6107
(213) 712-7360
FAX (818) 348-4507

David L. Glazer
(818) 713-1741
(818) 521-8037
FAX (818) 713-1741
www.davidglazer.net

Rick Gleitsman
(Underwater)
(818) 222-4292
(818) 489-4476
FAX (818) 222-4292

Jon Gold
(Art Director)
(818) 625-4408

Peter N. Griffith
(818) 692-0900

Mikel Hands
(818) 802-1196
FAX (818) 842-3501
www.mikelhandsreel.com

Rufus Herrick
(805) 496-0249
(206) 232-7100

Glen Houghton
(310) 779-8100
(760) 436-0287

Jim Johnson
(805) 497-7209
(213) 760-5491

Jeneffer Jones
(323) 445-4910
(415) 824-4423
www.artists-services.com

Jonathan Lee
(Set Decorator)
(818) 731-7724
(818) 907-7231
FAX (818) 986-4856

Priscilla Levy
(Set Decorator & Underwater)
(415) 669-7777
(916) 296-5037
FAX (415) 669-7777

Douglas C. Lewis
(562) 424-5476
(213) 700-7424
FAX (562) 424-5603

Ronnie Lombard
(818) 613-8705

Tony Maccario
(661) 268-1953
(818) 422-6887

David Marais
(213) 712-6011

Tom Margules
(818) 225-7767
(818) 519-7767

Neil Marquis
(818) 780-0118
(213) 280-4552

Daniele Maxwell
(323) 445-4910
www.artists-services.com

Robin L. Miller
(213) 400-6045

Joseph R. Olsen
(323) 899-1492
FAX (323) 257-1500

Craig Osler
(818) 702-0075
www.propertymaster.biz

Tim Perovich
(Prop Stylist & Set Decorator)
(805) 526-2780
(818) 596-6458

John Puhara
(Set Decorator)
(323) 663-7320
FAX (323) 663-7320

Steven Renick
(310) 422-5177

Jacqueline Sartino
(Set Decorator)
(760) 320-0724
FAX (323) 653-2979

Gary Shartsis (818) 957-0620
(818) 398-1728

Bjarne Sletteland (310) 770-8223
(505) 466-1436
(Set Decorator) FAX (505) 466-1436

Dan Spaulding (310) 993-2850
FAX (818) 845-9259

Michael Storosh (310) 753-3110
(Prop Stylist) FAX (310) 305-9994

Zeev Tankus (310) 499-6737

John Vonk (323) 462-7854
(310) 632-8931
(Set Decorator)

Jon Douglas West (818) 761-4488
(310) 888-4592
(Set Decorator) FAX (818) 761-2112

Jeff White (213) 500-1119
(310) 398-4172

Randy Young (310) 864-4075
(310) 323-3326
FAX (310) 323-3352

1313FX (818) 441-3797
www.1313fx.com

All Crew Agency (818) 206-0144
2920 W. Olive Ave., Ste. 201 FAX (818) 206-0169
Burbank, CA 91505 www.allcrewagency.com
(Reps for Prosthetics Artists)

Almost Human, Inc. (310) 838-6993
3650 Eagle Rock Blvd. FAX (310) 838-6999
Los Angeles, CA 90065 www.almosthuman.net

American Makeup and FX (336) 264-2302
(818) 780-5002
13536 Saticoy St. FAX (818) 780-5002
Van Nuys, CA 91402 www.amefx.com

Anatomorphex/The Sculpture Studio (818) 768-2880
8210 Lankershim Blvd., Ste. 14 www.anatomorphex.com
North Hollywood, CA 91605

Michele Burke (818) 574-7111

Michael Burnett (818) 768-6103
FAX (818) 768-6136
www.mbpfx.com

The Character Shop (805) 306-9441
4735 Industrial St., Ste. 4-B FAX (805) 306-9444
Simi Valley, CA 93063 www.character-shop.com

Bari Dreiband-Burman (818) 980-6587
www.burmanstudio.com

Nick Dudman (310) 285-0303
www.marshbest.com

Dynamic Design International, LLC/ Darren Perks (818) 923-8798
(818) 439-8447
FAX (623) 386-6826
www.dynamicdesignintl.com

Edward French (818) 340-4852
(818) 317-9997
FAX (818) 340-4837
www.edwardfrench.com

Alan Friedman (818) 881-1473

Gary J. Tunnicliffe's Two Hours in the Dark, Inc. (818) 837-1045
12473 Gladstone Ave., Ste. Q FAX (818) 837-1842
Sylmar, CA 91342 www.2hoursinthedark.com

GM Foam, Inc. (818) 908-1087
FAX (818) 908-1262
www.gmfoam.com

Byrd Holland (818) 558-1954
FAX (818) 558-1954

Trisha Kelley (818) 508-1533
(818) 809-9980

Kevin Marks (818) 613-2746

Masters FX, Inc./Todd Masters (818) 834-3000
(604) 683-5311
FAX (818) 834-9755
www.mastersfx.com

Multivision FX (818) 843-3266
(818) 288-6839
1112 N. Glenoaks Blvd. FAX (818) 843-3266
Burbank, CA 91504 www.multivisionfx.com

Deborah Patino (818) 371-9719
www.deborahpatino.com

Ralis Special Makeup Effects (818) 209-8046
(213) 622-3936
3727 W. Magnolia Blvd., Ste. 407 FAX (213) 622-3987
Burbank, CA 91505 www.ralisfx.com

Rick Stratton's (Strat-Tatts) Temporary Tattoos (818) 951-1051
6942 St. Estaban St. FAX (818) 951-8051
Tujunga, CA 91042
home.roadrunner.com/~bludney/index.html

Bob Romero (818) 981-3338
(818) 953-6625
FAX (818) 981-3339
www.bobromero.com

Smith FX, Inc. (818) 601-8800
www.shaunsmithfx.com

Stevie FX (818) 915-3615
(818) 206-0144
FAX (818) 206-0169
www.steviefx.com

Annie Adams (818) 294-2608 / (818) 453-8296

Yvette Alcala (310) 927-2404

All Crew Agency (818) 206-0144
2920 W. Olive Ave., Ste. 201 FAX (818) 206-0169
Burbank, CA 91505 www.allcrewagency.com
(Reps for Script Supervisors)

Robin Anderson (310) 396-5063 / (310) 210-0823
(Spanish & Visual FX) FAX (310) 399-8473

Sheryl Appleton (818) 762-5272 / (818) 422-0612
(Spanish) FAX (818) 755-5511
www.sherylappleton.com

Suzanne Armstrong (310) 745-4444 / (310) 766-2738
FAX (310) 745-4600

Karolyn Austen (323) 952-4067 / (323) 770-6418

Barbara Babchick (310) 927-3055 / (818) 908-2466
(Computer Frame Capturing, Motion Control & Visual FX)

Patricia Baker (818) 886-7503

Cassandra Barrère (323) 654-3445
(Spanish)

Elizabeth Barton (310) 301-6021 / (808) 823-6156
(Motion Control & Visual FX) FAX (808) 823-6840

Lisa Bemel (310) 600-9625 / (212) 452-2314

Ana Birch (310) 864-5131
FAX (509) 562-8781
(Computer Frame Capturing, Motion Control, Visual FX; Portuguese & Spanish)

Towie Bixby (818) 206-0144
www.allcrewagency.com

Joanie Blum (310) 657-1900 / (503) 392-3437
(Italian)

Lisa Bobonis (323) 377-9866

Mellanie Bradfield (323) 459-7260 / (323) 953-8767
FAX (323) 663-8796

Georgia Bragg (310) 398-8150 / (310) 345-8817
FAX (310) 398-4340

Janine M. Brauns (818) 326-7707

Jeanne Byrd-Hall (310) 822-2961 / (213) 220-9247

Maggie Causey (818) 416-4972 / (310) 457-2384

Ulyssa Childs (818) 429-7980 / (818) 865-8765
FAX (818) 865-8318

Laurie Cohn (818) 985-7788

Patti Dalzell (818) 761-3800 / (818) 523-0403
(Computer Frame Capturing)

Sarah Dart (323) 856-0380 / (213) 247-8811

Susan Dear (310) 398-2711 / (310) 922-2822
FAX (310) 398-5521
(Computer Frame Capturing & Motion Control)

Carol De Pasquale (213) 920-4816 / (510) 339-6352
(French)

Dawn 'DeDe' Dreiling (323) 658-7704 / (323) 547-4484
FAX (323) 658-7704

Diane Durant (310) 641-1302 / (310) 989-5082

Karen Kirkpatrick Eachus (818) 559-3499 / (818) 427-2955
FAX (818) 559-2499

Denise Eldridge (310) 562-7358 / (310) 305-1922

Monica Fernandez (310) 251-1415 / (310) 656-0366
(Spanish; Motion Control & Visual FX)

Veronica Flynn (310) 390-6311 / (310) 367-7653
(French & Spanish)

Jennifer Jurwich Freudenberg (805) 497-1797 / (818) 512-2990

Sandra Gainsforth (818) 957-3446
FAX (818) 475-1346

Sherry Gallarneau (213) 247-2113

Dawn Gilliam (626) 357-4820 / (626) 298-2119
(Computer Frame Capturing, Motion Control & Visual FX)

Laurie E. Gilson (310) 286-2640

Cori Glazer (310) 455-3343 / (310) 962-2404
(Computer Frame Capturing, Motion Control & Visual FX)

Jane Goldsmith (323) 467-4439 / (323) 697-3795
(Computer Frame Capturing, Motion Control & Visual FX)

Pauline Gray (626) 355-1682 / (626) 831-2290

Jill Gurr (323) 467-9039
(French, Italian & Spanish) FAX (323) 467-9642

Sharon Hagen (310) 306-5225 / (310) 396-1210
FAX (310) 306-5225

Jane Hampton (310) 544-6682 / (310) 569-1769
FAX (310) 544-4034

Heather Harris (818) 383-6265 / (661) 254-8625

Dora Hopkins (310) 488-5003

Ira Hurvitz (626) 300-8123

Catherine Jelski (310) 398-7504
(310) 386-8624
(Computer Frame Capturing; German)

Jessica Jordan (310) 979-8889
www.script-supervisors.com
(Computer Frame Capturing, Motion Control & Visual FX)

Iwona Kanclerz (310) 435-7642

Veda Kaplan (310) 849-9598

Bridgette Kelley (323) 934-2034
FAX (323) 934-2034

Kelly Kelley (323) 861-0913

Kristy Kelly (310) 475-6537
(310) 922-6537
www.kristykelly.net

Sandra King (323) 893-3866
(909) 866-0992
FAX (909) 866-0992

Marie Lamotte (310) 396-3737
(French)

Louann Lightfoot (818) 599-3288
(818) 889-4917

Christine Loss (818) 366-2043
(Spanish)

Cara Lowe (310) 562-4021

Kathy Lubinsky (323) 650-6875
(323) 260-0130

Cheryl Malat (310) 663-8336
(212) 799-9160

Lauren Malkasian (323) 225-1874
(323) 229-0333

Mary Manix (818) 216-2228

Tina Marrie (818) 753-2089
(818) 590-0996

Britta Martinez (213) 503-5777
(German, Motion Control & Visual FX)

J. Kelly Mayes (310) 418-7228
(818) 249-5899

Agnes Mazzola (310) 569-1506

Sandy Mazzola (310) 649-3472
(310) 795-4826

Lyn McKissick (323) 363-1953

Tracey Merkle (310) 393-5712
(310) 849-3837
FAX (310) 393-0097

Hilary D. Momberger (310) 709-4967

Morgan (323) 466-5500
(323) 466-7426
FAX (323) 466-4282

Jennifer Morris (310) 961-0077

Kathleen Mulligan (310) 312-6578
FAX (310) 312-6578

Jennifer J. Mullins (213) 716-0409
(626) 794-4603

Beth Multer (818) 206-0144
www.allcrewagency.com

Jora Nelstein (323) 933-5272
(323) 363-9956
(Dutch; Motion Control & Visual FX) FAX (323) 933-5272

Nila Neukum (310) 351-2777
(310) 839-7488

Mary Ann Newfield (323) 463-9570
(213) 819-9570
FAX (323) 461-5856

Kathleen Newport (818) 509-1935
(818) 426-3804
FAX (818) 509-8956

Monica Ochoa (714) 892-5480
(714) 815-0097
(Spanish) FAX (714) 892-5480

Kristina Palmer (310) 440-4001

Donna Parish (626) 798-2329
(323) 829-6557
FAX (626) 798-3666

Paulette Pasternack (818) 999-9796
(818) 943-9736
FAX (818) 999-9796

Mary M. Patton (310) 455-1519
(Spanish)

Victoria Peters (310) 545-8118

Daria Price (323) 962-7536
(212) 683-1266

Ana Maria Quintana (818) 548-5296
(213) 712-1909
(Computer Frame Capture, Motion Capture, Motion Control, Spanish & Visual FX)

Bruce Resnik (818) 206-0144
www.allcrewagency.com

Tricia Ronten (310) 829-0434
(310) 990-8346

Linda Salazar (310) 375-4008

Melisa Sanchez-Schmieder (310) 569-3345
(Italian, Russian & Spanish)

Debbie Sannes (310) 316-4034
(310) 415-4454
FAX (310) 540-2763

Mary Seward (818) 265-4040
(Motion Control & Visual FX) FAX (818) 265-4044

Shatsy (323) 464-8081
(323) 646-4730
FAX (323) 464-5575
(Motion Control & Visual FX; French & Spanish)

K. Rocco Shields (818) 642-0396
(818) 206-0144
www.allcrewagency.com

Susan Shparago-VanDernoot (310) 213-7708
(480) 206-8085
www.hollywoodscripty.com

Laura Shrewsbury (310) 301-8385
(310) 591-9551
(French) FAX (310) 301-8385

Beth A. Smith (818) 206-0144
www.allcrewagency.com

Catherine Smythe-Grasso (310) 455-7169
(310) 455-7169

Nancy Solomon (818) 753-1193
(818) 321-3719

Gretchen Somerfeld (323) 655-5308
(212) 330-7013
(French)

Lisa Soulé (310) 849-5472

Leslie Steadman (310) 459-0083
(310) 413-7285
FAX (310) 459-5415

Rooh Steif (213) 200-7700
(818) 500-9215
(Motion Control & Visual FX)
FAX (818) 500-0558

Scott Stephens (818) 281-7852
FAX (818) 776-8546

Susan B. Stroh (818) 541-7668
(818) 497-7486
FAX (818) 541-7669

Michele Tedlis (818) 398-4291
(Computer Frame Capturing)
www.micheletedlis.com

Mark Thomas (310) 453-1700

Marion Tumen (310) 459-1146

Ingrid Urich-Sass (310) 205-0659
(French & Spanish)
FAX (310) 205-8911

Judith Vogt (626) 798-7470

Marvel Wakefield (310) 876-2303

Tracey Weddle (916) 201-6989
(916) 359-4759
FAX (916) 359-4759

Denise A. Woods-Jordan (310) 710-5275
(310) 316-2342
(Computer Frame Capturing, Motion Control & Visual FX)

Linda Aliber-Karson (323) 936-7938

C.C. Barnes (310) 344-4327

Roger Barth (310) 877-3063

David Berke (310) 305-2428
(310) 344-2676
FAX (310) 305-2428

Mike Bocek (213) 344-6050
www.mikebocek.com

Rick Brown (310) 922-1946

Lori Berk Chapman (213) 700-7180
(818) 980-9040
FAX (818) 980-9788

Debbie Collura (818) 955-7730

Eugene Davis (818) 209-5486

Seth Edelstein (310) 535 5595
(310) 595-4198

John Elmore (323) 855-4420
(310) 839-0708

Brad Ewing (213) 220-0175

Maureen Gibson (818) 381-7810
FAX (818) 352-2280
www.mospace.net

Niles Goodsite (818) 998-6455

Chris Hayden (818) 889-0828
(Underwater) (310) 989-8226
FAX (818) 889-5483

Jamie Haynes (310) 305-7139
FAX (310) 827-7367

Glen A. Hettinger (661) 255-0953
(661) 400-4577
www.glenhettinger.com

John R. Hunstable (626) 797-1774
(818) 371-1566

Michael M. LaBohn (818) 244-3848
(818) 419-0613

Sharon Lorick (310) 440-3404
FAX (310) 440-3454

Kevin McNamara (310) 633-0602

Anita Miller (805) 927-3566
FAX (805) 927-3566

Jennifer Miller (661) 251-3250
(310) 739-1322

Lucille OuYang (310) 837-7776
FAX (310) 837-7780

Piazzie (323) 937-1096

Steve Ruggieri (310) 503-6911
(818) 368-0666
FAX (818) 360-0237

Chad Saxton (310) 659-1947
(310) 739-1935

Patricia M. Soto (310) 641-1300

Judy Trotter (805) 695-0499
(805) 705-2150

Eric Archer (310) 733-2550
www.photogenicsmedia.com

Michelle Ashley (323) 449-1538
FAX (323) 851-2249

Sharon Bonney (310) 804-7097
(310) 823-9191

Ruth Bracken (707) 495-7667
(707) 829-7957
FAX (707) 581-2046
www.ruthbdesigns.com

Dawn Carver (323) 937-1010
www.zenobia.com

Célestine Agency (310) 998-1977
1548 16th St.
Santa Monica, CA 90404
(Reps for Set Decorators)
FAX (310) 998-1978
www.celestineagency.com

Becket Cook (310) 998-1977
www.celestineagency.com

Kenneth Dean (818) 783-5904
(661) 251-0170

Robin del Pino (323) 937-1010
www.zenobia.com

Caryl Eagle (323) 937-1010
www.zenobia.com

Suzy Eaton (323) 937-1010
www.zenobia.com

Diane Ewing (323) 937-1010
www.zenobia.com

John Geary (310) 998-1977
www.celestineagency.com

Stefanie Girard (818) 558-6878
(818) 618-6878

Emily Henderson (323) 937-1010
www.zenobia.com

Jennifer Herwitt (310) 652-3681
(213) 220-8698
FAX (310) 360-1029
www.herwitt.com

Derek Hughes (310) 733-2550
www.photogenicsmedia.com

Kathleen Devlin Hughes (818) 767-8686
(213) 400-7223
FAX (818) 767-8646

Molly Hurd (310) 246-0446
www.workgroup-ltd.com

John M. Kelly (818) 769-4950
(213) 999-1303
(Prop Master)
FAX (818) 769-4950

Jerie Kelter (323) 933-6329

Shane Klein (310) 246-0446
www.workgroup-ltd.com

Anne Kuljian (310) 285-0303
www.marshbest.com

Melody LaVigna (818) 996-2855
FAX (818) 996-4181

Lisa Lupo (310) 998-1977
www.celestineagency.com

Loren Lyons (310) 274-0032
www.artistsbytimothypriano.com

Tracy McCandless (310) 399-6058

Deborah McLean (323) 937-1010
www.zenobia.com

Jules Moore (323) 937-1010
www.zenobia.com

Elizabeth Nicole (323) 937-1010
www.zenobia.com

Erin O'Brien (323) 937-1010
www.zenobia.com

Stephen Pappas (310) 998-1977
www.celestineagency.com

Marjolijn Reuter (323) 937-1010
www.zenobia.com

Rachel Roderick-Jones (310) 457-3029
(310) 430-0494

Carla Roley (323) 937-1010
www.zenobia.com

Viktoria Ruchkan (310) 246-0446
www.workgroup-ltd.com

Rob Scruggs (805) 581-7046
(805) 231-7532

Jane Shirkes (323) 344-0487

Jean Simone (818) 242-1790
(818) 434-1881
FAX (818) 242-1798

Joyce Artman Smith (661) 254-5445
(818) 434-3224
www.joyceartmansmith.com

Gary Spain (415) 722-3510
www.garyspaindesign.com

Christine Staggs (323) 790-0440

Kris Starr-Davila (818) 884-6068
(818) 968-7212
FAX (818) 884-6085

Jen Tauritz Gotch (323) 937-1010
www.zenobia.com

Ann G. Troy (805) 729-1923

Erinn Valencich (310) 274-0032
www.artistsbytimothypriano.com

Katherine Vallin (323) 493-5533
(323) 822-9401

Julia Weinberg (310) 274-2383
FAX (310) 821-0232
www.foodstylists.com

Donna Willinsky (323) 828-2280
picasaweb.google.com/donnawillinsky/
examplesofmywork#

Kira Wolman (323) 937-1010
www.zenobia.com

Jon Ailetcher (818) 516-5185
(818) 830-1647
www.indamix.tv

Lee Alexander (831) 428-2794

All Crew Agency (818) 206-0144
2920 W. Olive Ave., Ste. 201 FAX (818) 206-0169
Burbank, CA 91505 www.allcrewagency.com
(Reps for Sound Production Mixers)

Bryan Apolinar (310) 594-3940
www.crewavenue.com/bryan

Beau Baker (818) 505-8908
(818) 398-4119
FAX (818) 505-8998

Steve Bedaux (888) 246-3589
www.cinelux.tv

Gerald Beg (661) 296-8222
(805) 407-4945
(French)

Izak Ben-Meir (310) 829-7037
(213) 999-5959
FAX (310) 829-6237

Glenn E. Berkovitz (310) 902-1148
(310) 313-2776
FAX (310) 398-2776

Jack Bornoff (818) 905-0356

Steve Bowerman (805) 496-1716
(818) 522-9943

Forrest Brakeman (818) 952-2589
(818) 384-1491
FAX (818) 952-2587

Mark D. Burton, C.A.S. (818) 419-7571

Crew Chamberlain (714) 447-8090
FAX (714) 525-6028

Moe Chamberlain (323) 871-0413
(213) 281-0537
FAX (323) 871-0623

David B. Chornow (323) 428-8887
(Spanish)

John S. Coffey (323) 876-7525
FAX (323) 876-4775
www.coffeysound.com

Ron Cogswell (818) 368-6450

Peter Commans (714) 323-0438

Tim Cooney (818) 206-0144
www.allcrewagency.com

Garry K. Cunningham (818) 985-5641
(818) 216-7921
FAX (818) 985-5642
www.cinemagraphicaudio.com

Thomas Curley, C.A.S. (323) 304-4962
(518) 253-1879
FAX (786) 549-5971
www.curleysound.com

Roger Daniell (760) 771-8090
(310) 418-5689
FAX (760) 771-2055

James Dehr (310) 455-2308
(818) 424-2290

Dave Diamond (310) 430-9376
FAX (323) 913-9141

Bob Dreebin, C.A.S. (310) 629-2476
(623) 561-9204
FAX (623) 561-5813
www.rollsound.biz

Robert Eber (310) 450-8164
(310) 913-1707
FAX (310) 450-8264

Andrew Edelman (310) 499-6199
www.imdb.com/name/nm0248973/

Joseph Ekins (818) 720-7436

Farr Out Productions, LLC (310) 902-5944
(Reps for Sound Mixers) FAX (818) 830-3608
www.farroutpro.com

Chuck Fitzpatrick (818) 249-6667
(818) 731-5030
FAX (818) 249-6668

Joe Foglia, C.A.S. (818) 633-4449
(800) 562-8346
FAX (818) 276-8480
www.southeastaudio.com

Kirk Francis (310) 285-0303
www.marshbest.com

Devin Golub (323) 365-7480
(Boom Operator)

Courtney M. Goodin (323) 937-4978
(323) 465-9441
FAX (323) 935-6698
www.bwfwidget.com

Richard Bryce Goodman (310) 474-1100
(310) 600-0222
(French) FAX (310) 474-1003
www.imdb.com/name/nm0329208/

Albee Gordon (323) 666-1331
(323) 363-2773
FAX (323) 666-1331

Gary Gossett, C.A.S. (805) 732-7946
FAX (805) 522-5231

Brett Grant-Grierson (818) 606-5700
www.ears4hire.com

Steven Grothe, C.A.S. (310) 528-2887
(Japanese & Spanish)

Dennis Grzesik (818) 388-7358
FAX (503) 214-7521
www.moviebizsound.com

Clifford (Kip) Gynn (310) 397-7758
(216) 496-1555
www.imdb.com/name/nm0350484

John Halaby, C.A.S. (310) 312-8810
FAX (310) 312-9910

Don Hale, C.A.S. (619) 710-6858
FAX (619) 482-1834

Cameron Hamza, C.A.S. (310) 390-3520
(310) 430-9046
www.imdb.com/name/nm0359118/

Mark Hanes (323) 466-4803
(949) 494-7870

Patrick Hanson, C.A.S. (310) 374-3887
(310) 406-6511
FAX (213) 303-1543

Scott Harber (323) 662-0912
(323) 459-6691

Steve Hawk, C.A.S. (213) 448-9322
(818) 761-5091
FAX (818) 761-5091

Michael Emeric Hayes (818) 681-6879
www.emeric.com

Tim Hays (818) 789-8799
(877) 737-6863
FAX (818) 789-8329
www.planet3soundco.com

Jim Hilton (818) 988-4969

Michael Hoffman (818) 206-0144
www.allcrewagency.com

Ken Isley (818) 782-3072
(818) 509-0582

Bob Israel, C.A.S. (714) 843-1990
(888) 799-2202
FAX (714) 843-6345

Randy Johnson (818) 508-0374
(818) 281-5573

Fred Johnston (818) 752-0813
(520) 907-1155

Marty Kasparian (818) 788-8234
(818) 943-3723
(Armenian & Spanish)

Charles Kelly (323) 664-1658
(323) 528-9479
FAX (323) 664-1658

David M. Kelson (310) 560-2430
www.imdb.com/name/nm0447093/

Daniel G. Kent (310) 375-5952
(310) 502-6116
FAX (310) 378-2642

Joe Kenworthy (818) 606-6800
FAX (818) 782-8447

Theodore Kerhulas (818) 784-9025
FAX (818) 784-9383

David Kirschner (818) 314-8225
(818) 906-3534
FAX (818) 906-8806

C. Darin Knight (818) 700-0633
(818) 389-4851

Alex Lamm (818) 540-5979
(818) 772-2601
(Spanish)

B.J. Lehn (310) 379-9131
(310) 600-1445

Christopher Lennon (323) 459-6997
FAX (818) 766-9250

Darryl Linkow, C.A.S. (818) 597-8855
(818) 585-1495

Jim W. Machowski (310) 266-7086
(303) 949-9090

William Macpherson (213) 200-9401
(415) 518-0796
FAX (415) 668-2681
www.soundspeed.com

Itzhak Ike Magal, C.A.S. (323) 314-0948
(928) 282-2043
(Hebrew) www.ikemagal.com

Erik Magnus, C.A.S. (310) 902-3735
web.mac.com/emagnus

Jim Mansen (818) 599-2974
(480) 816-1380

Marsh, Best & Associates (310) 285-0303
9150 Wilshire Blvd., Ste. 220 FAX (310) 285-0218
Beverly Hills, CA 90212 www.marshbest.com
(Reps for Sound Production Mixers)

William Martel Jr., C.A.S. (213) 494-9492
(800) 323-0490
FAX (323) 225-1389
www.impactaudioinc.com

David McJunkin (310) 874-3355
(562) 598-0301
www.locationdigital.com

Kenneth McLaughlin (562) 420-3999
(800) 773-7962
FAX (562) 421-2008

Frank Menges, C.A.S. (818) 621-6150
(888) 877-6863
FAX (818) 767-9778

Richard Mercado (323) 253-2066
(323) 461-4290
FAX (323) 461-4292
www.actionaudioandvisual.com

Sunny Meyer (818) 989-3721
(Spanish)

Senator Mike Michaels (213) 389-7372
(888) 389-7372
(Japanese) FAX (213) 389-3299
www.mandy.com/stu001.html

Daniel D. Monahan, C.A.S. (661) 299-9000
(818) 307-6462

Michael C. Moore (310) 729-1920

Oliver Moss (310) 412-2399

Peter Navarro (310) 383-8039
FAX (310) 383-8039

Steve Nelson (818) 612-1383

Rob Newell (310) 963-3201
(310) 828-2017
FAX (310) 399-9227

Jacques Nosco (805) 241-6931
(805) 794-0476

Paul Oppenheim (310) 659-6744

Kim Ornitz (818) 206-0144
www.allcrewagency.com

Phillip W. Palmer (818) 206-0144
www.allcrewagency.com

Bruce Perlman (213) 359-9187
(323) 933-4489
FAX (323) 933-0249

Doc Pierce, C.A.S. (310) 629-9437

Roger Pietschmann (323) 668-0203
(323) 810-4910

Lisa Pinero (310) 422-5735
(Spanish)

D'Marco Ray (213) 923-0200
www.napalmsound.com

Michael Reilly (310) 600-0298
(310) 473-7142
FAX (310) 473-7142

Morteza Rezvani (310) 471-6667
(310) 497-0790
(Farsi) eatnet.tv

Lewis Rosen (818) 763-2882

Jamie Scarpuzza, C.A.S. (323) 774-9368
www.soundwavesurfer.com

David Schneiderman (805) 963-8240
(805) 637-3758

Jan Schulte (310) 374-2629
(310) 850-9077
(Dutch)

Wolf Seeberg (310) 822-4973
(French & German) FAX (310) 305-8918
www.wolfvid.com

Mark Sheret (818) 516-2797
FAX (360) 824-7362

David Silver (818) 415-9572
FAX (805) 531-0079
www.silverpixelproductions.com

Cabell Smith (310) 573-9295
(310) 776-0550
(French & Spanish) FAX (310) 230-1222

Roger V. Stevenson (310) 770-4630
FAX (323) 464-3311

Scott D. Stolz (310) 993-3303

Lee Strosnider (323) 851-5456
FAX (323) 851-5456

J. Woody Stubblefield (323) 595-8191
(323) 595-8191

Jim Stuebe (310) 994-2090

Jim Tanenbaum (323) 654-2076
(323) 497-7949

Joe Thompson, C.A.S. (858) 581-3366
(619) 995-1552

Pat Toma (818) 842-8662
(818) 295-8662
(Hebrew & Spanish) FAX (818) 842-8662

Paul Trautman (818) 438-8698

Janet Urban (805) 300-2039
(French & Spanish)

Video Tech Services (310) 574-9385
(310) 505-4015
10866 Washington Blvd., Ste. 513 FAX (310) 577-0850
Culver City, CA 90232 www.videotechservices.com
(Reps for Sound Production Mixers)

Ed White (805) 581-5551
(800) 537-7566
FAX (805) 581-5552

Marc Wielage (818) 486-7747
www.cinesound.tv

Ken Willingham (805) 545-9889
FAX (805) 545-0714

Jerry Wolfe (818) 624-7116
(Spanish) www.imdb.com/Name?Wolfe,+Gerald+B.

David Wyman (310) 435-4915
www.thesounddept.com

Studio Teachers/Welfare Workers

A.S.A. Medical Services Division (323) 662-9787
P.O. Box 125 FAX (323) 662-1569
La Cañada, CA 91012 www.asatalent.com/crew
(Reps for Studio Teachers/Welfare Workers)

Ⓐ **A.S.A. Studio Teachers Association** (323) 662-9787
P.O. Box 125 FAX (323) 662-1569
La Cañada, CA 91012 www.asatalent.com/crew
(Baby Nurses, Baby Wranglers, Studio Teachers & Welfare Workers)

Maxine Abarbara (818) 518-7115
FAX (818) 347-9347
(Baby Wrangler, Studio Teacher & Welfare Worker)

Kathy Abbott (818) 464-5390
(818) 464-5425

Franci Agajanian (310) 379-9989
(310) 480-9898
FAX (310) 379-4098

Juel Anderson (818) 249-2920
(818) 559-9600

Apple Entertainment/Lucas Moore (310) 526-7328
(818) 288-4259

Adria August (310) 471-5000
(818) 378-6882

Ⓐ **@baby! baby!/Lynn Raines** (818) 905-0790
(818) 216-8666
2830 S. Robertson Blvd. FAX (818) 501-0768
Los Angeles, CA 90034 www.atbabybaby.com
(Referral for Baby Wranglers and Studio Teachers/Welfare Workers)

Barbara L. Bass (818) 905-0766
FAX (818) 906-2242

Josie Batorski (310) 458-7941
(310) 428-1704

Joe Bauer (213) 501-4168

Kathy Berk (818) 399-3206
(336) 294-0228

Charmaine A. Boos (818) 222-2090
(818) 372-3762
FAX (818) 222-2095

Helen Bricker (310) 473-3302

Maxine Brooks (310) 306-5126
(213) 618-0816
(Studio Teacher & Welfare Worker) FAX (310) 306-6457
www.studioteachers.com

Judith M. Brown (310) 836-1366
(310) 487-1772

Mike Bujko (323) 662-9787
FAX (323) 662-1569
www.asatalent.com/crew

Polly Businger (310) 652-5330
(818) 559-9600

Cecilia Cardwell (310) 714-3101
(310) 398-6454
FAX (310) 398-6454

Casala, Ltd. (818) 780-7180
6539 Colbath Ave. FAX (818) 780-8262
Valley Glen, CA 91401 www.childreninfilm.com
(Referral for Studio Teachers/Welfare Workers)

A. Kathleen Chambers-Schelhorse (415) 680-0809
(Baby Wrangler & Studio Teacher)

John Chisholm (213) 392-1564
(Baby Wrangler) FAX (626) 403-3320
www.sharesomeknowledge.com

Bill Clark (818) 371-6722

Kathy Cornell (818) 404-1237
(818) 789-1114
FAX (818) 789-1112

Marsha Craig (760) 214-7475
(760) 436-8874
FAX (323) 857-7273

Ruth Ann Crudup-Brown
(323) 296-3422
(818) 389-3905
FAX (626) 568-9909

Cheryl Diamond
(310) 452-8271
(310) 804-3381
FAX (310) 452-8986

Phil Eisenhower
(310) 829-5869
(310) 428-7287

Dr. Caren M. Elin, D.C.
(805) 344-1414
(805) 448-1424
FAX (805) 344-4255

Steve Elster
(925) 324-2159
(310) 837-7542

Karen Erlich
(310) 454-9643
(310) 286-5785

Rhoda C. Fine
(818) 363-6736
(800) 936-8130
FAX (818) 360-8139
www.studioteacher.com

Nancy A. Flint
(818) 505-1993
(818) 415-2461

Terry Foley
(626) 824-2963

Mandy Friedrich
(818) 981-8388
(818) 486-6958
FAX (818) 981-8386

Elise Ganz
(310) 275-8524
(415) 517-5456
FAX (415) 459-5352
www.thestudioteachers.com
(Baby Wrangler & Studio Teacher)

Rhona Gordon
(818) 501-6468
(818) 486-4542

Claudette Grand
(310) 392-0772
(310) 990-0026

Leslie Hall
(310) 839-4222

Carol Hart
(Baby Wrangler)
(323) 663-3512
(323) 841-9192
FAX (323) 661-2124

Monique Hernandez-Fisher
(Studio Teacher)
(661) 718-2274
(661) 917-0336

Allison Hindin
(Baby Wrangler)
(310) 418-8446
(310) 474-6500
FAX (310) 476-3268
www.studioteacherbabywrangler.com

Cliff M. Hirsch
(310) 457-7935
(805) 573-9442
FAX (310) 457-7935

Millie Lucas Hirsch
(562) 372-4196
(562) 243-0612

Gloria Hoffman
(626) 446-3592
(818) 559-9600

Dwight Hovey
(310) 677-0514
(310) 692-8003

Judy Jennings
(805) 544-4474
(818) 648-6500
FAX (805) 544-2601
www.studioteachers.com

Eva Jensen
(714) 525-5005
(714) 746-7241
FAX (714) 525-5005

Alicia Kalvin
(310) 980-0290
(310) 459-6875
www.studioteacher.org
(Baby Wrangler, Studio Teacher & Welfare Worker)

Helen Karagozian
(310) 454-3426
(310) 922-1496
FAX (310) 454-3426

Jill Kimmel
(818) 865-9065
(818) 429-9399
FAX (818) 865-8260

Nancy Klein
(818) 981-8479
(818) 497-8880
FAX (818) 981-1601

Hermine Kosta
(310) 820-8152
(818) 559-9600

Carole Levine
(Studio Teacher)
(323) 650-5821
(323) 810-2310

Abby Logan
(818) 516-5972

Chavonne Long
(626) 665-9149
(626) 296-9006

Bonnie Mackie (626) 622-3006
(619) 435-8710

Jill McKay (310) 836-8877
(310) 617-8245
(Baby Wrangler, Studio Teacher & Welfare Worker)

Beth McManigill (818) 807-3163
(Studio Teacher & Welfare Worker) **www.setteacher.com**

Michael Thomas Carter Company (323) 656-3075
(323) 717-5545

Kevin Moll (323) 385-1313
FAX (419) 715-9741
www.kevinmoll.com
(Japanese; Studio Teacher & Welfare Worker)

Cynthia R. Nakane (805) 924-0678
(323) 573-1970
(Baby Wrangler, Studio Teacher & Welfare Worker)

Ⓐ **On Location Education** (818) 541-9077
(800) 800-3378
400 Columbus Ave., Ste. 7S FAX (914) 747-2750
Los Angeles, CA 90046 **www.onlocationeducation.com**
(Referral for Studio Teachers/Welfare Workers)

Stella Pacific/Terrific Teachers (818) 464-5425
(562) 867-0700
www.stellapacificandassociates.com

James Panger (310) 968-7210
(310) 452-7210

Cheryl Parker (818) 768-3739
(818) 377-2621
FAX (818) 768-1204

Stacey Parzik (818) 385-0000
(818) 648-1667
(Baby Wrangler) **www.partiesbystacey.com**

Caryl Pine-Crasnick (310) 306-0685
(310) 780-5528

Heather Poundstone (310) 699-8323

Nancy Pyne-Hapke (818) 782-2311
(818) 497-2441
FAX (818) 782-2322
(Baby Wrangler, Studio Teacher & Welfare Worker)

Jana Raines (909) 989-3111

Jeffrey Raines (818) 203-2674
(818) 906-3315
(Baby Wrangler, Studio Teacher & Welfare Worker)

Cyndi Raymond (323) 428-2906
FAX (323) 938-7714
www.cyndiraymond.com
(Baby Wrangler, Studio Teacher & Welfare Worker)

Linda Resnick (310) 476-6355
(310) 749-6700
FAX (310) 476-2620

Myra Rosenthal (818) 886-1108
FAX (818) 407-8985

Bobbie Ross (323) 650-7422
(888) 460-3270
FAX (323) 650-6321

Gail A. Ruckel (818) 744-9373
www.studioteacher.net

Sharon Sacks (323) 933-4226
(213) 713-7256
FAX (323) 935-7384

Suzy Salerno (310) 858-7853
(310) 387-7458
FAX (310) 858-7853

Margaret L. Schlaifer (805) 492-6574
(818) 984-1696
FAX (805) 492-6584

Craig Schoenfeld (818) 907-8703
FAX (818) 907-8703

Linda Stone Shure (310) 837-7542
(310) 488-1826
(Baby Wrangler) FAX (310) 204-5683

Missy Simms/StudioTeachersOnCall (619) 405-5050
(Welfare Worker)

Mike Simon (818) 357-3154
(Studio Teacher & Welfare Worker) FAX (419) 735-8829
www.teachingthestars.com

Arlene Singer-Gross (818) 506-5591
(818) 424-5513
FAX (818) 506-1709

Linda Stanley (310) 372-1449
(602) 740-5598
(Baby Wrangler & Studio Teacher)

Jack Stern (818) 970-7540
(Baby Wrangler)

Julie Stevens (323) 848-7719
www.educatingyoungstars.com
(Baby Wrangler, Studio Teacher & Welfare Worker)

Lorraine Hendricks Stewart (310) 219-0191
(661) 805-3999

Ⓐ **The Studio Teachers (IA Local 884)** (818) 559-9600
(818) 559-9797
www.thestudioteachers.com
(Referral for Baby Wranglers, Studio Teachers and Welfare Workers)

Roberta Sutter (805) 205-0600
(Studio Teacher)

Ⓐ **@Teacher! Teacher!** (310) 559-1918
(310) 880-2310
FAX (818) 501-0768
(Baby Wranglers, Studio Teachers/Welfare Workers & Tutors)

Janie Teller (310) 820-4522
(646) 331-9456
(Baby Wrangler)

Jack Tice (818) 363-5573
(818) 363-3247
FAX (818) 363-5573

Jimmy Wagner (818) 755-0076
(Baby Wrangler) FAX (818) 762-5156
www.jimmywagner.us

Marsha Whittaker (310) 822-9496
(310) 963-0644

Richard Wicklund (323) 681-9394
(213) 841-3666
FAX (323) 681-9394

Lois Yaroshefsky (323) 650-6956
(323) 394-1233
(Studio Teacher & Welfare Worker)

Saena Yi (310) 801-7921
(Baby Wrangler, Studio Teacher & Welfare Worker)

Academy of Interactive Arts & Sciences (AIAS) (818) 876-0826
236 Calabassas Rd., Ste. 220
Calabassas, CA 91302
www.interactive.org

Academy of Motion Picture Arts & Sciences (AMPAS) (310) 247-3000
8949 Wilshire Blvd.
Beverly Hills, CA 90211
FAX **(310) 859-9619**
www.oscars.org

Academy of Television Arts & Sciences (ATAS) (818) 754-2800
5220 Lankershim Blvd., Second Fl.
North Hollywood, CA 91601
FAX **(818) 761-2827**
www.emmys.org

Advertising Age (310) 860-6420
6500 Wilshire Blvd., Ste. 2300
Los Angeles, CA 90048
www.adage.com

Affiliated Property Craftspersons (IA Local 44) (818) 769-2500
12021 Riverside Dr.
North Hollywood, CA 91607
FAX **(818) 769-3111**
www.local44.com

American Federation of Musicians/West Coast (213) 251-4510
3550 Wilshire Blvd., Ste. 1900
Los Angeles, CA 90010
FAX **(213) 251-4520**
www.afm.org

American Federation of TV & Radio Artists (AFTRA) (323) 634-8100
5757 Wilshire Blvd., Ste. 900
Los Angeles, CA 90036
FAX **(323) 634-8246**
www.aftra.com

American Society of Cinematographers (ASC) (323) 969-4333
(800) 448-0145
1782 N. Orange Dr.
Hollywood, CA 90028
FAX **(323) 882-6391**
www.theasc.com

American Society of Composers, Authors & Publishers (ASCAP) (323) 883-1000
7920 Sunset Blvd., Ste. 300
Los Angeles, CA 90046
FAX **(323) 883-1049**
www.ascap.com

The Animation Guild (818) 766-7151
4729 Lankershim Blvd.
North Hollywood, CA 91602
FAX **(818) 506-4805**
www.mpsc839.org

Art Directors Guild/Scenic, Title & Graphic Artists (IA Local 800) (818) 762-9995
11969 Ventura Blvd., Ste. 200
Studio City, CA 91604
FAX **(818) 762-9997**
www.artdirectors.org

Association of Film Commissioners International (406) 495-8040
314 N. Main, Ste. 307
Helena, MT 59601
FAX **(406) 495-8039**
www.afci.org

Association of Independent Commercial Producers (AICP) (323) 960-4763
650 N. Bronson Ave., Ste. 223B
Los Angeles, CA 90004
FAX **(323) 960-4766**
www.aicp.com

Association of Independent Creative Editors (AICE) (310) 587-2400
1222 Sixth St.
Santa Monica, CA 90401
www.aice.org

Casting Society of America (CSA) (323) 463-1925
606 N. Larchmont Blvd., Ste. 4B
Los Angeles, CA 90004
www.castingsociety.com

Commercial Casting Directors Association (CCDA) (818) 782-9900
13425 Ventura Blvd., Ste. 200
Sherman Oaks, CA 91423
FAX **(818) 782-0030**
www.ccdala.com

Costume Designers Guild (IA Local 892) (818) 752-2400
11969 Ventura Blvd., First Fl.
Studio City, CA 91604
FAX **(818) 752-2402**
www.costumedesignersguild.com

Directors Guild of America (DGA) (310) 289-2000
7920 Sunset Blvd.
Los Angeles, CA 90046
FAX **(310) 289-2029**
www.dga.org

Directors Guild of America, Inc./ Producers Pension & Health (310) 289-2000
8436 W. Third St., Ste. 900
Los Angeles, CA 90048
FAX **(323) 653-2375**
www.dga.org

Film Independent (FIND) (310) 432-1200
9911 West Pico Blvd., 11th Fl.
Los Angeles, CA 90035
FAX **(310) 432-1203**
www.findfilm.org

Hollywood Post Alliance (213) 614-0860
846 S. Broadway, Ste. 601
Los Angeles, CA 90014
FAX **(213) 614-0890**
www.hpaonline.com

IATSE & MPTAAC/ West Coast (AFL-CIO) (818) 980-3499
10045 Riverside Dr., Second Fl.
Toluca Lake, CA 91602
FAX **(818) 980-3496**
www.iatse-intl.org

IATSE (IA Local 122) (619) 640-0042
3737 Camino Del Rio South, Ste. 307
San Diego, CA 92108
FAX **(619) 640-0045**
www.iatse122.com

IATSE (IA Local 442) (805) 898-0442
www.iatse442.org

IATSE (IA Local 504) (714) 774-5004
FAX **(714) 774-7683**
www.isatse504.com

Illustrators & Matte Artists (IA Local 790) (818) 784-6555
13245 Riverside Dr., Ste. 300-A
Sherman Oaks, CA 91423
FAX **(818) 784-2004**

International Cinematographers Guild (IA Local 600) (323) 876-0160
7755 Sunset Blvd.
Los Angeles, CA 90046
FAX **(323) 876-6383**
www.cameraguild.com

International Sound Technicians (IA Local 695) (818) 985-9204
(323) 877-1052
5439 Cahuenga Blvd.
North Hollywood, CA 91601
FAX **(818) 760-4681**

International Stunt Association (ISA) (818) 501-5225
4454 Van Nuys Blvd., Ste. 214
Sherman Oaks, CA 91403
FAX **(818) 501-5656**
www.isastunts.com

Makeup Artists & Hair Stylists (IA Local 706) (818) 295-3933
828 N. Hollywood Way
Burbank, CA 91505
FAX **(818) 295-3930**
www.local706.org

A Minor Consideration (310) 532-1345
(310) 344-9686
14530 Denker Ave.
Gardena, CA 90247
FAX **(310) 523-3691**
www.minorcon.org

Motion Picture Association of America (MPAA) (818) 995-6600
15503 Ventura Blvd.
Encino, CA 91436
FAX **(818) 382-1790**
www.mpaa.org

Motion Picture Costumers (IA Local 705) (818) 487-5656
4731 Laurel Canyon Blvd., Ste. 201
Valley Village, CA 91607
FAX **(818) 487-5663**
www.motionpicturecostumers.org

Motion Picture Editors Guild (IA Local 700) (800) 705-8700
7715 Sunset Blvd., Ste 200
Los Angeles, CA 90046
FAX **(323) 876-0861**
www.editorsguild.com

Motion Picture First Aid Employees (IA Local 767) (818) 842-7670
P.O. Box 6309 FAX (818) 474-1570
Burbank, CA 91510 www.iatse767.org

Motion Picture Industry Pension & Health Plan (818) 769-0007 (888) 369-2007
11365 Ventura Blvd., First Fl. FAX (818) 508-4714
Studio City, CA 91604 www.mpiphp.org

Motion Picture Set Painters (IA Local 729) (818) 842-7729
1811 W. Burbank Blvd. FAX (818) 846-3729
Burbank, CA 91506 www.ialocal729.com

Motion Picture Studio Grips & Crafts Service (IA Local 80) (818) 526-0700
2520 W. Olive Ave., Ste. 200 www.iatselocal80.org
Burbank, CA 91505

Motion Picture Studio Mechanics (IATSE Local 495) (619) 275-0125 (619) 518-7442
1717 Morena Blvd. FAX (619) 275-2578
San Diego, CA 92110 www.ia495.org

Music Video Production Association (MVPA) (213) 387-1590
201 N. Occidental Blvd. FAX (213) 385-9507
Los Angeles, CA 90026 www.mvpa.com

Ornamental Plasterers, Sculptors & Modelers (AFL-CIO Local 755) (818) 379-9711
13245 Riverside Dr., Ste. 300E FAX (818) 379-9985
Sherman Oaks, CA 91423 www.local755.com

Producers Guild of America (PGA) (310) 358-9020
8530 Wilshire Blvd., Ste. 450 FAX (310) 358-9520
Beverly Hills, CA 90211 www.producersguild.org

Professional Musicians Local 47 (AFM) (323) 462-2161
817 Vine St. FAX (323) 461-3090
Hollywood, CA 90038 www.promusic47.org

Screen Actors Guild (SAG) (323) 954-1600
FAX (323) 549-6603
www.sag.org

Script Supervisors/Continuity, Coordinators, Accountants & Allied Production Specialists Guild 871 (818) 509-7871
11519 Chandler Blvd. FAX (818) 506-1555
North Hollywood, CA 91601 www.ialocal871.org

Set Decorators Society of America (323) 462-3060
1646 N. Cherokee Ave. FAX (323) 462-3099
Hollywood, CA 90028 www.setdecorators.org

Set Designers & Model Makers (IA Local 847) (818) 784-6555
13245 Riverside Dr., Ste. 300-A FAX (818) 784-2004
Sherman Oaks, CA 91423

Society of Camera Operators (SOC) (818) 382-7070
P.O. Box 2006 www.soc.org
Toluca Lake, CA 91610

Southern California Broadcasters Association (310) 444-1412
1849 Sawtelle Blvd., Ste. 543 FAX (310) 444-1463
Los Angeles, CA 90036 www.scba.com

Stagehands for Theater & TV (IA Local 33) (818) 841-9233
1720 W. Magnolia Blvd. FAX (818) 567-1138
Burbank, CA 91506 www.ia33.org

Studio Electrical Lighting Technicians (IA Local 728) (818) 985-0728
11500 Burbank Blvd. FAX (818) 985-5288
North Hollywood, CA 91605 www.iatse728.org

Studio Transportation Drivers (Teamsters Local 399) (818) 985-7374
P.O. Box 6017 FAX (818) 985-0097
North Hollywood, CA 91603

Stuntmen's Association of Motion Pictures (818) 766-4334
FAX (818) 766-5943
www.stuntmen.com

Stuntwomen's Association of Motion Pictures (818) 762-0907
12457 Ventura Blvd., Ste. 208 FAX (818) 762-9534
Studio City, CA 91604 www.stuntwomen.com

TAF/TP (214) 561-7330 (877) 256-9298
2727 Inwood Rd. FAX (214) 561-7332
Dallas, TX 75235 www.shoottexas.org

United Stuntwomen's Association, Inc. (USA) (818) 508-4651
FAX (818) 508-7074
www.usastunts.com

Visual Effects Society (818) 981-7861
5335 Balboa Blvd., Ste. 205 FAX (818) 981-7861
Encino, CA 91316 www.visualeffectssociety.com

Women in Animation (WIA) (818) 759-9596
P.O. Box 17706 www.womeninanimation.org
Encino, CA 91416

Women in Film (WIF) (323) 935-2211
6100 Wilshire Blvd., Ste. 710 FAX (323) 935-2212
Los Angeles, CA 90048 www.wif.org

Women's Image Network (310) 229-5365
2118 Wilshire Blvd., Ste. 144 www.winfemme.com
Santa Monica, CA 90403

Writers Guild of America West (WGAw) (323) 951-4000
7000 W. Third St. FAX (323) 782-4800
Los Angeles, CA 90048 www.wga.org

William Coleman (323) 791-7055

Bruce Comtois (818) 262-5353

Chris Cordola (310) 339-3394
FAX (310) 313-0298

Noah Vincent Ford (818) 421-1361

Joe Gonzalez (661) 510-7650
FAX (661) 513.9776
www.buboosky.com

J. Bud Graves (818) 335-2130
(415) 336-6257
FAX (818) 761-8383

Keeldar S. Hamilton (310) 613-2494
FAX (310) 919-2844

Mark D. Hysen (818) 261-9288
(818) 846-7999
FAX (818) 846-5657

Michael Ingold (661) 993-5393
FAX (661) 554-5497
www.alohastudiorentals.com

Brian Jelloe (213) 792-9052

John Kvammen (626) 255-9114
FAX (626) 441-6430

Mel Langford (661) 857-3177

Kevin McBride (805) 498-0624
(805) 701-7249

Dale McDowell (323) 459-1278

Ed Melendez (909) 322-4392
FAX (909) 861-2505

Tom Oberlin (818) 266-9911

Moses Paskowitz II (818) 424-1312
FAX (818) 343-5432

Blake Steelgrave (818) 652-7377
(661) 298-8912
FAX (661) 298-8912
www.pmfarms.biz
(Car Coordinator, Driver & Picture Car Coordinator)

John Yarbrough (310) 210-9272

Lance Acquasanta (310) 863-4626
www.videotechservices.com
(Camera Operator, Director of Photography & Safety Diver)

Robert Anderson (562) 433-2863
(562) 688-3038
FAX (562) 433-2863
www.aquavision.net
(Director of Photography, Grip, Marine Coordinator, Producer & Safety)

Ronald Anderson (520) 419-1490
(800) 577-9635
(Gaffer) FAX (520) 623-3144
www.mistyproductionservice.com

Wayne Baker (818) 991-9676
(818) 472-1780
(Camera Operator) FAX (818) 991-9677

Tom Boyd (818) 623-8255
(818) 974-1937
(Camera Operator) www.taboyd.com

Devon Clark (310) 453-5250
(310) 795-0237
(Production Manager)

Jack Cooperman (909) 336-1535
(Director of Photography)

Customs by Eddie Paul, A Division of EP Industries, Inc. (310) 643-8515
(310) 259-0542
2305 Utah Ave. FAX (310) 643-8520
El Segundo, CA 90245 www.deadlinetv.net
(Marine Coordinator & Producer)

John Pierre Dechene (818) 889-6749
(818) 889-6749
(Camera Operator)

Dan Donley (805) 493-5990
(213) 200-2810
(Prop Master)

Gary Dorf (310) 476-8380
(First AD & Producer) FAX (818) 789-6435

James Doudna (818) 889-8865
(818) 321-6064

Joly Erickson (818) 701-1963
(Gaffer)

Michael Ferris (310) 456-1530
(310) 749-5850
(Director of Photography) FAX (310) 456-1433

Steven Guerrero (310) 864-2000
www.aquaticcinema.com

Jorge Guzman (310) 836-4323
FAX (310) 836-4307

Chris Hayden (818) 889-0828
(310) 989-8226
(Second AD) FAX (818) 889-5483

Bob Hayes (310) 390-9190
(310) 717-6625
(Director of Photography) www.floatinglantern.net

Rene Herrera (323) 707-3411
(323) 707-3415
(Grip) FAX (818) 293-0049
www.aquarescue.com

Joshua Humphrey (310) 270-7032
(Key Grip) www.aquamonsters.com

C. Hardy James (503) 702-3544
(310) 472-4734
(First AD) FAX (503) 824-2751

Capt. Lance Julian (808) 224-0801
(323) 856-3000
(Marine Coordinator) FAX (323) 856-3009
www.thegelleragency.com

Michael Kari (805) 647-0650
(310) 303-3700
(Marine Coordinator) FAX (310) 406-3001
www.bakercorp.com

Jim Kimura (323) 559-1110
FAX (626) 398-1387
www.tdnartists.com
(Camera Operator & Director of Photography)

Priscilla Levy (916) 296-5035
(415) 669-7777
(Prop Master) FAX (415) 669 7777

Thomas Levy (415) 515-5547
(415) 669-7777
(Key Grip) FAX (415) 669 7777

Tim McArdle (818) 368-8143
(818) 414-2367
(Gaffer) FAX (818) 368-8143

Doug Merrifield (310) 545-2119
(310) 503-1631
(Producer & Production Manager) FAX (310) 545-5350

Patrick M. Murray (818) 632-6320
(Gaffer) FAX (818) 301-2591

Michael Neipris (562) 594-9276
FAX (562) 594-9242
www.nauticalfilmservices.com

Jimmy O'Connell (310) 968-0549
(310) 452-5774
FAX (310) 452-5774

Jim Pearson (661) 222-7342
(877) 877-9605
(Coordination, Safety & Training) FAX (661) 253-3643
www.cinemarineteam.com

Ascanio Pignatelli (310) 913-2313
(310) 395-8004
(Camera Operator) FAX (267) 295-8152

Tim Pogoler (818) 700-9005
(818) 281-1616
(Grip) FAX (818) 700-9005
www.timcoworks.com

Cynthia Pusheck (323) 497-8489
(Camera Operator)

Scott M. Robinson (310) 544-6682
(310) 617-7241
(Key Grip) FAX (310) 544-4034

Pete Romano (310) 301-8187
(310) 282-9940
(Director of Photography) FAX (310) 301-3065

Karen Roseme (760) 935-4086
(323) 697-8382
(Gaffer) FAX (760) 935-4086

Roger Sassen (818) 348-5909 / (818) 429-2413
(Gaffer) FAX (818) 702-0689

Suzanne E. Sebastian (805) 452-0561 / (805) 687-0354
(Production Coordinator)

Capt. Chris Shearman (818) 610-1103 / (310) 650-4455
(Marine Coordinator) FAX (818) 610-1128
www.on-screenmarine.com

Mike Thomas (714) 761-4163
(Director of Photography)

Michael G. Uva (310) 901-3287 / (310) 366-5822
(Key Grip) www.kastandkrew.com

Ronald Vidor (818) 766-6868 / (800) 759-5722
(Camera Operator) www.ronvidor.com

Jean-Pierre Visier (310) 670-2265
(Key Grip)

Mark Vollmen (310) 567-8218

Jon Douglas West (818) 761-4488 / (310) 888-4592
(Producer & Prop Master) FAX (818) 761-2112

Jon Zarkos (310) 798-5265 / (310) 365-7856
(Camera Assistant)

Rob Abbey (310) 991-0884 (310) 589-5838

Peter Albert/On-Set Digital, Inc. (562) 633-2333 (800) 495-7328

Leonardo Arterberry III (323) 466-7232
www.videorama.com

Steve Beach (323) 578-6133

Jeff Benard/Videodrone (818) 508-6214 (323) 855-4278
(Digital) FAX (818) 508-6214

Jason Bittinger (805) 300-9797
FAX (310) 391-0550

Christopher Blakely (323) 466-6660 (213) 509-7798
FAX (310) 399-9227

Kevin Boyd/K.P.B Digital For Film (323) 350-3446
(Digital) www.kpbdigitalforfilm.com

Tim Bruns (818) 889-9655
(Digital) www.videohawks.com

Jeff Burrage/Digital Split (310) 791-7278 (310) 614-3920
FAX (310) 378-7299

Mike Carlson (310) 947-1673

Bob Chambers (805) 777-1779 (818) 486-7707
(Digital) FAX (805) 777-1799

Steve Chambers/ Industry Assist Digital (310) 398-3344 (323) 547-0557
(Digital) FAX (310) 398-3344
www.industryassist.com

Mark Chapman (323) 466-7232 (213) 610-7746
www.videorama.com

Sam Cherroff (818) 772-4777 (818) 359-3589
(Digital) www.videoassist.com

Keith Collea (310) 823-0508 (520) 907-2211
FAX (815) 642-4444
www.imdb.com/name/nm0007205/

Leo Coltrane (323) 466-7232
www.videorama.com

Glenn Derry (818) 889-9655
(Digital) www.videohawks.com

Anthony DeSanto/DVassist (805) 279-1016 (805) 499-6602
(Digital)

Michael Dorfman/Dorfman Digital (818) 404-5179
FAX (323) 843-9730
www.dorfmandigital.com

Tim Flugum (818) 212-8660
(Digital)

Scott M. Goldman/Video Systems (310) 441-9836 (310) 292-9284
FAX (310) 474-5282

Tom L. Greger (310) 418-2963 (310) 750-6477
FAX (208) 445-0926

Scott Hammar (310) 770-0377 (818) 346-5362

Jim Harling (818) 889-9655
(Digital) www.videohawks.com

Sam Harrison/Play It Again Sam (661) 263-6070 (661) 803-9372
(Digital)

Kevin Hawks/ Circle Take Video Assist (805) 241-0457 (805) 490-3621
FAX (805) 241-6050

Dean Hendler (818) 508-9155 (818) 601-1177
(Digital) www.deanhendler.com

Kurt Herbal (818) 889-9655
(Digital) www.videohawks.com

Chris B. Hill (818) 445-9211 (818) 353-9211
(Digital & Tape Based) FAX (520) 843-7147
www.hilldigital.com

John Hill (818) 506-5293 (818) 606-8901
(Digital) FAX (818) 506-3049
www.videoassistsystems.com

Brad Huffman (805) 750-0401

Rich Jackson/Lucky Jackson DV (818) 262-7505 (818) 753-0533
www.luckyjackson.com

Tom Janetzke (626) 255-7523
www.videorama.com

Willow Jenkins (323) 810-3456
(Digital) FAX (310) 395-1920
www.chillowvision.com

Jeb Johenning/Ocean Video (310) 859-7573 (213) 300-2000
FAX (310) 275-8676
www.oceanvideo.com

Brett Kelly/Kelly Video (818) 883-7932 (818) 389-1583

Robert Kenworthy (818) 825-0077

Tom Loewy/Video Hawks (818) 889-9655
(Digital) FAX (818) 889-9755
www.videohawks.com

Chris Lum (818) 889-9655
(Digital) www.videohawks.com

Bob Lund/Awesome Playback (310) 391-0550 (310) 365-2305
(Digital & Tape Based)

Brian Maris (562) 708-6429 (562) 866-5178
(Digital)

William Martel Jr. (213) 494-9492 (800) 323-0490
FAX (323) 225-1389

Steven Mikolas (818) 679-9091
(Digital)

Andy Minzes/Ready To Roll Video (818) 842-2977
(818) 321-2117
FAX (818) 842-5273

Dan Moore (818) 957-8040
(818) 517-2022
FAX (818) 957-7457
www.videohawks.com

Robert Morales/
Director's Choice Video (818) 766-9050
(323) 854-3236
FAX (818) 766-9250
www.directorschoicevideo.com

Michael Moretti/Lost Dog Video (310) 722-8351
FAX (310) 483-7872
www.lostdogvideo.com

Tom Myrick (310) 378-3103
(310) 387-2858
(Digital) FAX (310) 378-3154

Gaylen Nebeker (801) 550-1648
(801) 467-1920
(Digital) FAX (801) 467-0307
www.nebtek.com

Sean Newhouse (310) 890-7480

Richard Northcutt (310) 589-2211
(310) 293-7661
(Digital) FAX (310) 589-2211

Robert Panza (310) 729-0108
(Digital) www.videorama.com

Mike Pickel (818) 621-2594
(818) 343-6808
(Digital) www.videohawks.com

John Placencia (323) 466-7232
(818) 667-1396
www.videorama.com

Finnian Riley (818) 371-5376
www.maccool.net

Andrew Rozendal (213) 598-1056
(818) 366-3784
(Digital) www.nebtek.com

Dave Schmalz (323) 225-5091
(213) 308-0702

Bob Schmidt (310) 222-8614
(310) 488-8410
(Digital) FAX (310) 222-8624
www.hoodmanusa.com

Mike Schmidt (310) 222-8614
(310) 488-8410
(Digital) FAX (310) 222-8624
www.hoodmanusa.com

Erick H. Schultz/EZ Video (310) 542-3202
(310) 430-2468
FAX (310) 542-3202

Wolf Seeberg (310) 822-4973
FAX (310) 305-8918
www.wolfvid.com

Jeffery Shafer (310) 678-7269
(310) 836-7892
(Digital)

Mike Shaheen (805) 520-4989
(818) 202-1177
(Digital & Tape-Based)

Bryce Shields (818) 425-7960
(Digital)

Randall Sudbury (801) 557-4454
(818) 782-5466
FAX (818) 782-9907
www.nebtek.com

Gary Taillon (805) 443-3806

Terrence Tally (818) 378-8073
(Digital) FAX (818) 951-1744

Brian Thesing (310) 704-1080

Thomas Thonson (323) 466-7232
www.videorama.com

Dempsey Tillman/
Man In The Box Video Assist (818) 517-8865
FAX (818) 887-0682
www.maninthebox video.com

Ira D. Toles (310) 457-2830
(310) 560-5555

Mike Uguccioni/PreFX (310) 403-1556

Howard Van Emden/
Videorama! Industries, LLC (323) 697-6221
(323) 466-7232
FAX (323) 466-7232
www.videorama.com

Thomas Vanasse/
TV Productions, Inc. (818) 763-4098
(Digital)

Lance Jay Velazco (818) 848-2852
(818) 298-3666
(Digital) www.imdb.com/name/nm1100854/

Video Tech Services (310) 574-9385
(310) 505-4015
10866 Washington Blvd., Ste. 513 FAX (310) 577-0850
Culver City, CA 90232 www.videotechservices.com
(Reps for VTR Operators)

Allen Waggoner (626) 338-1806
(626) 736-8959
(Digital)

Bill Weiss (310) 770-7915
(310) 479-3496
(Digital)

Charlie Westfall/
Chas. Westfall Video (818) 509-7800
(818) 970-8962
(Digital) FAX (818) 769-1773

Eric Williams (323) 466-7232
www.videorama.com

Adam Yoblon (310) 738-7548
(Digital)

Angela Aaron (323) 664-6494
www.therexagency.com

Ashley Abercrombie (323) 906-9600
www.crystalagency.com

Marie Abma (323) 856-3000
www.thegelleragency.com

Aimee Acord (323) 297-0250
www.magnetla.com

Julie Adams (310) 995-1111
(323) 660-3838
FAX (323) 660-3800

Wess Albrecht (310) 403-8986
www.wessalbrecht.com

Mary Beth Alessandri (323) 937-1010
www.zenobia.com

All Crew Agency (818) 206-0144
2920 W. Olive Ave., Ste. 201 FAX (818) 206-0169
Burbank, CA 91505 www.allcrewagency.com
(Reps for Costume Designers)

Jason Alper (310) 273-6700
www.unitedtalent.com

Charlie Altuna (310) 822-2898
www.rougeartists.com

Shannon Amos (323) 933-0200
www.artistuntied.com

Deana Anais (310) 274-0032
www.artistsbytimothypriano.com

Michael Angel (310) 998-1977
www.celestineagency.com

Johanna Argan (310) 288-8000
www.paradigmagency.com

Arnelle (323) 299-4043
www.dionperonneau.com

Artist Untied (323) 933-0200
(415) 957-0500
(Reps for Wardrobe Stylists) FAX (415) 957-0555
www.artistuntied.com

Artists by Timothy Priano (310) 274-0032
345 N. Maple Dr., Ste. 397 FAX (310) 278-7520
Beverly Hills, CA 90210
www.artistsbytimothypriano.com
(Reps for Wardrobe Stylists)

artists' services (323) 445-4910
(415) 824-4423
8581 Santa Monica Blvd., Ste. 437
West Hollywood, CA 90069 www.artists-services.com
(Reps for Wardrobe Stylists)

ArtMix Beauty (310) 943-8102
2332 S. Centinela Ave., Ste. C FAX (310) 943-8101
Los Angeles, CA 90064 www.artmixbeauty.com
(Reps for Wardrobe Stylists)

Victoria Auth (310) 656-5151
www.innovativeartists.com

Varya Avdyushko (310) 652-8778
www.lspagency.net

Agnes Baddoo (323) 935-8455
www.ms-management.com

Hala Bahmet (323) 845-4144
www.montanaartists.com

Eileen Baker (323) 856-3000
www.thegelleragency.com

Inanna Bantu (818) 206-0144
www.allcrewagency.com

Britt Bardo (323) 297-0250
www.magnetla.com

Sarah Bardo (818) 242-7778

Kirk Bardole (323) 937-1010
www.zenobia.com

Chathene Barrow (323) 512-8002
www.karleeartist.com

Pauline Barry (415) 290-9532
www.paulinebarry.com

Shawn Barton (310) 652-8778
www.lspagency.net

Linda Bass (310) 656-5151
www.innovativeartists.com

Carol Beadle (323) 664-6494
www.therexagency.com

Jenny Beavan (310) 273-6700
www.utaproduction.com

Angee Beckett (323) 650-8187
(213) 484-9307
FAX (323) 650-8187

Nicole Beckett (323) 804-4550
www.nicolebeckett.com

Sarah Beers (323) 845-4144
www.montanartists.com

Robert Behar (323) 913-1566
(323) 251-4046
FAX (323) 660-3909
www.rowbinc.com

Jami Bele (310) 874-9119

Fifi Bell (323) 299-4043
www.dionperonneau.com

Alycia Belle (323) 460-4767
www.jacobandkoleagency.com

Erin Benach (310) 652-8778
www.lspagency.net

Marlene Jaye Benson (310) 306-1084
(310) 998-5400
FAX (310) 578-8204

Eric Berg (323) 664-6494
www.therexagency.com

Kate Bergh (818) 567-4723
(213) 706-9254

Christine Bieselin Clark (323) 578-0895
FAX (323) 660-2356
www.christinebieselin.com

Anna Bingemann (323) 297-0250
www.magnetla.com

Micah Bishop (323) 933-0200
www.artistuntied.com

Tim Bitici (310) 274-0032
www.artistsbytimothypriano.com

Heidi Bivens (310) 652-8778
www.lspagency.net

Marlene Blackwell (310) 435-2814
(310) 454-9440
www.mmblackwell.com

Izabel Blanca (323) 549-3100
www.beautyandphoto.com

Phillip Bloch (310) 394-8813
www.cloutieragency.com

Bénédicte Bodard-Willis (818) 783-6215

Johnetta Boone (818) 284-6423
www.italentco.com

Marissa Borsetto (310) 656-5151
www.innovativeartists.com

Liz Botes (310) 822-2898
www.rougeartists.com

Vincent Boucher (323) 436-7766
www.eamgmt.com

Gwen Bouzon (415) 695-1254
FAX (415) 695-1254

Kim Bowen (323) 297-0250
www.magnetla.com

Michael T. Boyd (310) 656-5151
www.innovativeartists.com

Mark Bridges (310) 273-6700
www.utaproduction.com

Tom Broecker (310) 274-6611
www.gershagency.com

Heather Brooks (310) 274-0032
www.artistsbytimothypriano.com

Margo Brumme (323) 445-4910
www.artists-services.com

Melissa Bruning (323) 377-5353
(323) 665-5775
www.melissabruning.com

Katherine Jane Bryant (323) 856-3000
(323) 463-0022
www.thegelleragency.com

Marie H. Burk (323) 663-8509
(323) 481-2931
FAX (323) 667-0135

Roger K. Burton (818) 284-6423
www.italentco.com

Dana Campbell (310) 652-8778
www.lspagency.net

Leslie Campbell (310) 614-2695

Poppy Cannon-Reese (310) 477-5116
(707) 292-6957
www.poppycannonreese.com

Connie Cappos (310) 837-8797
(808) 966-4890
www.conniecappos.com

Sophie Carbonell (323) 297-0250
www.magnetla.com

Susie Carlson (818) 888-9117
(818) 212-9117
FAX (818) 888-7723

Ruth Carter (310) 656-5151
www.innovativeartists.com

Debbie Castaldi (310) 503-7107
(310) 398-2375
FAX (310) 398-2375

Daniel Caudill (310) 998-1977
www.celestineagency.com

Célestine Agency (310) 998-1977
1548 16th St. FAX (310) 998-1978
Santa Monica, CA 90404 www.celestineagency.com
(Reps for Wardrobe Stylists)

Lisa Cera (310) 274-0032
www.artistsbytimothypriano.com

Catherine Chambaret (323) 937-7877
FAX (323) 937-8053

Tim Chappel (310) 274-6611
www.gershagency.com

Patric Chauvez (310) 274-0032
www.artistsbytimothypriano.com

Cherie Represents (323) 937-9095
845 S. Mansfield Ave., Ste. 1 FAX (323) 937-3300
Los Angeles, CA 90036 www.cheriereps.com
(Reps for Wardrobe Stylists)

Michelene Cherie (323) 937-9095
www.cheriereps.com

Wendy Chuck (310) 656-5151
www.innovativeartists.com

Michael Cioffoletti (310) 998-1977
www.celestineagency.com

Michael Clancy (323) 468-2240
www.nyoffice.net

Kecia Clark (310) 998-1977
www.celestineagency.com

Cloutier (310) 394-8813
1026 Montana Ave. FAX (310) 394-8863
Santa Monica, CA 90403 www.cloutieragency.com
(Reps for Wardrobe Stylists)

Cat Coffin (310) 977-2250

Garth Condit (310) 274-0032
www.artistsbytimothypriano.com

Kate Corrigan-Lee (310) 578-6756
(310) 702-2884

Carole Cotten (323) 937-1010
www.zenobia.com

Jamie Coulter (323) 937-1010
www.zenobia.com

Betsy Cox (310) 656-5151
www.innovativeartists.com

Ane Crabtree (310) 652-8778
www.lspagency.net

Marcy Craig (310) 600-5211

Crystal Agency (323) 906-9600
(323) 788-1336
4237 Los Nietos Dr. FAX (323) 443-3752
Los Angeles, CA 90027 www.crystalagency.com
(Reps for Wardrobe Stylists)

Carol Cutshall (310) 652-8778
www.lspagency.net

Deborah Dapolito (323) 933-0200
www.artistuntied.com

Dawn to Dusk Agency (323) 850-6783
(212) 431-8631
8306 Wilshire Blvd., Ste. 412
Beverly Hills, CA 90211 www.dawn2duskagency.com
(Reps for Wardrobe Stylists)

Tracie Delaney (310) 458-7800
www.partos.com

Sarah de Sa Rego (310) 274-6611
www.gershagency.com

Melissa Des Rosiers (310) 458-7800
www.partos.com

Louise de Teliga (310) 770-8558
(310) 777-8343
www.louisedeteliga.com

Marie-Sylvie Deveau (310) 274-6611
www.gershagency.com

Dion Peronneau Agency (323) 299-4043
5482 Wilshire Blvd., Ste. 1512 FAX (323) 299-4269
Los Angeles, CA 90036 www.dionperonneau.com
(Reps for Wardrobe Stylists)

Jane Doctor (818) 501-1217
FAX (818) 501-8178

Susan Doepner-Senac (323) 937-1010
www.zenobia.com

Jean-Pierre Dorléac (818) 206-0144
www.allcrewagency.com

Mynka Draper (310) 274-6611
www.gershagency.com

Jenna Drobnick (323) 445-4910
www.artists-services.com

Justin Ducoty (323) 436-7766
www.eamgmt.com

Laura Duncan (323) 856-8540
www.opusbeauty.com

Tere Duncan (310) 652-8778
www.lspagency.net

John Dunn (310) 274-6611
www.gershagency.com

Shannon Dunn (323) 933-0200
www.artistuntied.com

Chrisi Karvonides Dushenko (323) 845-4144
www.montanartists.com

Patti Early (818) 762-9908

Lauren Ehrenfeld (310) 998-1977
www.celestineagency.com

Ennis, Inc. (310) 587-3512
www.ennisinc.com
(Reps for Wardrobe Stylists/Costume Designers)

Epiphany Artist Group, Inc. (323) 660-6353
9903 Santa Monica Blvd., Ste. 480 FAX (323) 660-0094
Beverly Hills, CA 90212
(Reps for Wardrobe Stylists)

Nicoletta Ercole (310) 822-9113
www.murthaagency.com

Mary Erickson (877) 242-6878
www.lamakeup.com

Eleanor Estes (310) 822-2898
www.rougeartists.com

Leesa Evans (323) 463-0100

Jennifer Eve (323) 468-2240
www.nyoffice.net

Deborah Everton (310) 288-8000
www.paradigmagency.com

Exclusive Artists Management (323) 436-7766
7700 Sunset Blvd., Ste. 205 FAX (323) 436-7799
Los Angeles, CA 90046 www.eamgmt.com
(Reps for Wardrobe Stylists)

Caroline Fahrer (323) 462-5000
www.traceymattingly.com

Gamila M. Fakhry-Smith (818) 506-1683
(818) 653-5958
FAX (818) 506-5756

Lynn Falconer (323) 468-2240
www.nyoffice.net

Ellen Falguiere (310) 393-3597
(310) 403-3831

Deborah Ferguson (310) 943-8102
www.artmixbeauty.com

April Ferry (310) 273-6700
www.utaproduction.com

Trayce Field (310) 822-2898
www.rougeartists.com

Jordanna Fineberg (818) 206-0144
www.allcrewagency.com

FIRE House Management (888) 839-0101
(Reps for Wardrobe Stylists) FAX (888) 839-2943
www.firehousemanagement.com

Tietjen Fischer (323) 933-0200
www.artistuntied.com

Frank Fleming (323) 845-4144
www.montanartists.com

Maureen Fletcher (818) 985-0086
(818) 681-1324

Chaz E. Foley (310) 822-2898
www.rougeartists.com

Geren Ford (323) 297-0250
www.magnetla.com

Hank Ford (213) 482-5057
(323) 633-6817
FAX (213) 482-5057
www.hankford.net

Leah Forester (310) 733-2550
www.photogenicsmedia.com

Sharman Forman-Hyde (323) 876-6317
www.sharmanformanhyde.com

Mary Jane Fort (310) 274-6611
www.gershagency.com

Marie France (310) 282-9940
www.mirisch.com

Fred Segal Beauty (310) 550-1800
9250 Wilshire Blvd., Ste. 210
Beverly Hills, CA 90212
(Reps for Wardrobe Stylists)
FAX (310) 550-1501
www.fredsegalbeauty.com

Scott Free (323) 664-6494
www.rexagency.com

Leslie Fremar (323) 297-0250
www.magnetla.com

Louise Frogley (310) 273-6700
www.utaproduction.com

Michele Gampel (818) 883-3339
(818) 515-7890
FAX (818) 883-3339
www.mgampel.com

Sue Gandy (323) 856-3000
www.thegelleragency.com

Pierre-Yves Gauraud (310) 652-8778
www.lspagency.net

Vanessa Geldbach (323) 436-7766
www.eamgmt.com

The Geller Agency (323) 856-3000
1547 Cassil Pl.
Hollywood, CA 90028
(Reps for Costume Designers)
FAX (323) 856-3009
www.thegelleragency.com

Jenny Gering (323) 468-2240
www.nyoffice.net

The Gersh Agency (310) 274-6611
(212) 997-1818
P.O. Box 5617
Beverly Hills, CA 90210
(Reps for Costume Designers)
FAX (310) 274-4035
www.gershagency.com

Jean Lee Getson (323) 664-6494
www.therexagency.com

Becca Glesby (213) 509-9975

Beth Goodman (323) 972-5655
www.bethgoodmanstylist.com

Sarah Gore-Reeves (323) 856-8540
www.opusbeauty.com

Louisa Gravelle (310) 779-8977
(310) 798-8841
FAX (310) 798-3801

Ellen Greenberg (310) 273-9596
FAX (310) 271-2114

Justin Greenburg (323) 845-9421
(310) 656-5153

Lee Grenrock-Viles (818) 556-1557
(818) 355-1433

Mia Gyzander (310) 559-0570
FAX (310) 559-0580
www.miagyzander.com

Jonas Hallberg (323) 462-5000
www.traceymattingly.com

Mary Claire Hannan (310) 474-4585
www.ddatalent.com

Jessica Hansen (323) 445-4910
www.artists-services.com

Suzie Hardy (323) 935-8455
www.ms-management.com

Michelle Hartnett (310) 246-0446
www.workgroup-ltd.com

Roemehl Hawkins (310) 288-8000
www.paradigmagency.com

Dawn Haynes (323) 850-6783
www.dawn2duskagency.com

Sanja Hays (310) 656-5151
www.innovativeartists.com

Hazel & Diana (323) 664-6494
www.therexagency.com

Cathleen Healy (310) 274-0032
www.artistsbytimothypriano.com

Betsy Heimann (310) 273-6700
www.utaproduction.com

Frank Helmer (310) 656-5151
www.innovativeartists.com

Lindy Hemming (310) 273-6700
www.utaproduction.com

Sandra Hernandez (310) 656-5151
www.innovativeartists.com

Carla Hetland (818) 284-6423
www.italentco.com

Sid Hicks (323) 447-1701
www.sidhicks.com

Roberta Hoeft (310) 274-0032
www.artistsbytimothypriano.com

Michael Holdaway (323) 385-6113
www.michaelholdaway.com

Sarah Holden (310) 652-8778
www.lspagency.net

Eric Hollis (310) 733-2550
www.photogenicsmedia.com

Cliff Hoppus (310) 274-0032
www.artistsbytimothypriano.com

Aimee House (310) 429-2012

Seth Howard (310) 274-0032
www.artistsbytimothypriano.com

Judy Ruskin Howell (310) 652-8778
www.lspagency.net

Beverley Hyde (323) 468-2240
www.nyoffice.net

Mary Iannelli (818) 206-0144
www.allcrewagency.com

Innovative Artists (310) 656-5151
1617 Broadway, Third Fl. FAX (310) 656-5156
Santa Monica, CA 90404 www.innovativeartists.com
(Reps for Wardrobe Stylists/Costume Designers)

International Creative Management - ICM (310) 550-4000
10250 Constellation Blvd. www.icmtalent.com
Los Angeles, CA 90067
(Reps for Costume Designers)

Sheila Irwin (818) 489-5089
(818) 889-7733

Janine Israel (310) 998-1977
www.celestineagency.com

iTalent Company (818) 284-6423
9701 Wilshire Blvd., 10th Fl. FAX (866) 755-0708
Beverly Hills, CA 90212 www.italentco.com
(Reps for Wardrobe Stylists/Costume Designers)

Francine Jamison-Tanchuck (310) 273-6700
www.utaproduction.com

Jane Janiger (310) 288-8000
www.paradigmagency.com

Lisa Jensen (818) 284-6423
www.italentco.com

Jessica & Kelly (323) 436-7766
www.eamgmt.com

Zoe Joeright (310) 274-0032
www.artistsbytimothypriano.com

Darryle Johnson (310) 288-8000
www.paradigmagency.com

Jane Johnston (323) 468-2240
www.nyoffice.net

Betsy Jones (805) 969-5501
FAX (805) 969-5224

Carlton Jones (323) 937-1010
www.zenobia.com

Gary Jones (310) 273-6700
www.utaproduction.com

Jeneffer Jones (323) 445-4910
(415) 824-4423
www.artists-services.com

Stacey Jones (310) 274-0032
www.artistsbytimothypriano.com

Michael Kaplan (310) 273-6700
www.utaproduction.com

Karlee Artist Management (323) 512-8002
(323) 913-0700
2658 Griffith Park Blvd., Ste. 171 FAX (323) 878-0068
Los Angeles, CA 90039 www.karleeartist.com
(Reps for Wardrobe Stylists)

Katie & Lindsey (310) 274-0032
www.artistsbytimothypriano.com

Faye Poliakin Katske (310) 486-0196

Daniell Kays (323) 297-0250
www.magnetla.com

Jayne Marie Kehoe (818) 216-1154
FAX (818) 715-9970

Kool Keita (310) 733-2550
www.photogenicsmedia.com

Mary Kate Killilea (323) 856-3000
www.thegelleragency.com

Perri Kimono (323) 856-8000
(310) 701-0448
FAX (323) 856-8000

Holli Kingsbury (310) 274-0032
www.artistsbytimothypriano.com

Jill A. Kliber (323) 468-2240
www.nyoffice.net

George Kotsiopoulos (323) 556-3455
(212) 404-4527

Paula Kowalczyk (323) 937-1010
(212) 242-7284
www.paulakowalcyzk.com

Susan Kowarsh Hall (323) 656-7574
(310) 200-4138

Gini Kramer-Goldman (310) 403-0409
FAX (310) 398-1221

Christopher Kreiling (310) 822-2898
www.rougeartists.com

Christina Kretschmer (917) 553-7622
FAX (323) 932-0806
www.ckretschmer.com

Azan Kung (310) 804-2469
www.electricacid.com

Rachel Sage Kunin (310) 656-5151
www.innovativeartists.com

Jeffrey Kurland (310) 273-6700
www.utaproduction.com

Kurt & Bart (323) 549-3100
www.beautyandphoto.com

Kelle Kutsugeras (323) 845-4144
www.montanartists.com

LA Rep (213) 446-1720
(Reps for Wardrobe Stylists) FAX (323) 656-1756

Wallace G. (Woody) Lane Jr. (323) 856-3000
www.thegelleragency.com

Sylvia Lantz (323) 856-3000
www.thegelleragency.com

Erin Lareau/Topaz (323) 851-9444
www.topazwardrobe.com

Suttirat Larlarb (323) 845-4144
www.montanartists.com

Lauren & Nina (310) 943-8102
www.artmixbeauty.com

Stacy Lauwers (323) 896-2845
www.stacylauwers.com

Valerie Laven-Cooper (310) 457-1796
(310) 251-2172
FAX (310) 457-1796

Christopher Lawrence (310) 656-5151
www.innovativeartists.com

Donald Lawrence (323) 856-8540
www.opusbeauty.com

Francine Lecoultre (323) 664-1636
FAX (323) 664-1676

Derek Lee (323) 299-4043
www.dionperonneau.com

Sara Leete (310) 246-0446
www.workgroup-ltd.com

Sara Lete (310) 246-0446
www.workgroup-ltd.com

Jennifer Levy (323) 468-2240
www.nyoffice.net

Thea Lewis (323) 937-1010
www.zenobia.com

George Liddle (310) 822-9113
www.murthaagency.com

Marylou Lim (323) 661-8335
(213) 944-3021

Kate Lindsay (818) 783-2822
FAX (818) 905-6669

Mandi Line (310) 282-9940
www.mirisch.com

George Little (310) 656-5151
www.innovativeartists.com

Marc Littlejohn (888) 839-0101
www.firehousemanagement.com

Elin Litzinger (323) 646.9581
www.stylestar-la.com

Pie Lombardi (818) 769-9006
(213) 617-0118
FAX (818) 985-8417

Pipi Loose (310) 274-0032
www.artistsbytimothypriano.com

Betty Pecha Madden (323) 681-9394
FAX (323) 681-9394

Molly Maginnis (310) 656-5151
www.innovativeartists.com

Magnet LA (323) 297-0250
6363 Wilshire Blvd., Ste. 650 FAX (323) 297-0249
Los Angeles, CA 90048 www.magnetla.com
(Reps for Wardrobe Stylists)

Kasia Walicka Maimone (323) 460-4767
www.jacobandkoleagency.com

Ann Somers Major (310) 288-8000
www.paradigmagency.com

Maryam Malakpour (323) 556-3455
FAX (323) 556-3456
www.maryammalakpour.com

Karen Mann (310) 822-2898
www.rougeartists.com

Bobbie Mannix (310) 995-0803
FAX (661) 251-9321
www.bobbiemannix.com

Dana Marasca (310) 998-1977
www.celestineagency.com

Donna Marie (310) 274-0032
www.artistsbytimothypriano.com

Marsh, Best & Associates (310) 285-0303
9150 Wilshire Blvd., Ste. 220 FAX (310) 285-0218
Beverly Hills, CA 90212 www.marshbest.com
(Reps for Costume Designers)

Bernard Martinez (323) 935-8455
www.ms-management.com

Ernesto Martinez (323) 845-4144
www.montanartists.com

Ramona Martinez (323) 934-4375
(323) 842-4373
FAX (323) 937-6887
www.ramonamartinez.com

Michelle Martini (323) 297-0250
www.magnetla.com

Agata Maskiewicz (323) 856-3000
www.thegelleragency.com

Nonja McKenzie (323) 299-4043
www.dionperonneau.com

Jim McKinney (323) 856-3000
www.thegelleragency.com

Gail McMullen (310) 282-9940
www.mirisch.com

Heidi Meek (310) 394-8813
www.cloutieragency.com

Melissa Meister (323) 436-7766
www.eamgmt.com

Gitee Meldgaard (323) 549-3100
www.beautyandphoto.com

Mimi Melgaard (310) 656-5151
www.innovativeartists.com

Melissa Melvin (323) 937-1010
www.zenobia.com

Albert Mendonca (310) 998-1977
www.celestineagency.com

Lynette Meyer (323) 845-4144
www.montanartists.com

Michele Michel (310) 652-8778
www.lspagency.net

Louise Mingenbach (310) 273-6700
www.utaproduction.com

The Mirisch Agency (310) 282-9940
1925 Century Park East, Ste. 1070 FAX (310) 282-0702
Los Angeles, CA 90067 www.mirisch.com
(Reps for Costume Designers)

Susan Monaster (310) 306-8936

Elaine Montalvo (323) 856-3000
www.thegelleragency.com

Montana Artists Agency (323) 845-4144
7715 W. Sunset Blvd., Third Fl. FAX (323) 845-4155
Los Angeles, CA 90046 www.montanartists.com
(Reps for Wardrobe Stylists/Costume Designers)

Beth Morgan (323) 856-3000
www.thegelleragency.com

Kathryn Morrison (310) 656-5151
www.innovativeartists.com

Chrissy Morton (310) 458-7800
www.partos.com

MS Management (323) 935-8455
(Reps for Wardrobe Stylists) FAX (323) 935-3143
www.ms-management.com

The Murtha Agency (310) 822-9113
4240 Promenade Way, Ste. 232 FAX (310) 822-6662
Marina del Rey, CA 90292 www.murthaagency.com
(Reps for Costume Designers)

April Napier (323) 297-0250
www.magnetla.com

New York Office (323) 468-2240
(212) 545-7895
6605 Hollywood Blvd., Ste. 200 FAX (323) 468-2244
Los Angeles, CA 90028 www.nyoffice.net
(Reps for Costume Designers)

Jill Newell (310) 288-8000
www.paradigmagency.com

Ha Nguyen (310) 274-6611
www.gershagency.com

Eric Niemand (310) 274-0032
www.artistsbytimothypriano.com

Nikko (323) 856-8540
www.opusbeauty.com

Martina Nilsson (323) 856-8540
www.opusbeauty.com

Susan Nininger (323) 222-6217

Kathryn Nixon (323) 468-2240
www.nyoffice.net

Patricia Norris (310) 822-9113
www.murthaagency.com

Rosanna Norton (818) 206-0144
www.allcrewagency.com

Carol Oditz (310) 656-5151
www.innovativeartists.com

Ray Oliveira (323) 664-6494
www.therexagency.com

Danny O'Neill (323) 933-0200
www.artistuntied.com

Opus Beauty (323) 856-8540
6442 Santa Monica Blvd., Ste. 200B FAX (323) 871-8311
Los Angeles, CA 90038 www.opusbeauty.com
(Reps for Wardrobe Stylists)

Kathy O'Rear (310) 822-9113
www.murthaagency.com

Daniel Orlandi (310) 273-6700
www.utaproduction.com

Kendrick Osorio (323) 935-8455
www.ms-management.com

Richard Owings (310) 282-9940
www.mirisch.com

Rob Oxenham (323) 933-0200
www.artistuntied.com

Lydia Paddon (310) 458-7800
www.partos.com

Nina Padovano (818) 881-4358
(323) 497-7128
FAX (818) 881-3208

Partos Company (310) 458-7800
227 Broadway, Ste. 204 FAX (310) 587-2250
Santa Monica, CA 90401 www.partos.com
(Reps for Wardrobe Stylists)

Wendy Partridge (310) 288-8000
www.paradigmagency.com

Jessica Paster (310) 998-1977
www.celestineagency.com

Beth Pasternak (310) 274-6611
www.gershagency.com

Beatrix Aruna Pasztor (310) 274-6611
www.gershagency.com

Gretchen Patch (213) 709-1797
www.gretchenpatch.com

Karen Patch (310) 273-6700
www.utaproduction.com

Gaelle Paul (310) 998-1977
www.celestineagency.com

Christopher Peterson (310) 458-7800
www.partos.com

Gersha Phillips (310) 288-8000
www.paradigmagency.com

Photogenics (310) 733-2550
8549 Higuera St. FAX (310) 815-8632
Culver City, CA 90232 www.photogenicsmedia.com
(Reps for Wardrobe Stylists)

Juliet Polcsa (323) 468-2240
www.nyoffice.net

Romeo Pompa (323) 654-8065
(323) 620-8554
FAX (323) 654-8065

Joseph Porro (310) 274-6611
www.gershagency.com

Candy Poskin (323) 664-6494
www.therexagency.com

Milka Price (310) 998-1977
www.celestineagency.com

Brian Primeaux (310) 943-8102
www.artmixbeauty.com

Tiffany Puhy (310) 430-9902
www.9-agency.com

Nissa Quanstrom (415) 647-8105

LeeAnn Radeka (310) 288-8000
www.paradigmagency.com

Tiffani Rae (323) 906-9600
www.crystalagency.com

Rita Rago (310) 822-2898
www.rougeartists.com

Julie Ragolia (323) 856-8540
www.opusbeauty.com

Christann C. Rawls (888) 242-6355
FAX (888) 242-6313
www.christannrawls.com

Marina Ray (323) 377-0933
www.marinaray.com

Agga B. Raya (310) 274-0032
www.artistsbytimothypriano.com

Alysia Raycraft (917) 685-2236
(310) 656-5151
www.alysiaraycraft.com

Michele Rede (323) 856-3000
www.thegelleragency.com

Noel Reghanti (323) 933-0200
www.artistuntied.com

Swinda Reichelt (310) 401-3211
www.jeannineangelique.com

Luke Reichle (310) 656-5151
www.innovativeartists.com

Maude Retchin-Feil (310) 545-0882
(310) 738-1318
FAX (310) 546-5512

Marjolijn Reuter (323) 937-1010
www.zenobia.com

Edgar Revilla (323) 289-5988
www.edgarrevilla.com

The Rex Agency (323) 664-6494
4446 Ambrose Ave.
Los Angeles, CA 90027
(Reps for Wardrobe Stylists)
FAX (323) 664-6112
www.therexagency.com

Sally Rice (310) 729-8861
(949) 581-0583
FAX (949) 581-0583

Basia Richards (310) 274-0032
www.artistsbytimothypriano.com

Katie Riney (323) 935-8455
www.ms-management.com

David Robinson (310) 273-6700
www.unitedtalent.com

Aggie Rodgers (323) 460-4767
www.jacobandkoleagency.com

Neil Rodgers (323) 462-5000
www.traceymattingly.com

Nola Roller (323) 459-4447
(323) 222-3939
FAX (323) 342-0546
www.nolaroller.com

Kiersten Ronning (310) 458-7800
www.partos.com

Sena Rosenberg (310) 274-0032
www.artistsbytimothypriano.com

Anne Ross (310) 968-0007
www.anneross.com

Rouge Artists, Inc. (310) 822-2898
(310) 570-1150
2433 Boone Ave.
Venice, CA 90291
(Reps for Wardrobe Stylists)
FAX (310) 827-7367
www.rougeartists.com

Shoshana Rubin (310) 656-5151
www.innovativeartists.com

Viktoria Ruchkan (310) 246-0446
www.workgroup-ltd.com

Bon Russell (323) 309-1615
FAX (323) 654-4772

Alexa Ryan (310) 274-0032
www.artistsbytimothypriano.com

Sam Saboura (310) 822-2898
www.rougeartists.com

Robert Saduski (818) 206-0144
www.allcrewagency.com

Sharon Taylor Sampson (818) 206-0144
www.allcrewagency.com

Vicki Sanchez (310) 282-9940
www.mirisch.com

Cory Savage (323) 445-1560
www.corysavage.com

Eddie Schachnow (310) 998-1977
www.celestineagency.com

Peggy Schnitzer (310) 274-6611
www.gershagency.com

Nicole Christine Schott (818) 693-9618
www.nicolechristinedesign.com

Deborah Scott (310) 656-5151
www.innovativeartists.com

Mark Seabaugh (323) 937-1010
www.zenobia.com

Zeca Seabra (323) 656-6117

Justine Seymour (310) 849-2417
www.justine-seymour.com

Mychael Shandra (310) 994-3154
www.mychaelshandra.com

Laura Jean Shannon (212) 634-8114
(310) 458-7800
www.partos.com

Elizabeth Shelton (818) 284-6423
www.italentco.com

Shinko (323) 664-6494
www.therexagency.com

Charmaine Simmons (323) 465-7289

Shari Simonsen (323) 549-3100
www.beautyandphoto.com

Sarah Jane Slotnick (323) 856-3000
www.thegelleragency.com

Jules Smith (818) 662-7057
(213) 999-5110
www.clothesmith.com

Sally D. Smith-McCardle (310) 545-6196
(310) 619-6390

Sam Sok (310) 274-0032
www.artistsbytimothypriano.com

Kristin Spear (323) 937-1010
www.zenobia.com

Sean Spellman (323) 297-0250
www.magnetla.com

Alberto Spiazzi (310) 288-8000
www.paradigmagency.com

Sarah Stanley (310) 923-5149
(310) 943-8102
www.artmixbeauty.com

Katia Stano (310) 656-5151
www.innovativeartists.com

April Steiner (323) 436-7766
www.eamgmt.com

Nancy Steiner (323) 297-0250
www.magnetla.com

Jodie Stern (818) 761-4488
(818) 807-6707

Miriam Sternoff (323) 436-7766
www.eamgmt.com

Amy Stofsky (323) 856-3000
www.thegelleragency.com

Jennifer Stone (818) 571-6114
www.jenstonestyling.com

Neysa Stone (310) 476-6890
(310) 962-9260
FAX (310) 471-1638

Casey Storm (323) 297-0250
www.magnetla.com

Sonja Streater (818) 434-3113

Pamela Sullivan (310) 251-9097
www.pamelasullivan.com

Cynthia Summers (310) 288-8000
www.paradigmagency.com

TAMU Artist Agency (310) 721-0735
137 S. Robertson Blvd., Ste. 111 FAX (323) 571-3498
Beverly Hills, CA 90211 www.tamuartistagency.com
(Reps for Wardrobe Stylists)

Machiko Tanaka (323) 664-5948

Julieta Tapia (323) 632-0532
(323) 468-9222
FAX (323) 468-9221
www.rootbeercostumer.com

Sheree Thiel (818) 679-3756

Catherine Thomas (323) 845-4144
www.montanartists.com

David Thomas (323) 856-8540
www.opusbeauty.com

Joey Tierney (323) 856-8540
www.opusbeauty.com

Lisa Tilney (323) 258-2664
(323) 314-7474

Michi Tomimatsu (310) 458-7800
www.partos.com

Tracey Mattingly, LLC (323) 462-5000
(Reps for Wardrobe Stylists) FAX (323) 462-5001
www.traceymattingly.com

Sue Tsai (310) 998-1977
www.celestineagency.com

Joan Tucker (323) 731-7088
(323) 365-2001
FAX (323) 732-1808
www.joantucker.com

Heidi Tuininga (323) 937-1010
www.zenobia.com

Arianne Tunney (323) 462-5000
www.traceymattingly.com

Vivian Turner (323) 697-0773

Tracy Tynan (310) 282-9940
www.mirisch.com

Genevieve Tyrrell (323) 845-4144
www.montanartists.com

United Talent Agency (310) 273-6700
9560 Wilshire Blvd., Ste. 500 FAX (310) 247-1111
Beverly Hills, CA 90212 www.utaproduction.com
(Reps for Costume Designers)

Valade (818) 929-4313
(818) 484-8028
(Wardrobe Stylist)

Antonio Vega (310) 405-5649
www.antoniovegastyling.com

Mia Velez (310) 274-0032
www.artistsbytimothypriano.com

Paula Vila (310) 403-7330

Julie Vogel (917) 520-7490

Mary Vogt (310) 274-6611
www.gershagency.com

Keith Wager (323) 356-2682
www.keithwager.com

Ariyela Wald-Cohain (818) 371-7568
www.ariyela.com

Sarah Wallner (818) 252-7800
(213) 618-3636
FAX (818) 527-7803
www.sarahwallner.com

Melissa Walsh (323) 549-3100
www.beautyandphoto.com

Abram Waterhouse (310) 288-8000
www.paradigmagency.com

Michelle Wendell (310) 403-6929
www.chiclittledevilstylehouse.com

Jacqueline West (310) 274-6611
www.gershagency.com

Ise White (310) 274-0032
www.artistsbytimothypriano.com

Cindy Whitehead (310) 379-2112
www.cindywhitehead.com

Michael Wilkinson (310) 273-6700
www.utaproduction.com

Daren Willis (818) 601-0489
FAX (818) 980-2248

Christie Wittenborn (323) 468-2240
www.nyoffice.net

Lizz Wolf (818) 284-6423
www.italentco.com

Albert Wolsky (310) 458-7800
www.partos.com

Johnny Wujek (323) 297-0250
www.magnetla.com

Jeanne Yang (310) 394-8813
www.cloutieragency.com

Hiroshi Yoshida (323) 933-0200
www.artistuntied.com

David Zambranna (888) 839-0101
www.firehousemanagement.com

Marie Zelenka-Hootsmans (310) 237-6438
www.baesjou.net

Zenobia Agency, Inc. (323) 937-1010
(888) 639-6917
130 S. Highland Ave.
Los Angeles, CA 90036
FAX (323) 937-1133
www.zenobia.com
(Reps for Wardrobe Stylists)

Rachel Zoe (323) 297-0250
www.magnetla.com

Mary Zophres (310) 273-6700
www.utaproduction.com

Alison Zukovsky (310) 717-4810
www.alisonzukovsky.com

The following has been kindly provided by Paul Petersen, president of A Minor Consideration, www.minorcon.org, (310) 532-1345. The editors would like to thank Paul for his help with this section. The contact info for the State Labor Commission (DLSE) is: San Francisco (415) 703-5300, Los Angeles (213) 620-6330 and San Diego (619) 220-5451.

There have been a number of changes in the world of working children, some major, most just technical in nature. The Young Performer's Data Base, compiled by the American Humane Association and funded by a grant from SAG and the IACF no longer appears on the Screen Actors Guild website and is being up-dated. For the latest "State-by-State" information we suggest you contact On Location Education (www.onlocationeducation.com) or Children In Film, (www.childreninfilm.com).

The use of minor-age children appearing on reality shows has finally come to the attention of the Department of Labor. Age-appropriate limitations and common sense should always guide your employment practices.

On union productions be aware that the theatrical unions' contracts travel with union children no matter where they work, and employers must remember this important contractual language: "Wherever there is a conflict in law or regulation pertaining to minors, the strictest interpretation shall apply."

Mandatory education and mandatory Coogan Accounts are now in place in New York State, Louisiana and, of course, California. Coogan set-asides are pending in New Jersey and Connecticut. Make sure your payroll company knows the requirements of the 15% Coogan set-aside and the parental obligation to supply this account information.

Safety and education are important elements whenever a minor is employed. You have two IATSE locals willing and able to help your production company. Don't be shy about calling the Studio Teachers, Local 884, IATSE, or Studio First Aid, Local 767, IATSE. Tell them how you plan to employ the minor, especially if you're using infants, and they will supply the information you need.

In California, the Department of Labor Standards and Enforcement has oversight and issues both the Permit to Employ and the child's Work Permit. The Department of Industrial Relation's Web site provides a complete listing under this heading:
California Code of Regulations, Title 8
Chapter 6. Division of Labor Standards Enforcement
Subchapter 2. Employment of Minors in the Entertainment Industry

8 CCR Section 11755.3—Studio Teacher's Authority.
The studio teacher, in addition to teaching, shall also have the responsibility for caring and attending to the health, safety and morals of minors under 16 years of age for whom they have been provided by the employer, while such minors are engaged or employed in any activity pertaining to the entertainment industry and subject to these regulations. In the discharge of these responsibilities, the studio teacher shall take cognizance of such factors as working conditions, physical surroundings, signs of the minor's mental and physical fatigue, and the demands placed upon the minor in relation to the minor's age, agility, strength and stamina. The studio teacher may refuse to allow the engagement of a minor on a set or location and may remove the minor there from, if in the judgment of the studio teacher, conditions are such as to present a danger to the health, safety or morals of the minor. Any such action by the studio teacher may be immediately appealed to the Labor Commissioner who may affirm or countermand such action.

8 CCR Section 11755.4—Studio Teacher's Remuneration.
The remuneration of the studio teacher shall be paid by the employer.

(continued)

Paul Peterson
A Minor Consideration
(310) 532-1345
www.minorcon.org

CHILD LABOR LAWS—SUMMARY CHART

<table>
<tr><th>AGE</th><th>WORK TIME
SCHOOL <u>IN</u>
SESSION</th><th>WORK TIME
SCHOOL <u>NOT</u>
IN SESSION</th><th>CONCURRENT
REQUIREMENTS</th></tr>
<tr><td rowspan="2">15 days
to
6 months</td><td></td><td>20 minutes work activity

2 hrs. max at employment site</td><td>Permits to work and employ required. [8 CCR 11751]

Parent or guardian must be present. [8 CCR 11757]

1 studio teacher and 1 nurse must be present for each 3 or fewer infants 15 days to 6 weeks old. [8 CCR 11760, 11755.2]

1 studio teacher and 1 nurse must be present for each 10 or fewer infants 6 weeks to 6 months old. [8 CCR 11760, 11755.2]

May not be exposed to light exceeding 100 footcandles for more than 30 seconds. [8 CCR 11760]</td></tr>
<tr><td colspan="2">May only be employed between 9:30 a.m. and 11:30 a.m. or between 2:30 p.m. and 4:30 p.m. [8 CCR 11764] Mandatory Time Windows.</td><td></td></tr>
<tr><td rowspan="2">6 months
to
2 years</td><td></td><td>2 hours work activity

4 hours max at employment site

Balance for rest and recreation</td><td>Permits to work and employ required unless the minor is a high school graduate or equivalent. [8 CCR 11751] High School graduates may be employed as adults.</td></tr>
<tr><td colspan="2">May only be employed between 5 a.m. and 12:30 a.m. [LC 1308.7]</td><td>Parent or guardian must be present. [8 CCR 11757]</td></tr>
<tr><td rowspan="2">2 years
to
6 years</td><td></td><td>3 hours work activity

6 hours max at employment site

Balance for rest and recreation</td><td>Studio teacher must be present. [8 CCR 11751.1]

1 studio teacher required per 10 minors. [8 CCR 11755.1]</td></tr>
<tr><td colspan="2">May only be employed between 5 a.m. and 12:30 a.m. [LC 1308.7]</td><td>1 studio teacher per 20 minors on weekends, holidays, and school breaks and vacations. [8 CCR 11755.1]</td></tr>
<tr><td>6 years
to
9 years</td><td>4 hours work activity

3 hours school

1 hour rest and recreation

8 hrs. max at employment site</td><td>6 hours work activity

1 hour rest and recreation</td><td>Studio teachers are responsible for the health, safety, and morals of the minor. [8CCR 11755.2]</td></tr>
<tr><td></td><td colspan="2">May only be employed between 5 a.m. and 12:30 a.m. (to 10 p.m. preceding schooldays $\geq$4 hours).[LC 1308.7]</td><td>Minors in grades one through six must be tutored between the hours of 7 a.m. and 4 p.m. Minors in grades seven through twelve must be tutored between the hours of 7 a.m. and 7 p.m. [EC 48225.5]</td></tr>
</table>

9 years to 16 years	5 hours work activity 3 hours school 1 hour rest and recreation 9 hrs. max at employment site	7 hours work activity 1 hour rest and recreation	Permits to work and employ required unless a high school graduate or equivalent. High school graduates may be employed as adults.
	May only be employed between 5 a.m. and 12:30 a.m. (to 10 p.m. preceding schooldays ≥4 hours).[LC 1308.7]		
16 years to 18 years	6 hours work activity 3 hours school 1 hour rest and recreation 10 hrs. max at employment site	8 hours work activity 1 hour rest and recreation	Studio teacher need only be present for minors' schooling if minor still required to attend school.
	May only be employed between 5 a.m. and 12:30 a.m. (to 10 p.m. preceding schooldays ≥4 hours).[LC 1308.7]		
Regular School Attendance and Work Hours	Compute work hours for each age group by subtracting 6 hours from the max time at employment site for tutored minors when school in session. The difference is the maximum work hours for these minors. Thus, 9 to16 year-olds who attend regular school may only work up to 3 hours on a schoolday. The 1-hour of rest and recreation is not required, but the workday may be extended one-half hour by a meal period. No work permitted during regular school hours. **Exception:** Minors 14 and over may work up to 8 hours during regular school hours for each of 2 consecutive days if excused with the school's written permission. [8 CCR 11760]		
Max Day/Week	No minor may be employed over 8 hours in a day. [LC 1308.7, 1392] or over 48 hours in a week. [LC 1308.7] **No exceptions**.		
Meal Periods	Meal periods are not work time. Workdays extended up to one-half hour for a meal period. [8 CCR 11761] Meals must be within 6 hours of call time and/or previous meal period. Teachers may require an earlier meal period.		
Travel Time	Travel between studio and location is work time. Up to 45 minutes travel from on-location, overnight lodging to work site is not generally considered work time. Travel between school or home and studio is not work time. [8 CCR11759]		
Day's End	12 hours must elapse between dismissal and next day's call time. **No exceptions.** [8 CCR11760]		
Make-up Off Set	Make-up in minor's home by persons employed on the same project is work time, and may not begin before 8:30 a.m. 12 hours must elapse between dismissal and the beginning of the next day's make-up/hairdressing. [8 CCR 11763]		
Out of State	California employers who employ resident minors outside of California under contractual arrangements made within California, must comply with all California child labor laws and regulations. [8 CCR 11756]		

Note: Daily work and school hour schedules for tutored minors of all age groups are provided in 8 CCR 11760.

Signatory Requirements

Who is the Signatory to a union contract?

A production company producing a bonafide commercial project that wishes to hire union labor should be a signatory to the union. Legally a company is not required to sign a union contract. However, union employees are barred by their union from accepting work offered by a production company that has not signed the union agreement. Some unions have separate agreements for AICP and non-AICP companies.

A production company may become a union signatory in three ways:

Production Company Signs Directly

Commits the production company to observe all aspects of the union contract. DGA, SAG, Local 600 East and the IATSE Commercial Production Agreement require direct signatory. The advertising agency or client is usually the SAG signatory; rarely is the production company a SAG signatory. (SAG signatory issues are covered in greater depth in the introduction to the SAG Contracts.) In certain circumstances, a union might offer the production company a Letter of Adherence (LOA) that covers a single project rather than a Term Agreement, which covers all projects, but this is becoming less common.

The following unions require production companies to sign agreements directly with them:

DGA (if Non-AICP)
IATSE Commercial Production Agreement (Covers L.A. County and rest of U.S. except New York and San Francisco; covers Local 600 Nationwide)
IATSE Local 16 - San Francisco
IATSE Local 52 Studio Mechanics (Non-AICP Independent version)
IATSE Local 600 Cinematographers - Single Production Agreements when available
IATSE Local 829 Set Designers, Scenic Artists & Stylists
Teamsters Local 399 - Separate Driver and Location Scout Agreements (Non-AICP Independent version)

Production Company Signs Via AICP

Association of Independent Commercial Producers member companies are not automatically signatories to any contract. To become a signatory, a company must sign an agreement through the AICP:

DGA (AICP member companies)
IATSE Commercial Production Agreement (Covers L.A. County and rest of U.S. except New York and San Francisco; covers Local 600 Nationwide)
IATSE Local 52 - Studio Mechanics (Must sign Trust Acceptance)
IATSE Local 476 - Chicago (Agreement for locally based companies only)
Teamsters Local 399 - Separate Driver and Location Scout Agreements (AICP version)

Payroll Service Acts as Signatory

In the past, some unions have allowed the payroll service to function as the signatory. This means that the production company need not sign a union contract before hiring union personnel. This is a rare exception.

Union Responsibilities of Production Company

Whichever form of signatory is used, producers are required to follow all terms and conditions of the applicable union contract(s). In general these provisions include, but are not limited to:

Staffing requirements
Wage rates
Overtime
Meal penalties
Turnaround

In general, all employees working in classifications covered by a collective bargaining agreement are entitled to receive the wages, benefits and other terms specified in the collective bargaining agreement regardless of whether they are members of a union.

Right to work laws do not permit an employer to avoid union terms and conditions; they only give the employee the right not to join the union (not withstanding any union security provisions contained in the collective bargaining agreement; see Right to Work Laws information contained later in this guide).

As a practical matter, most union agreements do not permit the mixing of crews. It should be noted that in many situations IATSE is allowing the hiring of qualified non-union workers as long as the producer covers them under the full provisions of the contract. You should check with your payroll service in the event that it becomes necessary to utilize a mixed crew.

Premium Day Guidance - Commercial Union Agreements

Many union contracts allow for a flexible workweek, usually referred to as "Any 5 of 7". This means that the workweek can start on any day of the week and that Saturday and Sunday are not necessarily Premium days. As a result of these flexible workweek provisions, questions arise in regard to defining 6th or 7th Premium days and what constitutes the start of a new week.

While all the agreements discussed here provide for the "Any 5 of 7" flexible workweek, they fall into two categories in the interpretation of the determination of the 6th and 7th Premium days.

1. Per the AICP, for the following agreements, accepted practice is that 6th and 7th Premium rates are assigned when a 6th or 7th day is worked within a 7 day week as established by the first day of work. Thus if there is a day off within the workweek, there is no possibility of a 7th day Premium within that week.

   Commercial Production Agreement - Except NE Corridor
   Local 399 Teamsters
   Local 16 – San Francisco
   Local 399 - Location Scouts/Managers
   Note: Exempt category – 12 hr Flat rate. No OT except 1.5x for 7th day on same project.

2. Per the AICP, for the following agreements, accepted practice is that 6th and 7th Premium rates are assigned when work is performed on the 6th or 7th consecutive day of a week as established by the first day of work. Thus a day off within the workweek does not change the assignment of 6th or 7th day Premiums to the 6th or 7th consecutive day of that week.

   Local 829 - Scenic Artists
   DGA - Director's Guild of America
   Local 52* - NY
   NE Corridor - Commercial Production Agreement
   - Local 600 East
   - Local 161 - Script
   - Local 798 - Hair & Makeup

   *Local 52 Notes
   36 hours off ends a 6-day workweek.
   Tracking by department starts at the Pre-light and includes replacement hires.
   New function hires are tracked individually.
   Sunday work "other than photography" requires 5-hour call at double time.
   In a week where Sunday is not worked (34 hours turnaround) , 7th day is paid at 1.5x.
   In both situations, two consecutive days off with no work and no travel start a new workweek.

SAG and NY Teamsters Local 817 do not have flexible workweeks. For these contracts, Saturday and Sunday are premium days, as specified in their agreements.

IATSE COMMERCIAL PRODUCTION AGREEMENT (CONT'D)

Working Rules & Conditions

Term of Contract		10/1/07 - 9/30/2010
Contracted Day		8 consecutive hours
Contracted Workweek		Any 5 or 6 consecutive days of 7
Calls	Day/Night	Anytime — Time begins at Set Call Time
	Partial Day	No — Except Travel Days - Min. 4 hours/ Max. 8 hrs @ 1x
Overtime	**1.5x**	9-12 hrs, 6th day up to 12 hours
	2x	After 12 hrs, 7th day, Holidays
	3x	6th day after 12 hrs worked
	4x	7th day after 12 hrs worked
	Increments	¼ hr increments
Turnaround	Daily	10 hours (9 hrs overnight location, portal-to-portal. DP/Camera Operator: 10 hrs.)
Penalty	If rest at least 6 hrs	Base or OT rate when released plus 1x for invaded hours
	If rest less than 6 hrs	Base or OT rate when released plus 1x for day until 10 hr rest period provided
Meals	Intervals	6 hr intervals, 1st meal no earlier than 3 hrs
	Lengths	½ hr to 1 hr
	Penalties	1st ½ hr or fraction - $7.50, 2nd ½ hr or fraction - $10, Each additional - $15
	Second Meal	May be deducted if it is outside min call
	Extensions	1st may be extended 15 min to complete setup. 2nd may be extended 30 min to complete setup or wrap
	Walking Meal	Any second meal, excluding NDB, may be a non-deductible walking meal, provided crew is dismissed within 1 hr from time meal was due
Production Zone		Within a circular 30 mile zone from intersection of City Hall for designated production centers
Location Rules		Per Diem allowance and housing or housing allowance to be provided Air Transportation: Coach or better
Work Time/ Travel Time Provisions		Overnight locations: Work: Set call to set dismissal. 1 hr allowable travel time. Excess paid as work time. Travel Days: Min 4 hrs, Max 8 hrs Straight Time. Mileage at current IRS rate.
Cancellation of Call		By 3pm of prior non-work day; By end of prior work day Penalty: Work Day - 8 hrs pay Travel Day - 4 hrs pay
Minimum Staffing		No requirements. Staffing must be consistent with past practices. There is practical interchangeability within the production crafts. Covers classifications traditionally covered by IATSE. Excludes office clerical, PA's and guards. Commercial stylists are not included in the agreement, but Costume Designers and Costumers are.
Payment of Wages		No special provisions. Most states require payment within 2 weeks. CA has severe late payment penalties
Hazardous Work		No special provisions, except in NE Corridor. See NE Corridor Notes page.
Jurisdiction		Throughout U.S., Puerto Rico and U.S. Virgin Islands. See Jurisdiction: Within LA rates page for exceptions.
Pension Health & Welfare		Rates vary geographically. See AICP - IATSE Commercial Production Agreements - PH & W rates page. Travel and Idle Days on location: 8 hrs PH & W contribution
Holidays		New Year's Day, Martin Luther King Day, President's Day, Memorial Day Independence Day, Labor Day, Thanksgiving Day, Christmas Day
Union Security TV Commercial Roster		Preference of employment: First consideration to those referred by local unions. Workers who are not current members of the union may be hired based on advertiser or agency requirements or documented industry experience. All are covered by all of agreement's provisions. Marine coordinators, boat handlers & operators covered, if not covered by another union.
Notes		>Outside LA County, NY & Phila Zones, producers must notify LA or NY IA office prior to shoot. >Producers must be direct signatory to full agreement. No letters of adherence. >Excludes PSAs and spec commercials. P&W contributions optional on PSAs. >Excludes traditional low budget commercials w/ single day cost of $75K or less and total cost of $225K or less. >Excludes Non-Trad low budget commercials with single day cost of $50K or less and total cost of $750K or less. >For ALL low budget, wage rates subject to individual negotiation. P&W normal. >IATSE or crew may appoint a Job Steward for each production. >Scope of Agreement - Where Employer has no effective control portions of pre and post production not covered. Employers not prevented from subcontracting for services consistent with industry practice. >Higher Classification - Two or more hours work in higher classification requires higher rate for day. >Recognize jurisdiction over commercials made by traditional means for any medium including Internet. >Internet commercials by non-traditional means to be negotiated, all but wages & work rules apply.
Phone numbers		LA IATSE: 818-980-3499, NY: 212-730-1770 — LA AICP: 323-960-4763, NY: 212-929-3000

IATSE COMMERCIAL PRODUCTION AGREEMENT (CONT'D)

L.A. County Minimum Rates 10/1/08 - 9/30/09

Classification	Hourly	8-hour Day	Daily On Call	Weekly On Call
LOCAL 600				
Director of Photography	92.43	739.46		
Camera Operator	56.58	452.62		
First Assistant Cameraman	40.93	327.46		
Second Assistant Camera	37.60	300.76		
Camera Loader/Utility	32.17	257.34		
Digital Imaging Technician	53.38	427.04		
LOCAL 695				
Sound Mixer	63.14	505.11		
Boom Operator	42.62	340.97		
Sound Utility	42.62	340.97		
VTR/Video Playback	42.62	340.97		
LOCAL 80				
Key Grip	39.62	316.99		
2nd Grip	35.48	283.87		
Dolly Grip	36.75	294.00		
Grip	33.87	270.93		
Entry Level Grip	29.64	237.15		
Craft Service	28.72	229.73		
LOCAL 728				
Lighting Gaffer	39.62	316.99		
2nd Electrician	35.48	283.87		
Dimmer Operator	34.65	277.19		
Electrician	33.87	270.93		
Entry Level Electrician	29.64	237.15		
LOCAL 44				
Property Master	39.62	316.99		
2nd Prop	34.65	277.19		
3rd Prop	32.47	259.72		
Propmaker Foreman	39.80	318.39		
Propmaker	34.65	277.19		
Set Decorator (On Call)			570.32	2,407.73
Special Effects Foreperson	39.80	318.39		
Lead Effects	36.75	294.00		
Effects	34.65	277.19		
Lead Set Dresser	34..65	277.19		
Set Dresser	32.47	259.72		
Construction Coordinator (On Call)			554.18	2,342.53
LOCAL 892				
Costume Designer (On Call)			536.08	2,234.13
LOCAL 705				
Key Costumer	37.65	301.17		
2nd Costumer	35.04	280.32		
3rd Costumer	32.75	262.03		
Entry Level Costumer	25.55	204.43		
LOCAL 706				
Key Makeup Artist	45.10	360.83		
2nd Makeup Artist	38.39	307.10		
3rd Makeup Artist	34.79	278.35		
Key Hair Stylist	44.47	357.95		
2nd Hair Stylist	39.24	313.94		
3rd Hair Stylist	33.45	267.64		

Classification	Hourly	8-hour Day	Daily On Call	Weekly On Call
LOCAL 871				
Script Supervisor	30.58	244.65		
LOCAL 767				
First Aid	28.58	228.66		
LOCAL 800				
Art Director (On Call)				2,914.79
Assistant Art Director (On Call)				2,170.73
LOCAL 729				
Paint Foreperson	53.95	431.60		
Painter	32.04	256.35		
LOCAL 800				
Lead Scenic Artist	47.48	379.86		
Scenic Artist	42.93	343.44		
LOCAL 884				
Studio Teacher/Welfare Worker	39.79	318.31		

Note: Marine Coordinators, boat handlers and operators are covered, if not covered by another agreement. Wages are negotiable.

IATSE COMMERCIAL PRODUCTION AGREEMENT (CONT'D)

Outside L.A. County Minimum Rates 10/1/08 - 9/30/09

Classification	Hourly	8-hour Day	Daily On Call	Weekly On Call
LOCAL 600				
Director of Photography	92.43	739.46		
Camera Operator	56.58	452.62		
First Assistant Cameraman	40.93	327.46		
Second Assistant Camera	37.60	300.76		
Camera Loader/Utility	32.17	257.34		
Digital Imaging Technician	53.38	427.04		
LOCAL 695				
Sound Mixer	58.38	467.04		
Boom Operator	39.40	315.18		
Sound Utility	39.40	315.18		
VTR/Video Playback	39.40	315.18		
LOCAL 80				
Key Grip	36.64	293.10		
2nd Grip	32.81	262.44		
Dolly Grip	33.98	271.84		
Grip	31.31	250.50		
Entry Level Grip	27.40	219.18		
Craft Service	26.55	212.43		
LOCAL 728				
Lighting Gaffer	36.64	293.10		
2nd Electrician	32.81	262.44		
Dimmer Operator	32.04	256.35		
Electrician	31.31	250.50		
Entry Level Electrician	27.40	219.18		
LOCAL 44				
Property Master	36.64	293.10		
2nd Prop	32.04	256.35		
3rd Prop	30.01	240.11		
Propmaker Foreman	36.79	294.33		
Propmaker	32.04	256.35		
Set Decorator (On Call)			527.01	2,226.09
Special Effects Foreperson	36.79	294.33		
Lead Effects	33.98	271.84		
Effects	32.04	256.35		
Lead Set Dresser	32.04	256.35		
Set Dresser	30.00	240.03		
Construction Coordinator (On Call)			512.38	2,165.80
LOCAL 892				
Costume Designer (On Call)			495.65	2,065.57
LOCAL 705				
Key Costumer	34.81	278.51		
2nd Costumer	32.40	259.23		
3rd Costumer	30..27	242.17		
Entry Level Costumer	23.64	189.11		
LOCAL 706				
Key Makeup Artist	41.68	333.47		
2nd Makeup Artist	35.49	283.95		
3rd Makeup Artist	32.16	257.25		
Key Hair Stylist	41.36	330.92		
2nd Hair Stylist	36.29	290.30		
3rd Hair Stylist	30.91	247.28		

Classification	Hourly	8-hour Day	Daily On Call	Weekly On Call
LOCAL 871				
Script Supervisor	30.58	244.65		
LOCAL 767				
First Aid	28.58	228.66		
LOCAL 800				
Art Director (On Call)				2,914.79
Assistant Art Director (On Call)				2,170.73
LOCAL 729				
Paint Foreperson	53.95	431.60		
Painter	32.04	256.35		
LOCAL 800				
Lead Scenic Artist	47.48	379.86		
Scenic Artist	42.93	343.44		
LOCAL 884				
Studio Teacher/Welfare Worker	39.79	318.31		

Note: Marine Coordinators, boat handlers and operators are covered, if not covered by another agreement. Wages are negotiable.

LOCAL 399 TEAMSTERS - AICP & INDEPENDENT (CONT'D)

Working Rules & Conditions

Term of Contract		8/1/05 - 7/31/10
Contracted Day		8 consecutive hours
Contracted Workweek		Any 5 or 6 consecutive days of 7
Calls	Day/Night	Not mentioned
	Partial Day	No Except Travel Days - Min. 4 hours/ Max. 8 hrs @ 1x
Overtime	1.5x	9-12 hrs, 6th day up to 12 hours
	2x	After 12 hrs, 7th day, Holidays
	3x	6th day after 12 hrs worked
	4x	7th day after 12 hrs worked
	Increments	¼ hr increments Overtime premiums not compounded
Turnaround	Daily	9 hours (8 hrs overnight location)
Penalty	If rest at least 8 hrs	1x for invaded hours
	If rest at least 6 hrs	Premium rate for invaded hours
	If rest less than 6 hrs	Premium rate for day until 9 hr rest period is provided
Meals	Intervals	6 hr intervals, 1st meal no earlier than 3 hrs, except for early call crew provided w/ Non-Deductible Breakfast
	Lengths	½ hr - 1 hr
	Penalties	1st ¾ hr or fraction - $8.00, 2nd ¾ hr and each additional - $12.00
	Second Meal	
	Extensions	1st may be extended 15 min to complete setup. 2nd may be extended 30 min to complete setup or wrap
	Walking Meal	Any second meal, excluding NDB, may be a non-deductible walking meal, provided crew is dismissed within 1 hr from time meal was due
Studio Zone		>Within a circular 30 mile zone from intersection of Beverly Blvd. and La Cienega Blvd. in Los Angeles
Location Rules		>Per Diem allowance and housing or housing allowance to be provided. >Air Transportation - Domestic: Coach or better, International: Business Class >Local Hires: Fair consideration shall be given to those referred by affiliated local unions. > Not required to transport teamster drivers to distant locations to drive motorhomes/housecars
Work Time/ Travel Time Provisions		Travel Days: Min 4 hrs, Max 8 hrs Straight Time. Mileage at current IRS rate.
Cancellation of Call		By 3pm of prior non-work day; By end of prior work day Penalty: Work Day - 8 hrs pay Travel/Wrap Day - 4 hrs pay
Minimum Staffing		>If there is covered equipment, One Gang Boss for each production hired from Group 1 or 2 of Industry Experience Roster. Gang Boss may not be a Driver/Grip or Driver/Electrician or drive any Exempt Equipment (Such as Production Vans, Motorhomes, Chapman Cranes Camera Cars, etc.-See App. B) >No Gang Boss needed if four or less production vehicles. (Teamster or Non Teamster) (See list Art. 5) >Gang Boss may not work on more than one production at a time. >Gang Boss: 1. Must call/clear members within 2 hours of call or hire; 2.Must supervise parking of all vehicles; 3. Must travel on every job w/covered vehicle taken from LA; 4. May be released after 10hrs on STAGE day when no work to perform. >Operators of regulated vehicles requiring Class A or B comml license are subject to agrmt. >Preference of Employment (Roster) does not apply to drivers of Motorhomes, Exempt Vehicles and hyphenate drivers. >One driver to be assigned to each piece of covered equipment, will help with load, unload and fueling. >On Shoot Day only Teamster must shuttle cast and crew (not agency) to and from parking lot and set. >15 passenger vans driven by Teamsters only on shoot days.
Payment of Wages		No special provisions, but CA requires payment on same schedule as staff. Penalties are high.
Hazardous Work		No special provisions
Jurisdiction		CA. AR, HI, NV
Pension Health & Welfare		Follows IATSE Commercial Production Agreement. Rates vary geographically. See AICP - IATSE Commercial Production Agreements - PH & W rates page. Travel and Idle Days on location: 8 hrs PH & W contribution
Holidays		New Year's Day, Martin Luther King Day, President's Day, Memorial Day Independence Day, Labor Day, Thanksgiving Day, Christmas Day

(Cont'd next page)

<table>
<tr><td>Covered Vehicles</td><td colspan="2"><u>Non-Exempt Vehicles - Subject to Seniority Grouping</u>
10 Ton Trucks Driveable Generators (Class B) 200 Amps bolted to truck
Fuel Trucks Passenger Vans
Vehicles towing three axled trailers, generator, trailers w/three or more rooms or any trailer exceeding 10,000 lbs
>Five-Ton enclosed trucks are covered on Shoot and Wrap days only. (Does not include Cube and Super Cube trucks traditionally driven by Production Assistants.
> Stake bed trucks not requiring A or B License are covered by Independent agreement
Specialized Equipment - Exempt from Seniority Grouping Only
Production Vans - (400 Amp Gen Min.) Camera Cars
Chapman Cranes Catering Trucks
Car Carriers (4 vehicles or more) Water Trucks
Highway Buses (38+ Pass. Incl. Driver) Hydro-cranes (5 Ton or more)
Honeywagons Motorhomes/Housecars
Mobile Kitchens - Driver/Cooks (Class A), but NOT assistants
5 Ton trucks w/covered box not requiring a Class A or B license</td></tr>
<tr><td>Notes</td><td colspan="2">>Producers must be direct signatory to full agreement.
>Location Scouts and Managers - Paid under separate agreement.
>Higher Classification - 2 or more hours work in higher classification requires higher rate for day.
>Non-rostered drivers may be hired when designated by advertiser or agency due to special conditions.
>Where Employer has no effective control portions of pre and post production, they not covered.
>Employers not prevented from subcontracting for services consistent with industry practice.
>No use of non-covered equipment to deliberately avoid terms of agreement.
>See Agreement for new No-Hire, Hyphenate and Safety Passport provisions.
>AICP Members are not required to sign the Wrangler Sideletter. Terms are same as this agreement.
>Excludes public service announcements, spec commercials and low budget commercials whose aggregate shooting schedule is two days or more. Single day not more than $75K and. total costs do not exceed $225K
>On low budget commercials, wage rates subject to individual negotiation. P&W normal.</td></tr>
<tr><td>Phone numbers</td><td>Local 399: 818-980-3499</td><td>LA AICP: 323-960-4763</td></tr>
</table>

LOCAL 399 LOCATION SCOUTS/ MANAGERS - AICP ONLY

Working Rules & Scale Rates

Term of Contract		8/1/05 - 7/31/10
Contracted Day		12 hours "On call" consecutive hours
Contracted Workweek		Not specified, but state law requires premium pay for 6th and 7th days
Calls	Day/Night	Not mentioned
	Partial Day	No
Overtime (Calculated on 10 hr day rate)	**1.5x**	1.5x for 7th day of same project
	2x	N/A - Considered exempt under wage & hour law
	3x	N/A
	4x	N/A
	Increments	Not covered
Turnaround	Daily	9 hrs
	Weekly	
Penalty		1.5x for invaded hours
Meals	Intervals	CA law: No more than 6 hour intervals
	Lengths	CA law: ½ hr - 1 hr
	Penalties	Not covered
	Extensions	Not covered
	Walking Meal	Not covered
Studio Zone		Not covered
Location Rules		Not covered
Work Time/ Travel Time Provisions		Not covered
Cancellation of Call		Not covered
Minimum Staffing		Any Location Scouts or Location Managers needed
Payment of Wages		CA law requires payment on same schedule as staff. Penalties are high.
Hazardous Work		No special provisions
Jurisdiction		Los Angeles County and when transported out of L.A. County. Not required to transport out of L.A.
Pension Health & Welfare		Follows IATSE Commercial Production Agreement. Rates vary geographically. See AICP - IATSE Commercial Production Agreements - PH & W rates page. Travel and Idle Days on location: 8 hrs PH & W contribution
Holidays		2x for work on recognized SAG Agreement holidays
Scale Rates		(see below)
Notes		>Industry Roster: All employees must be listed on Roster unless less than 16 are available on 1st day of job >Effective August 1, 2008: Location Mgr. MUST be employed on any non-self contained location Self Contained Locations include: studio Lots, warehouses, stages, filming ranches and any private property with off-street parking sufficient that no equipment is parked on public property >Min. Kit rental $50 per day. Mileage at IRS allowable rates >Excludes public service announcements, spec commercials. Also excludes low budget commercials whose aggregate shooting schedule is two days or more and single day cost does not exceed $75K nor aggregate production costs do not exceed $225K >On low budget commercials, wage rates subject to individual negotiation. P&W normal
Phone numbers		Local 399: 818-985-7374 — AICP LA: 323-960-4763, NY: 212-929-3000

Scale Rates

Daily	8/1/05	8/1/06	8/1/07	8/1/08	8/1/09
Loc.Scout/Manager:	$515.00	$530.45	$546.36	$562.75	$579.64

LOCAL 399 LOCATION SCOUTS/ MANAGERS - INDEPENDENT

Working Rules & Scale Rates

Term of Contract		8/1/05 - 7/31/10
Contracted Day		12 hours "On call" consecutive hours
Contracted Workweek		Any 7 consecutive day commencing with the first day
Calls	Day/Night	Not mentioned
	Partial Day	No
Overtime (Calculated on 10 hr day rate)	**1.5x**	Over 12 hrs or 6th day (12.5% of 12 hr rate = 1.5x based on 12 hr rate)
	2x	7th Day - Considered exempt under wage & hour law
	3x	N/A
	4x	N/A
	Increments	"...major portion" of hour
Turnaround	Daily	9 hrs
	Weekly	
Penalty		1.5x for invaded hours
Meals	Intervals	CA law: No more than 6 hour intervals
	Lengths	CA law: ½ hr - 1 hr
	Penalties	Not covered
	Extensions	Not covered
	Walking Meal	Not covered
Studio Zone		30 mile zone from Beverly Blvd. and La Cienega Blvd.
Location Rules		Per Diem and housing or allowance to be provided
Work Time/ Travel Time Provisions		Travel days are at minimum rate
Cancellation of Call		Not covered
Minimum Staffing		Any Location Scouts or Location Managers needed Location Manager MUST be employed on any non-self-contained location. Self-contained locations include: studio lots, warehouses, stages, filming ranches and any private property with off-street parking sufficient that no equipment is parked on public property.
Payment of Wages		CA law requires payment on same schedule as staff. Penalties are high.
Hazardous Work		No special provisions
Jurisdiction		AZ, CA, CO, HI, NV, NM, OR, UT, WA
Pension Health & Welfare		Follows IATSE Commercial Production Agreement. Rates vary geographically. See AICP - IATSE Commercial Production Agreements - PH & W rates page. Travel and Idle Days on location: 8 hrs PH & W contribution
Holidays		2x for work on recognized SAG Agreement holidays

Scale Rates

Daily	**8/1/05**	**8/1/06**	**8/1/07**	**8/1/08**	**8/1/09**
Location Scout/ Manager:	$592.25	$610.02	$628.32	$647.17	$666.58
Asst. Loc. Manager	$283.25	$291.75	$300.50	$309.51	$318.80

Notes

>Definition of Work: Locating sites, Contacting property owners, Negotiating property rentals, Obtaining permission & permits, Maintaining conditions of rental agmt., Liaison with film councils & driving others if does not interfere with their duties.

>Industry Roster: For LA work or hired in LA to work anywhere else. All employees must be listed on Roster unless less than 16 are available on 1st day of job or are requested by advertiser or agency due to special abilities or training. L399 to be notified.

>Min. Kit rental $50 per day. Mileage at IRS allowable rates. Reimbursment of other expenses.

>Excludes public service announcements, spec commercials. Also excludes low budget commercials whose aggregate shooting schedule is two days or more and single day cost does not exceed $75K nor aggregate production costs do not exceed $225K.

>On low budget commercials, wage rates subject to individual negotiation. P&W normal.

Phone numbers	Local 399: 818-985-7374	AICP LA: 323-960-4763, NY: 212-929-3000

DGA NATIONAL COMMERCIALS AGREEMENT (CONT'D)

Working Rules & Conditions

Term of Contract		11/1/05 - 10/31/09
Contracted Day		12 consecutive hours
Contracted Workweek		Any 5 or 6 consecutive days of 7
Calls	Day/Night Partial Day	Anytime 1st & 2nd AD Calls must begin at earliest of cast and crew calls No
Overtime (Based on Contracted Day)	**13th & 14th hour** **Over 14 hrs** **Over 15 hrs** **6th day** **7th day & holidays**	1/8 of day rate for each hour invaded 1/6 of day rate for each hour invaded 1 day's pay for each 5 hour period; 5 hours computed starting at the 13th hour 150% of day rate/ 200% on distant location if work is performed 200% of day rate
	Increments	Whole hours
	Additional	Work on 5th day which extends into 6th day before completion of 12 hrs is paid at 2x 1st AD cannot be dismissed prior to crew 2nd AD cannot be dismissed until AD duties are completed Over 18 hrs - Producer must offer 1st class hotel or car service to employee's home or hotel
Turnaround	Daily	8 hrs
Penalty	If short	1 day's pay for each 5 hr period until 8 hr rest is achieved
Meals	Intervals	
	Lengths	Reasonable time provided - Meal time is work time
	Penalties	If no dinner provided by 7:30pm and day started 9am or earlier - $30.00
Location Rules		Lodging - 1st Class Air Transportation - Coach, but 1st or Business Class if over 5 hrs. - Always same class as Director. Layovers - Non-worked days on location are paid at straight time. Members shall not be required to drive transportation vehicles. Producer must provide minimum $100K travel insurance for travel to or from location. Proof must be provided.
Work Time/ Travel Time Provisions		Travel time is work time. Travel to distant loc. on 6th, 7th or holidays is 1x time, if no work performed. Except Report to studios: East - Within 5 Boroughs of NYC ---- West - LA County
Cancellation Fee		One day's pay if Agency cancels or postpones less than 48 hrs prior to call and AD makes best effort to replace work. See contract for additional rules. Does not apply to work reduced by accelerated schedule or after prod. has started. No PH&W on Fee. Cancellation or termination of job being worked on by 2 PM or owe for the next day.
Minimum Staffing *See AICP Provisions below*		>Director >1st AD: Whenever a Director is employed, including screen tests >2nd AD: Not less than one shooting day of each commercial When need to control background or crowds When 12 or more persons are photographed. >Must include Dir. & 1st AD on all location shoot days when shoot is 4 days or more and cast and crew is 10 or more >When Director sent out of U.S., 1st AD must be sent, unless destination country refuses work permit or production subsidy would be lost. (See special AICP Provisions below) >UPM shall be hired if UPM duties are being performed, but there is no min. staffing. >Southern CA and Third Area qualification lists to be established in addition to current NY list. >If 2nd AD member works as Location Scout, must be treated as DGA member. Does not apply in LA County or where other unions have jurisdiction.
Payment of Wages		Per state and federal timely payment requirements
Hazardous Work	Insurance Pay	$500K death and/or dismemberment. $500 per week total disability coverage Pay $150 per incident - Max $300 per day
Jurisdiction		U.S. based companies: Wherever they work.
Pension Health & Welfare		See rates page
Holidays		New Year's Day, Martin Luther King Day, President's Day, Memorial Day Independence Day, Labor Day, Thanksgiving Day, Christmas Day

Notes	>Staffing violations subject to triple damages >1st AD may not be dismissed prior to his/her crew. >Commercial Project Listing Form must be submitted prior to 1st day of production, incl. foreign productions >Minimum 1st AD Prep: 1 day for 1-2 day shoot, 2 days for 3+ day shoot or two or more significantly different or distant locations. >Special provisions for Spec Spots, Internet and Public Service Announcements. - See Contract. >Excludes low budget commercials with single day production of $75K or less and aggregate cost of $225K or less. Wage rates subject to individual negotiation. PH&W based on scale rates. >Signatory Producers may not subcontract to non-signatory producers. >Signatory Producers may be contracted by non-signatory producers, but must notify DGA within 10 days or project will be considered signatory. >DGA will consider requests for signatory employers to provide production services to non-signatory foreign prod. co's producing commercials for non-US/Canada markets. 1st & 2nd ADs must be hired. >Signators are bound to Basic Agmt. and other DGA agreements including production of scripted and reality TV shows, feature films, documentaries, industrials and internet projects. Does not cover music videos.
AICP Special Work Rules	>No 1st AD needed unless crew is more than6 and cast no more than 1. (Dir. not incl.) >No 1st AD prep day needed if shoot is less than 5 hours. If goes over 5 hrs - 1 AD owed for prep day >No 1st on prep day for 1 day shoot if: Limbo product shots w/no talent or Minor reshoots or >Stop Motion photography or Pick-up shots >No 2nd AD needed for "table top" production, if not required by needs of the production. >UPM shall be hired if UPM duties being handled substantially by one employee, but there is no min. staffing. >No need to travel US 1st AD to foreign countries outside No. America if shoot is 3 or fewer shoot days and is awarded less than 10 bus. days prior to first Shoot day. Local 1st AD to be given preference of employment >Projects in Canada and Mexico require sending of US 1st AD unless destination country refuses work permit or production subsidy would be lost. >Special provisions apply AICP to companies located in the Midwest. Contact DGA for info. >DGA members employed as Location Scouts within 75 miles of Chicago paid as DGA 2nd Ads.
AICP Pension Health & Welfare	Presumed Salaries for P&W Calculation: Principal (Owner) Director:*$150,000* per calendar year (or actual earnings if elected by*1/20* each year). Principal (Owner) or Staff UPM or 1st AD: *$120,000* per calendar year. Staff 2nd AD: $70,000 per calendar year. Other Directors: $7000 per shoot day. Other UPMs or Ads: Actual gross earnings including profits etc.
AICP Director-Deferred Membership	Directors may defer membership not later than 10 shoot days or one year from Director's first shoot day. Applies to director regardless of number of companies worked for. Producers must notify Guild. All other provisions, including PH&W apply.
DGA Office Phone numbers	Los Angeles: 310-289-2000, New York: 212-581-0370, Chicago: 312-644-5050

SCREEN ACTORS GUILD
COMMERCIALS CONTRACT DEPARTMENT
5757 Wilshire Blvd., Los Angeles, CA 90036
(323) 549-6858 for commercial queries only.
All other questions, call (323) 954-1600.
www.sag.org

The following is a brief interpretation of the Screen Actors Guild 2009 Commercials Contract relating to principal performers. This digest is possible due to the generous assistance of the Screen Actors Guild. For more complete information, LA 411 recommends that the reader review the full text of the 2009 Contract, or contact the Screen Actors Guild's Commercials Department.

Auditions

The first two auditions are allowed without compensation if one hour or less. Additional time is paid in 30 minute units @ $37.00 per unit. Third callbacks are $148.10 for the first two hours and $37.00 per half hour thereafter. Fourth callbacks are $296.10 for the first four hours and $37.00 per half hour thereafter. Please note that a Producer is allowed to call Performer for a 3rd or 4th audition without payment for the first 2 hours if Producer limits the audition to 3 Performers or fewer per role and none of the Performers brought back to audition for the role are on their 1st audition.

Bookings & Cancellations

A Performer is booked when:

1. Given written notice of acceptance.
2. A form contract signed by the Producer is delivered to the Performer or when a form contract unsigned by the Producer is delivered to a Performer and is executed by Performer and returned to Producer within 48 hours.
3. A script is delivered to the Performer (does not include delivery for auditions or for the Performer to review for possible employment).
4. Fitted (does not include wardrobe tests).
5. Given a verbal call which he/she accepts.
6. Told he/she will be used but no date is set.
7. Told not to accept an engagement for a spot advertising a competitive product or service.

The Producer shall have the right to cancel any call without payment because of impossibility of production due to "Force Majeure." Postponement of a call to a mutually acceptable date may be made by the Producer upon 24 hours notification (except on Saturdays, Sundays and holidays), as long as the new booking date is made within 15 working days of original date and payment of one half day of the session fee is paid. If production does not take place within 15 days, another half session payment is due and the Performer is thereupon released. None of these payments are creditable toward any session fees payable to the Performer if production should take place at a later date.

Employment

1. Session fees must be paid and postmarked within 12 working days.
2. On-camera principals/stunt performers' session fee is $592.20 for an 8-hour day. The voice-over session fee is $445.30 for a 2-hour session.
3. Performer is paid for each commercial shot on the same day. Performer is paid for each day whether or not the commercial is completed. In other words, the Performer is paid a session fee for the number of days or the number of commercials, whichever is greater.
4. If Performer is called in to re-shoot, session fees are due and payable depending on quantity of commercials and number of days.
5. For each tag or dealer identification made beyond one, the voice over rate is $126.85 for each tag numbered 2 through 25. $73.50 is paid for each tag numbered 26 through 50. $40.05 is paid for each tag 51+. If called in for the sole purpose of making tags, a session fee and a specified rate applies for each tag beyond one. (Contact SAG for the specific tier-step rate and whether any other session fee rate is applicable.)
6. Commercials made initially for use on the Internet or in New Media: Producer may bargain freely with Performer and shall pay Performer compensation in such amount as shall be agreed by direct bargaining with the Performer or the Performer's agent.
7. Pension & Health contribution is 15.5%.

(continued)

Work Time

1. All on-camera Principals' sessions are based on an 8-hour day. That does not include their meal periods. Off-camera (voice over) Performers' sessions are based on 2-hour engagements.
2. Performer's rate for the 9th and 10th hours of work is time-and-one-half, and the 11th hour of work is paid at double the Performer's hourly rate.
3. Overtime for Principals earning more than 2x the session fee per commercial per day shall be paid 1 1/2 x (instead of double time) after 10 hours.
4. Principal Performers making more than double scale for the session (over $1,184.40 per commercial) shall receive 1 1/2 x their session rate for Saturdays and Sundays. Performers making $1,184.40 or less shall receive double their session rate.
5. Rest periods from time of dismissal to first call thereafter must be 12 hours. Exceptions to this are made when the last shot of the day is an exterior shot on a nearby location and the next day's shooting begins with exterior photography. Then the rest period may be reduced to 10 hours. The reduced rest period pertains only to those performers who are in the respective scenes.
(Contact SAG for other exceptions.)

Night Work

Night work is defined as work between 8 p.m. and 6 a.m., except that a first call for the day at 5 a.m. or thereafter shall not constitute night work.

Except as above provided, the Performer shall receive premium pay for each hour of night work equal to 10% of his/her hourly rate for such hours. In the computation of such premium pay, the hourly rate of the Performer for such hours is first determined, and 10% thereof is added as the night work premium.

Travel Time

1. The Los Angeles Studio Zone is defined as that area within a radius of 30 miles of the intersection of Beverly and La Cienega Boulevards.
2. Travel to and from location when no services are rendered requires a full session fee. There are no half day or hourly rates.
3. Travel time shall be paid as work time if Performer is working. Overtime caused by travel to and from location is paid at straight time in quarterly units.
4. All travel past midnight shall be paid at 1 1/2 x Performer's rate, in quarterly units.
5. If traveling to and from LAX and JFK, add one hour. If traveling to and from La Guardia, add 1/2 hour.

(continued)

Meals & Meal Penalties

1. Meal periods must be within 6 hours of first call in-studio or on location. Second meal period must be within 6 hours following completion of first meal period.
2. Meal penalty is $25.00 for first 1/2 hour violation, second 1/2 hour is $25.00, third 1/2 hour and each 1/2 hour thereafter is paid at $50.00.
3. If makeup, wardrobe or hairdress preparation time will disrupt the Performer's normal meal period, the Producer may provide that Performer with a working meal (e.g., coffee, sandwiches) before the Performer's set call if no deduction is made from work time for meal periods.

Mileage & Parking

Mileage based on rate which IRS provides may be paid as a travel expense allowance not reported as income. The Producer shall provide supervised or secured parking.

Travel, Transportation & Accommodations

1. All travel expenses and lodging accommodations shall be furnished by the Producer including first class transportation to and from location for air travel of 1,000 or more air miles. For air travel of less than 1,000 miles, coach service may be provided. Producer shall provide a reasonable single room accommodation.
2. Necessary traveling expenses and meal per diem at breakfast ($10.95), lunch ($16.40), and dinner ($30.25).

Holidays

New Year's Day, Martin Luther King Jr.'s Birthday, Washington's Birthday (Presidents' Day), Memorial Day, July 4, Labor Day, Thanksgiving, Christmas. Holidays that fall on a Sunday will be attributed to the following Monday.

Principals working on a holiday are entitled to double time for all hours worked.

Visit www.sag.org for more information.

NOTES:

NOTES:

LA 411